THE ENCYCLOPEDIA OF NORTH AMERICAN SPORTS HISTORY

THE ENCYCLOPEDIA OF NORTH AMERICAN SPORTS HISTORY

Ralph Hickok

Facts On File

New York • Oxford

THE ENCYCLOPEDIA OF NORTH AMERICAN SPORTS HISTORY

Facts On File, Inc.   Facts On File Limited
460 Park Avenue South   Collins Street
New York NY 10016   Oxford OX4 1XJ
USA   United Kingdom

Library of Congress Cataloging-in-Publication Data
Hickok, Ralph.
    The encyclopedia of North American sports history / Ralph Hickok.
        p.   cm.
    Includes bibliographical references and index.
    ISBN 0-8160-2096-5 (alk. paper)
    1. Sports—North America—Encyclopedias.   I. Title.
GV567.H518   1991
796.′097—dc20   91-6667

A British CIP catalogue record for this book is available from the British Library.

Facts On File books are available at special discounts when purchased in bulk quantities for businesses, associations, institutions or sales promotions. Please call our Special Sales Department in New York at 212/683-2244 (dial 800/322-8755 except in NY, AK or HI) or in Oxford at 865/728399.

Text design by Ron Monteleone
Jacket design by Soloway/Mitchell Design Associates
Composition by the Maple-Vail Book Manufacturing Group
Manufactured by the Maple-Vail Book Manufacturing Group
Printed in the United States of America

10 9 8 7 6 5 4 3 2 1

This book is printed on acid-free paper.

CONTENTS

ACKNOWLEDGMENTS

A work of this sort obviously requires a great deal of assistance and cooperation from many people. Above all, I have to thank a good friend, Joan Bisbee, whose intelligence, persistence, and perseverance enabled her to dig out many, many facts without which this book would be much poorer. Joan also did much of the photo research. My son, Evan, helped save my eyesight by reading lists of winners so that I could transcribe them. He and my daughter, Colette, stuffed and labeled many of the letters of inquiry I sent out in pursuit of facts.

The many other helpful people who responded to those inquiries are listed here alphabetically. If I've inadvertently omitted someone who should have been included, I offer my sincere apologies.

Maurice Allan, secretary, Canadian Olympic Association; Wilbur Ammon, executive secretary, American Rubberband Duckpin Bowling Congress; Deborah S. Anderson, executive director, Women's Sports Foundation; Ian Anderson, executive director, U.S. Figure Skating Association; Luella Ansorge, U.S. Women's Curling Association; Jan Armstrong, curator, International Tennis Hall of Fame and Tennis Museum; Margie Baddely, assistant to the commissioner, American Indoor Soccer Association; Pat Baggett, business manager, National Bench Rest Shooters Association; Vaughan L. Baird, Q.C., president, Aquatic Hall of Fame and Museum of Canada, Inc.; Gerald W. Baltz, executive director, National Bowling Hall of Fame and Museum; John P. Barry, communications coordinator, Edmonton Northlands; R. H. Belanger, director general, Canadian Amateur Speed Skating Association; Martin Belsky, secretary-treasurer, American Athletic Association for the Deaf; Tim Berry, director of publicity, International Hot Rod Association; Jim Blake, executive director, New England Sports Museum; Kevin E. Boller, public relations officer, Canadian Cricket Association; David D. Bopp, general manager, Amateur Trapshooting Association; Nicole Bouchard, public relations director, Quebec Nordiques; Cindy Brickner, executive director, U.S. Hang Gliding Association; Chris Browning, director of public relations, Pennsylvania International Raceway; Sean Callahan, public relations, U.S. International Speedskating Association.

Vicki Capoccioni, director of publicity, Pittsburgh Civic Arena Corporation; Bob Carroll, Professional Football Researchers Association; Stephen Carroll, manager, education and administration, Canadian Professional Golfers' Association; Al Cartwright, executive director, Association of Sports Museums and Halls of Fame; Pete Cava, The Athletics Congress of the U.S.A.; Clayton W. Chapman, secretary-treasurer, Intercollegiate Fencing Association; Caroline Chartrand, administrative assistant, Canadian Colleges Athletic Association; Wes Clark, executive director, Ringette Canada; Nancy A. Colasurdo, public relations director, Babe Ruth League, Inc.; Michael J. Cole, director of marketing and communications, American Hockey League; LuAnn Collins, promotions manager, International Jet Skiboating Association, Inc.; Steve Combs, executive director, American Water Ski Association; Anthony Constantino, secretary, National Soccer League; Donald M. Cooper, president, Arctic Winter Games Corporation; Greg Cortopassi, co-director, World Footbag Association; Dr. Conrad P. Cotter, president, U.S. Powerlifting Federation; Bob Cronkwright, president, ACUC International; P. K. Debergo, executive assistant, Canadian Baseball Hall of Fame and Museum; Don R. DeBolt, executive director, International Swimming Hall of Fame; Ivor G. Dent, president, The Commonwealth Games Association of Canada, Inc.; Mavis Derflinger, chairman, U.S. Youth Soccer Association; Pat Dewire, U.S. Fencing Association.

Bob Dill, International DN Ice Yacht Racing Association; Ron Doornbos, promotion director, Canadian Ball Hockey Association, Inc.; Vincent dePaul Draddy, chairman, National Football Foundation and Hall of Fame; Joan Duncan, executive director, Canadian Sportive Rhythmic Gymnastics Federation; Linda Edmondson, public relations manager, Women's International Bowling Congress; Anne E. Eggebrecht, marketing manager, St. Louis Arena; Fred C. Engh, president, National Youth Sports Coaches Association; Bob Ericson, director of public relations, U.S. Badminton Association; Michael W. Everman, archivist, American Alliance for Health, Physical Education, Recreation and Dance; Anna Fabbri, public relations, Montreal Olympic Park; John Falzone, president, Ladies Pro Bowlers Tour; Dr. Gary F. R. Filosa II, president, American Surfing Association; Anne K. Fisher, assistant curator, Curling Hall of Fame and Museum of Canada, Inc.; Tom Fleetwood, general secretary, American Darts Organization; Steve Fleming, publication director, Professional Rodeo Cowboys Association; Lynn Fons, membership services, Soaring Society of America, Inc.; Ronald W. Forrester, president, Canadian Jiu-Jitsu Association; Gilbert Frey, corresponding secretary, The National Crossbowmen; Sue D. Friend, secretary, American Amateur Baseball Congress; Diane Fritschner, U.S. Cycling Federation; John H. Fritz, assistant secretary-treasurer, U.S. Equestrian Team; Andre Gallant, consultant, Canada Games Council.

Scoop Gallelo, president, International Veterans Boxing Association; Lee Gardner, vice-president marketing and public relations, International Motor Sports Association; Merli Garvis, commodore, American Canoe Association; Jan Gaspar, office manager, International Kart Federation; Henley Gibble, president, Road Runners Club of America; Roy Gillespie, president, PONY Baseball, Inc.; Margaret H. Gordon, executive secretary, American Tennis Association; Marguerite Grant, administrative assistant, Softball Canada; Jim Gruenwald, executive director, Soccer Association for Youth; Julie Gumlia, director of Communications, Ladies Professional Golf Association; Rick Haefner, membership director, International Motor Contest Association; Lori Hafen, membership coordinator, American Swimming Coaches Association; Dr. Creighton J. Hale, president, Little League Baseball; Dr. Ralph Hale, president, U.S.A. Water Polo; William T. Halls, secretary-treasurer, Professional Basketball Writers Association of America; Ann Hamilton, program coordinator, Canadian Academy of Sport Medicine; John Hamilton, executive director, Canadian Federation of Amateur Baseball; Frank Hannigan Sr., executive director, U.S. Golf Association; Jonathan R. Harley,

Olympic director, U.S. Sailing Foundation; Sandra Ifland, Greyhound Hall of Fame; Jerilyn Harris, editor/publisher, Charioteer Publications.

Armin Heiken, international secretary, George Khoury Association of Baseball Leagues, Inc.; Marvin Hess, executive vice-president, National Wrestling Coaches Association; Susan Hiller, director of communications, College Football Association; Will M. Holsberry, executive secretary, National Intramural-Recreational Sports Association; Al Hong, executive director, Canadian 5 Pin Bowlers' Association; Trudy Hughes, executive assistant, Montreal Canadiens; Sandy Inglis, National Museum of Racing and Hall of Fame; Jeff Iula, general manager, All-American Soap Box Derby; Carl C. James, commissioner, Big Eight Conference; Roger Jaynes, director public relations, Road America, Inc.; Bob Johnson, executive director, Amateur Hockey Association of the U.S.; Karen W. Johnstone, assistant communications director, U.S. Yacht Racing Union; Ghislaine Joly, executive director, Canadian Association for the Advancement of Women and Sport; Dick Jordan, news bureau director, United States Auto Club; Hamilton Jordan, executive director, Association of Tennis Professionals; Penny Joyce, marketing/media services coordinator, Swimming Canada; Karen Kast, United States of America Rugby Football Union; Bill Keating, commissioner, Major Indoor Soccer League; Lolly Keys, national director of public affairs, American Youth Soccer Organization; George E. Killian, executive director, National Junior College Athletic Association; Eric King, vice-president of operations, Coaching Association of Canada; Leslie A. King, Director of Communications, U.S.A. Amateur Boxing Federation, Inc.

Colin Kirk, executive director, Canadian Orienteering Federation; Jack Kyle, president, Canadian Cricket Association; Michael R. Lachapelle, technical program director, Canadian Lacrosse Association; Bernard Lacourciere, Cross Country Canada; Rick Lalor, director of communications, National Hot Rod Association; Noreen Landis-Tyson, director of public relations and fund development, U.S. Field Hockey Association; Nicki H. Lang, national secretary, Maccabi Canada; Dale E. Lanser, executive secretary, American Casting Association; Walter Latzko, registrar, Hall of Fame of the Trotter; Barbara C. Lockert, program coordinator, National Sportscasters and Sportswriters Association; Max O. Lundberg, director, Professional Ski Instructors Association Education Foundation; Tanja Mackin, Rowing Canada; Brian MacPherson, technical administrator, Federation of Canadian Archers Inc.; Barry Mano, president, National Association of Sports Officials; Wally Marr, executive director, U.S. Judo Association; Michael May, executive director, Boosters Clubs of America; Christine McCartney, executive secretary, National Archery Association of the U.S.; Fritz McGinness, assistant director, National Federation of State High School Associations; John McKeon, executive director, National Soccer Coaches Association of America; Ronald E. McMinn, executive director, National Amateur Baseball Federation; Tom Mee, director of media relations, Minnesota Twins.

Volney Meece, executive director, The Football Writers Association of America; Anne Merklinger, executive director, Canadian Federation of Sport Organizations for the Disabled; Thomas Miller, executive director, American College of Sports Medicine; Joseph F. Mitch, executive director, U.S. Basketball Writers Association; Linda L. Mojer, public relations director, American Amateur Racquetball Association; Gary D. Montgomery, executive director, Arizona Veterans' Memorial Coliseum; Marian Muhammad, executive secretary, International Boxing Federation; Don Murphy, the Chicago Blackhawks; Edward H. Murray, president, Horseshoe Canada; Nancy Nault, executive secretary, Soaring Association of Canada; Randy L. Neil, president, International Cheerleading Foundation, Inc.; Lyle Nelson, vice-president, U.S. Biathlon Association; Elgie Noble, secretary, U.S. Curling Association; Susan Noyes, executive director, U.S. Boardsailing Association; Bob O'Leary, founder, World Arm Wrestling Federation; Jack R. Osborn, president, U.S. Croquet Association; Virginia Oualline, Archives, The Ninety-Nines, Inc.; George Packard, executive secretary, U.S. Amateur Confederation of Roller Skating; Peter Pastorek, technical director, Canadian Team Handball Federation; Wayne Patterson, research specialist, Naismith Memorial Basketball Hall of Fame; John Pawlak, publicity and public relations director, U.S. Trotting Association; Ginny Peifer, public relations coordinator, American Birkebeiner Ski Foundation, Inc.

Beryl Peterson, administrator, Field Hockey Association of America; Howard Peterson, secretary general, U.S. Ski Association; Patricia Planques, director of communications and development, Canadian Special Olympics, Inc.; Bill Plummer III, communications director, Amateur Softball Association of America; N. R. "Bud" Poile, commissioner, International Hockey League; Carl Porter, Jr., president, U.S. Handball Association; Cheryl A. Rielly, assistant curator, Canada Sports Hall of Fame; Donnie Roberts, secretary-treasurer, The National Horseshoe Pitchers Association; Nicholas Rodis, executive director, U.S. Collegiate Sports Council; Ronald Rossi, executive director, U.S. Luge Association; Milt Roth, chairman, National Association of Jai Alai Frontons;

Jim Saccomano, director of media relations, Denver Broncos; Diane St-Denis, administrative coordinator, Canadian Weightlifting Federation; Laura Saunders, services manager, Canadian Figure Skating Association; Timothy D. Schmad, assistant general manager, Ak-Sar-Ben; Rick Schulhoff, director, service bureau, Thoroughbred Racing Associations; Steven Schwartz, executive director–media relations, New York Racing Association; Herb Shannon, executive vice-president, Canadian Trotting Association; Adham Sharara, president, Canadian Table Tennis Association; Pam Sherer, coordinator of public relations, National Baseball Congress; Kevin Shippey, public relations director, Professional Bowlers Association.

B. James Shubert, president, American Archery Council; Michael C. Sifton, president, Polo Canada; Becky Sjoberg, president, U.S. Korfball Federation; Rick Skaggs, director of public relations, Calgary Flames; Dan Skahill, Continental Motosport Club; Alan Smith, executive director, Canadian Squash Racquets Association; C. Jack Smith, president, Professional Bowhunters Society; Nancy Smith, Buffalo Memorial Auditorium; Carrie Snider, administrative assistant, Football Canada; Brenda Spencer, administrative secretary, Hockey Canada; Milt Stark, executive director, International Softball Congress; Forrest F. Steinlage, National Historian, American Turners; Linda Stelley, Professional Skaters Guild of America; Steve Stenerson, executive officer, The Lacrosse Foundation, Inc.; Joseph P. Steranka, director of communications and public relations, The Professional Golfers Association of America; Peter Ross Stilwell, director, PGA World Golf Hall of Fame; Toni Stokes, executive director, Canadian Amateur Wrestling Association; Kevin Sullivan, director of media services, Dallas Mavericks; Roger H. Tessman, executive secretary-treasurer, American Bowling Congress; James A. Thompson, president, Balloon Federation of America; Earl S. Torango, secretary-treasurer, American Lawn Bowls Association.

Naomi J. Torrey, executive secretary-treasurer, Pope and Young Club; Patricia M. Trinkle, administrative assistant, American Horse Shows Association, Inc.; Michelle Trueman-Gajoch, director of marketing, TrueSports, Inc.; Joe Tsao, director of marketing and events, Pontiac Silverdome; Gloria Urbin, executive administrator, American Power Boat Association; William H. Wadsworth, board chairman, National Bowhunter Education Foundation; William L. Wall, executive director, Amateur Basketball Association of the U.S.A.; Wilf Wedman, president, Canadian Sport and Fitness Administration Centre Inc.; Ben Weider, president, International Federation of Body Builders; Donna White, Judo Canada; Robert M.

Whitelaw, commissioner, Eastern College Athletic Conference; Chip Williams, director of public relations, National Association for Stock Car Auto Racing; Douglas Wilton, executive director, Office of Sport for the Physically Disabled; Ken Winner, president, U.S. Boardsailing Association; Carol Ann Wis-

hart, Canadian Fencing Association; Beth Wood, director of marketing, U.S. Dressage Federation, Inc.; Shirley A. Yates, executive secretary, Amateur Skating Union; Dr. Frank Zarnowski, executive director, DECA.

INTRODUCTION

This reference work is designed to provide fast, easy access to a wide variety of information about the history of North American sports. To that end, it contains numerous relatively short entries. The entry on baseball, for example, is only about 3,000 words long; it outlines the general history of the sport's development. More detailed information on baseball can be found in several other places. Each major league has its own entry, and there are also entries on such specialized subjects as the reserve clause and the World Series.

This book is not a history of great teams and great players. It focuses on the evolution of sports and of sports government and administration, along with other issues of interest to the growing number of sports historians and to the fan who is now exposed to many stories about contract negotiations, lawsuits, labor unrest, strikes and strike threats, gambling and recruiting scandals, and drug problems on sports pages that used to be devoted almost entirely to game results and highlights.

The entries in *The Encyclopedia of North American Sports History* fall into several broad categories:

1. Sports. Every modern organized competitive sport has its own entry, with an emphasis on its growth and development in North America. In many cases, the history of the sport before its arrival in North America is briefly summarized. There are also entries for obsolete sports of historic importance, such as rounders, the ancestor of American baseball.

   Since the emphasis is on history, I've made every attempt to be very specific about dates and places of important events. In most cases, I've assumed that the reader knows something about how the sport is played. There's no attempt to include detailed rules summaries, although ob-

scure sports are briefly described. However, historically important rules changes, such as the legalization of the forward pass in American football, are included in the text.

2. General history. There are many entries covering broad subjects such as amateurism, blacks in sports, gambling, players' associations, television, and women in sports.

3. Biography. The biographical emphasis is on sports figures of genuine historic importance: for example, Dr. James Naismith, who invented basketball; Kenesaw Mountain Landis, the first authoritative commissioner of baseball; James Gordon Bennett, Jr. and John Cox Stevens, both of whom contributed greatly to several different sports during the 19th century. Some athletes have to be included because they reached historic milestones or because they seem to be representative of an entire era, but this is not a biographical encyclopedia; most members of the major sports halls of fame are not included, and several of those who are included have never been inducted into a hall of fame. There is a certain emphasis on blacks and on women.

4. Sporting events. This category includes such well-known events as the World Series, the Stanley Cup playoffs, the Super Bowl, the Kentucky Derby, and the Indianapolis 500, as well as lesser-known events such as the Gold Cup powerboat race, airplane racing's "Powder Puff Derby," and quarterhorse racing's All-American Futurity. Again, the emphasis is on the history of an event: when, how, and where it originated, and how it has changed. Lists of winners are included in some, but not all, of these entries.

5. Major awards. There is obviously some overlapping between this category and the previous category. The Stanley Cup, for example, is an

award as well as an event. But there are many other awards covered, such as the Lombardi Trophy, which is presented to the Super Bowl winner. For several major awards, such as the Sullivan Trophy, all past winners are listed.

6. Cities. Every North American city that has ever had a major professional sports franchise is included, with a brief history of each of its teams, past or present. Some historically important amateur and semiprofessional teams are also included.

7. Stadiums, fields, and arenas. Every existing major-league sporting facility is included in this category, along with historically important places such as the Elysian Fields and the Polo Grounds.

8. Sports organizations, including governing bodies, sanctioning bodies, leagues, colleage conferences, halls of fame, museums, and research centers. These entries include information on when, where, and why the organization was established, where it is presently located, and so on. Most governing and sanctioning bodies are covered under the sports they represent; only those that have genuine histories of their own appear as separate entries. Every major professional league is included, along with NCAA Division I-A football conferences and a few major NCAA basketball conferences that are not also football conferences.

There's been a remarkable proliferation of sports halls of fame in recent years, many of them of limited scope. I've tried to include those that are of interest to the sports historian/researcher or to the average fan.

The Encyclopedia of North American Sports History is arranged alphabetically, with many cross-references. Some entries exist for cross-reference only; for example, **AFL** See AMERICAN FOOTBALL LEAGUE. Many such abbreviations are included, but only those that are commonly seen in publications.

Biographical sketches are alphabetized by last name and the most commonly used first name or nick-

name, followed by the complete first name and middle initial. For example, Red Grange appears as **Grange, "Red" Harold C.**

However, where a nickname is simply a natural shortening of the athlete's real first name, in general it is not shown. For example, Ty Cobb appears as **Cobb, Tyrus R.**

Some athletes, especially boxers, used professional names. In such cases, the athlete's real name is shown in parentheses. For example, Joe Louis was the ring name of Joseph Lewis Barrows. His entry appears as **Louis, Joe (Joseph Louis Barrows).**

A woman athlete may have been known by her maiden name at one stage of her career and by her married name at another stage. In such cases, I have tried to use the name by which the athlete is best known, with a cross-reference from the other name. For example, Glenna Collett Vare's biography appears under **Vare, Glenna Collett** and there is a cross-reference, **Collett, Glenna** See VARE, GLENNA COLLETT.

If a woman is listed under her maiden name, her married name (if she has one) is shown in parentheses for example, **Didrikson, "Babe" Mildred (Mrs. Zaharias).** And, again there is a cross-reference: **Zaharias, Babe** See DIDRIKSON, "BABE" MILDRED.

Many entries include brief bibliographies. These bibliographies are not meant to be exhaustive. They include only those books that I actually consulted and that I found to be most helpful in preparing an entry. There is also a general bibliography of works that either provided me with overall guidance in planning and research for the Encyclopedia or helped to direct me to other books on specific subjects.

Because of the scope of this work, most research was done through secondary sources. In cases where sources disagreed or important specifics weren't available from those sources, the *New York Times* microfilm in the New Bedford, MA, Free Public Library was invaluable, and many people who are listed in the acknowledgments responded either to leisurely letters or frantic phone calls with the information I needed.

AAA

See AMERICAN AUTOMOBILE ASSOCIATION.

AAFC

See ALL-AMERICA FOOTBALL CONFERENCE.

Aaron, "Hank" Henry L. (1934–   )
Baseball

Born February 5, 1934, Mobile, AL; Baseball Hall of Fame

Aaron made baseball history at 9:07 P.M. EST April 8, 1974, when he hit his 715th career home run to break Babe Ruth's 39-year-old record. Playing for the Atlanta Braves, Aaron hit the home run before a standing-room-only crowd of 53,775 at Atlanta Stadium off pitcher Al Downing of the Los Angeles Dodgers.

Aaron began the season with 713 home runs, and Atlanta owner Bill Bartholomay created a contro-

Hank Aaron made baseball history when he hit his 715th career home run on April 8, 1974, breaking Babe Ruth's record. He retired with 755 home runs, still the major-league record. Courtesy of the Milwaukee Brewers

versy by announcing that Aaron would not play in the team's first three games at Cincinnati so that the record could be broken in Atlanta. Baseball Commissioner Bowie Kuhn ordered that Aaron must play in Cincinnati. Aaron responded by hitting a home run off Jack Billingham in his first at-bat of the season, tying Ruth's record. Then he broke the record in Atlanta's first home game.

When Aaron retired after the 1976 season, he had hit 755 home runs. Aaron is also the all-time leader in extra base hits (1,477), total bases (6,856), and runs batted in (2,297). He is second in at-bats (12,364), third in games played (3,298) and runs scored (2,174, tied with Ruth), eighth in doubles (624), and twelfth in slugging percentage (.555). His career batting average is .305.

As with Ruth, Aaron's great hitting ability distracted attention from his all-around skills. He was a fine defensive outfielder with a strong arm, and he had speed. In 1963, he became only the third player in history to hit more than 30 home runs and steal more than 30 bases in a single season.

Aaron joined the Milwaukee Braves in 1954 as their starting right fielder, and established himself as a power hitter in 1957 by leading the National League with 44 home runs, 118 runs scored, and 132 runs batted in, while batting .322. The Braves won the pennant that season, and Aaron was named the National League's Most Valuable Player. He hit .393, with three home runs and seven RBIs, in the Braves' seven-game World Series victory over the New York Yankees.

Aaron never came close to Ruth's big single-season home run totals, but he had consistently high numbers for 20 seasons, from 1955 through 1974. He hit 20 or more home runs in each of those seasons, 30 or more in 15 of them, and 40 or more in 8 of them. His best home run season was 1971, when he hit 47. Fourteen times he batted over .300, with a high of .355 in 1959.

The Braves moved to Atlanta in 1966, and Aaron played there until after the 1974 season, when he went to a new Milwaukee team, the Brewers, in the American League. He finished his career as a designated hitter for Milwaukee. After retiring as a player, Aaron returned to the Braves as vice-president of player development.

Further Reading: Aaron, Henry, *Aaron*, New York: Thomas Y. Crowell Publishers, 1974.

AAU
See AMATEUR ATHLETIC UNION.

ABA
See AMERICAN BASKETBALL ASSOCIATION.

Abbott, Senda B.
See BERENSON, SENDA (MRS. ABBOTT).

ABC
See AMERICAN BOWLING CONGRESS.

ABC Masters
See MASTERS TOURNAMENT (BOWLING).

Abdul-Jabbar, Kareem (Lew Alcindor)
(1947–   )
Basketball
Born April 16, 1947, New York City

Abdul-Jabbar was born Lew Alcindor, and was the center on the great UCLA NCAA championship teams from 1967 to 1969. He was College Player of the Year in 1967 and in 1969. At 7 feet 2 inches and 235 pounds, he was remarkably agile. He could run the court on the fast break, and he was a great passer from the pivot position, especially when double-teamed, which he often was.

He began his NBA career with the Milwaukee Bucks in 1969–70, and was Rookie of the Year. He led the Bucks to the NBA championship in 1971, averaging 31.7 points a game and winning his first Most Valuable Player (MVP) Award. In 1975, he was traded to the Los Angeles Lakers. He then shocked many fans by becoming a Black Muslim and adopting his new name, the Muslim for "powerful servant." Because of the adverse publicity, Abdul-Jabber became suspicious of many sportswriters and sportscasters and refused to talk to many of them, further damaging his image during his early years. But his remarkable physical skills and a gradual warming of his demeanor eventually won back the fans—even in competing cities. When he passed Wilt Chamberlain's record of 32,419 career points in 1984, Boston fans gave Abdul-Jabbar a standing ovation that lasted more than 10 minutes. When he made his final tour of league cities in the spring of 1989, he received standing ovations and farewell gifts from fans and opposing players everywhere. And when he played his last regular-season game at the Los Angeles Forum on April 23, 1989, his teammates presented him with a Rolls Royce as a retirement present.

He played more seasons (20), more games (1,560), and more minutes (57,448) than anyone else in history. He also scored more points (38,387), made more field goals (15,837), and blocked more shots (3,189).

In Abdul-Jabbar's 14 seasons with the Lakers, the team won championships in 1980, 1982, 1985, 1987, and 1988. He won his second MVP award in the playoffs in 1985, and was the NBA's regular-season MVP in 1971, 1972, 1974, 1976, 1977, and 1980. He was the league's first-team all-star center in 1971, 1972, 1973, 1974, 1976, 1977, 1980, 1981, 1984, and 1986.

Further reading: Abdul-Jabbar, Kareem. *Kareem*. New York: Random House, 1990.

ABL
See AMERICAN BASKETBALL LEAGUE.

ACCUS
See AUTOMOBILE COMPETITION COMMITTEE FOR THE UNITED STATES.

Adams Award
Hockey
The National Hockey League Coach of the Year Award has been presented annually by the NHL Broadcasters' Association since 1974. It is named in honor of Jack Adams, coach of the Detroit Red Wings from 1927 to 1947.

Adams Award Winners

1974	Fred Shero, Philadelphia
1975	Bob Pulford, Los Angeles
1976	Don Cherry, Boston
1977	Scott Bowman, Montreal
1978	Bobby Kromm, Detroit
1979	Al Arbour, New York Islanders
1980	Pat Quinn, Philadelphia
1981	Red Berenson, St. Louis
1982	Tom Watt, Winnipeg
1983	Orval Tessier, Chicago
1984	Bryan Murray, Washington
1985	Mike Keenan, Philadelphia
1986	Glen Sather, Edmonton
1987	Jacques Demers, Detroit
1988	Jacques Demers, Detroit
1989	Pat Burns, Montreal
1990	Bob Murdoch, Winnipeg
1991	Brian Sutter, St. Louis

Adams Cup
Yachting
Awarded for the Women's North American Sailing Championship, this trophy originated in 1924 as the Hodder Cup. The one-time award was won by Ruth

Sears of the Cohasset (MA) Yacht Club. In 1925, Charles Francis Adams offered a permanent trophy for the championship. It was retired in 1929, when the Cohasset Yacht Club won it for the third time, and Adams replaced it. The second Adams Cup was retired when the Indian Harbor Yacht Club won it for the third time. Mrs. Charles Francis Adams then presented a perpetual challenge trophy, which was destroyed in a fire in 1951. Henry S. Morgan, Mrs. Adams' son-in-law, replaced it, and this fourth trophy has been contested since then.

Adios Butler
Harness Racing

Adios Butler won pacing's triple crown in 1959 and was the first horse ever to break 2 minutes in the Little Brown Jug. Bought in 1960 by a 19-man syndicate for $600,000, he won 14 of 17 starts and was named Horse of the Year. He won the honor again in 1961, when he lost his first start but then won 13 in a row. In a time trial at Lexington, KY in October 1960, he set a new record by pacing a mile in 1:54 ⅗. He set a record for a half-mile track in 1961 by doing a mile in 1:55 ⅗ at Delaware, OH.

Aerobatics

The barnstorming pilots of the 1920s and 1930s did aerial stunts for show, but aerobatics didn't become a competitive sport until after World War II, with a variety of local and regional contests, each with its own set of rules. The Precision Flying Division of the Experimental Aircraft Association was established in 1965 to develop uniform rules. It was succeeded in 1968 by the Aerobatic Club of America, which also sanctioned contests. In 1970, Bob Heuer organized the International Aerobatic Club to establish rules for four categories of competition: sportsman, intermediate, advanced, and unlimited, and a national contest was held in Fond du Lac, WI. The National Aeronautics Administration awarded sanctioning power to the IAC in 1981. The club has about 3,500 members and conducts more than 30 competitions annually.

Address: International Aerobatic Club, Wittman Field, P.O. Box 3086, Oshkosh, WI 54903 (901) 756–7800.

AFL
See AMERICAN FOOTBALL LEAGUE.

African-Americans in Sports
See BLACKS IN SPORTS.

Agents

The first sports agent was probably Christy Walsh, who began ghostwriting newspaper columns for Babe Ruth in 1921. Walsh quickly saw that there were many other possibilities for the baseball superstar; he lined up a vaudeville tour for $3,000 a week, set up Ruth's off-season barnstorming tours, and gained commercial endorsements for him. He was, however, more theatrical agent than sports agent.

C. C. "Cash and Carry" Pyle acted as agent and manager for football superstar Red Grange in 1925. Immediately after Grange's career ended at the University of Illinois, Pyle signed Grange to a personal services contract and leased his services to the Chicago Bears for a postseason barnstorming tour. He also booked a vaudeville tour for Grange and founded the American Football League in 1926 to showcase Grange with his own team, the New York Yankees.

But the modern sports agent didn't exist until the 1960s, when rival professional football and basketball leagues began competing for players. As teams got involved in bidding wars for top athletes, the athletes began to use lawyers and other representatives to handle negotiations. The idea wasn't popular with most teams. When All-Pro center Jim Ringo told Green Bay Packer coach and general manager Vince Lombardi that he had hired an agent, Lombardi left the room for a few minutes and returned to tell Ringo he had been traded to the Philadelphia Eagles.

A pioneer agent, Steve Arnold, said of those days, "The owners resent us because we stand in the way of them getting a guy cheap. I know they make us sound like leeches and bloodsuckers, but there's a need for us." The need became even greater as salaries escalated and long-term contracts with deferred payments became more common. The standard player contract was replaced by much more complicated contracts that virtually required a player to have professional help in negotiations, and owners gradually came to accept the player's agent as a necessity.

During the 1970s, professional athletes became more aware of the need for financial security after their sports careers ended. At the same time, more opportunities for commercial endorsements, personal appearances, and other off-the-field enterprises opened up. Sports agents began doing more than just negotiating contracts with the athlete's team; they became, in effect, theatrical agents and financial counselors.

While "agent" is the term commonly used, many of those working in the field don't like the word. Bob Woolf, a Boston attorney who is among the best known and most highly respected "agents" in the business, has said, "I'm no agent . . . As a lawyer, I take no fixed percentages, nothing off the top and only a reasonable fee." Nevertheless, Woolf sold his business to Marvin Josephson Associates, the owner of International Famous Agency, which represents actors and models on a percentage basis, and Robert Woolf Associates now operates in many respects as an agency, not a law firm.

The consensus is that a player's representative should probably be an attorney first. The NFL Players Association recommends that its members should be represented by attorneys. But, because part of the job is working out what amount to show business deals, a representative also needs to be part theatrical agent, and the theatrical agent does traditionally get 15 percent of the client's earnings. The solution to the dilemma, many athlete's representatives have decided, is to form a separate business that includes specialists in law, investments, and endorsements.

The tremendous amount of money now available to athletes has led inevitably to abuses. A few agents have taken enormous amounts of money, as much as 25 percent of the client's contract. The most common abuse has been signing a college athlete to a contract, a violation of NCAA rules governing amateurism. Such signings are kept secret, often by postdating contracts. In 1989, sports agents Norby Walters and Lloyd Bloom were found guilty of federal racketeering charges for those practices, but their convictions were overturned in 1990.

Several attempts have been made to regulate sports agents. The National Football League, National Basketball Association, and organized baseball certify agents judged to be effective and scrupulous. More than 100 agents belong to the Association of Representatives of Professional Athletes, formed in 1978 with the help of the NFL Players Association. ARPA members subscribe to a strict code of ethics covering reasonable fees, conflicts of interest, and client confidentiality.

See also LAW, SPORTS.

AGTOA

See AMERICAN GREYHOUND TRACK OPERATORS ASSOCIATION.

AIAW

See ASSOCIATION FOR INTERCOLLEGIATE ATHLETICS FOR WOMEN.

Airplane Racing

As with the automobile, airplane racing originated as an effort "to improve the breed." Prizes were awarded for speed, altitude, distance, and time of flight to encourage designers and manufacturers to produce better planes. The first major international competition was for the James Gordon Bennett Trophy, which included a $5,000 prize, donated by the publisher of the New York Herald-Tribune for the fastest two laps at a 1909 air meet held August 22–28 in Rheims, France. It was won by Glenn H. Curtiss of the United States, who averaged 47.65 miles per hour for 20 kilometers, about 12 miles, in a plane that he designed and built.

The Aero Club of America held the first international air meet in the United States during October 22–31, 1910, at Belmont Park in Elmont, NY, featuring the second Bennett Trophy race. Bennett Trophy racing continued annually through 1913 and resumed in 1920, when the French won for the third time and took permanent possession of the trophy.

The Pulitzer Trophy was offered in 1919 for an international air race to be held in the United States. The first race, at Mitchel Field, Long Island, on November 25, 1920, drew an estimated crowd of 25,000 to 40,000. Beginning in 1921, Pulitzer racing was the major event at an annual air meet. Other races were added to the program, and the meet became known as the National Air Races in 1924. Starting in 1930, the Thompson Trophy was offered for a closed-circuit race, and the following year a transcontinental race for the Bendix Trophy was added.

During the 1920s, the National Air Races were remarkably popular. The 1929 event in Cleveland drew more than 500,000 paid spectators over a ten-day period. Even during the Depression, crowds were good—more than 100,000 watched the Thompson Trophy race in 1937. But the program was cut back from ten days to four in 1933, and lack of money often limited the number of new planes entered. Suspended in 1940 by World War II, the races were resumed in 1946 under the auspices of the War Department. In 1949, one of the planes crashed in a residential area, killing a woman and child as well as the pilot, and races were not held in 1950. From 1951 through 1957, a National Air Show included air racing primarily for military planes, although there was a Continental Trophy race for civilian midget planes. That ended when the Department of Defense withdrew its support.

During that period, many less formal races were being contested in smaller planes, usually war surplus craft flown by veteran pilots. They formed the Professional Race Pilots Association in 1964 and began the Reno National Championship Air Races, with closed-circuit competion in four categories: unlimited, formula one, AT-6/SNJ (a World War II training plane), and sports biplane. The organization is now known as the National Air-Racing Group.

Probably the best known of all events is the annual International Air Race for Women, informally named the "Powder Puff Derby," established in 1947 by the

Specially-built planes compete in the formula one category in modern air racing. Ray Cote won seven consecutive national championships in this plane, Shoestring. Courtesy of the National Air Racing Group

Ninety-Nines, an organization of more than 7,000 licensed women pilots throughout the world. This cross-continent race follows a different route of about 2,500 air miles each year.

See also AEROBATICS; POWDER PUFF DERBY; SOARING.

Address: National Air-Racing Group, 1313 Los Arbales, Sunnyvale, CA 94087 (408) 733–7967.

Akron, OH
Football   The Akron Pros were one of the founding teams of the American Professional Football Association in 1920; they won the first APFA championship with a 6–0–3 record. The team didn't allow a point in 13 games that season, including three exhibitions. The APFA became the National Football League in 1921, and Akron dropped out after the 1926 season.
Basketball   Akron had two teams in the National Basketball League, the Firestone Non-Skids and the Goodyear Wingfoots. The Non-Skids won championships in 1939 and 1940. Both teams folded

when the league merged with the Basketball Association of American to form the National Basketball Association in 1949.

Alabama International Speedway
See TALLADEGA SUPERSPEEDWAY.

Alamo Bowl
Football
Hardin-Simmons beat the University of Denver 20–0 on January 4, 1947, in the only Alamo Bowl, played in San Antonio, TX.

Albright, Tenley E. (1935–   )
Figure Skating
Born July 18, 1935, Boston, MA; Figure Skating Hall of Fame

Exceptional grace and virtually flawless skating won nine major singles championships for Albright, including six consecutive U.S. national titles, from 1951 through 1956. She won world championships in 1951 and 1953 and the Gold Medal at the 1956 Winter Olympics. Her greatest success, however, may have been her exhibition program, skated to music from Richard Strauss' *Der Rosenkavalier*.

Alcindor, Lew

See ABDUL-JABBAR, KAREEM.

Alexander, "Ol' Pete" Grover C. (1887–1950)
Baseball

Born February 26, 1887, Elba, NE; died November 4, 1950; Baseball Hall of Fame

Nearing the end of his career, Alexander was dozing in the St. Louis Cardinals' bullpen on October 10, 1926, when he was suddenly awakened and told to warm up. It was the seventh game of the World Series against the New York Yankees. The right-hander had already pitched and won two complete games, 6–2 and 10–2. After his victory in the sixth game the previous day, he had celebrated, thinking the World Series was over for him. But now, suffering from a hangover, he was suddenly brought in with the bases loaded and two outs in the seventh inning to pitch to the dangerous Tony Lazzeri. The Cardinals led 3–2.

Alexander struck out Lazzeri on four pitches. He retired the next five batters before walking Babe Ruth with two outs in the ninth. But Ruth was thrown out attempting to steal second, and the Cardinals won the Series. The strikeout of Lazzeri was the most dramatic moment in a brilliant but often troubled career.

Alexander won 28 games, a record for a rookie, with the Philadelphia Phillies in 1911, and he won 20 or more in each of next three seasons. But that was just the prologue to a remarkable three years. He had 30 or more victories each year from 1915 through 1917, with earned-run averages of 1.22, 1.55 and 1.83. Even more remarkable, he compiled those statistics for a team that played in cozy Baker Bowl, known as a hitter's park because of its small dimensions.

Alexander was drafted into the army shortly after being traded to the Chicago Cubs in 1918. When he returned, he had lost the hearing in one ear and suffered the first of several epileptic seizures, and he had become an alcoholic. Nevertheless, he had a few more fine seasons, leading the league in shutouts and earned-run average in both 1919 and 1920, when he won 27 games. He had a 22–12 record in 1923 and was 21–10 in 1927, after the Cubs had sent him to the Cardinals. But in 1929 he was suspended for drinking, and the following year he lost all three of his decisions with Philadelphia, his only losing season, and he retired.

Alexander ranks third in career victories with 373 against 208 losses, and his total of 90 shutouts is second only to Walter Johnson's. His lifetime earned-run average is 2.56.

Ali, Muhammad (Cassius Clay) (1942–   )
Boxing

Born January 27, 1942, Louisville, KY

As Cassius Clay, he became an American hero by beating a Russian fighter to win the light-heavyweight championship in the 1960 Olympic Games. Then he became known as the "Louisville Lip" for his braggadocio and prefight predictions, often in doggerel. Finally, as Muhammad Ali, heavyweight champion of the world and a Black Muslim who refused to be drafted, he became a symbol of a country polarized by the Vietnam War, an antiestablishment hero hated, and adored, by many.

Clay's fight against heavyweight champion Sonny Liston at Miami Beach on February 25, 1964, seemed to be a mismatch. Liston was big, strong, and ferocious; Clay was smaller, boyish-looking, and still relatively unproven, but he won the championship when Liston didn't come out of his corner for the seventh round, and he knocked out Liston in the first round of a rematch at Lewiston, ME on May 25, 1965.

When Clay became a Black Muslim, he changed his name to Muhammad Ali. He had been classified 1-Y in 1963 for failing the army's intelligence test, but was reclassified 1-A after standards were lowered in 1967. On April 1, 1967, he refused induction while black students picketed outside the courthouse. The World Boxing Association took away his title, the New York Athletic Association revoked his boxing license, and Ali was sentenced to five years in prison for draft evasion. But he was supported by a growing minority, including antiwar protesters and other black athletes.

Ali appealed, and his lawyers worked to get him a boxing license. Finally, the city of Atlanta granted him a license for a fight against a promising white boxer, Jerry Quarry. Ali won on a third-round knockout on October 26, 1970; the fight was watched by more than half a million people on closed-circuit television. A Manhattan district court judge ordered the New York Athletic Commission to restore Ali's license, and he fought heavyweight champion Joe Frazier on March 8, 1971, at Madison Square Garden. It was described by Arthur Daley of the *New York Times* as "a wildly exciting exhibition of primitive savagery," with both fighters landing many blows. Frazier knocked Ali down with a left hook in the 15th round and won a unanimous decision.

On June 29, 1971, the U.S. Supreme Court set aside Ali's conviction. In the meantime, he had won the North American Boxing Federation's heavyweight title by knocking out Jimmy Ellis in the 12th round on July 26, 1971. He lost it on a surprising 12th-round knockout by Ken Norton on March 31, 1973, but regained it on September 10 of that year with a 12-round decision over Norton. He also avenged his loss to Frazier by winning a 12-round decision on January 28, 1974. And then, at last, he fought once again for the world championship, against George Foreman, who had won the title from Frazier.

The match was staged October 30, 1974, in Kinshasa, Zaire, the first heavyweight championship fight ever held in Africa. Ali developed a new strategy that he called "rope–a–dope," leaning against the ropes with his gloves in front of his face. Foreman kept flailing at him with little effect, and eventually wore himself out. Ali knocked him out in the eighth round. He defended the title three times in 1975 before the celebrated "Thrilla in Manila" against Frazier on October 1; Ali knocked out Frazier in the 14th round.

He was becoming a national hero again. The war in Vietnam had ended, and was seen as a tragic mistake even by many of those who had once supported it. Ali was named Fighter of the Year in 1974 and shared the 1975 award with Frazier. He appeared on television's "Face the Nation." He lost the title to Leon Spinks on February 15, 1978, but regained it on September 15 by winning a 15-round decision. And he was praised by Illinois Senator Charles Percy as "the symbol of racial pride to millions of blacks in the heat of the civil rights movement" and "a hero to the thousands of young people during the tumultuous Sixties because of his stand against the Vietnam war."

In 1979, Ali announced his retirement. He made an ill-considered comeback attempt, losing two fights, and retired for good in 1981. In 61 professional fights, Ali had 56 victories, 37 of them by knockouts; he lost four decisions and was knocked out once.

Further Reading: Ali, Muhammad. *The Greatest: My Own Story.* New York: Random House, 1975.

All-American Bowl
Football

This December bowl game, played at Legion Field in Birmingham, AL was founded in 1977 as the Hall of Fame Classic. It was renamed the All-American Bowl in 1985.

Winners

1977 Maryland 17, Minnesota 7
1978 Texas A & M 28, Iowa State 12

1979 Missouri 24, South Carolina 14
1980 Arkansas 34, Tulane 15
1981 Mississippi State 10, Kansas 0
1982 Air Force 36, Vanderbilt 28
1983 West Virginia 20, Kentucky 16
1984 Kentucky 20, Wisconsin 19
1985 Georgia Tech 17, Michigan State 14
1986 Florida State 27, Indiana 13
1987 Virginia 22, Brigham Young 16
1988 Florida 14, Illinois 10
1989 Texas Tech 49, Duke 21

All-America Football Conference (AAFC)

Arch Ward, sports editor of the *Chicago Tribune*, conceived the idea of a new football league in 1944, when World War II was still going on. Ward lined up a number of wealthy investors, including actor Don Ameche, singer and movie star Bing Crosby, movie producer Louis B. Mayer, and former heavyweight boxing champion Gene Tunney.

The All-America Football Conference began operation in 1946. Many college stars had served in the war without signing contracts with NFL teams, and the AAFC signed a number of them, including All-American halfbacks Glenn Dobbs from Tulsa and Otto Graham from Northwestern, and All-American quarterback Frankie Albert from Stanford. There were eight AAFC franchises: Brooklyn Dodgers, Buffalo Bisons, Chicago Rockets, Cleveland Browns, Los Angeles Dons, Miami Seahawks, New York Yankees, and San Francisco 49ers. The Miami franchise lasted just one season, becoming the Baltimore Colts in 1947.

The Cleveland Browns dominated the league, winning all four AAFC titles. Spectator interest dwindled in most other AAFC cities. In 1950, the AAFC and NFL agreed to a merger but only Baltimore, Cleveland, and San Francisco moved into the NFL. The other five teams were disbanded, and their players were dispersed to other clubs in a special draft.

AAFC Championship Game

1946 Cleveland 14, New York 9
1947 Cleveland 14, New York 3
1948 Cleveland 49, Buffalo 7
1949 Cleveland 21, San Francisco 7

See also NATIONAL FOOTBALL LEAGUE.

All-American Futurity
Quarterhorse Racing

The richest horse race in the world until the Breeder's Cup races for Thoroughbreds were established in 1984, the All-American Futurity is run by quarterhorses at Ruidoso Downs in Ruidoso, NM. The race originated in 1959. The total purse is well over $1 million; entrants run a series of quarter-mile elimination trials, with the ten fastest horses going into the final.

All American Girls Professional Baseball League (AGPBL)

When the United States entered World War II, many team owners were afraid that professional baseball might be banned by the government as nonessential to the war effort. As a possible replacement, Philip K. Wrigley of the Chicago Cubs invested $250,000 in the All American Girls Professional Baseball League. Most of the women who showed up at Wrigley Field in the spring of 1943 to try out for the league had played organized softball. They were carefully screened. Athletic ability wasn't enough to ensure a job; a proper "feminine" appearance was also required, and the training program included practice by day and charm school at night. The uniform consisted of a dress, cut no more than 6 inches above the knee, worn over shorts, with wool knee socks, and specially designed baseball shoes. The league's priorities in attracting fans are shown by one of its posters: "Beautiful Girls Plus Appealing Costumes Plus Grade A Baseball."

The sport wasn't quite baseball. The ball itself was larger than a baseball but smaller than a softball; the baselines were 85 feet long, rather than 90 feet; the pitcher's rubber was 55 feet from home plate instead of 60 feet 6 inches, as in regulation baseball, and pitches had to be thrown underhand, as in softball. The league had four teams in small cities for its first season: Kenosha (WI) Comets; Racine (WI) Belles; Rockford (IL) Peaches; and South Bend (IN) Blue Sox. The AGPBL drew about 200,000 fans and was pronounced a success.

The long-term plan was to expand into other areas and larger cities. But after President Roosevelt declared that major-league baseball would continue during the war, the AGPBL was largely confined to smaller cities in the Upper Midwest. However, other teams were added: the Milwaukee Chicks and Minneapolis Millerettes played during the 1944 season and became the Grand Rapids Chicks and Fort Wayne Daisies in 1945; the Muskegon Lassies and Peoria Redwings were added in 1946; and the Chicago Coleens and Springfield Sallies played in 1948. In 1951, the Racine Belles moved to Battle Creek, and the Muskegon Lassies to Kalamazoo. The AGPBL played before nearly one million spectators in 1948, but then attendance began to decline, and the league folded after the 1954 season.

All-American Teams

Although the original college football All-American teams are inevitably associated with Walter Camp, the idea originated with Caspar W. Whitney, a good friend of Camp's and part owner of a magazine, *This Week's Sport.* Evidently Whitney asked Camp to help select the first two All-American teams, which appeared in the magazine in 1889 and 1890.

Whitney went to *Harper's Weekly,* which listed All-American teams under his name from 1891 through 1896. When he went on a world tour in 1897, Camp picked the team, but Whitney was back to name All-Americans for *Harper's* in 1898 and 1899. Meanwhile, Camp began selecting All-American teams for *Collier's* in 1898 and he continued through 1924. Whitney chose teams for *Outing* magazine from 1900 through 1909.

It has been suggested that Camp may have tried to steal credit for originating the All-American idea. When his 1898 selections were published in *Collier's,* Camp also listed the teams Whitney had picked from 1889 through 1896, without crediting Whitney. Camp later apologized, in print, for that oversight. But in 1900, he did exactly the same thing without apology. As time went on, the legend grew that Walter Camp had created and selected the first All-American teams. Yet Whitney lived until 1929, and there's no record that he ever complained about the Camp legend. Since they were friends, and since Camp was the leading authority on football in his time, it seems likely that he selected most of the teams that appeared under Whitney's name.

All-American teams began to proliferate in the 1920s. Major selectors today include the Associated Press, United Press International, *Football Weekly, Sporting News,* the Football Writers Association, and the American Football Coaches Association. In addition, All-Americans are selected in a wide variety of other collegiate sports, including some quasi-sports such as baton twirling.

See also ALL-PRO TEAMS.

All-Around Track and Field

A forerunner of the decathlon, the all-around comprised nine track and field events in a single day, compared with the decathlon's ten events over a two-day period. The events were the 100-yard dash, the mile run, the 880–yard walk, the 120-yard hurdles, the high jump, the broad jump, the hammer throw, the pole vault, and the 56–pound weight throw. The first U.S. national championship was held in 1884. The event was discontinued after 1976.

See also DECATHLON.

Allen, "Phog" Forrest C. (1885–1974)
Basketball

Born November 18, 1885, Jamesport, MO; died September 16, 1974; Basketball Hall of Fame

Allen played basketball at the University of Kansas under the game's inventor, James Naismith. Naismith called himself a teacher, saying that basketball couldn't be coached. Allen replied, "Well, you can coach them to pass at angles and run in curves." In his senior year, he got a chance to prove his point. In that 1908–09 season, he not only replaced Naismith at Kansas, he also coached Baker University and Haskell Indian Institute. The three teams combined to win 74 games while losing only 10.

After attending the Kansas College of Osteopathy, Allen returned to coaching at Warrensburg Teachers College (now Central Missouri State) from 1912 through 1919, then went back to the University of Kansas for 37 seasons (1919–56). Allen's 1923 and 1924 teams were named national champions by the Helms Athletic Foundation, and his 1952 team won the NCAA tournament. In 46 seasons of coaching, he had a 770–233 record, a .768 percentage. He ranks third all-time in wins.

Allen's players gave him his nickname because of his foghorn-like voice; why it was spelled "Phog" has never been explained.

When the rules committee in 1927 proposed limiting the dribble to only one bounce, Allen led a move to form the National Association of Basketball Coaches to lobby against the change, and he became the NABC's first president. He was also a driving force behind having basketball added to the Olympic Games program in 1936.

All-Pro Teams
Football

Professional football's equivalent of the All-American college football team began in 1931. All-Pro teams were chosen by the National Football League until 1943, when both the Associated Press and United Press began making selections. From 1946 through 1949, the AP All-Pro teams included players from both the NFL and the All-American Football Conference, while the UP selected separate All-NFL and All-AAFC teams. The AAFC also made its own official all-league selections.

When the American Football League was organized in 1960, All-AFL teams were chosen by player vote. In 1964, the player vote was discontinued, and the wire services selected All-AFL teams through 1969. With the AFL-NFL merger in 1970, creating the American and National Football Conferences, All-Conference teams were chosen by AP, UPI, and *Sporting News.*

In 1977, while UPI and *Sporting News* continued to name All-Conference teams, the Associated Press began selecting a single All-Pro team made up of players from both conferences. Since 1951, All-Pro teams have been made up of offensive and defensive units. In 1970, punters and placekickers were added to the teams.

All-Star Games

It was only fitting that Babe Ruth, near the end of his career, hit a home run in the third inning to drive in the winning run in the first all-star game of any kind. The game attracted 40,000 fans to Chicago's Comiskey Park on July 6, 1933. Connie Mack of the Philadelphia Athletics managed the American League team, and John McGraw, long-time manager of the New York Giants, came out of retirement to serve as National League manager.

Baseball's all-star game has been an annual event ever since, played near the midpoint of the season at a major-league park. There was no game in 1945 because of World War II. From 1958 through 1962, two games were scheduled annually to raise extra money for the players' pension fund. However, the second game in 1961 was canceled by rain. Since 1970, the game has been played at night for prime-time television exposure.

Other major sports have followed baseball's lead. The National Hockey League played a special, unofficial all-star game in early 1934 to benefit Ace Bailey, who had suffered a serious head injury late in 1933, but there was no annual game until 1947, when the NHL began playing one before the beginning of the season, matching the defending Stanley Cup champion against all-stars from other teams in the league. The NHL all-star game is now played in midseason between eastern and western division teams.

The National Basketball Association's first all-star game was played March 2, 1951, at Boston Garden between teams representing the eastern and western divisions. The game has become a major television spectacle, played on a Sunday afternoon in late January or early February.

At the urging of Arch Ward, sports editor of the *Chicago Tribune,* the National Football League in 1934 began the preseason college all-star game in Chicago's Soldier Field, between the defending NFL champion and a squad of college players, to benefit the newspaper's charity fund. The game was discontinued after 1976, largely because many college stars were unwilling to play, fearing injury that might jeopardize their careers before they even began. The NFL's first Pro Bowl game, between all-star teams from the eastern and western divisions, was played in 1951 at Memorial Coliseum in Los Angeles. Now teams representing the American and National Football Conferences play in the game, one week after the Super Bowl.

All-Star Tournament
Bowling

This invitational match-game tournament was first held on December 7, 1941, under the sponsorship of the *Chicago Tribune*. The Bowling Proprietors Association of America took it over in 1943 and merged it with its own match-game tournament, which in turn had grown out of the Petersen Tournament. The All-Star used the Petersen points system of scoring. Competitors bowled matches against one another, receiving one point for each game won, one point for each 50 pins scored, and a half-point for outscoring an opponent in a series while losing the majority of the games. In 1971, the tournament was replaced by the BPAA Open.

All-Terrain Vehicle Racing
See OFF-ROAD RACING.

Aloha Bowl
Football

This postseason bowl game originated in 1982 and is played in late December in Honolulu, Hawaii.

Results

1982	Washington 21, Maryland 20
1983	Penn State 13, Washington 10
1984	Southern Methodist 27, Notre Dame 20
1985	Alabama 24, Southern California 3
1986	Arizona 30, North Carolina 21
1987	UCLA 20, Florida 16
1988	Washington State 24, Houston 22
1989	Michigan State 33, Hawaii 13
1990	Syracuse 28, Arizona 0

Altoona, PA

Altoona briefly had a major-league baseball team in the 1884 Union Association. Owned by Henry V. Lucas, Association president, the team was backed by the Pennsylvania Railroad. It lasted only six weeks and was replaced by Kansas City.

Alworth, Lance (1940–   )
Football
Born August 3, 1940, Houston, TX; Pro Football Hall of Fame

In 1978, Alworth became the first American Football League player elected to the Pro Football Hall of Fame. Known as "Bambi" because of his graceful running style, he joined the San Diego Chargers out of the University of Arkansas in 1962 and was an All-AFL wide receiver from 1963 through 1969. He played with the Chargers in 1970, after they joined the NFL, then spent two seasons with the Dallas Cowboys. In his 11 professional seasons, Alworth caught a total of 542 passes for 10,266 yards and 85 touchdowns. He led the AFL in pass receptions three times, with 73 for 1,383 yards and 13 touchdowns in 1966, 68 for 1,312 yards and 10 touchdowns in 1968, and 64 for 1,003 yards and 4 touchdowns in 1969.

Amateur Athletic Foundation of Los Angeles

W. R. "Bill" Schroeder in 1936 persuaded Paul Helms to fund the Helms Athletic Association for a variety of purposes. One of the foundation's first projects was the World Trophy, to recognize the outstanding athlete of the year from each of the six continents, retroactive to 1896. Schroeder, managing director of the foundation, collected a large number of trophies and other sports memorabilia through the years, and in 1948 the foundation moved into its own building in Los Angeles to display the collection. It also had a sports library, and in 1949 it began establishing halls of fame for a number of sports.

The United Savings and Loan Association of California took over the foundation in 1970 and three years later merged with Citizens Savings; the organization then became known as the Citizens Savings Athletic Foundation. For some years, the foundation stagnated, but in 1985 it became the Amateur Athletic Foundation of Los Angeles, with funds given to Southern California from the proceeds of the 1984 Los Angeles Olympic Games.

Address: 2141 West Adams Boulevard, Los Angeles, CA 90018 (213) 730–9600

Amateur Athletic Union (AAU)

The original governing body for track and field sports in the United States, the National Association of Amateur Athletes of America, came under fire in 1884 for refusing to suspend runner Lon Myers of the Manhattan Athletic Club, despite evidence that he had violated the amateur code. The Myers case was the most visible of a number of conflicts over what constituted amateurism. The NYAC, the Athletic Club of the Schuylkill Navy, and a dozen other clubs in 1888 left the NAAAA to form the Amateur Athletic Union, which held its first meet that year in Detroit. The AAU adopted a rule that any athlete competing in an NAAAA event would be banned. The NAAAA was dissolved in 1889, and its members joined the AAU.

By 1898, the AAU had 45,000 active members in eight districts, and an allied membership of more than 250,000 in its affiliates, the League of American Wheelmen, the Intercollegiate Association of Amateur Athletes of America, the North American Gymnastics Union, and the Western Intercollegiate Athletic Association. At first, the AAU was concerned only with track and field sports, boxing, fencing, gymnastics, and wrestling. In 1895, however, the YMCA asked the AAU to take over amateur basketball, which was just four years old at the time. That began the organization's expansion into many amateur sports, most of which did not have their own governing bodies at the time, including water polo in 1906, handball in 1919, volleyball in 1925, weight lifting in 1928, ice hockey in 1930, and bobsledding in 1931.

As college sports grew in importance, the organization became embroiled in almost continuous battle with the National Collegiate Athletic Association over the control of amateur sports, especially track and field. After U.S. track and field athletes won only 8 of 27 events in the 1920 Olympics, the NCAA called for a reorganization of the American Olympic Committee, which was dominated by the AAU. The AOC became the American Olympic Association in 1921, with increased NCAA representation. Controversy arose again in 1923, when the AAU ruled that no U.S. athletes were to compete in Europe. Charles Paddock of the University of Southern California tied a world record in the 150–meter dash in a Paris meet, declaring, "the AAU hasn't any authority over members of the National Collegiate Athletic Association," and he was suspended until 1924.

Avery Brundage became president of the AAU in 1928 and declared at the annual meeting in 1929: "There is an uplift that comes from doing something for its own sake without thought of material reward. The amateur gets an exhilaration from the game well played that the professional who engages in sport as a means of livelihood never experiences." It was a point of view, typical of the AAU hierarchy, that was to create further controversy. But Brundage did work out a reconciliation with the NCAA in 1930, and peace reigned until the late 1950s.

The 1936 Olympic Games were to be held in Germany. When Hitler came to power in 1933 and Jews were thrown out of German sports clubs, the president of the American Jewish Congress protested to Brundage, who was also head of the AOA. The AAU voted in 1934 to delay accepting the German invitation to the Games. Judge Jeremiah T. Murphy,

who was strongly opposed to religious and racial discrimination, became AAU president in 1935 and called for a boycott of the Olympics. But on December 6 the AAU voted narrowly, 58¼ to 55¾, to accept the German invitation. Murphy resigned in protest and Brundage replaced him.

In 1937, the AAU expelled hockey teams sponsored by commercial rinks, on the grounds that they were professional. The teams responded by forming the Amateur Hockey Association and asking to be recognized by the Ligue Internationale de Hockey sur Glace (LIHG) as the national governing body for the sport. After a long battle, the LIHG ruled in 1946 that a national governing body could control no sports other than ice hockey, and replaced the multi-sport AAU with the AHA.

The AAU had taken two more Olympic sports, field handball and modern pentathlon, under its umbrella in 1939, and in 1943 it added synchronized swimming to the list. A major step toward developing young athletes was the AAU's first Junior Olympics in 1948, for boys and girls aged 10 to 15. The AAU was also involved in establishing the Pan-American Games, a kind of Olympics for the Western Hemisphere. Led by Brundage, AAU officials began discussing the possibility in 1937, but plans were delayed by World War II. When the first games were held in Buenos Aires, Argentina, in 1951, the AAU supplied $50,000 of the $200,000 needed to send the U.S. team.

The battle with the NCAA flared up again before the 1964 Olympics. General Douglas MacArthur acted as a mediator and worked out a truce, but the battle wasn't over. The NCAA backed a movement to develop sports-governing bodies that could take control away from the AAU. The first was the Amateur Basketball Association of the U.S.A., which was recognized as the national governing body for that sport in 1975. Later, the U.S. Gymnastics and Wrestling Federations were recognized by the International Olympic Committee.

Congress settled the dispute by passing the Amateur Sports Act of 1978. The act required that each Olympic sport have its own independent national governing body by November of 1980, and gave overall jurisdiction over those sports to the U.S. Olympic Committee. By the end of 1980, the AAU had lost most of its power. Its chief function now is conducting the Junior Olympics.

Address: Amateur Athletic Union, 3400 86th Street, Indianapolis, IN 46268 (317) 872–2900.

See also AMATEURISM; ATHLETIC CLUBS; NATIONAL ASSOCIATION OF AMATEUR ATHLETES OF AMERICA; NEW YORK ATHLETIC CLUB; SULLIVAN AWARD; THE

ATHLETICS CONGRESS; TRACK AND FIELD; U.S. OLYMPIC COMMITTEE.

Amateur Basketball Association of the U.S.A. (ABA-USA)

The ABA-USA was organized on October 28, 1975, as the national governing body for amateur basketball. It conducts national championship tournaments and selects individuals and teams to represent the United States in international competition, except for the Olympics and Pan-American Games; for those events, the ABA-USA recommends players to the U.S. Olympic Committee, which makes the final selection. There are eight active members of the ABA: the Amateur Athletic Union, the National Association of Basketball Coaches, the National Association of Intercollegiate Athletics, the National Collegiate Athletic Association, the National Federation of State High School Associations, the National Junior College Athletic Association, the U.S. Armed Forces, and the Women's Basketball Coaches Association.

Address: 1750 E. Boulder Street, Colorado Springs, CO 80909 (719) 632–7687

Amateur Golf Association of the U.S.

See U.S. GOLF ASSOCIATION.

Amateur Hockey Association of the U.S. (AHA-US)

Originally known simply as the Amateur Hockey Association, this organization created a crisis in the Olympic movement when it was organized in 1937 by rink-sponsored teams that had been expelled from the AAU. According to Avery Brundage, these teams "had become little more than farm teams for the professional league, and this led to the formation of the outlaw leagues, which had the effrontery to call themselves amateurs although they admittedly pay their players." The AHA petitioned the Ligue Internationale de Hockey sur Glace (LIHG), hockey's international governing body, for recognition as the national hockey federation for the United States, with support from Great Britain and Canada.

In 1946, the LIHG ruled that national governing bodies for the sport could rule only hockey, and no other sports, in their countries. The AAU, which governed many other sports, was therefore replaced by the AHA. However, the U.S. Olympic Committee, headed by Brundage, still recognized the AAU. Both organizations sent U.S. teams to the 1948 Winter Olympics in St. Moritz, Switzerland. The International Olympic Committee decided not to allow either team in the Olympic tournament, but the Swiss protested, and ultimately the AHA team was accepted. In 1950, it was decided that the 1952 Olympic team would be chosen jointly by a committee with four members from the AHA, four from the USOC, and two from the National Hockey League.

Address: 2997 Broadmoor Valley Road, Colorado Springs, CO 80906 (719) 576–4990

Amateur Skating Union of the U.S. (ASU)

The national governing body for speed skating in the United States was originally the American Skating Congress, founded in 1868. It was replaced by the National Amateur Skating Union in 1886. On February 3, 1907, the organization was merged with the International Skating Union of America (ISUA), which governed both speed skating and figure skating in the United States and Canada. However, the U.S. Figure Skating Association was established in 1921, and the Amateur Skating Association of Canada became a separate entity in 1927. The ISUA was then replaced by the Amateur Skating Union of the United States, which governs speed skating in that country.

Address: 1033 Shady Lane, Glen Elyn, IL 60137 (708) 790–3230

Amateur Softball Association of America (ASA)

Softball grew rapidly during the 1920s and 1930s, and virtually every state had its own version of the rules. In 1933, sportswriter Leo Fischer and sporting goods salesmen Michael J. Pauley got the idea of holding a national tournament as part of the Century of Progress Exposition in Chicago, and they standardized rules for tournament competition. Fifty-five teams entered, and more than 70,000 spectators saw the first round of action. As a result, the Amateur Softball Association of America was organized. The ASA now has more than 100 member state and metropolitan associations, representing more than 220,000 teams. It conducts national championships for men and women in fast-pitch, modified fast-pitch, and slow-pitch softball.

Address: 2801 NE 50th Street, Oklahoma City, OK 73111 (405) 424–5266

Amateur Sports Act

A long battle between the Amateur Athletic Union and the National Collegiate Athletic Association threatened to create havoc with U.S. Olympic teams, resulting in congressional action in 1978. Against AAU opposition, the Amateur Sports Act was passed and signed into law in October. The act made the

U.S. Olympic Committee the coordinating authority for all Olympic and Pan-American Games sports and required that each such sport have its own autonomous national governing body by November of 1980. At the time, the AAU was recognized as the international representative for the United States in eight sports, including track and field. The first autonomous body organized under the act was The Athletics Congress, formed in August 1979 to govern track and field.

Amateurism

Walter Camp, the "father of American football," wrote in 1893: "A gentleman never competes for money, directly or indirectly. Make no mistake about this. No matter how winding the road may be that eventually brings the sovereign into the pocket, it is the price of what should be dearer to you than anything else,—your honor." That was the reason behind the idea of amateurism, first in England and then in North America. It was created primarily as a class distinction and as a way for the middle and upper middle classes to exclude the lower classes from their sports. As Paul Weiss put it in *Sport: A Philosophic Inquiry*, "By and large the line between amateur and professional is mainly a line between the unpaid members of a privileged class and the paid members of an underprivileged class."

Amateur means "lover" in French, and the original amateurs were gentlemen who enjoyed watching boxing matches, without participating, in early 19th century England—although some of those amateurs might take boxing lessons and even do a little sparring. In England, the word came to mean one who took part in a sport for love rather than money, drawing on the Renaissance ideal of the well-rounded courtier who acquired a variety of skills without specializing in one.

As late as 1920, John B. Kelly of the United States was barred from rowing in the Henley Regatta because he was a bricklayer; the Henley regulations specifically stated that an oarsmen could not be considered an amateur if he "is or has been by trade or employment for wages, a mechanic, artisan or laborer." Rowing in the United States also developed a very strict view of amateurism under the leadership of the Schuylkill Navy in 1872, when half the applicants for a major regatta were rejected because they had bet on themselves to win at one time or another.

The New York Athletic Club, an early leader in track and field, in 1876 defined an amateur as "any person who has never competed in an open competition for public or admission money, or with professionals for a prize. . . ." Those who taught or coach sports "as a means of livelihood" were also proscribed.

The amateur ideal has never been particularly successful. Attempts to keep team sports "pure" were especially ineffective. The gentleman's baseball clubs gave way to professional teams by 1872. College football, while theoretically amateur, has been plagued with problems of recruiting, undercover payments, and special favors for star players ever since the sport began charging admission and drawing large crowds.

In 1904, Brown University president William Faunce said before the National Education Association, "We are living in a time when college athletics are honeycombed with falsehood, and when the professions of amateurism are usually hypocrisy." James Hogan, the Yale football captain that year, lived free of charge in a luxurious dorm, was given free meals and a scholarship of $100 a year, shared the profits from sales of the baseball team's scorecards, received a commission from the American Tobacco Company on each pack of cigarettes sold in New Haven, and was rewarded with a vacation in Cuba when the season ended.

Professionalism in basketball plagued YMCAs shortly after the game was invented in 1891, and in 1896 the YMCA asked the AAU to supervise the sport. The problem didn't go away immediately. Many athletes, especially basketball players, were given free room and board in YMCAs and some had their dues remitted. The Trenton YMCA team "graduated" into the National Basketball League in 1898–99 and won the league's first two championships. New York City's 23rd Street Branch YMCA went professional as the Wanderers, one of the first barnstorming teams. The Buffalo German YMCA won the championship at the St. Louis Olympic Games in 1904, when it was a demonstration sport involving only U.S. teams, and later traveled as far as Kansas City for games. The Germans eventually became openly professional and played until 1929.

Most of the best basketball teams of the 1930s and 1940s were industrial teams such as the Phillips Oilers, the Peoria Caterpillars, and even the Fibber McGee and Mollies, sponsored by the popular radio show. Companies recruited top college players and gave them jobs. The fact that an employee/player might spend a good part of his working day practicing basketball didn't seem to bother anyone. These teams were considered amateur and participated in the annual AAU tournament.

Baron Pierre de Coubertin, the founder of the modern Olympic movement, felt it should be for "pure amateurs." Coubertin, a Frenchman, had spent much time in England, and his ideals of amateurism and fair play were very British. But those ideals conflict with the Olympic motto, "Citius, Altius, Fortius." If athletes are to run faster, jump higher, and be stronger, they need to train, they need coaching, and they need periodic top-flight competition, which usually requires travel. The time involved makes it difficult to earn a living, and without earning a living an amateur athlete can't afford the travel and expenses involved. This was a dilemma for the Olympic sports as they sought to remain amateur.

Socially exclusive athletic clubs depended on top athletes to maintain club prestige and to help attract new members, so they bid for talent. The National Association of Amateur Athletes of America, the first governing body for track and field, was destroyed by the conflict and replaced by the Amateur Athletic Union. However, controversies over professionalism and eligibility continued, since the wealthier clubs controlled the AAU and could afford to offer more money for expenses and travel, as well as better facilities for the athlete.

During the early 20th century, more and more track and field athletes came out of colleges and were not affiliated with athletic clubs. Meets became more popular, and the clubs that sponsored them wanted the best athletes to compete in order to attract larger crowds. The result was "shamateurism." Athletes were given inflated sums as travel and expense money. When the AAU set limits on expense money, meet sponsors simply began making illegal, under-the-table payments to track and field stars. The practice continued for many years. Distance runner Bill Rodgers claimed to have made more than $100,000 a year while running as an amateur in the 1970s.

Shamateurism entered tennis during the 1920s for the same reasons. In its early years, tennis had been a sport for the elite, and the best players were true amateurs. But then the public playgrounds began producing top-notch players, facilities were built to hold larger crowds, attendance became a factor, and, as in track and field, promoters began to make secret payments to athletes to take part in tournaments.

Yet some athletes were punished for relatively minor offenses. Jim Thorpe, who won both the pentathlon and the decathlon in the 1912 Olympics, was stripped of his medals for having played semiprofessional baseball for a brief period. Charles Paddock, a sportswriter who was also a top-ranked sprinter, was suspended by the AAU several times for writing about meets in which he had taken part. Similarly, tennis great Bill Tilden, who wrote many newspaper and magazine articles, was suspended by the U.S. Lawn Tennis Association in 1928 for covering tournaments in which he played. But the U.S. ambassador to France intervened to have the suspension lifted because the French wanted Tilden to play in the Davis Cup rounds in their country.

After World War II, amateurism was in chaos because there was no international standard. The International Olympic Committee allowed individual sports-governing bodies to determine eligibility; they, in turn, usually passed responsibility on to national governing bodies. In some countries, especially British Commonwealth nations, athletes could be paid by the companies they worked for when they were training or competing. In Communist countries, athletes were usually subsidized by the government. In North America, many world-class amateur athletes were college students receiving full scholarships or grants-in-aid based solely on their athletic skills. Standards varied not only from country to country, but from sport to sport. Skiers in many countries, for example, were allowed to endorse products for large sums without losing their amateur standing.

In tennis, not an Olympic sport at the time, shamateurism gave way to open professionalism in the late 1960s, when pro tours became firmly established and the major national tournaments were opened to professional players. When tennis did become an Olympic event in 1988, professionals were allowed to compete. That followed a complete change in the Olympic movement, which virtually abandoned the amateur ideal, while still allowing individual nations to set their own standards. In North America, those standards were relaxed considerably. Both the United States and Canada established resident training centers in many sports, allowing athletes to live and train together, subsidized by private money.

The beginning of the end for amateurism on the international scene was Canada's decision in 1971 to withdraw from the annual world hockey championship tournament because players from the National Hockey League weren't allowed to represent the country. In 1977 the International Ice Hockey Federation gave in and declared NHL players eligible; Canada reentered the world championships and was also allowed to use professional players in the Winter Olympics. The final step toward dismantling the facade of amateurism came in 1989, when the International Olympic Committee announced that players from the National Basketball Association would be eligible to play in the 1992 Olympics.

See also AMATEUR ATHLETIC UNION; ATHLETIC CLUBS; NATIONAL ASSOCIATION OF AMATEUR ATHLETES OF AMERICA; NEW YORK ATHLETIC CLUB; OLYMPIC GAMES.

American Alliance for Health, Physical Education, Recreation and Dance (AAHPERD)

Founded by 49 physical educators and medical doctors as the American Association for the Advancement of Physical Education in 1885, the alliance has had several name changes. It became the American Physical Education Association in 1903 and the American Association for Health and Physical Education and Recreation in 1933. "Association" became "Alliance" in 1974, and "Dance" was added to the title in 1979.

The alliance has more than 30,000 members and is actually a group of six associations: Association for the Advancement of Health Education; American Association for Leisure and Recreation; Association for Research, Administration, Professional Councils and Societies; National Association for Girls and Women in Sport; National Association for Sport and Physical Education; and National Dance Association. The first five were originally committees, but they became separate associations with a major reorganization in 1974. The National Dance Association was formed in 1979.

Address: 1900 Association Drive, Reston, VA 22091
(703) 476–3400

American Amateur Baseball Congress (AABC)

Amateur baseball flourished in the late 1920s with the growth of town teams and company-sponsored teams. It remained popular even during the Great Depression. The American Baseball Congress was created to govern the sport on March 31, 1935, at a meeting in Chicago. The word "amateur" was added in 1955. The ABC held a national tournament for its 16 member teams in Dayton, OH in 1935, and it has been held annually ever since, except for a four-year hiatus during World War II. In 1954, the ABC added its Connie Mack division for ages 18 and under, with regional championships. A national championship, the Connie Mack World Series, was first played in 1959. Other age groups were added later: The Mickey Mantle division (16 and under) in 1968, the Pee Wee Reese division (12 and under) in 1970, the Sandy Koufax division (14 and under) in 1972, and the Willie Mays division (10 and under) in 1976. The original senior division became known as the Stan Musial division in 1963. Each has its own "world series," preceded by regional championships. The AABC has a membership of more than 7,000 teams throughout the country and in Puerto Rico.

Address: 118–19 Redfield Plaza, Marshall, MI 49068
(616) 781–2002

American Association Baseball

The first of several upstart baseball leagues to challenge the National League, the American Association was officially organized November 2, 1881, in Cincinnati and began playing in the 1882 season. Four of the original six cities in the association had once had teams in the National League. Philadelphia had been expelled for not completing its 1876 schedule, St. Louis and Louisville had dropped out in 1877, and Cincinnati had been thrown out after the 1880 season for playing Sunday games and allowing the sale of liquor at its park.

These cities still had independent professional teams. Talk of forming a new league began as early as 1880, and in 1881, Philadelphia manager Horace B. Phillips invited several teams to a meeting in Pittsburgh on October 10 to discuss the idea. Only three men showed up at the meeting, all of them from Cincinnati. They were Justin Thorner of the J. G. Sohn brewery, who had been president of the Cincinnati team when it was in the National League, and O. P. Caylor and Frank Wright of the Enquirer. (Phillips had been fired after the season and had lost interest in baseball.)

They met Denny McKnight, who had been president of Pittsburgh's Allegheny Baseball Club in the International Association of Professional Baseball Players. McKnight liked the idea of a new league, and several other teams were invited to the organizational meeting in Cincinnati. Brooklyn, Cincinnati, Louisville, Pittsburgh, and St. Louis were the original association members. Philadelphia joined soon after the organizational meeting. Brooklyn dropped out and was replaced by Baltimore shortly before the inaugural season.

From the typical spectator's standpoint, the association had three major advantages over the National League: A 25–cent admission price, compared to the National League's mandatory 50 cents; Sunday games were allowed; and alcoholic beverages could be sold in the ballparks—hardly surprising, since three of the six teams were backed at least in part by money from brewers, and Chris von der Ahe, the colorful owner of the St. Louis franchise, was a saloonkeeper.

The National League and some sportswriters derided the Association as "the beer and whiskey circuit," but its policies and the fact that its six cities actually had a larger total population than the National League's eight cities made it a success. The association developed some fine young stars, attracted a number of established National League players, and had a very successful 1882 season. Reportedly, five of its six teams drew more fans than Chicago, the National League's strongest franchise.

The brief war between the new league and the old permanently changed the structure of major league baseball. Before the 1883 season, the association added teams in New York City and Columbus, Ohio. In response, the National League dropped two of its smallest cities, Troy and Worcester, and added Philadelphia and New York, setting up head-to-head competition for the first time.

On February 17, 1883, the association, the National League, and the minor Northwestern League held a "harmony conference" in New York. They adopted the Tripartite Pact drafted by National League president A. G. Mills. Under the pact, each team was allowed to reserve 11 players, who were not to be signed by any other team; players who were released could not be signed by another team for ten days; and existing teams were granted exclusive rights to professional baseball in their cities. The association formally accepted the Tripartite Pact at its annual meeting on March 17. The pact was later renamed the National Agreement to allow other minor leagues to join.

For the 1884 season, the association expanded to 12 teams, adding Brooklyn, Indianapolis, Richmond, and Toledo. But it was a disastrous year because of competition from a third league, the Union Association, which lasted just that season. The smaller cities—Columbus, Indianapolis, Richmond, and Toledo—dropped out, and the Association was back to eight teams, concentrated in larger cities. In 1887, Pittsburgh was replaced by Cleveland; in 1888 New York City dropped out and Kansas City was added; in 1889, Cleveland left the association and Columbus rejoined.

The revolt of the Brotherhood of Professional Base Ball Players, which led to the formation of the Players League in 1890, was the beginning of the end for the American Association. To meet the competition, the National League took over two of the Association's strongest franchises, Brooklyn and Cincinnati. Two other cities, St. Louis and Baltimore, dropped out. The association started a new team in Brooklyn and added three smaller cities, Rochester, Syracuse, and Toledo. But the Brooklyn team, faced with competition from both the National League and the Players League, moved to Baltimore in midseason.

The Players League lasted only one season. Under a "peace plan" proposed by Allan W. Thurman of the association's Columbus team, the three leagues would merge into two leagues with eight teams each. This idea led to long negotiations over consolidation

of existing teams. When the dust finally settled, the association still had its teams in Philadelphia, Louisville, St. Louis, Baltimore, and Columbus, Cincinnati rejoined, and there were new teams in Boston and Washington. On paper, this looked like a good arrangement. But the Association had lost several stars who had jumped to the Players League and were now in the National League. And its Boston, Cincinnati, and Philadelphia franchises were in direct competition with the National League.

Because of the dispute over former association players now in the National League, the association withdrew from the National Agreement. The result was disastrous. National League teams raided the association for several more players. The association's Cincinnati franchise moved to Milwaukee in August, and Columbus, Louisville, and Boston were all facing serious financial problems. A peace conference in Indianapolis on December 15 marked the end of the American Association. Its Baltimore, Louisville, St. Louis, and Washington teams were absorbed by the National League, and the other Association owners were bought out.

See also NATIONAL AGREEMENT; PLAYERS LEAGUE; UNION ASSOCIATION.

American Association Champions		W	L	Manager
1882	Cincinnati	55	25	Pop Snyder
1883	Philadelphia	66	32	Lew Simmons
1884	New York	75	32	Jim Mutrie
1885	St. Louis	79	33	Charles Comiskey
1886	St. Louis	93	46	Charles Comiskey
1887	St. Louis	95	40	Charles Comiskey
1888	St. Louis	92	43	Charles Comiskey
1889	Brooklyn	93	44	Bill McGunnigle
1890	Louisville	88	44	Jack Chapman
1891	Boston	93	42	Arthur Irwin

American Automobile Association (AAA)
Auto Racing

Organized as the American Automobile Club in 1902, it was the governing and sanctioning body for automobile racing in the United States from 1902 through 1955, when the United States Auto Club was organized.

See also AUTO RACING; U.S. AUTO CLUB.

American Basketball Association (ABA)

The ABA was organized on February 2, 1967, and began play in the 1967–68 season. Its goal from the beginning was to force a merger with the established National Basketball Association within a few years. The original franchises were in Anaheim, Dallas,

Denver, Houston, Indiana, Kentucky, Minnesota, New Jersey, New Orleans, Oakland, and Pittsburgh. George Mikan, a former NBA great, was the ABA's commissioner; the association's trademark, a red, white, and blue ball was his idea. The new league borrowed the idea of a three-point shot from its short-lived predecessor, the American Basketball League. The ABA rule awarded three points for a shot taken from 25 feet or more.

The ABA aggressively went after some established NBA stars and college All-Americans. Rick Barry, the NBA's leading scorer in 1966–67, signed with Oakland but was forced to sit out a year when a court ruled that he had to honor the one-year option clause in his contract with the San Francisco Warriors. Mel Daniels, an All-American from the University of New Mexico, was the ABA's first draft choice; he signed with Minnesota.

The inevitable franchise shuffling took place after the ABA's first season. The Minnesota franchise moved to Miami, the Pittsburgh franchise moved to Minnesota, the New Jersey team moved to Long Island and became known as the New York Americans, and the Anaheim franchise went to Los Angeles. The league gained further respectability in 1968 by landing two successful NBA coaches, Bill Sharman and Alex Hannum.

The 1969–70 season was pivotal for the ABA in several respects. Jack Dolph, formerly of CBS, became commissioner and persuaded his former network to televise the ABA's all-star game and some of its playoff games. The league adopted a new policy of signing so-called "hardship" cases, college undergraduates who could demonstrate financial need. The immediate purpose was to sign University of Detroit sophomore Spencer Haywood, who had become well known by leading the United States Olympic team to victory in 1968. Again, there was some franchise shuffling: the Minnesota team moved back to Pittsburgh, the Oakland franchise moved to Washington, D.C., and the Houston team became the Carolina Cougars.

Merger talks between the ABA and NBA began early in 1970, and an agreement was reached. But on April 16 a federal court granted the NBA Players Association a restraining order on the grounds that the merger would violate antitrust laws. During the next several years, it sometimes seemed that there was more basketball action in the courts than on the court. Competition for players heated up before the 1970–71 season, accompanied by suits and countersuits. Haywood jumped to Seattle of the NBA, and the ABA's Denver team sued him for breach of contract. Milwaukee of the NBA then sued Seattle for damages because Haywood's college class hadn't

graduated, a violation of NBA bylaws. The NBA suspended Haywood, who sued the league; his case went all the way to the U.S. Supreme Court, which ruled that he had a right to play.

The ABA scored a major coup by signing three college All-Americans: Dan Issel of Kentucky, Rick Mount of Purdue, and Charlie Scott of North Carolina. Issel edged Rick Barry for the league scoring championship, and he and Scott shared the Rookie of the Year award. The ABA signed three more All-Americans for the 1971–72 season: Artis Gilmore of Jacksonville University, Jim McDaniels of Western Kentucky, and John Roche of South Carolina. Just as important were three undergraduates signed as hardship cases: Julius Erving from the University of Massachusetts, George McGinnis from the University of Indiana, and Johnny Neumann from the University of Mississippi.

For the first time, ABA and NBA teams played preseason exhibition games, but interleague play didn't signal the end of the battle. Three of the ABA's best players signed future contracts with NBA teams—McDaniels with Seattle, Scott with Phoenix, and Erving with Atlanta, and in March of 1972 the league filed a $6 million antitrust suit against the NBA.

The ABA won two major victories. Billy Cunningham of the Philadelphia 76ers had signed with the Carolina Cougars in 1972–73 and then attempted to renege on the deal, but was ordered by a court to honor his contract. The NBA refused to let Erving play for Atlanta, because he had been drafted by the Milwaukee Bucks, so he returned to his ABA team, the Virginia Squires. Meanwhile, congressional action to allow a merger was stalled, and the ABA's antitrust suit, now combined with the NBA Players Association suit, was still dragging on. ABA owners had expected a merger within four or five years, and time was running out for many of them in the league's fifth season. The Florida and Pittsburgh franchises folded in 1972, the financially troubled Carolina team moved to St. Louis in 1974, and in early 1975 the San Diego franchise was taken over by the league, to be disbanded at the end of the season.

In September of 1975 came the shocking announcement that two ABA teams, the New York Nets and the Denver Nuggets, had applied for membership in the NBA. The other seven remaining teams quickly followed suit, but the NBA refused to act on the applications. When the Utah franchise collapsed in December, the end of the ABA was in sight. The result was called a merger by the ABA, an expansion by the NBA. Four ABA teams—Denver, Indiana, New York, and San Antonio—joined the NBA at an admission price of $3.2 million apiece, and the New York Nets had to pay the Knickerbockers $4 million for entering the NBA team's territory. The three other ABA teams were disbanded, and their players were distributed in a special draft.

The NBA Players Association emerged as a major winner of the long conflict. Competition between the two leagues had driven the average player salary up from about $35,000 in the 1969–70 season to nearly $150,000 in 1975–76. The association received $5 million in damages from the NBA in exchange for dropping its antitrust suit. And players were also granted more freedom in negotiating contracts.

ABA Champions

1968	Pittsburgh
1969	Oakland
1970	Indiana
1971	Utah
1972	Indiana
1973	Indiana
1974	New York
1975	Kentucky
1976	New York

See also NATIONAL BASKETBALL ASSOCIATION.

American Basketball League (ABL)

There have been two American Basketball Leagues. The first, organized in 1926 by George Preston Marshall, was made up of existing professional teams that had been playing exhibition games. Marshall owned one of these teams, the Washington Palace Five. The Original Celtics, the outstanding team of the day, refused to join because they were making more money touring than they could by playing in the league. After being blacklisted by the ABL, however, the Celtics did enter the league during the 1926–27 season. They won 19 of 20 games to win the second-half title, and they easily won the 1927–28 ABL championship.

The Celtics' dominance hurt ABL attendance, and the league finally decided to break up the team. Three of the top players ended up with the Cleveland Rosenblums, who won almost as easily as the Celtics had, and the ABL suspended operations in 1929. In 1933, the league was revived and continued operating through the 1945–46 season, when the Basketball Association of America was organized.

The second ABL was the brainchild of Abe Saperstein, founder–owner of the Harlem Globetrotters. Saperstein's league had franchises in Chicago, Cleveland, Hawaii, Kansas City, Los Angeles, Pittsburgh, San Francisco, and Washington. The ABL introduced the idea of the three–point shot, taken from a distance of 30 feet or more from the basket. Saperstein was the ABL's commissioner and its only

major backer. Most of the teams faced financial problems from the very beginning. The Washington franchise moved to Long Island midway through the season, and the Los Angeles franchise folded. Cleveland won the 1961–62 championship. That was the only ABL championship. The league disbanded before completing its second season.

American Bowling Congress (ABC)

Bowling had an image problem in the 19th century because of its association with taverns and gambling. To counter the problem, the ABC was founded on September 9, 1895, at a meeting in New York City's Beethoven Hall. The original membership included 10 leagues, 60 teams, and 300 bowlers. One purpose was to standardize the rules of ten-pin bowling, but the ABC was also concerned with policing the sport to prevent gambling and the possibility of fixed matches. The organization's goal, it has been said, was to move bowling "out of the alley and into the lanes," and it achieved that goal by the early 20th century, when bowling became a sport for women as well as men, in clean, well-lighted, modern lanes. The first ABC tournament, in 1901, had total prize money of $1,592; 41 teams took part. By 1986, prize money totaled $1,857,710 and 10,019 teams entered the tournament, but the numbers declined to $1,511,205 and 7,480 teams in 1987. ABC membership has also dropped after a long period of growth. It reached a peak of 4,799,195 members in 1979–80, but that was down to 3,424,205 in 1986–87.

The annual tournament, held at a different site each year, lasts from early February until late May. There is no direct head-to-head competition. Teams and individuals roll their games on a specified day and wait until the tournament is over to learn whether they've won. Titles are awarded for teams, doubles, singles, and all-events, which is based on the bowler's total pin count in the three other events.

Address: 5301 S. 76th Street, Greendale, WI 53129 (414) 421–6400

See also BOWLING.

American Canoe Association (ACA)

The oldest national canoeing organization in the world, the ACA was founded on August 3, 1880, by 23 canoeists taking part in a National Canoe Congress at Lake George, NY. It oversees most canoe and kayak racing in the United States and selects competitors for international events, including the Olympic Games.

One of its major activities is the annual National Encampment, at which canoeists gather to camp, cruise, race, and exchange ideas. The encampment was held at various sites from 1880 through 1902. In 1901, the ACA bought Sugar Island near Gananoque, Ontario, and the encampment has been held there, with a few exceptions, since 1903.

Separate committees oversee different types of competition. The National Paddling Committee is responsible for flat-water racing, the National Sailing Committee for canoe sailing. Because of the growth of white-water racing in the early 1950s, the National Slalom Committee was formed in 1954. Now called the National Slalom and Wildwater Committee, it has jurisdiction over white-water racing in closed boats. A National Whitewater Open Canoe Committee was formed in 1975 to oversee white-water racing in open boats.

Address: P.O. Box 1190, Newington, VA 22122 (703) 550–7523

See also CANOEING AND KAYAKING.

American Collegiate Athletics

After a three-year study of sports programs in 130 colleges and universities, the Carnegie Foundation for the Advancement of Teaching released its report, *American Collegiate Athletics*, in 1929. The report documented a wide range of abuses. Virtually every major football school, it found, actively recruited athletes from high schools and offered them incentives, including academic scholarships for those who could meet the standards and make-work jobs, usually within the athletic department itself. (At the time, only the Southeastern and Southwest Conferences actually gave out athletic scholarships.)

In general, the report focused on the commercialization of college sports and urged that it be ended, or at least cut back. The rather weak conclusion was that college presidents ought to step in and make the necessary changes. Many critics pointed out that it's virtually impossible for the president of a college to change policies that have been approved, implicitly or explicitly, by its trustees or regents. The report had little effect. Indirectly, it probably helped spur an increase in intramurals, as colleges turned more attention to sports for students who don't have the ability to play on the intercollegiate level.

See also INTERCOLLEGIATE SPORTS; NATIONAL COLLEGIATE ATHLETIC ASSOCIATION.

American Eclipse
Horse Racing

The first widely known thoroughbred, sometimes identified simply as Eclipse, took part in the first major horse race in 1823, when Sir Henry was brought from the South to challenge him at the recently opened Union Race Course at Jamaica, Long Island.

The "race of the century" was held on Tuesday, May 27, before a crowd estimated from 50,000 to 100,000. Each side bet $20,000 on the race; bets among spectators were said to have totaled at least $250,000. Sir Henry won the first of three 4-mile heats in a world record time of 7 minutes 37 seconds. However, Eclipse won the second heat in 7:49 and the third in 8:24.

American Football League (AFL)

The first American Football League was created in 1926 by Charles C. "Cash and Carry" Pyle, Red Grange's agent-manager. After Grange's successful postseason tour with the Chicago Bears, Pyle hoped to get a National Football League (NFL) franchise in New York. But the New York Giants refused to waive their territorial rights, so Pyle set up a rival league. The Rock Island Independents moved from the NFL to the AFL and new teams were established in Boston, Brooklyn, Chicago, Cleveland, Los Angeles, Newark, New York, and Philadelphia. Grange was the AFL's chief attraction, but the AFL also signed some other well-known college stars, including Harry Stuldreher and Elmer Layden, two of the Four Horsemen of Notre Dame, who played for the Brooklyn Horsemen. The AFL folded after that one season, and Pyle's New York Yankees joined the NFL in 1927.

The second AFL began play in 1936 with teams in Boston, Brooklyn, Cleveland, New York, Pittsburgh, and Rochester. In 1937, Cincinnati and Los Angeles replaced Brooklyn and Cleveland, but Pittsburgh folded during the season and the AFL went out of business after playing an abbreviated schedule.

Yet another AFL began operating in 1940 with teams in Boston, Buffalo, Cincinnati, Columbus, Milwaukee, and New York. In its two years of existence, the league's only well-known player was Tom Harmon, a halfback for the New York Americans in 1941. The AFL blamed World War II for its demise, but it probably wouldn't have lasted much longer anyway.

Oil multimillionaire Lamar Hunt in 1959 attempted to buy the Chicago Cardinal franchise in order to move it to Dallas, and discovered that at least three other men had also tried to buy the team. When his offer was turned down, he contacted one of them, K. S. "Bud" Adams of Houston, to discuss the idea of forming a new professional league. The result was the fourth AFL. In addition to Hunt's Dallas Texans and Adams' Houston Oilers, the original teams were to be the Denver Broncos, Minnesota Vikings, Buffalo Bills, Boston Patriots, New York Titans, and Los Angeles Chargers.

The NFL responded by awarding Dallas a franchise and persuading Max Winter of Minnesota to put his team into the NFL instead of the AFL. The Oakland Raiders replaced Minnesota. One of the AFL's innovations was the optional two-point conversion used in college football. The league began play in 1960 and lost an estimated $3 million that season. The three teams competing head to head with the NFL, in Dallas, Los Angeles, and New York, were all in serious financial difficulty. The Chargers went to San Diego in 1961 and Hunt moved his team to Kansas City after the 1962 season, renaming it the Chiefs. In 1963, New York owner Harry Wismer went bankrupt.

The bidding war for players drove salaries up, straining team budgets in both leagues. But after the NFL signed an exclusive contract with CBS television in 1964, NBC decided to take a chance on the new league with a five-year, $36 million contract. In 1965, the AFL added its first expansion team, the Miami Dolphins, and the New York Jets won the biggest bidding war of all, for Alabama quarterback Joe Namath, who got a $225,000 bonus for signing a four-year contract at $25,000 a year.

The leagues formally announced a merger on June 8, 1966. They agreed to hold one college player draft and to play a championship game, which became known as the Super Bowl. The AFL was to pay $26 million for the privilege of joining the NFL, and NFL commissioner Pete Rozelle was to become commissioner of the new league. The actual merger didn't take place until 1970, when the AFL's television contract expired.

In 1968, the Cincinnati Bengals became the AFL's second, and last, expansion franchise. After the merger, the AFL became known as the American Football Conference. To help it gain parity in television audiences, three former NFL teams, Cleveland, Baltimore, and Pittsburgh, moved into the AFC. And parity on the field also arrived in 1970, when the New York Jets stunned the Baltimore Colts 16–7 in Super Bowl III.

AFL Championship Results

1960 Houston 24, Los Angeles 16
1961 Houston 10, San Diego 3
1962 Dallas 20, Houston 17
1963 San Diego 51, Boston 10
1964 Buffalo 20, San Diego 7
1965 Buffalo 23, San Diego 0
1966 Kansas City 31, Buffalo 7
1967 Oakland 40, Houston 7
1968 New York 27, Oakland 23
1969 Kansas City 17, Oakland 7

AFC Championship Results

1970 Baltimore 27, Cincinnati 17
1971 Miami 21, Baltimore 0
1972 Miami 21, Pittsburgh 17
1973 Miami 27, Oakland 10
1974 Pittsburgh 24, Oakland 13
1975 Pittsburgh 16, Oakland 10
1976 Oakland 24, Pittsburgh 7
1977 Denver 20, Oakland 17
1978 Pittsburgh 34, Houston 5
1979 Pittsburgh 27, Houston 13
1980 Oakland 34, San Diego 27
1981 Cincinnati 27, San Diego 7
1982 Miami 14, New York 0
1983 Los Angeles 30, Seattle 14
1984 Miami 45, Pittsburgh 28
1985 New England 31, Miami 14
1986 Denver 23, Cleveland 20
1987 Denver 38, Cleveland 33
1988 Cincinnati 21, Buffalo 10
1989 Denver 37, Cleveland 21
1990 Buffalo 51, Los Angeles 3

See also NATIONAL FOOTBALL LEAGUE; SUPER BOWL.

American Indians
See NATIVE AMERICAN SPORTS.

American Indoor Soccer Association

This professional indoor soccer league began play in the fall of 1984 with six teams: Canton Invaders, Chicago Vultures, Columbus Capitals, Kalamazoo Kangaroos, Louisville Thunder, Milwaukee Wave. Canton, Chicago, and Milwaukee are still in the league, along with the Dayton Dynamo, Ft. Wayne Flames, Hershey Impact, and Memphis Storm.

Address: 229 Third Street, N..W. Canton, OH 44702 (216) 455–4625

American Jockey Club

Wall Street broker Leonard W. Jerome and banker August Belmont led the formation of the American Jockey Club in 1863 to build Jerome Park in Westchester County, NY. It opened in 1866. Because Jerome and Belmont belonged to top New York society, the club and its park brought many wealthy men into horse racing as breeders, owners, and aficionados, among them Marshall Field, W. Averill Harriman, Pierre Lorillard, William R. Travers, and William C. Whitney. The club went out of existence after Jerome Park was closed in 1888.

American Lacrosse League

This short-lived attempt to establish lacrosse as a professional sport in the United States began in December 1987 with teams in Baltimore, Boston, Denver, Long Island, New Jersey, and Syracuse. Average attendance was only about 2,000 per game, and the league folded because of financial problems in July 1988.

American Lawn Croquet
See CROQUET.

American League (AL)
Baseball

The National League was challenged by four other leagues in its first 25 years of existence. Only one of them, the American Association, lasted for any time. But the American League, which formally claimed major league status in 1901, won a brief war largely because of the leadership and persistence of Byron Bancroft "Ban" Johnson. In 1894 Johnson became president of the Western League, a reorganized version of the minor Northwestern League. The league had teams in Detroit, Grand Rapids, Indianapolis, Kansas City, Milwaukee, Minneapolis, Sioux City, and Toledo. Johnson persuaded Charles Comiskey to buy the Sioux City franchise in 1895 and move it to St. Paul. The Western League did well, and in October 1899 Johnson made his first move toward major league status. The name was changed to the American League, the Grand Rapids franchise moved to Detroit, Comiskey moved his team to Chicago, and a new team was established in Cleveland.

The timing was excellent. National League owners were worried about an attempt to revive the old American Association. The formation in 1900 of a union, the Protective Association of American Baseball Players, further distracted attention from the American League's threat. Johnson's next move came in December 1900, with a decision to expand into the East. This time, the National League was alerted, and struck back by awarding minor-league franchises to Kansas City and Minneapolis. That only helped Johnson. He abandoned Minneapolis, Kansas City, and Indianapolis, establishing new teams in Baltimore, Boston, Philadelphia, and Washington.

The American League quickly leaped ahead of the National in attendance, growing from 1,683,584 in 1901 to 2,206,457 in 1902, while the National League's attendance declined from 1,920,031 to 1,683,012. One reason for the its success was Johnson's strong backing of his umpires, eliminating the rowdyism that plagued the National League and alienated many fans. But when Johnson suspended Baltimore manager John McGraw indefinitely for fighting with umpires, McGraw and John T. Brush, owner of the Cincinnati National League team, gained control of the Baltimore franchise and sold it to the New York Giants. McGraw went to the Giants as manager, taking four of Baltimore's top players, and two other players went to Cincinnati. Johnson put Wilbert Robinson in charge of what was left of the Baltimore team, then moved it to New York in 1903.

On January 9, 1903, the National League accepted the American as a major league. A new National Agreement was signed by both major leagues and by the National Association of Professional Baseball Leagues, representing the minors. The first World Series was played that year, with the AL's Boston team beating the Pittsburgh Pirates. There was no World Series in 1904, because John McGraw, still angry at Johnson, refused to allow his Giants to play Boston. In 1905, the two leagues formally agreed that the World Series would become an annual event.

Johnson's strong control over the league he had created began to weaken in 1919, when he ruled that pitcher Jack Quinn belonged to the New York Yankees, not Charles Comiskey's Chicago White Sox. Comiskey, his long-time friend, became an enemy. Later that year, Johnson suspended pitcher Carl Mays, who had been traded from Boston to New York after having left the Boston team for two weeks. The Yankees got a temporary injunction allowing Mays to play, and Yankee co-owner Jake Ruppert called a meeting of the league's five-member executive committee, of which he, Comiskey, and Boston owner Harry Frazee, also a Johnson opponent, were members. The committee reinstated Mays. In October of 1919, the temporary injunction became permanent, and Judge Robert Wagner ruled that Johnson couldn't suspend a player, because it interfered with the contract between player and team. At the league meeting in February of 1920, Johnson was stripped of most of his powers.

But he still had the support of five club owners, who joined him in a fight against a proposed new government for baseball. The National Commission was then made up of the two league presidents and a third person, who served as chairman. Under a proposal by Albert D. Lasker, a new National Commission would be made up of three men not financially involved in baseball. The eight National League owners and the three anti-Johnson American League owners met on October 18, agreed on the Lasker plan, and said that if the other five American League owners didn't agree to it, they would form an 11-team National League. Johnson and his backers were forced to give in.

Ultimately, Judge Kenesaw Mountain Landis was named the commissioner of baseball, with no associate commissioners. He was given virtually absolute powers to police baseball, which he soon exercised by banning the eight "Black Sox" players who had been acquitted by a jury of charges that they had conspired to fix the 1919 World Series. Johnson hung on as president of the American League until 1927, then resigned.

The American League had become clearly dominant by 1910. Beginning in that year, the AL won 35 of 55 World Series, largely because of the New York Yankees, who won 17 of them. The AL also won 12 of the first 17 all-star games, beginning in 1933. However, the balance of power began to shift during the 1950s, at least in part because AL teams were much slower to sign black players than were NL teams.

The league remained unchanged from 1903 until 1954, when the St. Louis Browns moved to Baltimore and became the Orioles. In 1955 the Philadelphia Athletics moved to Kansas City. Expansion began in 1961, when the Washington Senators became the Minnesota Twins and were replaced in Washington by a new franchise. The Los Angeles Angels, now the California Angels, also joined the league that season.

The league grew to 12 teams in 1969, when the Athletics moved again, this time to Oakland. They were replaced by the Kansas City Royals, and Seattle was also given a franchise. Both the American League and the National League split into two divisions that season and began playing postseason league championship series between the division champions to determine the pennant winner. The series was five games until 1985, when it became a best-of-seven series, like the World Series. Seattle's troubled franchise lasted just a year, moving to Milwaukee in 1970. The most recent expansion was in 1977, when the Seattle Mariners and Toronto Blue Jays joined the American League.

Pennant Winners		W	L	Managers
1901	Chicago	83	53	Clark Griffith
1902	Philadelphia	83	53	Connie Mack
1903	Boston	91	47	Jimmy Collins
1904	Boston	95	59	Jimmy Collins
1905	Philadelphia	92	56	Connie Mack
1906	Chicago	93	58	Fielder Jones
1907	Detroit	92	58	Hughie Jennings
1908	Detroit	90	63	Hughie Jennings
1909	Detroit	98	54	Hughie Jennings
1910	Philadelphia	102	48	Connie Mack
1911	Philadelphia	101	50	Connie Mack
1912	Boston	105	47	Jake Stahl
1913	Philadelphia	96	57	Connie Mack
1914	Philadelphia	99	53	Connie Mack
1915	Boston	101	50	Bill Carrigan
1916	Boston	91	63	Bill Carrigan
1917	Chicago	100	54	Pants Rowland
1918	Boston	75	51	Ed Barrow
1919	Chicago	88	52	Kid Gleeson
1920	Cleveland	98	56	Tris Speaker
1921	New York	98	55	Miller Huggins
1922	New York	94	60	Miller Huggins
1923	New York	98	54	Miller Huggins
1924	Washington	92	62	Bucky Harris
1925	Washington	96	55	Bucky Harris
1926	New York	91	63	Miller Huggins
1927	New York	110	44	Miller Huggins
1928	New York	101	53	Miller Huggins
1929	Philadelphia	104	46	Connie Mack
1930	Philadelphia	102	52	Connie Mack
1931	Philadelphia	107	45	Connie Mack
1932	New York	107	47	Joe McCarthy
1933	Washington	99	53	Joe Cronin
1934	Detroit	101	53	Mickey Cochrane
1935	Detroit	93	58	Mickey Cochrane
1936	New York	102	51	Joe McCarthy
1937	New York	102	52	Joe McCarthy
1938	New York	99	53	Joe McCarthy
1939	New York	106	45	Joe McCarthy
1940	Detroit	90	64	Del Baker
1941	New York	101	53	Joe McCarthy
1942	New York	103	51	Joe McCarthy
1943	New York	98	56	Joe McCarthy
1944	St. Louis	89	65	Luke Sewell
1945	Detroit	88	65	Steve O'Neill
1946	Boston	104	50	Joe Cronin
1947	New York	97	57	Bucky Harris
1948	Cleveland	97	58	Lou Boudreau
1949	New York	97	57	Casey Stengel
1950	New York	98	56	Casey Stengel
1951	New York	98	56	Casey Stengel
1952	New York	95	59	Casey Stengel
1953	New York	99	52	Casey Stengel
1954	Cleveland	111	43	Al Lopez
1955	New York	96	58	Casey Stengel
1956	New York	97	57	Casey Stengel
1957	New York	98	56	Casey Stengel
1958	New York	92	62	Casey Stengel
1959	Chicago	94	60	Al Lopez
1960	New York	97	57	Casey Stengel
1961	New York	109	53	Ralph Houk
1962	New York	96	66	Ralph Houk
1963	New York	104	57	Ralph Houk
1964	New York	99	63	Yogi Berra
1965	Minnesota	102	60	Sam Mele
1966	Baltimore	97	63	Hank Bauer
1967	Boston	92	70	Dick Williams
1968	Detroit	103	59	Mayo Smith

Eastern Division Champions

1969	Baltimore	109	53	Earl Weaver
1970	Baltimore	108	54	Earl Weaver
1971	Baltimore	101	57	Earl Weaver
1972	Detroit	86	70	Billy Martin
1973	Baltimore	97	65	Earl Weaver
1974	Baltimore	91	71	Earl Weaver

1975	Boston	95	65	Darrell Johnson
1976	New York	97	62	Billy Martin
1977	New York	100	62	Billy Martin
1978	New York	100	63	Bob Lemon
1979	Baltimore	102	57	Earl Weaver
1980	New York	103	59	Dick Howser
1981	New York	34	22	Gene Michael (first half)
	Milwaukee	31	22	Buck Rodgers (second half)

(New York won divisional playoff)

1982	Milwaukee	95	67	Harvey Kuenn
1983	Baltimore	98	64	Joe Altobelli
1984	Detroit	104	58	Sparky Anderson
1985	Toronto	99	62	Bobby Cox
1986	Boston	95	66	John McNamara
1987	Detroit	98	64	Sparky Anderson
1988	Boston	89	73	Joe Morgan
1989	Toronto	89	73	Cito Gaston
1990	Boston	88	74	Joe Morgan

Western Division Champions

1969	Minnesota	97	65	Billy Martin
1970	Minnesota	98	64	Billy Martin
1971	Oakland	101	60	Dick Williams
1972	Oakland	93	62	Dick Williams
1973	Oakland	94	68	Dick Williams
1974	Oakland	90	72	Alvin Dark
1975	Oakland	98	64	Alvin Dark
1976	Kansas City	90	72	Whitey Herzog
1977	Kansas City	102	60	Whitey Herzog
1978	Kansas City	92	70	Whitey Herzog
1979	California	88	74	Jim Fregosi
1980	Kansas City	97	65	Jim Frey
1981	Oakland	37	23	Billy Martin (first half)
	Kansas City	30	23	Dick Howser (second half)

(Oakland won divisional playoff)

1982	California	93	69	Gene Mauch
1983	Chicago	99	63	Tony LaRussa
1984	Kansas City	84	78	Dick Howser
1985	Kansas City	91	71	Dick Howser
1986	California	92	70	Gene Mauch
1987	Minnesota	85	77	Tom Kelly
1988	Oakland	104	58	Tony LaRussa
1989	Oakland	99	63	Tony LaRussa
1990	Oakland	103	59	Tony LaRussa

League Championship Series Winners

1969	Baltimore
1970	Baltimore
1971	Baltimore
1972	Oakland
1973	Oakland
1974	Oakland
1975	Boston
1976	New York
1977	New York
1978	New York
1979	Baltimore
1980	Kansas City
1981	New York
1982	Milwaukee
1983	Baltimore
1984	Detroit
1985	Kansas City
1986	Boston
1987	Minnesota
1988	Oakland
1989	Oakland
1990	Oakland

Addresses: American League, 350 Park Avenue, New York, NY 10022 (212) 371–7600

Baltimore Orioles, Memorial Stadium, Baltimore, MD 21218 (301) 243–9800

Boston Red Sox, 4 Yawkey Way, Boston, MA 02215 (617) 267–9440

California Angels, P.O. Box 2000, Anaheim, CA 92803 (714) 937–6700

Chicago White Sox, 324 West 35th Street, Chicago, IL 60616 (312) 924–1100

Cleveland Indians, Cleveland Stadium, Cleveland, OH 44114 (216) 861–1200

Detroit Tigers, Tiger Stadium, Detroit, MI 48216 (313) 962–4000

Kansas City Royals, P. O. Box 419969, Kansas City, MO 64141 (816) 921–2200

Milwaukee Brewers, County Stadium, 201 South 46th Street, Milwaukee, WI 53214 (414) 933–4114

Minnesota Twins, 501 Chicago Avenue South, Minneapolis, MN 55415 (612) 375–1366

New York Yankees, Yankee Stadium, Bronx, NY 10451 (212) 293–4300

Oakland Athletics, Oakland Alameda County Coliseum, Oakland, CA 94621 (415) 638–4900

Seattle Mariners, P.O. Box 4100, Seattle, WA 98104 (206) 628–3555

Texas Rangers, P.O. Box 1111, 1250 Copeland Street, Arlington, TX 76010 (817) 273–5206

Toronto Blue Jays, 300 The Esplanade West, Suite 3200, Toronto, Ontario, Canada M5V 3B3 (416) 341–1000

See also NATIONAL AGREEMENT; NATIONAL LEAGUE; WORLD SERIES.

American Legion Baseball

H. L. Chaillaux of Indianapolis started the first American Legion Junior League, for players 17 and younger. American Legion baseball is now played nationwide, and more than 3,800 local posts sponsor teams, with a total of about 75,000 players. Regional and district playoffs lead to the Junior Legion World Series, which determines the national champion.

Address: P.O. Box 1055, Indianapolis, IN 46206 (317) 635–8411

American Olympic Committee

See U.S. OLYMPIC COMMITTEE.

American Physical Education Association (APEA)

See AMERICAN ALLIANCE FOR HEALTH, PHYSICAL EDUCATION, RECREATION AND DANCE.

American Power Boat Association (APBA)

Informal powerboat racing began on Long Island Sound about 1900, but virtually every boat was unique, so there was a need for ratings and time allowances to equalize competition. The American Power Boat Association, founded on April 22, 1903, drew up rather sketchy rules that led to frequent disputes, so the association formed a racing commission in 1913 to study the problem. The commission established five categories of competition: cruisers, express cruisers, open boats, displacement racers, and hydroplanes.

Within ten years, many new types of boats were on the water, and on October 25, 1923, the APBA adopted the rules of the Mississippi Valley Power Boat Association, establishing classes based on engine displacement for hydroplanes and runabouts. The following year, four classifications were added for outboards. The APBA now sanctions more than 400 races for more than 200 member clubs and more than 8,000 individual members, although the races are actually conducted by individual clubs.

The APBA is organized into 18 geographical regions, each with its own chairperson, and recognizes nine major categories of racing: unlimited hydroplane, offshore, inboard, drag racing, sportsman, outboard performance, stock outboard craft, modified outboard, and professional outboard. There's also a special-events category for unusual craft, such as inflatable boats. The APBA has joint operating agreements with the national boating federations of Canada and Mexico, allowing drivers licensed in one of the countries to compete in another. The

three groups also conduct annual North American championships.

Address: P.O. Box 377, 17640 E. Nine Mile Road, E. Detroit, MI 48021 (313) 773–9700

See also POWERBOAT RACING.

American Professional Football Association

See NATIONAL FOOTBALL LEAGUE.

American Professional Slo-Pitch League (APSPL)

Organized in 1977, the APSPL had 12 teams, each playing 56 games. There were three divisions: East, Central, and Midwest. The Detroit Caesars won the 1977 championship, beating the Baltimore Monuments in the playoff final, and they repeated in 1978 by defeating the Minnesota Norsemen. The Milwaukee Schlitz beat the Caesars for the championship in 1979, the league's last season.

American Skating Congress (ASC)

See AMATEUR SKATING UNION OF THE U.S.

American Soccer League (ASL)

A low-budget, low-profile operation, the ASL began play on April 8, 1988, with ten teams: Ft. Lauderdale, Miami, Orlando, Tampa, and Washington in the southern division and Albany, Baltimore, Boston, Fairfax, VA, and Paterson, NJ, in the northern division. Each team was allowed only three foreign players on its 18-player roster. The team salary limit for all players was only $50,000, or about $2,800 per player, for a 20-game season. In 1989, the league limited teams to two foreign players.

Address: 10620 Guilford Road, Jessup, MD 20794 (301) 498–4990

American Stud Book

Colonel Saunders D. Bruce published the first American Stud Book in 1868. Each major racing country has its own stud book, which lists the pedigree of every Thoroughbred horse born in the country, and only horses listed in the stud book can run as Thoroughbreds in sanctioned races. A horse is listed only if its sire and dam were both Thoroughbreds. In 1896, the Jockey Club took over the American Stud Book.

See also JOCKEY CLUB.

American Swimming Coaches Association (ASCA)

A small group of coaches founded the ASCA in 1958, at the Amateur Athletic Union's short-course national swimming championships in Dallas, TX. There are now more than 3,000 members from every level of coaching. The association offers a variety of educational programs and, since 1985, has conducted a coaches' certification program with five levels. With funding from the National Swimming Foundation, the ASCA also provides managerial and coaching assistance to new and emerging clubs. The association maintains a hall of fame, presents several awards, including Coach of the Year, and it offers a placement service for members.

Address: One Hall of Fame Drive, Ft. Lauderdale, FL 33316 (305) 462–6267

American Tennis Association (ATA)

Because they were barred from membership in the U.S. Lawn Tennis Association, black players organized the ATA on November 30, 1916, at a meeting in Washington, D.C. Its first national championship tournament was held in August of 1917. There were three events: men's singles, women's singles, and men's doubles. Women's doubles, mixed doubles, and juniors and seniors championships were added later. In 1950, ATA representatives met with the USLTA to urge the acceptance of qualified black players. As a result, Althea Gibson was allowed to play in the U.S. National Clay Court Championship that year, and in 1951 she played at Wimbledon.

In addition to its own national championships, the ATA conducts a spring-summer circuit of tournaments, primarily in the Northeast, although Norfolk, Memphis, New Orleans, and Los Angeles are also stops. The association in 1988 began a fund raising drive to build a permanent headquarters and national training center.

Address: P.O. Box 3277, Silver Spring, MD 20901 (301) 681–4832.

American Turf Register and Sporting Magazine

Largely because of John Stuart Skinner, its editor from 1829 to 1836, the *American Turf Register* pioneered in supporting outdoor sports and recreation as healthy practices. Skinner had previously edited *American Farmer* magazine, which strongly backed horse racing and harness racing as ways of improving stock. Partly because of its editorials, harness racing became a staple at many agricultural fairs during the 19th century. In 1839, Henry William Herbert, writing as Frank Forester, began a series of poetic articles on hunting and fishing for *American Turf Register* that did a great deal to popularize those

recreational sports. The magazine went out of business in 1845.

American Turners

See TURNER MOVEMENT.

American Youth Soccer Organization (AYSO)

Established in 1964 as a local organization with nine teams in Torrance, CA, the AYSO grew rapidly. It now has more than 325,000 players, boys and girls, ages 5 to 18, in more than 20,000 leagues in 36 states. The AYSO motto is "Everyone Plays," because one of its rules is that every player has to play at least half of every game. It also requires sanctioned organizations to distribute experienced and inexperienced players equally in order to ensure well-balanced teams.

Address: P.O. Box 5045, Hawthorne, CA 90251 (213) 643–6455

America's Cup
Yachting

The oldest international trophy in sports is a silver ewer that stands 2 feet 3 inches high and weighs 8 pounds 6 ounces. It originated as the Hundred Guinea Cup, commissioned by the Royal Yacht Club in 1851 at a cost of about $510 as the prize for a 58-mile race around the Isle of Wight. The British had invited Americans to enter a yacht in a regatta to be held in conjunction with the 1851 World's Fair. In response, John Cox Stevens, Commodore of the New York Yacht Club, put together a syndicate of six men to finance a new racing schooner.

Designed by George Steers, *America* cost $30,000. Launched on May 3, 1851, the ship sailed from New York on June 21 and arrived at Le Havre, France, on July 10 to be repainted and fitted with racing sails. On August 1, it arrived in Cowes, England, and Stevens issued a challenge to any British vessel that wanted to race. There were no takers, partly because of the ship's unique design. *America* boasted a sharp clipper bow and raked masts, and it was equipped with cotton racing sails, which were much more efficient than the baggy flax sails used by British sailships of the era.

Stevens decided to enter *America* in the Isle of Wight race against 17 British vessels. The race began at 10 A.M. on August 22. *America* finished at 8:37 P.M., 18 minutes ahead of its closest competitor. The syndicate sold *America* for $25,000 and returned to New York with the cup. In 1857 they gave it to the NYYC, with a deed of gift specifying that it was to be offered as a trophy to be challenged for by any foreign yacht club. The first challenge came in 1868 from England's James Ashbury. He offered to race his schooner *Cambria* against any American vessel. But the NYYC replied that the race would be conducted just as the Isle of Wight race had been—a single challenger against an entire fleet. The first America's Cup race took place on August 8, 1870, in Lower New York Bay, *Cambria* versus 14 U.S. yachts. The schooner *Magic* won, and *Cambria* finished eighth.

The race format has changed several times. It was a four-out-of-seven series in 1871, when Ashbury challenged again with *Livonia*, and a single U.S. yacht sailed each race, but the NYYC reserved the right to change vessels. *Columbia* won the first two races handily, but lost the third after her steering gear was broken. *Sappho* then beat *Livonia* in the next two races. The format was two out of three from 1876 through 1887, three out of five from 1893 through 1903, and four out of seven from 1930 to 1987. There were no limitations on the type of vessel until 1927, when the yachts were Universal Rule J Class boats. After World War II, J-boats were replaced by the smaller 12-meter yachts. Races were held in the open sea for the first time in 1893 and they moved to Newport, RI in 1927.

Several controversies have marred cup challenges through the years. The first arose in 1895, when the Earl of Dunraven's *Valkyrie III* was disqualified after apparently winning the second race. Dunraven then deliberately defaulted in the third race and charged the NYYC with with irregularities in ballasting. His protest was disallowed, and he was stripped of his honorary NYYC membership. In 1934, T. O. M. Sopwith of England won the first two races and narrowly lost the third. He had his protest flag flying after losing the fourth race, but the protest was disallowed by the NYYC because he hadn't raised the flag immediately after the alleged violation. The incident led a British writer to comment, "Britannia rules the waves, but America waives the rules."

America's *Intrepid* and Australia's *Gretel II* collided shortly after the start of their second race in 1967. *Gretel* crossed the finish line first, but was disqualified and the race was awarded to *Intrepid*. Telegrams, phone calls, and letters poured in from Americans who felt the NYYC was being unfair to the visitors, and an Australian legislator demanded that the country recall its ambassador to protest. *Intrepid* won the series, four races to one. The next controversy also involved Australia, but this time the NYYC did the protesting. The 1983 challenger, *Australia II*, was unique. It was the smallest yacht ever to compete for the cup. The secret was a bulging keel fitted with fins, which increased its speed and made it exceptionally maneuverable. The NYYC asked

The yacht America is portrayed shortly after her launching in 1851 in this Currier & Ives drawing.

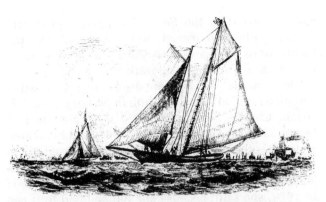

The America's Cup was originally the Hundred-Guinea Cup, won by America in an 1851 race against the Royal Yacht Squadron. The race was depicted some years later by Currier & Ives.

the International Yacht Racing Union to change Australia's rating, which would have resulted in either disqualification or a penalty, but the IYRU declined to intervene. After being behind, three races to one, the challenger won the final three races, and the longest winning streak in sports history, 132 years, encompassing 25 challenges, was over.

The successful 1970 America's Cup Defender was Intrepid, skippered by Bill Ficker.

Dennis Conner, who had lost the cup in 1983, went to Australia to win it back for the San Diego Yacht Club in 1987. Then New Zealand and the courts entered the picture. The SDYC had planned to accept a challenge in 1989, but Michael Fay, heading a New Zealand syndicate, won a court ruling that the cup should be defended against a New Zealand challenge in 1988. The SDYC responded by building a catamaran, a multihulled vessel, that easily beat the single-hulled New Zealand challenger in September of 1988. However, Judge Carmen Ciparick of the New York Supreme Court ruled that the Deed of Gift required races between similar boats and that the 1988 race was "a gross mismatch." She awarded the cup to Fay's Mercury Bay Boating Club, which hoped to defend in April of 1991. The SDYC appealed the decision.

America's Cup Results
(First yacht listed is the winner)

	Yacht	Country	Score
1851	America	United States	1–0
	19 yachts	England	
1870	Magic	United States	1–0
	Cambria	England	
1871	Columbia and Sappho	United States	4–1
	Livonia	England	
1876	Madeleine	United States	2–0
	Countess of Dufferin	Canada	
1881	Mischief	United States	2–0
	Atalanta	Canada	
1885	Puritan	United States	2–0
	Genesta	England	
1886	Mayflower	United States	2–0
	Galatea	England	
1887	Volunteer	United States	2–0
	Thistle	Scotland	
1893	Vigilant	United States	3–0
	Valkyrie II	England	
1895	Defender	United States	3–0
	Valkyrie III	England	
1899	Columbia	United States	3–0
	Shamrock	Northern Ireland	
1901	Columbia	United States	3–0
	Shamrock II	Northern Ireland	
1903	Reliance	United States	3–0
	Shamrock III	Northern Ireland	
1920	Resolute	United States	3–2
	Shamrock IV	Northern Ireland	
1930	Enterprise	United States	4–0
	Shamrock V	Northern Ireland	
1934	Rainbow	United States	4–2
	Endeavour	England	

1937	Ranger	United States	4–0
	Endeavour II	England	
1958	Columbia	United States	4–0
	Sceptre	England	
1962	Weatherly	United States	4–1
	Gretel	Australia	
1964	Constellation	United States	4–0
	Sovereign	England	
1967	Intrepid	United States	4–0
	Dame Pattie	Australia	
1970	Intrepid	United States	4–1
	Gretel II	Australia	
1974	Courageous	United States	4–0
	Southern Cross	Australia	
1977	Courageous	United States	4–0
	Australia	Australia	
1980	Freedom	United States	4–1
	Australia	Australia	
1983	Australia	Australia	4–3
	Liberty	United States	
1987	Stars & Stripes	United States	4–0
	Kookaburra	Australia	
1988	Stars & Stripes	United States	2–0
	Kiwi	New Zealand	

Further Reading: Bavier, Robert N. *The America's Cup: An Insider's View*. New York: Dodd Mead, 1986; Fairchild, Tony. *The America's Cup Challenge*. London: Nautical Books/Macmillan London, Ltd., 1983; Fanta, J. Julius. *Winning the America's Cup*. New York: Sea Lore Publishing, 1969.

See also NEW YORK YACHT CLUB.

Americas Golf Cup

This trophy was donated by Jerome P. Bowes for competition among six-man teams of amateur golfers from Canada, Mexico, and the United States. Competition has been held in even-numbered years from 1952 through 1960 and in odd-numbered years since 1961. The one-day event rotates among the three countries and is held immediately before the host country's national amateur tournament.

See U.S. GOLF ASSOCIATION.

Anabolic Steroids

When Canadian sprinter Ben Johnson was stripped of an Olympic Gold Medal in 1988 because of a positive drug test, anabolic steroids were suddenly front-page news. Nine other Olympic competitors lost medals because of steroid use, but Johnson was one of the most famous athletes in the world. Millions had watched on live television when he set a record in the 100-meter dash during the 1987 world championships in Rome, and millions watched him win the event in the Seoul Olympics, apparently breaking his own record. But the medal and the record were taken away two days later, and Johnson flew back to Canada in disgrace.

The Canadian government set up an investigative commission that heard more than 50 witnesses. His coach, Charlie Francis, testified that Johnson had begun using steroids as early as 1981, and he named a dozen other Canadian athletes who used them regularly, including sprinter Angella Taylor Issajenko, who also testified. She started taking steroids in 1979, she said, because she felt she had to if she was to remain competitive; virtually everyone she ran against was using steroids.

Largely because of the Johnson case, the U.S. Congress in October 1988 passed the Omnibus Anti-Substance Abuse Act, toughening penalties for steroid trafficking. The *New York Times* ran a series of five articles on steroids, documenting their widespread use among athletes. Experts said that at least half of the 9,000 athletes at the 1988 Olympics had probably used steroids at one time or another. The National Football League reported that about 6 percent of its players had tested positive for steroids during the 1988 season, but that figure was discounted as much too low by other experts. A former NFL linebacker told the *Times*, "If I had it to do all over, I would use them so fast I wouldn't think about it twice." At a Senate judiciary hearing on steroids in May 1989, two players testified that as many as 75 percent of the NFL's players had used steroids. Senator Joseph Biden of Delaware, chairman of the committee, commented, "Steroid abuse in football may have reached epidemic proportions."

The first anabolic steroid was the male sex hormone, testosterone, which was isolated in 1935. It was found to have anabolic powers; that is, it promotes the conversion of food into body tissue, which can be helpful in the treatment of serious injuries and debilitating illness. But it also masculinizes by producing more facial and body hair, deepening the voice, and increasing aggressiveness and libido. Some men began to use it to increase the sex drive, and also because it produces a general feeling of strength and well-being.

Testosterone was used by athletes as early as 1954. John B. Ziegler, physician for the U.S. weight lifting team, became friendly with the Soviet doctor at the world championships that year in Vienna and learned that at least half the Russian lifters were on testosterone. Dr. Ziegler experimented with it and discovered that it increased the size of the prostate, in addition to its other side effects. Nevertheless, he made it available to some members of the York Barbell lifting team, which was in effect, the U.S.

team. At the same time, Bob Hoffman (the owner of York Barbell) began promoting the use of isometric exercises in his magazine, *Strength and Health.* Weightlifters from around the country came to York to learn the exercise program, and many of them went home with supplies of testosterone. Word spread quickly, and so did testosterone use.

Because of its legitimate medical uses, chemists began working to develop synthetic derivatives of testosterone to reduce the undesirable side effects. The first such anabolic steroid was methandrostenolone, introduced by Civa Pharmaceutical under the trade name Dianabol. Many weight lifters switched from testosterone to Dianabol.

During the 1960s and 1970s, other athletes began using steroids—evidently football players first, followed by track and field athletes. Testing for steroid use was initiated at the 1976 Olympics in Montreal, but athletes discovered they could pass the tests by switching from synthetic steroids to testosterone in advance. Because testosterone is naturally produced by the body, it was not banned and it helped the athletes maintain their gains in weight and strength. In 1982, methods of distinguishing between natural testosterone and that which has been administered were developed, and administered testosterone was added to the list of banned substances.

Nevertheless, hurdler Edwin Moses said in 1983 that at least half of the U.S. Olympic track and field athletes were using drugs, mostly anabolic steroids. Federal officials estimated in 1988 that black-market steroids constituted a $100 million a year business. While tests had been developed for 16 anabolic steroids, it was believed that underground laboratories were producing others that could not yet be identified by testing.

Many medical experts have called for extensive education to warn athletes of the dangers involved in steroid use, which may include kidney and liver damage, heart disease, high blood pressure, sterility, and problems with blood clotting. They also point out, however, that clinical evidence is still scanty, and more research is needed.

There are doubts that education will be enough to end the problem. Angella Taylor Issajenko told the Dubin Commission that she and many other athletes feel that they have to use steroids to remain competitive, because of the perception that "everybody else is doing it." Dr. George "Jamie" Astaphan, who admitted furnishing steroids to Ben Johnson, Issajenko, and many other athletes, favors legalizing their use, under strict medical control.

In a 1976 survey, U.S. Olympians were asked if they would take a pill that could guarantee a Gold Medal, even if it would mean certain death within a year. More than half of them said they would. Charles E. Yesalis, a professor of health and human development at Pennsylvania State University, has said: "If there were drugs for investment bankers, journalists, teachers and scientists that made them more successful, they would use them, too."

Further Reading: Goldman, Bob, with Patricia Bush and Ronald Klatz. *Death in the Locker Room: Steroids & Sports.* South Bend: Icarus Press, 1984; Todd, Terry. "Anabolic Steroids: The Gremlins of Sport," in *The Journal of Sport History,* Volume 14, Number 1 (Spring, 1987), pp. 87–107.

See also HOFFMAN, BOB; DRUGS IN SPORTS.

Anaheim, CA
See CALIFORNIA.

Anaheim Stadium
Anaheim, CA

Opened in 1966 as the home of the California Angels, Anaheim Stadium's three-tiered stands originally seated 43,204 spectators, although nearly 45,000 were shoehorned in at times. Most of the stadium's seats are concentrated behind home plate and along the foul lines. The unique scoreboard, in left-center field, is shaped like an A and encircled by a halo, the Angels' logo. The stadium was expanded to a capacity of 64,593 in 1980, when the Los Angeles Rams of the National Football League began playing there.

Anderson, IN

The Anderson Duffey Packers, backed by a local business, won the National Basketball League championship in 1947 and entered the new National Basketball Association for the 1949–50 season. The franchise folded after that season.

Anderson, Paul (1932–   )
Weight Lifting
Born October 17, 1932, Toccoa, GA

America's greatest weight lifter, Anderson didn't take up the sport until 1952. In December of that year, he won the Tennessee state heavyweight championship and set a new world record of 660½ pounds in the squat, a power lifting event. Then he beefed up from a mere 285 pounds to more than 360, though he was only 5 feet 9 inches tall. He was the U.S. heavyweight champion in 1955 and in 1956, when he set a world record of 1,145 pounds for the three lifts. He won the world championship in 1955 and the Olympic title in 1956, and then became a professional.

Anderson, Willie (1880–1910)
Golf
Born May, 1880, North Berwick, Scotland; died 1910; World Golf Hall of Fame

The first great American professional golfer, Anderson came to the United States with his family in 1895. Two years later, at the age of 17, he finished second in the U.S. Open. He went on to become the first player to win the tournament four times, in 1901, 1903, 1904, and 1905. He's still the only golfer ever to win three Opens in a row. Anderson was also a four-time winner of the Western Open, then the second most important professional tournament in North America. He died suddenly of arteriosclerosis at the age of 30; he had played three 36-hole matches the previous week. For the centennial celebration of American golf, Anderson was named player of the decade for 1898–1907.

Andretti, Mario (1940–   )
Auto Racing
Born February 28, 1940, Montona, Italy

Andretti ranks with A. J. Foyt for versatility as a race driver. He's the only driver in history to win both the Formula One World Driver's Championship and the Indy Car Championship, which he has won four times (1965, 1966, 1969, and 1984). He's also the only man to win the Driver of the Year Award in three different decades (1967, 1978, and 1984). And he's one of only three drivers ever to win races on paved tracks, dirt tracks, and road courses in one season. He accomplished that in four consecutive years (1966–69). Andretti's total of 47 career wins is second to Foyt, and he shares the record of six victories in a season with three other drivers. His son, Michael, began driving Indy cars in 1983, and father and son were teammates in the 1989 Indy 500.

Angell Conference
American football faced a dual crisis during 1905–06. Deaths and injuries caused by mass momentum plays were to lead to major changes in the playing rules. But many college leaders were more concerned about the lack of control over the sport. As a result, James G. Angell, the president of the University of Michigan, called a meeting of Western Conference members in 1906 to resolve the problem.

The Angell Conference proposed several radical changes. Freshmen and graduate students were to be ineligible to compete; the football season was to be limited to five games; preseason practice and the training table for players were to be abolished; coaches were to be employed as faculty members, with comparable pay; ticket prices were to be limited to 50 cents; and financial management of football was to be transferred from student to faculty control. The conference further agreed to suspend football competition for two years if member institutions did not agree to modify their rules.

Ironically, Angell's school didn't like the new rules. The University of Michigan regents replaced the faculty athletic committee with a Board of Athletic Control. When this change was disapproved in 1908, the university withdrew from the conference, but rejoined in 1917.

See also BIG TEN CONFERENCE.

Angling
See CASTING; FISHING.

Animal Baiting
Bull baiting and bear baiting, popular amusements in Elizabethan England, were also popular on the American frontier during the late 18th and early 19th centuries. During the second half of the 19th century, virtually every state banned the sports.

See also COCKFIGHTING.

Anson, "Cap" Adrian C. (1852–1922)
Baseball
Born April 17, 1852, Marshalltown, IA; died April 14, 1922; Baseball Hall of Fame

A great player and manager, Anson was also a major reason that blacks were banned from major-league baseball from 1887 until 1947. He refused to let his team take the field for an 1883 exhibition game against Toledo, which had a black player, Moses Fleetwood Walker, but finally let the game go on because he didn't want to forfeit the ticket money. However, in 1888 he protested furiously when the New York Giants tried to sign George Stovey, a black, and as a result the National League owners entered into an agreement that no blacks would be allowed to play.

Anson began his long major-league career in 1871 with Rockford of the National Association, then went to the Philadelphia team from 1872 through 1875. When the National League was organized in 1876, he joined the Chicago team, the league's first champion. He became team captain and manager, and acquired the nickname "Cap," in 1879. He continued as player-manager until 1897. In 1898, he briefly managed the New York Giants.

Anson batted over .300 twenty times, had a lifetime batting average of .329, and was the first player to get more than 3,000 hits. As a manager, he was a very tough disciplinarian. He instituted a $100 fine for drinking—he had become a teetotaler after spending a night in jail for drunkenness—and he also fined players for being overweight. Anson is often credited with inventing the hit and run play, and he was probably the first manager to teach his fielders to back up other fielders to stop overthrows. His teams won pennants in 1880, 1881, 1882, 1885, and 1886. His career record was 1,297 wins and 957 losses, a .575 percentage.

Ante-Bellum Period

Sports and outdoor recreations grew rapidly during the period before the Civil War, especially in and around eastern cities. Immigration from the British Isles and northern Europe had a major impact. English weavers brought cricket to textile cities in the Northeast, and refugees from the failed 1848 revolution in Germany introduced gymnastics. Scottish immigrants organized Caledonian clubs and held annual Caledonian or Highland games, beginning in Boston in 1853. Boxing grew in large part because of its popularity among the first great wave of Irish immigrants, who also helped to create an urban sporting fraternity passionate about gambling on prizefights, horse racing, race walking, running, and rowing.

The growth of a merchant middle class, with leisure time and money, was another important factor. Ocean bathing, ice skating, rowing, and sleighing became popular urban pastimes. The sons of the middle class, at northeastern colleges, particularly enjoyed rowing. The first recorded intercollegiate contest was the Harvard-Yale Regatta of 1852. The New York Knickerbocker Club's version of baseball, created by Alexander Cartwright in 1845, began as a sport for young men of means. But it was soon taken up by others, including Irish and German immigrants, and it was rapidly carried across the country by the westward expansion.

Writers had their impact, too. Thomas Hughes' *Tom Brown's Schooldays*, about life at England's Rugby School, with its emphasis on spiritual growth through sports, helped introduce "muscular Christianity" to North America at the very time when many writers were publicly worrying about the lack of physical fitness among urbanites. Oliver Wendell Holmes, Sr. and Thomas Wentworth Higginson encouraged physical fitness through gymnastics and outdoor exercise and recreation, while *Harper's Weekly* editorialized in favor of physical education in schools and colleges. This movement was strongest after the Civil War, but the stage was set during the 1850s.

Antitrust Laws

Any league or college conference is a group of competitors who have allied to regulate their own competition. This type of alliance has been challenged repeatedly in courts under federal antitrust laws. The first major decision was handed down by Oliver Wendell Holmes on behalf of the U.S. Supreme Court in 1922 in a case brought by the Baltimore team of the defunct Federal League against organized baseball. Holmes wrote that baseball was not "a trade or commerce in the commonly-accepted use of the words," principally because a baseball player's activity is not really productive.

Many lawyers saw this ruling as a rather flimsy straw. In 1951, major-league baseball owners avoided the possibility of an adverse decision by repealing their television blackout rule when threatened by the Justice Department with antitrust action. The following year, the National Football League bylaws were amended to give Commissioner Bert Bell complete control over televised games; the intent was to let Bell negotiate a single TV contract for the entire league. The Justice Department brought suit, charging restraint of trade. In 1953, Judge Alan K. Grim ruled in favor of the NFL on the grounds that professional football was "a unique kind of business" that would be devastated by uncontrolled competition.

Two Supreme Court decisions, in 1953 and 1955, reaffirmed baseball's exemption from antitrust regulation, but in both cases the Court specifically said that the exemption did not apply to other professional sports. That left both the NFL and the National Basketball Association vulnerable. The NFL's first encounter came in a 1957 suit brought by former player Milo Radovich, who had jumped to the rival All-America Football Conference in 1946, and was later blocked by the NFL from taking a job as an assistant coach. The case eventually went to the Supreme Court, which ruled that the league was not exempt.

When the NFL signed a contract in 1961 giving television broadcast rights exclusively to CBS, the Justice Department sued again, and this time Judge Grim ruled that the contract was an undue restraint of trade. Congress then passed the Sports Broadcasting Act, specifically allowing professional leagues to negotiate broadcasting packages.

Fear of antitrust problems led major-league baseball to expand in 1967, several years before planned. When the Kansas City Athletics announced they were moving to Oakland, Missouri Senator Stuart Symington threatened to introduce a bill that would end baseball's immunity to antitrust action. To avoid that, the American League put a new team in Kansas City—the Royals—and added a franchise in Seattle to keep the divisions balanced. That virtually forced the National League to expand, and it added teams in San Diego and Montreal.

The most publicized antitrust action was brought by Curt Flood against major-league baseball in 1970. Flood, a center fielder for the St. Louis Cardinals, was traded to the Philadelphia Phillies after the 1969 season, but refused to report to his new team. Instead, he brought suit under the Sherman and Clayton Antitrust Acts, and alleged that the reserve system constituted a form of peonage and involuntary servitude—in a word, slavery. After ten weeks of testimony, Judge Irving B. Cooper of the U.S. District Court ruled against Flood and said that baseball should remain exempt from antitrust laws until either the Supreme Court or Congress took action.

When the American and National Football Leagues announced their plans to merge in 1966, the NFL Players Association threatened to sue. However, Congress was persuaded to pass the Football Merger Act, granting the league a limited exemption from antitrust action. The National Basketball Association was sued by its players in 1970 to prevent a merger with the American Basketball Association. The suit dragged on for five years, the merger was stalled, and the NBA unsuccessfully sought congressional action. It was finally dropped when the players won extensive changes in the league's reserve system.

In 1974, John Mackey, former president of the Players Association, sued the NFL over the "Rozelle rule," a decree by Commissioner Pete Rozelle that if a free agent moved from one team to another, the new team would have to compensate the old team with a player of equal skill, to be selected by the commissioner. A federal court in 1975 found against the NFL, and the Rozelle rule was dead. The league's policy of forbidding owners from holding a franchise in any other professional league was challenged in 1980 by the North American Soccer League, again on the grounds that the rule violated antitrust laws. Two NFL owners, Lamar Hunt of the Kansas City Chiefs and Joe Robbie of the Miami Dolphins, testified for the NASL, as did former owner Edward Bennett Williams, who had been forced to sell his interest in the Washington Redskins in order to acquire the Baltimore Orioles baseball team. The court ruled in favor of the NFL on the grounds that it is a "single economic entity," specifically exempted from action by the Sherman Antitrust Act.

Then, shockingly, the NFL was sued by one of its own members, the Oakland Raiders, seeking $160 million in damages because the league was attempting to block a move to Los Angeles. Under the NFL constitution, any franchise move had to be approved by a majority vote of the owners, and Davis' request for permission had been turned down. The Sherman Act was once again the issue. The suit was settled out of court in 1988.

The specter of antitrust action has forced both the NFL and the NBA to grant major concessions in negotiations with their player associations, especially on the issue of free agency. In the absence of a collective bargaining agreement after the NFL player strike in 1987, the NFL unilaterally adopted a new policy on free agency after the 1988 season, allowing its teams to protect just 37 of its 47 players, freeing the others to go to any other team.

See also OPTION CLAUSE; RESERVE CLAUSE.

APFA

See AMERICAN PROFESSIONAL FOOTBALL ASSOCIATION.

Aquaplaning

See WATER SKIING.

Aquatic Hall of Fame and Museum of Canada, Inc.

The Pan-Am Natatorium, one of the largest indoor swimming complexes in the world, was built in Winnipeg, Manitoba, for the 1967 Pan-American Games. It then became the site of the Aquatic Hall of Fame and Museum. Several major swimming competitions have taken place at the complex, which covers 13 acres of land on Poseidon Bay. The Hall of Fame itself honors competitors in diving, swimming, synchronized swimming, and water polo. The museum has a fine collection of sports stamps and many works of art, artifacts, and memorabilia related to aquatic sports.

Address: 436 Main Street, Winnipeg, Manitoba, Canada R3B 1B2 (204) 947–0131

Aqueduct
New York, NY

Built at a cost of $33 million and operated by the New York Racing Association, the new Aqueduct racetrack opened in 1959 to replace a track that had hosted racing from 1894 to 1955. Its most important races are the Wood Memorial, which had previously been run at Jamaica, and the Bold Ruler Stakes. While Belmont Park was closed for renovation from 1963 through 1968, Aqueduct also hosted the Belmont Stakes, the Woodward Stakes, the Jockey Club Gold Cup, and the Man O'War Stakes. The 110-foot-high grandstand seats 27,000 spectators. Aqueduct has a 1⅛-mile oval main course, a 1–mile inner dirt course, and an inner turf course that is 7 furlongs plus 43 feet long.

Address: New York Racing Association, P.O. Box 90, Jamaica, NY 11417 (718) 641–4700

Arcaro, "Eddie" George Edward (1916–   )
Horse Racing
Born February 19, 1916, Cincinnati, OH; Racing Hall of Fame

Eleven horses have won the Triple Crown. Arcaro is the only jockey to have ridden two of them, Whirlaway in 1941 and Citation in 1948. He originally trained on tracks in Mexico, where rough riding was tolerated. Then he came to New York and won a reputation for a bad temper and questionable tactics, although it was obvious he was also an excellent handler of horses.

In 1943, another jockey cut him off and Arcaro retaliated by riding him into the rail. "I'd have killed him if I could," he told the investigating stewards, and he was suspended for a year. Later he said it was the best thing that ever happened to him, because it taught him to control his temper and use his head. After the suspension ended, he developed a new reputation for his poise and his willingness to help young jockeys learn their trade.

Arcaro rode more than 4,000 winners and earned more than $3 million. He won 17 Triple Crown Races: the Belmont Stakes and the Preakness six times each and the Kentucky Derby five times. Many wondered why he kept riding in the late 1950s. Arcaro had a simple answer: "I like being a celebrity. Once I retire, I'm just another little man." But he did retire in 1962, and retained celebrity status by becoming a television commentator on major races.

Archery

Modern target archery developed in England during the 14th century. Beginning in 1330, English monarchs periodically prohibited other sports because they interfered with target practice. Even after firearms began to replace the bow, archery was considered a required sport for the courtier, along with fencing. The sport of archery apparently was not brought to North America by the English colonists, but it was already here, among native Americans. The artist Titian Ramsey Peale studied the Plains Indians and learned to use the bow and arrow from them. In 1828, he organized the first archery club on the continent, the United Bowmen of Philadelphia. The club conducted various tournaments and matches among its members before dissolving in 1859.

After the Civil War, Maurice and Will Thompson rediscovered archery. As former Confederate soldiers, they were not allowed to have firearms, so they began hunting with bow and arrow in the Florida wilderness. They then went to Crawfordsville, IN, and Maurice began writing lyrical articles about the joys of archery, followed by a book, *The Witchery of Archery*, in 1878. By 1879, there were at least 25 archery clubs in the United States, and the National Archery Association was created at a meeting of club representatives in Crawfordsville. The first national tournament was held later that year in Chicago's White Stocking Park, with championships for men and women.

Archery was added to the Olympic Games in 1900, when Margaret Abbott became the first American woman to win a Gold Medal, and it remained an Olympic sport through 1920, but there were no standard international rules until 1931, when the Federation Internationale de Tir l'Arc (FITA) was organized in Paris. By 1972, enough countries had their own governing bodies for archery to be restored to the Olympic program.

A professional archery tour began in 1963, under the auspices of the Professional Archers Association. The PAA tour now has more than 20 tournaments annually, with total prize money approaching $100,000. Most of the tournaments are indoors, where much smaller targets are used because the range is only 20 yards, as compared to up to 100 yards in outdoor archery.

Modern target archery equipment is very different from that used by Maurice and Will Thompson. Recurve bows, in which the limbs curve away from the archer for increased leverage, are equipped with stabilizers to reduce torque when the arrow is released. Strings are usually made of Kevlar or a patented hydrocarbon product, Fast Flight, and they are often fitted with "kisser buttons," which touch the archer's lips when at full draw. In unlimited competition, sights are used, but they are not permitted in barebow competition.

In addition to target shooting, there is competition in flight archery—shooting for distance—and in field archery, which simulates hunting animals in the wild. In clout shooting, the target is a circle drawn on the ground, and archers launch the arrow on a high trajectory so that it will drop onto the target.

Addresses: National Archery Association, 1750 East Boulder, Colorado Srings, CO 80909 (719) 578–4576; Federation of Canadian Archers, 333 River Road, Vanier, Ontario, Canada K1L 8H9 (613) 748–5604; Professional Archery Association, 26 Lakeview Drive, Stansbury Park, UT 84074 (801) 882–3817

ARCO Arena
Sacramento, CA

The original ARCO Arena was a temporary facility, the home of the National Basketball Association's Sacramento Kings after they moved from Kansas City in 1985. It was replaced by a new 17,500-square-foot ARCO Arena in September of 1988. Built by the Sacramento Sports Association, which also owns the team, the arena is partially subsidized by the Atlantic Richfield Corporation (ARCO). There are plans for a complete sports complex, including a baseball field, at the site.

Arctic Winter Games

Athletes from northern Canada did not do well in the 1967 Canada Winter Games, largely because of a lack of training facilities and regular competition. As a result, the Yukon and the Northwest Territories met with representatives from Alaska to plan the Arctic Winter Games for athletes from the three jurisdictions. The first competition was held in 1970 in Yellowknife, Northwest Territories. Northern Ontario began to participate in 1972, when the games were held in Whitehorse, but dropped out after 1976. Northern Alberta entered competition in 1986 and is expected to host the 1996 games.

A unique feature of the games is that they include traditional sports of Inuit Eskimos and native Americans from the area. At a meeting of the Arctic Winter Games Corporation in August 1988, directors decided to invite Eskimos from Greenland and the Soviet Union's Magadan Peninsula to take part in 1990, because of their close cultural ties with Canada's Inuits.

Address: Arctic Winter Games Corporation, c/o Don Cooper, Box 818, Yellowknife, Northwest Territories, Canada X1A 2N5

Arena Football

A made-for-TV sport, arena football was invented in 1987 by James Foster, who founded Arena Sports Ventures Un Limited to operate the Arena Football League. Arena football is played indoors on a 50-yard field, with eight players per team. The sport incorporates several gimmicks, including a field-wide net at each end of the playing area. On kickoffs and missed field goals, the ball remains in play when it hits the net. A dropkicked field goal is worth four points and a dropkicked conversion is worth two points. The league was organized as a single corporation, with each team owner holding a limited partnership.

A "preview season" was played in 1987, with teams in Chicago, Denver, Pittsburgh, and Washington and a total of just 12 games. In 1988, only Chicago and Pittsburgh remained, but Detroit, Los Angeles, New England (Providence), and New York were added. Disappointed at low attendance and television ratings, owners attempted to wrest control of the league from Foster early in 1989, but were

unsuccessful. With teams in Chicago, Denver, Detroit, Maryland, and Pittsburgh, the league played another abbreviated season that year, with a five-week schedule and three playoff games.

Arenas

There have been three great waves of arena building. The first, beginning about 1920, was brought about by boxing and hockey. As the National Hockey League became entrenched, new arenas were built in many NHL cities, including the Ottawa Arena in 1923, the Montreal Forum in 1924, and the Boston Garden in 1929. And because boxing was legalized in many states, entrepreneurs built new arenas in which to hold matches. Among them was the third Madison Square Garden, which opened in May 1925.

College basketball's growing popularity fueled the second wave, beginning after World War II. One of the biggest arenas built during the period was the Allen Field House at the University of Kansas, which opened in 1954 with a capacity of 16,740 spectators.

Then came the formation of the American Basketball Association in 1967 and the expansion of the National Hockey League, beginning in 1968. Those moves led to major arenas being built, usually with public money. Among them were the Omni in Atlanta; the Coliseum in Richfield, OH; McNichols Sports Arena in Denver; the Pontiac (MI) Silverdome; Oakland Coliseum Arena; the Summit in Houston; Market Square Arena in Indianapolis; the Spectrum in Philadelphia; HemisFair Arena in San Antonio; the Kingdome in Seattle; the Salt Palace in Salt Lake City; the Capital Centre in Washington, D.C.; and the fourth Madison Square Garden. Most of these arenas are used for professional basketball and hockey, and many are also sometimes used for college sports.

See also BASEBALL PARKS; STADIUMS.

Arizona Veterans' Memorial Coliseum
Phoenix, AZ

Construction of the coliseum began in August of 1964, and it was dedicated on October 23, 1965. Located on the Arizona State Fairgrounds, it cost $6.9 million. Capacity was increased by 2,000 seats in 1981, and in 1988 a completely new ice floor was installed. Since 1968, the coliseum has been the home of the Phoenix Suns of the National Basketball Association, and many other sports events have taken place there, including boxing, figure skating, gymnastics, hockey, indoor soccer, midget auto racing, polo, tennis, and wrestling. Seating capacity is 14,471 for basketball and 13,800 for hockey.

Arlington Park
Chicago, IL

Opened on October 13, 1927, Arlington pioneered racing on grass in North America and also built a strong program of stakes races after World War II. Among its major races are the American Derby, the Secretariat Stakes, the Arlington Classic, and the Arlington-Washington Futurity. A fire on July 31, 1985, destroyed most of the grandstand, but the track remained open through the 1987 racing season, after which it was closed for construction of a $110 million facility that opened on June 28, 1989. The park has a 1⅛-mile oval track, with a 1-mile turf course and an inner turf course of 7 furlongs.

Address: P.O. Box 7, Arlington Heights, IL 60007 (312) 255–4300

Arlington Stadium
Arlington, TX

Originally Turnpike Stadium, located just about halfway between Dallas and Ft. Worth, this baseball park was built in 1965 in hopes that it would eventually be the home park for a major-league team. That happened in 1972, when the Washington Senators became the Texas Rangers. The opening game was played on April 21 before a crowd of 20,105. The park seats 35,698 and has a scoreboard shaped like the state of Texas. It's symmetrical, 330 feet down the right-field and left-field lines and 400 feet to straightaway center field.

Armstrong, Henry (Henry Jackson) (1912–1988)
Boxing
Born December 12, 1912, Columbus, MS; died October 22, 1988; Boxing Hall of Fame

The only boxer ever to hold world championships in three different weight classes at the same time, Armstrong is thought by many to be the best fighter, pound-for-pound, in boxing history. Born in Mississippi, he grew up in a slum section of St. Louis. After graduating from high school, he hopped a freight train to Los Angeles and began his boxing career. He fought as Melody Jackson until 1935, when he adopted the ring name Henry Armstrong.

Armstrong won the world featherweight championship on October 29, 1937, with a sixth-round knockout of Petey Sarron. While still holding that title, he won the welterweight championship with a 15-round decision over Barney Ross on May 31, 1938. Less than three months later, on August 17, he added the lightweight title by winning a 15-round decision over Lou Ambers.

He voluntarily gave up the featherweight title late in 1938 and lost the lightweight championship to Ambers on a 15-round decision on August 22, 1939. However, he defended his welterweight championship 20 times before losing to Fritzie Zivic in a 15-round decision, October 4, 1940. Armstrong's rematch with Zivic in Madison Square Garden on January 17, 1941, drew 23,190 spectators, then the largest crowd ever for an indoor sports event. Zivic won with a knockout in the 12th round. Armstrong also challenged for the middleweight championship, but failed to win it in a 10–round draw with Ceferino Garcia on March 1, 1940.

He had 174 professional fights and won 145 of them, 98 by knockouts. He lost 20, 2 by knockouts, and also fought 8 draws and 1 no-decision. Armstrong's relentless, aggressive fighting style is described by the many nicknames he acquired: "Hammerin' Henry," "The Human Buzzsaw," "Homicide Hank," "Hurricane Henry," and "Perpetual Motion."

Arm Wrestling

Arm wrestling of a sort was a frontier sport during the 18th and 19th centuries, but has more recently been associated with bar rooms. It began to acquire a measure of respectability in 1964, when Bob O'Leary drew up a set of formal rules and founded the American Arm Wrestling Association to supervise the sport and sanction tournaments. At first, the only form of competition was sit-down, but standing arm wrestling has since been added, and there are national championships in both events. The 1988 world championships in Eskilstuna, Sweden, attracted about 200 competitors from 20 countries.

Address: American Arm Wrestling Association, c/o Bob O'Leary, P.O. Box 132, Scranton, PA 18504 (717) 342–4984

Arrowhead Stadium
Kansas City, MO

Part of the Harry S. Truman Sports Complex, Arrowhead was built by Jackson County, MO at a cost of about $33 million. Ground breaking took place in July of 1968, and the stadium was dedicated on August 12, 1971, with a Kansas City Chiefs' exhibition game. Since its opening, the Chiefs have invested another $9.5 million in additions, including a computerized scoreboard. Seating is 78,097.

Artificial Turf

The Houston Astrodome in 1965 became the first stadium to have artificial turf, AstroTurf, developed by the Monsanto Chemical Company. The idea quickly spread to other stadiums and other sports. Its two major advantages over "natural turf" are that the maintenance costs are lower and that it doesn't become muddy in the rain. Artificial turf also dries much more rapidly. But it has many disadvantages. Increased heat, with field-level temperatures going as high as 130 degrees, was a major problem in Miami's Orange Bowl. In 1985 the turf was replaced with real grass. The "mod sod" also causes new types of injuries, including infected "rug burns" and "turf toe," caused by stubbing the toe against the relatively hard surface.

Artificial turf has changed the nature of baseball considerably. Because it's much livelier than grass, ground balls are more likely to get past infielders, and drives hit to the outfield often take very high bounces over the fielder's head. Bunting is also much more difficult because it's harder to "kill" the ball on artificial turf. The 3M company, which developed Tartan Turf, also came up with a related Tartan surfacing material, widely used on running tracks. The surface is demonstrably faster than the old cinder and gravel tracks, especially in the sprint events. Similar surfacing is used for tennis courts.

Artistic Skating Union (ASU)

See ROLLER SKATING.

Ashe, Arthur R., Jr. (1943–   )
Tennis

Born July 10, 1943, Richmond, VA; International Tennis Hall of Fame

The first black male tennis player to win a major title, Ashe began training at the age of 10 with Dr. R. Walter Johnson, who had helped Althea Gibson develop into a champion. Awarded a tennis scholarship by UCLA, Ashe won the National Collegiate Athletic Association singles championship in 1965 and teamed with Ian Crookenden to win the doubles title. He went on to win the first U.S. Open in 1968, the Australian Open in 1970, and the Wimbledon championship in 1975. Ashe also won the USLTA hard courts title in 1963 and the clay courts championship in 1967, and was the first black chosen for the U.S. Davis Cup team, in 1963. He retired after suffering a mild heart attack in 1978. Ashe has spent much time telling young blacks that they should choose education, not sports, as their road to a future, and in 1988 he published a three-volume history of black athletes, *A Hard Road to Glory.*

Further Reading: Ashe, Arthur. *Off the Court.* New York: New American Library, 1981.

Arthur Ashe was the first black male to win the U.S. Open tennis championship, in 1968, and Wimbledon, in 1975. Courtesy of the U.S. Tennis Association

Association for Intercollegiate Athletics for Women (AIAW)

The first organization to conduct women's collegiate championships, the AIAW grew out of the Commission of Intercollegiate Athletics for Women, formed in 1966. The commission held its first championships in 1969, and in 1971 it became the AIAW. Many of its leaders opposed the emphasis on winning of men's intercollegiate athletics, and athletic scholarships for women were not allowed. However, a 1973 suit by a woman athlete charging sex discrimination forced the AIAW to allow member colleges to offer athletic grants-in-aid. In 1981, the National Collegiate Athletic Association, supervisory body for men's collegiate sports, also began offering national championships for women. The AIAW became inactive in 1985.

See also WOMEN IN SPORTS.

Association of College Unions-International (ACU-I)

An organization of about 1,000 student unions, the ACU-I conducts regional and national collegiate tournaments in billiards, bowling, and table tennis. It was founded in 1914 as the Association of College Unions and added "International" to its name in 1961.

Address: 400 East Seventh Street, Bloomington, IN 47405 (812) 332–8017

Association of Professional Ball Players
Baseball

Major- and minor-league players banded together in October 1924 to form the APBP, an organization to help sick and needy players. Former players and some umpires also joined, paying dues of $5 a year, and several owners donated money to the cause. The baseball all-star game originated in 1933 to benefit the APBP, although the proceeds now go to the Major League Players Association. The APBP still takes private contributions to assist indigent former players, primarily those whose major-league service was too short to qualify them for pensions.

Address: 12062 Valley View Street, Suite 211, Garden Grove, CA 92645 (714) 892–9900

Association of Sports Museums and Halls of Fame (ASMHF)

William F. "Buck" Dawson, executive director of the International Swimming Hall of Fame in Ft. Lauderdale, FL, conceived the idea of the ASMHF in 1971, and invited about a dozen fellow directors to discuss the idea. Only two showed up. Nevertheless, the group was informally organized, and a second meeting was held at the Naismith Memorial Basketball Hall of Fame in Springfield, MA in October 1972. This time 19 organizations were represented. By 1989, membership had grown to 85, including museums in Australia, Israel, Singapore, Spain, and Switzerland.

Address: 101 West Sutton Place, Wilmington, DE 19810 (302) 475–7068

Association of Tennis Professionals (ATP)

The ATP calls itself one of the most exclusive clubs in the world, with some right. Founded in 1972 by four professional players, Arthur Ashe, Cliff Drysdale, Jack Kramer, and Stan Smith, the organization has members in two divisions. Division I includes male professionals ranked in the top 200 in singles or the top 100 in doubles, and Division II includes those ranked in the top 500 in singles or the top 250 in doubles.

The primary goals of the ATP are to improve conditions on the men's professional tour, specifically to increase prize money. The association's first major action was a boycott of the 1973 Wimbledon tournament to protest the suspension of Nikki Pilic by the Yugoslavian National Federation. The International Tennis Federation recognized the ATP and

formed a Grand Prix Committee to oversee men's professional tennis; Ashe, Kramer, and Donald Dell of the ATP were among the six members of the committee.

The ATP now works closely with tournament organizers and sponsors to develop the ATP tour, which began in 1990 with 77 tournaments throughout the world. The tour includes an eight-week break at the end of the year and an ATP finals tournament for the top-ranked players.

Address: 200 Tournament Player Road, Ponte Vedra Beach, FL 32082 (904) 285–8000

Astrodome
Houston, TX

The Astrodome was the world's first domed stadium. Built by Harris County, where Houston is located, at a cost of $43 million, it opened in 1962 as the home of the Colt .45s (now the Astros) of baseball's National League and the Houston Oilers of the American Football League. Originally, the roof was made of 4,796 panes of glass to allow the sun to shine through so grass could grow, but the glass created a terrible glare problem. The roof was painted over and sealed, and an artificial surface was installed, the first of its kind; the developer, Monsanto Chemical, named it AstroTurf.

The Astrodome boasts a $3 million dollar scoreboard about as high as a 4-story building, and the domed roof is more than 18 stories high. An air-conditioning system keeps the temperature about 72 degrees. The stadium has been used for other sports from time to time, most notably the "Battle of the Sexes" tennis match between Billy Jean King and Bobby Riggs in 1973, which drew 30,472 spectators, the largest crowd ever to watch tennis, and the Houston-UCLA basketball game of 1965, which set a record for an indoor crowd with 52,693 fans.

As a baseball park, the Astrodome is 330 feet down each foul line and 400 feet to center field. The stadium seats 52,000 for baseball and 62,000 for football.

Athletic Clubs

The New York Athletic Club was founded in 1866 to bring together young athletes interested in track and field events. It soon inspired imitators, first in New York City and then throughout the country. Baltimore, Buffalo, Chicago, Detroit, New Orleans, Philadelphia, Providence, St. Louis, and San Francisco had athletic clubs by 1879, and an observer wrote in 1887 that, "scarce a city can be found having a population of more than 30,000 inhabitants, in which there is not at least one club of this class."

Track and field was the original focus of the athletic clubs, but they quickly became involved in other sports as well. Gymnasiums were used for boxing, fencing, gymnastic exercises, and wrestling. The NYAC and the Athletic Club of the Schuylkill Navy, among others, had facilities for rowing, and some clubhouses included swimming pools, billiard rooms, bowling alleys, and rifle ranges.

During the late 19th and early 20th centuries, most outstanding amateur athletes, especially in track and field, came from athletic clubs. But many of the clubs began to change their emphasis from sports to social activities, and membership in an athletic club became a badge of prestige. Prospective members were carefully screened, and dues were increased to discourage applications from anyone below the upper middle-income level. Good athletes were still welcomed; often, their dues were waived, and they were given free room and board, but most club members were no longer active athletes. They were more interested in the club dining rooms, ballrooms, and wine cellars than in the gymnasium.

At the same time, other organizations were becoming heavily involved in sports. Ethnic groups excluded from the socially oriented clubs formed their own athletic clubs, which remained genuinely sports-oriented. YMCAs built their own gyms and formed their own teams in many sports. College athletic programs expanded greatly, and the balance of power in intercollegiate athletics began to shift from the exclusive private colleges of the Northeast to the newer, fast-growing land-grant colleges to the west.

The result was a struggle over the control of amateur sports that continued well into the 1970s between the club-dominated AAU, led largely by wealthy men with elitist views of amateurism, and the National Collegiate Athletic Association. The AAU and the clubs eventually lost.

See also AMATEUR ATHLETIC UNION; NEW YORK ATHLETIC CLUB.

Athletic League of North America

After its invention in 1891, basketball became so popular that many YMCAs seemed to be turning into one-sport athletic clubs, and the specter of professionalism haunted the gymnasiums. YMCA teams furiously scheduled games with amateur, semipro, and even professional teams; to lure top players, many YMCAs offered special privileges, including remission of membership fees and free room and board. To counter this trend, the Athletic League of North America was formed in 1895, with Luther H. Gulick as its secretary. The goal was to promote regional and state competition among YMCA teams,

eliminating games with outside competition, but the goal was never reached. It was estimated in 1905 that YMCA teams were playing more than 2,000 games against non-YMCA teams. The league was dissolved in 1911, and the YMCA's national leadership began to promote a variety of athletic activities designed to reach large numbers of young men, not merely the outstanding athletes.

Athletics Congress
See THE ATHLETICS CONGRESS.

Atlanta, GA

Baseball Atlanta entered major professional sports in 1966, when the Braves of the National League moved from Milwaukee. The team had hoped to relocate a year earlier, but the threat of litigation because there was one year left on its stadium lease in Milwaukee forced a postponement. The Braves won the western division title in 1969, but lost to the New York Mets in the league championship series.

Basketball Before the 1968–69 season, the Hawks of the National Basketball Association moved from St. Louis to Atlanta. They won a central division championship in 1980, but have never been in the championship finals.

Hockey The Flames became an expansion franchise in the National Hockey League in 1972. The team moved to Calgary, Alberta, in 1980, after eight seasons of mediocre play and poor attendance.

Football In 1966, the same year that the Braves moved, the Atlanta Falcons began play as an expansion franchise in the National Football League. They won a western division championship in 1980.

See also ATLANTA–FULTON COUNTY COLISEUM; OMNI.

Atlanta-Fulton County Coliseum
Atlanta, GA

One of the first circular baseball parks, Atlanta–Fulton County Stadium was built in less than a year, at a cost of about $18 million. Groundbreaking took place on April 15, 1964, and the first game, an exhibition, was played on April 9, 1965. However, the Milwaukee Braves, who had been expected to move into the park that year as the Atlanta Braves, were forced by litigation to play one last season in Milwaukee. The year they finally arrived, 1966, the Atlanta Falcons football team came into existence. Both teams use the stadium, which seats 52,007 for baseball and 59,643 for football. The baseball home run distances are 330 feet down the lines and 402 feet to center field.

Atlanta International Raceway
Atlanta, GA

Called "the Big A" by race car drivers, Atlanta has a 1.522-mile oval track with turns of about a half-mile each and quarter-mile straightaways. Seating capacity is about 70,000. The track hosts two NAS-CAR Winston Cup races annually.

Address: P.O. Box 500, Hampton, GA 30228; (404) 946–4211

Atlantic City Raceway
Atlantic City, NJ

Major Thoroughbred races at Atlantic City are the Matchmaker Stakes and the United Nations Handicap. The track, which opened in 1946, also conducts a harness racing meet. Its main course is a 1⅛-mile oval, with a 1-mile turf course in the infield. Grandstand capacity is 16,000.

Address: Atlantic City Racing Association, P.O. Box 719, Atlantic City, NJ 08404 (609) 641–2190

Atlantic Coast Conference (ACC)

Seven members of the Southern Conference withdrew in 1953 to form the Atlantic Coast Conference. The original members were Clemson, Duke, Maryland, North Carolina, North Carolina State, South Carolina, and Wake Forest. The following year, the University of Virginia, which had left the Southern Conference in 1937, joined the ACC. South Carolina withdrew in June of 1971, and Georgia Tech moved into the ACC from the Southeastern Conference in April 1978.

Address: P.O. Drawer ACC, Greensboro, NC 27419–6199 (919) 854–8787

Attell, Abe (1884–1970)
Boxing

Born February 22, 1884, San Francisco, CA; died February 6, 1970; Boxing Hall of Fame

Although he was one of the great boxers of all time, Attell is unfortunately best known for his role in the Black Sox scandal of 1919. He was apparently both the payoff man and the front man for gambler Arnold Rothstein in the infamous attempt to fix the World Series between the heavily favored Chicago White Sox and the Cincinnati Reds. When a grand jury was called to investigate the scandal in 1920, Attell fled to Canada to avoid being subpoenaed.

Attell won the lightweight title with a 15-round decision over George Dixon on October 28, 1901. He held the championship until February 22, 1912, when he lost a decision to Johnny Kilbane. He retired in 1915 with a record of 90 wins, 47 by knock-out; 10 losses, 3 by knockout; 17 draws and 50 no-decisions.

See also BLACK SOX SCANDAL.

ATV (All-Terrain Vehicle)

See OFF-ROAD RACING.

Auerbach, "Red" Arnold (1917–   )
Basketball

Born September 20, 1917, Brooklyn, NY; Basketball Hall of Fame

The winningest coach in NBA history, Auerbach played basketball at George Washington College, then spent four years as a high school coach and saw military service during World War II. In 1946, he became coach of the Washington Capitols in the newly formed Basketball Association of America, and compiled a 123–62 record in three seasons. After one season with the Tri-Cities Blackhawks, where he had a 29–35 record, Auerbach went to the Boston Celtics in 1950 as coach and general manager.

The BAA had become the NBA, and the Celtics were a poor team that had never had a winning season. Auerbach eventually created a dynasty, but it took time. The Celtics became winners as soon as he arrived, but success in the NBA playoffs eluded them until the 1956–57 season, when Auerbach traded all-star "Easy Ed" Macauley to the St. Louis Hawks for the rights to Bill Russell. Russell, an All-American out of the University of San Francisco, missed more than half of his rookie season while playing with the U.S. Olympic team. But, when he finally did join the Celtics, Russell's rebounding and superlative defensive play led them to their first NBA championship in 1957.

After losing to St. Louis in the 1958 finals, the Celtics won eight consecutive championships from 1959 to 1966. Perhaps the most dramatic was the last one, after Auerbach had announced he would retire after the season. The Celtics finished second in their division, but beat Philadelphia in the Eastern Division finals, four games to one, and then defeated Los Angeles in a seven-game championship series.

As a coach, Auerbach stressed team play and strong defense. As a general manager, he had a knack for finding a player no one else wanted who could fit into the Celtics' concept. Among them, through the years, were Bailey Howell, Don Nelson, Clyde Lovellette, and Willie Naulls. Auerbach also pioneered the idea of a "sixth man" who could come off the bench to ignite the team. Two of them, Frank Ramsey and John Havlicek, are in the Basketball Hall of Fame.

After retiring as coach, Auerbach continued as Celtics' general manager through the 1985–86 season, and the Celtics won NBA championships in 1968, 1969, 1974, 1976, 1981, 1984, and 1986. With 1,037 wins, including 99 in the playoffs, Auerbach is the only coach to compile more than 1,000 victories. He was named NBA Coach of the Year in 1965 and Executive of the Year in 1980, when he was also chosen by the Professional Basketball Writers Association as the greatest coach in NBA history.

Augusta National Golf Course

One of the most famous courses in the world, Augusta was conceived by golfer Bobby Jones, who also helped design it. In 1934, Jones and Cliff Roberts held the first Masters tournament, an invitational event that is now one of the four tournaments in golf's "grand slam." It has wide fairways, few bunkers, and large greens, and is not a particularly difficult course most of the time, but it's made much tougher for the Masters, largely through pin placements.

See also MASTERS TOURNAMENT (GOLF).

Auto Racing

Formal auto racing began in 1894 with a race of about 78 miles from Paris, France, to Rouen. It arrived in North America two years later when H. H. Kohlsaat, publisher of the *Chicago Times-Herald*, sponsored a 54.36-mile race from downtown Chicago to a suburb and back. The race was won by Frank Duryea, who averaged just 7.5 miles per hour, while driving through a heavy snowstorm.

Henry Ford saw auto racing as "advertising of the only kind that people care to read." Ford won a match race against Alexander Winton in 1902, then built what was probably the first car designed for sheer speed, the 80-horsepower "999." He hired Barney Oldfield, a bicycle racer who had never driven before, and Oldfield set a new world record of 91.37 miles per hour in 1904. The same year, William K. Vanderbilt set up a 28-mile road course on Long Island for the 300-mile Vanderbilt Cup race. The Vanderbilt Cup series continued until World War I. In 1905, Charles Glidden established the "Glidden tour," a long-distance highway race designed to test the durability of cars, and held annually until 1914.

Because the automobile was still new and people were interested in testing its limits, there were many attempts at the land speed record beginning in the early part of the century and continuing well into the 1930s. The sandy beach at Daytona was the most common site for such attempts, but on September 3, 1935, Sir Malcolm Campbell of England became the first to travel more than 300 miles per hour, at Bonneville Salt Flats in Utah, and that is still where most such runs are made, although they're much less frequent now. The current record is 633.6 miles an hour.

The Automobile Club of America, later the American Automobile Association, was the first U.S. governing body for the sport. On Thanksgiving Day in 1908 the club sponsored a Grand Prize Race at Savannah, GA that drew more than 200,000 spectators. A racing tour was established the following year with 24 races, including three at the newly opened Indianapolis Motor Speedway. The track was paved with brick in 1911, and the first Indianapolis 500-mile race was held on Memorial Day. An estimated 80,000 spectators saw Ray Harroun win with an average speed of 74.59 miles per hour. By 1929, attendance was up to 160,000, and the record for average speed was over 100 miles an hour.

In the early years, foreign cars dominated at Indianapolis, but in 1922 Jimmy Murphy drove his own specially built car to victory, and the custom racing car began to replace more or less standard production cars on the race tracks. During the Great Depression, most tracks were forced to close down. In 1938, there were only two races on the tour, the Indy 500 and a 100-mile race at Syracuse; there were just three races a year from 1939 through 1941, and then auto racing was discontinued entirely because of the gasoline shortage during World War II.

The midget race car was developed as a low-cost alternative to the larger racing cars, and the first midget race was held in 1934. Another important development was the Offenhauser engine, designed specifically for racing. An Offy-powered car won for the first time in 1935. In 1949, every winning car on the tour had an Offy engine, and the domination lasted until 1965, when rear-engine cars began to take over.

The tour resumed after World War II with 12 or 13 races a year for so-called Indy cars. Sprint car racing, which has begun in 1929, became popular, especially on short tracks at county fairs, and the AAA established a national championship for midget racing, as well. Stock car racing formally began in 1948 under the auspices of the new National Association for Stock Car Auto Racing, and the AAA also added a stock car division.

In 1956, the AAA decided to get out of auto racing in order to concentrate on services for motorists; the U.S. Auto Club was organized as the new governing body for the sport. Under USAC, the Indy car tour expanded rapidly in the late 1960s to 21 races in 1967 and 28 in 1968, before dropping back to 24 in 1969. By 1975 it was down to the previous level of 12 or 13 races a year.

Meanwhile, the Indy car itself had drastically changed. The first cars were two-seaters, carrying a driver and a mechanic. During the 1930s, a special type of race car evolved: A sleek, low-slung roadster that had most of the weight of the engine and power train on the left side, since the car constantly turned to the left. This remained the basic Indy car design after World War II, although the aerodynamics were considerably improved. In 1961, a small rear-engine vehicle called the Cooper-Climax appeared. Driven by Jack Brabham, a formula one driver from Australia, it finished ninth at Indy. Jimmy Clark, another Formula One driver, finished second at Indy in 1963 and later won the Milwaukee 200, the first victory for a rear-engine car. A revolution was underway. There were 12 rear-engine cars at Indianapolis in 1964 and 27 of them in 1965, when Clark won in a Lotus-Ford. Now all Indy cars have rear engines, limited to 750 horsepower. They burn a mixture of nitromethane and methyl alcohol.

Two race car owners, Roger Penske and U. E. "Pat" Patrick founded a new organization, Championship Auto Racing Teams, Inc., in 1978 because they were unhappy with the USAC bureaucracy. Gordon Johncock won the first CART race, a 150-mile event at Phoenix International Raceway on March 11, 1979. When USAC banned owners who entered that race from entering the Indy 500, CART brought suit, and a federal judge ruled that USAC must accept the entries. In 1980, CART and USAC jointly formed the Championship Racing League, but that ended after just five races, and CART sanctioned the remaining events. CART now controls all racing for Indy cars, except for the Indy 500, which is still run by USAC.

Further Reading: Cutter, Robert, and Bob Fendell. *The Encyclopedia of Auto Racing.* Englewood Cliffs, NJ: Prentice-Hall, 1973; Engle, Lyle K., with the editorial staff of *Auto Racing Magazine. The Complete Book of Auto Racing.* New York: Bantam, 1970; G. N. Georgano, editor. *The Encyclopedia of Motor Sport.* New York: Viking, 1971.

See also AUTOMOBILE COMPETITION COMMITTEE FOR THE U.S.; CHAMPIONSHIP AUTO RACING TEAMS; DRAG RACING; INDIANAPOLIS MOTOR SPEEDWAY; INTERNATIONAL MOTOR CONTEST ASSOCIATION; INTERNATIONAL MOTOR SPORTS ASSOCIATION; SPORTS CAR RACING; STOCK CAR RACING; U.S. AUTO CLUB.

Automobile Club of America
See AMERICAN AUTOMOBILE ASSOCIATION.

Automobile Competition Committee for the United States (ACCUS)

The Federation Internationale d'Automobile (FIA), which supervises international racing, allows a country to be represented by just one organization. The many U.S. organizations involved in international auto racing formed ACCUS in 1957 to serve as the country's representative to the FIA.

Address: 1500 Skokie Boulevard, Suite 101, Northbrook, IL 60062 (708) 272–0090

Aviation Bowl
Football

This bowl game was played just once, on December 9, 1961, when New Mexico beat Western Michigan 28–12 at Dayton, OH.

BAA

See BASKETBALL ASSOCIATION OF AMERICA.

Babe Ruth Baseball

Babe Ruth Baseball was founded in 1951 in Hamilton Township, NJ for boys 13 to 15 years old. Its first World Series was held the following year in Trenton, NJ. There are now well over 400,000 players on more than 23,000 teams throughout the United States, Canada, and Guam. The 16–18 age group was added in 1966, a prep league for 13-year-olds in 1976, and the Bambino Division for the 12-and-under age group in 1981. Teams play seven-inning games on regulation diamonds, except that the Bambino Division plays six innings on a 60-foot-square diamond. Tournament teams from leagues enter district competition, with district champions moving on to state tournaments, followed by eight regional tournaments. The eight regional champions and a host team then take part in a world series. A softball program was added for girls from 6 to 18 years of age in 1984.

Address: P.O. Box 5000, Trenton, NJ 08638 (609) 695–1434

See also LITTLE LEAGUE; PONY BASEBALL.

Bacardi Bowl
Football

A special feature of the Cuban National Sports Festival at Havana, this bowl game was played on New Year's Day, 1937. Auburn and Villanova played to a 7–7 tie.

Bachelor Subculture

The phrase, coined by Ned Polsky in his book, *Hustlers, Beats and Others* (1969), refers to groups of men, married and unmarried, who spent virtually all of their leisure time together, usually in gambling places, pool halls, or saloons, during the last quarter of the 19th century. In most cities, the majority of its members were Irish-Americans or recent Irish immigrants, but the subculture also attracted some "slummers," young men from the wealthier classes. Gambling, especially on boxing, was a popular pursuit, and many professional boxers came out of the subculture, often after having worked as "pugs" for a political machine.

Badminton

Badminton originated as a game called *poona* in India, where it was discovered by English army officers, who brought it to England. In 1873 the Duke of Beaufort played it with friends at his country place, Badminton, and it became known as "that sport at Badminton." The Bath Badminton Club, organized in 1887, was the first governing body. That role was taken over by the Badminton Association (of England) when it was founded in 1895. The association held the first All-England championships in 1899 and added a tournament for women the following year.

Badminton apparently arrived in Canada about 1890 and in the United States a few years later, but

The greatest U.S. woman badminton player, Judy Devlin Hashman won the All-England singles title 10 times and the U.S. singles 12 times. Courtesy of the American Badminton Association

"The new game of badminton in India" was portrayed in this English engraving of 1875, two years after the sport was introduced to England.

it became popular in Canada much more rapidly. The Ladies' Montreal Tennis and Badminton Club, the oldest in North America, was formed in 1907, and the Canadian Badminton Association was founded in 1921 at the University Club in Montreal. The following year the first Canadian Closed Championships took place. The American Badminton Association was organized in 1937.

World championships were planned by the International Badminton Federation in 1939, but they were postponed until the 1948–49 season because of World War II. The championships are held in odd-numbered years. The IBF also conducts a series of Grand Prix tournaments worldwide, with total prize money for a single tournament ranging from $15,000 to $125,000 and more. More than 80 tournaments are scheduled each year, about 20 of them in North America.

According to the ABA, badminton is second only to soccer in the number of participants. More than 6 million rackets are sold annually, and 93 national organizations with a total of more than a million and a half members now belong to the IBF. Badminton was offered as a demonstration sport at the 1972 Olympics.

Addresses: Canadian Badminton Association, 1600 James Naismith Drive, Gloucester, Ontario, Canada K1B 5N4 (613) 748–5605; U.S. Badminton Association, 501 West Sixth Street, Papillion, NE 68046 (402) 592–7309

Bailey, "Ace" Irvin W. (1903–   )
Hockey
Born July 3, 1903, Bracebridge, Ontario; Hockey Hall of Fame

One of the most shockingly violent incidents in hockey history occurred on December 12, 1933, when the Toronto Maple Leafs were playing the Boston Bruins at Boston Garden. Bruin defenseman Eddie Shore was checked hard into the boards by Toronto's King Clancy. Upset that no penalty had been called, he charged into Bailey from behind, flipping him into the air with a shoulder. Bailey landed on his head and lay motionless on the ice.

The doctor who attended him reportedly said, "If this boy is a Roman Catholic, we should call a priest right away." Bailey eventually recovered after two brain operations. Shore was suspended by the NHL and given a leave of absence by the Bruins, partly to protect him from possible violence in other rinks, but his suspension was rescinded because he had never before received a match penalty for deliberately injuring an opponent. On February 14, 1934, the Maple Leafs played an all-star team as a fundraiser for Bailey, and Shore was one of the all-stars. When the starting lineups were introduced before the game, Bailey and Shore shook hands and then embraced one another.

Bailey joined the Maple Leafs in 1926 and played for them until his near-fatal injury. He led the National Hockey League in scoring in the 1928–29 season with 22 goals and 10 assists, and in his eight-year career he had 112 goals and 82 assists.

Baker Bowl
Philadelphia, PA

Built by Albert G. Reach, owner of the Philadelphia Phillies, Baker Bowl was formally opened on April 30, 1887, when a capacity crowd of 18,800 fans saw the Phillies beat the Giants 15–9. In 1894, a fire destroyed the main grandstand, but the team kept using the park, and major renovations were completed in 1896. Seven years later, a railing on the top of the grandstand collapsed from the weight of fans leaning on it to watch a fight outside the park. Twelve people were killed, and more than 100 were injured. While the park was closed for repairs, the Phillies played in Columbia Park. On June 29, 1938, the Phillies played their last game in Baker Bowl, then moved into the Athletics' Shibe Park.

Baker Bowl was the first park to have a cantilevered stand, which stretched all the way from the left-field corner to the right-field corner. The field was only 272 feet down the right-field line, 408 feet to center, and 335 feet down the left-field line.

Baker, "Home Run" Frank (1886–1963)
Baseball

Born March 13, 1886, Trappe, MD; died June 28, 1963; Baseball Hall of Fame

A third baseman for the Philadelphia Athletics, Baker won his nickname during the 1911 World Series against the New York Giants. The second game was tied 1–1 when Baker hit a two-run home run, in the sixth inning to win the game 3–1. Baker tied the next game with a ninth-inning home run, and the Athletics went on to win in extra innings.

Baker joined the Athletics in 1908 and became a starter in 1909. Beginning in 1912 he was a member of Connie Mack's "$100,000 infield." The others were Stuffy McInnis at first base, Eddie Collins at second base, and Jack Barry at shortstop. Baker sat out the 1915 season because he was denied a raise, and the following year he was sold to the New York Yankees. He played there through 1919, sat out 1920 after the death of his wife, then returned to the Yankees for two more years, 1921–22. Baker led the American League in home runs with 11 in 1911, 10 in 1912, and 12 in 1913. He tied for the lead in 1914 with 9. Baker also led the league in triples in 1909 with 19. His .347 average in 1912 is a record for third basemen, and he had a career average of .307, with 93 home runs in 13 major-league seasons.

Baker, "Hobey" Hobart A. H. (1892–1918)
Football, Hockey

Born January 15, 1892, Bala-Cynwyd, PA; died December 21, 1918; National Football Foundation, Hockey Hall of Fame

The Princeton hockey team was known as "Baker and six other players" during his tenure, from 1910 through 1913. The "rover" in the days of seven-player hockey, he was the same type of player as Bobby Orr, a superb skater who could do everything at top speed. He also captained the Princeton football team in 1912. After graduating, he played amateur hockey for the St. Nicholas Arena team, scoring eight goals in his first two games, and he won high praise from Canadian observers. One of them wrote, "Uncle Sam has the cheek to develop a first-class hockey player who wasn't born in Montreal." To F. Scott Fitzgerald, who went to Princeton at the same time, Baker was the athlete as romantic hero; Fitzgerald never forgot seeing Baker striding across the campus with a bandage wrapped around his head, the souvenir of a football injury. True to his heroic image, Baker became a pilot during World War I, winning France's Croix de Guerre, and he died in a crash while testing a plane after the war had ended.

Balloon Racing

The hot-air balloon was invented by Etienne and Joseph Montgolfier of France. Their first balloon,

The first great U.S. hockey player, Hobey Baker, was also a third-team All-American football player for Princeton in 1913. Courtesy of the U.S. Hockey Hall of Fame

launched on June 5, 1783, at Annonay, France, flew about a mile and a half in 10 minutes. On November 21, Pilatre de Rozier and the Marquis d'Arlandes became the first men to fly, traveling about 9,000 yards in a Montgolfier balloon.

Balloon racing became a sport in the late 19th century. The Aero Club de France, founded in 1898, was the first regulatory body.

The sport was similar to early airplane racing, with duration, distance, and accuracy events. James Gordon Bennett, the publisher of the *New York Herald*, in 1906 established a trophy for an international balloon race. The annual competition continued until 1938, with six years off for World War I. But there were relatively few balloons and balloonists during that period.

The sport was revived in the early 1960s because of the development of the propane burner and synthetic fabrics. Edward Yost of the United States built the first modern hot-air balloon in 1961, using nylon. The Balloon Federation of America was founded that year to oversee local and regional competition leading up to the national championships in August. Since 1973, the BFA has also conducted the World Hot Air Balloon Championship in Albuquerque, NM. Biennial world championships are

conducted by the International Aeronautical Federation.

Address: Balloon Federation of America, P.O. Box 400, Indianola, IA 50125 (515) 961–8809

Baltimore, MD

Baseball A team called the Lord Baltimores was one of the original members of the National Association when it was formed in 1871. The association folded after the 1875 season, and Baltimore didn't have a major-league team until joining the American Association in 1882. It also had a team in the Union Association, which played only during 1884. Baltimore moved into the National League in 1891 and won three consecutive pennants, 1894–96, but in 1899 Ned Hanlon, the team's president, became manager of the Brooklyn team, and he took several of Baltimore's top players with him. When the National League cut down from 12 teams to 8 the following year, Baltimore was dropped.

The Baltimore Orioles were in the American League in its first major-league season, 1901, with John McGraw as manager. McGraw feuded with league president Ban Johnson, and went to the New York National League team in 1902, taking some players with him, as Hanlon had done. After the season, the franchise went to New York, where it eventually became known as the Yankees.

The St. Louis Browns of the American League moved to Baltimore in 1954 and became the Orioles, who won American League pennants in 1966, 1969, 1970, 1971, 1979, and 1983, and were eastern division champions in 1973, and 1974. The Orioles won the World Series in 1966, 1970, and 1983.

Basketball The Baltimore Bullets entered the Basketball Association of America for the 1947–48 season and immediately won a championship, beating Philadelphia four games to two in the final playoffs. The team broke up after playing just 14 games in the 1954–55 season. The BAA had become the National Basketball Association, and another team called the Bullets joined the NBA in 1963. The Bullets won the eastern division championship in 1969 and the central division title in 1971. They became the Capital Bullets, playing in Landover, MD, in 1973.

Football The Miami Seahawks of the All America Football Conference moved to Baltimore in 1947 and became the Colts, who joined the National Football League when the leagues merged in 1950. The franchise folded after that season. In 1953, the Dallas Texans moved to Baltimore and were renamed the Colts. They beat the New York Giants 23–17 for the 1958 NFL championship in the first sudden-death overtime game ever played. The Colts were division

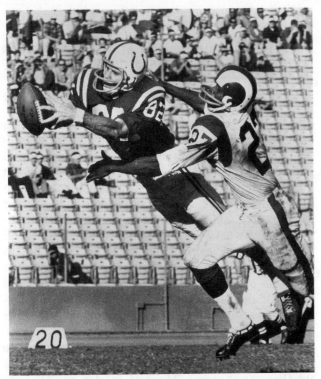

Raymond Berry of the Baltimore Colts was one of the stars of the first overtime game in professional football history, catching 12 passes in the Colts' 23–17 championship victory over the New York Giants in 1958. Courtesy of the Pro Football Hall of Fame

champions in 1959, 1964, and 1968 and won the NFL title in 1949 and 1968. They lost 16–7 to the New York Jets of the American Football League in Super Bowl III.

When the NFL and AFL merged in 1970, Baltimore, Cleveland, and Pittsburgh joined the former AFL teams in the American Football Conference. The Colts won the AFC championship in 1970 and beat the Dallas Cowboys 16–13 in Super Bowl IV. The franchise moved to Indianapolis in 1984.

Hockey Baltimore briefly had a team, the Blades, in the World Hockey Association. The franchise moved from Michigan midway through the 1974–75 season but lasted less than a year.

See also CAPITAL CENTRE; BALTIMORE MEMORIAL STADIUM; WASHINGTON, DC.

Baltimore Memorial Stadium
Baltimore, MD

Built as the home of the Baltimore Orioles in baseball's minor International League, this stadium opened in 1949, with a capacity of 31,000. When the St. Louis Browns of the American League moved to Baltimore and became the Orioles in 1954, the stadium was extensively remodeled and capacity was increased about 50 percent by adding a second deck to the grandstand. Later expansions increased capacity to 52,137. The baseball park has dimensions of 309 feet down each foul line, 385 feet in left center and right center, and 410 in center field.

Baltusrol Golf Club
Springfield, NJ

The original Baltusrol course, opened in 1895, was replaced in 1920 by two new courses, the upper and lower. The lower course has a 623-yard 17th hole, the longest ever in a U.S. Open. The Open was played on the old course in 1903 and 1915, on the lower course in 1936, 1954, and 1967.

Banff Springs Hotel Golf Course
Banff, Alberta

Generally considered the finest course in Canada, the Banff Springs layout is 6,704 yards long and plays to a par 71. The seventh hole was carved out of the face of a mountain in the Canadian Rockies, which surround the entire course.

Banks, Ernie (1931–   )
Baseball

Born January 31, 1931, Dallas, TX; Baseball Hall of Fame

The man called "Mr. Cub" genuinely loved playing baseball. Banks once walked onto the field before a game, looked at the sky, and said, "It's such a great day, let's play two games." He became the Chicago Cubs' starting shortstop in 1953 without any minor-league experience and played 424 consecutive games before being sidelined for 15 games in 1956; he then returned to the lineup for 717 consecutive games. Banks set a record for shortstops with 44 home runs in 1955 and broke that in 1958, when he led the league with 47. He also drove in 129 runs, batted .313, and was named the league's Most Valuable Player that year. Banks was MVP again in 1959 with a .304 average, 45 home runs, and 143 runs batted in. He set records for shortstops that season with only 12 errors and a fielding percentage of .985.

In 1962, Banks was moved from shortstop to first base, where he spent his last seven seasons. In his career, he hit .274 with 512 home runs, breaking Mel Ott's National League record of 511.

Barber, "Red" Walter L. (1908–   )
Sportscaster

Born February 17, 1908, Columbus, MS; Sportswriters and Sportscasters Hall of Fame

Barber attended the University of Florida, where he broadcast his first baseball game for the college radio station in 1929. He went to Cincinnati as the Reds' announcer in 1934, then became the Brooklyn Dodgers' broadcaster in 1939. In Brooklyn, Barber popularized the word "rhubarb" to refer to a baseball argument or fight, but denied coining the term. He commonly used unusual expressions from his native Mississippi, such as "sittin' in the catbird seat," meaning to be in a very good position, and "tearin' up the ol' pea patch." A believer in strict impartiality, he was criticized in 1947 for violating baseball tradition by mentioning that Yankee pitcher Bill Bevens was working on a no-hitter against the Dodgers. He replied that he was hired to be a reporter, not "a purveyor of superstition."

Barber was the announcer on the first major-league game ever telecast, between the Dodgers and the Reds in August of 1939. In the late 1940s, he began doing both television and radio, and at the end of his career he was strictly a TV broadcaster. He left the Dodgers after the 1953 season and did the New York Yankees' pre- and post-game shows for the next 12 years. He then became the Yankees' play-by-play announcer. Late in the 1966 season, attendance at a Yankee game was little more than 400; Barber mentioned the fact and asked cameramen to pan the empty seats. He was fired a few days later, creating a controversy over whether a sportscaster should be partial to his team's interests.

After his firing, Barber told a TV interviewer, "Radio and television have forgotten all about the most beautiful thing I know next to human love, and that's the English language." He later worked for a Miami radio station, made occasional network appearances on special sports events, and wrote a syndicated newspaper column. He also wrote a number of books, including *The Broadcasters* (1970).

Further Reading: Barber, Red, with Robert Creamer. *Rhubarb in the Catbird Seat*. Garden City, NY: Doubleday, 1968.

Barrel Jumping

During the 19th century, skaters sometimes took part in obstacle races, with barrels placed along the course. Barrel jumping probably grew out of that sport. It became rather popular in the 1930s, virtually died out, then returned in the 1950s. The object is to jump over a series of barrels lying on their sides; the person with the longest jump wins. North American and U.S. championships have been held since 1951.

Barrow, Joseph Louis

See LOUIS, JOE.

Baseball

Baseball descended from rounders, an English game also called "base ball" or "goal ball." An American soldier recorded playing "base" at Valley Forge on April 7, 1778, and a Princeton student in his diary mentioned "baste ball" in 1786. By the early 19th century, there were several forms of the game in North America. They had many elements in common: four bases or goals; a batter swinging at a pitched ball and trying to advance from base to base after hitting it; fielders attempting to put runners out by "soaking"—that is, hitting them with a thrown ball while between bases; and a run, or "ace," being scored when a runner reached the fourth base.

A group of young gentlemen in 1842 began to play baseball regularly at 27th Street and 4th Avenue in New York. In 1845 they organized the Knickerbocker Base Ball club, limited to 40 members who agreed to play every Monday and Thursday. Alexander Cartwright drafted a set of rules as the club bylaws. He specified four bases in a square 42 paces (just about 90 feet) on a side, three strikes for an out, and three outs in an inning. He also did away with "soaking" by requiring that a runner be tagged out. A batted ball caught on the fly or first bounce was also an out, and the first team to score 21 aces (runs) was the winner.

Although baseball's rules changed considerably over the next 50 years, the Knickerbocker Club bylaws, adopted on September 23, 1845, essentially created the modern form of the sport. The first recorded game was on October 7 at the Elysian Fields in Hoboken, NJ, and the club played at least 13 more games that fall. The first game against another team took place on June 19, 1846, when the New York Club beat the Knickerbockers 23–1.

Other clubs were soon formed, all made up of well-to-do young gentlemen. One club, the Aesculapians, was composed entirely of physicians from Brooklyn. On March 10, 1858, 22 clubs organized the National Association of Base Ball Players, and a series of three games between all-star teams from Brooklyn and New York at the Fashion Race Course drew crowds of about 1,500 that year.

Baseball had already spread into upstate New York, Cleveland, Detroit, and Chicago, and by 1859 California had a club. The sport was also played in some areas in the South; it was especially popular in New Orleans. The Brooklyn Excelsiors went on tour in 1860 through New York State and into Delaware, Maryland, and Pennsylvania, playing local teams.

Although the Civil War slowed growth, it also helped introduce baseball to many Southerners, who saw northern soldiers playing in prison camps. Thousands of Northerners also learned the game while training with New Yorkers. Growth was explosive after the war. Sixteen clubs from Illinois, Indiana, Iowa, Michigan, Minnesota, Missouri, Ohio, and Wisconsin formed the Northwestern Association of Base Ball Players on December 6, 1865, and associations were organized in Ohio and Iowa in 1867. By the following year, the National Association had nearly 350 clubs from all over the country. One of the major purposes of the association was to preserve amateurism, but the very popularity of baseball defeated that purpose. Teams secretly began paying some players as early as 1860, when pitcher Jim Creighton of the Excelsiors became the first known professional.

An English-born cricket instructor, Harry Wright, in 1869 organized the first openly all-professional team, the Cincinnati Red Stockings. They toured the East, then went to the West Coast, winning 56 of their 57 games (the other was a tie) and playing before an estimated 200,000 spectators. In March of 1871, ten clubs formed the National Association of Professional Base Ball Players and established a series of games leading to a championship. The original teams were the Boston Red Stockings, the Chicago White Stockings, the Forest Citys of Cleveland, the Forest Citys of Rockford, the Kekiongas of Fort Wayne, the New York Mutuals, the Philadelphia Athletics, the Unions of Troy, the Washington Nationals, and the Washington Olympics.

This association was supplanted in 1876 by the first true major league, the National League of Professional Base Ball Clubs, an association of owners, not players. Within ten years of the National League's founding, *Harper's Weekly* remarked, "the fascination of the game has seized upon the American people, irrespective of age, sex, or other condition." Baseball was already being called "the national game."

Between 1858 and 1890, many rules changes were made, most of them attempts to balance offense and defense. When the National Association was formed in 1858, it called for nine-inning games. Pitchers threw underhand from a distance of only 45 feet. The batter told the umpire whether he wanted a high or low pitch, and the umpire then told the pitcher. If the pitcher threw three pitches that were not in the right area, the umpire would call "unfair ball," and after three unfair balls the batter was awarded first base. If a batter did not swing at a good pitch, the umpire would call it a strike—unless the batter already had two strikes, in which case he would be warned that the next good pitch would be called a strike. In effect, a walk required nine balls, a strikeout four strikes.

In 1880, eight balls were required for a walk. The following year, the pitching distance was moved to 50 feet, with seven balls for a walk and three strikes for an out. The walk was reduced to six balls in 1884, when pitchers were allowed to throw overhand or sidearm, and it was cut to five balls in 1885.

Major changes were made in 1887. The pitcher was no longer allowed to take a run and jump before throwing the ball, and the batter was no longer allowed to specify the kind of pitch he wanted. Seven balls or being hit by a pitch put the batter on base, and four strikes were allowed. Batting averages were inflated that season, because walks counted as hits. In 1888, walks were no longer hits, and the batter was given only three strikes. The following year, the walk was reduced to four balls. That created the game almost as we know it. The last major change was the increase in the pitching distance to 60 feet 6 inches in 1893. (It was supposed to be 60 feet 0 inches, but a surveyor misread the number.)

Equipment also evolved. At first, the flat cricket-type bat was used, but in 1862 the rules specified that the bat had to be round. From 1885 through 1891, a bat with one flat side was permitted, but the round bat came back in 1892. Charles G. Waite, in 1875, began using an ordinary glove with the fingertips cut off to protect his hand. He was first regarded as a sissy, but soon other players wore similar gloves and a heavily padded glove for catchers was introduced in 1891. Fred W. Thayer of Harvard modified a fencing mask for use by catchers in 1875, the chest protector was invented in 1877, and Hall of Fame catcher Roger Bresnahan added the last major piece of equipment, shin guards, in 1907.

Collegiate baseball flourished during this period. The Lawrence Baseball Club, organized at Harvard in 1858, played under National Association rules, and Princeton formed a club later that year. Amherst and Williams played the first intercollegiate game on July 1, 1859, Amherst winning 73–32. Harvard went on tour in 1870, traveling as far west as St. Louis and winning 17 games while losing 8, mostly against professional teams.

The American College Baseball Association was established in 1879 by Amherst, Brown, Dartmouth, Harvard, Princeton, and Yale, but the league disbanded in 1888 after a series of disputes. Baseball was second only to football as an intercollegiate sport until early in the 20th century, when its popularity was diminished by the growth of minor-league baseball.

The National League faced several challenges from other leagues during the 19th century. The American Association, which began play in 1882, signed some of the league's players and had a successful year; its six cities actually had a greater total population than the National League's eight, and it offered Sunday games, the sale of liquor, and a 25-cent admission, compared to the League's 50 cents. Before the 1883 season, the two leagues and the minor Northwestern League signed the Tripartite Pact, later known as the National Agreement, agreeing to honor one another's contracts.

The two major leagues lived in peace for seven years, overcoming a relatively minor challenge in 1884 from the Union Association, which lasted just one season. A much more significant challenge was the Players' League, organized in 1890 by the Brotherhood of Professional Base Ball Players. The new league attracted many National League stars, but everyone lost money in the bloodbath that followed, and the Players' League, like the Union Association, was defunct after one season. Most of its teams simply merged with their counterparts in the National League.

The war left the American Association in bad shape. Most of its former players who had jumped to the Players' League were now in the National League, and after two association players were signed by the League's Pittsburgh team, the American Association repudiated the National Agreement. The result was another brief war, which ended after the 1891 season, when the National League absorbed four association teams to become a 12-team circuit, and the American Association was gone.

By 1900, the National League was down to eight teams again, and a new challenger was emerging to the west. Under the leadership of Ban Johnson, the minor Western League was renamed the American League in 1900. It expanded into eastern cities in 1901 and lured at least 70 players from the National League. Before the 1902 season began, the two leagues made peace and signed a new National Agreement, along with the National Association of Professional Leagues, an alliance of minor leagues. The agreement created a three-man National Commission to govern organized baseball. The first World Series was played between Pittsburgh of the National League and Boston of the American League in 1903, Boston winning five of nine games. There was no series in 1904, but the leagues formally agreed in 1905 to play a championship series, and it's been played annually ever since.

In 1913, six teams made up of free agents formed the Federal League without joining the National Agreement. The following year, it expanded to eight teams and signed more than 80 players from the

In 1866, baseball was already being called "The American National Game," the title of this Currier & Ives lithograph of a game at the Elysian Fields.

existing major leagues and more than 100 from the minor leagues. The Federal League lasted through the 1915 season, then agreed to go out of business in exchange for $600,000 from organized baseball. Two of its owners were permitted to buy existing major-league franchises.

The last real threat to major-league baseball was internal. After the heavily favored Chicago White Sox of the American League lost the 1919 World Series to the Cincinnati Red Stockings, there were widespread rumors of a fix, and a Chicago grand jury began investigating in 1920. Eight White Sox players, who became known as the "Black Sox," were indicted, along with 11 gamblers. No convictions resulted, but major-league baseball was forced into an extensive reorganization. The three-man National Commission was replaced in late 1920 by a single commissioner, Judge Kenesaw Mountain Landis, and a new National Agreement in 1921 gave him almost unlimited powers to take any actions necessary to protect the sport. Landis promptly banned the eight players. He ruled organized baseball until his death in 1944, at the age of 78.

Babe Ruth did at least as much as Landis to rescue baseball from the scandal. A brilliant left-handed pitcher with the Boston Red Sox for five seasons, Ruth became a full-time outfielder after being traded to the New York Yankees in 1920. He hit 54 home runs that season, shattering his own record of 29, set the year before. He was helped by the livelier ball introduced that season to make baseball more exciting and more enticing to fans, but he was still far ahead of his nearest rival, George Sisler, who hit only 19. The game changed remarkably in a 15-year period. Home runs per team per game climbed from 0.33 in 1915 to 1.26 in 1930, while stolen bases per game declined from 2.20 to 0.87.

The two major leagues remained stable until 1953, when the National League's Boston Braves moved to Milwaukee, setting a precedent for other financially troubled franchises. The St. Louis Browns became the Baltimore Orioles in 1954, the Philadelphia Athletics moved to Kansas City in 1955, and major-league baseball finally arrived on the West Coast in 1958, when the Brooklyn Dodgers moved to Los Angeles and the New York Giants to San Francisco. Then came expansion, originally spurred by the announcement that a new major league was to be formed. The Washington Senators became the Minnesota Twins in 1961, and were replaced by a new Washington Senators franchise. The Los Angeles Angels also joined the American League that year. In 1962, the Houston Colt .45s (now the Astros) and the New York Mets were added to the National League.

Both leagues expanded to 12 teams in 1969. The Athletics moved from Kansas City to Oakland, and the new Kansas City Royals and the Seattle Pilots joined the American League, while the National League added the San Diego Padres and the first Canadian franchise, the Montreal Expos. The Seattle franchise was in trouble immediately, and moved to Milwaukee as the Brewers in 1970. (The National League's Braves had moved to Atlanta in 1966.) The leagues were now organized into eastern and western divisions, each with its own champion, requiring a postseason playoff to determine the pennant winner. The playoffs were best-of-five games until 1985, when they become best-of-seven games. The most recent expansion was in 1977, when the Seattle Mariners and Toronto Blue Jays became American League teams.

Labor unrest marked the 1970s and early 1980s. The Major League Players Association went on strike on April 5, 1972, which was supposed to be opening day. Owners quickly assented to the association demand for increased pension benefits, and the season finally opened on April 15. The following year, the basic agreement between the players and owners was amended to allow outside arbitration on grievances and on salary negotiations for any player with more than two years of major-league service.

But the association's chief goal was to win free agency for as many players as possible. The first major victory came in 1975, when an arbitrator ruled that pitchers Dave McNally and Andy Messersmith were free agents because they had played a full season without contracts. In effect, that decision meant that the reserve clause, which supposedly bound a player to a team for life, was really effective for only one year. A second strike, which began on June 12, 1981, and lasted eight weeks, resulted in an agreement allowing any player to become a free agent after six seasons in the major leagues. For the first time since owners had adopted the reserve system in 1879, a sizable number of players were free to sell their services on the open market. The average salary nearly tripled in just five years, from $46,000 in 1975 to $135,000 in 1980, and the balance of power had apparently shifted to the players for the first time in more than a century.

Further Reading: Henderson, Robert W. *Baseball: Notes and Materials on Its Origin.* New York: New York Public Library, 1940; Leitner, Irving A. *Baseball: Diamond in the Rough.* New York: Criterion, 1972; Seymour, Harold. *Baseball: The Early Years.* New York: Oxford University Press, 1960; ———, *Baseball: The Golden Age.* New York: Oxford University Press, 1971; Voigt, David Quentin. *American*

Baseball: From Gentleman's Sport to the Commissioner System. Norman: University of Oklahoma Press, 1966.

See also AMERICAN LEAGUE; BASEBALL HALL OF FAME AND MUSEUM; CARTWRIGHT, ALEXANDER; MINOR LEAGUES; NATIONAL AGREEMENT; NATIONAL COMMISSION; NATIONAL LEAGUE; WORLD SERIES.

Base Ball Players Fraternity

Some major-league players began talking about organizing a union in 1910, and Jack Fultz, a lawyer who had once played major-league baseball, was hired to help. The Base Ball Players Fraternity was chartered in September of 1912. The fraternity at first was occupied primarily with keeping spectators from abusing players and ensuring that a player traded from one team to another would not have his salary cut. But on November 8, 1913, 17 demands were presented to the sport's governing body, the National Commission, and the nearly 500 players who signed the petition threatened not to play in 1914 unless the demands were met.

In January of 1914, Fultz and a committee of five players met with the National Commission to discuss their demands, and they worked out an agreement generally favorable to the players. However, when Clarence Kraft was sent by Brooklyn to its minor-league team, he was claimed by Nashville in a lower minor league, and the claim was granted. Kraft refused to report, because it would have meant a salary cut, and the fraternity threatened to strike on July 22 if Kraft wasn't allowed to play for Newark. Finally, the Dodgers paid Nashville $2,500 for the rights to Kraft so that he could stay with Newark, and the strike was averted.

One reason for the fraternity's success was the Federal League, which sought major-league status. Owners feared that fraternity members might jump en masse to the Federal if they weren't satisfied. But the would-be third league lasted only two seasons, 1914–15. In January 1916, the National Commission announced it would no longer recognize the fraternity, the 1914 agreement was rescinded, and the Base Ball Players' Fraternity was effectively defunct.

See also FEDERAL LEAGUE.

Baseball Hall of Fame and Museum

Dedicated on June 12, 1939, at Cooperstown, NY by Commissioner Kenesaw Mountain Landis, the Baseball Hall of Fame was inspired by the Hall of Fame for Great Americans at New York University. The place and year were chosen because of the myth that Abner Doubleday had invented baseball at Cooperstown in 1839—a myth created in 1907 by a committee established by organized baseball and chaired by A. G. Mills.

In 1936, the first five players were chosen: Ty Cobb, Walter Johnson, Christy Mathewson, Babe Ruth, and Honus Wagner. When the hall opened, 13 players were enshrined. The others, selected by the Baseball Writers Association of America, were Grover Cleveland Alexander, Eddie Collins, Lou Gehrig, Willie Keeler, Napoleon Lajoie, George Sisler, Tris Speaker, and Cy Young. The next election was not held until 1942, when Rogers Hornsby was chosen.

A player becomes eligible for election by the BWAA five years after retirement. He must have played at least ten major-league seasons, and his name has to appear on 75 percent of the ballots. Twenty years after retirement, a player can no longer be elected by the BWAA, but a veterans' committee, made of former players, retired writers, and baseball executives, can elect players of the past who have been overlooked by the writers. Because many great black players had been banned from major-league baseball until 1947, a seven-man committee was formed in 1971 to select players from the Negro leagues. That committee named nine players before being disbanded in 1977.

In addition to plaques of inductees, the museum has a collection of baseballs, bats, and other equipment, cigarette and bubble gum baseball cards, trophies, and pictures. Its library includes a complete set of baseball guides, record books, scrapbooks, newspaper clippings, photographs, phonograph records, and tapes.

Baseball Parks

The original baseball fields were just that, open fields, ringed by standing spectators. On May 15, 1862, William Cammeyer opened the first enclosed baseball park, the Union Grounds, at Rutledge Street and Lee Avenue in Brooklyn. Cammeyer let teams use it rent-free, but collected 10 cents admission. Among the teams who played at the Union Grounds were the Brooklyn Atlantics and the New York Mutuals.

By 1871, all of the cities in the National Association had enclosed wooden parks. The only seating was on benches, often reserved for women spectators, and seating capacity was generally less than 2,000. The use of grandstands and bleachers, which began with Chicago's West Side Park in 1885, increased seating to a maximum of about 15,000. There were no dugouts; the players sat on plain wooden benches. The dugout originated when box seats did. The boxes were generally placed about 6 feet above field level, and the dugouts were tucked under them.

Baseball began to draw much larger crowds after 1900, and that brought the need for larger parks, built of concrete. The first was Forbes Field in Pittsburgh, opened in 1909. By 1923, when Yankee Stadium opened, every major-league team had a concrete stadium. At first, they usually had grandstand seating behind home plate and along the base lines, with bleachers along the outfield foul lines. There were no seats behind the outfield walls, which were often as much as 500 feet away from plate. But as attendance increased, teams began putting seats in front of the outfield walls, and eventually these seats were fenced in. That changed the nature of baseball by creating the home run hit out of the park.

These stadiums were owned by the baseball teams themselves, though they were often rented out for boxing, football, and other events. The next great trend in stadium building was largely the result of major-league expansion, beginning in 1960. Cities that wanted franchises offered to build parks themselves, often with county and/or state aid. Because of the enormous cost, most of these new stadiums were also designed for football. Of the major-league parks in use now, only five are owned by the teams that play in them: Comiskey Park and Wrigley Field in Chicago, Fenway Park in Boston, Tiger Stadium in Detroit, and Dodger Stadium in Los Angeles.

See also STADIUMS.

Baseball Writers Association of America (BWAA)

Like many organizations of sportswriters, the BWAA was formed to help improve working conditions in press boxes. Its main function now is selecting winners of a number of awards, including the Cy Young Award for the outstanding pitcher in each major league, and the Most Valuable Player and Rookie of the Year Awards. The BWAA also elects former players, who have been retired for more than 5 years but less than 21 years, to the Baseball Hall of Fame.

Address: 36 Brookfield Road, Fort Saratoga, NY 11768 (516) 757–0562

Basketball

Luther H. Gulick, Jr., the head of the physical education department at the International Young Men's Christian Association Training School in Springfield, MA in the late fall of 1891 asked instructor James Naismith to come up with an indoor game to occupy students during the winter. Naismith tried adapting football, soccer, and lacrosse for indoor play, but they just weren't suitable. Then it occurred to him that a game in which a player could not run

with the ball might be the answer, and that a horizontal goal would force players to throw the ball in an arc, rather than trying to hurl it through a wall of opponents.

Naismith asked the janitor to find him a couple of boxes. The janitor returned with two peach baskets. Naismith nailed the baskets to the lower rail of the balcony runnning around the top of the gym, got a soccer ball, and wrote down 13 rules for his new sport. The rules stated that the ball could be thrown or batted in any direction, but not hit with the fist; that a player could not run with ball; that the ball must be held with the hands only, without using the arms or body; that bodily contact would be considered a foul, and when a player committed his second foul, he would have to leave the game without being substituted for until the next goal; and that if either side committed three consecutive fouls, the other team would be awarded a goal. A game would consist of two 15-minute halves. Naismith even made a provision for sudden-death overtime after a tie, if both captains agreed.

The first game was played in middle to late December of 1891. The class had 18 members, so there were 9 players on each team. Just one goal was scored. Nevertheless, Naismith wrote, "The game was a success from the time the first ball was tossed up. . . . Word soon got around that they were having fun in Naismith's gym class, and only a few days after the first game we began to have a gallery." That led to Naismith's first major change: He had backboards put up to keep fans in the balcony from kicking the ball away from the basket. A student named Frank Mahan suggested that the sport should be called "Naismith ball," but the modest Naismith quickly parried with "basket ball" (usually spelled as two words until 1921).

There was a lot of tinkering with the rules through the early years of the sport. Players realized that they could pass the ball to themselves, either by tossing it into the air or by bouncing it. Juggling and double dribbling were banned in 1898, but the dribble itself was allowed. Teams at first ranged from 3 to 40 players. Naismith and Gulick in 1893 decided to allow five or nine players, and in 1894 they decided seven players was all right, too. The number was standardized at five for the 1897–98 season. A basket counted as only one point until 1894–95, when it was raised to three points, with one point awarded for every foul committed by an opponent. In 1896–97 the value of a field goal was reduced to two points. The free throw, from 20 feet, was introduced in 1894–95, and the following season the distance was cut to 15 feet. Until 1923, each team designated one player to shoot all of its free throws. The game was extended to two 20-minute periods in 1893–94, and in 1907–08 the 5-minute overtime period replaced the sudden-death overtime.

The game was played with a soccer ball until a bicycle manufacturer, the Overman Wheel Company, introduced a basketball in 1894. The peach basket was replaced in 1892 by a wire basket with a hole in the bottom so that a pole could be used to push the ball back out; until then, someone had to climb a ladder to get it. In 1893, a basket with iron rims and a cord netting was made, with a chain at the bottom that, when pulled, released the ball. The first open-bottom nets were made as early as 1906, but they weren't approved for championship play until the 1912–13 season. Backboards were usually made of wood or wire mesh until 1908, when the plate-glass backboard was introduced.

Because of the network of YMCAs all across North America, basketball spread with amazing speed. A Canadian student, William H. Ball, brought the sport to Montreal during Christmas vacation, just a week or so after its invention. By the summer of 1892, it was being played on the Sioux Indian reservation in South Dakota. That fall, Walter E. Magee brought the sport to the University of California, where it became especially popular among women students.

Women began playing basketball very early. Teachers from a Springfield girls' school watched a game early in 1892, and in March they arranged a game between their girl students and women teachers. Senda Berenson, director of physical education at Smith College, visited Naismith that fall to learn the sport and she organized the first women's college game on February 22, 1893, between two teams of Smith students. Stanford and the University of California played the first recorded women's intercollegiate game on April 4, 1895. One of the first great touring teams was made up of women. The Edmonton Commercial Grads of Alberta, Canada, traveled an estimated 125,000 miles through North America and Europe between 1915 and 1940, winning 522 games while losing 20, beating men's teams seven times in nine tries. They also won 14 Canadian national championships.

Women played by men's rules until 1899, when the women's rules committee made a whole series of changes designed to reduce physical exertion and prevent rough play. The court was divided into three sections, and each player was assigned to a specific section, which she could not leave. A player was allowed to hold the ball for no more than 3 seconds, the dribble was limited to one bounce, and stealing the ball was forbidden. A team could consist of anywhere from five to ten players. The number was set at six in 1937.

The first men's collegiate team to play outside competition was apparently the University of Toronto, which beat the Toronto YMCA 2–1 on January 25, 1893. The first intercollegiate game was played between two small schools, the Minnesota State School of Agriculture and the Minnesota State School of Agriculture-Hamline, on February 9, 1895. Hamline won 9–3.

Columbia, Cornell, Harvard, Princeton, and Yale founded the Eastern Intercollegiate Basketball League in 1901, and Yale won the first championship. The college sport was governed by the AAU from 1894 until 1905, when the newly formed Intercollegiate Athletic Association, now the National Collegiate Athletic Association, took over. Three sets of rules were evolving in somewhat different ways, so in 1915 the AAU, the YMCA, and the NCAA created the Joint Rules Committee to work out a unified code.

Professional basketball began as an outgrowth of YMCA basketball. Some YMCA directors decided that a sport using such a large area for a relative handful of players wasn't such a good idea after all, and they dropped basketball. The teams often remained together, but had to rent gyms to play in. To raise the rent money, they began charging admission or passing a hat among spectators. The first professional game is believed to have been played in 1896 in the Trenton (NJ) Masonic Hall, although some claim there was a pro game as early as 1893 at the Fox Opera House in Herkimer, NY.

The first National Basketball League was formed in 1898 with teams from Camden, NJ; Germantown, PA; Hancock, PA; Millville, PA; Philadelphia, and Trenton, NJ. It was replaced in 1902 by the Philadelphia League, which had several of the same teams. In 1908–09, the league expanded and was renamed the Eastern League, which played through the 1922–23 season. Other early professional leagues included the Central (1906), the Hudson River (1909), the New York State (1911), the Western Pennsylvania (1912), the Pennsylvania State (1914), the Inter-State (1915), and the Metropolitan Basketball League (1926).

Naismith had meant basketball to be a noncontact sport, but it was very rough early in the century, especially on the professional level, where the court was often surrounded by a wire cage to protect the fans from the players, and vice versa. One pioneer pro player, Barney Sedran, recalled, "Players were thrown against the wire. Most of us were cut several times. The court was covered with blood. Ninety percent of the fellows I played with had broken

The team that won the first basketball game ever played, in December of 1891, is enshrined as a unit in the Hall of Fame. The sport's inventor, James Naismith, is on the right in the middle row. Courtesy of the Basketball Hall of Fame

noses." Money wasn't good, and most of the early professionals played for several different teams in different leagues; some of them played as many as 200 games in a season.

The greatest of the early professional teams signed their players to exclusive contracts and barnstormed,

Basketball was also being played outdoors in 1892, less than a year after its invention. Note that there is no backboard; that wasn't added until 1896, primarily to prevent fans in the balcony from interfering with play. Courtesy of the A.A. Stagg Lecture Material, Basketball Hall of Fame

taking on all comers, rather than playing in a league. First came the Original Celtics, named for the New York Celtics, a pre–World War I settlement house team. Organized in 1918, the original Celtics were probably the best team in basketball during the 1920s. The New York Whirlwinds challenged them in 1921, and they split two games, but the Celtics then hired the two best players from the Whirlwinds. In 1922–23, they won 194 of 205 games.

Another great barnstorming team, the Harlem Renaissance Big Five, better known as the "Rens," was organized in 1922 by Bob Douglas and named for the Harlem Renaissance Casino, a nightclub. This all-black team went on the road in the late 1920s, and won 2,318 games while losing 381 in 22 seasons. The Rens inspired the formation of the best-known and most traveled basketball team of all time, the Harlem Globetrotters, organized in 1926 as the Savoy Big Five. After a few difficult years on the road, the Globetrotters caught on big, although they didn't really become globetrotters until after World War II.

The AAU held its first national championship tournament in 1897. It was won by New York City's 23rd Street YMCA, which later became a professional team, the Wanderers. The tournament was not held from 1902 through 1909; it resumed in Chicago in 1910, was suspended for two more years, and became permanently reestablished in 1913. YMCA teams dominated the early tournaments, colleges took over in the early 1920s, and then industrial teams such as the Hillyard Chemical Company, the Cook Paint Company, Henry Clothiers, the Diamond D-X Oilers, Denver Safeway Stores, and the Phillips 66 Oilers became dominant. Industrial teams won every AAU championship from 1929 through 1956.

The first women's national championship was played in 1926 at Pasadena, CA, using men's rules. The Pasadena Athletic and Country club won the tournament. It wasn't played in 1927 or 1928, but it resumed in 1929. Industrial teams dominated here, too.

By then, the sport was truly international. Three games in China in as many nights drew a total of 75,000 spectators in 1931. YMCA workers and missionaries had introduced the sport throughout Asia and in parts of Africa, as well as in Europe. By World War II, basketball was being played in more than 75 countries. American teams demonstrated the sport at the 1904, 1924, and 1928 Olympics, and in 1936 it became an official Olympic sport. Women's basketball became an Olympic sport in 1976.

Collegiate play was pretty much regional until 1934, when sportswriter Ned Irish began promoting doubleheaders in Madison Square Garden, usually

A wire net, or cage, surrounded many early basketball courts, such as this one at the Paterson (NJ) Armory. Basketball players are still sometimes called "cagers." Courtesy of the Basketball Hall of Fame

matching good New York area teams against teams from elsewhere in the country. The first double-header, on December 29, 1934, pitted New York University against Notre Dame and St. John's against Westminster College of Missouri, attracting 16,138 spectators. During the season, Irish promoted eight doubleheaders that drew a total of 99,955. In December of 1936, Stanford ended a Long Island University winning streak at 43 games, and Hank Luisetti introduced the one-hand shot to 17,263 fans, starting a basketball revolution. Within a few years, everyone was using the one-hand shot.

Irish's success led to the first National Invitation Tournament at Madison Square Garden after the 1937–38 season, and the National Collegiate Athletic Association launched its national championship tournament the following year. The NIT was the premier tournament until the early 1950s, when the NCAA tournament gained supremacy.

Meanwhile, professional basketball struggled. George Preston Marshall, owner of a team called the Washington Palace Five, organized the American Basketball League in 1925. Teams represented Brooklyn, Chicago, Cleveland, Detroit, Ft. Wayne, Rochester, and Washington. The Original Celtics joined in the middle of the 1926–27 season and won two straight championships. The team was broken up, but three Celtics ended up with the Cleveland Rosenblums and won another title there. The ABL became dormant in 1931 and was reorganized for another try in 1933, but despite its name it was only a regional league. The Philadelphia Sphas, named for the South Philadelphia Hebrew Association, where they had begun play in 1918, won 7 championships in 13 seasons. This all-Jewish team was coached by Eddie Gottlieb, who later founded the Philadelphia Warriors. The Sphas played most of the top independent teams of the era, and won many more games than they lost.

The beginning of modern professional basketball was the founding of the National Basketball League in 1937. The chief movers were three teams from the Midwest Industrial Basketball Conference, the Akron Firestone Non-Skids, the Akron Goodyear Wingfoots, and the Ft. Wayne General Electrics. They were joined by teams in Buffalo, Columbus, Dayton, Ft. Wayne, Kankakee, IL, Indianapolis, Pittsburgh, Oshkosh, WI, Richmond, IN, Warren, OH, and Whiting, IN. In 1938–39, several college stars entered the league, and the NBL continued to operate with moderate success through World War II.

The NBL was suddenly confronted by competition in 1946, when a group of arena owners organized the Basketball Association of America. The NBL still had most of the stars, but the BAA had much larger arenas. A bidding war for college players began. The NBL won the first major battle, signing George Mikan of DePaul, the pro sport's first outstanding big man (6 feet 10 inches), for the 1946–47 season. Mikan led the Chicago American Gears to the league championship that year, while the Philadelphia Warriors won the BAA title.

The BAA went from 11 franchises to 8 in the 1947–48 season, and almost every team in both leagues lost money. But four NBL franchises moved into the BAA in the summer of 1948, and the following year the two leagues merged as the National Basketball Association, with 17 teams. There were only eight teams by the beginning of the 1954–55 season, when a rule requiring a team to shoot within 24 seconds of gaining possession of the ball went into effect. That rule is generally considered the salvation of the professional sport, because it eliminated the kind of stalling that had led to a 19–18 victory by Ft. Wayne over Minneapolis on November 22, 1950, in the lowest-scoring game in NBA history.

That began an almost uninterrupted climb in attendance, which reached nearly 2 million in 1960 and more than 5 million in 1970. The NBA's success led to the formation of the American Basketball Association in 1967. In the ensuing battle for college stars, the average salary leaped from $20,000 in 1967 to more than $100,000 in 1975. The leagues agreed to merge in 1970, but they were blocked by an antitrust suit brought by the NBA's players. The merger finally took place in 1976, and 4 ABA teams joined the NBA, creating a league of 22 teams in four divisions. By 1989, there were 27 teams, with a total attendance of more than 15 million, and CBS and the Turner Broadcasting System were paying the league a total of about $100 million a year for television rights. But the biggest basketball show on TV was the NCAA tournament, televised by both ESPN and CBS over a three-week period, with a prime-time championship game and television revenue of about $60 million.

Further Reading: Hollander, Zander, editor. *The Modern Encyclopedia of Basketball*. Garden City, NY: Dolphin, 1979; Isaacs, Neil. *All the Moves: A History of College Basketball*. Philadelphia: Lippincott, 1975; Jares, Joe. *Basketball: The American Game*. Chicago: Follett, 1971; McCallum, John D. *College Basketball U. S. A. Since 1892*. New York: Stein & Day, 1978; Naismith, James. *Basketball: Its Origins and Development*. New York: Association Press, 1941; Weyand, Alexander M. *The Cavalcade of Basketball*. New York: Macmillan, 1960.

See also AMERICAN BASKETBALL ASSOCIATION; AMERICAN BASKETBALL LEAGUE; NAISMITH, JAMES; NAISMITH MEMORIAL BASKETBALL HALL OF FAME; NATIONAL BASKETBALL ASSOCIATION; NATIONAL BASKETBALL LEAGUE; NATIONAL INVITATION TOURNAMENT.

Basketball Association of America
See NATIONAL BASKETBALL ASSOCIATION.

Baugh, "Slingin' Sammy" Samuel A.
(1914–   )
Football
Born March 17, 1914, Tyler, TX; National Football Foundation, Pro Football Hall of Fame

Another charter member of the Pro Football Hall of Fame, Johnny "Blood" McNally, once said that if he were to choose up sides for a game, Sammy Baugh would be his first choice. "He could beat you in every possible way," he said, "on offense or on defense." Hall of Fame center Mel Hein agreed, saying that Baugh came closer to being a one-man team than anyone else who'd ever played. He's the only player ever to lead the NFL in passing, punting, *and* interceptions—and he did that in a single season, 1943.

Baugh went to Texas Christian on a baseball scholarship, but became a varsity football player in 1934, when "Dutch" Myers began coaching and installed the spread formation, which emphasized a passing attack. "Slingin' Sammy" was a consensus All-American as a senior, in 1936, when he completed 109 of 219 passes for 1,890 yards and 11 touchdowns. During his college career, he had 274 completions in 599 attempts for 3,439 yards and 39 touchdowns.

He signed a baseball contract with the St. Louis Cardinals, but George Preston Marshall offered him $5,000 to play for the Washington Redskins—a very high salary in 1937—so Baugh opted for pro football. Baugh spent his entire 16-year professional career with the Redskins, as a single-wing tailback for the

"Slinging Sammy" Baugh was the only player ever to lead the National Football League in passing, punting, and interceptions, in 1943. He played for the Washington Redskins from 1937 through 1952. Courtesy of the Pro Football Hall of Fame

first seven seasons, then moving to quarterback in 1944 when the team installed the T-formation.

Baugh's actual pro debut came before the 1937 season, in the college all-star game against the NFL champion Green Bay Packers. His 47-yard touchdown pass to Gaynell Tinsley was the only score in a 6–0 victory. Then he led the Redskins to the Eastern Division championship. In the NFL championship game, the Chicago Bears had a 14–7 halftime lead, but Baugh threw a 55-yard touchdown pass to Wayne Millner in the third quarter to tie the score. The Bears then scored to take the lead again. Baugh took over in the fourth quarter, with touchdown passes of 78 yards to Millner and 35 yards to Ed Justice, and the Redskins won, 28–21.

The Redskins played the Bears in the championship game three more times, in 1940, 1942, and 1943. They suffered the worst defeat in NFL history, 73–0, in 1940. Baugh threw what looked like a touchdown pass on the first play of the game, but his receiver dropped the ball. Asked afterward if that had made a difference in the outcome, Baugh drawled,

"Yes, we would have lost 73–7." In the 1942 game, he threw a 25-yard touchdown pass to Wilbur Moore as the Redskins beat the previously undefeated Bears, 14–6. And he had touchdown passes of 17 yards and 26 yards in 1943, but the Bears overwhelmed the Redskins 41–21.

For the rest of his career, he played for mediocre or downright bad teams, but he still had some outstanding days. When Washington played the Chicago Cardinals in 1947, the Redskins and their fans staged "Sammy Baugh Day." He passed for 355 yards and six touchdowns in a 45–21 upset victory that afternoon, against a team that went on to win the NFL championship.

Baugh was the NFL passing champion six times: 1937, 1940, 1943, 1945, 1947, and 1949. He led the league in pass attempts in 1937 (171), 1943 (239), 1947 (354), and 1948 (313); in completions in 1937 (81), 1943 (133), 1945 (128), 1947 (210), and 1948 (185); in completion percentage in 1940 (62.7), 1942 (58.7), 1943 (55.6), 1945 (70.3), 1947 (59.3), 1948 (58.7), and 1949 (56.9); in passing yards in 1937 (1,127), 1940 (1,367), 1947 (2,938), and 1948 (2,599); and in touchdown passes in 1940 (12) and 1947 (25). During his career, he completed 1,693 of 2,995, a percentage of 56.5, for 21,886 yards and 186 touchdowns. His career punting average of 44.9 yards is an NFL record.

Baylor, Elgin (1934–   )
Basketball
Born September 16, 1934, Washington, D.C.; Basketball Hall of Fame

When Baylor joined the Minneapolis Lakers of the NBA in 1958, he represented a new kind of basketball player—big and strong (6 feet 5 inches and 225 pounds) yet quick and agile. Baylor could go to the basket with power or finesse, and he could pull up for an accurate jump shot. According to Bob Short, who owned the Lakers, Baylor's signing saved the franchise from bankruptcy, because ticket sales immediately increased.

At Seattle University, Baylor led the nation in rebounding as a junior and was an All-American as a senior in 1958. In 80 college games, he scored 2,500 points for a 31.3 average and had 1,559 rebounds. The Lakers' first choice in the college draft, he was the NBA's Rookie of the Year in 1959.

He spent 13 seasons in the NBA, all with the Lakers—11 of them after they moved to Los Angeles in 1960—and was named All-NBA nine times. Baylor set the league's single-game scoring record with 64 points against Boston on November 8, 1959, and extended it to 71 points against New York on November 15, 1960. (The record was broken in 1962 by Wilt Chamberlain.) In 1962, he scored 2,719 points, an average of 38.2 per game, but finished second to Wilt Chamberlain.

Baylor retired after playing just a few games in the 1971–72 season. At the time, he was the NBA's third all-time leading scorer with 23,149 points in 846 games, a 27.4 average, and he had 11,463 rebounds. He added 3,623 points in 134 playoff games, including a record 61 in 1962. Baylor was one of the ten players named to the NBA's Silver Anniversary Team in 1972.

B.C. Place Stadium
Vancouver, British Columbia

B.C. Place was built at a cost of nearly $100 million in connection with EXPO 86, Vancouver's World's Fair. The stadium, which has the world's largest air-supported roof, was one of the first projects completed in the 224-acre complex. Since opening in 1983, it has been the home field of the Canadian Football League's British Columbia Lions. It seats 59,478.

Beacon Race Course

Built at a cost of more than $60,000, the Beacon Race Course in Hoboken, NJ was the first luxurious race track in North America, but it was a failure. Cadwallader R. Colden, who had formerly operated the Union Course on Long Island, oversaw its construction, but the new owners of the Union Course, Alexander L. Botts and David H. Branch, outbid Colden and leased the new track. It opened in November 1837, during a depression, didn't attract many racing fans, and soon became primarily a trotting track. In 1844, the course was the site of three major pedestrian races that helped establish that sport in the New York area. The Beacon Course closed early in 1845.

Beamon, "Bob" Robert (1946–   )
Track & Field

Born August 29, 1946, New York, NY; National Track and Field Hall of Fame

Although an inconsistent long jumper who often fouled, Beamon turned in one of the most incredible leaps in history at the 1968 Olympic Games in Mexico, with a jump of 29 feet 2½ inches, the first time anyone had jumped more than 28 feet. His personal best until then had been 27 feet 4 inches. Early in 1969, Beamon suffered a severe hamstring pull, forcing him to change his takeoff foot, and he never again jumped more than 27 feet. Beamon won the U.S. outdoor long jump championship in 1968 and 1969.

Beckman, John (1895–1968)
Basketball

Born October 22, 1895, New York, NY; died June 22, 1968; Basketball Hall of Fame

"The Babe Ruth of basketball" spent 27 years as a professional without any college experience. After playing for the Hudson County Opals, the Troys of Union Hill, and Hoboken, Beckman joined the Original Celtics in 1922. He was the best foul shooter of his era, an important asset since each team then selected one player to take all of its free throws. In 1927, his contract was sold to the Baltimore Orioles of the Eastern Basketball League for an unheard-of $10,000, a tribute not only to his basketball skills but to his ability to draw fans. The New York Basketball Old-Timers in 1950 named him the greatest professional player of his era.

Bednarik, "Chuck" Charles A. (1925–   )
Football

Born May 1, 1925, Bethlehem, PA; National Football Foundation, Pro Football Hall of Fame

The two-platoon system, using offensive and defensive specialists, began in 1950. Yet Bednarik, at the age of 35, played both offensive center and defensive linebacker for the Philadelphia Eagles for much of the 1960 season and logged 58 minutes in the NFL championship game against the Green Bay Packers. With time running out in the game and the Eagles leading 13–10, Green Bay fullback Jimmy Taylor caught a pass and seemed to be headed for a touchdown, but Bednarik made a game-saving tackle at the Eagles' 9-yard line.

Bednarik served in the air force during World War II, then entered the University of Pennsylvania, where he was an All-American center in 1947 and 1948. The Eagles' bonus pick in the 1949 draft, he missed the first two games of the season with an injury, but missed only one more game in the rest of his 14-season career. He was All-Pro center in 1950 and an All-Pro linebacker for the next five seasons. During his career, he had 20 interceptions, returning them for 268 yards and one touchdown.

Beliveau, Jean A. (1931–   )
Hockey

Born August 31, 1931, Three Rivers, Quebec; Hockey Hall of Fame

The Montreal Canadiens coveted Beliveau for several years, while he was playing in the amateur Quebec Senior League, but they delayed signing him because of fears that Quebec legislators would have the Montreal Forum liquor license taken away in retaliation. Finally, the Canadiens bought the entire league to get Beliveau, and he joined the team for the 1953–54 season.

Six feet 3 inches, 210 pounds, and known as "Le Gros Bill" ("Big Bill") by his French-Canadian fans, Beliveau was one of the largest forwards ever in the National Hockey League. He won the Hart Trophy as the league's Most Valuable Player in 1956 and 1964 and was a ten-time All-Star. Beliveau led the league in scoring in the 1955–56 season with 88 points on 47 goals and 41 assists. An exceptionally smooth, effortless skater with speed, he was well liked by his teammates, partly because of his unselfish play. Linemate Dick Duff once said of him, "He had great moves, that great range, and anyone playing on a line with him was certain to wind up with a lot of goals."

Beliveau remained with the Canadiens through the 1970–71 season, scoring 482 goals and 661 assists in 1,955 games. He is the only player besides Gordie Howe and Wayne Gretzky to score more than 1,000 career points.

Bell, "Bert" De Benneville (1895–1959)
Football

Born February 25, 1895, Philadelphia, PA; died October 11, 1959; Pro Football Hall of Fame

Bell bought the Philadelphia Eagles of the National Football League in 1933 and lost large amounts of money during the next eight seasons. Before the 1941 season, he sold the Eagles and became a part owner of the Pittsburgh Steelers.

With the NFL facing a major challenge from the All America Football Conference, Bell succeeded Elmer Layden as the league's commissioner in 1946. His greatest contribution to pro football was his television policy. In 1952, he persuaded owners to agree to bylaw changes that blacked out telecasting of home games into a team's home territory and gave the commissioner the right to negotiate a package television contract for the entire league rather than letting each franchise work out its deal. As an owner, Bell also had proposed the idea of an annual draft of college players. He died of a heart attack while watching a game between his two former teams, the Eagles and the Steelers.

Bell, "Cool Papa" James T. (1903–   )
Baseball

Born May 17, 1903, Starkville, MS; Baseball Hall of Fame

Satchel Paige once said of Bell, "He was so fast he could turn out the light and be in bed before the room got dark." He may have been the fastest man ever to play baseball. In a game against a major-league all-star team, he scored from first base on a sacrifice bunt. And in 1945, when he was 42 years old, he was still among the stolen-base leaders in the Negro National League. His speed allowed him to play such a shallow center field that he could catch a runner at second on a pickoff play.

Bell began his professional career with the St. Louis Stars of the Negro National League in 1922, and stayed there for ten seasons. In 1932, he was with the Detroit Wolves, and the following year he joined the Pittsburgh Crawfords for four seasons. After playing in the Dominican Republic in 1937 and in Mexico from 1938 through 1941, he was with the Chicago American Giants in 1942 and the Homestead Grays from 1943 through 1946. Bell was player-manager of the Detroit Senators in 1947 and the Kansas City Stars from 1948 through 1950.

A left-handed throwing switch hitter, Bell reportedly hit over .300 virtually every season he played, and over .400 several times. Unfortunately, the Negro leagues did not keep good records, but it is known that he batted .437 in Mexico in 1940, and he was credited with 175 stolen bases in 1933, when he played about 200 games.

Belmont Park
Elmont, NY

When it opened in 1890, the Belmont Stakes, previously run at Jerome Park, became Belmont Park's most famous race. The track became known internationally in 1923, when Joseph Widener suggested a match race between Zev, winner of the Belmont, and Papyrus, who had won the English Derby. On a muddy track, Zev took an easy 8-length victory. The international tradition continues with a major turf event that often attracts top European horses, the Man o'War Stakes. The $300,000 Turf Classic was also formerly held at Belmont, but has moved to Aqueduct.

Belmont's Fall Championship Series has three events: the Marlboro Cup, the Woodward Stakes, and the Jockey Club Gold Cup. There's also an important fall series for fillies: the Maskette, the Ruffian Handicap, and the Beldame. In 1963, Belmont closed for major renovations, including a completely new grandstand that seats 30,000. The park reopened in 1968. The main course is a 1½-mile oval. Belmont also has the Widener Turf Course, 1^{15}/16 mile plus 27 feet, and an inner turf course of 1³/16 mile.

Address: P.O. Box 90, Jamaica, NY 11417 (718) 641-4700

See also NEW YORK RACING ASSOCIATION.

Belmont Stakes
Horse Racing

The third race in the Triple Crown for three-year-olds is the oldest and longest of the three. First run in 1867 at Jerome Park, it moved to Morris Park in 1889 and to Belmont Park in 1890. The distance was 1⅝ miles until 1874; 1¼ miles from 1890 through 1892 and in 1895; 1⅛ miles in 1893 and 1894; 1⅝ miles from 1896 through 1925; and 1½ miles from 1874 to 1889 and from 1896 to the present.

Bennett Trophy

James Gordon Bennett donated trophies for air racing, auto racing, and balloon racing. The Bennett Trophy auto race for three-car teams from competing countries, first run in 1900, was replaced by the French Grand Prix in 1906. The ballooning trophy was established in 1906 for an international race, held annually through 1938. Bennett also donated a trophy for the first international air meet at Reims, France, in 1909. It was in competition through 1913, and there was a final race in 1920.

Bennett, James Gordon, Jr. (1841–1918)
Patron

Born May 10, 1841, New York, NY; died May 14, 1918

Bennett was the successor to John Cox Stevens as a rather eccentric but important patron and promoter of sports. His father made a fortune as owner of the *New York Herald*, but was never part of New York society. At the age of 16, the younger Bennett owned a 77-foot yacht, and became the youngest member of the New York Yacht Club. Nine years later, in 1866, he won the first transatlantic race, for $60,000 in bets, losing six crew members to a violent storm in the process.

During an 1875 visit to England, Bennett discovered polo. The following year, he hired an English player to teach the game to his friends, with mallets and balls imported from England and a carload of cow ponies from Texas. Then he organized the Westchester Polo Club and introduced the sport to other society friends in Newport, RI, a summer colony for the wealthy. In Newport, he built the Casino Club, a sports complex that hosted the U.S. national tennis championships from 1881 through 1914 and is now the home of the International Lawn Tennis Hall of Fame.

To promote his name and his newspaper, Bennett also donated trophies for several sports, beginning in 1873, when he put up a challenge cup for the 2-mile race that was on the first intercollegiate track and field program, at the Saratoga regatta. He exiled himself to France in 1878, after creating a scandal by urinating in a fireplace at his fiancee's New Year's party, which broke the engagement and led to a harmless duel with her brother. Bennett established trophies for auto racing in 1900, balloon racing in 1906, and air racing in 1909, and also contributed money to the United States Olympic movement.

Bennett was not just a patron. In 1874, he and a lawyer named John Whipple had a walking race from Bennett's home on 38th Street in Manhattan to Jerome Park, more than ten miles, for a $3,000 bet. Others bet an estimated $50,000 on the race. Bennett won in one hour 46 minutes and 55 seconds.

Benoit, Joan (Mrs. Samuelson) (1957–   )
Distance Running

Born March 16, 1957, Eugene, OR

Benoit set a U.S. record of 2 hours 22 minutes 43 seconds in the 1983 Boston Marathon, and she won the Gold Medal in the first women's Olympic marathon in 1984. Then she was troubled by injury. Just two weeks before the 1988 Olympic trials, she had arthroscopic surgery on a knee, and ran in almost constant pain after that. Nevertheless, she continues to compete in marathons, explaining that she wants to run one in less than 2 hours and 20 minutes before retiring. Representing Bowdoin College, Benoit won the 10,000-meter run at the 1979 championships of the Association of Intercollegiate Athletics for Women, and she also won the event at The Athletics Congress national championships in 1981.

Further Reading: Benoit, Joan, and Sally Baker. *Running Tide*. New York: Alfred A. Knopf, 1987.

Berenson, Senda (Mrs. Abbott) (1868–1954)
Basketball

Born March 19, 1868, Vilna, Lithuania; died February 16, 1954; Basketball Hall of Fame

The first director of physical education at Smith College, Berenson visited the nearby Springfield Training School in 1892 to learn a new sport called basketball. On March 21, 1893, she coached and officiated the first women's collegiate game at Smith. Like most educators of her day, she seriously underestimated women's physical abilities and endurance, so she developed a totally different sport, in which each player was assigned an area of the court in which she had to remain throughout the game. To eliminate physical contact, attempting to steal the ball was forbidden. Dribbling was limited to just three bounces. Her rules were formally adopted by the Physical Training Conference in 1899. Berenson originated the Women's Basketball Guide in 1901 and edited it for 12 years. She was also the chief organizer of the Basketball Committee for Women in 1905. Berenson and Margaret Wade were the first two women elected to the Basketball Hall of Fame.

Berg, "Patty" Patricia J. (1918–)
Golf
Born February 13, 1918, Minneapolis, MN; World Golf Hall of Fame

Berg and Babe Didrikson were the first great professional women golfers. She didn't begin playing until 1932, but she was runner-up in the U.S. Women's Amateur in 1935 and 1937, and she won it in 1938. During her professional career, which began in 1940, she won more than 80 tournaments, including the U.S. Women's Open in 1946. During the celebration of golf's centennial in the United States, she was named player of the decade for 1938–47, and the Associated Press named her the woman athlete of the year in 1938 and 1943.

Among Berg's other major victories were seven Western Opens and seven Titleholders championships. Somehow she also found time to conduct more instructional clinics than any other golfer in history, introducing the sport to thousands of women throughout the world.

Berra, "Yogi" Lawrence P. (1925–)
Baseball
Born May 12, 1925, St. Louis, MO; Baseball Hall of Fame

Though he's probably best known for his "Yogi-isms," such as "Ninety percent of this game is half mental," Berra didn't get into the Baseball Hall of Fame for the way he talked. In 17 seasons with the New York Yankees, he played in 14 World Series, a record, and he also holds Series records for most games, 75, most times at bat, 259, most hits, 71, and most times playing on the winning team, 10. He got the first pinch-hit home run in Series history in 1947. Berra was named the American League's Most Valuable Player in 1951, 1954, and 1955, and he played in 15 all-star games.

Berra originally won a job with the Yankees primarily for his hitting, at the end of the 1946 season, but he became an outstanding defensive catcher. He led league catchers in fielding percentage and assists three times and in putouts eight times, and from 1957 to 1959 he caught 148 consecutive games without making an error. He was also an excellent handler of pitchers. Casey Stengel, who managed the Yankees for 12 of Berra's seasons, called him "my assistant manager." A left-handed hitter, Berra hit 30 home runs, an American League record for catchers, in 1952 and in 1956. Five times he had more than 100 runs batted in. For his career, Berra hit .285, with 385 home runs and 1,430 RBIs.

In 1964, the year after he retired as a player, Berra managed the Yankees to their fifth straight pennant, but he was fired after they lost the World Series to the St. Louis Cardinals in seven games. He became the New York Mets' manager in 1973, won a pennant with them the following year, and was fired late in the 1975 season. Berra served as a coach with the Yankees and the Houston Astros before retiring from baseball after the 1990 season.

Further Reading: Berra, Yogi, with Tom Horton. *Yogi: It Ain't Over. . . .* New York, McGraw-Hill, 1989.

Berwanger, "Jay" John J. (1914–)
Football
Born March 19, 1914, Dubuque, IA; National Football Foundation Hall of Fame

The first winner of the Heisman Trophy, in 1935, Berwanger was an All-American quarterback at the University of Chicago. At 6 feet 1 inch and 190 pounds, he was a big back for his time, and he could run the 100-yard dash in just over 10 seconds. His teammates called him "the man in the iron mask," because he wore a face protector after suffering a broken nose in his freshman year. Berwanger was best known as a runner. He had touchdown runs of 97 yards against Iowa in 1934, 85 yards against Ohio State in 1935, and 65 yards against Dartmouth in 1933, and in his three years as a starter he gained more than 5,000 yards. But he was also an excellent passer; in 1934 he threw three game-winning touchdown passes. The Philadelphia Eagles made him their first choice in the 1936 college draft, then traded the rights to the Chicago bears, but Berwangter chose not to play professionally.

Betsy Ross Bowl
Yachting
Inaugurated in May 1989 as part of New York City's second annual Fleet Week, the Betsy Ross Bowl is a series of six races over a three-day period for women sailors in 24-foot sloops, each with a crew of five.

Betting
See GAMBLING.

Betts, John R. (1917–1971)
Sports Historian
Born July 1, 1917, Bloomsbury, NJ; died August 9, 1971

Betts was the first professional historian to concentrate on sports history. A 1938 graduate of Princeton, he became interested in the history of sports while studying for his doctorate at Columbia University, but he had doubts because it was not considered a suitable field for serious study. Fortunately, his adviser was John A. Krout, author of *Annals of American Sport*, who told him there should be no limits to intellectual curiosity. The result was Betts' 757-page thesis, *Organized Sport in Industrial America*, completed in 1951. Betts began teaching at South Dakota State College in 1946, went to Tulane University in 1948, and to Boston College in 1954. At his death, he was preparing the manuscript for *American's Sporting Heritage: 1850–1950*, published posthumously in 1974 by Addison-Wesley.

Biathlon

Also known as the military biathlon, this sport grew out of exercises by European military ski patrols. It was on the Winter Olympic program as "military ski patrol" in 1924, 1928, 1936, and 1948. Then it was dropped, but it became an Olympic event again in 1960. The first world championships were held in 1958. Competitors race on skis over a long-distance course, periodically stopping to shoot at targets with rifles. If a target is missed, 2 minutes is added to the racer's time. The sport was formerly governed in the United States by the U.S. Modern Pentathlon and Biathlon Association, but a separate U.S. Biathlon Association was spun off in 1980 and now has about 1,000 members. The Canadian governing body is Biathlon Canada.

Addresses: Biathlon Canada, 333 River Road, Vanier, Ontario, Canada K1L 8H9 (613) 748-5608; U.S. Biathlon Association, P.O. Box 5515, Essex Junction, VT 05453 (802) 655-4524

Bicycle Polo

This less expensive alternative to polo was developed in England in 1897, but didn't achieve much popularity in the United States until the late 1960s. The U.S. Bicycle Polo Association, formed in 1942, now has about 20 member clubs.

Address: 107 East 99th Street, Suite 2B, New York, NY 10128 (212) 369-3599

Bicycle Racing
See CYCLING.

Big East Conference

The Big East, founded in 1979, is a basketball conference only. The original members were Boston College, Georgetown, Providence, St. John's (New York), Seton Hall, Syracuse, and the University of Connecticut. Villanova was added to the conference in 1980, and Pittsburgh in 1982. The conference has been highly successful, largely because it includes four of the country's top ten television markets and a quarter of the 90 million homes that have TV. In the 1988–89 season, 110 Big East games were televised, many of them nationally on CBS and ESPN, and the conference earned more than $6 million from television. The exposure not only helps financially, it helps Big East schools recruit players. In 1985, it became the first conference in history to have three teams in the NCAA Final Four, and Villanova beat Georgetown in an all–Big East final.

Facing the prospect of losing its three major football schools, Boston College, Pittsburgh, and Syracuse, to another conference, the Big East in 1990 announced that the University of Miami (FL) would become a member effective with the 1991–92 school year. Miami is a major football school with a mediocre basketball program. The move will allow the Big East to have its own miniconference of four major football teams, while also spurring Miami to improve its basketball program in order to become competitive in the Big East.

Address: 321 South Main Street, Providence, RI 02903 (401) 272-9108

Big Eight Conference

The Missouri Valley Intercollegiate Athletic Association was organized on January 12, 1907, by the Universities of Iowa, Kansas, Missouri, and Nebraska, Washington University of St. Louis, and Ames College (now Iowa State University). Drake University was added in 1908, and Iowa dropped out in 1911. The Kansas College of Applied Science and Agriculture, now Kansas State University, entered the conference in 1913, followed by Grinnell College in 1919, the University of Oklahoma in 1920, and Oklahoma A & M, now Oklahoma State, in 1925. At an association meeting on May 19, 1928, six of the seven state universities reorganized as the Big Six. It became the Big Seven on December 12, 1947, when the University of Colorado was added, and the Big Eight on June 1, 1957, when Oklahoma State joined.

Address: 104 West Ninth Street, Suite 408, Kansas City, MO 64105 (816) 471-5088

Big Four
See INTERPROVINCIAL RUGBY UNION.

Big Ten Conference

The Big Ten originated as the Intercollegiate Conference of Faculty Representatives, attended in 1895 by representatives of the Universities of Chicago, Illinois, Michigan, Minnesota, and Wisconsin, as well as Northwestern and Purdue. At the time, intercollegiate sport was largely under student control. The conference set a precedent for faculty control of athletics, voting to allow only bona fide undergraduates who were not delinquent in their studies to compete. The faculty representatives also decided that a transfer student would have to wait for half a year before becoming eligible.

Shortly afterward, the group became known as the Western Intercollegiate Conference. Indiana University and the University of Iowa entered the conference on December 1, 1899. Michigan withdrew on January 14, 1908, Ohio State joined on April 6, 1912, and Michigan rejoined on November 20, 1917, bringing membership to ten. The University of Chicago dropped football after the 1939 season and withdrew from the conference in 1946, when it became known as the Big Nine. It became the Big Ten when Michigan State was admitted on May 20, 1949.

Address: 1111 Plaza Drive, Suite 600, Schaumburg, IL 60173 (708) 605-0110

See also ANGELL CONFERENCE.

Billiards

Billiards in a rather primitive form was played by the Dutch in New Amsterdam in the 1650s and by southern gentry as early as 1710, when William Byrd II (1674–1744) had a table on his Virginia plantation. Wealthy New Yorkers also played billiards in the 1730s. The table at that time looked much like the modern pocket billiards table. Surrounded by a low railing and covered with green cloth, it had six pockets, called "hazards." The game itself was very different, though. There was an ivory wicket, the "port," at one end of the table and an ivory peg, the "king," at the other end. Each player had a small ivory ball and used a kind of miniature hockey stick. Points could be scored by knocking the ball through the port, by touching the king without knocking it down, or by knocking the opponent's ball against the king or into a hazard.

A different version if the game, developed in France, was introduced in the late 18th century, possibly by French officers during the American Revolution. This version was similar to modern carom billiards in that it was played on a pocketless table, and players tried to score "billiards" by hitting all of the object balls with the cue ball on a single shot. Billiards is now played with only two object balls, but at that time there were usually three. In 1808, New York City had eight public billiard tables in hotels and coffeehouses, and there were undoubtedly many more in private homes. By 1850, the sport had developed something of a split personality. It was played by

gentlemen in homes and private clubs, while public billiard rooms "were always associated with gambling and various forms of low life", as Ned Polsky put it.

Michael Phelan, the owner of a New York billiard parlor, set out to change the sport's image. In 1850, he challenged English champion John Roberts to play matches in England and the United States for $500 a match. Roberts didn't respond, but Phelan recieved a lot of free publicity for his challenge. His book, *Billiards without Masters*, was published that year and went through ten editions between 1850 and 1875. In 1855, Phelan and Hugh Collender began making billiard tables, and in 1856 he founded a four-page monthly publication, *Billiard Cue*. He played the first recorded U.S. match in 1858, beating Ralph Benjamin for $1,000.

Meanwhile, Dudley Kavanagh emerged as a top professional player. He won the $2,000 prize in a winner-take-all tournament in New York in 1858 and, on April 10, 1859, he beat Michael Foley in the first match at which admission was charged. Just two days later, Phelan beat John Seereiter at Fireman Hall in Detroit, in a match billed as "the billiard championship of the United States." This match attracted much attention in the press, and all 500 seats were sold. Reportedly, Phelan won $15,000, $10,000 in a bet with Seereiter and $5,000 from the promoter.

Kavanagh and Phelan never played one another, but they were rivals nevertheless, since they both manufactured equipment. Phelan retired in 1863 and Kavanagh won a tournament to become the new U.S. champion. In September of 1865, Phelan organized the American Billiard Players Association to supervise the sport. The following year, Kavanagh became president of the new National American Billiards Association. Billiards was also gaining popularity in Canada. On November 21, 1864, the first championship tournament for Upper Canada (now Ontario) was held in the Toronto Music Hall. The first official U.S. billiards championship tournament was played in 1870, when John Deery and A. P. Rudolphe tied.

But the sport became boring as expert players learned how to keep all the balls in the same area of the table, near a cushion, and score billiards repeatedly by making the same shot over and over, so balklines were introduced. The lines, drawn a specified distance from the cushions, define balk areas. A player is allowed to make only one or two points while the balls are in a balk area. The first form of this game was 8-inch balkline, in 1883. The following year, 14.2 balkline billiards, in which the lines are 14 inches from the cushions and two points

All 500 seats at Fireman Hall in Detroit were sold for the championship billiards match between Michael Phelan and John Seereiter on April 12, 1859. Phelan's victory was illustrated in the New York Clipper.

are allowed in a balk area, was invented. In 1897, 18.1 balkline became the championship sport, and 18.2 was introduced in 1902.

Pocket billiards was created during the 1870s. Its common name, "pool," derives from the fact that it was usually played in pool parlors, where gambling pools were organized. The first world championship was held in 1878, when three-cushion carom billiards was introduced. In this game, the cue ball has to hit three cushions before striking the second object ball. By 1935, the balkline games were obsolete, replaced by three-cushion carom and pocket billiards.

The Billiard Congress of American, established in 1948, was the single governing body for both carom billiards and pocket billiards until 1964, when the National Pocket Billiards Association was founded. The NPBA sanctions league and tournament competition in its sport and issues weekly statistical reports. The Professional Pool Players Association, founded in 1976, sponsors the sport's major tournament, the World Open Pocket Billiards Championship. Some three-cushion tournaments are sponsored by the U.S. Billiard Association, which was formed in 1989 by a merger of the American Billiard Association and the Billiard Federation of the U.S.A.

Addresses: Billiard Congress of America, 1901 Broadway Street, Suite 310, Iowa City, IA 52240 (319) 351-2112; National Pocket Billiards Association, 2635 West Burnham Street, P.O. Box 15365, Milwaukee, WI 53215 (414) 672-3935; Professional Pool Players Association, 422 North Broad Street, Elizabeth, NJ 07206 (201) 355-1302; U.S. Billiard Association, 757 Highland Grove Drive, Buffalo Grove, IL 60089 (708) 459-7042

Blacks in Sports

Little is known about how black slaves amused themselves, but they were often used to amuse their owners. Slaves crewed in rowboat races, trained fighting cocks and horses, rode as jockeys, and may sometimes have been matched against one another in boxing. The first American athlete to compete internationally was Bill Richmond, a freeborn black who went to England at the age of 14. He won at least six fights before losing to Tom Cribb in 1805. Tom Molineaux, a former slave who may have been freed because of his boxing prowess, also won several fights in England before losing to Cribb in December of 1810.

Before the Civil War, slaves were occasionally given holidays to help relieve tensions. According to Frederick Douglass, "the majority spent the holidays in sports, ball-playing, wrestling, boxing, foot races, dancing and drinking whiskey." After the war, some emancipated slaves became professional horse trainers and many more became jockeys. The greatest jockey of the 19th century was Isaac Murphy, who rode Kentucky Derby winners in 1884, 1890, and 1892. When the Jockey Club began licensing riders in 1894, the number of new black jockeys was limited, and eventually none were licensed. By 1930, there were only about a dozen blacks among the 950 licensed jockeys, although Charlie Smoot was riding in steeplechases well into the 1930s.

One of the greatest of the early black athletes was Marshall W. "Major" Taylor, a bicycle racer during the 1890s, when cycling was a very popular sport. Blacks were excluded from the League of American Wheelmen in 1894 because many southern clubs threatened to leave the organization, and the National Racing Association was also an all-white group. However, Taylor was such a drawing card that race promoters in the North usually welcomed him. Taylor won the national sprint championship from 1898 through 1900.

Sports developed in black colleges much as they had in white colleges. Biddle College (now Johnson C. Smith) and Livingstone College played the first football game between black schools on Thanksgiving Day of 1892. Hampton Institute, Lincoln University, Union University, and Wilberforce University had basketball teams before 1911, when many black colleges added the sport, and baseball became popular at black schools after 1910. Two black collegiate conferences, the Colored Intercollegiate Athletic Association and the North Carolina Inter-Collegiate Athletic Association, were organized in 1912. They were followed by the Southern Intercollegiate Athletic Association (1913), the Southwestern Athletic Conference (1920), the South-Central Athletic Conference (1923), the Middle Atlantic Athletic Association (1931), and the Mid-Western Athletic Association (1932).

Before black colleges had football teams, there were some black players at predominantly white colleges. William H. Lewis played center for Amherst from 1888 through 1891, then went to Harvard Law School and became the first black All-American in 1892. Charles Follis was the first black professional football player, with the Shelby (OH) Athletic Club in 1904. Fritz Pollard, an All-American halfback at Brown, was the first black to play in the National Football League. He joined the Akron Pros in 1919, the year before the league was organized as the American Professional Football Association, and became the team's player-coach in 1921. He was the only black head coach in NFL history until Art Shell took over the Los Angeles Raiders during the 1989 season.

Other early black players were Paul Robeson of Rutgers, who played two seasons in the NFL, and Duke Slater, an All-Pro tackle in 1928 and 1929. In 1933, Ray Kemp was with the Pittsburgh Pirates (now the Steelers) and Bill Lillard played for the Chicago Cardinals, but both were released after the season, and there were no more blacks in pro football until 1946. In 1935, Cardinal Coach Les Schissler admitted that Lillard, an outstanding runner, had been cut because of his color.

Baseball was popular among blacks very early. The sport was played in 1871 at the first fair held by the Middle Tennessee Colored Agricultural and Mechanical Association. The National Association of Professional Base Ball Players in 1867 specifically excluded blacks, indicating that there may have been some black professional players. Certainly there were two black teams in Brooklyn, the Monitors and the Uniques, and one in Philadelphia, the Excelsiors. They played for the "colored championship" in Brooklyn that October.

The first black player known to get paid was John W. "Bud" Fowler, who played for a white team in New Castle, PA, in 1872. Moses Fleetwood "Fleet" Walker began playing for Toledo in the minor Northwestern League in 1883 and he became the first black major leaguer when Toledo joined the American Association in 1884. Teams in Baltimore, Boston, Cincinnati, Louisville, New York, Philadelphia, Pittsburgh, and Washington in 1897 formed the League of Colored Baseball Clubs, which was accepted into organized baseball. However, the league lasted only one week, and professional leagues began to draw the color line. On July 14, 1887, the

International League decided to approve no more contracts with black players. Five days later, Cap Anson of the Chicago White Stockings refused to let his team play an exhibition game against Newark if George Stovey, a black, was allowed to pitch. In September, the St. Louis Browns refused to play against a black barnstorming team, the Cuban Giants.

The Giants were probably the best of the early black teams. In 1887 they played 150 games throughout the Northeast and Midwest, including contests against three major-league teams. The Giants and another black team, the New York Gorhams, were in the Middle States League in 1899 with six white teams. The MSL beame the Eastern Interstate League in 1890, when the Gorhams dropped out, the Giants became the York (PA) Monarchs, and two of its black players jumped to Harrisburg. Renamed the Big Gorhams, the Giants played for Ansonia in the Connecticut State League, which didn't finish the season. There were no blacks in organized baseball from 1892 through 1894, but in 1895 the Page Fence Giants were organized in Adrian, MI as a barnstorming team, and five of its black players briefly joined the Adrian team in the Michigan State League. The last black team in organized baseball was the Acme Colored Giants, who represented Celeron, NY in the Iron and Oil League in 1898.

Blacks formed the National Negro Baseball League in 1920 and the Eastern Colored League in 1923; they played their own World Series in 1924. The ECL became the American Negro League in 1929 but folded after that season, and the NNBL went out of business after the 1931 season. A new Negro National League was formed in 1933, and the Negro American League was founded in 1937. They reestablished the Black World Series in 1942. Among the great players in the black major leagues were pitcher Satchel Paige, catcher Josh Gibson, outfielders Oscar Charleston and "Cool Papa" Bell, shortstop John Henry Lloyd, and first baseman Buck Leonard, all of whom are in the Baseball Hall of Fame.

Boxing and track and field were integrated early. Before track and field was an important sport, a black "pedestrian," Frank Hart of Boston, finished fourth and won $2,730 in the 1879 Astley Belt race. Blacks organized their own athletic clubs during the 1890s, and a few also took part in intercollegiate track and field. John B. "Doc" Taylor of the University of Pennsylvania won the IC4A 440-yard championship in 1904, 1907, and 1908 and was the first black to win an Olympic Gold Medal, as a member of the United States 1,600-meter relay team in 1908. Howard Drew won the AAU 100-yard dash in 1912, and he won both the 100- and 220-yard dashes in 1913.

Two black long jumpers, De Hart Hubbard of the University of Michigan and Edward Gourdin of Harvard, appeared in the early 1920s. Gourdin in 1921 became the first to jump more than 25 feet, and he was the national pentathlon champion in 1921 and 1922. Hubbard, national long jump champion from 1922 through 1927, won the 1924 Olympic Gold Medal in the event.

During the 1930s, great black sprinters emerged. Eddie Tolan and Ralph Metcalfe had some legendary races. Tolan won the national 100-yard dash in 1928 and 1930 and the 220-yard dash in 1929 and 1931. Metcalfe won the 100 meters from 1933 through 1935 and the 200 meters from 1932 through 1936. In the 1932 Olympics, Tolan barely edged Metcalfe in both events. The greatest of all was Jesse Owens, who broke five world records and tied a sixth in the 1935 Big Ten championship meet and won four Gold Medals at the 1936 Berlin Olympics. He was the leader of the "Black Auxiliaries," as Nazi propagandists called the black members of the U.S. track team. Other black Gold Medalists in 1936 were Archie Williams in the 400 meters, John Woodruff in the 800 meters, and Cornelius Johnson in the high jump.

Ivy Wilson was the first black woman to win a national title, in the 50-meter dash in 1936. Alice Coachman, who won 23 national championships in the high jump and sprints between 1939 and 1948, became the first black woman to win an Olympic Gold Medal, in the 1948 high jump.

George Dixon of Halifax, Nova Scotia, became the first black boxing champion when he won the world bantamweight title in 1890. He was followed by Joe Walcott, welterweight champion from 1901 to 1904 and 1905 to 1906, and Joe Gans, lightweight champion from 1902 to 1908. The heavyweight title, though, was off limits to black fighters until Jack Johnson literally chased Tommy Burns halfway around the world and was finally matched against him on December 26, 1908, in Sydney, Australia. Johnson won the title with a 14th-round knockout.

The search for a "great white hope" brought former champion Jim Jeffries out of retirement to fight Johnson on July 4, 1910, but Johnson knocked him out in the 15th round. Johnson's love of the fast life and his predilection for white women made him a controversial figure. In 1912, he was sentenced to a year and a day in federal prison for abduction and transporting a woman across state lines for immoral purposes, and he fled the country while his appeal

was pending. On April 5, 1915, he lost the title to Jess Willard on a 26th-round knockout in Havana.

After Johnson, there were four outstanding black heavyweights: Joe Jeannette, Sam Langford, Sam McVey, and Harry Wills. Wills was probably the best of them. In 1925 the New York State Athletic Commission ordered heavyweight champion Jack Dempsey to defend his title against Wills; Dempsey instead fought Gene Tunney. But there were black champions in lower divisions, led by Henry Armstrong, who held the featherweight, lightweight, and welterweight titles in 1938. Panama Al Brown was bantamweight champion from 1929 to 1935 and John Henry Lewis was light-heavyweight titlist from 1935 until he retired in 1939.

Finally, the second black heavyweight champion arrived on June 22, 1937, when Joe Louis knocked out James Braddock in the 12th round at Chicago. Louis had been groomed to be acceptable to most whites, and the success of American black athletes in the Olympics, combined with a reaction against Hitler and Nazism, helped improve the racial atmosphere. When he avenged his only professional defeat by knocking out Germany's Max Schmeling in the first round, he became a national hero.

Because basketball was a YMCA sport, blacks were playing it soon after its invention in 1891. The YMCA established its first "colored branch" in 1853 in Washington, D.C., and by 1891 there were many such branches throughout the country. Black athletic clubs also adopted the sport. One of the greatest early pro basketball teams was the Harlem Renaissance Big Five, organized in 1923. The Rens won 1,588 games and lost only 239 in 17 seasons.

In "social sports" such as bowling, golf, and tennis, blacks were forced to create their own governing bodies. John Shippen, believed to be the son of a black father and an American Indian mother, finished fourth in the 1913 U.S. Open, but the U.S. Golf Association soon adopted a whites-only policy. Black golfers set up their own tournament in 1926 and two years later formed the United Golfers Association. The Professional Golf Association accepted black members until 1943, but the country clubs that sponsored its tournaments didn't allow blacks to play. The American Tennis Association was founded by blacks in 1916 and held its first national championships the following year. Black bowlers from Illinois, Indiana, Michigan, Ohio, and Wisconsin formed the National Bowling Association in 1939.

World War II helped to open doors for blacks. The Fair Employment Practices Commission was established by President Roosevelt in 1941, and in 1944 the New York Assembly passed a law prohibiting discrimination by employees. In August of that year, New York Mayor Fiorello LaGuardia formed a baseball subcommittee as part of his Anti-Discrimination Committee. Shortly afterward, A. B. "Happy" Chandler became commissioner of baseball and announced, "I don't believe in barring Negroes from baseball just because they are Negroes."

On October 23, 1945, Jackie Robinson signed a contract with the Montreal Royals of the International League, the Brooklyn Dodgers' top farm club. Pro football was actually reintegrated before major-league baseball, but not many people noticed, because baseball was truly the national pastime then. In 1946, the Los Angeles Rams of the NFL signed Woody Strode and Kenny Washington from UCLA, and the Cleveland Browns of the new All America Football Conference signed Bill Willis and Marion Motley. Meanwhile, Robinson broke into organized baseball with Montreal on April 18, 1946, and a year later he was the Dodgers' starting first baseman. Robinson batted .297, stole 29 bases, scored 125 runs, and was named National League Rookie of the Year.

Robinson was not alone in the major leagues in 1947. Larry Doby joined the Cleveland Indians in July, and in August Henry Thompson and Willard Brown signed with the St. Louis Browns. Catcher Roy Campanella came up to the Dodgers in 1948 and the legendary Satchel Paige won six games and lost only one with the Indians, who won the American League pennant that season. There were 20 blacks in the major leagues by 1953, and the Boston Red Sox became the last team to integrate in 1959.

Pro basketball, which has become the preeminent sport for blacks, was integrated in 1950 when the Boston Celtics signed Chuck Cooper of Duquesne University. Shortly afterward, Nat "Sweetwater" Clifton of the Harlem Globetrotters joined the New York Knicks. By the early 1980s, about 80 percent of the players in the National Basketball Association were black. Not surprisingly, professional basketball led the way in giving blacks more important positions. John McLendon became the first black professional coach with the Cleveland Pipers of the American Basketball Association in 1961, and Wayne Embry was named general manager of the NBA's Milwaukee Bucks ten years later, becoming the first black to hold that position in any sport.

There was progress in other sports, as well. The ABC allowed blacks to use its lanes in 1949. Althea Gibson became the first black to play in the U.S. National tennis tournament in 1950. She won that tournament and England's Wimbledon title in both 1957 and 1958. The first black men to play in the U.S. National were Reginald Weir and George Stewart in 1952, and Arthur Ashe was the first to win the tournament, in 1968, when it became the U.S. Open. The PGA admitted Charlie Sifford to membership in 1959, and he won his first tournament, the Los Angeles Open, ten years later. Lee Elder was the first black golfer to be invited to the prestigious Masters tournament in 1975.

So many black athletes have followed Robinson, Willis, Motley, and Cooper into professional sports that it's pointless to attempt a list. But it is worth naming some blacks who made their marks in lesser-known sports, among them fencer Peter Westbrook, who won seven national saber championships; Ron Galimore, who scored the only perfect ten in the history of the NCAA gymnastics championships; weight lifter John Davis, who won ten national, seven world, and two Olympic heavyweight championships; Debi Thomas, U.S. figure skating champion in 1986 and 1988; and George Branham III, who in 1986 became the first black to win a tournament on the Professional Bowlers Association tour.

But problems have persisted, especially in team sports. Blacks were generally limited to certain positions, and they had to outperform white players to make it. A Rand Corporation study showed that from 1966 to 1970 black major-league players hit 20.8 percentage points better than white players, and they were much more likely to play the outfield or first base than to be pitchers, catchers, or infielders. Black football players were also "slotted" into the wide receiver, running back, and defensive back positions.

Money has also been a racial issue in professional sports. While black superstars were generally well paid, other blacks were usually not paid as well as white players of comparable ability. And even the superstars were denied extra income from personal appearances, endorsements, and commercials. Carl Yastrzemski, a white, estimated that winning the American League's Most Valuable Player award in 1967 was worth $200,000 over a three-year period. But Frank Robinson, a black, won the award in 1966 and received only $1,000 for two speaking engagements.

"The Revolt of the Black Athlete" began with Muhammad Ali, who became a Black Muslim shortly after winning the heavyweight championship in 1964. Two years later, he refused induction into the armed services for religious reasons. In 1967, black college athletes began to protest. All of Syracuse's black football players were suspended by Coach Ben

Schwartzwalder after walking out of spring practice because he wouldn't hire a black assistant. Black football players at Wyoming were also suspended for planning to wear black armbands in a game against Brigham Young to protest the Mormon Church's antiblack bias.

Harry Edwards, a sociology instructor at San Jose State, organized the Olympic Project for Human Rights (OPHR) to boycott the 1968 Olympics. The boycott didn't take place, but the OPHR attracted a lot of attention, picketing the indoor track meet of the all-white New York Athletic Club in February, calling for the resignation of Avery Brundage as president of the International Olympic Committee, and demanding that Muhammad Ali's championship be restored. At the Olympics in Mexico City, two of Edwards' followers, Tommie Smith and John Carlos, raised black-gloved fists in the Black Power salute while on the victory podium, and were almost instantly suspended from the team and banned from further Olympic competition.

The movement, and changing times, brought some improvements during the 1970s. Colleges became more sensitive to the needs of black athletes, who were often recruited out of urban ghettos and plunged into alien environments on rural campuses. The Universities of Kansas and Nebraska led the way in hiring academic advisors to work with athletes, and many colleges began hiring black assistant coaches.

There was further progress in the 1980s. Doug Williams, a black quarterback, started for the Washington Redskins in the 1988 Super Bowl, passed for a record 340 yards and four touchdowns, and was named the game's Most Valuable Player. Warren Moon of the Houston Oilers and Randall Cunningham of the Philadelphia Eagles were also black starting quarterbacks. Blacks in general became much more visible on television, and black athletes began to cash in on their fame. Michael Jordan of the NBA's Chicago Bulls by 1988 was earning more than $4 million a year for endorsements, and one company even named a basketball shoe, the Air Jordan, for him.

Off the playing field, however, there was not much improvement. The only black professional football coach after Fritz Pollard was Willie Wood with the Philadelphia team in the short-lived World Football League until Art Shell was named coach of the Los Angeles Raiders during the 1989 season. Frank Robinson became baseball's first black manager with the San Francisco Giants in 1975, and he later managed the Cleveland Indians and Baltimore Orioles. But there was only one other black manager during the next 13 seasons. Al Campanis, general manager of the Los Angeles Dodgers, touched off a furor in

April of 1987 when he suggested on national television that blacks weren't equipped for managerial or front-office positions. Campanis was fired for his remarks, and baseball commissioner Peter Ueberroth hired Harry Edwards as a consultant to study the problem. Not much seemed to happen until Cito Gaston was hired to manage the Toronto Blue Jays in 1989. Another milestone was reached that year when Bill White, a former major-league player and broadcaster, was named president of the National League.

Further Reading: Ashe, Arthur. *A Hard Road to Glory: A History of the African-American Athlete.* New York: Warner Books, 1988, three vols.; Chalk, Ocania. *Pioneers of Black Sport: The Early Days of the Black Professional Athlete in Baseball, Basketball, Boxing and Football.* New York: Dodd, Mead, 1975; Henderson, Edwin B. *The Negro in Sports.* Washington, D.C.: Associated Publishers, 1949, revised edition; Jones, Wally, and Jim Washington. *Black Champions Challenge American Sports.* New York: David McKay, 1972; Olsen, Jack. *The Black Athlete: A Shameful Story.* New York: Time, Inc., 1968.

See also ALI, MUHAMMAD; ASHE, ARTHUR; BLACK WORLD SERIES; CUBAN GIANTS; DAVIS, ERNIE; DOUGLAS, BOB; EASTERN COLORED LEAGUE; EDWARDS, HARRY; FOSTER, "RUBE"; GIBSON, ALTHEA; HARLEM GLOBETROTTERS; HARLEM RENAISSANCE BIG FIVE; JOHNSON, "JACK"; LOUIS, JOE; MURPHY, ISAAC; NEGRO AMERICAN LEAGUE; NEGRO NATIONAL LEAGUE; RICKEY, BRANCH; ROBINSON, "JACKIE"; RUSSELL, "BILL"; TAYLOR, "MAJOR"; UNITED GOLFERS ASSOCIATION.

Black Sox Scandal
Baseball

After his heavily favored White Sox lost five of eight games to the Cincinnati Reds in the 1919 World Series, manager Kid Gleason said, "Something was wrong. I didn't like the betting odds." Less than a year later, on September 28, 1920, a Chicago grand jury indicted eight White Sox players for agreeing to throw the Series in exchange for $100,000 in bribes. The eight were pitchers Eddie Cicotte and Claude "Lefty" Williams, outfielders "Shoeless Joe" Jackson and Oscar "Happy" Felsch, shortstop Charles "Swede" Risberg, third baseman George "Buck" Weaver, first baseman Arnold "Chick" Gandil, and utility player Fred McMullin. They became known as the "Black Sox."

The charges against McMullin were dropped, but the other seven went on trial, along with three gamblers, in July of 1921, and most of the story gradually emerged. "Sleepy Bill" Burns, a former major-league player, testified that he had been told by Cicotte and Gandil in September of 1919 that they would be willing to fix the World Series if their team won the pennant. Burns then met with Abe Attell, a former featherweight boxing champion; Hal Chase, a former major leaguer who had himself been indicted for allegedly fixing games in 1919; and David Zelser, a gambler. They arranged a meeting with another gambler, Arnold Rothstein, who agreed to put up $100,000 in bribe money.

Burns and Attell met with seven of the players, all but Jackson, and worked out an arrangement. In 1919, the World Series had a best five-out-of-nine format; the players were to arrange to lose five games, and were to receive $20,000 after each loss. According to Burns' testimony, "Cicotte said he'd throw the first game if he had to throw the ball clear out of the Cincinnati park." As it turned out, Cicotte lost the first game, 9–1; he had won 29 and lost only 7 games during the regular season. In the second game, Williams, who had won 23 and lost 11, averaging only about two walks per game, walked three hitters and gave up three runs in the fourth inning, as Cincinnati won again, 4–2. The *Chicago Tribune* called it "almost criminal wild pitching."

The White Sox won the third game, but they lost the fourth 2–0, when Cicotte made two throwing errors in the fifth inning to allow both Cincinnati runs. Williams pitched well for five innings, then gave up four runs in the sixth as the White Sox lost 5–0. Ironically, Gandil drove in Weaver with the winning run in a 5–4 victory and Jackson drove in the winning run the following day to give Cicotte a 4–1 victory. The Reds now led the series only four games to three. The "Black Sox" at this point had seen little, if any, of the bribe money, and they may have decided not to go through with the plan. But they had put themselves in a dangerous position. There were already rumors that the Series had been fixed, and when Cicotte lost the final game, 10–5, those rumors became much louder. American League President Ban Johnson began an investigation that ultimately led to the indictments and the trial.

The players and gamblers were found not guilty. But because of the scandal, the three-man National Commission was replaced by a single commissioner, Judge Kenesaw Mountain Landis, in 1921, and Landis banned all eight players from baseball for life. Cicotte had received $10,000 for his role, Jackson $5,000. Evidently none of the other players ever got paid, but there were reports that Gandil had been given all the money, and hadn't shared it with the others. He retired to California after the Series.

Further Reading: Asinof, Eliot. *Eight Men Out: The Black Sox and the 1919 World Series.* New York: Holt, 1963; Luhrs, Victor. *The Great Baseball Mystery.* New York: A. S. Barnes, 1966.

Black World Series
Baseball
The first Black World Series was played in 1924 between the champions of the Negro National League and the Eastern Colored League. It continued through 1927. The Eastern League folded early in the 1928 season, and there was no Black World Series until 1942, when the Negro American League and a new Negro National League began postseason play. This Series continued through 1948, after which the Negro National League went out of business.

Blaik, "Red" Earl H. (1897–1989)
Football
Born February 15, 1897, Detroit, MI; died May 6, 1989; National Football Foundation Hall of Fame

Blaik played on undefeated Miami (OH) University football teams in 1916 and 1917, then was appointed to the U.S. Military Academy, graduating in 1920. He became head coach at Dartmouth in 1934 and remained there through 1940, winning 45 games while losing 15 and tying 4. At one point, his teams went undefeated for 22 consecutive games. He was then named Army's first civilian football coach. In 18 seasons, he compiled a 121–33–10 record; from 1944 through 1950, his teams won 57 games while losing only 3 and tying 4. Led by the "Touchdown Twins," halfback Glenn Davis and fullback Doc Blanchard, Army won the national championship in 1944 and 1945, and Blaik was named Coach of the Year in 1946, when Army won every game except for the scoreless tie against Notre Dame.

The Army team was decimated in 1951, when 44 football players were expelled for violating the Honor Code. Blaik had his only losing team that year. In his final season, 1958, Blaik produced his third undefeated team, using the "lonesome end" offense. It was so called because one end, Bill Carpenter, was flanked wide and never entered the team's huddle. He was given the plays through hand signals.

Blake, "Toe" Hector (1912–   )
Hockey
Born August 21, 1912, Victorian Mines, Ontario; Hockey Hall of Fame

Blake was with the Montreal Canadiens as a player and coach for 26 seasons, and they won ten Stanley Cup championships during that time. In his playing days, he was known as the "Old Lamplighter" for his goal-scoring ability. He played just three games for the Montreal Maroons in 1934, then joined the Canadiens late in the 1935–36 season and was one of the top left wingers in the National Hockey League until 1948, when he had to retire because of a broken ankle. "Chunky, quick-tempered, and durable," according to Brian McFarlane, Blake led the league in scoring in 1939 with 47 points, and won the Lady Byng Trophy for gentlemanly play in 1946, when he had 29 goals. He teamed with Elmer Lach and Joe Benoit on the high-scoring "punch line" that led the Canadiens to Stanley Cup titles in 1944 and 1946, when Blake scored the winning goal in the deciding game against the Boston Bruins. During his career, he had 253 goals and 292 assists in 19 seasons, and 25 goals and 37 assists in 57 playoff games.

Blake became the Canadiens' coach in 1955 and was an immediate success. The team won five consecutive Stanley Cups in his first five seasons. After a four-year hiatus, the Canadiens won two more cups in a row, 1965–66, and another in 1968, Blake's final season.

Blanchard, "Doc" Felix (1924–   )
Football

Born December 11, 1924, Bishopville, SC; National Football Foundation Hall of Fame

Called "Little Doc" by his family because his father was a doctor, Blanchard spent his freshman year at the University of North Carolina, then enlisted in the army and was sent to West Point. He became one of the greatest college fullbacks of all time, an All-American in 1944, 1945, and 1946. His best season was 1945, when he scored 19 touchdowns, three of them in a 32–13 victory over Navy. Blanchard won the Heisman Trophy and became the first football player ever to win the Sullivan Award as the outstanding amateur athlete of the year.

Blanchard was not only an outstanding runner, he was also a devastating blocker and a fine pass receiver. At 6 feet 1 inch and 208 pounds, he was exceptionally strong, and he had speed. In 1945 he won the 100-yard dash in 10 seconds flat against Cornell, and he was IC4A indoor shotput champion. After graduating from West Point, Blanchard became an army jet pilot. His plane caught fire in 1959 near London, and he brought it down safely rather than parachuting and risking the chance that the plane would crash in a densely populated area.

Blanda, George (1927–   )
Football

Born September 17, 1927, Youngwood, PA; Pro Football Hall of Fame

Some pro football fans hoped he would play until he was at least 50. But, after a 26-year career, Blanda announced his retirement in August of 1976, one month before he turned 49. A quarterback and placekicker at the University of Kentucky, Blanda spent ten seasons with the Chicago Bears of the NFL (1949–58), except for one game with Baltimore in 1951. He was used primarily as a kicker, but started at quarterback in 1953 and 1954. Blanda retired after the 1958 season.

Then came the new American Football League, and a call from the Houston Oilers. Blanda spent seven seasons, from 1960 to 1966, as Houston's starting quarterback and compiled some astounding numbers. He was the AFL's passing champion and player of the year in 1961, when he set a new

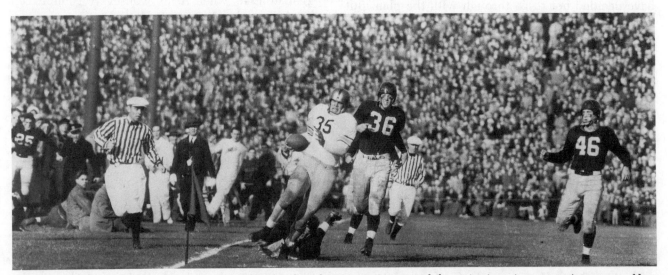

Winner of the 1945 Heisman Trophy, Doc Blanchard is shown scoring a touchdown in Army's 21–18 victory over Navy in 1946. Courtesy of the Public Broadcasting Service

professional record by throwing 36 touchdown passes. He led the league in attempted passes in 1963 (423), 1964 (505), and 1966 (442); in completions in 1963 (224), 1964 (262), and 1965 (186); and in yards gained passing in 1961 (3,330) and 1963 (3,003). Blanda led Houston to three consecutive division titles, from 1960 to 1962, and the first two AFL championships.

He went to the Oakland Raiders as backup quarterback and kicker in 1967. When the American and National leagues merged into a single NFL in 1970, Blanda rescued the Raiders from apparent defeat five weeks in a row. He began by coming off the bench to throw three touchdown passes against Pittsburgh. His 48-yard field goal with 3 seconds left tied Kansas City. Against Cleveland, he threw a touchdown pass and kicked a 52-yard field goal in the last 96 seconds to win the game. The following week, his fourth-quarter touchdown pass beat Denver, and then he kicked a last-second field goal for a victory over San Diego. He was named AFC Player of the Year and the Associated Press Male Athlete of the Year.

When he retired after the 1975 season, Blanda held the record for most career points with 2,002. He completed 1,911 of 4,007 passes, a 47.7 percentage, for 26,920 yards and 236 touchdowns; scored 9 rushing touchdowns; and kicked 943 of 957 extra points and 335 of 638 field goals.

Bluebonnet Bowl
Football

The first Bluebonnet Bowl was played at Rice Stadium in Houston on December 19, 1959. From 1968 through 1984, the game was played at the Houston Astrodome. It went to Rice again in 1985, then returned to the Astrodome. The game was discontinued after 1987.

Results

1959   Clemson 23, Texas Christian 7
1960   Texas 3, Alabama 3
1961   Kansas 33, Rice 7
1962   Missouri 14, Georgia Tech 10
1963   Baylor 14, Louisiana State 7
1964   Tulsa 14, Mississippi 7
1965   Tennessee 27, Tulsa 6
1966   Texas 19, Mississippi 0
1967   Colorado 31, Miami (FL) 21
1968   Southern Methodist 28, Oklahoma 27
1969   Houston 36, Auburn 7
1970   Alabama 24, Oklahoma 24
1971   Colorado 29, Houston 17
1972   Tennessee 24, Louisiana State 17
1973   Houston 47, Tulane 7

1974   North Carolina State 31, Houston 31
1975   Texas 38, Colorado 21
1976   Nebraska 27, Texas Tech 24
1977   Southern California 47, Texas A & M 28
1978   Stanford 25, Georgia 22
1979   Purdue 27, Tennessee 22
1980   North Carolina 16, Texas 7
1981   Michigan 33, UCLA 14
1982   Arkansas 28, Florida 24
1983   Oklahoma State 24, Baylor 14
1984   West Virginia 31, Texas Christian 14
1985   Air Force 24, Texas 16
1986   Baylor 21, Colorado 9
1987   Texas 32, Pittsburgh 27

Bluegrass Bowl
Football

There was just one Bluegrass Bowl game, on December 13, 1958, in Louisville, when Oklahoma State defeated Florida State, 15–6.

Blue-Gray All-Star Classic
Football

Played annually at Montgomery, AL, the Blue-Gray game is the oldest of the postseason bowl games for college seniors. The first was played on January 2, 1939. Since then, games have taken place in December. As the name suggests, teams represent the North (Blue) and the South (Gray).

Boardsailing

The sailboard is similar to a surfboard, but longer, and it has a single triangular sail, usually about 59 square feet. The U.S. Boardsailing Association, an affiliate of the U.S. Yacht Racing Union, was organized in 1980 to govern the sport. After being inactive for several years, it was revived in 1987. In addition to course racing, competition is conducted in slalom and in freestyle.

Address: U.S. Boardsailing Association, P.O. Box 978, Hood, OR 97031

Bobsledding

Sledding and sleighing were very popular pastimes in North America as early as the 17th century among the Dutch in New Amsterdam. In Canada, the French *coureurs des bois* adopted a sled called a "tobaakum" by the native Americans; we now call it a "toboggan." At first used to haul supplies, it also became a form of transportation, and the French occasionally held informal races.

For the most part, though, sledding was simply a form of amusement. In the 19th century, the horse-

Bobsledding in North America has been hampered by the lack of facilities. The only world-class bobsled run in the United States is this one, built at Lake Placid, NY, for the 1932 Winter Olympics and upgraded for the 1980 Games. Courtesy of F. Kelly MacNeill

drawn sleigh ride became a social event, often an occasion for courting. The Quebec Tandem Club, organized about 1830, went on sleigh rides every Sunday during the winter, and in New York City Sunday sleighing was popular even during the Civil War. The original bobsled appeared during the 1850s; it was actually two sleds connected by a plank. The racing bobsled was developed about 1895 by Americans vacationing in Switzerland, who built a heavier type of toboggan to increase stability, and put runners on it. The first formal competiton was held on a natural slide, the Cresta Run in the Alps, on January 5, 1898, with five-passenger bobsleds. An artificial bobsled run was built at St. Moritz in 1902.

Bobsledding was included in the 1924 Winter Olympics, and the first world championships were held in 1927. American sleds finished first and second in the 1928 Olympic event, for a four-man team, and the United States won both the four-man and the new two-man competition in 1932 at Lake Placid, NY. The first bobsled run in North America was built at Mt. Van Hoevenberg for those games, and it was greatly upgraded for the 1980 Olympics, also at Lake Placid.

Addresses: Canadian Amateur Bobsleigh and Luge Association, 333 River Road, Vanier, Ontario, Canada K1L 8H9 (613) 748-5610; U.S. Bobsled and Skeleton Federation, Box 828, Lake Placid, NY 12946 (518) 523-1842

See also LUGE.

Boccie

Played in only a few areas of North America, boccie is an Italian sport similar to lawn bowls. It's played on a hard dirt court enclosed by wooden boards that allow carom shots. New York City and San Francisco both have public courts, but in most places where the game is played, the courts are owned by Italian-American clubs. The U.S. Boccie Federation, founded in 1976, has about 2,000 members.

Address: 2239 Orange Street, Martinez, CA 94553 (415) 646-5300

Bobybuilding
See POWERLIFTING.

Boston, MA

Baseball When the first professional league, the National Association of Professional Base Ball Players, was formed in 1871, Boston was a charter member with a team called the Red Stockings. Boston won four of the National Association's five pennants. The National Association of Professional Baseball

Clubs replaced the old National Association in 1876, and the Boston team joined. They were still called the Red Stockings, but by 1882 they had become known as the Beaneaters. Later they were the Bees, and finally the Braves, who won only two National League pennants, in 1914 and 1948. They also won the 1914 World Series. The franchise moved to Milwaukee for the 1953 season.

Boston has had a team in every other major league: the Union Association, in 1884; the Players' League, in 1890; the American Association, in 1891; and, of course, the American League, since it achieved major league status in 1901. That team was originally known as the Pilgrims, but became the Red Stockings, or Red Sox, in 1908. They won American League pennants in 1903, 1912, 1915, 1916, 1918, 1946, 1967, 1975, and 1986, and were World Series champions in 1903, 1912, 1915, 1916, and 1918. The

Boston won National League pennants from 1891 through 1893 with this team. Frank Selee's suit and derby were typical attire for managers of that era. Courtesy of the Boston Public Library

1988 and 1990 teams won the eastern division title, but the Oakland Athletics beat them in four straight games in both league championship series.

Basketball The Celtics joined the Basketball Association of America in 1946, when it was organized. The BAA became the National Basketball Association, and Boston won 11 NBA chamionships in 13 years, from 1957 through 1969. They also won titles in 1974, 1976, 1981, 1984, and 1986.

Football Professional football has never been successful in Boston. The Boston Bulldogs were in the first American Football League, which played for just the 1926 season. Another team called the Bulldogs joined the National Football League in 1929 and dropped out the following year. In 1933, the Boston Redskins joined the NFL. They won the eastern division championship in 1936, but attendance was so bad that the championship playoff game was moved to the Polo Grounds in New York, and the Green Bay Packers beat the Redskins, 21–6. The following season, the team moved to Washington, D.C. The Boston Shamrocks played in the second American Football League in 1937, but this league folded after one season.

The Boston Yanks joined the NFL in 1944 and became the New York Bulldogs for the 1949 season. Finally, the Boston Patriots helped found the third American Football League in 1960. The team played its home games at Fenway Park, Harvard Stadium, Boston University's Nickerson Field, and Boston College's Alumni Stadium until 1971, when Schaefer Stadium (now Sullivan Stadium) opened in Foxboro, MA. The franchise then became known as the New England Patriots.

Hockey After watching the Stanley Cup finals in 1924, Charles F. Adams of Boston decided he wanted a National Hockey League franchise, and his Bruins entered the league that fall as the NHL's first U.S.-based team. The Bruins were Stanley Cup champions in 1929, 1939, 1941, 1970, and 1972. They also reached the finals in 1927, 1930, 1943, 1946, 1953, 1957, 1958, 1974, 1977, 1978, 1988, and 1990.

See also BOSTON GARDEN; FENWAY PARK; NEW ENGLAND; SULLIVAN STADIUM.

Boston Athletic Association (BAA)

Organized in 1877, the BAA was at first a kind of federation of athletic clubs to enable them to pool their resources and build a clubhouse. The clubhouse opened on December 29, 1888, and the association soon absorbed many of the smaller clubs. When the first modern Olympic Games were held in Athens in 1896, the BAA raised money to send a team of five men, who won 7 of the 12 Gold Medals given in track and field events. The following year, the BAA conducted the first Boston Marathon, inspired by the 25-mile run which had been created for the Olympics. The association is now best known for the annual marathon, although it still operates as a year-around athletic club.

Address: 131 Clarendon Street, Boston, MA 02190 (617) 236-1652

See also BOSTON MARATHON.

Boston Game
Football

When the Harvard College Football Club was organized in 1871, it revived a form of the sport known as the "Boston game," which allowed a player to catch or pick up the ball and even to run with it. This was quite different from the soccerlike forms of football played at other colleges, in which handling the ball was generally forbidden. When Yale called a convention to form an intercollegiate football league, Harvard refused to attend. The team captain, Henry Grant, wrote: "Our game depends upon running, dodging, and position playing. . . . We even went so far as to practice and try the Yale game. We gave it up at once as hopeless."

Unable to play other American colleges, Harvard in 1874 played two games in Cambridge, MA against McGill University of Montreal, the first under Harvard's rules, the second under McGill's version of English rugby rules. In 1875, Harvard and Yale played a game that was essentially rugby. Princeton then decided to take part, and in the fall of 1876 Columbia, Harvard, Princeton, and Yale formed an Intercollegiate Football Association to play the rugbylike game. That was the beginning of American football.

Boston Garden
Boston, MA

Built as the home of the National Hockey League's Boston Bruins, the Boston Garden opened on November 20, 1928. The famous parquet basketball floor was pieced together of short hardwood strips, the only wood available immediately after World War II, when the Boston Celtics were founded in 1946. The garden seats 14,890 for hockey and 14,451 for basketball.

Boston Marathon

The first modern marathon was run in 1896 at the Olympics in Athens. John Graham and Arthur Burnham of the Boston Athletic Association were there, and they decided to introduce the marathon to the United States. Fifteen men ran in the first Boston

Marathon, on Patriot's Day, April 19, 1897. Although the standard marathon course then was 25 miles, the Boston race covered only about 24½ miles, from outside the city to the Irvington Street Oval, where runners had to do a 220-yard lap to finish. The winner was John J. McDermott of New York City, despite the fact that he was delayed by a funeral procession near the end of the race.

The official marathon distance became 26 miles and 385 yards in 1908, but the Boston course didn't reach that distance until 1924, after several adjustments. The starting point is now Hopkinton, west of Boston. The finish line has been at the John Hancock Building since 1986, when the John Hancock Insurance Company signed a ten-year contract to sponsor the race for $1 million a year, since extended to 2003 at $1.3 million a year.

The first woman to run in the marathon was Kathy Switzer in 1967. She entered as "K. Switzer," with her hair pushed up under a cap, and she was accepted as a man. When John D. "Jock" Semple, known as "the angry overseer of the Marathon," realized she was a woman, he tried to push her off the course, and the news photograph was printed all over the world. Women were finally accepted as official entrants in 1972.

In his book about the marathon, Joe Falls wrote: "This is the one simon-pure athletic event left in the United States. . . . This is the charm of the old race. That it is devoid of commercialism." That changed in 1986, because other marathons throughout the United States had been offering prize money for several years, and many runners were passing up the Boston race. In 1986, there was $250,000 in prize money, with the first-place man and woman each getting $30,000. That increased to a total of $313,500 in 1989, with $45,000 to each of the first-place finishers and $100,000 to the open division champion.

Further Reading: Falls, Joe. *The Boston Marathon.* New York: Macmillan, 1977.

See also BOSTON ATHLETIC ASSOCIATION.

Boston, Ralph (1939–   )
Track and Field
Born May 9, 1939, Laurel, MS; National Track and Field Hall of Fame

When Boston won the Olympic Gold Medal with a long jump of 26 feet 7¾ inches in 1960, he broke the world record set by Jesse Owens 25 years before. He became the first ever to jump more than 27 feet on May 27, 1961, when he did 27 feet ½ inch. Less than two months later, he extended the record to 27 feet 2 inches. Boston tied the new record of 27 feet

3¼ inches the following year, and on August 12, 1964, he broke that with a jump of 27 feet 4¼ inches. His best jump, also a world record, was 27 feet, 5 inches on May 29, 1965. Boston was the NCAA champion in 1960, representing Tennessee A & I, and he won the AAU outdoor championship six years in a row (1961–66).

Boucher, Frank (1901–1977)
Hockey
Born October 7, 1901, Ottawa, Ontario; died December 12, 1977; Hockey Hall of Fame

He was nicknamed "Raffles," after the gentleman burglar in E. W. Hornung's stories, because he was a great puck stealer who won the Lady Byng trophy for gentlemanly play so often—seven times in eight seasons—that it was presented to him permanently in 1935, and a new one was donated for future winners. A Montreal sportswriter recalled, "He would take the puck away from the enemy with the guile and smoothness of a con man picking the pockets of yokels at a country fair."

In his 14-year career as a National Hockey League center, Boucher had only one fight. Playing for the Rangers in their first game at Madison Square Garden on November 16, 1926, Boucher got so exasperated at the rough play of "Bad Bill" Phillips that he knocked him down with a punch. Then, being a gentleman, he helped Phillips to his feet—and immediately knocked him down again.

Boucher played briefly for the Ottawa Senators in the 1921–22 season, then spent four seasons with Vancouver in the Pacific Coast League before returning to the NHL with the Rangers, where he played from 1926 through 1938. He coached the Rangers 1939–48, and played 15 games in a brief comeback during the 1943–44 season. In 557 games, Boucher had 161 goals and 262 assists, with 18 goals and 18 assists in 67 playoff games.

Boudreau, Louis (1917–   )
Baseball
Born July 17, 1917, Harvey, IL; Baseball Hall of Fame

Boudreau in 1942 became the youngest manager ever to open the season with a team. He was 24 years old, and he was also the Cleveland Indians' starting shortstop. The Indians and Boston Red Sox tied for first place in 1948, when Boudreau was named Most Valuable Player. He got four hits, including two home runs, in the playoff game at Boston, won by the Indians 8–3. Cleveland then beat the Boston Braves in six games in the World Series.

As a sophomore at the University of Illinois, Boudreau was named captain of the basketball team, but he decided to play professional baseball and gave up his college eligibility. Late in the 1939 season he was called up by the Indians. In 1940, his first full season, he batted .295, driving in 101 runs. He led the league in hitting in 1944 with a .327 average, and in 1948 he had 18 home runs and 106 runs batted in, along with a .355 batting average.

A seven-time all-star, Boudreau was a graceful fielder who led league shortstops in fielding percentage eight times, setting a record with .978 in 1944, and breaking his own record with a percentage of .982 in 1947. His lifetime .973 percentage is also a record for shortstops. As a manager, he's known for developing the "Boudreau shift" to be used against Ted Williams, an extreme pull hitter. Boudreau stationed three infielders, including the shortstop, on the rightfield side of second base, a move imitated by several other managers.

Released by the Indians in 1951, he played for a year with the Boston Red Sox, then became their manager for three seasons. In 1955, Boudreau was named the first manager of the Kansas City Athletics, who had just moved from Philadelphia. Fired in 1957, he became a broadcaster with the Chicago Cubs, and managed the Cubs in 1960 before returning to broadcasting.

Bowling

Skittles, a form of bowling, was played in the Plymouth Colony as early as 1621, and Dutch colonists in New Amsterdam enjoyed a type of skittles called nine-pins. The Dutch game was apparently derived from a German bowling game that was originally a religious ceremony, in which a churchgoer rolled a stone down the aisle of the church to knock down a club called "the heathen." If he succeeded, it proved his faith.

In the early part of the 19th century, nine pins were usually used, and they were tall and thin, much like modern candlepins. About 1820, ten-pin bowling began in New York City. Like billiards, the sport was commonly associated with drinking and gambling—the original bowling alleys actually were alleys, usually next to a tavern—and was in some disrepute. In 1847, the Gothic Hall Bowling Saloon tried to overcome that image by advertising itself as "the largest and most magnificent establishment of the kind in the city, (or world) . . . visited only by the most respectable company."

By 1850 New York City had an estimated 400 alleys. Between then and the Civil War, however, the sport lost ground, and larger, bottle-shaped pins were introduced to increase scoring. Bowling began to boom again after the war. In 1875, representatives from nine bowling clubs in New York and Brooklyn formed the National Bowling Association, which was superseded by the American Amateur Bowling Union, organized in 1890. The association that now governs the men's sport, the American Bowling Congress, was established in 1895.

Bowling had already begun to move out of the saloons, and some women had taken up the sport. In 1892, *Harper's Weekly* said bowling "generally conduces to a more perfect *entente cordiale* between the sexes." The process speeded up after formation of the ABC, with the construction of larger lanes where bowling was the primary activity, not just an afterthought. By 1900, Chicago had 20,000 bowlers, and there were more than 100 bowling clubs in New York City. More and more women were participating. The ABC originally ruled the women's sport, but in 1916 the Women's National Bowling Association was organized; it was renamed the Women's International Bowling Congress in 1971.

Bowling's growth continued well into the 20th century, with a slight pause during the depression. The number of teams registered with the ABC increased from 12,000 in 1925 to 43,000 in 1930. That declined somewhat to 41,000 in 1935, but the number leaped to 132,000 in 1940. ABC membership reached a peak of 4,799,195 bowlers in 1979–80, but dropped to 3,424,205 in 1986–87. WIBC tournament participation shows a similar pattern of growth, from 8 teams in 1916 to 1,189 in 1940, 2,600 in 1950, 4,491 in 1960, 4,894 in 1970, and 8,429 in 1980. It peaked at 14,430 teams in 1983, then went down to 9,840 in 1986 and 7,147 in 1987.

Professional bowling, meanwhile, has shown phenomenal financial growth. The men's Professional Bowlers Association was founded in 1958 with 33 members, and the professional tour began the following year with three tournaments and total prize money of $49,500. In 1960, there were seven tournaments worth a total of $150,000. By 1974, four of the PBA tournaments had prize money of $100,000 or more apiece. Earl Anthony in 1975 became the first bowler to win more than $100,000 in a season. Expanded television coverage and increased sponsorship of individual tournaments pushed average prize money per tournament to $118,000 in 1980. In 1988, prize money averaged $188,000 per tournament.

The Professional Women Bowlers Association began its own championship tournament in 1960 and offered a three-tournament tour in 1962. Some dissatisfied players broke away in 1974 to form the Ladies' Professional Bowlers Association. In 1978, the groups merged into the Women's Professional Bowlers Association, which became the Ladies Professional Bowlers Tour in 1981. Because of the lack

An early version of indoor bowling was illustrated in the New York Atlas in 1842.

of television money, prizes have not come close to those offered on the men's tour, although they've shown steady growth. In 1974, the top prize for first place was $12,500. That had increased to $40,000 by 1988.

See also AMERICAN BOWLING CONGRESS; PROFESSIONAL BOWLERS ASSOCIATION OF AMERICA; LADIES PROFESSIONAL BOWLERS TOUR; WOMEN'S INTERNATIONAL BOWLING CONGRESS.

Bowling Proprietors Association of America (BPAA)

During the 1932 American Bowling Congress tournament in Detroit, a group of lane owners formed the BPAA to exchange ideas and promote the sport.

When the Prince of Wales visited Canada in 1860, he went bowling at Niagara Falls. This illustration is from Frank Leslie's Illustrated Weekly.

In 1933, the BPAA took over sponsorship of the match-game tournament that had been initiated in 1922 by Louis B. Peterson. The BPAA Tournament in 1943 was merged with the *Chicago Tribune's* All-Star Tournament, and in 1971 the All-Star was replaced by the BPAA U.S. Open, an event on the Professional Bowlers' Association tour. The BPAA Women's All-Star Tournament, which began in 1949, became the BPAA Women's U.S. Open in 1971. The association now has about 4,200 member lanes.

Address: P.O. Box 5802, Arlington, TX 76011 (817) 649–5105

When bowling began moving out of saloons and billards parlors into its own lanes, it became popular among women, as shown in this drawing from Frank Leslie's Illustrated Weekly of December 9, 1882.

Bowling on the Green
See LAWN BOWLING.

Boxing

According to Nat Fleischer, "the first authentic ring fight or contest in America where rules were partially, if not wholly, observed" took place in 1816, when Jacob Hyer beat Tom Beasley and claimed the American heavyweight championship. No one challenged him, and he never fought again. During the 1820s, some gyms began to offer boxing as a gentlemanly exercise in self-defense, and there were a few prizefights, but in general the sport was viewed negatively, if not ignored entirely. Nevertheless, the number of bouts increased continuously into the 1840s. Tom Hyer, the son of Jacob, beat "Country McCloskey" (George McChester) in 101 rounds on September 9, 1841, and was acclaimed American heavyweight champion. This widely publicized fight stirred interest in the sport.

But to most observers boxing was, if anything, less reputable than ever. In 1842, Philip Hone noted in his diary that "the amusement of prize fighting, the disgrace of which was formerly confined to England, . . . has become one of the fashionable abominations of our loafer-ridden city." Hone was probably in the majority, because many fighters were associated with gambling parlors and taverns, and most of them were "pugs" for political factions. Christopher Lilly and Thomas McCoy, representing different factions, fought for 120 rounds near Yonkers on September 13, 1842. McCoy died after being hit by 81 punches in the final round. The *New York Tribune*, long critical of boxing, editorialized that "the promoters of the sport are gamblers, brothelkeepers, and saloonkeepers," and other newspapers agreed. Boxing was not quite as dead as McCoy, but it seemed moribund.

Tom Hyer, Jacob's son, came to the rescue. Billed as the "Great American Hope," Hyer was matched against the Irish-born and English-trained Yankee Sullivan on February 7, 1849, at Rock Point, MD. Public interest was so high that news of Hyer's 16-round victory was wired to New York newspapers—the first time the telegraph was used to carry a sports story. Once again, boxing became popular. But its very popularity stirred public opposition, and many states passed laws prohibiting prizefighting, while others began stricter enforcement of existing laws. When John Morrissey beat Sullivan on October 12, 1853, the fight was held at Boston Corners, NY, just across the border from Massachusetts, so fighters and fans alike could escape across the state line if authorities intervened. Similarly, his victory over John C. Heenan on October 20, 1858, took place at Long Point, Canada, just across the border from New York.

Many consider the match between Joe Goss of England and Irish-born Paddy Ryan as the first true American championship fight. It took place on May 30, 1880, in Collier Station, WV, near the Pennsylvania and Ohio borders. Ryan knocked out Goss in the 87th round. Although he held the title for nearly two years, Ryan defended it only once, losing to John L. Sullivan in just 10½ minutes on February 7, 1882, at Mississippi City, MS. The fight had been scheduled for New Orleans, but was moved to Mississippi at the last minute because of the fear of legal action.

For Sullivan's next major fight, against Jake Kilrain on July 8, 1889, the site was kept secret until the last minute. Both Mississippi and Louisiana had outlawed boxing, and the governors of both states issued executive orders prohibiting the fight. The fighters and spectators gathered in New Orleans, then took three special trains to Richburg, MS, for the match. It was the first ever in North America under the new Marquis of Queensbury rules; gloves

replaced bare knuckles, and the timed 3-minute round was used. (Under London Prize Ring rules, a round ended whenever a fighter was knocked down.) Tickets sold for as much as $15 and virtually every major newspaper carried extensive prefight stories. Sullivan won when Kilrain's manager threw in the sponge after 75 rounds.

Laws of the time usually distinguished between prize fighting and sparring. Many private athletic clubs had long had boxing instructors for their members, there were many private gyms where boxing was taught, and the sport was even included in some college physical education programs. On those levels, it was an amateur sport for gentlemen, much like fencing. The reformers objected only to prizefighting. Yet the fame of the prize fighter Sullivan spurred the growth of private boxing clubs. And some of them, such as the Southern Athletic Club and the Young Men's Gymnastic Club, both in New Orleans, began to stage professional fights that were advertised as "clean and decorous."

Reformers objected, and Louisiana in 1889 passed a new law, supposedly to strengthen the 1882 law against prizefighting. However, this law allowed "glove contests" sponsored by chartered clubs. New York passed a similar law in 1900. As a result, the structure of boxing changed. Clubs were organized for the sole purpose of staging fights. In effect, the promoter-matchmaker had arrived. Instead of clandestine bouts arranged by the boxers or their managers and staged in hastily built rings in out-of-the-way locations, major prizefights were now arranged by clubs, and they took place in indoor auditoriums or gyms in major cities.

The Olympic Club of New Orleans in 1890 built the first modern boxing arena, complete with electric lights and a canvas mat, and offered a $12,000 purse for a middleweight championship fight between Jack "the Nonpareil" Dempsey and Bob Fitzsimmons. From September 5 through 7, 1892, the club offered a "Carnival of Champions": The Jack McAuliffe-Billy Myer lightweight championship fight, the George Dixon-Jack Skelly featherweight championship fight, and then the showpiece, John L. Sullivan defending his title against "Gentleman Jim" Corbett for a $25,000 purse. Corbett knocked out the overweight Sullivan in the 21st round.

The next heavyweight championship fight, between Corbett and Bob Fitzsimmons, had trouble finding a home. Texas was originally to be the site, but the state legislature passed a law providing a jail term of two to five years for prize fighting. Promoter William A. Brady then tried the Indian Territory, but was turned away by the federal government. In Arkansas, the fight was blocked by an injunction.

Carson City, NV finally hosted the bout on March 17, 1897, and Fitzsimmons knocked out Corbett in the 14th round. James J. Jeffries won the title from Fitzsimmons with an 11th-round knockout on June 9, 1899; he retired in 1905. The title changed hands twice more before Jack Johnson became the first black heavyweight champion by knocking out Tommy Burns in the 14th round on December 26, 1909, in Sydney, Australia. The victory created a search for a "great white hope" who could beat Johnson, but none could. Convicted of a Mann Act violation in 1912, he fled to Canada, then Europe. Eventually, he lost the title to Jess Willard, in Havana in 1915.

Most boxing had moved to the West after New York's Frawley Act of 1910 prohibited the sport in that state. In a way, it proved to be a blessing for boxing in New York, because it produced Tex Rickard. Rickard promoted the 1906 lightweight championship fight between Joe Gans and Battling Nelson in Goldfield, NV, as well as Johnson's 1910 fight against Jeffries in Reno for a purse of $100,000. After making an unknown Jack Dempsey the heavyweight champion in a 1919 fight against Willard, he came to New York, which legalized boxing in 1920. Rickard leased Madison Square Garden and turned it into a profit center, largely by making boxing more than respectable. He transformed it into a sport attended by women, by celebrities, and by New York society men, who wore tuxedos to sit in ringside seats and be seen. He promoted the first fight with a $1 million gate, Dempsey versus Georges Carpentier on July 2, 1921, and the first with a $2 million gate, the second Dempsey–Gene Tunney fight on September 22, 1927.

After Tunney beat Dempsey in that second fight, the heavyweight division fell into the doldrums for more than a decade. But there were some very good fighters in other weight divisions, and there were more weight divisions. Until 1855, the only champion was the English champion, regardless of weight. Then the lightweight division was created, followed by bantamweight in 1856, featherweight in 1860, middleweight in 1867, welterweight about 1880, light heavyweight in 1903, and flyweight in 1910. The New York Athletic Commission, established in 1920, drew up the first official weight limits and initiated prefight weigh-ins to ensure that neither fighter is over the limit.

Among the top fighters of the era were Mickey Walker, middleweight champion 1926–31; Barney Ross, lightweight champion 1933–35 and welterweight champion in 1934 and 1935–38; and Henry Armstrong, the only fighter to hold three world championships at the same time, as featherweight, welterweight, and lightweight. There were also some

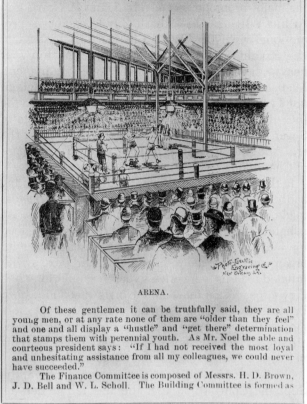

The first indoor boxing arena was built in 1890 by the Olympic Club of New Orleans. Courtesy of the Louisiana Collection, Tulane University Library

very good black heavyweights who were never given a chance to win the championship, among them Harry Wills, who was backed by Nat Fleischer, editor of *Ring* magazine, as a serious challenger to Dempsey and then to Tunney.

A virtual unknown, James J. Braddock, became heavyweight champion in 1935. Braddock decided to go for one last big payday by facing Joe Louis, the "Brown Bomber." On June 22, 1937, Louis knocked Braddock out in the eighth round to become the second black heavyweight champion. Louis reigned longer (nearly 12 years) and defended his title more times (25) than any other heavyweight champion. He retired in 1949, though he later fought unsuccessfully to regain the title.

Boxing began to enter a new boom era, largely created by television, even before World War II ended. The Gillette Safety Razor Company in 1944 began sponsoring weekly telecasts of Madison Square Garden fights on NBC. In 1947, CBS set up a subsidiary, the Tournament of Champions, Inc., to promote fights on Wednesday nights, putting the network in direct competition with the Twentieth Century Sporting Club, which promoted the Garden fights. But the International Boxing Club of New York soon became the major promoter. Formed by James D. Norris and Arthur Wirtz in 1948, the IBC held exclusive promotional rights to Ezzard Charles, Gus Lesnevich, Lee Savold, and Jersey Joe Walcott, the top four heavyweight contenders after Louis' retirement. Madison Square Garden in March of 1949 bought out Twentieth Century and assigned its rights to the IBC; that included exclusive rights to the fights of Sugar Ray Robinson, the most exciting boxer of the era. And in May the IBC bought out the Tournament of Champions.

In the long run, television and the IBC hurt boxing badly. TV fight fans wanted winners; a single loss made a fighter unacceptable to TV promoters. As congressional investigations later revealed, the need for winners, along with the IBC's association with organized crime, led to fixed fights, and boxers with inflated records were often exposed as inferior when they appeared on television. Norris' greed also hurt. Because major fights in large stadiums drew more money than televised fights, he began using closed-circuit TV in theaters for the best fights, leaving network TV with second-rate fighters.

Norris' empire eventually crumbled. In 1955, the Supreme Court ruled that the IBC fell under the Sherman Act, and a district court judge in 1957 ordered that the monopoly must be broken up. After the civil charges came criminal charges. Frankie Carbo, who got payoffs from the IBC because he controlled many managers and fighters, was sent to prison for 2 years in December 1959, and in February of 1961 he was sentenced to 25 years in prison. Truman Gibson, who had replaced Norris as president of the IBC, was sentenced to two concurrent five-year terms. In the meantime, NBC in 1960 had stopped televising fights, leaving only the Gillette Friday night fights on network television. They went off the air in 1964.

Most top fighters during this period were not connected with organized crime. Among them was Rocky Marciano, who won the heavyweight title by knocking out Jersey Joe Walcott in the 13th round on September 23, 1952. Marciano defended his title six times before retiring in 1956 as the only heavyweight champion never to have lost a professional fight. He was succeeded by Floyd Patterson, who lost the championship to Sweden's Ingemar Johansson in 1959, but won it back the following year.

The sport was not helped when Sonny Liston won the heavyweight championship by knocking out Patterson in the first round on September 25, 1962. Liston was an ex-convict controlled by Carbo and Frank "Blinky" Palermo. He lost the title to Cassius Clay when he refused to come out of his corner for the seventh round, claiming a shoulder injury. Many suspected a fix. In a rematch in Lewiston, ME, Clay scored a first-round knockout with a punch that most observers never even saw, fueling further suspicions. Clay then revealed he had become a Black Muslim and changed his name to Cassius X. Shortly afterward, he became Muhammad Ali. When Ali was sentenced to five years in prison for draft evasion in 1967, his title was taken from him.

The heavyweight division was again in disarray. New York and several other states recognized Joe Frazier as champion, while the World Boxing Association held an eight-man tournament that was won by Jimmy Ellis. Frazier knocked out Ellis in the fifth round on February 16, 1970, to win world recognition. Ali had meanwhile won an appeal of his conviction and was back in business. He met Frazier in one of the most publicized fights in history on March 8, 1971, in Madison Square Garden. Frazier won a close decision, refused to give Ali a rematch, and lost the title on a surprising second-round knockout by George Foreman on January 22, 1973. Ali reclaimed the title by knocking out Foreman in the eighth round on October 30, 1974, in Zaire.

Don King, a black, had emerged as the top fight promoter in the United States. He had promoted the Zaire fight, the first heavyweight championship bout ever held in Africa, and he was Ali's promoter. The war in Vietnam over, Ali had become something of a hero for his antiwar stand, and he was clearly the best attraction in the fight business. King was hired in 1978 as fight promoter by Madison Square Garden.

Ali lost the title to Leon Spinks in 1978, regained it in a rematch later that year, then retired. As usual after the retirement of a great champion, confusion reigned, and it was compounded by the fact that three different groups recognized champions: the World Boxing Association, the World Boxing Council and the International Boxing Federation. There were often three different "world champions" in each weight division. Even Larry Holmes, who was generally considered the real heavyweight champion from 1978 until 1985, was at first recognized only by the WBC, and was stripped of that title in 1984. He was the IBF champion when he lost to Michael Spinks, Leon's brother, the following year.

Turmoil in the sport continues. Mike Tyson won the WBC heavyweight title with a second-round knockout of Trevor Berbick on November 22, 1986, and was generally recognized as world champion after he beat WBA titlist James "Bonecrusher" Smith on a 12-round decision, March 7, 1987. But his personal and professional problems distracted attention from his great boxing ability. In 1988, he fired his long-time trainer, sued his manager, ran into a tree with his car, got involved in a street fight, and was sued for divorce by actress-model Robin Givens after less than six months of marriage.

Tyson was generally considered invincible in the ring, however, until little-known James "Buster" Douglas knocked him out in the 10th round on February 11, 1990, in Tokyo. Douglas lost the title in his first defense on October 25, when Evander Holyfield KOed him in the third round at the Mirage Hotel and Casino in Las Vegas, NV.

Further Readings: Fleischer, Nat. *Heavyweight Championship: An Informal History of Heavyweight Boxing from 1719 to the Present Day.* New York: Putnam, 1961; Gorn, Elliot J. *The Manly Art: Bare-Knuckle Prize Fighting in America* Ithaca: Cornell University Press, 1986; Riess, Steven A. "In the Ring and Out: Professional Boxing in New York, 1896–1920," in Donald Spivey, editor, *Sport in America: New Historical Perspectives.* Westport, CT: Greenwood Press, 1985; Sammons, Jeffrey T. *Beyond the Ring: The Role of Boxing in American Society.* Urbana: University of Illinois Press, 1988.

See also CARNIVAL OF CHAMPIONS; FRAWLEY ACT; HORTON LAW; INTERNATIONAL BOXING FEDERATION; INTERNATIONAL BOXING LEAGUE; RICKARD, TEX; WORLD BOXING ORGANIZATION.

Box Lacrosse
See INDOOR LACROSSE.

BPAA
See BOWLING PROPRIETORS ASSOCIATION OF AMERICA.

Bradley Center
Milwaukee, WI
This sports and entertainment arena, built at a cost of more than $71 million, is named for Harry Lynde Bradley. It was a gift of his daughter and her husband. Opened in 1988, the center is the home of the National Basketball Association's Milwaukee Bucks, the Marquette University basketball team, and minor-league hockey and indoor soccer teams. It seats about 18,600 for basketball and 17,800 for hockey.

The center also hosts wrestling, motor sports, ice shows, and entertainment events.

Bradshaw, Terry (1948–   )
Football
Born September 2, 1948, Shreveport, LA; Pro Football Hall of Fame
Although Bradshaw played at a small college, Louisiana Tech, the Pittsburgh Steelers made him the first player chosen in the 1970 National Football League college draft, and Bradshaw became the only quarterback ever to lead a team to four Super Bowl victories. He became a starter in 1971. The following year, the Steelers were champions of the Central Division in the American Football Conference. In the playoff game against Oakland, Bradshaw threw the famous "immaculate reception," a pass that bounced off an Oakland defensive back and was caught by fullback Franco Harris, who ran it in for a touchdown with 5 seconds left to give Pittsburgh a 13–7 win. But Bradshaw missed most of the championship game after being knocked dizzy in the first quarter, and the Steelers lost to the unbeaten Miami Dolphins 21–17.

A shoulder separation kept Bradshaw out of several games in 1973, and the Steelers dropped to second place. Joe Gilliam took over the starting job in 1974, but Bradshaw replaced him about halfway through the year and took the Steelers to their first Super Bowl victory, built primarily on running. He attempted only 14 passes, completing 9, in a 16–7 win over the Minnesota Vikings. Bradshaw followed that with a sensational 1975 season, completing 58 percent of his passes and throwing for 18 touchdowns with only 9 interceptions. The Steelers won their second straight Super Bowl, 21–17 over the Dallas Cowboys, on a 64–yard touchdown pass from Bradshaw to Lynn Swann with a little more than 3 minutes left in the game.

The Steelers were AFC champions again in 1978 and 1979. They won both Super Bowls, and Bradshaw was named the Most Valuable Player both times. Against Dallas in Super Bowl XIII, he completed 17 of 30 passes for 318 yards and 4 touchdowns in a 35–31 win. The following year, he completed 14 of 21 for 309 yards and 2 touchdowns, as the Steelers beat the Los Angeles Rams 31–16.

Bradshaw retired after the 1983 season. For his career, he had 2,205 completions in 1,901 attempts for 27,989 yards and 212 touchdowns. He holds postseason records for attempts (417), completions (233), yards (3,508), and touchdown passes (58). He was named Player of the Year by the Associated Press and *Sport* magazine in 1978.

Further Reading: Bradshaw, Terry, with David Diles. *Terry Bradshaw: Man of Steel.* Grand Rapids, MI, 1979.

Breeders Crown
Harness Racing

The Breeders Crown began in 1984 as a series of eight major races for two- and three-year-old trotters and pacers, both colts and fillies. In 1985, races for aged trotters and pacers were added, and the following year the number of races increased to 12, with separate events for aged mares and horses. The Breeders Crown differs from Thoroughbred racing's Breeders' Cup in that the races are held over a period of time at different tracks; purses range from more than $200,000 to about $500,000. In the current format, the first race is the aged horse and gelding trot in early August and the last two, the two-year-old colt pace and two-year-old filly pace, are run on the same card in mid-November.

Address: 1 Pear Tree Plaza, 289 Route 33 East, Manalapan, NJ 07726 (201) 446–5151

Breeders' Cup
Horse Racing

Featuring seven races with a total of $10 million in purses, the Breeders' Cup was inaugurated in 1984 by a newly formed organization, Breeders' Cup Limited. The feature race is the $3 million, 1¼-mile Breeders' Cup Classic. There's also a $2 million, 1½-mile turf race. The other five races have purses of $1 million each: A 6-furlong sprint, a 1¹⁄₁₆-mile race for juvenile fillies, a 1⅛-mile race for mares and fillies, a 1-mile race, and a 1¹⁄₁₆-mile juvenile race. The Breeders' Cup was held at Hollywood Park in 1984 and 1987, Aqueduct in 1985, Santa Anita in 1986, Churchill Downs in 1988, Gulfstream Park in 1989, and Belmont Park in 1990.

Address: Breeders' Cup Limited, P.O. Box 4230, Lexington, KY 40544–4230 (203) 629–2229

Bret Hanover
Harness Racing

The first two-year-old to be named Harness Horse of the Year, in 1964, Bret Hanover repeated in 1965 and 1966, winning an incredible 62 races in 68 starts over the three-year period. He was never out of the money, finishing second five times and third once. Bret Hanover won pacing's Triple Crown and became the first horse to win more than $300,000 in a single season in 1965. He ran a record 1:55 mile at Indianapolis that year and also set a world record of 1:57 for a half-mile track. In 1966, Bret Hanover won $407,534, with 17 victories in 20 starts, and paced

a time trial in 1:53.3, another record. He was then purchased for $2 million and put out to stud.

Briggs Stadium
See TIGER STADIUM.

Brimsek, "Mr. Zero" Francis C. (1915–)
Hockey
Born September 26, 1915, Eveleth, MN; Hockey Hall of Fame

The Boston Bruins players and their fans were doubtful. Management thought so highly of Brimsek that they sold their veteran Hall of Fame goaltender "Tiny" Thompson to Detroit to make way for him. Brimsek, called up from the Providence farm team in November of 1938, was not only a rookie, but a native of the United States. He quickly made believers of the doubters. He had a shutout in his second National Hockey League Game, another in his third, and still another in his fourth. Finally, a goal was scored on him after he'd set a league record: 231 minutes and 54 seconds of scoreless goaltending. He

Known as "Mr. Zero" because of his 40 career shutouts, Frank Brimsek played in the National Hockey League for ten seasons. Courtesy of the U.S. Hockey Hall of Fame

followed that with three more shutouts and 220 minutes, 24 seconds without being scored upon. Now the fans called him "Mr. Zero."

Brimsek had ten shutouts and a remarkable 1.6 goals-against average that season, winning both the Vezina Trophy as top goaltender and the Calder Trophy as Rookie of the Year, while the Bruins won the Stanley Cup. He collected his second Vezina Trophy in 1942. After serving in the Coast Guard during World War II, he returned to the Bruins in 1945 and remained with them through the 1948–49 season, then was traded to Chicago, where he played just one season before retiring. During his career, he allowed 1,402 goals in 478 games, a 2.94 goals-against average, and had 40 shutouts; in Stanley Cup play, he gave up 186 goals in 68 games, a 2.74 average, with 2 shutouts.

Brinker, Maureen Connolly
See CONNOLLY, MAUREEN.

Bristol International Raceway
Bristol, TN

Opened in 1961, Bristol is considered the fastest half-mile auto racing track in the world. It hosts two NASCAR Winston Cup championship events.

Address: P.O. Box 3966, Bristol, TN 37625 (615) 764–1161

British Columbia
See VANCOUVER.

British Columbia Sports Hall of Fame and Museum

Housed in the former British Columbia Pavilion on the Pacific National Exhibition grounds, this hall opened in 1966. Its 5,000 feet of display space includes exhibits on the history of sports in the province, and it also houses the provincial sports archives. A fund drive is currently underway to move into a larger facility at B.C. Place Stadium, home of the British Columbia Lions of the Canadian Football League.

Address: P.O. Box 69020, Station K, Vancouver, British Columbia, Canada V5K 4W3 (604) 253–2311

Broadcasting
See RADIO; TELEVISION.

Broad Jump
See LONG JUMP.

Brock, Lou (1936–   )
Baseball
Born June 18, 1936, El Dorado, AR; Baseball Hall of Fame

Ty Cobb's record of 890 stolen bases seemed as if it would stand forever. But it was broken by Lou Brock, who ended his career after the 1979 season with 838 stolen bases, including a record 118 in 1974 (broken in 1982 by Ricky Henderson). Brock arrived in the major leagues with the Chicago Cubs late in the 1961 season, and was traded to the St. Louis Cardinals in 1964. He led the National League in stolen bases eight times, from 1966 to 1969 and, again, from 1971 to 1974. A left-handed batter and thrower, he had a career batting average of .293, with 3,022 hits and 1,610 runs scored. Brock played in the World Series in 1964, 1967, and 1968, and tied Series records for career stolen bases (14), stolen bases in a game (3, twice, on October 12, 1967 and October 5, 1968), and stolen bases in one inning (2).

Brooklyn, NY
Baseball   Brooklyn was an early hotbed of baseball. Its top team, the Atlantics, won the "whip pennant" as the champion of the United States six times from 1859 through 1866, and the Brooklyn Eckfords won it the other two years. The Eckfords joined the first professional league, the National Association, in the middle of the 1871 season, replacing the Kekiongas of Fort Wayne. The Brooklyn Atlantics also entered the association in 1872. The Eckfords dropped out in 1873, but the Atlantics remained in the league until it folded after the 1875 season.

Brooklyn next had a team in American Association from 1884 through 1889. After winning the 1889 pennant, the team moved into the National League; the association hastily put together another Brooklyn team, but it moved to Baltimore before the 1890 season ended. The National League team became known as the Robins, for Manager Wilbert Robinson, in 1916. Later, they were the Trolley Dodgers, then simply the Dodgers. They won pennants in 1890, 1899, 1900, 1916, 1920, 1941, 1947, 1949, 1952, 1953, 1955, and 1956, and the World Series in 1955. The Dodgers moved to Los Angeles in 1958.

Football   There were two professional football teams in Brooklyn in 1926: the Lions in the National Football League and the Dodgers in the American Football League. The AFL folded after that season. From 1930 through 1940, another team called the Dodgers was in the NFL.

See also EBBETS FIELD.

Brotherhood of Professional Baseball Players
On October 22, 1885, the New York Giants formed the original chapter of the Brotherhood of Professional Baseball Players, the first union of professional athletes. There were nine charter members, and shortstop John Montgomery Ward was elected

president. Ward, who was studying law at Columbia University, drew up the brotherhood charter, stating that its purpose was "to protect and benefit its members collectively and individually, to promote a high standard of professional conduct, and to advance the interests of the 'National Game'."

Chapters were organized in other National League cities during the 1886 season. The brotherhood attracted members rapidly because players had some very definite grievances about how major league baseball was run. They especially disliked the reserve clause, which in effect turned a player's one-year contract into a contract for his entire career.

Ward decided against affiliating with the Knights of Labor, a national organization roughly equivalent to the modern American Federation of Labor. But in 1887 he asked the National League to recognize the brotherhood as a union with power to negotiate on behalf of the players. The owners refused, although they did agree to meet with a committee of players headed by Ward to discuss grievances. Little resulted from that meeting.

After the 1888 season, the owners adopted a Classification Plan, under which players were assigned to classifications ranging from A to E. Class A players were to be paid no more than $2,500 a season, Class E players no more than $1,500. Ward met on June 25 with Albert G. Spalding, president of the Chicago team, and told Spalding that the players wanted the classification plan to be thrown out. Spalding said the issue would have to wait until the National League's annual meeting, after the season.

The players talked about striking on July 4, but voted against it, probably because Ward had a bigger idea in mind. He held a meeting on July 14 with leaders of the brotherhood and Albert L. Johnson, owner of a Cleveland streetcar line. The idea was to start a new league, a cooperative of players and backers, not owners. Johnson agreed to back a Cleveland team. Other backers were lined up with Johnson's help. The Players' National League of Base Ball Clubs, usually known as the Players' League, was formally established on November 4, 1889; the official announcement was made two days later. Although the Players' League attracted most of the National League's players, it lasted just one season. Its failure marked the end of the brotherhood.

See also CLASSIFICATION PLAN; PLAYERS' LEAGUE; WARD, "MONTY."

Brown, Doris (1942–   )
Distance Running
Born September 17, 1942, Gig Harbor, WA; National Track and Field Hall of Fame

The first great American woman distance runner, Brown began as a very good middle-distance runner. In 1959, she set an American record in the 440-yard run at 59.4 seconds, and she also set a record of 2 minutes 2 seconds in the 800 meters in 1968. But her best event was cross-country. She won the U.S. women's championship, in 1966 and from 1968 through 1971, and the world women's cross-country championship the first five years it was held (1967–71). Because there weren't any longer events in the Olympics, she ran the 1,500 meters in 1972, but tripped on a lane curb and broke her foot. In 1976, she also tried the marathon, running 2:47:34.8, then a world record for a first-time runner in the event.

Brown, Jim (1936–   )
Football
Born February 17, 1936, St. Simons, GA; Pro Football Hall of Fame

Possibly the greatest running back of all time, Brown was remarkably fast for someone his size, 6 feet 2 inches and 228 pounds. He was not a genuine breakaway runner, but he was elusive enough to throw defenders off balance so he could use his power to break through tackles. He once said, "I'm not Superman," prompting an opponent to respond, "What he really means is that Superman isn't Jimmy Brown."

An All-American running back at Syracuse in 1956, Brown was also an All-American lacrosse player in 1957 and a three-year starter in basketball. He joined the Cleveland Browns in the 1957 season and played for nine years before retiring abruptly at the age of 30. He was an All-Pro for eight of those years, missing out only in 1962, and he gained more than 1,000 yards seven times, falling just 4 yards short in 1962. Perhaps most remarkable, he never missed a game.

In his rookie season, he gained 942 yards on 202 carries, a 4.7 average, and scored 10 touchdowns. *Sporting News* named him Player of the Year and Rookie of the Year. Brown won the Jim Thorpe Trophy as the NFL's Most Valuable Player in his second season, when he gained 1,527 yards and scored 18 touchdowns, and in his final season, when he had 1,544 yards and 21 touchdowns. He led the NFL in rushing attempts in 1958 (257), 1959 (290), 1961 (305), 1963 (291), 1964 (280), and 1965 (289); in yards gained in 1957 (942), 1958 (1,527), 1959 (1,329), 1960 (1,257), 1961 (1,408), 1963 (1,863), 1964 (1,446), and 1965 (1,544); in rushing average in 1963 (6.4) and 1964 (5.2); and in touchdowns rushing in 1957 (9), 1958 (17), 1959 (14), 1963 (12), and 1965 (17).

During his pro career, Brown gained 12,312 yards on 2,359 carries, a 5.2 average, and scored 106 rushing touchdowns; he caught 262 passes for 2,499 yards, a 9.5 average, and 20 touchdowns; and he returned 29 kickoffs for 648 yards, a 22.3 average.

Brown, Paul (1908–1991)
Football

Born September 7, 1908, Norwalk, OH; died August 5, 1991; Pro Football Hall of Fame

As coach of the Cleveland Browns, who were named for him, in the All America Football Conference 1946–49 and the National Football League 1950–62, Brown made professional football truly professional. He used detailed studies of game films to grade his players, hired a full-time coaching staff, tested players for intelligence and used classroom lectures as well as practices to teach them, and initiated the idea of sending plays in from the sidelines rather than having the quarterback call them. Brown's teams practiced things that had never been practiced before, such as forming interference after an interception and catching tipped balls. Both drills were part of his philosophy that a good team should always be ready to capitalize on opportunity.

Brown played quarterback at Miami University (OH), graduating in 1929, then coached high school football before taking over at Ohio State in 1941. In his second season, the team won won nine games and lost one. After the 1943 season, Brown was in the service, coaching the team at the Great Lakes Naval Training Station. When World War II ended in 1945, the AAFC was being formed, and Cleveland owner Mickey McBride offered Brown $20,000 a year and 15% of the profits to coach the new team. Brown brought blacks back into professional football for the first time since 1933, signing guard Bill Willis, who had played for him at Ohio State, and Marion Motley, a big, fast fullback from the University of Nevada. (About the same time, the Los Angeles Rams also signed two black players, Woody Strode and Kenny Washington, from UCLA.)

The AAFC lasted four years, and the Browns won all four championships, compiling a record of 47 wins, 4 losses, and 3 ties during the regular season. When the leagues merged in 1950, the Browns were one of only four AAFC teams that actually survived. They won the NFL championship that year, beating the Los Angeles Rams 30–28. The Browns lost the title game to Los Angeles 24–17 in the following year, but they won consecutive championships in 1954 and 1955, beating Detroit 56–10 and Los Angeles 38–14.

Although he had only one losing season in 17 years, he was fired after the 1962 season. In 1968, a year after he was elected to the Pro Football Hall of Fame, he reappeared as part owner, general manager, and coach of the Cincinnati Bengals in the American Football League. They joined the National Football League in the 1970 merger and won a division title in just their third year of existence. The Bengals won another division title under Brown in 1973, and the next two years they finished second to the powerful Pittsburgh Steelers. Brown retired from coaching after the 1975 season.

Further Reading: Brown, Paul. *PB: The Paul Brown Story.* New York: Atheneum, 1979.

Brown, "Three-Finger" Mordecai P. C. (1876–1948)
Baseball

Born October 19, 1876, Nyesville, IN; died February 14, 1948; Baseball Hall of Fame

When he was seven years old, Brown lost most of his right index finger when his hand was cut in a corn chopper, and his thumb and middle finger were badly mangled. The injury helped him become one of the best pitchers in baseball, because it turned his fastball into a natural sinker. Brown joined the St. Louis Cardinals in 1903 and was traded to the Chicago Cubs the following year. He achieved real stardom in 1906, when he won 26 and lost 6, with 9 shutouts and a 1.04 earned run average. In the World Series against the Chicago White Sox, Brown won one game 1–0 and lost two, one of them by a 2–1 score. He had a 20–6 record in 1907 and won the fifth game of the World Series 2–0 over the Detroit Tigers to give the Cubs the championship.

In 1908, the Giants and Cubs finished in a tie for first place, and had to replay a tied game in New York. Brown had appeared in 6 of the team's last 13 games, but he was called in against the Giants in the first inning; he posted a 4–2 win, giving him 29 wins against 9 losses for the season. He beat the Tigers in relief in the first game of the World Series, then pitched a 3–0 shutout in the fourth game as the Cubs again won in five games.

Brown led the league in wins with 27 in 1910, when the Cubs finished second, and he was 25–14 in 1910, but won just one game and lost two in the World Series, won by the Philadelphia Athletics in five games. In 1911, he was 21–11, his sixth straight season with more than 20 victories. Because of a knee injury in 1912, he was ineffective for the last few years of his career, although he had a 17–8 record with the Chicago Federal League team in 1915.

Brown won 239 games and lost 130 in 14 seasons, with 57 shutouts and a 2.06 earned run average, the third lowest in history.

Brundage, Avery (1887–1975)
Olympics, Track & Field
Born September 28, 1887, Detroit, MI; died May 8, 1975

A long-time, controversial leader in the U.S. and international Olympic movements, Brundage was a track star at the University of Illinois, graduating in 1909. He finished sixth in the 1912 Olympic decathlon, and he won the national all-around championship in 1914, 1916, and 1918. When the American Olympic Committee was restructured as the American Olympic Association (AOA) in 1921, Brundage was one of its original members. He served as president of the Amateur Athletic Union from 1928 through 1932 and initiated a 1930 peace settlement with the National Collegiate Athletic Association, temporarily ending a feud that had begun more than 20 years before. He succeeded General Douglas MacArthur as president of the AOA in 1928.

In 1934, a movement began to boycott the 1936 Berlin Olympics, led by Judge Jeremiah T. Murphy, president of the AAU. Brundage sailed to Europe in late July and returned with assurances from German leaders that there would be no discrimination against Jews, but the AAU annual convention in December voted to postpone accepting the invitation to the Games. Alarmed, Brundage published a pamphlet favoring participation and issued a statement as AOA president, saying in part: "Many of the individuals and organizations active in the present campaign to boycott the Olympics have Communist antecedents. Radicals and Communists must keep their hands off American sport." On December 6, 1935, the AAU voted to accept the invitation. Murphy resigned as president and Brundage replaced him, serving through 1936.

He was embroiled in controversy again in 1936, when Eleanor Holm Jarrett, the swimmer, allegedly got drunk on the ship carrying U.S. athletes to the Games, and was suspended from the team. Brundage rejected a petition signed by 220 U.S. coaches and athletes asking that she be reinstated, and newspapers had a field day with the story. But he scored a personal triumph on July 30, when the International Olympic Committee chose him to a replace a U.S. representative who had favored the boycott. The following year, he was placed on the IOC's executive board.

The idea for the Pan-American Games came to Brundage in 1937, when he discussed it with AAU officials. After the 1940 Helsinki Olympics were canceled because of the German invasion of Finland, Brundage went to Buenos Aires for a meeting of 16 Latin-American countries, and games were tenta-tively scheduled for 1942. However, they were also canceled when the Japanese attacked Pearl Harbor. (They were first held in 1951 in Buenos Aires.)

In 1952, Brundage was elected president of the IOC and immediately spoke out for absolute ama-teurism in the Olympic Games; for the next 20 years he adhered strictly to that principle. Brundage consistently opposed any practice that smacked of professionalism, including athletic scholarships, payments in lieu of wages for the time an athlete spends training, commercial endorsements by athletes, and money made from books and articles written by an athlete about sports. He also fought against nationalism in the Olympic movement (he wanted bugle fanfares, not national anthems, to be played at medal ceremonies) and tried unsuccessfully to keep international politics out of the Games.

Brundage retired from the IOC after the 1972 Olympics in Munich, at which 11 Israeli athletes were murdered by Palestinian terrorists. His last major decision as IOC president was that the games should continue after one day of mourning. At the memorial service in the Olympic stadium, he said, "The Games must go on and we must continue our efforts to keep them clean, pure and honest and try to extend the sportsmanship of the athletic field into other areas."

Further Reading: Guttmann, Allen. *The Games Must Go On: Avery Brundage and the Olympic Movement.* New York: Columbia University Press, 1984.

Budge, "Don" J. Donald (1915–   )
Tennis
Born June 13, 1915, Oakland, CA; International Tennis Hall of Fame

Trained on gravel courts in public parks, Budge was an outstanding all-around tennis player with no weaknesses, and it was universally agreed that he had the best backhand ever seen. By 1936, he was America's top-ranked player, though he was narrowly defeated by England's Fred Perry in the national championship. Perry became a professional the following year, and Budge took over as the best amateur in the world. He won the men's singles, the men's doubles (with Gene Mako), and the mixed doubles (with Alice Marble) at Wimbledon, the first player ever to win all three events in one year. He also won the U.S. singles title.

In 1938, he repeated his three-championship performance at Wimbledon and became the first man to win the "Grand Slam"—the Australian, English, French, and U.S. championships—in one year. Budge then became a professional, and in 1939 he beat Ellsworth Vines, 21 matches to 18, and Fred Perry,

18 to 11, to win the championship. He won the U.S. professional singles championship in 1940 and beat the aging Bill Tilden, 51 matches to 7, on the 1941 pro tour. Budge won the professional singles title again in 1942. After service during World War II, he lost to Bobby Riggs, 23 matches to 21, on the pro tour, and he retired from competition.

Buffalo, NY

Baseball Buffalo had a National League team for seven seasons, 1879–85, and was also represented in the Players' League in 1890.

Basketball The Buffalo Braves entered the National Basketball Association for the 1970–71 season. The team moved to San Diego, as the Clippers, after the 1977–78 season.

Football When the American Football League was founded in 1960, the Buffalo Bills were one of its eight original teams. The Bills won AFL championships in 1964 and 1965. Since the AFL merger with the National Football League in 1970, the team has been in the eastern division of the NFL's American Football Conference. The Bills won division championships in 1980, 1981, 1988, 1989, and 1990, and the AFC championship in 1990. They lost Super Bowl XXV to the New York Giants, 20–19.

Hockey In 1970, Buffalo got a National Hockey League franchise, the Sabres, which for years had been the name of its team in the American Hockey League. The Sabres were in the Stanley Cup finals in 1975, losing to the Philadelphia Flyers, four games to two.

See also BUFFALO MEMORIAL AUDITORIUM; RICH STADIUM.

Buffalo Memorial Auditorium
Buffalo, NY

The Buffalo Memorial Auditorium was built by the federal government's Works Progress Administration at a cost of $2,650,000. It opened in 1940. In 1971, it became the first arena to have its roof raised, adding more than 4,500 seats at a cost of $11 million. The home of the Buffalo Sabres of the National Hockey League, the auditorium was also the home floor of the former Buffalo Braves of the National Basketball Association, and it hosts college basketball games, boxing and wrestling matches, and entertainment events. Capacity is 17,900 for hockey and 16,433 for basketball, including standees.

Busch Stadium
St. Louis, MO

One of the completely enclosed superstadiums, Busch Memorial Stadium opened on May 12, 1966. The name was changed to Busch Stadium in 1983. The stadium is owned by the Civic Center Redevelopment Corporation, which has several other income-generating properties on the site that make enough money to cover operating losses on the stadium itself. The field was originally grass, but AstroTurf was installed in 1970. Home run distances are 330 feet down the lines and 414 feet to center field. The stadium, which has a capacity of 50,222, is the home park of the St. Louis Cardinals in baseball's National League, and was also the home of the National Football League team of the same name until 1988, when the franchise moved to Phoenix, AZ.

See also SPORTSMAN'S PARK.

Butcher, Susan (1954–   )
Sled Dog Racing
Born December 26, 1954, Cambridge, MA

Butcher won the Iditarod Sled Dog Race, called the "last great race on earth," three consecutive years, 1986, 1987, and 1988. She had a close call in the 1985 race, which was won by another woman, Libby Riddles. Butcher was leading the race when a pregnant moose attacked her team, killing two dogs and wounding seven others, and she was forced to drop out. After barely losing in 1989, Butcher claimed her fourth victory in five years by setting a new record of 11 days, 1 hour, 53 minutes, and 23 seconds in 1990, breaking her own record by more than 12 minutes. Butcher views herself as more coach than athlete, saying that she does the training, but the dogs do the work. Nevertheless, driving a sled dog team on a 1,162-mile race, with temperatures as low as 50 degrees below zero, often in the face of blizzards, obviously requires athletic skills.

Butkus Award
Football

The Downtown Athletic Club of Orlando, FL presents the Butkus Award to the player chosen as the outstanding collegiate linebacker. The award is named for Dick Butkus, Chicago Bears' middle linebacker from 1965 through 1973, six times an All-Pro and twice an All-American at the University of Illinois.

Butkus Award Winners

1985 Brian Bosworth, Oklahoma
1986 Brian Bosworth, Oklahoma
1987 Paul McGowan, Florida State
1988 Derrick Thomas, Alabama
1989 Percy Snow, Michigan State
1990 Alfred Williams, Colorado

Button, "Dick" Richard T. (1929–   )
Figure Skating
Born July 18, 1929, Englewood, NJ; Figure Skating
Hall of Fame

Until Button arrived by winning the U.S. men's
singles title in 1946, figure skating was not very
athletic, although Sonja Henie had certainly brought
some athleticism to the sport years before. Button
was incredibly athletic, and used the entire surface
of the ice to build up speed for his spectacular leaps.
He was the first skater to perform the double Axel,
which requires two and a half turns in the air. His
skating was so exciting to watch that he revolutionized the sport for women as well as men. After his
example, every figure skater began to do leaps. Button was the U.S. singles champion seven consecutive years, 1946–52, and he won the world championship five times, 1948–52.

Calder Memorial Trophy
Hockey

Frank Calder, the president of the National Hockey League, in 1933 began presenting a trophy to the league's outstanding rookie player. After his death in 1943, the league established the Calder Memorial Trophy, which also carries a $3,000 prize. The winner is selected by vote of the Professional Hockey Writers' Association.

Calder Trophy Winners

1933   Carl Voss, Detroit
1934   Russ Blenko, Montreal Maroons
1935   Dave Schriner, New York
1936   Mike Karakas, Chicago
1937   Syl Apps, Toronto
1938   Cully Dahlstrom, Chicago
1939   Frank Brimsek, Boston
1940   Kilby MacDonald, New York
1941   Johnny Quilty, Montreal
1942   Grant Warwick, New York
1943   Gaye Stewart, Toronto
1944   Gus Bodnar, Toronto
1945   Frank McCool, Toronto
1946   Edgar Laprade, New York
1947   Howie Meeker, Toronto
1948   Jim McFadden, Detroit
1949   Pentti Lund, New York
1950   Jack Gelineau, Boston
1951   Terry Sawchuck, Detroit
1952   Bernie Geoffrion, Montreal
1953   Loren Worsley, New York
1954   Camille Henry, New York
1955   Ed Litzenberger, Chicago
1956   Glenn Hall, Detroit
1957   Larry Regan, Boston
1958   Frank Mahovlich, Toronto
1959   Ralph Backstrom, Montreal
1960   Bill Hay, Chicago
1961   Dave Keon, Toronto
1962   Bobbie Rousseau, Montreal
1963   Kent Douglas, Toronto
1964   Jacques Laperriere, Montreal
1965   Roger Crozier, Detroit
1966   Britt Selby, Toronto
1967   Bobby Orr, Boston
1968   Derek Sanderson, Boston
1969   Danny Grant, Minnesota
1970   Tony Esposito, Chicago

1971   Gilbert Perreault, Buffalo
1972   Ken Dryden, Montreal
1973   Steve Vickers, New York Rangers
1974   Denis Potvin, New York Islanders
1975   Eric Vail, Atlanta
1976   Bryan Trottier, New York Islanders
1977   Willie Plett, Atlanta
1978   Mike Bossy, New York Islanders
1979   Bobby Smith, Minnesota
1980   Ray Bourque, Boston
1981   Peter Stastny, Quebec
1982   Dale Howarchuk, Winnipeg
1983   Steve Larmer, Chicago
1984   Tom Barrasso, Buffalo
1985   Mario Lemieux, Pittsburgh
1986   Gary Sutter, Calgary
1987   Luc Robitaille, Los Angeles
1988   Joe Nieuwendyk, Calgary
1989   Brian Leetch, New York Rangers
1990   Sergei Makarov, Calgary
1991   Ed Belfour, Chicago

Caledonian Games

Annual track and field games were traditional in the towns of Scotland. The tradition was carried on by Scottish immigrants through their Caledonian clubs. Clubs were established in Boston in 1853, New York in 1856, Montreal in 1857, and Philadelphia in 1858; by the 1880s, there were more than 100 of them throughout North America. Their goal was to perpetuate a variety of Scottish customs, including bagpipe playing and the Highland costume, but the Caledonian Games were their most visible feature. Among the events were tossing the caber (a long, heavy pole), sledge and heavy stone throwing, shot-putting, pole vaulting, running, hurdling, jumping, steeplechasing, and the tug-of-war.

In many areas, the Caledonian Games became very popular outside the Scottish community. Clubs began to charge admission, opening the games to all athletes and offering cash prizes for the winners. This popularity inspired the growth of track and field events in colleges and paved the way for the creation of the New York Athletic Club. When the NYAC held its first open track and field meet in 1868, the New York Caledonian Club was offered a special invitation to participate, and many of the events were taken directly from the Caledonian Games. As Scottish-Americans became assimilated, the Caledonian Clubs and their games began to die out; by 1900, most of them had disbanded. However, Highland Games are still played annually in Canada.

Address: Canadian Highland Games Council, P.O. Box 1992, Brantford, Ontario, Canada N3T 5W5 (519) 753–5027

Calgary, Alberta

Football   The Calgary Bronks joined the Western Interprovincial Football Union when it was organized in 1936. They dropped out before the 1941 season, but continued playing independently. Renamed the Stampeders, they entered the Union again in 1946. The Stampeders won the Grey Cup in 1948, 1968, and 1971.

Hockey   The Atlanta Flames of the National Hockey League became the Calgary Flames before the 1981–82 season. The Flames won the Stanley Cup in 1989, beating the Montreal Canadians, 4 games to 2, in the finals.

See also MCMAHON STADIUM; OLYMPIC SADDLEDOME.

California

Baseball   The Los Angeles Angels entered the American League in 1961. They moved to Anaheim in 1966 and became known as the California Angels. The Angels won the American League's western division championship in 1979, 1982, and 1986, but lost the league championship series all three years.

Hockey   In the National Hockey League expansion of 1968, the California Seals were created. They were renamed the Oakland Seals in midseason and the California Golden Seals in 1971. The franchise moved to Cleveland before the 1976–77 season.

See also ANAHEIM, CA; LOS ANGELES; OAKLAND.

California Raisin Bowl
Football

The first California Bowl, between the champions of the Mid-American Conference and the Pacific Coast Athletic Association, was played on December 19, 1981, in Fresno, CA. The name was changed to the California Raisin Bowl in 1989.

Results

1981   Toledo 28, San Jose State 25
1982   Fresno State 29, Bowling Green 28
1983   Northern Illinois 20, Cal State-Fullerton 13
1984   Nevada-Las Vegas 30, Toledo 13*
1985   Fresno State 51, Bowling Green 7
1986   San Jose State 37, Miami (OH) 7
1987   Eastern Michigan 30, San Jose State 27

1988   Fresno State 35, Western Michigan 30
1989   Fresno State 27, Ball State 6
1990   San Jose State 48, Central Michigan 24

*1984 game was later forfeited to Toledo because Nevada-Las Vegas used an ineligible player

Calumet Farm
Horse Racing

Originally a breeder of standardbreds, Calumet Farm produced many top horses, including Calumet Butler, who won the Hambletonian in 1931. Owner Warren Wright then decided to breed Thoroughbreds. After several lean years, Bull Lea won the Widener Stakes in 1939. Retired to stud, the horse became an outstanding sire. Under trainer "Plain Ben" Jones, Calumet Farms was the top money-winner among owners in 1941, 1943–44, 1946–49, 1952, and 1956–59. The stable holds the record for the most stakes races won in a single year, with 46 in 1952.

Camellia Bowl
Football

Hardin-Simmons beat Wichita State 49–12 at Lafayette, LA on December 30, 1948, in the only Camellia Bowl.

Camp, Walter (1859–1925)
Football

Born April 7, 1859, New Haven, CT; died March 14, 1925; National Football Foundation Hall of Fame

The "Father of American football" entered Yale University in 1875 and promptly helped organize a team to play a new kind of football, which was much closer to rugby than soccer. He graduated in 1880, but enrolled in medical school and continued playing football. A halfback, he was team captain in 1878, 1879, and 1881. Camp dropped out of medical school in 1882 and took a job in New Haven.

While still a student, Camp was Yale's delegate to the Intercollegiate Football Association. In 1880, he suggested a major rules change that began the metamorphosis of English rugby into American football. Rugby, like soccer, is essentially a continuous action sport. When a player is downed, the teams fight for possession of the ball in a kind of mass melee called the "scrimmage," or "scrum." Camp proposed allowing the team with the ball to retain possession, using a scrimmage to put the ball in play by having the player who was downed snap it back with his foot to the quarterback. The change was adopted, along with another Camp proposal, to reduce the number of players from 15 to 11. But the scrimmage allowed a team to keep possession of the ball indefinitely, a strategy called the "block game." In 1882, Camp came up with the idea of allowing a team just three downs to gain 5 yards or lose 10 yards.

Until 1884, there was no real numerical scoring. At first, a touchdown counted nothing at all; it simply allowed the team to have a free try at a goal. In 1876, four touchdowns equaled one goal, and in 1882 the rule was changed so that a team scoring four touchdowns would be given the victory against a team that scored only one goal. The following year, Camp devised a numerical scoring method, with a safety worth one point, a touchdown two points, a goal following a touchdown (what we now call a conversion, or extra point) four points, and a field goal five points. The numbers changed several times until 1912, when the present scoring method was adopted.

Camp served as secretary of the rules committee from 1894 through 1905, and was also its chairman in 1896 and 1897. He lost much of his influence at the end of 1905, when there was a national furor over violence in the sport. President Theodore Roosevelt got involved, meeting with two representatives each from Harvard, Princeton and Yale. Camp was the leader of the group, and he drew up a kind of gentleman's agreement, assuring the president that the three colleges would take the lead in carrying out "in *letter* and in *spirit* the rules of the game of football, relating to roughness."

Many college leaders felt that rules changes, not empty words, were needed to curb violence. On December 8, 1905, representatives of 13 colleges met in New York to discuss the problem. Harvard was trying unilaterally to reform the rules and refused an invitation; its president, Charles W. Eliot, blamed Camp for "the degradation and ruin of the game," saying that he was "deficient in moral sensibility—a trouble not likely to be cured at his age."

A resolution to abolish the sport was narrowly defeated, and a committee was established to reform the rules. On December 28, 68 colleges attended a meeting to establish the Intercollegiate Athletic Association, now the National Collegiate Athletic Association. Camp was invited to merge his committee, which now included only Cornell, the University of Chicago, the Naval Academy, Princeton and Yale, with the IAA, but he opposed all the proposed changes, except the one requiring the offensive team to gain 10 yards in three downs. Finally, however, Camp gave in, and the two committees were merged into the American Intercollegiate Football Rules Committee.

The "Father of American Football," Walter Camp is shown here in his 1879 college uniform. Courtesy of Yale University

In addition to the rules that he proposed, Camp made many contributions to football. Beginning about 1885, he served as unofficial advisor to the Yale football captain. Because of his business, he couldn't usually attend the afternoon practices, but his wife did, taking notes, and Camp met with the captain of the team in the evenings to give advice. He continued as advisor even after Yale appointed its first official head coach in 1893. During his period as an advisor, through the 1906 season, Yale won 218 games while losing only 11 and tying 8.

A tireless promoter of football, Camp wrote many articles and several books about the sport. In 1889, he helped Caspar Whitney select the first All-American team, and from 1898 through 1924, he chose the All-American teams for *Collier's* magazine. In 1911, Camp once again became secretary of the Rules Committee, and he served until his death, which occurred while he was attending the committee's 1925 meeting.

Further Reading: Powell, Hartford Jr. *Walter Camp.* Boston: Little, Brown, 1926.

Campanella, Roy (1921–   )
Baseball
Born November 19, 1921, Philadelphia, PA; Baseball Hall of Fame

The first black catcher in the major leagues, Campanella joined the Baltimore Elite Giants of the Negro National League in 1937. He played with them through the 1945 season, when the Brooklyn Dodgers signed him to a minor league contract, and he became the Dodgers' starting catcher in 1948. A stocky, powerful hitter, "Campy" batted .325 in 1951, with 33 home runs and 108 runs batted in, and was named the league's Most Valuable Player. He also won the MVP award in 1953, when he hit 41 home runs, a record for catchers, and in 1955, when he batted .318 with 32 home runs.

On January 28, 1958, shortly after the Dodgers had announced they were moving to Los Angeles, Campanella was driving when his car skidded on a curve and hit a telephone pole. His back was broken, and he was paralyzed from the chest down. The Dodgers continued to pay his salary and made him a spring training instructor. The largest crowd ever to attend a baseball game, 93,103, turned out in Los Angeles Coliseum in 1959 when the Dodgers and Yankees played an exhibition game in his honor. Campanella batted .276 in 10 major-league seasons, with 242 home runs.

Further Reading: Campanella, Roy. *It's Great to Be Alive*. Boston: Little, Brown, 1959.

Canada Cup
See WORLD CUP (GOLF).

Canada's Cup
Yachting

The sloop *Canada*, representing Toronto's Royal Canadian Yacht Club, won a trophy at an 1896 regatta in Toledo, OH, and the RCYC offered the trophy as a challenge cup for a series of match races between yachts representing Canada and the United states in 1899. Competition was held biennially through 1907 and from 1930 through 1934. There was a series in 1954, followed by a 15-year hiatus. The rules were changed to allow racing by yachts with a Cruising Club of America rating of not more than 37 feet—originally, the cup had been offered for the larger 8-meter boats—and competition resumed in 1969. The Canada's Cup series began as a best three-out-of-five match race. Since 1969, though, there have been only four races in the series. Three of the races are conducted over a 30-mile Olympic course, and the fourth is a long-distance race that counts as two.

Canada Games

The Canada Games are held biennially, in odd-numbered years, and they alternate between summer and winter games. The idea originated at the annual meeting of the Amateur Athletic Union of Canada in 1924 when Norton Crowe, retiring as secretary of the AAUC, proposed "what might be styled a 'Canadian Olympics'" to help develop young athletes for the Olympic Games.

The proposal was frequently discussed in future years, but there was no way of funding it. On March 30, 1963, a Winter Games Corporation was formed by several prominent Quebec sports figures to lobby for government funding. About the same time, the Canadian Amateur Sports Federation was looking at the possibility of periodic national games. In February 1964 a third group, the Centennial Commission, recommended that the games be held in 1967, Canada's centennial year. An agreement for funding was signed on March 30, 1965, and the first Canada Winter Games opened on February 1, 1967, in Quebec City.

The sports in the first winter games were badminton, basketball, figure skating, gymnastics, hockey, shooting, skiing, speed skating, synchronized swimming, table tennis, volleyball, and wrestling, conducted over a ten-day period. More than 1,800 athletes took part. The federal government contributed $700,000 of the $776,000 operating budget, and the rest was raised through private donations.

The first Canada Summer Games were held August 16–24, 1969, in Halifax-Dartmouth, Nova Scotia. The sports were baseball, canoeing, cycling, field hockey, lacrosse, lawn bowling, rowing, soccer, softball, swimming, tennis, track and field, water polo, water skiing, and yachting. More than 2,500 athletes participated and about 600,000 fans attended.

Hosts for the Canada Games since 1973 have been New Westminster/Burnaby, British Columbia, in 1973; Lethbridge, Alberta, in 1975; St. John's, Newfoundland, in 1977; Brandon, Quebec, in 1977; Thunder Bay, Ontario, in 1979; Saguenay/Lac St. Jean, Ontario, 1983; St. John, Ontario, in 1985; Cape Breton, Nova Scotia, in 1987; and Saskatoon, Saskatchewan, in 1989. The 1991 Canada Winter Games will be held in Charlottetown, Prince Edward Island, and the 1993 Canada Summer Games are scheduled to take place at a still undetermined site in British Columbia.

Address: Canada Games Council, c/o Fitness and Amateur Sport, 385 Laurier Avenue W. Ottawa, Ontario, Canada K1A 0X6

Further Reading: McLaughlin, Paul, and David McDonald. *Jeux Canada Games: The First Decade.* Ottawa: Fitness and Amateur Sport, 1978.

Canada Olympic Hall of Fame

Established in 1988 in Canada Olympic Park, Calgary, where the 1988 Winter Olympic Games were held, this hall of fame includes information on every medal winner since the Winter Olympics began in 1924. The 10,000-square-foot structure, built at a cost of about $5 million, also has a complete record of how the 1988 Games were organized.

Address: Canada Olympic Park, S.S. #1, Calgary, Alberta, Canada T2M 4N3 (403) 286–2632

Canada Sports Hall of Fame

Harry I. Price, chairman of the Canadian National Exhibition's Sports Committee, in 1947 began gathering support for a national sports hall of fame. On June 10, 1955, he became chairman of the newly established Canada Sports Hall of Fame, located in the old Stanley Barracks in Toronto. The hall moved to Exhibition Place, Toronto, in 1957. A new building was constructed in 1967 and a major renovation in 1988 tripled the exhibition space, which is organized into eight theme areas: all rounders, aquatic, equine, lifestyle, strength and science, team, track and field, and winter sports. Each area has a computer terminal where a visitor can call up a biography of any inductee, often including an action videotape. The hall also has more than 3,000 sports artifacts and memorabilia.

Address: Exhibition Place, Toronto, Ontario, Canada M6K 3C3 (436) 595–1046

Canadian Amateur Football Association (CAFA)

The Canadian Rugby Union was renamed the Canadian Amateur Football Association, also known as Football Canada, in 1967. Despite its name, the CRU was the national governing body for Canadian football, which evolved from rugby. It was originally the Canadian Rugby Football Union, formed on October 21, 1882. When the Ontario Rugby Football Union withdrew in a dispute over rules in 1886, the CRFU dissolved and was succeeded by the CRU five years later.

The CRU controlled both amateur and professional football in Canada until 1958, when the Canadian Football Council, later known as the Canadian Football League, withdrew. In 1909, the Grey Cup was established for the championship of Ca-

nadian football, and only teams registered with the CRU were eligible to compete. The CRU gave the cup to the Canadian Football League in 1966, and the name change the following year reflects the fact that the association now governs only the amateur sport.

Address: Football Canada, 333 River Road, Vanier, Ontario, Canada K1L 8H9 (613) 748–5636

Canadian Amateur Speed Skating Association (CASSA)

The Amateur Skating Association of Canada, founded in 1887, originally governed both speed skating and figure skating. That group was absorbed in 1907 by the International Skating Union of America, which governed figure skating, speed skating, hockey, and roller skating in Canada and the United States. The Canada Amateur Skating Association was organized in 1914, and held its first national speed skating championships. Later, the word "Speed" was added to its name.

Address: 1600 James Naismith Drive, Gloucester, Ontario, Canada K1B 5N4 (613) 748–5669

Canadian Amateur Sports Federation

See SPORTS FEDERATION OF CANADA.

Canadian Association for the Advancement of Women and Sport (CAAWS)

Women leaders in national, provincial, and local sports organizations founded the CAAWS in March of 1981. In 1983 the association held a national leadership seminar for coaches, sports administrators, teachers, and students to discuss issues facing women in sports. The following year, the "Walk and Roll" project was initiated as part of National Physical Activity Week to encourage girls and women to walk, roll, run, jump, hop, skip, ride a bike, or take part in some other exercise. The "Breakthrough Celebration" recognizes individual women or groups who have broken traditional barriers. One of the major goals of the CAAWS is to achieve equality in the media for women athletes. On "Media Equinox Day," held on March 21 and September 21 each year, members are asked to monitor media coverage of sports and to complain to media that are devoting unfair amounts of space or time to men. (The dates were chosen because night and day are of equal length on the equinoxes.)

Address: 323 Chapel Street, Ottawa, Ontario, Canada K1N 7Z2 (613) 233–5204

Canadian Baseball Hall of Fame and Museum

Located in Ontario Place Theme Park, across the street from the Toronto Blue Jays' park, the Canadian Baseball Hall of Fame and Museum was founded in 1983 and now attracts more than 400,000 visitors a year. In addition to inducting several players each year, the Hall of Fame gives the Tip O'Neill Award to the Canadian Player of the Year. The award is named for the Canadian-born outfielder who won National League batting championships in 1887 and 1888.

Address: P.O. Box 4008, Station A, Toronto, Ontario, Canada M5W 2R1 (416) 597–0014

Canadian Canoe Association (CCA)

The organization responsible for sprint and marathon canoe racing in Canada, the CCA was founded in 1900 by nine canoeing clubs. It was restructured in 1984, with the creation of two councils, for sprint racing and marathon. Now made up of 42 clubs from throughout Canada, the CCA conducts an annual Championships Regatta for canoeing and kayaking. The Canadian White Water Association and the Canadian Recreational Canoeing Association are affiliated members.

Address: 1600 James Naismith Drive, Gloucester, Ontario, Canada K1B 5N4 (613) 748–5623

See also CANOEING AND KAYAKING.

Canadian Colleges Athletic Association (CCAA)

The CCAA, organized in 1973, held its first national collegiate championships in 1975. The association has 88 member institutions with a total of more than 275,000 students, and it conducts championships in men's and women's badminton, basketball, curling, and volleyball; men's hockey; and men's soccer.

Address: 1600 James Naismith Drive, Gloucester, Ontario, Canada, K1B 5N4 (613) 748–5626

Canadian Federation of Amateur Baseball (CFAB)

The Canadian Amateur Baseball Association was organized in 1893 to establish a national championship tournament. In 1896 it was renamed the Canadian Baseball Association. It took its present name in 1967, when it organized the first national team to play in the Pan-American Games in Winnipeg. The CFAB established the National Baseball Institute at Vancouver in 1986 for high-performance training of outstanding players. The federation conducts na-

tional championships in four age classifications: senior, junior (21 and under), bison (18 and under), and midget (16 and under).

Address: 1600 James Naismith Drive, Gloucester, Ontario, Canada K1B 5N4 (613) 748–5606

Canadian Fencing Association (CFA)

The National Fencing Committee of the Amateur Athletic Union of Canada held the first Canadian national championships in 1902. In 1966 the committee became the independent Canadian Fencing Association, which hosted the world championships in Montreal the following year. Membership has increased from just over 1,500 in 1980 to nearly 3,000 in 1989. The CFA also selects national teams for the Olympics, the Pan-American Games, and other international events.

Address: 1600 James Naismith Drive, Gloucester, Ontario, Canada K1B 5N4 (613) 7485633

Canadian Figure Skating Association (CFSA)

The Amateur Skating Association of Canada, founded in 1887 to govern figure skating and speed skating, formed a figure skating department 1914. In 1939 the department became the Canadian Figure Skating Association, an affiliate of the ASAC. In 1947 it was reorganized as an independent body. The CFSA is the largest figure-skating organization in the world, with about 150,000 members in more than 1,400 clubs.

The association has 13 geographical sections, each of which holds its own championship events. The top four finishers in each section advance to regional championships. From the regionals, the top three in the senior class and the top four in the novice and junior classes go to the national championships. Competition is conducted in singles, pair skating, and ice dancing for all classes, and there is a fours event in the seniors class.

Address: 1600 James Naismith Drive, Gloucester, Ontario, Canada K1B 5N4 (613) 748–5635

Canadian Football

Like American football, the Canadian version of football evolved from rugby, but took a somewhat different direction. The first recorded rugby game in Canada was played in 1865 between British troops stationed in Montreal and a Canadian team made up mostly of students from McGill University. The sport grew rapidly, and on October 21, 1882, the Canadian Rugby Football Union was organized as the governing body. It held the first championship game in 1883, with Montreal beating Toronto 30–0. But the

Ontario and Quebec Rugby Unions played under different sets of rules, and in 1886 the Ontario union withdrew from the CRFU, which then folded. It was reorganized on December 19, 1891, as the Canadian Rugby Union.

The first major change from English rugby rules came in 1882, when the rugby scrum was replaced by the scrimmage used in American football. In 1897, the offensive team was given three downs in which to gain 10 yards and keep possession of the ball for another set of downs, and the number of players was reduced from 15 to 14 in 1902. Two years later, the value of a try (touchdown) was increased from four to five points.

The Ontario Rugby Football Union in 1905 adopted a new set of rules, proposed by "Thrift" Burnside. The number of players was cut to 12, and the snapback from center used in American football replaced the rugby method of heeling the ball back. The CRU decreed that the championship game would be divided into four 15-minute quarters, with the first half played under rules chosen by the team winning the toss, and the second half under rules chosen by the other team. The ORFU abandoned the Burnside rules after one season.

Frank Shaughnessy, an American who began coaching at McGill University in 1912, developed a new type of offense, putting the wingback in motion at the snap of the ball and often using the player as a blocker. That brought frequent charges of interference, because Canadian football at the time did not allow blocking ahead of the ball carrier. Other teams began using the tactic, and in 1914 the Intercollegiate Rugby Football Union legalized interference up to 3 yards beyond the line of scrimmage. That was changed to 4 yards in 1920, when the CRU decided to adopt the college rules, and to 10 yards in 1946. Downfield blocking became legal at any point on the field in 1966.

The forward pass was always legal in the Western Canada Rugby Football Union, organized in 1911. In 1921, the WCRFU joined the CRU in order to challenge for the Grey Cup, and the CRU cut the number of players from 14 to 12 and began using the snapback. In 1929, the forward pass was legalized on an experimental basis for the WCRFU, two major intercollegiate leagues, and the Grey Cup finals. Two years later, the forward pass was made legal for all leagues.

Canadian football is a more open offensive sport than American football in several ways. The twelfth player is a fifth offensive back, and backs are allowed to be moving forward when the ball is snapped. A team has only three downs in which to gain 10 yards for a first down, which encourages more passing.

The field is 110 yards long, from goal line from goal line, and 65 yards wide; end zones are 25 yards deep. A team can score a single (one point) by punting the ball over the end zone; it is a rouge, also one point, if a punt goes into the end zone and is not run out by the receiving team.

Further Reading: Cosentino, Frank. *Canadian Football: The Grey Cup Years.* Toronto: Musson Book Company, 1969.

See also GREY CUP; RUGBY.

Canadian Football Hall of Fame and Museum
Hamilton, Ontario.

The Hall of Fame's building was formally opened on November 28, 1972, but members had been elected annually since 1963. The hall includes exhibits on the history of Canadian football and a library, in addition to material on its inductees.

Address: 58 Jackson Street West, Hamilton, Ontario, Canada L8P 1L4 (416) 528–7566.

Canadian Football League (CFL)

The CFL was organized as the Canadian Football Council on January 22, 1956, in a merger of the Eastern Interprovincial League and the Western Interprovincial Football Union. The name was changed to the Canadian Football League in 1958. The original teams were Hamilton, Montreal, Ontario, and Toronto of the EIL and British Columbia, Calgary, Edmonton, Saskatchewan, and Winnipeg of the WIFU. The EIL became the Eastern Conference in 1960, and the WIFU became the Western Conference a year later.

At first, each conference played its own schedule, but in 1961 partial interconference play was introduced. The conferences were renamed the eastern and western divisions in 1981, when a full schedule of interdivisional play was established. There have been only a few changes in the makeup of the league since its beginning. The Montreal Alouettes were replaced after the 1981 season by a new franchise, the Montreal Concordes. The team name was changed back to the Alouettes in 1986. In 1987, Montreal dropped out of the league, and the Winnipeg Blue Bombers moved into the eastern division.

The Grey Cup, symbolic of the Canadian football championship, was turned over to the CFL by the Canadian Rugby Union in 1966.

Addresses: Canadian Football League, 1200 Bay Street, 12th floor, Toronto, Ontario, Canada M5R 2A5 (416) 928–1200

British Columbia Lions, 765 Pacific Boulevard South, Vancouver, BC, Canada V6B 4Y9 (604) 681–5466

Calgary Stampeders, 1817 Crowchild NW, Calgary, Alberta, Canada T2M 4R6 (403) 289–0205

Edmonton Eskimos, 9023 111 Avenue, Edmonton, Alberta, Canada T5B 0C3 (403) 429–2821

Hamilton Tiger-Cats, P.O. Box 172, Hamilton, Ontario, Canada L8N 3A2 (416) 547–2418

Ottawa Rough Riders, Coliseum Building, Lansdowne Park, Ottawa, Ontario, Canada K1S 3W7 (613) 563–4551

Saskatchewan Roughriders, 2940 10th Avenue, P.O. Box 1277, Regina, Saskatchewan, Canada S4P 3B8 (306) 569–2323

Toronto Argos, Exhibition Place, Toronto, Ontario, Canada M6K 3C3 (416) 595–9600

Winnipeg Blue Bombers, 1465 Maroons Road, Winnipeg, Manitoba, Canada R3G 0L6 (204) 786–2583

See also CANADIAN FOOTBALL; GREY CUP.

Canadian Lacrosse Hall of Fame

Because the New Westminster Salmonbellies have won more Canadian amateur lacrosse championships than any other team, the Canadian Lacrosse Association in 1964 awarded the town a charter for the sport's hall of fame. Selection committees from eastern and western Canada met on January 19, 1966, in Montreal and named 48 Hall of Fame members. The hall was officially opened on May 17, 1967, in New Westminster's Centennial Community Centre.

Address: P.O. Box 308, New Westminster, British Columbia, Canada V3L 4Y6 (604) 526–4281

Canadian Olympic Association (COA)

Canada became the 10th nation to take part in the modern Olympics in 1904, when the Amateur Athletic Union of Canada formed a special Olympic Committee. Etienne Desmarteau won Canada's first gold medal, in the 56-pound weight throw. In 1907, the committee became the National Olympic Committee of Canada. It took its present name in 1946 and became an independent organization with its own constitution in 1951.

The organization selects and funds the country's teams for the Olympics and Pan-American Games. About 20 percent of its income is derived from a Sports Canada grant, and the rest is raised from the private sector by the Olympic Trust of Canada, an affiliate formed in 1970. The COA gives financial grants to national sports-governing bodies, administers the Royal Bank Junior Olympics, and holds an annual one-week Olympic Academy of Canada, at which athletes and coaches discuss the history and goals of the Olympic movement. Affiliates include Olympic Club Canada, made up of former Olympic team members; the Olympic Athlete Career Centre in Toronto, which offers career counseling and placement services to Canadian athletes; and an Information Centre.

Address; Olympic House, Cite du Havre, Montreal, Quebec, Canada H3C 3R4 (514) 861–3371

Canadian Polo Association

Canadian polo clubs have full membership in the U.S. Polo Association, which governs the sport in both countries. However, Canada had to have its own national organization to participate in the International Polo Federation's world tournaments, so the Canadian Polo Association, also known as Polo Canada, was formed in 1985 to select and oversee national teams.

Address: c/o Armadale Ltd., Toronto Buttonville Airport, Markham, Ontario, Canada L3P 3J9 (416) 477–8000

Canadian Professional Golfers Association (CPGA)

The CPGA was organized at the Royal Ottawa Golf Club on July 11, 1911, five years before its U.S. counterpart. It held its first national championship in 1912. The organization, which has about 1,750 members, also conducts championships for seniors, club professionals, and assistant professionals. In October 1978, the CPGA bought the Royal Oak Country Club Resort in Titusville, FL as a winter home.

Address: 430 Signet Drive, Unit D, Weston, Ontario, Canada M9L 2T6 (416) 744–2212

Canadian Professional Rodeo Association (CPRA)

Led by Arnold Montgomery and Ken Thomson, a group of Canadian rodeo cowboys met in Vancouver in June of 1944 to discuss their need for insurance. A month later, they formed the Cowboys' Insurance Association. Each contestant was to pay $1 for each rodeo he entered to establish an insurance fund. The CIA became the Cowboys' Protective Association in 1945, and the association adopted three major rules: (1) Every rodeo would offer a minimum purse of $100 per event; (2) contestants' entry fees would be added to the purse; and (3) the CPA itself would name the judges. The CPA changed its name to the Canadian Rodeo Cowboys Association in 1965 and took its current name in late 1980, when it became a sanctioning and governing body for the sport. Under the CPRA, prize money has grown from just over $1 million in 1981 to nearly $3 million by 1989. The association has about 1,600 members.

Address: 2116 27th Avenue, Calgary, Alberta, Canada T2E 7A6 (403) 250–7440

Canadian Rugby Union

See CANADIAN AMATEUR FOOTBALL ASSOCIATION.

Canadian Sport and Fitness Administration Centre Inc.

In response to a 1969 report that Canadian sports associations were in need of professional help, the Administrative Centre for Sport and Recreation was established in July of 1970 to offer office space, furniture, secretarial assistance, printing, mailing and shipping, and conference rooms. Accounting, bulk purchasing, audiovisual services, computer services, public relations, management counseling, and translation were made available later.

The centre housed 43 national associations in 35,000 square feet of space by 1973, and was incorporated as the National Sport and Recreation Centre in January 1974. The centre took its present name in 1988, when it moved into a new $22 million building, Place R. Tait McKenzie. The centre currently houses 65 organizations in 139,000 square feet.

Address: 1600 James Naismith Drive, Gloucester, Ontario, Canada K1B 5N4 (613) 746–0060

Canadian Trotting Association (CTA)

The Canadian Trotting and Pacing Horse Association and the Dominion Harness Horse Association merged in 1939 to form the CTA, which supervises harness racing throughout Canada. Its membership includes tracks, horse owners, drivers, trainers, grooms, officials, and organizations that sponsor major stakes and futurities. All tracks under its jurisdiction are connected on-line to a central computer so that records of horses, drivers, trainers, and owners can be updated immediately upon completion of a race. The CTA sanctions race meetings and licenses officials, drivers, trainers, and grooms. It also publishes the monthly *Trot* magazine, gives annual awards for outstanding horses and horsemen, and maintains the Standardbred Canada Library and Archives.

Address: 233 Evans Avenue, Toronto, Ontario, Canada M8Z 1J6 (416) 252–3565

Candlepin Bowling

Candlepin bowling is similar to the ten-pin bowling of the 19th century, which used almost-cylindrical pins. To increase scoring and attract more bowlers, bowling lane owners introduced the larger, bottle-shaped pins, and the original form of the sport became known as candlepin bowling. It still survives in New England and eastern Canada, but is virtually unknown elsewhere.

Candlestick Park
San Francisco, CA

Named for its location on Candlestick Point, the park opened in 1960 as the home of baseball's San Francisco Giants, who had moved from New York in 1958. For its first two seasons, the team played in Seals Stadium, which had been the home of the city's Pacific Coast League team. Baseball fans nationwide learned that wind was a big problem in Candlestick Park, when it hosted the 1961 all-star game and pitcher Stu Miller was blown off the mound. The wind tends to blow in from left field, circle around the stands, and blow out toward right center. The problem was alleviated in 1970 when all the stands were enclosed. At the same time, grass was replaced with AstroTurf and the seating capacity was expanded from 45,774 to 59,091, making it the largest park in the National League. The San Francisco 49ers of the National Football League began playing at Candlestick that season.

Cane Pace
Harness Racing

The Cane Pace, named for William H. Cane, was inaugurated as a 1¹⁄₁₆-mile dash for pacers in 1955, and became a 1-mile dash in 1963. One of the events in pacing's Triple Crown, it is run at Yonkers Raceway, where Cane was president from 1950 until his death in 1956.

Canoeing and Kayaking

French explorers and *coureurs des bois* began using the birchbark canoe almost immediately upon arriving in North America, because it could navigate shallow waters and river rapids. About 1855, George W. R. Strickland and J. S. Stephenson began building wooden canoes, using plank and rib construction, near Peterborough, Ontario, and racing began soon afterward. When the Prince of Wales visited Canada in 1860, canoe races were included in a rowing regatta staged for him on August 30.

The New York Canoe Club was founded in 1871, and the Point St. Charles Club was organized in Montreal in 1875. Although most canoe club members were, and still are, recreational canoeists, an NYCC sailing race in 1879 attracted more than 200 entrants. On August 3, 1880, the American Canoe Association was founded and held sailing and paddling races at its first encampment. The ACA had many Canadian members until 1900, when the Canadian Canoe Association was organized.

John MacGregor, an English attorney, discovered the Eskimo kayak design in Greenland and built a boat called the *Rob Roy*. MacGregor cruised in Europe and the Holy Land, using both paddle and sail, and wrote a popular book, *A Thousand Miles in the Rob Roy Canoe*. The kayak became very popular in Europe. In 1907, Johann Klepper of Germany invented a folding kayak that was brought into North America in quantity in the 1930s. At the same time, the "Peterborough" canoe, now often made of canvas stretched tightly over a wooden frame, was spreading throughout the world. After World War II, the Grumman Aircraft Corporation developed an aluminum canoe, and canoes of molded fiberglass construction were introduced in 1962.

Sail racing in decked sailing canoes was very popular in the late 19th and early 20th centuries, although paddle racing in canoe or kayak is now predominant. The NYCC offered the Seawanhaka International Challenge Cup for decked sailing canoes, with the first race in August of 1886. A world championship race for these vessels has been held since 1961. The Associated Canoe Clubs of Sheepshead Bay began sail races in open canoes in 1931 and joined the ACA in 1934. Open canoe racing is now conducted in three classes, A, B, and C, with sail areas of 3, 5, and 7 square meters, respectively. The decked sailing canoe has a sail area of 10 square feet.

Paddle racing in kayaks developed in Europe and arrived in North America in the late 1920s. The International Canoe Federation was established in 1924 to govern canoe and kayak racing, and the Washington Canoe Club demonstrated the sport at the Olympic Games in Paris that year. Both kayak and canoe paddling races were held at the 1936 Berlin Olympics; Frank Amyot of Canada won the Gold Medal in the 1,000-meter canoe singles. Kayak singles racing for women was added to the program in 1948, and the women's kayak pairs event was added in 1960.

Canada's national championship races began in 1900, when the CCA was formed. Canada has a unique event, the "war canoe" race, in which a team of 15 paddlers propels a heavy dugout canoe. The ACA began national championship races for canoe and kayak paddling in 1930, and kayak races for women were added in 1958.

Both white-water slalom races and "wild-water" races down rivers developed in Europe, although there was some informal racing in North America. In slalom events, paddlers in kayaks or decked canoes race down a river and have to pass through

In kayak racing, the canoeist uses a double-bladed paddle. Wielding it here is Marcia Jones Smoke, who won ten national singles championships. Courtesy of the National Paddling Committee

gates. The International Canoe Federation conducted the first world slalom championships in 1949 on the Rhone River at Geneva, Switzerland. That event is held every two years. The first organized slalom race in North America took place at Salida, CO in 1953, and the following year there was slalom racing on the Brandywine River in Delaware. The ACA established a National Slalom Committee in 1954 to oversee the sport, and the first national championships were held in 1956. The Canadian White Water Association, established on November 18, 1963, became affiliated with the Canadian Canoe Association, and the two groups conducted the first Canadian National Slalom and White Water Championships in 1967.

In 1959, the ACA added national championships in white-water racing, a series of time trials over a short stretch of rapids. The canoes specified by the ACA are now the same as those used in marathon racing, because many canoeists compete in both sports. In the Northeast, white-water racing in open canoes was popular. Under an ACA sanction, the Penobscot Paddle and Chowder Society of Bangor, ME, in 1970, conducted the first national championships, with 132 participants.

Marathon racing, often with folding kayaks, was popular in Canada and the Midwest in the 1930s. A major event at the 1932 regatta of the Radisson Club of Three Rivers, Ontario, was a 125-mile race over a three-day period. The sport expanded rapidly after

World War II, largely fostered by the U.S. Canoe Association.

See also CANADIAN CANOE ASSOCIATION; U.S. CANOE ASSOCIATION.

Canton, OH

Before professional football was really organized, Canton had the Bulldogs, a semipro team founded in 1905, when there were already at least eight teams in Ohio. The team folded after 1907 amid rumors that the coach had thrown a game against arch rival Massillon. In 1915, the Bulldogs reorganized under new management and signed Jim Thorpe for $250 a game. The American Professional Football Association was organized in Canton in 1920, and Thorpe was named president of the APFA, which became the National Football League in 1922. Canton won the championship in 1922 and 1923. The team moved to Cleveland and won a third championship the following year. Canton rejoined the NFL for the 1925 and 1926 seasons, then dropped out for good. The city became the home of the Pro Football Hall of Fame in 1963.

Capital Centre
Landover, MD

An unusual saddle-shaped structure, the Capital Centre opened in 1973. It was the first arena to show instant replays on giant television screens. The four 12-by-16-foot screens, suspended 49 feet above the arena floor, also give spectators closeups of the action taking place beneath them. The Centre is the home of the Washington Bullets of the National Basketball Association, the Washington Capitals of the National Hockey League, and the Georgetown University basketball team. It seats 19,035.

Capitoline Grounds
Brooklyn, NY

Inspired by the success of the first enclosed ballpark, the Union Grounds, Brooklyn's Capitoline Grounds opened in 1864, and the New York Herald enthused that it was the "most extensive and complete ball grounds in the United States." A game betweeen the Brooklyn Atlantics and the defending champion Athletics drew 15,000 fans in 1869. On January 14, 1870, the touring Cincinnati Red Stockings lost to the Atlantics 8–7 at the park, and more than 9,000 paid 50 cents apiece to watch the game. The Atlantics joined the National Association in 1871 and played all their home games at the Capitoline Grounds. Several other Brooklyn teams used the park from time to time until 1884, when Washington Park opened.

Carnival of Champions
Boxing

The first Carnival of Champions was held September 5–7, 1892, at the Olympic Club of New Orleans. On September 5, Jack McAuliffe defended his light-weight championship with a 15th-round knockout of Billy Myer. The following day, featherweight champion George Dixon knocked out Jack Skelly in the eighth round. James J. Corbett won the heavyweight title on the third day of the carnival by knocking out John L. Sullivan in the 21st round. The Dixon-Skelly fight was notable because Dixon was black and Skelly was white, and it was the first interracial fight ever staged in the South.

Four fights were offered on a single card in the second Carnival of Champions, September 23, 1937, at the Polo Grounds in New York. The first three were 15-round decisions: Harry Jeffra won the world bantamweight title from Sixto Escobar, Lou Ambers defended his lightweight championship against Pedro Montanez, and Barney Ross retained the welterweight title against Ceferino Garcia. The fourth fight, between Marcel Thil and Fred Apostoli, was billed as a world middleweight championship fight, but the New York State Athletic Commission refused to recognize it as a title match. Apostoli knocked out Thil in the 10th round.

Carr, Joseph F. (1880–1939)
Football

Born October 22, 1880, Columbus, OH; died May 20, 1939; Pro Football Hall of Fame

The manager of the semiprofessional Columbus Panhandles since 1904, Carr represented the team when the American Professional Football Association was organized in Canton, OH in 1920. Jim Thorpe, the greatest player of his era, was named president because of his public relations value, but the owners decided in 1921 that they needed a real administrator, and Carr replaced Thorpe.

The APFA was renamed the National Football League in 1922, and Carr was instrumental in transforming it from an organization of basically semi-professional teams in small cities to a genuine major league. At first, players were usually hired for just one game, and could jump from one team to another at any time during the season. To prevent that practice, Carr developed a standard contract binding a player to one team for the entire season, and insisted that every player in the league had to sign that type of contract to be eligible. He also established strict rules to prevent college players from competing under assumed names.

Carr's greatest asset may have been his ability to sell the idea of professional football to potential owners in big cities. In 1925, he decided the league needed a New York franchise to get maximum exposure in the press, and he persuaded Tim Mara to pay $500 for a franchise. Later that year, halfback Red Grange signed for a postseason tour with the Chicago Bears, just ten days after playing his final game at the University of Illinois. While the Grange tour helped publicize the NFL—a game with the Giants drew 70,000 fans to the Polo Grounds—Carr realized the danger of antagonizing colleges, and established a rule that no player could be signed until his class had graduated.

When Carr became NFL president, the league had teams in Akron, Buffalo, Canton, Chicago (where there were two teams, the Bears and the Cardinals), Cincinnati, Cleveland, Columbus, Dayton, Detroit, Green Bay, Rochester, and Rock Island. Among the big cities only the two Chicago franchises were stable. When Carr died in May of 1939, Green Bay was the only small city left in the NFL; the other teams were Brooklyn, Chicago, Cleveland, Detroit, New York, Philadelphia, Pittsburgh, and Washington, D.C. The price for a new franchise was $50,000, and 48,120 fans had attended the 1938 championship game in the Polo Grounds, compared with 26,000 for the first playoff in 1933.

Carr Trophy
Football

The National Football League's official Most Valuable Player Trophy, named for Joseph F. Carr, longtime league president, was awarded from 1938 through 1946.

Carr Trophy Winners

1938	Mel Hein, New York Giants	
1939	Parker Hall, Cleveland Rams	
1940	Ace Parker, Brooklyn Dodgers	
1941	Don Hutson, Green Bay Packers	
1942	Don Hutson, Green Bay Packers	
1943	Sid Luckman, Chicago Bears	
1944	Frank Sinkwich, Detroit Lions	
1945	Bob Waterfield, Cleveland Rams	
1946	William Dudley, Pittsburgh Steelers	

CART

See CHAMPIONSHIP AUTO RACING TEAMS, INC.

Carter, Don (1926–   )
Bowling

Born July 29, 1926 St. Louis, MO; American Bowling Congress, Professional Bowlers Association Halls of Fame

Voted the greatest bowler of all time in a 1970 poll, Carter was a charter member of the Professional Bowlers Association and its president twice. Bowler of the Year in 1953, 1954, 1957, 1958, 1960, and 1962, Carter won the BPAA All-Star Tournament in 1953, 1954, 1957 and 1958; the World Invitational in 1957, 1959, 1960, 1961, and 1962; and the ABC Masters in 1961.

Cartwright, Alexander (1820–1892)
Baseball

Born April 17, 1820, New York, NY; died July 12, 1892; Baseball Hall of Fame

When a commission proclaimed in 1907 that baseball had been invented by Abner Doubleday in Cooperstown, NY in 1839, Bruce Cartwright produced the diaries of his grandfather to disprove the theory. Baseball was actually "invented" in 1845 by Alexander Cartwright. Although the Baseball Hall of Fame was established in Cooperstown in 1939, the supposed centennial of the sport, Cartwright was duly enshrined and Doubleday was not. That year Babe Ruth visited Hawaii and placed flower leis on Cartwright's grave in Honolulu.

Baseball existed in several forms before 1845. It was derived from an English game that was usually called rounders, although it was also known as "baseball" in England as early as 1744. In the versions played in North America, fielders attempted to put a runner out by hitting him with a thrown ball, called "soaking," while he was between bases, and the distances from base to base varied. In the "Massachusetts game," also known as "town ball," the batter, or striker, stood about halfway between home and first base, and had to run only about 30 feet to get to first. The other bases were 60 feet apart. The "New York game" was similar, except that what we now call the diamond was a pentagon rather than a square; the batter ran at an angle to first base, 45 feet away. The distance from first base to second was 60 feet, from second to third it was 72 feet, and from third to home, it was 72 feet.

This was the game played by Cartwright and his friends in the Murray Hill section of Manhattan in 1845. Cartwright was apparently not pleased with the asymmetry of the layout. At his suggestion, the Knickerbocker Base Ball Club was formed on September 23, 1845, complete with a constitution and bylaws. The bylaws were actually 20 rules for a new version of baseball, with 90-foot base paths and the batter stationed at home plate. Soaking was abolished. Rule 13 stated: "A player running the bases shall be out, if the ball is in the hands of an adversary on the base, or the runner is touched with it before he makes his base; it being understood, however that in no instance is a ball to be thrown at him." Another departure was that three outs constituted an inning; in most previous forms of baseball, every player on a team had to be retired before the side was out.

Johnny Kucks, a former major-league pitcher who grew up near the site of the Elysian Fields, recalled being told that Abner Doubleday had invented the game in Hoboken. He told interviewer Harold Peterson, "You know, every guy who ever plays baseball seriously seems to stop and meditate about the precision of the game. . . . I decided whoever figured out the measurements so exactly must have been a genius. . . . The distance to the bases, for example, is just perfect. Or if they ever made the angle between the foul lines wider than 90 degrees, there would be many, many more home runs."

The Knickerbocker version of baseball was an instant success in New York, and it soon spread elsewhere. Cartwright didn't stay in the United States long enough to see the sport flourish. On March 1, 1849, he joined the gold rush and left for San Francisco. During the trip, Cartwright and his party often played baseball and introduced the sport to several major cities. Shortly after he arrived in California, he came down with dysentery, and was told to go to Hawaii for his health. He arrived in Honolulu on August 10, 1849, and lived in Hawaii for the rest of his life. Cartwright became friendly with King Kamehaha and often served as the king's personal diplomat. But he didn't leave baseball behind. In 1852, he stepped off the first baseball field in Hawaii, at Makiki Park, and he taught baseball throughout the islands, while others were spreading the sport in North America. When Cartwright died in 1892, baseball had been long established as "the national game."

Further Reading: Peterson, Harold. *The Man Who Invented Baseball.* New York: Charles Scribner's Sons, 1973.

See also BASEBALL; KNICKERBOCKER BASEBALL CLUB.

Casino Club
Newport, RI

There is a story that James Gordon Bennett, Jr. had his guest privileges revoked by the exclusive Reading Room in Newport, RI because he persuaded a British officer to ride a horse into the club. To retaliate, Bennett built the Casino Club a short distance away. The Newport Casino, as it is now known, hosted the U.S. national tennis championships from their beginning in 1881 through 1914. It is now the home of the International Tennis Hall of Fame and Museum.

See also INTERNATIONAL TENNIS HALL OF FAME.

Casting

The basic purpose of casting is to help a fisherman catch more fish, but it became a sport in its own right in 1861 with an annual tournament held by the New York Sportsmen's Club. The National Rod and Reel Club controlled the sport from 1882 through 1889, and from 1890 through 1906 there were many tournaments held by member clubs of the NRRC. The Chicago Fly-Casting Club, organized in 1893, held the first genuinely national tournament at that year's World's Fair in Chicago. The National Association of Scientific Angling Clubs was formed in 1906 and took over the national tournament the following year. It became the National Association of Angling and Casting Clubs in 1939 and the American Casting Association in 1960.

There are two types of casting competition—accuracy and distance—and four basic kinds of tackle—bait (artificial lure) casting, fly casting, spin casting and spinning. A major casting tournament has an almost bewildering variety of events, including various types of flies, various weights of bait, various weights of line, and both one-handed and two-handed events in distance casting.

Further Reading: Netherton, Cliff. *History of the Sport of Casting, Early Times* and *History of the Sport of Casting, Golden Years.* Lakeland, FL: American Casting Education Foundation, Inc., 1981 and 1983.

Address: American Casting Association, c/o Dale Lanser, 1739 Praise Boulevard, Fenton, MO 63026 (314) 225–9443

Catholic Youth Organization (CYO)

In 1930, Bishop Bernard Sheil told George Cardinal Mundelein, Archbishop of Chicago, "Your eminence, I want to run the biggest boxing tournament this city has ever seen." The tournament was to be run by a new organization, the CYO, which was chartered later that year as "a recreational, educational and religious program that will adequately meet the physical, mental and spiritual needs of out-of-school Catholic boys and girls . . ." The first boxing tournament, held in 1931, drew more than 2,000 entrants.

The CYO expanded its program in 1932 to include basketball and speed skating, and in June of that year the first CYO center, with bowling alleys and gymnasiums for training boxers, was opened. By the late 1940s, the CYO was conducting league play and tournaments in badminton, bowling, gymnastics, softball, table tennis, tumbling, volleyball, weight lifting, and wrestling. In addition to sports, there are activities in arts and crafts, music and drama, as well as youth retreats, nature clubs, and service programs to involve young people in assisting the ill and the elderly. The organization spread across the country after World War II. An estimated 4 million youngsters now belong to CYOs.

Address: National Federation for Catholic Youth Ministry, 3900-A Harewood Road, Washington, D.C. 20017 (202) 636–3825

Chadwick, Florence (1917–   )
Swimming
Born November 9, 1917, San Diego, CA; International Swimming Hall of Fame

Chadwick was the first woman to swim the English Channel in both directions. On August 8, 1950, she swam from France to England in 13 hours and 20 minutes and on September 11, 1951, she swam from England to France in 16 hours, 22 minutes. She later made two other France-to-England channel swims. Chadwick swam from Catalina Island to Palos Verdes, CA, a distance of 21 miles, in 13 hours 47 minutes and 32 seconds on September 21, 1952, breaking a record that had been set by George Young of Canada in 1927.

Chadwick, Henry (1824–1908)
Baseball
Born October 6, 1824, St. Thomas Exeter, England; died April 24, 1908; Baseball Hall of Fame

An Englishman was the first chronicler of America's national pastime. When he was 12 years old, Chadwick's family emigrated to Brooklyn. He saw a baseball game for the first time when he was 23, just two years after the modern form of the sport was created, and he saw the original team, the Knickerbocker Base Ball Club, playing at the Elysian Fields in Hoboken, NJ.

Chadwick was a prolific writer. He often covered cricket matches early in his career, and he was a Civil War correspondent for the *New York Tribune*. He edited the first glossary of baseball slang, *Our Boys Base Ball Guide*, in 1877 and 1878, and he wrote instructional handbooks on baseball, chess, cricket, and handball. He adapted the cricket box score for baseball, and he also created the play-by-play scoring system that is still being used, with some revisions. In 1869, he compiled the first written book of rules, which helped to standardize the sport throughout the country, and he published the first list of professional players, complete with heights, weights, birthdates, and birthplaces, in 1872.

From 1858 until 1889, Chadwick was associated with the *New York Clipper,* the first daily newspaper to follow baseball closely. Later, he was a sportswriter for the *New York Tribune* and sports editor of the *Brooklyn Eagle.* He founded and published the *Ball Player's Chronicle,* the first weekly devoted to baseball, from 1867 to 1869, and from 1882 to 1884 he edited *The Metropolitan,* a weekly devoted entirely to baseball at the Polo Grounds.

Chadwick also edited the *Official Baseball Guide* for the Spalding Publishing Company from 1881 to 1908. The *Guide,* now published by Spink Publications, is an annual compilation of statistics for teams and individual players. Many of the statistical categories still in use, such as the batting average, were invented by Chadwick as early as 1860, when he edited *Beadle's Dime Base Ball Guide,* a forerunner of the *Official Guide.*

He and his publisher, Albert G. Spalding, had a long-standing argument about the origin of baseball. Chadwick insisted that it was derived from rounders, which he had played as a boy in England, while Spalding was equally insistent that the sport was purely American in origin. Because of their debate, a commission was established in 1905 to investigate the origin of baseball, and it was this commission that created the myth that Abner Doubleday was the inventor, Cooperstown, NY the place, and 1839 the year.

While Chadwick loved baseball—he once wrote that it was a "remedy for the many evils resulting from the immoral associations (that) boys and young men of our cities are apt to become connected with"—he was not blind to its problems. He constantly inveighed against gambling, because it contained the threat of fixed games, and he strongly opposed rowdyism among players and fans alike.

Chadwick went to the opening day game at the Polo Grounds in 1908, although he had a fever. He developed pneumonia. When he died later that month, flags in baseball parks all over the country were flown at half-mast.

See also BASEBALL; SPALDING, ALBERT G.

Chalmers Award
Baseball
This award originated in 1910 when Hugh Chalmers, an automobile manufacturer, announced that for the next five years he would present a new car to the player who led the major leagues in hitting. With one day left in the 1910 season, unofficial figures showed that Ty Cobb of Detroit was hitting .383, Napoleon Lajoie of Cleveland .376. Cobb missed the

final game, while Lajoie played in a doubleheader against the St. Louis Browns. The result was controversy. Lajoie collected eight hits in eight at-bats, including six bunt singles.

League president Ban Johnson, pressured by newspapers and Tiger management, investigated. As a result, St. Louis Manager Jack O'Connor was fired for having told his third baseman to play deep, allowing the bunt hits. When the official figures were finally tabulated, nearly six weeks later, Cobb had won the batting title, .385 to .384. (Those figures have since been revised downward to .383 and .382.)

Chalmers gave cars to both Cobb and Lajoie and announced that he was changing the contest: An automobile would be awarded to the player in each league who was chosen by a panel of sportswriters "as the most important and useful player to his club and the league at large in point of deportment and value for services rendered . . ." Using those criteria, the Chalmers Award was presented from 1911 through 1914, and the winners are often included in lists of major-league most valuable players.

See also MOST VALUABLE PLAYER.

Chamberlain, Wilton (1936–   )
Basketball
Born August 21, 1936, Philadelphia; PA; Basketball Hall of Fame

The 7-foot-1, 275-pound "Wilt the Stilt," also known as the "Big Dipper," has sometimes been called a scoring machine, but he was also a rebounding machine. In his first game at the University of Kansas in 1956, he scored 52 points and had 31 rebounds. He was an All-American center in 1957 and 1958, then left school after his junior year to play one season with the Harlem Globetrotters.

He joined the Philadelphia Warriors in 1959. As a rookie, Chamberlain set National Basketball Association records with 2,707 points, an average of 37.6 points per game, 2,311 field goals attempted, 1,065 field goals scored, 1,941 rebounds, an average of 26.9 rebounds per game, and most games scoring 50 or more points in a single season, 5. He was named Rookie of the Year and Most Valuable Player.

That was just the beginning. The following season, he broke his own records, scoring 3,033 points for a 38.4 average and pulling down 2,149 rebounds, a 27.2 average. And in 1961–62, he scored 4,029 points, an average of 50.4 a game, although his rebounding fell off to "only" 25.6 a game—still good enough to lead the league. Against the New York Knicks on March 2, 1962, he scored 100 points, hitting 36 of 63 field goal attempts and 28 of 32 free throws. He scored 60 or more points in 15 games and more than 50 points in 44 games.

The Warriors moved to San Francisco in 1962, and Chamberlain was traded to a new Philadelphia team, the 76ers, during the 1964–65 season, when he led the NBA in scoring for the seventh year in a row. He led again in 1966 and won the Most Valuable Player Award for the second time. But Chamberlain was being criticized by sportswriters and many fans as a loser, and he was constantly compared unfavorably to his nemesis, Bill Russell of the Boston Celtics. His teams lost to Boston five times in five tries in the playoffs until 1967, when the 76ers beat the Celtics in the 1967 semifinals and went on to win the championship series against the Warriors. For the first time since he had joined the league, Chamberlain didn't lead in scoring, but he did lead in rebounding, he played excellent defense, and he also learned to pass the ball to the open man when he was double-teamed. He was the league's MVP for the second year in a row.

Chamberlain was named MVP again after leading in rebounding and assists in the 1967–68 season, but the 76ers lost to Boston in the playoffs, and he was traded to the Los Angeles Lakers. His scoring went down—he wasn't even among the top five—but he led the NBA in rebounding for the eighth time. Because of a knee injury, he played only 12 games in the regular 1969–70 season, but returned full-time the following season. The long-awaited Lakers' championship finally arrived in 1972, when Chamberlain became the first player to score more than 30,000 career points. Los Angeles won 12 of 15 playoff games, polishing off New York four games to one in the championship series. After one more season, Chamberlain retired. In 1981, he was named to the NBA's 35th anniversary all-time team.

In 14 seasons and 1,045 games, Chamberlain scored 31,419 points, a 30.1 average, and collected 23,924 rebounds. He was a first team All-NBA center 7 times, had the highest single-season field goal percentage ever, 72.7 in 1973, was scoring leader seven times, rebounding leader 11 times, and assist leader once. In the playoffs, he averaged 22.5 points in 160 games, and had 3,913 rebounds.

Championship Auto Racing Teams, Inc. (CART)
Two racing car owners, Roger Penske and U. E. "Pat" Patrick, founded CART in 1978 because they were dissatisfied with the U.S. Auto Club and they felt that owners should have more to say about the sport's rules and the way it was administered. Gordon Johncock won CART's first race, a 150-mile

event at Phoenix International Raceway on March 11, 1979, televised by NBC..

USAC struck back by refusing entries for the Indianapolis 500 from owners who had entered their cars in the Phoenix race, but a federal judge ruled that USAC had to accept the entries. A Penske car won the race. CART and USAC briefly got together as the Championship Racing League to sanction races in early 1980, but the wedding broke up after five races, and CART sanctioned the rest of the events. In 1981, CART put together an 11-race schedule that was the richest ever. The organization had taken over control of Indy car racing. CART now sanctions all Indy car races except the Indianapolis 500, which is still governed by USAC.

Address: 390 Enterprise Court, Bloomfield Hills, MI 48013 (313) 334–8500

See also AUTO RACING; INDIANAPOLIS 500; U. S. AUTO CLUB.

Chance, Frank (1877–1924)
Baseball
Born September 9, 1877, Fresno, CA; died February 15, 1924; Baseball Hall of Fame

He was the first baseman in the double-play combination immortalized in 1910 by Franklin P. Adams, "Tinkers to Evers to Chance." He was also the "Peerless Leader" who led the Chicago Cubs to four pennants, including three in a row, and two World Series victories. Chance joined the Cubs in 1898 as a catcher. He moved to first base during the 1902 season. He batted .327 and stole 67 bases in 1903 and hit .310 with 42 stolen bases the following year.

He was named manager in July of 1905, and the Cubs won the pennant in 1906, when he hit .319 with 103 runs scored and 57 stolen bases. They lost the World Series to the Chicago White Sox, but in 1907 they won the pennant again and swept the World Series in four games against the Detroit Tigers. The Cubs won a third straight pennant and second straight World Series, again beating Detroit in 1907, and they claimed their fourth pennant under Chance in 1910, but lost the World Series in five games to the Philadelphia Athletics.

Chance became manager of the New York Yankees in 1913. They finished seventh that year, and he was fired late in the 1914 season. He returned as a major-league manager with the Boston Red Sox in 1923; during spring training, he predicted the team would finish last, and he was right. He was also fired again. Chance batted .296 in 17 major-league season and had 932 wins and 640 losses, a .593 percentage, as a manager.

Chariot Racing
Ranchers near Thane, WY often staged horse-drawn sled races during the winter to see who had the fastest work horses. Eventually, sleds called "cutters" were scaled down for speed, and smaller, faster saddle horses replaced the work horses. The sport spread from Wyoming into Colorado, Idaho, Montana, and Utah, with regular racing from early December to late March. Then wheels were put on the cutters to extend the racing into spring and summer, and the chariots replaced the cutters entirely in 1965, when the first world championships were held.

Charlotte, NC
Basketball The Charlotte Hornets became an expansion franchise in the National Basketball Association for the 1988–89 season. There were some doubts about whether a professional team could succeed in a state that is known for its college basketball, but the Hornets sold out virtually every home game in their first two seasons of operation.

See also CHARLOTTE COLISEUM.

Charlotte Coliseum
Charlotte, NC
Built in part to compete with two other major basketball arenas in North Carolina, Dean Smith Center and Greensboro Coliseum, this arena was a major reason for Charlotte's acquisition of a National Basketball Association franchise in 1988. The third largest basketball arena in North America and the largest in the NBA, it seats 23,500. The University of North Carolina-Charlotte and Davidson University play some of their home games in the Coliseum.

Charlotte Motor Speedway
Harrisburg, NC
This speedway is a 1½-mile track that seats nearly 160,000 spectators and has its own 40-unit condominium within view of the first turn. In 1988 a $20 million Speedway Club/office complex was completed. The track, which opened in 1960, hosts two major NASCAR races each year.

Address: P.O. Box 600, Concord, NC 28026–0600 (704) 455–2121

Cherry Bowl
Football
There were two Cherry Bowl games in Pontiac, MI. Army beat Michigan State 10–6 on December 22, 1984, and Maryland beat Syracuse 35–18 on December 21, 1985.

Chicago, IL

Baseball The Chicago White Stockings were charter members of the first professional league, the National Association of Professional Base Ball Players, in 1871. After the Association folded, they joined the new National League in 1876. The team later became known as the Colts, then the Broncos, and finally the Cubs in 1900. They were very successful in the early years, winning pennants in 1876, 1880, 1881, 1882, 1885, and 1886. In this century, they were league champions in 1906, 1907, 1908, 1910, 1918, 1932, 1935, 1938, and 1945, and they won the World Series in 1907 and 1908. The Cubs were also eastern division champions in 1984 but lost to the San Diego Padres in the league championship series.

Chicago had a team in the Union Association in 1884 and in the Players' League in 1890. When the American League achieved major league status in 1901, another team called the Chicago White Stockings, now the White Sox, joined. They won pennants in 1901, 1906, 1917, 1919, and 1959, the World Series in 1906 and 1917.

See also BLACK SOX SCANDAL

Basketball In 1947, the Chicago American Gears won the National Basketball League championship, and the Chicago Stags finished first in the western division of the Basketball Association of America in 1947, but lost the championship playoffs to Philadelphia. When the two leagues merged into the National Basketball Association in 1949, the Stags survived for one season. Chicago had another NBA franchise, the Packers, for two seasons beginning in 1961. The Chicago Bulls, who entered the league in 1966, won the midwest division championship in 1975 and they were NBA champions in 1991.

Football Although the Bears are by far better known, the Cardinals were the original Chicago team in the National Football League, in 1920, when the NFL was known as the Professional Football Association of America. The Decatur Staleys were also in the

The famous Tinker-to-Evers-to-Chance double-play combination was performed by this Chicago Cubs team that won National League pennants from 1906 through 1908. Joe Tinker is number 18, Johnny Evers is number 12, and Frank Chance is number 10. Courtesy of the Boston Public Library

PFAA that year. They moved to Chicago in 1921 and became the Bears in 1922. The Cardinals, who won NFL championships in 1925 and 1947, moved to St. Louis in 1960. The Bears won titles in 1921, 1932, 1933, 1940, 1941, 1944, 1946, and 1963, and were Super Bowl champions in 1986.

Hockey   The Chicago Black Hawks entered the National Hockey League in 1927 and won the Stanley Cup in 1934, 1938, and 1961. The 1938 team had eight U.S.-born players, a record for a Stanley Cup winner.

See also CHICAGO STADIUM; COMISKEY PARK; SOLDIER FIELD; WRIGLEY FIELD.

Chicago Stadium
Chicago, IL

Built at a cost of $7 million, Chicago Stadium opened on March 29, 1929, with a boxing match between Mickey Walker and Tom Loughran. It hosted the first indoor championship game in the history of the National Football League on December 18, 1932, when the Chicago Bears beat the Portsmouth Spartans 9–0. The home of the National Hockey League's Chicago Black Hawks and the National Basketball Association's Chicago Bulls, the stadium seats 17,458 for basketball and 17,317 for hockey. Several major boxing matches have taken place in the stadium, including Sugar Ray Robinson's knockout victory over Rocky Graziano, which drew 28,500 spectators in 1953.

Churchill Downs
Lexington, KY

Joe Palmer wrote, "To men who have never seen a horse race, and never will, the twin towers of Churchill Downs and the roaring lane to the finish of the Kentucky Derby have symbolized racing." The famous twin spires were not added until 1895, 21 years after the track was built on the old Churchill farm. The man who built it was Colonel M. Lewis Clark, who went to England in 1872 to study racing and tracks. Churchill Downs is the oldest track in North America to have had continuous annual racing since its opening. The Kentucky Derby, which made Churchill Downs so famous, was first run in 1875, but didn't become nationally known until the early 20th century, when Colonel Matt Winn took over. Winn, who watched the very first Derby as a young boy, saw 75 in a row before his death in 1949. He began operating the track in 1902, and set out to interest New York owners in the race, with great success. In 1906, he introduced pari-mutuel betting, which was also a great success.

A 7-furlong turf course and a $2.6 million paddock/toteboard complex were added in a $25 million renovation that began in 1984 and was completed in 1988. The main track is a 1-mile oval. It has seating for 42,250 spectators, but the Derby draws well over 100,000 people, most of whom crowd into the infield.

See also KENTUCKY DERBY.

Cincinnati, OH

Baseball   The first all-professional baseball team was the Cincinnati Red Stockings, organized in 1869 by Harry Wright, a former player-instructor with the Union Cricket Club who had taken up baseball in 1867. The Red Stockings won 56 games and tied 1 on a national tour, and they won 63 consecutive games in 1870 before losing 8–7 to the Brooklyn Atlantics.

Cincinnati had a team in the National League when it was organized in 1876. It was expelled after the 1880 season, but returned in 1890. After having been the Redlegs for a time, the Cincinnati team is now called the Reds. The Reds won pennants in 1919, 1939, 1940, 1970, 1972, 1975, 1976, and 1990, and they were World Series champions in 1919, 1940, 1975, 1976, and 1990.

The American Association had a team in Cincinnati from 1882 through 1889 and in 1891, and there was a Cincinnati team in the Union Association in 1884, the only year that league operated.

Basketball   The National Basketball Association's Royals moved from Rochester, NY to Cincinnati in 1957, and they became the Kansas City-Omaha Kings in 1972.

Football   Cincinnati had teams in the National Football League for two seasons, the Celts in 1921 and the Reds in 1933. There was also a team called the Bengals in the American Football League in 1940. The team died, along with the league, but the name didn't. The Cincinnati Bengals entered the American Football League as an expansion franchise in 1968, just two years before the AFL was merged into the National Football League. The Bengals won the Central Division title in the American Football Conference in 1973 and 1981. They were conference champions in 1988.

See also CROSLEY FIELD; RIVERFRONT STADIUM.

Citation
Horse Racing

Trained by Jimmy Jones at Calumet Farm and ridden by Eddie Arcaro, Citation won the Triple Crown in 1948. In five years of racing, Citation started 45 races, winning 32, finishing second 10 times and third twice. He was the first horse to win more than $1 million.

Thoroughbred racing's Triple Crown winner in 1948, Citation, was the first horse to win more than $1 million. Courtesy of the National Museum of Racing

Citizens Savings Athletic Foundation

See AMATEUR ATHLETIC FOUNDATION OF LOS ANGELES.

Citrus Bowl
Football

This postseason game originated as the Tangerine Bowl on January 1, 1947, at Orlando, FL. It moved into December in 1958, was played on New Year's Day in 1960, and went back to a December date from 1960 through 1985. The name became the Citrus Bowl in 1983, and it has been played on January 1 since 1987. In the list of results, when two games are listed for a year, the first game was played in January, the second in December.

Results

1947 Catawba 31, Maryville 6
1948 Catawba 7, Marshall 0
1949 Murray State 21, Sul Ross State 21
1950 St. Vincent 7, Emory & Henry 6
1951 Morris Harvey 35, Emory & Henry 14
1952 Stetson 35, Arkansas State 20
1953 East Texas State 33, Tennessee Tech 0
1954 East Texas State 7, Arkansas State 7
1955 Nebraska-Omaha 7, Eastern Kentucky 6

1956 Juniata 6, Missouri Valley 6
1957 West Texas State 20, Southern Mississippi 13
1958 East Texas State 10, Southern Mississippi 9
1959 East Texas State 26, Missouri Valley 7
1960 Middle Tennessee State 21, Presbyterian 12
1960 Citadel 27, Tennessee Tech 0
1961 Lamar 21, Middle Tennessee State 14
1962 Houston 49, Miami (OH) 21
1963 Western Kentucky 27, Coast Guard 0
1964 East Carolina 14, Massachusetts 13
1965 East Carolina 31, Maine 0
1966 Morgan State 14, West Chester 6
1967 Tennessee-Martin 25, West Chester 8
1968 Richmond 49, Ohio 42
1969 Toledo 56, Davidson 33
1970 Toledo 40, William & Mary 12
1971 Toledo 28, Richmond 3
1972 Tampa 21, Kent State 18
1973 Miami (OH) 16, Florida 7
1974 Miami (OH) 21, Georgia 10
1975 Miami (OH) 20, South Carolina 7
1976 Oklahoma State 49, Brigham Young 21
1977 Florida State 40, Texas Tech 17
1978 North Carolina State 30, Pittsburgh 17
1979 Louisiana State 34, Wake Forest 10

1980 Florida State 35, Maryland 20
1981 Missouri 19, Southern Mississippi 17
1982 Auburn 33, Boston College 26
1983 Tennessee 30, Maryland 23
1984 Georgia 17, Florida State 17
1985 Ohio State 10, Brigham Young 7
1987 Auburn 16, Southern California 7
1988 Clemson 35, Penn State 10
1989 Clemson 13, Oklahoma 6
1990 Illinois 31, Virginia 21
1991 Georgia Tech 45, Nebraska 21

Clark, "Dutch" Earl H. (1906–   )
Football
Born October 11, 1906, Fowler, CO; died August 5, 1978; National Football Foundation, Pro Football Hall of Fame

An All-American quarterback at Colorado College in 1929, Clark joined the Portsmouth Spartans of the National Football League in 1931, when he led the NFL in rushing touchdowns with nine and threw eight touchdown passes. He was named All-Pro quarterback in both 1931 and 1932, partly because of his play-calling ability. An NFL coach said of him, "If he stepped on the field with Red Grange, Jim Thorpe, and George Gipp, Dutch would be the general." After retiring temporarily to coach at the Colorado School of Mines, he returned in 1934, when the Spartans had become the Detroit Lions. Clark averaged 6.3 yards a carry, scored 8 touchdowns, 14 extra points, and 4 field goals, and was named an All-Pro for the third time in his three seasons.

In 1935, he led the league in scoring with 55 points. The Lions won the western division championship, and Clark scored on a 40-yard run in their 26–7 championship victory over the New York Giants. He averaged 5.1 yards a carry in 1936, scoring 7 touchdowns, and completed a remarkable 53.5 percent of his passes—the league completion percentage that year was only 36.5. He also led the NFL in scoring and was named to the All-Pro team for the fifth time. A player-coach in his final two seasons with Detroit, Clark was an All-Pro again in 1937. He retired as a player after the 1938 season and coached the Cleveland Rams from 1939 through 1942. In his seven NFL seasons, Clark gained 2,296 yards on 498 carries, an average of 4.9 yards, and scored 24 touchdowns; completed 97 of 197 passes for 2,235 yards and 8 touchdowns; and kicked 57 extra points and 12 field goals for a total of 350 points.

Classification Plan
Baseball
The Classification Plan was adopted by league owners in late 1888 to go into effect during the 1889 season. Each player was assigned one of five classifications from A to E, to determine his maximum salary. Maximums were: A—$2,500; B—$2,250; C—$2,000; D—$1,750; E—$1,500. Classification was based on the player's "habits, earnestness, and special qualifications," with owners and managers as judges. The Classification Plan was a major cause of the "Brotherhood War," which led to the formation of the Players' League in 1890. It was abolished after 1890.

See also BROTHERHOOD OF PROFESSIONAL BASE BALL PLAYERS; LIMIT AGREEMENT; PLAYERS' LEAGUE.

Clay, Cassius
See ALI, MUHAMMAD.

Clemente, Roberto (1934–1972)
Baseball
Born August 18, 1934, Carolina, Puerto Rico; died December 31, 1972; Baseball Hall of Fame

Clemente got his 3,000th major league hit on September 30, 1972. It was his last. On New Year's Day of 1972, he got onto a small plane to help take supplies from Puerto Rico to Managua, Nicaragua, which had been devastated by an earthquake. The plane exploded shortly after takeoff, and Clemente was killed. The Baseball Writers Association of America held a special meeting later that year, waived the usual five-year waiting period, and elected him to the Hall of Fame.

Clemente joined the Pittsburgh Pirates late in the 1955 season. He batted .311 in 1956 and was on his way to stardom. The Pirates won the National League pennant in 1960, when Clemente hit .314 with 16 home runs, and he batted .310 in the seven-game World Series victory over the New York Yankees. He led the league in hitting in 1961 with a .351 average, collecting 201 hits. He also won batting titles in 1964 (.339), 1965 (.329), and 1967 (.357). Clemente was named the league's Most Valuable Player in 1966, after hitting .317 with 29 home runs and 119 runs batted in.

The Pirates won another championship in 1971, when Clemente batted .341. He was named MVP of the World Series, hitting .414 and making some outstanding defensive plays as the Pirates beat the Baltimore Orioles in seven games. In his final season, he hit .312. It was the thirteenth time he batted over .300, including eight consecutive seasons, 1960 through 1967. He also led National League outfielders in assists five times.

Cleveland, OH
Baseball Cleveland had a rather fitful existence in major league baseball in the 19th century. There was

a National League team in the city from 1879 through 1884 and an American Association team from 1887 through 1888. That team moved into the National League in 1889. The Players' League had a rival team in Cleveland for its only season, 1890. When the National League cut down from 12 teams to 8 in 1900, Cleveland was dropped, but promptly found a home in the new American League, which became a major league in 1901. The team was known as the Spiders until 1903, when it was renamed the Naps, in honor of star second baseman Napoleon Lajoie. They became the Indians in 1915. The Indians won pennants in 1920, 1948, and 1954, and they were World Series champions in 1920 and 1948.

Basketball The Cleveland Cavaliers joined the National Basketball Association as an expansion franchise in 1970. The team won the central division championship in 1976.

Football There have been several teams from Cleveland in the National Football League at one time or another, beginning with the Panthers in 1920 and 1921. Then there were the Indians, 1923–25, the Bulldogs in 1927, the Indians again in 1931, and the Rams from 1937 through 1942 and 1944 through 1945. The Rams moved to Los Angeles before the 1946 season, when the All America Football Conference was organized. The Cleveland Browns won all four AAFC championships before the league became part of the NFL, and they won the NFL title in 1950, 1954, 1955, and 1964. After the merger with the American Football League, the Browns moved into the American Football Conference. They won division titles in 1967, 1969, 1971, and 1980.

Hockey The California Golden Seals of the National Hockey League became the Cleveland Barons in 1977. The team was merged with the Minnesota North Stars in 1978.

See also CLEVELAND STADIUM; COLISEUM, THE.

Cleveland Stadium
Cleveland, OH

The Cleveland Indians began using two baseball parks in 1932, when Cleveland Stadium opened. Most of their games were in League Park, built in 1910, but they played in the new stadium on Sundays and holidays. Lights were installed in 1939, and in 1947 the Indians abandoned League Park. The Cleveland Rams of the National Football League played in the stadium from 1937 until they moved to Los Angeles in 1946, when they were replaced by the Cleveland Browns. The stadium seats 80,098.

Cliff Diving

Cliff divers in Mexico and the Caribbean islands often amused tourists by performing breathtaking dives into the ocean. Some American divers were inspired to make a competitive sport of it, with subjective judging as in springboard and platform diving. Divers from Mexico and the United States compete in the International Cliff Diving Championship, in which contestants perform dives from heights of 65 feet and 85 feet into a narrow, shallow body of water.

Coaching Association of Canada (CAC)

The 1969 Task Force on Sport for Canadians recommended establishing a national coaches association, and the CAC was formed in 1971 to supervise a national coaching certification program for more than 50 sports. Courses in coaching theory are offered through various colleges and universities, while technical, sport-specific courses are given by national sport-governing bodies. The CAC also conducts a national coaching seminar each October, provides grants through its coaching apprentice program, and offers scholarships for work toward level 4 or level 5 certification.

Address: 1600 James Naismith Drive, Gloucester, Ontario, Canada K1B 5N4 (613) 748–5624

Coachman, Alice (Mrs. Davis) (1919–   )
Track and Field

Born January 6, 1919, Richton, MS; National Track and Field Hall of Fame

The first black woman to win a Gold Medal, Coachman was the high jump champion at the 1948 London Games with an Olympic record of 5 feet 6⅛ inches. She won the national women's outdoor high jump ten consecutive years, 1939–48, the 50-meter dash from 1943 to 1947, and the 100-meter dash in 1942, 1945, and 1946. Coachman was also the indoor high jump champion in 1941, 1945, and 1946 and the indoor 50-meter champion in 1945 and 1946.

Cobb, Tyrus R. (1886–1961)
Baseball

Born December 18, 1886, Narrows, GA; died July 17, 1961; Baseball Hall of Fame

Cobb was "the most feared man in the history of baseball," according to Rube Bressler, who played against him. He was especially feared as a base runner. He led the American League in stolen bases six times and was often accused of using sharpened spikes to intimidate opponents. Cobb may also have been the most disliked man in the history of the game. He roomed alone, ate alone, and rarely spoke to his teammates off the field. Some thought he was crazy. Others thought it was because he was a Southerner with an ingrained hatred of Northerners.

Ty Cobb had a major-league record career batting average of .367 in 24 seasons, most of them with the Detroit Tigers. Courtesy of the National Baseball Library, Cooperstown, NY

Cobb arrived in the major leagues with the Detroit Tigers in 1905 and batted .316 the following year, the first of a record 23 consecutive seasons in which he hit over .300. He batted over .400 three times and won nine consecutive batting championships, from 1907 through 1915. The Tigers won the American League pennant in 1907, when Cobb hit .350 and led the league in runs batted in with 119. The following year, he led in hits, doubles, triples, and runs batted in while hitting .324. The Tigers won the pennant again, but lost the World Series for the second straight year. Cobb's .377 average led the league once more in 1909, and the Tigers again won the pennant and lost the World Series.

After hitting .383 in 1910 and .420 in 1911, when he was named Most Valuable Player, Cobb held out for more money. He eventually got a raise to more than $11,000 and batted .410. His streak of consecutive batting titles ended in 1916, when he hit .371 but Tris Speaker of Cleveland led with .386. Cobb then hit .368, .369, and .371 to win three more batting championships. In two of his best seasons, Cobb finished second in hitting. He had a .389 average in 1921, but Harry Heilmann batted .394. And in 1922, Cobb hit .401 but George Sisler led with a .420 average.

Baseball fans were surprised when Cobb was named player-manager in 1921. They were shocked when the Tigers suddenly released him after he hit .339 in 1926. Then Baseball Commissioner Kenesaw Mountain Landis announced that Cobb and Tris Speaker, who had just resigned as player-manager at Cleveland, may have been involved in a fixed game. On the last day of the 1919 season, the Tigers could finish third by beating the Indians. According to retired pitcher Hubert "Dutch" Leonard, who had played for Detroit that season, he and Cobb met with Speaker and pitcher "Smokey" Joe Wood of Cleveland before the game, and were assured by Speaker that the Tigers would win—as they did. The players then placed bets on the Tigers. Leonard had letters from both Cobb and Wood that backed up his charges, but Landis ultimately cleared both players. Cobb went to the Philadelphia Athletics for two seasons. He retired from baseball after batting .323 in 1928.

In 24 seasons, Cobb collected 4,190 hits, including 724 doubles, 294 triples, and 118 home runs. He scored 2,245 runs and had 1,933 runs batted in. His career batting average of .366 is a record. Cobb also had held the records for most stolen bases in a season, 96, broken by Maury Wills in 1961, and in a career, 892, broken by Lou Brock in 1979. Pete Rose broke his record for career hits in 1985 and his career record for runs scored in 1987.

Further Reading: Alexander, Charles C. *Ty Cobb.* New York: Oxford University Press, 1984.

Cochran, Jacqueline   (1910–1980)
Air Racing
Born 1910, Pensacola, FL; died August 9, 1980

Cochran was the first woman to compete in the London-to-Melbourne air race, in 1934, and the Bendix Trophy transcontinental race, in 1935. She won the Bendix Trophy in 1938. In 1957 she became the first woman to fly faster than the speed of sound, and on May 11, 1964, she set a women's speed record of 1,429 miles per hour. In 1962, after having set 33 national and international records, she put in a claim for 49 more point-to-point records, based on a series of flights from New Orleans to Germany in a four-engine Lockheed Jet Star.

Further Reading: Cochran, Jacqueline. *The Stars at Noon.* Boston: Little, Brown, 1954.

Cochrane, "Mickey" Gordon S.   (1903–1962)
Baseball
Born April 6, 1903, Bridgewater, MA; died June 28, 1962; Baseball Hall of Fame

Connie Mack of the Philadelphia Athletics coveted Cochrane so much that he paid $50,000 to a minor-league team for his contract. He became the Athletics' starting catcher in 1925 and was named the American League's Most Valuable Player in 1928, when he hit .293. The Athletics won the pennant in 1929, when Cochrane batted .331 and drove in 95 runs. He hit .400 in the five-game World Series victory over the Chicago Cubs.

The Athletics repeated as pennant winners in 1930 and 1931, Cochrane batting .357 and .349. He hit two home runs in the 1930 World Series against the St. Louis Cardinals, when the Athletics won four games to two. He hit 23 home runs and drove in 121 runs in 1932, and batted .322 in 1933. Cochrane then became the Detroit Tigers' player-manager. The team had finished fifth the year before, but they won the pennant in 1934; however, they lost the World Series to St. Louis in seven games. In 1935, they won the World Series by beating the Cubs in six games.

Cochrane suffered a nervous breakdown during the 1936 season, and on May 26, 1937, he lay unconscious in a hospital for ten days after being hit on the head by a pitch. That was the end of his playing career but he returned as manager in 1937 and for part of the 1938 season. Cochrane's lifetime batting average was .320 in regular-season play, and he had 413 victories and 297 losses as a manager, a .582 percentage.

Cockfighting

One of the cruel amusements popular in Elizabethan and Restoration England, cockfighting was particularly popular in the American South during the 18th century, but it was not unknown in the North. Cotton Mather denounced its practice in Boston in 1705, and a cockfighting pit was documented in New York City at about the same time. Reportedly, hundreds of people, of all classes, attended cockfights in Hampton County, VA in 1787.

During the 19th century, it was featured with dog fighting and ratting by sporting halls in New York and other large cities. The best known site in New York was Kit Burns' Sportsman Hall, which could seat up to 400 spectators. All such sports were banned by New York State in 1856, but in 1861 the New York *Clipper* reported that cockfighting was "becoming more popular than formerly." Although it was apparently less common in rural areas, a visitor to northern Virginia in 1872 saw people sleeping outside a cockfighting pit, awaiting the next day's matches.

By the turn of the century, cockfighting was prohibited virtually everywhere, but it didn't com-

pletely die out. There is a cockfighting scene in Nathanael West's *The Day of the Locust* (1950) that was probably based on real life, and immigrants from Mexico and Cuba have reintroduced the sport in Texas and Florida.

Codeball

Codeball is two sports, codeball on the green and codeball in the court, both played with a ball 6 inches in diameter and weighing 12 ounces. They were invented by Dr. William E. Code of Chicago about 1930. Codeball on the green is similar to golf, except that the player kicks the ball, and codeball in the court is like handball, but it's played with the feet. The court game was popular for a time during the 1930s on playgrounds in many midwestern cities, but both versions of codeball are now virtually unknown.

Colisee, Le
See QUEBEC COLISEUM.

Coliseum, The
Richfield, OH

The $32 million Coliseum is located about halfway between Cleveland and Akron, OH. Groundbreaking took place on March 16, 1973, and the grand opening was on October 26, 1974. The home of the Cleveland Cavaliers of the NBA, the Coliseum also hosts wrestling, auto racing, indoor soccer, ice shows, and entertainment. Seating capacity is 19,500.

Collectibles

The most popular sports collectible is the baseball trading card. The first trading cards were issued in 1886 by Goodwin and Company as premiums in packets of Gypsy Queen and Old Judge cigarettes. Other cigarette, cigar, and plug tobacco manufacturers issued baseball cards until 1895, when the American Tobacco Trust was organized. The trust was a virtual monopoly and didn't need premiums to sell cigarettes. After it was broken up by a federal court, the American Tobacco Company in 1910 began to offer cards portraying baseball players and boxers in exchange for coupons in the cigarette packages. The rarest of them is a Honus Wagner card issued in 1910. A nonsmoker, Wagner sued to stop the company from using his name. Only about 30 of the cards are in existence, and one in mint condition is worth more than $20,000.

Goudey was the first gum company to issue baseball cards, from 1933 through 1936 and in 1938 and 1941. Both the Bowman Company and the Leaf Gum Company packaged baseball cards in 1948. Bowman dropped out after 1949, but in 1951 the most famous of them all, Topps Chewing Gum Company, entered the market. When Fleer issued a set of cards in 1963, Topps won a restraining order because it had contracts for rights with most major leaguers and Fleer was temporarily out of the card business. But Fleer sued on antitrust grounds, and in 1980 a federal judge ruled that Topps was guilty of restraint of trade.

Both Fleer and Donruss, another bubble gum maker, issued baseball cards in 1981, and many other companies got into the act, including Squirt Soda, Coca-Cola, Drake's Bakery, and Kellogg's, which came out with three-dimensional cards. Confusion was compounded late that year when a judge ruled that Topps did have exclusive rights to baseball cards distributed with confectionery products. Fleer responded in 1982 by issuing baseball cards with stickers containing team logos, and Donruss sold cards with pieces of a jigsaw puzzle showing an artist's rendering of great moments in baseball.

Card collecting really became a hobby in the 1960s. For many, it's a business. Baseball card shops are found in virtually any sizable city, there are at least ten periodicals aimed at collectors, and hundreds of shows devoted to baseball cards are held throughout the country. The top publication, *Beckett's Baseball Card Monthly*, has a paid circulation of more than 150,000. *Sports Collectors Digest* had to become a tabloid in June of 1989 because in its smaller size it would have grown beyond 300 pages, which is all the printer's stapling machine can handle. And many companies sell cards by mail.

Topps, Fleer, and other companies also issue basketball, football, and hockey cards, but they are not considered particularly collectible because neither the sports nor the cards themselves have enough history behind them. Many other sports items are collectible, though. Foremost, perhaps, are autographs. Some collectors specialize in Hall of Fame members, while others collect autographs of players from a single team, pitchers who threw no-hitters, and so forth.

Among other sports collectibles are uniforms and other items of equipment, baseball "coins" containing player's likenesses (which, like cards, have been distributed as premiums by a variety of companies), college homecoming badges, press pins, team media guides and yearbooks, programs, scorecards, ticket stubs, posters, and figurines. There are also collectors of sports magazines and books.

Most collectors specialize, but some collect a wide range of sports memorabilia. The "King of the Sports Collectors" is Barry Halper of Livingston, NJ. His collection includes Babe Ruth's polo coat, Ruth's 1932 contract, a wax figure of Ruth that was once in Madame Tussaud's London Wax Museum, Ty Cobb's contract for the 1914 and 1915 seasons, Lou Gehrig's glove, and more than 150 World Series bats, cartoons, photographs, autographs.

Further Reading: Sugar, Bert Randolph. *The Sports Collectors Bible*. New York: Bobbs-Merrill, 1979; Sullivan, George. *The Complete Book of Baseball Collectibles*. New York: Arco Publishing, 1983.

College All-Star Game
See ALL-STAR GAMES.

College Football Association (CFA)
Twenty-five major football colleges met in October of 1975 to discuss an attempt to reorganize the National Collegiate Athletic Association. After their reorganization plan was defeated at the 1976 convention, they formed the College Football Association, which now has 66 members. One of the CFA's first actions, at its 1977 annual meeting, was to form a committee to develop tougher academic standards. The result was the NCAA's Proposition 48, which requires that incoming freshmen receiving athletic scholarships or grants-in-aid must have passed a core curriculum in high school.

Beginning in 1981, the CFA has conducted an annual survey of its members to determine the graduation rate of college football players receiving grants-in-aid. The school with the highest graduation rate is given the CFA Academic Achievement Award. The CFA survey reveals that the graduation rate for college football players is slightly higher than the rate for the general student population, allowing five years to graduate.

In 1983, a CFA suit against the NCAA went to the Supreme Court, which ruled that the NCAA's policy of negotiating a single network contract for all of its member schools violated antitrust laws, thereby allowing the CFA to negotiate its own contracts. ABC and ESPN televised CFA games from 1984 through 1986, and the association in 1987 entered into contracts with CBS and ESPN. However, it received a blow in 1990. After the CFA had signed five-year contracts with ABC for $210 million and with ESPN for $140 million to begin the 1991 season, Notre Dame pulled out and negotiated its own five-year $37.5 million contract with NBC. The CFA had to take a cut to $175 million from ABC and $125 million from ESPN, a loss of $50 million.

Address: 6688 Gunpark Drive, Suite 201, Boulder, CO 80301 (303) 530-5566

College Union Regatta Association

The first known intercollegiate sports association was organized by Brown, Harvard, Trinity, and Yale in 1858, but the association's planned regatta that year was canceled because a Yale crew member drowned shortly before the event was to be held. The association held two successful regattas on Lake Quinsigamond, near Worcester, MA. The 1859 regatta attracted nearly 20,000 spectators and was reported on the front page of the *New York Herald*. But the Civil War intervened, and only Harvard and Yale competed from 1864 through 1871.

College World Series
Baseball

Formally the National Collegiate Baseball Championship Game, conducted by the NCAA, the first College World Series was held on June 21, 1947, at Kalamazoo, MI. The Division II championship was added in 1968, the Division III championship in 1976.

Collegiate Sports

See INTERCOLLEGIATE SPORTS.

Collett, Glenna

See VARE, GLENNA COLLETT.

Colonial Cup
Steeplechase

The first steeplechase ever to offer as much as $100,000 in prize money, the Colonial Cup originated in 1972. It's run at Camden, SC over a 2-mile, 6 ½-furlong course with 17 obstacles.

Colonial Era

North American colonists brought with them the amusements they had learned in England. For the most part, these were folk games that enlivened English village life on religious and secular holidays and on Sunday afternoons. But the rigors of life in a new land and Puritan suspicion of recreation as a form of idleness did not allow much play in the early colonial years. The Puritan outlook was not confined to New England. Sir Thomas Dale saw a game of bowls in Jamestown shortly after he arrived in 1611 to become governor of Virginia, and was not amused. He banned "gaming" on the Sabbath, prescribing the death penalty for the third offense.

On Christmas Day, 1621, Governor William Bradford of Plymouth saw colonists playing games in the street, "pitching at the barre" and stoolball among them. Since the Pilgrims did not recognize Christ-

The first illustration of sports in the Colonies appeared in John Smith's Description of New England *in 1619. It shows hunting, fishing, and falconry.*

mas as a holiday, he ordered them to get to work and confiscated their equipment. Massachusetts in 1640 forbade fasting, feasting, or refusing to work on Christmas, and in 1648 passed a law that no one "shall spend his time idly or unprofitably." Even the Dutch in New Amsterdam, who were generally more tolerant of play, in 1656 banned a variety of amusements on Sunday mornings, including ball playing, cricket, nine-pins and tennis. Two years later, Boston prohibited football, and Quaker-ruled Pennsylvania outlawed "rude and riotous sports" in 1682.

Of course, the fact that these prohibitions were necessary means that some people were playing games. And, as villages were formed and life became somewhat less toilsome, play increased and was even tolerated, to a certain extent, by the authorities. One Puritan minister noted, "We daily need some respite and diversion, without which we dull our powers"—the equivalent of "all work and no play makes Jack a dull boy."

During the late 17th and early 18th centuries, games enlivened the increasing number of informal secular holidays, including harvest festivals, commencements, election days, and county fairs. In 1737, prizes were offered for a cudgeling match, a horse race, and a wrestling match at the Hanover County Fair in Virginia. Taverns in towns and along major highways were centers for a variety of amusements, including skittles and billiards. The very association with taverns and drinking brought those sports into disrepute. A Virginia clergyman complained about taverns "where prohibited and unlawful games, sports and pastimes are used, followed, and practiced, almost without intermission, namely cards, dice, horse-racing, and cock-fighting.''

See also DUTCH COLONIAL SPORTS; FOLK GAMES; FRONTIER SPORTS; GENTRY SPORTS; PURITANISM; TRAINING DAYS.

Colorado Rockies
See DENVER, CO.

Columbus, OH
Baseball Columbus had a team in the American Association in 1883 and 1884 and from 1889 through 1891, the association's last year of existence.
Football The Columbus Panhandles, originally an independent semiprofessional team, joined the American Professional Football Association in 1921, its second year. The APFA became the National Football League in 1922, and the Panhandles were in the league through the 1926 season.

Comiskey, Charles A. (1859–1931)
Baseball
Born August 15, 1859, Chicago, IL; died October 26, 1931; Baseball Hall of Fame

As a player, Comiskey joined the first union of professional athletes and jumped to another league. As an owner, he fought unions, helped organize a new league, and persuaded players to jump to it; later he inveighed against ''outlaw'' leagues and players who joined them. Comiskey was generous with charities, but paid his players so little that many blame him for the ''Black Sox Scandal'' of 1919, when eight of his White Sox players were bribed to throw the World Series.

Comiskey became the first baseman for the American Association's St. Louis Browns in 1882 and was named player-manager late in the 1883 season. The Browns won four straight pennants from 1885 through 1888. In 1890, Comiskey went to the Chicago team in the Players' League as player-manager, but he returned to the Browns in 1891. The American Association folded after that season and Comiskey went to Cincinnati, again as player-manager. When Ban Johnson became president of the minor Western League in 1895, Comiskey bought the Sioux City (IA) team and moved it to St. Paul, MN. It became the Chicago franchise in the renamed American League in 1900.

Before the 1901 season, Comiskey persuaded pitcher Clark Griffith of the National League's Chicago Cubs to join his White Stockings as player-manager. The White Stockings, who became better known as the White Sox, won the pennant that season and in 1906, 1917, and 1919. Amid rumors and hints in the press that the 1919 World Series had been fixed, Comiskey denied that anything had been wrong. But, after a grand jury began investigating in late 1920, he issued a statement that he had suspected a fix after the first game. Ultimately eight players were indicted by the grand jury. Though found not guilty in a jury trial, they were banned from baseball for life by Commissioner Kenesaw Mountain Landis.

The White Sox, considered the best team in baseball in 1919, were probably the worst paid. ''Shoeless Joe'' Jackson, one of the implicated players, was a great hitter, base runner, and fielder. He was paid $6,000 that year, whereas his Cincinnati counterpart, Edd Roush, earned $11,000. Claude ''Lefty'' Williams, who won 23 games in 1919, was paid only $3,000. When stories appeared about the low salaries the White Sox received, Comiskey paid $1,500 bonuses to the rest of his players, the difference between the winner's share and loser's share of the Series money, and made sure that it was well publicized. From 1920 until his death in 1931, the White Sox were a second-division team.

See also BLACK SOX SCANDAL.

Comiskey Park
Chicago, IL
The owner of the Chicago White Sox, Charles Comiskey, named this concrete and steel park for himself. It opened on July 1, 1910. The park had a single-deck grandstand extending from the left-field to the right-field corner, with bleachers in left and right fields. Seating capacity was about 30,000. In 1926, a second deck was added to the grandstand and the existing bleachers, and a small bleacher section was built in center field. The bullpens were moved into center field in 1950. Capacity is now 44,087 and the home run distances are 347 feet down the lines and, 409 feet to center field. The stadium was called White Sox Park from 1962 through 1975 and then reverted to its original name.

The White Sox played in the stadium during the 1990 season while a new Comiskey Park was being build a short distance away. The team moved into the new park in 1991.

Commission of Intercollegiate Athletics for Women
See ASSOCIATION FOR INTERCOLLEGIATE ATHLETICS FOR WOMEN.

Commonwealth Games
Sir Astley Cooper of England in 1891 proposed a ''Pan-Brittanic-Pan-Anglican Contest and Festival''

to be held every four years. Twenty years later, his proposal was acted upon when the Inter-Empire Championships were held in conjunction with the Festival of Empire to honor the coronation of King George V. Teams from the United Kingdom, Australia, Canada and South Africa competed in boxing, swimming, track and field, and wrestling. Tentative plans to stage championships quadrennially were canceled by World War I and were virtually forgotten until 1928, when M. M. "Bobby" Robinson, manager of Canada's Olympic track and field team, called a meeting of representatives from British Empire countries to propose that games be held in 1930.

The first British Empire Games were staged in Hamilton, Ontario. London hosted the games in 1934 and Sydney, Australia, in 1938. War again intervened, but in 1950 the renamed British Empire and Commonwealth Games were hosted by Auckland, New Zealand. There have been two name changes since then, to the British Commonwealth Games in 1966 and to the Commonwealth Games in 1974. Games were held in Vancouver, British Columbia, in 1954; Cardiff, Wales, in 1958; Perth, Australia, in 1962; Kingston, Jamaica, in 1966; Edinburgh, Scotland, in 1970 and 1986; Christchurch, New Zealand, in 1974; Edmonton, Alberta, in 1978; and Brisbane, Australia, in 1982. The 1990 games were held in Auckland, and Victoria, British Columbia, will be the host city in 1994.

Sports include badminton, boxing, cycling, diving, lawn bowling, rowing, shooting, swimming, synchronized swimming, track and field, weight lifting, and wrestling. The Commonwealth Games Association of Canada, Inc., selects and supervises the Canadian team.

Address: Commonwealth Games Association of Canada, 1600 James Naismith Drive, Gloucester, Ontario, Canada K1B 5N4

Commonwealth Stadium
Edmonton, Alberta

Built to host the 1978 Commonwealth Games, this stadium is the home field of the Canadian Football League's Edmonton Eskimos. It seats 61,356.

Conacher, Lionel P. (1901–1964)
Canadian Football, Hockey
Born May 24, 1901, Toronto; died May 26, 1964; Hockey Hall of Fame

An all-around athlete, Conacher played both professional Canadian football and professional hockey. University of Illinois Coach Bob Zuppke called him the finest punter he ever saw. He was also a minor-league baseball player, a sprinter, a boxer, wrestler, and a lacrosse player. He died of a heart attack at the age of 62 after hitting a triple in a sandlot baseball game.

Conacher was known as a very rough hockey player. In 1936, he got into a fight with his brother Charlie of the Toronto Maple Leafs; the fight went from the ice up a ramp and into the lobby of the arena before it was broken up. He played for the North Toronto Athletic Club in 1919 and the Toronto Canoe Club in 1920. He then became captain and manager of the Pittsburgh Yellow Jackets. He joined the Pittsburgh Pirates of the National Hockey League in 1925 and was traded during the 1926–27 season to the New York Americans, where he served as player-coach in 1928–29. Conacher then spent three seasons with the Montreal Maroons, one with the Chicago Black Hawks, and three more with the Maroons. He retired after the 1936–37 season.

Connie Mack Stadium
Philadelphia, PA

When it opened as baseball's first concrete and steel stadium on April 12, 1909, it was named Shibe Park for Ben Shibe, president of the Philadelphia Athletics. There was a double-deck grandstand behind home plate, with bleachers along the foul lines, and capacity was about 20,000. Home run distances were 360 feet down the lines and 420 feet to center field. On July 4, 1938, the Philadelphia Phillies moved into Shibe Park under a rental agreement with the Athletics. Lights were installed the following year, and the first night game in American League history was played on May 16, 1939. The park was renamed Connie Mack Stadium in 1953, three years after Mack retired as manager of the Athletics. After the Athletics moved to Kansas City in 1955, the Phillies bought the park and played there until the 1971 season, when Veterans Stadium opened.

Connie Mack Stadium was torn down after a fire seriously damaged its grandstand in August 1971.

Connolly, Harold (1931–   )
Track and Field
Born August 1, 1931, Somerville, MA; National Track and Field Hall of Fame

Connolly took up the hammer throw to strengthen his left arm, which had been slightly withered at birth. He became a four-time U.S. Olympic team member, winning the Gold Medal in 1956 with a record throw of 207 feet, 3½ inches. During the Olympics, he met Olga Fikotova, the Czechoslovakian winner of the women's discus throw; they were married later that year. On November 2, 1956, Connolly set a world record of 224 feet 10 inches. He extended that to 225 feet 4 inches on May 29, 1958, and to 233 feet 9 inches, on June 20, 1958. Both Harold and Olga Connolly were on the U.S. Olympic teams in 1960, 1964, and 1968, and she was also an Olympian in 1972.

Connolly, Maureen (Mrs. Brinker) (1934–1969)
Tennis

Born September 17, 1934, San Diego, CA; died June 21, 1969; International Tennis Hall of Fame

"Little Mo" was only 5 feet 4 inches and 130 pounds, but she was a powerful, accurate shotmaker who rarely made an unforced error. She won a total of nine Grand Slam championships, even though her career ended before she was 20 years old when her left leg was badly broken in a fall from a horse. She was the first woman to win all four Grand Slam events (the Australian, English [Wimbledon], French, and U.S. titles) in a single year, 1953. Connolly was also the U.S. champion in 1951 and 1952, the Wimbledon champion in 1952 and 1954, and the French champion in 1954.

Shortly before her death from cancer in 1969, she established the Maureen Connolly Brinker Foundation to offer financial assistance to promising junior tennis players.

Continental League
Baseball

New York attorney William Shea and former major-league executive Branch Rickey announced in 1960 that they were forming the Continental League with teams in Atlanta, Buffalo, Dallas-Ft. Worth, Denver, Houston, Minneapolis-St. Paul, New York, and Toronto. Many thought the announcement was only a ploy to force the existing major leagues to expand. If so, it worked. On August 2, 1960, the American and National Leagues announced that they would each add two teams immediately, and that all eight cities named by the Continental League would ultimately have major-league teams. The Continental then faded away. Of the eight cities, Buffalo and Denver still do not have major-league franchises, but the Colorado Rockies, representing Denver, will join the National League in 1993.

Cooperative Sports

The pioneer in developing noncompetitive sports and games was the Peace Research Laboratory in the late 1940s. The idea was adopted by many others in the early 1970s. Although aimed primarily at children, cooperative sports are designed, as Terry Orlick has put it, as "games of acceptance, cooperating, and sharing that can bring children, families, and communities together in the spirit of cooperative play."

The "long, long, long jump" resembles the relay long jump. A team of children try to jump, collectively, as far as possible, with each starting where the previous jumper left off. In crossover dodgeball, an adaptation of a popular grade-school gym sport, a player is not eliminated when hit by the ball, but goes to the other team. Deacove rounders, invented by Jim Deacove, is a kind of reverse baseball. The fielders try to make what would be putouts in baseball in order to allow hitters to get on base. A fielded grounder gives the batter one base, an infield fly two bases, and an outfield fly three bases. If the hitting team has five players, the object is to score five runs, and the fielding team is then rewarded by getting a chance to bat.

Further Reading: Orlick, Terry. *The Cooperative Sports and Games Book.* New York: Pantheon, 1978; Weinstein, Matt, and Joel Goodman. *Playfair.* San Luis Obispo, CA: Impact Publishers, 1980.

Corbett, James J. (1866–1933)
Boxing

Born September 1, 1866, San Francisco, CA; died February 18, 1933; Boxing Hall of Fame

Known as "Gentleman Jim" and the "Dancing Master," Corbett was the first man to win the heavyweight title under the Marquis of Queensbury rules when he knocked out John L. Sullivan on September 7, 1892. In the 21st round, Corbett "shot his right across the jaw and Sullivan fell like an ox," as one writer described it. Corbett spent most of 1893 in a show called "Gentleman Jim." He knocked out Peter Courtney in the first fight ever filmed on September 7, 1894, and lost the title on March 17, 1897, when Bob Fitzsimmons knocked him out in the first round at Carson City, NV.

Cosell, Howard (Cohen) (1920–   )
Sportscaster

Born March 25, 1920, Winston-Salem, NC

His nasal voice, his overaggressive approach to interviews, and his hyperbolic, polysyllabic speech made him famous as "the man you love to hate" on ABC television's "Monday Night Football." Cosell worked in relative obscurity for years before he was suddenly thrust into fame. A practicing attorney, he began doing 5-minute sports broadcasts for ABC Radio in 1955. He broke into television by producing a documentary special about Babe Ruth on August 18, 1962, the 14th anniversary of Ruth's death. The show was a success, and in 1964 Cosell began to make frequent appearances on "Wide World of Sports." Beginning in 1966, he worked every fight televised by ABC for seven years, while continuing to produce documentaries.

Cosell first collided with controversy by backing Muhammad Ali's right to keep the heavyweight championship after he had refused to report for induction into the army in 1967. But that was mild compared to what "Monday Night Football" did when it debuted in 1970. There were three broadcasters, play-by-play announcer Keith Jackson, former Dallas Cowboys' quarterback Don Meredith, and Cosell. To many, three people in the broadcast booth seemed like too many, especially when one of them was Cosell. But the byplay between the abrasive Cosell and the laid-back Meredith worked.

Many fans said they watched the games with the sound turned off so that they wouldn't have to listen to Cosell. But Frank Deford of *Sports Illustrated* wrote, "Feel sorry for the people who turn off the sound. The poor bastards missed the game." Cosell did "Monday Night Football" through the 1983 season, when ratings suddenly dropped. He had stopped covering boxing, amid much publicity, the year before. Cosell also had a pioneering show, "Sports-Beat," that went on the air on August 30, 1981, and often probed drug use, racism, sexism, and other issues generally ignored by television sports. Now semiretired, Cosell still does a daily sports report on radio for the American Contemporary Network.

Further Reading: Cosell, Howard, with the editorial assistance of Mickey Herskowitz. *Cosell.* Chicago: Playboy Press, 1973; Cosell, Howard, with Peter Bonventre. *I Never Played the Game.* New York, William Morrow, 1985.

Cotton Bowl
Football

The fourth of the four major college football bowl games, the Cotton Bowl was first played in Dallas, TX on January 1, 1937. In most years, one team has been from Texas, but six times the University of Arkansas has been the host team.

Results

1937	Texas Christian 16, Marquette 6
1938	Rice 28, Colorado 14
1939	St. Mary's (CA) 20, Texas Tech 13
1940	Clemson 6, Boston College 3
1941	Texas A & M 13, Fordham 12
1942	Alabama 29, Texas Texas A & M 21
1943	Texas 14, Georgia Tech 7
1944	Texas 7, Randolph Field 7
1945	Oklahoma State 34, Texas Christian 0
1946	Texas 40, Missouri 27
1947	Arkansas 0, Louisiana State 0
1948	Southern Methodist 13, Penn State 13
1949	Southern Methodist 21, Oregon 13
1950	Rice 27, North Carolina 13
1951	Tennessee 20, Texas 14
1952	Kentucky 20, Texas Christian 7
1953	Texas 16, Tennessee 0
1954	Rice 28, Alabama 6
1955	Georgia Tech 14, Arkansas 8
1956	Mississippi 14, Texas Christian 13
1957	Texas Christian 28, Syracuse 27
1958	Navy 20, Rice 7
1959	Texas Christian 0, Air Force 0
1960	Syracuse 23, Texas 14
1961	Duke 7, Arkansas 6
1962	Texas 12, Mississippi 7
1963	Louisiana State 13, Texas 0
1964	Texas 28, Navy 6
1965	Arkansas 10, Nebraska 7
1966	(Jan.) Louisiana State 14, Arkansas 7
1966	(Dec.) Georgia 24, Southern Methodist 9
1968	Texas A & M 20, Alabama 16
1969	Texas 36, Tennessee 13
1970	Texas 21, Notre Dame 17
1971	Notre Dame 24, Texas 11
1972	Penn State 30, Texas 0
1973	Texas 17, Alabama 13
1974	Nebraska 19, Texas 3
1975	Penn State 41, Baylor 20
1976	Arkansas 13, Georgia 10
1977	Houston 30, Maryland 21
1978	Notre Dame 38, Texas 10
1979	Notre Dame 35, Houston 34
1980	Houston 17, Nebraska 14
1981	Alabama 30, Baylor 2
1982	Texas 14, Alabama 12
1983	Southern Methodist 7, Pittsburgh 3
1984	Georgia 10, Texas 9
1985	Boston College 45, Houston 28
1986	Texas A & M 36, Auburn 16
1987	Ohio State 28, Texas A & M 12
1988	Texas A & M 35, Notre Dame 10
1989	UCLA 17, Arkansas 3
1990	Tennessee 31, Arkansas 27
1991	Miami 46, Texas 3

Country Club, The
Brookline, MA

Best known as the site of Francis Ouimet's stunning victory in the 1913 U.S. Open, the Country Club was founded in 1882, the first in the country, and became the model for the socially exclusive country clubs that followed it. Two members who wrote a history of the club said it was "a denial of the spirit of democracy, since a small group sets itself apart from the majority, building, as it were, a wall around its pastimes. . . ." At first, the chief sports were hunting and steeplechasing. The golf course was built in 1892, and the club became a charter member of the U.S. Golf Association in 1894. It hosted the U.S. Open in 1913, 1963, and 1988.

Further Reading: Curtiss, Frederick H., and John Heard. *The Country Club, 1882–1932.* Brookline, MA: Privately printed, 1932.

Country Clubs

Nostalgia for the English country home and life outside the city created the country club movement of the late 19th century. Country clubs originally concentrated on outdoor sports, especially horsemanship, with such activities as fox hunting, horse shows, steeplechasing, and cross-country riding, although many also had billiard rooms. They also certified social prestige and offered a respite from the pressures of city business. As golf became prestigious late in the century, most country clubs built courses.

The first was The Country Club in Brookline, MA, built in 1882. In 1886 the New York Athletic Club built its own country club at Travers Island. The greatest of them was Tuxedo Park, really a resort community developed around a club. Built by Pierre Lorillard III on 5,000 acres in Orange County, NY, Tuxedo Park had an enormous clubhouse with a ballroom, dining room, billiard room, and theater. The grounds included a race track and facilities for pigeon shooting and steeplechasing, as well as winter sports such as skating, sleighing, tobogganing, and ice yachting. Tuxedo Park opened in 1885, and a golf course was added in 1889.

In the 1920s, country clubs sprang up all over North America, built around golf as a sport with the clubhouse as a center for social activities. These clubs were generally exclusive only because of the initiation fees and dues that they charged. The members were not usually from old-money society; they were more likely to be upper middle-class businessmen, and membership now conferred social prestige, rather than prestige being a prerequisite for membership. Ironically, the growth of golf as a country club sport turned the sport into an extension of business rather than a respite from it: Business deals were often discussed during a round of golf and sealed at "the 19th hole," the club's bar, afterward.

During the Great Depression, nearly one third of the country clubs went out of business, and many became municipally or privately owned. And as golf became more accessible to the general public through municipal and daily-fee courses, it lost some of its social luster. By the early 1960s, most country clubs were simply golf courses that also offered some social events for their members.

See also GOLF.

Coursing

See GREYHOUND RACING.

Court Tennis

Also called "real" or "royal" tennis, this sport originated in France during the 12th century, when it was played in courtyards and monasteries. At first, it was a kind of handball. Then a paddle was used, followed by something like the modern racket, with strings drawn over a framework. Court tennis was a favorite sport of Henry VIII. It declined in England toward the end of the 18th century, but regained some popularity in the middle of the 19th century. Court tennis arrived in the United States in 1876, when Hollis Hunnewell and Nathaniel Thayer built a court in Boston.

Other courts were built at the Newport Casino, the Boston Athletic Association, the New York Racquet and Tennis Club, the Chicago Athletic Association, the Tuxedo Club at Tuxedo Park, NY, the Myopia Hunt Club in Hamilton, MA, and the Racquet Club in Philadelphia, among others. The first U.S. national singles championship, in 1892, was won by Richard Sears, seven-time national lawn tennis champion.

Because of the high cost of building a court and the incredible complexity of its rules, the sport is now virtually extinct.

Cousy, "Bob" Robert J. (1928–   )
Basketball

Born August 9, 1928, New York, NY; Basketball Hall of Fame

Sportswriters called him "the Houdini of the hardwood" for his uncanny dribbling and passing ability. An All-American at Holy Cross in 1950, Cousy was drafted by the Chicago Stags. The franchise folded, and in the dispersal draft of Stags' players the Boston Celtics picked his name out of a hat. Red Auerbach, the Celtics' coach, later said that Cousy "was one of the greatest all-around basketball players in the game, and undoubtedly he was the best backcourt player."

He became known for behind-the-back and over-the-shoulder passes. At first, his passing confused his teammates as well as the defense, but they soon learned to be ready for a pass whenever Cousy had the ball, and he led the NBA in assists eight years in a row, 1953 through 1960. He could also score. On March 21, 1953, he had 50 points in a playoff victory over Syracuse, a record at the time, and he averaged 18.4 points a game during his professional

In a contest of superstar guards, Bob Cousy of the Boston Celtics drives past Jerry West of the Los Angeles Lakers during the 1966 National Basketball Association finals. Courtesy of the Public Broadcasting Service

career. But, as Jimmy Cannon wrote, "If Cousy never put the ball in the basket, he'd still be the most respected player in the league."

In 13 seasons with the Celtics, Cousy played for seven NBA champions, was named Most Valuable Player in 1957, and was an All-Star ten times. When he retired after the 1962–63 season, he held career records for most assists and most minutes played and was fourth in scoring. Cousy coached Boston College from 1964 to 1969, compiling a 117–54 record, then went to the Kansas City Kings of the NBA for three seasons and part of a fourth. In his NBA career, Cousy played 924 games, scored 16,960 points, and had 6,955 assists. He added 2,008 points and 937 assists in 109 playoff games.

Crawford, Samuel E. (1880–1968)
Baseball
Born April 18, 1880, Wahoo, NE; died June 15, 1968; Baseball Hall of Fame

Although he retired after the 1917 season, "Wahoo Sam" still holds the major-league record with 309 career triples. A left-handed center fielder who could hit for power in the dead-ball era, Crawford was also an outstanding base runner and a good defensive

player. He joined the Cincinnati Reds in 1899 and got five hits in his first major-league game. Crawford led the National League in home runs with 16 in 1901, when he batted .330. He was traded to the Detroit Tigers in 1903 and led the American League with 25 triples.

The Tigers won three straight pennants, 1907–09. Crawford led the league in runs scored with 102 in 1907, in home runs with 7 in 1908, and in doubles with 35 in 1909. The Tigers lost all three World Series, despite having Crawford in center and Ty Cobb in right field. The two great players didn't speak to one another for years. Crawford believed that Cobb stopped speaking to him after he had hit into four double plays in one game, with Cobb on first base each time.

He led the league in triples three consecutive years with 23 in 1913, 26 in 1914, and 19 in 1915. Crawford was also the league leader in runs batted in with 120 in 1910, 104 in 1914, and 112 in 1915, and in home runs with 8 in 1914. He retired after 1917 with a lifetime .309 average, 2,961 hits, 1,391 runs scored, and 1,525 runs batted in.

Cricket

A primitive form of cricket was played in the American Colonies through most of the 18th century, but it apparently all but disappeared by the time of the Revolution, perhaps because of anti-British sentiment. In Canada, a more modern version was introduced by British soldiers in 1759, and matches were recorded in Quebec in 1785. George A. Barber, the "father of Canadian cricket," helped to found the Toronto Cricket Club, and in 1829 introduced the sport at Upper Canada College. Matches between the Toronto club and the college began in 1836 and have continued intermittently ever since.

In 1838, teams made up of emigrants from Nottingham and Sheffield played a match in New York City for $100. Later that year, a Long Island team played a team from Manhattan, which included several of the Sheffield players. On St. George's Day, April 23, 1840, the St. George Cricket Club of New York was founded, and in August of that year the club played a match in Canada against the Toronto Cricket Club. When the Toronto club visited New York in 1844, about 5,000 spectators turned out and an estimated $50,000 was bet on the match. The New York Cricket Club was organized that year. All-star teams from Montreal and New York played matches against one another in 1845 and 1846, but a fight interrupted the 1846 match and the Canadian team refused to continue.

Textile workers from England introduced the sport to other northeastern cities during the 1840s, and it became very popular in Philadelphia. The "beef and ale" style of cricket played by the English immigrants was basically an excuse for masculine cameraderie, and a match was always followed by drinking. Philadelphians took a more genteel approach. The Young America Cricket Club, open only to native-born Americans, was formed in 1855, a symbol of dissociation from the English.

During the 1850s, cricket flourished in the New York and Philadelphia areas. In 1853, the Canadian-American all-star game resumed in New York and continued as an annual event, alternating between New York and Montreal, until the Civil War. Cricket got a big publicity boost in 1859, when the All-England Eleven played a New York all-star team at the Elysian Fields in Hoboken, NJ before an estimated 25,000 spectators. By 1860, there were 13 teams in Brooklyn and Manhattan and 6 in Philadelphia. However, the Civil War and the sudden growth in baseball's popularity slowed the growth of the sport in the 1860s.

Prime Minister John A. McDonald declared cricket the national sport when Canada became a nation in 1867, and Philadelphia cricket clubs built large clubhouses after the Civil War. An all-star team from Philadelphia won a trophy in competition against Canada and Great Britain at Halifax, Nova Scotia, in 1874. The trophy, called the Halifax Cup, became the chief prize for Philadelphia clubs.

Intercollegiate cricket began in 1875 when Haverford College played the University of Pennsylvania. Twelve years later, the Intercollegiate Cricket Association was founded. In 1890, there were at least 50 teams in the United States, and Baltimore, Boston, Chicago, Detroit, New York, Philadelphia, and Pittsburgh formed the Inter-City Cricket League.

However, baseball was taking over in popularity while cricket was becoming an amateur sport to be played by an elite few in private clubs. All sports suffered during World War I, but those that were to be major sports in the 20th century rebounded immediately afterward. Cricket was not one of them.

Although virtually unknown in the United States, cricket is still played by some enthusiasts in Canada, and a Canadian national team is occasionally assembled to play against teams from Australia, Great Britain, or New Zealand.

Address: Canadian Cricket Association, c/o Jack Kyle, 2041 West 63rd Avenue, Vancouver, BC, Canada V6P 2J2

Cromwell, Dean (1879–1962)
Track and Field

Born September 20, 1879, Turner, OR; died August 3, 1962; National Track and Field Hall of Fame

A 1902 graduate of Occidental College, Cromwell became track coach at the University of Southern California in 1909. His teams won 12 NCAA team championships, including 9 in a row, and from 1930 through 1948 the team lost only three dual meets. Known as the "Maker of Champions," Cromwell coached 33 NCAA and 38 AAU individual winners,

The St. George Club of New York lost to an All-Canada team at the Elysian Fields in Hoboken, NJ in 1844.

36 U.S. Olympic team members, and 10 Gold Medalists.

As co-coach with Lawson Robertson of the 1936 Olympic track and field team at Berlin, Cromwell was involved in controversy when two Jewish runners, Marty Glickman and Sam Stoller, were replaced on the 400-meter relay team by Jesse Owens and Foy Draper. The new relay team won the Gold Medal, but Cromwell and Robertson were accused of anti-Semitism and of giving in to pressure from Nazi officials. However, it's likely that Owens was added so that he would have a chance at a fourth Gold Medal, and Draper may well have been put on the team because he was one of Cromwell's college athletes. Cromwell also coached the Olympic track team in 1948.

Cronin, Joseph E. (1906–1984)
Baseball

Born October 12, 1906, San Francisco, CA; died September 7, 1984; Baseball Hall of Fame

Cronin played in just 50 games for the Pittsburgh Pirates in the National League in 1926 and 1927, and hit only .242 in 63 games with the Washington Senators in 1928. But he became the Senators' starting shortstop the following season, and was suddenly a star in 1930, when he batted .346, drove in 126 runs, and was named the American League's Most Valuable Player. Cronin drove in 126 runs again in 1931 and in 1932 he led the league in triples with 18. He became manager in 1933 and promptly led the Senators to the American League pennant, hitting .309 and leading the league with 45 doubles.

Cronin was the starting shortstop and manager for the American League All-Star team in 1934. But the Senators fell all the way to seventh place, and Cronin was sold to the Boston Red Sox for $250,000 after the season. He was player-manager with Boston from 1935 through 1945, then retired as a player but managed for two more seasons. The Red Sox won the pennant in 1946, losing to St. Louis in the World Series. He was the team's general manager from 1948 until 1959, when he became president of the American League. He retired in 1974.

Cronin had a record of 1,236 wins and 1,055 losses as a manager. In 20 seasons as a player, he hit .302 with 515 doubles, 117 triples, 171 home runs, and 1,423 runs batted in.

Croquet

A French doctor adapted croquet from a medieval game known as *paille-maille* (ball-mallet) in the 1830s. It soon became popular at spas in Southern France, where English visitors discovered it. In 1862,

a sporting goods dealer advertised croquet equipment in the *New York Clipper,* and the game became a craze after the Civil War. The *Nation* printed a complete set of rules in 1866, and in 1867 the *New York Chronicle* said, "never in the history of outdoor sports in this country had any game achieved so sudden a popularity with both sexes, but especially with the ladies, as Croquet has."

By the 1870s, many companies were manufacturing equipment, and each company had its own set of rules. The National Croquet Association was formed in 1879 to standardize rules, and in 1882 it held the first national tournament. American croquet had become very different from the English version of the sport. It was played on a hard dirt court surrounded by a boundary board, using short-handled mallets with rubber heads, hard rubber balls, and very narrow wickets. The rules were revised in 1899, and the first and last letters of the name were clipped off. The new American form of the sport was called "roque," and the American Roque League was organized in 1916.

Traditional lawn croquet declined for a time, but it became popular again during the 1920s, when it was played both by wealthy people on large permanent courts at private estates and by families on impromptu layouts in backyards. It waned during the Great Depression, then regained some popularity after World War II, and the National Croquet Association was reorganized in 1950 to codify rules and govern the sport. A new group, the U.S. Croquet Association, came into being in 1976, and has helped to spur the sport's recent growth. Originally, there were five clubs with about 100 members; there are now more than 300 clubs in the USCA, representing more than 3,500 members. Many resorts have built permanent croquet courts. Among them is Miami's Fisher Island development, where Gardnar Mulloy serves as croquet and tennis director. According to Mulloy, the rules are so complicated that "if you learn them, you're automatically ranked in the first ten in the world."

Addresses: American Roque League, P.O. Box 2304, Richmond, IN 47375 (317) 962-7191; U.S. Croquet Association, 500 Avenue of the Champions, Palm Beach Gardens, FL 33418 (407) 627-3999

Crosley Field
Cincinnati, OH

After the Cincinnati Reds' wooden park burned down in 1911, a new Redland Field was built of concrete and steel, and it was ready for opening day in 1912. Like many parks built at the time, it had a two-tiered grandstand behind home plate and along the base

In 1866, Harper's Weekly said that croquet was the greatest outdoor sport invented for women.

lines, with bleachers extending to the fences. Home run distances were 420 feet to center and 360 feet down each line. Powel Crosley bought the team in 1934 and renamed the park Crosley Field. To increase attendance during the Great Depression, the Reds installed lights, and the first night game in major-league history was played at Crosley Field on May 24, 1935. Upper decks were added over the foul-line bleachers, and home plate was moved in 1939, cutting the dimensions to 328 feet down the left-field line, 366 feet down the right-field line, and 387 feet to center. The park was replaced by Riverfront Stadium after the 1970 season.

Crosley Field was subsequently dismantled, and many of its pieces were sold as souvenirs.

Cross-Country

Students at British public schools during the middle of the 19th century enjoyed a game called "hare and hounds," in which one runner laid a trail by dropping pieces of paper or other markers and other runners followed the trail, trying to catch the hare. In 1878, William C. Vosburgh of New York introduced the sport to the United States. The Westchester Hare and Hounds Club held a well-publicized race on Thanksgiving Day of that year. The sport became something of a fad, but soon turned into cross-country racing over courses laid out in advance.

The National Cross-Country Association was formed in 1887 and held its first race that year. At the same time, cross-country running was introduced at Harvard as training for track and field athletes. In 1890, City College of New York, Cornell, and the University of Pennsylvania took part in the first intercollegiate meet, and Cornell led in the formation of the Intercollegiate Cross-Country Association in 1899. Although most top cross-country runners also run distance events in track and field, cross-country is a separate sport, held in the fall.

Distances for the event have varied considerably through the years. Major races are now standardized at 10 kilometers (6.2 miles) for men and 5 kilometers (3.1 miles) for women.

The Amateur Athletic Union held the first men's national championship race in 1890 and added the national women's championship in 1966. The Athletics Congress has conducted the championships since 1980, when it replaced the AAU as the national governing body for track and field.

World champions were inaugurated for men in 1903 and for women in 1967.

See also MARATHON; PEDESTRIANISM.

Crowley, "Sleepy Jim" James H. (1902–1986)
Football

Born September 10, 1902, Chicago, IL; died January 15, 1986; National Football Foundation Hall of Fame

Crowley was one of the Four Horsemen of Notre Dame, and he coached the Seven Blocks of Granite at Fordham in 1936 and 1937. He got his nickname from Notre Dame Coach Knute Rockne, who described him as "a sleepy-eyed lad who looked as though he were built to be a tester in an alarm clock factory." Crowley was Notre Dame's top passer in 1922 and 1923, and led the team in scoring in 1924, his senior year. In his career he averaged 6.3 yards per rushing attempt. He played with Green Bay and Providence in the National Football League in 1925.

Crowley coached Michigan State from 1929 through 1932 and Fordham from 1933 through 1941. His 1937 Fordham team won seven games and tied one without a loss and was ranked third in the country in the Associated Press poll. Under Crowley, Fordham went to two major bowl games, losing 13–12 to Texas A & M in the 1941 Cotton Bowl and beating Missouri 2–0 in the 1942 Sugar Bowl.

Cuban Giants
Baseball

Black waiters at the Argyle Hotel in Babylon, Long Island, in 1885 formed a baseball team called the Cuban Giants. They won an 1888 tournament involving the best four black teams in the East. The *Sporting News* correspondent who covered the tournament wrote, "This club . . . would play a favorable game against such clubs as the New Yorks or Chicagos," meaning the National League teams in those cities.

The Giants in 1889 joined the Middle States League, which had one other black team, the New York Gorhams, and six all-white teams. They moved to York, PA in 1890, when the MSL became the Eastern Interstate League, and late in the season the team was renamed the York Monarchs. After representing Ansonia in the Connecticut State League, the Giants went on tour in 1891. According to one source, they won 100 of 104 games that year. They were renamed the Genuine Cuban Giants in 1895, because there was another black team called the Cuban X Giants. The team broke up after the 1900 season.

Cummings, "Candy" William A. (1848–1924)
Baseball

Born October 17, 1848, Ware, MA; died May 17, 1924; Baseball Hall of Fame

Cummings is generally considered the inventor of the curveball. One story is that he threw a clamshell at the beach one day, saw that it curved, and decided he could do the same thing with a baseball. Fred Goldsmith, a Yale graduate who pitched in the National League from 1877 through 1884, claimed to have invented the curve, but baseball writer Henry Chadwick disputed that, saying he saw Cummings throwing curves in 1866, "long before Goldsmith was known in the baseball world."

Cummings joined the Brooklyn Excelsiors in 1866. In 1868, with the Brooklyn Stars, he was the winning pitcher over the New York Mutuals in a game that was billed as the "battle of champions." He also beat the Mutuals 14–3 in 1871, when giving up only three runs in a game was as good as a shutout is today. He played for the Mutuals in 1872, winning 34 games and losing 19, and he was 29–14 with the Lord Baltimores in 1873, 28–26 with the Philadelphia Athletics in 1874, and 34–11 with Hartford in 1875. Hartford joined the National League in its first season, 1876, when Cummings became the first pitcher ever to win two complete games in one day. His final major-league season was in 1877, when he pitched briefly for Cincinnati while serving as president of the first minor league, the International Association.

Cunningham, Glenn (1909–1988)
Track and Field

Born August 4, 1909, Atlanta, KS; died March 10, 1988; National Track and Field Hall of Fame

Voted the outstanding athlete in the history of Madison Square Garden in 1979, Cunningham was one of America's first great milers. His legs were badly burned in a household accident when he was seven years old. Doctors said he would never walk again and recommended amputation, but his parents refused. Cunningham not only walked again, he began running as therapy. At the University of Kansas, he was the NCAA 1,500-meter champion in 1932 and the mile champion in 1933. He also won the AAU outdoor 800- and 1,500-meter runs in 1933, when he won the Sullivan Award as the nation's outstanding amateur athlete.

Running in the 1934 Princeton Invitational meet, Cunningham set a world record of 4 minutes 6.7 seconds in the mile. Cunningham was the AAU outdoor 1,500-meter champion four consecutive years, 1935–38, and he won the indoor 1,500-meter in 1934, 1935, 1938, and 1939.

Cup of the Americas
Polo

This trophy for polo competition between the United States and Argentina was offered in 1928, when the U.S. won two out of three matches. Argentina won two straight matches in 1932, and the U.S. regained the cup by winning two of three matches in Buenos Aires in 1936. The 1940 competition was canceled because of World War II, and the two countries played for the cup just one more time, in 1950, with Argentina winning two straight matches.

Curling

Curling, a team sport in which players slide 42½-pound stones along the ice at a target, was played in Scotland as early as the 16th century, and Scottish immigrants brought the sport to Canada in the late 18th century. The Montreal Curling Club, founded in 1807, held its first formal match April 11 on the St. Lawrence River. In 1835, Montreal and Quebec City played the first interclub match at Three Rivers. A French-Canadian farmer who saw the sport near Quebec about this time wrote, "Today I saw a band of Scotchmen who were throwing large balls of iron like tea-kettles on the ice, after which they cried, 'Soop! Soop!' and then laughed like fools. I really believe they *are* fools."

The sport was established in the United States by 1820, when the Orchard Lakes club was formed in Pontiac, MI, and other clubs sprang up in northern New York and the upper Great Lakes states before the Civil War. On February 10, 1866, the United States and Canada played the first international match. Sir William Elliott in 1870 challenged any Scottish rink to play a match with Canada for a prize of 500 pounds sterling. That offer was denounced by a delegate to the sport's Grand National Convention in 1871; he said that playing for money "would drag curling down to the level of baseball."

Competition between Canada and the United States resumed in 1884, when Robert Gordon of New York donated the Gordon International Medal as a trophy. There was no competition from 1885 through 1887, but it resumed in 1888 and has been held annually ever since, except for breaks during the two world wars. By 1900, curling had become very popular throughout Canada and the northern United States. A Scottish team visited Canada in January of 1903 and in the winter of 1908–09 a Canadian team won 23 of 26 matches in Scotland to claim the Strathcoma Cup, which had been established for the competition. Canada retained the cup in 1911–12 against visiting Scottish rinks, but in 1920–21 Scotland won the cup back.

In 1927, the W. C. Macdonald Company of Montreal donated the Macdonald Briar Tankard for the Canadian championship. The first national governing body for the sport was the U.S. Women's Curling Association, organized in 1947 with just five clubs and about 130 members. The USWCA held its first

Brought to Canada by Scottish immigrants in the early 18th century, curling has spread across the northern United States. This is action from a tournament in Milwaukee, WI. Courtesy of Mrs. C.F. Pollen

national tournament in 1949. The U.S. didn't have national championships for men until 1958, when the U.S. Curling Association was founded in Chicago.

Curling was a demonstration sport at the 1932 Winter Olympics in Lake Placid, NY, but there was no international governing body until April 1, 1966, when the International Curling Federation was founded in Vancouver, and the Air Canada Silver Broom Trophy was established for the world championship. In 1988, curling became a Winter Olympic sport.

Addresses: Curl Canada, 333 River Road, Vanier, Ontario, Canada K1L 8H9 (613) 748-5628; U.S. Curling Association, 1100 Center Point Drive, Box 971, Stevens Point, WI 54481 (715) 344-1199; U.S. Women's Curling Association, 4114 North 53rd Street, Omaha, NE 68104 (402) 453-6574

Curtis, Ann (1926–   )
Swimming
Born 1926; International Swimming Hall of Fame

Curtis won two Gold Medals in the 1948 Olympics, swimming the 400-meter freestyle in a record 5 minutes 17.8 seconds, and anchoring the U.S. 400-meter relay team to another record, 4:29.2. She was the national outdoor champion in the 100-meter event in 1944, 1945, 1947, and 1948, in the 400-meter and 800-meter freestyle six years in a row, 1943–1948, and in the 1,500-meter in 1944 and 1946. She also won 12 national indoor championships, in the 100-yard freestyle in 1945 and 1947, and in both the 220-yard and the 440-yard freestyle from 1944 through 1948.

Curtis Cup
Golf

The first Curtis Cup matches were held in 1932 between six-woman teams of amateur golfers from the United States and the British Isles, and competition has been held every two years since, except for 1940–46. Teams play three 18-hole foursomes the first day and six 18-hole singles matches the second. The trophy was donated by Harriot and Margaret Curtis, both former U.S. Women's Amateur champions.

Cy Young Award
Baseball

Named for the pitcher who holds the all-time records for most career victories and shutouts, the award was established in 1956 by the Baseball Writers Association of America. It was given to the major-league pitcher of the year until 1967, when separate awards was established for each league.

Cy Young Award Winners

1956	Don Newcombe, Brooklyn Dodgers
1957	Warren Spahn, Milwaukee Braves
1958	Bob Turley, New York Yankees
1959	Early Wynn, Chicago White Sox
1960	Vernon Law, Pittsburgh Pirates
1961	Whitey Ford, New York Yankees
1962	Don Drysdale, Los Angeles Dodgers
1963	Sandy Koufax, Los Angeles Dodgers
1964	Dean Chance, Los Angeles Angels
1965	Sandy Koufax, Los Angeles Dodgers
1966	Sandy Koufax, Los Angeles Dodgers

American League

1967	Jim Lonborg, Boston Red Sox
1968	Denny McLain, Detroit Tigers
1969	Mike Cuellar, Baltimore Orioles
	Denny McLain, Detroit Tigers (tie)
1970	Jim Perry, Minnesota Twins
1971	Vida Blue, Oakland Athletics
1972	Gaylord Perry, Cleveland Indians
1973	Jim Palmer, Baltimore Orioles
1974	Jim "Catfish" Hunter, Oakland Athletics
1975	Jim Palmer, Baltimore Orioles
1976	Jim Palmer, Baltimore Orioles
1977	Sparky Lyle, New York Yankees
1978	Ron Guidry, New York Yankees
1979	Mike Flanagan, Baltimore Orioles
1980	Steve Stone, Baltimore Orioles
1981	Rollie Fingers, Milwaukee Brewers
1982	Pete Vukovich, Milwaukee Brewers
1983	LaMarr Hoyt, Chicago White Sox
1984	Willie Hernandez, Detroit Tigers
1985	Bret Saberhagen, Kansas City Royals
1986	Roger Clemens, Boston Red Sox
1987	Roger Clemens, Boston Red Sox
1988	Frank Viola, Minnesota Twins
1989	Bret Saberhagen, Kansas City Royals
1990	Bob Welch, Oakland Athletics

National League

1967	Mike McCormick, San Francisco Giants
1968	Bob Gibson, St. Louis Cardinals
1969	Tom Seaver, New York Mets
1970	Bob Gibson, St. Louis Cardinals
1971	Ferguson Jenkins, Chicago Cubs
1972	Steve Carlton, Philadelphia Phillies
1973	Tom Seaver, New York Mets
1974	Mike Marshall, Los Angeles Dodgers
1975	Tom Seaver, New York Mets
1976	Randy Jones, San Diego Padres
1977	Steve Carlton, Philadelphia Phillies
1978	Gaylord Perry, San Diego Padres
1979	Bruce Sutter, Chicago Cubs
1980	Steve Carlton, Philadelphia Phillies
1981	Fernando Valenzuela, Los Angeles Dodgers
1982	Steve Carlton, Philadelphia Phillies
1983	John Denny, Philadelphia Phillies
1984	Rick Sutcliffe, Chicago Cubs
1985	Dwight Gooden, New York Mets
1986	Mike Scott, Houston Astros
1987	Steve Bedrosian, Philadelphia Phillies
1988	Orel Hershiser, Los Angeles Dodgers
1989	Mark Davis, San Diego Padres
1990	Doug Drabek, Pittsburgh Pirates

Cycling

The first pedal-driven bicycle was built in 1861 by Pierre Michaux, owner of a blacksmith shop and builder of coaches. A Michaux mechanic, Pierre Lamellent, came to New Haven, CT in 1866 to manufacture the new vehicle, but it didn't catch on until it was modified by the Hanlon Brothers, acrobats who used it in their act. They popularized it in 1869. It became a craze that summer, but only briefly, because the vehicle was uncomfortable and unsafe.

During the next decade, the design was improved in several ways. James Stanley of the Coventry Sewing Machine Company in England in 1871 invented a gear that permitted the drive wheel to make two revolutions for every turn of the pedal. His bicycle had spoked wheels, and the front wheel was huge, while the rear wheel was small. This became known as the "ordinary" or "penny-farthing." It was displayed at the 1876 Centennial Exhibition in Philadelphia, and Albert A. Pope in 1877 founded a company in Hartford, CT to import bicycles. The following year, he began manufacturing them, and he helped organize the Boston Bicycle Club. In 1880, a group of clubs met at Newport, RI and formed the League of American Wheelmen.

Racing began in the 1870s, when many clubs held "centuries," 100-mile races. Manufacturers hired top racers, called "scorchers," to advertise their bicycles, and the LAW conducted many races. After the LAW banned scorchers from its races because they were professionals, scorchers organized the American Cyclists Union in 1886 to promote their own races.

The bicycle didn't become truly popular until the Rover was introduced in 1885. This was a "safety bike" with equal-sized wheels and a simple chain drive. When the pneumatic tire replaced the hard rubber tire in 1890, the safety bike had replaced the penny-farthing, and bicycling became a national fad. By 1896, there were more than 250 companies manufacturing bikes, and more than 1 million were in use. Racing on closed tracks began to replace road racing as a sport.

Six-day racing, imported from England in 1889, become very popular at Madison Square Garden beginning in 1895. New York City in 1898 passed an ordinance limiting riders to 12 hours a day, and two-man teams began competing. The Garden was filled with spectators every night, and promoters throughout the country went to two-man, six-day races. Shorter track races also thrived. The International Cyclists Association, formed in 1893, held its first world championships in Chicago that August.

LAW officials opposed racing on Sunday, when the largest crowds turned out, so racers and promoters formed the National Cycling Association in 1898 to govern professional racing. The LAW got out of racing entirely in 1900, and the cycling craze ended about the same time. Several tracks went out of business, prize money dwindled at those that were still operating, and many top American cyclists began racing in Europe.

A former racer, John M. Chapman, in 1908 conceived the idea of a franchised racing circuit to include Boston, Newark, New Haven, Philadelphia, and Providence. He persuaded the owner of the Newark Velodrome to put up the money, and he also persuaded some top cyclists from Europe and Australia to race on the circuit. It was an immediate success, and bicycle racers became the highest-paid athletes in the country. The American world champion, Frank Kramer, made $20,000 in 1911, compared to $10,000 for baseball star Ty Cobb. But when Floyd MacFarland, another former cyclist, took charge of the Newark Velodrome and the circuit in 1914, the pay went even higher. MacFarland paid appearance fees to top riders, in addition to race prizes. He was killed in a fight with a Newark concessionaire in April of 1915, and Chapman replaced him.

Chapman and Tex Rickard of Madison Square Garden began to promote two six-day races a year in the Garden in 1920, and Chapman also took over the New York Velodrome, which opened in 1921 with seating for 20,000 spectators. In addition to his eastern track circuit, Chapman operated an international circuit of six-day races in Buffalo, Chicago, Cleveland, Detroit, Indianapolis, Kansas City, Montreal, Philadelphia, Pittsburgh, St. Louis, and Toronto. He paid the top racer, Alf Goullet, $1,000 a day in appearance money for the New York and Chicago races. Bicycle racing was a big part of the "Golden Age of Sports," and one of the most golden. When Frank Kramer rode his last race, on July 26, 1922, it was front-page news. Kramer had earned about $500,000 in 22 years as a professional. Rickard opened his new Madison Square Garden in November of 1925 with a six-day race that drew 15,475 spectators the first night, and he gave a $10,000 retirement gift to Goullet after the race.

Then came the Great Depression. Attendance had already begun dropping at Newark in 1929, and the decline continued in 1930. A new velodrome opened at Coney Island on July 19, but just two weeks later the New York Velodrome burned down, and the Newark track went out of business in December. By the end of 1931, the only major velodrome left was Coney Island. Six-day racing continued at Madison Square Garden until December of 1939, when a final, five-day race was held. Professional racing in North America was extinct.

There was still amateur racing, though it was virtually invisible. The Amateur Bicycle League of America, formed in 1920, wasn't allowed to use the professional tracks, so its races were held on roads in out-of-the-way areas, usually early in the morning to avoid auto traffic. The ABL held the first national road championship in 1921, and a women's road race was added in 1937.

After World War II, many American racers went to Europe. Ted Smith was the first American to compete for the world professional road championship, in 1950, and Jack Heid raced in the professional track championships that year. Nancy Neiman Baranet of the U.S. began racing in Europe in 1955, and the following year she became the first American cyclist, male or female, to compete in a European stage race, finishing 14th out of 40 finishers in the eight-day Women's Criterium from Lyonnaise to Auvergne.

Racing expanded greatly during the 1960s. In 1965, the ABL added pursuit and 10-mile races for men to

Many cycling sprint records were set on the ⅛–mile track at the old Salt Palace velodrome in Salt Lake City. Races were staged at the velodrome from 1899 until 1914. Courtesy of the Utah State Historical Society

After a long decline, U.S. cycling gained dramatically in popularity during the 1980s, largely because of an infusion of money into the U.S. Cycling Federation. This is the start of a national championship road race. Courtesy of Robert F. George/Cyclenews

the national championship program; sprint and pursuit races for women were added the following year. With more opportunities to compete and more reason to train extensively, U.S. cyclists improved. In 1968, Audrey McElmury became the first American to win the world road racing championship. Bicycle sales increased from 3.7 million in 1960 to 8.5 million in 1971, and ABL membership grew from 3,000 in 1968 to 8,600 in 1973. Two American women were among the top cyclists in the world during the early 1970s. Sheila Young won the world match sprint championship in 1973, but lost to Sue Novara in the U.S. championships in 1974. Novara was the 1975 world sprint champion and in 1976 Young and Novara finished first and second in the event.

The ABL changed its name to the U.S. Cycling Federation in 1976. Corporate sponsorship and development money from the U.S. Olympic Committee increased its budget to $235,000, up from $38,500 in 1973. Eddie Borysewicz was hired in 1977 as the first full-time national coach to work with cyclists at the Olympic Training Center in Squaw Valley, CA. He helped produce two top racers, Greg LeMond and George Mount, both of whom went to Europe to race as professionals after the U.S. boycott of the 1980 Olympic Games. LeMond won the 1983 world championship road race, and in 1986 he became the first American to win the Tour de France, the best-known famous race. He won it again in 1989 and 1990.

Women's cycling events were on the Olympic program for the first time in 1984. Connie Carpenter and Rebecca Twigg of the U.S. won the Gold and Silver Medals in the road race. The same day, Alexi Grewal of the United States edged Steve Bauer of Canada for the Gold Medal in the men's road race. Later, Steve Hegg of the U.S. won the 4,000-meter individual pursuit race, and teammate Mark Gorski won the sprint.

Those medals gave cycling even more impetus. USCF membership reached more than 30,000 licensed riders and 1,091 clubs in 1988, when there were more than 1,600 sanctioned races in the country, many of them with major corporate sponsorship. In addition, several large companies sponsored cycling teams, including Campbell Soup, Alfa-Romeo, Lowry's Seasonings, Plymouth, 7–Eleven stores, Coors, and Weight Watchers. There were more than 20 hours of bicycle racing on television, up from just one hour in 1983. And American races were

attracting European cyclists. Greg LeMond, after visiting President Reagan to be congratulated on his Tour de France victory, told a reporter, "I think my future in cycling is in America."

Further Reading: Nye, Peter. *Hearts of Lions: The History of American Bicycle Racing.* New York: W. W. Norton, 1988.

See also LEAGUE OF AMERICAN WHEELMEN; SIX-DAY RACES.

Cyclo-Cross

Cyclo-cross is bicycle racing over trails in difficult terrain. Racers usually have to carry their bikes across a body of water at least once during the race. The sport reached some degree of popularity in the late 1960s and early 1970s, but has since declined.

Cyr, Louis (1863–1912)
Weight Lifting
Born October 11, 1863, St. Cyprien de Napierville, Quebec; died November 10, 1912

A professional strongman who did much to popularize weight lifting, Cyr was matched against David Michaud in a stone-lifting contest in 1881. Michaud called himself the strongest man in Canada, but Cyr won the match by lifting a 480-pound granite boulder. As a Montreal policeman, he achieved some fame when he disarmed two thugs who were having a knife fight and carried them, one under each arm, to the police station. Richard Kyle Fox, publisher of the *National Police Gazette*, then became Cyr's promoter, billing him as the "Strongest Man in the World" and offering $5,000 to anyone who could match one of his feats. No one ever did.

Cyr, who stood 5 feet 8½ inches and weighed 270 pounds, specialized in lifting a dumbbell that could be loaded with shot to adjust its weight. In 1892, he set a record of 273¼ pounds for that lift, with both hands, and four years later he set records of 258 pounds with the right hand and 254 pounds with the left hand. One of his most spectacular stage performances was lifting a platform carrying 18 men onto his back. The total weight was said to have been 4,300 pounds. He also lifted a 445-pound barrel of sand and water to his shoulder, using one hand and his right knee. And in 1896, using just the middle finger of his right hand, he picked up a weight of 552½ pounds.

D

Dallas, TX

Baseball See TEXAS RANGERS.

Basketball The Dallas Chapparals joined the American Basketball Association when it was organized in 1967. They moved to San Antonio and became the Spurs after the 1972–73 season. A second Dallas team, the Mavericks, entered the National Basketball Association as an expansion franchise in 1980.

Football Dallas briefly had a team in the National Football League in 1952. The Texans were created when the NFL bought the assets of the New York Yanks and gave the players to a new Dallas franchise. However, attendance in Dallas was very poor, and the team finished its one season by playing all of its games on the road. In 1953, Carroll Rosenbloom gave the franchise a new home in Baltimore, as the Colts.

One of the founders of the American Football League in 1960 was Lamar Hunt, who established the Dallas Texans. To counter that, the NFL placed the Cowboys in Dallas. Although the Texans won the 1962 AFL championship, they moved to Kansas City and became the Chiefs the following season.

The Cowboys soon became one of the most successful franchises in the NFL, winning the eastern division championship in 1966 and 1967 and the National Football Conference championship in 1970, 1976, and 1979. They won the 1971 NFL championship by beating the Miami Dolphins 24-3 in Super Bowl VI.

See also REUNION ARENA; TEXAS STADIUM.

Daly, Charles D. (1897–1959)
Football
Born October 31, 1880, Roxbury, MA; died February 12, 1959; National Football Foundation Hall of Fame

A dangerous runner and excellent kicker, Daly is the only person ever to play for a Harvard team that beat Yale and an Army team that beat Navy. He became Harvard's starting quarterback as a sophomore in the 1898 season. The team won 32 consecutive games, losing to Yale in 1900 when Daly was sidelined by a knee injury. He was an All-American in 1899 and 1900 at Harvard and in 1901 at Army. In an 11–5 win over Navy, he scored all of Army's points with a 98-yard kickoff return, the conversion, and a 35-yard field goal. He also averaged more than 40 yards punting. Because of public criticism for playing at Army after having graduated from Harvard, he sat out most of the 1902 season, but returned for the Navy game and Army won again, 22–8.

Daly became Army's head coach in 1913. In four years, he produced two undefeated teams, in 1914 and 1916, and beat Navy all four years. After serving as an officer in World War I, he coached Army four more years, 1919–22, and had an unbeaten team in his final season.

Dancer, Stanley R. (1927–)
Harness Racing
Born July 25, 1927, Edinburg, NJ; Hall of Fame of the Trotter

Dancer was the first harness driver to win more than $1 million in a season in 1964, he was also the leading money-winner among drivers in 1961, 1962, and 1966. He trained and drove seven Horses of the Year: Su Mac Lad in 1962; Nevele Pride in 1967, 1968, and 1969; Albatross in 1971 and 1972; and Keystone Ore in 1976. In his career, Dancer won 3,720 dashes and $26,684,756 in purses.

Dan Patch
Harness Racing

He was more famous than most human athletes of his era. Cigars, chewing tobacco, a sled, a hobby horse, a wagon, a washing machine, and even a dance, the Dan Patch two-step, were named after him. He traveled in his own railroad car with his picture on the side, and thouands of people came to see him whenever the train stopped.

Foaled in 1896, Dan Patch tied the pacing world record of 1 minute 59¼ seconds in 1902. By the end of that year, he had paced 56 heats, winning 54 of them without losing a race. He was then purchased for $60,000 by Marion W. Savage, who raced him all over the country, often in exhibitions or time trials. In 1903, Dan Patch set a world record of 1:56 ¼, and he lowered it to 1:56 the following year at Memphis. Dan Patch also set track records at Allentown, PA and at the Minnesota State fair, where 60,000 people cheered him on. He then lowered the world record again, to 1:55 ¼, in a time trial at Lexington. Dan Patch retired undefeated in 1909, but still made occasional appearances, his last on Thanksgiving Day, 1913, at New Orleans. It has been estimated that he earned more than $3 million from stud fees and appearances. He died on July 11, 1916, and Savage died the next day.

Darlington International Raceway
Darlington, SC

The first superspeedway, Darlington opened on Labor Day, 1950, with the running of NASCAR's Southern 500. The 1.366-mile track hosts two NASCAR Winston Cup races annually, and is also the home of the National Motorsports Press Association Stock Car Hall of Fame and Joe Weatherly Museum.

Address: P.O. Box 500, Darlington, SC 29532-0500 (803) 393-4041

Darts

Imported from English pubs, darts began to catch on in North America in the early 1970s, and the American Darts Organization was founded in 1975 to govern the sport. It now has more than 300 affiliated local chapters representing about 100,000 darters in the U.S., Puerto Rico, and Guam. The ADO runs a circuit of sanctioned tournaments with more than $1 million in prize money, conducts annual nationwide playoffs to select teams for international competition, and chooses a national team for the biennial World Cup competition. In 1979, the organization hosted the World Cup, the first major international darts competition held outside of England, and in 1982 it held the first annual All-Star Playoffs for women.

Address: American Darts Organization, 13841 Eastbrook Avenue, Bellflower, CA 90706 (213) 925-1205

Davies, "Bob" Robert E. (1920–1990)
Basketball
Born January 15, 1920, Harrisburg, PA; died April 22, 1990; Basketball Hall of Fame 1969

The "Harrisburg Houdini" invented the behind-the-back dribble and was also an excellent passer, the National Basketball Association's leader in assists six consecutive seasons. Davies led Seton Hall to 43 consecutive victories from 1939 into 1941 and was an All-American in 1941 and 1942. He played for the Great Lakes Naval Training Station team that won the 1943 armed services championship.

In 1945 he joined the Rochester Royals of the Basketball Association of America (now the National Basketball Association) and played there for ten seasons. He was an All-Pro four straight years, 1949–52, and played for championship teams in 1946, 1947, and 1951. During the 1946–47 season, he also coached Seton Hall to a 24–3 record. In 569 profes-

sional games, Davies scored 7,770 points, an average of 13.7 per game, and had 2,250 assists. He scored 904 points, a 13.5 average, and had 182 assists in 67 playoff games. Davies was named to the NBA's Silver Anniversary team.

Davis, Alice Coachman
See COACHMAN, ALICE.

Davis Cup
Tennis
Formally the International Lawn Tennis Challenge Cup, the trophy was donated in 1900 by Dwight F. Davis. The defending champion simply waited for a tournament to determine the challenger until 1972, but since then a full-scale tournament, including the champion country, has determined the cup winner.
See also TENNIS.

Davis, Ernest (1939–1963)
Football
The first black to win the Heisman Trophy, Davis was an All-American halfback at Syracuse three years in a row, 1959–61. The 6-foot-2, 210-pound Davis broke Jimmy Brown's school records for total yards gained, touchdowns, and points. He was the first player chosen in the National Football League draft by the Washington Redskins. They traded him to the Cleveland Browns, but Davis contracted leukemia in the summer of 1962 and died without ever playing professional football.

Davis, Glenn W. (1925–   )
Football
Born December 25, 1925, Claremont, CA; National Football Foundation Hall of Fame

"Mr. Outside" of Army's famous "Touchdown Twins" (Doc Blanchard was "Mr. Inside"), Davis was an exceptional all-around athlete who won 13 letters in four sports in high school. He became Navy's nemesis in 1944, when he intercepted a pass to stop a scoring threat, then ran 52 yards for a touchdown to ensure a 23–7 win. The following year, he scored on runs of 49 and 33 yards in a 32–13 victory. In 1946 Davis caught a 30-yard pass, scored on a 14-yard run, and threw a 27-yard touchdown pass to Blanchard as Army won for the third time in a row, 21–18. In three baseball victories over Navy, Davis had five hits in ten at-bats, stole five bases, and scored five runs. Immediately after the 1947 game, he changed into his track uniform and won the 100- and 220-yard dashes in a dual meet against Navy.

His finest football performance came in 1946 against Michigan, when he completed seven out of eight passes for 160 yards, scored on a 59-yard touchdown run, threw a 41-yard touchdown pass to Blanchard, and caught a 31-yard touchdown pass as Army won 20–13. Davis accounted for 265 yards in total offense that day. He was named an All-American for the third time and won the Heisman Trophy. After graduating from West Point, Davis served in the Army until 1950, then joined the Los Angeles Rams of the National Football League. In the NFL championship game against the Cleveland Browns, he scored on an 82-yard pass play from Bob Waterfield. Davis played little because of a knee injury in 1951, and retired after that season.

Dayton, OH

Football The Dayton Triangles were one of the founding teams of the American Professional Football Association when it was organized in 1920. They played through the 1929 season, after the APFA had become the National Football League.

Daytona Beach, FL
Auto Racing

A 10-mile racing strip at Daytona Beach was used for attempts at the world land speed record from 1903 to 1935. Alexander Winton set the first record of 68.198 miles per hour in 1903. The last record set at Daytona Beach was 276.082 miles per hour by Sir Malcolm Campbell of England on March 7, 1935. The quest for land speed records then shifted to the Bonneville Salt Flats in Utah. The Daytona Beach course was used for stock car racing in the late 1930s, and from 1949 through 1958 the National Association for Stock Car Auto Racing held an annual race on a 4.1-mile beach and road course.

Daytona International Speedway
Daytona Beach, FL

This 2.5-mile superspeedway opened in 1959. It hosts the Daytona 500, the world's richest stock car race with total prize money of about $1.5 million. The track has permanent seating for about 90,000 spectators. The Firecracker 500, another NASCAR Winston Cup race, is also run at Daytona.

Address: P.O. Drawer S, Daytona Beach, FL 32015 (904) 253-6711

D. C. Stadium

See ROBERT F. KENNEDY MEMORIAL STADIUM.

Dean, "Dizzy" Jay H. (1911–1974)
Baseball

Born January 16, 1911, Lucas, AR; died July 17, 1974; Baseball Hall of Fame

Dean was a great pitcher and a colorful player who proved to be just as colorful a broadcaster. A right-hander, he joined the St. Louis Cardinals in 1930 and became a full-time starter in 1932, when he won 18 games and lost 15, leading the National League in strikeouts with 191. He was the strikeout leader again in 1933 with 199, and he won 20 games that year, losing 18. On July 18, he set a major-league record by striking out 17 Chicago Cubs. (The record is now 20.)

Dean was named the National League's Most Valuable Player in 1934, when he won 30 games and lost only 7, with 7 shutouts and an earned run average of 2.66. For the third year in a row, he led the league in strikeouts. His brother Paul was a rookie pitcher with the Cardinals that season. On September 21, Dizzy pitched a three-hit shutout in the first game of a doubleheader against the Brooklyn Dodgers, and Paul pitched a no-hitter in the second game. Dizzy remarked afterward, "If I'd known Paul was gonna do that, I'd have pitched one, too." The Cardinals won the pennant in the last series of the year, when Dizzy beat the Cincinnati Reds 4–0 on Friday, Paul beat them 6–1 on Saturday, and Dizzy won 9–0 on Sunday.

Asked for a World Series prediction, Dean brashly responded, "Me and Paul will win two games each." He was right. Dizzy beat the Detroit Tigers 8–3 in the first game and Paul won the third 4–1. After Dizzy lost the fifth game, Paul won 4–3 the next day and Dizzy came back to beat the Tigers 11–0 in the final game.

Dean won 28 and lost 12 in 1935, when he led the league in complete games for the third straight year and in strikeouts for the fourth year in a row. He had his last good season in 1936. He won 23, lost 13, had an earned run average of 3.17, and led the league in complete games and innings pitched. The beginning of the end came in the 1937 all-star game, when Earl Averill hit a line drive that broke the big toe on Dean's right foot. He insisted on pitching with the toe in a splint, but that altered his delivery and he developed arm trouble.

Dean was traded to the Cubs in 1938, but saw only part-time duty, compiling a 7–1 record and a 1.80 earned run average. During the next three seasons, he won just 9 games while losing 7, and he retired in 1941. However, Bill Veeck of the St. Louis Browns signed Dean for one game in 1947 as a promotional stunt, and he pitched four scoreless innings.

After retiring from the Cubs, Dean broadcast the Cardinals' and Browns' games and quickly became a fan favorite because of his ungrammatical speech and his sense of humor. "He slud into second," a

Deanism, became a baseball catch phrase. On one occasion, when a fielder made a lazy play, Dean commented, "Look at him nonchalant that ball." During the 1950s, he did the nationally televised game of the week. He retired from broadcasting in the 1960s.

Decathlon

The decathlon originated as a modern Olympic sport in 1912, patterned after a similar event in the ancient Olympics. It consists of ten track and field events during two days of competition. The first-day events are the 100-meter dash, long jump, shot put, high jump, and 400-meter run. On the second day, athletes compete in the 110-meter hurdles, discus throw, pole vault, javelin throw, and 1,500-meter run. Scoring tables awarding from 1 to 1,200 points in each event are used. Jim Thorpe of the United States won the first Olympic decathlon with a score of 6,756, a record for 15 years. Akilles Jarvinen of Finland was the first to score more than 7,000 points, in 1930, and Rafer Johnson of the United States went over 8,000 points in 1960.

Address: DECA, c/o Dr. Frank Zarnowski, Mount St. Mary's College, Emmitsburg, MD 21727 (301) 447-6122

Decatur, IL

Football George Halas was hired in 1919 by the Staley Starch Company in Decatur, and he assembled a company football team, the Decatur Staleys. The team entered the American Professional Football Association in 1920. In 1921, Halas moved the Staleys to Chicago.

Decker, Mary (Mrs. Slaney) (1958–   )
Track and Field
Born August 4, 1958, Flemington, NJ; National Track and Field Hall of Fame

Though her career has been dogged by injury and controversy, Decker holds American records at eight different distances ranging from 800 to 10,000 meters. She began running in 1969, when she entered a cross-country race for grade-school pupils and won by a big margin. "After that," she said later, "all I wanted to do was run." In 1971, at the age of 13, she ran the mile in 4 minutes and 55 seconds and the 800 meters in 2:12.7. Three years later she set world records of 2:26.7 in the 1,000-yard run, 2:02.4 in the 880-yard run, and 2:01.8 in the 800 meters.

Then her problems began. From late 1974 to 1976, she suffered an ankle injury, shin splints, and stress fractures in her lower legs. Decker had grown 6 inches and gained 25 pounds in little more than a year, which created another problem known as compartment syndrome, a condition in which the calf muscles grow too large for their sheaths. An operation in 1977 cured that, and the following February she broke her record for the 1,000 yards, running it in 2:23.8.

Tendinitis limited her to six races in 1979, but she came back strong in 1980, setting world records in the mile (4:21.7), the indoor 1,500 meters (4:08), and the 880-yard run (1:59.7). After a ten-week layoff because of a sprained tendon, she set an Olympic trials record of 4:04.91 in the 1,500 meters, and she established new American records of 4:01.17 in the 1,500 and 8:38.73 in the 3,000-meter run, the first time she ever attempted that distance. But she tore an Achilles tendon in August and underwent two operations.

It was 1982 before she returned to form. Decker set world records in the indoor mile, 2,000 meters, and 3,000 meters early in the year. After another bout with tendinitis, she set a world record of 15:08.26 in the 5,000-meter run in June and she won the national outdoor 1,500 meters in 4:03.37, more than 3 seconds better than the previous record. In Europe that summer, she won all five races she entered, with a world record in the mile, 4:18.08, and an American record for 3,000 meters, 8:29.71. Back in the United States, Decker tried the 10,000 meters for the first time, running an incredible 31:35:23 to shatter the previous American record by 42 seconds. She won the Sullivan Award as the outstanding amateur athlete of the year.

At the first world championships in 1983, she won both the 1,500 meters and the 3,000. Having missed the 1976 Olympics because of her physical problems and the 1980 Olympics because of the U.S. boycott, she was now looking forward to 1984. She qualified for the 1,500- and 3,000-meter runs, but decided to concentrate on the 3,000. Decker led early in the race, but Zola Budd, a transplanted South African running for Great Britain, passed her at the 1,600-meter mark. About 1,000 meters later, Decker bumped Budd's left leg, throwing her off stride. Decker then tripped over the leg and fell onto the infield, suffering a hip injury.

She rebounded again in 1985, setting world records of 5:34.2 in the indoor 2,000 meters and 4:16.7 in the outdoor mile. She did some running while pregnant in 1986, and said she expected to be even stronger after the baby was born. But 1987 was a poor year for her, and in 1988 she ran a disappointing tenth in the Olympic 3,000-meter run. Her career seemed to be over, but with her previous record of coming back from adversity, no one is quite ready to write her off.

Mary Decker, center, drives for the lead in the 800–meter run during the 1976 U.S.-U.S.S.R. meet. Running beside her are Robin Campbell (number 154) and Valentina Gerasimova (number 57). Courtesy of W.J. Wallace/Duke University

Deerfoot (Lewis Bennett) (1830?–1895)
Distance Running
Born 1830?, Cattaraugus Reservation, NY; died in 1895

One of a number of Seneca Indians from upstate New York who were leading runners during the 19th century, Lewis Bennett became famous in England as "Deerfoot." He was first mentioned in 1856, when he won a 5-mile race at Fredonia, NY in 25 minutes, an outstanding time for the period. During most of his running career here, however, he was overshadowed by Albert Smith, John Steeprock, and other fellow Senecas. But he did beat Smith and two other runners in a 15-mile race at Boston in May of 1858 and he won a 5-mile race at North Bridgewater, MA a week later.

A series of races in 1861, in which he competed against three English runners, brought him to the attention of George Martin, a British promoter. Martin took him to England, renamed him Deerfoot (he was also sometimes known as "Red Jacket") and launched a publicity campaign that excited English newspapers and the public. In publicity appearances, Deerfoot wore a wolfskin blanket, a headband, and eagle feather. He never said a word in public, because Martin had told the press that Deerfoot couldn't speak English. The London *Sporting News* breathlessly reported that before his first race ". . . his appearance caused a great rush to obtain a peek at him, as he stalked in stately manner, with his wolf skin wrapped around him, looking the very model of one of Fenimore Cooper's Mohicans or Pawnees."

Deerfoot lost that race, but the crowd of 4,000 cheered him anyway. He raced virtually every week to the end of the year, winning most of the time. But early in 1862 some English newspapers charged that his victories had been fixed, and attendance dropped when Deerfoot began another racing schedule in February. A tour of the country had to be cut short because of disappointing crowds, but tours of Scotland and Ireland during the summer were successful, and an estimated 4,000 people saw him set a record of 11 miles, 720 yards in a one-hour race after his return to London. He extended the record to 11 miles, 970 yards early in 1863, but his performances were erratic, probably because of his heavy schedule. A few days after dropping out of a 10-mile race in May, he sailed for the United States. He continued to compete, mostly in local races in upstate New York, until 1870.

Del Mar Park
Del Mar, CA

The photofinish camera was first used at Del Mar Park in 1937, shortly after the track opened. Invented by an optical engineer at Paramount, the camera is now used at virtually every track in the world, for harness and greyhound racing as well as Thoroughbred racing. When Del Mar opened on July 3, 1937, the event was like a movie premiere, with hundreds of Hollywood celebrities on hand. Bing Crosby, the track's first president, collaborated on its theme song, "Where the Turf Meets the Surf." Del Mar fell on hard times in the late 1960s, and it was taken over in 1970 by a non-dividend-paying corporation, the Del Mar Thoroughbred Association. The park, which seats 15,300 people, has a 1-mile oval main track and a 7½-furlong turf course.

Address: P.O. Box 700, Del Mar, CA 92014 (619) 755-1141

Delta Bowl
Football

Hosted by Memphis, the Delta Bowl was played only twice. Mississippi State beat Texas Christian 13–9 on January 1, 1948, and William and Mary defeated Oklahoma State 20–0 one year later.

DeMar, Clarence (1888–1958)
Marathon

Born June 7, 1888, Madeira, OH; died June 11, 1958

"Clarence the Great" won seven Boston Marathons, the first in 1911, when he set a record of 2 hours 21 minutes and 39 seconds. Then he was diagnosed as having a heart murmur and was told to stop running. In 1917 he decided to take up the sport again. He won at Boston in 1922 in 2:18:10, a record for the 24.5-mile course. After his victory in the 1923 event, the course was lengthened to the standard distance of 26 miles, 385 yards. DeMar won at that distance in 1924, finishing more than 5 minutes ahead of the runner-up. He also won in 1927, 1938, and 1930, at the age of 42. DeMar was the AAU marathon champion in 1926, 1927, and 1928.

Dempsey, "Jack" William H. (1895–1981)
Boxing

Born June 24, 1895, Manassa, CO; died May 31, 1983; Boxing Hall of Fame

The managerial genius of Doc Kearns and the promotional genius of Tex Rickard created the Dempsey legend. Kearns became his manager in 1917, when Dempsey was little more than a brawler. He brought his fighter to the East in 1918, and teamed with Rickard the following year to ballyhoo Dempsey's bout with the heavyweight champion, Jess Willard. Willard, 6-foot-6 and about 250 pounds, was known as the "Pottawatomie Giant"; Dempsey was only 6-foot-1 and 187 pounds. But he knocked Willard out in the third round to win the title, and Kearns and Rickard billed him as "Jack the Giant Killer."

Dempsey held the title for seven years, but defended it only six times. After knocking out Billy Miske and Bill Brennan in 1920, he was made the villain for his defense against Georges Carpentier of France. Nicknamed "the Orchid Man" by Rickard, Carpentier was a debonair war hero, while Dempsey was the scowling, vicious "slacker" who had somehow avoided serving in World War I. The result was the first $1 million gate in the history of boxing. It was also a mismatch. Dempsey knocked out the Frenchman in the fourth round on July 2, 1921, at Jersey City, NJ. He fought seven exhibitions in 1922, and then Kearns broke away from Rickard temporarily to promote a fight against middleweight Tommy Gibbons in Shelby, MT on July 4, 1923. That turned into a financial fiasco. Kearns personally took over the box office to make sure he collected Dempsey's $200,000 guarantee. Dempsey won a 15-round decision in a dull fight.

Rickard promoted Dempsey's next defense. It was "Jack the Giant Killer" again, fighting Luis Firpo, a gigantic, awkward Argentinian known as the "Wild Bull of of the Pampas." The fight produced another $1 million gate on September 14, 1923, at the Polo Grounds in New York. Dempsey knocked down Firpo seven times in less than two minutes, but Firpo then landed a tremendous right that sent Dempsey out of the ring. He landed on a sportswriter's typewriter, was helped back into the ring, and managed to finish the round. In the second round, Dempsey knocked down Firpo twice more, then knocked him out. The fight produced a change in New York boxing regulations that would have an impact on the second Dempsey-Tunney fight in 1927. Every time he knocked down Firpo, Dempsey simply stood there, waiting for his opponent to get up again so he could attack immediately. The new rule required a boxer to go to a neutral corner after knocking down his opponent. Illinois also adopted the rule.

Dempsey was basically inactive for three years, fighting only exhibitions and appearing in vaudeville. Finally, Rickard found a suitable challenger in Gene Tunney, former light-heavyweight champion of the Allied Expeditionary Forces. The clever Tunney avoided the bull-like rushes of the champion, who was badly out of shape, and landed enough of his own blows to win a 10–round decision in Philadelphia's Sesquicentennial Stadium on September 23, 1926.

A rematch took place on September 22, 1927, at Soldier Field, Chicago. It produced the only $2 million gate in boxing history, as 104,943 spectators turned out and an estimated 50 million listened to the radio broadcast. In the seventh round, Dempsey knocked Tunney down. The referee began to count, at the same time waving Dempsey to a neutral corner. When Dempsey finally obeyed, the referee started the count again. Tunney got to his feet at the count of nine, avoided Dempsey for the rest of the round, and then boxed his way to another decision. Most sportswriters said that Tunney had been on the canvas for 14 or 15 seconds. Dempsey's manager protested to the Illinois Athletic Commission, but the protest was rejected. Dempsey announced his retirement from the ring shortly afterward.

Further Reading: Dempsey, Jack. *Round by Round: An Autobiography.* New York: McGraw-Hill 1940; Roberts, Randy. *Jack Dempsey: The Manassa Mauler.* Baton Rouge: Louisiana State University Press, 1979.

See also RICKARD, TEX.

Denver, CO
Basketball A charter member of the American Basketball Association in 1967, the Denver Nuggets joined the National Basketball Association when the leagues merged in 1975. They won the midwest division championship in 1977, 1978, and 1985, but have never made it to the finals.
Football The Denver Broncos were one of the original eight franchises in the American Football League, and they joined the American Football Conference in 1970, when the AFL and the National Football League merged. The Broncos won AFC championships in 1977, 1986, and 1987.
Hockey Denver was home for a National Hockey League team, the Colorado Rockies, from 1977 to 1982. The franchise, which had moved from Kansas City, left to become the New Jersey Devils for the 1982–83 season.

See also MILE HIGH STADIUM; MCNICHOLS ARENA.

Detroit, MI
Baseball Detroit had a National League team from 1881 through 1888 and won the 1887 pennant. In 1894, the city joined the minor Western League, which became the American League in 1899 and assumed major-league status in 1901. The Detroit Tigers won pennants in 1907, 1908, 1909, 1934, 1935, 1940, 1945, 1968, and 1984, and they were World Series champions in 1935, 1968, and 1984.
Basketball The Ft. Wayne Pistons of the National Basketball Association moved to Detroit before the 1957–58 season. The Pistons won the NBA championship in 1989.
Football George Richards bought the Portsmouth (OH) Spartans of the National Football League in 1934, moved the team to Detroit, and renamed it the Lions. The Lions have been in the NFL championship game five times, winning in 1935, 1952, 1953, and 1957.
Hockey The Detroit Cougars joined the National Hockey League in 1927. They became known as the Falcons in 1931 and the Red Wings in 1934. The Red Wings won Stanley Cup championships in 1936, 1937, 1943, 1950, 1952, 1954, and 1955.

See also JOE LOUIS SPORTS ARENA; THE PALACE; PONTIAC SILVERDOME; TIGER STADIUM.

Dickey, "Bill" William M. (1907–   )
Baseball
Born June 6, 1907, Bastrop, LA; Baseball Hall of Fame

Perhaps the greatest catcher in history, Dickey joined the New York Yankees' "Murderer's Row" in 1929, after playing just ten games in 1928. A left-handed batter, he hit .324 in his first full season and led the league's catchers in assists with 95. He followed with a .339 average in 1930 and a .327 average in 1931, when he had a remarkable .996 fielding percentage to lead all catchers.

The Yankees won the pennant in 1932, when Dickey hit .310 with 15 home runs and 84 runs batted in, and he batted .438 in a four-game World Series victory over the Chicago Cubs. He had the best season of his career in 1936 with a .362 average, 22 home runs, and 107 runs batted in, and he hit over .300 with more than 20 home runs and more than 100 runs batted in each season from 1937 through 1939. Dickey led the league's catchers in putouts and assists in both 1937 and 1938 and in fielding percentage in 1939. The Yankees won four pennants and four World Series during the period; Dickey hit .400 in the 1938 Series, tying a record with four hits in one game. After catching more than 100 games in 1941 for the 13th consecutive season, a major-league record, Dickey began to see less playing time in 1942, but his home run gave the Yankees a 2–0 victory in the fifth and deciding game of the 1943 World Series.

Dickey served in the army in 1944 and 1945, returned as a backup catcher in 1946, and managed the team for part of the season, winning 57 games and losing 48. He retired in 1947. Dickey had a career batting average of .313, with 202 home runs and 1,209 runs batted in, and he batted .255, hit 5 home runs, and drove in 24 runs in eight World Series.

Didrikson, "Babe" Mildred (Mrs. Zaharias)
(1914–1956)
Golf, Track and Field
Born June 26, 1914, Port Arthur, TX; died September 27, 1956; World Golf Hall of Fame, National Track and Field Hall of Fame

She was named female athlete of the half-century by Associated Press in 1950 and will probably go down in history as the best of the century. She was also AP's Woman Athlete of the Year six times, in three different decades. Didrikson was nicknamed for Babe Ruth after hitting 13 home runs in a neighborhood softball game with boys. At Beaumont (TX) High School, she competed in basketball, golf, swimming, tennis, and volleyball. She was an AAU All-American basketball player three times, from 1930 through 1932, and she led the Golden Cyclones of the Employers Casualty Company of Dallas to the AAU title in 1931. Didrikson also won the 80-meter hurdles and the baseball throw in the AAU outdoor track championships.

In 1932, she won the 80-meter hurdles, the high jump, the broad jump, the shot put, the javelin throw, and the baseball throw, and the Golden Cyclones won the team championship, even though she was the only member of the team. Her javelin throw of 139 feet 3 inches was a U.S. record until 1955. She said after making the throw, "I coulda throwed it farther, but I slipped." Didrikson won Olympic Gold Medals in the 80-meter hurdles and the javelin that year and was deprived of another, in the high jump, when officials ruled she had used an illegal technique, the "Western roll." After returning to the United States and claiming her first athlete of the year award, she capitalized on her fame by appearing in vaudeville and barnstorming with her own basketball team.

Babe Didrikson excelled at basketball, softball, and track and field before becoming an outstanding professional golfer. She was named Associated Press Woman Athlete of the Year in three different decades, 1932, 1945–1947, 1952, and 1954. Courtesy of the U.S. Golf Association

Then she got serious about golf. After winning the Texas state championship in 1935, she was declared a professional by the U.S. Golf Association. She was earning up to $1,000 a week on an exhibition tour with Gene Sarazen when the USGA said she could regain her amateur status if she stayed out of competition for three years, so she did. In the meantime, she met and married George Zaharias, a professional wrestler. Reinstated, she won the U.S. Amateur Championship in 1946, and the following year she became the first American to win the British Ladies' Amateur. She was named athlete of the year for the third straight year.

Didrikson turned professional again in 1948 and won the U.S. Women's Open by eight shots. She also won it in 1950, when she was once again named athlete of the year. Stricken by cancer in 1953, she underwent an operation. She returned to the tour to win the 1954 Open by a record 12 strokes. That year she won four other tournaments and the Vare Trophy for the lowest average strokes per round, and she had two victories early in 1955. But the cancer had recurred, she was forced to leave the tour again, and the disease claimed her life in 1956.

Further Reading: Johnson, William Oscar, and Nancy P. Williamson. *"Whatta-Gal": The Babe Didrikson Story.* Boston: Little, Brown, 1977; Zaharias, Babe Didrikson. *This Life I've Led.* New York: A. S. Barnes, 1955.

DiMaggio, Joseph (1914–   )
Baseball
Born November 25, 1914, Martinez, CA; Baseball Hall of Fame

Many baseball fans think that DiMaggio's 56–game hitting streak, in 1941, is among the records that will never be broken. The streak ended when he was robbed of two hits by Cleveland third basemen Ken Keltner, and DiMaggio then started another streak of 17 consecutive games. If it hadn't been for Keltner, the record might well be 74.

The "Yankee Clipper" was a very graceful center fielder with a strong arm. He led American League outfielders in assists with 22 as a rookie in 1936, when he hit .323 with 29 home runs and 125 runs batted in. He batted .346 in the World Series that year. In 1937, he led the league with 46 home runs, hit .346, and drove in 167 runs. After "slumping" to .324, 32 home runs, and 140 runs batted in in 1938, he came close to hitting over .400 in 1939. He was at .412 in September, but an eye infection caused his average to drop to .381, still good enough to lead the league. He also had 30 home runs and 126 runs batted in and was named the league's Most Valuable Player. DiMaggio hit .311 when the Yankees swept the Cincinnati Reds in a four-game World Series.

He won another batting title with a .352 average in 1940, and he led the league in runs batted in with 125 in 1941, the year of his streak, when he hit .357 and won his second Most Valuable Player award. After a .305 average in 1942, DiMaggio spent three years in the army. On his return in 1946, he hit only .290, but he rebounded with a .315 average in 1947 and was named Most Valuable Player again.

DiMaggio led the league in home runs with 39 and runs batted in with 155, while hitting .320 in 1948. A bone spur on his right heel had to be operated on after the season and he couldn't play until June of 1949. In his first series of the year, he hit four home runs in three games against the Boston Red Sox, and he ended the season with a .345 average. DiMaggio had his last great season in 1950, hitting .301 with 32 home runs and 122 runs batted in. His tenth-inning home run won the second game 2–1 in the Yankees' four-game World Series sweep of the Philadelphia Phillies.

The bone spur limited his playing time in 1951 and he retired after the season. DiMaggio had a career .325 batting average with 389 doubles, 131 triples, 361 home runs, 1,390 runs scored, and 1,537 runs batted in. He played in 10 World Series, batting .271 with 8 home runs and 30 runs batted in.

Disabled, Sports for the
The Akron (OH) Club of the Deaf in 1945 hosted a basketball tournament for teams of deaf players from Buffalo, Kansas City, Los Angeles, and Philadelphia. On April 13, 1945, the American Athletic Union of the Deaf was formed to make the tournament an annual event. The group became the American Athletic Association of the Deaf in 1947. Since 1976, the association has also held a national softball tournament, and it selects and funds national teams for the World Summer Games for the Deaf, the World Winter Games for the Deaf, and the Pan-American Games for the Deaf. The Canadian Deaf Sports Association, made up of ten provincial associations, also conducts competitions and selects national teams.

Shortly after the end of World War II, disabled veterans began playing wheelchair basketball, which was very important in publicizing the need for sports and recreation for the disabled. Many teams toured the country, playing exhibitions against nondisabled athletes. The National Wheelchair Basketball Association, founded in 1948, has 185 member teams in 28 conferences across the country and conducts a national tournament.

It was followed in 1958 by the National Wheelchair Athletic Association, which sponsors regional championships leading up to the National Wheelchair Games, with competition in archery, slalom, swimming, table tennis, target shooting, and track and field. The Canadian Wheelchair Sports Association conducts similar championships. The American Wheelchair Bowling Association was organized in 1962, the National Wheelchair Softball Association in 1976, and the National Foundation of Wheelchair Tennis 1980. The International Wheelchair Road Racers Club concentrates its efforts on helping organizations and race directors establish wheelchair divisions. As a result, most major distance road races now also offer competition and trophies for wheelchair "runners."

Many sports are promoted by the U.S. Association for Blind Athletes, founded in 1976. The organization conducts national championship events and the North American Games for the Blind, with competition between the United States and athletes selected by the Canadian Blind Sports Association, Inc. The American Blind Bowling Association, established in 1951, was the first sports organization for the visually impaired. Volunteer ski instructors make up the American Blind Skiing Foundation, which sponsors international competition with Canada and selects a national team to take part in the World Cup for the Disabled in Switzerland. Recreational sports for the blind, including biking, camping, fishing, hiking, horseback riding, skating, and skiing, are promoted through local clubs established by the Blind Outdoor Leisure Development organization.

The largest and best known organization for disabled sports is the International Special Olympics, founded in 1968 to provide fitness, recreation, and competitive sports programs for the mentally handicapped. The organization, which has more than 1,200,000 members in about 60 countries, conducts local, regional, state, and national competition in many sports. International championships are held every two years.

Both Canada and the United States have Amputee Sports Associations. In addition to supervising national championships, the associations select national teams for competition conducted by the International Sports Organization for the Disabled. The National Amputee Golf Association, with nearly 2,000 members, promotes mental and physical rehabilitation through recreational golf in addition to sponsoring tournaments. Several groups promote horseback riding for disabled persons, including the National Foundation for Happy Horsemanship for the Handicapped, the North American Riding for the Handicapped Association, and the National Center for Therapeutic Riding.

The Canadian Federation of Sport Organizations for the Disabled, founded in 1981 as the Office of Sport for the Physically Disabled, took its present name in 1987. Its membership includes the Canadian Amputee Sports Association, the Canadian Blind Sports Association, the Canadian Deaf Sports Association, the Canadian Disabled Ski Association, the Canadian Wheelchair Sports Association, the Ontario Amputee Sports Association, the Ontario Blind Sports Association, the Ontario Cerebral Palsy Sports Association, and the Ontario Wheelchair Sports Association.

Addresses: Canadian Federation of Sport Organizations for the Disabled, 333 River Road, Vanier, Ontario, Canada K1L 8H9 (613) 748-5630; National Association for Disabled Athletes, 17 Lindley Avenue, Tenafly, NJ 07670

See also SPECIAL OLYMPICS.

Discus Throw

The discus throw was one of the major events in the ancient Olympics in Greece and it was recreated for the modern Olympic Games. The first Olympic champion, in 1896, was Robert S. Garrett of Princeton University with a throw of 95 feet, 7½ inches. Charles Henneman of the U.S. increased the record to 118 feet 9 inches in 1897, and it inched toward the 200-foot mark until Al Oerter of the U.S. broke the barrier in 1962. Women didn't compete in the discus until the early 1920s, and the event was added to the Olympic program in 1928. Liesel Westermann of West Germany was the first woman to surpass 200 feet, in 1967. Women throw a 1-kilogram discus, about 2 pounds and 3 ounces, while men throw a 2-kilogram discus.

See also OERTER, AL.

Diving

Modern diving, with its gymnastic-like movements, was developed by Earnest Brandsten while coaching at Stanford. A member of the 1908 Swedish Olympic team, Brandsten went to Stanford in 1912. At the time, competitive diving emphasized precision of body form, with a minimum of movement. Brandsten's divers were trained to do somersaults and spins, and the style spread throughout North America and then the world.

Platform diving was on the Olympic program in 1904, and "elastic board" diving, now called springboard diving, was added in 1908. The first diving meet in North America wasn't held until 1907, at the University of Pennsylvania. The AAU began conducting a national championship for platform diving in 1909 and for springboard diving in 1923. Women's diving became an Olympic sport in 1912, but there was no AAU championship for women until 1916.

When the Canadian Amateur Swimming Association was organized in 1909, it also governed diving, but the Canadian Diving Council broke away in 1966 to become an independent body, the first in the world. It's now the Canadian Diving Association. In the United States, the sport was governed by the Amateur Athletic Union until 1977, when U.S. Diving, Inc., took over jurisdiction.

Since 1920, United States men have dominated the Olympics, winning all but two Gold Medals in the springboard event and 12 out of 17 in the platform. American women have won 11 of 17 Gold Medals in the springboard, and they won 8 out of 9 in the platform from 1920 through 1964. Eastern European countries and China have dominated women's diving at recent Olympics, but Sylvie Bernier of Canada won the springboard Gold Medal in 1984.

Addresses: Canadian Amateur Diving Association, Inc., Tower A, 3rd floor, 333 River Road, Vanier, Ontario, Canada K1L 8H9 (613) 748-5631; U.S. Diving, Inc., 201 South Capitol Avenue, Suite 430, Indianapolis, IN 46225 (317) 237-5252

Division of Girls' and Women's Sports
See ASSOCIATION FOR INTERCOLLEGIATE ATHLETICS FOR WOMEN.

Dixie Bowl
Football
The Dixie Bowl was played twice, in Birmingham, AL. Arkansas beat William and Mary 21–19 on January 1, 1948, and Baylor beat Wake Forest 20–7 on January 1, 1949.

Dixie Classic
Football
The Dixie Classic was the third bowl game, after the Rose Bowl and the San Diego East-West Christmas Classic, but it was played only three times, irregularly, in Dallas. On January 1, 1922, Texas A & M beat Centre 22–14; West Virginia Wesleyan defeated Southern Methodist 9–7 on January 1, 1925, and Arkansas and Centenary tied 7–7 on January 1, 1934.

Dobie, Gilmour (1879–1948)
Football
Born January 21, 1879, Hastings, MN; died December 23, 1948; National Football Foundation Hall of Fame

He was called "Gloomy Gil" because he was always pessimistic about his team's chances. Yet, in 33 years of college coaching, he produced a record 14 undefeated teams and had a winning percentage of .781. Dobie played for the University of Minnesota, graduating in 1903, and he got his first coaching job in 1906 at North Dakota State, where he had two unbeaten teams in two seasons. Then he went to the University of Washington in 1908. Washington never lost a game under Dobie, winning 58 and tying 3 over nine seasons.

Dobie suffered his first defeat in his 12th season of coaching, at Navy in 1917. After winning 17 and losing 3 in three years there, he went to Cornell in 1920. His 1921, 1922 and 1923 teams were unbeaten and untied, and Dobie was given the first ten-year contract in college football history. He spent a total of 16 seasons at Cornell, winning 82, losing 36, and tying 7. In 1936, he went to Boston College, where his teams were 16–6–5 in three seasons. He retired after the 1938 season.

Dodger Stadium
Los Angeles, CA
Much controversy surrounded Dodger Stadium before it was even built. To get the Dodgers to move from Brooklyn, the city of Los Angeles provided 300 downtown acres known as Chavez Ravine, which had been planned as a public housing project for the poor. A 1958 referendum to prevent the city from giving the land to the Dodgers was defeated by a narrow margin. Los Angeles also spent about $5 million preparing the site for construction, but the Dodgers paid for the stadium. Opened in 1962, it seats 56,000 and has parking for 24,000 cars. Its triple-decker grandstand surrounds about two thirds of the field and there are bleachers in left center and right center. Home run distances are 330 feet down the lines and 385 feet to center field.

Dog Racing
See GREYHOUND RACING; SLED DOG RACING.

Dogsled Racing
See SLED DOG RACING.

Dorais, "Gus" Charles E. (1891–1954)
Football
Born July 2, 1891, Chippewa Falls, WI; died January 4, 1954; National Football Foundation Hall of Fame

Dorais and his Notre Dame roommate, Knute Rockne, became football's first famous passing combination on November 1, 1913. Though Notre Dame had been unbeaten the year before, it wasn't given a chance to beat Army that afternoon, but Dorais completed 13 of 17 passes for 213 yards in a 35–13 victory. He went on to become a successful college coach. Dorais had a 17–9–2 record at Dubuque College from 1914 through 1917. After serving in the U.S. Army, he went to Gonzaga University, where he won 20 games, lost 13 and tied 3 in five seasons. His University of Detroit teams won 19 consecutive games from 1927 into 1929 and had an overall mark of 113–48–7 through 1942. Dorais coached the Detroit Lions of the National Football League for five seasons, 1943–47, but had only 20 victories against 31 losses and 2 ties.

Douglas, "Bob" Robert L. (1882–1979)
Basketball
Born November 4, 1882, St. Kitts, BWI; died July 16, 1979; Basketball Hall of Fame

The first black inducted into the Basketball Hall of Fame, Douglas was founder, owner, and coach of the Harlem Renaissance Big Five. He organized the team in 1922 to play in the ballroom of the Renaissance Casino in Harlem. In 1925, he added some outstanding players and took the team on the road. The Rens won 2,318 games in 22 seasons, making Douglas the winningest coach of all time, and they beat the Harlem Globetrotters to win the 1939 World Professional Tournament in Chicago.

See also HARLEM RENAISSANCE BIG FIVE.

Dover Downs International Speedway
Dover, DE

This 1-mile track opened in 1969 and has expanded its capacity four times since then. It now seats more than 60,000 spectators and has the distinction of hosting the first and last NASCAR Winston Cup races of the season in the Northeast: the Budweiser 500 (the Mason-Dixon 500 until 1984) and the Delaware 500.

Address: P.O. Box 843, Dover, DE 19903 (302) 674-4600

Draft

See PLAYER DRAFTS.

Drag Racing

Drag racing began with informal matches among teenagers in souped-up cars after World War II, and the National Hot Rod Association was formed in 1951 to govern the sport. It now has 175 member tracks and sanctions more than 3,000 events, including 18 national championships, in a variety of classes. With sponsorship from the R. J. Reynolds Tobacco Company, total prize money for the national championship series reached $17 million in 1989. Another group, the International Hot Rod Association, was organized in 1970 as a regional sanctioning association, but has expanded considerably in recent years. It conducts 12 national professional championships and sanctions tracks in 21 states.

Addresses: International Hot Rod Association, P.O. Box 8018, Waco, TX 76714 (917) 776-7733; National Hot Rod Association, 2035 Financial Way, Glendora, CA 91740 (818) 914-4761

Dressage

See EQUESTRIAN SPORTS.

Drugs in Sports

"Doping," the use of drugs to improve performance, was first reported in 1865, when some swimmers in an Amsterdam canal race were accused of it. Six-day bicycle racers were taking "speedballs," a mixture of cocaine and heroin, as early as 1869, and late in the century some athletes used caffeine tablets, brandy, sugar cubes soaked in ether, strychnine,

Top fuel dragsters are the fastest vehicles in drag racing. Don "Big Daddy" Garlits drove this one to many victories during the 1970s. Courtesy of the National Hot Rod Association

heroin, cocaine, and nitroglycerine in attempts to enhance their performances. The first major drug scandal arose in 1904, when Tom Hicks of the United States collapsed after winning the Olympic marathon. It was discovered he'd taken a mixture of brandy and strychnine.

The word "dope" first appeared in an English dictionary in 1889; it was defined as an opium mixture given to Thoroughbred horses. (The word comes from the Bantu *dop*, a type of hard liquor, and it arrived in English through the Dutch language.) Testing horses' saliva for possible doping was instituted in 1910, and shortly afterward racing dogs were also being tested.

Amphetamines were in wide use among cyclists during the 1950s and 1960s. They also spread into the National Football League, which banned them in 1971. Yet, Redskin players in 1979 told the *Washington Post* that about one third of the them took amphetamines. Dr. Arnold J. Mandell revealed that he had given large quantities of amphetamines to San Diego Charger football players, beginning in 1968, and he said that many players in the league used the drugs. He interviewed 87 players, of whom 48 said they took amphetamines every week during the football season, and 9 said they occasionally took them.

A major drug problem, often overlooked, is the use of painkillers to allow an athlete to perform after an injury. One such drug, an anti-inflammatory, is phenylbutazone, usually called "bute," a shortening of Butazolidin, one of its trade names. It's most commonly given to horses, although humans also use it. Some racing commissions ban its use, others don't. Bute became headline news in 1968, when Dancer's Image was disqualified after finishing first in the Kentucky Derby, because he tested positive for the drug. Among human athletes, commonly used painkillers range from local anesthetics sprayed on a minor injury during a game to injected cortisones, often used for joint pains.

While painkillers mask pain, they don't cure the damage already done, and continued exertion may aggravate the original injury. Charlie Krueger, who played for the San Francisco 49ers for 15 years, in 1989 won a settlement of about $1.5 million from his former team because, according to the California Supreme Court, the medical staff "fraudulently concealed" the extent of a knee injury and kept him playing by giving him painkillers and steroids. In a case that's still pending, Ken Easley claims that the Seattle Seahawks gave him large doses of a painkiller that caused serious kidney disease.

"Blood doping" was a kind of fad in sports for a time. Blood is removed from an athlete's body, stimulating the production of more blood, and is then given back by transfusion. Theoretically, this should increase the supply of oxygen, which is carried by red blood cells. Several American cyclists used blood doping before the 1984 Olympics. However, recent studies have cast doubt on whether it really improves performance.

In some sports, such as target shooting and archery, some athletes use relaxing drugs, including alcohol, tranquilizers, and "beta blockers," commonly used to control high blood pressure. At the 1984 Olympics, athletes using beta blockers for medical reasons had to submit declarations stating the dosage used. In modern pentathlon, which involves target shooting, some countries submitted declarations for every team member.

A related problem is the "recreational" use of drugs, which may overlap with their use to improve performance. Gene "Big Daddy" Lipscomb, an All-Pro defensive tackle, died of a heroin overdose in 1963, but cocaine has been the drug most often mentioned on the sports pages. It's a stimulant that induces feelings of euphoria, which is why cyclists used it in the 19th century. But it's also a social drug that has become prevalent among well-to-do, fast-track achievers, including professional athletes.

The dam broke in 1982, when former National Football League player Don Reese told his story to *Sports Illustrated*. Reese had been sentenced to a year in prison for selling cocaine in 1977, but was welcomed back to football by the New Orleans Saints in 1978. He said that cocaine use was common on all three NFL teams he'd played for—the Miami Dolphins, the Saints, and the San Diego Chargers. He and *Sports Illustrated* were denounced by the NFL, NFL Players' Association, and individual players—among them Mercury Morris of the Dolphins, who was later sentenced to 15 years in prison for selling cocaine.

But Carl Eller, who played in the NFL from 1964 through 1979, said that 40 percent of the league's players were using cocaine. Suddenly, many of them confessed and others were arrested. It spread beyond the NFL. Three National Basketball Association players were suspended for drug use, and three members of baseball's Kansas City Royals were imprisoned for trying to buy cocaine. Two former Heisman trophy winners, George Rogers of the Saints and Charles White of the Cleveland Browns, admitted that they were cocaine-dependent. Most shocking, Maryland basketball star Len Bias and Cleveland Browns defensive back Don Rogers died of cocaine poisoning nine days apart in June of 1986.

Professional leagues adopted substance-abuse policies, generally offering rehabilitation to first-time offenders who agreed to submit to random testing afterward. The NBA gives a player two chances to be rehabilitated, with a lifetime suspension for the third offense. In the NFL, a player is subject to a 30-day suspension for failing a test the first time and an indefinite suspension for a second failure. Major-league baseball has a similar program.

In 1968, the International Olympic Committee began random testing for antidepressants, painkillers, stimulants, and some tranquilizers. Since then, testing on the international level has expanded to include many more drugs and more sophisticated test procedures. Drug testing in the United States, however, has not been totally successful because of the privacy issue. Players associations oppose mandatory testing as a violation of the right to privacy.

The National Collegiate Athletic Association began mandatory random testing in November of 1986 for athletes involved in postseason championship play and football bowl games, and more than 100 colleges and universities also test their athletes. That policy has been challenged in court several times with conflicting results. A federal district court in February of 1988 decided that testing is constitutional, but in August a California judge ruled that mandatory testing is unconstitutional in that state. The fate of testing, on both the professional and the collegiate levels, probably rests on a future decision by the U.S. Supreme Court.

Further Reading: Burk, Thomas F., "Drug Use in Athletics," in *Federation Proceedings* 40 (October 1981, Federation of American Societies for Experimental Biology); Donohue, Tom, and Neil Johnson. *Foul Play: Drug Abuse in Sports* New York: Basil Blackwell, 1986.

See also ANABOLIC STEROIDS.

Duckpin Bowling

Baseball managers Wilbert Robinson and John McGraw were the owners of the Diamond Alleys in Baltimore in 1900, when ten-pin bowling was strictly a winter sport. During the off-season, bowlers often used small balls, 6 inches in diameter, for informal competition. Frank Van Sant, manager of the alleys, decided that small pins could be used with the small ball, and he had a set of ten-pins trimmed down. The smaller pins flew around so wildly that Robinson and McGraw, both duck hunters, said they looked like a "flock of flying ducks," and the new sport was named duckpin bowling.

At first, it was a summer sport for ten-pin bowlers, but leagues were organized for the winter season in Baltimore in 1903 and in Washington, D.C. the fol-

lowing year. The Washington City Duckpin Association, formed on February 23, 1910, held the first tournament that year. In the fall of 1927, the National Duckpin Bowling Congress was founded. The first national championships were held under NDBC auspices in the spring of 1928. By 1938, there about 200,000 league bowlers and about 400,000 recreational bowlers throughout the Northeast. After World War II, ten-pin bowling became more popular in the region, and duckpin bowling essentially stopped growing, although it still has its share of loyal followers.

Address: National Duckpin Bowling Congress, 4609 Horizon Circle, Baltimore, MD 21208 (301) 636-BOWL

See also RUBBERBAND DUCKPIN BOWLING.

Dudley, "Bullet Bill" William M. (1921–   )
Football

Born December 24, 1921, Bluefield, VA; National Football Foundation, Pro Football Hall of Fame

Johnny "Blood" McNally once said that the ideal backfield would be four Bill Dudleys, because he could do everything so well. At the University of Virginia, Dudley was second in the nation in rushing in 1940, his junior year. He captained the team in 1941, led the nation in scoring with 134 points, was a unanimous All-American, and won the Maxwell Trophy. Dudley gained 968 yards rushing, with an average of 6.3 yards per carry, and passed for 856 yards.

With the Pittsburgh Steelers in 1942, "Bullet Bill" scored on a 55-yard touchdown run in his first game and returned a kickoff for a touchdown in his second. He led the National Football League in rushing with 696 yards on 162 carries, a 4.3-yard average, and was named an All-Pro. After serving in the Army Air Corps during World War II, he played part of the 1945 season with the Steelers. He again led the NFL in rushing in 1946, gaining 604 yards in 146 attempts, a 4.1 average. He also led in interceptions with 10 and in punt returning with an average of 14.3 yards and was named the league's Most Valuable Player.

Traded to the Detroit Lions in 1947, he was used primarily as a pass receiver for two seasons, then went to the Washington Redskins in 1949. He played three seasons in Washington, retired in 1952, and returned to the Redskins in 1953. He retired permanently after seeing little action that season. Dudley shows up in practically every statistical category. In nine seasons, he rushed for 3,057 yards, averaging 4.0 yards per carry and scoring 20 touchdowns; caught 123 passes for 1,383 yards, an 11.2-yard average, and 18 touchdowns; passed for 985 yards and 6 touchdowns; returned 124 punts for 1,515 yards, a 12.2-yard average, and 3 touchdowns; returned 78 kickoffs for 1,743 yards, a 22.3-yard average, and 1 touchdown; intercepted 23 passes, returning them for 459 yards, a 20.0-yard average, and 2 touchdowns; and punted 193 times for a 38.2-yard average. All told, Dudley scored 44 touchdowns and kicked 121 extra points and 33 field goals for a total of 484 points.

Duffy, Hugh (1866–1954)
Baseball

Born November 26, 1866, River Point, RI; died October 19, 1954; Baseball Hall of Fame

He batted .440 in 1894, the highest average ever under modern rules. (In 1887, a walk was counted as a hit, and Tip O'Neill was credited with a .492 average. However, if walks are subtracted from his totals, O'Neill hit .435.) Duffy is the only player to hit over .300 in four major leagues. He became the starting right fielder for Chicago's National League team in 1888 and batted .312 in 1889, his first full season. He then jumped to the Chicago team in the new Players' League, where he hit .320 in 1890.

After that league dissolved, he joined Boston in the American Association, then a major league. Duffy finished second in hitting with a .336 average and stole 87 bases as Boston won the pennant, but the association also folded and Boston moved into the National League. Duffy led the league with a .363 average in 1893, then had his remarkable 1894 season, when he won the Triple Crown, leading not only in average but also in home runs with 18, runs batted in with 145, and hits with 237. His teammates advised him to sit out the final game of the season to protect his lead in the batting race, but he played anyway, and got five hits.

Duffy batted over .300 four of the next six years, then became player manager of the American League's Milwaukee team, where he hit .302 in 1901. The franchise moved to St. Louis in 1902, but Duffy remained in Milwaukee, managing a minor-league team, until 1904, when he became player-manager of the Philadelphia Phillies in the National League. He appeared in 34 games with the Phillies during the next three seasons. Later, he owned and managed minor-league teams, and he managed the Chicago White Sox in 1910 and 1911 and the Boston Red Sox in 1921 and 1922.

In his 17 seasons in the majors, Duffy batted .324, stole 574 bases, and scored 1,553 runs.

Duluth, MN

The Kelley-Duluths, named for a hardware store that originally sponsored the team, entered the National Football League in 1923. The players ran the team as a kind of cooperative but sold the franchise for a dollar to Ole Haugsrud after losing $44 apiece in 1925. The NFL faced its first challenge in 1926, from the American Football League, starring Red Grange. Haugsrud had gone to high school with Ernie Nevers, the All-American fullback from Stanford and the only player who could compete with Grange at the box office. He signed Nevers to play for Duluth, renaming the team "Ernie Nevers' Duluth Eskimos." After playing their first game at home, the Eskimos spent the rest of the season on the road. According to Haugsrud, they played 29 games in 110 days, although researchers have been able to find newspaper accounts of only 23 games. More recent research has shown that they may have had 30 games scheduled, and played 28 of them, but that hasn't been established. After the 1927 season, the Eskimos dropped out of the NFL.

Dune Buggy
See OFF-ROAD RACING.

Dutch Colonial Sports

The Dutch in New Amsterdam were much more amenable to play than the English colonists. They brought a wide variety of winter sports from the Netherlands, including skating, ice boating, and sledding, and they staged winter carnivals that included silver and pewter prizes for speed skating. They also played a game called Kolf, which used heavy clubs; it may have been something like golf, but more probably it was a kind of hockey. The Dutch enjoyed a variety of ball games, including Kaetzen, in which a ball filled with horsehair was bounced off a wall, a tree, or a post, often in tavern yards. While men used their hands, women played kaetzen with rackets of netting, similar to modern tennis rackets.

Another favorite game was Klootban or Klos, in which players tried to throw a round disk through a wicket at the end of a long alley. And, of course, the Dutch were fond of bowling games, including skittles, nine-pins, and bowling on the green. The colony lasted 40 years, 1624–64, after which the Dutch were gradually assimilated into the New York community. Aside from their general love of sports, in particular bowling, they had no lasting impact on North American sports.

See also COLONIAL ERA.

Eagan, Edward P. F. (1898–1967)
Bobsledding, Boxing
Born April 26, 1898, Denver, CO; died June 14, 1967

Eagan is the only athlete ever to win Gold Medals in both the Summer and Winter Olympics. He won the light-heavyweight boxing championship in 1920, and in 1932 he was a member of the winning four-man bobsled team at the Winter Olympics. Eagan was also the AAU heavyweight boxing champion in 1919. His idol was Frank Merriwell, a fictional sports hero. Eagan wrote in 1932, "To this day I have never used tobacco, because Frank didn't. My first glass of wine, which I do not care for, was taken under social compulsion in Europe. Frank never drank."

Eagleson, R. Alan (1933–   )
Hockey
Born April 24, 1933, St. Catherines, Ontario

Eagleson has been called the most powerful man in hockey. His first involvement with the sport was as Bobby Orr's agent in 1966, when he negotiated a $40,000 contract with the Boston Bruins for his 18-year-old client. A year later, Eagleson organized the National Hockey League Players Association and became its executive director.

In 1970, Canada withdrew from the world hockey championships because it wasn't allowed to use its professional players, and Eagleson capitalized on that by organizing the "Summit Series" between Canada and the Soviet Union in 1972. Two years later, he was named chief negotiator for Hockey Canada to make arrangements for the Canada Cup tournament, the successor to the Summit Series. He also helped persuade the International Ice Hockey Federation that professionals should be allowed in the world championships. As a result, Hockey Canada resumed sending a team to the championships in 1977.

Professional hockey salaries have not kept pace with salaries in other major professional sports, and in 1980 the Boston Bruins player representative, Mike Milbury, challenged Eagleson for leadership of the Players Association. Eagleson's response was that the National Hockey League is a "peanut stand" that can't pay as much because it's not on network television in the United States. Bryan Trottier, president of the association, said of Eagleson, "He cares for the players. He started the union. He's very tough

in negotiations with the owners. He represents our side very well." Milbury's challenge failed, and in 1987 Eagleson was given a contract extension through 1993.

Eastern College Athletic Conference (ECAC)

The largest athletic conference in the United States, the ECAC is not a league but an administrative body that helps coordinate scheduling, assigns officials, and manages a variety of tournaments and championship events. Founded by 53 schools in 1938 as the Central Office for Intercollegiate Athletics, the ECAC took its present name in 1947. It now has more than 255 members from throughout New England and the Mid-Atlantic States. Among the conferences belonging to the ECAC are the Atlantic Ten, the Big East, the Colonial Athletic Association, the East Coast Conference, the Ivy League, and the Metro Atlantic.

The ECAC helps manage championships in track and field for the IC4A, in crew for the Eastern Association of Rowing Colleges, in fencing for the Intercollegiate Fencing Association, in gymnastics for the Intercollegiate Gymnastics League, in swimming for the Eastern Intercollegiate Swimming League, and in wrestling for the Eastern Intercollegiate Wrestling Association. It also conducts the Holiday Basketball Festival at Madison Square Garden.

Address: P.O. Box 3, 1311 Craigville Road, Centerville, MA 02632 (508) 771-5060

Eastern Colored League
Baseball

Organized by five teams on December 16, 1923, the league was formally called the Mutual Association of Eastern Colored Baseball Clubs. A sixth team was added before the 1924 season began. Some of the top players from the Negro National League jumped to the ECL because its salaries tended to be higher, but the two leagues agreed to a truce before the season ended and their champions played in the first Negro World Series that fall. The ECL broke up early in the 1928 season.

East-West Shrine Classic
Football

Commonly known as the East-West game, the Classic is played between all-star teams of college seniors to benefit the Shriners' burn hospitals. The first game was played on December 26, 1925, at Ewing Field in San Francisco. The game has sometimes been played in January, sometimes in December. Except for one game in New Orleans in 1942, the East-West game was in San Francisco until 1969, when it was played at Stanford Stadium in Palo Alto. It moved to the Oakland Coliseum in 1971, to Candlestick Park in San Francisco in 1973, and back to Palo Alto in 1974.

Ebbets Field
Brooklyn, NY

When Ebbets Field opened in 1913, its cost greatly exceeded estimates, and Charles Ebbets, formerly the sole owner of the Brooklyn Dodgers, had to give shares in the team to the contractors, Steve and Ed McKeever. On the brighter side, the park was within easy access of 90 percent of Brooklyn's population and its two-tiered grandstand could seat 22,000 people. The left-field fence was a mammoth 418 feet 9 inches, from home plate down the line. Later, bleachers were added, cutting the distance to 383 feet 9 inches, and in the 1930s, the bleachers were replaced by a double-deck stand, further reducing the distance to 348 feet. The right-field fence was only 301 feet from home plate, but center field was an immense 476 feet 9 inches. The Dodgers played at Ebbets field until moving to Los Angeles in 1958. The park was torn down and replaced by a housing development the following year.

ECAC

See EASTERN COLLEGE ATHLETIC CONFERENCE.

Eckersall, Walter H. (1886–1930)
Football

Born June 17, 1886, Chicago, IL; died March 24, 1930; National Football Foundation Hall of Fame

Eckersall was the first All-American from the University of Chicago and only the second from the Western Conference (now the Big Ten). In high school, he tied the national interscholastic records for the 50- and 100-yard dashes, and his speed made him a dangerous runner. He was also an excellent drop-kicker and when the forward pass was legalized in 1906, Coach Alonzo Stagg designed a pass-run option play to take advantage of Eckersall's skills.

As a freshman in 1903, Eckersall scored two touchdowns, one of them on a 52-yard run, and kicked a 45-yard field goal in a 34–0 victory over Indiana. He kicked three field goals against Wisconsin in a 15–6 win (field goals counted five points at that time). He returned the first kickoff of the 1904

season 107 yards against Texas. He also had a 95-yard touchdown run against Iowa and a 106-yard kickoff return against Wisconsin that year. Walter Camp decided he should be an All-American, but listed him as an end.

His kicking ability came to the fore in 1905. Against Wisconsin, his 23-yard field goal on a muddy field brought a 4–0 victory. Chicago ended Michigan's 56-game winning streak 2–0, largely because of Eckersall's great punting. Against Purdue he kicked two field goals, and against Illinois he scored a touchdown and kicked five field goals, tying the collegiate record. In his senior season, Eckersall kicked five field goals against Nebraska, becoming the only college player ever to accomplish it twice. He was the All-American quarterback in 1905 and 1906, and in 1920 he was named to the All-Time All-American team.

Eclipse Awards
Horse Racing

The *Daily Racing Form*, the National Turf Writers Association, and the Thoroughbred Racing Associations elected Thoroughbred champions separately until 1971, when they combined to establish the Eclipse Awards. The awards are named for the great English horse, Eclipse, who was undefeated in 18 starts beginning in 1759. They're given to Thoroughbreds in 12 categories: Horse of the Year, older colt, horse or gelding, older filly or mare, three-year-old colt, three-year-old filly, two-year-old colt, two-year-old filly, turf horse, female turf horse, male turf horse, sprinter, and steeplechase or hurdle horse. Awards are also given for trainers, jockeys, apprentice jockeys, owners, breeders, and owner-breeders.

Horse of the Year (age)

1971	Ack Ack (5)
1972	Secretariat (2)
1973	Secretariat (3)
1974	Forego (4)
1975	Forego (5)
1976	Forego (6)
1977	Seattle Slew (3)
1978	Affirmed (3)
1979	Affirmed (4)
1980	Spectacular Bid (4)
1981	John Henry (6)
1982	Conquistador Cielo (3)
1983	All Along (4)
1984	John Henry (9)
1985	Spend A Buck (3)
1986	Lady's Secret (4)
1987	Ferdinand (4)

1988 Alydar (4)
1989 Sunday Silence (3)

Ederle, Gertrude (1906–   )
Swimming

Born October 23, 1906, New York, NY; International Swimming Hall of Fame

When she was 15 years old, in 1922, Ederle entered the 3-mile swim in New York Bay for the J. P. Day Cup. She had never competed in a race longer than 220 yards, but she won over more experienced opponents. She was the AAU outdoor champion in the 440-yard freestyle in 1922 and 1923, in the 880-yard freestyle in 1923 and 1924, and she won the indoor 220-yard freestyle in 1923. Then she began to specialize in distance swimming.

About 7 A.M. on August 6, 1926, she entered the English Channel on the French shore and 14 hours 23 minutes later she arrived in England, becoming the first woman to swim the Channel and breaking the men's record by more than 2 hours. When she returned to the United States, an estimated 2 million people turned out for a ticker-tape parade in her honor. Ederle then joined the vaudeville circuit, touring North America and Europe with a huge collapsible swimming tank in which she performed. She suffered a nervous breakdown in 1928, in part because of her hectic schedule, and became deaf because of damage to her eardrums suffered during the Channel swim. After her recovery, Ederle taught swimming to deaf children.

Edmonton, Alberta

Football The Edmonton Eskimos joined the new Western Canada Rugby Football Union in 1911 and they became the first Western team to play in the Grey Cup finals in 1921, losing to the Toronto Argonauts 23–0. The WCRFU was reorganized as the Western Interprovincial Football Union in 1936. Edmonton joined the new league in 1938, dropped out in 1940, and rejoined in 1949.

The Eskimos won the Grey Cup in 1954, 1955, 1956, 1975, 1978, 1979, 1980, 1981, 1982, and 1987. They're the only team to win five consecutive Grey Cups.

Hockey The Edmonton Oilers were one of the original teams in the World Hockey Association when it was formed in 1972. When the WHL merged into the National Hockey League in 1979, Edmonton entered the NHL. The Oilers won the Stanley Cup in 1984, 1985, 1987, 1988, and 1990.

See also COMMONWEALTH STADIUM; NORTHLANDS COLISEUM.

Edwards, Harry (1942–   )
Sports Sociologist

Born November 22, 1942, East St. Louis, IL

Edwards played basketball and threw the discus at San Jose State University, graduating with a degree in sociology in 1964. While a part-time instructor at San Jose State, he led a drive to organized a boycott of the Olympics by black athletes. The Olympic Project for Human Rights, as the organization was called, picketed the New York Athletic Club's indoor track meet in February of 1968 because the club was all white. Attendance dropped by more than 50 percent as a result.

During 1968, the OPHR also called for the resignation of Avery Brundage, head of the International Olympic Committee, and demanded that the heavyweight championship be returned to Muhammad Ali. None of these things happened, and the Olympic boycott didn't come to pass, but two of Edwards' supporters, Tommie Smith and John Carlos, gave black power salutes with gloved hands while on the Olympic victory podium to receive medals for the 220-meter dash. They were suspended from the team and expelled from the Olympic village.

After completing the course work toward his Ph.D. at Cornell, Edwards went to the University of California at Berkeley to teach sociology. His doctoral dissertation was published in book form as *The Sociology of Sport* in 1973. When baseball commissioner Peter Ueberroth announced in 1987 that the sport would attempt to hire more blacks in management and front-office positions, Edwards was hired as a consultant.

Further Reading: Edwards, Harry. *The Struggle That Must Be: An Autobiography.* New York: Macmillan, 1980.

See also BLACKS IN SPORTS.

Eisenhower Trophy
Golf

This is a perpetual trophy for golf's World Amateur Team Championship. The winning country receives a silver replica of the trophy as a permanent prize and temporary custody of the trophy itself for two years. Established in 1948, it was named for Dwight D. Eisenhower.

Elysian Fields

In 1946, a plaque was dedicated in Hoboken, NJ, to mark the 100th anniversary of the first modern baseball game. The plaque is at the site of the Elysian Fields, just across the Hudson River from New York City, which also hosted many other sports in the

Cricket and baseball coexisted for many years at the Elysian Fields in Hoboken, as this Currier & Ives lithograph of 1859 shows. A cricket match is portrayed in the top panel.

19th century. The Elysian Fields was established by John Cox Stevens in 1831 as an amusement park on the family estate. New York Scots held their annual Caledonian Games there. After the New York Yacht Club was formed aboard Stevens' yacht in 1844, its clubhouse was built on a piece of the property. The site was also the home of the St. George Cricket Club, which drew large crowds to matches with Canadian teams during the 1840s and 1850s; the cricket match between the United States and an English team in 1859 drew an estimated 25,000 spectators. In the late 1860s, the Elysian Fields was used by the New York Athletic Club for track and field meets.

See also STEVENS, JOHN COX.

Embry, Wayne R. (1937–)
Basketball
Born March 26, 1937, Springfield, OH

Embry became the first black executive in professional sports in 1972, when he was named general manager of the Milwaukee Bucks. He became a vice-president of the team in 1977. Embry was briefly vice-president and consultant for the Indiana Pacers from 1985 until he went to the Cleveland Cavaliers as vice-president and general manager in June of 1986. The team had won just 29 games while losing 53 the previous season. Embry engineered a series of trades that made them contenders in the 1988–89 season, when they finished second to the Detroit Pistons in the powerful central division. A graduate of Miami University (OH), Embry played for Cincinnati (1959–66), Boston (1966–68), and Milwaukee (1968–69) averaging 12.5 points a game.

English Channel Swim

The first person to propel himself across the English Channel was Paul Boynton of the United States on April 10, 1875, but he did it in a most unusual way. Wearing an inflatable lifesaving suit, he paddled across the channel in 23 hours 30 minutes. A little more than four months later, on August 24–25, Matthew Webb of England swam, unaided, from Dover,

England, to Cap Gris Nez, France, in 21 hours 45 minutes. In the 1920s and 1930s, there were 22 successful channel swims. The first was by an American, Henry Sullivan, on August 6, 1923. Exactly three years later, Gertrude Ederle became the first woman to do it, setting a new record. The feat almost became a fad after World War II. There was an annual race across the channel from 1948 through 1959, with a high of 18 finishers in 1951. The shortest distance across the Channel is about 21 miles, but currents and tides can make the actual swim much longer.

See also CHADWICK, FLORENCE; EDERLE, GERTRUDE.

Entertainment and Sports Programming Network (ESPN)

ESPN wasn't given much chance for success when it went on the air in September of 1979 as a 24-hour, all-sports cable channel. The idea was conceived by William Rasmussen of Hartford, CT, and it was made possible by satellite communications. Rasmussen persuaded Getty Oil to pay $10 million for 85 percent of the network seven months before its first broadcast, and Chet Simmons, president of NBC Sports, was hired to run the new network. ESPN at first paid local cable stations 5 cents per subscriber to carry its programming to build an audience.

The network started by broadcasting minor sports events that cost little or no money, including hurling and slow-pitch softball, and much of its programming was rebroadcast in the early morning for sports junkies who worked the late shift. In some cases, the sponsor of an event actually paid ESPN to broadcast it. When Bill Grimes succeeded Simmons in 1982, he stopped paying local systems and began charging them 7 cents per subscriber.

The number of cable systems grew from about 625 in 1979 to nearly 14,000 in 1985. As cable penetration increased, so did advertising revenue, giving ESPN more money to spend on rights fees for major sports. ESPN developed the strategy of sharing major events with the networks—for example, broadcasting the early rounds of the NCAA basketball tournament, leaving the regional and national finals for CBS. The network also picked up events for the rabid fan, among them the professional leagues' college player drafts.

In 1983, ESPN covered the America's Cup races in their entirety. The United States lost the cup for the first time, to Australia, and in 1987 the network invested $2 million in coverage of the races when the United States won it back. The investment paid off in more than $4 million of advertising from sponsors looking for the upscale yachting audience—Domaine Chandon champagne, for example. The coverage won rave reviews because of the use of miniaturized cameras mounted on masts, camera locations on helicopters, blimps, and boats, and microphones mounted throughout the yachts.

That was a breakthrough year for ESPN. The network had finally turned a small profit in 1985, and a somewhat larger profit in 1986. By the end of 1987, it had a larger prime-time audience than any other cable channel, and it moved into really big-time sports with Sunday night pro football. In 1989, ESPN signed a contract with major-league baseball to telecast 175 games in 1990, and ESPN officials were talking about tackling the 1992 Olympic Games. The network at the end of 1989 was available to about 52 million viewers, and advertising revenue was well over $200 million a year.

See also TELEVISION.

Equestrian Sports

One equestrian event, individual jumping, was on the 1900 Olympic program along with two now obsolete events that were held only that year, the high jump and the long jump. The three-day event, team jumping, and individual dressage were added in 1912, team dressage in 1928.

Dressage, from the French *dresser*, to train, is a test of how well a horse has been schooled. It involves performing a variety of complex movements in a limited area, with subjective judging, as in figure skating and gymnastics. Jumping, or the *Prix des Nations*, is competition over a course including a variety of jumps. Penalty points are deducted for failing to clear an obstacle cleanly and for exceeding a specified time limit. The three-day event, also called combined training, has a test of dressage on the first day, an endurance run over a cross-country course on the second day, and jumping on the third day. North America hosts four major international competitions annually, in New York City, Washington, D.C., Toronto, and Calgary.

U.S. Army Cavalry teams represented the United States in international competition until after World War II. To fill the gap left by the army's withdrawal from the sport, International Equestrian Competitions, Inc., was formed in 1949. The name was changed to the U.S. Equestrian Team the following year. The USET selects, trains, equips, and finances teams for the Olympic Games, the Pan-American Games, the World Championships, and other international events. Training centers are maintained at Gladstone, NJ, and Hamilton, MA. The U.S. Combined Training Association sanctions and oversees scheduling of combined training competitions, distributes rule books and manuals, and sponsors clinics and conferences. The U.S. Dressage Federation, organized in 1973, is made up of about 96 local dressage groups. It's basically a promotional and educational association that works with the USET and the USCTA.

Since 1978, the American Grandprix Association has conducted a professional show jumping tour. The 1990 tour offered total prize money of more than $1.5 million for 31 events.

Addresses: American Grandprix Association, P.O. Box 495, Wayne, PA 19087 (215) 438-8383; Canadian Equestrian Federation, 333 River Road, Tower B-12, Vanier, Ontario, Canada K1L 8H9 (613) 748-5606; U.S. Combined Training Association, 292 Bridge Street, S. Hamilton, MA 01982 (508) 468-7133; U.S. Dressage Federation, P.O. Box 80668, Lincoln, NE 68501 (402) 474-7632; U.S. Equestrian Team, Gladstone, NJ 07934 (201) 234-1251.

See also HORSE SHOWS.

Equitation
See EQUESTRIAN SPORTS.

Erving, Julius "Dr. J" (1950–   )
Basketball
Born February 22, 1950, Roosevelt, NY

The "slam dunk" was invented by giant centers, but none of them could do it the way Dr. J did. He would take off from near the foul line and glide through the air for 12 or 15 feet before jamming the ball into the basket. Erving was the biggest single drawing card in professional basketball for more than a decade, and, as sportswriter Tony Kornheiser put it, he was "the first black athlete regarded with such esteem that white fathers confidently recommended him as a role model for their sons."

Though he was only 6 feet 6 inches, Erving played center at the University of Massachusetts. He left school before his senior year to play for the Virginia Squires in the American Basketball Association and was the league's Rookie of the Year in 1972, averaging 27.2 points and 15.7 rebounds a game. He jumped briefly to the National Basketball Association's Atlanta Hawks the following season, but was ordered by a court to return to the Squires before the season started. In 1974, Erving was traded to the New York Nets, and he played there through the 1975–76 season, then went to the Philadelphia 76ers, where he played for 11 seasons. In his final regular-season game, in 1987, he scored 38 points for a career total of 30,002, mak-

ing him the third player in history with more than 30,000 points. Erving was the ABA's Most Valuable Player three times, and he won the NBA award in 1981.

Eskimo Sports
Like the other native Americans of North America, the Eskimo enjoyed a wide variety of sports and games. Many tribes played a kind of football, using a sealskin ball stuffed with hair or moss, and they often used the same ball for handball. The Eskimo of Kotzebue Sound played "stickball," which was somewhat similar to baseball.

Tug-of-war and similar games were also played. Among the Iglulik, tug-of-war was a woman's game, and both the Netsilik and the Polar Eskimo had a two-man version, using two rounded pieces of wood joined by a strip of leather or sealskin. Many other tests of strength were spread through the Eskimo regions, including rock throwing, pulling locked arms or fingers, waist wrestling, and throwing hunting equipment for accuracy and distance. The Iglulik and the Labrador Eskimo both had friendly kinds of boxing, in which the competitors took turns striking one another on the shoulder or temple until one of them conceded defeat.

The Kotzebue Sound Eskimo were particularly competitive. They held contests in carpentry, carving, dancing, sewing, and storytelling, and when groups of men went hunting, they competed to see which group could bring home the most game. The Aleut had similar hunting competitions. The Iglulik and Labrador Inuit held target archery contests, and the Netsilik played an indoor archery game in which competitors shot at suspended prizes.

Many Eskimo games were tests of dexterity, played by both men and women. In the cup-and-pin game, a wooden or ivory pin was attached by string to a cup, and the player tossed the pin into the air and tried to catch it in the cup. The ring-and-pin game was similar, but the object was to get the pin through a ring. The Netsilik had an unusual game in which a piece of ivory pierced with small holes was attached to a wall with one string, while a person twirled it at high speed with a second string. The other players then tried to stop the ivory by inserting a small pick into one of the holes.

Further Reading: Damas, David, volume editor. *Handbook of North American Indians, Volume 5: Arctic.* Washington, D.C.: Smithsonian Institution, 1984.

See also NATIVE AMERICAN SPORTS; WORLD ESKIMO-INDIAN OLYMPICS.

Espirito Santo Trophy
Golf

This trophy is awarded for the Women's World Amateur Team Championship, which has been held every two years since 1964 under the auspices of the World Amateur Golf Council.

ESPN

See ENTERTAINMENT AND SPORTS PROGRAMMING NETWORK.

Esposito, Philip A. (1942–   )
Hockey

Born February 20, 1942, Sault Ste. Marie, Ontario; Hockey Hall of Fame

One of the most dangerous scorers in National Hockey League history, Esposito got many of his goals by firing a quick wrist shot without looking at the net. A center, Esposito began his NHL career with the Chicago Black Hawks in 1963, and in 1967 he was traded to the Boston Bruins. He led the league in scoring in 1969, 1971, 1972, 1973, and 1974, and won the Hart Trophy as the league's Most Valuable Player in 1969 and 1974. Esposito and Bobby Orr led the Bruins to Stanley Cup championships in 1970 and 1972. The Bruins in 1975 traded him to the New York Rangers, where he played through the 1979–80 season. In 18 seasons as a player, Esposito scored 717 goals and 873 assists for a total of 1,590 points in 1,282 games.

Ethnicity in Sport

Studying the names of athletes can reveal a great deal about the history of ethnic groups in North America. The first sports were introduced by immigrants, of course. The Dutch in New Amsterdam brought nine-pin bowling, a type of billiards called "truck" and ice skating, and the first English colonists played skittles and stoolball. Cavalier immigrants fleeing to Virginia after the execution of Charles I in 1649 introduced sports of the British gentry, including horse racing. Rounders, which was to evolve into baseball, came from England during the 18th century, along with football (actually a primitive form of soccer).

Scottish immigrants in the 19th century banded together in Caledonian clubs, and their annual Highland, or Caledonian, games led to the birth of track and field. And the Turners, who came to North America after the failure of Germany's 1848 revolution, formed their own clubs, the Turnverein, where gymnastics and fencing were important components of a total program of mental, spiritual, and physical training. Although modern boxing came from England, Irish immigrants were instrumental in its early development as a professional sport.

Modern baseball originally developed as an amateur sport among clubs made up of upper middle-class English-Americans, typified by its "inventor," Alexander Cartwright, and its first chronicler, Henry Chadwick, a native of England. But when it became a professional sport, Irish- and German-Americans were so predominant among the best players that some speculated they had a special inborn talent for the game, just as some speculate today that blacks have a natural aptitude for basketball. In the 20th century, several other ethnic groups invaded the national sport. Napoleon Lajoie, called "the first superstar of modern baseball," was French-American, as were Charles "Deacon" Phillippe, a top pitcher early in the century, and Jeff Tesreau, a pitcher with the New York Giants from 1912 through 1918. Harry Coveleski became a major-league pitcher in 1907, followed by his brother Stan in 1912 and the great hitter, Al Simmons (Aloysius Szymanski) in 1924. In the 1920s came Tony Lazzeri, followed by Frank Crosetti, the three DiMaggio brothers, Tony Cuccinello, Cookie Lavagetto, Ernie Lombardi, and Dolph Camilli.

American football, which sprang from the Canadian version of English rugby, was embraced by college students from upper middle-class families and was confined in its early years to a handful of schools in the Northeast. The names of the early All-Americans are typically English, although there's a sprinkling of Irish and German names. But as the sport spread to the land-grant colleges of the Midwest, Scandinavian, Jewish, German, Slavic, and Italian names began to appear. One of the first great passing combinations, at the University of Michigan, had Benny Friedman, a Jew, throwing to Bennie Oosterbaan, a Dutch-American. Notre Dame's famous coach, Knute Rockne, was a native of Norway, and Coach Bob Zuppke at the University of Illinois was born in Germany. During the 1930s, the "Fighting Irish" of Notre Dame had stars named Schwartz, Carideo, Metzger, Vlk, Terlzak, Hoffman, Jaskwich, Lukats, Sheeketski, LaBorne, Pivarnik, Melinkovich, Pfefferle, Schiralli, Mazziotti, Carideo, Solari, Canali, Schrenker, Pojman, Steinkemper, Wijcikovski, Kuharich, Skoglund, Tonelli, Zontini, DeFranco, Sitko, and Gubanich.

Professional football originated largely in mining areas and steel manufacturing centers. Many of the early professional players were of Eastern European descent. The South Bend Athletics, who were undefeated in 12 games and claimed the professional football championship in 1915, had players named Sobieraski, Sokolowski, Klosinski, Ruszkowski,

Greenburg, Schaefer, and Brakeman. George Halas, who founded the Chicago Bears (originally the Decatur Staleys) was of Slavic descent, and Jim Thorpe, whose name was almost synonymous with pro football when it became organized in 1920, was part Sac-Fox Indian and part Irish-German. Thorpe played college football at Carlisle Institute in Pennsylvania, an Indian school that produced great teams under Glenn "Pop" Warner.

Boxing, because it was a predominantly lower-class sport that offered an escape from ghettos, reflected the changing ethnic patterns in urban America. Until the early part of the century, Irish-Americans dominated the sport, although there were also many outstanding black fighters, including George Dixon, who in 1890 became the first black champion, in the bantamweight division. Jewish boxers began to emerge about 1900. The first Jewish champion was Abe Attell, who won the featherweight title in 1901, and many other Jews won championships, including Louis "Kid" Kaplan, Harry Greb, Benny Leonard, Barney Ross, and Max Baer, who became heavyweight champion in 1934. About 1920, a wave of Italian contenders and champions arrived, including Pete Herman (Peter Gulotta), Johnny Dundee (Joseph Carrora), Tony Canzoneri, Frankie Genaro, and Rocky Graziano. Canada contributed three French-Canadian champions, Johnny Coulon, Jack Delaney (Ovila Chapdelaine), and Albert "Frenchy" Belanger. The sport in North America is now dominated by black and Hispanic fighters.

Basketball was urban-centered after its invention in 1891, partly because it was fostered by YMCAs, but also because it required little space and there was an abundance of gyms in the big cities. The first top professional teams had many Jewish players, among them Barney Sedran, Benny Borgman, and Nat Holman. One of the great barnstorming teams, the Sphas, originated at the South Philadelphia Hebrew Association. Another, the Harlem Renaissance Big Five, was an all-black team. The Rens inspired Abe Saperstein, a Jew, to organize the Harlem Globetrotters in 1926. As with boxing and baseball, many Italian-Americans later entered the sport, including Hank Luisetti, who revolutionized basketball by displaying amazing precision with the one-handed shot in a 1936 game at Madison Square Garden.

During the late 19th and early 20th centuries, sport was seen as a way of Americanizing the children of immigrant families. Walter Camp's view was typical of many leaders in sports: "Americanization is more possible . . . through the medium of American sport than in almost any other way." The physical education movement in the public schools and the playground movement in major cities both had their roots in this outlook. Foreign-born parents didn't necessarily agree. Rube Marquard, who became a Hall of Fame pitcher, ran away from home as a teenager because his father, a German-born engineer, didn't want him to play baseball. And the Italian-born father of Joe, Vince, and Dom DiMaggio, all of whom became major-league outfielders, wanted his sons to play boccie, an Italian version of lawn bowling, instead of baseball.

Despite parental opposition, most immigrant children did take up American sports. As Oscar Handlin put it, "Increasingly the thoughts of the children were preoccupied with the events of the world of sport within which were played out the vivid dramas of American success and failure." And professional sports brought players of different ethnic groups in contact with one another. In 1939, Franklin D. Roosevelt could say, with some truth, "Baseball has become, through the years, not only a great national sport but also the symbol of America as a melting pot." But he ignored the fact that black players were banned from playing at the highest level of the national sport, as they were banned from the National Football League and the National Basketball League. That deserves its own story.

See also BLACKS IN SPORTS.

Evansville, IN

The Evansville Crimson played in the National Football League for just one season, 1922.

Ewry, Ray C. (1873–1937)
Track and Field

Born October 14, 1873, Lafayette, IN; died September 29, 1937; National Track and Field Hall of Fame

As a boy, Ewry contracted polio and was confined to a wheelchair. He began exercising, regained the use of his legs, and then started jumping to strengthen them. He went on to win ten Olympic Gold Medals in the standing jumps, which were discontinued after 1912. He won the standing long jump, standing high jump, and standing triple jump in 1900 and 1904. The triple jump was eliminated, but he won the other standing jumps at the "Intercalated Games" of 1906 and the regular Olympics of 1908.

Exterminator
Horse Racing

Exterminator looked like a scarecrow and was known as "Old Bones" or the "Galloping Hat Rack." As a two-year-old in 1917, he started four races, winning two, then came up lame. He was bought by Willis Kilmer to help train another horse, Sun Briar, for the 1918 Kentucky Derby. However, Sun Briar was held out of the race because of a muddy track and Exterminator was entered instead. He won the Derby and went on to become one of the greatest handicap horses of all time. Often carrying as much as 138 or 140 pounds, he won 50 of 100 starts, finishing second 17 times and third 17 times. Four years in a row, from 1919 through 1922, he was the top money-winner among horses four years old and up. Among his major victories were the Brooklyn Handicap in 1922, the Pimlico Cup in 1919, 1920, and 1921, and the Saratoga Cup in 1919, 1920, 1921, and 1922.

Fairs

English country fairs were outdoor markets at which farmers and artisans could sell their wares, but they also offered recreation, furnishing the pattern for 18th century colonial fairs. Among the sports commonly associated with fairs were running, wrestling, cudgeling, and greased pig chases, usually for prizes of merchandise such as a pair of shoes or gloves, a hat, or silver buckles. In Virginia and Maryland, horse races were often held.

About the middle of the 19th century, the country market fair was replaced by county and state fairs to promote agriculture, with prizes for livestock, poultry, and crops, but entertainment remained important. Harness racing, justified because it could help improve horse breeding, has been the major sport of county and state fairs from their beginning. The famous pacers of the 19th century raced at many fairs, and some fairs have also featured auto racing.

Fashion Race Course
Long Island, NY

The Fashion Jockey Club took over the National Race Course in Newtown, Long Island, and reopened it under its new name on June 17, 1856. Thoroughbred racing failed, but it became a successful harness track in 1862. Historically, it is best known as the site of three all-star baseball games between Brooklyn and New York City teams in 1858.

Faurot, Don (1902–   )
Football

Born June 23, 1902, Mountain Grove, MO; National Football Foundation Hall of Fame

Faurot invented the split-T formation at the University of Missouri in 1941. The key to the formation is an option play, in which the quarterback slides down the line of scrimmage with a trailing half back and watches the defensive end. If the end heads for the quarterback, he pitches the ball to the half back; if the end chooses to cover the half back, the quarterback keeps the ball and runs upfield. By the early 1950s, most major college teams were using the split T. A 1925 graduate of Missouri, Faurot coached at Northeast Missouri state from 1926 through 1934, then returned to his alma mater in 1935 and coached there through the 1946 season. His overall record was 164–92–13.

Feathers, Beattie (1908–1979)
Football

Born August 4, 1908, Bristol, VA; died March 11, 1979; National Football Foundation Hall of Fame

Feathers, an All-American half back at the University of Tennessee in 1933, joined the Chicago Bears in

This is a view of the Fashion Race Course on Long Island when it opened in 1856 as it appeared in Frank Leslie's Illustrated Weekly.

1934, and became the first National Football League player ever to rush for more than 1,000 yards. Despite missing two games, he gained 1,004 yards in 101 carries. That was his only big professional season. After three more years with the Bears, he played for the Brooklyn Dodgers in 1938–39 and the Green Bay Packers in 1940 before retiring. In seven seasons, he rushed for 1,979 yards, a 5.5-yard average, with 16 touchdowns.

Federal Baseball Case

When the National and American Leagues worked out a peace settlement with the Federal League after the 1915 season, the Baltimore team of the Federal League was left out. On March 29, 1916, the team filed a suit against organized baseball under the Sherman Anti-Trust Act. A judge in the District Court of Columbia ruled in 1919 that organized baseball was a monopoly, and a jury set damages at $80,000. The case went to the Supreme Court and Oliver Wendell Holmes, writing a 1922 opinion for a unanimous court, said that baseball did not fall under the Sherman Act because "personal effort, not related to production, is not a subject of commerce."

See also FEDERAL LEAGUE.

Federal League
Baseball

Organized in 1913, the Federal League had teams in Chicago, Cincinnati, Cleveland, Indianapolis, Pittsburgh, and St. Louis. The Cincinnati team moved to Kansas City in midseason. Although it invaded territories belonging to National Agreement teams, the league didn't raid them for players and was essentially ignored by organized baseball at first. But in 1914 the league expanded to eight teams, dropping Cleveland and moving into Baltimore, Brooklyn and Buffalo. It also acquired some wealthy investors and announced that its teams would not honor the reserve clause.

The Federal League operated as a single corporation, with each team owning ten shares of stock. The league was given the leases or sole rights to all ball parks used by its teams. Players were entitled to automatic 5 percent salary increases each year, and a player who had been in the league for any part of ten different seasons was entitled to become a free agent upon request. The Federal League signed only 81 established major-league players in its two years of existence, but the competition forced salaries up. For example, Rabbit Maranville of the National League's Boston team got a raise from $1,800 to $6,000 to prevent his jumping to the new league.

A variety of suits and a bewildering array of court opinions followed. Teams in organized baseball sued to keep players from performing for Federal League teams, while Federal League teams sued to regain players who had signed their contracts and then gone back to their original teams. A Chicago judge found that the reserve clause was binding, but was overruled by a higher court. A federal district court in Maryland declared that the standard player contract lacked mutuality, because it bound a player, in effect, for life, while the team could release him with ten days' notice. Hal Chase was enjoined from playing with the Federal League Buffalo team, but a higher court dissolved the injunction on the grounds that the contract produced "a species of quasi-peonage."

After good attendance early in the 1914 season, the Federal League began to suffer, and several teams were forced to lower ticket prices. The league's losses were estimated at $176,000. Nevertheless, it kept going in 1915, and there were periodic peace talks throughout the year. On December 13, National League owners met with two of the Federal League's chief backers and worked out a tentative settlement. A committee appointed by the American League then went to New York for a December 17 meeting and an agreement was signed five days later. Organized baseball agreed to pay $600,000 to the Federal League for dissolving, and the owners of the Chicago and St. Louis Federal League team were allowed to buy the National League and American League teams, respectively, in those cities.

See also FEDERAL BASEBALL CASE.

Federation Cup
Tennis

The women's equivalent of the Davis Cup, the Federation Cup was established by the International Lawn Tennis Federation in 1963. The idea of a trophy for international team competition among women had been in the air for some time. The U.S. Lawn Tennis Association in 1961 agreed to sponsor international competition, but a year later the ILTF preempted the idea. The United States won the first Federation Cup tournament, in London.

Federation Movement

During the late 1960s, the National Collegiate Athletic Association and the Amateur Athletic Union resumed their long-standing struggle for control of amateur sports after a temporary truce. The NCAA adopted the strategy of forming independent federations for the many sports controlled by the AAU. Two of them, the U.S. Gymnastics Federation and the U.S. Wrestling Federation, won recognition from the International Olympic Committee as the national governing bodies for those sports. In 1978, Congress passed the Amateur Sports Act, requiring that each Olympic sport should have its own independent governing body under the overall supervision of the U.S. Olympic Committee.

See also AMATEUR ATHLETIC UNION; AMATEURISM; NATIONAL COLLEGIATE ATHLETIC ASSOCIATION.

Feller, "Bob" Robert W. A. (1918–)
Baseball

Born November 3, 1918, Van Meter, IA; Baseball Hall of Fame

Feller's fastball, once timed at more than 98 miles an hour, made him one of the great strikeout pitchers of all time. He joined the Cleveland Indians in 1936, at 17. Though used sparingly, he tied Dizzy Dean's record with 17 strikeouts in a game. After the season, he went back to Iowa for his senior year in high school. Feller became a full-time starter in 1938 and led the American League in strikeouts four years in a row. He pitched the only opening-day no-hitter in history on April 16, 1940, against the Chicago White Sox. After records of 24–9 in 1939, 27–11 in 1940, and 25–13 in 1941, he joined the navy shortly after the start of the 1942 season.

Feller had his greatest season in 1946, winning 26 games, with a league-leading 10 shutouts and a major-league record 348 strikeouts (later broken by Sandy Koufax and Nolan Ryan). He also threw a no-hitter on April 30 against the New York Yankees. He won 20 games in 1947, when he again led the league in shutouts with 5 and strikeouts with 196. Feller was no longer the ace of the Cleveland staff in 1948, when the Indians won the pennant, but he had one more 20-victory season, in 1951, when he pitched his third no-hitter against the Detroit Tigers on July 1.

Feller retired after the 1956 season. In his 18 years with the Indians, he won 266 games, lost 162, struck out 2,581 hitters, and had 42 shutouts and a 3.25 earned run average.

Fencing

A required skill for the gentry, fencing was practiced in Virginia in the mid-17th century. A century later, John Rievers advertised fencing lessons in New York City, and there were fencing masters in New Orleans at the time of the Louisiana Purchase in 1803. A Mr. Girard ran an advertisement in the March 16, 1816, *Montreal Herald* announcing "that he will open a FENCING SCHOOL, for the purpose of teaching the Small Sword, Cut and Thrust, and Broad Sword exercises in the modern style." However, it was the German Turner movement that brought modern fencing to North America. The New York Turnverein, established in 1850, hired Franz Siegel as its

fencing master the following year. As the Turner system of gymnastics was adopted by athletic clubs and colleges after the Civil War, fencing often accompanied it.

The New York Fencers Club was established in 1883 and five years later the Amateur Athletic Union held the first national championships in the sport. A group of New York fencers, unhappy with the AAU, formed the Amateur Fencers League of America in 1891 and the AFLA took over the national tournament the following year. It was renamed the U.S. Fencing Association in 1981. Columbia, Harvard, and Yale formed the Intercollegiate Fencing Association (IFA) in 1894 and held a championship tournament in foils.

Fencing was on the first modern Olympic program in 1896, but no Americans competed until 1912. Women's foil became a national championship event in 1912 and was added to the Olympic program in 1924. (Women fence only with foil; men with foil, epee, and saber.) Bryn Mawr, Cornell, New York University, and Pennsylvania in 1929 founded the Intercollegiate Women's Fencing Association, which became the National Intercollegiate Women's Fencing Association in 1972.

Addresses: Canadian Fencing Association, 333 River Road, Vanier, Ontario, Canada K1L 8H9 (613) 748-5633; Intercollegiate Fencing Association, P.O. Box 3, Centerville, MA 02632 (508) 771-5060; National Intercollegiate Women's Fencing Association, 235 McCosh Road, Upper Montclair, NJ 07043 (201) 783-9871; U.S. Fencing Association, 1750 East Boulder, Colorado Springs, CO 80909 (719) 578-4511

Fenway Park
Boston, MA

The Boston Red Sox played at the Huntington Avenue Grounds, a wooden ballpark that opened in 1901, when the team came into existence. They moved to Fenway in 1912, and the park was extensively renovated in 1934. The wooden left-field wall was replaced with the present "Green Monster," 37 feet high. Home run distances are 315 feet down the left-field line, 420 feet to center, and 302 feet to right-field. Seating capacity is 33,583.

Field Handball

See TEAM HANDBALL.

Field Hockey

Field hockey evolved from an English schoolboy sport called bandy. Princeton University prohibited bandy in 1787, calling it "low and unbecoming gentlemen and scholars," and it was played at North Carolina's Trinity College (now Duke University) in

The New York Fencers Club was conducting classes for women as early as 1888, as this lithograph shows.

the early-19th century. It seems to have died out, because modern field hockey was reintroduced by English troops in Canada during the mid-19th century.

The sport was evidently tried and abandoned by U.S. college men late in the century, but Canadian women were playing field hockey in British Columbia as early as 1896. Field hockey became a major women's sport in the United States largely because of Constance M. K. Applebee from the British College of Physical Education. At Harvard in 1901, she was surprised to find that field hockey was unknown here. "An English woman cannot be judged athletically until she performs in field hockey," she said, and demonstrated the sport to a group of physical educators, using ice hockey sticks and a softball.

Applebee taught the sport that fall at Vassar and later at Bryn Mawr, Mount Holyoke, Smith, and Wellesley. She presided over the meeting at which the U.S. Field Hockey Association was organized on January 21, 1922, and many women learned the sport at her hockey camp in Mt. Pocono, PA. Interest flagged somewhat before and shortly after World War I, but a U.S. team visited England in 1920 and an English team reciprocated the following year.

American men also learned the sport from an Englishwoman in 1926, when Louise Roberts, a coach at Rosemary Hall School in Greenwich, CT demonstrated it to a group headed by Henry K. Greer of Rye, NY. (She later became Mrs. Greer.) The first men's match was played October 28, 1928, between the Rye Field Hockey Club and a team from the Germantown Cricket Club of Philadelphia. The Field Hockey Association of America was organized in 1930 to govern the men's sport and to select a team for the 1932 Olympic Games. Field hockey has never won much popularity among men in North America, but it is a major fall sport for high school and college women in the United States. Canada during the 1920s developed a form of the sport with five men and six women on a team, but field hockey on the whole never really caught on in Canada. The Canadian Women's Field Hockey Association wasn't organized until 1962, and there is no governing body for the men's sport in Canada.

Addresses: Canadian Women's Field Hockey Association, 333 River Road, Vanier, Ontario, Canada K1L 8H9 (613) 748-5634; Field Hockey Association of America, 1750 East Boulder, Colorado Springs,

CO 80909 (719) 578-4587; U.S.A. Field Hockey Association, 1750 East Boulder, Colorado Springs, CO 80909 (719) 578-4567

Field Trials

The field trial is for hunting dogs what dressage is for a horses: a test to see how well the animal has been trained. The first field trial in North America was held in 1874 at Memphis, TN. Dogs are judged on a variety of skills, including pointing, backing, keenness of nose, and running style. Trials are held for several different breeds under the auspices of the American Kennel Club and the Amateur Field Trial Club of America.

Address: Amateur Field Trial Club of America, R.R. 1, Box 185, Stanton, TN 38069 (901) 548-6076

Fiesta Bowl
Football

The first Fiesta Bowl was played on December 27, 1971, at Tempe, AZ, home of Arizona State University, which won four of the first five games. Since 1978, the Fiesta Bowl has invited two of the best college teams in the country not committed to other bowls. The game has been played on January 1 since 1982.

Results

1971	Arizona State 45, Florida State 38
1972	Arizona State 49, Missouri 35
1973	Arizona State 28, Pittsburgh 7
1974	Oklahoma State 16, Brigham Young 6
1975	Arizona State 17, Nebraska 14
1976	Oklahoma 41, Wyoming 7
1977	Penn State 42, Arizona State 30
1978	Arkansas 10, UCLA 10
1979	Pittsburgh 16, Arizona 10
1980	Penn State 31, Ohio State 19
1982	Penn State 26, Southern California 10
1983	Arizona State 32, Oklahoma 21
1984	Ohio State 28, Pittsburgh 23
1985	UCLA 39, Miami (FL) 37
1986	Michigan 27, Nebraska 23
1987	Penn State 14, Miami (FL) 10
1988	Florida State 31, Nebraska 28
1989	Notre Dame 34, West Virginia 21
1990	Florida State 41, Nebraska 17
1991	Louisville 34, Alabama 7

Figure Skating

Figure skating, as it originated in England, was simply the cutting of various figures and patterns into the ice, and the skaters were usually stiff and ungainly. The *Treatise of Skating* by Robert Jones, published in 1772, describes some simple figures. In the early 19th century, a French group, known as the *Gilets Rouges* because they wore red vests, added pirouettes and a jump. While the British were inventing new figures, Jackson Haines, an American ballet master, added dance movements. He toured Europe in 1864 and was well received, especially in Vienna, where he settled down to teach.

As skating became popular in North America, covered rinks were built in the late 1850s and early 1860s. They gave rise to organized clubs. A Philadelphia club sponsored a competitive exhibition as early as 1862, and Canadian skating carnivals often featured figure skating competition in fancy dress. One of the first was the Montreal Masquerade Skating Carnival in 1865. Rules were formulated in 1868 by the American Skating Congress, but the first national championships weren't held until 1886, when the National Amateur Skating Association was organized.

The first great North American figure skater was Louis Rubinstein of Montreal, who studied with Haines in the early 1870s. Rubinstein taught skating and helped organize the Amateur Skating Union of Canada in 1887. Like the NASA, it controlled both figure and speed skating. Rubinstein was the Canadian champion 12 years in a row, 1878–89, and he won the U.S. championship in 1888 and 1889. Because of his influence, the Viennese style of figure skating became predominant in North America.

The Canadian and U.S. organizations formed the International Skating Union of America on February 1, 1907. In 1914, the Amateur Skating Union of Canada established a separate Figure Skating Department. It was renamed the Canadian Figure Skating Association in 1939 and became an independent body in 1947. Similarly, the U.S. Figure Skating Association became independent in 1921, leaving the parent group to oversee speed skating only.

The International Skating Union was organized in 1892 as the governing body for both figure and speed skating and held the first world championships at St. Petersburg (now Leningrad) in 1895. Competitive figure skating was for men only until 1902, when Madge Syers-Cave of England entered the championship and finished second. A separate women's championship was established in 1906, and pairs skating was added the following year.

The 1908 Olympics in London featured figure skating, and the sport was on the program of the first Winter Olympics in 1920. But it was still a sport for the few, to be watched by a few, until Sonja Henie of Norway burst onto the scene. She combined grace and technique with an athletic approach that had never been seen before. Henie, who won three

The figure skating champion at the 1976 Winter Olympics, Dorothy Hamill, was also a two-time U.S. champion in 1974 and 1976. Courtesy of the U.S. Figure Skating Association

Gold Medals, drew crowds whenever she skated and inspired many young people to begin figure skating.

Austria and the Scandinavian countries dominated world figure skating until after World War II. The first North American to win a world championship was Barbara Ann Scott of Canada, in 1947. The following year, Dick Button of the United States did for men what Henie had done for women, only more so. Button leaped higher than the rink barriers in an unprecedented display of power skating, winning the first of his five consecutive world championships. He also won three Olympic Gold Medals.

Athleticism was suddenly in. Donald Jackson of Canada brought it to a peak when he did three triple jumps, a Lutz, a Salchow, and a loop, while winning the 1962 world championship. Another Canadian, Petra Burka, on February 24, 1966, became the first woman to do a triple Salchow. But athleticism was displayed only during the free-skating portion of the competition, which counted just 40 percent of the skater's score. Crowds were often displeased when a spectacular free skater didn't win because of low scores on the compulsory figures. The ISU in 1967 changed the scoring ratio to 50-50, and in 1973 a short program with compulsory free-skating move-

ments was added to the competition, for 20 percent of the score, with school figures and free skating each counting 40 percent. The trend continued in 1976, when the figures were cut down to 30 percent, while free skating went up to 50. The school figures were eliminated completely shortly before the 1988 Winter Olympics.

Ice dancing dates to the 1880s, when it was popular in Austria and England. The first world championship was held in 1950, and ice dancing became an Olympic sport in 1976. In Canada, two other types of figure skating are very popular. Fours skating is similar to pairs, except that a team is made up of two men and two women. The event was on the Canadian championship program from 1914 through 1964, and was added to the program again in 1981. Canada also holds a national championship in precision skating, in which teams of 12 or more skaters perform synchronized maneuvers to music.

See also CANADIAN FIGURE SKATING ASSOCIATION; ICE SKATING; WINTER OLYMPICS; WORLD FIGURE SKATING HALL OF FAME.

Filion, Herve (1940–   )
Harness Racing
Born February 1, 1940, Angers, Quebec; Hall of Fame of the Trotter

The all-time leading driver with 11,193 career wins, Filion was the youngest person ever elected to the Hall of Fame of the Trotter, at 35. Only a handful of drivers have won more than 400 races in a year; Filion has done it 15 times. He has been the top driver in victories 13 times, including seven years in a row, 1968–74. One reason Filion has accumulated so many victories is that since 1970 he's usually raced on two programs a day, at Freehold, NJ in the afternoon and then, after a helicopter ride, at Roosevelt or Yonkers at night.

Firestone Tournament of Champions
Bowling

The first big-money professional bowling tournament, the Firestone Tournament originally offered $100,000 in prize money in 1965. First place was worth $25,000. The purse has since increased to $250,000, with $50,000 for the winner.

Tournament of Champion Winners

1965	Billy Hardwick
1966	Wayne Zahn
1967	Jim Stefanich
1968	Dave Davis
1969	Jim Godman
1970	Don Johnson

1971	Johnny Petraglia
1972	Mike Durbin
1973	Jim Godman
1974	Earl Anthony
1975	Dave Davis
1976	Marshall Holman
1977	Mike Berlin
1978	Earl Anthony
1979	George Pappas
1980	Wayne Webb
1981	Steve Cook
1982	Mike Durbin
1983	Joe Berardi
1984	Mike Durbin
1985	Mark Williams
1986	Marshall Holman
1987	Pete Weber
1988	Mark Williams
1989	George Pappas
1990	Dave Ferraro

Fisherman's Challenge Cup
Yachting

Nova Scotia fishermen often took part in informal races in their sail-powered fishing boats during the early part of this century. In 1920, A. H. Dennis of the *Halifax Herald* donated the International Fisherman's Challenge Cup, with a prize of $7,000, for competition between fishing schooners from Canada and the United States. To the chagrin of the Nova Scotians, the United States won the cup. Then the schooner *Bluenose* was built, and she won every race in the series from 1921 through 1938, except for 1923. The series ended after 1938.

Fishing

While fishing may be a necessity, a business, or a recreation, it is also a competitive sport. Countless fishing derbies and tournaments are held on the local, national, and international levels. And some fishermen go game fishing in the hope of catching a world record. Among the major competitive events are the Cat Cay (FL) Tuna Tournament, the Bay Shore (Long Island) Mako Tournament, the Metropolitan Miami Fishing Tournament, the Ocean City (MD) Cup tournament, the International Light Tackle Tournament, and the International Billfish Tournament.

Salmon Unlimited conducts a series of tournaments, and U.S. Bass also sponsors a variety of international, national, regional, and local tournaments. The largest fishing organization in the world is the Bass Anglers Sportsman Society (BASS), with more than 400,000 members, which has been de-

scribed as "one big tournament." Hundreds of tournaments are run by its local chapters and affiliated organizations to select the finalists for the Bass Masters Classic, which offers $500 for the largest fish caught each day. In most of these tournaments, fish have to be released after they're caught, and in several of them the fish are tagged so their feeding patterns and migratory routes can be traced.

The International Game Fish Association, founded in 1939, registers records for about 50 species of saltwater fish caught on revolving spool or spinning tackle, using lines of various test strengths. The International Spin Fishing Association and the Salt Water Fly Rodders of America are two of the largest of the other organizations that compile records.

Address: International Game Fish Association, 3000 East Las Olas Boulevard, Ft. Lauderdale, FL 33316 (305) 467-0161

See also CASTING.

Fitzsimmons, James (1874–1966)
Horse Racing
Born July 23, 1874, Brooklyn, NY; died March 11, 1966; National Racing Hall of Fame

He was known as "Sunny Jim" because, as Red Smith put it, he was "kindly, spritely, gentle, generous, gracious, humble, wise, and brimming with life." Fitzsimmons was involved with Thoroughbred racing for 78 years, first as a water boy, then as exercise boy, stable hand, jockey, and trainer. He is the only man ever to have trained two Triple Crown winners—Gallant Fox in 1930 and Omaha in 1935—and he saddled ten other horses that won one or two of the Triple Crown races. Fitzsimmons led trainers in money winnings in 1936, 1939, and 1955, and he trained Bold Ruler, Horse of the Year in 1955.

Five-Pin Bowling

In 1905, Thomas F. Ryan opened the Temperance Street Bowling Club, the first regulation-sized alley in Toronto. Many of its members asked the pinboys to set up only five pins so they could get back to work on time after bowling on their lunch hours. In 1909, Ryan decided to make it a sport in its own right. He had five ten-pins whittled down and established a new scoring system, with each pin assigned a certain number of points. The first league was formed in 1910, the first women's league in 1921. The Canadian Bowling Association was organized in 1927, but western Canada used a different scoring system and formed its own group, the Western Canada Fivepin Bowling Association, in 1943. Ten years later, the two associations met and agreed on a compromise method of scoring. The Canadian Bowling Council was the governing body from 1964 to 1978, when it was replaced by the Canadian Five Pin Bowlers' Association.

Address: 1475 Star Top Road, #3, Gloucester, Ontario, Canada KIB 3W5 (613) 744-5090

Flag Football
See TOUCH FOOTBALL.

Flat-Water Racing
See CANOEING AND KAYAKING.

Fleischer, "Nat" Nathaniel S. (1887–1972)
Boxing
Born November 3, 1887, New York, NY; died June 24, 1972

"Mr. Boxing" covered every major championship fight for more than 50 years. Fleischer became a sportswriter after graduating from City College of New York in 1908. In 1922, he founded *Ring* magazine, known as the "Bible of boxing." Fleischer was not just a boxing reporter, he was a crusader for the sport. His articles and editorials spurred many improvements, including better ring padding and thorough prefight physical examinations. At a time when black fighters were unofficially banned from heavyweight championship fights, he mounted an unsuccessful campaign in 1922 to get Jack Dempsey to fight Harry Wills, a black who was certainly the top contender. During Fleischer's 50-year tenure at *Ring*, the magazine's monthly ratings of fighters were accepted as authoritative and helped to prevent mismatches.

Flora Temple
Harness Racing

It has been written that Stephen Foster's "Camptown Races" was a tribute to Flora Temple, since she was a "bob-tailed nag." She won 95 of 112 starts and was the first trotter to break the 2:20 mark. Foaled in 1845 in Oneida County, NY, she was sold for $350 in 1850, but after trotting a 2:36 mile her price was $4,000. Between 1853 and 1859, she broke the world record six times. The final record was 2:19¾, which stood until 1867.

Florida Citrus Bowl
See CITRUS BOWL.

Folk Games

By analogy with folk tales and folksongs, folk games are passed down among common people by oral tradition. As used in North American sports history,

the term applies primarily to games and amusements brought by colonists from their country villages in England. Among them were a variety of quasi-athletic games, including stoolball, a primitive version of cricket; quoits; wrestling and cudgeling; footracing and jumping; target shooting; skittles and lawn bowls; shinty and bandy, the ancestors of field hockey; and football. There were also such amusements as dice, card playing, and dancing, as well as blood sports like animal baiting and cockfighting. Folk games tended to be celebratory, involving an entire community, and were usually associated with Sunday afternoons, with holidays such as May Day and Shrove Tuesday, and with parish feasts, harvest festivals, and the Easter and Christmas seasons.

Further Reading: Brailsford, Dennis. *Sport and Society: Elizabeth to Anne*. London: Routledge & Kegan Paul, 1969; Malcolmson, Robert W. *Popular Recreations in English Society, 1700–1850*. London: Cambridge University Press, 1973.

See also COLONIAL ERA; PURITANISM.

Footbag

The footbag is a small, round beanbag filled with plastic pellets, and used for several games in which the bag can be touched only with the foot or the knee. The chief competitive sport is footbag net, which combines the playing rules of tennis with the scoring rules of volleyball. The World Footbag Association was founded in 1983 as a promotional and educational organization.

Address: World Footbag Association, 1317 Washington Avenue, Suite 7, Golden, CO 80401 (303) 278-9797

Football

A football game between two towns was recorded as early as 1685 in Massachusetts. College students began playing it in the late 18th century, and about 1840 an interclass contest became an annual event at Yale. Freshmen were given the ball, and they formed a kind of flying wedge to protect the ballcarrier, while sophomores tried to break through. A similar game was played at Harvard. Football was banned at both schools in 1860, as it had been at Brown, West Point, and Williams. The game was popular among schoolboys in Boston, where an annual match was played between Boston Latin School and Dixwell's private Latin school. Throwing the ball and striking it with the hand were permitted; in English soccer football, both were prohibited.

The first intercollegiate "football" game, played between Princeton and Rutgers on November 6, 1869, was really soccer. Under Rutgers' rules, there were

The earliest known portrayal of football in North America is this 1807 etching of Yale, with students kicking the ball in the foreground.

25 players on a team, and the ball could be advanced only by kicking. Rutgers won 6–4. A week later, Princeton won 8–0 under its own rules, which allowed batting the ball with hands or head.

Princeton, Rutgers, and Yale met to standardize rules in October of 1873, but Harvard refused to attend the meeting because its students preferred "the Boston Game." As a result, a Canadian team played in the most important game in the early history of American football. Harvard challenged McGill University of Montreal to two games, one under Harvard's rules and one under McGill's rules. Harvard won the first, 3–0 at Cambridge on May 14, 1874 and the next day they played a scoreless tie

under McGill's rules. McGill played a form of rugby, and the Harvard players decided they liked that sport even better than the Boston game.

In 1875, Yale and Harvard agreed to play under a set of "concessionary rules," actually pretty much Harvard's, and Harvard won, four goals and four touchdowns to nothing. Columbia, Harvard, Princeton, and Yale formed the Intercollegiate Football Association in a meeting at Springfield, MA in the fall of 1876. They agreed to play McGill's version of rugby, with some modifications.

In this early version of American football, there were 15 players per team: eight forwards on the "rush line," four halfbacks behind them, and three

A football game between freshmen and sophomores was an annual event at several colleges dating to the early 19th century. This Winslow Homer illustration from Harper's Weekly shows the 1857 "Bloody Monday" game at Harvard.

American football was brutal from the beginning until early in the 20th century, when rules changes opened up the game. This cartoon is from the Harvard Lampoon of November 21, 1879.

fullbacks farther back. The first major rules changes leading toward modern American football were made in October of 1880, when the number of players was reduced to 11 and rugby's "scrum" was replaced by a scrimmage. Instead of the two teams struggling for the ball after the runner was downed, the offensive team kept possession, and put the ball in play by having one of the forwards snapping it to a back with his foot. Both changes were suggested by Walter Camp of Yale.

Many colleges began to use the "block game" by simply holding onto the ball without attempting to advance it. The climax came in the championship game between Yale and Princeton on Thanksgiving Day, 1882, when Princeton held the ball for the first half and Yale held it for the second half. In 1883, also at Camp's suggestion, a rule was adopted requiring a team to gain 5 yards or lose 10 in three downs in order to keep possession of the ball.

This is a scene from the Yale-Princeton football game of 1879. The drawing by A.B. Frost appeared in Harper's Weekly on December 20.

Football was so rough in the early 1880s that the Harvard faculty banned it in 1885, saying it was "brutal, demoralizing to the players and to the spectators, and extremely dangerous." It became even more brutal in 1888, when tackling below the waist was allowed for the first time. Parke Davis wrote of this rule change, "Open field running disappeared and in its place came heavy interference, . . . flying wedges, turtle backs, mass play, momentum plays, flying interference. . . ."

Harvard dropped out of the IFA in 1890 and Pennsylvania and Wesleyan withdrew in 1893. The following year, Harvard, Pennsylvania, Princeton, and Yale formed a new rules committee and adopted a rule allowing only three members of the offensive team to be moving forward at the snap of the ball. But injuries were still a problem.

Football was no longer confined to the East. The University of Michigan had organized a team in 1879, followed by Minnesota in 1882, Northwestern in 1886, Indiana and Purdue in 1887, Iowa and Wisconsin in 1889, Illinois in 1890, and the University of Chicago in 1892. On February 8, 1896, Chicago, Illinois, Michigan, Minnesota, Northwestern, Purdue, and Wisconsin formed the Intercollegiate Conference of Faculty Representatives, primarily to establish eligibility rules.

After 18 college and high school players were killed in 1905, there was a widespread demand for the reform or abolition of football. President Theodore Roosevelt invited representatives from Harvard, Princeton, and Yale to discuss the problem in October of 1905. They promised to abide by the rules against roughness, but took no concrete action. The death of a Union College player after a game against New York University spurred others to action, however. Thirteen colleges were represented at a meeting on December 8, 1905, in New York City and they appointed a committee to propose rules changes. A second meeting, on December 28, was attended by 68 representatives.

In January of 1906, the new committee merged with the existing Intercollegiate Football Rules Committee to form the Intercollegiate Athletic Association, which became the National Collegiate Athletic Association in 1910. The rules of football were completely revised. A neutral zone was established between the offensive and defensive lines, the offense was required to have six men on the line of scrimmage, the yardage required for a first down was increased from 5 to 10 yards, the forward pass was legalized, and the number of officials was increased from two to four.

The changes didn't open up the game as much as hoped. Passing was hedged in by rules: A pass had

Serious injuries, even deaths, led colleges to consider doing away with football. This dramatic illustration was in the August 31, 1891, Harper's Weekly.

to be thrown at least 5 yards to either side of the center, could not be thrown more than 20 yards beyond the line of scrimmage, and, worst of all, if it wasn't caught, the ball was awarded to the defense. Because of the 5-yard rule, the field was marked in a gridiron pattern, with chalked lines at 5-yard intervals both across the field and from goal line to goal line.

Coaches developed a new kind of interference, in which blockers linked their arms in front of the ballcarrier. In 1909, there were 33 deaths in college football, and the rules makers made more changes, requiring seven men on the offensive line of scrimmage and forbidding interlocked interference. American football came very close to its present form in 1912, when the 20-yard limit on the forward pass was removed, the length of the field was reduced from 110 to 100 yards, the offense was given four downs in which to gain 10 yards, the 10-yard end zones were added, and the kickoff was moved from the 50- to the 40-yard line. A forward pass could now cross the line of scrimmage at any point, but the passer had to be at least 10 yards behind the line.

The present method of scoring (except for the two-point conversion) was also reached in 1912, after much evolution. Originally, a touchdown only entitled the team to a free try for a goal. In 1876, four touchdowns were made equal to field goal. The rule was amended in 1883 to give a victory to a team scoring four touchdowns over a team scoring a single goal. The touchdown increased to two points in 1883, four points in 1884, and five points in 1897, when the field goal was also worth five points; however, the touchdown allowed the scoring team a free try at goal, worth one point. The field goal was reduced to four points in 1904 and to three points in 1909. The touchdown reached its present value, six points, in 1912.

Meanwhile, professional football had begun. It started as an amateur sport conducted by athletic clubs in large cities, often sponsored by businesses in the small towns. At first, the players were local but, as time went on, some players were brought from outside, which inevitably led to professionalism. The teams often accused one another of paying players during the 1890s, but proof didn't emerge until about 70 years later, when a page from the Allegheny Athletic Association's account book revealed that Yale All-American "Pudge" Heffelfinger had been paid $500 for a game on November 12, 1892, against the Pittsburgh Athletic Club.

This kind of semiprofessional football spread rapidly through Pennsylvania and into upstate New York and Ohio. A major rivalry developed in Ohio between Canton and Massillon. The outstanding professional player during the early era was Jim Thorpe, who signed with Canton for $250 a game in 1915. Canton crowds had averaged about 1,200 until then. For the game with Massillon, 8,000 were on hand, and in 1916 the game in Massillon attracted 10,000 people.

In 1920, 13 teams founded the American Professional Football Association, which became the National Football League in 1922. But pro football was still played in small towns and cities while college football drew the crowds and got the coverage. During the 1920s, the football players fans read and talked about were Red Grange of Illinois, Ernie Nevers of Stanford, the Four Horsemen of Notre Dame, Brick Muller of California, Bennie Friedman of Michigan, Chris Cagle of Army, and other college stars. The Green Bay Packers were still playing on an open field, passing the hat among fans at halftime, in 1924, when Harvard Stadium, seating 38,000, was 21 years old; the Yale Bowl, with a capacity of 67,000, was 11 years old; and Ohio State University had a 2-year-old stadium seating more than 75,000.

Professional football got a boost in 1925. First, a franchise was established in New York City. Second, Red Grange went on a postseason tour with the Chicago Bears and drew some unprecedented crowds. Grange and his manager, C. C. Pyle, in 1926 formed the American Football League with 9 teams, and the NFL expanded to 22. Virtually every team lost money. The AFL folded after the season, and so did a dozen NFL franchises.

After being in a state of flux early in the century, with rules changes forcing coaches to develop new strategies and tactics, football had become pretty well stabilized by the 1920s. The 1906 rules prohibited the player who took the snap from running with the ball within 5 yards of the center, so the T-formation was developed, with a quarterback taking the snap and handing the ball off or lateraling it to another back. Then teams began to line up in the T and shift to other formations. By the early 1920s, three basic formations were being used: the single wing, perfected by Glenn "Pop" Warner at Carlisle; the double wing, invented by Warner; and the Notre Dame Box, a variation of the single wing, created by Jess Harper and perfected by Knute Rockne.

That changed in 1940 when Clark Shaughnessy recreated the T-formation at Stanford. Shaughnessy split his linemen, forcing the defensive line to spread out, and built an offense based on quick-hitting plays, with backs running through the holes created by the line splits. Deceptive ball handling was an important feature of the T, and Shaughnessy made it a good passing formation by having the quarterback bring the ball away from the center to make or fake handoffs. After faking, he was in a good position to throw the ball. Passing was also easier because the circumference of the ball had been reduced in 1934 from a maximum of 23 inches to a maximum of 21¼ inches.

After World War II, college and professional football took sharply different paths. The three-end formation became standard in the pros, and passing was definitely in during the 1950s. The free-substitution rule, adopted in 1950, helped by creating offensive and defensive specialists. Most major colleges, though, went to formations that emphasized the run. The average number of passes by both teams per game declined from a high of 37.7 in 1951 to 27.1 in 1955. College football had adopted the free-substitution rule in 1941, but substitutes could be sent in only during a time out. In 1948, the referee was required to call time out whenever the ball changed hands, allowing the use of specialized offensive and defensive players, and by 1950 three quarters of the major colleges were platooning at times. However, free substitution went out again in 1953 and wasn't restored to college football until 1961.

The NFL faced its first real threat from another league in 1946, when the well-financed All-America Football Conference began play. As in 1926, most teams lost money, and in 1950 the NFL and AAFC merged. Another rival, the American Football League, began operating in 1960. The NFL and AFL formally merged in 1970.

The professional game changed considerably during the 1960s, with the most successful teams going to run-oriented offenses. Ironically, colleges began passing more often, in part because defenses had adjusted to the running formations. Between 1960 and 1969, the number of passes per college game increased from 31.5 to an all-time high of 50.9; average yards gained by passing went up from 187.1 to 314.1 during the same period.

A whole series of rules changes during the 1970s encouraged more passing in professional football, but the best teams worked for balance between running and passing. College teams returned to the run, reaching a peak in 1975, when they averaged 103.8 rushes and 408.9 yards rushing per game, while the average number of passes was down to 36.7. The pendulum began to swing back again during the 1980s. The number of passes per game hit an all-time high of 55.2 in 1982, while rushes were down to 90.2, and the average number of yards gained passing reached a record 372.2 in 1985. By 1987, colleges showed much the same balanced approach to offense that the pros did, with an average per game of 346.4 yards rushing and 367.1 yards passing.

Further Reading: Claasen, Harold. *Ronald Encyclopedia of Football.* New York: Ronald Press, 1960; Davis, Parke H. *Football: The American Intercollegiate Game.* New York: Scribner's, 1912; Kaye, Ivan N. *Good Clean Violence: A History of College Football.* Philadelphia: Lippincott, 1973; McCallum, John, and Charles H. Parson. *College Football U.S.A., 1869–1972.* Greenwich, CT: Hall of Fame Publishing, 1971.

See also AMERICAN FOOTBALL LEAGUE; CAMP, WALTER; INTERCOLLEGIATE FOOTBALL ASSOCIATION; NATIONAL FOOTBALL FOUNDATION AND HALL OF FAME; NATIONAL FOOTBALL LEAGUE; PRO FOOTBALL HALL OF FAME; SUPER BOWL; TOUCH FOOTBALL.

Football Canada
See CANADIAN AMATEUR FOOTBALL ASSOCIATION.

Football Merger Act
When the American and National Football Leagues agreed in 1966 to merge, they were threatened with antitrust action from their players' associations. The Football Merger Act, specifically exempting the merger from antitrust action, was quickly passed by Congress. It raised some eyebrows, because the chief backers of the legislation, Senate Whip Russell Long and House Whip Hale Boggs, were both from Louisiana and shortly afterward New Orleans was given an NFL franchise.

See also AMERICAN FOOTBALL LEAGUE; NATIONAL FOOTBALL LEAGUE.

Football Writers Association of America (FWAA)
When it was founded in Chicago in 1941, the chief goal of the FWAA was to improve working conditions in press boxes. The association in 1944 began selecting a college All-America team. It has presented the Outland Trophy to the outstanding collegiate interior lineman since 1947 and the Grantland Rice Trophy to the national championship college team since 1954. The FWAA began selecting the college coach of the year in 1957.

Address: Box 1022, Edmond OK 73083 (405) 341-4731

Forbes Field
Pittsburgh, PA
Baseball's second concrete and steel park and the National League's first, Forbes Field opened on June 10, 1909. Called "the baseball palace," it had elevators, telephones, and electric lights in the triple-decked stands and maids in the ladies' rooms. Double-decked stands were added in right field in 1925, and several additions through the years brought the park's capacity to about 35,000 by 1959. On June 28, 1970, Forbes Field hosted its last major-league game. The Pirates played their next home game in newly opened Three Rivers Stadium, and Forbes Field was torn down.

Forego
Horse Racing
The Horse of the Year for three years in a row, 1974–76, Forego won 34 of 57 starts, including 31 handicaps despite carrying the top weight every time. He retired with a total of $1,938,957 in winnings. An amazingly versatile horse, he won the 1½-mile Woodward Stakes, the 7-furlong Vosburgh Handicap, and the 2-mile Jockey Club Gold Cup in a five-week period in 1974. Forego carried the top weight of 129 pounds in the Widener Handicap that year and was dead last going into the final turn, but he passed the field and won at the wire.

In 1975, he won the Seminole, Carter, Widener, Brooklyn, and Suburban Handicaps, setting a new track record in the Brooklyn despite a 132-pound handicap, and he beat the three-year-old champion, Winona, in the Woodward Stakes to win his second Horse of the Year award. Forego won the Metropolitan, the Brooklyn, and the Woodward in 1976 and beat Honest Pleasure in the Marlboro Cup, carrying 137 pounds. He won four out of seven starts in 1977, including the Metropolitan and the Woodward for the fourth time. After winning his first start in 1978, Forego finished fifth in the Suburban Handicap and was retired because of calcium chips in a leg.

Forest City Baseball Club
Baseball
Rockford, IL produced one of the first outstanding baseball teams, in 1867. The National Baseball Club of Washington went on tour that summer, playing nine games in five states. Their only loss was to the Forest City's 17-year-old pitcher, Albert G. Spalding. In 1870, Rockford businessmen raised $7,000 to send the team on a tour of the eastern states; Forest City won 13 of 16 games, losing only to the New York Mutuals and the Philadelphia Athletics, with one tie. Success led to the team's demise, as some of its

top players, including Spalding and shortstop Ross Barnes, were signed by other teams.

Forest Hills, NY
Tennis

After having been played at the Newport (RI) Casino since its beginning in 1881, the U.S. National tennis championships moved to the West Side Tennis Club at Forest Hills in 1915. From 1921 through 1923, the tournament was held at the Germantown Cricket Club in Philadelphia, while Forest Hills hosted the Davis Cup challenge round. The club in 1923 built the first modern tennis facility, with seating for 14,000 people, and the national championships returned the following year. In 1978, the tournament was moved to the new National Tennis Center in Flushing Meadow.

See also U.S. OPEN (TENNIS).

Ft. Wayne, IN
Basketball   Ft. Wayne had a team in the American Basketball League from its founding in 1925 until the league disbanded in 1931. The Hoosiers won the western division in 1928, 1929, and 1931, but lost all three championship playoffs. The Ft. Wayne General Electrics joined the National Basketball League when it was formed in 1937, but dropped out after one season.

The Ft. Wayne Pistons were in the National Basketball League after World War II, but left to join the Basketball Association of America for its third season in 1948–49. After the BAA had become the National Basketball Association, the Pistons won western division titles in 1955 and 1956, losing in the finals both year. The franchise moved to Detroit in 1957.

The Indiana Pacers were one of the original teams in the American Basketball Association in 1967, and they won ABA championships in 1970, 1972, and 1973. The Pacers moved into the National Basketball Association when the leagues merged in 1976.

Ft. Worth Classic
Football

This bowl game was played just once, on January 1, 1921, when Centre College beat Texas Christian University, 63–7.

Fosbury, "Dick" Richard (1947–   )
Track and Field
Born March 6, 1947, Portland, OR; National Track and Field Hall of Fame

The man who invented the "Fosbury flop" began experimenting with it at the age of 16. His best jump increased from 5 feet 3¾ inches to 6 feet, 6¾ inches by the time he graduated from high school. (In the "flop," technically a back layout, the jumper approaches the bar at an acute angle, twists just before takeoff, and goes over the bar headfirst and backward.) Fosbury had an outstanding year in 1968 while a student at Oregon State. He became the first ever to jump 7 feet indoors, in the NCAA championships. He also jumped a record 7 feet 2½ inches in the NCAA outdoor meet, and he won the Olympic Gold Medal with a jump of 7 feet 4¼ inches. Because of his success, virtually every world-class high jumper now uses some version of the Fosbury flop.

Foster, "Rube" Andrew (1879–1930)
Baseball
Born September 17, 1879, Calvert, TX; died December 9, 1930

Foster was the guiding force behind the National Negro League, the first major league for blacks. A pitcher, Foster got four victories when the Cuban X Giants won the 1903 "colored championship of the world" with five wins over the Philadelphia Giants. He joined the Philadelphia team the following year and got both of the team's wins in a three-game series over the Cuban X Giants, striking out 18 hitters in one and pitching a two-hitter in the other. Foster managed the Leland Giants of Chicago to a record of 123 wins and 6 losses in 1910 and then organized the Chicago American Giants.

Writing in 1919 for the *Chicago Defender*, Foster proposed organizing two black leagues patterned after the all-white major leagues. The result was the National Negro League, established on February 13, 1920. While it had its problems, Foster kept it going, sometimes by sheer willpower. He gave money to teams that needed it and at times paid for transportation or hotel bills for stranded teams. Foster was hospitalized for mental illness in 1926; the league struggled on through the 1931 season, then went out of business.

See also NEGRO NATIONAL LEAGUE.

Four Horsemen
Football

Although Grantland Rice made them famous, the "Four Horseman" idea came from George Strickler, a student sports publicist at Notre Dame in 1924. Strickler rounded up the four backs, Jim Crowley, Elmer Layden, Don Miller, and Harry Stuldreher, and had a publicity photo taken of them on horseback. Sportswriter Rice liked the idea and, after Notre Dame beat Army 13–7, he immortalized the backfield in his lead: "Outlined against a blue-grey

October sky, the Four Horsemen rode again. In dramatic lore they are known as Famine, Pestilence, Destruction and Death. These are only aliases. Their real names are Stuldreher, Miller, Crowley and Layden."

Fox Hunting

Foxhounds were brought to America in 1650 by Robert Brooke, who fled to Maryland after Cromwell's Glorious Revolution, but formal fox hunting didn't begin until 1749, when Thomas, Lord Fairfax, arrived at Greenway Court, VA with a pack of English foxhounds. George Washington in 1751 visited Greenway Court and wrote in his diary, "as I was never tired of the saddle, we were much engaged in the hunting of wild foxes." The sport virtually disappeared during the Revolutionary War but began to flourish again during the 1830s in Maryland, Virginia, and Washington, D.C.

The Civil War also ended fox hunting for a decade. It resumed on a small scale in the early 1870s. Archibald Bevan introduced drag hunting, in which a bag of scent is used to lay down a trail, in Clarke County, VA in 1887. The same year, the first formal foxhunt was founded in Warrenton, VA. While Virginia is the center of American fox hunting, well-known hunts were also established in Massachusetts and New York, particularly on Long Island. Since a hunt is essentially a cross-country race on horseback, requiring jumps over fences, hedges, and other obstacles, fox hunting has long been associated with steeplechasing. The National Steeplechase and Hunt Association, founded in 1895 to govern both sports, is now chiefly concerned with steeplechasing. Most formal hunts are sanctioned by the American Masters of Foxhounds Association, established in 1907.

Address: American Masters of Foxhounds Association, 294 Washington Street, Boston MA 02108 (617) 542-9109

See also STEEPLECHASE.

Foxx, "Jimmy" James E. (1907–1967)
Baseball

Born October 22, 1907, Sudlersville, MD; died July 21, 1967; Baseball Hall of Fame

A right-handed hitter, Foxx was the only player ever to hit a ball over the outfield stands at Chicago's Comiskey Park, and one of a handful to hit a home run into the left-field upper deck in Yankee Stadium. But "Double X" wasn't an immediate success in the major leagues. He joined the Philadelphia Athletics as a backup catcher in 1924 and played in only 99 games during his first four years. In 1928, he batted .328 with 13 home runs, and he became the Athlet-

ics' starting first baseman in 1929, when he had a .354 average, 33 home runs, and 117 runs batted in, beginning a streak of 12 consecutive seasons in which he hit 30 or more home runs. Foxx hit .350 with two home runs when the Athletics beat the Chicago Cubs in a five-game World Series.

Foxx hit 37 home runs, drove in 156 runs, and batted .335 in 1930. In the World Series against the St. Louis Cardinals, his two-run home run gave the Athletics a 2–0 victory in the fifth game, and they won the Series in six. He slumped to .291 in 1931, but still had 30 home runs and 120 runs batted in, and he batted .348 in a five-game World Series loss to St. Louis.

If it hadn't been for two rainy days in 1932, Foxx would have tied Babe Ruth's single-season record of 60 home runs. He hit 58, but two others didn't count because the games were rained out before five innings. Foxx also led the league with 158 runs batted in, was second in batting average with .364, and was named the league's Most Valuable Player. He won the MVP award and the Triple Crown in 1933, with a .356 average, 48 home runs, and 163 runs batted in.

After hitting 44 home runs in 1934 and 36 in 1935, Foxx was traded to the Boston Red Sox. He batted .338 with 41 home runs in 1936 and .285 with 36 home runs in 1937, then won his third MVP award in 1938 with a .349 average, 50 home runs, and 175 runs batted in. After leading the league in home runs for the fourth time with 35 in 1939, he hit 36 in 1940, but dropped to only 19 in 1941, his final year as a starter. He played for the Chicago Cubs in 1942 and retired temporarily after that season. After brief comebacks with the Cubs in 1944 and with the Philadelphia Phillies in 1945, he retired permanently. Foxx had a .325 batting average in 20 seasons, with 2,546 hits, 1,751 runs scored, 534 home runs, and 1,921 runs batted in.

Foyt, "A. J." Anthony Joseph (1935–   )
Auto Racing

Born January 16, 1935, Houston, TX; Indianapolis 500 Hall of Fame

Foyt is the only man to win the Indianapolis 500 four times, in 1961, 1964, 1967, and 1977, and is the all-time leader in Indy car victories with 67. He's also the only driver ever to win the Indy 500, the Daytona 500 for stock cars (in 1972), and the 24 Hours of LeMans (in 1968, 1983, and 1985), and one of only three to win races on oval speedways, road courses, and dirt tracks in a single season, in 1968. He was the USAC national driving champion in 1960, 1961, 1963, 1964, 1967, 1975, and 1979. Foyt won 41 races in USAC stock cars, 7 in NASCAR stock cars, 29 in sprint cars, 21 in midget cars, 7 in sports cars, and 2 in championship dirt cars. He was the USAC dirt car champion in 1971 and the USAC stock car champion in 1968, 1978, and 1979.

Frankford Yellowjackets
See PHILADELPHIA.

Fraser, Gretchen K. (1919–   )
Skiing
Born February 11, 1919, Tacoma, WA; National Skiing Hall of Fame

Fraser was selected for the U.S. Olympic ski team in 1940, but because of World War II she had to wait until 1948 to become the first Gold Medalist in the women's slalom. She also won a Silver Medal in the alpine combined. Fraser was the U.S. downhill and Alpine combined champion in 1941 and the slalom champion in 1942.

Frawley Act
Boxing

An attempt to legalize boxing, as opposed to prize-fighting, the Frawley Act went into effect in New York State in 1911. It created the New York State Athletic Commission to control the sport and allowed ten-round exhibition fights with no decisions. But newspapers began reporting unofficial decisions, and boxing fans made bets on the basis of those decisions. The law was repealed in 1917.

See also BOXING; HORTON LAW.

Freedom Bowl
Football First played on December 26, 1984, in Anaheim, CA, the Freedom Bowl has taken place on December 30 since 1985.

Results

1984 Iowa 56, Texas 17
1985 Washington 20, Colorado 17
1986 UCLA 31, Brigham Young 10
1987 Arizona State 33, Air Force 28
1988 Brigham Young 20, Colorado 17
1989 Washington 34, Florida 7
1990 Colorado State 32, Oregon 31

Freestyle Skiing

Like many modern competitive sports, freestyle skiing originated as a recreational sport when skiers began performing gymnastic stunts and tricks. It was originally known as "hot dog" skiing. The first competitive meet was held in 1971, and two years later the International Freestyle Skiers Association was formed; women organized their own group, the World Hot Dog Ski Association, the same year. The sport was demonstrated at the 1988 Winter Olympics. Because of the prospect that it might become an Olympic sport, it is now controlled by the national governing bodies for skiing and the specialized groups are defunct.

See also SKIING.

Freestyle Wrestling
See WRESTLING.

Frisbee

The original Frisbee was a pie plate manufactured by the Frisbie Pie Company in New Haven, CT, where Yale students began playing catch with the tin plates during the early 1920s. The company's truck drivers threw the plates, and during World War II they introduced the pastime to soldiers all over the country. In 1948, Fred Morrison invented a plastic disk, the Flying Saucer, and he developed an improved version, the Pluto Platter, in 1951. Four years later he sold his patent to the Wham-O Manufacturing Company, which renamed the product the Frisbee in 1959.

The Frisbee is used for many different games, including Ultimate Frisbee, invented at Columbia High School in Maplewood, NJ in 1967. Rutgers and Princeton played the first intercollegiate match in 1972. This is a seven-player team sport on a 60- by 40-yard field with 30-yard end zones. The disk is passed from player to player, and a catch in the end zone is worth one point. Other games include Frisbee golf, netbee, double disk court, discathon, circle Frisbee, goal-line Frisbee, and courtsbee. In freestyle Frisbee, competitors are judged on tricks and style in throwing and catching.

Frontier Sports

Eighteenth century frontiersmen worked hard and played hard. Among their favorite amusements were brutal fights, sometimes impromptu but often the result of a challenge. Philip Fithian described such fighting in Virginia in 1773–74: "Every diabolical strategem for Mastery is allowed and practised, of bruising, kicking, scratching, pinching, biting, butting, tripping, throtling, gouging, cursing, dismembring, howling, etc." A Canadian observer described a similar fight early in the 19th century: "they attack each other with the ferociousness of bull-dogs, and seem in earnest only to disfigure each other's faces and to glut their eyes with the sight of blood."

Less violent amusements emphasized physical ability and skills needed for survival. Community gatherings often included primitive track and field events such as running, broad jumping, high jumping, pole vaulting (for distance rather than height), throwing the maul, and pitching heavy stones. Hunting was a necessity, not a pleasure sport, but target shooting was popular on the frontier. Some contests, such as logrolling and cornhusking, drew directly on work skills. During the 19th century, more traditional sports were adapted to frontier conditions, including town ball (an early version of baseball), quoits, horseshoe pitching, weight lifting, and tug-of-war.

Gaines, "Big House" Clarence E. (1923–   )
Basketball

Born May 21, 1923, Paducah, KY; Basketball Hall of Fame 1981

The first black college coach inducted into the Basketball Hall of Fame, Gaines graduated from Morgan State in 1945 and began coaching at Winston-Salem State College in 1947. His team won the NCAA college division championship in 1967, when he was named Coach of the Year. He ranks second to Adolph Rupp in all-time victories with 785.

Gambling

A few sports owe their very existence to gambling. Horse racing in North America began with match races in Virginia during the 17th Century, usually for bets of tobacco. During the 18th Century, inns and taverns were centers for gambling on cockfighting, animal baiting, shuffleboard, billiards, skittles, and sometimes horse racing.

As early as 1756, there was a newspaper report of a rowing race in New York for a $20 bet. Side bets of up to $10,000 were made on an 1820 race, and in 1824 the New York Whitehallers beat a crew from an English frigate for a $1,000 bet before a crowd variously estimated at between 20,000 and 50,000. When a crew from St. John's, New Brunswick, beat a New York crew in 1856, the *Clipper* said that more than $50,000 was wagered by spectators.

Gambling was conducted by pool sellers who paid the track operator for the privilege when harness and Thoroughbred racing became popular sports. All betting money went into a pool, with a payoff only on the winning horse. As William Robertson put it, "The pure concept of sport for sport's sake had to be tempered with the realities of economic necessity, and gambling exchanged its stool in the corner for a seat at the main table."

Beginning in the 1840s bettors could also make their wagers at taverns, saloons, and billiard parlors. (The phrase "pool hall," which now means a billiard parlor, was originally a place where gambling pools were operated.) By the 1870s many establishments had telegraph receivers so they could also post results almost immediately.

During its early years, baseball suffered from its association with gambling. The first major scandal arose after a game between the New York Mutuals and Brooklyn Eckfords on September 28, 1865, when three players on the Mutuals were accused of throwing the game to the Eckfords. Two of them were banned, but they were reinstated by 1870. The Troy Haymakers, owned by John Morrissey, were known for fixing games. It was said that Morrissey, who also owned gambling houses in Saratoga, used the team "like loaded dice and marked cards." When the Haymakers played the Cincinnati Red Stockings in 1869, they left the field in the sixth inning so Morrissey wouldn't lose the money he'd bet on the game, which went down as a tie.

One of the goals of the National Association of Professional Base Ball Players, organized in 1871, was to control gambling, but it was unsuccessful. The National League did a better job. When the Louisville club fired four players for fixing games in 1877, the league banned them from playing for any other team. The standard player's contract, introduced in 1878, included a clause prohibiting any type of gambling. Nevertheless, there were several scandals that resulted in lifetime suspensions for players. The culmination was the "Black Sox" scandal, when eight Chicago White Sox were accused of taking bribes to throw the 1919 World Series. Seven of them were tried and acquitted, but all eight were banned from baseball for life.

Fixes were also suspected in Thoroughbred and harness racing. Tracks tried barring admission to professional gamblers, but the fact that they were dependent on professional pool operators and bookmakers still made them vulnerable. The sports were ultimately saved by the introduction of pari-mutuel betting, allowing the track itself to control gambling, with the added benefit of increasing revenue and therefore prize money.

Boxing has had a long association with gambling. Boxers and their managers often operated out of gambling establishments. Frank Stuart, who owned a gambling parlor, was Yankee Sullivan's promoter when he fought Tom Hyer in 1849, and gambler Bud Renau promoted the last bareknuckle heavyweight championship fight between John L. Sullivan and Jake Kilrain in 1889. Although there were periodic suspicions of the sport early in the century, the first major scandal arose in 1947, when Rocky Graziano withdrew from a fight, claiming a back injury. Graziano subsequently testified that he had been offered

$100,000 to throw the fight, and faked the injury because he was afraid of the consequences if he didn't accept the bribe. He also said he'd been offered bribes on three earlier occasions. And in 1960 Jake LaMotta told a Senate committee that he had thrown a fight against Billy Fox in 1947 because of death threats.

College basketball has been the sport most seriously damaged by gambling. In the early 1940s, the point spread system of betting on basketball and football was introduced. One team is favored by a certain number of points, and a bettor who wagers on that team wins only if the team wins by more. In 1949, gamblers began bribing players to "shave points," that is, to keep the winning margin under the point spread. The scandal broke in 1951 when Junius Kellogg of Manhattan College reported a bribe attempt to his coach, who contacted the district attorney's office. Players at Manhattan, Long Island University, City College of New York, the University of Kentucky, and Bradley University were implicated. Ten years later, it happened again, with players from Brooklyn College, New York University, St. John's University, Seton Hall, and the University of Connecticut.

Football and hockey have been relatively free of scandal. However, two New York Giants' players, Merle Hapes and Frank Filchock, were suspended in 1946 for failing to report bribe attempts. And in 1963 Paul Hornung of the Green Bay Packers and Alex Karras of the Detroit Lions were suspended for having bet on games, although both bet on their own teams to win. They were reinstated in 1964.

The most recent gambling scandal in sports involved Pete Rose, manager of baseball's Cincinnati Reds. Rose was accused of betting with bookmakers over a period of several years. On August 26, 1989, Rose was suspended from baseball for life, with a chance to apply for reinstatement.

Social attitudes toward gambling have seesawed. Because of a nationwide reform movement, bookmaking was outlawed in all states except Kentucky, Maryland, and New York in 1900. New York in 1910 prohibited betting at race tracks, which killed Thoroughbred racing until 1913, when a new law was passed permitting "oral betting" between friends. Bookmakers took advantage of the new law by making friends with everyone. In 1940, the state legalized pari-mutuel betting at tracks. Nevada since 1931 has allowed gambling in licensed establishments, and Atlantic City has been licensing casinos since 1977, but only pari-mutuel betting on greyhound, harness, and Thoroughbred racing is allowed in most other states. Three states, Connecticut, Florida, and Rhode Island, also allow pari-mutuel betting on jai alai.

See also BLACK SOX SCANDAL.

Garden State Bowl
Football

The Garden State Bowl was played at Giants Stadium in East Rutherford, NJ from 1978 until 1981. The New Jersey Sports and Exhibition Authority, which sponsored the game, dropped it after losing $400,000 in four years.

Results

1978   Arizona State 34, Rutgers 16
1979   Temple 28, California 17
1980   Houston 35, Navy 0
1981   Tennessee 28, Wisconsin 21

Gator Bowl
Football

Played in Jacksonville, FL, the Gator Bowl was inaugurated on January 1, 1946. It has been played in late December through most of its history. In the list of results, when two games are shown for a single year, the first game was played on January 1 and the second in December.

Results

1946   Wake Forest 26, South Carolina 14
1947   Oklahoma 34, North Carolina State 13
1948   Maryland 20, Georgia 20
1949   Clemson 24, Missouri 23
1950   Maryland 20, Missouri 7
1951   Wyoming 20, Washington & Lee 7
1952   Miami (FL) 14, Clemson 0
1953   Florida 14, Tulsa 13
1954   Texas Tech 35, Auburn 13
1954   Auburn 33, Baylor 13
1955   Vanderbilt 25, Auburn 13
1956   Georgia Tech 21, Pittsburgh 14
1957   Tennessee 3, Texas A & M 0
1958   Mississippi 7, Florida 3
1960   Arkansas 14, Georgia Tech 7
1961   Penn State 30, Georgia Tech 15
1962   Florida 17, Penn State 7
1963   North Carolina 35, Air Force 0
1965   Florida State 36, Oklahoma 19
1965   Georgia Tech 31, Texas Tech 21
1966   Tennessee 18, Syracuse 12
1967   Penn State 17, Florida State 17
1968   Missouri 35, Alabama 10
1969   Florida 14, Tennessee 13
1970   Auburn 35, Mississippi 28

1971 Georgia 7, North Carolina 3
1972 Auburn 24, Colorado 3
1973 Texas Tech 28, Tennessee 19
1974 Auburn 27, Texas 3
1975 Maryland 13, Florida 0
1976 Notre Dame 20, Penn State 9
1977 Pittsburgh 34, Clemson 3
1978 Clemson 17, Ohio State 15
1979 North Carolina 17, Michigan 15
1980 Pittsburgh 37, South Carolina 9
1981 North Carolina 31, Arkansas 27
1982 Florida State 31, West Virginia 12
1983 Florida 14, Iowa 6
1984 Oklahoma State 21, South Carolina 14
1985 Florida State 34, Oklahoma State 23
1986 Clemson 27, Stanford 21
1987 Louisiana State 30, South Carolina 13
1988 UCLA 17, Arkansas 3
1989 Clemson 27, West Virginia 7
1990 Michigan 35, Mississippi 3

Gehrig, "Lou" Henry Louis (1903–1941)
Baseball

Born June 19, 1903, New York, NY; died June 2, 1941; Baseball Hall of Fame

On June 2, 1925, New York Yankee first baseman Wally Pipp complained of a headache and Gehrig took his place. It was the first of a major-league record 2,130 consecutive games for the "Iron Horse." He was overshadowed by teammate Babe Ruth for most of his career, but Gehrig compiled some remarkable numbers, leading the American League in runs batted in five times and setting the major-league record with 184 in 1931. He was named the American League's Most Valuable Player in 1927, when he hit .373 with 47 home runs and a league-leading 175 runs batted in, and in 1936, when he batted .354, led the league with 49 home runs, and drove in 152 runs. Gehrig hit four consecutive home runs on June 2, 1932, the first time it was accomplished in the 20th century.

Gehrig was a great clutch player, as his World Series statistics show. He hit four home runs and had nine runs batted in 1928, when the Yankees beat St. Louis in four games. In another four-game series in 1932, he batted .529 with three home runs, nine runs scored, and eight runs batted in. He played a total of 34 World Series games, batting .361 with 8 doubles, 3 triples, 10 home runs, 30 runs scored and 35 runs driven in.

In the spring of 1939, Gehrig had obviously lost weight and he appeared slow and clumsy in the field. He was batting only .143 when he told Manager Joe McCarthy, "I think I'm hurting the team. Maybe it would be better if I took a rest for a while." He never played again. In June, he was diagnosed as having amyotrophic lateral sclerosis, a rare disease that causes hardening of the spinal cord. The Yankees held a day in his honor on July 4, 1939, and he died less than two years later.

In 16 seasons, Gehrig had a .340 batting average with 2,721 hits, including 535 doubles, 162 triples, and 493 home runs. He scored 1,888 runs and drove in 1,990.

Gentry Sports

Virginia remained loyal to King Charles I during Oliver Cromwell's civil war, and hundreds of English loyalists fled there in the early 1650s, joining with wealthy tobacco planters to form a gentry class that mimicked England's landed nobility. Horse racing, usually on a quarter-mile straightaway, was the most popular sport, allowed only among the gentleman.

There were billiard rooms in many of the great mansions, and some planters, such as William Byrd II, played lawn bowls and cricket. In the courtly tradition, a gentleman was also expected to learn fencing, along with dancing and conversational skills, but fencing was considered a graceful exercise rather than a sport. "The better sorts of Virginians only, who are Bachelors" were invited to a field day proclaimed in 1691 by the governor, Sir Francis Nicholson, and prizes were awarded for horseback and foot races, target shooting, wrestling, and "playing at backswords." Cockfighting and hunting were also popular pastimes among the gentry.

Geoffrion, "Boom Boom" Joseph A. B. (1931–   )
Hockey

Born February 14, 1931, Montreal; Hockey Hall of Fame

Geoffrion got his nickname, "Boom Boom," from the sound of his explosive slap shot: The first "Boom" is the stick hitting the ice, and the second is the puck hitting the boards. A right wing with the Montreal Canadiens from 1950 through 1964 and 1966 through 1968, Geoffrion totaled 393 goals, and was the second player, after "Rocket" Richard, to score 50 goals in a season, in 1960–61. Geoffrion coached the New York Rangers in 1968 and was the first coach of the Atlanta Flames, 1972 to 1975.

George Halas Trophy
See HALAS TROPHY.

Giants Stadium
See MEADOWLAND SPORTS COMPLEX.

Gibson, Althea (1927–   )
Tennis
Born August 25, 1927, Silver, SC; International Lawn Tennis Hall of Fame

The first black to play in major tennis tournaments, Gibson grew up in Harlem, where she played stickball, basketball, and street tennis with a solid wooden paddle. At 14, she began taking lessons at the Cosmopolitan Tennis Club. She recalled in her autobiography: "After a while I began to understand that you could walk out on the court like a lady, all dressed up in immaculate white, be polite to everybody, and still play like a tiger and beat the liver and lights out of the ball."

Beginning in 1947, Gibson won ten consecutive national singles championships of the American Tennis Association, the black counterpart of the U.S. Lawn Tennis Association. In 1950 she won the USLTA's Eastern Indoor title and finished second in the National Indoor championship. But there was still some doubt about whether she would be allowed to play in the national tournament. The tide turned with a guest editorial by former champion Alice Marble in the July 1950 *American Lawn Tennis* magazine. If Gibson was kept out of major tournaments, Marble wrote, "there is an ineradicable mark against a game to which I have devoted most of my life, and I would be bitterly ashamed." Shortly afterward, Gibson played in the Eastern Grass Court Championships at South Orange, NJ and was subsequently invited to play in the national championships.

The 5-foot-10 Gibson probably had the most powerful serve ever in women's tennis, and she played aggressively, constantly following her serve to the net. Inconsistency troubled her during the early 1950s, but in 1956 she won 21 tournaments, including the French national title, her first major championship. The following year, she beat Darlene Hard in the finals at Wimbledon, and was given a ticker-tape parade on her return to New York City. She won the U.S. championship later that year. After winning both championships again in 1958, she signed a $100,000 contract to play halftime exhibitions at Harlem Globetrotter games. Gibson later played on the women's professional golf tour for several years before beginning a third career as a singer and actress.

Further Reading: Gibson, Althea. *I Always Wanted To Be Somebody*. New York: Harper & Brothers, 1958.

Gibson, "Bob" Robert (1935–   )
Baseball
Born November 9, 1935, Omaha, NE; Baseball Hall of Fame

Gibson set a record with an earned run average of 1.12 in 1968, bettering Grover Cleveland Alexander's 1916 mark of 1.15. He had a 22–9 record that season, leading the league with 13 shutouts and 268 strikeouts. Gibson had established himself as a star in 1964, his sixth season with the St. Louis Cardinals, when he won 19 games and lost 12 with a 3.01 earned run average and pitched three complete games against the New York Yankees in the World Series. He lost the second game but won the fifth 5–2 in 10 innings and came back with just two days' rest to win the seventh and deciding game 7–5. He struck out 31 hitters in 27 innings. He had an even better World Series in 1967, when he beat the Boston Red Sox three times, 2–1 in the first game, 1–0 in the fourth, and 7–2 in the seventh, striking out 26 hitters in 27 innings.

A strong right-handed thrower, Gibson pitched a no-hitter against the Philadelphia Phillies on August 14, 1971. He won 20 or more games five times, and his lifetime record was 251 wins and 174 losses, with 56 shutouts, a 2.91 earned run average, and 3,117 strikeouts. In three World Series, he had a 7–2 record with 2 shutouts, a 1.89 earned run average, and 92 strikeouts in 91 innings.

Further Reading: Gibson, Bob. *From Ghetto to Glory: The Story of Bob Gibson*. Englewood Cliffs, NJ: Prentice-Hall, 1968.

Gibson, Joshua (1911–1947)
Baseball
Born December 21, 1911, Buena Vista, GA; died January 20, 1947; Baseball Hall of Fame

Probably the greatest black player of his era, Gibson died of a cerebral hemorrhage shortly before Jackie Robinson broke major league baseball's color barrier. A catcher, the 6-foot-1, 215-pound Gibson was an incredibly strong hitter. Reportedly, he once hit a ball out of Yankee Stadium; if so, he was the only player ever to do it. Gibson got his start with the Homestead Grays under odd circumstances on the night of July 25, 1930. He was a spectator at a game between the Grays and the Kansas City Monarchs when the Pittsburgh catcher quit because he said the lighting wasn't good enough. Gibson came out of the stands to replace him and was the Grays' starting catcher from then until 1932.

He hit 75 home runs for the Grays in 1931, then went to the Pittsburgh Crawfords, where he caught for the legendary Satchel Paige. The Crawfords broke up after the 1936 season, and he rejoined the Grays until 1940, when he jumped to the Mexican League for two seasons. He went back to the Grays from 1942 through 1946. The Negro leagues unfortunately did not keep good records, but some say that he once hit 89 home runs in a season. Roy Campanella, the Hall of Fame catcher who played against Gibson in the late 1930s, said he was "not only the greatest catcher but the greatest ballplayer I ever saw."

Gipp, George (1895–1920)
Football
Born February 18, 1895, Laurium, MI; died December 12, 1920

When Walter Camp selected him as fullback on the 1920 All-American team, he cited Gipp for "his versatility and power, able as he is to punt, drop-kick, forward-pass, run, tackle—in fact, do anything that any backfield man could ever be required to do, and do it in a well-nigh superlative fashion." After leaving high school, Gipp was offered a contract by the Chicago White Sox, but he decided to attend Notre Dame on a baseball scholarship, which he supplemented by playing cards and billiards for money. Gipp was persuaded to play football in 1917, his sophomore year. Called on to punt in one game that season, he drop-kicked a 62-yard field goal instead.

Knute Rockne took over as coach in 1918, when the team played only six games that didn't count against a player's eligibility, so Gipp was still considered a junior in 1919. Notre Dame was undefeated that season. In the big game of the year, Army was winning 9–0 near the end of the first half, but Gipp completed passes totaling 75 yards to move the ball to the 10-yard line, then scored on a run. In the second half, he threw a long pass to Eddie Anderson to set up the winning touchdown.

Gipp scored on runs of 95 yards against Purdue and 70 yards against Nebraska in 1920. He was heroic once more against Army, gaining 124 yards rushing, running back kicks for 112 yards, and passing for 96 yards in a 27–17 victory. Gipp suffered a dislocated shoulder against Indiana, but with Notre Dame losing and time running out, he went back into the game and scored the winning touchdown. In the final game of the season the following week against Northwestern, Gipp sat on the bench because of the shoulder injury and a severe cold, but he entered the game in the fourth quarter and threw a 45-yard touchdown pass. That was Notre Dame's second straight 9–0–0 season.

Suffering from strep throat and pneumonia, Gipp was accepted into the Roman Catholic Church shortly before his death in December. In 1928, Notre Dame was tied with Army 0–0 at halftime. Rockne told his players that Gipp, on his deathbed, had said, "when the team is up against it, tell them to win just one for the Gipper." Notre Dame won the game 12–6. Whether true or not, the story was immortalized in the movie, "The Knute Rockne Story," in which Ronald Reagan played Gipp.

Gliding
See SOARING.

Go-Kart Racing
See KART RACING.

Gold Cup
Powerboat Racing
Established in 1904 for a race on the Hudson River, the Gold Cup is the major North American trophy for unlimited hydroplanes. Held under the auspices of the American Power Boat Association, the race has been held at several sites, most often at Detroit, where it has drawn as many as 600,000 spectators, and at Seattle.

See also AMERICAN POWER BOAT ASSOCIATION; POWERBOAT RACING.

Gold Glove
Baseball
The Rawling Sporting Goods Company since 1957 has given Gold Glove awards to the players chosen as the best defensively at their positions in both the American and National Leagues. Major-league managers and coaches elect the winners.

Golden Gloves Association of America
Boxing
The original Golden Gloves competition for amateur boxers was held by the *New York Daily News* in 1927, and the *Chicago Tribune* also sponsored competition in 1928. The *Tribune* then began an annual tournament to benefit charity. During the 1930s, other newspapers started sponsoring local and regional tournaments leading to the championship finals in Chicago. Proceeds from the final went to *Chicago Tribune* Charities and a committee of sportswriters oversaw the tournament until 1963, when the Golden Gloves Association of America was formed to take over the job. Most local tournaments are still sponsored by newspapers, and net proceeds are distributed among a variety of charities. Many professional champions got their starts in the Golden Gloves, including Sugar Ray Robinson, Joe Louis, Ezzard Charles, and Rocky Marciano.

Address: P.O. Box 190, Hutchinson, KS 67504 (316) 662-3311

Golden State

Basketball The San Francisco Warriors of the National Basketball Association moved to Oakland and became known as the Golden State Warriors in the 1970–71 season. They won the 1975 NBA championship.

See also OAKLAND; SAN FRANCISCO.

Goldsmith Maid
Harness Racing

Until it was discovered that she could trot when she was eight years old, she was a farm horse named Nellie. She was sold in 1865 to Alden Goldsmith, who raced her against Dexter, the top harness horse of the time. She narrowly lost. Trainer-driver Budd Doble then bought her for $20,000 and gave her the name that was to become famous in harness racing. During an 11-year period, she broke the world trotting record seven times and won 97 of 123 races. On September 6, 1871, she beat Lucy in a $4,000 match race at Milwaukee, trotting the second heat in 2:15 to break the world record by a quarter of a second. Her all-time best was 2:14 in 1874.

Golf

Golf was evidently played in North America during the 18th century. In 1729, the inventory of New York Governor William Burnet's estate listed "nine gouff clubs, one iron ditto and seven dozen balls." The sport was prohibited on Sunday in Albany, NY

in 1760, and a golf club in Charleston, SC held an anniversary meeting in 1795. The first course whose location is definitely known was built in 1873 by the Montreal Golf Club, and there was a match between the Montreal and Quebec City clubs in 1876. Robert Lockhart of Yonkers, NY visited his native Scotland in 1887, returned with some clubs and balls, and taught the sport to a friend, John Reid. Reid laid out a three-hole course in a cow pasture on February 22, 1888, and he and some friends founded the St. Andrews Golf Club, named after the famed Scottish club.

The sport spread rapidly. The Shinnecock Hills Golf Club built a nine-hole course at Southampton, Long Island, in 1891, the Chicago Golf Club was organized in 1893, and there was a course in Riverside, CA by 1894, when two national championships were held, at Newport, RI and at Yonkers. In December of that year, representatives of five clubs founded the Amateur Golf Association, now the U.S. Golf Association. The first official amateur and open championships were held in October, 1895, at Newport and the women's national amateur was inaugurated a month later at Meadowbrook, Long Island. The Royal Canadian Golf Association also held its first national amateur championship that year, but didn't conduct an open tournament until 1904.

By 1900, there were more than 1,000 clubs in North America. Amateurs dominated the sport. Professionals, many of them Scottish, gave lessons and repaired equipment, and were looked down upon

Goldsmith Maid's 1869 victory over American Girl at the Buffalo (NY) Driving Park was one of her 97 wins in 123 races.

by their well-to-do patrons. Harry Vardon, a great English professional, toured the continent in 1900 to publicize a new ball, the "Vardon Flyer," manufactured by A. G. Spalding. His exhibitions helped to popularize golf. But it really became front-page news in 1913, when Vardon and Ted Ray were co-favorites in the U.S. Open. A 20-year-old amateur from Massachusetts, Francis Ouimet, beat them in an 18-hole playoff.

Ouimet changed golf's image. Like tennis, the sport was viewed by many as an effete amusement for the upper class. Theodore Roosevelt cautioned his successor, William Howard Taft, "photos on horseback, yes; tennis no. And golf is fatal." Ouimet, a modest former caddie from a lower-class family, had great popular appeal. Golf historian Herbert Warren Wind wrote of his victory, "Had a pleasant young man from a good Fifth Avenue family or some stiff and staid professional defeated Vardon and Ray, it is doubtful if his victory would have been the wholesale therapeutic for American golf that was Ouimet's."

The prosperity of the 1920s also helped create a boom in golf, which became a middle-class sport as country clubs and golf clubs blossomed all over the continent. By 1930, there were about 6,000 courses in North America, including about 500 municipal courses and about 700 public-fee courses. Country club membership and a golf bag were status symbols for businessmen.

The professional tour had begun in a small way in 1916, when Rodman Wanamaker donated $2,580 in prize money for a match play tournament. That led to the formation of the Professional Golfers' Association on April 10. "Long Jim" Barnes won the first PGA championship, October 10–16 at Bronxville, NY. The winter circuit began in 1922 with the $5,000 Texas Open and later added tournaments in Florida and California. But the summer circuit didn't get started until 1930, when St. Paul, MN hosted a tournament with $10,000 in prize money.

The first great American-born professional was Walter Hagen, who won the Open in 1914 and later won five PGA championships, including four in a row. In 1922, he became the first U.S. native to win the British Open, and he went on to win three more. There wasn't much money on the pro tour, but the colorful Hagen made a fortune playing exhibitions throughout North America in the 1920s, and he also made professional golf respectable by forcing clubs to open their locker rooms and clubhouses to the pros, who had previously been excluded. Hagen was rivaled in popularity by Bobby Jones, an amateur. Jones won all four major tournaments, the U.S. and British Opens and Amateur Championships, in 1930, after which he retired with a total of 13 major titles

to Hagen's 11. Most of the top women golfers were British, but Glenna Collett Vare of the United States won five National Amateur titles between 1922 and 1930, and added a sixth in 1935.

Probably no nonmechanized sport has been more affected by improvements in equipment. The original feather-stuffed ball was replaced by the solid gutta percha ball about 1848. A ball with rubber thread wrapped around a rubber center and covered with gutta percha entered the market in 1899. The harder balata cover was introduced in 1905 and dimples were added in 1908.

Nineteenth-century clubs were long and slender, with whippy shafts of ash and thick grips. After the harder gutta percha ball was introduced, shafts were made of hickory and leather insets were added to protect wooden club heads. In the rubber ball era, laminated club heads of persimmon were developed. The steel shaft was approved for use in 1924.

Golf suffered during the Great Depression. About a third of the country clubs went out of business, and others were converted to municipal or public fee courses. However, Bobby Jones built the Augusta National Course and conducted the first Masters Tournament in 1934, and two years later Fred Corcoran became the full-time tournament director for the PGA. In ten years, he increased the number of tournaments from 11 to more than 30, and prize money went up from about $50,000 to $750,000.

As a prelude to the great expansion of professional golf after World War II, Byron Nelson arrived on the scene in 1937 by winning the Masters. He also won the U.S. Open in 1939 and the PGA Championship in 1940. In 1944 and 1945, Nelson won 26 of 51 tournaments, including 18 in 1945. He didn't get rich in the process. His big payoffs were in the 1944 and 1945 World's Championships, which paid more than $13,000 in bonds, but most of his first-place finishes paid between $1,000 and $2,000.

The average purse increased to $23,108 in 1954 and to $47,550 in 1963; it went over $100,000 in 1967. Television money was an important factor, but competition among several great golfers also helped. Ben Hogan and Sammy Snead were the stars during the late 1940s and early 1950s, along with Jimmy Demaret, Lloyd Mangrum, and Cary Middlecoff. Then came Arnold Palmer, who was made for television. He had a spectacular victory in the 1960 U.S. Open, when he shot a 65 on the last round to come from seven shots back, holding television audiences spellbound. He added four more wins in which he shot 67 or lower on the final round, collecting a hero-worshipping gallery known as "Arnie's Army."

But Palmer was not alone. He, Gary Player, and Jack Nicklaus formed the "Big Three" during the 1960s, and Nicklaus eventually emerged as the greatest of them all, with victories in 17 major tournaments, 4 more than Bobby Jones' former record, and total earnings of more than $4 million. During this period, television and commercial sponsorship of major tournaments pushed total prize money from about $1.5 million in 1958 to more than $10 million in 1978. In 1962 Palmer became the first golfer to win more than $100,000 in a single season. Ten years later, Nicklaus won more than $300,000. Tom Watson, another charismatic figure, took over in the late 1970s and surpassed the $500,000 mark in 1980.

Women's professional golf also grew, though not quite so dramatically. Their tour was created with the formation in 1946 of the Women's Professional Golfers' Association, which held the first Women's Open that year. The Ladies' Professional Golf Association replaced the WPGA in 1948. Babe Didrikson Zaharias and Patty Berg were the early stars. Zaharias was the top money winner in 1948 with just $3,400, and Berg led in 1956 with $20,235. The men's leader that year won $72,835. Mickey Wright led in winnings five years in a row, 1960–64. Her best year was 1963, with $31,269.

In the late 1970s, both corporate sponsorship and television money increased dramatically, as did the number of tournaments. Total prize money climbed from $345,000 for 21 tournaments in 1970 to $5.1 million for 39 tournaments in 1980. Judy Rankin in 1976 became the first woman to win more than $100,000 in a season; her total was $150,734, nearly twice Sandra Palmer's $76,374, which led in 1975. Nancy Lopez won more than $200,000 in 1980, JoAnne Carner more than $300,000 in 1982, and Lopez went over the $400,000 mark in 1985. Women's golf, like women's tennis, had indeed come a long way in a short time.

Further Reading: Grimsley, Will. *Golf: Its History, People and Events.* Englewood Cliffs, NJ: Prentice-Hall, 1966; Kavanagh, L. V. *History of Golf in Canada.* Toronto: Fitzhenry & Whiteside, 1973; Ross, John M., editor. *Golf Magazine's Encyclopedia of Golf.* New York: Harper and Row, 1979; Wind, Herbert Warren. *The Story of American Golf,* third revised edition. New York: Alfred Knopf, 1975.

See also CANADIAN PROFESSIONAL GOLFERS ASSOCIATION; COUNTRY CLUBS; LADIES PROFESSIONAL GOLF ASSOCIATION; PROFESSIONAL GOLFERS ASSOCIATION OF AMERICA; U.S. GOLF ASSOCIATION; UNITED GOLFERS ASSOCIATION; WORLD GOLF HALL OF FAME.

Good Will Games

After the United States boycott of the 1980 Olympic Games in Moscow and the Soviet boycott of the 1984 Olympic games in Los Angeles, Ted Turner of the Turner Broadcasting System decided to try to bring the two countries closer together with a privately operated sports festival. Called the Good Will Games, the festival was held in Moscow in 1986 with competition in 21 sports. TBS put together a cable network to broadcast the games, but ratings were disappointingly low and losses ran to more than $20 million. Nevertheless, Turner decided to go ahead with the second Good Will Games four years later in Seattle. With more time to prepare for 1990, TBS expected losses of about $3.5 million, based on anticipated revenues of $80 million and costs of $83.5 million. Largely because of low TV ratings, actual losses were well over $30 million, raising doubts that TBS management would go ahead with the 1994 Games, scheduled for Moscow and Lenningrad.

Gotham Bowl
Football

The Gotham Bowl was played twice in New York City. Baylor beat Utah State 24–9 on December 9, 1961, and Nebraska beat Miami (FL) 36–34 on December 15, 1962.

Graham, Otto E., Jr. (1921–)
Football

Born December 6, 1921, Waukegan, IL; National Football Foundation, Pro Football Hall of Fame

An All-American basketball player at Northwestern University, Graham was also named the single-wing tailback on some All-American football teams in 1943. After serving in the U.S. Navy, Graham played for the Rochester Royals, who won the National Basketball League championship in 1946. Then he signed with the Cleveland Browns of the new All America Football Conference and became a T-formation quarterback.

The Browns won all four AAFC championships. Graham was named Most Valuable Player the first three years and shared the award with San Francisco's Frankie Albert in 1949. During those four seasons, he completed 592 of 1,051 passes for 10,085 yards and 86 touchdowns. The AAFC merged into the National Football League in 1950, and Cleveland beat the Los Angeles Rams 30–28 in the NFL championship game, with Graham completing 22 of 33 passes for 296 yards and 4 touchdowns. The Browns also won conference titles in 1951, 1952, and 1953, losing the championship game each year, but they beat Detroit 56–10 in the 1954 title game. Graham retired after the season, but Coach Paul Brown talked him into coming out of retirement in 1955, and he led the Browns to another championship victory, 38–14 over the Los Angeles Rams, passing for two touchdowns and running for two more.

Graham was the All-Pro quarterback five years in a row, 1951–55, and was the NFL's Player of the Year in 1953 and 1955. In 10 seasons, he completed 1,464 of 2,626 passes for 23,584 yards and 174 touchdowns. He coached football at the Coast Guard Academy from 1959 through 1965, then went to the Washington Redskins as head coach and general manager. In three seasons, he had a 17–22–3 record.

Grand American
Auto Racing

Established as the Grand Touring division of the National Association for Stock Car Auto Racing in 1968, this form of stock car racing was for small, sporty sedans. It was discontinued after 1983.

Grand American Handicap
Trapshooting

First held in 1893 as an event in the national trap shooting championships at Dexter Park, Long Island, the Grand American Handicap is the premier championship in the sport. Since 1924, it has been held at the American Trap Shooting Association's headquarters in Vandalia, OH.

See also TRAPSHOOTING.

Grand Circuit
Harness Racing

Established by four tracks in 1873 as the Quadrilateral Trotting Combination, the Grand Circuit includes most of the sport's major stakes races for colts. The four original tracks were the Buffalo Driving Park, Hampden Park at Springfield, MA, the Cleveland Driving Park, and the Utica (NY) harness track. In 1875, the group was renamed the Central Driving Circuit, and it became known as the Grand Circuit in 1888. More than 60 tracks have belonged at one time or another. The chief features of the circuit are major races at fairs, such as the Little Brown Jug at Delaware, OH, and the Kentucky Futurity at the Red Mile in Lexington. Many of the members have three- or four-day meetings, which are coordinated to allow drivers and horses to travel from one meet to the next.

Grand National
Auto Racing

Originally the top prize in stock car racing, the Grand National championship was created by the National Association for Stock Car Auto Racing in 1949. It was replaced in 1970 by the Winston Cup championship, with a Winston Racing Series for Grand National racing.

See also WINSTON CUP.

Grand National
Motorcycle Racing

In 1954, the American Motorcycle Association established the Grand National series to choose a national champion based on selected races of various types, including flat track, short track, dirt track, road course, and speedway.

Grand Prix
Auto Racing

The original Grand Prix, from the French for "great prize," was a 1906 race that replaced Bennett Trophy competition. Eventually, the Grand Prix turned into a circuit of important road races for formula one cars. There are two major prizes in Grand Prix racing: the Driver's Championship and the Manufacturers' Championship.

Grand Prix de Dressage
See EQUESTRIAN SPORTS.

Grand Prix of Tennis

Jack Kramer, a long-time advocate of organized professional tennis, persuaded the International Lawn Tennis Association to establish the Grand Prix circuit in 1970. The circuit awards bonus points for many major international tournaments, culminating in the Masters Tournament for the top point winners. In 1974, the Men's International Tennis Council (now the Men's Tennis Council) was formed to administer the circuit. By 1989, there were more than 70 Grand Prix tournaments offering total prize money of $37 million, with bonus money of $4.6 million.

Grange, "Red" Harold E. (1903–1991)
Football

Born June 13, 1903, Forksville, PA; died January 27, 1991; National Football Foundation, Pro Football Hall of Fame

As a sophomore at the University of Illinois in 1923, Grange gained 1,260 yards, scored 12 touchdowns, and was named an All-American. In his first game, against Nebraska, he played just 39 minutes, but scored all three Illinois touchdowns, one of them on a 65-yard punt return. He ran back an interception 43 yards to the 3-yard line, then scored a touchdown against the University of Chicago. He had a 92-yard interception return against Northwestern, and scored winning touchdowns against Iowa, Ohio State, and Wisconsin. During the season, Grange gained more than 100 yards in seven games, with a high of 251 against Northwestern.

Red Grange helped make professional football respectable when he went on tour with the Chicago Bears shortly after finishing his collegiate career in 1925. A three-time All-American at the University of Illinois, the "Galloping Ghost" was one of the most exciting runners of all time. Courtesy of the Pro Football Hall of Fame

By his junior year, Grange was nationally known by three nicknames: The "Wheaton Iceman," because he delivered ice in Wheaton, IL during the summer; the "Galloping Ghost," coined by Grantland Rice; and "Number 77." Against Michigan, he had one of the most celebrated days in football history, scoring touchdowns the first four times he touched the ball. After returning the opening kickoff 95 yards, he scored on runs from scrimmage of 67, 56, and 45 yards, all in the first 12 minutes. Then he was taken out until the third quarter, when he scored his fifth touchdown on a 5-yard run. He totaled 402 yards in 21 carries in the 39–14 victory.

Grange began his senior season by returning the first kickoff 85 yards against Iowa and he had a 70-yard run against Butler. But he saved his best for Pennsylvania. Eastern football fans were still dubious about Grange. Playing against the unbeaten Penn team on a muddy field, he ran 55 and 25 yards for touchdowns, returned a kickoff 59 yards to set up another, and totaled 363 yards in 36 runs during a 24–2 victory. In the final game of the season, against Ohio State, he gained 235 yards, giving him 4,085 yards and 31 touchdowns in 20 games during his collegiate career.

He then joined the National Football League's Chicago Bears for a postseason tour. College football was king, and pro football was hardly noticed, but Grange helped make it popular and, just as important, respectable for other college stars, who began to enter professional football more frequently after his example. He reportedly earned $125,000 for the tour, vaudeville appearances, and three movies.

His manager, C. C. Pyle, in 1926 created the American Football League to showcase Grange with a team called the New York Yankees. The league folded after one season, but the Yankees joined the National Football League in 1927. Grange missed six games with a torn tendon and was forced to sit out the 1928 season. After that, he said, "I was just another halfback." But he rejoined the Bears in 1929 and was named to the first official All-Pro team in 1931. He retired after the 1933 season.

Further Reading: Grange, Red, with Ira Morton. *The Red Grange Story*. New York: G. P. Putnam's Sons, 1953.

Grape Bowl
Football

The Grape Bowl was played twice at Lodi, CA. College of the Pacific beat Utah State 35–21 on December 13, 1947, and tied Hardin-Simmons 35–35 on December 11, 1948.

Great Depression

Although most sports suffered during the Great Depression, a few benefited. And many of them gained in the long run because of the federal government's spending on public works. The Works Progress Administration built athletic fields, golf courses, handball and tennis courts, skating rinks, and swimming pools across the country, and the Public Works Administration spent an estimated $40 million on athletic facilities.

Thoroughbred racing was probably the chief beneficiary. To raise more tax revenues, ten states legalized pari-mutuel betting during the Great Depression. College basketball also benefited. Because of the decline in boxing, many arena owners turned to basketball as an alternative. Madison Square Garden held a series of college triple-headers to benefit the New York City Relief Fund in 1931, 1932, and 1933, and they were so popular that Ned Irish began promoting interregional double-headers at the Garden in 1934. That led to the creation of the National Invitation Tournament in 1938.

Golf was the hardest-hit sport because of its cost. About one third of the nation's country clubs were forced to close, and many others became private or municipal daily-fee courses. The number of member clubs in the U.S. Golf Association dropped from 1,154 in 1927 to 767 in 1935. Major-league baseball revenues went from about $17 million in 1929 to less than $11 million in 1933. To boost interest in the sport, the annual all-star game was inaugurated that year, and in 1935 the Cincinnati Reds installed lights and began playing some games at night in an effort to increase attendance. By 1942, 11 of the 16 major-league parks were lighted.

Several colleges were forced to drop their football programs. Attendance in the Big Ten was down nearly 40 percent in the early 1930s, and professional football teams, if they survived, did it by moving from small towns to big cities. By 1935, Green Bay was the only small city that still had a National Football League franchise.

The worst was over by 1936, although the Depression was not. In 1937, college football attendance was up to an estimated 20 million, twice what it had been in 1930. Night games helped to bring major-league baseball attendance close to the levels of the 1920s, and professional football was more popular and better-publicized than ever. Like other leisure-time industries such as moviemaking and publishing, big-time sports had survived and were poised to reach new heights in the prosperous era after World War II.

Great Lakes Bowl
Football

Kentucky beat Villanova 24–14 at Cleveland in the only Great Lakes Bowl on December 6, 1947.

Greco-Roman Wrestling
See WRESTLING.

Green Bay, WI

Football With a population of about 90,000, Green Bay is the smallest city with a professional sports franchise. The Packers were organized in 1919 and joined the American Professional Football Association (now the National Football League) in 1921. They won three consecutive NFL championships in 1929, 1930, and 1931. Since the league's playoff system originated in 1933, they have won titles in 1936, 1939, 1944, 1961, 1962, 1965, 1966, and 1967.

See also LAMBEAU FIELD; MILWAUKEE COUNTY STADIUM.

Greene, Nancy (1943–   )
Skiing

Born May 11, 1943, Ottawa, Ontario; Canada Sports Hall of Fame

Her idol, France's Jean-Claude Killy, said of her, "She attacks the course, instead of concentrating on *le style.*" Greene attacked courses well enough to win skiing's World Cup the first two years the competition was held, in 1967 and 1968. She also won a Gold Medal in the giant slalom at the 1968 Winter Olympics. Greene was the U.S. downhill champion in 1960 and 1967, and she won four titles—the downhill, slalom, giant slalom, and alpine combined—in 1965.

Grey Cup
Canadian Football

The governor general of Canada, Lord Earl Grey, in 1909 donated a trophy for the Canadian rugby football championship. The first Grey Cup game was played on December 4, 1909, between the University of Toronto and the Parkdale Canoe Club in Toronto. The university won 26–6. The Western Canada Rugby Football League joined the Canadian Rugby Union in 1921 and the Edmonton Eskimos became the first western team to play in a Grey Cup championship game, losing to the Toronto Argonauts 23–0. By then, a series of rules changes had turned rugby into Canadian football. Originally, any team registered with the CRU could challenge for the cup, including college and amateur teams, but the Eastern Intercollegiate Union withdrew from competition in 1934 and the amateur Quebec Rugby Football Union stopped challenging in 1937. At that point, the Grey Cup became symbolic of the Canadian professional championship and the final Grey Cup playoff was between the champions of the two major professional leagues, the Western and Eastern Interprovincial Rugby Unions. In 1956, they formed the Canadian Football Council, renamed the Canadian Football League in 1958. The CRU formally turned the cup over to the league in 1966.

Grey Cup Results

1909	University of Toronto 26, Parkdale 6
1910	University of Toronto 16, Hamilton Tigers 7
1911	University of Toronto 14, Toronto 7
1912	Hamilton Alerts 11, Toronto 4
1913	Hamilton Tigers 44, Parkdale 2
1914	Toronto 14, University of Toronto 2
1915	Hamilton Tigers 13, Toronto RAA 7
1916–1919	Not Played
1920	University of Toronto 16, Toronto 3
1921	Toronto 23, Edmonton 0
1922	Queen's University 13, Edmonton 1
1923	Queen's University 54, Regina 0
1924	Queen's University 11, Balmy Beach 3
1925	Ottawa Senators 24, Winnipeg 1
1926	Ottawa Senators 10, University of Toronto 7

1927	Balmy Beach 9, Hamilton Tigers 6
1928	Hamilton Tigers 30, Regina 0
1929	Hamilton Tigers 14, Regina 3
1930	Balmy Beach 11, Regina 6
1931	Montreal AAA 22, Regina 0
1932	Hamilton Tigers 25, Regina 6
1933	Toronto 4, Sarnia 3
1934	Sarnia 20, Regina 12
1935	Winnipeg 18, Hamilton Tigers 12
1936	Sarnia 26, Ottawa Rough Riders 20
1937	Toronto 4, Winnipeg 3
1938	Toronto 30, Winnipeg 7
1939	Winnipeg 8, Ottawa 7
1940	(Two-game total point series)
	Ottawa 8, Balmy Beach 2
	Ottawa 12, Balmy Beach 5
1941	Winnipeg 18, Ottawa 16
1942	Toronto RCAF 8, Winnipeg RCAF 5
1943	Hamilton Flying Wildcats 23, Winnipeg RCAF 14
1944	Montreal St. H-D Navy 7, Hamilton Flying Wildcats 6
1945	Toronto 35, Winnipeg 0
1946	Toronto 28, Winnipeg 6
1947	Toronto 10, Winnipeg 9
1948	Calgary 12, Ottawa 7
1949	Montreal Alouettes 28, Calgary 15
1950	Toronto 13, Winnipeg 0
1951	Ottawa 21, Saskatchewan 14
1952	Toronto 21, Edmonton 11
1953	Hamilton Tiger-Cats 12, Winnipeg 6
1954	Edmonton 26, Montreal 25
1955	Edmonton 34, Montreal 19
1956	Montreal 27, Edmonton 15
1957	Hamilton 32, Winnipeg 7
1958	Winnipeg 35, Hamilton 28
1959	Winnipeg 21, Hamilton 7
1960	Ottawa 16, Edmonton 6
1961	Winnipeg 21, Hamilton 14 (overtime)
1962	Winnipeg 28, Hamilton 27
1963	Hamilton 21, British Columbia 10
1964	British Columbia 34, Hamilton 24
1965	Hamilton 22, Winnipeg 16
1966	Saskatchewan 29, Ottawa 14
1967	Hamilton 24, Saskatchewan 1
1968	Ottawa 24, Calgary 21
1969	Ottawa 29, Saskatchewan 11
1970	Montreal 23, Calgary 10
1971	Calgary 14, Toronto 11
1972	Hamilton 13, Saskatchewan 10
1973	Ottawa 22, Edmonton 18
1974	Montreal 20, Edmonton 7
1975	Edmonton 9, Montreal 9
1976	Ottawa 23, Saskatchewan 20
1977	Montreal 41, Edmonton 6
1978	Edmonton 20, Montreal 13
1979	Edmonton 17, Montreal 9
1980	Edmonton 48, Hamilton 10
1981	Edmonton 26, Ottawa 23
1982	Edmonton 32, Toronto 16
1983	Toronto 18, British Columbia 17
1984	Winnipeg 47, Hamilton 17
1985	British Columbia 37, Hamilton 24
1986	Hamilton 39, Edmonton 15
1987	Edmonton 38, Toronto 36
1988	Winnipeg 22, British Columbia 21
1989	Saskatchewan 43, Hamilton 40
1990	Winnipeg 50, Edmonton 11

See also CANADIAN FOOTBALL.

Greyhound
Harness Racing

Foaled in 1932, Greyhound was bought at auction for $900 by E. J. Baker. As a two-year-old, he trotted a mile in 2 minutes 4 ¾ seconds, a record for the age, and in 1935 he won the Hambletonian in two heats, timed at 2:02 ¼ and 2:02 ¾. Greyhound set a new record of 2 minutes flat that year at Springfield, IL. In 1937, he set a track record of 1:59 ¾ at the Historic Track in Goshen; that stood until 1966. His all-time record was 1:55 ¼, run in 1938 at Lexington. Retired in 1940, Greyhound continued to make money for his owner by being exhibited from coast to coast.

Greyhound Hall of Fame and Museum

This hall of fame, located in Abilene, KS, is the headquarters for the National Greyhound Association. Opened in 1973, it has historic exhibits on greyhound racing from 400 B.C. to modern times, and it also honors outstanding greyhounds and persons who have contributed to the sport. Exhibits occupy about 20,000 square feet; an adjoining auditorium was opened in 1984.

Address: 407 South Buckeye, Abilene, KS 67410 (913) 263-3000

Greyhound Racing

Coursing, an ancient sport in which greyhounds race after live animals, was codified in England in 1776. It began as a sport in the United States in 1878, with hounds chasing antelopes. Coursing was also a pastime with a purpose in the Midwest, where farmers were troubled by hares and rabbits eating their crops. But formalized greyhound racing originated with Owen Patrick Smith, director of the Chamber of Commerce in Hot Springs, SD. He organized a coursing meet in 1905 to attract visitors to the town and was impressed by the number of spectators who

Greyhound racing was often staged at fairs in the late 19th century. This illustration shows an 1884 race at the State Agricultural Society fair in Philadelphia.

showed up. Smith knew that greyhounds have a poor sense of smell and will chase anything that looks even remotely like prey. He stuffed a rabbit skin, hitched it to a motorcycle, and used it as a lure in a race at Salt Lake City, UT in 1907. Shortly afterward, he built a circular course near Salt Lake City.

In 1910, Smith patented an improved "unanimate rabbit conveyor." This was something like a trolley, with the fake rabbit carried along a single track by an overhead arm. With financial backing from a group of Oakland businessmen, he built a track at Emeryville, CA in 1919, but attendance was poor. One of his backers, George Sawyer, convinced Smith that betting was the solution. They set up a five-week meet at Tulsa, OK with track bookmakers, and it was a success. Then they moved on to East St. Louis, IL, but their track there went bankrupt despite good attendance.

The sport finally became successful in 1922, when Smith built a track at Humbuggus, FL, now Hialeah. By 1932, seven tracks were operating in Florida alone, and Smith had also helped to establish greyhound racing at Erlanger, KY, New Orleans, Butte, MT, and Milwaukee, WI. Pari-mutuel betting was legalized in Florida that year and in 1934 it was introduced at two tracks in Massachusetts. Pari-mutuel betting on greyhounds is now legal in 18 states.

The American Greyhound Track Operators Association, organized by Florida track owners in 1947, became the national supervisory body for the sport in 1960. Racing greyhounds are registered by the National Greyhound Association, which is headquartered at the Greyhound Hall of Fame and Museum in Abilene, KS.

Address: American Greyhound Track Operators Association, 1065 N.E. 125th Street, Suite 219, North Miami, FL 33161 (305) 893-2101; Canadian Greyhound Racing and Breeders Association, c/o Mrs. C. McIlveen, Alexander Boulevard, Baldwin, Ontario, Canada L0E 1A5 (416) 722-5394

See also GREYHOUND HALL OF FAME AND MUSEUM.

Griffith Stadium
Washington, D.C.

The Washington Senators had two homes before Griffith Stadium. The first was American League Stadium, which opened on April 29, 1901. The team moved in 1903 to National Park, which had been the home of a National League team from 1892 through 1899. That park burned down early in 1911, and a new stadium, at first known as American League Park, was built. It was little more than a grandstand when the Senators began the 1912 season. Clark Griffith became team president in 1920, added new upper deck stands, and renamed the park after himself. Griffith Stadium had home run distances of 402 feet in left field, 421 feet to center, and 328 in right. Its largest capacity was about 30,000. The Senators played there until after the 1960 season, when they moved to Minneapolis and became the Minnesota Twins. They were replaced by an expansion franchise, also known as the Senators. They spent two years in Griffith Stadium before moving into new D.C. Stadium, now Robert F. Kennedy Stadium. That franchise moved to Arlington, TX in 1972 and became known as the Texas Rangers.

Grove, "Lefty" Robert M. (1900–1975)
Baseball

Born March 6, 1900, Lonacoming, MD; died May 22, 1975; Baseball Hall of Fame

Voted the greatest left-handed pitcher in history in 1969, the 100th anniversary of major-league baseball, Grove spent four and a half years with the minor-league Baltimore Orioles before the Philadelphia Athletics bought his contract for $100,000 in 1925. He led the American League in strikeouts seven consecutive years, 1925–31, in earned run average nine times, in victories four times, and in shutouts twice. From 1927 through 1933, he won 172 games while losing only 53, including a 31–4 record in 1931, when he had 16 consecutive victories from June 8 to August 19 and was named the league's Most Valuable Player.

Traded to Boston in 1934, he developed a sore arm but rebounded with his final 20-victory season in 1935. Grove retired in 1941 after collecting his 300th win against just 141 losses, giving him a percentage of .680, seventh best among pitchers with 100 or more wins and the highest among winners of 300 or more games, ahead of Christy Mathewson's .667. His career earned run average was 3.06, and he had 2,266 strikeouts and 32 shutouts. In three World Series, 1929 through 1931, he won four games while losing two, with a 1.75 earned run average.

Groza, Lou (1924–   )
Football
Born January 25, 1924, Martins Ferry, OH; Pro Football Hall of Fame

"The Toe" was professional football's first kicking specialist. Groza played for Paul Brown at Ohio State, served in the army during World War II, then rejoined Brown with the Cleveland Browns in the new All-American Football Conference in 1946. He was at first a second-string tackle but a first-string placekicker, leading the AAFC in extra points (45), field goals (13), and total points (84). In 1948 he became a starting tackle as well.

The Browns joined the National Football League in 1950, and Groza was an All-Pro tackle from 1951 through 1955 and in 1957. He led the league in field goals in 1950, 1952, 1953, 1954, and 1957, and in scoring in 1955. Because of a back injury, he didn't play in 1960, but he came back in 1961 as a kicker only and remained with the Browns through the 1967 season.

Groza was the first to take a specialist's approach to kicking. He designed a 6-foot measuring tape that he used to find the starting point for a kick, and he practiced mechanics constantly. In 21 professional seasons, he kicked 810 extra points and 264 field goals for a total of 1,608 points. He was the first to kick more than 200 field goals, and the first to score more than 1,000 points.

Gulick, Luther H. (1865–1918)
Basketball, Physical Education
Born December 4, 1865, Honolulu; died August 13, 1918; Basketball Hall of Fame

Gulick is best known for asking James Naismith to come up with an indoor game that turned out to be basketball, but Gulick was a major figure in physical education throughout his career. He got a medical degree from New York University in 1889, then became chairman of physical training at the YMCA's training school in Springfield, MA. In 1891 he called Naismith into his office and suggested that calisthenics and workouts weren't enough during the colder months because they bored the students. After basketball was invented, Gulick worked with Naismith for several years to refine the sport's rules.

A strong believer in "muscular Christianity," Gulick created the YMCA logo, an inverted triangle symbolizing spiritual development supported by development of the body and the mind. His course in the psychology of play, emphasizing competitive sport appropriate to the maturity and ability of the players, inspired William Morgan to invent volleyball at the YMCA in Holyoke, MA. Under Gulick's leadership, both the Springfield school and the YMCA organization became very involved in competitive sports, moving away from individual physical and gymnastic training. During the late 19th century, YMCAs throughout North America organized teams to compete in a wide variety of sports. That created a problem, because they were playing many outside teams, including semiprofessionals, and Gulick headed the Athletic League of North America when it was founded in 1895 to try to keep YMCA teams competing against one another only. The league failed, however, and in 1900 Gulick left to become a high school principal in Brooklyn.

In 1903, he was named director of physical training for public schools in Greater New York and he helped found the Public Schools Athletic League, the first major interscholastic sports league in the country. One of the basic ideas of the PSAL was that it would help to Americanize second-generation ethnic students and reduce juvenile delinquency in the city. But Gulick's own version of muscular Christianity also lay behind it. He had worked with G. Stanley Hall of Clark University in Worcester, MA, developing an "evolutionary theory of play." The theory said, basically, that the kind of play boys enjoy, or should enjoy, at certain ages recapitulates evolution. (Girls were left out.)

The essential feature of the theory was that male instincts would lead to group activity, based on group hunting in human history. If this group activity wasn't channeled into competitive team sports, it would lead to youth gangs instead, so team sports were to be encouraged. The theory had a powerful influence on the youth sports and playground movements. Gulick was a founder and the first president of the Playground Association of America, and a cofounder with his wife of the Campfire Girls of America. His hundreds of articles, speeches, and books also had a profound impact on the boys' and youth's sports movements of the early 20th century.

See also NAISMITH, JAMES; PLAYGROUND MOVEMENT; PUBLIC SCHOOLS ATHLETIC LEAGUE.

Gurney, Daniel S. (1931–)
Auto Racing
Born April 13, 1931, Long Island, NY

In 1967, Gurney became the first driver ever to win races in sports cars, stock cars, Indy cars, and formula one cars. Gurney began as a sports car driver in 1955, concentrated on formula one racing during the late 1950s and early 1960s, and also drove Indy cars from 1962 through 1970. He won 18 races in sports cars, seven each in formula one and Indy cars, and five in stock cars. Gurney was also a pioneer as a car builder. He helped introduce the rear-engine car at the Indianapolis 500 in 1963. After foreign cars threatened to take over the sport entirely, Gurney designed the American Eagle, which won the Indianapolis 500 three times and carried the national championship driver in 1968 and 1974. In 1973, 21 of the 33 starters in the Indianapolis 500 were Eagles.

Guthrie, Janet (1938–)
Auto Racing
Born March 7, 1938, Iowa City, IA

Guthrie became the first woman driver ever to race in the Indianapolis 500, on March 29, 1977. Her car's engine blew in the 27th lap. She also raced at Indianapolis in 1978, finishing ninth, and in 1979, when a piston problem forced her out of the race after only three laps. Guthrie started 11 Indy car races from 1976 through 1979. Her highest finish was fifth in the 1979 Milwaukee 200.

Gymnasium Movement

There was a gymnasium in North America in 1825 at the Round Hill School in Northampton, MA, and in 1826 the city of Boston built a gym. As cities began to grow during the 1840s, concern for the physical condition of city dwellers also grew. In his *Plea for Amusements* (1847), Frederick W. Sawyer called for regular recreation as a necessary balance to work, and the *New York Clipper* in 1857 urged schools to make gymnasiums "as important as blackboards" to improve the health of their pupils. The Turners who emigrated from Germany in the late 1840s established their own gyms in many major cities, but the gymnasium movement didn't really get underway until after the Civil War.

Soviet gymnast Olga Korbut, shown here on the uneven parallel bars, dazzled and charmed millions of television viewers during the 1972 Olympics. Courtesy of the Nissen Company

In 1869, the first YMCA gymnasiums were built in New York and San Francisco; there were 348 of them by 1891. Yale had a gym in 1872, run by Dudley A. Sargent, who went to Harvard in 1879 as director of its new Hemenway Gymnasium. Most of the athletic clubs that began to spring up in the 1880s had gymnasiums and many colleges added gyms during the same period. Sargent opened the Sanatory Gymnasium in Cambridge, MA in 1881, offering free instruction to anyone who wanted to teach gymnastics.

During the 1880s, several schools of physical education opened, and in 1892 Ohio passed a law requiring physical education in primary schools.

The increasing demand for physical education in schools, along with the growth of school systems and the tremendous amount of new building in the early part of the century, made the gymnasium standard in high schools and junior high schools by 1930.

See also PHYSICAL EDUCATION.

Gymnastics

The sport of gymnastics originated in calisthenics and exercises on gymnastic equipment. A pioneer in the field was Catherine E. Beecher, who founded the Western Female Institute in Ohio in 1837. She called her program "grace without dancing." Students exercised to music, progressing from simple limbering movements to more strenuous movements as their condition improved.

The parallel bars and the vaulting horse were developed in Germany by Frederick Ludwig Jahn, founder of the Turner movement, and were introduced to North America when Turners emigrated in the late 1840s and early 1850s. During the 1880s, the Turners became actively involved in promoting their system of gymnastics in the public schools. At the same time, the Swedish system of gymnastics was also being promoted for schools. This system of free exercise was originally developed in 1814 by Peter Henry Ling, a Swedish physician. Ling's disciples expanded on his ideas by promoting aesthetic gymnastics, using feelings and emotions to guide bodily movements.

In 1885, the first U.S. championship meet was held with competition in the flying rings, horizontal bars, parallel bars, and Indian clubs. Tumbling was added to the program in 1886 and the rope climb in 1888. Gymnastics was on the program of the first modern Olympic games in 1896. As a result, the long horse, side horse, and all-around competition were added to the national championships the following year. The floor exercise, then called free calisthenics and based on Swedish aesthetic gymnastics, didn't become part of the program until 1921. Ten years later, the first women's championships were held.

New York University hosted the first intercollegiate gymnastics meet on March 24, 1899. Eight of the colleges that competed afterward formed the Intercollegiate Gymnastics Union. However, national competition didn't take place until 1938, when the National Collegiate Athletic Association held its first championships in the sport.

Addresses: Canadian Gymnastics Federation, 1600 James Naismith Drive, Gloucester, Ontario, Canada K1B 5N4 (613) 748-5637; U.S. Gymnastics Federation, 201 South Capitol, Suite 300, Indianapolis, IN 46225 (317) 237-5050

See also RHYTHMIC GYMNASTICS; TRAMPOLINE AND TUMBLING.

H

Hagen, Walter (1892–1969)
Golf
Born December 21, 1892, Rochester, NY; died October 6, 1969; World Golf Hall of Fame

British golf expert A. C. M. Croome wrote of Hagen, "He makes more bad shots in a single season than Harry Vardon did from 1890 to 1914, but he beats more immaculate golfers because 'three of those and one of them counts 4' and he knows it." Known as "Sir Walter," Hagen was a great champion because of his ability to make recovery shots and important putts. Probably his most remarkable feat was winning the PGA championship four consecutive years,

"Sir Walter" Hagen was not only a great golfer, he fought to gain acceptance for professionals. Hagen in 1922 became the first U.S.-born player to win the British Open. Courtesy of the U.S. Golf Association

1924 through 1927, when it was a match play tournament. He had also won the championship in 1921.

Hagen arrived at The Country Club in Brookline, MA to play in the 1913 U.S. Open, dressed in white flannels, a striped silk shirt, white bucks with red rubber soles, and a checkered cap, with a red bandanna around his neck. He told defending champion John McDermott, "I've come down here to help you fellows stop Vardon and Ray," the British golfers who were favored to win. As it turned out, U.S. amateur Francis Ouimet won the title in a playoff with Vardon and Ray, but the following year Hagen became the first American-born professional to win the Open. He also won it in 1919. Hagen was the first U.S. native to win the British Open, in 1922, and he also won it in 1924, 1928, and 1929.

Although professional golf didn't pay much at the time, Hagen claimed he was the first golfer to make more than $1 million and spend more than $2 million. He played exhibitions all over the country, touring in a caravan of three limousines with his chauffeur, his manager, his caddie, and suitcases full of money.

Hagen won first-class status for professional golfers, who were not allowed to use locker room and clubhouse facilities at the country clubs where most tournaments were played. Hagen broke the barrier at the Midlothian in Chicago during the 1914 U.S. Open by simply pretending he didn't know the rule and making himself at home. During the 1920 British Open at Deal, he wasn't allowed to use the locker room, so he parked his limousine in front of the clubhouse and changed his clothes in the car. The same year, he and British professional George Duncan threatened to boycott the French Open unless the host club lifted its social restrictions on professionals. The French knew that Hagen could draw big crowds, so they complied. Hagen won the tournament as well as the point.

Halas, George S. (1895–1983)
Football
Born February 2, 1895, Chicago, IL; died October 11, 1983; Pro Football Hall of Fame

"Papa Bear" had hopes of being a major-league baseball player. But after hitting only .091 in a brief trial with the New York Yankees in 1919, he decided to concentrate on football instead. Halas played for the

Founder and long-time coach of the Chicago Bears, George Halas, was a founder of the American Professional Football Association in 1920, and it was his idea to change the name to the National Football League two years later. Courtesy of the Pro Football Hall of Fame

Hammond (IN) Pros in 1919 and then was hired as athletic director at the A. E. Staley Starch Company in Decatur, IL. He formed a team called the Decatur Staleys and got a franchise in the American Professional Football Association in 1920. The following year, he and Edward "Dutch" Sternaman bought the franchise and moved it to Chicago. Halas was involved in two important name changes in 1922. He suggested that the APFA should be called the National Football League, and he renamed his team the Bears.

Halas played end and coached the team from 1920 through 1929, winning the league championship in 1921. He coached again from 1933 through 1942. The Bears won championships under Ralph Jones in 1932 and under Halas in 1933, 1940, and 1941. While Halas was in the navy, the Bears won the 1943 championship, and Halas was back in charge in 1946 to win another title.

In 1956, Halas again left coaching, but after the Bears had two poor seasons without him he took over once more and won his final championship in 1963. He retired permanently from coaching after the 1967 season. Halas has been called the inventor

of the man in motion, but that honor is actually Ralph Jones'. He's also been called the inventor of the modern T-formation, but that was Clark Shaughnessy, who installed the system for the Bears in 1941, a year after he'd done so at Stanford University. As a coach, Halas was more interested in hard physical play than in strategy.

Halas Trophy
Football

The National Football League's Defensive Player of the Year Award, established in 1966, was named for George Halas after his death in 1983. The award is based on a poll of sportswriters conducted by the Newspaper Enterprise Association.

Halas Trophy Winners

1966 Larry Wilson, St. Louis Cardinals
1967 David "Deacon" Jones, Los Angeles Rams
1968 David "Deacon" Jones, Los Angeles Rams
1969 Dick Butkus, Chicago Bears
1970 Dick Butkus, Chicago Bears
1971 Carl Eller, Minnesota Vikings
1972 Joe Greene, Pittsburgh Steelers
1973 Alan Page, Minnesota Vikings
1974 Joe Greene, Pittsburgh Steelers
1975 Curley Culp, Houston Oilers
1976 Jerry Sherk, Cleveland Browns
1977 Harvey Martin, Dallas Cowboys
1978 Randy Gradishar, Denver Broncos
1979 Lee Roy Selmon, Tampa Bay Buccaneers
1980 Lester Hayes, Oakland Raiders
1981 Joe Klecko, New York Jets
1982 Mark Gastineau, New York Jets
1983 Jack Lambert, Pittsburgh Steelers
1984 Mike Haynes, Los Angeles Raiders
1985 Howie Long, Los Angeles Raiders
     Andre Tippett, New England Patriots (tie)
1986 Lawrence Taylor, New York Giants
1987 Reggie White, Philadelphia Eagles
1988 Mike Singletary, Chicago Bears
1989 Tim Lewis, Green Bay Packers
1990 Bruce Smith, Buffalo Bills

Hall of Fame Bowl
Football

Initiated in 1986 to benefit the National Football Foundation Hall of Fame, this bowl game is played in Tampa, FL. The first game was on December 23, 1986, but the date was then changed to January, so the second game wasn't played until 1988.

Results

1986 Boston College 27, Georgia 24
1988 Michigan 28, Alabama 24

1989 Syracuse 23, Louisiana State 10
1990 Auburn 31, Ohio State 14
1991 Clemson 30, Illinois 0

Hall of Fame of the Trotter

This hall of fame was established by the Trotting Horse Club of America in 1951; it became an independent entity in 1961, when the THCA dissolved. It's located in the former Good Time Stable in Goshen, NY, next door to the Historic Track, the oldest operating race track in North America. In addition to statues of its inductees, the hall has a large collection of Currier and Ives prints of harness racing and an exhibit showing the evolution of the sulky.

Address: 240 Main Street, Goshen NY 10924 (914) 294-6330

Halls of Fame

The Hall of Fame of Great Americans at New York University was the inspiration for the Baseball Hall of Fame. Conceived in 1936 to celebrate baseball's supposed 100th anniversary in 1939, this was the first sports hall of fame. The building, at Cooperstown, NY, was dedicated on June 12, 1939. The Helms Athletic Foundation, also created in 1936, established halls of fame for many sports beginning in 1948. During the 1950s and 1960s, sports halls of fame proliferated, although many of them existed only on paper for years. The National Football Foundation Hall of Fame, for example, began as an organization in 1947 in Syracuse, NY and inducted its first members in 1951, but it didn't have a building until 1978. Now most sports have a hall of fame of some kind, and there are also sports halls of fame in several states, provinces, and cities. Other halls honor ethnic groups, among them the Hellenic Sports Hall of Fame, the International Jewish Sports Hall of Fame, the National Italian American Sports Hall of Fame, and the National Polish-American Sports Hall of Fame and Museum.

See also ASSOCIATION OF SPORTS MUSEUMS AND HALLS OF FAME.

Hambletonian
Harness Racing

Hambletonian was the greatest sire in harness racing history. Foaled on May 5, 1849, he trotted a mile in 2 minutes, 48½ seconds in 1852, a world record at the time. He had already begun his stud career a year earlier and he sired 1,331 foals before his death in 1876. Almost all of today's harness horses trace their ancestry to Hambletonian.

John C. Bauer, C. W. Leonard, Joseph I. Markey, and Harry O. Reno formed the Hambletonian Society in 1924 and announced that the Hambletonian Stake for three-year-old trotters would be held during the 1926 New York State Fair at Syracuse. The Hambletonian was held in Lexington in 1927, Syracuse in 1928, and Lexington again in 1929. From 1930 through 1956, it was run at Goshen, NY, except for 1943, when it was held at the Empire City track in New York City. It moved to the Du Quoin (IL) State Fair from 1957 through 1980, and since 1981 has been run at Meadowlands Race Track in East Rutherford, NJ.

Hamilton, Ontario

Football Hamilton had a team in the Ontario Rugby Football Union when the ORFU was organized in 1883. The team became known as the Tigers when it entered the new Interprovincial Rugby Football Union in 1907. Another Hamilton team, the Alerts, merged with the Tigers in 1914. During World War II, the Tigers suspended play and were replaced by the Hamilton Flying Wildcats, originally made up of members of the Royal Canadian Air Force. That team, manned by civilians and renamed the Wildcats, remained in the IRFU after the war, while the Tigers were reorganized as a member of the ORFU. The two teams merged in 1950 as the Hamilton Tiger-Cats in the IRFU. Hamilton won the Grey Cup for the Canadian football championship in 1912, 1913, 1915, 1928, 1929, 1932, 1953, 1957, 1963, 1965, 1967, 1972, and 1986.

Hockey Hamilton also had a team called the Tigers in the National Hockey League from 1920 until 1925, when the franchise became the New York Americans.

See also IVOR WYNNE STADIUM.

Hammer Throw

Throwing the maul or hammer—actually a heavy sledgehammer—was an event in the Scottish Highland games and in Irish and Welsh field games. By 1860, the hammer had become stylized as an iron ball with a short wooden handle. At that time, a competitor could run as far as he wanted before throwing it. In 1876, the hammer had to be thrown from between two lines, 7 feet apart, and from 1878 to 1886 a 7-foot circle was used. The circle was enlarged to 9 feet in 1887, but reduced to 7 feet again in 1908. The hammer is now a metal ball connected by a spring steel wire to a double grip, weighing 16 pounds all told. The first man to throw the hammer more than 130 feet was James Mitchel of the United States in 1890; he broke the 140-foot mark two years later. John Flanagan of the United States threw it more than 150 feet in 1897, more than 160 feet in 1899, more than 170 feet in 1901, and more than 180 feet in 1909, increasing the world record by nearly 44 feet in a 14-year period. Patrick Ryan of the United States set a world record with a throw of 189 feet, 6½ inches in 1913, and that stood until 1936. The record was held by Europeans from then until 1958, when Harold Connolly made a throw of 225 feet, 4 inches. Connolly surpassed 230 feet in 1965. The current American record of 265 feet 4 inches was set by Jud Logan in 1986. Yuriy Syedikh of the Soviet Union holds the world record, 284 feet 7 inches, also set in 1986.

See also CONNOLLY, HAROLD.

Hammond, IN

Football The Hammond Pros joined the American Professional Football Association in its first season, 1920, dropped out in 1921, and rejoined in 1922, when the APFA was renamed the National Football League. Hammond left the league for good after the 1926 season.

Handball

Various forms of handball were played by Dutch and English colonists. John Bentley of Massachusetts noted in his diary for 1791 that "those of better education" preferred handball to football, which was considered "rather disgraceful." But the modern version of the sport was developed in Ireland, and Irish immigrant Phil Casey built the first American four-wall court in Brooklyn in 1886. Casey won the U.S. championship in 1887 and defeated John Lawlor, the Irish champion, the following year. He beat all challengers before retiring in 1900.

Many YMCAs built handball courts early in this century and an informal one-wall version of the sport became popular on bathing beaches in the New York area and on the playgrounds of Catholic schools in Montreal. The Amateur Athletic Union assumed control of the sport in 1897 and held its first tournament that year. Chicago realtor Bob Keindler founded the U.S. Handball Association in 1951, and the USHA held a tournament in competition with the AAU tournament that year. In 1952, the two groups held a joint tournament, and the following year they signed an agreement to work together.

The USHA has held exhibitions throughout the country to popularize the sport, and it also developed a "family ball," softer than the regulation ball, to encourage women and children to play. There are now about 2,000 private and 1,000 public courts throughout North America, used by an estimated 2.5 million players. The USHA sanctions 50 state tournaments and 9 regional tournaments, leading to the national championships. The Gatorade/Spalding Pro Tour is a series of tournaments offering prize money for men and women.

Address: U.S. Handball Association, 930 North Benton Avenue, Tucson, AZ 85711 (602) 795-0434

See also TEAM HANDBALL.

Handicapped
See DISABLED, SPORTS FOR THE.

Hang Gliding

A type of hang glider was invented in 1921 by Alexander Lippisch of Germany, but the modern hang glider was originally based on the "Rogallo wing." Designed by Francis M. Rogallo of NASA during the late 1950s, its original purpose was to allow planes or spacecraft to drop large payloads safely to earth. The large flexible wing was soon scaled down by hobbyists and equipped with a seat so it could carry a passenger. By 1970, a rigid, more easily controllable design had largely replaced the Rogallo wing, and hang gliding became a popular sport in California. The Peninsula Hang Glider Club, organized in December of 1971, became the Southern California Hang Gliding Association early in 1972. At the end of 1973, the name was changed to the U.S. Hang Gliding Association. The USHGA, an autonomous division of the Federal Aeronautics Administration, conducts 12 regional meets leading to the national championships.

Address: U.S. Hang Gliding Association, P.O. Box 8300, Colorado Springs, CO 80933 (719) 632-8300

See also SOARING.

Hanson, Victor A. (1903–1982)
Basketball, Football
Born July 30, 1903, Watertown, NY; died April 10, 1982; Basketball, National Football Foundation Hall of Fame

A nine-letter man at Syracuse University, Hanson was an All-American in football in 1926 and in basketball in 1925, 1926, and 1927. He played professionally with the Cleveland Rosenblums of the American Basketball League, then coached football at Syracuse from 1930 through 1936, compiling a 33–21–5 record. Grantland Rice named Hanson as an end on his all-time All-American football team in 1952, and in 1960 he was selected by the Helms Athletic Foundation as an all-time All-American in basketball. He was named the best amateur athlete in the history of New York State in 1953.

Harbor Bowl
Football

The Harbor Bowl was played at San Diego three times, all on New Years Day. New Mexico and Montana State tied 13–13 in 1947, Hardin-Simmons beat San Diego State 53–0 in 1948, and Villanova beat Nevada-Reno 27–7 in 1949.

Harlem Globetrotters
Basketball

Originally the Savoy Five, this famous black team was organized by Abe Saperstein in 1926 and played in Chicago's Savoy Ballroom. When the ballroom became a skating rink in 1927, Saperstein renamed the team the Harlem Globetrotters and took it on the road. They played serious basketball in those days, traveling from town to town in a dilapidated car, taking on all comers and beating most of them. They won the World Basketball Tournament in 1940. By then, they were so good that it was hard to find opponents, so the Globetrotters turned their game into a show full of clowning, dribbling, and trick-shot exhibitions.

After World War II, they became real Globetrotters, traveling to Europe, where they drew 75,000 fans to Berlin's Olympic Stadium on August 22, 1951. They made a round-the-world cruise in 1952, playing in Africa and Asia. Among the team's stars were Reece "Goose" Tatum, the "Clown Prince of Basketball," and Marques Haynes, one of the greatest dribblers in history. In 1953, the Globetrotters began touring with the Washington Generals, a team put together to furnish token opposition. The typical Globetrotter game features several 2- or 3-minute periods of serious basketball followed by 10 or 12 minutes of clowning.

See also SAPERSTEIN, ABRAHAM.

Harlem Race Course
New York, NY

The first recorded race by a trotter took place on an unnamed Harlem race course, believed to have been a one-mile oval track, on June 10, 1806, and the first track exclusively for harness horses was built next to the Red House Tavern in Harlem in 1813. The tracks were used primarily for training the horses, which did most of their racing on paved roads at that time. The second track was also unnamed but was usually known as the Red House track.

Harlem Renaissance Big Five
Basketball

Organized by Bob Douglas, the "Rens" are one of the few teams inducted into the Basketball Hall of Fame as a unit, and Douglas was the first black person inducted. From 1922 to 1925, the team played most of its games in the ballroom of the Harlem Renaissance Casino, but in 1925–26 Douglas added three fine players, Clarence "Fat" Jenkins, James "Pappy" Ricks, and Eyre "Bruiser" Saitch, and the team began barnstorming. By 1932, the Rens had four more stars, Charles "Tarzan" Cooper, John "Casey" Holt, "Wee Willie" Smith, and Bill Yancey. From then through 1936, they won 473 games while losing only 49, and they had an 88-game winning streak in 1933–34. In 1926–27, the Rens split a six-game series with the Original Celtics, and they beat the Celtics seven out of eight games in 1933. In 22 seasons, they won 2,318 games and lost 381.

Harmsworth Trophy
Powerboat Racing

Sir Alfred Harmsworth donated this trophy for international powerboat racing in 1903. English boats won three of the first four races, and a French boat won the fourth, but E. J. Schroeder of the United States was the winner in 1907 and 1908. There was no competition in 1909; F. K. Burnham of the United States won in 1910 and 1911. After two more English victories, racing was suspended until 1920, when Garfield A. Wood of the United States won the first of ten consecutive races. Competition was again suspended in 1934. Harmsworth Trophy races were next held in 1949, 1950, and 1956, after which the event was discontinued.

Harness Racing

Trotting and pacing horses were raced under saddle in the 18th century. The sport was banned in Maryland in 1747, and New Jersey restricted it to certain days of the year in 1748. The Narragansett pacer, bred in Rhode Island, was the most prized breed. George Washington owned one that was raced at Accotink, VA on September 20, 1768. Pacers were valued as saddle horses because of their gait: In the pace, both legs on one side move forward at the same time, making for a smoother, more comfortable ride.

The most important event in the early history of harness racing was the arrival in 1788 of the Thoroughbred Messenger, who sired many trotters. All trotting horses trace their ancestry to Messenger through Abadallah, his grandson, who is the first horse listed in the American Trotting Register. As roads improved in the late 18th Century, the trotter became popular. In the trot, the right front and left rear foot move forward at the same time, which minimizes swaying when the horse pulls a vehicle.

The Harlem Renaissance Big Five, commonly known as the "Rens," were organized in 1922 by Bob Douglass. The team won 127 of 134 games in the 1933–34 season. Courtesy of the Basketball Hall of Fame

The first record of a race, probably just a time trial, appeared in the *New York Commercial Advertiser* of June 11, 1806: "A horse named Yankee trotted a mile yesterday in 2:59 in Harlem, N.Y."

Harlem was an early center for harness racing. In 1813, the first track exclusively for trotters was built next to Harlem's Red House Tavern. However, the horses did most of their racing on roads; tracks were used primarily for training and time trials. The second recorded trotting race was a time trial in 1818. During a dinner at the New York Jockey Club, William Jones bet a Colonel Bond of Maryland $1,000 that his trotter, Boston Blue, could run a mile in less than 3 minutes. Jones won the bet. Several tracks were built on Long Island, including one at Centerville that was constructed by the New York Trotting Club, founded in 1825. The first one-mile track for trotters was Hunting Park in Philadelphia, which opened in 1821. Other early tracks were the Cambridge Course in Boston and the Eagle Course in Trenton.

During the 1840s, the sport began to develop stars. The first of them was Lady Suffolk, who inspired the song "The Old Gray Mare." On October 7, 1844, she became the first trotter to run the mile in less than 2 minutes 30 seconds, running heats of 2:28, 2:29, and 2:30 to win a five-heat race against two other horses. In 16 seasons, she ran 162 races and may have won as much as $60,000.

Trotting races became a staple at county and state fairs beginning in the late 1840s. In 1858, it was estimated that there were more than 70 harness tracks in the United States. The sulky, a two-wheeled vehicle pulled by the horse, which had been used for racing as early as 1810, replaced the saddle except in occasional time trials. Harness racing gradually became commercialized, as tracks were built to hold large crowds and admission money became important to the sport. The process continued even during the Civil War.

In February 1870, the National Trotting Association for the Promotion of the Interest of Trotting Turf

The Union Course on Long Island, built for Thoroughbred racing in 1821, became a major trotting track during the late 1840s. This illustration shows an 1851 race at the track.

was founded; the name was shortened to the National Trotting Association in 1878. The National Association of Trotting Horse Breeders was organized in 1876 and on November 19, 1879, the group agreed on a definition for a trotting breed to be called the Standardbred. The "standard" referred to a mile done in 2:30, and essentially any horse that had met the standard, or had sired or foaled a horse that had met the standard, was declared a member of the new breed.

In the meantime, the pacer had been rediscovered. Pacers were brought out of Canada in the early 19th century to be used on the frontier, where roads were poor or nonexistent. As early as June 21, 1855, Pocahontas set a world record by pacing a mile in 2:17½, nearly 10 seconds faster than any trotter. The pacer was scorned by most horsemen, but pacing races were popular at county fairs in the Midwest. The first major race for pacers in the East was run at Mystic Park in Boston on August 30, 1875, with a purse of $5,000. It drew only a small crowd.

A pace was held at Cleveland during the 1877 Grand Circuit meeting. Established by four tracks in 1873 as the Quadrilateral Trotting Combination, the Grand Circuit coordinated major stakes races to make it easy for drivers and horses to travel from one meet to the next. Once pacing made the Grand Circuit, it was almost certain to succeed, and it did. The speed of the horses certainly helped. The 2-minute mark was first broken in 1897 by Star Point, who paced a 1:59¼ mile.

A major step toward new speed records was the introduction of the "bicycle sulky" in 1892. The original sulkies had broad, heavy wooden wheels and weighed 100 pounds or more. In the late 1820s,

the high-wheeled sulky was introduced. The first weighed 108 pounds, but that was cut down to 46 pounds by 1843. The bike sulky used bicycle wheels with ball bearings and pneumatic tires. The fastest time by a trotter pulling a high-wheeled sulky was 2:08¼ in 1891. Pulling a bike sulky, Nancy Hanks lowered that mark by a full 3 seconds in 1892, and the pacing record was reduced from 2:06 to 2:04 between 1891 and 1892.

During the 1890s, colt racing began to increase. Until then, most harness horses weren't allowed to race until they were five or six years old. The Kentucky Futurity, for three-year-olds, was established in 1874 but that was an isolated event. Leland Stanford then developed the Palo Alto system of training, which emphasized early speed and was widely adopted by other trainers. Breeders and owners naturally wanted to win prize money as soon as possible, so races were inaugurated for two- and three-year-olds. The length of the usual heat was cut to 1 mile for these younger horses. That allowed tracks to have more races on a single card, which helped to attract more spectators.

Dan Patch, the most famous harness horse of all, began racing in 1900 and he helped attract fans, too. In three years, he won 54 of 56 heats and never lost a race. A pacer, he lowered the world record to 1:59 in 1903, 1:56 in 1904, and 1:55¼ in 1905. That record stood until 1938.

Harness racing continued to boom early in the century and into the 1920s. The first $50,000 race, the American Trotting Derby, was run August 25, 1908, at Readville, MA. The Grand Circuit expanded from 4 tracks to 17 by 1911. Similar regional circuits were established by smaller tracks in eastern Iowa, the Illinois Valley, southern Michigan, southern Indiana, Ohio, Illinois, California, and southern Indiana–Kentucky.

The Great Depression hurt harness racing, but in the late 1930s it regained ground. The sport was in some disarray, however. The American Trotting Association had been formed in 1887 to govern harness racing in much of the Midwest, and during the 1920s the United Trotting Association began governing the sport in Ohio, which had 78 tracks. The three groups met November 11–13, 1938, and agreed to form a single governing body. The United States Trotting Association was formally organized on January 6–7, 1939. The Canadian Trotting Association was also formed in 1939 through a merger of the Canadian Trotting and Pacing Horse Association and the Dominion Harness Horse Association.

Like Thoroughbred racing, harness racing prospered after World War II, when the sport began to move from small tracks and county fairs in rural

One of the most popular sports during the 1850s was harness racing. This is the finish of a June 5, 1855, race at the Union Course. From a Nathaniel Currier lithograph.

areas to metropolitan areas. The number of tracks increased for a short period, from 485 in 1945 to a high of 612 in 1948. By 1958, however, there were only 454 tracks, but total prize money had nearly tripled, from $9,805,079 in 1948 to $27,572,830 in 1958, and on-track betting more than tripled, from $194,771,307 to $712,487,454.

Harness racing originated with informal matches on town and city roads. This is a view of trotting on Harlem Lane in 1870.

The upward trend generally continued into the late 1970s, when competition from state lotteries, along with off-track and simulcast betting on Thoroughbreds, began to hurt. From a high of $2,833,126,601 in 1980, on-track betting dropped to $2,228,968,320 in 1988, and the number of racing dates went down from 5,731 to 5,381 during the same period. Harness racing also faced one problem that Thoroughbred racing didn't: While most people have heard of the Kentucky Derby and can name at least one of the other two races in the Thoroughbred Triple Crown, harness racing has two Triple Crowns, for trotters and pacers, and few people can name one of the three races.

Harness racing's Triple Crowns are relatively recent developments. The Trotting Triple Crown was established in 1955, when the Yonkers Trot was inaugurated, to go with the Kentucky Futurity (1896) and the Hambletonian (1926). The Pacing Triple Crown was created the following year, when the Messenger Stakes was founded. The other two races are the Little Brown Jug (1946) and the Cane Pace (1955).

Further Reading: Akers, Dwight. *Drivers Up: The Story of American Harness Racing.* New York: G. P. Putnam & Sons, 1938; Hervey, John. *American Trotter.* New York: Coward-McCann, 1947; Pines, Philip A. *The Complete Book of Harness Racing.* New York: Arco, 1978; 3rd edition; Wrench, Frank A. *Harness Horse Racing in the United States and Canada.* New York: Van Nostrand, 1948.

See also BREEDERS' CROWN; CANADIAN TROTTING ASSOCIATION; GRAND CIRCUIT; HALL OF FAME OF THE TROTTER; HARNESS TRACKS OF AMERICA; NATIONAL TROTTING ASSOCIATION; TROTTING REGISTER.

Harness Tracks of America

Established in 1954, the HTA is a trade organization of major pari-mutuel harness racing tracks in North America. The association sponsors the North American Junior Driving Championship, produces promotional and advertising material for its members, and conducts periodic seminars on track management.

Address: 35 Airport Road, Morristown, NJ 07960 (201) 285-9090

Hart Memorial Trophy
Hockey

Given to the National Hockey League's Most Valuable Player, the original Hart Trophy was donated by Dr. David A. Hart, father of Cecil Hart, former general manager and coach of the Montreal Canadiens. It was given to the Hockey Hall of Fame in 1960 and replaced by the Hart Memorial Trophy, donated by the National Hockey League. The trophy winner is selected by the Professional Hockey Writers' Association.

Trophy Winners

1924	Frank Nighbor, Ottawa
1925	Billy Burch, Hamilton
1926	Nels Stewart, Montreal Maroons
1927	Herb Gardner, Montreal Canadiens
1928	Howie Morenz, Montreal Canadiens
1929	Roy Worters, New York Americans
1930	Nels Stewart, Montreal Maroons
1931	Howie Morenz, Montreal Canadiens
1932	Howie Morenz, Montreal Canadiens
1933	Eddie Shore, Boston
1934	Aurel Joliat, Montreal Canadiens
1935	Eddie Shore, Boston
1936	Eddie Shore, Boston
1937	Babe Siebert, Montreal Canadiens
1938	Eddie Shore, Boston
1939	Toe Blake, Montreal Canadiens
1940	Ebby Goodfellow, Detroit
1941	Bill Cowley, Boston
1942	Tom Anderson, New York Americans
1943	Bill Cowley, Boston
1944	Babe Pratt, Toronto
1945	Elmer Lach, Montreal Canadiens
1946	Max Bentley, Chicago
1947	Maurice Richard, Montreal Canadiens
1948	Buddy O'Connor, New York Rangers
1949	Sid Abel, Detroit
1950	Charlie Rayner, New York Rangers
1951	Milt Schmidt, Boston
1952	Gordie Howe, Detroit
1953	Gordie Howe, Detroit
1954	Al Rollins, Chicago
1955	Ted Kennedy, Toronto
1956	Jean Beliveau, Montreal Canadiens
1957	Gordie Howe, Detroit
1958	Gordie Howe, Detroit
1959	Andy Bathgate, New York Rangers
1960	Gordie Howe, Detroit
1961	Bernie Geoffrion, Montreal Canadiens
1962	Jacques Plante, Montreal Canadiens
1963	Gordie Howe, Detroit
1964	Jean Beliveau, Montreal Canadiens
1965	Bobby Hull, Chicago
1966	Bobby Hull, Chicago
1967	Stan Mikita, Chicago
1968	Stan Mikita, Chicago
1969	Phil Esposito, Boston
1970	Bobby Orr, Boston
1971	Bobby Orr, Boston
1972	Bobby Orr, Boston
1973	Bobby Clarke, Philadelphia
1974	Phil Esposito, Boston
1975	Bobby Clarke, Philadelphia
1976	Bobby Clarke, Philadelphia
1977	Guy LaFleur, Montreal
1978	Guy LaFleur, Montreal
1979	Bryan Trottier, New York Islanders
1980	Wayne Gretzky, Edmonton
1981	Wayne Gretzky, Edmonton
1982	Wayne Gretzky, Edmonton
1983	Wayne Gretzky, Edmonton
1984	Wayne Gretzky, Edmonton
1985	Wayne Gretzky, Edmonton
1986	Wayne Gretzky, Edmonton
1987	Wayne Gretzky, Edmonton
1988	Mario Lemieux, Pittsburgh
1989	Wayne Gretzky, Los Angeles
1990	Mark Messier, Edmonton
1991	Brett Hull, St. Louis

Hartford, CT

Football   The Hartford Blues played in the National Football League only in the 1926 season.

Hockey The New England Whalers of the World Hockey Association, originally based in Boston, moved to Springfield, MA in 1974 and to Hartford in 1975. The Whalers joined the National Hockey League in 1979 when the WHA and NHL merged, and they dropped the "New England" name because the Boston Bruins objected to it.

See also HARTFORD CIVIC CENTER; NEW ENGLAND.

Hartford Civic Center
Hartford, CT

The $70 million Hartford Civic Center, built as part of a major downtown renewal project, opened in 1976. It was the home of the New England Whalers in the World Hockey Association. The arena's roof collapsed under the weight of snow on January 16, 1978, and the Whalers played in nearby Springfield, MA while a $31 million rebuilding took place, expanding seating capacity from 10,700 to 15,100. The center reopened on February 7, 1980. In addition to Whalers' games, the arena hosts two Boston Celtics' basketball games each season.

Harvey, Douglas N. (1924–   )
Hockey

Born December 19, 1924, Montreal; Hockey Hall of Fame

Toe Blake, his long-time coach, called Harvey "the greatest defenseman who ever played, bar none." He joined the Montreal Canadiens in 1947 and played with them through the 1960–61 season, then went to the New York Rangers, the Detroit Red Wings, and the St. Louis Blues, retiring in 1969. An excellent rusher who could take the puck the full length of the ice to score, Harvey won the Norris Trophy as the outstanding defenseman in the NHL seven times, 1955–58 and 1960–62. He served as player-coach with the Rangers for one season, 1961–62, but quit coaching because, he said, "I couldn't be one of the boys. This way, if I want a beer with them, I get a beer."

Haughton, Percy D. (1876–1924)
Football

Born July 11, 1876, Staten Island, NY; died October 24, 1924; National Football Foundation Hall of Fame

As a coach, Haughton helped modernize football, creating an open style of play that emphasized speed and deception. He played tackle and fullback at Harvard, graduating in 1899. After coaching Cornell to a 16–5 record in two seasons, he became a bond broker. The Harvard Athletic Association hired him as the school's first full-time professional coach in 1908. Haughton immediately transformed Harvard

football. In nine seasons, his teams won 71 games, lost 7, and tied 5, outscoring their opponents 1,427 to 106. From 1911 into the 1915 season, Harvard had a 39-game unbeaten streak.

After serving in World War I, Haughton entered business again, but went to Columbia as football coach in 1923. He died of a heart attack after a practice the following season. His record there was 8–5–1. Haughton developed the modern system of using a coordinated staff of coaching specialists, with a military chain of command from the head coach through his assistants to the players. Among his innovations were the running pass, the "mouse-trap" play, and the five-man defensive line with three linebackers.

Haymaker Club
See TROY, NY.

Hayes, "Bob" Robert (1942–   )
Football, Track and Field

Born December 20, 1942, Jacksonville, FL; National Track and Field Hall of Fame

Hayes didn't begin sprinting until he was 16, but two years later he tied the world record of 9.3 seconds in the 100-yard dash. In 1962, he tied the new world record, 9.2 seconds, and he lowered it to 9.1 in 1963. Hayes became the first man in history to break the 6-second barrier in the 60-yard dash, running it in 5.9 seconds in 1964. That year he set an Olympic record of 10.0 seconds in the 100 meters, and he anchored the winning United States 400-meter relay team, gaining 5 yards on the last lap to win his second Gold Medal.

Hayes played football at Florida A & M, and in 1965 he became a wide receiver for the Dallas Cowboys of the National Football League. He was with Dallas through 1974, then joined the San Francisco 49ers for one season. In 11 years, he caught 371 passes for 7,414 yards, averaging 20 yards per catch, and he scored 71 touchdowns. He also returned 104 punts for 1,158 yards and 3 touchdowns.

Heffelfinger, "Pudge" William W. (1867–1954)
Football

Born December 20, 1867, Minneapolis, MN; died April 5, 1954; National Football Foundation Hall of Fame

The first known professional football player, Heffelfinger was paid $500 for one game with the Duquesne Athletic Club in Pittsburgh on November 12, 1892. A remarkable physical specimen, he played his last game at the age of 65. At 6-foot-3 and 206 pounds, he was unusually fast. He became a starting guard as a freshman at Yale in 1888. Teams often used a "guards-back" formation, in which the guards dropped back behind the line of scrimmage to get a good running start for their blocks, but Yale devised several plays on which Heffelfinger would get the snap from center and run with the ball.

Heffelfinger broke up Princeton's feared "flying wedge" play time after time by taking a running jump at the lead man, hitting him on the chest with his knees. Because of his speed, Coach Walter Camp in 1890 came up with the idea of having Heffelfinger take a step back and run behind the line of scrimmage to lead a back around end, making Heffelfinger the first pulling guard. He was named to the All-American team the first three years it existed, 1889–92, and as late as 1950 he was still being listed on most all-time All-American teams.

After coaching at Lehigh in 1894 and Minnesota in 1895, Heffelfinger became a stockbroker. He returned to Yale briefly as an assistant coach in 1916. Showing the linemen how it should be done during a scrimmage, he knocked two starters out of action. In 1922, at the age of 54, Heffelfinger played 51 minutes in a charity game for a team of all-stars against the Ohio State alumni. His final game was in Minneapolis on November 11, 1933.

Heiden, Eric (1958–)
Speed Skating

Born June 14, 1958, Madison, WI

During the 1980 Winter Olympics, Heiden became the first athlete ever to win five individual Gold Medals, when he swept the men's speed-skating events, setting five Olympic records and two world records. Whenever he broke a world record that year, it was his own, because he already held the records in all six standard distances from 500 to 10,000 meters. In 1976, Heiden turned down a chance to play for the U.S. national junior hockey team in order to continue his training, and it paid off the following year, when he had an unprecedented sweep of the world sprint, overall, and the junior overall championships. He also got his first world record, 38.80 seconds in the 500 meters.

"It was like a dream," Heiden said of his victories. "All the time I was looking up at all those guys, those Russians and Scandinavians, and suddenly it's me." He swept the three world championships again in 1978, setting world records of 1 minute, 14.99 seconds in the 1,000 meters and 4:07.10 in the 3,000 meters. In 1979 he won all four events at the world overall championships, once again won the world sprint title, and set a world record of 14:43.11 in the 10,000 meters. Heiden was still much better known in Europe, where speed skating is a major

sport, than in the United States. One of Norway's popular songs that year was "The Ballad of Eric Heiden."

But television made him famous in his own country in 1980. After winning the world overall and world sprint championships for the fourth year in a row, setting records of 1:13.60 in the 1,000 meters and 1:54.79 in the 1,500 meters, Heiden was spotlighted at the Winter Olympics and came through brilliantly. He won the 500 meters in a world record 38.03, the 1,000 in an Olympic record 1:15.18, the 1,500 in an Olympic record 1:55.40, and the 5,000 in an Olympic record 7:02.29. He climaxed his performance by skating the 10,000 meters in 14:28.13, 6.20 seconds faster than the previous record. Heiden won the 1980 Sullivan Award as the outstanding amateur athlete of the year.

Heisman, John W. (1869–1936)
Football

Born October 25, 1869, Cleveland, OH; died October 3, 1936; National Football Foundation Hall of Fame

Heisman played football at Brown from 1887 through 1889 and at Pennsylvania from 1890 through 1891, then began coaching at Oberlin College. It was only the school's second year of football, but Heisman's team won all seven of its games, beating Ohio State twice, 40–0 and 50–0. He coached the University of Akron in 1893, returned to Oberlin for one year, then went to Clemson from 1900 through 1903. Heisman's longest stay was at Georgia Tech, from 1904 through 1919. He produced unbeaten teams there in 1905 (5–0–1), 1915 (7–0–1), 1916 (8–0–1), and 1917 (9–0–0). From 1914 into the 1918 season, Georgia Tech had a 32-game unbeaten streak, including a 222–0 victory over Cumberland, the highest score ever recorded.

Heisman then went to Pennsylvania for three seasons, 1920–22, to Washington and Jefferson in 1923, and to Rice from 1924 through 1927. His overall record was 185–70–17 in 37 seasons. At his death, he was the trainer at the Downtown Athletic Club in New York City.

Among Heisman's innovations were the use of the word "hike" or "hip" to signal that the ball was to be centered, the double lateral, the spin buck play, and having the center toss the ball back rather than snapping it with his foot. He invented the "jump shift," also known as the "Heisman shift," in which players would move quickly into new positions just before the snap of the ball. That led to the rule that offensive players have to be set for one second before the snap.

See HEISMAN MEMORIAL TROPHY.

Heisman Memorial Trophy
Football

Originally the Heisman Trophy, this award was initiated by the Downtown Athletic Club of New York City in 1935, named for John W. Heisman. After his death in 1936, it was renamed the Heisman Memorial Trophy. It's given to the college player voted the best in the country by the Football Writers Association of America.

Heisman Trophy Winners

1935 Jay Berwanger, Chicago HB
1936 Larry Kelley, Yale E
1937 Clint Frank, Yale HB
1938 Davey O'Brien, Texas Christian QB
1939 Nile Kinnick, Iowa HB
1940 Tom Harmon, Michigan HB
1941 Bruce Smith, Minnesota HB
1942 Frank Sinkwich, Georgia HB
1943 Angelo Bertelli, Notre Dame QB
1944 Les Horvath, Ohio State HB
1945 "Doc" Blanchard, Army FB
1946 Glenn Davis, Army HB
1947 John Lujack, Notre Dame QB
1948 Doak Walker, Southern Methodist HB
1949 Leon Hart, Notre Dame E
1950 Vic Janowicz, Ohio State HB
1951 Dick Kazmaier, Princeton HB
1952 Billy Vessels, Oklahoma HB
1953 John Lattner, Notre Dame HB
1954 Alan Ameche, Wisconsin FB
1955 Howard Cassady, Ohio State HB
1956 Paul Hornung, Notre Dame QB
1957 John David Crow, Texas A & M HB
1958 Pete Dawkins, Army HB
1959 Billy Cannon, LSU HB
1960 Joe Bellino, Navy HB
1961 Ernie Davis, Syracuse HB
1962 Terry Baker, Oregon QB
1963 Roger Staubach, Navy QB
1964 John Huarte, Notre Dame QB
1965 Mike Garrett, Southern California HB
1966 Steve Spurrier, Florida QB
1967 Gary Beban, UCLA QB
1968 O. J. Simpson, Southern California HB
1969 Steve Owens, Oklahoma FB
1970 Jim Plunkett, Stanford QB
1971 Pat Sullivan, Auburn QB
1972 Johnny Rodgers, Oklahoma HB
1973 John Cappelletti, Penn State HB
1974 Archie Griffin, Ohio State HB
1975 Archie Griffin, Ohio State HB
1976 Tony Dorsett, Pittsburgh HB
1977 Earl Campbell, Texas HB
1978 Billy Sims, Oklahoma HB
1979 Charles White, Southern California HB
1980 George Rogers, South Carolina HB
1981 Marcus Allen, Southern California HB
1982 Herschel Walker, Georgia HB
1983 Mike Rozier, Nebraska HB
1984 Doug Flutie, Boston College QB
1985 Bo Jackson, Auburn HB
1986 Vinny Testaverde, Miami (FL) QB
1987 Tim Brown, Notre Dame HB-WR
1988 Barry Sanders, Oklahoma State RB
1989 Andre Ware, Houston QB
1990 Ty Detmer, Brigham Young QB

HemisFair Arena
San Antonio, TX

Built in 1968 as part of San Antonio's Hemisfair, a world's fair dedicated to friendship between North America and Latin America, the arena originally seated 10,000 and was expanded to 15,800 in 1973, when the Dallas Mavericks of the American Basketball Association became the San Antonio Spurs. The Spurs are now in the National Basketball Association.

Henderson, Robert W. (1888–1985)
Sports Historian
Born December 25, 1888, South Shields, England; died August 19, 1985

As baseball was preparing for its "centennial" in 1939, based on the myth that Abner Doubleday had invented the sport in Cooperstown, NY a century earlier, Henderson found proof that baseball had actually evolved from the British game of rounders. A researcher at the New York Public Library, Henderson discovered that *The Boy's Own Book* by William Clarke, published in London in 1829, contained the rules for rounders. They were copied in Robin Carver's *The Book of Sports*, published in Boston in 1834, but the heading was changed from "Rounders" to "Base, or Goal Ball."

Henderson published his discovery, with additional early references to the sport, in *Baseball: Notes and Materials on Its Origins* (New York: New York Public Library, 1940). His book, *Ball, Bat and Bishop: The Origin of Ball Games* (New York: Rockport, 1947) traces modern ball games, including baseball, field hockey, and football, to ancient Egyptian fertility rites. He also published an account of Colonial sports, *Early American Sport* (Rutherford, NJ: Fairleigh Dickinson, 1976, 3rd edition).

Henie, Sonja (1912–1969)
Figure Skating
Born April 8, 1912, Oslo, Norway; died October 12, 1969; World Figure Skating Hall of Fame

The 11-year-old Henie finished last in women's figure skating at the 1924 Winter Olympics. But she went on to win Gold Medals in three consecutive Olympics, in 1928, 1932, and 1936. She also changed figure skating forever and made it popular worldwide. Henie, who had studied ballet, created the idea of free skating as a series of moves and turns flowing smoothly into one another, as in a dance, and she combined grace with an athleticism unmatched by any male skater of the period. When she went for her third Gold Medal in 1936, 200,000 spectators crowded into the rink in Garmisch-Partenkirchen, Germany. The *New York Times* described her winning performance as "a brilliant execution of spins, twirls, and jumps."

In addition to her Olympic victories, Henie won the world championship ten years in a row, 1927–1936. After the 1936 Olympics, she began touring North America with her own ice show. Until her retirement in 1950, Henie skated before audiences totaling between 15 and 20 million people.

Heptathlon

The women's scaled-down version of the decathlon, the heptathlon is a seven-event competition conducted over a two-day period. It replaced the five-event pentathlon on most track and field programs in 1981. Athletes compete in the 100-meter hurdles, shot put, high jump, and 200-meter run on the first day, and the long jump, javelin throw, and 800-meter run on the second day.

Heston, "Willie" William M. (1878–1963)
Football
Born September 9, 1878, near Galesburg, IL; died September 9, 1963; National Football Foundation Hall of Fame

Heston took a roundabout route from his Illinois birthplace to football stardom at the University of Michigan. His family moved to Oregon and in 1898 he played guard for a teacher's college in California. "Hurry-Up" Yost, coaching at Stanford in 1900, was asked to help prepare the team for an important game. Yost moved Heston to halfback and was impressed by his talents.

When Yost became coach at the University of Michigan the following year, he persuaded Heston to attend law school and play some more football. That marked the beginning of a great collegiate career. In Heston's four years at Michigan the team was undefeated, with just one tie. He scored his first touchdown on defense, by intercepting a lateral and carrying it for a score. In the next game, he scored four touchdowns as a substitute, and from that time on he was a starting halfback. When Michigan beat Stanford 49–0 in the first Rose Bowl in 1902, Heston gained 170 yards on 18 carries.

Heston was relatively small but solidly built at 5 feet 8 inches and 184 pounds and he was an explosive starter with breakaway speed; he once did the 100-yard dash in 10.2 seconds. Yost said that he scored at least 100 touchdowns, but Heston modestly claimed only 93. He was an All-American in 1903 and 1904. After graduating, he coached Drake to a 4–4 record in 1905, and he played for the Canton Bulldogs for one game, receiving $600 and expenses. In 1906, he suffered a leg injury while playing for a college all-star team against Massillon, and his career was over.

Hewitt, Foster (1903–1985)
Sportscaster
Born November 21, 1903, Toronto; died April 21, 1985; Hockey Hall of Fame

Hewitt was the first man ever to broadcast a hockey game, although he was reluctant to do it. At 18, he was working on the radio desk of the *Toronto Daily Star* when he was assigned to do the broadcast on March 22, 1923. Radio Station CFCA then began regular programming of hockey with Hewitt at the microphone. His trademark, "He shoots—he scores!" became a catch phrase among fans and Hewitt became a national celebrity. In his 50-year career, Hewitt broadcast about 3,000 hockey games on radio and television. He also wrote several books, including *Hockey Night in Canada: The Maple Leafs' Story*.

Hialeah Race Course
Hialeah, FL

Opened near Miami Beach on January 15, 1925, Hialeah attracted many owners and trainers from the Northeast because it was virtually the only place where they could race their horses during the winter. Facing competition from nearby Calder and Gulfstream, the track ran into financial difficulties during the 1980s and closed in early 1990. Hialeah's best-known race was the Flamingo Stakes for three-year-olds, an important stepping stone to the Kentucky Derby. The track had a 1⅛-mile main course and a turf track 7 furlongs and 171 feet long.

High Jump

The first man to high jump more than 6 feet was Marshall Brooks of England, who reached 6 feet and 1 inch in 1876. Charles Dumas of the United States surpassed 7 feet in 1956. Jean Shiley was the first

American woman to high jump more than 5 feet, in 1929, and Audri Reid bettered 6 feet in 1972.

Highland Games
See CALEDONIAN GAMES.

High School Sports

In the late 19th century, high school sports followed the collegiate model and faced many of the same problems that college sports faced. Students ran the teams, hired the coaches, and handled the finances, and the win-at-all-costs philosophy often resulted in the recruiting of ineligible players. The 15th Educational Conference of Academies and High Schools in 1902 recommended strict faculty control of sports and the establishment of state associations to oversee competition. By 1923 all but three states had associations.

Beginning about 1890, the traditional classics-oriented high school began to give way to the comprehensive high school, meant to prepare students for citizenship and careers rather than college, and team sports were encouraged as an important part of social education along with other extracurricular and social activities. Educators also saw sports as a means of reducing juvenile delinquency and helping to Americanize children of immigrant families.

The Public Schools Athletic League (PSAL) was formed in Greater New York in 1903 to supervise interscholastic sports. By 1910, it was being praised as "the world's greatest athletic organization," and many other cities had established similar leagues, including Baltimore, Birmingham, Buffalo, Cleveland, Kansas City, Newark, New Orleans, San Francisco, Tacoma, and Troy.

Teachers found that the popularity of sports gave them a carrot to use for discipline, rather than a stick, because students had to have certificates of good conduct and good grades in order to compete. A 1909 survey of Nebraska high schools revealed that 95 percent of them had interscholastic sports; 91 percent of those said that discipline was improved, 92 percent that scholastic standards became higher, and 97 percent that school spirit was better.

State high school basketball tournaments were especially popular. Wisconsin held the first in 1905; Illinois, Kansas, and Utah followed in 1908, Louisiana and Ohio in 1909. Half of the states had basketball tournaments by 1920. In 1929, a writer noted of basketball, "In many schools, especially in the Middle West, it has driven baseball out of existence."

Despite increased faculty control, there was a serious problem with events organized by outside promoters, including colleges and universities, at which eligibility rules were frequently ignored. L. W. Smith, secretary of the Illinois High School Athletic Association, called a meeting in 1920 of representatives from the Indiana, Iowa, Michigan, and Wisconsin associations to discuss the problem and they organized the Midwest Federation of State High School Athletic Associations. It became a national federation in 1922.

With the tremendous growth of sports during the 1920s, many high schools built expensive stadiums, gymnasiums and other athletic facilities with an eye toward increased attendance and larger gate receipts, and state championship events were established in a variety of sports. High school football became a major spectator sport in smaller towns and cities far from college campuses. But even in Chicago, which had both college and professional football, more than 120,000 fans turned out for the city championship series in the early 1930s.

Growth slowed during the Great Depression, when more emphasis was placed on intramural sports and physical education. But the baby boom after World War II, combined with high levels of federal funding for construction, led to the building of many new comprehensive high schools and vocational-technical schools that contained large auditoriums and gymnasiums, along with outdoor facilities such as tennis courts and adjoining fields for team sports.

As at the college level, girls' competitive sports lagged far beyond boys' until Title IX of the Educational Amendments Act went into effect in 1972. Pressured to increase programs for girls, most schools added several more girls' sports during the 1970s. The women's movement and the increased visibility of women athletes also encouraged more girls to participate. In 1971, there were 3,666,917 boys playing interscholastic sports, but only 294,015 girls. The number of boys taking part declined to 3,425,777 in 1987–88, while the number of girls increased to 1,849,684.

See also NATIONAL FEDERATION OF STATE HIGH SCHOOL ASSOCIATIONS; PUBLIC SCHOOLS ATHLETIC LEAGUE.

Hill, Phil (1927–   )
Auto Racing
Born April 20, 1927, Miami, FL

In 1961, Hill became the first American ever to win the World Championship of Drivers in formula one races. He began his racing career driving sports cars in 1949 and joined the Ferrari racing team in Europe in 1956. Hill got his first formula one starts two years later and scored his first victory in the 1960

Grand Prix of Europe. In his championship season, he won the Grand Prix of Belgium and Grand Prix of Italy, was second in the Grand Prix of Holland and the Grand Prix of England, and finished third in the Grand Prix of Monaco and the Grand Prix of Europe.

Historic Track
Goshen, NY

The oldest harness racing track in existence, it opened in 1838 as Westcott's Meadow. The original ⅓-mile track was replaced by a ½-mile oval in 1858. Historic Track joined the Grand Circuit in 1911 and was the first New York State harness track to have pari-mutuel racing, in 1940. The track in 1966 became the first sports facility to be registered as a national historic landmark.

History, Sports

Although there were many books on sports history before John R. Betts, he was the first professional historian to concentrate on the field. His doctoral thesis at Columbia University was *Organized Sport in Industrial America*, and his book *America's Sporting Heritage: 1850–1950* was published posthumously in 1974. By that time, several historians had entered the field. The North American Society for Sports History, founded in 1972 with fewer than 100 members, now has more than 900 members.

The first scholarly history of a single sport was Harold Seymour's *Baseball: The Early Years* (1960), followed by his *Baseball: The Golden Years* (1971). Scholarly works have proliferated since Betts and Seymour. There have been general histories, such as Douglas Rader's *American Sports: From the Age of Folk Games to the Age of Spectators*, and studies of a specific community during a specific period, such as Melvin L. Adelman's *A Sporting Time: New York City and the Rise of Modern Athletics, 1820–70*.

There have also been specialized studies of individual sports, including Elliott J. Gorn's *The Manly Art: Bare-Knuckle Prize Fighting in America*. And the typically bland, as-told-to sports biography is giving way to scholarly biographies of sports figures, among them Randy Roberts' *Papa Jack: Jack Johnson and the Era of White Hopes* and William J. Baker's *Jesse Owens: An American Life*. Other books have examined particular aspects of sports, among them *Sport and Political Ideology*, by John M. Hoberman, and *Sports and Freedom: The Rise of Big-Time College Athletics*, by Ronald A. Smith.

Scholarly articles about the history of sports have spread beyond the *Journal of Sport History* and the *Journal of the Canadian Association for Health,* *Physical Education and Recreation*. They appear frequently in periodicals such as the *New England Quarterly*, *Research Quarterly*, the *Journal of American History*, and the *Journal of American Culture*. Popular interest in the subject led to the publication of two magazines, both founded in 1987. *Sports History* is still publishing, but *Sports Heritage* went out of business in mid-1988.

Hitchcock, "Tommy" Thomas, Jr. (1900–1944)
Polo

Born February 11, 1900, Aiken, SC; died April 19, 1944

Unquestionably the greatest American polo player, Hitchcock was known for absolute fearlessness. He demonstrated his courage as a member of the Lafayette Escadrille during World War I. Shot down behind German lines, he spent four months in hospitals and then was put in a prison camp. While being moved to another camp, he leaped through a train window into a river and spent eight nights walking to the Swiss border, 100 miles away. Besides courage, Hitchcock had superb riding ability and a strong, accurate shot. He was ranked at 10 goals, the top handicap rating, for 18 years. He played for the U.S. team that won the 1921 Westchester Cup and for the teams that defended the cup in 1924, 1927, and 1930. He was also on two National Open champions: Meadow Brook in 1923 and the Sands Point Club in 1924. He was killed in the crash of a military plane during World War II.

Hockey

A committee appointed by the Amateur Hockey Association of Canada in 1941 decided that hockey was first played in 1855 by the Royal Canadian Rifles, British troops who were stationed at Kingston, Ontario. It is likely that the soldiers, far from inventing ice hockey, simply brought a primitive version of it from England. Types of field hockey known as bandy, hurley, shinny, or shinty often moved to the ice during the winter, especially in East Anglia. The village of Bury Fen was playing "ice bandy" as early as 1813 and its team demonstrated the sport at London's Crystal Palace in 1860.

Two nine-man teams played hockey at McGill University, Montreal, on March 3, 1875, and the first formal rules for hockey were written by McGill students W. F. Robertson and R. F. Smith in 1879. The rules called for nine players on a team, prohibited forward passing and body checking, and required offensive players to remain behind the puck at all times. A. P. Low brought the sport from McGill to

Ottawa in 1885, when a league was established by the Kingston Athletics, the Kingston Hockey Club, Queen's University, and the Royal Military College. The Amateur Hockey Association of Canada was founded in 1886 by five clubs, three in Montreal, one in Quebec, and one in Ottawa.

For a game at the Montreal Winter Carnival in 1886, one team showed up with only seven players and the other agreed to use just seven men, too. The game turned out to be so much faster and more exciting than nine-player hockey that seven-player teams became the rule. Also during the 1880s, field hockey equipment turned into modern ice hockey equipment. According to one story, someone created a puck by slicing the top and bottom off the rubber field hockey ball that had been used. The stick was made longer and the blade was flattened to allow better stick handling. The hockey goal was simply two posts with a crossbar, and the goalie was required to stand up, because the puck always slid along the ice and it would have been simple to shut out a team by simply lying down in front of the goal.

In 1892, a Montreal resident complained that the city was "hockey mad" because the number of teams made it impossible to get skating time on local rinks. There were leagues throughout the country by 1893, when the Stanley Cup was presented for the Canadian championship. It was awarded that year to the Montreal Amateur Athletic Association. Hockey also entered the United States in 1893. A Canadian student organized a team at Johns Hopkins University in Baltimore and the sport was also introduced at Yale by Malcolm G. Chace and Arthur E. Foote, who had seen a hockey game while playing in a tennis tournament in Canada.

The United States Amateur Hockey League was formed by four New York City teams in 1896 and a Baltimore Hockey League was organized in January of 1897. Brown, Columbia, Harvard, Princeton, and Yale founded the Intercollegiate Hockey League in 1898. Meanwhile, professionalism had become a problem in Canada. When the AHA accepted the Ottawa Capitals in 1899, three teams withdrew in protest, claiming that the Capitals paid their players. Those teams, Quebec, Ottawa, and the Victorias, joined with the Montreal Shamrocks to form the Canadian Amateur Hockey League.

The Portage Lakers were organized in Houghton, MI in 1903 as the first all-professional team. They joined the International Professional Hockey League in 1904, along with teams representing Calumet, MI, Pittsburgh, and both Sault Ste. Maries, in Michigan and Ontario. The IHL folded in 1907, when many of its Canadian players returned to their former teams because the Eastern Canada Amateur Hockey Asso-

In this informal 1884 version of hockey on a frozen pond, a rubber ball was used instead of a puck. The sketch appeared in Harper's Young People.

ciation had decided that professionals could play, as long as each team listed the players who were being paid. The ECAHA had originated in 1904 as the Federal Amateur Hockey League.

In 1907, the Ontario Professional League was formed by teams in Berlin (now Kitchener), Brantford, Guelph, and Toronto, and two years later the ECAHA dropped the word "amateur" from its name because its only members were four professional teams. It lasted less than a year under its new name, becoming the Canadian Hockey Association in 1909. But more important was the formation in 1910 of the National Hockey Association, with teams in Cobalt, Haileybury, and Renfrew, and two in Montreal, the Wanderers and the Canadiens. Two of the ECHA teams, Ottawa and the Montreal Shamrocks, replaced Cobalt and Haileybury in 1911, when three 20-minute periods of play replaced two 30-minute

Hockey was being played by roller skaters at least as early as 1888, as shown in this newspaper illustration of a game in Jersey City, NJ.

periods and the number of players was cut from seven to six.

Professional leagues sprang up all over Canada after 1910. The best of them was the Pacific Coast Hockey League, organized with teams in New Westminster, Vancouver, and Victoria. From 1911 through 1917, the NHA and PCHL champions played an annual series for the Stanley Cup. When Portland, OR entered the PCHL in 1914, cup trustees ruled that the trophy was for the world championship and that teams from the United States could compete. The Seattle Metropolitans in 1917 became the first U.S. team to win the Stanley Cup. The same year, the NHA was disbanded and replaced by the National Hockey League, formed by the Canadiens, Ottawa, Quebec, and the Wanderers. However, Toronto replaced Quebec for the league's first two seasons.

The NHL struggled through several years, but had unquestionably become a success by 1923, when a new 10,000-seat arena opened in Ottawa. The Montreal Forum opened the following year, and the Boston Bruins became the first U.S. team in the league. In 1926, the New York Americans and Pittsburgh joined the NHL, followed by the Chicago Black Hawks, Detroit Cougars, and New York Rangers in 1927. The league was split into the American and Canadian Divisions, and the Stanley Cup became the NHL's championship trophy.

Hockey had changed considerably since 1911. In 1917, goaltenders were allowed to fall to the ice to make a save, and in 1918 penalty rules were established, sending a player to the penalty box for 3 minutes on a minor foul, 5 minutes on a major foul, and for the rest of the game on a match penalty. The center, or neutral, zone was created that year, with blue lines drawn 20 feet from the center of ice, and forward passing was allowed in this zone only. Beginning in 1921, goaltenders were allowed to pass the puck forward as far as the blue line, and the minor penalty was cut from 3 minutes to 2.

The delayed penalty was introduced in 1925, providing that each team had to have at least four players on the ice, no matter how many penalties had been called. To encourage offense, the NHL in 1925 passed a rule that only two defensemen could remain behind their team's blue line once the puck had advanced beyond it. The blue lines were moved in 1926 to 60 feet from each goal line, increasing the size of the neutral zone.

The league continued to experiment with ways to speed up the game and increase scoring for several years. Although these are NHL rules, most of them were eventually adopted by other professional leagues and by amateur hockey, sometimes with minor changes. Forward passing in the defensive zone was allowed in 1927, and in 1928 a forward pass into the offensive zone was permitted if the player receiving the pass was in the neutral zone when the puck left his teammate's stick.

The following year, forward passing was allowed in all three zones, but no pass could cross a blue line. That more than doubled scoring, so in midseason a rule was added prohibiting a player from entering the offensive zone before the puck—the beginning of the modern offside rule. Although penalty rules were changed somewhat, and the penalty shot was introduced in 1934, the next major change came in 1943 when the red line at center ice was created. The NHL considers that the beginning of its modern era.

After 25 years as a six-team league, the NHL decided in 1967 to expand dramatically, adding six new teams, all in the United States: Los Angeles, Minneapolis-St. Paul, Oakland, Philadelphia, Pittsburgh, and St. Louis. In 1970, Buffalo and Vancouver were added, and Atlanta and the New York Islanders joined the league two years later. The NHL's first rival, the World Hockey Association, was also organized in 1972, with teams in Alberta, Chicago, Cleveland, Houston, Los Angeles, Minnesota, New England (Hartford, CT), New York, Ottawa, Philadelphia, Quebec, and Winnipeg.

Meanwhile, hockey had become a truly international sport. The world amateur championship, first held in 1930, was dominated by Canada until 1952. The Canadians won 14 of the first 18 world titles (in Olympic years, the Winter Olympic Games champion is the world champion). But, from 1953 through 1972, Russia won 11 championships, including 9 in a row, to Canada's four. Canada withdrew from international competition in 1971 because its best players were professionals and weren't allowed to take part, while the government-subsidized players of the Communist-bloc countries were considered amateurs.

A showdown came in 1972, when a team of NHL all-stars met the Russian national team in a series of eight games, four in Canada and four in Moscow. Russia won two and tied one in Canada and won the first game in Moscow to take a commanding lead, but Canada scrambled back with three straight victories. The result was reversed in 1974, when Russia won four, lost three, and tied one against a WHA all-star team. The "Summit Series" led to the Canada Cup tournament in 1976. Six countries took part in the tournament, and Canada beat Czechoslovakia for the championship.

In 1974, the WHA and NHL agreed to a settlement in a $50 million antitrust suit brought by the WHA.

The NHL paid a $1.75 million indemnity, and the leagues agreed to honor one another's contracts. They also arranged for a series of interleague exhibition games beginning in 1975. However, they were still competing to sign amateur players and the financial strain was particularly hard on WHA teams and the newer NHL teams. The WHA went out of business in 1979, and four of its teams moved into the NHL.

Of the major professional sports, hockey is the least popular. It doesn't come across well on television, because it's difficult to see the puck. Although there are weekly network telecasts in Canada, and each team has its own local television coverage, the lack of nationwide network television in the United States has kept hockey, in general, and the NHL, in particular, from gaining a broad-based group of fans. The league in 1988 landed a three-year contract with SportsChannel America at $18 million a year, more than double the $8 million that ESPN had been paying. That gives each team only about $800,000 a season, compared to $16 million a team for the National Football League, nearly $8 million a team in major-league baseball, and more than $1.5 million a team for the National Basketball Association.

Further Reading: Beddoes, Richard, Stan Fischler, and Ira Gitler. *Hockey! The Story of the World's Fastest Sport.* New York: Macmillan, 1973, new expanded edition; Eskenazi, Gerald. *Hockey.* Chicago: Follett, 1971; Fischler, Stan, and Shirley Fischler. *Fischler's Ice Hockey Encyclopedia.* New York: Crowell, 1979, revised edition; Isaacs, Neil D. *Checking Back.* New York: W. W. Norton, 1977; Ronberg, Gary. *The Hockey Encyclopedia.* New York: Macmillan, 1974.

See also AMATEUR HOCKEY ASSOCIATION OF THE U.S.; HOCKEY CANADA; HOCKEY HALL OF FAME; NATIONAL HOCKEY LEAGUE; STANLEY CUP; U.S. HOCKEY HALL OF FAME; WORLD HOCKEY ASSOCIATION.

Hockey Canada

Established in 1969, Hockey Canada is the national governing body for the country's most popular sport. The organization is responsible for developing young players and for selecting, training, and supporting national teams for international competition. In 1970, Hockey Canada withdrew from the world championship because the country was not allowed to use players from the National Hockey League. The international federation changed its rules in 1977, and Canada returned to the competition with a team made up of NHL players. Through a committee headed by Alan Eagleson, Hockey Canada also manages the international Canada Cup series between Canadian and Soviet all-star teams, held every three years.

The National Training Centre, operated by Hockey Canada at the Olympic Saddledome in Calgary, Alberta, is the home of the Canadian national team. Officially opened in September of 1985, the complex includes the Father Bauer Olympic Arena and the International Hockey Centre of Excellence.

Address: 1600 James Naismith Drive, Gloucester, Ontario, Canada K1B 5N4 (613) 748-5613

Hockey Hall of Fame

Although it held its first elections in 1943, the Hockey Hall of Fame didn't have a home until August 26, 1961, when it opened in a new building on the Canadian National Exhibition Grounds in Toronto. Construction was funded by the six National Hockey League teams. In 1990, the hall of fame moved into 50,000 square feet of space in the Bank of Montreal building in downtown Toronto.

Address: Exhibition Place, Toronto, Ontario, Canada M6K 3C3 (416) 595-1345

See also U.S. HOCKEY HALL OF FAME.

Hockey Skating Union
See U.S.A. CONFEDERATION OF AMATEUR ROLLER SKATING.

Hoffman, Bob (1898–1985)
Weight Lifting
Born November, 1898, Tiffin, GA; died July 18, 1985

From 1946 through 1956, the United States weight lifting team won 7 of 11 world championships, and Hoffman was the major reason for that success. The co-owner of an oil burner company in York, PA, Hoffman began making barbells there in 1929. In 1932 he founded the York Barbell Company and began publishing *Strength and Health* magazine, which promoted both the sport and the company. Determined to make the United States a world power in the sport, he recruited weight lifters as employees and put together a company team that virtually became the national team.

When the United States won its first world championship in 1946, four of its six lifters worked for York. In 1947, the world championships were held in Philadelphia, largely because Hoffman paid $10,000 in travel expenses for foreign competitors and donated $25,000 for running the meet. The American team won again. Hoffman spent $20,000 on the team's training in York before the 1948 Olympic Games, where the United States won four individual Gold Medals and the team championship.

When the Cold War began, Hoffman turned it into a weight-lifting contest. He continued to subsidize lifters and teams and to help them train, but at the 1952 Olympics he began to realize that his resources couldn't match those of the Soviet government, which subsidized its weight lifters, and he sought gimmicks that would ensure victory. The first was a "miracle food" called "Hi-Proteen," developed after Russia won the 1953 world title. But Russia won again in 1954. The United States did win one final team title at the 1956 Olympics, along with five individual Gold Medals. That was the last hurrah.

Hoffman's final gimmick was an exercise technique called functional isometric contractions, which seemed to produce astounding results with some of the York lifters. What Hoffman apparently did not know was that those lifters were also using anabolic steroids, which had been introduced to them by Dr. John Ziegler, the team physician. Even that did not help, because the Communist bloc countries were ahead in steroid use. By the late 1960s, Hoffman was more interested in promoting softball than weight lifting.

One of Hoffman's great strengths was that he completely ignored race, creed, and color when putting together the York team. Among his champions were two Jews, Frank Spellman and Isaac Berger; two blacks, John Davis and James Bradford; three Japanese-Americans, Emerick Ishikawa, Tommy Kono and Yas Kuzuhara; an Italian-American, Charles Vinci; three Polish-Americans, Frank Kay, Stanley Stanczyk, and Norbert Schemansky; a Ukrainian-American, John Terpak; and a Bulgarian-American, Pete George. As Hoffman himself wrote, "No country or color has a monopoly on strength. There are good men in every nation."

Further Reading: Fair, John D., "Bob Hoffman, the York Barbell Company, and the Golden Age of American Weightlifting, 1945–1960," in *Journal of Sport History*, Volume 14, Number 2 (Summer, 1987), pp. 164–184.

See also ANABOLIC STERIODS; WEIGHT LIFTING.

Hogan, "Ben" William Benjamin (1912–   )
Golf
Born August 13, 1912, Dublin, TX; World Golf Hall of Fame

Chosen the player of the 1948–57 decade during golf's centennial celebration, Hogan became a star relatively late in his career. From 1946 through 1953 he compiled an astounding record in major championships. He is one of only four players to win all four Grand Slam events (the U.S. and British Opens, the PGA Championship, and the Masters tourna-

Ben Hogan won four U.S. Opens, two Masters tournaments, two PGA Championships, and the British Open. Courtesy of the U.S. Golf Association

ment). He won three of them in 1953 and nine overall. Even more remarkable, he won the British Open the only time he ever entered, in 1953, breaking the course record at Carnoustie in the process.

Hogan won his first major tournament, the PGA, in 1946. He repeated in the PGA in 1948 and also won the U.S. Open for the first time that year. He won the Open three more times, in 1950, 1951, and 1953, and the Masters in 1951 and 1953. Between 1940 and 1960, he finished in the top ten in every Open he entered, and from 1941 through 1956 he was never worse than seventh in the Masters. Hogan was PGA Player of the Year in 1948, 1950, 1951, and 1953, and he won the Vardon Trophy for lowest scoring average in 1940, 1941, 1942, 1946, and 1948.

Sportswriters dubbed him "the mechanical man" because of his silence and grim intensity while playing, but Hogan simply explained it was the price he had to pay to maintain his concentration. In 1949, he was almost killed in an auto accident, suffering serious leg injuries, which forced him to limit his schedule and often hurt him in the late stages of a tournament, when it became difficult for him to walk the course. Nevertheless, in 1960, at the age of 47, he set a record in the Masters by shooting a 30 on the back nine.

Holiday Bowl
Football

The first Holiday Bowl, at San Diego, was played in 1978. The home team is the Western Athletic Conference champion and the visiting team is selected from among the top teams in the country. The Big Ten has been represented 5 times in 11 games.

Results

1978 Navy 23, Brigham Young 16
1979 Indiana 38, Brigham Young 37
1980 Brigham Young 46, Southern Methodist 45
1981 Brigham Young 38, Washington State 36
1982 Ohio State 47, Brigham Young 17
1983 Brigham Young 21, Missouri 17
1984 Brigham Young 24, Michigan 17
1985 Arkansas 18, Arizona State 17
1986 Iowa 39, San Diego State 38
1987 Iowa 20, Wyoming 19
1988 Oklahoma State 62, Wyoming 14
1989 Penn State 50, Brigham Young 39
1990 Texas A&M 65, Brigham Young 14

Hollywood Park
Inglewood, CA

Perennially the leading U.S. track in attendance and purses, Hollywood Park opened on June 10, 1938. After being used by the military during World War II, it reopened in 1944, then was closed by a fire in 1949 and its major races were held at Santa Anita. The rebuilt Hollywood Park opened in 1951, when Citation won the Hollywood Gold Cup to become the first horse ever to earn more than $1 million. In 1979, Affirmed won the race, becoming the first to surpass the $2 million mark. The track has a 1-mile main course and a turf course 7 furlongs and 45 yards long. It seats 31,000.

Address: P.O. Box 369, Inglewood, CA 90306 (213) 419-1500

Holm, Eleanor (1913–   )
Swimming

Born December 6, 1913, New York, NY; International Swimming Hall of Fame

The glamorous Holm was a cause célèbre before the 1936 Olympics, when she reportedly drank too much champagne while the U.S. team was sailing to Europe. Avery Brundage, chairman of the U.S. Olympic Committee, refused to let her participate, despite a petition signed by virtually every America athlete asking that she be reinstated. Holm was the U.S.

Champion swimmer, singer, and actress, Eleanor Holm won a Gold Medal at the 1932 Olympics, but was thrown off the 1936 team for allegedly drinking too much champagne when sailing to Germany. Courtesy of the International Swimming Hall of Fame

outdoor champion in the 220-yard backstroke in 1929, 1930, 1931, 1932, 1933, and 1936, and she won the event at the 1932 Olympics. She also won the indoor 100-yard backstroke in 1930, 1931, 1932, 1934, 1935, and 1936. She married musician Art Jarrett in 1933 and sang with his band, and in 1938 she played Jane in the movie *Tarzan's Revenge*. After divorcing Jarrett, she married theatrical promoter Billy Rose and swam in his Aquacade at the 1939–40 World's Fair.

Holman, Nat (1896–   )
Basketball

Born October 18, 1896, New York, NY; Basketball Hall of Fame 1964

An outstanding shooter, passer, and ball handler, Holman attended the Savage School of Physical Education and New York University, then began his professional career in Hoboken, NJ, where he once scored 23 points in a 28–25 victory. He also played for Bridgeport, Scranton, and Germantown before joining the New York Whirlwinds. The Whirlwinds played a long awaited series with the Original Celtics in 1921, winning the first game 40–27 and losing the second 26–24. The Celtics then hired Holman and Chris Leonard, and the third game of the series was never played.

During his eight years with the Celtics, they won 720 games while losing only 75, and were generally considered the greatest basketball team in the world, with Holman and Johnny Beckman ranked the greatest players. The Celtics were broken up in 1928, and Holman then played for Syracuse and Chicago. He retired in 1933. He had been coaching City College of New York since 1919, and he remained there until his retirement in 1960, compiling a 423–190 record. In 1950, CCNY became the only team ever to win both the National Invitational Tournament and the NCAA tournament in the same year. Red Holzman, the Hall of Fame coach who played under Holman, wrote of him, "His understanding of the game was one of his strong traits. . . . He had good theories about team defense, and I picked up a lot of insights in that area from him."

Hoosier Dome
Indianapolis, IN

The Hoosier Dome opened on May 3, 1984, adjacent to the Indiana Convention Center. It was built at a cost of about $77 million. The stadium, which has an inflatable, translucent dome, seats 61,127. Since 1984, it has been the home of the Indianapolis Colts of the National Football League. The stadium has hosted the 1985 National Basketball Association all-star game, the first World Indoor Track and Field Championships in 1987, and the 1987 Pan-American Games.

Hoppe, "Willie" William F. (1887–1959)
Billiards

Born October 11, 1887, Cornwall-on-Hudson, NY; died February 1, 1959; Billiards Congress of America Hall of Fame

Sportswriter Joe King summed up Hoppe's longtime domination of billiards: "His personality, his reputation, his remorseless play, his integrity and gameness created a shimmering fear which danced across the nerves of his opponents. . . . His rivals tried to beat Hoppe, just as the golfers tried to beat (Bobby) Jones. But Hoppe and Jones never had any antagonist except the game itself."

His first major victory was in the 1904 Young Masters tournament in Paris. He won the world 18.1 balkline championship in 1906 and the 18.2 championship a year later. He lost both titles to Jake Schaefer, Sr., but regained the 18.1 championship in 1909 and the 18.2 championship in 1910. After losing the 18.1 title in 1912, he won it back in 1914 and held it through 1926. When Jake Schaefer, Jr.

won the 18.2 championship in 1921, the *New York Telegram* wrote, "At 34, Hoppe is an ex-champion. . . . There is a new era dawning." The obituary notice was premature. Although he lost to Schaefer again early in 1922, he regained the title in November of that year and he won three major challenge matches in 1924, beating Schaefer in Chicago, Edouard Horemans in New York, and Welker Cochran in Boston.

Despite a record run of 200 billiards, Hoppe lost the 18.1 balkline title to Schaefer in 1926. The following year, he ran the last 41 points to beat Erich Hagenlacher for the 18.2 balkline championship, and he regained the 18.1 title from Schaefer in 1937. Balkline billiards was losing its popularity, so Hoppe began to play three-cushion. He held that championship in 1936, from 1940 to 1944, and from 1947 through 1952, when he retired at 65.

Hornsby, Rogers (1896–1963)
Baseball

Born April 27, 1896, Winters, TX; died January 5, 1963; Baseball Hall of Fame

Perhaps the greatest right-handed hitter of all time, "the Rajah" batted .402 and had 1,078 hits over a five-year period, 1921–25. His averages were .397, .401, .384, .424 and .403 in those seasons. The .424 average in 1924 is the highest ever in the 20th century, and his career average of .358 is a National League record. He hit 42 home runs in 1922, a record for second basemen until 1973, and he was named Most Valuable Player in 1925.

Hornsby entered the big leagues as a shortstop and third baseman with the St. Louis Cardinals in 1916. He hit over .300 in three of his first four years. He moved to second base in 1920, when he led the league in hitting (.370), runs batted in (94), and hits (218). Named player-manager during the 1925 season, Hornsby led the Cardinals to a World Series victory in 1926, then was traded to the New York Giants. After hitting .361 there, he went to the Boston Braves in 1928 and became player-manager early that season.

The Braves sent him to the Chicago Cubs for five players and $200,000 in 1929, when he hit .380 with 39 home runs and 149 runs batted in, winning the MVP award again. He was named player-manager of the Cubs late in 1930 and was fired during the 1932 season. After returning to the Cardinals for part of the 1933 season, Hornsby became manager of the St. Louis Browns in the American League, playing occasionally until he was fired midway through 1937.

After managing the Browns briefly in 1952, he took over the Cincinnati Reds late in the 1953 season. In 23 seasons as a player, Hornsby had 2,930 hits, including 541 doubles, 168 triples, and 301 home runs. He scored 1,579 runs and drove in the same number.

Hornung, Paul (1935–)
Football
Born December 23, 1935, Louisville, KY; Pro Football Hall of Fame

Hornung's selection for the 1956 Heisman Trophy was widely criticized, largely because he played quarterback for a Notre Dame team that won only two games. The Green Bay Packers made him the first player chosen in the National Football League's college player draft. Hornung was not very productive in his first two seasons, as the Packers tried him at quarterback, halfback, fullback, and tight end.

In 1959, Vince Lombardi became the Packers' coach and made Hornung the starting left halfback. Before the season ended, the "Golden Boy" was recognized as one of the finest all-around players in football. He rushed for 681 yards and led the National Football League in scoring with 94 points, on 7 touchdowns, 31 extra points, and 7 field goals. He was also an excellent blocker, a good pass receiver, and a threat to throw the ball on Lombardi's halfback option play.

Hornung set a single-season scoring record with 176 points in 1960, when he also led the league with 13 rushing touchdowns and was named Player of the Year. He won the award again in 1961, when he was the scoring leader for the third year in a row with 146 points. Hornung set a playoff record with 19 points in the Packers' 37–0 victory over the New York Giants in the NFL championship game.

He missed much of the 1962 season while serving in the army, then was suspended in 1963 for betting on games. He returned in 1964 to score 107 points, but a neck injury limited his playing time the next two seasons and finally forced his retirement in 1967. During his nine seasons, Hornung gained 3,711 yards on 893 attempts, a 4.2-yard average; caught 130 passes for 1,480 yards; completed 24 of 55 passes for 383 yards and 5 touchdowns; scored 62 touchdowns and kicked 190 extra points and 66 field goals for a total of 760 points. He was an All-Pro in 1960 and 1961.

Horse Racing

Formal racing in North America began in 1665, when Governor Richard Nicolls of New York established races to improve the breed, and a course was laid out on Salisbury Plain, now the site of Garden City. But racing reached its greatest popularity during the 17th and 18th centuries in Virginia, beginning with match races on straight stretches of road.

There were more than a dozen race courses in Virginia before 1700, and periodic attempts were made to restrict or ban the sport. In 1696, the House of Burgesses heard complaints that Saturday races in Northumberland County often resulted in all-night partying and rematches on Sunday, and in 1747 racing was banned during Quaker meetings in Virginia. William and Mary College in 1752 prohibited its students from owning horses or "making races." There had been restrictions even earlier. Boston prohibited the sport within 4 miles of the city in 1677, and the Philadelphia City Council in 1695 asked the state legislature to ban racing entirely.

Racing spread rapidly in the years before the Revolutionary War. The first mile track was laid out at Williamsburg in 1739. Other early tracks were the York Course (1758) and Blake Track (1760), both near Charleston, SC, where a jockey club was organized as early as 1735. The Annapolis Jockey Club, founded in 1745, included horsemen from Virginia and Pennsylvania and by 1770 it was conducting an annual four-day spring meet. During the 1760s, Philadelphia's meeting attracted many owners and breeders from the South. The track at Salisbury Plain in New York, called "Newmarket," was rebuilt in 1764 in imitation of the famous English track of the same name.

During the early years of racing, no particular attention was paid to breeding. The horses raced on straightaways in Virginia were the ancestors of modern quarterhorses. Trotters and pacers, the forerunners of today's harness horses, were raced under saddle. The term "thoroughbred" wasn't in general use until 1808, when the first British Stud Book was published, but horses later listed as Thoroughbreds came to North America before that. The first was probably Bulle Rock, in 1730. Samuel Ogle, who became governor of Maryland in 1747, was the first person to breed horses for speed. He brought the stallion Sparke and the mare Queen Mab from England and began to develop a racing stable. Several other English horses were imported for breeding purposes during the 1750s and 1760s.

The Revolution temporarily ended racing, but the sport resumed almost as soon as the war was over. In 1792 the South Carolina Jockey Club opened the Washington Course, and ten years later the Washington, D.C. Jockey Club built the National Course. Meets were held "almost at every town and considerable place in Virginia" in 1784, according to an English visitor. Many of the gentry from Virginia, Maryland, and the Carolinas moved into Kentucky and Tennessee, bringing their horses and the racing tradition with them. Sportsman's Hill near Louisville, laid out in 1788, was the first circular track west of the Alleghenies. Lexington had a course about 1790 and formed a jockey club in 1797. By 1800 there was also regular racing in Kentucky at Bardstown, Danville, Georgetown, and Shelbyville.

Breeding also resumed on a larger scale. Diomed, the winner of the first English Derby in 1780, was imported by Colonel John Hoomes of Bowling Green, VA in 1798. At 21, he was thought to be impotent, but he sired more than 50 foals and founded a great line of American racehorses, including Sir Archy, American Eclipse, Sir Henry, Boston, and Lexington.

Public racing was banned in New York in 1802, but it was legalized in Queens County in 1821, and the New York Association for the Improvement of the Breed was organized. The Union Race Course opened on Long Island in October of 1821. The first major intersectional race took place there on May 27, 1823, between two of Diomed's descendants, American Eclipse representing the North and Sir Henry representing the South. As usual at the time, they raced 4-mile heats. Sir Henry won the first, but American Eclipse came back to win the last two heats and the $20,000 bet. Newspapers claimed that as many as 60,000 spectators attended the race and that more than $1 million was wagered.

Horse racing boomed during the 1830s. The Maryland Jockey Club was organized in 1830, and St. Louis had a track by 1835. The number of meets increased from 56 on 40 tracks in 1830 to 153 on 106 tracks in 1839. But after the Panic of 1837, many owners and breeders dispersed their stock and track attendance declined, along with purses. By 1849, there were only 38 race meetings on 27 tracks. Two more major North-South races were held at the Union Course, though. On May 20, 1842, the North's Fashion beat Boston in straight heats before a crowd of 50,000 to 70,000, including 40 U.S. Senators. A year later, an estimated 70,000 to 100,000 people saw Peytona defeat Fashion in two heats.

Despite the general decline during the 1840s, the sport spread across the country. The Chicago Jockey Club was founded in 1844; a visitor who saw horse racing in Texas in 1846 called it "the national sport"; Sacramento formed a jockey club in 1850, and the Pioneer Race Course was opened at San Francisco a year later. Racing also became popular in Metairie, LA, and the bluegrass area of Kentucky took over as the country's breeding capital.

The oldest existing race, the Queen's Plate, was first held June 27, 1860, at the Toronto Turf Club, with a trophy donated by Queen Victoria to encourage horse breeding in Canada. And breeding helped the Confederacy early in the Civil War, when its cavalry was clearly superior to the Union cavalry

because so many southerners sold their entire racing stables to the government. Yet the war itself had little effect on the sport. Northern tracks kept operating, Lexington missed only its 1862 meeting, and a new track opened in August 1863 at Saratoga, NY.

August Belmont, Leonard Jerome, and W. R. Travers led the way in establishing the American Jockey Club, which opened its first meet on September 25, 1866, at Jerome Park in Westchester County. Intoxicants and professional gamblers were prohibited and the track attracted a wealthy, respectable clientele. Other tracks opened within ten years after the war in Baltimore, Boston, Cincinnati, Memphis, Mobile, New Orleans, and St. Louis. The most famous track of all, Churchill Downs in Louisville, opened in 1875.

During the final quarter of the 19th century, the nature of racing changed. Postwar prosperity created a wealthy leisure class interested in the kind of conspicuous consumption that racing stables offered. Shorter races began to replace 4-mile heats, allowing more races per day. A Board of Control, organized on February 16, 1891, was replaced by the Jockey Club three years later. The club was given authority to license jockeys and trainers, to appoint officials, and to codify the rules. In 1896 it took over the American Stud Book.

Major tracks began to conduct stakes races, in which horse owners pay an entry fee that becomes part of the purse. The first was the Travers, inaugurated at Saratoga in 1864. That was followed by the Saratoga Cup (1865), the Belmont and the Champagne (1867), the Alabama (1872), the Preakness (1873), the Withers (1874), and the Kentucky Derby (1875). Stakes races helped contribute to the financial stability of tracks, which had formerly depended on admission charges for all the prize money.

Just as it was reaching new heights, Thoroughbred racing was threatened by a nationwide reform movement directed at gambling, particularly at bookmakers, who handled betting at the tracks, paying a fee to the track owner for the privilege. The Kentucky law, passed in 1908, specifically prohibited bookmaking. Churchill Downs stayed open by adopting pari-mutuel betting, which was legal. Other tracks in Kentucky and Maryland, which had a similar law, also began to take pari-mutuel bets. In New York, however, racing shut down for two years after bookmaking and the use of gaming devices was prohibited in 1910. It resumed in 1913, when pari-mutuel betting was legalized there.

Total purses in the United States dropped from $4,351,691 in 1908 to $2,337,957 in 1911, when many tracks were shut down. By 1927, pari-mutuel betting was legal in five states, and the money climbed to a high of $13,935,619. At the depth of the Great Depression in 1933, however, it was back down to $8,516,325. Ironically, the depression was a long-term boon to Thoroughbred racing. As Damon Runyon put it, "the states needed money, and they found that racing could be made to pay huge sums of taxes." Pari-mutuel betting was legalized in Florida in 1931, and in ten states, California, Michigan, New Hampshire, New Mexico, North Carolina, Ohio, Oregon, Texas, Washington, and West Virginia, in 1933. Several tracks reopened, and many new ones were built. By 1940, total purses stood at $15,911,167, well above the pre-Depression high.

During World War II, using gasoline to transport horses was prohibited, but the sport still gained popularity after a couple of years of stagnation. The Thoroughbred Racing Associations of North America, Inc., was founded in March of 1942 by 32 tracks to represent their interests. In January of 1946, the TRA created the Thoroughbred Racing Protective Bureau as a private investigatory agency to police the sport. The TRPB introduced lip tattooing to identify horses, and worked to keep undesirables away from member tracks.

Thoroughbred racing took off after the war, as track attendance increased from 18,900,000 in 1945 to 26,834,218 in 1946, total purses climbed from $32,300,060 to $49,291,024, and betting went from $1.4 billion to just under $1.8 billion. By 1980, attendance had reached 75 million, with total bets of $10.5 billion. However, the sport has declined since then, at least in part because of other legalized forms of gambling. Attendance was down to 50 million, and total betting declined to $7.6 billion by 1985. The share of the legal gambling dollar dropped sharply in the same period, from 28 percent to 10 percent.

A major factor was the burgeoning of state lotteries. While serious horse players will always go to the track to make their bets, the casual bettor who is more interested in gambling than in horse racing can find it at a neighborhood pharmacy or grocery store in many states, without the trouble of going to the track. Off-track betting, first legalized in New York in 1970, allows the bettor to make a wager on a horse race at a state-operated betting shop. While the track gets a share of the money, OTB does cut into attendance, which is seen as a long-term problem by many track operators. Related to OTB is simulcasting: Bettors gather at another track or OTB center to place their bets and watch a live telecast of the race. In 1988, $1.1 million was bet on the Kentucky Derby at Churchill Downs, and $1.89 mil-

The intersectional race between Peytona and Fashion on May 13, 1845, attracted a crowd estimated at more than 70,000. From a Nathaniel Currier lithograph.

lion was bet on simulcasts. Again, while simulcasting increases the betting intake, it tends to cut track attendance. As Gerald Lawrence, general manager of Churchill Downs, said, "This is a disaster waiting to happen, if we're not careful."

Further Reading: Hedges, David. *Horses and Courses.* New York: Viking Press, 1972; Herbert, Ivor, editor. *Horse Racing: The Complete Guide to the World of the Turf.* New York: St. Martins, 1981; Hervey, John. *Racing in America, 1665–1865.* New York: Jockey Club, 1944, 2 volumes; Robertson, William H. P. *A History of Thoroughbred Racing in America.* Englewood Cliffs, NJ: Prentice-Hall, 1964.

See also BREEDERS CUP; ECLIPSE AWARDS; HARNESS RACING; JEROME PARK; NATIONAL COURSE; NATIONAL MUSEUM OF RACING AND HALL OF FAME; NEWMARKET COURSE; QUARTER-HORSE RACING; THOROUGHBRED RACING ASSOCIATIONS; UNION GROUNDS.

Horse Shows

The horse show is a kind of hybrid of equestrian sports and the horse fair, at which horses were displayed and demonstrated by their owners for potential buyers. The first modern horse show was held in 1853 in Upperville, VA. Thirty years later the first National Horse Show was held at Gilmore's Gardens in New York City. That became the model for other shows in Atlanta, Boston, Kansas City, Newport, Philadelphia, Saratoga, and St. Louis.

The American Horse Shows Association, Inc., was founded by representatives of 50 horse shows on January 20, 1917, in New York City. The AHSA sanctions and promotes more than 2,500 shows for 23 types of horses. A horse show includes three basic types of competition: Breeding, in which a horse is judged on appearance, conformation, and way of moving; performance, in which horses are displayed under saddle or in harness; and equitation, in which the rider's skills are judged.

Address: American Horse Shows Association, 220 East 42nd Street, Suite 409, New York, NY 10017 (212) 972-2472

See also EQUESTRIAN SPORTS.

Horseshoe Pitching

Since horseshoes can be pitched virtually anywhere domesticated horses are found, the sport was probably played on an informal basis in the 17th century, but it wasn't recorded until the American Revolution, when soldiers whiled away their time pitching horseshoes on Boston Common. During the early 19th century, horseshoes became popular along the

frontier. Organization of the sport began in 1899, when a club was formed in Meadville, PA, and rules were codified for the first time for a 1909 tournament in Bronson, KS.

Five years later, the Grand League of American Horseshoe Pitchers was founded, and rules were standardized nationally. The organization was renamed the National Horseshoe Pitchers of the U.S. in 1921 and the National Horseshoe Pitchers Association of America in 1925. The first national tournament for women was held in 1920. Organized competition began in Canada at Toronto's Royal Winter Fair, in 1927, and the Dominion of Canada Horseshoe Pitchers Association was established two years later. It became the Canadian National Horseshoe Players Association in 1967 and Horseshoe Canada in 1979.

Addresses: Horseshoe Canada, P.O. Box 548, Raymore, Saskatchewan, Canada S0A 3J0 (306) 746-4535; National Horseshoe Pitchers Association of America, Box 278, Munroe Falls, OH 44262 (216) 650-2234

Horton Law
Boxing

The financial success of prizefighting in the Western United States led New York to pass the Horton Law in 1896, permitting "boxing bouts" to be staged by athletic clubs. As a result, James J. Jeffries won the heavyweight championship from Bob Fitzsimmons in an 1899 match at Coney Island and successfully defended the title twice at Coney Island. Several clubs were formed for the sole purpose of staging fights, including the Twentieth Century Athletic Club, which leased Madison Square Garden and promoted several bouts. The law, which contained no provision for controlling the sport, was repealed in 1900, largely because of an apparently fraudulent bout between Kid McCoy and Jim Corbett.

See also FRAWLEY ACT.

Hotchkiss, Hazel V. (Mrs. Wightman) (1886–1974)
Tennis

Born December 20, 1886, Healdsbury, CA; died December 5, 1974; International Tennis Hall of Fame

Hotchkiss won 45 national tennis titles, the last at the age of 68 in 1954. She was also the U.S. women's squash racquets champion in 1930, when she was 44, and she finished second in the national mixed doubles badminton championship when she was 50. Barely 5 feet tall, Hotchkiss used her exceptional speed to develop a strong volleying game. One journalist wrote of her, "She went up into the air to volley a ball like a fox terrier after a butterfly." Hotchkiss won the U.S. national singles, doubles, and mixed doubles titles three years in a row, 1909, 1910, and 1911. She married George Wightman in 1912, had children, then returned to win another singles championship in 1919. She also won the national indoor singles that year.

Her quickness, volleying skill, and great sense of anticipation made Hotchkiss a superb doubles player. She won the outdoor women's doubles title in 1915, 1924, and 1928, the outdoor mixed doubles in 1915, 1918, and 1920, and the indoor women's doubles in 1919, 1921, 1924, 1927, 1928, 1929, 1930, 1931, 1933, and 1943. During the 1940s and 1950s, she won many senior doubles titles for players over 40. In 1919, she donated the Wightman Cup for international competition play among women's teams.

Hot Dog Skiing
See FREESTYLE SKIING.

Houston, TX

Baseball The Houston Colt .45s joined the National League as an expansion franchise in 1962. They were called the Astros after moving into the Astrodome in 1965. The Astros won the league's western division championship in 1980 and 1986, losing in both league championship series.

Basketball The San Diego Rockets of the National Basketball Association moved to Houston in 1971. They won the midwest division championship in 1981 and 1986.

Football K. S. "Bud" Adams of Houston, like Lamar Hunt of Dallas, wanted a franchise in the National Football League. They eventually helped to found the American Football League and Adams' Houston Oilers won the league's first two championships, in 1960 and 1961. The Oilers won their third straight eastern division championship in 1962, but lost to Dallas, 30–17, in the first double-overtime game in football history. They were also division champions in 1967.

Hockey When the World Hockey Association was created in 1972, the Houston Aeros were one of the original teams. They won the WHA championship in 1974 and 1975, but folded after the 1976–77 season.

See also ASTRODOME; SUMMIT, THE.

Howe, Gordie (1928–   )
Hockey
Born March 31, 1928, Floral, Saskatchewan; Hockey Hall of Fame

After four years of retirement, Gordie Howe joined the Houston Aeros of the World Hockey Association for the 1973–74 season and was named the league's Most Valuable Player. Courtesy of the Houston Aeros

Dave Keon of the Toronto Maple Leafs once said there were four strong teams in the National Hockey League, "Toronto, Montreal, Chicago, and Gordie Howe." Teammate Bill Gadsby said that Howe "was not only the greatest hockey player I've ever seen, but the greatest athlete." And his coach, Tommy Ivan, said, "Howe has the ability and the knack for making the difficult plays look easy."

A right winger, Howe was an an outstanding stick handler and a very tough player with a very hard shot. He began his NHL career with the Detroit Red Wings in 1946 and seemed to be little more than a journeyman his first three seasons. But in 1949 he was the top scorer in the playoffs with eight goals and three assists, and his career took off. He was the first player to win three scoring titles, in 1951, 1952, and 1953. Howe won the scoring championship for the fourth straight time in 1954, and led again in 1957 and 1963.

Howe was the league's Most Valuable Player in 1952, 1953, 1957, 1958, 1960, and 1963. He was a first-team all-star in 1951, 1952, 1953, 1954, 1957,

1958, 1960, 1966, 1968, 1969, and 1970. In 25 seasons, he played 1,687 games, scored a total of 1,809 points on 786 goals and 1,023 assists, and served 1,643 penalty minutes, all NHL records.

He retired after the 1970–71 season but in 1973, at the age of 45, he joined the Houston Aeros of the World Hockey Association, playing alongside his two sons, Mark and Matt. He scored a goal in the first minute of the season and finished third in WHA scoring with 100 points on 31 goals and 69 assists. Houston won the 1974 and 1975 WHA championships, and Howe was named Most Valuable Player in the 1975 playoffs. Houston dropped out of the league in 1977, and Howe and his sons went to the Hartford Whalers. He played there through the 1979–80 season.

Further Reading: O'Reilly, Don. *Mr. Hockey: The World of Gordie Howe.* New York: Henry Regnery, 1975.

Hubbard, "Cal" Robert Calvin (1900–1977)
Baseball, Football

Born October 31, 1900, Keytesville, MO; died October 17, 1977; Baseball, National Football Foundation, Pro Football Hall of Fame

The New York Giants, trying to sign fullback Clarke Hinkle out of Bucknell, made the mistake of taking him to a game between the Giants and the Green Bay Packers. Hinkle later said, "I decided to sign with the Packers because I wanted to play with Cal Hubbard, not against him." By then the 6-foot-5 Hubbard weighed 265 pounds; he had played in college at 240 pounds. He was not only big but aggressive, mobile, and remarkably fast for his size.

Hubbard played at both Centenary and Geneva Colleges under Coach Bo McMillin, who called him the greatest football player he'd ever seen. He was a tackle at Centenary in 1922, moved to end the following year, and played both positions in 1924. McMillin went to Geneva in 1925, and Hubbard dropped out of school. He rejoined McMillin in 1926.

He played tackle for the Giants in 1927 and 1928 and for the Packers from 1929 through 1935. Green Bay won National Football League championships in his first three seasons. Hubbard is called the first middle linebacker because teams refused to run at him, so he frequently dropped out of the line in order to meet the play wherever it was directed. Hubbard was an All-Pro in 1930, 1931, 1932, and 1933.

He became an American League umpire in 1936 and also played one game for the New York Giants that fall. After the Giants sold him to Pittsburgh,

though, he retired from football again. Hubbard became the American League's umpire-in-chief in 1958. He is the only man in both the Baseball Hall of Fame and the Pro Football Hall of Fame.

Hubbell, Carl (1903–1988)
Baseball

Born June 22, 1903, Carthage, MO; died November 21, 1988; Baseball Hall of Fame

Hubbell, who put the word "screwball" permanently into baseball's lexicon, spent his entire major-league career with the New York Giants, from 1928 to 1943, winning 253 games while losing 154, with a career earned run average of 2.97. He won 21 or more games for five consecutive seasons, 1933–37, and was named the National League's Most Valuable Player in 1933 and 1936. A left-handed pitcher, Hubbell spent more than six seasons in the minor leagues. Attempting to develop a sinker by snapping his wrist, Hubbell accidentally threw a screwball—a pitch that breaks in the opposite direction from a curve, that is, away from a right-handed hitter when thrown by a left-handed pitcher.

Hubbell was acquired by the Giants in 1928 and on May 8, 1929, he pitched a no-hitter against the Pittsburgh Pirates and went on to an 18–11 record. He was a steady but not exceptional starting pitcher until 1932, when he won 23 games while losing 12. He had 10 shutouts that season, including an 18-inning, 1–0 victory over the St. Louis Cardinals. In the Giants' five-game World Series victory over Washington, he won the first and last games without allowing an earned run.

Hubbell is probably best remembered for the 1934 all-star game; after giving up a hit and a walk to the first two batters, he struck out Babe Ruth, Lou Gehrig, and Jimmie Foxx to end the inning, then struck out Al Simmons and Joe Cronin in the next inning to make it five in a row—five of the greatest hitters in baseball history. Hubbell won his last 16 decisions in 1936 and his first 8 decisions in 1937 for an all-time record of 24 consecutive victories.

After a 26–6 record in 1936, he ended the New York Yankees' 12-game World Series winning streak in the first game, but lost his other start, and the Yankees won four games to two. He was 22–8 in 1937, but elbow trouble began to plague him in 1938, when he won just 13 games, and he had 11 victories in each of the next four years. He retired with a 4–4 record in the middle of the 1943 season.

Hubert H. Humphrey Metrodome
See METRODOME.

Huggins, Miller (1880–1929)
Baseball
Born March 27, 1880, Cincinnati, OH; died September 25, 1929; Baseball Hall of Fame

The 5-foot-4, 140-pound Huggins was called "Rabbit" and "Little Mister Everywhere" during his playing days, and then became known as the "Mite Manager" with the St. Louis Cardinals and the New York Yankees, where he helped to create one of the greatest dynasties in sports history. After receiving a law degree from the University of Cincinnati, Huggins became the Reds' starting second baseman in 1904. He was traded to St. Louis in 1910, was named manager in 1913, and retired as a player after the 1916 season.

Huggins went to the Yankees in 1917. At his suggestion, the team purchased Babe Ruth from the Boston Red Sox in 1920 for $100,000 in cash plus a $300,000 loan. Ruth had been a pitcher in Boston, though he sometimes played in the outfield or at first base, but Huggins installed him as the Yankees' starting right fielder and Ruth began hitting home runs in record numbers. The Yankees won pennants in 1921, 1922, and 1923, losing the first two World Series to the New York Giants and beating the Giants in their third try.

In 1925, Ruth was badly out of shape and playing sluggishly. Huggins fined him $5,000 and suspended him indefinitely. Ruth appealed to Yankee management, but they backed Huggins and Ruth finally apologized. His suspension lasted just one week, and after his return he was considerably subdued. The Yankees won three consecutive pennants in 1926, 1927, and 1928, and they won the World Series the last two years, both in four-game sweeps. Late in 1929, Huggins left the team because of illness. He died of blood poisoning caused by an infected carbuncle. The following season, the Yankees dedicated a monument to Huggins in deep centerfield of Yankee Stadium; later, monuments to Ruth and Lou Gehrig were added.

As a player, Huggins had a batting average of .265, and he stole 324 bases. His record as a manager was 1,413 victories and 1,134 losses, a .555 percentage.

Hula Bowl
Football
The Hula Bowl, played in Honolulu, began in 1947 as a game between the college all-stars and the Hawaiian all-stars. Beginning in 1950, some National Football League players were added to the Hawaiian team. From 1960 through 1962, it was an East-West college all-star game. It became a North-South game in 1963 and went back to the East-West format in 1974.

Hull, "Bobby" Robert M. (1939–   )
Hockey
Born January 3, 1939, Point Anne, Ontario; Hockey Hall of Fame

Known as "The Golden Jet" because of his blond hair and skating speed, Hull won four major awards during his career with the Chicago Black Hawks in the National Hockey League: The Art Ross Trophy as the league's leading scorer in 1960, 1962, and 1966; the Hart Memorial Trophy as Most Valuable Player in 1965 and 1966; the Lester Patrick Trophy for outstanding service to United States hockey in 1969; and the Lady Byng Trophy for sportsmanship in 1966. He was a first-team all-star at left wing in 1960, 1962, 1963, 1964, 1965, 1966, 1967, 1968, 1969, and 1972.

After the 1972 season, Hull jumped to the Winnipeg Jets of the new World Hockey Association. He finished fourth in WHA scoring with 103 points, despite missing 20 games, was named Most Valuable Player and led the Jets into the World Cup finals, where they lost to the New England Whalers. Hull retired before the 1978–79 season. In 16 seasons and 1,063 games, he scored 610 goals and had 560 assists for a total of 1,170 points.

Further Reading: Hull, Bobby. *Hockey Is My Game.* New York: David McKay, 1967.

Hunting
New Englanders hunted for food, not sport, during the 17th century. Rhode Island passed the first game law to protect deer in 1646. Massachusetts established a deer hunting season in 1694 and appointed the first game wardens in 1739. Hunting was a popular sport among the Virginia gentry in the 18th century. It had the practical purpose of ridding the countryside of unwanted animals, especially wolves, and shooting wild turkey and deer furnished delicacies for the table.

Hunting was popularized as a sport after the American Revolution. *The Sportsman's Companion,* published in 1783, was written by an unidentified author "who has made shooting his favorite amusement upwards of 26 years in Great Britain, Ireland, and North America." *The American Shooter's Manual, by a Gentleman of Philadelphia County* appeared in 1827, and in 1839 Henry William Herbert began writing passionately and lyrically about hunting and fishing in *The American Turf Register,* using the pseudonym Frank Forester. During the second half of the century, many wealthy Easterners established deer parks on their estates, stocked not only with deer but with elk, antelope, wild boars, and American bison.

As the turn of the century approached, hunters began to organize in the interests of conservation. The Massachusetts Fish and Game Association was formed in 1874, and Theodore Roosevelt founded the Boone and Crockett Club for big-game hunters in 1887. They were followed by such groups as the League of American Sportsmen, the American Bison Society, and the American Game Protective and Propagation Association. By 1900, big-game hunting was banned in virtually every state and territory.

Ironically, urbanization helped save big game. Small farms were abandoned in the Northeast and the land reverted to forest. Many deer park owners sold or gave their animals to organizations and agencies who operated restocking programs. The programs were too successful, in a sense. Deer were virtually extinct in Pennsylvania in 1900, but the population was more than 1 million by 1924, and thousands of deer died of starvation. The state adopted a model game law developed by the International Association of Game, Fish and Conservation Commissioners and for the first time allowed hunters to shoot antlerless deer as well as antlered bucks. Though criticized by many, the liberalized hunting regulations brought the deer population into line with what the habitat could support. Many other states adopted the model law during the 1920s.

Small game birds were imported in the early part of the century, including the Chinese and Iranian ringneck pheasant, Turkish, Spanish, and Hungarian partridge, bobwhite quail from Mexico, chukar partridge from Asia, and Asiatic jungle fowl. Migratory game birds were taken under federal jurisdiction in 1913, and a treaty was negotiated with Canada in 1916 to cooperate on conservation. The Norbeck-Andresen Migratory Bird Conservation Act of 1929 authorized appropriations over a ten-year period of almost $8 million to acquire feeding, nesting, and resting areas. In 1934, the Duck Stamp Law required hunters of waterfowl to pay $1 for a federal stamp to fund the program.

Modern wildlife management, pioneered by the University of Wisconsin in 1933, recognizes hunting as an important element in population control and as a source of funding for conservation programs. The 1937 Pittman-Robertson Act imposed an excise tax on hunting firearms and ammunition and the money was given to states for research and land acquisition and development. All participating states were required to use their own hunting license revenues to fund game departments. By the late 1940s, virtually every state had a game commission autho-

Don Hutson's National Football League record of 99 career touchdown receptions stood until 1989. Here he catches a touchdown pass despite having a defender draped all over him. Courtesy of the Pro Football Hall of Fame

rized to regulate hunting based on changing animal populations and other conditions.

Hunting, as sport, is usually recreational rather than competitive. However, trophies are given for record animals killed by firearms and by bow and arrow. The Boone and Crockett Club gives trophies for a variety of animals exceeding certain standards, among them antelope, mountain sheep, deer, and bears. The Pope and Young Club offers trophies for bow and arrow hunting.

Hutson, Don (1913–   )
Football

Born January 31, 1913, Pine Bluff, AR; National Football Foundation, Pro Football Hall of Fame

Although he played in an era when there were only 12 games in a season and the forward pass wasn't emphasized, Hutson's record of 99 career touchdown receptions stood for 44 years, until Steve Largent broke it in 1989. Known as the "Alabama Antelope" because of his deceptively smooth stride, Hutson didn't become a starting end at the University of Alabama until late in his junior year, but he was an All-American as a senior in 1934, and he caught six passes for 165 yards and two touchdowns in a 29–13 win over Stanford in the 1935 Rose Bowl.

Hutson joined the Green Bay Packers in 1935. He was held out of the first game so he could be used as a surprise weapon against the arch-rival Chicago Bears. It worked. On his first play as a professional, Hutson caught an 83-yard touchdown pass and the Packers beat the Bears 7–0. The Bears' founder and coach, George Halas, later said, "Hutson is so extraordinary that I concede him two touchdowns a game and hope we can score more." Hutson played 11 seasons, all with the Packers, and was an All-Pro nine times. He led the National Football League in receptions eight times and in scoring five times and was named Most Valuable Player in 1941 and 1942.

When he retired after the 1945 season, Hutson held 20 records, including most receptions in a career (489), in a season (74 in 1942), and in a game (14 against the New York Giants in 1942); most touchdown receptions in a career (99), in a season (17 in 1942), and in a game (4 in 1945); most yards receiving in a career (8,010), in a season (1,211 in 1942), and in a game (237 on eight catches in 1943); most years leading the league in receiving and most years leading in scoring; most points in a career (825) and in a season (138 in 1942); most consecutive games scoring one or more points (41); and most touchdown receptions in championship playoff games (nine in four games). He had the second highest-scoring game in NFL history with 31 points against the Detroit Lions in 1945.

Iba, "Hank" Henry P. (1904–   )
Basketball
Born August 6, 1904, Easton, MO; Basketball Hall of Fame 1968

Coaching at Oklahoma A & M (now Oklahoma State), Iba became the first coach to guide a team to two straight NCAA championships, in 1945 and 1946. He taught a very slow, deliberate style of play, emphasizing strong defense and a great deal of passing on offense while players maneuvered to get free. It was successful, but it was also criticized by writers and fans who found it boring.

He attended Westminster College, Missouri, and graduated from Maryville Teachers College, now Northwest Missouri State, in 1919. After playing AAU basketball with Sterling Milk and the Hillyards, Iba became coach at Maryville and began his career with a 43-game winning streak. After four seasons, he went to the University of Colorado for one season, 1933–34, and then moved on to Oklahoma A & M, where he remained until his retirement in 1970. He had an overall collegiate record of 767 wins and 338 losses. Iba also coached three U.S. Olympic teams, winning the Gold Medal in 1964 and 1968, but losing to Russia in the 1972 finals on a much-disputed last-second basket.

ICAAAA
See INTER-COLLEGIATE ASSOCIATION OF AMATEUR ATHLETES OF AMERICA.

Ice Boating
See ICE YACHTING.

Ice Dancing
See FIGURE SKATING.

Ice Hockey
See HOCKEY.

Ice Skating

Skating originated in Scandinavia about 1600 years ago; the skates were animal bones, and skaters propelled themselves with poles. The sport had reached England by 1180, when William FitzStephen in his *Description of the Most Notable City of London* wrote of young men playing on the ice, "some tye bones to their feet and under their heels. . some stryding as wide as they may and shoving them-selves with little picked staff, doe slide as swiftlie as a bird flyeth in the air." Skating also developed on Holland's frozen canals, and the Dutch invented the metal skate in the early 17th century. Royalists who fled to Holland after Cromwell's Glorious Revolution brought metal skates back after the Restoration.

Dutch colonists introduced skating to North America in 1624 and English troops brought it to Canada late in the century. The sport really began to develop when the grooved blade was invented about 1770. The last major advance was the invention of the all-metal skate by E. V. Bushnell of Philadelphia in 1848. Bushnell attached the skate permanently to a boot, allowing skaters to make new intricate moves that had been impossible when skates were simply strapped on.

Skating became very popular during the 1850s, especially in Canada, where several covered rinks were built to keep skating areas clear of snow. The first was in Toronto in 1858 and Montreal had one the following year. Skating clubs were also established. The Philadelphia Skating Club and Humane Society, founded in 1849, was at first primarily involved in patroling the Schuylkill River to rescue skaters who had fallen through the ice, but by 1860 the club was also holding events for its members. The Montreal Skating Club was organized in 1859, the New York Skating Club in 1863.

The Glaciarium, the first artificial ice rink, was opened in London in 1876 by W. A. Parker. The surface, only 24 by 40 feet, was reserved for nobility.

New York's Central Park rink was mobbed with skaters during the 1880s. This drawing appeared in Frank Leslie's Illustrated Weekly in 1883.

As refrigeration methods improved during the next several years, more indoor rinks opened throughout the world, but it wasn't until after World War II that equipment was efficient enough to maintain ice during the summer.

The popularity of skating, the growth of clubs, and the advent of formal competition in both figure and speed skating led to the establishment of national governing bodies. The National Amateur Skating Association of the United States was founded in 1886, the Amateur Skating Association of Canada in 1887. The organizations governed both sports until early in the 20th century, when separate bodies were established for figure skating and speed skating.

See also FIGURE SKATING; SPEED SKATING.

Ice Yachting

The Dutch began traveling in sailboats on ice early in the 17th century, and Dutch colonists probably sailed iceboats on the Hudson River. The first record, however, is from 1790, when Oliver Booth sailed a Dutch type of boat on the frozen Hudson. Dutch iceboats were large sleds with four runners and a single large sail. Shortly after the Civil War, several iceboat clubs were formed in the New York area. The first was organized in Poughkeepsie in 1865; it was followed by the New Hamburgh and Hudson

Ice boats raced and beat an express train from New York City to Poughkeepsie in 1871. From a Currier & Ives lithograph.

River Ice Yacht Clubs. The Hudson River Boat, a large ice yacht with a T-shaped frame, three runners, and two sails (a jib and a main), was developed in 1870. There were two small runners at each end of the crossbar; the major runner, in the center of the boat, was connected to a tiller at a rear pivot to allow steering. These yachts were about 60 feet long, carried about 1,000 square feet of sail, and could travel nearly 60 miles an hour.

A major race on the Hudson began in 1881, with boats sailing from Poughkeepsie to a marker 8 miles down the river and back. The Ice Yacht Challenge Pennant was introduced in 1883 for a race at Red Bank, NJ. Competition was discontinued after 1902, but it resumed in 1951 for smaller boats. Ice yachting was a sport for the wealthy until 1937, when the *Detroit News* held a contest for a smaller boat design. The result was a 12-foot ice boat, the DN, which had about 60 square feet of sail. Like other designs developed during the 1930s, the DN used bow steering, introduced by the Joy brothers of Milwaukee in 1931, and a relatively small sail for stability.

The International DN Ice Yacht Racing Union has held an annual North American championship since its founding in 1953. The Union began the Gold Cup world championships in 1973 at Gull Lake, MI. The event alternates between North America and Europe. The 1988 Gold Cup was held in Leningrad.

IMCA

See INTERNATIONAL MOTOR CONTEST ASSOCIATION.

IMSA

See INTERNATIONAL MOTOR SPORTS ASSOCIATION.

Independence Bowl
Football

First played on December 13, 1976, this game was created to showcase little-known small colleges with good football teams. Since 1981, however, major-college teams have met in the Independence Bowl, which is played at Shreveport, LA.

Results

1976	McNeese State 20, Tulsa 18
1977	Louisiana State 24, Louisville 14
1978	East Carolina 35, Louisiana Tech 13
1979	Syracuse 31, McNeese State 7
1980	Southern Mississippi 16, McNeese State 14
1981	Texas A&M 33, Oklahoma State 16
1982	Wisconsin 14, Kansas State 3
1983	Air Force 9, Mississippi 3
1984	Air Force 23, Virginia Tech 7
1985	Minnesota 20, Clemson 13
1986	Mississipi 20, Texas Tech 17
1987	Washington 24, Tulane 12

1988 Southern Mississippi 38, Texas-El Paso 18
1989 Oregon 27, Tulsa 24
1990 Louisiana Tech 34, Maryland 34

Indiana Pacers
See INDIANAPOLIS.

Indianapolis, IN

Baseball Indianapolis had a team in the National League in 1878 and from 1887 through 1889 and in the American Association in 1884.

Basketball The Indiana Pacers, based in Indianapolis, joined the American Basketball Association when the league began play in 1967. They won ABA championships in 1970, 1972, and 1973. The Pacers entered the National Basketball Association when the leagues merged in 1976.

Football The Baltimore Colts of the National Football League became the Indianapolis Colts in 1984.

See also HOOSIER DOME; MARKET SQUARE ARENA.

Indianapolis Motor Speedway

Indianapolis businessmen James A. Allison and Carl G. Fisher were the major financiers of the speedway when it was built in 1909. A 2½-mile oval track, it was originally surfaced with macadam. After two races in 1909, the track was in such bad shape that a race scheduled for 300 miles was stopped after a death and several other serious accidents in the first 235 miles. The track was resurfaced with 3.2 million paving bricks and it hosted nine races in 1910. The Indy 500, North America's most famous auto race, was first held on Memorial Day, 1911.

Because grooves had been worn in the paving bricks, asphalt was laid over the turns in 1937. Unused during World War II, the track was in poor shape when Anton "Tony" Hulman, Jr., bought it in 1945, but he got it back into shape and continually plowed profits into further improvements, including a complete resurfacing of the track with asphalt, except for a 1-yard-wide strip where the bricks are still exposed. Hulman was also a tireless promoter, who made the Indy 500 auto racing's equivalent of the Kentucky Derby—a race known by almost everyone, which attracts an enormous number of people (more than 500,000 at Indianapolis). Total prize money had gone over $1 million by 1970, and in 1986 the winner alone received nearly $1½ million.

The Indianapolis Motor Speedway Hall of Fame was created on paper by the American Automobile Association in 1952 but it was basically defunct two years later. However, Hulman in 1956 set up the Speedway Foundation, Inc., to fund a building for the hall of fame and accompanying museum in the track infield. In 1963 the foundation began inducting new hall of fame members. The museum exhibits many cars of the past, including the Marmon Wasp in which Ray Harroun won the first Indy 500.

Year	Indy 500 Winners Driver	Speed (mph)
1911	Ray Harroun	74.59
1912	Joe Dawson	78.72
1913	Jules Goux	75.933
1914	Rene Thomas	82.47
1915	Ralph DePalma	89.84
1916	Dario Resta	83.26[a]
1917–18	Not held	
1919	Howard Wilcox	88.05
1920	Gaston Chevrolet	88.16
1921	Tommy Milton	89.62
1922	Jimmy Murphy	94.48
1923	Tommy Milton	90.95
1924	L. I. Corum–Joe Boyer	98.23
1925	Peter DePaolo	101.13
1926	Frank Lockhart	95.904[b]
1927	George Souders	97.545
1928	Louis Meyer	99.482
1929	Ray Keech	97.585
1930	Billy Arnold	100.448
1931	Louis Schneider	96.629
1932	Fred Frame	104.144
1933	Louis Meyer	104.162
1934	William Cummings	104.863
1935	Kelly Petillo	106.240
1936	Louis Meyer	109.069
1937	Wilbur Shaw	113.580
1938	Floyd Roberts	117.200
1939	Wilbur Shaw	115.035
1940	Wilbur Shaw	114.277
1941	Floyd Davis–Mauri Rose	115.117
1942–45	Not held	
1946	George Robson	114.820
1947	Mauri Rose	116.338
1948	Mauri Rose	119.814
1949	Bill Holland	121.327
1950	Johnny Parsons	124.002[c]
1951	Lee Wallard	126.244
1952	Troy Ruttman	128.922
1953	William Vukovich	128.740
1954	William Vukovich	130.840
1955	Robert Sweikert	128.209
1956	Pat Flaherty	128.490
1957	Sam Hanks	135.601
1958	Jimmy Bryan	133.791
1959	Rodger Ward	140.293
1960	Jim Rathmann	138.767
1961	A. J. Foyt	139.139
1962	Rodger Ward	140.293
1963	Parnelli Jones	143.137
1964	A. J. Foyt	147.350

1965	Jim Clark	150.686
1966	Graham Hill	144.317
1967	A. J. Foyt	151.207
1968	Bobby Unser	152.882
1969	Mario Andretti	156.867
1970	Al Unser	155.749
1971	Al Unser	157.735
1972	Mark Donohue	163.465
1973	Gordon Johncock	159.014[d]
1974	Johnny Rutherford	158.589
1975	Bobby Unser	149.213[e]
1976	Johnny Rutherford	144.499[f]
1977	A. J. Foyt	161.331
1978	Al Unser	161.363
1979	Rick Mears	158.899
1980	Johnny Rutherford	142.862
1981	Bobby Unser	139.085
1982	Gordon Johncock	162.026
1983	Tom Sneva	162.117
1984	Rick Mears	163.621
1985	Danny Sullivan	152.982
1986	Bobby Rahal	170.722
1987	Al Unser	162.175
1988	Rick Mears	144.809
1989	Emerson Fittipaldi	167.581
1990	Arie Luyendyk	185.984

[a] 300 miles
[b] 400 miles
[c] 345 miles
[d] 332.5 miles
[e] 435 miles
[f] 255 miles

Further Reading: Reed, Terry. *Indy: Race and Ritual.* San Rafael, CA: Presidio Press, 1980.

Indoor Lacrosse

Also known as box lacrosse or "boxla," indoor lacrosse was developed in Canada about 1930. Usually played on a hockey rink without ice, boxla became so popular that Canadian field lacrosse was almost extinct by 1935. Boxla is a very fast sport because there are only six players on a team and the ball is played off the boards, as in hockey, so it doesn't often go out of bounds. Although the sport declined in popularity after World War II, there have been three attempts to make indoor lacrosse a professional sport. The National Lacrosse Association, organized in 1968, lasted just one season and the National Lacrosse League operated in 1974 and 1975. The Major Indoor Lacrosse League has been in existence since 1986.

Indoor Polo

North America's first polo match was played indoors during the winter of 1876, at Dickel's Riding Academy in New York City, by teams of men learning the sport, but the indoor form of the sport was not formally organized until 1915, when the Indoor Polo Association of the United States was established. Indoor polo is played on a field 100 by 50 yards, surrounded by a wooden fence 4 to 4½ feet high to keep the ball from going out of bounds. There are only three players on a team, and the ball is similar to a small soccer ball, 5¼ inches in diameter and weighing at least 6 ounces.

See also POLO.

Indoor Soccer

Although outdoor soccer hasn't prospered as a professional sport in North America, indoor soccer has succeeded reasonably well. The sport was developed in the early 1920s, probably out of indoor practice on rainy days. It seems to have been invented in Chicago, where the International Soccer League (now the National Soccer League) held weekend tournaments in the early 1920s. But the first full-season schedule of indoor games began on January 1, 1950, under the auspices of the National Soccer League, and the first game was locally televised in Chicago.

Like indoor lacrosse, The sport is played on a court, often a hockey rink, about 200 feet long and 85 feet wide, surrounded by dasher boards topped by Plexiglass, so that the ball rarely goes out of bounds. There are just six players per team, including a goalkeeper, but substitution is allowed freely in the course of the game. The goal, 6 feet 6 inches high and 12 feet wide, is set into the boards at the end of the court. Players go to a penalty box for fouls, as in hockey, but power-play goals count only one point, regular goals and penalty shots two points, and a goal from the mid-area is worth three points.

See also MAJOR INDOOR SOCCER LEAGUE.

Industrial Sports

The pioneer in industry-sponsored sports was George Pullman, inventor and manufacturer of the railroad sleeping car that was named for him. In the 1880s, he built an $8 million company town outside Chicago that included athletic facilities, and the Pullman Athletic Association offered many sports, including baseball, cricket, sailing, track and field, and a road bicycle race. But that was unique until World War I, when the labor shortage forced many companies to offer incentives, including sports programs, to help retain employees.

After the war, industrial sports expanded, mainly because of new ideas in personnel management. Most sports were intramural. A company would organize its own bowling league, its own softball league, its own golf tournament, to improve employee morale. However, many communities, led by Oakland, CA and Akron, OH, organized recreational and competitive programs for industrial teams. By 1925, such large companies as Borden's Milk, General Electric, Johnson and Johnson, Macy's, Metropolitan Life, Michelin Tire, U.S. Steel, and Wanamaker's, to name just a few, had organized athletic clubs. The Great Depression caused cutbacks in these programs, but a 1940 survey of 600 companies revealed that 40 percent had athletic programs. Bowling was the most popular, followed by softball, basketball, golf, baseball, tennis, table tennis, horseshoe pitching, target shooting, volleyball, swimming, roller skating, billiards, and badminton.

Some companies also sponsored top-flight teams as a means of advertising. AAU basketball from 1920 until about 1950 was dominated by industrial teams such as the Phillips 66ers and the Cook Paint Company. Because professional basketball wasn't well organized and pay was low during that period, many college All-Americans chose to take a job with a company in order to play basketball. Company teams have ruled the Amateur Softball Association's tournament from its beginning in 1933, and most of the team bowling champions at the ABC tournament have also been industry-sponsored.

Women's sports benefited greatly from industrial sponsorship. Babe Didrikson first became known as the star of the Golden Cyclones, of the Employers Casualty Company of Dallas, who won the 1931 AAU women's basketball championship. And the winning team in the first AAU women's track and field championship, in 1923, was the Athletic Association of the Prudential Insurance Company of New Jersey.

During the 1930s, labor unions began to criticize industrial sports programs as paternalistic, and they launched their own programs in opposition. By 1950, about 70 locals and other labor organizations were involved in competitive sports, but that didn't cut into company sponsorship. The *Industrial Sports Journal* in 1951 reported that more than 20 million employees were involved in sports. During the 1960s and 1970s, though, involvement declined, in part because the proportion of blue-collar workers declined. Another major factor was the new emphasis on physical fitness. Many companies dismantled their competitive sports programs in favor of gyms and outdoor facilities, allowing individuals to work out on their own.

Inter-Allied Games

World War I ended in 1918, but in 1919 there were still many troops in Europe, eager to be discharged and sent home. Edwood S. Brown, director of ath-letics for the Allied Expeditionary Force in France, decided that a kind of military Olympics would be a good distraction. The 25,000-seat Pershing Stadium, named for the U.S. general, was built outside Paris for the games, and about 1,500 athletes from 18 countries competed in 24 events, some of them at Columbes Stadium, which had been the site of the 1900 Paris Olympics. The United States won 12 of the 24 championships.

Inter-Collegiate Association of Amateur Athletes of America

Usually known as the IC4A, the association was formed on December 14, 1875, at a meeting of track and field competitors from ten colleges in Springfield, MA. The first three intercollegiate track meets had been held, on a small scale, in conjunction with the annual rowing regatta at Saratoga, NY. The IC4A decided to hold an annual meet the day after the Saratoga regatta. The two-day meet, on July 20–21, 1876, included the baseball throw and a three-legged race, along with track and field events that are now standard.

The regatta was discontinued after that year, and the second IC4A meet was held in 1877 at the New York Athletic Club's facility at Mott Haven. Until the National Collegiate Athletic Association inaugurated its track and field meet in 1921, the IC4A meet was the equivalent of the national championships, although few western schools participated. It's still a major meet for eastern colleges.

Intercollegiate Athletic Association

See NATIONAL COLLEGIATE ATHLETIC ASSOCIATION.

Intercollegiate Football Association (IFA)

The real beginning of American college football was a meeting of students from Columbia, Harvard, Princeton, and Yale in 1876, when the Intercollegiate Football Association was formed and a set of rules based on the Rugby Union rules used by McGill University in Montreal was adopted. The IFA arranged a schedule and instituted an annual Thanksgiving Day championship game. In the first game, Yale beat Princeton two goals to none in Hoboken, NJ, before a crowd of about 1,000 fans.

Eligibility rules became a major problem for the association. In 1882, the IFA decided to set a limit of five years of competition; previously, some athletes had competed all the way through their undergraduate and graduate careers, for as long as seven years. Harvard and Yale had a major conflict over eligibility in 1889. Walter Camp of Yale offered a resolution that would prohibit subsidies and ban part-time students from competition. An amendment to make transfer students ineligible, offered by Princeton and aimed at Harvard, was voted down and Camp's resolution passed. Harvard then claimed that 15 Princeton students should be declared ineligible, and Princeton countered with a list of four Harvard players. After a ten-day adjournment, all protests were tabled. Harvard withdrew from the association, and it became defunct in 1894.

Intercollegiate Sports

The first college sports were sporadic and intramural. Students played baseball, cricket, football, and bandy or shinty, primitive versions of field hockey, during the 18th century. Future president John Adams, who graduated from Harvard in 1755, said in his diary that freshmen had to provide "batts, balls and footballs for the use of the students." At times the authorities stepped in. Yale banned scrimmaging at football in 1765, though punting the ball was specifically approved, and Princeton prohibited bandy in 1787.

Although several eastern colleges began using football as a way of "rushing" or "hazing" freshmen in the early 19th century, rowing was the first major intercollegiate sport. Boat clubs were formed at Yale in 1843 and at Harvard the following year, and in 1852 the two schools rowed at Lake Winnepesaukee, NH in the first intercollegiate athletic contest.

In 1858, the College Union Regatta was organized by Brown, Harvard, Trinity College and Yale, and regattas were held in 1859 and 1860 at Lake Quinsigamond near Worcester, MA, with prizes of $100 for first place and $75 for second. A crowd estimated at 10,000 attended. During the Civil War, Brown and Trinity dropped out of the regatta, but Harvard and Yale continued to compete. Yale became the first college to hire a professional coach in 1864, and won the event for the first time.

The Rowing Association of American Colleges in 1871 held its first annual regatta at Springfield, MA; it moved to Saratoga Lake, NY in 1874. The following year, 13 colleges participated, at least in part because the host Saratoga Rowing Association paid their transportation and offered expensive prizes. Intercollegiate track and field developed as an outgrowth of the regatta. In 1873 James Gordon Bennett offered a silver trophy, worth perhaps $500, for a 3-mile run in conjunction with the Springfield regatta. At Saratoga in 1874, Bennett donated silver prizes for five track events.

That created the impetus for several colleges to form track and field clubs, culminating in the founding of the Inter-Collegiate Association of Amateur Athletes of America in December of 1875. The IC4A held its first meet, including three field events, at the 1876 Saratoga regatta.

In the meantime, baseball and football had emerged as major college sports. Harvard and Princeton both formed baseball clubs in 1858 and Amherst and Williams played the first intercollegiate game in 1859. The College Baseball Association was organized in 1879. The famous first collegiate football game between Princeton and Rutgers in 1869 was actually a soccer match, but the Intercollegiate Football Association began the development of American football by adopting the rules of rugby, with a few modifications, when it was organized in 1876.

Other sports were added to college programs after the Civil War, and associations sprang up to standardize rules and arrange competitive events: the Intercollegiate Lacrosse Association in 1882, the Intercollegiate Rowing Association and Intercollegiate Lawn Tennis Association in 1883, the Intercollegiate Fencing Association in 1895, and the Intercollegiate Golf Association in 1897.

All of these intercollegiate associations were formed by students for students. At numerous colleges, the single sport clubs began to give way to schoolwide athletic associations, also made up of students and headed by a student athletic manager or student treasurer. The Harvard Athletic Association, organized in 1874, was the first and it set the pattern for others, collecting dues from student members and engaging in other fund-raising activities to support athletic programs. During the late 1880s, alumni began to make major contributions to the associations and in most cases they also took control of the treasury. A prime example was Walter Camp, who had been the most important single member of the football rules committee as a student at Yale; after graduation, Camp not only served as ex officio coach of the football team, he also handled the Yale Athletic Association's finances.

With students and alumni in control, winning became paramount, creating all of the problems that are familiar in big-time college sports today: Overzealous recruiting, illegal payments, and overcommercialization. There were actually even more problems in 19th-century collegiate sport because there was no central governing body. For example, constant squabbles about eligibility could not be settled. In 1855, Yale complained about Harvard's use of a graduate to coxswain its crew. But, with no authority to appeal to, Yale's only options were to accept the coxswain or withdraw from the race. Yale decided to go ahead with the race.

During the 1870s, college baseball teams routinely played against professionals. The practice actually began in 1869, when Harvard beat the Philadelphia

Athletics but lost to the Cincinnati Red Stockings, the first openly all-professional team, and in 1870 Harvard went on a 25-game tour, traveling as far west as St. Louis and playing mostly professional teams. Harvard president Charles W. Eliot in 1882 called for a meeting of New England colleges to ban playing against professionals, but the other colleges weren't interested; as a result, Harvard continued the practice to avoid being at a disadvantage.

After football replaced baseball as the premier college sport during the 1880s, competition among colleges became more intense in recruiting as well on the field. Football could be a big money-maker for athletic programs, as it is today, and colleges wanted winning teams to attract bigger crowds. Graduate students were allowed to play, and many stars had six- or seven-year college careers. In some cases, a player from one college was recruited to attend graduate school at another. Other players were persuaded to transfer from one college to another. The students and alumni who controlled athletic treasuries didn't hesitate to offer special inducements to good players. In one of the most celebrated cases, Fielding H. Yost, a law student at West Virginia University, transferred to Lafayette College during the 1896 season. After Lafayette upset Pennsylvania 6–4, Yost quietly returned to West Virginia to resume his law studies. Later, he built great teams at the University of Michigan, partly through his skill at recruiting graduates from other schools.

John Bascom, president of the University of Wisconsin, in 1876 said that if sport was important, "we should hire a few persons, as we do clowns, to set themselves apart to do this work." His disdain was typical of school authorities during the formative years of college sport, but there were only a few, generally unsuccessful, attempts by administration and faculty to control sports until the 1880s, when abuses became public knowledge. As early as March of 1880, *Popular Science Monthly* noted "a serious evil of athleticism is, that it tends to become a power in the schools, rivaling the constituted authorities."

On April 29, 1881, a Faculty Committee on Athletics and the Musical Clubs was established at Princeton, and the following year Harvard appointed an athletic committee made up of two professors and the gymnasium director, Dudley A. Sargent. The committee immediately prohibited competition against professionals and gave Sargent veto power over student appointment of coaches. The committee also fired the school's baseball coach, over student protests, and two years later the rowing coach was dismissed. This was the beginning of a long

battle over whether colleges should use professional coaches. The battle was joined at Princeton in 1884, when the faculty committee banned professional coaches entirely.

The Harvard Athletic Committee went too far in 1885, when it persuaded the faculty to ban football. Shortly afterward, the committee was reorganized to include two students, one alumnus, a physician, and Sargent, the only faculty representative. This new committee restored football to the athletic program in 1886. Two years later, the committee was reorganized once again, with three representatives each from the alumni, the faculty, and the student body. It had become obvious that the faculty could not take complete control of the students' extracurricular activities, and the new Harvard committee became the model for athletic control at many other colleges.

The first attempt at intercollegiate control came on December 8, 1883, when faculty members from Columbia, Harvard, Pennsylvania, Princeton, Trinity, Wesleyan, Williams, and Yale met in New York City and adopted eight resolutions, including a prohibition on professional coaches, a ban on competition against noncollegiate teams, and control by faculty athletic committees. The resolutions were sent to 21 colleges, but only Harvard and Princeton approved them.

Representatives of Northwestern, Purdue, and the Universities of Chicago, Illinois, Michigan, Minnesota, and Wisconsin, meeting in 1895 as the Intercollegiate Conference of Faculty Representatives, voted to limit eligibility to bona fide undergraduates with good academic records and to require a transfer student to spend half a year at his new college before participating in athletics. The ICFA, later the Western Intercollegiate Conference, is now known as the Big Ten.

Eastern colleges once again got together to discuss athletics problems on February 18, 1898, at Brown University. A committee of faculty members was appointed to issue a report on intercollegiate athletics. The report, issued that spring, spoke out strongly against professionalism and commercialization and again called for faculty control. But faculty naivete about the meaning of sports to students and alumni was revealed in the statement, "there is very little fun in watching a college team which has been so trained and perfected that it can win every game during the season." That, in fact, was the very kind of team that students, alumni, and the growing number of professional coaches wanted to create.

The report caused some action by individual colleges but didn't lead to any kind of central authority.

That had to await the football crisis of 1905, which seemed to center on brutality in football. But when Harvard President Eliot was asked to call a conference of eastern schools to reform football in order to eliminate brutality, he replied, "Deaths and injuries are not the strongest argument against football. That cheating and brutality are profitable is the main evil." The Western Intercollegiate Conference agreed. At a special meeting in 1906, the conference decided to bar freshmen and graduate students from competition, to eliminate preseason practice and the training table, to limit the season to five games and ticket prices to 50 cents, and to bring financial management under faculty control.

Meanwhile, a group of 13 eastern schools had met in December of 1905 to form the National Intercollegiate Football Conference, which soon became the Intercollegiate Athletic Association of the United States and, in 1910, the National Collegiate Athletic Association. The group made several football rules changes, including legalization of the forward pass, but didn't take control of intercollegiate sports. It was limited to suggesting guidelines on eligibility, recruiting, and athletic scholarships, and it spoke out in favor of faculty control. During the next 40 years, the NCAA standardized rules and established national championships in many sports, but it didn't become a powerful central governing body until after World War II.

While many schools adopted NCAA guidelines in whole or part, most of the old abuses continued or crept back into athletic programs. A three-year study by the Carnegie Foundation for the Advancement of Teaching resulted in a 1929 report that said, "The paid coach, the gate receipts, the special training tables, the costly sweaters and extensive journeys in special pullman cars, the recruiting from the high school, the demoralizing publicity showered on the players, the devotion of an undue proportion of time to training, the devices of putting a desirable athlete, but a weak scholar, across the hurdles of the examination—these ought to stop."

The report had little noticeable effect, although a number of schools dropped football during the 1930s, primarily because of the Great Depression. Most colleges either eliminated the sport or cut way back on the number of games because of travel restrictions during World War II. After the war, football came back stronger than ever, and basketball also became a major sport, as many colleges built large field houses. Basketball also began to attract gamblers, resulting in the scandal of 1951, when it was revealed that at least 32 players from seven colleges had been paid to "shave points."

The NCAA during this period was struggling to find sensible methods of enforcing its own rules, but as a voluntary member organization it had problems. Expulsion of a member institution, requiring a two-thirds vote, seemed the only recourse, but it proved impossible to get the necessary votes even if a college was clearly in violation of the rules. Ironically, the flow of television money, beginning in the late 1960s and increasing rapidly during the 1970s, gave the NCAA the enforcement stick, but it also proved to be a carrot that led to even worse abuses.

Attendance at collegiate football games grew from 20 million to 30 million during the 1960s, and money from the NCAA's football television contract increased from $3 million in 1968 to $16 million in 1976, $29 million in 1979, and more than $65 million in 1981. Basketball lagged behind football, but gained ground rapidly during the 1980s. Each of the final four teams in the NCAA basketball tournament received nearly a half-million dollars in 1981, most of it from television networks, and that was up to nearly $1.5 million by 1990. Major postseason bowl games were worth $1 million to a team, and a team good enough to get into a bowl game would undoubtedly earn large amounts of money for regular-season television coverage, too.

The NCAA had the threat of cutting off the cash flow by banning a college from television during the regular season and from postseason play. But the possibility of collecting all that money led to some major scandals. To cite just a few: Arizona State football players in 1980 were given credit for off-campus extension courses that they never went to; a University of New Mexico basketball coach was convicted of forgery for altering transcripts; many of the schools in the Pacific Ten Conference altered transcripts and gave "student-athletes" credit for courses they never took; the football program at Southern Methodist University was so fraught with illegal payments from alumni that the school was given the NCAA's "death penalty"—banned entirely from intercollegiate sports for two years.

And those weren't the only problems. Athletes at many campuses, especially youngsters from black ghettos, faced problems coping with an alien environment. Given full scholarships for athletic ability alone, they had little or no spending money. College athletes were being convicted of theft, rape, assault, drunken driving, and drug abuse in unprecedented numbers. At a single college, seven football players were convicted of various criminal charges in a period of less than six months. And in 1990 basketball coach Jim Valvano of North Carolina State was paid $212,000 to leave the school because of a host of problems with the program. Many of his fellow coaches felt that Valvano was being blamed for events entirely beyond his control.

The brightest spot in the intercollegiate picture was the rise of women's sports, although that was in large part forced on the colleges by Title IX of the Educational Amendments Act of 1972. Title IX, which was opposed by the NCAA and athletic directors at most major basketball and football schools, prohibits sexual discrimination in the allocation of money by any educational institution that receives federal aid— meaning virtually every educational institution in the country. There was a long battle over what Title IX actually meant to sports programs, but many colleges moved quickly to organize varsity teams for women in a variety of sports. In 1972, women's programs were given less than 1 percent of the total money spent on intercollegiate sports; that had increased to at least 16 percent by 1987.

Further Reading: Cady, Edwin H. *The Big Game: College Sports and American Life.* Knoxville: University of Tennessee Press, 1978; Atwell, Robert N., *et al. The Money Game: Financing Collegiate Athletics.* Washington, DC: American Council on Education, 1980; Durso, Joseph. *The Sports Factory: An Investigation into College Sports.* New York: Quadrangle/New York Times, 1975; Smith, Ronald A. *Sports and Freedom: The Rise of Big-Time College Athletics.* New York: Oxford University Press, 1988.

See also AMERICAN COLLEGIATE ATHLETICS; COLLEGE FOOTBALL ASSOCIATION; INTER-COLLEGIATE ASSOCIATION OF AMATEUR ATHLETES OF AMERICA; NATIONAL ASSOCIATION OF INTERCOLLEGIATE ATHLETICS; NATIONAL COLLEGIATE ATHLETIC ASSOCIATION; NATIONAL JUNIOR COLLEGE ATHLETIC ASSOCIATION; TITLE IX; WHITE HOUSE CONFERENCE ON FOOTBALL.

International Boxing Federation (IBF)

The IBF was originally the U.S. Boxing Association, organized in September 1976 because of dissatisfaction with the World Boxing Association. Most members were state boxing commissioners. The name was changed to the U.S. Boxing Association International in April of 1983, and to the IBF in May of 1984. The IBF is one of three major bodies that sanction fights and recognize world champions.

Address: 20 Clinton Street, Newark, NJ 07102 (201) 621-7200

International Boxing League (IBL)

Sportscaster Jack Drees and Chicago businessman Joe Kellman founded the IBL in 1969. The league had eight teams with 15 boxers per team, three in each of five weight divisions: Lightweight, welterweight, middleweight, light-heavyweight, and heavyweight. Teams competed in six-round fights in each weight division, and standings were based on rounds won and lost. The teams were the Chicago Clippers, Denver Rocks, Milwaukee Bombers, and St. Louis Saints in the western division and the Detroit Dukes, Louisville Pacers, Miami Barracudas, and New York Jolters in the eastern division. The IBL operated only during the 1969–70 season.

International Hot Rod Association (IHRA)

Organized in 1970 as a regional sanctioning association for drag racing, the IHRA expanded greatly in 1988, after moving to headquarters in Waco, TX. Its series of professional championship races was increased from 8 to 12, and a new contract with the Entertainment and Sports Programming Network guaranteed at least 48 hours of coverage on cable television. The association now sanctions tracks in 21 states and conducts world championship events for nonprofessional drivers, as well as regional championship programs for both professionals and nonprofessionals.

See also DRAG RACING.

International Ladies' Games

Because there were no track and field events for women on the Olympic program, the Federation Sportive Feminine Internationale was founded in 1920 to organize the first Women's Olympic Games, held in Paris in 1922. When the International Olympic Committee agreed to add five women's events for the 1928 games, the FSFI changed the name to the International Ladies' Games. They were held every four years through 1934.

International League
Baseball

Baseball's first minor league, the International was organized in 1877 with teams in Columbus, OH; Guelph, Ontario; London, Ontario; Lynn, MA; Manchester, NH; Pittsburgh, PA; and Rochester, NY. After the 1878 season, the league was renamed the National Association, which folded in 1879. A new International League was founded in 1884. In 1946, it was classified as a top minor league, AAA, along with the American Association and the Pacific Coast League. The league has had teams in Canada and Havana through the years, but is now made up of only U.S. teams, in Columbus, OH; Pawtucket, RI; Richmond, VA; Rochester, NY; Scranton/Wilkes-

Barre, PA; Syracuse, NY; Tidewater, VA; and Toledo, OH.

See also MINOR LEAGUES.

International Motor Contest Association (IMCA)

IMCA was founded in March of 1915, when it held its first auto race at the Michigan State Fairgrounds in Detroit. The association now sanctions more than 50 tracks in Arkansas, Florida, Illinois, Iowa, Kansas, Michigan, Minnesota, Missouri, Nebraska, Oklahoma, Texas, and Wisconsin, and it conducts championships in modified, midget, sprint, and stock car divisions. In 1989, IMCA Canada was established to oversee modified division racing in Alberta. The division was expanded into British Columbia and Saskatchewan in 1990.

Address: 1800 West D Street, Vinton, IA 52349 (319) 472-4763

International Motor Sports Association (IMSA)

John Bishop founded IMSA in Fairfield, CT as a race sanctioning organization in 1969. He introduced two major series in 1971, GT (grand touring) racing for small domestic production cars such as Mustangs and Camaros and European production sports cars, and small sedan racing on street radial tires. The current IMSA schedule includes five major series with races in 12 states, a total attendance of about 1 million spectators, and television coverage by ESPN, Turner Broadcasting, and NBC.

Address: P.O. Box 3465, 860 Clinton Avenue, Bridgeport, CT 06604 (203) 336–2116

International Motor Sports Hall of Fame

Located next to Alabama International Motor Speedway in Talladega, this hall of fame opened in May of 1983. The three-building complex contains many cars that have set land speed records, as well as championship stock cars. One room focuses on the history of racing at Daytona, FL, another on international racing.

Address: P.O. Box 3465, 860 Clinton Avenue, Bridgeport, CT 06604 (203) 336-2116

International Race of Champions (IROC)
Auto Racing

Roger Penske, Mike Phelps, and Les Richter founded the IROC series in 1973 as an attempt to determine the world's best race car driver. The idea was to give each driver the same kind of car and run one race

each on an Indy car track, a stock car track, and a road course. For the first 15 years, only three drivers were invited, the champions in Indy car, stock car, and road racing, but in 1988 special invitations were extended to A. J. Foyt and Richard Petty, and in 1989 there were 12 drivers and a fourth race, on a one-mile track, was added.

Porsches were raced in the first year of competition and Chevrolet Camaros for the next three years. Since 1977, the car has been equipped with the type of chassis used in Winston Cup stock car racing. The all-time leader in the series is stock car racer Cale Yarborough, with five victories in eight appearances.

International Skeet
See SKEET SHOOTING.

International Softball Congress (ISC)

Although the ISC has held a "world tournament" for fast–pitch softball teams every year since its founding in 1946, it is not an international organization. Most of the teams in the tournament are from the United States, although teams from Canada and Mexico have been entered. When a New Zealand team was invited in 1988, the ISC agreed for the first time to pay a sanctioning fee to the Amateur Softball Association, the sport's national governing body, which has control over any U.S. event involving foreign teams.

At one time, the ASA didn't allow member teams to play in the ISC World Tournament at all. But another group, the U.S. Slo-Pitch Softball Association, won a suit against the ASA in 1976 on antitrust grounds, and since then several teams have won both the ASA and the ISC tournament, which is for fast-pitch softball teams.

See also AMATEUR SOFTBALL ASSOCIATION OF AMERICA.

International Swimming Hall of Fame

A major international swimming meet in a new $1 million pool was on the program when this hall of fame held its grand opening in 1965. Ft. Lauderdale, FL owns the building and grounds, and the hall is operated by a chartered nonprofit corporation. The idea originated with the Amateur Athletic Union, but more than 100 countries agreed to give the hall of fame international status, and in 1968 it was dedicated by Harold Henning, secretary of the Federation Internationale de Natation Amateur. In addition to exhibits on each of its more than 200 inductees, the Hall of Fame has a library with more than 5,000 volumes about aquatic sports, a movie and videotape library, and an art collection. In 1988, plans were announced for an $11 million expansion and renovation project.

Address: 1 Hall of Fame Drive, Fort Lauderdale, FL 33316 (305) 462-6536

International Tennis Hall of Fame

The Newport Casino, which hosted the U.S. national tennis championships from their beginning in 1881 through 1915, is the home of this hall of fame. Sanctioned by the U.S. Lawn Tennis Association in 1954, it originally took up just one room, but it now occupies the entire building. The site includes 13 grass courts, where two professional tournaments are played annually. The building itself houses a court tennis court, one of only nine in the United States, and rooms devoted to the Davis Cup, the early history of tennis, women in tennis, a collection of art, trophies, and other memorabilia, and displays on the history of tennis equipment and fashion. In addition, the Hall of Fame has a 2,500-volume library on racquet sports and a 400-seat theater.

Address: 194 Bellevue Avenue, Newport RI 02840 (317) 638-9155

International Track Association (ITA)

This professional track organization was announced by Michael O'Hara on November 14, 1972, and it held its first meet on March 3, 1973, at Pocatello, ID, attracting 10,480 spectators. A number of stars, including miler Jim Ryun, pole-vaulter Bob Seagren, shot-putter Randy Matson, and middle-distance runner Lee Evans, signed with the ITA, which paid $500 for a first-place finish, with a $500 bonus for breaking a world record. Its second meet, on March 24 in Los Angeles, drew the ITA's largest-ever crowd. After that, attendance became sporadic, and the association folded in 1976.

International Trapshooting

See TRAPSHOOTING.

International Trophy
Golf

Awarded to the player with the best individual score in the World Cup golf matches for professionals, the International Trophy was established in 1954, one year after the matches began.

International Volleyball Association (IVA)

The IVA was a professional, co-ed league that played just one season, in 1974. Its chief drawing card was

former basketball star Wilt Chamberlain. The league's 12 teams were all in the West: Albuquerque Lasers, Denver Comets, El Paso-Juarez Sol, Orange County Stars, Phoenix Heat, Salt Lake City Stingers, San Diego Breakers, San Jose Diablos, Santa Barbara Spikers, Seattle Smashers, Southern California Rangers, and Tucson Sky.

International Women's Professional Softball League (IWPSA)

The IWPSA began play in May of 1976 with ten teams: Buffalo Breskis, Chicago Ravens, Connecticut Falcons, Michigan Travelers, Pennsylvania Liberties, Phoenix Birds, San Diego Sandpipers, San Jose Sunbirds, Santa Ana Lionettes, and Southern California Gems. All players were paid $100 a week for a 120-game season. During the 1976 season, the Phoenix team moved to Prescott, AZ, and after the season Michigan, Pennsylvania, San Diego and Southern California dropped out. The IWPSA operated for just one more season.

Interprovincial Rugby Union (IRU)

The Hamilton Tigers and Toronto Argonauts of the Ontario Rugby Union joined with the Ottawa Rough Riders and Montreal Football Club of the Toronto Rugby Union in 1907 to form the IRU, also known as the Big Four. In 1956, the IRU joined the Canadian Football Council, which was renamed the Canadian Football League in 1958, and in 1960 the IRU became the eastern conference of the CFL.

See also CANADIAN FOOTBALL LEAGUE.

Intramural Sports

The new emphasis on physical education and the increase in college gymnasiums shortly after the turn of the century led to the beginning of modern intramurals, particularly in the East. According to a 1910 survey, intramural participation had reached about 80 percent at Amherst and Princeton, 75 percent at Harvard, and 67 percent at Yale, compared to only 35 to 40 percent at the University of Chicago and 10 to 12 percent at the University of California. Another survey of 142 schools with a total of 111,600 male students in 1913 revealed that 40.3 percent took part in intramural sports, even though 37 percent of the colleges didn't even offer intramurals.

World War I revealed a nationwide need for physical fitness programs and, at the urging of Secretary of War Newton D. Baker, the National Collegiate Athletic Association in 1920 voted to encourage the continued development of intramural programs among its members. The University of Michigan led the way in 1921 by requiring that all male students take part in some kind of outdoor sports, and other colleges adopted similar requirements during the 1920s. By 1930, many colleges reported that more than 90 percent of their male students were playing intramurals. The movement also began to filter down to high schools, where participation in intramural sports increased from only 5.7 percent of boys in 1922 to 50.7 percent in 1934.

Intramural sports weren't as severely affected by the Great Depression as were intercollegiate and interscholastic sports, and they came back stronger than ever in both schools and colleges after World War II. Educators also began adding intramural sports for girls. Beginning in the 1960s, there has been a trend toward co-ed intramurals, in which both sexes are represented in team sports.

See also HIGH SCHOOL SPORTS; INTERCOLLEGIATE SPORTS; PHYSICAL EDUCATION.

Irish, "Ned" Edward S. (1905–1982)
Basketball
Born May 6, 1905, Lake George, NY; died January 21, 1982; Basketball Hall of Fame

In 1931, New York Mayor Jimmy Walker asked a group of sportswriters to organize a college basketball triple-header to benefit the city's relief fund. Irish was one of the organizers. The "Relief Games" filled Madison Square Garden three years in a row, and in 1934 Irish rented the Garden to promote his own double-headers. That was the real beginning of intersectional basketball, because he usually scheduled New York area teams against strong teams from other areas, including the Pacific Coast. Eight dou-ble-headers drew a total of 99,528 fans in the first season, inspiring the establishment of the National Invitation Tournament in 1935. After World War II, Irish also promoted double-headers in Philadelphia and Buffalo, so that teams visiting the East could be guaranteed three games during the trip. By 1950, 25 double-headers in the three cities attracted more than 600,000 fans.

Irish was one of the founders of the New York Knickerbockers and the Basketball Association of America in 1946, and he was president of the team until his retirement on July 1, 1974.

Ivor Wynne Stadium
Hamilton, Ontario
The oldest stadium in the Canadian Football League, this field opened in 1932. The home of the league's Hamilton Tiger-Cats, it seats 29,183. The stadium is named for a former Hamilton player and coach.

Ivy League
Although the Ivy League was not formally organized until 1954, the term was used as early as the 1920s. Robert Harron wrote in 1938, "Close bonds of similarity, athletic standards, eligibility rules, etc., have caused a group of ten homogeneous colleges in the East to become known as the 'Ivy League.'" The schools were Army, Brown, Columbia, Cornell, Dartmouth, Harvard, Navy, Pennsylvania, Princeton, and Yale. The two military academies are not members of the present Ivy League.

Address: Council of Ivy Group Presidents, Room 22, 70 Washington Road, Princeton, NJ 08540 (609) 452-6246

Jack Murphy Stadium
San Diego, CA

The only major stadium named after a sportswriter, Jack Murphy Stadium was built by the city of San Diego at a cost of about $27 million. It opened in 1967 as the home of the San Diego Chargers of the National Football League, and since 1969 has also been the home field of the National League's San Diego Padres. The stadium seats 60,100 for football, 58,433 for baseball. Its home run dimensions are 330 feet down the lines and 405 feet to center field. Originally San Diego Stadium, it was renamed San Diego/Jack Murphy Stadium in 1982, but is generally known by the shorter name.

Jackrabbit Ski League

Named for Herman "Jackrabbit" Smith-Johannsen (1975–1987), an active skier for more than 90 years, the Jackrabbit Ski League is a cross-country skiing program for children administered by Cross Country Canada. It began in 1975 as a pilot program in Manitoba and gained national status in 1980. The largest ski league in North America, it offers a series of badges for technique, speed, and distance. Programs are operated by local ski clubs, schools, and recreation centers.

Address: 1600 James Naismith Drive, Gloucester, Ontario, Canada K1B 5N4 (613) 748-5662

Jackson, "Shoeless Joe" Joseph J. (1887–1951)
Baseball

Born July 16, 1887, Brandon Mills, SC; died December 5, 1951

The greatest player who is not in the Baseball Hall of Fame, Jackson was banned from baseball in 1921 for his involvement in the "Black Sox" scandal. A right-handed thrower and left-handed hitter, Jackson compiled a career .356 batting average, third highest in history, in 13 major-league seasons. He was also a fine defensive outfielder with an exceptionally strong throwing arm. After playing briefly for the Philadelphia Athletics in 1908 and 1909 and appearing in 20 games with the Cleveland Indians in 1910, Jackson became a star in 1911, when he hit .408 with 233 hits, 45 doubles, 41 stolen bases, and 126 runs scored. He led the league in triples with 26 in 1912, and hit .395, and in doubles in 1913

while hitting .373. After hitting .338 in 1914, Jackson was traded to the Chicago White Sox during the 1915 season. He batted only .308 that year, but hit .341 with a league-leading 21 triples in 1916. The White Sox won the American League pennant and the World Series in 1917, with Jackson hitting .301 for the season and .304 in the Series.

Wartime work in a shipyard limited him to just 17 games in 1918, but he hit .351 in 1919, when the White Sox won the pennant again. They were heavily favored in the World Series, but the Cincinnati Reds beat them five out of eight games. Jackson's 1920 season was one of his finest: He batted .382 and again led the league in triples with 20. But, before the season ended, a Cook County grand jury was investigating charges that the 1919 World Series had been fixed, and Jackson was one of eight White Sox players indicted. They were all acquitted in 1921, but the new commissioner of baseball, Judge Kenesaw Mountain Landis, had already declared them "outlaws" and banned them. There are many questions about Jackson's involvement, especially since he batted .375 and fielded flawlessly during the Series, and there have been several unsuccessful attempts to have him reinstated so that he can be elected to the Hall of Fame.

Further Reading: Gropman, Donald. *Say It Ain't So, Joe! The Story of Shoeless Joe Jackson.* Boston: Little, Brown, 1979.

See also BLACK SOX SCANDAL.

Jai Alai

A kind of handball in which players use long, curved wicker baskets to propel a very hard rubber ball, jai alai originated in the Basque region of Spain. It was introduced to North America during the 1904 St. Louis World's Fair, and became a popular betting sport in Chicago and New Orleans until gambling was made illegal in those cities. In 1924, a jai alai fronton (court) opened in Miami, and Florida legalized pari-mutuel betting on the sport in 1933. Betting on jai alai also became legal in Connecticut in 1971 and in Newport, RI in 1976. There are now 14 frontons in the United States, 10 of them in Florida and 3 in Connecticut. Most of the best players are still Basques, but some Mexicans and Americans became successful professionals during the 1980s.

Address: National Association of Jai Alai Frontons, P.O. Box 2630, Daytona Beach, FL 32115 (904) 255-7398

Javelin Throw

Although the javelin was on the 1908 Olympic program, it wasn't added to the Amateur Athletic Union's national championships until 1922. The event was dominated by Scandinavians until 1953, when Dick Held of the United States studied the javelin's flight characteristics and developed a new aerodynamic model that allowed his brother, Franklin "Bud" Held, to make the first throw of more than 260 feet. Held extended his world record to 268 feet 2½ inches in 1955, but that was shattered the following year by Egil Danielsen of Norway with a throw of 281 feet 2 inches. The women's javelin throw was added to the Olympic program in 1932, when Mildred "Babe" Didrikson of the United States won the Gold Medal. Since then, the event has been dominated by European women.

Jennings Trophy
Hockey

Established for the 1981–82 season by the National Hockey League, this trophy honors William M. Jennings, long-time president of the New York Rangers. It's awarded to "the goalkeeper(s) having played a minimum of twenty-five games for the team with the fewest goals scored against it." Because most NHL teams use two goalies, there have been two winners each year.

Jennings Trophy Winners

1982　Dennis Herron and Rick Wamsley, Montreal
1983　Bill Smith and Roland Melanson, New York Islanders
1984　Pat Riggin and Al Jensen, Washington
1985　Bob Sauve and Tom Barrasso, Buffalo
1986　Darren Jensen and Bob Froese, Philadelphia
1987　Brian Hayward and Patrick Roy, Montreal
1988　Brian Hayward and Patrick Roy, Montreal
1989　Brian Hayward and Patrick Roy, Montreal
1990　Rejean Lemelin and Andy Moog, Boston

Jerome Park
Westchester County, NY

Built by the American Jockey Club on 230 acres, Jerome Park opened on September 25, 1866, with General Ulysses S. Grant as the guest of honor. The track was named for Leonard W. Jerome, a millionaire financier and horseman who was one of the club's founders. Jerome Park, which had seating for

Opening day at Jerome Park in 1876 was celebrated in this newspaper illustration. Courtesy of the National Museum of Racing

more than 7,000, made Thoroughbred racing a sport for fashionable society, with New York as its capital. The track also led the change from multiple-4-mile-heat racing to a number of shorter races on a single card. The Belmont Stakes was originally held at Jerome Park in 1867. The race moved to Morris Park in 1890, after Jerome Park closed.

Jet Ski Boating

A jet ski boat is a kind of water motorcycle, introduced about 1980. Competition was formalized in 1982 when the International Jet Ski Boating Association, Inc., was founded to sanction and promote races. The association has about 12,000 members in a dozen countries. The top event is the international championship held annually at Lake Havasu City, NV as the culmination of the World Jet Ski Tour for professional racers. The IJSBA sanctions competition for novices, experts, and professionals in stock, superstock, and modified classes. In addition to closed-course racing, there's competition in slalom, freestyle, drag racing, and jumping over a 6-foot water ski jump.

Address: International Jet Ski Boating Association, Inc., 1239 East Warner Avenue, Santa Ana, CA 92705 (714) 751–4277

Jiujitsu

From the Japanese for the "art of flexibility," jiujitsu was developed more than 2,000 years ago by the Japanese warrior class. The better-known martial arts, judo and karate, both grew out of jiujitsu, which stresses maximum results with minimum effort. Jiujitsu became a competitive sport during the 1960s, but the first international tournament wasn't held until 1975. The first world championships took place in 1984 in Niagara Falls, Ontario. Jiujitsu is much more popular in Canada than in the United States. The Canadian Jiu-Jitsu Association was organized in 1963, and Canadian teams won the first three world championships. There is no national organization in the United States.

Address: Canadian Jiu-Jitsu Association, 1309 Falgarwood Drive, Oakville, Ontario, Canada L6H 2L7 (416) 844-8750

Jim Thorpe Trophy

See THORPE TROPHY.

Jockey Club
Horse Racing

Incorporated in February of 1894, the Jockey Club developed rules of racing, patterned after the British rules, which are used with a few local variations by all state racing commissions. Since 1896, the club has controlled the registration of Thoroughbreds through its ownership of the American Stud Book.

Address: 380 Madison Avenue, New York, NY 10017 (212) 599-1919

Joe Louis Sports Arena
Detroit, MI

Named for the long-time heavyweight boxing champion who grew up in Detroit, this arena opened in 1979. The home rink of the National Hockey League's Detroit Red Wings, it seats 19,275.

Joe Robbie Stadium
Miami, FL

Dissatisfied with the Orange Bowl, owner Joe Robbie of the Miami Dolphins spent $102 million to build the stadium named for him. It opened in 1987 with a seating capacity of 74,930. The stadium hosted Super Bowl XXIII in 1989.

John Hancock Bowl
Football

The Sun Bowl, inaugurated in El Paso, TX in 1936, became the John Hancock Bowl in 1989. From 1958 through 1975 and 1977 through 1988, it was played in December. The game was played on New Year's Day from 1936 through 1958 and in 1977. The site was Kidd Field from 1936 until 1963, when Sun Bowl Stadium opened.

Sun Bowl Results

1936	Hardin-Simmons 14, New Mexico State 14
1937	Hardin-Simmons 34, Texas-El Paso 6
1938	West Virginia 7, Texas Tech 6
1939	Utah 26, New Mexico 0
1940	Catholic University 0, Arizona State 0
1941	Western Reserve 26, Arizona State 13
1942	Tulsa 6, Texas Tech 0
1943	2nd Air Force 1, Hardin-Simmons 7
1944	Southwestern Texas 7, New Mexico 0
1945	Southwestern Texas 35, New Mexico 0
1946	New Mexico 34, Denver 24
1947	Cincinnati 18, Virginia Tech 6
1948	Miami (OH) 13, Texas Tech 12
1949	West Virginia 21, Texas-El Paso 12
1950	Texas Western 33, Georgetown 20
1951	West Texas 14, Cincinnati 13
1952	Texas Tech 25, Pacific 14
1953	Pacific 26, Southern Mississippi 7
1954	Texas Western 37, Southern Mississippi 14
1955	Texas Western 47, Florida State 20
1956	Wyoming 21, Texas Tech 14
1957	George Washington 13, Texas Western 0
1958	(Jan.) Louisville 34, Drake 20
1958	(Dec.) Wyoming 14, Hardin-Simmons 6
1959	New Mexico State 28, North Texas 8
1960	New Mexico State 20, Utah State 13
1961	Villanova 17, Wichita 9
1962	West Texas 15, Ohio 14
1963	Oregon 21, Southern Methodist 14
1964	Georgia 7, Georgia Tech 0
1965	Texas Western 13, Texas Christian 12
1966	Wyoming 28, Florida State 20
1967	Texas-El Paso 14, Mississippi 7
1968	Auburn 34, Arizona 10
1969	Nebraska 45, Georgia 6
1970	Georgia Tech 17, Texas Tech 9
1971	Louisiana State 33, Iowa State 15
1972	North Carolina 32, Texas Tech 28
1973	Missouri 34, Auburn 17
1974	Mississippi State 26, North Carolina 24
1975	Pittsburgh 33, Kansas 19
1977	(Jan.) Texas A & M 37, Florida 14
1977	(Dec.) Stanford 24, Louisiana State 14
1978	Texas 42, Maryland 0
1979	Washington 14, Texas 7
1980	Nebraska 31, Mississippi State 17
1981	Oklahoma 40, Houston 14
1982	North Carolina 26, Texas 10
1983	Alabama 28, Southern Methodist 7

1984 Maryland 27, Tennessee 26
1985 Arizona 19, Georgia 13
1986 Washington 14, Texas 7
1987 Alabama 28, Washington 6
1988 Oklahoma State 35, West Virginia 33
1989 Alabama 29, Army 28
1990 Michigan State 17, Southern California 16

Johnson, Benjamin S., Jr (1961–)
Track and Field
Born December 30, 1961, Falmouth, Jamaica

Johnson was the world's fastest human for four years, but when he tested positive for steroid use after apparently winning the Olympic 100-meter dash, he was stripped of the Gold Medal. And, when an investigation revealed that he'd begun using steroids as early as 1981, his world records were also vacated. Representing Canada, Johnson won the event at the 1985 World Cup meet after tying the world record in 10.00 seconds during a preliminary heat. He also won the 100 meters in the 1986 Commonwealth Games with a Games record 10.07, and in 1987 his explosive start in the World Championships gave him a victory over Carl Lewis of the United States in a record 9.83 seconds. His 9.79 in the 1988 Olympics would also have been a new world record, but the medal was awarded to Lewis, who had finished second. Because of his steroid use, Johnson was suspended for life by the International Amateur Athletic Federation. However, he was reinstated after 2½ years, and he began competing again in January 1991.

Johnson, "Jack" Arthur John (1878–1946)
Boxing
Born March 31, 1878, Galveston, TX; died June 10, 1946; Boxing Hall of Fame

The first black heavyweight champion began boxing professionally in 1897. His first major fight was a 20–round decision in 1902 over George Gardner, who won the light-heavyweight title the following year. By 1905, Johnson was clearly one of the best boxers in the world, but he spent most of the next two years fighting other blacks, especially Joe Jeannette; they had eight bouts in 1905 and 1906. But in 1907 Johnson knocked out former heavyweight champion Bob Fitzsimmons in the second round, and later that year his first-round knockout of Jim Flynn inspired a *St. Louis Post-Dispatch* writer to comment, ". . . he is the greatest living exponent of the art of hit-and-getaway and as such, is the outstanding challenger for the title."

Tommy Burns (Noah Brusso) of Canada had won the championship in 1906. When he went to En-gland to fight in 1908, Johnson followed him, and he also followed when Burns sailed to Australia later that year. Burns had said he would fight Johnson for $30,000, and promoter Hugh McIntosh came up with the money for a bout in Sydney on December 26. Johnson controlled the fight completely, and when police stopped it during the 14th round, McIntosh declared Johnson the winner.

The search for a "Great White Hope" who could beat Johnson began almost immediately. Johnson was not only black, he was an "uppity nigger," in the ugly phrase of the day, arrogant, boastful, fond of white women and a fast lifestyle. Retired champion James J. Jeffries was finally persuaded to come out of retirement, but Johnson knocked him out in the 15th round at Reno, NV on July 4, 1910. Race riots broke out throughout the country, a number of blacks were killed by white assailants, and the film of the fight was banned by local authorities almost everywhere. (Two years later, after Johnson knocked out Jim Flynn, Congress passed a law prohibiting the interstate transportation of fight films, to prevent the public from seeing a black fighter beating a white fighter.)

Jeffries was really the last hope. There were no white heavyweights who could beat Johnson. But the law could. The mother of his white mistress, Lucille Cameron, in 1912 accused him of abducting her daughter, and a federal prosecutor charged Johnson with a violation of the Mann Act, which prohibited transporting a woman across state lines for sexual purposes. That case fell through, but Johnson was convicted of violating the act with another white woman, and he was sentenced to a year and a day in prison. While out on bail awaiting an appeal, Johnson fled to Canada. From there he went to England and then France. After defending his title four times in Paris and once in Buenos Aires, Johnson was knocked out by Jess Willard in the 26th round at Havana, Cuba, on April 5, 1915.

Johnson continued fighting in Spain and Mexico until July 20, 1920, when he reentered the United States and was arrested at the border. He served a little less than a year in prison. He had several meaningless fights through 1933, when he formally retired from the ring, although he returned to fight a couple of exhibitions in 1945. On June 10, 1946, Johnson was killed in an automobile crash while on his way to watch the second black heavyweight champion, Joe Louis, defend his title against Billy Conn.

Further Reading: Roberts, Randy. *Papa Jack: Jack Johnson and the Era of White Hopes*. New York: The Free Press, 1983.

Johnson, Rafer (1934–)
Track and Field
Born August 18, 1934, Hillsboro, TX; National Track and Field Hall of Fame

Johnson was a hurdler and long jumper until a knee injury slowed him somewhat, and he took up the decathlon. The fourth time he competed in the event, in 1955, he set a world record with 7,985 points. He finished second in the 1956 Olympics, set another world record with 8,302 points in 1959, and increased that to 8,683 points in 1960, when he won the Olympic Gold Medal. During his career, Johnson won 9 of the 11 decathlons in which he competed.

Johnson, Walter (1887–1946)
Baseball
Born November 6, 1887, Humboldt, KS; died December 10, 1946; Baseball Hall of Fame

Sam Crawford compared Johnson to a pitching machine. "You hardly see the ball at all. But you *hear* it. *Swoosh*, and it smacks into the catcher's mitt . . . He threw so nice and easy—and then *swoosh*, and it was by you." Although he pitched for mediocre Washington Senators' teams for most of his career, he won 417 games, second only to Cy Young, and he was one of the first five players named to the Baseball Hall of Fame.

"The Big Train," as Grantland Rice nicknamed him because of the speed of his fastball, joined the Senators late in the 1907 season. In 1908, he set a record by starting three consecutive games and pitching shutouts in all three, against the New York Yankees. Johnson won 20 games for the first time in 1910, when he was 25–17 with eight shutouts and a league-leading 313 strikeouts. He went on to win 11 more strikeout titles, and from 1910 through 1919 he averaged 26 victories a season for a team that averaged only 76. He had a 33–12 record in 1912 and was 36–7 in 1913, when he pitched 11 shutouts and five one-hitters. He won the Chalmers award as the American League's Most Valuable Player that year.

Although he won only 8 games in 1920 because of a sore arm, he pitched a no-hitter against the Boston Red Sox on July 1. After three more subpar seasons, he returned to form with a 23–7 record and another Most Valuable Player Award in 1924, when the Senators won their first pennant. He had a 1–2 record in the World Series, but his one victory won the Series against the New York Giants. The Senators repeated in 1925, when Johnson had a 20–7 mark, and he was 2–1 in the World Series against Pittsburgh, but the Pirates won in seven games.

Bobby Jones retired from competitive golf after winning the Grand Slam—the U.S. and British Open and amateur tournaments—in 1930. He later built the Augusta (GA) National Course and helped establish the Masters tournament. Courtesy of the U.S. Golf Association

Johnson retired after mediocre seasons in 1926 and 1927. He managed the Senators from 1929 through 1932 and the Cleveland Indians from 1933 until August of 1935. In his 21-season career, he won 417 games against 279 losses, with 3,506 strikeouts and only 1,359 walks in 5,925 innings. He had 110 shutouts, an all-time record, and an earned run average of 2.17. As a manager, Johnson won 530 games and lost 432.

Jones, "Bobby" Robert T., Jr. (1902–1971)
Golf
Born March 17, 1902, Atlanta, GA; died December 18, 1971; World Golf Hall of Fame

Jones was a child prodigy golfer who won the Atlanta junior championship at the age of 9 by beating a 16-year-old. But he had a terrible temper that held him back for several years. The temper was directed at himself, as British professional George Duncan recognized when he said, "Jones will never be a champion. He is too fine an artist. Only the perfect shot ever suits him." But he conquered the temper when he was 21, winning the 1923 U.S. Open, and he went on to win to win 13 major titles—4 U.S. Opens, 3 British Opens, 5 U.S. Amateurs, and 1 British Amateur. He retired at the age of 28 after winning all four championships in 1930.

After retiring, Jones made a great deal of money from golf through endorsements of equipment, instructional films, and a radio show. He helped design the Augusta National Golf Course and, with Clifford Roberts, inaugurated the Masters tournament there in 1934. Jones played in the Masters until 1947, when he had to quit after the second round because of a sore shoulder, which was eventually diagnosed as the result of a spinal disease that confined him to a wheelchair. He was named the player of the 1928–37 decade during the celebration of golf's centennial in the United States.

See also AUGUSTA NATIONAL GOLF COURSE; MASTERS TOURNAMENT (GOLF).

Journalism, Sports

The first "sports story" printed in North America was a paragraph about an English prizefight, copied from a London newspaper by the *Boston Gazette* on March 5, 1733. It reported that John Faulconer had knocked out Bob Russel after 8 minutes of fighting before "as great a Concourse of People as ever was known on such an Occasion."

That, however, was an isolated incident. Sports didn't attract much attention from the press until horse racing began to get some coverage in the early 19th century, and even that coverage was confined to brief notices in magazines such as the *American Farmer*, which in 1825 introduced the first sports column, "The Sporting Olio," which was devoted entirely to racing. The magazine's editor, John Stuart Skinner, in 1829 founded the first successful sports publication, the *American Turf Register*.

During the 1830s, some newspapers began reporting on races and boxing matches, among them the *New York Sun* and *Transcript* and the *Philadelphia Public Ledger*. The first sports newspaper, *Spirit of the Times*, was introduced on December 10, 1831, by William Trotter Porter. It wasn't successful at first, and in 1832 it was merged into the *Traveller*, but Porter purchased the *Traveller* and began publishing the *Spirit* again on January 3, 1835. Because there was no way of transmitting news rapidly, newspapers copied freely from one another and from other publications, and the *Spirit* was accepted as an authority, widely copied and quoted throughout the country. Extracts of its account of the horse race between Boston and Fashion in 1842 appeared in more than 100 publications.

Sports coverage expanded rapidly in the next decade, though it still focused on boxing and racing. The *New York Herald* led the way, sending eight reporters to cover the race between Fashion and Peytona in 1845 and using a team of relay riders to bring news of the 1847 fight between Yankee Sullivan and Bob Caunt from Harpers Ferry, WV.

Thanks to Henry Chadwick, the first newspaper to cover baseball was the *New York Clipper*, founded by Frank Queen in 1853. Chadwick volunteered to cover cricket and baseball matches without pay, and Queen accepted his offer. He also covered the sports for other papers. ". . . the New York papers had been giving no attention to athletics," Chadwick later recalled, "and I was merely endeavoring to interest them." He was finally hired in 1862 by the *New York Herald*. Chadwick, who created the batting average, the box score, and the system of baseball scorekeeping still in use, occasionally wrote about other sports, but concentrated chiefly on baseball.

The *National Police Gazette*, later an important popularizer of sport, was founded in 1845 by George Wilkes. He sold that publication in 1856 and bought *Spirit* from Porter, though he kept Porter as editor. During the 1850s, saloons, betting parlors, and barbershops routinely kept copies of *Spirit* and a similar English publication, *Bell's Life of London*, on hand for their customers to read.

The invention of the telegraph in 1844 led to the establishment of the first wire service, Associated Press, in 1848. The result of the heavyweight match between Tom Hyer and Yankee Sullivan in 1849 was wired to New York newspapers from Maryland, but the telegraph didn't have a major impact on journalism until after the Civil War, when lines expanded along with the growing railroad network.

The first major international sports event was the Harvard-Oxford boat race in 1869; moments after the race ended, the news that Oxford had won flashed across the Atlantic cable. Collegiate rowing became a major spectator sport in the Northeast during the 1870s, and most newspapers in the region regularly covered crew races and regattas. Then college football entered the picture, and a host of other sports were organized and modernized.

The perfection of the high-speed web press, the reduced cost of paper, and increased literacy made newspapers a genuine mass medium in the 1880s.

The result was called the "New Journalism" by its proponents, "yellow journalism" by its critics. It combined crusades against "fraud and sham . . . public evils and abuses," as Joseph Pulitzer put it, with lively writing and sensationalism. Pulitzer's *New York World* reached a circulation of 100,000 in 1884 and surpassed 250,000 two and a half years later. The *World* was probably the first newspaper to have a page devoted exclusively to sports, in 1883. Until then, sports stories had been scattered here and there throughout the paper. Pulitzer also created the first sports department with writers specializing in sports coverage. William Randolph Hearst, who had discovered that sports could help boost circulation with his first newspaper, the *San Francisco Examiner*, bought the *New York Journal* in 1895 and went one step further than Pulitzer, hiring writers to specialize in specific sports.

The leading national publication during the period was the *National Police Gazette*, purchased in 1877 by Richard Kyle Fox, who turned it into a forerunner of today's supermarket tabloids. Printed on shocking pink paper, the *Gazette* was read wherever men gathered, as *Spirit of the Times* had been 20 years before. It featured crime, scandal, and sex at first, but when an account of the Paddy Ryan-Joe Goss fight in 1880 helped to sell 400,000 copies, Fox made boxing a staple. A regular column on baseball, "Our National Game," and a column of general sports news were soon added.

Virtually every major paper had a "sporting editor" by 1890 and the amount of space devoted to sports grew from 0.6 percent in 1878 to 4.2 percent in 1898. Baseball was the major beneficiary, but newspapers also covered billiards, boxing, college football, cycling, horse racing, rowing, track and field, and yachting. And they not only reported on events, they ran advance publicity with the latest news on training, injuries, possible trades, and off-field gossip.

There were also specialized publications devoted to sports. *Outing* magazine, founded in 1882, focused at first on camping and outdoor recreation, but it soon began to carry stories on competitive sports and built an average circulation of 88,000 a month. Francis C. Richter's *Sporting Life*, founded in 1883 in Philadelphia, drew on regional correspondents throughout the country to cover a variety of sports, although baseball was its primary subject. By 1888, it had a circulation of about 45,000 a week. It also had a similar competitor, *Sporting News*, a St. Louis–based publication established in 1886 by Albert and Charles Spink. *Sporting Life* died in 1903, but *Sporting News* is still the self-styled "Bible of Baseball."

Now that they were specialists, sportswriters began to develop their own jargon, which became the fans' jargon as well. A baseball shutout became a "whitewash" or a "calcimine job." A hit was a "bingle," a stolen base an "embezzlement," and a player who made an out was described in deathly terms—he "was smothered," or "expired in anguish." Writers both led and followed fans in glorifying athletes, but they also reported on the players' private lives much as Hollywood gossip columnists later reported on the private lives of the movie stars.

When the "Golden Age of Sports" arrived in the 1920s, though, that changed. Led by Grantland Rice, sportswriters became "gee whizzers." Coaches and managers were compared to Napoleon and Julius Caesar, and athletes were great warriors. Purple prose and extravagant nicknames, usually alliterative, filled the sports pages. Jack Dempsey was the "Manassa Mauler," Babe Ruth the "Sultan of Swat," Red Grange the "Galloping Ghost," the 1924 Tulane line was the "Seven Wonders of the World," the 1927 New York Yankee batting order was "Murderer's Row." Sports coverage expanded incredibly. In 1929, 20 million words of European news crossed the Atlantic cable; but four years before, more than 2 million words had been wired out of Chicago on the Dempsey-Tunney fight. Major sports stories moved to the front page, even in the staid *New York Times:* On July 3, 1921, the *Times* devoted three fourths of its front page and all of the following 12 pages to the mismatch between Jack Dempsey and French champion George Carpentier.

Feet of clay were no longer exposed. Babe Ruth's drinking and promiscuity were common knowledge to sportswriters, but not to their readers. When Ruth missed much of the 1925 season with an intestinal ailment, many writers thought he had a venereal disease, but the story they unanimously told their readers was that he had eaten a gargantuan number of hot dogs and washed them down with an ocean of soda pop. Paul Gallico, a confessed "gee whizzer", said later, "We had an overwhelming innocence in those days. . . . Everybody was happy. There was a big boom. There were no problems. You could let yourself go on sports. A heavyweight championship fight, the build-up, was tremendous. It was like the Israeli-Arab war . . ."

There were exceptions. The *Times*, among others, covered sports in a subdued style, as it covered other kinds of news. Westbrook Pegler, who later became a right-wing political columnist, belonged to what Gallico called the "aw-nuts" school of sportswriting, scornful of the events and athletes he wrote about. And Ring Lardner portrayed baseball players as ignorant, semiliterate, boastful bumpkins in many of his columns, as well as in "You Know Me, Al" and other writings.

The Great Depression and World War II made sports less important to readers and writers alike. The most publicized college football player of the 1930s, Michigan halfback Tom Harmon, was not as celebrated as Grange or the Four Horsemen, and is not nearly as well known today. The top players of the 1940s were Glenn Davis and Doc Blanchard of the U.S. Military Academy, whose careers began during the war. They and many other athletes, especially black heavyweight champion Joe Louis, were used as public relations tools for the Allied cause.

The postwar boom in sports was accompanied by a new style in sportswriting, led by Red Smith of the *New York Herald-Tribune* and *Times*. Smith described his approach: "I've always had the notion that people go to spectator sports to have fun and then they grab the paper to read about it and have fun again. . . . Sports isn't Armageddon. These are just little games that little boys can play, and it really isn't important to the future of civilization whether the Athletics or the Browns win. If you can accept it as entertainment, and write it as entertainment, then I think that's what spectator sports are meant to be."

Smith's example and the mood of the era inspired a group of sportswriters who called themselves "the Chipmunks;" they took an irreverent, tongue-in-cheek approach to their subject. While the Chipmunks saw sports as show business, with the emphasis on "show," other writers began to emphasize "business" during the 1960s, led by Leonard Koppett of the *New York Times*. The trend increased with the growing importance of players' associations, labor unrest, interleague competition, and escalating salaries during the 1970s. Many journalists wrote disillusioned books about sport as business: Joseph Durso's *The All-American Dollar* (1971), Larry Merchant's . . . *And Every Day You Take Another Bite* (1971), Ken Denlinger and Leonard Shapiro's *Athletes for Sale* (1975), John Underwood's *Spoiled Sport* (1982).

The growing problems of drug and alcohol abuse among athletes also led to a new emphasis on players' private lives. In the 1988 Associated Press poll of sportswriters, heavyweight champion Mike Tyson's marital problems and Boston Red Sox third baseman Wade Boggs' sexual involvement with Margo Adams were among the top ten sports stories of the year. That emphasis reflected a growing trend in journalism, which increasingly focused on the private lives of politicians, beginning with the sexual peccadillos of one-time presidential candidate Gary Hart. In a sense, journalism in general and sports-

writing in particular had returned to their modern roots in the 1890s, the era of sensationalism, although with a more somber tinge.

Further Reading: Holtzman, Jerome, editor. *No Cheering in the Press Box.* New York: Holt, Rinehart and Winston, 1974.

See also CHADWICK, HENRY; LARDNER, RING; NATIONAL POLICE GAZETTE; RADIO; RICE, GRANTLAND; SMITH, RED; SPIRIT OF THE TIMES; TELEVISION.

Jousting

Before the Civil War, many southern plantation owners viewed slavery as a kind of feudalism; they saw their mansions as castles and themselves as nobles. As an outgrowth of this romantic view, modern jousting began in 1840, with young men in armor trying to catch suspended rings on their lances while they rode full tilt on horseback. The first such tournament was evidently held in Fauquier County, VA; it was inspired by an 1839 tournament at Eglinton Castle in England. "Knights" from as far away as Texas competed in a tournament on August 28, 1841, at Warrenton Springs, VA, and the sport spread rapidly into neighboring states and even into New Jersey, New York, Ohio, and Pennsylvania. Jousting died out during the Civil War, but it was revived in the mid-Atlantic soon afterward. It is now the state sport of Maryland, and the National Jousting Association was founded in 1968 to conduct an annual championship tournament in Washington, D.C.

Address: National Jousting Association, c/o Sandy Iszer, The Imporium Creekside, 112 East Patrick, Frederick, MD 21701 (301) 223–9468.

Judo

Judo was introduced to North America in 1902, when a Japanese expert demonstrated the sport to many Americans, including President Theodore Roosevelt, but it didn't catch on. However, a Japanese immigrant, Shigetaka Sasaki, organized a judo club in Vancouver, British Columbia, in 1924, and Jigoro Kano, who had invented judo in 1882, came to the United States in 1932 and established several associations, most of them made up of Japanese-Americans. The sport got its biggest boost after World War II from the U.S. Strategic Air Command, which required its bomber crews to spend nine weeks of training in judo. Many of the crew members organized judo clubs on SAC bases and at YMCAs. By 1950, there was enough interest for the AAU's National Wrestling Committee to form a subcommittee on judo, and the first national championships were held in 1953 at San Jose, CA. The same year Sasaki organized the Canadian Kodokan Black Belt Association.

The Amateur Judo Association of the U.S., founded in 1954, became the Judo Black Belt Federation in 1955 and the U.S. Judo Federation in 1961. In the meantime, the SAC Judo Association, which had been organized in 1954, went through several name changes, to the U.S. Air Force Judo Association, the Armed Forces Judo Association, and finally the U.S. Judo Association. The two groups struggled for some time to control the sport, but in 1979 U.S. Judo was founded as the national governing body. The USJA and USJF still operate as sanctioning organizations. The Canadian Judo Association, now known as Judo Canada, was organized in 1956.

The International Olympic Committee voted to include judo in the 1940 Olympic Games, which were canceled because of World War II. Judo finally became an Olympic sport in 1964.

Addresses: Judo Canada, 333 River Road, Vanier, Ontario, Canada K1L 8H9 (613) 748–5640; U.S. Judo, P.O. Box 10013, El Paso, TX 79991 (915) 565–8754; U.S. Judo Association, 19 North Union Boulevard, Colorado Springs, CO 80909 (719) 633–7750; U.S. Judo Federation, c/o Yosh Uchida, 50 West San Fernando, Suite 804, Cranford, NJ 95113 (201) 298–7551

Jules Rimet Trophy

See WORLD CUP (SOCCER).

Junior Legion Baseball

See AMERICAN LEGION BASEBALL.

Junior Olympics

To help develop young athletes, the Amateur Athletic Union inaugurated the Junior Olympics in 1948. Originally for boys and girls ages 10 to 15, the annual championships now embrace age groups from under 11 to under 19, with competition in baseball, basketball, field hockey, gymnastics, karate, soccer, swimming, synchronized swimming, taekwondo, and track and field. More than 4,000 youngsters competed in the national championships in 1988.

K

Kahanamoku, Duke P. (1890–1968)
Surfing, Swimming

Born August 24, 1890, Honolulu, HI; died January 22, 1968; International Swimming Hall of Fame

The "crawl," based on a swimming stroke used by Australian aborigines, was still relatively new to North America in 1912, when Kahanamoku began his competitive swimming career in California, using a version of the crawl which Hawaiians had known for centuries. He won two Olympic Gold Medals in the 100-meter freestyle, in 1912 and 1920, and he was the U.S. outdoor 100-yard champion in 1916, 1917, and 1920, and the indoor 100-meter titlist in 1912 and 1920. Kahanamoku was also a superb surfer, who did a great deal to popularize the sport by giving demonstrations in California and Australia.

Kansas City, MO

Baseball Kansas City had teams in the Union Association in 1884, the National League in 1886, and the American Association in 1888 and 1889, but didn't have another major-league franchise until 1955, when the Athletics moved from Philadelphia. The A's went to Oakland, CA, in 1967, but two years later the Kansas City Royals joined the American League as an expansion team. The Royals won western division championships in 1976, 1977, 1978, 1980, 1984, and 1985 and pennants in 1980 and 1985. They beat the St. Louis Cardinals in a seven-game World Series in 1985.
Basketball The Cincinnati Royals of the National Basketball Association became the Kansas City–Omaha Kings in 1972 and split their home games between the two cities until the 1975–76 season, when they became a full-time Kansas City team. The Kings moved to Sacramento, CA in 1985.
Football The Kansas City Cowboys were in the National Football League from 1924 through 1926, when they played almost all of their games on the road. In 1963, the Dallas Texans of the American Football League moved to Kansas City and became the Chiefs. They were AFL champions in 1966 and 1969. They lost the first Super Bowl but won the fourth. When the leagues merged in 1970, the Chiefs entered the American Football Conference of the NFL. They won the AFC's western division championship in 1971.

Hockey The Kansas City Scouts entered the National Hockey League in 1974 and lasted just two seasons, becoming the Colorado Rockies in 1976.

See also ARROWHEAD STADIUM; KANSAS CITY MUNICIPAL STADIUM; ROYALS STADIUM.

Kansas City Municipal Stadium
Kansas City, MO

Originally built in 1923, it was known as Ruppert Stadium and then Blues Stadium until it underwent a complete rebuilding that increased its capacity from 17,456 to 32,561. It was then renamed Kansas City Municipal Stadium and became the home of the American League's Kansas City Athletics, who moved from Philadelphia in 1955. The team went to Oakland in 1967. The Royals, a new team established in 1969, played at the stadium until 1973, when they moved into Royals Stadium in the new Harry S. Truman Sports Complex. Municipal Stadium was also the home of football's Kansas City Chiefs from 1963 until 1973.

Karate

From the Japanese for "open hand," karate is the art of self-defense by striking blows with the feet and hands. It became fairly popular in North America during the 1960s and 1970s, but there are several different forms of the sport, each with its adherents, and as a result karate has become fragmented among several different organizations. As a competitive sport, karate was originally noncontact—fighters stopped their blows just before making contact and were awarded points by judges—but full-contact karate fighting for men developed in the 1970s. Women usually compete in *kata* karate, in which a series of blows is demonstrated against various opponents with subjective judging. The American Amateur Karate Association, founded in 1961, has 241 member clubs representing about 20,000 individuals, and it conducts the annual All-American Karate championships. The U.S.A. Karate Federation, founded in 1986, selects national teams for international competition. Other organizations include the Feminist Karate Union (1971), which teaches self-defense to women and people who are potential victims, such as the elderly; the International Traditional Karate Federation (1974); the Pan-American Union of Karatedo Organizations (1975); the Professional

Karate Association (1974), which sanctions and promotes full-contact competition; and the U.S.A.–Korean Karate Association (1982).

Address: U.S.A. Karate Federation, 1300 Kenmore Boulevard, Akron, OH 44314 (216) 753–3114

Kart Racing

The go-kart was invented in 1956 by Art Ingels, a hot rodder and racing car builder, who mounted a 2½-horsepower, one-cylinder, two-cycle engine on a tubular chassis, with a bicycle chain driving semi-pneumatic tires. He was surprised to find that the little car could travel nearly 30 miles an hour. The following year, three other Southern California men, Roy Debrow, Duffy Livingstone, and Bill Rowles, began building and selling the vehicles. A writer for *Rod and Custom* magazine called them "Go Karts," and the company quickly adopted the name and began offering kits as well as assembled cars. Ingles himself soon started his own company to manufacture what he called "Carettas." Within a few months, several other companies were in the business.

In December of 1957, the Go Kart Club of America was founded to establish specifications. The club divided karts into three classes, based on engine displacement. There are now many classes, ranging from 80–cc, 215-pound vehicles for the 8 through 11 age group to unlimited, which may have engines up to 200–cc and weigh as much as 425 pounds, for ages 18 and up. There are also five types of racing: Two-cycle and four-cycle sprint, two-cycle and four-cycle speedway, and road racing.

The sanctioning body, now called the International Kart Federation (IKF), has about 5,000 members, but estimates that there are about 30,000 people involved in kart racing.

Address: 4650 Arrow Highway, Suite 84, Montclair, CA 91763 (714) 625–5497

Kayaking

See CANOEING AND KAYAKING.

Keeneland Race Track
Lexington, KY

Keeneland opened in 1936, but it was built on a rich legacy of racing in Lexington, dating back at least to 1787, when horses raced along Main Street to Henry Clay's home. The first track was built in 1797, and in 1828 the Kentucky Association opened a downtown racetrack that operated until 1933, to be replaced by Keeneland three years later. The best-known race at Keeneland is the Blue Grass Stakes, a major stepping-stone to the Kentucky Derby. The 1⅛-mile Spinster Stakes is one of the country's

major races for fillies and mares. Keeneland is perhaps best known for its five annual Thoroughbred auctions, which now gross about $400 million. The track's main course is 1¹/₁₆ mile, and there is a 7½-furlong turf course. Keeneland has seating for 10,000 spectators.

Address: Keeneland Association, Inc., P.O. Box 1690, Lexington, KY 40592-1690 (606) 254–3412

Kekionga Club
See FT. WAYNE, IN.

Kelly, John B. Sr. (1889–1960)
Rowing
Born October 4, 1889, Philadelphia, PA; died June 21, 1960

Kelly won the national Association singles sculls in 1914, the championship and quarter-mile singles in 1919 and 1920. He won the Olympic Gold Medal in the singles in 1920, and he and his cousin, Paul V. Costello, won the Gold Medal in the doubles in both 1920 and 1924. Kelly was not allowed to compete in the Diamond sculls at England's Henley Regatta in 1920 because he was a bricklayer; the regatta's rules explicitly said that anyone who "is or has been by trade or employment for wages, a mechanic, artisan or laborer" was not an amateur. His son, John B., Jr., won the Diamond sculls in 1947 and 1949, and his daughter Grace was the movie star who became Princess of Monaco.

Kelly, "King" Michael J. (1857–1894)
Baseball
Born December 1, 1857, Troy, NY; died November 8, 1894; Baseball Hall of Fame

One of sports' first truly colorful stars, Kelly was nicknamed "King" by Chicago fans, but reached his pinnacle of popularity in Boston. During his 16-year career, he played every position, but was chiefly a catcher and an outfielder. He played with Cincinnati in the National League in 1878 and 1879, when he batted .348, then went to Chicago for seven seasons, including five pennants. In 1886, he led the league in hitting with a .388 average and in runs scored with 155. He was then sold to Boston for the unprecedented price of $10,000. After he hit .322 with 84 stolen bases in 1887, Boston fans gave him a house and a carriage with two white horses.

Kelly was player-manager for the Boston team that won the Players' League pennant in 1890, and he was briefly with Cincinnati and Boston in the American Association in 1891 before returning to the Boston National League team. After playing the 1892 season in Boston, he finished his career with one year in New York. Kelly is generally credited with inventing the hook slide and the headfirst slide. During his baseball years, he also performed in vaudeville, usually reading "Casey at the Bat." He led a high life, dressing expensively, drinking too much—he said it was good for him—and betting heavily on horse races. He died of pneumonia contracted on a boat trip to Boston to make another vaudeville appearance in 1894. Kelly had a lifetime .308 average.

Kelso
Horse Racing

The only Thoroughbred ever to win five consecutive Eclipse Awards as horse of the year, Kelso won 39 of 63 starts despite the fact he usually carried the highest weight in handicaps. He won the Jockey Club Gold Cup five times, the Woodward Stakes three times, and the Aqueduct stakes and Stymie Handicap twice each. Retired because of an injury, he had amassed $1,977,896 in winnings. Bred at Woodstock Farm in Maryland, Kelso won his first start as a two-year-old in September of 1959, coming from seventh place in the stretch to win by 1¼ lengths. He had two more starts that year, finishing second both times. In 1960, he won eight of nine starts and his first Eclipse Award.

Kelso became the third horse in history to win the Handicap Triple Crown, in 1961. With Eddie Arcaro riding, he won the Metropolitan, carrying 130 pounds, the Suburban, carrying 133 pounds, and the Brooklyn, carrying 136 pounds. He also won the Woodward Stakes and the Jockey Club Gold Cup that year. Arcaro retired, and Kelso had a slow start in 1962, winning only one of his first four starts. Ishmael Valenzuela then replaced Willie Shoemaker as his jockey, and Kelso won the Woodward Stakes by 10 lengths, setting a track record. He also won the Jockey Club Gold Cup. He was unanimously named Horse of the Year, his fourth Eclipse Award, in 1963, when he won 9 of 12 starts, including the Woodward and the Jockey Club Gold for the third consecutive year.

After narrowly losing the Suburban Handicap, while carrying the top weight of 136 pounds, Kelso won the 1964 Aqueduct Stakes, was second in a photofinish in the Woodward, then broke his own track record while winning the Jockey Club Gold Cup. In the Washington International, he set another track record of 2 minutes 23⅘ seconds. He had just six more races, winning three, including the Whitney Stakes and the Stymie Handicap in 1965. An eye injury shortened his season, and the following year he suffered a hairline fracture to a leg bone and had to be retired.

Kennedy Stadium
See ROBERT F. KENNEDY STADIUM.

Kenosha, WI
Football The Kenosha Maroon were in the National Football League only during the 1924 season.

Kentucky Derby
Horse Racing

Irwin S. Cobb, the humorist from Paducah, KY, once said, "Until you've been to the Kentucky Derby, you ain't never been nowhere and you ain't never seen nothing." When it began on May 17, 1875, the Kentucky Derby was a relatively minor, regional horse race. It was the idea of Meriwether Lewis Clark, Jr., grandson of William Clark of Lewis and Clark Expedition fame. He wanted his new Churchill Downs track to have a race that would equal England's famed Epsom Derby. However, by 1890 the track was in financial trouble, and in 1902 the future of the Kentucky Derby looked bleak. Its unlikely savior was a tailor, Matt J. Winn, who had seen every race since the beginning, but otherwise knew little or nothing about the racing business. Winn not only raised the money to save the track, he persuaded New York owners to enter their horses in the Derby. In 1911, Meridian came from New York to win and was named the best three-year-old of the year. That was the beginning of the Derby's real fame.

When Regret became the first filly to win the Derby in 1915, it was also a publicity coup. And in 1922 Winn persuaded the owner of Morvich, who had been undefeated as a two-year-old, to run the horse at Louisville. That attracted reporters from all over the country, and Morvich won the race. When Winn died in 1949, at the age of 88, he had seen 75 consecutive Kentucky Derbies.

Run on the first Saturday in May, the Derby is the first race in Thoroughbred racing's Triple Crown. The other two are the Preakness and Belmont. It's now 1¼ miles, as it was in its first four years, but it was run at 1½ miles from 1879 through 1895. Crowds of well over 100,000 attend, and wagering at the track has grown to more than $13 million. Called "the greatest two minutes in sports," the Derby is more than a race, it's the center of a week-long festival that includes mint julep parties, the National Turf Writers Association dinner, the Kentucky Derby Museum Gala, which is a black-tie dinner dance, the Kentucky Colonels banquet, the Knights of Columbus Charity Dinner, a steamboat race, and various concerts. The day before the Derby, Churchill Downs hosts the Kentucky Oaks, a major race for fillies.

Further Reading: Hirsch, Joe. *Kentucky Derby: The Chance of a Lifetime.* New York: McGraw-Hill, 1988.

See also CHURCHILL DOWNS.

Kentucky Futurity
Harness Racing

The Kentucky Futurity, first run in 1893, is the oldest race in the Triple Crown for Trotters. It's run at the Red Mile track in Lexington, KY.

King, Billie Jean (1943–   )
Tennis

Born November 22, 1943, Long Beach, CA; International Tennis Hall of Fame

Besides being a great tennis player, King has been an articulate and outspoken advocate of equal rights and equal pay for women athletes. After Bobby Riggs had beaten Margaret Court in their match on Mother's Day, 1973, King challenged Riggs and beat him 6–4, 6–3, 6–3, on September 30 at the Houston Astrodome. The match, billed as "the Battle of the Sexes," drew the largest crowd ever to watch tennis, 30,472, and was also seen on television by millions in 36 countries. King wrote afterward, ". . . if I had done nothing sensational in beating Riggs, I had shown thousands of people who had never taken an interest in women's sports that women were skillful, entertaining, and capable of coming through in the clutch."

Erasing Riggs' claim that a middle-aged man could beat a woman in her prime was just one of her contributions to the women's movement. In 1970, she and other top women players threatened to boycott a West Coast tournament that offered $12,500 to the men's winner and only $1,500 to the women's

Billie Jean King won a record 20 Wimbledon championships and was also a strong supporter of women's sports; she is a founder of the Virginia Slims circuit, the Women's International Tennis Association, and womenSports maga-zine. Courtesy of the U.S. Tennis Association

champion. Gladys Heldman, publisher of *World Tennis* magazine, organized an alternative women's tournament in Houston, with sponsorship from Phillip Morris. The tournament, called the Virginia Slims Invitation, offered $7,500 in prize money for eight players. They were suspended by the U.S. Lawn Tennis Association for competing, but that was the beginning of the Virginia Slims Circuit. In 1971, the circuit had 24 tournaments, offering $250,000 in prizes, and King became the first woman tennis player ever to win more than $100,000 in a year. By 1975, the circuit had nearly $1 million in total prize money.

In 1973, King was instrumental in forming the Women's Tennis Association. The USLTA and the WTA signed a truce, and women's prize money at the U.S. Open was equal to men's for the first time. She was also a founder of *womenSports* magazine and of the Women's Sports Foundation.

With her vigorous, aggressive, athletic play, King also transformed the image of women's tennis. An irony of her victory over Riggs was that she played "like a man," going to the net to volley after her service, while Riggs played "like a woman," staying at the baseline and hitting soft shots with a lot of spin. Her style brought her the record for most Wimbledon championships with 20; she won the singles in 1966, 1967, 1968, 1972, 1973, and 1975; the women's doubles in 1961, 1962, 1965, 1967, 1968, 1970, 1971, 1972, 1973, and 1979, and the mixed doubles in 1967, 1971, 1973, and 1974. In the U. S. Nationals, she won the singles in 1967, 1971, 1972, and 1974; the women's doubles in 1964, 1967, 1974, 1978, and 1980; and the mixed doubles in 1967, 1971, 1973, and 1976.

Further reading: King, Billie Jean, with Frank Deford. *Billie Jean.* New York: Viking, 1982.

See also WOMEN'S INTERNATIONAL TENNIS ASSOCIATION.

Kingdome
Seattle, WA

King County, where Seattle is located, built this domed stadium at a cost of about $60 million. The original contractor was dismissed in December of 1974 because of cost overruns, and a second contractor finished the project. The county subsequently recovered $12 million in a suit against the first contractor. Opened in April of 1976, the Kingdome seats 64,752 for football 59,438 for baseball, and 40,000 as an arena. It's the home of the National Football League's Seahawks, the American League's Mariners and the National Basketball Association's Supersonics.

Klem, "Bill" William J. (1874–1951)
Baseball

Born February 22, 1874, Rochester, NY; died September 1, 1951; Baseball Hall of Fame

The first umpire elected to the Baseball Hall of Fame, and possibly the greatest, was Bill Klem. In 1905, his first year of umpiring in the National League, Klem threw the great New York Giants' manager, John McGraw, out of a game. "I'll get your job for this," McGraw yelled, and Klem responded, "Mr. McGraw, if you can get my job, I don't want it." McGraw didn't get Klem's job; he held it until 1941, when he became supervisor of National League umpires.

Umpiring was still rather primitive. Only one umpire worked, calling balls and strikes and plays at all bases. Fans often threw bottles when they didn't like a call, and the National League didn't offer their umpires much protection from players and managers. Klem helped to change that, and he also virtually created modern umpiring. He was the first to use the now familiar signals to indicate a strike, a ball, an out, or safe. He was the first to wear a whalebone chest protector under his coat instead of the inflated, external protector. And he was the first to stand slightly to the side of the catcher in order to see pitches better. He also led umpires in a successful drive for better dressing rooms, and he was the leader of a strike before the 1917 World Series that resulted in the umpires getting $650 instead of $400.

When the Chicago Cubs and New York Giants tied for the pennant in 1908 and had to replay a tie game, Klem was assigned to umpire the playoff. Klem reported to the league president that the Giants' team physician, Dr. Joseph M. Creamer, had offered him a bribe of first $2,500 and then $3,000 to see to it that the Giants won. Creamer denied the story, but was banned from all parks in organized baseball.

Klem umpired 18 World Series, his first in 1908 and his last in 1940. He was also an umpire for the first all-star game, in 1933. In late 1940, he was hit by a grounder, and he realized he had finally slowed down at the age of 66. He retired after that season, but he was called on to work some important games in 1941. He was supervisor of umpires until his death in 1951.

Knickerbocker Baseball Club

A group of young New York City businessmen, clerks, and other professionals began in 1842 meeting regularly at 27th Street and 4th Avenue to play baseball, then still a rather primitive sport more often played by boys. One of them, Aexander Cartwright, proposed forming an exclusive club. As a result, the Knickerbocker Baseball Club was organized in 1845. Membership was limited to 40, annual dues were set at $5, and members had to show up to play baseball every Monday and Thursday. They were to be fined for disobeying the captain, arguing with an umpire, and using profanity, and they had to furnish their own uniforms of white flannel shirts, blue pantaloons, and straw hats. More important, Cartwright drew up a set of rules for the club that virtually created modern baseball at a single stroke.

See also CARTWRIGHT, ALEXANDER.

Koufax, "Sandy" Sanford (1935–   )
Baseball

Born December 30, 1935, Brooklyn, NY; Baseball Hall of Fame

After a year at the University of Cincinnati, Koufax was pitching for the Brooklyn Dodgers without ever playing in the minor leagues. A hard-throwing but wild left-handed pitcher, he won only 38 games and lost 40, striking out 684 batters while walking 405 in 691⅔ innings during his first six seasons. He did show signs of his future when he tied the major-league record with 18 strikeouts against the Chicago Cubs on August 31, 1959. The Dodgers, who had moved to Los Angeles after the 1957 season, faced the Chicago White Sox in the 1959 World Series, and Koufax lost 1–0 in his only Series start.

Finally, Koufax learned to control his pitches, and he also developed an exceptional curve to go with his fastball. He spent only six more seasons in the major leagues, but he was the best pitcher in baseball during that period. He won 18 and lost 13 in 1961, striking out 269 batters in 255⅔ innings to lead the National League. The following year, he won 14 and lost 7, but in June he was hit by a pitch that broke an artery in his pitching hand, and he missed the rest of the season. Nevertheless, his 2.54 earned run average led the league, and he had 216 strikeouts in just 184⅓ innings.

The Dodgers won three pennants in his last four seasons. Koufax won the Cy Young Award as the best pitcher in the major leagues and was also named the National League's Most Valuable Player in 1963, when he won 25 games, losing only 5, and led the league in earned run average (1.88), strikeouts (306), and shutouts (11). He beat the New York Yankees twice in the World Series, allowing just 12 hits and 3 earned runs while striking out 23 batters in 18 innings.

Koufax was on his way to an equally brilliant year in 1964 when adhesions ripped in his pitching arm,

and he missed the last month of the season. He still had a 19–5 record, leading the league in earned run average (1.74) and shutouts (7). The injury led to chronic arthritis, but he had two more great seasons. He was 26–8 in 1965, with a 2.04 earned run average, again the best in the league, and he had 382 strikeouts, a single-season record. On September 9, he pitched a perfect game against the Chicago Cubs, retiring all 27 hitters he faced. It was his fourth no-hitter, another major-league record. (Both the strikeout record and the no-hitter record were later broken by Nolan Ryan.)

A Jew, Koufax didn't pitch in the first game of the 1965 World Series because it was played on Yom Kippur, and he lost the second game, 3–0, to the Minnesota Twins. But he pitched a 4-hit, 7–0 victory, striking out 10, in the fifth game and a 3-hit, 2–0 win in the seventh game, working on just two days of rest.

For the fifth year in a row, Koufax led the National League in earned run average in 1966, at 1.73, winning 27 games and losing 9, and he struck out 317 hitters. However, he lost his only World Series start, 1–0, against the Baltimore Orioles, who swept the Dodgers in four games. After the season, doctors told him that his left arm would be permanently crippled if he continued to pitch, and he announced his retirement. Five years later, he became the youngest man ever elected to the Baseball Hall of Fame, at 36, and only the sixth to be elected the first year he was eligible. In 12 seasons, he won 165 games, including 40 shutouts, lost only 87, had an earned run average of 2.76, and struck out 2,396 in 2,324⅓ innings. His World Series record was 4–3, with a 0.95 earned run average, and 61 strikeouts in 57 innings.

Kraenzlein, Alvin (1876–1928)
Track and Field

Born December 12, 1876, Milwaukee, WI; died January 6, 1928; National Track and Field Hall of Fame

Until Kraenzlein came along, hurdling was a rather clumsy sport. Competitors simply depended on running at top speed and hoping that they would somehow get over the hurdles without falling down. But Kraenzlein developed the art of taking a hurdle at a single stride with minimum loss of speed, and his technique revolutionized the event. The record for the 110-yard high hurdles was 16.0 seconds until Kraenzlein lowered it to 15.2 in 1898; that record stood until 1918. He also cut a full second off the 220-yard low hurdles record, from 24.6 to 23.6. That record wasn't broken until 1925.

In the 1900 Olympic Games, Kraenzlein became the only man ever to win four individual Gold Med-

The national singles champion in 1946 and 1947, Jack Kramer in 1954 began promoting the professional tour and was an outspoken advocate of open tennis tournaments. He established the Grand Prix of tennis in 1970. Courtesy of the International Tennis Hall of Fame

als in track and field events. (Jesse Owens won three individual Gold Medals and one in the 400-meter relay in 1936.) He set Olympic records in the 110-meter high hurdles (15.4 seconds) and the long jump (23 feet 6⅞ inches), and he also won the 60-meter dash and the 200-meter hurdles. He was the AAU national champion in the long jump in 1898, in the 120-yard hurdles in 1898 and 1899, and in the 220-yard hurdles in 1897, 1898, and 1899. Representing Princeton, Kraenzlein won both the 120-yard and 220-yard hurdles at the IC4A meet three years in a row, 1898–1900, and he also won the long jump in 1899.

Kramer, "Jack" John A. (1921–   )
Tennis
Born August 1, 1921, Las Vegas, NV; International Tennis Hall of Fame

Kramer and Ted Schroeder won the national doubles titles in 1940 and 1941. Kramer then spent three of his best years in the service during World War II. In 1946, he returned to win the national singles championship and formed a two-man team with Schroeder to crush defending champion Australia 5–0 in the Davis Cup finals. After winning both the U.S. and Wimbledon titles in 1947, Kramer became a professional and won the pro tour four years in a row. In 1954 he became the tour's promoter and made it more successful than ever through aggressive promotion.

Kramer was often criticized for signing top young amateur players, making them ineligible for major tournaments and Davis Cup play. His reply was that tournaments ought to be open to professionals as well as amateurs. He finally won his point in 1968, when Wimbledon became an open tournament, and other major international tournaments quickly followed. In 1970, Kramer established the Grand Prix circuit, which awards points to players for high finishes in major tournaments and pays bonus money to the top point-winners.

Kurland, "Bob" Robert A. (1924–   )
Basketball
Born December 23, 1924, St. Louis, MO; Basketball Hall of Fame

A couple of 7-footers had played before Kurland, but Kurland was the first to be a genuine star. Nicknamed "Foothills," he was not an exceptional athlete, but he did have excellent timing that made him the first of the great shot blockers. His ability to get above the rim to knock the ball away was the major reason the goaltending rule was adopted in 1944. He led Oklahoma A & M to the NCAA championship in 1945, scoring 65 points in three games to win the tournament MVP award. Kurland led the nation in scoring with 643 points in the 1945–46 season and was named College Player of the Year. He was again MVP in the NCAA tournament, as Oklahoma A & M won its second title in a row.

After graduating, Kurland played AAU basketball with the Phillips 66ers for six seasons. Phillips won AAU national championships in 1947, 1948, and 1950, and Kurland was named to the All-AAU team six times. He was also the first man ever to play on two Olympic Gold Medal basketball teams, in 1948 and 1952.

Lacrosse

When Europeans began exploring North America in the early 16th century, they discovered a wide variety of ball-and-stick games. In some areas, players held a stick in each hand; in others, women played alongside men; in still others, women had their own version of the sport. Like European football at the time, the game usually resembled a melee, often pitting one entire village against another and covering an enormous area with no apparent boundaries except for a goal at each end, sometimes miles part. The distinctive feature of all these games was the stick, which had a net or pouch of leather on one end, allowing a player to scoop the ball from the ground and carry or throw it.

It is usually said that the game was named by a French missionary who thought the stick resembled a bishop's crozier—*la crosse* in French. However, it seems more likely that the name came from a French version of field hockey, *jeu de la crosse*. (*La crosse* means "hockey stick" as well as "crozier.")

Modern lacrosse grew out of the game played by the Iroquois tribes of northern New York, eastern Ontario, and southwestern Quebec; the natives called it baggataway or tewaraathon. By the 19th century, many of the tribes had stopped playing, but the Caughnawagee and St. Regis Indians still carried on the tradition, and Montrealers learned the game from them. The first lacrosse club was formed in Montreal in 1839. By the late 1850s there were numerous clubs in Quebec and Montreal, and migrating settlers brought lacrosse to the Western provinces. In the

Teams from the Middle Atlantic region have long dominated club and collegiate lacrosse. Here Johns Hopkins and the University of Maryland meet in NCAA tournament action. Courtesy of Jeff Wagner/Intercollegiate Lacrosse Association

Action from a game between the New York Lacrosse Club and the Yale team is shown in this 1883 newspaper illustration.

meantime, the Onondaga Indians in upstate New York, influenced by the St. Regis tribe, revived the sport, and other people in the area became interested. It soon spread to New York City, Brooklyn, and Philadelphia.

Lacrosse had by now become semimodernized. It was played by teams of 12 on a field about 125 yards long, with 4-foot-long sticks and a rubber ball, but rules varied greatly from one region to another. In 1867, Dr. W. George Beers of Montreal developed a standard set of rules, based loosely on the rules of field hockey, and representatives from throughout Canada met at the Kingston Conference that year to form the National Lacrosse Association. Dr. Beers, now known as "the father of Canadian lacrosse," also introduced the sport at Upper Canada College in Toronto.

Lacrosse spread rapidly in the northeastern United States, especially among colleges. The National Lacrosse Association was founded in 1879 and adopted the Canadian rules. Harvard, Princeton, and New York University established an intercollegiate association in 1882, and teams were also formed at Boston University, Columbia, Cornell, and Stevens Institute. The Intercollegiate Lacrosse League, established in 1905, included Columbia, Cornell, Harvard, Hobart, Johns Hopkins, Lehigh, Stevens and

Swarthmore. It was succeeded by the U.S. Intercollegiate Lacrosse Association in 1929.

Lacrosse was probably Canada's most popular sport at the turn of the century. Many of the early stars were also professional hockey players. Sir Donald Mann of the Canadian Northern Railway in 1910 donated a challenge cup for the country's senior amateur championship. Quarreling between amateur and professional teams during the 1920s led to the breakup of Canada's National Lacrosse Association, and the Canadian Lacrosse Association was formed in 1925 to govern the amateur form of the sport. The association took possession of the Mann Cup and began conducting an annual championship tournament for the trophy.

About 1930, an indoor version, box lacrosse or "boxla," was developed, and it became so popular by the middle 1930s that it virtually replaced field lacrosse in Canada. Boxla, typically played on an iceless hockey rink, has only 6 players on a team, as opposed to field lacrosse's 11, and it's a very fast game because the ball rarely goes out of bounds. With field lacrosse nearly extinct, the Mann Cup was transferred to box lacrosse as the national championship trophy. After World War II, box lacrosse declined in popularity, and field lacrosse gained somewhat in Canada in the late 1960s. Canada won the third annual World Lacrosse Games in 1978, the only time the United States hasn't taken the championship.

Women field hockey players discovered lacrosse during the 1920s, and the U.S. Women's Lacrosse Association was formed in 1931 by clubs from Baltimore, Boston, New York, and Philadelphia. There are now about 2,500 clubs in the USWLA, representing about 70,000 players. The association sponsors national championships, chooses an All-American team, and selects teams for international play. The U.S. Intercollegiate Lacrosse Association was reorganized in 1926 and began selecting All-American teams in 1927. Since 1956, the USILA has given the Wingate Trophy to the national collegiate champion. The National Collegiate Athletic Association began national championship tournaments for men in 1971, for women in 1982.

Addresses: Canadian Lacrosse Association, 333 River Road, Vanier, Ontario, Canada K1L 8H9 (613) 748–5628; U.S. Intercollegiate Lacrosse Association, P.O. Box 928, Washington & Lee University, Lexington, VA 24450 (703) 463–8670; U.S. Women's Lacrosse Association, 20 East Sunset Boulevard, Philadelphia, PA 19118 (215) 248–3771

See also INDOOR LACROSSE; LACROSSE HALL OF FAME FOUNDATION, INC.; MAJOR INDOOR LACROSSE LEAGUE.

Lacrosse Hall of Fame Foundation, Inc.

Founded in June 1959, the Foundation's chief goal originally was to build a hall of fame for lacrosse, but it also operates a library and reference bureau and raises money to promote the sport and to help develop young players. In 1964, Johns Hopkins University offered the foundation space in the Newton H. White, Jr. Athletic Center, then under construction on its Homewood campus in Baltimore. It was dedicated on June 10, 1966. The foundation sponsors U.S. national teams in international competition, awards scholarships for lacrosse camps, and gives grants to help promote youth lacrosse in potential growth areas.

Address: Newton H. White Jr. Athletic Center, Homewood, Johns Hopkins University, Baltimore, MD 21218 (301) 235–6882

Ladies Professional Bowlers Tour (LPBT)

The LPBT was originally the Women's Professional Bowlers Association, formed in 1978 by a merger of the Professional Women Bowlers Association and the Ladies' Professional Bowlers Association. It took its present name in 1981. The LPBT sanctions about 15 major national tournaments, as well as regional tournaments in the Midwest, Northwest, and Southeast.

Address: 7171 Cherryvale Boulevard, Rockford, IL 61112 (815) 332–5756

Ladies Professional Golf Association (LPGA)

Three women founded and incorporated the Women's Professional Golf Association in 1944 to develop a tour, but without much success. In 1948 Wilson Sporting Goods offered some funding, and the group was reorganized as the Ladies Professional Golf Association, with Fred Corcoran as marketing director. Corcoran had helped to found the men's Professional Golf Association, and had also been Babe Didrikson Zaharias' personal manager. By 1952, the LPGA tour had grown to 21 tournaments, but as pioneer Betsy Rawls said, "You couldn't make money doing it."

However, stars such as Zaharias, Rawls, Louise Suggs, and Patty Berg helped the tour gain popularity; by 1959, there were 26 tournaments offering a total of $200,000 in prizes. Television finally discovered women's professional golf in 1963, covering the final round of the U.S. Women's Open. By 1970, at least two tournaments were being televised annually, the number of events had increased to 34, and total prize money had reached $600,000.

As television money and tour sponsorship increased, undoubtedly spurred by the feminist movement of the 1970s, prize money escalated dramatically, reaching about $5 million in 1980 and growing to $13 million in 1989. In 1976, Judy Rankin became the first women golfer to win more than $100,000 in a season; in 1988, Pat Bradley won $492,021. There are now 16 women who have earned more than $1 million in their careers, led by Bradley, with nearly $3 million.

The LPGA owns the Sweetwater Country Club in Sugar Land, TX, which opened in October 1983. Built at a cost of $28 million, it houses LPGA headquarters, the LPGA Hall of Fame, and a championship golf corse, as well as tennis courts, racquetball, basketball, and volleyball courts, and banquet facilities.

Address: 4675 Sweetwater Boulevard, Sugar Land, TX 77479 (713) 980–5742

Lady Byng Trophy
Hockey

Lady Byng, wife of the Governor-General of Canada, presented this trophy to the National Hockey League in 1925, to be given "to the player judged to have exhibited the best type of sportsmanship and gentlemanly conduct combined with a high standard of playing ability." Frank Boucher won the trophy seven times in eight years, and it was given to him permanently. Lady Byng then donated a new trophy. The winner is chosen by the Professional Hockey Writers Association.

Byng Trophy Winners

1925	Frank Nighbor, Ottawa
1926	Frank Nighbor, Ottawa
1927	Billy Burch, New York Americans
1928	Frank Boucher, New York Rangers
1929	Frank Boucher, New York Rangers
1930	Frank Boucher, New York Rangers
1931	Frank Boucher, New York Rangers
1932	Joe Primeau, Toronto
1933	Frank Boucher, New York Rangers
1934	Frank Boucher, New York Rangers
1935	Frank Boucher, New York Rangers
1936	Doc Romnes, Chicago
1937	Marty Barry, Detroit
1938	Gordie Drillon, Toronto
1939	Clint Smith, New York Rangers
1940	Bobby Bauer, Boston
1941	Bobby Bauer, Boston
1942	Syl Apps, Toronto
1943	Max Bentley, Chicago
1944	Clint Smith, Chicago
1945	Bill Mosienko, Chicago
1946	Toe Blake, Montreal
1947	Bobby Bauer, Boston
1948	Buddy O'Connor, New York Rangers

1949	Bill Quackenbush, Detroit
1950	Edgar Laprade, New York Rangers
1951	Red Kelly, Detroit
1952	Sid Smith, Toronto
1953	Red Kelly, Detroit
1954	Red Kelly, Detroit
1955	Sid Smith, Toronto
1956	Earl Reibel, Detroit
1957	Andy Hebenton, New York Rangers
1958	Camille Henry, New York Rangers
1959	Alex Delvecchio, Detroit
1960	Don McKenney, Boston
1961	Red Kelly, Toronto
1962	Dave Keon, Toronto
1963	Dave Keon, Toronto
1964	Ken Wharram, Chicago
1965	Bobby Hull, Chicago
1966	Alex Delvecchio, Detroit
1967	Stan Mikita, Chicago
1968	Stan Mikita, Chicago
1969	Alex Delvecchio, Detroit
1970	Phil Goyette, St. Louis
1971	John Bucyk, Boston
1972	Jean Ratelle, New York Rangers
1973	Gilbert Perreault, Buffalo
1974	John Bucyk, Boston
1975	Marcel Dionne, Detroit
1976	Jean Ratelle, New York Rangers-Boston
1977	Marcel Dionne, Los Angeles
1978	Butch Goring, Los Angeles
1979	Bob MacMillan, Atlanta
1980	Wayne Gretzky, Edmonton
1981	Rick Kehoe, Pittsburgh
1982	Rick Middleton, Boston
1983	Mike Bossy, New York Islanders
1984	Mike Bossy, New York Islanders
1985	Jari Kurri, Edmonton
1986	Mike Bossy, New York Islanders
1987	Joe Mullen, Calgary
1988	Mats Naslund, Montreal
1989	Joe Mullen, Calgary
1990	Brett Hull, St. Louis
1991	Wayne Gretzky, Los Angeles

Laguna Seca Raceway
Monterey, CA

A 1.9-mile road racing course with nine turns, Laguna Seca opened in 1983. It hosts a 300-kilometer CART race for Indy cars.

Address: P.O. Box SCRAMP, Monterey, CA 93940 (408) 373–1811

Lajoie, Napoleon (1874–1959)
Baseball

Born September 5, 1874, Woonsocket, RI; died February 7, 1959; Baseball Hall of Fame

When a Cleveland newspaper held a contest in 1904 to choose a new name for the city's American League team, fans voted for the "Naps," from Napoleon Lajoie, the team's second baseman. Although he's almost forgotten now, Lajoie was called "the king of ballplayers" in his time, and his biographer justly calls him "modern baseball's first superstar." He was a superb fielder—Arthur Daley called him "the most graceful ballplayer who ever lived"—and an excellent hitter.

Called up by the Philadelphia Nationals late in the 1896 season, Lajoie batted .326 in 39 games at first base. The following season, he played both first base and the outfield, hitting .361 and leading the league with 9 home runs. In 1898, he was moved to second base, and he hit .324 again, leading the league in doubles with 43. Injured in a collision, he missed much of the 1899 season, playing in only 77 games and batting .378. His last season with the Nationals was 1900, when he hit .337.

He jumped to the Philadelphia Athletics in the new American league and had a sensational 1901 season, winning the triple crown by hitting .426 with 14 home runs and 125 runs batted in. He also led the league in doubles with 48, and in runs scored with 145. In the meantime, the Philadelphia Nationals had filed suit against Lajoie for violating the reserve clause in his contract, and on April 21, 1902, the Pennsylvania Supreme Court prohibited him from playing for any team other than the Nationals.

Lajoie was inactive for nearly two months and was then sent to Cleveland, because the court order was effective only in Pennsylvania. He played only 87 games that year, hitting .378. Early in 1903, the leagues signed a truce in the form of a new National Agreement, and Lajoie was permitted to play for Cleveland, even in Pennsylvania. He led the league in hitting once more, at .355.

Near the end of the 1904 season, Lajoie became player-manager of the team now nicknamed for him. They finished fourth that year, with Lajoie batting .376 to win his third batting title in four years; he led the league in hits with 208 and doubles with 49. On July 1, 1905, Lajoie was spiked in a play at second base. The injury became infected, and he developed blood poisoning. He was out of the lineup until August 28, and batted .329 in just 65 games.

Lajoie managed Cleveland to a third-place finish in 1906 and batted .355, again leading the league in doubles (48) and hits (214). But he was spiked again in 1907, missed a month of the season, and hit only .299. And he batted only .289 the following season, when Cleveland came close to winning the pennant, finishing second to Detroit. Both teams had 90 victories, but Detroit had 63 losses to Cleveland's 64. The team slumped in 1909, and Lajoie resigned as

manager late in the season. He remained with Cleveland as a player and hit .324. He was now 35 years old, and it looked as if his career might be coming to an end.

But he came back strongly in 1910, amid controversy over his "automobile race" with Ty Cobb of Detroit. George Chalmers, owner of an automobile company, had announced he would give a car to the top hitter in each league. At the end of August, Cobb was hitting .362 to Lajoie's .359, and the race continued through September and into October. Cobb sat out the final two games of the season, believing he had a safe lead. But in a double-header against St. Louis on the last day of the season, Lajoie got eight hits in eight times at bat. Six of the hits were bunt singles. League president Ban Johnson investigated, decided that the Browns had deliberately let Lajoie bunt for base hits, and ordered St. Louis to fire their manager, Jack O'Connor. The final league figures showed Cobb winning the title by one point, .385 to .384. Lajoie led in hits, with 227, and doubles, with 53. Chalmers decided to give cars to both of them. (Recent research has shown that for the season Lajoie actually hit .383, Cobb .382, although those figures have not been officially recognized.)

Injury again forced him to miss much of the 1911 season, though he hit .366. But he was healthy for most of 1912, when he batted .368. He hit .335 in 1913, his last season over .300. On September 17, 1914, he got the 3,000th hit of his career. He was the third player in history to reach that mark. The first two were "Cap" Anson and Honus Wagner, who had done it earlier that year. Lajoie was traded back to Philadelphia in 1915, and finished his career with two seasons as a part-time player there.

In 21 big-league seasons, Lajoie had a .338 batting average, with 3,242 hits, including 657 doubles, 163 triples, and 83 home runs. He also scored 1,502 runs and drove in 1,599. He was one of the first eight players elected to the Baseball Hall of Fame.

Lalonde, "Newsy" Edouard C. (1887–1970)
Hockey, Lacrosse
Born October 31, 1887, Cornwall, Ontario; died November 21, 1970; Hockey Hall of Fame

Lalonde was chosen Canada's outstanding lacrosse player in the first half of the century. He began his hockey career in 1905 in Cornwall and later played for several teams in Ontario and Vancouver. With Toronto in 1908, he led the Ontario Professional League in scoring with 29 goals in nine games. After playing for the Montreal Canadiens, he joined Renfrew of the National Hockey Association late in the 1910–11 season, and in 1911–12 he scored 38 goals in 11 games to lead the league. Lalonde was the Pacific Coast Hockey League scoring champion in

1912–13 with Vancouver. In 1917 he became player-manager of the Canadiens, and in the 1919 Stanley Cup finals he scored all of the Canadiens' goals in a 4–2 win over Seattle in the second game, and he had five goals in the third game.

His final season was 1922–23 as player-manager for Saskatoon in the WCHL. He returned to hockey briefly to coach the Canadiens in the 1932–33 and 1933–34 seasons. In his 18 years in professional hockey, Lalonde scored 441 goals in 365 games.

Lambeau, "Curly" Earl L. (1898–1965)
Football
Born April 9, 1898, Green Bay, WI; died June 1, 1965; Pro Football Hall of Fame

Lambeau played fullback at Notre Dame in 1918, and was the only freshman to win a letter. But tonsillitis forced him to leave school and go back to Green Bay, where he was offered a job at the Indian Packing Corporation after he recuperated. In 1919 he persuaded his employer to put up $500 to buy equipment and uniforms for a semipro team, to be called the Packers. The team in 1921 joined the American Professional Football Association, which became the National Football League in 1922. The Packers, which Lambeau played for and coached, were a respectable team for eight seasons, but Lambeau wanted a championship. Before the 1929 season, he signed three players, guard Mike Michalske, tackle Cal Hubbard, and halfback Johnny "Blood" McNally; all three were named to the first All-Pro team in 1931, and all are now in the Pro Football Hall of Fame.

Using the pass much more than most teams, the Packers won three consecutive championships, 1929–31. They were undefeated in 13 games in 1929, with one tie. In 1930 they were 10–3–1, and in 1931 they won 12 and lost 2. Under the modern system, the Packers would have won a fourth straight title in 1932, when they won 10, lost 3, and tied 1, as in 1930. The Chicago Bears won the championship with a 7–1–6 record. At the time, ties were not counted at all. Now, a tie is counted as a half-win, half-loss. Using that method, the Packers would have had 10½ wins and 3½ losses, while the Bears would have had 10 wins and 4 losses.

Lambeau had retired as a player after the 1928 season, but he remained as coach until 1950. The Packers won NFL championships in 1936, 1939, and 1944, giving them a total of six titles in 24 seasons. But the team sank into mediocrity and, finally, hopelessness. In Lambeau's last two years as their head coach, Green Bay won only 5 of 24 games. He resigned and coached the Chicago Cardinals for two years, then the Washington Redskins for two years, without success. Despite those losing seasons at the end, Lambeau had a record of 229 wins, 134 losses, and 22 ties.

Lambeau Field
Green Bay, WI
Named for "Curly" Lambeau and opened in 1967, the home field for the Green Bay Packers originally had a seating capacity of 32,150. Expansions in 1961, 1963, 1966, 1967, and 1985 have brought capacity to 57,063. The stadium has a network of electric heating coils six inches beneath the playing surface to keep it free of snow and ice.

Land Speed Record
The quest for the land speed record began in France in 1898 as a way for automobile manufacturers to show how fast their cars could go. The first record was an average 39.24 miles per hour over 1 kilometer. Henry Ford, driving his famous "999," was the first American to hold the record, at 91.370 miles per hour on January 4, 1903, and William K. Vanderbilt broke that just less than a year later, with 92.307. Vanderbilt set his record on the hard sand beach at Daytona, FL, and that was the site for most attempts at the land speed record until September 3, 1935, when Sir Malcolm Campbell of England averaged 301.13 miles per hour on the Bonneville Salt Flats in Utah.

By then, special cars were being built for record attempts. Another Englishman, John Cobb, set a record of 394.2 miles per hour at Bonneville in 1947, and that stood for 16 years. Then Craig Breedlove of the United States used a jet-propelled car to travel 407.49 miles per hour on August 5, 1963. Art Arfons broke that with 536.71 miles per hour the following year, but Breedlove came back with 600.601 miles per hour in 1965. Since then, the record has only inched upward. The current mark is 633.6 miles per hour, set by Richard Noble of Great Britain in 1983.

Landis, Kenesaw Mountain (1866–1944)
Baseball
Born November 20, 1866, Millville, OH; died November 25, 1944; Baseball Hall of Fame

Landis was a baseball fan who became a U.S. district judge in 1906. He won some fame the following year when he fined Standard Oil more than $29 million, though the decision was overturned by the Supreme Court. Landis also won a reputation in legal circles for having many decisions overturned by higher courts. When the Federal League sued organized baseball for breaking antitrust laws in 1914, Landis was the judge. He said during the trial that "any blows at the thing called baseball would be regarded by this court as a blow to a national institution." He took the case under advisement, and the Federal League folded a year later, before he handed down a decision.

Late in 1920, the major-league owners decided to replace the three-man National Commission with a single commissioner. Landis was formally offered a seven-year contract at $50,000 a year on November 12; he said he would take the job only if he was given absolute authority and allowed to hold his judgeship. The owners agreed. A new National Agreement, signed on January 12, 1921, gave the new commissioner the authority to investigate "any act, transaction, or practice . . . suspected to be detrimental to the best interests of the national game of baseball." He would also be allowed to impose punishment on players, teams, team officers, or leagues. The owners agreed to submit to the commissioner's disciplinary authority, waiving their rights to legal action. (Landis was attacked by the American Bar Association, members of Congress, and others for remaining on the federal bench while also serving as commissioner. Under pressure, he resigned from the judiciary, effective March 1, 1922.)

The "Black Sox" scandal was one reason, though not the only one, for hiring a "czar" to oversee the sport. The Black Sox were eight Chicago White Sox players accused of accepting bribes to throw the 1919 World Series. Charges against one of them were dismissed, and the other seven players came to trial on June 27, 1921, along with two gamblers. On August 2, all nine defendants were acquitted. However, Landis had already declared all eight players ineligible, and the trial didn't change his mind. "Regardless of the verdict of juries," he declared, "no player that throws a ball game; no player that undertakes or promises to throw a ball game; no player that sits in a conference with a bunch of crooked players and gamblers where the ways and means of throwing games are planned and discussed and does not promptly tell his club about it, will ever play professional baseball."

The Black Sox weren't the only players banned by Landis. In March of 1921 he banished Eugene Paulette of the Philadelphia Phillies for associating with gamblers. Three months later Cincinnati pitcher Ray Fisher was blacklisted for taking a college coaching job after his request for a two-year contract was turned down. And New York Giant outfielder Benny Kauff was put on the blacklist after being indicted for car theft. He was acquitted in May of 1921, but, as with the Black Sox, Landis refused to reinstate him.

Other players banned from baseball less controversially were "Shuffling Phil" Douglas, an alcoholic pitcher who wrote a letter offering to leave his team if members of another team paid him; shortstop Jim

O'Connell and coach Cozy Dolan of the New York Giants, who were apparently involved in an attempt to bribe a player on another team. A less serious but more publicized case arose after the 1921 season. The owners had adopted a rule that players involved in the World Series could not go on barnstorming tours immediately after the Series. Babe Ruth, Bob Meusel, and Bill Piercy of the Yankees ignored the rule. Landis held back their shares of the World Series money and suspended them until May 20, 1922. Several American League owners appealed to him to reduce the suspension, because Ruth was the biggest attraction in baseball, and they stood to lose money during his suspension, but again the commissioner held firm. He did finally give the players their World Series money, though.

In 1926, Landis faced the biggest scandal since the Black Sox. In November, Ty Cobb was released as player-manager of the Detroit Tigers, and about a month later, Tris Speaker resigned as player-manager of Cleveland. They were two of the biggest names in baseball—both are now in the Hall of Fame. Then Landis announced that the two stars had been "permitted to resign" because of evidence that they may have been involved in fixing a game on September 25, 1919. A former Detroit pitcher, Hubert "Dutch" Leonard, claimed that Speaker and pitcher "Smokey" Joe Wood had assured Cobb and Leonard that Detroit would beat Cleveland that day. Cleveland had clinched second place, and Detroit could finish third by winning. Leonard had letters he'd received from both Cobb and Wood to help support his story. Finally, on January 27, 1927, Landis cleared Cobb and Speaker of the charges. Cobb then went to the Philadelphia Athletics, Speaker to the Washington Senators.

An inveterate foe of gambling in any form, Landis refused to allow baseball owners to be involved in horse racing. When he became commissioner in 1921, he ordered Charles A. Stoneham and John McGraw, both part owners of the New York Giants, to get rid of their interest in a Havana race track and casino. He also ordered Stoneham to stop inviting gambler Arnold Rothstein to his private box at the Polo Grounds. Rothstein was allegedly the man who put up the money that caused the Black Sox scandal. Much later, in 1943, when he discovered that Philadelphia Phillies owner William Cox had been betting on his own team, Landis ordered him to sell his stock and blacklisted him permanently.

Landis also opposed the "farming out" of players to minor-league teams. This practice allowed a major-league team owning an excellent shortstop, for example, to keep him at the minor-league level and away from other teams if it already had an even better shortstop. Landis wanted a free market that would allow a player to advance to the major leagues if he had the ability. After Branch Rickey established the first farm system for the St. Louis Cardinals by buying minor-league teams, other clubs began to follow his lead. Landis kept attacking the practice, and now and then he "freed" a player for a technical violation of organized baseball's rules, but he was essentially powerless to stop the practice. It had been forbidden under the National Agreement of 1903, but not under the 1921 agreement that had given Landis so many other powers.

While his tactics were often high-handed and would unquestionably be impossible today, when every player has agents, lawyers, and other advisors, Landis did rid baseball of the gambling specter that had hung over it almost from its very beginning as a professional sport. After the Cobb-Speaker case of 1926—which dated to before the time Landis became commissioner—there was no major scandal involving gambling until the Pete Rose furor in 1989.

Further Reading: Spink, J. G. Taylor. *Judge Landis and Twenty Five Years of Baseball.* New York: Thomas Y. Crowell, 1947.

See also BLACK SOX SCANDAL; NATIONAL COMMISSION.

Lansdowne Park Stadium
Ottawa, Ontario

The home of the Ottawa Rough Riders of the Canadian Football League, this stadium opened in 1967. It seats 30,927. The nearby Civic Center, also in Lansdowne Park, hosts the annual Canadian National Figure Skating Championships.

Lapchick, Joe (1900–1970)
Basketball

Born April 12, 1900, Yonkers, NY; died August 10, 1970; Basketball Hall of Fame

The son of immigrant parents from Czechoslovakia, Lapchick was 6 feet tall by the time he was 12; he eventually grew to 6 feet 5 inches. He dropped out of high school at 17 to play professional basketball in order to help support his family. From 1917 to 1923 he played in the Western Massachusetts League, the Metropolitan League, and the New York State League, then became the center for the Original Celtics. After the Celtics were broken up by the American Basketball League for being too good, he went to the Cleveland Rosenblums of the ABL. The league suspended operations in 1931, and Lapchick put another Celtics team together to barnstorm until 1936.

Lapchick had two coaching stints at St. John's University in New York, 1936–47 and 1956–65,

compiling a record of 335 wins and 129 losses. His teams won the National Invitational Tournament in 1943, 1944, 1959, and 1965. But he was more than a winning coach. Red Smith wrote in *Women's Wear Daily,* shortly after Lapchick's death, that he "lectured the kids at St. John's on the importance of education and breathed down their necks to make sure they kept up academically." He also coached the New York Knicks in the NBA 1947–56, compiling a 326–247 record.

Lardner, "Ring" Ringgold W. (1883–1933)
Sportswriting

Born March 6, 1883, Niles, MI; died September 25, 1933

Led by Grantland Rice, a school of sportswriters who called themselves the "gee whizzers" emerged in the 1920s; they made athletes larger than life. But Ring Lardner, who was writing a syndicated sports column during that period, wasn't one of them. He was a very strong antidote. Lardner took a sardonic view of athletes and fans alike, portraying both as "wise boobs" who thought they knew much more than they actually did. Despite this approach—or maybe because of it—he was remarkably popular. At its peak, his syndicated column was carried by more than 150 newspapers with a total readership of about 8 million. Beginning in 1908, Lardner covered the White Sox and the Cubs for the *Chicago Tribune,* the *Chicago American,* and the *Chicago Examiner,* and in 1913 he began writing the Tribune's sports column, "In the Wake of the News." Shortly afterward, he began writing fiction, mostly for the *Saturday Evening Post.* His first published story was "A Busher's Letters Home," in the March 7, 1914 *Post,* about a pitcher named Jack Keefe.

Keefe, like most players in later Lardner stories, was cocky, immature, semiliterate and always blaming his own failures on someone else. Lardner wrote six stories about Keefe, collected in 1916 in *You Know Me Al.* After losing a game, Keefe could write to his friend Al, "This should ought to of gave me a record of 16 wins and 0 defeats because the only games I lost was throwed away behind me but instead of that my record is 10 games win and 6 defeats and that don't include the games I finished up and helped the other boys win which is about 6 more alltogether but what do I care about my record Al?"

Lardner wrote seriously at times, especially early in his career, but he later began to present much the same image of himself as sportswriter. The World Series became the "World Serious" when he was a syndicated columnist, from 1919 into 1927, and he wrote the column "Weekly Letter," in semiliterate style, although there were usually shrewd observations disguised in that style. After the advent of Babe Ruth as a home run hitter, baseball owners decided more home runs would excite fans, and a livelier ball was introduced. Lardner wrote, "the master minds that controls baseball says to themselfs that if it is home runs that the public wants to see, why leave us give them home runs, so they fixed up a ball that if you don't miss it entirely it will clear the fence, and the result is that ball players which used to specialize in hump back liners to the pitcher is now among our leading sluggers."

In addition to the Jack Keefe stories, Lardner wrote many short stories about baseball and baseball players. He also wrote a long short story, "Champion," about a boxer named Midge Kelly, which was much darker than any of his baseball fiction. The opening paragraph sets the tone: "Midge Kelly scored his first knockout when he was seventeen. The knockee was his brother Connie, three years his junior and a cripple."

Most of the stories Lardner wrote after 1920 were not about sports. They often satirized the boorishness and stupidity of the ordinary American. Besides the stories, Lardner published a collection of satiric verse, *Bib Ballads* (1915), a novel, *The Big Town* (1921), and a tongue-in-cheek autobiography, *The Story of a Wonder Man* (1921). He also collaborated with George S. Kaufman on a comedy, *June Moon*, that ran during the 1929–30 Broadway season.

Further Reading: Yardley, Jonathan. *Ring: A Biography of Ring Lardner*. New York: Random House, 1977.

Laurel Raceway
Laurel, MD

Laurel opened in 1911 and was a well-known, successful race track until World War II. However, the track was in financial trouble in 1947, when the Maryland Jockey Club bought it. The club sold it to Morris Schapiro in 1950, and Laurel prospered almost immediately. Schapiro built a new $3 million clubhouse and turf club, refurbished the grandstand, and on October 18, 1952, he inaugurated the Washington, DC, International, now one of the top races in the world. Horses from 23 countries, including New Zealand, Singapore, and the Soviet Union have run in the International. In 1954, when Queen Elizabeth's horse, Landau, was entered, it became the first race outside of Great Britain in which a rider wore the royal colors. Another major race is the Laurel Futurity. Laurel has a 9-furlong main course and an 8-furlong turf course. It seats 19,400 people.

Address: P.O. Box 130, Laurel, MD 20707 (301) 725–0400

Law, Sports

Sports law involves several special areas, which are not necessarily related to one another. Some of the issues are much older than modern sports, such as tort liability and contract law. Others have arisen more recently, including the conflict between drug testing and invasion of privacy, player-agent relations, and antitrust litigation. In 1972 the Boston College School of Law offered the first sports law course, "Regulation of Professional Athletics." Sports law programs are now offered by more than 40 colleges and universities, and several firms specialize in the field. The Sports Lawyers Association, which has a membership of 400, has developed a code of ethics for sports lawyers.

Further Reading: Weistart, John C., and Cym H. Lowell. *The Law of Sports*. Indianapolis: Bobbs-Merrill, 1979.

Lawn Bowling

Modern lawn bowling is derived from a medieval game called *boule* in France and bowls in England, in which a bowler attempted to roll a ball as near as possible to a target—a line in the dirt, an upright stake, or another ball. Those games, in turn, may have sprung from kegels, a German sport dating at least to the third century A.D., in which the target was a single pin that had to be knocked down by the ball. Lawn bowling is different from pin bowling in that the first ball rolled, the jack, becomes the target, and other bowlers attempt to come as close to it as possible. ("Jack" is a shortening of *jacut lapidum*, the Latin for "throwing the stone," because the first balls were made of stone.)

The sport was fairly widespread in colonial Virginia; a Williamsburg bowling green was built in 1632, and in 1670 a Colonel Hoomes built a green in what is now Bowling Green. It spread to other colonies in the 18th century. A bowling green was advertised in 1714 in the *Boston News Letter*. In 1732, a green was established at what is now Battery Park in New York City. Lawn bowling seems to have become dormant for most of the 19th century—the New York green went out of use about 1820—but it was revived in the last quarter of the century. The Dunellen (NJ) Bowling Club was organized in 1879, and the sport soon spread into other areas of northern New Jersey and metropolitan New York City. Buffalo also became a lawn bowling center. Teams from the United States and Canada took part in an international tournament there in 1914, and on July 27, 1915, the American Lawn Bowls Association was formed at a meeting in Buffalo by clubs from Boston, Brooklyn, and Buffalo.

The first U.S. national championships, for rinks (four-man teams), were held in 1918. The doubles event was added in 1920, singles in 1929. Another major tournament, the Open National Marl, began at St. Petersburg, FL in 1926. And in 1957 the Spalding Inn of Whitefield, NH established a new round-robin tournament for the Spalding Inn Trophy. Canada's major lawn bowling championship is the Interprovincial Match between teams from Ontario and Quebec, inaugurated in 1950. The governing bodies are Lawn Bowls Canada, formerly the Canadian Lawn Bowling Council and the Canadian Ladies Lawn Bowling Council.

Addresses: American Lawn Bowls Association, 8710 Tern Avenue, Fountain Valley, CA 92708 (714) 962–6820; Lawn Bowls Canada, 1600 James Naismith Drive, Gloucester, Ontario, Canada K1B 5N4 (613) 748–5643

Lawn Tennis
See TENNIS.

League Alliance
Baseball

After the National League's first season, 1876, non-league baseball clubs planned a convention in Pittsburgh in February of 1877. William L. Hulbert, league president, A. G. Mills, and Albert G. Spalding then worked out a plan under which outside teams could become affiliated with the league. Under the plan, affiliate members agreed to respect other teams' contracts, to not play any team that used a player expelled from another team, and to notify the league when signing or releasing any player. Nevertheless, 17 non-league clubs formed the International Association of Professional Base Ball Players (IAPBBP).

About 13 teams affiliated themselves with the National League in 1877, and the plan became known as the "League Alliance." Rules for admission became stricter. As in the league itself, only one team was admitted from any one city, two negative votes could keep a team out of the alliance, and games between league teams and non-alliance teams were not allowed in cities represented in the alliance. The League Alliance was abolished in 1883.

See also MINOR LEAGUES.

League Championship Series (LCS)
Baseball

When the American and National Leagues expanded to 12 teams apiece in 1969, each of them split into two divisions, and the League Championship Series between division champions was established to determine the league pennant winner. Originally best-of-five, the LCS became a best-of-seven series in 1985.

League of American Wheelmen (LAW)

Soon after the "safety bike" made bicycling popular, the LAW was formed in 1880 by 29 bicycle clubs meeting in Newport, RI. One of the chief purposes of the new organization was to share information on road networks that could be used for cycling. Membership reached 18,000 in 1890 and then shot up to 102,600 in 1898. The LAW held the first national championship race, at 1 mile, at its 1882 convention in Boston. It was won by George M. Hendee. The following year, the association became the de facto governing body for most bicycle racing in the United States.

In the 1890s, the LAW became involved in two controversies. Some of its southern affiliates withdrew, or threatened to withdraw, because the league had black members. At its 1894 convention, the delegates voted to ban blacks from membership rather than lose southern members. In 1898, a National Cycling Association was formed, primarily to promote racing. Professional bicycle racing was a popular and lucrative sport, and Sunday was a big day for it. The LAW opposed racing on Sunday. In 1900, the league gave up its involvement in racing in order to concentrate on touring.

Address: 6707 Whitestone Road, Suite 209, Baltimore, MD 21207 (301) 944–3399

Leahy, "Frank" Francis W. (1908–1973)
Football
Born August 27, 1908, O'Neill, NE; died June 21, 1973; National Football Foundation Hall of Fame

Leahy was a starting tackle as a junior for Notre Dame's unbeaten 1929 team, but a knee injury that kept him from playing in 1930 might have been the best thing that ever happened to him. When he went to the Mayo Clinic for an operation on the knee, he shared a room with Coach Knute Rockne, who discussed football strategy and tactics with him during the entire stay. Rockne then invited Leahy to come to all the team's practices that fall to learn more about football. He learned well. Leahy's winning percentage of .864, on 107 victories, 13 defeats, and 9 ties, is second only to Rockne's among coaches with ten or more seasons.

He served as a college line coach for eight years, the last six of them at Fordham under "Sleepy Jim" Crowley, a former member of Notre Dame's Four Horsemen, and became head coach at Boston College in 1939. His 1939 team won nine games while losing one, and lost to Clemson 6–3 in the Cotton Bowl. In

1940, Boston College was undefeated in ten games, and upset Tennessee 19–13 in the Sugar Bowl. Leahy then returned to Notre Dame and had a second consecutive unbeaten season, with one tie in nine games. In 1942, he installed the T-formation, replacing Rockne's "Notre Dame box" formation. The team was 7–2–2 that season, and in 1943 the Fighting Irish went 9–1–0.

After two years in the U.S. Navy, Leahy resumed coaching at Notre Dame and had four straight undefeated seasons, with 37 wins and 2 ties. One of the ties was a 0–0 game against undefeated Army in 1946. The other was a 14–14 game against Southern California in 1948. Notre Dame slumped to a 4–4–1 record in 1950, went 7–2–1 in each of the next two seasons, then had a 9–0–1 record in 1953. That was Leahy's last season. Suffering from pancreatitis, he collapsed during halftime of one game that season, and retired when the season was over.

Further Reading: Twombly, Wells. *Shake Down the Thunder: The Official Biography of Notre Dame's Frank Leahy.* Radnor, PA: Chilton, 1974.

Le Colisee
See QUEBEC COLISEUM.

Liberty Bowl
Football Game

The Liberty Bowl was first played on December 19, 1959, in Philadelphia. The game moved to Atlantic City in 1964, and since 1965 has been in Memphis, where it's played in a stadium also called the Liberty Bowl. In 1988, the Liberty Bowl Committee decided that one of the three service academies (Army, Navy, or Air Force) would be given one of the berths beginning with the 1989 game.

Liberty Bowl Results

1959	Penn State 7, Alabama 0
1960	Penn State 41, Colorado 12
1961	Syracuse 15, Miami (FL) 14
1962	Oregon State 6, Villanova 0
1963	Mississippi State 16, North Carolina State 12
1964	Utah 32, West Virginia 6
1965	Mississipi 13, Auburn 7
1966	Miami (FL) 14, Virginia Tech 7
1967	North Carolina State 14, Georgia 7
1968	Mississippi 34, Virginia Tech 17
1969	Colorado 47, Alabama 33
1970	Tulane 17, Colorado 3
1971	Tennessee 14, Arkansas 13
1972	Georgia Tech 31, Iowa State 30
1973	North Carolina State 31, Kansas 18
1974	Tennessee 7, Maryland 3
1975	Southern California 20, Texas A & M 0
1976	Alabama 36, UCLA 6
1977	Nebraska 21, North Carolina 17
1978	Missouri 20, Louisiana State 15
1979	Penn State 9, Tulane 6
1980	Purdue 28, Missouri 25
1981	Ohio State 31, Navy 28
1982	Alabama 21, Illinois 15
1983	Notre Dame 19, Boston College 18
1984	Auburn 21, Arkansas 15
1985	Baylor 21, Louisiana State 7
1986	Tennessee 21, Minnesota 14
1987	Georgia 20, Arkansas 17
1988	Indiana 34, South Carolina 10
1989	Mississippi 42, Air Force 29
1990	Air Force 23, Ohio State 11

Lieberman, Nancy (1958–   )
Basketball
Born July 1, 1958, Brooklyn, NY

As a schoolgirl, the red-haired Lieberman took the A train to play basketball with black youths on Harlem playgrounds. She won their respect and two nicknames, "Flame" and "Big Red." While still in high school, she was chosen for the U.S. Olympic team that won a Silver Medal in 1976. At Old Dominion University, she was an All-American in 1978, 1979, and 1980. Old Dominion won national collegiate championships in 1979 and 1980, and Lieberman was awarded the Broderick Trophy as the outstanding woman college player of the year both seasons.

She was also selected for the Olympic team in 1980, but the United States boycotted the Games because of the Soviet Union's invasion of Afghanistan. Lieberman was one of the few athletes who supported the boycott. She became a professional with the Dallas Diamonds of the Women's Basketball League for the 1980–81 season, and scored 814 points in 36 games for a 22.6 average. Dallas lost to Nebraska in the league's championship series. In eight playoff games, Lieberman scored 176 points, 22.0 per game. The WBL folded after that season; Lieberman played in men's summer leagues and helped tennis great Martina Navratilova train. In 1987 she joined the Washington Generals, the team that plays against the Harlem Globetrotters on their tours. The only woman on the squad, she married teammate Tim Cline in 1988.

Limit Agreement
Baseball

Complaining about escalating major league salaries, owners of baseball teams in the National League and

American Association appointed a committee to solve the problem in 1885. Meeting in August at Saratoga, NY, the committee drew up a fairly simple plan under which no player would be paid more than $2,000 a season. The plan was approved by both leagues in October.

It didn't work simply because owners didn't abide by it. In one of the most flagrant violations of the Limit Agreement, King Kelly of Boston signed for the $2,000 in 1887, but the team paid him an additional $3,000 for the use of his picture in their advertising. Many other players were paid additional money under the table or given bonuses for specific types of of behavior. (Unlike the modern incentive payments, based on athletic performance, bonuses were more likely to be awarded for avoiding alcohol for a specific period.)

Albert G. Spalding later released figures showing that the 64 best players in the National League averaged $2,670 a season in 1889, well above the supposed limit. The failure of the Limit Agreement ultimately led to adoption of the Classification Plan in 1889.

See also CLASSIFICATION PLAN.

Little Brown Jug
Harness Racing

The oldest race in the Triple Crown of pacing, the Little Brown Jug was established in 1946. It is run at the Delaware (OH) County Fair in September in 1-mile heats.

Little League
Baseball

In 1939, Carl Stotz of Williamsport, PA and two of his friends found three local sponsors—a dairy, a lumber company, and a pretzel manufacturer—to outfit three baseball teams for boys. The first official game was played on June 6. The Little League, as they decided to call it, spread rapidly after World War II. The first World Series was played in Williamsport in 1947, and by 1951 there were more than 150,000 players; that grew to more than 1.6 million in 1966, and there are now more than 2.5 million players worldwide.

Originally organized for boys 9 through 12 years of age, Little League baseball now has programs in a variety of age groups. The Senior League, for 13- to 15-year-olds, began in 1961. There are now about 3,500 leagues, with an annual World Series in Kissimmee, FL. The Big League, for ages 16 through 18, was inaugurated in 1968, with a World Series in Ft. Lauderdale, FL. Junior League baseball was established in 1979 as a transitional program for 13-year-

olds. The Junior League World Series is played in Taylor, MI. Little Leaguers play on a diamond with 60-foot base paths, but the other leagues play on regulation 90-foot diamonds.

In 1972, the parents of a Hoboken, NJ girl filed suit against the Little League because their daughter wasn't allowed to play. The National Organization for Women (NOW) intervened and made it a class action suit for girls 8 to 12. On November 8, 1973, an examination officer ruled that the Little League should admit girls. The Little League appealed. On March 29, 1974, the State Superior Court of New Jersey ruled, on a 2–1 vote, in favor of NOW. The Little League at first filed an appeal of that decision, but then withdrew the appeal; on June 12, 1974, girls were allowed to play Little League baseball for the first time. Since then, the organization has introduced Little League Softball for girls 9–12 and Senior League Softball for girls 13–15, both in 1974. Big League Softball, for girls 16–18, was added in 1980. Each has a World Series, in Kalamazoo, MI for Little League and Senior League, and in Ft. Lauderdale, FL for Big League.

See also BABE RUTH BASEBALL; PONY BASEBALL.

Lombardi, Vincent T. (1913–1970)
Football
Born June 11, 1913, Brooklyn, NY; died September 3, 1970; Pro Football Hall of Fame

A complex man, often misunderstood because of his statement, "Winning isn't everything. It's the only thing," Lombardi forged some of the greatest teams in football history as coach of the Green Bay Packers. In his book, *Distant Replay*, (1985), former Packers guard Jerry Kramer wrote of Lombardi, "He united us, initially, in our fear of him, our hatred for him." But on the next page he says, "We loved each other after we won. We loved Lombardi, too. We saw through him, and loved what we found."

Lombardi was a guard at Fordham, one of the Seven Blocks of Granite, in 1935 and 1936. As offensive coach with the New York Giants beginning in 1954, Lombardi created a powerful offense, using single-wing blocking out of the T-formation. During his five years there, New York won four division titles, and in 1956 they beat the Chicago Bears 47–7 for the National Football League championship.

In 1959, he became the Packers' general manager and head coach. The team had won only one game in 1958, and hadn't had a winning season since 1947. But in his first team meeting, he told the players, "I have never been on a losing team, gentlemen, and I don't intend to start now." He didn't. The Packers won 7 of their 12 games that year. In

1960, they won the western division title, but lost 17–13 to the Philadelphia Eagles in the NFL championship game. Over the next two seasons, they won 24 games while losing only 4, and they beat the Giants in the title game both times, 37–0 in 1961 and 16–7 in 1962.

After missing the playoffs in 1963 and 1964, the Packers won three consecutive championship games. (Starting with the 1965 season, the championship game was played in January of the following year, e.g., January 1966). They beat the Cleveland Browns 23–12 in 1966, the Dallas Cowboys 34–27 in 1967, and Dallas, again, 21–17 in 1968. The 1968 game was a classic. It was played in Green Bay, with the temperature as low as 13 degrees below zero. The Cowboys were winning 17–14, but the Packers had the ball on the Dallas 1-yard line with 13 seconds to play. It was third down, but Green Bay had no time-outs left and wouldn't have had time to get the field goal team out if they failed to score. Nevertheless, Lombardi called for a quarterback sneak rather than the field goal that would have sent the game into overtime, and Bart Starr scored on the play.

The Packers won the first two Super Bowls, beating the Kansas City Chiefs 35–10 in 1967 and the Oakland Raiders 33–14 in 1968. Lombardi retired as head coach after the second Super Bowl victory, remaining as general manager, but after a year out of coaching, he went to the Washington Redskins in 1969. He began to turn that team around, too, from a 5–9–0 record the previous year to 7–5–2. But he was diagnosed as having cancer in 1970, and he died shortly after the season started.

In his ten years of coaching, Lombardi's teams won 96 regular-season games, lost 34, and tied 6, a .728 percentage. Even more remarkable, they won 9 out of 10 playoff games.

Further Reading: Kramer, Jerry, editor. *Lombardi: Winning Is the Only Thing.* Cleveland: World, 1970; Lombardi, Vince, with W. C. Heinz. *Run to Daylight.* New York: Dunlap, 1967; O'Brien, Michael. *Vince: A Personal Biography of Vince Lombardi.* New York: William Morrow, 1987.

Lombardi Award
Football

Given by the Rotary Club of Houston, TX, this award is given to the outstanding interior lineman in college football. It is named for Vince Lombardi.

1970	Jim Stillwagon, Ohio State
1971	Walt Patulski, Notre Dame
1972	Rich Glover, Nebraska
1973	John Hicks, Ohio State
1974	Randy White, Maryland
1975	Lee Roy Selmon, Oklahoma
1976	Wilson Whitley, Houston
1977	Ross Browner, Notre Dame
1978	Bruce Clark, Penn State
1979	Brad Budde, Southern California
1980	Hugh Green, Pittsburgh
1981	Kenneth Sims, Texas
1982	Dave Rimington, Nebraska
1983	Dean Steinkuhler, Nebraska
1984	Tony Degrate, Texas
1985	Tony Casillas, Oklahoma
1986	Cornelius Bennett, Arkansas
1987	Chris Spielman, Ohio State
1988	Tracy Rocker, Auburn
1989	Percy Snow, Michigan State
1990	Chris Zorich, Notre Dame

Lombardi Trophy
Football

Beginning with Super Bowl V, in January of 1972, the permanent trophy presented to the winning team has been known as the Vince Lombardi Memorial Trophy, after the coach whose Green Bay Packer teams won the first two Super Bowls. For the first three Super Bowls, it was called the NFL-AFL Championship Trophy; for the fourth, it was the NFL Championship Trophy.

For trophy winners, see SUPER BOWL.

Long Island, NY
See NEW YORK, NY.

Long Jump

Formerly known in North America as the broad jump, the long jump was taken from the Scottish Highland, or Caledonian Games, but it's an old enough idea. Allegedly, Chionis of Sparta jumped 7.05 meters, or about 23 feet 1½ inches, in 656 B.C., a mark that wasn't matched in modern times until 1874. American Indians often competed in long jumping, and so did the French *coureurs des bois* in Canada during the 17th century and American frontiersman during the 18th century. When the first U.S. national championships were held in 1876, there were both standing and running long jumps, and both events were on the Olympic Games program from 1900 through 1912.

The first man to jump more than 24 feet was W. J. M. Newburn of Ireland in 1898. Edward Gourdin of the United States surpassed 25 feet in 1921, and Silvio Cator of Haiti went beyond 26 feet in 1928. Jesse Owens of the United States set a world record of 26 feet 8¼ inches in 1935, and that mark stood for 25 years until Ralph Boston of the United States broke 27 feet in 1960.

Then came the most incredible leap of all, at the 1968 Olympic Games in Mexico, when Bob Beamon jumped 29 feet, 2¼ inches. No one else had ever jumped more than 28 feet. During the 1980s, Carl Lewis did jump more than 28 feet several times, but no one has approached Beamon's record.

See also BEAMON, BOB.

Longboat, Tom (1888–1949)
Running

Born 1888, Onondaga Reserve, Toronto; died January 10, 1949; Canada Sports Hall of Fame

One of the greatest runners in the early part of the century, Longboat ran his first "marathon"—actually a 20-mile race—on Thanksgiving Day, 1906, when he was 18. His winning time of 1 hour 49 minutes 25 seconds was so incredible that the timer thought his watch had stopped. Less than a week later, Longboat won a 15-mile race by more than 500 yards over his nearest competitor. In the 1907 Boston Marathon, Longboat took the lead at the start and ran away from the field, winning in 2:24:20.4, more than 5 minutes better than the old record. Clarence DeMar, a perennial winner at Boston, said in 1947, "If Longboat had today's race conditions—macadam roads and no accompanying cars—he might have set a 2:06 record for the old 24½-mile course."

Longboat ran for Canada in the 1908 Olympics, winning a Bronze Medal in the marathon, although the United States challenged his amateur status. Immediately after the Olympics, Longboat turned professional. Displaying one of the many medals he'd won as an amateur, he said, "I've been running for these things long enough. Now I'm after all the money I can get. I'll run for a price against anything with two legs." During the next several years, he raced against many of the top professional runners in the world and won much more often than he lost.

Los Angeles, CA

Baseball The Brooklyn Dodgers moved to Los Angeles in 1958, creating a furor in New York City. But they were moving to what was then the third largest metropolitan area in the country, and they had no competition in that market, after having shared the New York market with both the Giants and the Yankees. And, while they couldn't find a good site in New York for a stadium, they were given 300 acres in downtown Los Angeles, and the city and county agreed to pay about $5 million to develop the site for construction. In 1959, the Dodgers won the National League pennant and the World Series, beating the Chicago White Sox. They also won pen-

nants in 1963, 1965, 1966, 1974, 1977, 1978, 1981, and 1988, and the World Series in 1963, 1965, 1981 and 1988.

Basketball The Minneapolis Lakers moved to Los Angeles before the 1960–61 season, making the National Basketball Association truly national. During the 1960s, the Lakers lost seven times in the NBA championship playoff, six times to the Boston Celtics and once to the New York Knicks. They finally won the championship in 1972, beating the Knicks. The Lakers were also NBA champions in 1980, 1982, 1985, 1987 and 1988.

Los Angeles got a second NBA team in 1984, when the Clippers moved from San Diego.

Football There was a Los Angeles franchise in the first American Football League in 1926, the league's one year of existence. The team was called the Wildcats because its star player was halfback George "Wildcat" Wilson. The second American Football League lasted two seasons, 1936 and 1937. The Los Angeles Bulldogs were in the league during its second season and won the AFL championship that year.

The Cleveland Rams moved to Los Angeles in 1946 and signed two black players from the University of California at Los Angeles, Kenny Washington and Woody Strode. They were the first blacks to play in the NFL since 1933. The Rams won the 1951 NFL championship by beating the Cleveland Browns 24–17. The Rams won seven consecutive western division titles in the National Football Conference, 1973 through 1979, but won the NFL championship only once, in 1979, and then lost to the Pittsburgh Steelers, 31–19, in the Super Bowl.

Los Angeles got a second NFL team in 1985, when the Raiders moved from Oakland.

When the the American Football League was organized in 1960, the Los Angeles Chargers were in the league. However, the Chargers moved to San Diego after one season.

Hockey The Los Angeles Kings joined the National Hockey League as an expansion franchise in 1968.

See also DODGER STADIUM; LOS ANGELES FORUM; LOS ANGELES MEMORIAL COLISEUM.

Los Angeles Christmas Festival Bowl
Football

Southern California beat Missouri 20–7 on December 25, 1924, the only time this bowl game was played.

Los Angeles Forum

Jack Kent Cooke bought the Los Angeles Lakers of the National Basketball Association in 1965. The following year he bought an expansion franchise in the National Hockey League and named his team the Kings. Both teams played in the Los Angeles Sports Arena, an adjunct to the Los Angeles Memorial Coliseum, but in 1967 Cooke built his own arena, the Fabulous Forum, as he named it. Cooke sold the teams in 1979, and the word "Fabulous" was dropped from the forum's title. However, the Kings' ownership usually refers to the arena as the Great Western Forum, while the Lakers simply call it the Forum.

Los Angeles Memorial Coliseum
Los Angeles, CA

Originally built in 1923, the Coliseum was extensively remodeled and expanded to 105,000 seats for the 1932 Olympic Games. Temporarily known as Olympic Stadium, it boasted probably the finest running track in the world. The Coliseum, since scaled back to about 95,000 seats, is now the home field for the University of Southern California and the Los Angeles Raiders of the National Football League. It was also the home of the Los Angeles Rams from 1946 through 1979, after which the Rams moved to Anaheim Stadium.

After the Brooklyn Dodgers moved to Los Angeles in 1958, they played in the Coliseum for four seasons while their own stadium was being built. In their first game, they drew 78,672 fans, still a record crowd for a regular-season baseball game. The 1959 World Series between the Dodgers and the Chicago White Sox set records for single-game attendance, 92,706, and total Series attendance, 420,784. The Coliseum was not well-suited for baseball, however. To create a left-field fence, the Dodgers installed a 42-foot-high screen from the foul line into left center field, and the home run distance down the line was only 251 feet. It was 333 feet down the right-field line and 420 feet to center field.

Louis, Joe (Joseph Louis Barrow) (1914–1981)
Boxing

Born May 13, 1914, Lafayette, AL; died April 12, 1981; Boxing Hall of Fame

The second black heavyweight champion, Louis was known as the "Brown Bomber." Columnist Red Smith wrote "Louis may very well have been the greatest fighter who ever lived. . . . At the top of his game he would have outboxed Rocky Marciano and perhaps taken him out. . . ."

Louis was carefully groomed by his black managers, Julian Black and John Roxborough, to be acceptable to the public at large, unlike the first black heavyweight champion, Jack Johnson. He was never to have his picture taken with a white woman, never

to enter a nightclub alone, never to gloat in victory, and he was to fight and live cleanly. In less than a year as a professional fighter, from July 4, 1934, to May 7, 1935, he won all 22 of his fights, 18 of them by knockout. His first big match was against former heavyweight champion Primo Carnera of Italy, on June 25, 1935, in Yankee Stadium. Louis knocked out Carnera in the sixth round. Italy had invaded Abyssinia, a black African nation, the year before, and Louis's victory was widely hailed as a symbolic victory for Emperor Haile Selassie of Abyssinia over Italy's Benito Mussolini.

On September 24, Louis knocked out another former champion, Max Baer, in the fourth round. After two more knockout victories, he had another symbolic confrontation, with former champion Max Schmeling of Germany. Although Schmeling was not a Nazi, he was used as an instrument of propaganda for Nazism. Having beaten a symbol of Fascist Italy, Louis was now being asked to beat a symbol of Hitler's Germany. But on June 19, 1936, Schmeling knocked out Louis in the 12th round. It was his first defeat.

Louis quietly went back to work. He knocked out yet another former champion, Jack Sharkey, in the third round on August 18, and won ten more fights in the next six months, nine of them by knockout. (Five of these fights were considered exhibitions.) On June 22, 1937, he became the first black heavyweight champion in 23 years by knocking out James J. Braddock in the eighth round in Chicago. He defended his title three times in 1937 and 1938 before a rematch with Schmeling on June 22, 1938. Louis avenged his only loss by battering the German fighter with a barrage of punches, knocking him out in just 2 minutes and 4 seconds of the first round. To most Americans, it was an impressive victory over the myth of Aryan supremacy.

After defending his title 16 times, including 15 knockouts, Louis enlisted in the U.S. Army in February 1942. He had one championship fight as a soldier, knocking out Abe Simon in the 13th round on March 27, and he donated his purse to the Army Emergency Relief Organization. For the rest of the war, he was used to help build morale among soldiers, both black and white. In 1943, he starred in a Frank Capra propaganda film, *The Black Soldier*, and he appeared in newsreels more often than any officer. Louis was awarded the Legion of Merit in 1945 for his wartime services.

On June 19, 1946, Louis had a long-awaited rematch with Billy Conn, who was the only fighter who had come close to winning the title from him. In their first fight, June 18, 1941, Conn had put on a marvelous display of boxing and was ahead on points when Louis knocked him out in the 13th round. The rematch was anticlimactic. Conn was out of shape and rusty, and Louis knocked him out in the eighth round. He defended his title three more times before announcing his retirement from the ring on March 1, 1949. He had held the heavyweight championship for 12 years and defended it 25 times, both records for any weight division.

Unfortunately, Louis learned in 1950 that he owed nearly $1 million in back taxes. He had theoretically earned nearly $5 million in the ring. But the federal tax rate at that time was 88 percent on annual earnings of $200,000 or more, and the Internal Revenue Service disallowed a number of deductions that Louis had claimed. He was forced to come out of retirement to try to pay his tax bill, but he was no longer the fighter he had been. On September 27, 1950, he lost a 15-round decision to Ezzard Charles in a championship fight. He then won eight matches against lesser opponents before being knocked out by Rocky Marciano in the eighth round on October 26, 1951. Louis retired again, and Marciano went on to win the championship a year later. In 70 professional fights, Louis had 67 victories, 53 of them by knockouts.

Further Reading: Edmonds, Anthony. *Joe Louis*. Grand Rapids, MI: Wm. B. Eerdmans, 1973; Louis, Joe. *Joe Louis: My Life*. New York: Harcourt Brace Jovanovitch, 1978; Mead, Chris. *Champion—Joe Louis: Black Hero in White America*. New York: Charles Scribner's Sons, 1985.

Louisiana Superdome
New Orleans, LA

The original cost estimate for the Superdome was $35 million, but by the time it opened in 1975 the price tag was $173 million. The domed stadium is 273 feet high and has a diameter of 680 feet. It seats 69,105 for football and nearly 19,000 for basketball. The Superdome is the home stadium for the New Orleans Saints of the National Football League and was formerly the home of the New Orleans Jazz of the National Basketball Association. The Jazz began as an expansion franchise in 1976 and moved to Utah in 1979.

Louisville, KY

Baseball A Louisville team was a founding member of the National League in 1876, but lasted just two seasons. From 1882 through 1891, Louisville had a team in the American Association; it won the 1890 pennant. When the Association folded after the 1891 season, Louisville moved into the National League again, remaining until 1899, when the League cut down from 12 to 8 teams.

Hank Luisetti of Stanford revolutionized basketball by making the one-hand shot a standard offensive weapon. He was College Player of the Year in 1937 and 1938. Courtesy of the Basketball Hall of Fame

Football The Louisville Brecks were in the National Football League in 1922 and 1923, and the Louisville Colonels played in the NFL in 1926.

LPBT
See LADIES PROFESSIONAL BOWLERS TOUR.

LPGA
See LADIES PROFESSIONAL GOLF ASSOCIATION.

Luge

The luge (French for "sled") developed out of the one-person toboggan. A sport similar to luging, called "skeleton toboggan," was on the Winter Olympic program in 1928 and again in 1948. However, the modern luge was created in the early 1950s, and the Fédération Internationale de Luge was organized in 1953 to conduct international competition. Although the AAU began national championships in 1972, the United States didn't have a quality luge track until one was built at Lake Placid, NY for the

1980 Winter Olympics. Since then, the sport has grown rapidly. U.S. lugers won five medals on the World Cup circuit in 1987, including a first-place finish by Bonny Warner, who was third in the Cup standings that year. The U.S. Luge Association, formed in 1979, now governs the sport in this country. The governing body in Canada is the Canadian Amateur Bobsleigh and Luge Association.

Addresses: Canadian Amateur Bobsleigh and Luge Association, 1600 James Naismith Drive, Gloucester, Ontario, Canada K1B 5N4 (613) 748–5631; U.S. Luge Association, P.O. Box 651, Lake Placid, NY 12946 (518) 523–2071

See also BOBSLEDDING.

Luisetti, "Hank" Angelo S. (1916–   )
Basketball
Born June 16, 1916, San Francisco, CA; Basketball Hall of Fame.

Luisetti may not have been the first to use the running, one-handed shot in basketball, but he certainly made it famous, and revolutioned the sport in the process. He developed the shot in high school, and some of his teammates at Stanford University also began using it, though not as consistently or effectively as Luisetti himself. A sophomore in the 1935–36 season, he scored 416 points in 29 games and was named an All-American.

In December 1936, Stanford played at Madison Square Garden against Long Island University, which had won 43 consecutive games. So many people wanted to see the game that riot squads were called out to keep order in the streets near the Garden. Those who didn't get to buy tickets missed quite a show, with Luisetti scoring 15 points in a 45–31 win. Up until then, there were only two types of shots in basketball, the two-handed set shot and the layup. According to Luisetti's biographer, two years after the famous game in the Garden, "every school kid coming to an Eastern college was firing one-handed shots off his ears."

Luisetti was an All-American in 1937 and 1938, and set a collegiate record by scoring 1,596 points in his four-year career. He was the second college player to score 50 points in one game, in 1938, and in 1960 he was named to the Helms All-Time All-American team. Although known primarily for his shooting, the 6-foot-2 forward was also an excellent ball handler and passer and a good defensive player. After graduating from Stanford, Luisetti was an AAU All-American in 1941 and 1942.

MacArthur Bowl
Football

Named for General Douglas MacArthur, this bowl was donated by the National Football Foundation and Hall of Fame in 1959 as a trophy for the top college team in the country.

MacArthur Bowl Winners

1959	Syracuse
1960	Minnesota
1961	Alabama
1962	Southern California
1963	Texas
1964	Notre Dame
1965	Michigan State
1966	Notre Dame
	Michigan State (tie)
1967	Southern California
1968	Ohio State
1969	Texas
1970	Ohio State
	Texas (tie)
1971	Nebraska
1972	Southern California
1973	Notre Dame
1974	Southern California
1975	Oklahoma
1976	Pittsburgh
1977	Notre Dame
1978	Alabama
1979	Alabama
1980	Georgia
1981	Clemson
1982	Penn State
1983	Miami (FL)
1984	Brigham Young
1985	Oklahoma
1986	Penn State
1987	Miami (FL)
1988	Notre Dame
1989	Miami (FL)
1990	University of Colorado

Maccabiah Games

The quadrennial Maccabiah Games grew out of a speech by Dr. Max Nordau at the 1898 Zionist Congress, in which he called for a "Jewry of muscles." Later that year, the first Jewish Turnverein was organized in Austria. In 1903 the Jüdische Turner-schaft was founded as an organization of all Jewish gymnastic clubs. It was replaced in 1921 by the Maccabi World Union, which held the first Maccabiah Games in Tel Aviv in 1933. Nearly 400 athletes from 14 countries took part, and that increased to more than 1,700 participants in 1935. However, World War II and the Holocaust intervened. The third Maccabiah Games were not held until 1950 in Israel. Although the games were open to all Jewish athletes, not just members of Maccabiah clubs, there were only 800 participants because of the persecution of European Jews.

Since 1957, the Maccabiah Games have been held in Israel every four years. Nearly 5,000 athletes now compete in most of the Olympic events. In addition to the world games, European Maccabiah Games are held every two years and the Pan-American Maccabiah Games, inaugurated in 1966, have taken place every four years since 1983. North American Maccabiah Youth Games have been held quadrennially since 1982.

Mack, Connie (Cornelius McGillicuddy)
(1862–1956)
Baseball
Born December 22, 1862, East Brookfield, MA; died January 8, 1956; Baseball Hall of Fame

Mack built two dynasties and disassembled both of them because his Philadelphia Athletics had chronic attendance and financial problems. He managed the team for 50 seasons, mainly because he also owned it. Although he won nine American League pennants and five World Series, he also finished last 17 times and had a losing record for his career.

A major-league catcher for 11 seasons, Mack was player-manager of Pittsburgh's National League team from 1894 through 1896, then managed Milwaukee in the minor Western League. When the Western became the American League in 1901, Mack was given 25 percent of its new team in Philadelphia, where he also became manager. The Athletics won the pennant in 1902, when there was no World Series, and they won both the pennant and the Series in 1905. His first dynasty began in 1910, when the A's won the first of four pennants in five years; they also won three of four World Series, in 1910, 1911, and 1913. But financial problems forced him to sell three quarters of his "$100,000" infield—shortstop Dave Bancroft, second baseman Eddie Collins, and

Connie Mack spent 11 seasons in the major leagues, but he's better known as manager of the Philadelphia Athletics for 50 years, 1901 through 1950. Courtesy of the National Baseball Library, Cooperstown, NY

third baseman "Home Run" Baker—and the team fell into last place in 1915 and stayed there for seven seasons.

The Athletics didn't challenge again until 1925, when they finished second to the Washington Senators, and they were also in second place in 1927 and 1928; then they won three straight pennants and two of three World Series. This time the Great Depression struck, and Mack once again sold his top players to raise cash. Al Simmons, Lefty Grove, Jimmy Foxx, and Mickey Cochrane, all now in the Baseball Hall of Fame, went to other teams by 1935, and the Athletics never again threatened to win a pennant while they were in Philadelphia. Mack gained majority control of the franchise in 1940. He retired after the 1950 season; his sons sold the team in 1954, and the Athletics were moved to Kansas City.

A quiet, soft-spoken man—in his 50 years of managing, he was never thrown out of a game—Mack always wore a suit and tie with a straw hat or derby. The sight of him standing on the top step of the dugout, gesturing with a scorecard to move his defensive players into new positions, was familiar to millions of baseball fans over two generations. Mack's overall managerial record was 3,776 victories and 4,025 defeats, both major-league records that will stand forever.

Madison Square Garden
New York, NY

The first Madison Square Garden didn't get that name until 1879. An abandoned railroad station between 26th and 27th Streets and Fourth and Madison Avenues, it was leased by P. T. Barnum in 1873 and rebuilt to become "Barnum's Monster Classical and Geological Hippodrome," which opened on April 27, 1874. After Barnum turned his show into a traveling circus, the lease was taken over by Patrick S. Gilmore, who renamed it Gilmore's Garden. Gilmore began holding boxing exhibitions in 1877. William K. Vanderbilt took over in 1879, renaming the building Madison Square Garden.

It was torn down in 1889 to make way for a new Madison Square Garden, designed by Stanford White. The 200- by 465-foot structure had a 320-foot tower topped by a copper statue of the goddess Diana. It included an 8,000-seat auditorium, a 1,200-seat theater, a 1,500-seat concert hall, a restaurant, and a roof garden where architect White was shot to death in 1906 by Harry K. Thaw.

Despite boxing, professional wrestling, six-day bicycle racing, the National Horse Show, and the Westminster Dog Show, the garden lost money annually until 1920, when boxing promoter Tex Rickard leased and refurbished it. Rickard quickly turned into a money-maker. When the owner, New York Life, announced that the building would be torn down in 1925 and replaced by an office building, Rickard decided to erect his own Madison Square Garden on Eighth Avenue between 49th and 50th Streets.

The third Garden was an 18,000-seat arena, built at a cost of about $6 million. A six-day bike race was held there in late November of 1925, followed by a professional basketball game and Paul Berlenbach's successful defense of his light-heavyweight title. The official opening was on December 15, when the New York Americans and Montreal Canadiens played a hockey game. Rickard also created the New York Rangers as a Garden-owned hockey team, and he added tennis and track and field as attractions.

Rickard died in 1929, and the Great Depression cut into Garden revenues. But in 1934, Ned Irish began promoting college basketball double-headers, which were immensely popular. The National Invitation Tournament, inaugurated in 1938, was the major event in college basketball until the early 1950s. Six-day racing died after 1937, but boxing and professional wrestling helped pick up the slack even during World War II. Immediately after the war, Irish organized the New York Knickerbockers, another Garden-owned team, in the new Basketball Association of America.

By 1960, the Madison Square Garden Corporation was looking for a new site. It settled on air rights over Penn Station, between Seventh and Eighth Avenues on 33rd Street. The arena, which seats 19,591 for basketball and 17,500 for hockey, opened February 11, 1968, as part of a complex including the 4,200-seat Felt Forum for boxing, a 48-lane bowling center, an art gallery, and a movie theater. The first sports event was a basketball game between the Knicks and the San Diego Rockets on February 14.

A $200 million renovation of Madison Square Garden began in September of 1989. Scheduled for completion in the fall of 1991, Felt Forum, now called the Paramount, will allow for more concerts and theatrical events, with seating increased to 6,000, while arena seating expands to 20,000.

Further Reading: Hollander, Zander. *Madison Square Garden: A Century of Sport and Spectacle on the World's Most Versatile Stage.* New York: Hawthorn Books, 1973.

Major Indoor Lacrosse League

Unique in that Kansas City businessmen Chris Fritz and Russ Cline own the entire league and all its teams, the MILL began play in 1987 with four teams: Baltimore Thunder, New Jersey Saints, Philadelphia Wings, and Washington Wave. In its second season, the New Jersey team moved to New York City, and the Detroit Turbos and New England Blazers joined the league. Players are paid on the basis of tenure, $100 a game for the first year, $150 the second, and $200 the third year. The season runs from January through March, and the teams play at major arenas such as the Spectrum in Philadelphia and the Meadowlands in New Jersey. In its third season, 1989, the league averaged about 6,000 spectators a game, well above its break-even point.

Major Indoor Soccer League (MISL)

The MISL had six teams in its first season, 1978–79: Cincinnati Kids, Cleveland Force, Houston Summit, New York Arrows, Philadelphia Fever, and Pittsburgh Spirit. The league went through a series of expansions and franchise moves, reaching a peak of 14 teams in the 1982–83 season. That dropped to 12 in 1983–84, went back up to 14 the following season, then went down to 12 again in 1985–86. That number held steady until 1987–88, when there were only 11 teams. That was a difficult season, as the Chicago, Cleveland, Minnesota, Pittsburgh, and St. Louis teams all suffered financial problems and were forced to drop out.

To save the league, the MISL Players' Association agreed to a four-year collective bargaining agreement, setting each team's total player salaries at a maximum of $850,000 and a minimum of $750,000 for 18 players. The league operated in 1988–89 with teams in Baltimore, Dallas, Los Angeles, San Diego, Tacoma, and Wichita. Los Angeles dropped out before the 1989–90 season, but the MISL added teams in Cleveland, Kansas City, and St. Louis.

Address: 7101 College Boulevard, Suite 320, Overland Park, KS 66210 (913) 339–6475.

Mallory Cup
Yachting

Donated in 1952 by the family of Clifford D. Mallory, first president of the North American Yacht Racing Union, this trophy is presented for the U.S. men's sailing championship. In various years, yachts have had crews of three or four. The skipper has to be a man, but women are allowed to be crew members.

Mann Cup
Lacrosse

Sir Donald Mann of the Canadian Northern Railway presented this cup in 1910 as a trophy for Canada's senior amateur lacrosse championship. Like the Stanley Cup, it was originally a challenge trophy; that is, a team could win the trophy only by challenging and beating the team that held it. In 1925, the Canadian Lacrosse Association took over the Mann Cup and began holding an annual tournament to determine the champion.

Man O' War
Horse Racing

The first Thoroughbred to become a matinee idol with the general public, Man O' War helped to popularize horse racing among people who only read about it in the newspapers. Raced for only two years, in 1919 and 1920, he won 19 of 20 starts and was pressed in only one of his victories. His only defeat, by the appropriately named Upset, came in the Sanford Memorial Stakes at Saratoga on August 13, 1919, when Man O' War had a bad start and was interfered with shortly afterward. He also carried 130 pounds to only 115 for the winner. Among his wins were the Preakness and Belmont, the last two legs of the Triple Crown in 1920. He didn't run in the Kentucky Derby, the first leg. In his next-to-last race, the Potomac Handicap on September 18, 1920, he carried the incredible weight of 138 pounds, yet won by 1½ lengths. Man O' War was put to stud at the age of four and died November 1, 1947. His son, War Admiral, won the Triple Crown in 1937.

Man O' War won 20 of 21 career starts, including the Preakness and Belmont in 1920. He didn't run in the Kentucky Derby. National Museum of Racing

Hall of Famer Mickey Mantle spent 18 seasons with the New York Yankees and was named the American League's Most Valuable Player in 1956, 1957, and 1962. Courtesy of the New York Yankees

Mantle, Mickey C. (1931–   )
Baseball
Born October 22, 1931, Spavinaw, OK; Baseball Hall of Fame

The greatest switch-hitter in history, Mantle holds the New York Yankees record for most games played, 2,401, despite several serious injuries. He played right field for the Yankees for part of the 1951 season and replaced the retired Joe DiMaggio in center field in 1952. Mantle led the American League in runs scored in 1954 with 129 and in home runs in 1955 with 37. He won the Triple Crown in 1956, when he batted .353 with 52 home runs and 130 runs batted in. He also led the league in runs scored, 132, and slugging percentage, .705.

After hitting .365 in 1957, Mantle led the league in home runs with 42 in 1958 and 40 in 1960. He hit 54 in 1961, but finished second to teammate Roger Maris, who set the major-league record with 61 that season. Mantle was named the American League's Most Valuable Player three times, in 1956, 1957, and 1962. Troubled by osteomyelitis caused by a high school football injury, a chronic knee injury suffered during the 1951 World Series, and a painful hip abscess, he retired after hitting only .237 in 1968. During his 18 seasons, the Yankees won 12 pennants and 7 World Series. Mantle holds career records for most World Series home runs (18), runs scored (42), and runs batted in (40). He had a career batting average of .298 with 536 home runs, 1,677 runs scored, and 1,509 runs batted in.

Maple Leaf Gardens
Toronto, Ontario

One sign that the National Hockey League was successful was the construction of Maple Leaf Gardens by Conn Smythe, owner of the Toronto Maple Leafs. The arena was budgeted at $1,200,000, but Smythe was unable to raise all the money, and the construction workers agreed to take stock in the Garden as partial payment of their wages. A capacity crowd of 13,542 fans saw the first game on November 12, 1931. The arena now has a capacity of 16,307.

Marathon

According to Greek legend, in 490 B. C. Pheidippides ran 25 miles to bring news of the Athenian victory at the Battle of Marathon to the elders in Athens. When the modern Olympic Games were inaugurated in Athens in 1896, the first marathon was run over approximately the same route; the surprise winner was Spiridon Loues, a Greek shepherd. The distance was 25 miles until the 1908 Olympics in London, when the original starting line was moved to Windsor Castle to give the royal family a better view, making the course 26 miles, 385 yards long. That has been the official distance ever since.

The first marathon in North America was run from Stamford, CT to Columbus Circle in New York City in October of 1896. The Boston Marathon, long the best-known and most prestigious of them all, was first held on April 19, 1897. John J. McDermott won both races. The marathon became a genuinely popular sport in the early 1970s, inspired both by the sudden craze in running for fitness and by Frank Shorter's victory in the 1972 Olympic race. Women began to be allowed to run the event about that time, and in 1984 the women's marathon was added to the Olympic program.

The New York Marathon, begun in 1970, and America's Marathon in Chicago, first held in 1985, now vie with Boston as the top North American events, and the Montreal International Marathon and San Francisco Marathon are not far behind. There are more than 500 marathons held worldwide, and a recent study showed that more than 700,000 Americans run at least one marathon a year.

Further Reading: Treadwell, Sandy. *The World of Marathons.* New York: Stewart, Tabori & Chang, 1987.

See also BOSTON MARATHON; NEW YORK MARATHON.

Marble, Alice (1913–)
Tennis
Born September 28, 1913, Plumas City, CA; International Tennis Hall of Fame

Marble won her first important tournaments in 1933, but her career suffered a setback in a tournament on Long Island when she was forced to play in both the semifinals and finals of the singles and doubles championships in one day—a total of 108 games in temperatures of over 100 degrees. She collapsed after losing in both finals, and the following year it was discovered that she had tuberculosis. However, she returned to win the national singles titles in 1936, 1938, 1939, and 1940. Marble also teamed with Sarah Palfrey to win the women's doubles four years in a row, 1937–40.

Marciano, Rocky (Rocco F. Marchegiano) (1923–1969)
Boxing
Born September 1, 1923, Brockton, MA; died August 31, 1969; Boxing Hall of Fame

The "Brockton Blockbuster" won all 49 of his professional fights, a remarkable 43 of them by knockout. Marciano didn't become a professional fighter until 1947. He won the heavyweight championship on September 23, 1952, by knocking out Jersey Joe Walcott in the 13th round at Philadelphia, and he defended the title six times before announcing his retirement on April 27, 1959. He was the only heavyweight champion ever to retire undefeated. The slow-moving Marciano stalked his opponents relentlessly, often taking many punches before managing to throw his almost inevitable knockout blow. Archie Moore, a clever boxer who was Marciano's last opponent, said ruefully after being knocked out in the ninth round, "This time the bull caught up to the matador."

Maris, Roger E. (1934–1985)
Baseball
Born September 10, 1934, Fargo, ND; died December 14, 1985

Although he hit only 275 career home runs, Maris in 1961 broke Babe Ruth's "sacred" record by hitting 61 home runs, one more than Ruth had hit in 1927. Commissioner Ford Frick declared that Maris's record would carry an asterisk because he played 162 games to Ruth's 154, but there is no asterisk in the record book. Both records are listed, Ruth's for a 154-game season, Maris's for a 162-game season.

It was a difficult season for Maris. A quiet, often moody person, he was troubled by all the attention from sportswriters and by the resentment of many Yankee fans, because he was locked in a race with his more popular teammate, Mickey Mantle, for most of the summer. At the end of July, Maris had 40 home runs, Mantle 39, and it looked as if both of them might break Ruth's record. However, Mantle was bothered by nagging injuries in September (he finished with 54 home runs), and Maris surged ahead. Despite the intense pressure, he tied the record on September 26 and broke it on the last day of the season, October 1, with a home run off Boston's Tracy Stallard.

A right-handed throwing, left-handed hitting outfielder who usually played right field because of his strong throwing arm, Maris began his major-league career with the Cleveland Indians in 1957. He was traded to the Kansas City Athletics during the 1958 season, and to the Yankees in 1960. He spent the 1967 and 1968 seasons with the St. Louis Cardinals. Maris had a career batting average of .260.

Market Square Arena
Indianapolis, IN
The city of Indianapolis built Market Square Arena for about $16 million. The 18,000-seat arena opened in 1976 under lease to a private company, Market Square Associates, which paid an additional $4 million for two parking garages under the arena. The home of the Indiana Pacers of the National Basketball Association, the arena has seating for 16,912.

Marshall, George Preston (1897–1969)
Basketball, Football
Born October 13, 1897, Grafton, WV; died August 9, 1969; Pro Football Hall of Fame

As the owner of the National Football League's Boston Braves, later the Boston Redskins, and then the Washington Redskins, Marshall used the same flamboyant promotional methods that made him a successful laundry owner. The Redskins were the first professional team to have their own band, taking part in extravagant halftime shows. When the Redskins signed Sammy Baugh of Texas Christian University in 1937, Marshall dubbed him "the Cowpoke Quarterback" and had him wear a cowboy hat and boots for a major press conference, the first of its kind to announce a player's signing. Marshall also proposed reorganizing the league into two divisions in 1933, with an annual championship game between the division titlists.

He first became involved in professional sports in 1926 when he organized the American Basketball League to showcase his team, the Washington Palace Five, and he hired Joe Carr, NFL commissioner, to head the league. The ABL folded in 1929. Three years later, Carr persuaded Marshall to buy a share of the new Boston franchise in the NFL. His partners bailed out when the team lost $46,000 in its first season, but Marshall held on, renaming the team the Redskins in 1933. The 1936 team won the eastern division title, but attendance was so poor that Marshall moved the championship game to the Polo Grounds in New York, where the Green Bay Packers beat the Redskins 21–6. Marshall transferred the franchise to Washington the following season. Between then and 1945, the Redskins won five more division titles and two NFL championships, in 1937 and 1942, but they became perennial also-rans after World War II.

Many writers suspect that Marshall was behind the NFL's unofficial ban on black players, which began in 1934. The color barrier was finally broken in 1946 by the Los Angeles Rams of the NFL and the Cleveland Browns of the new All-America Football Conference. As late as 1960, however, Marshall declared, "We'll start signing Negroes when the Harlem Globetrotters start signing whites." The Redskins finally signed black players in 1962 after the Kennedy Administration threatened to cancel the team's lease for federally owned D.C. Stadium.

Martinsville Speedway
Martinsville, VA

Originally a .526-mile dirt track that opened in 1947, Martinsville was paved in 1955. The track annually hosts two NASCAR Winston Cup races.

Address: P.O. Box 3311, Martinsville, VA 24115 (703) 956–3151

Massachusetts Game
Baseball

Also known as "town ball," this early form of baseball was popular throughout New England during the first half of the 19th century. The game used stakes for bases and had 60-foot base paths. The hitter stood halfway between home plate and first base, with the pitcher 30 feet away. Rules varied somewhat from one town to another; there were generally 10 to 14 players on a team, and runners were put out by being hit with a thrown ball while between bases. In at least one version of the game, the first team to score 100 runs was the winner. It

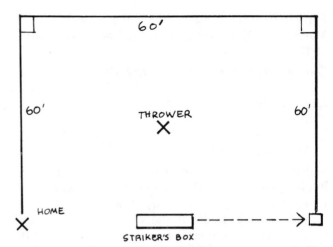

In the Massachusetts game, also known as "town ball," the striker stood halfway between home and first base.

had been supplanted by the New York Knickerbocker Club's modern game by 1860.

See also BASEBALL; NEW YORK GAME.

Masters Tournament
Golf

The Masters, inaugurated in 1934 at Bobby Jones's Augusta National Golf Club, is unusual among the major tournaments in that it is strictly invitational. A large number of players automatically receive invitations, including all previous Masters champions, the last five winners of the U.S. and British Opens and the PGA Championship, and the top 24 finishers in the previous Masters. Six touring professionals are chosen on the basis of their tournament records during the previous year, and several foreign players are invited, based on their play in international events. There are usually about 90 golfers in the starting field, which is cut down to the top 40 plus ties after the first two rounds.

Masters officials were widely criticized during the late 1960s and early 1970s because no black player was invited; Lee Elder became the first in 1975. Since then, two other blacks, Calvin Peete and Jim Thorpe, have played in the tournament.

Masters Winners

1934	Horton Smith
1935	Gene Sarazen
1936	Horton Smith
1937	Byron Nelson
1938	Henry Picard
1939	Ralph Guldahl
1940	Jimmy Demaret
1941	Craig Wood
1942–45	Not played
1946	Herman Keiser

1947	Jimmy Demaret			
1948	Claude Harmon			
1949	Sam Snead			
1950	Jimmy Demaret			
1951	Ben Hogan			
1952	Sam Snead			
1953	Ben Hogan			
1954	Sam Snead			
1955	Cary Middlecoff			
1956	Jack Burke, Jr.			
1957	Doug Ford			
1958	Arnold Palmer			
1959	Art Wall, Jr.			
1960	Arnold Palmer			
1961	Gary Player			
1962	Arnold Palmer			
1963	Jack Nicklaus			
1964	Arnold Palmer			
1965	Jack Nicklaus			
1966	Jack Nicklaus			
1967	Gay Brewer, Jr.			
1968	Bob Goalby			
1969	George Archer			
1970	Billy Casper			
1971	Charles Coody			
1972	Jack Nicklaus			
1973	Tommy Aaron			
1974	Gary Player			
1975	Jack Nicklaus			
1976	Ray Floyd			
1977	Tom Watson			
1978	Gary Player			
1979	Fuzzy Zoeller			
1980	Severiano Ballesteros			
1981	Tom Watson			
1982	Craig Stadler			
1983	Severiano Ballesteros			
1984	Ben Crenshaw			
1985	Bernhard Langer			
1986	Jack Nicklaus			
1987	Larry Mize			
1988	Sandy Lyle			
1989	Nick Faldo			
1990	Nick Faldo			
1991	Ian Woosnam			

Masters Tournament
Tennis

The Masters was inaugurated in 1970 as a round-robin tournament for the top six point winners on the Grand Prix circuit, with the six players also pairing off for doubles competition. Doubles competition was dropped in 1971, when the field was expanded to seven men. The format was changed again in 1972, with eight players divided into two groups for preliminary round-robin competition to pick four semifinalists. Doubles competition was restored in 1975.

The field was increased to 12 in 1983, and a straight elimination tournament was used, with the top four players getting first-round byes. The present format, adopted in 1986, again has eight players competing in round-robin preliminaries to determine four semifinalists. Also in 1986, the Masters doubles became a separate tournament, with eight teams qualifying on the basis of their Grand Prix finishes.

From 1970 through 1976, the Masters was played in December, but in 1977 the tournament was moved to January of the following year, and in 1986 it moved back to December. Thus, there was no tournament in 1977, and there were two in 1986.

Masters Singles Champions

1970	Stan Smith, United States
1971	Ilie Nastase, Rumania
1972	Ilie Nastase, Rumania
1973	Ilie Nastase, Rumania
1974	Guillermo Vilas, Argentina
1975	Ilie Nastase, Rumania
1976	Manuel Orantes, Spain
1978	Jimmy Connors, United States
1979	John McEnroe, United States
1980	Bjorn Borg, Sweden
1981	Bjorn Borg, Sweden
1982	Ivan Lendl, Czechoslovakia
1983	Ivan Lendl, Czechoslovakia
1984	John McEnroe, United States
1985	John McEnroe, United States
1986	Ivan Lendl, Czechoslovakia (Jan.)
1986	Ivan Lendl, Czechoslovakia (Dec.)
1987	Ivan Lendl, Czechoslovakia
1988	Boris Becker, West Germany
1989	Stefan Edberg, Sweden
1990	Andre Agassi, United States

Masterton Memorial Trophy
Hockey

Named for Bill Masterton, a Minnesota North Stars player who died of hockey injuries on January 15, 1968, this trophy is presented by the Professional Hockey Writers Association to "the National Hockey League player who best exemplifies the qualities of perseverance, sportsmanship and dedication to hockey." A donation of $1,500 is made to the Bill Masterton Scholarship Fund in the winner's name.

Masterton Trophy Winners

1968	Claude Provost, Montreal
1969	Ted Hampson, Oakland

1970	Pit Martin, Chicago
1971	Jean Ratelle, New York Rangers
1972	Bobby Clarke, Philadelphia
1973	Lowell MacDonald, Pittsburgh
1974	Henri Richard, Montreal
1975	Don Luce, Buffalo
1976	Rod Gilbert, New York Rangers
1977	Ed Westfall, New York Islanders
1978	Butch Goring, Los Angeles
1979	Serge Savard, Montreal
1980	Al MacAdam, Minnesota
1981	Blake Dunlop, St. Louis
1982	Glenn Reach, Colorado
1983	Lanny McDonald, Calgary
1984	Brad Park, Detroit
1985	Anders Hedberg, New York Rangers
1986	Charlie Simmer, Boston
1987	Doug Jarvis, Hartford
1988	Bob Bourne, Los Angeles
1989	Tim Kerr, Philadelphia
1990	Gordon Kluzak, Boston
1991	Dave Taylor, Los Angeles

Mathewson, "Christy" Christopher (1880–1925)
Baseball

Born August 12, 1880, Factoryville, PA; died October 7, 1925; Baseball Hall of Fame

A thinking man's pitcher, Mathewson left Bucknell University in 1899 to play professional baseball, and he joined the New York Giants in the National League during the following season. He had a unique pitch, the "fadeaway" or "reverse curve," now known as the screwball. Later in his career he developed another trick pitch that he called a "dry spitter," probably a knuckleball. In his first full season, 1901, Mathewson won 20 games, including five shutouts, for a seventh-place team. He pitched a no-hitter against St. Louis on July 15.

After a losing season in 1902, Mathewson won 30 games in 1903, 33 in 1904, and 31 in 1905. He pitched three shutouts against the Philadelphia Athletics in the Giants' five-game 1905 World Series victory, allowing just 14 hits and 1 walk while striking out 18 in 27 innings. Mathewson won 22 or more games in each of the next nine seasons, setting a 20th-century league record by winning 37 in 1908 and pitching 68 consecutive innings without giving up a walk in 1913. The Giants won three consecutive pennants, 1911–13, but lost all three World Series. Mathewson won only two while losing five Series games, despite a 1.51 earned run average.

Mathewson won only eight games in 1915 and was traded to Cincinnati to become player-manager during the 1916 season. He continued managing until entering the army in August 1918. His lungs were severely damaged by poison gas while serving in Europe, and he never completely recovered. Named president of the Boston Braves in 1923, he died of tuberculosis just before the 1925 World Series. In 19 seasons, Mathewson won 372 games, a National League record, and lost 187. He struck out 2,502 hitters while walking only 838 in 4,778 innings. His career earned run average was 2.13, fifth best of all time.

Mathias, "Bob" Robert B. (1930–)
Track and Field

Born November 17, 1930, Tulare, CA; National Track and Field Hall of Fame

At 17, Mathias was the youngest person ever to win the Olympic decathlon competition, in 1948, just two months after competing in the event for the first time, and he repeated this feat in 1952. He won all ten decathlons he entered between 1948 and 1956.

Maxwell Award
Football

Given by the Maxwell Football Club of Philadelphia to the nation's outstanding college football player, this award is named for Robert W. Maxwell, a guard at Swarthmore College who was a third-team All-American in 1905.

Maxwell Award Winners

1937	Clint Frank, Yale end
1938	Davey O'Brien, Texas Christian quarterback
1939	Nile Kinnick, Iowa halfback
1940	Tom Harmon, Michigan halfback
1941	Bill Dudley, Virginia halfback
1942	Paul Governali, Columbia quarterback
1943	Bob Odell, Pittsburgh halfback
1944	Tom Harmon, Michigan halfback
1945	Doc Blanchard, Army fullback
1946	Charlie Trippi, Georgia halfback
1947	Doak Walker, Southern Methodist halfback
1948	Chuck Bednarik, Pennsylvania center
1949	Leon Hart, Notre Dame end
1950	Reds Bagnell, Pennsylvania halfback
1951	Dick Kazmaier, Princeton halfback
1952	John Lattner, Notre Dame halfback
1953	John Lattner, Notre Dame halfback
1954	Ron Beagle, Navy end
1955	Howard Cassady, Ohio State halfback
1956	Tommy McDonald, Oklahoma halfback
1957	Bob Reifsnyder, Navy tackle
1958	Pete Dawkins, Army halfback
1959	Rich Lucas, Penn State quarterback

1960 Joe Bellino, Navy halfback
1961 Bob Ferguson, Ohio State fullback
1962 Terry Baker, Oregon State quarterback
1963 Roger Staubach, Navy quarterback
1964 Glenn Ressler, Penn State center
1965 Tommy Nobis, Texas linebacker
1966 Jim Lynch, Notre Dame linebacker
1967 Gary Beban, UCLA quarterback
1968 O. J. Simpson, Southern California halfback
1969 Mike Reid, Penn State tackle
1970 Jim Plunkett, Stanford quarterback
1971 Ed Marinaro, Cornell halfback
1972 Brad VanPelt, Michigan State defensive back
1973 John Cappelletti, Penn State halfback
1974 Steve Joachim, Temple quarterback
1975 Archie Griffin, Ohio State halfback
1976 Tony Dorsett, Pittsburgh halfback
1977 Ross Browner, Notre Dame end
1978 Chuck Fusina, Penn State quarterback
1979 Charles White, Southern California halfback
1980 Hugh Green, Pittsburgh defensive end
1981 Marcus Allen, Southern California halfback
1982 Herschel Walker, Georgia halfback
1983 Mike Rozier, Nebraska halfback
1984 Doug Flutie, Boston College quarterback
1985 Chuck Long, Iowa quarterback
1986 Vinnie Testaverde, Miami (FL) quarterback
1987 Don McPherson, Syracuse quarterback
1988 Barry Sanders, Oklahoma State halfback
1989 Andre Ware, Houston quarterback
1990 Ty Detmer, Brigham Young quarterback

Mays, Willie H. (1931–)
Baseball
Born May 6, 1931, Westfield, AL; Baseball Hall of Fame

Perhaps the most exciting baseball player of all time, Mays was an exuberant player who could hit for average and power, steal bases, and rob opponents of seemingly sure hits with his speed and instinct for the ball. Called up by the New York Giants during the 1951 season, he helped lead them to a pennant by hitting 20 home runs and driving in 68 runs. After spending most of the next two seasons in the army, he became a true superstar in 1954, leading the National League in hitting with a .345 average and in triples with 13. He also had 41 home runs and 110 runs batted in. In the Giants' four-game World Series sweep of the Cleveland Indians, Mays made one of the greatest clutch catches ever. With two men on and the score tied 2–2 in the ninth inning of the first game, the Indians' Vic Wertz hit a 440-foot drive to center field. Mays caught it in an outstretched glove while running at top speed with his back to home plate, sending the game into the tenth inning, when the Giants won.

After leading the league with 51 home runs in 1955, Mays led in stolen bases for four consecutive years and was the home run leader again with 49 in 1962, 47 in 1964, and 52 in 1965. The Giants, who had moved to San Francisco in 1958, traded him to the New York Mets in 1972, and Mays retired after the 1973 season. In 22 years, he batted .302 with 3,283 hits, 523 doubles, 140 triples, 680 home runs, 338 stolen bases, and 1,903 runs batted in. He ranks third in career home runs, ninth in hits, and fourth in extra base hits.

McCarthy, "Joe" Joseph V. (1887–1978)
Baseball
Born April 21, 1887, Philadelphia, PA; died January 13, 1978; Baseball Hall of Fame

"Marse Joe" spent 14 seasons playing in the minor leagues, the last two as a player-manager, and then became a full-time manager. In 1926, he took over the Chicago Cubs, who had finished last the previous season, and managed them to the 1929 pennant. He quit with four games left in the 1930 season, but the New York Yankees hired him almost immediately, and in 1932 McCarthy became the first manager to win pennants in both leagues. After three second-place finishes, the Yankees won pennants in 1936, 1937, 1938, 1939, 1941, 1942, and 1943, and they won the World Series each of those years except 1942.

McCarthy resigned early in the 1946 season, claiming ill health, but he became manager of the Boston Red Sox in 1948. They finished in a first-place tie, but lost a one-game playoff to the Cleveland Indians. After a second-place finish in 1949, he resigned and left baseball permanently during the 1950 season. In 24 seasons, his major-league teams won 2,126 games and lost 1,335, a .614 percentage.

McCormick, Patricia (Keller) (1930–)
Diving
Born May 12, 1930, Seal Beach, CA; International Swimming Hall of Fame

McCormick won Olympic Gold Medals in both platform and springboard diving in the 1952 Olympics, and she repeated in both events in 1956, just eight months after giving birth to her first child. She won the Sullivan Award as the outstanding amateur athlete of the year. McCormick also won 26 national diving championships, in the outdoor 1-meter springboard in 1950, 1951, 1953, 1954, 1955, and

1956, the outdoor 3-meter springboard in 1950, 1951, 1953, 1954, 1955, and 1956, the outdoor platform in 1949, 1950, 1951, 1954, and 1956, the indoor 1-meter springboard in 1951, 1952, 1953, 1954, and 1955, and the indoor 3-meter springboard in 1951, 1952, 1954, and 1955.

McGraw, John J. (1873–1934)
Baseball

Born April 7, 1873, Truxton, NY; died February 25, 1934; Baseball Hall of Fame

McGraw—always "Mr. McGraw" to his players— was a tough, fiery manager who could cuss out players, opponents, and umpires, as well as a cool, calculating tactician who could usually come up with just the right move at the right time. ". . . there has been only one manager," Connie Mack said in 1927, "and his name [is] McGraw." The "Little Napoleon" was a fine infielder who played for Baltimore in the American Association in 1891 and in the National league from 1892 through 1899, managing the team in his final season. After playing for St. Louis in 1900, he went to the new Baltimore team in the American League as player-manager in 1901. During the 1902 season, he went to the New York Giants in the National League. McGraw retired as a player after 1906, but managed the team until June of 1932, the longest tenure in the league's history and second only to Mack's American League record 50 years.

The Giants rose from last place in 1902 to second in 1903 and then won two consecutive pennants. Because of a feud with American League President Ban Johnson, McGraw refused to play a World Series in 1904, but his team beat the Philadelphia Athletics in five games in 1905. The Giants finished in a tie for first place with the Chicago Cubs in 1908, losing the playoff game. They won three consecutive pennants in 1911, 1912, and 1913, another in 1917, and then four in a row from 1921 through 1924, but could win only two World Series, in 1921 and 1922. McGraw had only four losing teams in his 33 seasons, winning 2,840 games to 1,984 losses, a .589 percentage. As a player, he had a career batting average of .334.

Further Reading: Alexander, Charles C. *John McGraw.* New York: Viking, 1988.

McLoughlin, Maurice (1890–1957)
Tennis

Born January 7, 1890, Carson City, NV; died December 10, 1957; International Tennis Hall of Fame

The "California Comet" learned tennis on the hard, fast cement and asphalt courts of California public playgrounds, and when he came to the East in 1909 he changed the sport permanently. McLoughlin was the first player to use a cannonball serve, the rush to net after service, and the overhand smash. Bill Tilden wrote of him, "Cyclonic, dynamic energy, embodied in a fiery-headed boy, transformed tennis to a game of brawn as well as brains," and John Kieran said, "He made it a game for the millions, for the young fellows at the small clubs about the country and the young stars just starting out on the courts in the public parks." McLoughlin won the national singles title in 1912 and 1913, and the doubles from 1912 through 1914.

McMahon Stadium
Calgary, Aberta

Opened on August 15, 1960, as the home field of the Canadian Football League's Calgary Stampeders, McMahon Stadium was named for the brothers Frank and George McMahon, who led the community effort to get it built. The stadium seats 38,400.

McNamee, Graham (1888–1942)
Sportscaster

Born July 10, 1888, Washington, DC; died May 9, 1942; National Sportscasters and Sportswriters Hall of Fame

McNamee's was probably the best-known radio voice in North America until Franklin D. Roosevelt began his "fireside chats." Originally a concert singer, he began his sportscasting career by doing the Harry Greb–Johnny Wilson middleweight championship fight on August 31, 1923, for New York's WEAF. That October, he was assigned to do color between innings of the World Series, with sportswriter Grantland Rice as the broadcaster. But Rice quit during the fourth inning of the third game, and McNamee took over.

He was so good at covering live events that he broadcast the Republican and Democratic National Conventions in 1924. McNamee did ten sports at one time or another, including the Rose Bowl football game, horse racing, and major boxing matches. An estimated 50 million people listened to his broadcast of the second Gene Tunney–Jack Dempsey fight on CBS in 1927. Sportswriter Heywood Broun wrote of him, "Graham McNamee has been able to take a new medium of expression and through it transmit himself—to give out vividly a sense of movement and of feeling. Of such is the kingdom of art."

But the travel, the workload, and the constant pressure of broadcasting live eventually wore McNamee down. He did his last sports broadcast in

1935 and finished his broadcasting career as a straight man for comedian Ed Wynn on the popular "Texaco Hour."

McNichols Arena
Denver, CO

The Denver Nuggets of the National Basketball Association began playing in McNichols Sports Arena when it opened in 1975. It was also the home rink of the National Hockey League's Colorado Rockies from 1976 until 1982, when the team became the New Jersey Devils. The arena seats 16,700.

Mead, Andrea (Mrs. Lawrence) (1932–   )
Skiing

Born April 19, 1932, Rutland, VT; National Ski Hall of Fame

The only American skier to win two Gold Medals in the Winter Olympics, Mead was the slalom and giant slalom champion in 1952, and she was leading in the downhill when she fell. The previous year, she had won 10 of 16 races on the international circuit. She was also a member of the 1956 Olympic team, and in 1960 she was chosen to ski into the stadium at Squaw Valley, CA with the Olympic torch. Mead was the U.S. downhill, slalom, and Alpine combined champion in 1952 and 1955, and the giant slalom champion in 1953.

Meadowlands Sports Complex
East Rutherford, NJ

Built on 588 acres at a cost of $350 million, this complex is operated by the New Jersey Sports and Exposition Authority. It includes Giants Stadium, Brendan Byrne Arena, and Meadowlands Race Track. The track opened on September 1, 1976. It has 10,000 fixed seats, a total capacity of 35,000, a 1-mile oval dirt track, and a 7-furlong inner turf track. In its first season, it was used for harness racing only; Thoroughbred racing began in 1977. Since 1981, the Meadowlands has hosted the Hambletonian, one of the races in the trotting triple crown.

Giants Stadium opened on October 10, 1976, as the home of the New York Giants of the National Football League, and the New York Jets have also played there since 1984. The stadium seats 76,800 and has two computerized scoreboards.

Brendan Byrne Arena is the home of the New Jersey Nets of the National Basketball Association and the New Jersey Devils of the National Hockey League. The arena seats 20,149 for basketball, 19,040 for hockey.

Medicine, Sports

There were a number of orthopedists and orthopedic surgeons who specialized in sports injuries, but sports medicine didn't exist as a discipline in North America until the American College of Sports Medicine was founded in 1955. It is unusual in that it concentrates on a certain type of patient, the athlete, rather than on a specific disease or part of the body. It combines orthopedics, cardiology, physiatrics, physical therapy, biomechanics, podiatry, osteopathy, pediatrics (for treating young athletes), and obstetrics and gynecology (for treating female athletes).

Medical problems at the 1968 Olympic Games in Mexico, many of them caused by the high altitude, led to the establishment of the Canadian Academy of Sports Medicine, which was incorporated in 1970. Its chief purpose is coordinating medical service to Canadian athletes at all levels of play in all sports through the Sport Medicine Council of Canada. In 1985, the academy established a research committee to plan and oversee a comprehensive program of research into sports medicine.

The sports doctor does much more than help to heal injuries. He or she works with an athlete to develop training and exercise programs that will help to prevent injury. Sports biomechanics uses videotape or film to analyze body movements to determine flaws in technique that may cause chronic pain. The technique can also be used to improve skills.

The development of sports medicine and the resultant pooling of knowledge have brought several major changes in the treatment of injuries. Heat, for example, is now rarely used in the early stages of an injury because it increases the blood supply to the treated area, which encourages inflammation. Instead, the standard formula is RICE—rest, ice, compression, and elevation, all of which reduce inflammation and swelling. After three or four days, however, heat is often used to speed the healing process.

Many new rehabilitation techniques have also been developed. It is now known, for example, that stressing a damaged bone or muscle leads to faster healing than simple immobilization. Special exercises and equipment have been developed to stress bone and muscle even when the injury is in a cast, and ultrasound and electricity can also be used to speed healing.

Memorial Coliseum
See LOS ANGELES MEMORIAL COLISEUM.

Memorial Stadium
See BALTIMORE MEMORIAL STADIUM.

Mercy Bowl
Football

Fresno State beat Bowling Green 36–8 in the only Mercy Bowl game, November 23, 1961, at Los Angeles.

Meredith, "Ted" James Edward (1892–1957)
Track and Field

Born November 14, 1892, Chester Heights, PA; died November 2, 1957; National Track and Field Hall of Fame

Meredith was a long-time world record holder in the 400-meter, 440-yard, 800-meter, and 880-yard runs. Winning the Gold Medal in the 1912 Olympics, he set a record of 1 minute 51.9 seconds for 800 meters and was also timed in a record 1:52.5 for 880 yards. Meredith lowered the 880-yard mark to 1:52.2 in 1916. Both of those records stood until 1926. His mark of 47.4 seconds in the 440-yard run, set in 1916, was tied twice in 1931 and finally broken in 1932, and his record in the 400 meters, also 47.4, stood from 1916 until 1928. Meredith was the AAU 440-yard champion in 1915 and 1916. Running for the University of Pennsylvania, he won the IC4A 440-yard title in 1914, 1915, and 1916 and the 880-yard run in 1915 and 1916.

Merion Golf Club
Ardmore, PA

Originally an offshoot of the Merion Cricket Club, the golf club's East Course, built in 1912, is one of the finest in the country. Relatively short at 6,694 yards and a par 70, Merion has more than 100 bunkers, many of them ringed by tall grass, requiring very accurate tee and fairway shots. The course hosted the U.S. Open in 1934, 1950, 1971, and 1981.

Messenger Stakes
Harness Racing

The second leg in pacing's Triple Crown, this race was the last of the three to begin, in 1956. Originally run at Roosevelt Raceway, it moved to Yonkers Raceway in 1988, after Roosevelt closed. The Messenger is the only one of the Triple Crown races that is a simple 1-mile dash, with no heat racing.

Metrodome
Minneapolis, MN

Formally the Hubert H. Humphrey Metrodome, this stadium is the home of the American League's Minnesota Twins, the National Football League's Minnesota Vikings, and the National Basketball Association's Minnesota Timberwolves. Construction began in December of 1979, and the Metrodome opened in April of 1982 with a Twins' game. Total cost was $75 million, including $7 million contributed by the Twins and the Vikings for exclusive space. The inflated, 10-acre roof is made of Teflon-coated fiberglass. Seating capacity is 35,000 for basketball, 55,000 for baseball, and 63,500 for football. Home run distances are 343 feet to left field, 408 to center, and 327 to right.

Metropolitan Conference

Formed in 1975, the Metropolitan is a strong basketball conference made up of the University of Cincinnati, Florida State, Louisville, Memphis State, South Carolina, Southern Mississippi, and Virginia Tech.

Address: One Ravinia Drive, Suite 1120, Atlanta, GA 30346 (404) 577–3700

Metropolitan Sports Center
Bloomington, MN

The Met Center opened in 1967 as the home of the Minnesota North Stars in the National Hockey League. It originally adjoined Metropolitan Stadium, which was the home field for the Vikings and Twins until 1982, when the Hubert H. Humphrey Metrodome opened. The center seats 15,499.

Miami, FL

Basketball The Miami Heat entered the National Basketball Association as an expansion team for the 1988–89 season.

Football Miami first entered major professional sports with a team called the Seahawks in 1946, the All-America Football Conference's first season. However, the franchise moved to Baltimore in 1947.

The city got another chance in 1966, when the Miami Dolphins were admitted to the American Football League as an expansion team. Since the merger with the National Football League in 1970, the Dolphins have been in the American Football Conference. They won AFC championships in 1971, 1972, 1973, 1982, and 1984. The Dolphins won all 17 of their games in 1972, the only team in NFL history to go undefeated through the regular season and the playoffs. They won Super Bowls VII and VIII.

See also JOE ROBBIE STADIUM; MIAMI ARENA.

Miami Arena
Miami, FL

Built at a cost of $52 million, this arena opened in 1988 as the home of the Miami Heat, an NBA expansion franchise. It seats 15,500.

Michigan International Speedway
Brooklyn, MI

This 2-mile oval opened on September 16, 1968; its first major event was a 250-mile race for Indy cars on October 13. NASCAR racing began in 1969. The track now hosts two 400-mile NASCAR races, a 250-mile CART race, and a 500-mile CART race. The speedway has a seating capacity of 40,000.

Address: 12626 U.S. 12, Brooklyn, MI 49230 (517) 592–6666

Mid-American Conference (MAC)

Probably the least known of the NCAA Division I conferences, the Mid-American was founded in 1947 by Bowling Green, the University of Cincinnati, Kent State, Marshall, Miami (OH), Ohio University, Toledo, and Western Michigan. Ball State, Central Michigan, and Eastern Michigan have since joined the MAC, while Cincinnati has dropped out.

Address: Four SeaGate, Suite 501, Toledo, OH 43604 (419) 249–7177

Mid-Ohio Sports Car Course
Lexington, OH

This 2.4-mile, 15-turn road course was originally opened in 1962. It has undergone extensive improvement in recent years, including a complete resurfacing of the track in 1990. In 1980, Mid-Ohio hosted a 150-mile Championship Auto Racing Teams event, and since 1983 it has been the site of a 200.5-mile CART race.

Address: P.O. Box 3108, Lexington, OH 44904 (419) 884–2295

Mikan, George L. (1924–   )
Basketball

Born June 18, 1924, Joliet, IL; Basketball Hall of Fame

Professional basketball's first truly dominating big man, the 6-foot-10, 248-pound Mikan was an All-American at DePaul in 1944, 1945, and 1946. He led the nation in scoring and was College Player of the Year in 1945 and 1946. During the 1945 National Invitation Tournament, he scored a record 53 points in one game and had a record total of 120 points in three games as DePaul won the tournament. The year he graduated, the Basketball Association of America was formed to compete with the established National Basketball League. Mikan signed a five-year, $60,000 contract with the NBL's Chicago American Gears, but left the team in the middle of the season when the financially troubled Gears tried to cut his salary. He returned in time to lift the team

At 6–foot-10 and 245 pounds, George Mikan was professional basketball's first truly big player. College Player of the Year at DePaul in 1945 and 1946, he was a National Basketball Association all-star from 1949 through 1954. Courtesy of the Basketball Hall of Fame

from fifth place into third, and he scored 78 points in a four-game championship playoff victory over Rochester.

The Chicago team folded, and Mikan went to the Minneapolis Lakers. He promptly led them to the NBL championship, averaging 21.3 points a game. The Lakers moved into the BAA for the 1948–49 season and won another title, Mikan leading the league with 28.4 points per game. The BAA became the National Basketball Association the following year, but that made no difference: The Lakers won the championship and Mikan won the scoring title again. He was the scoring leader once more in 1950–51 and finished second in rebounding (it was the first year rebounding statistics were kept), but the Lakers were eliminated in the semifinal round of the playoffs. However, they came back to win titles in 1952, 1953, and 1954. Mikan was only 30, but an accumulation of injuries, including two broken legs, a broken foot, and a broken wrist were making it painful to play, and he announced his retirement. He returned to the Lakers for part of the 1955–56 season, but was not effective, and he retired permanently.

Although not a great leaper, Mikan had the bulk and strength to get excellent rebounding position and to work his way toward the basket for relatively easy shots. He was a first-team all-star in two leagues for eight consecutive seasons and totaled 11,764 points, an average of 22.6 per game. He coached the Lakers for part of the 1957–58 season, winning just 9 games while losing 30, and in 1967 he was named the first commissioner of the American Basketball Association.

Mile High Stadium
Denver, CO

Built in 1948 as a baseball park for the minor-league Denver Bears, Mile High was originally called Bears Stadium. When the Denver Broncos joined the American Football League as a charter member in 1960, capacity was increased from about 20,000 to 34,657. A nonprofit group bought the stadium for $1.8 million in 1968 and gave it to the city of Denver. An upper deck was added that year, bringing capacity to 51,706, and in December it was renamed Denver Mile High Stadium. Voters in 1974 approved a $25 million bond issue for stadium improvement and expansion to 75,100 seats. Capacity grew to its present 76,273 with the addition of luxury suites in 1986. Mile High Stadium is unique in that it has movable east stands; the stand area can be retracted 145 feet to configure the field for baseball.

Military Biathlon
See BIATHLON.

Miller, Cheryl (1964–   )
Basketball
Born January 3, 1964, Riverside, CA

After leading Riverside Poly High School to a 132–4 record, Miller went to the University of Southern California, where she was an All-American four times, 1983 through 1986, and she won the Wade Trophy as the nation's top player in 1985. Southern Cal won the NCAA Division I championship in 1983 and 1984, and she was named tournament Most Valuable Player both times. In 128 games, she averaged 23.6 points and 12.0 rebounds per game, and she's one of only three women to have more than 3,000 career points and more than 1,500 rebounds. Miller led the U.S. team in scoring when it won the 1983 Pan-American Games championship and the 1984 Olympic title.

Milwaukee, WI
Baseball   Milwaukee had teams in the National League in 1878, the Union Association in 1884, the

American Association in 1891, and the American League in 1901. The city finally got another major-league baseball team when the National League Braves moved from Boston in 1953. They won pennants in 1957 and 1958 and beat the Yankees in the 1957 World Series, but lost to them in 1958. The Braves went to Atlanta in 1966, but four years later Milwaukee got an American League team, the Brewers, when a year-old expansion franchise failed to make it in Seattle and had to move. The Brewers won the American League pennant in 1982 but lost to the St. Louis Cardinals in the World Series.

Basketball   The Tri-Cities Blackhawks of the National Basketball Association became the Milwaukee Hawks in 1951. They moved to St. Louis in 1955. The NBA awarded Milwaukee an expansion franchise in 1968. The Bucks, as the new team was called, won the midwest division championship from 1971 through 1974 and the central division championship from 1981 through 1986. They were NBA champions in 1974.

Football   The Milwaukee Badgers were in the National Football League from 1922 through 1926. Milwaukee also had a team, the Chiefs, in the American Football League in 1939 and 1940.

See also BRADLEY CENTER; MILWAUKEE COUNTY STADIUM.

Milwaukee County Stadium

The home of the Milwaukee Brewers and part-time home of the Green Bay Packers opened in 1953 with a capacity of 35,911. Built by Milwaukee County, it was originally planned for the city's minor-league team (also the Brewers) in the American Association, but before it was completed the Boston Braves announced that they were moving to Milwaukee for the 1953 season. As a result, another $500,000 was added to the budget to bring the park up to major-league standards; the total cost was about $5 million. The Braves left for Atlanta in 1966 and were replaced by the American League Brewers, formerly the Seattle Pilots, in 1970. The stadium now seats 55,976 for football and 53,182 for baseball. Home run distances are 330 feet down the lines and 410 feet to center field.

Minneapolis, MN

Basketball   The Minneapolis Lakers, who moved into the National Basketball Association from the National Basketball League in 1948, dominated the NBA for six years, winning the league championship five times during that period. They missed only in 1951, when they finished first in the central division but lost to the Rochester Royals in the semifinals. The Lakers had previously won the 1947–48 NBL championship. After the retirement of the great George Mikan, though, the Lakers fell on hard times and moved to Los Angeles in 1960.

Football Minneapolis had two teams in the National Football League during its early days: the Marines from 1922 through 1924 and the Redjackets in 1929 and 1930.

See also METRODOME; METROPOLITAN SPORTS CENTER; MINNESOTA.

Minnesota

Baseball Most professional teams based in the Minneapolis-St. Paul area have used the state's name. The first of them, the Minnesota Twins, was named for the twin cities. That team moved from Washington, DC in 1961. The Twins won the American League pennant in 1965 and 1987 and the World Series in the latter year. They were the league's western division champions in 1969 and 1970.

Basketball After nearly 30 years without a major-league basketball team, Minnesota was awarded an expansion franchise in the National Basketball Association in 1989. The team is called the Timberwolves.

Football The Minnesota Vikings were originally organized to join the American Football League in its first season, 1960. However, the owners were persuaded to join the National Football League instead. The Vikings have been to the Super Bowl four times without winning. They were National Football League champions in 1969 and National Football Conference champions in 1973, 1974, and 1977. The Vikings also won central division titles in 1970, 1971, 1975, 1976, 1978, and 1980.

Hockey When the National Hockey League expanded from 6 to 12 teams in 1967, the Minnesota North Stars were one of the new franchises. In 1978, the North Stars were merged with the financially troubled Cleveland Barons. The team finished first in the Norris division in 1982 and 1984, and lost to the New York Islanders in the 1981 Stanley Cup finals.

See also MINNEAPOLIS, MN; ST. PAUL, MN.

Minor Leagues

Although the distinction between major and minor leagues wasn't made at the time, the first minor baseball league was the International Association of Professional Base Ball Players, organized at a convention of clubs in Pittsburgh in February 1877. It was a very loose organization; any team that paid $10 could join, but those that wanted to play for the championship had to pay an additional $15. By the end of the 1877 there were 23 members, only 7 of

which competed for the championship. The London (Ontario) Tecumsehs won the league's first pennant.

The Northwestern League, founded in 1879 with four teams, lasted just one season, but was reorganized as an eight-team league in 1883. Its leaders immediately asked for an agreement with the National League that its player contracts would be honored. The result was the Tripartite Pact, under which the Northwestern and National Leagues and the American Association (then a major league) agreed to respect each others' reserve lists and to uphold each others' suspensions and expulsions.

There were nine minor leagues in 1887: the California, Eastern, Interstate, New England, Northwestern, Ohio State, Pennsylvania, Southern, and Western Leagues. The Western absorbed the Northwestern League in 1888 and eventually became the only minor league ever to achieve major-league status, after a couple of reorganizations. Ban Johnson became president of the league in 1894 and made a success of it. In 1899 he renamed it the American League. After a brief struggle with the established National League, a truce was drawn up in 1902.

The minor leagues were badly wounded by the battle for players between the National and American Leagues, as they had been earlier by similar challenges to the National League from the Union Association, the Players' League, and the American Association. On September 5, 1901, eight of them formed the National Association of Professional Baseball Leagues. Membership grew to 13 before the 1902 season began and to 19 in 1903, when the National Association signed a new National Agreement with the two major leagues.

Minor leagues were grouped into four classifications, A, B, C, and D, based on the total population of each league's territory. The National Agreement allowed major-league teams to draft players from the minor leagues at set prices, from $750 for a Class A player to $200 for a Class D player, with the provision that no more than two players could be drafted from a Class A team. Minor-league teams were also allowed to draft players from teams in lower classifications. In 1906, the American Association, the International League, and the Pacific Coast League were moved into the new AA classification, and draft prices were increased to $2,500 for a Class AA player, $1,500 for Class A, $1,200 for Class B, $750 for Class C, and $500 for Class D.

While many individual franchises and a few leagues might have been financially shaky, minor-league baseball flourished under the new arrangement. By 1913, there were more than 40 minor leagues with teams in more than 300 cities across the country. Because of World War I, the number shrank to just 20 leagues in 1917, of which only 12 finished the season, and a mere 9 leagues played abbreviated schedules in 1918.

In 1919, the National Association withdrew from the National Agreement, although the majors and minors agreed to respect player contracts and territorial rights. A new agreement was finally reached in January 1921, when Organized Baseball replaced the old National Commission with a single, all-powerful commissioner, Judge Kenesaw Mountain Landis. Draft prices were once again increased; they ranged from $1,000 for a Class D player to $5,000 for a Class AA player. Major-league teams were allowed to "option out" up to eight players each for a maximum of two years, and minor-league teams were also allowed to option players to teams in lower classifications. Under the option arrangement, the player's contract remained the property of the higher-classified team, which had the option of calling the player back at any time.

The 1921 agreeement also allowed a minor league to become exempt from the draft if it gave up its own draft rights. All three AA leagues, the Class A Western Association, and the Class B Three-I League (Illinois, Indiana and Iowa) chose to become draft-exempt. As a result, many of their teams prospered during the early 1920s. Jack Dunn, the owner of the International League's Baltimore Orioles, had lost Babe Ruth for just $2,500 in 1914; he sold Jack Bentley to the New York Giants for $65,000 in 1923, and it was estimated that Dunn took in nearly $1 million through player sales during the 1920s.

Meanwhile, Branch Rickey was quietly changing the structure of organized baseball. While vice-president of the St. Louis Cardinals, he conceived the idea of the modern farm system, and began putting it into practice by buying a half-interest in a minor-league team in 1919. He continued buying some teams and developing working agreements with others. (Under a working agreement, the major-league team gives financial aid to the minor-league team and stocks it with players who remain the property of the parent team.) By 1940, St. Louis owned 15 teams and had working agreements with 17 others. The farm system not only kept the Cardinals supplied with players, it was a source of income through the sale of surplus players.

The idea worked so well that most other major-league teams began developing their own farm systems in the 1930s. That helped the minor leagues prosper through the Great Depression. The number of leagues increased from 14 in 1933 to 44 in 1940; that decreased to only 10 in 1945 because of the World War II manpower shortage, but it quickly bounced back to 43 in 1946, the first full season after the war.

The classification system was revised in 1946, when the American Association, International League, and Pacific Coast League were moved into a new Class AAA and the Southern and Texas Leagues were moved from Class A into AA. Another new classification, "open," was created for leagues whose cities had an aggregate population of more than 10 million. The Pacific Coast League reached that status in 1951, and it seemed that the PCL had a good chance of eventually becoming a third major league. But it lost its two largest cities in 1958, when the Brooklyn Dodgers moved to Los Angeles and the New York Giants moved to San Francisco, and the league reverted to AAA status.

The minor leagues had their best year in 1949, when an all-time high of 59 leagues drew more than 42 million spectators. But a rapid decline began in the early 1950s, primarily because of television. In 1953, more than 60 percent of all major-league games were televised into minor-league territories, and 38 leagues attracted just 21 million fans, a 50-percent decrease in four years.

Major-league franchise movement and expansion further hurt the minors. Between 1953 and 1977, 13 of the largest minor-league cities entered the major leagues. The classification system was overhauled during the 1960s: Classes B, C, and D were eliminated, and a Rookie League classification was added. There are now four AAA leagues, including the Mexican; three AA leagues, seven Class A leagues, and four Rookie Leagues. In 1989, minor-league attendance reached 23,103,593, up 7 percent over 1988 and the highest total since 1952.

See also INTERNATIONAL LEAGUE; NATIONAL AGREEMENT; NATIONAL ASSOCIATION OF PROFESSIONAL BASEBALL LEAGUES; NORTHWESTERN LEAGUE; PACIFIC COAST LEAGUE; WESTERN LEAGUE.

MISL

See MAJOR INDOOR SOCCER LEAGUE.

Missouri Valley Conference (MVC)

More than 20 colleges have belonged to the MVC at one time or another. Originally known as The Missouri Valley Intercollegiate Athletic Association, it was organized on January 12, 1907, by the Universities of Iowa, Kansas, Missouri, and Nebraska, and Washington University of St. Louis. The makeup of the conference changed several times until 1928, when six members—Iowa State, Kansas, Kansas State, Missouri, Nebraska, and Oklahoma—withdrew to form the Big Six, now the Big Eight. That left just Drake, Grinnell, Oklahoma A & M, and Washington University as members, but Creighton joined in time to compete in the 1928 football season.

Current MVC members are Bradley, Creighton, Drake, Illinois State, Indiana State, Southern Illinois, Tulsa, and Wichita State. The conference now conducts a championship schedule only in basketball.

Address: 200 North Broadway, Suite 1905, St. Louis, MO 63102 (314) 421–0339

Modern Pentathlon

The decathlon in the ancient Olympics was a test of military skills. Baron Pierre de Coubertin, founder of the modern Olympics, asked the Swedish Olympic Committee to design a similar test for the 1912 Stockholm Games. The modern pentathlon was based on the skills needed by a military courier: to deliver a message, he would begin on horseback, defend himself with sword and pistol, abandon his mount to swim a river, and finally arrive on foot.

A 1,000-meter cross-country horse race over 20 obstacles is held on the first day, followed by a round-robin fencing tournament, target pistol shooting, a 300-meter swimming race, and a 4,000-meter cross-country run on the fifth and final day. The modern pentathlon has been an Olympic event since 1912. The sport was largely dominated by the military until 1959, when the U.S. Modern Pentathlon and Biathlon Association was organized to involve civilian athletes. In 1981 the U.S. Biathlon Association was spun off as a separate organization. The Canadian Modern Pentathlon Association was founded in 1971.

Women were allowed to compete in the late 1970s, and the women's world championship was established in 1980. Lynn Chornobrywy of Canada in 1983 became the first North American to win a world title.

Addresses: Canadian Modern Pentathlon Association, 25 Chevrier, Laval, Quebec, Canada H7E 3Z7; U.S. Modern Pentathlon Association, P.O. Drawer 8178, San Antonio, TX 78208 (512) 246–3000.

Modern Sports

There are several definitions of modern sports. All agree that folk games (also called "premodern" games or sports) become modern by becoming more structured. Melvin L. Adelman, in *A Sporting Time*, lists six characteristics of modern sports: formal organization at local, regional, and national levels; standardized, written rules; national and international competition; emergence of specialists who take part in the sport full-time while most others are spectators; regular coverage in local and national media, along with the appearance of specialized sports publications; and keeping statistical records.

Most modern sports grew gradually out of folk games. Baseball, variously known as "base ball" or "goal ball," descended from rounders, a British folk game usually played by boys or young men. It existed in at least two distinct forms before the modernization process began in 1845, when the Knickerbocker Base Ball Club was founded in New York and Alexander Cartwright drew a diagram of the playing field and wrote a set of rules. By the 1860s, baseball was a de facto professional sport for the best players, and teams were charging admission to games. The founding in 1871 of the National Association of Professional Base Ball Players was a major step in the sport's modernization, but probably the modernization process couldn't be considered completed until 1876, when the National League brought strong central rule to the sport.

Even an invented sport such as basketball has to go through a premodern phase. Indeed, basketball spread so rapidly on several different levels that it was in chaos soon after its invention in 1891. Rules weren't standardized until 1915, when the Amateur Athletic Union, National Collegiate Athletic Association, and YMCA formed the Joint Rules Committee. Although the AAU held its first "national" tournament in 1897, only New York teams competed, and the tournament wasn't permanently established until 1919. Competition at the collegiate level didn't become truly national until the late 1930s, when the National Invitation Tournament and the NCAA's own national championship tournament were established.

Molineaux, Tom (1784–1818)
Boxing
Born 1784, Georgetown, SC; died August 4, 1818; Boxing Hall of Fame

A former slave who may have won his freedom through his boxing ability, Molineaux (or Molyneaux) went to New York City and won several impromptu fights before embarking for England in 1809. After beating Bill Burrows and Tom Blake, he was matched against Tom Cribb for 200 guineas on December 10, 1810. Molineaux apparently had the fight won when Cribb couldn't answer the bell for the 23rd round, but Cribb's followers stalled by claiming the American had lead weights in his gloves. By the time the dispute ended, Cribb had recovered. He knocked out Molineaux in the 33rd round. In a savage rematch on September 28, 1811, Cribb was "bleeding from every organ," according to one reporter, but he broke Molineaux's jaw in the 9th round and knocked him out in the 11th. Molineaux had just four more formal matches. He died while touring Ireland with a boxing show.

Monmouth Park
Oceanport, NJ

Now operated by the New Jersey Sports and Exposition Authority, Monmouth Park opened in 1946. It revived the Monmouth Handicap, which had been run from 1884 through 1893 at a previous Monmouth Park. The track's top race is now the Haskell Stakes, which has a purse of $500,000. Monmouth Park has a 1-mile oval main track and a ⅞-mile turf track. The grandstand seats 13,200, the clubhouse 4,900.

Address: P.O. Box MP, Oceanport, NJ 07757 (201) 222–5100

Montreal, Quebec

Baseball The Montreal Expos joined the National League in 1969 as the first major-league team outside the United States. They won their first game 8–7 over the St. Louis Cardinals in Montreal on April 14. The Expos won the second-half eastern division title in 1981, when the season was split because of a players' strike, and they beat the Philadelphia Phillies in the division playoff, but lost the league championship series to the Los Angeles Dodgers.

Football The Montreal Football Club, organized in 1868, was a charter member of the Quebec Rugby Football Union when it was founded in 1882. The QRFU and the Ontario Rugby Football Union formed the Canadian Rugby Union in 1891. Montreal lost 45–5 to Osgoode Hall in the first CRU championship game the following year. In 1907, Montreal joined Hamilton, Ottawa, and Toronto in the Interprovincial Rugby Football Union, also known as the "Big Four." After seven straight last place finishes, the MFC was replaced in 1946 by a new team, the Montreal Alouettes. The Alouettes were Grey Cup champions in 1949, 1974, 1977, 1979, 1981, and 1985, but the team folded in 1987.

Hockey Montreal teams dominated Stanley Cup play before the founding of the National Hockey League in 1917. The cup went to the Montreal Amateur Athletic Association in the first two years, 1893 and 1894, and in 1902; to the Montreal Victorias in 1895, 1896, 1897, and 1898; to the Montreal Shamrocks in 1899 and 1900; to the Montreal Wanderers in 1906, 1907, 1908, and 1910; and to the Montreal Canadiens in 1916. Montreal had two teams in the NHL in its first season, the Canadiens and the Wanderers, but the Wanderers lasted just one season. In 1925 the Montreal Maroons entered the league; they remained through the 1937–38 season. The Maroons won the Stanley Cup in 1926 and 1935, the Canadiens in 1924, 1930, 1931, 1944, 1946, 1953, 1956,

1957–60, 1965, 1966, 1968, 1969, 1971, 1973, 1976–79, and 1986.

See also MONTREAL FORUM; OLYMPIC STADIUM.

Montreal Forum

The original Montreal Forum opened on November 29, 1924. Built at a cost of $1.5 million, it had 9,000 seats, increased to 12,500 in 1949. A new Forum, with 16,500 seats, was built for $10 million and opened on November 2, 1968. The home of the Montreal Canadiens of the National Hockey League, the Forum also hosts ice shows, boxing and wrestling matches, and entertainment events.

Morenz, "Howie" William Howard (1902–1937)
Hockey

Born September 21, 1902, Mitchell, Ontario; died March 8, 1937; Hockey Hall of Fame

Because of his blazing speed, Morenz was called the "Mitchell Meteor" and the "Stratford Streak," but his career was still young when some sportswriters began calling him the "Babe Ruth of hockey." Sportswriter Andy O'Brien wrote, "He would challenge the opposing offenses by dazzling dash and deception. You didn't have to know anything about hockey to be lifted from your seat by Morenz—just as you didn't have to know anything about baseball to be thrilled by a towering home run by Babe Ruth."

Morenz joined the Montreal Canadiens in 1923. As NHL champions, they had to play two challengers for the Stanley Cup in 1924: Calgary of the Western Canadian Hockey League and Vancouver of the Pacific Coast Hockey Association. Morenz scored all Montreal's goals in a 3–2 victory and added another in a 2–1 victory as Montreal swept Calgary in two games. The Canadiens also swept Vancouver in two games. Morenz led the NHL in scoring in 1928 and 1931 and won the Hart Trophy as the league's Most Valuable Player in 1931 and 1932. He was traded to the Chicago Blackhawks in 1935, and spent one season there and one with the New York Rangers before returning to Montreal for the 1936–37 season. On January 28, 1937, Morenz suffered a badly broken leg in a game against Chicago. Worried about his future in hockey, he evidently had a nervous breakdown while in the hospital; he then developed heart disease which killed him. His funeral service was held at center ice in the Montreal Forum and thousands of hockey fans paid tribute.

Morrissey, John (1831–1878)
Boxing, Horse Racing

Born February 12, 1831, Templemore, Tipperary, Ireland; died May 1, 1878

John Morrissey beat John C. Heenan in the first major North American championship fight on October 20, 1858, at Long Point, Canada. From the New York Clipper.

Morrissey's family emigrated to Troy, NY when he was three years old, and as a teenager he became a gang leader. In the late 1840s, he went to New York City, walked into the Empire Club saloon, and offered to fight anyone; he was knocked unconscious by several willing volunteers. But he stayed in New York until 1851 when he went to California to seek gold. He made some money gambling, and he also fought his first formal match.

Returning to New York, Morrissey fought Yankee Sullivan on October 12, 1853, near the New York–Massachusetts border, for $1,000 a side. He was declared the winner when Sullivan failed to come up to scratch for the 38th round because he was busy fighting off some of Morrissey's backers who had entered the ring. Morrissey's next, and last, formal fight was an 11-round knockout of John C. Heenan on October 20, 1858. That made Morrissey the American heavyweight champion, but he immediately retired and went into gambling. In 1861 he opened a major gambling parlor in Saratoga Springs, and two years later he joined with two wealthy members of the city's elite, John R. Hunter and William R. Travers, to build a racetrack there. It was a success, and it helped inspire the formation of the American Jockey Club and the construction of Jerome Park in Westchester County. Morrissey served as a New York state legislator from 1873 through 1877, and was elected to the state senate just six months before his death.

Morris Park
Westchester County, NY

When it was announced in 1887 that New York City was going to take over the site of Jerome Park, Francis Morris and his son John built a new racetrack about 2 miles east. Morris Park opened in August 1889 and hosted most of the major races that had originated at Jerome Park, including the Belmont Stakes. The track closed after the 1904 meet and was replaced by the newly built Belmont Park in 1905.

Mosconi, "Willie" William J. (1913–   )
Billiards
Born June 21, 1913, Philadelphia, PA; Billiard Hall of Fame

Mosconi's father owned a billiard parlor, but wouldn't let his son play. Young Mosconi practiced in secret, using a broomstick and potatoes. When he was six years old, his uncle jokingly challenged him to a game of pocket billiards, and the youngster promptly ran 15 balls. He won his first world championship in league competition in 1941, and he won the world tournament the following year. He was also world champion in 1944, 1945, 1947, and 1948, 1950 through 1957. Mosconi once ran an incredible 526 balls during an exhibition.

Moses, Annie
See OAKLEY, ANNIE.

Moses, Edwin (1955–   )
Track and Field
Born August 31, 1955, Dayton, OH; National Track and Field Hall of Fame

Moses dominated his event, the 400-meter intermediate hurdles, longer than any other athlete has dominated any event. From 1976 into 1988, he won 176 out of 184 races, including 122 consecutive victories from September 2, 1977, through May 29, 1987. He was the first ever to break 48 seconds in the 400-meter hurdles in 1976; by the end of 1980, the event had been run in less than 48 seconds 14 times, 12 times by Moses. He was the second man in history ever to win two Gold Medals in the event, but he had to do it over an eight-year span, in 1976 and 1984, because the United States boycotted the 1980 Olympics in Moscow; the first double winner, Glenn A. Davis, had done it in consecutive Olympics, in 1956 and 1960. Moses also won the World Cup title in 1977, 1979, 1981, 1983, and 1987 (he missed the 1985 season with an injury).

He appeared likely to win a third Gold Medal in 1988 after finishing first in the U.S. Olympic trials, and some thought he might break the 47-second barrier, but he faltered in Seoul and finished third, his poorest showing since early 1976. Nevertheless, he was still planning to take part in the 1992 Games—possibly in bobsledding as well as track and field.

Most Valuable Player (MVP)

The notion of a Most Valuable Player award is a rather recent development. The oldest MVP award is the National Hockey League's Hart Memorial Trophy, originally presented in 1923. However, the idea originated with the Chalmers Award, which in 1910 went to the major leagues' top hitters; because of a controversy, from 1911 through 1914 the award was given to "the most important and useful player to his club" in each league. After the sponsoring Chalmers Automobile Company stopped presenting the award, there was a hiatus of eight years before the American League began naming an official MVP in 1922. The National League followed suit in 1924. *Sporting News* presented the award in the American League in 1929 and in both leagues in 1930. Since 1931, the Baseball Writers Association has given the award in both leagues.

Similarly, the National Football League presented the Joseph F. Carr Trophy to an official MVP from 1938 through 1946. The News Enterprise Association in 1955 established the Jim Thorpe Trophy for an MVP chosen by the league's players. Although the old National Basketball League named an MVP in 1948 and 1949, the National Basketball Association didn't offer its award, the Podoloff Trophy, until 1956.

There has often been controversy about the criteria for an MVP. Some writers feel that the winner should come from a championship team, or at least a team that finishes very high in the standings, arguing that a player can't really be very valuable if he plays for a losing team. Others say the award should simply go to the player who had the best all-around season. Both major wire services, the *Sporting News*, and several other publications select a player of the year in various sports, avoiding the controversial concept of "value." There are also MVP awards for specific games and events, such as the Super Bowl, the World Series, the NBA and NHL playoffs, the NCAA team championship tournaments, and the professional all-star games.

See also CARR TROPHY; CHALMERS AWARD; HART MEMORIAL TROPHY; PODOLOFF TROPHY; THORPE TROPHY.

Motley, Marion (1920–   )
Football
Born June 5, 1920, Leesburg, VA; Pro Football Hall of Fame

Professional football was reintegrated in 1946 when Motley and Bill Willis signed to play for the Cleveland Browns in the new All-America Football Conference. A 6-foot-1, 238-pound fullback, Motley had gone to South Carolina State and the University of Nevada before entering the Navy, where he played for Coach Paul Brown's Great Lakes Naval Training Station team. When Brown became coach and part owner of the Cleveland team after the war, he immediately signed Motley and designed a new kind of offense. The "pass-and-trap" attack used what is now called the draw play to keep defenses from concentrating entirely on Otto Graham's passing, and the fast, powerful Motley was the featured runner.

Motley was the AAFC's top ground-gainer during its four years of operation, and he led the NFL in rushing in 1950, the Browns' first year in the league after a merger between the AAFC and NFL. A chronic leg injury limited his playing time in 1951 and 1953. After missing the entire 1954 season, he joined the Pittsburgh Steelers in 1955 but carried the ball only twice. In nine seasons, Motley gained 4,720 yards on 828 carries, a 5.7 average; he caught 85 passes for 1,107 yards; and he returned 48 kickoffs for 1,122 yards, a 23.4 average. He scored 38 touchdowns, 31 of them rushing.

Motocross

The odd name for cross-country motorcycle racing comes from the French, who pioneered it as a sport after World War II. Races are run over difficult natural terrain, including gullies and holes, and uphill and downhill sections. The Swedish motorcycle manufacturer Husqvarna brought European riders to North America in the late 1960s to demonstrate the sport, and it caught on. The American Motorcycle Association began sanctioning motocross in 1969, and the sport became quite popular during the 1970s.

See also MOTORCYCLE RACING.

Motorboat Racing
See POWERBOAT RACING.

Motorcycle Racing

The early development of motorcycle racing closely paralleled that of automobile racing. Between 1895 and 1901, several varieties of motor-powered bicycles and tricycles were produced. The best of them was designed by Oscar Hedstrom, a Swedish-born professional bicycle racer, who teamed with George Hendee of Springfield, MA to form the Indian Motocycle Company in 1901. (The "r" wasn't added to the word until several years later.) To demonstrate the product, Hendee rode it 250 miles in 16½ hours that year, and then began regular racing, usually on harness racing tracks. Other manufacturers soon

Foreign manufacturers and their company racing teams helped popularize motorcycle racing in North America beginning in the 1950s. This is Heiki Mikkola of Finland in a U.S. motocross event. Courtesy of Rusty Rae/AMA News

sprang up and got involved in racing as a form of advertising.

During the early years of the century, the motorcycle was seen as a low-cost alternative to the automobile, and it became very popular. At one time or another, more than 100 companies manufactured motorcycles in North America between 1900 and 1920. The Federation of Motorcyclists was organized in 1906 to oversee the sport, but it split in a dispute over whether professionals should be allowed to race. Henry Ford's introduction of the Model T in 1914 suddenly made cars less expensive (and more reliable) than motorcycles. World War I ended racing, and after the war the sport was virtually extinct in North America. Every major American motorcycle manufacturer except Harley-Davidson was out of business by the 1930s.

The American Motorcycle Association was founded in 1924. Although the AMA did sanction races, it was a trade association controlled by manufacturers, and its local and regional affiliated clubs were made up of motorcyclists in general, most of whom weren't involved in competition. Between the wars, most North American motorcycle races were run on short dirt tracks as sideshows at fairs, rodeos, and auto shows, while Europe was concentrating on Grand

Prix road racing. However, "speedway" racing, as the English call short-track racing, also became popular in Australia and England, and several top American cyclists raced in England during the 1930s. In 1937, Jack Milne of the United States won the world speedway championship, countryman Wilbur Lamoreaux finished second, and Jack's brother, Cordy, was third for an unprecedented sweep of the top three places.

During the late 1930s, the AMA sanctioned nearly 1,000 race meets a year, but virtually all the races were for amateurs and the few professional races offered minuscule prizes. The AMA in 1936 began awarding national championships in a number of categories, including road racing (actually racing on long paved tracks) and Tourist Trophy (which is really road racing). After World War II, the sport was again nearly extinct in North America, although the AMA continued its national championships and important meets were staged by a few tracks in California, notably the 300-yard Lincoln Park course in Los Angeles.

There was a comeback during the 1950s. In 1954, the AMA began awarding a national championship to the rider accumulating the most points for major events in five different types of racing, with 150 points to the winner, 120 to the second-place finisher, on down to 1 point for 20th place. By the end of the decade, the AMA was sanctioning about 4,000 meets a year—again, most of them for amateurs.

Two foreign manufacturers discovered the American market during the 1960s: Husqvarna of Sweden and Honda of Japan. Husqvarna brought a team of European motocross racers over to demonstrate that version of racing, and it became popular. To help sell its low-cost bikes, Honda began investing money in racing, increasing purses and competition. As the sport became more popular, the AMA changed its structure to give racing members more say over the rules of competition. And the association also gave in to pressure from its members by joining the international governing body, the Fédération Internationale Motocycliste, in 1973.

Motorcycle racing still hasn't approached major status in North America. It is nowhere near as popular as auto racing, and few professional racers can earn a living at the sport. But the continent's biggest race, the Daytona 200, has become a major international event, attracting top European racers, and more Americans are also competing in major European races.

The American Motorcycle Association became the American Motorcyclist Association in 1976, reflecting its change in orientation. In 1989 it absorbed the

American All-Terrain Vehicle Association, which had governed off-road racing of all kinds since 1983.

Address: American Motorcyclist Association, P.O. Box 6114, Westerville, OH 43081 (614) 891–2425

Muncie, IN

Football The Muncie Flyers were represented at the organizational meeting of the American Professional Football Association (now the National Football League) in 1920, but they dropped out after losing their only game 45–0 to Rock Island.

Murphy, Isaac (1861–1896)
Horse Racing

Born January 1, 1861, Fayette County, KY; died February 12, 1896; National Racing Hall of Fame

Murphy was one of many black jockeys who rode during the late 19th century. Black jockeys won 13 of the first 27 Kentucky Derby winners, and Murphy was the first ever to win the race three times, with Buchanan in 1884, Riley in 1890, and Kingman in 1891. That record stood for 57 years, until Eddie Arcaro won his fourth Kentucky Derby in 1948.

Murphy's original name was Isaac Burns, but he later took the name of his maternal grandfather, Green Murphy, who brought him up after his father was killed fighting for the Union Army in the Civil War. Racing expert L. P. Tarlton wrote, "I have seen all the great jockeys of England and this country for years back but, all in all, Isaac Murphy is the greatest of them all." Murphy's record bears Tarlton out: 628 winners in 1,412 races, a remarkable 44 percent.

Murphy died of pneumonia, probably caused in part by constant dieting to keep his weight down. He is now buried in Lexington, KY near Man O' War's grave.

Muscular Christianity

A kind of Victorian echo of the classical "healthy mind in a healthy body," muscular Christianity arose in England in the 1850s as the notion that physical development could contribute to spiritual and moral development. It quickly arrived in North America, largely because of Thomas Hughes' *Tom Brown's School Days*, a novel about life at Rugby School in England under headmaster Thomas Arnold. The first major proponent of muscular Christianity was Thomas Wentworth Higginson, who preached the virtues of outdoor recreation and sport in a series of articles in the *Atlantic Monthly*.

However, the movement didn't reach its peak until after the Civil War, when increasing urbanization created concern about the health and physical fitness of American youth. The hero of muscular Christianity was epitomized by Frank Merriwell, a fictional character who appeared in a series of 208 books written between 1896 and 1916 by Gilbert Patten, using the pseudonym Burt L. Standish. Merriwell was the ideal amateur sportsman and gentleman. He was candid, courageous, and fair-minded, dedicated to justice, opposed to pretense—and an outstanding athlete as well.

The YMCA's growing emphasis on physical training toward the end of the century was inspired by muscular Christianity, the gymnasium and playground movements were strongly influenced by it, and the rationale that high school and college sports are desirable because they help build character is a modern residue.

Musial, Stanislaus F. (1920–)
Baseball

Born November 21, 1920, Donora, PA; Baseball Hall of Fame

Musial's unique "peek-a-boo" stance would never be recommended to a young player. Holding the bat straight up and down, he hunched his back and coiled his body so that he was virtually looking over his shoulder at the pitcher. It worked for him. He won seven National League batting titles and three Most Valuable Player Awards, and when he retired he held more than 50 records. A left-handed thrower and batter, "Stan the Man" was a minor-league pitcher until he hurt his throwing arm in 1940. He became an outfielder the following season; before it was over he was playing for the St. Louis Cardinals, and in 1942 he was their starting left fielder. The Cardinals won three consecutive National League pennants, beginning that season. After hitting .315 in 1942, Musial led the league with a .357 batting average in 1943, when he won the first of his Most Valuable Player Awards, and he hit .347 in 1944.

He missed the 1945 season because of military service, then won another MVP award in 1946, when he spent most of his time at first base, leading the league in batting (.365), hits, doubles, triples, and runs scored. The Cardinals won their fourth pennant in his fourth full season with the team, but it was Musial's last, though he played another 18 seasons. He was MVP for the third time in 1948, leading the league in batting (.376), doubles, triples, runs scored, and runs batted in. He won three consecutive batting titles from 1950 through 1952 and hit over .300 every season until 1959, when he fell all the way to .255. Two more mediocre seasons convinced most fans that Musial was at the end of his career, but he rebounded to hit .330 in 1962. He retired after seeing only part-time duty the following season.

In 22 seasons, Musial had a .331 average with 3,630 hits, 725 doubles, 177 triples, 475 home runs, 1,949 runs scored and 1,951 runs batted in. He walked 1,599 times and struck out only 696 times in 10,972 at-bats. He is the only man ever to play more than 1,000 games both at first base and in the outfield, and he played in 892 consecutive games between 1952 and 1957.

MVP
See MOST VALUABLE PLAYER.

Myers, "Lon" Lawrence E. (1858–1899)
Track and Field
Born February 16, 1858, Richmond, VA; died February 15, 1899; National Track and Field Hall of Fame

One of many track and field stars who began running at an early age because of poor health, Myers was an amazingly versatile runner. Although the 440- and 880-yard runs were his best events, he also excelled at the shorter sprints. At one time, he held American records at all five standard distances from 100 yards to 1 mile. Myers won the 100, 220, and 440, at the 1879 and 1881 national championship meets; the 100, 220, 440, and 880 in 1880; the 440 in 1882 and 1883; and the 440 and 880 in 1884. He set a world record of 49.2 seconds in the 440 in 1879, the first time it had ever been run in less than 50 seconds, and he lowered it to 48.6 in 1881. He also set world records in the 880 at 1 minute 56 seconds in 1881 and at 1:55.4 in 1884.

Controversy over Myers' amateur status helped lead to the formation of the Amateur Athletic Union. Myers belonged to the Manhattan Athletic Club, an arch rival of the older New York Athletic Club. At a hearing before the National Association of Amateur Athletes of America in 1884, Myers was charged with professionalism because he owned a roller skating rink, accepted pay to judge a six-day walking race and to write a sports column, held a paid position as secretary of the Manhattan AC, and had won a $20 gold piece at a meet. The charges were dismissed, but because of this incident and other conflicts the NYAC withdrew from the NAAAA in 1886 and two years later joined with a dozen other clubs to form the AAU.

Shortly after the hearing, Myers went to England with several other American athletes and drew large crowds at several meets. He missed the national championships in 1885 for another trip to England, where he competed in 35 races in two months, but failed to arrange a meeting with the English champion, Walter George. After a brief retirement, George began running professionally, and in February 1886 Myers also gave up his amateur status, saying, "Amateur athletic sport has now little or nothing to offer me. I have won prizes and honors enough to satiate any man's ambition." He and George had a series of three races, 1,000 yards, 1,320 yards, and 1 mile, at Madison Square Garden; Myers won all three, and the two runners split $4,500 in gate receipts. They tried another series of races in Australia in 1887, but attendance was disappointing. George returned to England, and Myers, after trying to promote races for more than a year, eventually gave up and retired from racing.

N

NAAAA

See NATIONAL ASSOCIATION OF AMATEUR ATHLETES OF AMERICA.

Nagurski, "Bronko" Bronislaw (1905–1990)
Football

Born November 1, 1905, Rain River, Ontario; died January 7, 1990; National Football Foundation, Pro Football Hall of Fame

His coach at the University of Minnesota, Clarence W. Spears, said that Nagurski "could be an All-American at any of the eleven positions," and in fact he was named an All-American at both fullback and tackle by the *New York Sun* in 1929. Nagurski played fullback, defensive tackle, and linebacker for the Chicago Bears from 1930 through 1937. After five years as a professional wrestler, he returned to the Bears in 1943, because so many of the team's players were serving in World War II, and he averaged 5.3 yards per rushing attempt in limited action. The 6-foot-2, 225-pound Nagurski was an exceptionally hard hitter as a runner, blocker, and tackler. Steve Owen of the New York Giants said, "Tacklers to the Bronk were like flies on the flank of a horse—a nuisance, but not serious."

One of Nagurski's biggest plays was a pass he threw in the 1932 National Football League championship game against the Portsmouth Spartans. On fourth down at the Portsmouth 2-yard line, Nagurski faked a run into the line, stepped back and threw a touchdown pass to Red Grange to give the Bears a 7–0 lead in the fourth quarter of a game they won 9–0. Portsmouth protested, to no avail, that Nagurski hadn't been the required 5 yards behind the line of scrimmage when he passed. Partly because of the controversy, the NFL changed the rule to allow a forward pass from anywhere behind the line of scrimmage for the 1933 season.

Nagurski also threw two touchdown passes in the Bears' 23–21 championship win over the New York Giants in 1933. And in 1934 his blocking helped rookie halfback Beattie Feathers become the first NFL player ever to gain more than 1,000 yards in a season. In 1935 and 1937, he didn't carry the ball as frequently as in other years because he was often used as a tackle on offense while Jack Manders played fullback. Incomplete statistics for his nine seasons show 772 rushes for 3,435 yards, a 4.4-yard average, and 25 touchdowns. (The NFL didn't begin keeping official statistics until 1932, but figures are available from some earlier games.)

NAIA

See NATIONAL ASSOCIATION OF INTERCOLLEGIATE ATHLETICS.

Naismith, James (1861–1939)
Basketball

Born November 6, 1861, near Almonte, Ontario; died November 28, 1939; Basketball Hall of Fame

The man who invented basketball was orphaned on his ninth birthday and went to live with a bachelor uncle. He worked as a lumberjack for nearly five years, then went back to high school at the age of 19 and graduated from McGill University in Montreal when he was 25. After three years in a Presbyterian seminary, in 1890 he became an instructor at the International YMCA Training School in Springfield, MA.

In the fall of 1891, the director of the school, Luther H. Gulick, asked Naismith to invent an indoor sport that would hold students' interest during the winter. Naismith recalled, nearly 50 years later,

James Naismith invented basketball in December 1891 at the International YMCA Training School in Springfield, MA. Courtesy of the Basketball Hall of Fame

that he thought about his boyhood games to get some ideas. He decided to use a large ball, because a small ball was usually propelled by a bat or a racket, and he decided that the ball would be advanced by passing only, since if a player were allowed to run with it, tackling would be involved.

He dismissed the idea of a vertical goal, as in soccer and lacrosse, because players would try to hurl the ball into the goal through sheer force. At this point, according to his recollection, he thought of a game called "duck on a rock." In that childhood game, a player would put a stone called the duck on a larger stone, and his opponent would try to knock it off by throwing his own duck at it. The best strategy in that game was to toss the missile into the air, trying to hit the target from above. That, in turn, reminded Naismith of a warm-up exercise he had invented when he was captain of the McGill rugby team, in which players tossed balls into a box—the kind of horizontal goal he had in mind.

"Now, a goal on the floor would be too easy to guard," he recalled, "so I decided on a box above the floor. The janitor couldn't find a box, but he offered a couple of peach baskets, which were nailed to the gymnasium railing." Naismith got a soccer ball, drew up 13 rules, split his class into two teams of nine players each—and basketball was invented. It was an immediate success, and Springfield-trained instructors and missionaries literally brought it all over the world—to China and India in 1894, to France in 1895, to Japan in 1900, and to Persia (now Iran) in 1901.

In 1894, Naismith married Maude Sherman, who had played in the first women's basketball game two years before. After getting a degree in medicine at Gross School in Denver, he went to the University of Kansas as director of physical education. He promptly organized an eight-team intramural league for students and teachers, and then established a university team, which he "coached" until 1912. (Naismith, who played basketball only twice, believed the fundamentals of the sport could be taught, but he didn't think coaching was required. He, along with many other YMCA-trained people, saw basketball as a pleasurable exercise, not as a full-fledged sport like baseball or football.)

Naismith never made any money from his invention, and he was never financially successful. In the meantime, Forrest C. "Phog" Allen, who had been one of his players, had become a very successful coach at Kansas and had lobbied successfully to get basketball on the 1936 Olympic program. He also launched a fund drive to send Naismith to Berlin for the Games. Colleges in 43 states held "Naismith Nights," with a penny from each ticket going to the fund, and nearly $5,000 was raised. Naismith tossed up the ball for the opening tipoff of the first official Olympic game, between Estonia and France, and he presented the Gold Medals to the United States team that, ironically, had defeated his native Canada in the championship game.

Further Reading: Naismith, James. *Basketball, Its Origin and Development*. New York: Association Press, 1941.

Naismith Award
Basketball

There are actually three Naismith Awards, all presented by the Atlanta Tip-Off Club. The first, established in 1969, is given to the outstanding men's collegiate basketball player of the year. In 1983 the club added a similar award for women, and since 1987 there has been a third award, for the nation's top college coach. Winners are chosen by a panel of broadcasters, coaches, and sportswriters.

Naismith Award Winners—Men

1969 Lew Alcindor (Kareem Abdul-Jabbar), UCLA
1970 Pete Maravich, Louisiana State
1971 Austin Carr, Notre Dame
1972 Bill Walton, UCLA
1973 Bill Walton, UCLA
1974 Bill Walton, UCLA
1975 David Thompson, North Carolina State
1976 Scott May, Indiana
1977 Marques Johnson, UCLA
1978 Butch Lee, Marquette
1979 Larry Bird, Indiana State
1980 Mark Aguirre, DePaul
1981 Ralph Sampson, Virginia
1982 Ralph Sampson, Virginia
1983 Ralph Sampson, Virginia
1984 Michael Jordan, North Carolina
1985 Patrick Ewing, Georgetown
1986 Johnny Dawkins, Duke
1987 David Robinson, Navy
1988 Danny Manning, Kansas
1989 Danny Ferry, Duke
1990 Lionel Simmons, LeSalle
1991 Larry Johnson, Nevada-Las Vegas

Naismith Award Winners—Women

1983 Anne Donovan, Old Dominion
1984 Cheryl Miller, Southern California
1985 Cheryl Miller, Southern California
1986 Cheryl Miller, Southern California
1987 Kamie Ethridge, Texas
1988 Teresa Weatherspoon, Louisiana Tech
1989 Clarissa Davis, Texas

1990 Venus Lacy, Louisiana Tech
1991 Dawn Staley, Virginia

Naismith Award Winners—Coaches

1987 Bobby Knight, Indiana
1988 Larry Brown, Kansas
1989 Mike Krzyzewski, Duke
1990 Jim Calhoun, Connecticut
1991 Mike Krzyzewski, Duke

Naismith Memorial Basketball Hall of Fame

This hall of fame began in October of 1949 as a two-room office on the campus of Springfield (MA) College, formerly the International YMCA Training School, where basketball was invented in 1891. Edward J. Hickox, formerly Springfield's basketball coach, served as the unpaid executive secretary for 14 years, gathering memorabilia and keeping the idea alive. The first members were inducted in 1959, but construction didn't begin until 1961, and it was stopped a year later for lack of funds.

The original Naismith Memorial Basketball Hall of Fame, a $650,000 building, finally opened on February 17, 1968. In 17 years of operation, it attracted 630,179 people, an average of about 37,000 a year. It was replaced by an $11 million building in a more accessible location on June 30, 1985. In addition to the Honors Court, where inductees are enshrined, the hall of fame features displays on the history of the sport, a movie theater, and a library and research center open by appointment only.

Address: 1150 West Columbus Avenue, P.O. Box 179, Springfield, MA 01101–0179 (413) 781–6500

Namath, Joseph W. (1943–   )
Football

Born May 31, 1945, Beaver Falls, PA; Pro Football Hall of Fame

The five-year-old American Football League won a large measure of respectability in 1965, when quarterback Joe Namath signed a contract with the New York Jets for a reported $400,000. Namath gave the league even more respectability when he led the Jets to a 16–7 win over the Baltimore Colts in Super Bowl III, after having "guaranteed" a victory to a scoffing banquet crowd.

Drafted out of Alabama in 1965, Namath became the Jets' starter during his rookie season. He attracted fans wherever he played, and his well-publicized swinging life-style, which earned him the nickname "Broadway Joe," kept Namath, his team, and the AFL in the news. He led the league in attempts, completions, and yardage in 1966 and 1967 and threw three touchdown passes in the Jets' 27–23

win over the Oakland Raiders for the 1968 AFL championship game. Then came Super Bowl III, the AFL's first victory over the NFL. Namath masterfully took apart the Colts' experienced defense by mixing inside runs with short passes, and the Jets controlled the game all the way.

The Jets won the eastern division title again in 1969, but lost 13–6 to the Kansas City Chiefs in the playoffs. Namath missed most of the next two seasons with injuries. He played six more seasons and posted good numbers most of those years, but continuing problems with his knees made him less mobile and more vulnerable to the pass rush. He retired after spending the 1977 season with the Los Angeles Rams.

Namath was the AFL Player of the Year in 1968, and he was named quarterback on the AFL's all-time team in 1969, the last year before its merger into the National Football League. He completed 1,886 out of 3,762 passes for 27,663 yards, with 173 touchdowns and 229 interceptions.

Further Reading: Namath, Joe Willie, with Dick Schaap. *I Can't Wait Until Tomorrow 'Cause I Get Better Looking Every Day.* New York: Random House, 1969.

NASCAR

See NATIONAL ASSOCIATION FOR STOCK CAR AUTO RACING.

National Agreement
Baseball

Now largely superseded by the collective bargaining contract between the Major League Players Association and the leagues, the National Agreement was the foundation of organized baseball for nearly a century. It originated as the Tripartite Pact, an 1883 peace treaty between the National League and the American Association, which was also signed by the minor Northwestern League. The pact established territorial rights for existing franchises and allowed each team to reserve 11 players, who could not be signed by any other team. (This was the first time the reserve clause was made explicit; it had previously been only a gentleman's agreement among National League owners.) The leagues agreed to honor one another's expulsions and suspensions of players. Minimum salaries for reserved players were set at $1,000 for major-leaguers and $750 for minor-leaguers. An arbitration committee made up of three representatives from each league was established to settle any dispute that might arise under the agreement.

After minor revision in 1885 and 1886, a totally new agreement was drawn up in 1890 among the two major leagues and the Western Association, which had replaced the Northwestern League. The arbitration committee was replaced by a three-member National Board with much broader powers. The board was given total responsibility for fining and suspending anyone involved in the sport, including players, teams, umpires, and official scorers. That lasted only a year. Unhappy about the loss of many players and a couple of franchises as a result of a year-long struggle with the Players' League, the American Association, in 1891, withdrew from the National Agreement and began to sign National League players. But the National League retaliated, and the greatly weakened Association folded after that season.

In 1892, the National League and several minor leagues entered into another National Agreement, which established two minor-league classes, A and B, and a player draft system. Major-league teams were allowed to draft Class A players for $1,000 apiece, and Class A teams were allowed to draft Class B players for $500 apiece.

A new war began in 1901, when the American League (formerly the Western League) claimed major-league status and refused to re-sign the National Agreement. Peace was reached in December of 1902 with a fourth National Agreement, signed by the American and National Leagues and the newly formed National Association of Professional Baseball Leagues. The National Board was replaced by a National Commission, made up of the two major-league presidents and a chairman selected jointly.

Even before the Black Sox Scandal, a major reorganization was considered. The National Agreement was temporarily abandoned in 1920, to be replaced by a plan proposed by Albert D. Lasker, a part-owner of the Chicago Cubs. The Lasker plan called for a new National Commission made up of three paid members with no financial interest in baseball. However, the new National Agreement finally ratified by both major leagues on January 12, 1921, called for a single, all-powerful commissioner. It also provided that interleague disputes be settled by a majority vote of the 16 major-league clubs; if there was no majority, each league would cast a single vote with the commissioner as tiebreaker. (A separate agreement was signed by the National Association on January 10.)

Kenesaw Mountain Landis, the first baseball commissioner, served until his death in 1944. The following year, the National Agreement was revised to increase the Advisory Council from three members to seven, greatly reducing the commissioner's powers; Landis had, in effect, controlled the council during his tenure, when he and the presidents of the two major leagues were its members. The presidents were also given much greater control over their league affairs. In 1968, the first basic agreement between the players and the owners was signed, incorporating most of the player relations issues previously governed by the National Agreement and now subject to collective bargaining.

See also MINOR LEAGUES; NATIONAL COMMISSION; RESERVE CLAUSE.

National Amateur Athletic Federation (NAAF)

The idea for the NAAF grew out of a kind of mini-revolt against the Amateur Athletic Union in 1907, when the YMCA and the Boy Scouts were joined by a number of schools and colleges in forming the Athletic Research Society. Their major complaint was that the AAU was interested only in elite athletes, not in making sports available to as many people as possible. As the result of an ARS report, the National Federated Committee was organized in 1911 "to unite the national organizations interested in play and recreation in a comprehensive educational campaign. . . ."

The committee disappeared during World War I, but dissatisfaction with the AAU lingered. After the war, the AAU-controlled Olympic movement became the chief bone of contention. The American Olympic Association was organized in 1921 to raise funds and manage the Olympic effort, but the AAU and its allied members had a total of 42 votes, to only 16 for the National Collegiate Athletic Association and 3 each for other groups. As a result, the NCAA, the YMCA, Army, and Navy refused to join. Both Palmer Pierce, head of the NCAA, and Secretary of War John W. Weeks called for a national association of all amateur sports organizations. The result was the National Amateur Athletic Federation, founded on May 8, 1922.

The NAAF offered to join the AOA if given voting power equal to the AAU's, but the AAU rejected the offer. A compromise was finally worked out, and the NAAF, along with its major members, did join the AOA. However, they dropped out again in 1926 because AAU member clubs were actively recruiting college undergraduates, in violation of NCAA rules. After General Douglas MacArthur became its president in 1927, the AAU agreed to stop recruiting college students, and the NAAF affiliates rejoined the AOA, while the federation itself quietly faded away.

See also NATIONAL COLLEGIATE ATHLETIC ASSOCIATION.

National Amateur Baseball Federation (NABF)

The National Amateur Baseball Association was founded in 1914 in Louisville, KY to conduct a national tournament for amateur teams. It became the National Baseball Federation in 1916 and took its present name in 1933. The NABF now oversees national championship tournaments for five age groups: major (unlimited age); college (under 21), established in 1982; senior (18 and under), established in 1975; junior (16 and under), established in 1962; and sophomore (14 and under), established in 1962.

Address: 12406 Keynote Lane, Bowie, MD 20715 (301) 262–0770.

National Amateur Challenge Cup

See NATIONAL CHALLENGE CUP.

National Amateur Skating Association of the United States (NASA)

The NASA, founded in 1886, governed both figure skating and speed skating in the United States until 1921, when it was replaced by two new organizations, the U.S. Figure Skating Association and the Amateur Skating Union of the United States (now the U.S. International Speed Skating Association). [Similarly, the U.S. Figure Skating Association became independent in 1921, leaving the parent group to oversee speed skating only.]

National Association for Stock Car Auto Racing (NASCAR)

Stock car racing had some small regional organizations before and immediately after World War II, but it wasn't a genuine organized sport until December 14, 1947, when NASCAR was founded in a meeting at Daytona Beach, FL. The man who called the meeting was William H. G. "Big Bill" France, a one-time service station attendant who made extra money racing souped-up cars against challengers. NASCAR held its first race February 15, 1948, on the beach course at Daytona, which had been used for informal racing since the early 1930s.

NASCAR grew rapidly. Superspeedway racing began in 1950 when the Darlington (SC) Raceway opened. Ten California tracks that had belonged to their own organization merged into NASCAR in 1954, and a year later a midwestern group, SAFE, also became part of NASCAR, adding convertible racing to its schedule. NASCAR racing passed other types of auto racing in popularity in 1976, with a total attendance of 1,431,292 for its Winston Cup

Series alone. A major reason for its success has been its ability to line up major sponsors from outside the automotive field, beginning with R. J. Reynolds Tobacco Company in 1970.

Address: P.O. Bin K, 1801 Speedway Boulevard, Daytona Beach, FL 32015 (904) 253–0611

See also STOCK CAR RACING; WINSTON CUP.

National Association of Amateur Athletes of America (N4A)

The New York Athletic Club ruled track and field and conducted an annual national championship meet open to members of other amateur clubs during the 1870s. As the number of clubs proliferated across the country, the need grew for a separate national organization to oversee the sport. The American Amateur Athletic Association was organized in 1878 by eight clubs, but the NYAC didn't join. On April 22, 1879, the AAAA was reorganized as the National Association of Amateur Athletes of America (N4A), with the NYAC as a member. The new organization took over the national meet and adopted the NYAC rule governing amateurism.

However, the N4A was soon torn apart by internal problems, particularly the power struggle between the New York and Manhattan Athletic Clubs. The struggle first surfaced in 1884 with charges that L. E. "Lon" Myers of the Manhattan AC was a professional. Among other things, Myers had accepted money for serving as a judge at a six-day walking race and for writing a sports column, he owned a roller skating rink, and he was the paid secretary of the club. Myers' amateur status was upheld, leading the weekly sports publication *Spirit of the Times* to suggest that the association's rules needed to be clarified.

In 1886, the NYAC lured Malcolm Ford away from the Brooklyn AC after he had won the 100- and 220-yard dashes and the running long jump at the N4A championship meet. The Brooklyn AC immediately charged that Ford had competed under an assumed name in a professional meet at Springfield, MA. After a long "trial," Ford was declared ineligible. The NYAC also recruited distance runner Edward C. Carter from England, hammer thrower W. L. Condon of Baltimore, and shot-putter George Gray of Toronto. The Manhattan AC then landed miler A. B. George of England and distance runner Patrick Conneff of Ireland, who had beaten Carter in a 4-mile race. The NYAC protested when Coneff was given a job with a company managed by the secretary of the Manhattan AC, but to no avail.

The NYAC then withdrew from the N4A and on October 1, 1887, called a meeting of clubs to form a new association. As a result, the Amateur Athletic Union was founded on January 21, 1888, and it was widely supported, while the N4A lost much of its membership. After the AAU announced it would hold a national championship meet on September 19 in Detroit, the N4A announced a western championship meet in St. Louis on September 9. But the AAU declared that any athlete competing in a non-AAU meet would be barred from the national championships. The N4A then postponed its meet, primarily to allow the Manhattan AC to take part in the national meet. Shortly afterward, the Inter-Collegiate Association of Amateur Athletes of America decided to withdraw from the N4A. The war ended abruptly with a "truce" that was really a surrender: The N4A was dissolved, and its members were accepted into the AAU.

See also AMATEUR ATHLETIC UNION.

National Association of Base Ball Players (NABBP)

A group of baseball clubs from New York met in January of 1857, elected officers, and appointed a committee to standardize rules. That was the beginning of the National Association of Base Ball Players, which was formally organized on March 10, 1858, by 22 New York area clubs. The association adopted the rules of the Knickerbocker Base Ball Club, with one major modification calling for seven-inning games, soon changed to nine innings. Under Knickerbocker rules, the first team to score 21 runs won the game.

The NABBP grew rapidly. By 1866, there were 202 member clubs from 17 states plus the District of Columbia. The following year, membership was limited to state associations, except for states that had fewer then ten clubs. The association at first prohibited professionals from playing for any member teams, but by 1868 there were so many professional players that a separate membership classification was established for them. In 1869, the professionals pretty much took over the NABBP convention, and most amateur associations and clubs dropped out as a result.

After the National Association of Professional Base Ball Players was organized in 1870, a group of 18 clubs tried to revive the association as the National Association of Amateur Base Ball Players, but the new organization was short-lived.

See also NATIONAL ASSOCIATION OF PROFESSIONAL BASE BALL PLAYERS.

National Association of Basketball Coaches (NABC)

Basketball's Joint Rules Committee in the spring of 1927 suddenly voted to limit the dribble to a single bounce. "Phog" Allen, basketball coach at the University of Kansas, criticized the action in a speech before the National Education Association and got letters and telegrams from more than 160 coaches supporting him. He asked them to meet with him at the Drake Relays in Des Moines, IA in May. A month later, the NABC was formally organized at a meeting in Chicago and Allen was elected president. A resolution opposing the rule change was passed and sent to the Joint Rules Committee, which agreed to postpone the change for a year. As it turned out, the new rule never went into effect.

About 100 coaches attended the NABC's first convention in 1928. There are now more than 1,200 member coaches. The association held the first national collegiate tournament in 1939; it was taken over by the NCAA the following year. The NABC names college and university division All-American teams and selects the winners of several awards, including a coach of the year.

Address: P.O. Box 307, Branford, CT 06405 (203) 488–1232.

National Association of Intercollegiate Athletics (NAIA)

The seed of the NAIA was planted in 1937 when Kansas City business leaders decided the city needed a college basketball tournament to replace the Amateur Athletic Union tournament, which had moved to Denver. After meeting with James Naismith, the sport's inventor, who was at the University of Kansas, and Emil S. Liston, athletic director at Baker University in Baldwin, KS, they organized the National Small College Basketball Tournament, featuring the champions of eight midwestern conferences. The tournament grew to 32 teams in 1938, and two years later the National Association of Intercollegiate Basketball was organized. The NAIB not only ran the tournament, it established standards of eligibility for member schools and conferences.

The NAIB became the NAIA in 1952, when it added national championships in golf, tennis, and track and field. The association expanded into baseball, cross-country, football, and swimming in 1956, wrestling in 1958, soccer in 1959, bowling in 1962, gymnastics in 1964, indoor track in 1966, hockey in 1968, and volleyball in 1969.

There are more than 500 NAIA member colleges and about 50 affiliated conferences. The association is organized into 32 geographical districts, each with its own chairman and executive committee. District championships are held in most sports, with winners advancing into area or national championships.

Address: 1221 Baltimore, Kansas City, MO 64105 (816) 842–5050

National Association of Professional Baseball Leagues (NAPBL)

Faced with the prospect of losing many players in the bidding war between the National and American Leagues, seven minor leagues met in Chicago on September 5, 1901, to form the NAPBL. The original members were the Eastern League, New England League, New York State League, Pacific Northwestern Association, Three-I League, Western Association, and Western League. The Southern Association joined the NAPBL later that year, and the Cotton States, Missouri Valley, North Carolina, Pennsylvania State, and Texas Leagues joined before the 1902 season began.

Leagues were classified from A to D, depending on the total population of the cities and towns represented. Class A teams were allowed to sell players directly to major-league teams, and a system was set up under which teams could draft players from leagues in lower classification for a set price. After the two major leagues made their peace in 1903, this system was incorporated into the new National Agreement, with some modifications.

Address: P.O. Box A, St. Petersburg, FL 33731 (813) 822–6937.

See also MINOR LEAGUES.

National Association of Professional Base Ball Players

Organized professional baseball began on March 17, 1871, when ten teams formed the National Association of Professional Base Ball Players. The original teams were the Boston Red Stockings, Chicago White Stockings, Cleveland Forest Cities, Ft. Wayne Kekiongas, New York Mutuals, Philadelphia Athletics, Rockford Forest Cities, Troy Unions, Washington Nationals, and Washington Olympics. The Ft. Wayne team was replaced by the Brooklyn Eckfords during the first season.

The National Association, as it is generally known, didn't set up a formal schedule, but it provided for "match games" among its members, with each series to consist of five games. The team winning the most games was to be champion; in case of a tie, the team with the highest percentage of victories would be the winner. The association was unstable because of the lack of parity among teams and the distances to

be traveled. Teams with poor records often simply refused to go on road trips, resulting in an imbalanced schedule. In 1872, for example, Boston won 39 of 47 games to finish first while Brooklyn was a dismal last with only 3 victories in 29 games.

During its five years of existence, 25 teams belonged to the National Association, and only 3 of them played every season. The association was also weak administratively and unable to deal with the problems associated with gambling and "revolving"—the practice of players moving from one team to another at will. In 1876, the National League of Professional Baseball Clubs was organized, and the National Association folded.

National Association Champions

1871 Philadelphia Athletics
1872 Boston Red Stockings
1873 Boston Red Stockings
1874 Boston Red Stockings
1875 Boston Red Stockings

See also NATIONAL LEAGUE.

National Baseball Players Association of the United States (NBPA)

The fourth attempt by major-league players to organize a union, the NBPA was founded in 1922. Raymond J. Cannon of Milwaukee was hired to head the group. Cannon, a lawyer and former professional player, was a long-time advocate of players' rights. He was the attorney for Black Sox scandal victim "Shoeless Joe" Jackson in his unsuccessful attempt to claim back pay, and in 1937, as a congressman from Wisconsin, he tried in vain to get the U.S. attorney general to investigate organized baseball for possible antitrust action.

The association's constitution pointed out that major-league owners were united (as organized baseball) and concluded that it was "necessary that the players shall deal with such owners and their organization as a unit." However, players apparently weren't yet ready for such action. One player was reported to have said, scornfully, "It would be a lot of satisfaction, now wouldn't it, to sit down and read over your union card after you'd struck out in the ninth with the bases full?" The association was defunct before the year ended.

National Basketball Association (NBA)

A number of arena owners, looking at the popularity of college basketball and the need for more money-making attractions, met in New York on June 6, 1946, to organize the Basketball Association of America. The original 11 franchises were in Boston,

Chicago, Cleveland, Detroit, New York, Philadelphia, Pittsburgh, Providence, St. Louis, Toronto, and Washington. Zone defenses were outlawed by the new league to encourage more scoring. Maurice Podoloff, who had been president of the American Hockey League, was named BAA president.

A salary war with the National Basketball League hurt several BAA teams. Cleveland, Detroit, Pittsburgh, and Toronto dropped out of the BAA after one season, but the Baltimore Bullets were added and the league was reorganized into two four-team divisions. After the 1947–48 season, Podoloff persuaded the Ft. Wayne Pistons and Indianapolis Jets to move from the NBL into the BAA, and the Minneapolis Lakers and Rochester Royals quickly followed. Before the 1949–50 season, the two leagues merged, and the BAA was renamed the National Basketball Association.

The result was a cumbersome 17-team league. Providence dropped out, while Anderson, Denver, Sheboygan, Syracuse, Tri-Cities, and Waterloo were added. The NBA was reorganized into three divisions, with four teams from each division qualifying for the playoffs. Minneapolis won the championship, its third in four years—the first having come in the NBL. Anderson, Chicago, Denver, St. Louis, Sheboygan, and Waterloo all folded after the 1949–50 season, and the NBA went back to two divisions.

The Washington Capitols disbanded on January 10, 1951, after winning just 10 of 35 games, leaving 10 teams. And the Tri-Cities Blackhawks (representing Davenport, IA and East Moline and Rockford, IL) became the Milwaukee Hawks after the season. The NBA remained stable during the 1952–53 season, but Indianapolis then dropped out, leaving just nine teams. At this point, the league was basically stagnant. While major-league baseball and professional football were riding the crest of postwar prosperity, professional basketball still lagged behind the college sport.

A major rules change in 1954 probably saved the NBA. The league adopted a rule requiring a team to take a shot within 24 seconds after gaining control of the ball. There was no immediate impact on attendance—indeed, the Baltimore franchise folded just 14 games into the 1954–55 season—but the increased scoring unquestionably stepped up public interest and, in the long run, greatly improved the sport's television appeal.

The Hawks moved from Milwaukee to St. Louis in 1955, the Rochester Royals went to Cincinnati in 1957, and the NBA became genuinely national when the Lakers moved to Los Angeles in 1960. The following year, a franchise was added in Chicago. The league got a second West Coast franchise in 1962,

the Philadelphia Warriors moving to San Francisco, and in 1963 Philadelphia acquired a new team, the 76ers, who had formerly been the Syracuse Nationals.

The 1963–64 season was doubly important to the NBA. Attendance climbed over 2 million for the first time, in part because the struggling Chicago franchise had moved to Baltimore. Maurice Podoloff retired and was replaced as president by J. Walter Kennedy, who was to guide the league through expansion and a battle with the American Basketball Association. Expansion began quietly when another Chicago franchise was established in 1966. The following season, San Diego and Seattle joined the league; Phoenix and Milwaukee were added in 1968, and Buffalo, Cleveland, and Portland in 1970. So, for its 25th season, the NBA once again had 17 teams, the number it had boasted after the merger with the NBL in 1949.

It also had a rival, the American Basketball Association. Founded in 1967 with teams in Anaheim, Dallas, Denver, Houston, Indiana, Kentucky, Minnesota, New Jersey, New Orleans, Oakland, and Pittsburgh, the ABA planned to force a merger with the NBA within five years. The leagues did agree in 1971 to merge, but they were blocked by an antitrust suit filed by the NBA Players Association. By the time the merger finally took place, in 1976, the ABA had only seven teams; the Denver Nuggets, Indiana Pacers, New York Nets, and San Antonio Spurs were accepted into the NBA while players from the three other went into a special dispersal draft.

The NBA was up to 22 teams—the New Orleans Jazz had joined the league in 1974—and it remained at that number until 1980, when the Dallas Mavericks were given an expansion franchise. In 1987, the NBA announced a two-phase, four-team expansion program, with Miami and Charlotte joining for the 1988–89 season and Minnesota and Orlando entering the following season.

During the early 1980s, financial ruin threatened several teams, largely because of escalating player salaries brought on by limited free agency. The NBA and its players association reached a landmark agreement in 1983, when the league guaranteed that players would receive 53 percent of gross profits. In exchange, the players accepted a "salary cap" under which each team's total player payroll was limited. By the 1989–90 season, the salary cap was $9.2 million a team, and some teams were again in financial trouble. However, under contracts signed in 1990, the NBA's television money increased from about $72 million a season to nearly $220 million for each of the next four seasons. The money is to come from two major sources, NBC and Turner Network Television. Season ticket sales also increased by 13.8 percent, from 247,396 in the 1988–89 season to 281,440.

NBA Champions

1947	Philadelphia
1948	Baltimore
1949	Minneapolis
1950	Minneapolis
1951	Rochester
1952	Minneapolis
1953	Minneapolis
1954	Minneapolis
1955	Syracuse
1956	Philadelphia
1957	Boston
1958	St. Louis
1959	Boston
1960	Boston
1961	Boston
1962	Boston
1963	Boston
1964	Boston
1965	Boston
1966	Boston
1967	Philadelphia
1968	Boston
1969	Boston
1970	New York
1971	Milwaukee
1972	Los Angeles
1973	New York
1974	Boston
1975	Golden State
1976	Boston
1977	Portland
1978	Washington
1979	Seattle
1980	Los Angeles
1981	Boston
1982	Los Angeles
1983	Philadelphia
1984	Boston
1985	Los Angeles
1986	Boston
1987	Los Angeles
1988	Los Angeles
1989	Detroit
1990	Detroit
1991	Chicago

Addresses:

National Basketball Association, Olympic Tower, 545 Fifth Avenue, New York, NY 10022 (212) 826–7000.

Atlanta Hawks, 100 Techwood Drive NW, Atlanta, GA 30303 (404) 827–3800

Boston Celtics, 150 Causeway Street, Boston, MA 02114 (617) 523–6050.

Charlotte Hornets, Two First Union Center, Suite 2600, Charlotte, NC 28282 (704) 376–6430.

Chicago Bulls, One Magnificent Mile, 960 North Michigan Avenue, Suite 1600, Chicago, IL 60611 (312) 943–5800.

Cleveland Cavaliers, 2923 Streetsboro Road, Richfield, OH 44286 (216) 659–9100.

Dallas Mavericks, 77 Sports Street, Dallas, TX 75207 (214) 748–1808.

Denver Nuggets, 1635 Clay Street, P.O. Box 4658, Denver, CO 80204 (303) 893–6700.

Detroit Pistons, 3777 Lapeer Road, Auburn Hills, MI 48057 (313) 377–0100.

Golden State Warriors, Oakland Coliseum Arena, Oakland, CA 94621 (415) 638–6300.

Houston Rockets, Ten Greenway Plaza, Houston, TX 77046 (713) 627–0600.

Indiana Pacers, Two West Washington, Suite 510, Indianapolis, IN 46204 (317) 263–2100.

Los Angeles Clippers, 3939 South Figueroa Street, Los Angeles, CA 90037 (213) 748–8000.

Los Angeles Lakers, The Forum, 3900 West Manchester Boulevard, P.O. Box 10, Inglewood, CA 90306 (213) 419–3100.

Miami Heat, The Miami Arena, Miami, FL 33136 (305) 577–4328.

Milwaukee Bucks, Bradley Center, 1001 North Fourth Street, Milwaukee, WI 53203 (414) 227–0500.

Minnesota Timberwolves, 500 City Place, 730 Hennepin Avenue, Minneapolis, MN 55403 (612) 337–3865.

New Jersey Nets, Meadowlands Arena, East Rutherford, NJ 07073 (201) 935–8888.

New York Knickerbockers, Madison Square Garden, Four Pennsylvania Plaza, New York, NY 10001 (212) 563–8000.

Orlando Magic, Orlando Arena, 1 Magic Place, Orlando, FL 32801 (407) 649–3200.

Philadelphia 76ers, P.O. Box 25040, Philadelphia, PA 19147 (215) 339–7600.

Phoenix Suns, 2910 North Central Avenue, Phoenix, AZ 85012 (602) 266–5753.

Portland Trail Blazers, Suite 950 Lloyd Building, 700 Multnomah Street, Portland, OR 92732 (503) 234–9291.

Sacramento Kings, One Sports Parkway, Sacramento, CA 95834 (916) 928–0000.

San Antonio Spurs, 600 East Market Street, Suite 102, San Antonio, TX 78205 (512) 224–4611.

Seattle Supersonics, 190 Queen Avenue N., Box C 900911, Seattle, WA 98109 (206) 281–5800.

Utah Jazz, 5 Triad Center, Suite 500, Salt Lake City, UT 84180 (801) 575–7800.

Washington Bullets, Capital Centre, Landover, MD 20785 (301) 773–2255.

See also AMERICAN BASKETBALL ASSOCIATION.

National Basketball League

Three major industrial basketball teams, the Goodyear Wingfoots and Firestone Non-Skids of Akron and General Electrics of Ft. Wayne, decided to become fully professional in 1937. They joined with ten other teams to form the National Basketball League. As their names indicate, most of the other teams were also commercially sponsored: Buffalo Bisons, Columbus Athletic Supply, Dayton Metros, Indianapolis Kautskys, Kankakee Gallagher Trojans, Oshkosh All-Stars, Pittsburgh Pirates, Richmond Comellos, Warren Penn Oilers, and Whiting Ciesar All-Americans.

As usual with a new league, several teams had financial problems. The Richmond team moved to Cincinnati during the season, and some teams didn't bother to complete their schedules because they were out of contention. Juggling of franchises went on almost constantly. After World War II, the NBL had some major cities, including Chicago and Minneapolis, but it also faced competition from the new Basketball Association of America. The NBL won the first major battle when the Chicago American Gears signed George Mikan of DePaul for the 1946–47 season. But it lost the war in 1948 when four of its teams (Ft. Wayne, Indianapolis, Minneapolis and Rochester) joined the BAA. The leagues merged into the National Basketball Association in 1949.

NBL Champions

1938	Oshkosh
1939	Akron Firestone
1940	Akron Firestone
1941	Oshkosh
1942	Oshkosh
1943	Ft. Wayne
1944	Ft. Wayne
1945	Ft. Wayne
1946	Rochester
1947	Rochester
1948	Minneapolis
1949	Anderson

National Bowling Hall of Fame and Museum

The American Bowling Congress, Professional Bowlers Association, and Women's International Bowling Congress each had its own hall of fame until June 2, 1984, when the three were amalgamated as

Steve Nagy, a member of the National Bowling Hall of Fame, was named to the modern All-Time All-American team by bowling writers in 1970. Courtesy of the American Bowling Congress

the National Bowling Hall of Fame in St. Louis. Built at a cost of about $7 million, the three-story facility has nearly 50,000 square feet of exhibit space near Busch Memorial Stadium. In addition to areas honoring inductees to the three halls of fame, the complex includes a 19th-century alley where visitors can bowl with old lignum vitae balls; Busch Theatre, which features the movie *The World of Bowling*; and Tenpin Alley, which has several life-size dioramas illustrating the history of the sport. There are also two hands-on exhibits, Hometown Heroics, where visitors can use computer terminals to look up members of local and state bowling halls of fame, and Star Talk, where famous bowlers talk about their careers, illustrated by old film footage, on videodisc.

The Hall of Fame had its roots in a display of historical material assembled by the ABC in 1939 to be exhibited at its annual tournament. The exhibit was given a temporary home in 1972 at Bowling Headquarters, the joint ABC/WIBC membership services operation in Greendale, WI. In 1977, the two organizations joined with the Bowling Proprietors Association of America and two major manufacturers of bowling equipment, AMF Incorporated and the Brunswick Corporation, to form the National Bowling Hall of Fame and Museum as a nonprofit corporation. St. Louis was selected as the site for the hall of fame and museum in 1979 from among 35 cities that applied.

Address: 111 Stadium Plaza, St. Louis, MO 63102 (314) 231–6340.

National Bowling League

Bowling was just becoming a television staple when the National Bowling League was organized in 1961. There were ten teams: the Dallas Broncos, Detroit Thunderbirds, Ft. Worth Panthers, Fresno Bombers, Kansas City Stars, Los Angeles Toros, New York Gladiators, Omaha Packers, San Antonio Spurs, and Twin Cities (Minneapolis-St. Paul) Skippers. The five bowlers on each team rolled in head-to-head competition for two games. A win was worth one point, with one point for a game over 210, and an added point for every 10 pins beyond 210. A 240 game, for example, would be worth four points.

The season was to run from October 1961 to May 1962. Kansas City, Omaha, and San Antonio dropped out in December, Los Angeles in January. Only 1,000 fans watched Detroit win the league championship match against Twin Cities, and the NBL was out of business after just one season.

National Boxing Association

See WORLD BOXING ORGANIZATION.

National Challenge Cup
Soccer

Sir Thomas R. Dewar of England donated this trophy in 1912 for the soccer championship of the United States. In a letter to T. W. Cahill of the American Amateur Football Association, Sir Thomas said, "I trust that one day foot ball will be found a formidable rival of that great national game, base ball, a game for which I also have a great respect, having been, in fact, for several years president of the Base Ball Association in England." Because semiprofessional teams began to dominate the competition, the National Amateur Challenge Cup was established in 1923 for amateur teams, and the original Challenge Cup was offered for open competition among amateur and professional teams.

National Collegiate Athletic Association (NCAA)

John D. Rockefeller, the meat-packing industry, and college sports were all targeted by "muckraking" journalists in 1905. Henry Beach Needham's two-part series in *McClure's* magazine exposed illegal payments to players, classroom cheating, the use of

"tramp athletes," and many other abuses, even at prestigious eastern colleges and preparatory schools. Brutality in football was also a major issue of the year. President Theodore Roosevelt's White House conference with representatives from Harvard, Princeton, and Yale produced nothing but a gentleman's agreement that the "Big Three" would do their best to observe the spirit as well as the letter of the football rules.

However, after a Union College player was killed in a game against New York University, NYU's chancellor, Henry M. MacCracken, invited 19 colleges to decide whether to reform football or abolish it. Thirteen schools attended the meeting on December 9, 1905, and 62 were represented at a second meeting on December 28, when the Intercollegiate Athletic Association of the United States was formally organized to reform the sport's rules, with Captain Palmer E. Pierce of the U.S. Military Academy as president. However, only 28 of the schools actually joined the organization.

The association worked with the existing American Intercollegiate Football Rules Committee, through intermediary William T. Reid of Harvard, to make several rules changes. Mass-momentum plays, which caused many serious injuries, were eliminated by requiring that six offensive players must be on the line of scrimmage at the snap of the ball; the forward pass was legalized, with a number of restrictions; and the number of yards to be gained in three downs was increased from 5 to 10.

The second major move by the IAAUS was an eligibility code limiting participation to four years for full-time students only. A bylaw required every athlete to sign a card attesting to his amateur status, even though the association had no enforcement powers. Cards were to be filed with the colleges, which had responsibility for enforcing eligibility requirements.

In 1907, the collegiate Basketball Rules Committee came under IAAUS jurisdiction and prohibited teams from playing noncollegiate opponents. The association established committees to standardize playing rules and set standards for competition in track and field in 1908, soccer in 1911, swimming and other aquatic sports in 1913, wrestling in 1917, and volleyball in 1918. In addition, rifle target shooting was recognized as an intercollegiate sport in 1917, and tennis followed in 1918.

The IAAUS had become a genuinely national organization in 1910, when its name was changed to the National Collegiate Athletic Association. By 1919, the NCAA had a membership of 170 colleges representing about 400,000 students, and it had begun two long struggles: an internal struggle over how collegiate sport should be controlled, and an external struggle with the Amateur Athletic Union over the control of American amateur sport.

Although the NCAA bylaws specified standards of amateurism and eligibility, its constitution stipulated that no legislation could be binding on a member if its "proper athletic authority" made a formal objection. In 1918, a committee was appointed to study the problem of institutional control, and the 1920 convention, after hearing the committee's report, established an arbitration committee to "deal with charges of proselytizing or eligibility" and a central committee to act as a final court of appeals on such charges. However, the committees were given little work.

The Carnegie Foundation for the Advancement of Teaching issued a report, "American Collegiate Athletics," in 1929, with detailed documentation of recruiting and subsidization of athletes, particularly in football. While the report caused concern, it resulted in no practical action. However, in 1933 an NCAA committee was appointed to study the problems, and the 1934 convention adopted a resolution calling almost every form of recruiting or subsidization "unjustifiable." Six years later, the association took its first move toward enforcement by giving its executive committee the power to investigate alleged violations. But the only possible punishment was expulsion, requiring a two-thirds vote of the annual convention.

The struggle to find a means of control continued after World War II. In 1948, the so-called sanity code became Article 3 of the NCAA constitution, but it was virtually obsolete in that it banned athletic scholarships, which were rapidly becoming commonplace. A constitutional compliance committee was established to investigate complaints. The first major test of the mechanism came in January 1950, when the committee recommended expulsion of seven NCAA members. A bare majority, well short of the required two thirds, voted in favor. The sanity code was repealed a year later and temporarily replaced by a 12-point code laying down general principles rather than specific rules. The new code implicitly allowed financial grants to athletes by recommending that they be limited in number and dollar amount.

In 1952 the convention voted to allow probation and suspension as penalties, and in 1954 it authorized hiring an assistant to the executive director specifically to work with the Subcommittee on Infractions for investigation and enforcement. The committee, in turn, was to report its findings to its parent Committee on Membership, which would report to the NCAA Council. That cumbersome approach was changed in 1964 to make the Subcommittee on Infractions a full committee reporting directly to the council. Finally, in 1973, the Committee on Infractions was given the power to impose penalties, with the council acting as a court of appeals, and a year later the number of investigators on the association staff was increased from two to eight.

Many penalties can now be imposed on an institution found guilty of violating NCAA regulations, ranging from reprimand and censure for a minor offense to the "death penalty"—being forced out of competition for a specified period. Southern Methodist University is the only school to have suffered the death penalty, when it was forced to drop football for the 1987 and 1988 seasons. Other possible penalties include probation, ineligibility for one or more championship events, postseason meets and tournaments, or television appearances, and a limitation on the number of athletic grants-in-aid that can be given during a specified period.

In recent years, the NCAA has focused much attention on athletes' grades and the predicted grades of incoming freshmen as eligibility standards, often with accompanying controversy. The first such rule, which went into effect on January 1, 1966, required that an incoming student have a predicted grade-point average of at least 1.6 (C- on the 4.0 scale) to receive a scholarship. It came under fire a few years later because of questions about the tests' validity, and was revised in 1971 to allow scholarships for genuine disadvantaged students. The rule was replaced in 1973 by the requirement that the student have a 2.0 average in high school.

Proposition 48, which became effective in 1985, said that a student-athlete who didn't have a 2.0 average and a minimum 700 combined score on the Scholastic Aptitude Test couldn't practice with the team as a freshman and would lose that year of eligibility. Proposition 42, effective in 1990, denied scholarships to such students, but it came under heavy attack as discriminatory, because most of the players affected were black basketball players. Because of the uproar, the proposition was amended in January of 1990 to allow need-based regular scholarships, but not athletic scholarships, to such students.

The NCAA's first major confrontation with the AAU was in 1921, when the AAU-controlled American Olympic Committee decided to form an American Olympic Association as a fund-raising and management body, with 33 votes for the AAU and 16 for the NCAA. Later, the NCAA representation was cut to three, and the association withdrew from the AOA. In 1922, the NCAA, YMCA, Army, Navy, and several other sports organizations organized the National Amateur Athletic Association as a direct challenge to the AAU's control of most amateur sports. However, after a compromise gave the AAU and NCAA three votes apiece on the AOA, the groups decided to join the new association.

Several skirmishes took place during the next few years, but in 1929 the AAU agreed that student-athletes could be certified as amateurs by their colleges rather than by an AAU club. A rather uneasy truce existed until 1961, when an NCAA special committee declared that the AAU was "no longer truly representative of all interests in certain sports and is certainly not the best representative group for NCAA interests in specific sports," and urged that new national organizations be formed to govern basketball and gymnastics. As a result, the U.S. Basketball, Gymnastics, and Track and Field Federations were formed in 1962.

That was the beginning of the end of the long battle. Another temporary truce was worked out in 1964 by mediator General Douglas MacArthur, but a year later the NCAA threatened to withdraw from the U.S. Olympic Committee because the AAU had once again been given control of the body. When the NCAA actually did withdraw in 1972 after several attempts at negotiation had failed, the action spurred passage of the Amateur Sports Act of 1978. The act requires that each Olympic sport have its own autonomous, separately incorporated, national governing body, effectively stripping the AAU of most of its power and opening the door for the NCAA-backed federations to govern their own sports and be represented on the U.S. Olympic Committee.

The NCAA has grown into an entirely different organization than was envisioned—or needed—in 1905. It held its first national collegiate championship, in track and field, in 1921, and soon moved into other sports, in several cases taking over championship events that already existed. The U.S. Lawn Tennis Association, for example, first held a national invitational collegiate tournament in 1893. The USLTA and NCAA began cosponsorship of the championship in 1938, and it became a full-fledged NCAA event in 1941. Similarly, the Central Intercollegiate Conference cross-country meet became the NCAA championship meet in 1938.

For more than 40 years, the NCAA depended primarily on volunteer workers. Its first paid staff members were hired in 1946 to operate the National Collegiate Athletic Bureau, which compiled statistics and records. On October 1, 1951, Walter Byers was chosen as the association's first full-time executive director. At that time, the NCAA was headquartered in Chicago, but it moved to Kansas City, MO on July 28, 1952. The staff and budget have grown enormously since then. The NCAA now has 185 full-time staff members, an annual budget of nearly $80 million, and its own building in Mission, KS. The building, erected at a cost of just over $1.5 million, was dedicated on April 28, 1973.

Until the association turned a profit of $146 on its 1921 national track and field meet, all of the NCAA's revenues came from dues. Now most of the money comes from its championship events, largely through television rights fees. In 1952, the NCAA sold its first football package to NBC for $1,144,000. The package increased to only $3 million by 1965, but it soared to $7.8 million in 1966, $12 million in 1970, $30 million in 1978 and an average of more than $60 million a year in 1982 and 1983. However, in 1983 the Supreme Court ruled that the television package violated antitrust laws, and the College Football Association, an organization of about 60 major college football powers, began negotiating its own television contracts. Television rights to the NCAA basketball tournament helped offset that loss, increasing from $55 million in 1990 to an average of more than $142 million from 1991 through 1997. Most television money is distributed among member schools, but the NCAA's share still accounts for most of its budget.

To allow smaller schools to take part in postseason play, the NCAA established separate university and college divisions in 1956, and the first NCAA college division basketball tournament was held in 1957. In 1973, the association adopted its present structure, with Divisions I, II, and III; each member school was allowed to decide which division to enter. A school may now choose to be in Division I for one sport, usually basketball, while remaining in Division II for other sports, and each division has its own rules regarding scholarships, eligibility, and other issues.

Further Reading: Fatta, Jack. *NCAA: The Voice of College Sports.* Mission, KS: National Collegiate Athletic Association, 1981.

Address: P.O. Box 1906, Mission, KS, 66201 (913) 384–3220.

See also INTERCOLLEGIATE SPORTS; NATIONAL ASSOCIATION OF INTERCOLLEGIATE ATHLETICS; SANITY CODE.

National Commission
Baseball

When the American and National Leagues ended their two-year battle by signing a new National Agreement in 1903, they established a three-man National Commission, the so-called "supreme court of baseball," to interpret and enforce it. The league presidents were ex officio members of the commission, and they chose a third person as its chairman. August "Garry" Herrmann chaired the commission for its entire 17 years of existence. Herrmann was an ideal compromise candidate, since he was president of the National League's Cincinnati team and a long-time friend of American League President Ban Johnson, who had once been a sportswriter in Cincinnati. In fact, because Johnson was much stronger-willed than his National League counterparts, he virtually ruled the sport during this period. As one sportswriter later put it, Johnson was "the real baseball authority, for Garry never did know much about it. He had been chosen chairman, like it so often happens, because he was so delightfully what they call innocuous."

Ironically, criticism of the National Commission usually focused on the fact that there were two National League members. However, in its adjudication of interleague, interteam, and team-player disputes, the commission seems to have been generally fair. To cite just one of many cases, the Cleveland team in 1911 sent William J. Ingerton to a minor-league team but agreed to pay his major-league salary. When the team moved into a lower classification, his salary was cut, but the commission ordered that he be moved to a team in a higher-classified league, and his salary was restored.

The commission was funded by both major leagues, a 10-percent share of World Series receipts, and a cut of gate receipts for other postseason games. In 1913, it negotiated a five-year contract with Western Union, allowing the company exclusive rights to telegraph reports of major-league games in exchange for $17,000 a year to each major league and $2,000 a year to the National Commission itself—a forerunner of modern television contracts.

By 1915, the National Commission was overburdened and under fire. Its case load had grown from 110 in 1903 to nearly 4,000, and the rival Federal League, which operated as a major league for two years, was bought out at an enormous cost after the 1915 season. Although the commission had imposed a lifetime ban on players who jumped to the league, the ban wasn't enforced, and Federal League owners were allowed to sell players back to their former teams, which antagonized many major-league owners. The minor leagues and the players periodically asked to be represented on the commission, and some owners felt that Herrmann should be replaced by someone from outside baseball.

The next-to-last straw for the commission was the Scott Perry case in 1918. A pitcher, Perry had been purchased by the National League's Boston team from the minor-league Atlanta Club, but he jumped from Boston to an independent team before the deal was completed. Subsequently, Atlanta sold him to the American League's Philadelphia Athletics, and he began playing for them. Boston protested to the National Commission. By a 3–2 vote (the president of Atlanta's minor league and the secretary of the National Association of Professional Baseball Leagues also took part), Perry was ordered to return to Boston. However, the Athletics' owner-manager, Connie Mack, got a court injunction allowing his team to keep Perry.

That angered National League President John K. Tener, who refused to take part in commission meetings and asked his league's owners to boycott the World Series if Perry wasn't returned to Boston. When the owners refused, Tener resigned and was replaced by John A. Heydler. Although a compromise was finally worked out, with Philadelphia paying Boston $2,500 for Perry, Heydler was also dissatisfied with the commission. In November 1918, a delegation of owners secretly offered the commission presidency to William Howard Taft, but he declined. However, the owners appointed a committee to search for a replacement for Herrmann.

The following year, Johnson got into trouble with some of the American League owners because of his handling of another player dispute. Carl Mays, a pitcher for the Boston Red Sox, quit the team and was subsequently traded to New York. Johnson suspended him indefinitely, but the Yankees went to court and won an injunction declaring that teams had a right to run their own businesses and the league president had no power to intervene.

National League owners in September 1919 voted unanimously for a neutral commission chairman, and Herrmann submitted his resignation on January 8, 1920, to take effect February 11. The day before it took effect, the American League executive committee, dominated by anti-Johnson owners, stripped the president of most of his powers. Although Johnson was backed by five of the league's eight owners, the three dissidents joined the eight National League owners to force the adoption of the Lasker plan. Originally proposed in 1918 by Albert D. Lasker, part owner of the Chicago White Sox, the plan called for a national commission made up of three members with no financial interest in baseball.

The 11 owners met on October 7, 1920, and agreed on a salary of $25,000 for the commission chairman, with salaries of $10,000 each for his two associates. They threatened to form a new 11-team National League if the other five owners refused to accept the plan. As a result, all 16 owners met on November 12. Instead of a three-member commission, they decided on a single commissioner with a salary of $50,000. Federal judge Kenesaw Mountain Landis accepted the job and was given virtually unlimited powers under a new National Agreement adopted on January 12, 1921.

See also LANDIS, KENESAW MOUNTAIN; NATIONAL AGREEMENT.

National Course
Newtown, NY

In an attempt to revive Thoroughbred racing in New York after after a five-year drought, a group of investors headed by S. J. Carter of New Orleans spent about $250,000 building the National Course on the 141-acre Willet farm at Newtown, Long Island, in 1854. William W. Boyden and Lovell Purdy were Carter's major backers in the enterprise. The course boasted a 12,000-seat grandstand and a total capacity of more than 25,000.

The track opened in June of 1854. Plans called for two six-day meetings a year, with two races a day— at the time, a race usually consisted of two or three heats of 4 miles each. The National Course was a pioneer in sports sponsorship, since several of its races were named for New York hotels that contributed money to the purses.

After a good beginning, attendance fell off sharply during the fall meeting. High ticket prices were partly to blame, but another important factor was that some announced races were never held. Mortgage holders foreclosed on the track in February of 1855. It was revived as the Fashion Race Course in 1856, but that venture folded after little more than a year.

National Federation of State High School Associations (NFSHSA)

L. W. Smith, secretary of the Illinois High School Athletic Association, invited representatives of nearby states to a 1920 meeting to discuss problems caused by sports events organized by outside promoters, including colleges and universities, many of whom ignored scholastic eligibility rules. Indiana, Iowa, Michigan, and Wisconsin were represented at the meeting, held on May 14 in Chicago. A year later, the Midwestern Federation of State High School Athletic Associations was formally organized by Illinois, Iowa, Michigan, and Wisconsin. When 11 states were represented at the 1922 meeting, it became a national federation.

The NFSHSA is now made up of state associations from all 50 states, the District of Columbia, and ten Canadian provinces, as well as the Philippines, Guam, St. Croix, and St. Thomas. Because many of its member associations are also responsible for overseeing nonathletic activities, such as music, speech, and debate, the word "Athletic" was dropped from its the federation's name in 1970.

One of the federation's chief concerns is still the sanctioning of interstate and international high school competition, under strict controls. In 1978, the NFSHSA joined the International Schoolsport Federation, which promotes competitions considered to be of educational value. In general, the NFSHSA doesn't approve of major championship events on regional, national, or international levels. In January 1978, its national council tentatively voted to sponsor national championships, but in July it voted to delay the events for a year, and a year later the council voted overwhelmingly against the idea.

The NFSHSA operates a variety of programs. It began recording high school track and field records in 1925, added swimming records in 1973, and since 1976 has published the annual *National High School Sports Record Book*, which now includes 15 sports. The federation conducts annual conferences for school athletic directors and publishes the quarterly professional journal, *Interscholastic Athletic Administration*. Its National Research Center has a collection of data on many subjects pertaining to extracurricular programs. The federation also promulgates rules for a wide variety of sports, produces officials' manuals and casebooks, and develops safety standards for athletic equipment.

Address: 11724 Plaza Circle, Box 20626, Kansas City, MO 64195 (816) 464–5400.

See also HIGH SCHOOL SPORTS.

National Finals Rodeo (NFR)

The "Cowboy World Series," held every December since 1959, usually determines the sport's world championships. The champion in an event is the cowboy who wins the most money in all the year's rodeos. Purses at the NFR are so large (totaling more than $2 million) that it's virtually impossible for a contestant to have won enough money before entering the finals to be assured of a championship. The top 15 cowboys in each of the seven major events take part in ten rounds of competition over a tenday period, and the NFR winnings are added to the regular season winnings to determine the champion. The top title, the all-around championship, is awarded to the cowboy who wins the most money by competing in two or more events.

The NFR was held in Dallas for its first three years, Los Angeles from 1962 through 1964, and Oklahoma

City from 1965 through 1984. Las Vegas has hosted the rodeo since 1985. Steer roping finals are held at a separate site; since 1984 it has been hosted by Guthrie, OK.

National Football Foundation and Hall of Fame

Arthur Evans led a group of Syracuse businessmen and football fans who organized the National Football Foundation in 1947, primarily as a fund-raising and promotional body to establish a college football hall of fame. Rutgers University, site of the first college football (actually soccer) game in 1869, was chosen as the site in a 1949 poll of sportswriters, coaches, and athletic directors. A mass induction of 52 former players and coaches was held in 1951. Evans died shortly thereafter, and his successor, George E. Little, also became gravely ill after taking on the job.

The foundation was reorganized in 1953 under the leadership of sportswriter Grantland Rice and Admiral William "Bull" Halsey, and plans were made to put up a hall of fame building at Rutgers. However, the funds weren't forthcoming until 1976, when the owners of the Kings Island Amusement Park near Cincinnati put up $5 million for construction. The hall opened in August of 1978.

Although the Hall of Fame is in Kings Island, the foundation is headquartered in Larchmont, NY. It sponsors two college football games, the postseason Hall of Fame Bowl in Tampa, FL and the Kickoff Classic, the first game of the year, at Giants Stadium in East Rutherford, NJ. The Kickoff Classic benefits the American Football Coaches Association and the National Association of Collegiate Directors of Athletics, as well as the Hall of Fame. The foundation annually presents two major awards: the MacArthur Bowl to the national championship football team, and the Gold Medal Award to a distinguished citizen who has been closely associated with college football.

Addresses: National Football Foundation, 1865 Palmer Avenue, Larchmont, NY 10538 (914) 834-0474; Hall of Fame, 5440 Kings Island Drive, Kings Island, OH 45034 (513) 398-5410.

See also MACARTHUR BOWL.

National Football League (NFL)

For more than 20 years, professional football was really a semiprofessional sport dominated by small-town teams manned largely by local players who practiced in the evenings after working all day, although a few stars might be brought in from outside for a game or two. Even after the American Professional Football Association was organized, the pattern remained much the same for several years. The APFA was informally established in 1919, according to some accounts. However, the NFL dates the founding to September 17, 1920, when ten team owners met at Ralph Hay's automobile showroom in Canton, OH. The original teams were the Akron Pros, Canton Bulldogs, Chicago Cardinals, Cleveland Tigers, Dayton Triangles, Decatur Staleys, Hammond Pros, Muncie Flyers, Rochester Jeffersons, and Rock Island Independents. They agreed not to tamper with one another's players and not to sign any players who had college eligibility remaining. Canton player Jim Thorpe was named president simply because his name was so well known.

It was years before the new professional league was genuinely organized, as the major baseball leagues were. There was no formal schedule and no provision for determining a champion. Teams scheduled games among themselves and with independent teams in their areas. Four independent teams—the Buffalo All-Americans, Chicago Tigers, Columbus Panhandles, and Detroit Heralds—played so many games against APFA teams in 1920 that they're usually listed in the year's standings. On the other hand, Rochester didn't play a single game against a league team, and the Muncie team disbanded after losing its only game 45–0. Akron, which won six games and tied three without being scored on, was awarded the 1920 championship.

Joseph F. Carr, long-time manager of the Columbus Panhandles, was named APFA president in 1921, when the number of teams grew to 21. George Halas's Staleys, who had moved from Decatur to Chicago, were declared champions, with a 9–1–1 record. Halas was instrumental in two important name changes in 1922. At his suggestion, the APFA was renamed the National Football League. And, to capitalize on the popularity of baseball's Chicago Cubs, he renamed his team the Bears. Seven teams dropped out before the season, but three others were added. The NFL was in a state of constant flux for the next ten seasons as it gradually evolved from a league of small-town teams to an organization of truly professional teams in larger cities.

Although there was still no official league schedule, the NFL took a step in the right direction in 1924 by declaring September 23 the beginning of the season and November 30 its end, with the championship to be decided by the best winning percentage in games played during that period. That created controversy, at least in Chicago. When the season ended, the Cleveland Bulldogs were in first place with a 7–1–1 record, Chicago second at 6–1–

4. The Bears then beat the Bulldogs 23–0 and claimed the championship. However, league owners in January of 1925 awarded the title to Cleveland because that final game had taken place after the November 30 deadline.

There was another controversy over the 1925 championship, but it went almost unnoticed at the time. Pottsville had a 10–2–0 record to the Cardinals' 9–2–1 mark with two weeks left in the season. The Cardinals won two games against makeshift teams from Milwaukee and Hammond, while Pottsville played an exhibition game against a team of Notre Dame all-stars in Philadelphia. The Frankford Yellowjackets, who played in a suburb of Philadelphia, protested the invasion of their territory, and Carr immediately suspended the Pottsville franchise, giving the Cardinals the championship.

But the event of the year was Red Grange's decision to join the Chicago Bears immediately after the University of Illinois' season ended. He drew a crowd of 36,000 in his first game, against the Cardinals on Thanksgiving Day, and on December 6 more than 73,000 fans packed the Polo Grounds to watch the Bears play the New York Giants. For the first time, professional football was getting crowds and publicity.

Grange was also responsible for the first challenge to the NFL. His manager, C. C. Pyle, wanted a franchise in New York but was turned down, so he formed the American Football League with a team called the New York Yankees to showcase Grange. The NFL expanded to 23 teams, admitting some independents primarily to keep them out of the AFL. Grange's Yankees drew fans, but none of the other AFL teams did, and the league folded after the season. So did a dozen NFL franchises, and the Yankees were allowed to join the league.

The NFL dropped from 12 to 10 teams in 1928, jumped back to 12 in 1929, dropped to 11 in 1930, was back to 12 in 1931, then dropped to only 8 in 1932. The Chicago Bears and Portsmouth Spartans tied for first place that season, and a championship playoff game was scheduled for December 18 in Chicago. Cold and snow forced the game indoors, at Chicago Stadium, which could accommodate a field only 60 yards long from goal line to goal line and only 45 yards wide. At the time, if a play went out of bounds or ended right next to a sideline, the next play started there and the offensive team usually had to waste a play just moving the ball toward the center of the field. For this game, the ball was to be brought in 10 yards from the sideline after going out of bounds. And, because the end lines were curved, the goalposts were put on the goal lines.

Despite the weather, 15,000 fans attended the game. The Bears broke a scoreless tie in the fourth quarter when fullback Bronko Nagurski faked a run into the line and threw a 2-yard pass to Red Grange. Portsmouth argued that he had been less than 5 yards behind the line of scrimmage, but the touchdown was allowed and the Bears added a safety for a 9–0 victory.

At their 1933 meeting, NFL owners decided to split the league into two divisions and stage an annual championship game between the division winners. They also voted to move the goalposts from the end lines to the goal lines, to have the ball moved in 10 yards from the sidelines when it went out of bounds, and to allow a forward pass from anywhere behind the line of scrimmage. The football was slimmed down to its present shape, making it easier to pass. Those changes, most of them inspired by the 1932 championship game, began pro football's modern era. Another major innovation was the college player draft, which began in 1936.

The NFL had become much more stable. It grew from eight to ten teams in 1933, and most of its franchises were in big cities. The eastern division had Boston, Brooklyn, New York, Philadelphia, and Pittsburgh; the western had the Chicago Bears, Chicago Cardinals, Cincinnati, Green Bay, and Portsmouth. In 1934 the Portsmouth Spartans became the Detroit Lions, and Cincinnati folded. In 1937 the Boston Redskins moved to Washington, and the Cleveland Rams joined the league.

Pro football's popularity was growing, as evidenced by two rival American Football Leagues that challenged the NFL. The first played during the 1936 and 1937 seasons, the second in 1940 and 1941, but neither was able to sign enough top college players to achieve true major-league status. World War II took its toll, but the NFL kept playing. The Cleveland franchise was inactive for lack of players in 1943 and the Pittsburgh and Philadelphia franchises temporarily merged that season; in 1944, Pittsburgh and the Chicago Cardinals had a similar merger.

When the war ended, the NFL faced its most serious challenge, the well-bankrolled All-America Football Conference. But it also became a truly national league when the Cleveland Rams moved to Los Angeles for the 1946 season and signed two black players, the first to enter the league since 1933 (the Cleveland Browns of the AAFC also had two black players in 1946). Bert Bell, former owner of the Philadelphia Eagles and part owner of the Pittsburgh Steelers, became the league's commissioner, replacing Elmer Layden, who had held the job since Joe Carr's death in 1939.

Virtually every professional team suffered financially because of the bidding for players, but the AAFC suffered most because the Cleveland Browns' domination of the league led to poor attendance in most other cities. After the 1949 season, the two leagues announced a merger, but only the Baltimore Colts, the Browns, and the San Francisco 49ers actually joined the NFL. The other four teams disbanded, and their players were distributed in a special draft. The league was realigned, with the Chicago Cardinals, Cleveland, New York Giants, Philadelphia, Pittsburgh and Washington in the American Conference and Baltimore, the Chicago Bears, Detroit, Green Bay, Los Angeles, New York Yankees and San Francisco in the National.

The Baltimore Colts folded after the 1950 season. The New York Yankees moved to Dallas in 1952, and became a new Baltimore Colts franchise the following season. But, in general, the 1950s represented a new era of prosperity for the NFL, as attendance climbed over 2 million in 1952 and over 3 million in 1958. More important, television entered the picture, although NFL owners had early doubts about the medium. When the Los Angeles Rams televised their home games in 1950, their attendance was cut almost in half, although the Rams had an exciting, pass-oriented team that won the National Conference title. The following year, they televised only road games and attendance returned to the 1949 level.

That persuaded Commissioner Bell that home games should be blacked out in a team's television territory, and an NFL bylaw to that effect was upheld by a federal judge. Bell died in October of 1959, when the NFL was facing a challenge from yet another American Football League, which was to begin play in 1960. In January, Pete Rozelle became the NFL's new commissioner. He oversaw the league's first expansion since the AAFC merger in 1950. A new franchise was added in Dallas in 1960 to go head-to-head with an AFL team there, and Minnesota, which had been slated to join the AFL, was persuaded to enter the NFL in 1961. Franchises were also added in Atlanta in 1966 and New Orleans in 1967, bringing about a major realignment into four divisions, each with four teams.

Rozelle's greatest success in his early years as commissioner was probably his handling of the league's television policy, which became vitally important as the bidding war between the NFL and AFL escalated. The 1961 contract with CBS was worth $4,650,000; that climbed to $14.1 million in 1964, plus $1.8 million for the championship game.

Despite the flow of television money, escalating salaries threatened teams in both leagues. They spent an estimated $25 million just signing draft choices in 1966. Secret peace talks were begun early that year, and on June 8 a merger was announced. The leagues agreed to begin a common draft and an interleague championship game in 1967, with a complete merger into a new NFL in 1970, after the leagues' existing television contracts expired. Rozelle was to be commissioner of the merged league, and AFL teams were to pay an indemnity of $18 million to the NFL over a 20-year period.

The first two interleague championship games went as expected, the NFL's Green Bay Packers winning both handily, 35–10 over the Kansas City Chiefs and 33–14 over the Oakland Raiders. But in the third game, the AFL's New York Jets stunned the Baltimore Colts 16–7. The championship game was officially named the Super Bowl the following year, when Kansas City evened the series for the AFL by beating the Minnesota Vikings 23–7.

The merger brought a major restructuring of the NFL. The Baltimore Colts, Cleveland Browns, and Pittsburgh Steelers joined the 10 former AFL teams in the American Football Conference, and the other 13 NFL teams went into the National Football Conference. Each conference had three divisions. In addition to the division champions, the second-place team with the best record in the conference went into the playoffs as a "wild-card" team.

One reason for the restructuring was to give the conferences parity in their television markets. CBS, which had long covered the NFL, was awarded rights to NFC home games; NBC won rights to AFC home games; and ABC also got into the act with "Monday Night Football," which was an immediate success.

The NFL expanded to 28 teams in 1976, adding the Tampa Bay Buccaneers to the NFC and the Seattle Seahawks to the AFC. In 1978 the playoff format was changed so that five teams from each conference qualified, two of them wild cards who had to meet in a preliminary game to determine which would advance into the semifinals.

The 1970s and early 1980s were marked by constantly increasing television money and by labor problems, as the NFL Players' Association sought a bigger piece of the pie. On July 1, 1974, the association went on strike—shortly before a new rival, the World Football League, began operating. The WFL, however, was underfinanced and was in trouble even before its season ended in August. The league folded in 1975, in the middle of its second season.

Meanwhile, the NFL players returned to work in 1974 after missing several exhibition games. But in 1975, without a contract settlement, the players struck again a week before the regular season. The strike lasted just four days, and the season once more went on as scheduled. One of the players' chief targets was the so-called Rozelle rule, which required that if a player went to another team after his option year, his former team had to be reimbursed, usually in the form of a player or draft choice named by the commissioner. That rule was declared illegal by a federal judge in 1975.

A new five-year collective bargaining agreement was finally signed in 1977, but the players staged a real strike before the third week of the 1982 season. It lasted 57 days. The season resumed on November 21, was extended into January, and the league temporarily went back to having just a single wild card team from each conference, to shorten the playoff schedule. Attendance at first suffered in several cities, but by the time the playoffs began, interest in the NFL seemed as strong as ever. Network television contracts signed in 1982 called for about $400 million a year from the three major networks over a five-year period. Despite a slight decline in ratings, the contracts negotiated in 1987 showed an increase to nearly $500 million a year for three years, with the ESPN cable network covering eight Sunday night games.

Although the average NFL salary had climbed from $90,000 to $242,000 in just five years, the players again went on strike during the 1987 season. This time, the owners were prepared. For three weeks, replacement teams made up of free agents and some regular players who refused to strike kept the schedule going. The strike once again ended without an agreement. One of the major issues was free agency. While the players association brought an antitrust suit against the league, team owners instituted "plan B free agency," which allowed teams to protect only 37 players; all others became free agents who could sign with any other team. Under that plan, more than 100 players did change teams between the 1988 and 1989 seasons.

The NFL also faced a major internal problem in 1980 when the Oakland Raiders asked permission to move to Los Angeles. The move was voted down by other owners, but the Raiders won an antitrust suit that struck down the league bylaw requiring a vote on any proposed franchise move, and the Raiders began playing in Los Angeles in 1982. That also paved the way for the Baltimore Colts to move to Indianapolis without seeking permission in 1984. And the St. Louis Cardinals moved to Phoenix in 1988 with league approval.

Early in 1989, Commissioner Rozelle announced his retirement, creating another internal problem. Although Jim Finks, general manager of the New Orleans Saints, seemed to be the heir apparent to the job, a group of dissident owners blocked his

hiring. After more than six months of wrangling that brought general scorn from the press, Paul Tagliabue was finally named as a compromise choice.

Despite the problems, professional football had replaced baseball as the most popular national sport, according to several polls. And television revenue soared to new heights in 1990, when the NFL signed contracts with NBC, CBS, ABC, and the cable networks ESPN and TBS for about $3.6 billion over a four-year period, $32 million a team per year as opposed to $17 million in 1989. To help justify the increased rights fees, the league agreed to expand to a 17-week regular season in 1990 and an 18-week season in 1991. The number of games per team remains at 16, with teams each drawing one week off in 1990 and a second week off in 1991.

NFL Champions 1920–1932

1920	Akron Pros	6–0–3
1921	Chicago Staleys	9–1–1
1922	Canton Bulldogs	10–0–2
1923	Canton Bulldogs	11–0–1
1924	Cleveland Bulldogs	7–1–1
1925	Chicago Cardinals	11–2–1
1926	Frankford Yellowjackets	14–1–2
1927	New York Giants	11–1–1
1928	Providence Steamroller	6–1–2
1929	Green Bay Packers	12–0–1
1930	Green Bay Packers	10–3–1
1931	Green Bay Packers	12–2–0
1932	Chicago Bears	7–1–6

NFL Championship Games 1933–1970

1933	Chicago Bears 23, New York Giants 21
1934	New York Giants 30, Chicago Bears 13
1935	Detroit Lions 26, New York Giants 7
1936	Green Bay Packers 21, Boston Redskins 6
1937	Washington Redskins 28, Chicago Bears 21
1938	New York Giants 23, Green Bay Packers 17
1939	Green Bay Packers 27, New York Giants 0
1940	Chicago Bears 73, Washington Redskins 0
1941	Chicago Bears 37, New York Giants 9
1942	Washington Redskins 14, Chicago Bears 6
1943	Chicago Bears 41, Washington Redskins 21
1944	Green Bay Packers 14, New York Giants 7
1945	Cleveland Rams 15, Washington Redskins 14
1946	Chicago Bears 24, New York Giants 14
1947	Chicago Cardinals 28, Philadelphia Eagles 21
1948	Philadelphia Eagles 7, Chicago Cardinals 0
1949	Philadelphia Eagles 14, Los Angeles Rams 0

1950   Cleveland Browns 30, Los Angeles Rams 28
1951   Los Angeles Rams 24, Cleveland Browns 17
1952   Detroit Lions 17, Cleveland Browns 7
1953   Detroit Lions 17, Cleveland Browns 16
1954   Cleveland Browns 56, Detroit Lions 10
1955   Cleveland Browns 38, Los Angeles Rams 14
1956   New York Giants 47, Chicago Bears 7
1957   Detroit Lions 59, Cleveland Browns 14
1958   Baltimore Colts 23, New York Giants 17
1959   Baltimore Colts 31, New York Giants 16
1960   Philadelphia Eagles 17, Green Bay Packers 13
1961   Green Bay Packers 37, New York Giants 0
1962   Green Bay Packers 16, New York Giants 7
1963   Chicago Bears 14, New York Giants 10
1964   Cleveland Browns 27, Baltimore Colts 0
1965   Green Bay Packers 23, Cleveland Browns 12
1966   Green Bay Packers 34, Dallas Cowboys 27
1967   Green Bay Packers 21, Dallas Cowboys 17
1968   Baltimore Colts 34, Cleveland Browns 0
1969   Minnesota Vikings 27, Cleveland Browns 7

(For champions since 1970, see SUPER BOWL.)

Further Reading: Harris, David. *The League: The Rise and Decline of the NFL*. New York: Bantam Books, 1986.

Addresses:

National Football League, 410 Park Avenue, New York, NY 10022 (212) 758–1500.

Atlanta Falcons, Suwanee Road at I-85, Suwanee, GA 30174 (404) 945–1111.

Buffalo Bills, One Bills Drive, Orchard Park, NY 14127 (716) 648–1800.

Chicago Bears, Halas Hall, 250 North Washington, Lake Forest, IL 60045 (312) 295–6600.

Cincinnati Bengals, 200 Riverfront Stadium, Cincinnati, OH 45202 (513) 621–3550.

Cleveland Browns, Tower B, Cleveland Stadium, Cleveland, OH 44114 (216) 696–5555.

Dallas Cowboys, Cowboys Center, One Cowboy Parkway, Irving, TX 75063 (214) 556–9900.

Denver Broncos, 5700 Logan Street, Denver, CO 80216 (303) 296–1982.

Detroit Lions, 1200 Featherstone Road, Box 4200, Pontiac, MI 48057 (313) 335–4131.

Green Bay Packers, 1265 Lombardi Avenue, P.O. Box 10628, Green Bay, WI 54307 (414) 494–2351.

Houston Oilers, 6910 Fannin Street, Houston, TX 77030 (713) 797–9111.

Indianapolis Colts, P.O. Box 535000, Indianapolis, IN 46253 (317) 297–2658.

Kansas City Chiefs, One Arrowhead Drive, Kansas City, MO 64129 (816) 924–9300.

Los Angeles Raiders, 332 Center Street, El Segundo, CA 90245 (213) 322–3451.

Los Angeles Rams, 2327 West Lincoln Avenue, Anaheim, CA 92801 (714) 535–7267.

Miami Dolphins, 2269 N.W. 199th Street, Miami, FL 33056 (305) 620–5000.

Minnesota Vikings, 9520 Viking Drive, Eden Prairie, MN 55344 (612) 828–6500.

New England Patriots, Route 1, Foxboro, MA 02035 (508) 543–7911.

New Orleans Saints, 1500 Poydras Street, New Orleans, LA 70112 (504) 733–0255.

New York Giants, Giants Stadium, East Rutherford, NJ 07073 (201) 935–8111.

New York Jets, 598 Madison Avenue, New York, NY 10022 (212) 421–6600.

Philadelphia Eagles, Brood Street and Pattison Avenue, Philadelphia, PA 19148 (215) 463–2500.

Phoenix Cardinals, P.O. Box 888, Phoenix, AZ 85001 (602) 967–1010.

Pittsburgh Steelers, 300 Stadium Circle, Pittsburgh, PA 15212 (412) 323–1200.

San Diego Chargers, P.O. Box 2066, San Diego, CA 92120 (619) 280–2111.

San Francisco 49ers, 4949 Centennial Boulevard, Santa Clara, CA 95054 (408) 562–4949.

Seattle Seahawks, 11220 N.E. 53rd Street, Kirkland, WA 98033 (206) 827–9777.

Tampa Bay Buccaneers, One Buccaneer Place, Tampa, FL 33607 (813) 870–2700.

Washington Redskins, Redskin Park, P.O. Box 17247, Washington, DC 20041 (703) 471–9100.

See also AMERICAN FOOTBALL LEAGUE; CARR, JOSEPH F.; PRO FOOTBALL HALL OF FAME; ROZELLE, "PETE" ALVIN R.; SUPER BOWL; THORPE TROPHY.

National Hockey League (NHL)

When the Renfrew (Ontario) Millionaires were denied admission to the Eastern Canada League in 1909, owner Ambrose O'Brien decided to form his own league, the National Hockey Association of Canada, Ltd. It began play in January 1910 with five teams: the Montreal Canadiens, Montreal Shamrocks, Montreal Wanderers, Ottawa Senators, and Renfrew. Hockey was played by seven-man teams at the time, but the NHA originated six-man teams in 1911 to speed up the game. The NHA was reorganized as the National Hockey League on November 22, 1917, with Frank Calder as president and secretary-treasurer. The charter members were the Canadiens, the Wanderers, the Senators, and the Quebec Bulldogs. However, Quebec temporarily suspended operations, and the Toronto Arenas were added to the league.

Westmount Arena, home of both Montreal teams, burned down in January, and the Wanderers were forced to drop out of the NHL while the Canadiens played their games in tiny Jubilee Rink. In its first two seasons, the league played a 22-game split schedule, with the first- and second-half winners meeting in a championship playoff. The NHL champion then played a western champion for the Stanley Cup.

The Quebec Bulldogs finally began play in the 1919–20 season, when the league went to a 24-game schedule. However, the franchise moved to Hamilton the following season. The split schedule was dropped in 1921, and the first- and second-place finishers began playing a postseason series for the league title. In 1924, the Boston Bruins and Montreal Maroons joined the NHL, and a 30-game schedule was adopted, with three of the six teams going into the playoffs, the second- and third-place finishers meeting in a semifinal series, and the winner playing the first-place team for the championship. The schedule increased to 36 games for 1925–26, after the Hamilton franchise folded and the New York Americans and Pittsburgh Pirates joined the league. NHL expansion into the United States continued in 1926 with the addition of the Chicago Blackhawks, Detroit Cougars (now the Red Wings), and New York Rangers. The NHL was now a ten-team league with American and Canadian divisions and a 44-game schedule, and the Stanley Cup had become the league's own championship trophy.

After this growth spurt, the Great Depression struck. The Pittsburgh team became the Philadelphia Quakers in 1930, but the Quakers dropped out in 1931 and Ottawa suspended play for a season. Ottawa rejoined the NHL in 1932, moved to St. Louis in 1934 and folded after a single season there. And in 1937 the Montreal Maroons withdrew from the league, reducing it to seven teams. That dropped to six in 1942, when the Brooklyn (formerly New York) Americans dropped out, but the schedule increased from 48 to 50 games. Four teams now entered the playoffs, with the first- and third-place teams and the second- and fourth-place teams matched against one another in the first round.

The six-team league remained intact until 1967. When the league announced plans to add six more teams for the 1967–68 season, 14 applications were received. Franchises were awarded to the California Seals (who became the Oakland Seals during the season), Los Angeles Kings, Minnesota North Stars, Philadelphia Flyers, Pittsburgh Penguins, and St. Louis Blues, with the new teams assigned to the western division, the six established teams to the eastern division.

The schedule was expanded to 74 games in 1967 and to 76 games in 1968. Although a couple of the new teams had attendance and financial problems, expansion was generally successful, and the Buffalo Sabres and Vancouver Canucks were added to the NHL's eastern division in 1970, while Chicago moved into the western division. The schedule went to 78 games, and in 1971–72 the playoff format was changed: The first-place team in each division was to play the fourth-place finisher, and the second- and third-place teams were to meet in the other semifinal series.

The NHL faced competition for the first time in 1972, from the World Hockey Association, which signed several long-time NHL stars. But expansion continued, as the Atlanta Flames entered the west division and the New York Islanders the east division. In 1973, the Kansas City Scouts and Washington Capitals were added, and the NHL was realigned into two conference and four divisions: The Smythe and Patrick Divisions in the Campbell Conference, the Adams and Norris Divisions in the Prince of Wales Conference.

Rising player salaries because of the WHA caused further problems for some borderline franchises. The California Seals became the Cleveland Barons, and the Kansas City Scouts went to Denver and were renamed the Colorado Rockies in 1976, but the Cleveland team was forced to merge into the Minnesota North Stars in 1978. The following year, the WHA went out of business and the NHL added four of its teams, the Edmonton Oilers, Hartford Whalers, Quebec Nordiques, and Winnipeg Jets. After two moves, the Atlanta Flames going to Calgary in 1980 and the Colorado Rockies becoming the New Jersey Devils in 1982, the NHL reached its present makeup.

An NHL players association was organized in 1957, but league owners refused to recognize it, and the association folded without accomplishing anything. Attorney Alan Eagleson, the agent for many of the sport's top players, organized a new players association in 1967. This one was recognized by the NHL, but it's limited in what it can accomplish due to lack of funding. Television brings only about $17 million a year to NHL teams, compared with about $240 million a year for professional basketball. NHL teams play about the same number of games in arenas of comparable size, so gate receipts are about the same as in the National Basketball Association. A few top players do command high-priced contracts, but the average player salary is considerably lower than in other professional sports.

Addresses:

National Hockey League, 1155 Metcalfe Street, Suite 960, Montreal, Quebec, Canada H3B 2W2 (514)

871–9220; 650 Fifth Avenue, 33rd Floor, New York, NY 10019 (212) 398–1100.

Boston Bruins, 150 Causeway Street, Boston, MA 02114 (617) 227–3206.

Buffalo Sabres, Memorial Auditorium, Buffalo, NY 14202 (716) 856–7300.

Calgary Flames, P.O. Box 1540, Station M, Calgary, Alberta, Canada T2P 3B9 (403) 261–0475.

Chicago Blackhawks, 1800 West Madison Street, Chicago, IL 60612 (312) 733–5200.

Detroit Red Wings, Joe Louis Sports Arena, 600 Civic Drive, Detroit, MI 48226 (313) 567–7333.

Edmonton Oilers, Northlands Coliseum, Edmonton, Alberta, Canada, T5B 4M9 (403) 474–8561.

Hartford Whalers, One Civic Center Plaza, Hartford, CT 06103 (203) 728–3366.

Los Angeles Kings, 3900 West Manchester Boulevard, Box 17013, Inglewood, CA 90306 (213) 419–3160.

Minnesota North Stars, 7901 Cedar Avenue South, Bloomington, MN 55425 (612) 853–9333.

Montreal Canadiens, 2313 St. Catherine Street W., Montreal, Quebec, Canada H3H 1N2 (514) 932–2582.

New Jersey Devils, P.O. Box 504, East Rutherford, NJ 07073 (201) 935–6050.

New York Islanders, Nassau Veterans' Memorial Coliseum, Uniondale, NY 11553 (516) 794–4100.

New York Rangers, Madison Square Garden, 4 Pennsylvania Plaza, New York, NY 10001 (212) 563–8000.

Philadelphia Flyers, Pattison Place, Philadelphia, PA 19148 (215) 465–4500.

Pittsburgh Penguins, Civic Arena, Pittsburgh, PA 15219 (412) 642–1800.

Quebec Nordiques, 2205 Avenue du Colisée, Quebec City, Quebec, Canada G1L 4W7 (418) 529–8441.

St. Louis Blues, 5700 Oakland Avenue, St. Louis, MO 63110 (314) 781–5300.

Toronto Maple Leafs, 60 Carlton Street, Toronto, Ontario, Canada M5B 1L1 (416) 977–1641.

Vancouver Canucks, 100 North Renfrew Street, Vancouver, British Columbia, Canada V5K 3N7 (604) 254–5141.

Washington Capitals, Capital Centre, Landover, MD 20785 (301) 350–3400.

Winnipeg Jets, 15–1430 Maroons Road, Winnipeg, Manitoba, Canada R3G 0L5 (204) 583–5387.

See also STANLEY CUP; WORLD HOCKEY ASSOCIATION.

National Invitation Tournament (NIT) Basketball

Inspired by the success of intersectional college basketball double-headers at Madison Square Garden, the Metropolitan Basketball Writers Association in 1938 established the NIT to showcase top teams from the New York area and other regions. At first, six teams were invited, with two getting byes into the semifinals. The Eastern College Athletic Conference took over in 1940, and the following year the field was expanded to eight teams. Four New York teams, CCNY, Manhattan, NYU, and St. John's— were all considered for the eighth spot in 1949; the selection committee finally decided to invite all four of them and add a 12th team. From 1964 through 1977, there were 16 teams in the tournament. The format changed in 1978, when the field was expanded to 32 teams, with the first three games played on the home courts of the top-seeded teams, and only the semifinals and the championship game at Madison Square Garden. A preseason tournament, the Big Apple NIT, was inaugurated in 1985.

National Junior College Athletic Association (NJCAA)

Representatives of several junior colleges met in Fresno, CA in 1937 to discuss the need for a national organization to supervise sports. As a result, the NJCAA was formally organized on May 14, 1938, in Fresno. The charter members were Bakersfield, Chaffey, Compton, Fullerton, Glendale, Los Angeles, Pasadena, Riverside, Sacramento, San Bernardino, San Mateo, Santa Monica, and Visalia, all of California. The association held a championship track and field meet in 1939 in Sacramento.

The first schools from outside California to join the NJCAA were Phoenix, AZ and Trinidad, CO in 1940. Trinidad hosted the 1941 track and field meet in Denver. The meet was discontinued from 1943 through 1945 because of World War II, but it resumed in 1946. The association sanctioned a national invitational basketball tournament in 1945 and took it over as a championship event in 1948. National championships in boxing, golf, gymnastics, tennis, and swimming were also inaugurated, but all were temporarily dropped after 1950 because of lack of entrants.

The NJCAA's general procedure since then has been to establish a national invitational tournament in a sport, making it a formal national championship after enough schools have shown interest. At one time or another, the association has awarded national championships in 23 sports for men and 16 sports for women.

The association also sanctions postseason football bowl games. The first, inaugurated in 1964, was the NJCAA Shrine Bowl, sponsored by the Alee Shrine Temple of Savannah, GA. The game became the Sunkist El Toro Bowl and moved to Yuma, AZ in 1972. It was discontinued after 1973. Postseason games currently sanctioned are the East Bowl, Jayhawk Bowl, Royal Crown Cola Bowl, Mid-America Bowl, Midwest Bowl, Texas Junior College Shrine Bowl, and the Valley of the Sun Bowl.

In 1949, the NJCAA was reorganized into 16 regions, each with its own regional vice-president. There have been 24 regions since 1983. The association's Women's Division was established in 1975, a year after the first invitational championships for women were offered in basketball, tennis, and volleyball. National championships currently offered, with the year established, are:

Baseball (1958), men's basketball (1945), women's basketball (1975), men's bowling (1971), women's bowling (1977), men's cross-country (1959), women's cross-country (1976), decathlon (1973), women's field hockey (1975), football (1956), men's golf (1959), women's golf (1976), men's gymnastics (1969), women's gymnastics (1976), ice hockey (1972), lacrosse (1970), men's marathon (1976), women's marathon (1986), men's Alpine skiing (1970), women's Alpine skiing (1976), men's Nordic skiing (1975), women's Nordic skiing (1980), men's soccer (1961), women's soccer (1982), women's fast-pitch softball (1977), women's slow-pitch softball (1983), men's swimming (1961), women's swimming (1976), men's tennis (1948), women's tennis (1975), men's indoor track and field (1973), women's indoor track and field (1980), men's outdoor track and field (1939), women's outdoor track and field (1976), women's volleyball (1974), and wrestling (1960).

Address: P.O. Box 7305, Colorado Springs, CO 80933 (719) 590–9788.

National League
Baseball

While the National Association of Professional Baseball Players was stumbling through its fifth season in 1875, William A. Hulbert decided that baseball needed a league made up of a few strong teams. A director of the Chicago team, Hulbert strengthened his own club by signing four top players from Boston and another from Philadelphia for 1876, in defiance of association rules. After the season, he met with representatives of St. Louis, Cincinnati, and Louisville to discuss formation of a new league.

Boston, Hartford, New York, and Philadelphia were then invited to join. On February 2, 1876, representatives of the eight teams met in New York City and founded the National League of Professional Baseball Clubs. The league gave a team territorial rights in its own city and for a radius of 5 miles around, and a club had to represent a city of at least 75,000

people. Every team was required to play ten games against each other team, five at home and five away.

The National League was the first attempt to turn a professional sport into a genuine business. It was governed by a five-man board of directors, which acted as the tribunal for cases involving interclub disputes or appeals by players who had been expelled or dismissed. The first directors were chosen by having their names drawn from a hat; the first name drawn was that of Morgan G. Bulkeley, who became the league's first president. Bulkeley was replaced after one season by Hulbert, who served until his death in April 1882.

Chances for survival seemed poor during the first several seasons. Virtually every team lost money. Philadelphia and New York were thrown out after the 1876 season for not playing the required number of games, and Hartford, Louisville, and St. Louis dropped out after the 1877 season. They were replaced by Indianapolis, Milwaukee, and Providence, but of those three only Providence remained in 1879, when Buffalo, Cleveland, Syracuse, and Troy were added.

Despite its problems, the National League got tough on its member teams during its first few years. At first, Sunday games were allowed but didn't count in the standings, a gentleman's agreement kept the admission price at 50 cents, and the sale of alcohol at games was frowned upon but allowed. In 1878, Sunday games were forbidden, in 1880 the 50-cent admission charge was added to the league's constitution, and after the 1880 season the constitution was again amended to prohibit the sale of alcohol. Cincinnati, which took in about $3,000 a year from beer and other refreshments, was expelled for refusing to go along with that amendment.

The league also tried to eliminate two serious problems that had plagued the National Association: gambling and "revolving"—the movement of players from team to team almost at will. When George Hall, Jim Devlin, Al Nichols, and Bill Craver of the Louisville team admitted throwing games in 1877, they were expelled by the team, and the league confirmed the lifetime expulsions at its winter meeting. While the National Association had occasionally suspended players involved in gambling or throwing games, the suspensions had never lasted long.

The problem of revolving was solved when the reserve was adopted by secret agreement among owners at a meeting on September 29, 1879. Under the reserve, each team was allowed to reserve five players, and the other teams agreed not to sign any of them. The number of players to be reserved increased to 11 in 1883, 12 in 1886, and 14 in 1887—

at a time when 14 was virtually a team's entire roster.

As the National League became relatively stable and most of its teams began to show profits, it also faced growing resentment from many professional teams that were left outside the circuit—especially those that had been expelled or forced to drop out. In 1882, the rival American Association began play with teams in Baltimore, Cincinnati, Louisville, Philadelphia, Pittsburgh, and St. Louis. The association charged only 25 cents admission, and allowed Sunday baseball and the sale of alcohol. During the season, association teams aggressively pursued National League players, signing many of them to future contracts for the 1883 season, thus honoring the contracts but not the reserve rule.

The war lasted only one season. In 1883, the American Association, the National League, and the minor Northwestern League met at a "harmony conference" and signed the Tripartite Pact, under which they agreed to honor one another's contracts, reserve lists, suspensions, and expulsions. Just a year later, there was another challenge, from the Union Association, which opened the 1884 season with teams in Altoona, Baltimore, Boston, Chicago, Cincinnati, Philadelphia, St. Louis, and Washington. The new league seemed to have solid financial backing, and its opposition to the reserve rule attracted some players who resented the rule. But its teams were all beset by financial problems, and association leaders agreed to disband the league after one season as part of a peace settlement.

As part of the settlement, the National League agreed to give Henry V. Lucas, the chief Union backer, a St. Louis franchise. That caused friction with the American Association, which already had a team in St. Louis. Lucas bought the Cleveland franchise and planned to move it, but St. Louis owner Chris Von der Ahe objected to the invasion of his territory. In the meantime, the association's Brooklyn team signed most of the Cleveland players on the grounds that they didn't go with the franchise. The National League charged that Brooklyn had violated the Tripartite Pact, and gave the association a choice: let Lucas have a team in St. Louis, or expel Brooklyn. Finally, Von der Ahe relented, and Lucas had his team.

A. G. Mills resigned the league presidency after the 1884 season, partly because he disapproved of the league's reinstatement of players who had been blacklisted for jumping to the association. He was replaced by Nicholas E. Young, secretary of the league since its beginning. Young soon faced baseball's first real labor movement, the Brotherhood of Professional Baseball Players. Organized late in 1885, the brotherhood had nearly 100 members by 1887, when it was formally recognized by the owners. A year later, the major leagues adopted the Classification Plan, under which players were to be graded in five classes from A to E, with salary determined by class. The Brotherhood objected and threatened to strike. After negotiations stalled, the players lined up financial backers and formed their own league for the 1890 season.

To combat the Players' League, the National League dropped its weakest franchises, Indianapolis and Washington, and took the American Association's two strongest franchises, Brooklyn and Cincinnati. After a disastrous season for all three leagues, peace was worked out in a series of meetings early in 1891. The National League's New York team, which had nearly been forced out of business, was merged with the Players' League team. Then the Pittsburgh franchises were also merged, and the Chicago National League team bought out the Players' League franchise in that city.

When the dust finally settled, the National League was much stronger than it had been in 1889, but the American Association was weaker. Many association players who had jumped to the Players' League were now in the National League. The Association declared war by pulling out of the National Agreement, and another salary war began. The leagues met in August of 1891 to discuss a truce, and they met again in Indianapolis on December 15. The association was dissolved; the National League, temporarily renamed the National League and American Association of Professional Base Ball Clubs, became a 12-team circuit, adding the former association franchises in Baltimore, Louisville, St. Louis, and Washington.

Clubs quickly moved to reduce payrolls, cutting rosters from 15 to 13 players and arbitrarily slashing salaries as much as 30 to 40 percent in the course of the season. The league used a split schedule in 1892, with a best five-of-nine playoff between first-half champion Boston and second-half champion Cleveland after the season. It was also the first year of Sunday ball in the National League, as a concession to the former association owners. Salaries were reduced even further. For example, "Sliding Billy" Hamilton, who had earned $3,400 in 1892 was paid $1,800 in 1893.

The league was troubled by internal squabbles through the rest of the 1890s. Gambling in the stands and among managers and owners again brought discredit to the sport, as did increasing rowdyism caused in part by Sunday ball, which attracted the frequently unruly working class, and New York owner Andrew Freedman didn't help the cause. He punched one New York sportswriter, banned others from the park for criticizing his team, and arbitrarily deducted "fines" from the salary of his top pitcher, Amos Rusie, who refused to play for an entire season as a result. League owners wanted Freedman to improve his poor team, but he said he would spend the money only after the league was reduced to eight teams.

He got his way after the 1899 season, when the league decided to drop its four weakest franchises: Baltimore, Cleveland, Louisville, and Washington. While that was probably a good financial move, it came at a bad time. The minor Western League had just changed its name to the American League, and in 1900 it expanded into Chicago and Cleveland; the following season it moved teams into Baltimore, Boston, Philadelphia, and Washington and claimed major-league status. Here at last was a rival that the National League couldn't conquer.

One problem was that National League owners were distracted. In August of 1901, Freedman met with owners Arthur Soden of Boston, John T. Brush of Cincinnati, and Frank Robison of St. Louis at his estate in Red Bank, NJ to discuss turning the league into an organization, called the National Baseball Trust, with each team holding stock. The trust would license players, assign them to teams, and hire managers. At the league's annual meeting in December, A. G. Spalding was nominated to replace Nick Young as president, but Freedman's group backed Young. The resulting vote was a four-to-four split.

The trust plan was then proposed as a constitutional amendment, but it failed to pass. On December 13, the fifth day of the meeting, Freedman's group left after repeated tie votes on the presidency, and the remaining four owners unanimously elected Spalding. But he was almost immediately served with a court order preventing him from acting as president. The matter was finally settled the following spring, when Spalding resigned, Brush sold his Cincinnati team and bought out Freedman, and Harry Pulliam was elected president.

In the fall of 1902, the National League proposed consolidation into a 12-team league, but the American League rejected that idea. Committees representing the two leagues met in Cincinnati on January 9, 1903, and worked out a truce. A new National Agreement was signed by the major leagues and the National Association of Professional Baseball Leagues, representing the minor leagues. It established a three-man National Commission made up of the two league presidents and a chairman to be chosen jointly by them.

The first World Series was played in 1903 under an informal agreement between the teams, Boston of the American League and Pittsburgh of the National League. However, Brush and his manager, John McGraw, both had grudges against American League president Ban Johnson and refused to play a series against Chicago in 1904. Ironically, it was Brush who drew up the procedure under which the World Series was permanently established in 1905.

The National League was still beset with internal problems, despite Freedman's departure. Although Johnson was a strong leader who worked under long-term contracts with the American League, the National chose a president annually. Harry Pulliam tried to resign the job early in 1909 because of conflicts with owners; given a leave of absence, he returned to the presidency shortly afterward but committed suicide in July. His interim replacement was John A. Heydler, the league's secretary-treasurer. After a deadlocked election at the end of the year, John T. Lynch, a former umpire, was chosen as a compromise candidate. Lynch angered several owners by frequently fining or suspending players and managers who fought with umpires. He lasted four terms, until John K. Tener, governor of Philadelphia, was chosen in 1913. In his farewell speech, Lynch said that Tener was the right man, but told the owners, " . . . I hope that you will inject some of the dignity expected of him into yourselves and be a help instead of a hindrance to him."

Tener, given a four-year contract, almost immediately faced another outside threat, the Federal League. After its first season in 1913, the league began signing some major-league players. It wasn't particularly successful in its raids, but the rivalry did drive up salaries, as several players signed with the Federal League and were then lured back to their original teams. The Federal League was dissolved after the 1915 season in exchange for a $600,000 indemnity. The Chicago owners were allowed to buy the Chicago team in the National League, with the league itself donating $50,000 for the purchase.

When his original contract expired, Tener signed a one-year deal, but he didn't finish the term. In 1918 the Boston National League team and Philadelphia American League team both claimed rights to pitcher Scott Perry. The National Commission awarded him to Boston, but Philadelphia got a restraining order against the decision. Tener resigned from the National Commission, said he would have no more dealings with the American League, and asked his owners to cancel the World Series. They refused, and he resigned the presidency on August 6, 1918. He was replaced by Heydler, who took the job on a permanent basis this time.

The National Commission was replaced by a single commissioner, Kenesaw Mountain Landis, in 1921, and the league president became much less important than in the past. However, the National League president had always been limited in his powers. As Tener put it, "What can a president accomplish who is authorized by the laws of the league (only) to preside over the meetings and to supervise the umpires?"

The lack of strong leadership and the National League's internecine warfare undoubtedly helped the American League become dominant on the field through the first half of the century. The New York Yankees also had a lot to do with it. The American League won 35 of the first 55 World Series, with the Yankees winning 19 times. The dominance also showed up in the annual all-star game, which began in 1933. The National League won 11 of the first 27. After the Brooklyn Dodgers broke the color barrier in 1947, however, National League teams moved faster in signing black players. As a result, the National League took the lead in overall talent beginning about 1960, winning a remarkable 26 of 30 all-star games, including 11 in a row from 1972 through 1982. Because of better balance within the league, however, the World Series has been almost evenly split, the National League winning 17 of 32 from 1959 through 1990.

After its streamlining to eight teams for the 1900 season, the league remained stable for more than a half-century, with franchises in Boston, Brooklyn, Chicago, Cincinnati, New York, Philadelphia, Pittsburgh, and St. Louis. But several of the teams that competed head to head with the American League had problems after World War II. In 1953, the Braves moved from Boston to Milwaukee, and in 1958 the Brooklyn Dodgers went to Los Angeles, and the New York Giants to San Francisco. The league reentered New York with a new franchise, the Mets, in 1962, when Houston was also added. The Braves went to Atlanta in 1966.

Further expansion took place in 1969 with the addition of Montreal and San Diego. The American League also expanded to 12 teams that season, and both leagues split into two divisions, with the division champions meeting in a league championship series to determine the pennant winners.

Further Reading: Allen, Lee. *The National League Story*. New York: Hill & Wang, 1961.

Addresses:

National League, 350 Park Avenue, New York, NY 10022 (212) 371–7300.

Atlanta Braves, P.O. Box 4064, Atlanta, GA 30302 (404) 522–7630.

Chicago Cubs, Clark and Addison Streets, Chicago, IL 60613 (312) 281–5050.

Cincinnati Reds, 100 Riverfront Stadium, Cincinnati, OH 45202 (513) 421–4510.

Houston Astros, P.O. Box 288, Houston, TX 77001 (713) 799–9500.

Los Angeles Dodgers, 1000 Elysian Park Avenue, Los Angeles, CA 90012 (213) 224–1500.

Montreal Expos, P.O. Box 500, Station M, Montreal, Quebec, Canada H1V 3P2 (514) 253–3434.

New York Mets, 126th Street & Roosevelt Avenue, Flushing, NY 11368 (718) 507–6387.

Philadelphia Phillies, P.O. Box 7575, Philadelphia, PA 19101 (215) 463–6000.

Pittsburgh Pirates, P.O. Box 7000, Pittsburgh, PA 15212 (412) 323–5000.

St. Louis Cardinals, 250 Stadium Plaza, St. Louis, MO 63102 (314) 421–4040.

San Diego Padres, P.O. Box 2000, San Diego, CA 92120 (619) 283–7294.

San Francisco Giants, Candlestick Park, San Francisco, CA 92120 (415) 468–3700.

See also AMERICAN LEAGUE; WORLD SERIES.

National Museum of Racing and Hall of Fame

The National Museum of Racing was in the Canfield Casino at Saratoga Springs, NY when it was founded in 1950. The museum moved into its own new building across the street from Saratoga Race Course in August of 1955. A wing was added in 1957 to house a sizable collection of art works related to horse racing.

The museum temporarily closed when a major renovation and modernization project began on September 1, 1987, financed by a $6 million fund drive. It reopened on July 14, 1989. As part of the project, the Widener Hall of Fame Auditorium was equipped with touch screen video monitors that allow visitors to access film clips from famous races and tracks, and a 15-minute movie shown on a curved screen gives a jockey's-eye view of racing at Aqueduct, Belmont Park, Churchill Downs, Keeneland, and Santa Anita.

Address: Union Avenue, Saratoga Springs, NY 12866 (518) 584–0400

National Period (1787–1840)

During the first half-century of the American republic, a handful of sports flourished in their different ways. On the expanding frontier, men competed in turkey shooting and other target sports, rail splitting, primitive athletic contests including sprinting and jumping, and impromptu brawls. In the growing cities, less reputable sports such as billiards, bowling, cockfighting, and shuffleboard clustered around inns and taverns. College students worked off excess energy by playing cricket, football (soccer), and rounders, and students in the academies that were spreading through the Northeast followed their example. Southern gentlemen fought duels, rode and raced horses, played billiards in their homes, and bowled on their own private greens. Northern aristocrats enjoyed both horse racing and driving, the precursor of harness racing.

Two divergent attitudes toward sports and recreation emerged during this period. The revival of Puritan attitudes in the form of Calvinism, sometimes called the "Second Great Awakening," led to renewed attempts to ban sports "and other dissipations," at least on the Sabbath. But many others, including Thomas Jefferson, advocated sports as a means toward health. Dr. Benjamin Rush, in the late 18th century, recommended any activities that would "import health, strength and elegance to the human body," and he was echoed by many other writers, especially educators, in the early part of the 19th century.

The seeds of the gymnasium, physical education, and playground movements were all planted during this period. Formal gymnastics exercises were imported from Germany and Switzerland, and gymnasiums were established at several schools and colleges. The *American Journal of Education* in 1826 called for city playgrounds and extolled the virtues of sports such as cricket, handball, and golf for the adult as well as for the student, and the *Journal of Health* in 1829 proposed that public baths and gymnasiums should be established and made available to the working class for a nominal fee.

None of these movements came to fruition during the National Period, but the thoughts and principles behind them were reinforced during the antebellum period by the ideas of muscular Christianity, and postwar concerns about the health of urban dwellers and the physical and moral welfare of children in the rapidly growing cities would eventually lead to the establishment of gymnasiums in the late 19th and early 20th centuries.

The late National Period also saw the first genuinely popular spectator sports emerge. Horse racing was the first. Although it had achieved some popularity during the colonial era, especially in New York and Virginia, the sport didn't begin to attract large numbers of spectators until after 1821, when horse racing was legalized in Queens County after having been prohibited in all of New York since 1802. The Union Course in 1821 began holding two three-day

meetings a year, but the biggest race by far was between Eclipse, representing the North, and Henry, the southern challenger, on May 27, 1823. An estimated 50,000 spectators turned out to see Eclipse win two of three 4-mile heats.

The first tentative steps toward organization also occurred in horse racing with the founding of the New York Association for the Improvement of the Breed in 1821. The NYAIB aimed to offer attractive purses to encourage breeders and to lure horses from the South. However, Thoroughbred racing fell on hard times late in the decade, and harness racing came to the fore. The New York Trotting Club, organized in the winter of 1824–25, was patterned after the NYAIB; it built a course on Long Island and held two meetings a year. The sport also moved onto several tracks where Thoroughbred racing was floundering.

Pedestrianism—professional walking and running—began in New York about 1820. The contests were often held in conjunction with horse races. The sport became very popular after the "Great Footrace" of 1835, when John Cox Stevens offered $1,000 to the winner of a 10-mile race, with a $3,000 bonus if he covered the distance in less than an hour. Diarist Philip Hone said that the crowd was "as great, I think, as at the famous *Eclipse* race." Henry Stannard won the race and collected the bonus with a time of 59 minutes 48 seconds.

Rowing races, featuring side bets of up to $10,000, were also occasionally popular. The Whitehallers, a New York crew organized about 1810, beat a crew from the English frigate *Hussar* in the fall of 1824 before a cheering crowd estimated by the press at between 20,000 and 50,000. Interest in professional rowing temporarily declined toward the end of the decade, but amateurs became involved in the early 1830s. In 1834, a group of clubs made up of young men from prominent families formed the Castle Garden Amateur Boat Club Association to conduct an annual regatta—another small step toward organized sport.

While sport was sporadic at best during the National Period, it was certainly much more common than it had been through the colonial period. There were more sports and more people participating. The frowns of the Puritans and Calvinists were giving way to moderate approval of exercise as a way to better health, and the idea that organization and scheduling could replace the impromptu, hastily organized games and matches was beginning to coalesce. And the great battle between amateurism and professionalism that was to continue almost to the present day was foreshadowed by the split between the professional, working Whitehallers and the well-to-do amateur oarsmen of the Castle Garden Association.

National Police Gazette

Until 1877, the *National Police Gazette* was a minor weekly scandal sheet. Then Richard Kyle Fox bought it and turned it into a sensation. The *Gazette* specialized in crime, scandal, and pictures of showgirls, and Fox marketed it aggressively. It became a staple in saloons, barbershops, clubs, and other all-male establishments. When an account of the May 30, 1880, bout between Joe Goss and Paddy Ryan helped to sell more than 400,000 copies, Fox decided to continue featuring boxing. He was aided by a well-publicized feud with the popular John L. Sullivan, who had snubbed him when Fox asked for an introduction.

The *Gazette* soon began campaigning for a fight between Sullivan and the champion, Paddy Ryan, with Fox offering to back Ryan with up to $10,000. When they finally agreed to fight for a bet of $2,500 apiece, Fox filled his newspaper with advance publicity about the match, and he made a lot of money from a special eight-page illustrated report after Sullivan won the title. The *Gazette* then began a search for someone who could beat the "Boston Strong Boy," culminating in the last bareknuckle heavyweight title fight, Sullivan's victory over Fox's challenger, Jake Kilrain, in 1887.

By that time, the *Gazette* had a circulation of more than 150,000, and its readership was considerably higher. Fox helped modernize boxing by offering championship belts in six different weight divisions. He ran a regular column on baseball, "Our National Game," and a summary of news from other sports. Fox also gave prizes for several sports and quasi-sports, ranging from women's weight lifting to one-legged clog dancing.

The *Gazette* began to decline in popularity around the turn of the century, with the rise of big-city tabloids that it had helped to inspire, but it held on until 1932, ten years after Fox's death, when it went into bankruptcy. It was revived as a monthly magazine that lasted into the 1970s.

Further Reading: Smith, Gene, and Jayne Barry, editors. *The Police Gazette.* New York: Simon & Schuster, 1972.

National Professional Soccer League (NPSL)

Shortly after the United Soccer Association announced that it would begin play in 1968, the National Professional Soccer League was organized and scheduled to play in 1967. NPSL backers included Jerry Hoffberger of baseball's Baltimore Orioles and Art Rooney, owner of football's Pittsburgh Steelers. Charter franchises were the Atlanta Chiefs, Baltimore Bays, California Clippers, Chicago Spurs, Los Angeles Toros, New York Generals, Philadelphia Spartans, Pittsburgh Phantoms, St. Louis Stars, and Toronto Falcons. Caught off guard, the USA also decided to play in 1967 by importing foreign teams. Because the USA had been sanctioned by the national and international soccer governing bodies, the NPSL had some problems lining up players, who faced possible suspension for competing in an unsanctioned league, but it played the season. The NPSL did have a television contract with CBS, but ratings were poor, as was attendance, and in 1968 it merged with the USA as the North American Soccer League.

National Rifle Association of America (NRA)

National Guard officers organized the NRA on November 17, 1871, with General Ambrose Burnside as its president. The primary purpose was to encourage and supervise shooting competitions. The association opened its Creedmoor range on Long Island on April 25, 1873, and held the first national championships there on October 8. The first major international competition, between teams representing Ireland and the United States, also took place at Creedmoor, on September 26, 1874. The NRA at first emphasized long-distance rifle marksmanship to train both soldiers and civilians, but it introduced pistol competition in 1906 and small-bore rifle shooting in 1908.

Hunting became popular shortly after the turn of the century, and many hunters formed shooting clubs for target practice. As these clubs became affiliates of the NRA, the association's orientation began to shift. Although it continued to sanction and conduct competition, the NRA also got involved in conservation and other issues of interest to hunters. More recently, it's been identified with the pro-gun lobby in its battle against laws that would prohibit or restrict ownership of handguns. The NRA's membership is now over 3 million.

Address: 1600 Rhode Island Avenue, N.W., Washington, DC 20036 (202) 828–6255

National Soccer Hall of Fame

A temporary soccer museum was established in 1980 in a former mansion at Oneonta, NY. Known as "Soccertown, U.S.A.," Oneonta is the home of two colleges that perennially have fine teams, Hartwick and Oneonta State, and the town has nearly 1,500 players in its youth soccer program, a remarkable figure for a city of only about 15,000. The hall of fame museum was sanctioned by the U.S. Soccer Federation in 1982, and four years later a 61–acre site was purchased for a permanent complex, to include a 54,000-square-foot museum, eight soccer fields, and a stadium. Current plans are to have the first phase of construction completed by 1994, when the U.S. hosts the World Cup tournament.

Address: 5–11 Ford Avenue, Oneonta, NY 13820 (607) 432–3351

National Softball Hall of Fame and Museum

Founded by the Amateur Softball Association in 1957, this hall of fame existed only on paper for years. The ASA moved from Newark, NJ to Oklahoma City in 1966, and in 1973 the hall of fame got its own 10,000-square-foot facility, with exhibits on the history of softball and the people who have been inducted into the hall. The nearby Hall of Fame Stadium, built in 1987 for about $2 million, seats 2,046 spectators and is the site of the ASA's national tournaments.

Address: 2801 N.E. 50th Street, Oklahoma City, OK 73111 (405) 424–5266

National Sport and Recreation Centre

See CANADIAN SPORT AND FITNESS ADMINISTRATION CENTRE INC.

National Steeplechase and Hunt Association (NSHA)

The NSHA was founded in 1895 to govern both fox hunting and steeplechasing, but is now chiefly concerned with steeplechasing. Most of its races are held on spring and fall circuits at local and regional hunt meetings, but the association also conducts steeplechases on Thoroughbred courses in Georgia, Kentucky, Maryland, Missouri, New Jersey, New York, Pennsylvania, Tennessee, and Virginia. In recent years, the NSHA has been very successful in rounding up corporate sponsorship; as a result, purses have increased from about $600,000 in 1983 to more than $3 million in 1990. A nonprofit organization, the NSHA has about 1,500 members.

Address: Box 308, Elmont, NY 11003 (516) 437–6666

National Track and Field Hall of Fame

This hall of fame was originally an independent organization, founded in 1974 and located in Charleston, WV. The Athletics Congress, the na-

tional governing body for the sport, took over the hall of fame in 1983 and moved it to Indianapolis, IN. It is now located in 3,500 square feet of space next to the TAC's headquarters in the Hoosier Dome.

Address: P.O. Box 120, Indianapolis, IN 46206 (317) 638–9155

National Trotting Association (NTA)

The Narragansett Trotting Association (of Rhode Island) called a convention of harness racing track operators in 1869 to adopt uniform rules. The meeting, on February 4, 1870, created one of the first genuine sports governing bodies, the National Trotting Association for the Promotion of the Interest of the Trotting Turf. The 46 tracks from 15 states that took part agreed on a set of rules and decided that a person suspended by one track in the organization would also be suspended at all other tracks subscribing to the rules. A board of appeals was appointed to rule on any disputes.

The name of the organization was shortened to the National Trotting Association in 1878, and, in the interests of the sport, the NTA also worked to coordinate its members' schedules to avoid conflicting dates for important stakes races. Later, the American Trotting Association was formed to govern races in the Midwest, and track operators in Ohio organized their own group, the United Trotting Association. The three merged in 1939 into the U.S. Trotting Association.

See also HARNESS RACING.

Native American Sports

Most European explorers and travelers commented on the prevalence of play among native Americans. Many of them also noted that games were often associated with religious ritual. Stickball, called "lacrosse" by the French, was played by many tribes from Ontario and Quebec in the North to the Gulf of Mexico. The sport varied somewhat from region to region—several tribes in the Southeast, for example, played a version in which each player had two sticks—but the essentials were the same: Teams of players, using sticks with leather nets or pouches, attempted to advance a ball to a goal. Players often prepared for the game as if they were about enter combat or go hunting. The Cherokees, Choctaws, and other tribes preceded the game with a night of ritual dancing. Among the Creeks, a stickball game was an important feature of the four-day Green Corn Festival in late summer, the approximate equivalent of our New Year's. Games resembling soccer were also popular, especially among western tribes that didn't play stickball. And at least one group of

Eskimos played a kind of stickball that somewhat resembled baseball.

Target shooting of one sort or another was also important in a culture that used the bow and arrow for hunting and warfare. Among many tribes, target practice for boys was formalized. The Natchez trained youngsters by having them shoot at a bundle of grass thrown into the air, and the best shot was rewarded with the title "young warrior." Hopi adults were spectators at target shooting contests among boys, encouraging them with loud applause whenever a shot hit the target. Competition among adult warriors was less formal, usually brought on by a challenge and accompanying wager. The Mandan tribe and others played a game called "arrows" in their language, in which a warrior shot as many arrows as he could into the air before the first one came back to earth.

Chunkey was a very popular sport in the Southeast, often played on an enclosed court built for the purpose or on a public square that could also be used for other games. A stone disk was rolled along the ground, and players attempted to hit it with a long slender pole. Explorer John Lederer in 1672 wrote of the Enos tribe in South Carolina: "Their town is built round a field, where in their sports they exercise with so much labor and violence, and in so great numbers, that I have seen the ground wet with the sweat that dropped from their bodies; their chief recreation is slinging of stones." This has usually been interpreted as a reference to chunkey, but it sounds more like a weight-throwing contest.

Many tribes enjoyed distance running. Artist George Catlin described a footrace among the Mandan Indians of the upper Missouri: A 3-mile course was laid out as the arc of a circle, and runners traversed the course three times. Running was particularly popular in the Southwest, but in the late 19th century it was the Senecas of upstate New York who became noted for their running ability. Lewis Bennett, one of several Senecas who competed against whites in formal contests, competed in England under the name of "Deerfoot." The Zuni, in the Southwest, had kicking-stick relay races in which a runner balanced a stick on his foot and threw it into the air as far as he could. The next player would then pick it up on his foot and throw it. The better players could throw the stick more than 100 feet, and races were "run" for as long as 25 miles.

"Snowsticks," sliding a stick or cane pole across the snow for distance, was popular among northern tribes, and one visitor found a kind of handball played by youngsters, especially girls, in Louisiana: "This consists in tossing a ball from one to the other with the palm of the hand, which they perform with

a tolerable address." Gambling was an important element in many native American sports, and there were also many gambling games, including a kind of dice, using seeds, stones, or grains of corn.

See also DEERFOOT; ESKIMO SPORTS; WORLD ESKIMO–INDIAN OLYMPICS.

Navin Field
See TIGER STADIUM.

Nazi Olympics
The 1936 Olympic Games were awarded to Germany before Hitler came to power. After his ascent, Jews were barred from membership in German sports clubs, which would prevent them from entering Olympic trials. The Amateur Athletic Union on November 21, 1933, voted to boycott the Olympics unless Germany changed its policy. Avery Brundage, president of the American Olympic Committee, traveled to Germany in 1935 and reported that the country was living up to the spirit and rules of the Olympics. By a narrow vote, the AAU finally decided to accept the invitation less than three months after the Nuremberg Laws were passed, depriving Jews of citizenship and civil rights.

Hitler set out to make the Berlin Olympics a showcase for his "New Order," Nazism, spending $30 million on facilities, including a 100,000-seat stadium, gyms and arenas, and housing for athletes. For the first time, photofinish equipment was used, and closed-circuit television carried events to 18 television halls and the Olympic Village. Noted German filmmaker Leni Riefenstahl was given a grant of $7 million to produce and direct a movie about the Games.

The U.S. track and field team had 18 black members, contemptuously dubbed the "Black Auxiliaries" by the German press. One of them, Jesse Owens, was unquestionably the hero of the Games, but the story that Hitler deliberately snubbed him is a myth. On August 2, the first day of competition, shot-putter Hans Wollke became the first German ever to win a Gold Medal in track and field, and Hitler personally congratulated him. He also congratulated the Finnish runners who swept the 10,000-meter run and the German women who finished first and second in the javelin. When an American black, Cornelius Johnson, won the high jump shortly afterward, Hitler was no longer in his box. The official explanation was that he had left because rain was threatening. Owens won the first of his four Gold Medals the following day, after Hitler had been told by the International Olympic Committee that he should congratulate all the winners or none of them.

His decision to stop offering public congratulations was undoubtedly based in large part on the fact that American blacks were likely to win more than their share of medals.

The story about Hitler's supposed snub of Owens has obscured the fact that Germany won the propaganda victory it hoped for. The country won 181 medals, including 33 Gold, to the United States' 124 medals and 24 Golds. And the whole spectacle was a foreshadowing of the athletic cold war that was to begin with the Soviet Union's entry into the Olympics in 1952, when the Olympics became a contest to determine which political system could produce the best athletes—a contest ultimately won, probably, by East Germany during the 1970s.

Further Reading: Mandell, Richard D. *The Nazi Olympics.* New York: Macmillan, 1971.

See also OWENS, JESSE.

NBA
See NATIONAL BASKETBALL ASSOCIATION.

NCAA
See NATIONAL COLLEGIATE ATHLETIC ASSOCIATION.

Negro American League (NAL)
Baseball

Because the Negro National League had withdrawn from the Midwest in 1936, H. G. Hall of the Chicago American Giants organized the Negro American League in 1937. The original teams were the American Giants, Birmingham Black Barons, Cincinnati Tigers, Detroit Stars, Indianapolis Athletics, Kansas City Monarchs, Memphis Red Sox, and St. Louis Stars. While Birmingham, Chicago, and Kansas City remained in the league for most of its existence, other franchises came and went annually. Among the other cities represented in the league from time to time were Atlanta, Baltimore, Cleveland, Jacksonville, Louisville, and New Orleans. The NNL went out of business in 1948, and the NAL then added some teams in the Northeast and reorganized into eastern and western divisions. The league kept operating through 1960, but was relegated to second-class status because the best black players were in the formerly all-white major leagues by then.

See also BLACK WORLD SERIES.

Negro National League (NNL)
Baseball

Andrew "Rube" Foster, the manager of the Chicago American Giants, in 1919 suggested that two six-team leagues of black players should be organized.

Because of Foster's proposal, the National Association of Colored Professional Baseball Clubs and the Negro National League, commonly called just the Negro National League, was founded at a meeting in Chicago on February 13, 1920. The original teams were the Chicago American Giants, Chicago Giants, Cuban Stars (who played all their games on the road), Dayton Marcos, Detroit Stars, Indianapolis ABCs, Kansas City Monarchs, and St. Louis Giants.

Although the league originally planned to begin operations in 1921, it played a kind of preview season in 1920. Official standings weren't published, but the Chicago American Giants were awarded the championship. The Dayton Marcos were replaced by the Columbus Buckeyes in 1921, the first of many franchise changes that would take place during the league's 12 years of existence, and the Cuban Stars found a home in Cincinnati. The NNL was troubled by the fact that five of its teams had to lease parks from white teams, and could use them only when the resident teams were out of town. The result was a skewed schedule. The Kansas City Monarchs played 81 games that season, the Chicago Giants only 42.

Like other new leagues in baseball and other sports, the NNL was also dominated by a few teams, and the others suffered at the gate. The Chicago American Giants and Kansas City Monarchs each won 5 of 12 pennants, the St. Louis Stars won one, and the outcome of the 1928 race is not known. Every year, weaker teams dropped out, to be replaced by other weak teams that could last only a season or two. And, in 1923, the NNL faced major competition from the Eastern Colored League. The ECL in 1924 lured ten players away from the Indianapolis ABCs; that team folded in midseason and was replaced by the Memphis Red Sox.

Despite the salary war, however, the NNL and ECL did play the first Black World Series in 1924, and the Kansas City Monarchs beat Hilldale of the ECL, five games to four. Meanwhile, Foster helped to keep the league going by lending money or giving it outright to shaky franchises. Unfortunately, he suffered a nervous breakdown and was hospitalized in 1926. Without Foster's strong leadership, the NNL struggled through five chaotic seasons; then disorganization and the Great Depression combined to force it out of business in 1932.

A second Negro National League was organized in 1932 by Gus Greenlee, owner of the Pittsburgh Crawfords, which had some of the greatest black players in baseball history, including Satchel Paige, Josh Gibson, Oscar Charleston, and "Cool Papa" Bell, all of whom are in the Baseball Hall of Fame. Greenlee's NNL included the Crawfords, the Chicago American Giants, Columbus Blue Birds, Detroit Stars,

Homestead Grays, and Indianapolis ABCs. The league played a split schedule, but Homestead and Indianapolis dropped out after the first half, and the second half was never completed.

Nevertheless, the NNL resumed play in 1933 with six teams and expanded to eight in 1935. The following season, the league pulled out of its two midwestern cities, Chicago and Columbus, to reduce travel expenses. For the first half of the season, the franchises were the Homestead Grays, Newark Eagles, New York Cubans, Philadelphia Stars, Pittsburgh Crawfords, and Washington Elite Giants. The New York Black Yankees joined the NNL for the second half. The Negro American League in 1937 moved into the vacuum in the Midwest and South, and the two leagues began playing a World Series in 1942. It continued through 1948, and then the NNL folded because so many black players were finally being accepted into the major leagues.

See also BLACK WORLD SERIES.

Neil Trophy
Boxing

Named for Edward J. Neil, an Associated Press sportswriter who was killed in 1938 while covering the Spanish Civil War, this trophy is given by the New York Boxing Writers' Association to "the person who did the most for boxing during the preceding year."

Nelson, "Byron" John Byron, Jr. (1912–)
Golf

Born February 4, 1912, Ft. Worth, TX; World Golf Hall of Fame

Nelson had the most incredible year in golf history in 1945, when he won 19 tournaments on the pro tour, including 11 in a row. That record is sometimes downplayed because most top golfers were in the service, but Nelson averaged just 68.33 strokes a round that year, the lowest ever recorded. Unquestionably one of the greatest golfers of all time, Nelson won the U.S. Open in 1939, the PGA in 1940 and 1945, and the Masters in 1937 and 1942. In his 1937 Masters victory, he was trailing Ralph Guldahl by four shots with seven holes to play, but he birdied the 12th hole and scored an eagle on the 13th to climb into first place for good. He had a similar burst in the 1945 PGA Tournament, which was then at match play. In the second round, he was down by 2 holes with just 4 left to play in his 36-hole match against Mike Turnesa. Nelson promptly won three holes with two birdies and an eagle, then parred the 18th to win the match by one hole.

Nelson was the Vardon Trophy winner in 1939 and 1945 and the tour's leading money-winner in 1944 and 1945. He was also named the Associated Press Athlete of the Year both years. Nelson retired from the tour after winning six tournaments and finishing second in the U.S. Open in 1946, but he continued to play in a few tournaments each year. Even as a part-timer, he tied for second in the Masters in 1947 and won the Texas PGA in 1948, the Bing Crosby Invitational in 1951, and the French Open in 1955.

Nevele Pride (1965–)
Harness Racing

By winning 26 of 29 starts and $222,923 in 1967, Nevele Pride became the first two-year-old ever named Harness Horse of the Year. He repeated in 1968 and 1969. As a three-year-old, he won 21 of 24 races, including the trotting Triple Crown, the Hambletonian, Kentucky Futurity, and Yonkers Trot. That year, he also set a record for his age by trotting a mile in 1 minute 56⅗ seconds on August 31 at Indianapolis. Originally named Thankful's Major, he was purchased in 1966 for $20,000 by Charles Slutsky of Nevele Farms, who renamed him. After the 1969 season, Nevele Pride was put out to stud. In 67 starts, he had 57 wins, 4 seconds, and 3 thirds.

Nevers, "Ernie" Ernest A. (1903–1976)
Football

Born June 11, 1903, Willow River, MN; died May 3, 1976; National Football Foundation, Pro Football Hall of Fame

He played only five seasons in the National Football League, but Nevers turned in enough remarkable performances to become a charter member of the Pro Football Hall of Fame. In 1925, he was an All-American fullback at Stanford, where he played for Glenn "Pop" Warner. Warner had also coached the great Jim Thorpe in college, but he considered Nevers the better player, saying, "Nevers can do everything Thorpe could do and he tries harder." An example of his trying harder came in the 1926 Rose Bowl game against Notre Dame. Playing on two badly injured ankles, Nevers gained 114 yards rushing and, according to one sportswriter who covered the game, made 75 percent of his team's tackles in a losing cause.

In early 1926, Nevers earned $25,000 from a Florida "all-star" team that played a few exhibition games, including one against the New York Giants and another against the Chicago Bears, who were on their barnstorming tour with Red Grange. Then he joined the St. Louis Cardinals as a pitcher and was contacted by a high school classmate, Ole Haugsrud, owner of the NFL's Duluth Eskimos. A rival American Football League had been organized around Grange, and Nevers was the only other drawing card available. Haugsrud offered him $15,000 plus a cut of the gate receipts to play for the Eskimos, and Nevers accepted. (The rest of the players got $75 for a victory, $60 for a tie, and $50 for a loss.)

To give every team in the league a home game against "Ernie Nevers' Duluth Eskimos," as they were billed, the Eskimos became a road team. According to Haugsrud, the team played 29 games that season, and Nevers played all but 27 minutes. As fullback in the Warner double-wing system that he taught the Eskimos, he handled the ball on every play, and was more than a triple threat. He could not only run, kick, and pass, he called the signals, returned kicks, and was an outstanding linebacker. Duluth didn't have a successful 1927 season, and Nevers suffered a broken vertebra that kept him out of action in 1928. However, he became player-coach of the Chicago Cardinals in 1929, and had the most prolific two weeks in pro football history that season. After scoring all his team's points in a 40–6 victory over the Chicago Bears—still the NFL record for a single game—Nevers scored every point in a 19–0 win over Dayton a week later.

After two more seasons with the Cardinals, Nevers retired. But he later claimed that he had played the equivalent of ten seasons during his five years in the NFL, and none of his former teammates ever disputed it.

Newark, NJ

Football The Orange (NJ) Tornadoes of the National Football League moved to Newark in 1930. After winning just one game while losing ten and tying one, the franchise folded.

New England

Football After years of moving from one stadium to another, the Boston Patriots moved into newly built Schaefer Stadium (now Sullivan Stadium) in Foxboro, MA in 1971 and became known as the New England Patriots. As a wild-card team in 1985, they beat the Miami Dolphins 31–14 for the AFC championship. The Patriots were defeated 46–10 by the Chicago Bears in Super Bowl XX.

Hockey The Boston Whalers of the World Hockey Association moved to West Springfield, MA in 1974 and became known as the New England Whalers. They played in Hartford, CT for the next three seasons, were forced to move back to Springfield after

the Hartford Civic Center's roof collapsed in 1978, and returned to Hartford in 1980. When the WHA merged with the National Hockey League for the 1979–80 season, they became the Hartford Whalers because the NHL's Boston Bruins objected to their use of the phrase "New England."

See also BOSTON, MA; HARTFORD, CT; HARTFORD CIVIC CENTER; SULLIVAN STADIUM.

New England Game
See MASSACHUSETTS GAME.

New Jersey

Although only two major-league teams, the Devils and the Nets, have "New Jersey" in their names, both of New York City's pro football franchises, the Giants and the Jets, play their home games at Giants Stadium in Meadowlands Sports Center. When the Giants moved into the stadium in 1976, the city threatened to bring suit to force the team to change its name to the New Jersey Giants, but no such suit was ever filed.

Basketball The New Jersey Nets, now in the National Basketball Association, originated as the New Jersey Americans of the American Basketball Association in 1967, but the franchise moved to Long Island as the New York Americans the following year. They became the New York Nets in 1969, and after moving into Brendan Byrne Arena at the Meadowlands for the 1976–77 season they became the New Jersey Nets.

Hockey The Colorado Rockies of the National Hockey League became the New Jersey Devils in 1982.

See also MEADOWLANDS SPORT COMPLEX; NEW YORK, NY.

Newmarket Course
Hempstead, NY

The first known racecourse in North America was laid out in 1665 at what is now Hempstead, Long Island, at the order of Richard Nicolls, who had arrived the year before to become the first English governor of New York. It was named the Newmarket Course after the famous English track. At least one race was undoubtedly held there in 1665, but the first documented race was in 1668; the prize was a silver porringer that still exists. Nicolls' successor, Frank Lovelace, sponsored a race at the course in 1669 for a subscription of one crown "or its equivalent in goode wheate." That was probably the first sweepstakes race in North American history.

New Orleans, LA

Basketball The New Orleans Jazz entered the National Basketball Association as an expansion franchise in 1974, but remained for only five seasons, moving to Salt Lake City as the inappropriately named Utah Jazz in 1979.

Football Shortly after the American and National Football Leagues announced their merger agreement in 1966, the NFL awarded an expansion franchise to New Orleans, and the new team, the Saints, began play in the 1967 season. The move was widely seen as a political payoff, since federal legislation clearing the way for the merger had been guided through Congress by Senator Russell Long and Representative Hale Boggs, both of Louisiana. The Saints have never won a division championship.

See also LOUISIANA SUPERDOME.

Newport Casino

See CASINO CLUB.

Newspapers

See JOURNALISM, SPORTS.

New York, NY

Baseball Modern baseball originated in New York with the Knickerbocker Base Ball Club in 1845, and most of the early teams were located in the city—although a few of the very best were in Brooklyn, which was then a separate city. Among the best were the Knickerbockers themselves; the Metropolitan Club, originally made up of schoolteachers; and the Mutual Club, made of firemen from the Mutual Hook and Ladder Company No. 1. By 1871, the Mutuals had become a professional team in the newly formed National Association of Professional Base Ball Players. After the league folded, the Mutuals moved into the new National League of Professional Base Ball Clubs in 1876—usually known simply as the National League.

They were expelled for not playing out their schedule, however, and New York didn't have another major-league team until 1883, when it suddenly had two. The New York Metropolitans, an independent professional team since 1880, joined the American Association, and another New York club, not yet nicknamed, entered the National League. Both were controlled by John B. Day. The Metropolitans won the American association championship in 1884, but were forced to drop out after the 1887 season because association owners suspected Day of being a spy for the National League.

Bobby Thomson's three-run home run in the ninth inning at the Polo Grounds gave the New York Giants a 5–4 victory over the Brooklyn Dodgers in the final game of a three-game playoff for the 1951 National League pennant. Courtesy of the Public Broadcasting System

The New York National League team was inadvertently nicknamed the Giants in 1885 when manager Jim Mutrie exulted in front of sportswriters, "These are my big guys! My giants!" The name has been with the team ever since, even in San Francisco. The Giants won National League pennants in 1888, 1889, 1904, 1905, 1911, 1912, 1913, 1917, 1921, 1922, 1923, 1924, 1933, 1936, 1937, and 1951. That last pennant came when Bobby Thomson hit his famous three-run, ninth-inning homer—"Miracle of Coogan's Bluff"—to beat the Brooklyn Dodgers 4–3 in the final game of a three-game playoff series. They were World Series champions in 1905, 1921, 1922, and 1933. The team moved to San Francisco in 1958, the same year the Dodgers went to Los Angeles.

New York reentered the National League with the Mets, short for Metropolitans, in 1962. They won National League pennants in 1969, 1973, and 1986, and were World Series champions in 1969 and 1986.

New York didn't have an American League team until 1903, its third season of operation, when the troubled Baltimore franchise was moved. The American League team was originally known as the Highlanders or Hilltoppers because they played at Hilltop Park at 186th Street and Broadway. Exactly when or why they became the Yankees is unknown, but the name was in frequent use by 1905. They became the dominant team in baseball, beginning in the 1920s. They won the World Series in 1923, 1927, 1928, 1932, 1933, 1936, 1937, 1938, 1939, 1941, 1943, 1947, 1949, 1950, 1951, 1952, 1953, 1956, 1958, 1961, 1962, 1977, and 1978. They also won American League pennants in 1921, 1922, 1926, 1942, 1955, 1957, 1960, 1963, 1964, 1976, and 1981.

Basketball The New York Knickerbockers, now known simply as the Knicks, joined the newly formed Basketball Association of America in 1946. The BAA became the National Basketball Association in 1949, and the Knicks won NBA titles in 1970 and 1973.

The New Jersey Americans of the American Basketball Association moved to Long Island in 1968. The team became known as the New York Nets the following season, and moved back to New Jersey in 1977, the year after the ABA merged with the NBA. The Nets won ABA championships in 1974 and 1976.

Football Named for the baseball team, the New York Giants entered the National Football League in 1925. The Giants won NFL championships in 1934, 1938, and 1956, and beat the Denver Broncos 39–20 in Super Bowl XXI in 1987, and the Buffalo Bills 20–19 in Super Bowl XXV in 1991.

The New York Yankees were in the first American Football League in 1926. The league lasted only one season, and the Yankees played in the NFL in 1927 and 1928. A second team called the Yankees played in the All-America Football Conference for its four seasons of operation, 1946 through 1949, and entered the NFL for two seasons before moving to Dallas in 1952.

The New York Titans, a charter member of the American Football League in 1960, were renamed the Jets in 1963. They beat the Baltimore Colts 16–7 in Super Bowl III.

Hockey The New York Americans entered the National Hockey League for the 1925–26 season. The Americans moved to Brooklyn in 1941.

Just a year after the Americans were born, the New York Rangers entered the NHL, and they're still there. The Rangers won the Stanley Cup in 1928, 1933, and 1940.

See also BROOKLYN, NY; MADISON SQUARE GARDEN; MEADOWLANDS SPORTS COMPLEX; NEW JERSEY; POLO GROUNDS; SHEA STADIUM; STATEN ISLAND, NY; YANKEE STADIIUM.

New York Athletic Club (NYAC)

John C. Babcock, Henry E. Buermeyer, and William B. Curtis were enthusiastic athletes who in 1866 turned the parlor of their New York City apartment

The first national track and field championship meet was held at the New York Athletic Club's Mott Haven grounds in 1876. Courtesy of the New York Athletic Club

into a small gym. On September 8, 1868, they joined with 11 fellow enthusiasts to organize the New York Athletic Club. The NYAC held an indoor track meet at the Empire Skating Rink on November 11, with members of the New York Caledonian Club also taking part. The program included four running races, from 75 to 880 yards, a hurdle race of unspecified distance, a 1-mile walking race, and eight field events. The NYAC followed that with an outdoor meet in the spring of 1869 near Central Park.

Membership grew to more than 100 the following year, and in 1871 the club bought land at Mott Haven, north of the Harlem River, as the site for a cinder track and a boat house. The NYAC's success led to the founding of similar clubs throughout the city and, by 1880, across the country, but the NYAC remained the leader, establishing the first national championships in track and field in 1876, swimming in 1877, boxing, fencing, and wrestling in 1878. The club also codified rules for these sports and developed standards of amateurism that were adopted by most other clubs. When the National Association of Amateur Athletes of America (N4A) was established in 1879, it adopted the NYAC amateur code.

About the same time, a feud began between the NYAC and its younger rival, the Manhattan Athletic Club, which won the national team track and field championship from 1880 through 1885. Manhattan star L. E. "Lon" Myers was charged with professionalism in 1884, but the N4A upheld his amateur status after an investigation. The rivalry between the two clubs escalated in 1886, when the NYAC recruited four top athletes, including one from England and one from Ireland, and the Manhattan AC responded by recruiting an English miler and an Irish distance runner.

The N4A declared one of the NYAC recruits ineligible for having competed as a professional under an assumed name, but dismissed an NYAC protest against the Manhattan AC's Irish runner. As a result, the NYAC in 1887 pulled out of the N4A and led a group of clubs that founded the Amateur Athletic Union the following year. In 1889, the N4A was dissolved, and its members, including the Manhattan AC, joined the AAU, which was largely controlled by the NYAC.

In the meantime, the NYAC was changing. Colonel William Van Wyck, who became the club's second president, was more interested in creating an upper-class social club than running an athletic club. In 1882, he recruited two very wealthy men, Herman Oelrichs and William R. Travers. They led the way for an invasion of the NYAC rolls by members of the social register. The club's initiation fee had been increased from $10 to $100, the annual dues from $5 to $50 to encourage the trend toward wealth. This trend angered many of the "Old Guard," including two of the club's founders, Curtis and Buermeyer, who resigned.

By 1885, the NYAC had 1,500 members and enough capital to spend $150,000 on a five-story clubhouse. The new clubhouse had a billiard parlor, bowling alley, gym, rifle range and swimming pool, and it boasted a well-stocked wine cellar, several dining rooms, and sleeping rooms for members. Three years later, the club built a country home at Travers Island with a boathouse, clubhouse, and tennis courts. And, with membership up to 2,500 in 1892, an even more sumptuous clubhouse was constructed in midtown Manhattan.

Many other athletic clubs followed suit. Sports, especially track and field, were important for the prestige that winning could bring; however, the NYAC and its imitators were no longer athlete-centered. Most members were akin to those wealthy fans of today who buy luxury boxes in professional sports stadiums. And since the best athletes were likely to come from a lower social class, they were more or less openly recruited, often given free room and board, and allowed to become club members without paying any intiation fee or dues.

The NYAC set the pattern for the structure of American amateur sport during most of this century. The club controlled the AAU for many years; as a result, the AAU was essentially run by wealthy men, and athletes were secondary. The U.S. Olympic Committee, originally a creature of the AAU, was much the same. Although the original NYAC amateur code was adopted by virtually every amateur-sport governing body, it was largely ignored in practice. As an example, the first international track and field meet was held on September 21, 1895, with the London Athletic Club meeting the NYAC. Beating the British became an important cause, and the NYAC team, made up of athletes recruited from throughout the Northeast, won all 11 events, setting three world records and tying a fourth. Ostensibly representing the NYAC, the assembled squad was actually a national team.

From 1893 through 1903, the NYAC dominated the national track and field championships, but then the Irish-American Athletic Club of New York took over. The Irish-American AC was exactly what the NYAC wasn't: a club devoted entirely to sports, especially track and field, and run by the athletes themselves. Other clubs more like the NYAC—the Chicago Athletic Association, the Los Angeles AC, the Illinois AC, and the Olympic Club of San Francisco, for example—dominated the sport after 1914, and the NYAC again took over leadership in 1932, winning 17 of the next 27 team championships and finishing second nine times.

During the late 1950s and early 1960s, many new clubs, concentrating solely on track and field, were organized. Most of them were on the West Coast, where the climate allows longer periods of training, and they were generally made up of college athletes and recent graduates. About the same time, the National Collegiate Athletic Association began urging the formation of individual sports federations, independent of the AAU. When Congress passed the Amateur Sports Act in 1978, the AAU lost virtually all of its power over amateur sports, and so did its long-time supporters, such as the NYAC.

Until 1968, the NYAC's indoor track and field meet at Madison Square Garden was still one of the most prestigious in the country. But the meet was picketed that year by Harry Edwards' Olympic Project for Human Rights, an outgrowth of the Black Power movement. Few black athletes took part in the meet, and the attendance fell by more than 50 percent. The NYAC subsequently dropped the meet entirely. NYAC teams and athletes were prominent in several sports besides track and field in the first half of the century. The club won 16 of the first 40 national team fencing championships, from 1906 through 1951, and also produced some fine boxing, rowing, swimming and wrestling champions. But, as in track and field, specialized clubs and college teams gained supremacy in most such sports beginning in the 1960s.

Further Reading: Considine, Bob, and Fred R. Jarvis. *The First Hundred Years: A Portrait of NYAC.* New York: Macmillan, 1969.

Address: 180 Central Park South, New York, NY (212) 247–5100

See also AMATEURISM; ATHLETIC CLUBS.

New York Game
Baseball

Though the version of baseball created by Alexander Cartwright of the Knickerbocker Club in 1845 became known as the New York game, there was an earlier form of the sport with the same popular name. Judging by an 1842 diagram, it was played on an asymmetrical field. The "striker" or batter had to run about 45 feet, at an angle of about 30 degrees, to first base, then 60 feet to second base, 60 feet to third base, and 72 feet to home plate, which was not where he had started out. As in the Massachusetts Game, runners were put out by being hit by a thrown ball while between bases. It was this game that the Knickerbocker Club played before Cartwright came up with his symmetrical diamond.

See also BASEBALL; CARTWRIGHT, ALEXANDER; MASSACHUSETTS GAME.

New York Marathon

Although it began in 1970, long after the better-known Boston Marathon, the New York Marathon is now probably the preeminent race of its kind in North America, if not the world, because of the prize money offered. There were only 127 entrants at the first running, which was open only to men; that grew to more than 11,000 men and women in 1979 and to nearly 25,000 runners in 1989. Prize money wasn't offered until 1976, when the total purse was just $60,000; it is now well over $20 million. In addition to standard prizes for high finishes, the marathon offers special incentives to top runners. Grete Waitz of Norway, for example, in 1988 received a $50,000 appearance fee, round-trip airfare from Norway for herself and her husband, and $20 for cab fare, as well as $26,385 in prize money and a Mercedes-Benz valued at about $30,000 for her first-place finish. Juma Ikangaa, the 1989 winner, was given a $10,000 prize for setting a course record, as well as $26,385 and a Mercedes-Benz. (The odd amount for first place is based on the marathon distance, 26 miles and 385 yards.) The race begins at the Verrazano-Narrows Bridge and winds through all five boroughs before finishing in Central Park.

New York Marathon Winners—Men

1970	Gary Muhrcke
1971	Norman Higgins
1972	Sheldon Karlin
1973	Tom Fleming
1974	Norbert Sander
1975	Tom Fleming
1976	Bill Rodgers
1977	Bill Rodgers
1978	Bill Rodgers
1979	Bill Rodgers
1980	Alberto Salazar
1981	Alberto Salazar
1982	Alberto Salazar
1983	Rod Dixon
1984	Orlando Pizzolato
1985	Orlando Pizzolato
1986	Gianni Poli
1987	Ibrahim Hussein
1989	Steve Jones
1990	Douglas Wakiihuri

New York Marathon Winners—Women

1970	No Finisher
1971	Beth Bonner
1972	Nina Kuscsik
1973	Nina Kuscsik
1974	Katherine Switzer
1975	Kim Merritt
1976	Miki Gorman
1977	Miki Gorman
1978	Greta Waitz
1979	Greta Waitz
1980	Greta Waitz
1981	Allison Roe
1982	Greta Waitz
1983	Greta Waitz
1984	Greta Waitz
1985	Greta Waitz
1986	Greta Waitz
1987	Priscilla Welch
1989	Greta Waitz
1990	Wanda Panfil

Address: New York Road Runners Club, 9 East 89th Street, New York, NY 10128 (212) 860–4455

New York Racing Association (NYRA)

With major New York tracks losing money and in disrepair under private ownership, the NYRA was organized as a nonprofit corporation in 1955 to buy Aqueduct, Belmont, Jamaica, and Saratoga for $20 million. About $8 million was spent in improvements at Belmont and Saratoga, and a completely new plant was built at Aqueduct, which reopened in 1959. Jamaica was sold that year to become a housing development. Belmont was almost completely rebuilt at a cost of about $7 million for the 1968 racing season. Under the NYRA, thoroughbred racing has flourished in New York. The total handle at the three tracks is now approaching $1 billion a year, an average of about $10.5 million per racing day, up from $2.9 million a day in 1980. The NYRA's only stockholders are trustees, who receive no compensation; they may sell shares only to succeeding stockholders at the same price paid for them.

Address: P.O. Box 90, Jamaica, NY 11417 (718) 641–4700

New York Yacht Club (NYYC)

Nine yachtsmen founded the NYYC aboard John Cox Stevens' *Gimcrack* on July 30, 1844. The club grew rapidly, to about 120 members within two years and to nearly 500 by 1860. Yachting was similar to horse racing: Just as wealthy men owned horses and hired professional jockeys to ride them, so wealthy yachtsmen bought yachts or had them built and, in most cases, hired professionals to sail them. The yachts of the time were large schooners requiring a number of crew members, not to mention professional knowledge of seamanship and navigation. Yachting was more a symbol of wealth and prestige than it was a genuine sport, and NYYC activities often centered on the social. Magnificent dinners and balls were held in its large clubhouse, built on Stevens's Elysian Fields in Hoboken, NJ, and the club's annual regatta at Newport, RI was a major social event rather than a major sporting event.

Nevertheless, NYYC members, led by Stevens, made a major contribution to sports history in 1851, when five of them commissioned the yacht *America* for a voyage to England in search of competition. The *America* won the Hundred-Guinea Cup in the Royal Yacht Squadron's race around the Isle of Wight, and the syndicate subsequently deeded the cup to the NYYC for an international challenge race. Although a letter outlining terms for the race was written in May of 1852, it was never delivered, and was found among Stevens' papers after his death in 1857. In the meantime, the NYYC in 1853 had offered a $500 prize for a race if a foreign vessel entered, without any takers, and America's Cup, as it was to become known, had to wait until 1870 for the first challenge.

The NYYC, as custodian of America's Cup, has been involved in an enormous amount of controversy, beginning with that first challenge. James Ashbury of England wanted to sail his *Cambria* against a single yacht selected by the NYYC, but the club ruled he had to race against an entire fleet, just as *America* had done to win the cup in 1851. He finally agreed. Racing against 23 NYYC yachts, *Cambria* finished tenth. (For further history, see AMERICA'S CUP.) Although the cup went to Australia in 1983 and to the San Diego Yacht Club in 1987, the NYYC's Deed of Gift still governs competition.

Probably the greatest golfer of all time, Jack Nicklaus won a record 18 major tournaments. His first was the 1962 U.S. Open, his last the 1986 Masters. Courtesy of the U.S. Golf Association

Address: 37 West 44th Street, New York, NY 10036 (212) 382–1000

See also AMERICA'S CUP; STEVENS, JOHN COX.

Nicklaus, Jack W. (1940–   )
Golf
Born January 21, 1940, Columbus, OH; World Golf Hall of Fame

Bobby Jones was widely considered the greatest golfer of all time, until Nicklaus reached his prime. Jones himself conceded, "Jack Nicklaus plays a game with which I am not familiar." An exceptionally long and accurate driver, Nicklaus also hit very accurate iron shots and was a superb putter. His single weakness was the sand shot, but his other skills kept him out of the sand most of the time. He won the Ohio Open as a 16-year-old amateur, was U.S. Amateur champ at 19, finished second in the U.S. Open at 20, and won the U.S. Amateur once again at 21 before becoming a professional.

He was an immediate success on the pro tour, winning the Los Angeles Open in 1962 and then beating Arnold Palmer 71–74 in a playoff at the U.S. Open. But he wasn't a popular champion at the time. Nicknamed the "Golden Bear" because of his pudginess, he was resented by the many Palmer fans who thronged golf courses and watched on television. His sheer skill and a trimmed-down figure ultimately won fans over, though. A student of golf history, Nicklaus geared himself up for the major events and won a record six Masters tournaments (1963, 1965, 1966, 1972, 1975, and 1986), five PGA Championships (1963, 1971, 1973, 1975, and 1980), four U.S. Opens (1962, 1967, 1972, and 1980), and three British Opens (1966, 1970, and 1978).

Nicklaus totaled 71 wins on the PGA tour, won over $5 million, and was named PGA Player of the Year in 1967, 1972, 1973, 1975, and 1976. Of all his victories, the most remarkable was probably the 1986 Masters, when he was tied for eighth after three rounds. Well past his prime at 46, Nicklaus shot 35 on the front nine and an incredible 30 on the back nine to win the tournament by one shot for his first major title since 1980. Nicklaus continues to earn money on the tour and has over 75 golf courses worldwide.

NIT
See NATIONAL INVITATION TOURNAMENT.

Norris, James D. (1906–1966)
Boxing, Hockey
Born November 6, 1906, Chicago, IL; died February 25, 1966; Hockey Hall of Fame

The son of the owner of the Detroit Red Wings, Norris became co-owner of Chicago Stadium with Arthur Wirtz in 1934, and they promoted Sonja Henie's very successful ice show. They also owned the National Hockey League's Chicago Black Hawks, and Norris inherited a large interest in Madison Square Garden, not to mention a fortune estimated between $40 million and $500 million. Early in 1948 he met with heavyweight champion Joe Louis and Louis's advisers Truman Gibson and Harry Mendel to discuss Mendel's plan to control the heavyweight championship after Louis's retirement. The idea was to have Louis obtain exclusive rights to the fights of the four leading contenders: Ezzard Charles, Gus Lesnevich, Lee Savold, and Jersey Joe Walcott.

After much bargaining, Norris and Wirtz paid Louis $150,000 and gave him a 20-percent share of the newly formed International Boxing Club. The IBC soon bought exclusive leases to Yankee Stadium and the St. Nicholas Arena, along with the contract for Sugar Ray Robinson's fights, from promoter Mike Jacobs, and then acquired the Tournament of Champions, which had exclusive rights to boxing in the Polo Grounds. In just over four years, from March 1949 to May 1953, the IBC promoted 36 of the 44 championship fights in the United States.

Boxing became a programming staple during the rapid growth of television in the early 1950s, and by 1955 the IBC was making $90,000 a week from television rights alone. But Norris did his best to kill the golden goose. He began putting the major fights on closed-circuit TV in theaters, leaving only second-rate bouts to home television. The public outcry, combined with complaints from some boxers that they were being kept out of good matches, led the Justice Department to bring an antitrust suit against the IBC in 1952. The suit was delayed by a 1954 district court ruling that boxing was entitled to the same antitrust exemption granted to baseball by the Supreme Court in 1922, but a year later the Supreme Court overruled that decision.

The IBC tried to avoid further action by abandoning its lease arrangements, but on July 2, 1957, a federal district court found Norris, Wirtz, the IBC, and the Madison Square Garden Corporation guilty of violating the Sherman Anti-Trust Act and ordered that the monopoly be dissolved. Norris responded by backing two new companies, National Boxing Enterprises and Title Promotions, Inc., both ostensibly led by Truman Gibson but under Norris's financial control.

A criminal investigation of the IBC began in 1958. Frankie Carbo, a gangster who controlled the Boxing Managers Guild of New York, had been receiving payments from the IBC since its formation. He and Blinky Palermo, another gangster, had taken over control of the exclusive contracts the IBC had relinquished as part of its supposed dissolution. Carbo, Palermo, and Gibson in 1961 received federal prison sentences for extortion. Although Norris was not tried, the testimony made it clear that he had been the power behind Gibson's presidential throne and that he had authorized payments to Carbo to help keep the Managers Guild in line.

Further Reading: Nagler, Barney. *James Norris and the Decline of Boxing.* New York: Bobbs-Merrill, 1964.

Norris Trophy
Hockey

Presented to the "greatest all-around" defenseman in the National Hockey League, this award was presented in 1953 by four children of James Norris, the former owner of the Detroit Red Wings.

Norris Trophy Winners

1954	Red Kelly, Detroit
1955	Doug Harvey, Montreal
1956	Doug Harvey, Montreal
1957	Doug Harvey, Montreal
1958	Doug Harvey, Montreal
1959	Tom Johnson, Montreal
1960	Doug Harvey, Montreal
1961	Doug Harvey, Montreal
1962	Doug Harvey, New York Rangers
1963	Pierre Pilot, Chicago
1964	Pierre Pilot, Chicago
1965	Pierre Pilot, Chicago
1966	Jacques Laperriere, Montreal
1967	Harry Howell, New York Rangers
1968	Bobby Orr, Boston
1969	Bobby Orr, Boston
1970	Bobby Orr, Boston
1971	Bobby Orr, Boston
1972	Bobby Orr, Boston
1973	Bobby Orr, Boston
1974	Bobby Orr, Boston
1975	Bobby Orr, Boston
1976	Denis Potvin, New York Islanders
1977	Larry Robinson, Montreal
1978	Denis Potvin, New York Islanders
1979	Denis Potvin, New York Islanders
1980	Larry Robinson, Montreal
1981	Randy Carlisle, Pittsburgh
1982	Doug Wilson, Chicago
1983	Rod Langway, Washington
1984	Rod Langway, Washington
1985	Paul Coffey, Edmonton
1986	Paul Coffey, Edmonton
1987	Ray Bourque, Boston
1988	Ray Bourque, Boston
1989	Chris Chelios, Montreal
1990	Ray Bourque, Boston
1991	Ray Bourque, Boston

North American Soccer League (NASL)

Professional soccer arrived in North America very suddenly in 1967. A league called the United Soccer Association announced plans to begin play in 1968, but the National Professional Soccer League appeared a short time later, ready to start operations in 1967. That began a kind of comic opera battle involving the U.S. Soccer Federation and the international governing body, the FIFA, as well as some of the world's best players and teams.

The USA, recognized by both the USSF and the FIFA, decided to start a year earlier than planned by importing entire teams. The Shamrock Rovers of Ireland, for example, became the Boston Rovers, and the Wolverhampton Wolves of England were the Los Angeles Wolves for the league's 12-game season. The NPSL, meanwhile, had to scramble for players, who faced the threat of lifetime suspension for competing in an unsanctioned league.

The USA and NPSL merged into the North American Soccer League in 1968. The NASL had 17 teams: Atlanta, Baltimore, Boston, Chicago, Cleveland, Dallas, Detroit, Houston, Kansas City, Los Angeles, New York, Oakland, St. Louis, San Diego, Toronto, Vancouver, and Washington. That was far too many. In the league's second season, only Atlanta, Baltimore, Dallas, Kansas City, and St. Louis remained. Baltimore dropped out in 1970, but Rochester and Washington were added, and in 1971 the NASL seemed on its way to success. Montreal, New York, and Toronto were given franchises, and Kansas City folded. New York won the championship that year, and having a strong team in the continent's biggest city helped the sport win a lot of media attention.

The Washington franchise moved to Miami in 1972, and the Philadelphia Atoms entered the NASL in 1973. The Atoms became a major success story, winning the championship in their first season. More important, they had the first American soccer star, Kyle Rote, Jr., who was both Rookie of the Year and Most Valuable Player. The Atoms also had an American coach, Al Miller, and Goalie of the Year Bob Rigby, another young American player. It seemed that soccer had genuinely become established as a North American sport. With average attendance at nearly 6,300 per game, the NASL grew to 15 teams in 1974. Franchises were added in Baltimore, Boston, Denver, Los Angeles, San Jose, Seattle, Toronto, and Vancouver, and Atlanta and Montreal dropped out.

The NASL expanded into Chicago, Hartford, Portland, San Antonio, and Tampa Bay in 1975, when the New York Cosmos signed the great Pele of Brazil to a three-year contract for more than $4 million. The best-known soccer player in the world, and the only one widely known among American sports fans, Pele was an incredible drawing card. The Cosmos' attendance increased from an average of just over 5,000 in 1974 to nearly 30,000 a game in 1977, the last year of his contract. His presence also allowed the NASL to increase the entry fee for a new franchise from $25,000 to $100,000.

There were 20 teams in the NASL in 1978, organized into two conferences and six divisions. That increased to 24 teams in 1979, but then attendance and television ratings began declining. The number of teams dropped to 21 in 1981, 14 in 1982, 10 in

1983, and only 6 in 1984. The league folded after that season.

See also SOCCER.

North American Society for Sports History (NASSH)

Founded in 1972 by a handful of sports historians, the NASSH now has nearly 1,000 members, most of whom teach sports history at the collegiate level. The association publishes *The Journal of Sports History* and an annual *Directory of Scholars Identifying with the History of Sports*. The NASSH convention, held in late May, features papers and symposiums on a variety of sports history topics.

Address: c/o Ronald A. Smith, 101 White Building, Penn State University, University Park, PA 16802

North American Turnerbund

See TURNER MOVEMENT.

North Carolina Motor Speedway
Rockingham, NC

The first racetrack to be designed with the help of computers, this speedway has a very wide, high-banked surface. The 1.017-mile oval opened in 1965 and was completely resurfaced in 1985. It hosts two major NASCAR races.

Address: P.O. Box 500, Rockingham, NC 28379 (919) 582–2861

Northlands Coliseum
Edmonton, Alberta

Built at a cost of about $16 million in support of Edmonton's bid for the 1978 Commonwealth Games, Northlands opened on November 10, 1974, as the home rink of the World Hockey Association's Edmonton Oilers, who are now in the National Hockey League. The Coliseum also hosts the Canadian Finals Rodeo, boxing, curling, skating, indoor soocer competition, and entertainment events. Seating capacity ranges from 17,312 for hockey to a maximum of 18,600.

North Wilkesboro Speedway
North Wilkesboro, NC

North Wilkesboro is a ⅝-mile track that opened in 1946. It is the oldest arena in NASCAR's Winston Cup series, hosting two 400-mile races annually.

Address: P.O. Box 500, North Wilkesboro, NC 27102 (919) 724–7932

Northwestern League
Baseball

The first minor league, the Northwestern had an up-and-down history. Founded in 1879, it lasted only one season, but was reorganized in 1883 and was instrumental in creating peace between the National League and American Association. Northwestern League president Elias Matter asked the National League for an agreement that the two leagues would respect one another's contracts, and the American Association was also brought into a February 17 meeting that resulted in the Tripartite Pact, later known as the National Agreement. The Northwestern folded after the 1884 season, when many of its best players were signed by a third would-be major league, the Union Association. Many of the cities that had been in the Northwestern were also in the Western League, organized in 1892, which eventually became the American League.

See also NATIONAL AGREEMENT.

Oak Hill Country Club
Rochester, NY

At 6,902 yards and a par 70, Oak Hill is considerably shorter than most championship golf courses. But its undulating fairways, thick rough, and small fairways make it a challenge that rewards good shot-making, as opposed to sheer strength off the tee. Oak Hill hosted the U.S. Open in 1956 and 1968.

Oakland, CA

Baseball   The Kansas City Athletics moved to Oakland in 1968. The A's won the American League pennant and the World Series three years in a row, 1972–74. They also won pennants in 1988, 1989, and 1990, and beat the San Francisco Giants in the 1989 Series.

Basketball   The Oakland Oaks were in the American Basketball Association when it began play in the 1967–68 season. They won the ABA's championship in 1968–69, but the franchise moved to Washington the following season.

Football   When the Minnesota Vikings decided to join the National Football League in 1961 rather than the new American Football League in 1960, they were replaced in the AFL by the Oakland Raiders. The Raiders were AFL champions in 1967, but lost to the Green Bay Packers in Super Bowl II. After the AFL merged into the NFL in 1970, the Raiders won the NFL's American Football Conference championship in 1976 and 1980, and they won Super Bowls XI and XV.

In 1980, the Raiders announced their intention to move to Los Angeles and refused to submit the proposed move to the NFL owners for a vote, as required by the league's constitution. The NFL threatened to block the move, but the Los Angeles Memorial Coliseum Commission brought suit against the league, contending that the constitution provision violated the Sherman Anti-Trust Act. The Raiders later joined the suit; after a hung jury and a new trial, the NFL in 1982 was found in violation of the act, and that fall the Raider franchise did go to Los Angeles. The Los Angeles Raiders won the 1983 AFC championship and beat the Washington Redskins 38–9 in Super Bowl XVIII.

Hockey   The California Golden Seals, based in Oakland, entered the National Hockey League in 1968. They were renamed the Oakland Golden Seals in the middle of their first season, and in 1971 they became the California Golden Seals again. The franchise was relocated to Cleveland in 1976.

See also GOLDEN STATE; OAKLAND-ALAMEDA COUNTY COLISEUM.

Oakland-Alameda County Coliseum
Oakland, CA

Alameda County and the city of Oakland jointly financed this round, three-tiered stadium and the adjoining Coliseum Arena in 1965. Although it was designed primarily for baseball, the Oakland Raiders began playing on the field in 1966, two years before the American League's Kansas City Athletics moved to Oakland. The Raiders moved to Los Angeles in 1982, largely because of the lack of luxury boxes in the stadium, which seats 48,219. Since 1971, the Golden State Warriors of the National Basketball Association have played their home games in the 15,025-seat arena.

Oakland Hills Country Club
Birmingham, MI

Originally built in 1918, this course was extensively redesigned by Robert Trent Jones in 1950. It boasts more than 100 traps containing 400 tons of sand. As with most Jones' designs, Oakland Hills rewards good strategy and tactics, along with good shotmaking, rather than merely penalizing poor shots. The U.S. Open was played at Oakland Hills in 1924, 1937, 1951, and 1961.

Oakley, Annie (Annie Moses) (1860–1926)
Shooting

Born August 13, 1860, Greenville, OH; died November 3, 1926; American Trapshooting Hall of Fame

The most famous American woman athlete until Babe Didrikson, Annie Moses learned to shoot game at the age of eight to help support her family. She soon became locally famous for her shooting ability. When she was 15, neighbors raised money to send her to Cincinnati for a match against Frank Butler, a well-known marksman who had a traveling show. After she won the match, Butler married her, gave her the stage name Annie Oakley, and added her to his troupe. They joined Buffalo Bill Cody's Wild West Show in 1884 and Oakley soon became the star attraction.

As a member of Buffalo Bill's Wild West Show, sharp-shooter Annie Oakley became the first famous woman athlete. Courtesy of the Amateur Trapshooting Association

Among her most celebrated trick shots were hitting a dime tossed into the air, shooting a cigarette from Butler's lips, and splitting a playing card held on edge from 30 paces away. Oakley was also an expert trapshooter. She broke 100 targets in a row on many occasions between 1887 and 1922, when she was 62 years old. Complimentary tickets to theatrical and sports events are still sometimes called "Annie Oakleys" because they have punched holes to differentiate them from purchased tickets.

O'Brien, Parry (1932–   )
Track and Field
Born January 28, 1932, Santa Monica, CA; National Track & Field Hall of Fame

O'Brien revolutionized shot-putting in 1951 by beginning his throw with his back to the field and making a 180-degree turn to increase momentum. During the next five years, he won 116 events in a row. O'Brien won Olympic Gold Medals in 1952 and 1956 and was the national champion from 1951 through 1955 and from 1958 through 1960. He also won the national discus title in 1955.

Oerter, Al (1936–   )
Track and Field
Born September 19, 1936, Astoria, NY; National Track and Field Hall of Fame

One of the greatest competitors in any sport, Oerter won four consecutive Gold Medals in the Olympic discus throw. Jay Silvester, a world record holder in the event, once commented, "When you throw against Oerter, you don't expect to win. You just hope." Oerter won his first Gold Medal in 1956, when he was just 20, quite young for a weight thrower. He repeated in 1960, and two years later he claimed the world record, becoming the first man to throw the discus more than 200 feet. His record was broken a short time later, but he took it back before the year was over.

Oerter was up against a new world record holder, Ludvik Danik, in the 1964 Olympics. A week before the competition, he ripped cartilage in his rib cage and was told by doctors the injury would take a month to heal. His chest wrapped in bandages holding ice packs in place to slow down the internal bleeding, Oerter got off four poor throws, but on his fifth attempt he beat Danik with a throw of just over 200 feet. "Don't play this up like I'm a hero," he told sportswriters afterward, "but I really gutted this one out." Silvester, whose world record was 12 feet better than Oerter's all-time best, was favored in 1968, but again Oerter came through to win with the longest throw of his career.

Oerter won the national championship in 1957, 1959, 1960, 1962, 1964, and 1966. Representing the University of Kansas, he was the NCAA champion in 1957, and he tied for the 1958 title.

Off-Road Racing

The origins of off-road racing are obscure, but the original off-road vehicles were Model T Fords using belts instead of rear wheels. Developed during the 1920s to carry smuggled liquor over sand dunes, it is possible that they were also used for informal races. The modern dune buggy was invented about 1960 by Bruce Meyers of Newport Beach, CA, who put a fiberglass body on a wrecked Volkswagen. Many other types of off-road vehicles were developed during the decade, chief among them the all-terrain vehicle (ATV), which has six large, very soft tires, and the swamp buggy, originally built for traveling through the Everglades.

The National Off-the-Road Racing Association was founded in 1968 to govern the sport. Among the major races are the Mile o' Mud, held near Naples, FL for swamp buggies; the national ATV championship, held near Monroe, MI; and the Mexico 1,000, held on the Baja Peninsula. Many events are now staged in indoor arenas. The NORRA was absorbed by the American Motorcyclist Association in 1989.

See also MOTORCYCLE RACING.

Oil Bowl
Football

The Oil Bowl was played just twice, in Houston on New Year's Day. Georgia beat Tulsa 20–6 in 1946, and Georgia Tech beat St. Mary's of California 41–19 in 1947.

Oldfield, "Barney" Berna Eli (1878–1946)
Auto Racing

Born January 29, 1878, Wauseon, OH; died October 4, 1946; Auto Racing Hall of Fame

A professional bicycle racer who had never driven a car, Oldfield was chosen by Henry Ford to drive his 80-horsepower "999" in 1902. After two weeks of practice, Oldfield got into the car to start the Detroit 5-mile Classic. As Ford was cranking the engine for the start, Oldfield said, "This chariot may kill me, but they will say after that I was going like hell when she took me over the bank." Oldfield and "999" won the race in 5 minutes 28 seconds.

He bought the car from Ford and went on tour with it. On May 30, 1903, he became the first American to travel more than 60 miles an hour—a mile a minute—in an automobile. A colorful figure who constantly had a cigar in his mouth, Oldfield was frequently suspended by the American Automobile Association, then the sport's ruling body, for unsanctioned racing, but he drew crowds to exhibitions and time trials at county and state fairs all over the country. In 1910, he set a world land speed record of 131.724 miles an hour at Daytona Beach.

Olympic Games

While traveling all over the world studying methods of physical education, Baron Pierre de Coubertin of France talked to many people about his idea for a modern Olympics. De Coubertin had spent much time in England, and was strongly influenced by the British ideals of gentlemanly amateurism and sportsmanship. He was also an enthusiast who aroused others to enthusiasm over his idea.

Plans were announced in 1892 for the first modern Olympics, which opened April 6, 1896, in a new stadium in Athens, Greece. Only eight countries were represented: Denmark, England, France, Germany, Greece, Hungary, Switzerland, and the United States. There was no official U.S. team. The Boston Athletic Association sent eight athletes and a coach. Two athletes, Robert Garrett of Princeton and James Connolly of Harvard, paid their own way to compete. Connolly became the first modern Olympic champion, winning the hop, step and jump (now known as the triple jump). In addition to 12 track and field events, there was competition in cycling, gymnastics, shooting, swimming, tennis, and weight lifting.

The next three regular Olympics were attached to, and largely overshadowed by, major attractions. In 1900, it was the Paris Universal Exposition. There were 55 U.S. athletes on hand, but no official national team. The New York Athletic Club and some colleges and universities sent athletes, and again a few athletes paid their own way. The exposition program didn't even mention the Olympics, only the "world's amateur track and field championships," and some competitors said afterward they didn't know they were taking part in the Olympics until they received their medals. Swimming and tennis were dropped, and there was just one gymnastics event.

In 1904, the Olympics were held in conjunction with the Louisiana Purchase Exposition in St. Louis. It was by far the most ambitious program to that point, with boxing, fencing, golf, lacrosse, roque, rowing, swimming, diving, tennis, water polo, weight lifting, and wrestling, along with a full schedule of gymnastics events and track and field. But participation and attendance were both disappointing. Australia, Canada, Cuba, Germany, Greece, Hungary, Ireland, and South Africa sent athletes, but England and France didn't take part.

An "intercalated" Olympics was held at Athens in 1906, the tenth anniversary of the modern Games. For the first time, the U.S. had an official team, selected by the American Olympic Committee and financed by private donations. Boxing was dropped

A former bicycle racer, Barney Oldfield did much to popularize auto racing by driving in exhibitions throughout North America. Courtesy of the Indianapolis Motor Speedway

from the program, and track and field was cut back somewhat, but archery, cycling, shooting, and soccer were added.

De Coubertin and his supporters had conceived of the Olympics as a step toward creating an international brotherhood of men by starting with an international brotherhood of sportsmen. It didn't seem to occur to them that international competition could just as easily inspire nationalism among athletes and teams, or that international tensions could arrive at the Games along with the Olympic torch. The first major problems arose in London in 1908, when the Olympics were staged in conjunction with the Franco-British Exposition. The Finnish team, told it would have to carry the Russian flag in the opening parade of athletes, refused to carry any flag at all, and Irish athletes were unhappy because they had to parade under the flag of Great Britain.

More controversy flared once the Games began. Several countries, especially the United States, ac-cused British officials of favoritism. Canada and France complained about rulings made in the cycling competition. Sweden's wrestlers pulled out of competition because of decisions they considered unfair. Italy complained bitterly when Dorando Pietro, who collapsed while leading the marathon a short distance from the finish line, was helped across the line by British officials and then disqualified because of the assistance he'd received. The biggest brouhaha, however, came in the 400-meter finals. With Americans J. C. Carpenter and W. C. Robbins leading British favorite Wyndham Halswelle coming down the stretch, there was a cry of "Foul!" and British judges leaped onto the track to stop the race. The claim was that Halswelle had been interfered with by one or both Americans. American runners refused to take part in a rerun on the last day of the Games, and Halswelle won in a walkover.

Because of all the fuss, the International Olympic Committee decided to take control of competition away from the host country; instead, the international governing bodies for each sport were to take charge. That format, which has been followed ever since, went into effect for the Stockholm Games in 1912, when the Olympics for the first time won front-page press coverage in North America. Twenty-six countries were represented, including Japan, the first Asian country to compete. Women had previously competed in figure skating (on the 1908 program, before there was a Winter Olympics) and gymnastics; in 1912, two women's swimming events were added, as were equestrian events and the modern pentathlon. The biggest newsmaker was Jim Thorpe, who won both the pentathlon and the decathlon and was hailed by Sweden's King Gustav as "the greatest athlete in the world." Unfortunately, the IOC later took Thorpe's medals away because he had been paid for playing semiprofessional baseball.

The 1916 Games, scheduled for Berlin, were canceled by World War I, and war-torn Antwerp, Belgium, was chosen to host the 1920 Olympics. Austria, Germany, Hungary, and Turkey, the aggressors, were not invited, and several other countries didn't take part because of the war's devastation. But the program expanded once again. Boxing, figure skating, and wrestling were restored; field hockey, ice hockey, and rugby were added; and weight lifting was offered in a variety of weight classes for the first time.

The United States sent about 300 athletes to the 1920 Games, and for the first time they were genuine national teams—a track and field team, a wrestling team, a boxing team, and so on. But the effort turned into a fiasco before the Olympics even began. Many of the athletes sailed on an army transport ship that offered limited accommodations and questionable food. Soon after arrival, Dan Ahearn was thrown off the track and field team because he rented his own room rather than stay in the uncomfortable abandoned schoolhouse allotted to the team. More than 200 athletes petitioned for Ahearn's reinstatement and better quarters; Ahearn was eventually reinstated, but the quarters remained the same. The United States won just eight Gold Medals in track and field, by far its poorest performance, and the American Olympic Committee was reorganized in 1921 because of all the problems that had arisen.

Ice hockey and figure skating were so popular in 1920 that the IOC decided to create the Winter Olympics in 1924 (see WINTER OLYMPICS). The summer Games, held in Paris, were an enormous success. Track and field events alone drew about 1,430 athletes from 45 countries, including 110 from the United States. In the unofficial newspaper scoring, the United States won the team title with ten Gold Medals in track and field, but competition was much

tougher than it had been in the early years. Finland, which had tied the U. S. with eight Gold Medals in 1920, won eight more in 1924.

In the meantime, women had been petitioning the IOC to have track and field events added. The Federation Sportive Feminine Internationale, founded in 1920, held its own Women's Olympic Games in 1922 and 1926. After women's track and field was added to the 1928 program, the FSFI agreed to change the name to the International Ladies' Games. The 1928 Olympic Games, in Amsterdam, attracted more than 4,000 athletes, and 40,000 spectators crowded into the stadium just to see the opening ceremonies, while another 75,000 stood outside hoping to get in. Again, the United States showing was disappointing—eight Gold Medals in track and field. A surprise double winner was Percy Williams, a 19-year-old high school student from Canada, who won the 100- and 200-meter dashes. A virtual unknown, Williams had hitchhiked across the country from Vancouver to take part in the Olympic trials.

The Great Depression cut participation in the 1932 Olympics to just 39 countries and about 2,000 athletes. Nevertheless, Los Angeles set the tone for future host cities by spending $2.5 million on facilities, including a 105,000-seat stadium, a 10,000-seat auditorium, a 12,000-seat swimming stadium, a 17,000-seat rowing course, and the first Olympic village, a 250-acre site with 55 buildings. The warm climate and the superb new track contributed to a host of new Olympic and world records in the track and field events. As the host country, the United States had by far the greatest number of competitors, about 500 in all, and won 11 Gold Medals.

Shortly after Berlin was chosen as the site for the 1936 Games, Adolph Hitler rose to power, touching off a debate within the United States over whether to send a team. Judge Jeremiah T. Murphy, president of the Amateur Athletic Union, in 1934 led the movement to boycott the Games. After postponing a formal answer to the invitation to participate, the AAU late in 1935 narrowly voted to accept. Murphy resigned and was replaced by Avery Brundage. Brundage, who was to become a major figure in the Olympic movement for more than 40 years, threw swimmer Eleanor Holm Jarrett off the team for allegedly drinking champagne on the voyage to Europe, and he also sent two boxers home for unknown reasons shortly after arrival.

But all that was overshadowed by the Nazi Olympics. Germany built a 150-cottage Olympic village and nine arenas with total seating of 237,000. More than 4.5 million tickets were sold, and the 110,000-seat stadium was filled daily for the track and field events, but the specters of anti-Semitism and racism hung over the entire spectacle like smog. The black

This 110,000-seat stadium was the centerpiece of the 1936 Berlin Olympics. Part of the aquatic sports complex can be seen at the left.

athletes on the U.S. track and field team were christened "the Black Auxiliaries" by the Nazi press. Hitler personally congratulated the first two Gold Medal winners in track, but after Cornelius Johnson, a black American, won the high jump, the Fuehrer suddenly left his box. The official explanation was that it looked like rain.

The 1936 Games, though, belonged to another black, Jesse Owens. He won four Gold Medals, in the 100- and 200-meter dashes, the long jump, and the 400-meter relay. U.S. Coach Lawson Robertson stirred some controversy of his own by adding Owens and Ralph Metcalfe to the relay team, replacing two Jewish sprinters, Sam Stoller and Marty Glickman. Some American sportswriters saw that as a concession to the Nazi hosts, but the fact that Owens and Metcalfe were both black helped defuse criticism, as did the world record 39.8-second time the team turned in to win the finals.

The 1940 Olympics were originally scheduled for Tokyo, but the Japanese decided in mid-1938 that the war with China made it impossible to host the Games, and Helsinki was chosen as a substitute.

Then Russia invaded Finland, and the Olympics were canceled entirely. With nearly the entire world at war, there was no the way the Games could go on in 1944, but London hosted the 1948 Olympics despite a desperate housing shortage, the aftermath of the German bombings. About 6,000 athletes from 59 countries took part. There was just one rather minor controversy, when the new nation of Israel wasn't allowed to participate, ostensibly because it didn't belong to the IOC but actually because the IOC feared a boycott by Arab nations.

The cold war entered the Olympics in 1952, when the Games were held in Helsinki and the Soviet Union was invited for the first time. Bob Mathias, who won his second consecutive Olympic decathlon title, said afterward that the Russians ". . . were in a sense the real enemies. You just loved to beat them." The press focused on the U.S.-Soviet rivalry to the point that the Games sometimes seemed like a dual meet rather than a gathering of nearly 6,000 athletes from 67 countries. Although the IOC refused to recognize team scoring, both countries kept their own unofficial scores. The Americans claimed victory, 614–553½, but the Russians said it was a 494–494 tie.

Avery Brundage became president of the IOC in 1952 and was almost immediately in the news. Melbourne had been selected to host the 1956 Olympics, but no government money was forthcoming, and early in 1953 Brundage expressed alarm at the lack of preparedness. He even suggested that Rome, the 1960 site, was so much farther ahead than Melbourne that it might even be asked to take over the 1956 Games as well. Finally, the Australian government agreed to lend the organizing committee $4.5 million to build the Olympic village. As late as April of 1955 Brundage was still talking about the possibility of transferring the Games from Melbourne, but by the end of the year it was clear Melbourne would be ready.

Many athletes weren't happy with the site because the Games were to be staged in November, which is the middle of spring in the Southern Hemisphere, and their training schedules were usually geared to achieving peak performance in late summer. Their complaints, however, were overshadowed by two major international incidents that affected the Olympics: the Soviet invasion of Hungary and the British-French takeover of the Suez Canal after Israel attacked Egypt. Egypt, Iraq, and Lebanon withdrew from the Games because of the Suez seizure, and the Netherlands, Spain and Switzerland pulled out in protest of the Russian invasion. Then the Australians made the mistake of hoisting the Nationalist Chinese flag in the Olympic Village, and Communist China also withdrew.

The tensions carried into the Games themselves. The water polo game between Hungary and the Soviet Union turned into a bloody brawl that had to be called off with Hungary leading 4–0, and a soccer match between the Russians and the Yugoslavians almost became another free-for-all. And, for the first time, complaints about subjective judging surfaced, especially in diving, where Hungarian and Russian judges consistently gave low scores to Americans. Joaquin Capilla of Mexico, who edged Gary Tobian of the U.S. in the platform event, lamented, "It amounted to a competition between the nationalities of the judges rather than a competition of divers." Although the U.S. had its best performance in men's track and field in a long time, winning 15 of the 24 Gold Medals, the Soviet Union won the unofficial championship, 722 to 593, even using the American scoring method.

The Rome Olympics in 1960 offered a welcome relief. The only really untoward incident involved Nationalist China, which had to parade as Formosa and did so under protest. There was also a contro-versy over the finish of the 100-meter freestyle when John Devitt of Australia was declared the winner even though all three timers gave Lance Larson of the U.S. a faster time. And the issue of drugs publicly emerged for the first time when a Danish cyclist collapsed and died after having taken a mixture of nicotinic acid and amphetamines. But attention was focused for the most part on the competition and the competitors, 5,902 of them from 84 countries, both records. Once again, the Soviet Union increased its superiority over the U.S., adding medals in equestrian sports and target shooting to go with its domination of gymnastics and weight lifting.

The major story before the 1964 Games in Tokyo was the IOC's expulsion of South Africa because of its practice of apartheid. The first Olympics to be held in Asia were also marred by an Asian dispute. The IOC had refused to sanction the Asian Games of 1962 because Indonesia, the host country, wouldn't allow Israel or Nationalist China to compete. Indonesia canceled the event but decided to hold its own "Games of the New Emerging Forces" in 1963. The world governing bodies for swimming and track and field both decreed that athletes who competed would be barred from the Olympics. Nevertheless, Indonesia and North Korea showed up in Tokyo with some of the suspended athletes; when they found out the suspensions would be upheld, both countries withdrew.

The Japanese spent more than $2 billion, perhaps as much as $3 billion, not only building new facilities but even redesigning the highway system around Tokyo. The opening ceremony was hailed as a stunning performance, and the Games produced a couple of remarkable American heroes. Billy Mills, an unknown native American distance runner, ran 50 seconds faster than his previous best to win the 10,000-meter run, and Al Oerter won his third consecutive Gold Medal in the discus, despite having torn cartilage in his rib cage during practice. In a remarkable display of spontaneous camaraderie, athletes broke ranks during the closing ceremony and, instead of marching in national teams, mingled with one another and finally carried the Japanese flag bearer and standard-bearer around the track. The indignity of it so disturbed Brundage that he limited the number of athletes who could march as a team.

Mexico City was a controversial choice for the 1968 Olympics, partly because of its altitude—more than a mile above sea level—and partly because Mexico was viewed as an underdeveloped country that simply couldn't spend the money necessary to stage the Games properly. But a deeper controversy arose over the IOC's decision to reinstate South Africa. In response, nearly 40 countries announced they would stay away from the Games, the Soviet Union threatened a boycott, and sociologist Harry Edwards organized a boycott by American black athletes. The IOC decided not to readmit South Africa after all. Then, about a month before the Games were to begin, student rioting broke out in Mexico. The uprising was ruthlessly repressed by the army. The IOC considered canceling the Olympics, but the Games went on while soldiers guarded major thoroughfares and the area around the stadium.

The "Revolt of the Black Athletes," as Edwards later called his movement, involved much more than South Africa. It was aimed at discrimination by colleges and professional teams and, among other things, sought to have Brundage removed from his IOC post because of his membership in an all-white social club. The revolt spilled over into the Olympics when Tommie Smith and John Carlos, Gold and Bronze Medal winners in the 200-meter dash, thrust black-gloved fists into the air and refused to look at the flag when the National Anthem was played at the medal ceremony. They were immediately thrown off the team and sent back to the United States.

Amid the turmoil, there were again some remarkable athletic performances. The most remarkable was Bob Beamon's long jump of 29 feet 2½ inches, nearly 2 feet farther than the former world record. Jim Hines of the United States became the first man to run the 100-meter dash in less than 10 seconds, and the Olympic pole-vault record was extended beyond 17 feet for the first time. In fact, nine vaulters exceeded that height, led by Bob Seagren of the United States at 17 feet 8½ inches. And American swimmer Debbie Myers became the first woman ever to win three Gold Medals in one Olympiad.

The political problems of the past seemed like nothing after the 1972 Munich Olympics. Again, African nations threatened to withdraw, this time in protest against white-ruled Rhodesia. The country had been allowed to compete in 1968 as a British colony, using the Union Jack as its flag and "God Save the Queen" as its anthem. The IOC had assumed the same arrangement would work in Munich, but Rhodesia was expelled because of the threatened boycott. Then came the tragedy of September 5, when Arab terrorists killed two Israeli athletes and took nine others hostage. The hostages, five terrorists, and a German policeman were killed during a rescue attempt at an airport near Munich. After a one-day suspension and a memorial service for the dead athletes, the Games continued, though many wondered why. For the first time, the whole notion of the Olympics was called into question. Some critics felt the Games had simply become too big

and too accessible an arena for those with political axes to grind.

The hero of the Games was U.S. swimmer Mark Spitz, who won seven Gold Medals and immediately capitalized on his fame with a series of commercial endorsements. But U.S. men won only six Gold Medals in track and field, their lowest total ever, and the basketball team lost to the Soviet Union in a controversial final after apparently having won 50–49. Officials ordered a replay of the final 3 seconds, and the Russian team scored the winning basket.

Lord Killanin of Ireland replaced Brundage as president of the IOC shortly after the Games, and he found himself confronted by more international political problems in 1976, when Montreal hosted the Olympics. Just a few weeks before the opening ceremony, Canadian Prime Minister Pierre Trudeau announced that athletes from Taiwan would not be allowed to compete under the name of the Republic of China. Killanin's protests were to no avail, and the Taiwanese team went home. Then the Supreme Council for Sport in Africa announced, the night before the opening ceremony, that its member countries would withdraw if New Zealand participated, because a New Zealand rugby team had toured South Africa earlier in the year. The IOC refused to eject New Zealand, and 26 African countries did pull out, much to the consternation of their own athletes. Again, the U.S. men's team won just six track and field Gold Medals, and the Soviet Union won a total of 125 medals to 94 for the United States.

The United States won no medals at all in 1980. In protest against the Soviet invasion of Afghanistan the previous year, President Jimmy Carter called for a boycott of the Moscow Games, and 65 countries refused to participate, but 61 took part. The Soviet Union and 13 of its Eastern Bloc allies reciprocated for the 1984 Games in Los Angeles, claiming they feared for the safety of their athletes, but a record 140 nations sent 7,800 competitors. The United States led the way with 174 medals, and Carl Lewis duplicated Jesse Owens' 1936 performance by winning the 100– and 200-meter dashes, the long jump, and anchoring the 400-meter relay team to victory. The Los Angeles event was unique among Olympics in that it was organized by a private committee with no direct government involvement, and it was probably the most successful of all time, making a profit of $222.7 million.

Internal political problems threatened the 1988 Games, in Seoul. Student riots in May and June led to some bloody battles with police and soldiers; an American bank and a U.S. Information Agency office were bombed, and there was some doubt about whether the United States would even send a team. But the riots were quelled, and the Olympics went on as planned in August, setting new records with 160 nations and 9,600 athletes. The biggest American stories of the Games were Florence Griffith-Joyner, who won four Gold Medals in track and field; her sister-in-law, Jackie Joyner-Kersee, who set a world record in the heptathlon; and Matt Biondi, who won seven medals in swimming, including four Golds.

By then, the original Olympic ideal of amateur sportsmen competing for the sheer joy of it had disappeared. Brundage had been a stubborn opponent of any taint of professionalism; he felt that American college students on athletic scholarships, European athletes subsidized by their governments, and athletes from British Commonwealth countries who were paid by their employers while in training were all professionals and, if he'd had his way, those practices would have been banned. But in 1974, at the urging of Lord Killanin, the word "amateur" was deleted from Olympic Rule 26, which governs eligibility.

Since the international governing body decides which athletes are eligible for its sport, the rule hadn't been effective for some time, anyway. Canada withdrew from international ice hockey competition because its best players, the professionals, were banned; in 1971 the international federation voted to allow National Hockey League players in the world championships, and a year later they were also allowed to compete in the Winter Olympics. Rules were similarly loosened in several other sports in ensuing years. When tennis was restored to the Olympic program in 1988, it was an open competition won by Steffi Graf, the top money-winning woman professional of the year. And in 1989 the international federation decreed that professionals from the National Basketball Association would be allowed to compete in the 1992 Olympics—probably the final blow against the amateur ideal that Brundage had fought to uphold during his 20 years as IOC president.

See also AMATEURISM; CANADIAN OLYMPIC ASSOCIATION; NAZI OLYMPICS; PAN-AMERICAN GAMES; U.S. OLYMPIC COMMITTEE.

Olympic Saddledome
Calgary, Alberta

The impetus behind the Saddledome was the need for a multipurpose facility to back Calgary's bid for the 1988 Winter Olympics. Construction began in 1980, with joint funding from the city of Calgary, the government of Alberta, the Canadian govern-

ment, and the Olympic Winter Games Organization Committee. The arena actually opened in 1983 as the home of the National Hockey League's Calgary Flames. Capacity, then 16,674, was increased to 20,002 for the Winter Olympics. The Saddledome is so named because its roof is saddle-shaped. Prestressed cable strands support 391 precast concrete slabs to form the 3-acre roof. The ice surface can be increased from NHL size (85 by 200 feet) to international size (100 by 200 feet) by removing the first two rows of seating.

Olympic Stadium
Montreal, Quebec

A series of labor stoppages almost kept the stadium from opening in time for the 1976 Olympics; the sod was installed on July 16, the day before the opening ceremonies. Overruns that brought construction costs of facilities, including the Olympic Village and a new subway line, to about $1 billion further delayed completion of the stadium. However, the National League's Montreal Expos opened the season there on April 15, 1977, the world roller skating championships were held in the stadium in September, and the Grey Cup game for the Canadian Football League championship took place in November. The retractable Kevlar roof wasn't installed until 1987, and the Expos played their first game under the roof on April 20. The world's tallest inclined tower, 626 feet high, supports the roof on guy wires, which are also used to retract it on sunny days. It takes about half an hour to raise or lower the roof. Stadium capacity was increased by 627 seats, bringing the total to 59,893, in 1989, when a new AstroTurf surface was also installed. The park's home run distances are 325 feet down the lines and 404 feet to center field.

Olympic Trench Shooting
See TRAPSHOOTING.

Omni, The
Atlanta, GA

Opened in 1972, the Omni seats 16,818. It is the home court of the National Basketball Association's Atlanta Hawks, and was also home to the Atlanta Flames of the National Hockey League from 1972 through the 1979–80 season, after which the team moved to Calgary.

Ontario Rugby Football Union

The ORFU was founded as Canada's second football League on January 4, 1883, a year after the Quebec Rugby Football Union. Both were members of the

Canadian Rugby Football Union, but the ORFU withdrew in a dispute over rules in 1886 and the CRFU disbanded. The Ontario and Quebec Unions got together once more in 1891 to agree on the rules and establish the Canadian Rugby Union. In a major departure, the ORFU in 1905 adopted rules proposed by Thrift Burnside, reducing teams to 12 players per side, using the scrimmage and snapback rather than the rugby scrum, and requiring the offensive team to gain 10 yards in three downs to retain possession of the ball. Although those rules remained in effect for only one ORFU season, they were later to form the basis of modern Canadian football.

Option Clause

Professional football's version of baseball's reserve clause is the option clause. That clause in the standard player's contract gave the team a one-year option on the player's services after the contract expired. By playing out his option—that is, playing one season without re-signing—the player could become a free agent. The reserve clause theoretically bound a player to his team perpetually, but an arbitrator's ruling in 1975 limited its effect to one year, as with the option clause, so there is no longer any great difference between the two. The National Hockey League during the 1974–75 season adopted the option clause because courts ruled that its reserve clause was not legally binding on players.

See also RESERVE CLAUSE.

Orange Bowl
Football

The Rose Bowl was permanently established in 1916, but there wasn't another college football bowl game until 1933, when Miami (FL) held a game in conjunction with its Palm Festival. That became the Orange Bowl in 1935. Like several other bowls, it accepted sponsorship in 1990 and is formally called the Federal Express Orange Bowl, though most listings and many press accounts omit the name of the sponsor. The game is played in a 75,500-seat stadium also called the Orange Bowl, built in 1935 and owned by the city of Miami. The stadium was the home of the National Football League's Miami Dolphins from 1966 through 1986; then the team moved to newly built Joseph F. Robbie Stadium.

Orange Bowl Results

1933 Miami (FL) 7, Manhattan 0
1934 Duquesne 33, Miami (FL) 7
1935 Bucknell 26, Miami (FL) 0
1936 Catholic University 20, Mississippi 19

1937 Duquesne 13, Mississippi State 12
1938 Auburn 6, Mississippi State 0
1939 Tennessee 17, Oklahoma 0
1940 Georgia Tech 21, Missouri 7
1941 Mississippi State 14, Georgetown 7
1942 Georgia 40, Texas Christian 26
1943 Alabama 37, Boston College 21
1944 Louisiana State 20, Texas A & M 14
1945 Tulsa 26, Georgia Tech 12
1946 Miami (FL) 13, Holy Cross 6
1947 Rice 8, Tennessee 0
1948 Georgia Tech 20, Kansas 14
1949 Texas 41, Georgia 28
1950 Santa Clara 21, Kentucky 13
1951 Clemson 15, Miami (FL) 14
1952 Georgia Tech 17, Baylor 14
1953 Alabama 61, Syracuse 6
1954 Oklahoma 7, Maryland 0
1955 Duke 34, Nebraska 7
1956 Oklahoma 20, Maryland 6
1957 Colorado 27, Clemson 21
1958 Oklahoma 48, Duke 21
1959 Oklahoma 21, Syracuse 6
1960 Georgia 14, Missouri 7
1961 Missouri 21, Navy 14
1962 Louisiana State 25, Colorado 7
1963 Alabama 17, Oklahoma 0
1964 Nebraska 13, Auburn 7
1965 Texas 21, Alabama 17
1966 Alabama 39, Nebraska 28
1967 Florida 27, Georgia Tech 12
1968 Oklahoma 26, Tennessee 24
1969 Penn State 15, Kansas 14
1970 Penn State 10, Missouri 3
1971 Nebraska 17, Louisiana State 14
1972 Nebraska 38, Alabama 6
1973 Nebraska 40, Notre Dame 6
1974 Penn State 16, Louisiana State 9
1975 Notre Dame 13, Alabama 11
1976 Oklahoma 14, Michigan 6
1977 Ohio State 27, Colorado 10
1978 Arkansas 31, Oklahoma 6
1979 Oklahoma 31, Nebraska 24
1980 Oklahoma 24, Florida State 7
1981 Oklahoma 18, Florida State 17
1982 Clemson 22, Nebraska 15
1983 Nebraska 21, Louisiana State 20
1984 Miami (FL) 31, Nebraska 30
1985 Washington 28, Oklahoma 17
1986 Oklahoma 25, Penn State 10
1987 Oklahoma 42, Arkansas 8
1988 Miami (FL) 20, Oklahoma 14
1989 Miami (FL) 23, Nebraska 3
1990 Notre Dame 21, Colorado 6
1991 Colorado 10, Notre Dame 9

Orange, NJ

The Orange Tornadoes played in the National Football League for just one season, 1929.

Organized Baseball

Although the phrase "organized baseball" didn't come into use until 1903, the reality it described was created in 1883, when the American Association, the National League, and the minor-league Northwestern Association entered into the Tripartite Pact, later known as the National Agreement. Under this pact, the three leagues agreed to honor one another's contracts, reserve lists, suspensions, and expulsions. Each team was also given exclusive rights to a territory including its home city and the area around it for a radius of 5 miles.

A few would-be major leagues challenged this arrangement, most notably the American League, which entered into the National Agreement in 1903 after a two-year battle with the National League. The National Association of Professional Baseball Leagues, a group of minor leagues, also signed the 1903 agreement, which used the phrase "organized baseball" to describe the leagues and teams that fell under its umbrella. The last major challenge to organized baseball came from the Federal League, which operated from 1913 through 1915, and a few "outlaw" minor leagues also sprang up from time to time.

After blacks were silently excluded from organized baseball in 1899, several black professional teams and leagues were organized. Since they didn't raid the white leagues for players, though, they weren't considered outlaws and were simply ignored by organized baseball. With the integration of organized baseball in 1946 and the subsequent demise of the black leagues, "organized baseball" has come to mean all of professional baseball, major and minor leagues alike, in North America.

See also MINOR LEAGUES; NATIONAL AGREEMENT.

Orienteering

Originally, orienteering was a ski sport that developed in the Scandinavian countries in the late 19th century as military training. Using a map and compass, skiers attempted to find their way over an unmarked course. It became a summer sport in Sweden shortly after World War I; competitors were now distance runners moving over wooded land and checking in at certain points marked on the map. It became an organized sport in Canada in 1967, when the Canadian Orienteering Federation was founded; the first Canadian national championship was held in 1968 and became a two-day event in 1969. The United States held its first national championship at the University of Southern Illinois in 1970, and a North American championship meet was inaugurated in 1971.

Addresses: Canadian Orienteering Federation, 333 River Road, Vanier, Ontario, Canada K1L 8H9 (613) 748–5649; United States Orienteering Federation, P.O. Box 1444, Forest Park, GA 30051 (404) 363–2110

Original Celtics
Basketball

The New York Celtics were organized as a settlement house team in an Irish neighborhood on the West Side in 1914. Among the players were Pete Barry and John Whitty. The team disbanded because of World War I, but after the war Jim and Tom Furey decided to reorganize it. The founder of the team, however, refused to let them use the name, so they called their team the Original Celtics. Whitty and Barry were on the squad. Jim Furey strengthened the team greatly by adding Johnny Beckman and Dutch Dehnert for the second season.

Another top team of the era was the New York Whirlwinds. In 1921 the Celtics and Whirlwinds agreed to play a three-game series at the 71st Street Armory. The Whirlwinds won the first easily, the Celtics won the second, and the third game was canceled because fans' emotions ran so high there was fear of violence. Furey then persuaded two of the Whirlwinds, Chris Leonard and Nat Holman, to jump to the Celtics. Before the 1922–23 season, he began to pay his players a guaranteed salary on the condition that they couldn't play for any other team. That was a revolutionary move, because at the time pro basketball paid so little that most players performed for two or more teams.

From that time on, the Celtics were almost unbeatable. Playing together virtually every night and often twice on Sunday, they developed unmatched team play, and because they were rarely in danger of losing they could afford to experiment with new ideas during a game. They made basketball a genuine team sport, creating the switching man-to-man defense, the give-and-go play, and the pivot play. Whitty, the coach, once told a young Joe Lapchick, "We know what you can do with the ball. It's how you are without the ball that determines how good a basketball player you are." Coaches and commentators still talk about "moving without the ball" as the key to genuinely good team play.

When the American Basketball League was organized in 1926, the Celtics refused to join because they could make more money barnstorming. But, after being blacklisted by the league's teams, they

ORIGINAL CELTICS

Johnny Beckman

Dutch Dehnert

Joe Lapchick

Nat Holman

Pete Barry

The Original Celtics, organized in 1919, were the first great professional basketball team. Courtesy of the Basketball Hall of Fame

finally entered the ABL in midseason and won 19 of 20 games and the championship. The team was dismantled after winning the title again the following season. The ABL folded in 1929, and a few of the Celtics put together a barnstorming team, but it wasn't quite the same.

Orlando, FL

Basketball The Orlando Magic entered the National Basketball Association as an expansion franchise for the 1989–90 season.

Orr, "Bobby" Robert G. (1948–   )
Hockey
Born March 20, 1948, Parry Sound, Ontario; Hockey Hall of Fame

He may have been supplanted by Wayne Gretzky, but many observers thought that Orr in his prime was the greatest hockey player ever. Although a defenseman, he was a superb offensive player and an outstanding skater and stickhandler. He had an uncanny knack for knowing where everyone was on the ice and could hit a teammate with a perfect pass at just the right moment. Harry Sinden of the Boston Bruins, where Orr spent most of his professional career, said of him, "Orr can do everything, *and* do it at top speed." And Chicago sports columnist Robert Markus wrote, "Orr is a stylish, graceful athlete who does everything extremely well, much in the manner of DiMaggio."

The Bruins spotted him when he was only 12 years old and playing midget hockey. They immediately put his name on their protected list, the only step necessary to get rights to an amateur player at that time. Orr joined the Bruins in 1966, when he was just 18, and he won the Calder Trophy as National Hockey League Rookie of the Year that season.

In 1970, Orr became the only defenseman ever to lead the NHL in scoring, and the second player to score more than 100 points in a season. He repeated in 1975. He won the Hart Trophy as the league's outstanding player three years in a row, 1970–72, and the Norris Trophy as best defenseman from 1968 through 1975. Orr and center Phil Esposito led the Bruins to Stanley Cup championships in 1970 and 1972, with Orr scoring the goal that clinched the cup both years. He was also named the Most Valuable Player of the playoffs both years, becoming the first player to win the Conn Smythe Trophy twice.

Knee injuries shortened Orr's career. Traded to the Chicago Black Hawks in 1978, he played only a few games there before retiring and moving into the front office. Orr appeared in just 657 games in his 12 NHL seasons. (By contrast, Brad Park, who is immediately behind Orr on the all-time scoring list, played 1,113 games in 17 seasons.) He totaled 270 goals and 645 assists for 915 points. His average of 1.393 points per game is the fifth best ever, and by far the highest for a defenseman.

Ott, Melvin T. (1909–1958)
Baseball
Born March 2, 1909, Gretna, LA; died November 21, 1958; Baseball Hall of Fame

Ott was a catcher with a semipro team in Patterson, LA in 1925, when he entered the office of New York Giants manager John McGraw with a letter of introduction from the team's owner. McGraw agreed to give the youngster a tryout, but decided he was too small to be a catcher. He asked if Ott could play the outfield. "Yes, Mr. McGraw," the baby-faced 16-year-old replied. "I played a little outfield when I was a kid."

The tryout was the beginning of a 22-year career, all with the Giants, and Ott became the first National League player to hit more than 500 home runs, despite his size. Only 5 feet 9 inches, Ott in his prime carried 170 pounds on a solid frame. A left-handed hitter, he had an unusual batting style, lifting his front foot high into the air and then putting it quickly down to launch his powerful swing after a stride of just a few inches.

Ott didn't become a regular until 1928, when McGraw made him the club's right fielder. The following season, he had career highs of 42 home runs and 151 runs batted in, though neither figure led the league. Ott did win or share six league home run

titles, and he led in runs batted in with 135 in 1934. He also batted over .300 ten times. One of his greatest performances came in the 1933 World Series. Playing in his first Series game, Ott got four hits in four times at bat, including a two-run homer, as the Giants won 4–2. He hit the winning home run in the tenth inning of the fifth and deciding game.

The Giants fell on hard times in the late 1930s, and Ott was named playing manager in 1942. The team finished third, but dropped to last place the following season. Ott was replaced by Leo Durocher in the middle of the 1948 season. After a stint as a minor-league manager, he became a radio broadcaster with the Detroit Tigers. He died in 1958 from injuries suffered in a car crash.

Ott had a lifetime .304 batting average, with 2,876 hits, 511 home runs, 1,859 runs scored, and 1,860 runs batted in.

Ottawa, Ontario
Football   One of the first rugby games recorded in Canada was played in 1867 between two Ottawa teams, the Rough Riders and the Senators. It is believed that the Rough Riders were named for lumberjacks who rode logs down the Ottawa River. Another Ottawa team, also called the Rough Riders, joined the Interprovincial Rugby Football Union when it was organized in 1907. The IRFU in 1960 became the eastern conference of the Canadian Football league. The Rough Riders won the Grey Cup in 1936, 1939, 1942, 1948, 1966, and 1981.

Hockey   The Ottawa Senators were in the National Hockey League from its founding in 1917 through the 1930–31 season. After skipping one season, the Senators rejoined the league in 1932, but the franchise moved to St. Louis after the 1933–34 season. The Senators won the Stanley Cup in 1920, 1921, 1923, and 1927. Before the formation of the NHL, the Ottawa Silver Seven were Cup champions from 1903 through 1905 and the Senators won the Cup in 1909 and 1911.

See also LANSDOWNE PARK STADIUM.

Ouimet, Francis D. (1893–1967)
Golf
Born May 8, 1893; died September 2, 1967; World Golf Hall of Fame

Golf won major headlines for the first time, and Ouimet became the sport's first popular hero in 1913 when he beat two top British professionals, Ted Ray and Harry Vardon, in the U.S. Open. Everyone had expected one of the Britons to win the title, but Ouimet, an amateur, was tied with them at the end of regulation play and in the playoff round, on a rain-soaked course, he beat Vardon by five strokes and Ray by seven. It was a terrific story, because Ouimet was a former caddy at The Country Club in Brookline, where the tournament was played. The son of French-Canadian immigrants, he helped change golf's image; it had previously been viewed as a sport for the idle rich. Ouimet also won the U.S. Amateur in 1914, 1920, and 1931, and he was on every Walker Cup team from 1921 through 1949.

Outland Award
Football

Presented by the Football Writers' Association of America to the nation's outstanding interior lineman, this award is named for John Outland, an All-American tackle at the University of Pennsylvania in 1897.

Outland Award Winners

1946 George Connor, Notre Dame
1947 Joe Steffy, Army
1948 William Fischer, Notre Dame
1949 Ed Bagdon, Michigan State
1950 Robert Gain, Kentucky
1951 James Weatherall, Oklahoma
1952 Richard Modzelewski, Maryland
1953 J. D. Roberts, Oklahoma
1954 William Brooks, Arkansas
1955 Calvin Jones, Iowa
1956 Jim Parker, Ohio State
1957 Alex Karras, Iowa
1958 Zeke Smith, Auburn
1959 Mike McGee, Duke
1960 Tom Brown, Minnesota
1961 Merlin Olsen, Utah State
1962 Bobby Bell, Minnesota
1963 Scott Appleton, Texas
1964 Steve Delong, Tennessee
1965 Tommy Nobis, Texas
1966 Loyd Phillips, Arkansas
1967 Ron Yary, Southern California
1968 Bill Stanfill, Georgia
1969 Mike Reid, Penn State
1970 Jim Stillwagon, Ohio State
1971 Larry Jacobson, Nebraska
1972 Rich Glover, Nebraska
1973 John Hicks, Ohio State
1974 Randy White, Maryland
1975 Lee Roy Selmon, Oklahoma
1976 Ross Browner, Notre Dame
1977 Brad Shearer, Texas
1978 Greg Roberts, Oklahoma
1979 Jim Ritcher, North Carolina State
1980 Mark May, Pittsburgh

1981 Dave Rimington, Nebraska
1982 Dave Rimington, Nebraska
1983 Dean Steinkuhler, Nebraska
1984 Bruce Smith, Virginia Tech
1985 Mike Ruth, Boston College
1986 Jason Buck, Brigham Young
1987 Chad Henings, Air Force
1988 Tracy Rocker, Auburn
1989 Mohammed Elewonibi, Brigham Young
1990 Russell Maryland, Miami (FL)

Owen, Stephen J. (1898–1964)
Football

Born April 21, 1898, Cleo Springs, OK; died May 17, 1964; Pro Football Hall of Fame

One of the biggest lineman of his day at 6-foot-2 and 235 pounds, Owen went on to become a successful professional coach who emphasized defense as the key to victory. After playing at little Phillips University in Kansas, "Stout Steve" joined the Kansas City Cowboys of the National Football League in 1924. He was with both Kansas City and Cleveland in 1925, then went to the New York Giants in 1926. He played for the Giants through 1931 and appeared in a few games in 1933.

Shortly before the 1931 season, Giants' owner Tim Mara called Owen to say he'd chosen a coach. "Who is he, Mr. Mara?" asked Owen. "You," Mara answered, and hung up. Owen remained in the job for 23 seasons, winning eight divisional titles and two NFL championships. The first championship came in a celebrated playoff against the Chicago Bears in 1934. On an icy field, the Bears took a 10–3 halftime lead. At Owen's suggestion, most of the Giants changed from football shoes to sneakers during the intermission. Although they fell behind 13–3 at the end of the third quarter, the sneakers gave them better traction on the ice and the Giants scored 27 points in the fourth quarter to win the game 30–13.

When the Cleveland Browns entered the National Football League in 1950, their pass-and-trap offense seemed unstoppable. But they managed a total of just 21 points in three games against Owen's "umbrella defense." It looked like a 6–1–4—a six-man line with one linebacker and four defensive backs—but Owen had his ends dropping off to defend against the pass—very similar to the 4–3–4 defenses that were used from the late 1950s to the present day. Despite the success of the defense, however, the Giants lost to the Browns 8–3 in the divisional championship game. After consecutive second-place finishes, the team plummeted into fifth in 1953 and Owen was replaced. He had 153 victories, 108 losses and 17 ties.

Owens, "Jesse" James C. (1918–1980)
Track and Field

Born September 12, 1918, Decatur, AL; died March 31, 1980; National Track and Field Hall of Fame

Although Owens is best remembered for winning four Gold Medals in the 1936 Olympics, his greatest performance may have come at the 1935 Big Ten meet. Then a sophomore at Ohio State, Owens was not sure he could compete because he'd wrenched his back a few days earlier, but he decided to try the 100-yard dash and tied the world record of 9.4 seconds. He then made one attempt at the long jump, setting a new record of 26 feet 8¼ inches. From the long jump pit he went to the 220-yard dash, where he set another record of 20.3 seconds. After resting during the 2-mile run, Owens ran the 220-yard low hurdles in 22.6 seconds, another record. In a little more than an hour, he had set three world records and tied a fourth.

The story that Hitler snubbed him at the 1936 Berlin Olympics because he was black has been told many times, but it is not accurate. In fact, Owens was wildly applauded by German fans, and he said later that when he passed Hitler's box one day, "he arose, waved his hand at me, and I waved back at him."

A naturally effortless runner, Owens won the AAU outdoor 100-yard dash in 1936 and the broad jump in 1933, 1934, and 1936. He was the indoor broad jump champion in 1934 and 1935. Owens won the NCAA 100-yard and 220-yard dashes in 1935, the 100– and 200-meter dashes in 1936, the 220-yard low hurdles and the broad jump in 1935 and 1936. He then became a very popular speaker who worked for civil rights in a low-key way. He once spoke of how he saw his role as a black leader: "The Negro people needed an image and Joe Louis and I came along. It gives you a real sense of responsibility to your fellow man."

Further Reading: Baker, William J. *Jesse Owens: An American Life.* New York: The Free Press, 1986.

See also NAZI OLYMPICS.

Pacific Coast Conference (PCC)

Formally the Pacific Coast Intercollegiate Athletic Conference, the PCC was organized on December 2, 1915, by the University of California, University of Oregon, Oregon State University, and the University of Washington. Stanford and Washington State were admitted the following year, the Universities of Idaho and Southern California in 1922, and Montana State and UCLA in 1927. Montana State pulled out in 1950. The conference folded in 1959, after California, Southern California, UCLA, and Washington withdrew to form the Athletic Association of Western Universities, now known as the Pacific Ten Conference.

Pacific Coast League
Baseball

The PCL seemed on the verge of becoming the third major league in 1951, when it was the first league granted the "Open" classification, placing it a notch above the AAA leagues and restricting the major leagues' drafting powers. The league's eight teams were independent, not bound to any major-league teams, and they owned most of their players outright. However, the PCL lost its two biggest cities in 1958, when the Brooklyn Dodgers moved to Los Angeles and the New York Giants moved to San Francisco. It then reverted to AAA status, where it remains.

The league originally operated as an "outlaw" league, outside of the National Agreement that governed the major leagues and most of the minors, and its teams lured many major-league players to the West Coast with high salaries. In February of 1904, Ban Johnson of the American League, Ned Hanlon of the National League's Brooklyn team, and Jim Hart of the Chicago Cubs worked out a settlement that brought the PCL under the National Agreement, but its teams were allowed to keep all players they had under contract.

Charges of gambling and fixes began after World War I, and in October 1920 a grand jury was told that a gambling syndicate controlled at least five of the PCL's eight teams. As a result, four players were banned from organized baseball, and several others were released by their teams. The league president, William H. McCarthy, also banned professional gamblers from PCL ballparks.

At its peak in the early 1950s, the PCL had teams in Hollywood, Los Angeles, Oakland, Phoenix, Sacramento, San Diego, San Francisco, and Seattle, five of which now have major-league franchises. The league currently has ten teams: Calgary, Edmonton, Portland, Tacoma, and Vancouver in the northern division, and Albuquerque, Colorado Springs, Las Vegas, Phoenix, and Tucson in the southern division.

Pacific Coliseum
Vancouver, BC

The Vancouver Canucks, now in the National Hockey League, have played in Pacific Coliseum since coming into existence as a World Hockey Association team in 1970. The Coliseum seats 16,160.

Pacific Ten Conference (Pac Ten)

California, Southern California, UCLA, and Washington pulled out of the Pacific Coast Conference in 1959 and founded the Athletic Association of Western Universities. The AAWU became the Pacific Eight in 1971 and the Pacific Ten in 1979. Current Pac Ten members are Arizona, Arizona State, California, Oregon, Oregon State, Southern California, Stanford, UCLA, Washington, and Washington State.

Address: 800 South Broadway, Suite 400, Walnut Creek, CA 94596 (415) 932–4411

Paddle Tennis

The Reverend Frank P. Beal of Albion, MI invented paddle tennis in 1898 as a kind of training for children too small to play lawn tennis. He cut the tennis court in half, to the size of 18 by 39 feet, and he replaced the racquet with a wooden paddle, and the tennis ball with a ball of hard sponge rubber. When he was transferred to a church in Greenwich Village in 1921, he introduced the sport to New York City, where it soon became very popular.

The American Paddle Tennis Association, founded in 1923, was renamed the U.S. Paddle Tennis Association three years later. Many adults who were playing the sport felt the court should be larger, and in 1937 the USPTA acquiesced, adopting a court of 20 by 44 feet for adults, while keeping the original size for children under 15.

The sport was extremely popular in California, where it was governed by the Western United States

Paddle Tennis Association. Differences in rules led to feuding between East and West, which probably prevented paddle tennis from becoming a truly national sport; it declined rapidly after World War II, although it made something of a comeback in the 1960s. Membership in the USPTA is currently about 200,000.

Address: U.S. Paddle Tennis Association, 189 Seeley Street, Brooklyn, NY 11218 (718) 788–2094
See also PLATFORM TENNIS.

Paddleball

Paddleball was invented in 1930 by Earl Riskey, Director of Intramural Sports at the University of Michigan. After watching varsity tennis players practice on handball courts on rainy days, he soaked a tennis ball in gasoline stripped the felt from it to get a less lively ball, and drew up a set of rules, patterned after those of handball. Within a short time, a wooden paddle replaced the tennis racquet.

Paddleball remained a local sport until World War II, when army recruits trained at the university and many of them learned the game. The National Paddleball Association was organized in 1952, although it didn't hold its first championship tournament until 1961. However, during the late 1960s many paddleball players began to switch to racquetball, and in 1973–74 the only supplier of official balls for paddleball stopped making them, causing even more players to switch. It is now played primarily in the Upper Midwest, although one-wall paddleball is popular in New York City, where there are many one-wall handball courts.

Address: National Paddleball Association, P.O. Box 91, Portage, MI 49081 (616) 323–0011

Paddock, Charles W. (1900–1943)
Track & Field
Born August 11, 1900, Gainesville, TX; died July 21, 1943; National Track and Field Hall of Fame

A rather plump 18-year-old, Paddock surprised people by winning the 100-meter dash at the Inter-Allied Games in 1919. He went on to win the event at the 1920 Olympics, and was a world-class sprinter for a remarkably long time, also competing in the 1924 and 1928 Games. While attending the University of Southern California, he became the third man to run 100 yards in 9.6 seconds. He did it three more times that year and twice more in his career. He also set world records of 10.4 seconds in the 100 meters and 20.8 seconds in the 200 meters in 1921. Paddock was the Olympic 100-meter champion in 1920, the U.S. 100-yard champion in 1921 and 1924, and the U.S. 220-yard champion in 1920, 1921, and 1924.

Colorful and often controversial, Paddock used a unique jump finish, leaving the ground about 10 feet from the finish line and flying through the tape. His style attracted fans. When he raced at the unusual distance of 175 yards in the Penn Relays, which required running down a straightaway into an inset in the grandstand, so many people crowded around the finish line that a wall collapsed and Paddock leaped through falling bricks to win the race.

His frequent trips to compete abroad often led to charges of professionalism. The Amateur Athletic Union in 1923 ruled that U.S. athletes were not to compete in Europe that year, but Paddock defied the ban, claiming "The AAU hasn't any authority over members of the National Collegiate Athletic Association," and he tied a world record in the nonstandard 150-meter dash in a Paris meet. The AAU suspended him, but he was reinstated in time to join the 1924 Olympic team. A sportswriter, Paddock was also in periodic trouble with the AAU for reporting on competitions in which he took part, and in 1928 he was suspended for making personal appearances to promote a film in which he appeared. When the suspension was lifted, allowing him to compete in the 1928 Olympics, one AAU director resigned in protest.

Paige, "Satchel" LeRoy R. (1906–1982)
Baseball
Born July 7, 1906, Mobile, AL; died June 5, 1982; Baseball Hall of Fame

Because he was black, Satchel Paige didn't get to pitch in the major leagues until he was 42 years old. He joined the Cleveland Indians in 1948 as the fifth black player, the first black pitcher in the American League, and the oldest rookie in major-league history. He won six games, lost only one, and had an outstanding 2.48 earned run average. But Paige was already famous, undoubtedly the most famous of the many blacks who had played in the obscurity of their own major leagues; in his first three starts, more than 200,000 fans turned out at Cleveland's Municipal Stadium.

The tall, lanky Paige began his career getting $1 a game for the Mobile Tigers in 1924. He threw only a fastball, but had exceptional control, and by 1926 he was pitching in the Negro Southern League. Two years later he was in the black version of the major leagues, with the Birmingham Black Barons. His great skills, combined with his showmanship, made him such a gate attraction that the owner of the team often "rented" Paige for a day to another team.

In 1929, Paige began playing baseball year-round, moving to the Caribbean during the winter, pitching as many as 200 games a year. He became nearly as well known among whites as among blacks in 1930, when he played for the Baltimore Black Sox against a barnstorming team of major-leaguers. Paige struck out 22 hitters in one of those games. (Roger Clemens set the major-league record of 20 in 1986.)

Paige made very good money during the 1930s—as much as $22,000 a year with the Kansas City Monarchs in 1938—but he resented the fact that he couldn't play in the major leagues. He finally got his chance when Bill Veeck, the flamboyant Cleveland owner, signed him in 1948. After a bad second season, when he was suffering from various illnesses, he was released. But Veeck signed him again, to play for the St. Louis Browns, in 1951. The Browns' bullpen was equipped with a rocking chair for Paige, who was going on 45, and most people thought this was just another Veeck publicity stunt. But Paige was an American League all-star in 1952 and 1953, winning a total of 15 games and saving 21.

After more barnstorming and some minor-league pitching, Paige was signed by the Kansas City Athletics to make one appearance, against the Boston Red Sox on September 25, 1965. At the age of 59, he pitched three scoreless innings, giving up just one hit and striking out a batter. Six years later, he became the first player named to the Baseball Hall of Fame by the Committee on Negro Leagues.

Palace, The
Auburn Hills, MI

The Detroit Pistons of the National Basketball Association built this arena at a cost of about $80 million and began playing there at the beginning of the 1988–89 season. The Palace is unique among basketball arenas in that it has luxury suites, like those in most major-league baseball parks and football stadiums. The 180 suites are leased for $30,000 to $120,000 a year, bringing in more money than the total box office revenues of about half the other teams in the NBA. The Palace seats 21,454.

Palmer, Arnold (1929–   )
Golf

Born September 10, 1929, Latrobe, PA; World Golf Hall of Fame

Arnold Palmer and nationally televised golf arrived at just about the same time, and they were made for each other. A great golfer with a natural sense of showmanship, Palmer in 1960 made a series of last-minute charges that had millions watching and rooting for yet another dramatic comeback victory. It began when he birdied the last two holes of the Masters to win by one shot. In the U.S. Open, he was in 15th place and trailing by seven strokes

Arnold Palmer was golf's first television star. His open display of emotion and dramatic last-round charges to victory made him the most popular golfer of the 1960s. Courtesy of the U.S. Golf Association

entering the final round. He shot a 65 to win. Another 65 on the final round won the Palm Springs Open. He followed that with a 67 to win at Pensacola; a 67 at Hartford that got him into a playoff, which he won; and another 67 to win the Mobile Open.

The son of a club professional, Palmer won the National Amateur championship in 1955 and joined the pro tour shortly afterward. His first major victory came in the 1958 Masters Tournament, which he also won in 1960, 1962, and 1964. He was the British Open champion two years in a row, 1961 and 1962, giving him a total of seven major titles. During the 1960s, Palmer, Jack Nicklaus, and Gary Player were known as the "Big Three," and the competition among these superb golfers helped build the sport's television audience to unprecedented levels.

His final-round charges and his open display of emotion attracted enormous galleries, known as "Arnie's Army," as well as television viewers. Palmer grimaced as if in pain after a poor shot, grinned widely and thrust his club into the air to celebrate a good shot, and the television cameras caught it all. Golf's first millionaire, he was turned into a virtual conglomerate by his manager, Mark McCormack. The pressures of his many businesses obviously affected his golf—he didn't win a major championship after 1964—but that didn't diminish the size of his galleries or his television appeal, and many resented the presence of Nicklaus, who had clearly surpassed Palmer as the world's best golfer during the mid-1960s.

Pan-American Games

Conceived as the Olympics of the Western Hemisphere, the Pan-American Games were apparently the brainchild of Avery Brundage, long-time Olympic leader. Formally, however, it was the Argentine Olympic Committee that called the 1940 meeting at which the plan for the Games was discussed and accepted. Buenos Aires was to host the first Games in 1942, but World War II intervened and the Games didn't begin until 1951.

Although not all Olympic sports are included, the Pan-American Games are patterned very closely after the Olympics, with the same sort of opening and closing ceremonies. Athletes even take the Olympic oath, and a country's Olympic committee usually also functions as a Pan-American Games committee. The Games have shown steady growth. In 1987, more than 6,000 athletes and officials from 38 countries took part, compared with 2,000 athletes from 20 countries in 1951. The number of sports has increased from 19 to 26: archery, baseball, basketball, boxing, canoeing and kayaking, cycling, equestrian events, fencing, judo, gymnastics, modern pentathlon, rhythmic gymnastics, roller skating, rowing, soccer, softball, swimming and diving, synchronized swimming, table tennis, tennis, track and field, volleyball, water polo, weight lifting, wrestling, and yachting.

Because of U.S. dominance, especially in swimming and track, some top American athletes have declined to take part in recent Pan-American Games, preferring to face better competition in European meets in order to prepare for the Olympics the following year. And some, led by Brundage himself in 1971, have proposed that the United States should be represented by younger athletes who are still developing their skills. Latin-American countries object to that idea, however, because the better-known athletes help to attract spectators and also offer Latin-American athletes a chance to improve their own skills and techniques by facing superior competition.

Buenos Aires was the site for the first Pan-American Games. Since then, host cities have been Mexico City, 1955; Chicago, 1959; Sao Paulo, Brazil, 1963; Winnipeg, Canada, 1967; Cali, Colombia, 1971; Mexico City, 1975; San Juan, Puerto Rico, 1979; Caracas, Venezuela, 1983; and Indianapolis, 1987. Cuba is scheduled to host the 1991 games.

See also OLYMPIC GAMES.

Parachuting
See SPORT PARACHUTING.

Paralympics

The Olympics for paraplegics, which began in 1960, are held in the same year and usually in the same country as the Olympic Games. Fifteen countries were represented at the first event, in Rome. By 1968, when the games were held in Israel, more than 700 athletes took part, representing 27 countries. Blind athletes and amputees competed for the first time in 1976 at Toronto. Among the sports are archery, basketball, fencing, shooting, swimming, track and field, and weight lifting.

See also DISABLED, SPORTS FOR THE.

Paris Crew
Rowing

One of Canada's finest moments in international sports came in July 1867, when a four-oared crew without cox from St. John, New Brunswick, won a world championship race at the Paris Exposition. The four crew members, who made their own boat and also wore homemade uniforms, were George Price, Samuel Hutton, Elijah Ross,and Robert Fulton. Coming shortly after Canada became a dominion, the victory appealed to nationalist feelings and was widely celebrated across the country. The "Paris Crew," as they became known, rowed against a crew from Tyne, England, on September 15, 1870, for 1,000 pounds, but Tyne won that race.

Parseghian, Ara R. (1923–   )
Football
Born May 21, 1923, Akron, OH; National Football Foundation Hall of Fame

One of several successful coaches to come out of Miami of Ohio, Parseghian revived Notre Dame's football program after six losing seasons. He went to the school in 1963, after Notre Dame had won just two games the previous year, and his first team won nine of ten games. In 1964, Parseghian was named Coach of the Year when Notre Dame won its first nine games, losing to Southern California 20–17 at the last minute in the final game of the season. His 1966 team was undefeated and was ranked first in the nation after a controversial 10–10 tie with Michigan State; Parseghian was widely criticized by the press for apparently playing for the tie rather than victory.

Parseghian retired after the 1974 season, complaining of burnout because of the pressures of the job. His record at Notre Dame was 95–17–4, and his teams finished in the top ten during 9 of his 11 seasons, winning national championships in 1966 and 1973. Notre Dame lost 21–17 to Texas in the 1970 Cotton Bowl, but beat Texas 24–11 in the 1971 game. In 1973, the Irish were whipped 40–6 by Nebraska in the Orange Bowl. They beat Alabama 24–23 in the 1974 Sugar Bowl. Parseghian's last game was a 13–11 victory over Alabama in the 1975 Orange Bowl.

A halfback at Miami, Parseghian was elected captain for the 1948 season, but his class had graduated and he chose to play with the Cleveland Browns instead. A hip injury during the 1949 preseason ended his career. He became head coach at Miami in 1951, succeeding Woody Hayes, and compiled a 39–6–1 record in five seasons, including nine victories in nine games in 1955. Parseghian went to Northwestern in 1956. In eight seasons there, he had a respectable 44–35–1 record, including four victories over Notre Dame in four games.

Pasadena Bowl
Football

Known as the Junior Rose Bowl in its first year, 1967, this bowl game skipped one year and was revived as the Pasadena Bowl in 1969. It was played just three times under that name.

Results

1967	West Texas State 35, California State-Northridge 13
1969	San Diego State 28, Boston University 7
1970	Long Beach State 24, Louisville 24
1971	Memphis State 28, San Jose State 9

Patrick, Lester (1883–1960)
Hockey

Born December 30, 1883, Drummondville, Quebec; died June 1, 1960; Hockey Hall of Fame

If it had anything to do with hockey, Patrick did it, beginning in his years at McGill University in Montreal, when he was a "rover"—the seventh player on the seven-man hockey team of the day. He then moved on to the outstanding Westmount team in the Canadian Amateur Hockey League in 1905 and the Montreal Wanderers in 1906 before becoming a professional with the Renfrew Millionaires in 1910. But Patrick wanted to be more than a player, and, with financial backing from his millionaire father, he and his brother Frank founded the Pacific Coast Hockey Association in 1911.

The Patricks built North America's first artificial ice rink in Victoria, British Columbia, and later added another in Vancouver. Patrick played for Victoria, Spokane, and Seattle in the PCHA while helping to run the league, then returned to Victoria as a

player-coach-manager. The team won the Stanley cup in 1924, when the contestants for the cup were the PCHA and National Hockey League champions.

In 1926, Patrick became the coach of the NHL's New York Rangers. He remained through the 1938–39 season, winning seven of the first eight Coach of the Year awards and guiding the Rangers to Stanley Cup championships in 1928 and 1933. The 1928 final with the Montreal Maroons created one of hockey's greatest legends. Montreal was heavily favored, and all five games were to be played in Montreal because a circus was in Madison Square Garden. The Maroons won the first game 2–0, and the second game was tied 1–1 when Ranger goalie Lorne Chabot was hit in the left eye by a shot early in the second period. Teams didn't carry backup goalies in those days, so the 44-year-old Patrick went into net. He shut out the Maroons until the Rangers won on a goal 7 minutes into overtime, and the team went on to win two of the next three games to claim the cup.

Both the Patrick Trophy, for outstanding service to U.S. hockey, and the Patrick Division of the NHL are named for him. Two of his sons, Lynn and Frederick M. "Muzz" Patrick, played, coached, and managed in the NHL.

Patrick Trophy
Hockey

Named for Lester Patrick, this trophy was presented by the New York Rangers in 1966, to be awarded for "outstanding service to hockey in the United States." The winner is chosen by an award committee that includes the president of the National Hockey League, a governor of the NHL, a nationally syndicated sports writer, a hockey writer for a national news service, a representative of a major network, and a former player who is in the Hockey Hall of Fame. More than one award may be presented annually.

PBA

See PROFESSIONAL BOWLERS ASSOCIATION OF AMERICA.

Peach Bowl
Football

Inaugurated in Atlanta in 1968, the Peach Bowl has usually been played in late December, but it took place on New Years Day in 1981 and 1988.

Peach Bowl Results

1968	Louisiana State 31, Florida State 27
1969	West Virginia 14, South Carolina 3
1970	Arizona State 48, North Carolina 26
1971	Mississippi 41, Georgia Tech 18

1972	North Carolina St. 49, West Virginia 13
1973	Georgia 17, Maryland 16
1974	Vanderbilt 6, Texas Tech 6
1975	West Virginia 13, North Carolina State 10
1976	Kentucky 21, North Carolina 0
1977	North Carolina State 24, Iowa State 14
1978	Purdue 41, Georgia Tech 21
1979	Baylor 24, Clemson 18
1981	(Jan.) Miami (FL) 20, Virginia Tech 10
1981	(Dec.) West Virginia 26, Florida 6
1982	Iowa 28, Tennessee 22
1983	Florida State 28, North Carolina 3
1984	Virginia 27, Purdue 24
1985	Army 31, Illinois 29
1986	Virginia Tech 25, North Carolina State 24
1988	(Jan.) Tennessee 27, Indiana 22
1988	(Dec.) North Carolina State 28, Iowa 23
1989	Syracuse 19, Georgia 18
1990	Auburn 27, Indiana 23

Pearson Award
Hockey

The National Hockey League's outstanding player, as chosen by the players themselves, is given this trophy, which was presented to the league in 1970 by the NHL Players' Association. It's named for Lester B. Pearson, former prime minister of Canada.

Pearson Award Winners

1971	Phil Esposito, Boston
1972	Jean Ratelle, New York Rangers
1973	Phil Esposito, Boston
1974	Bobby Clarke, Philadelphia
1975	Bobby Orr, Boston
1976	Guy Lafleur, Montreal
1977	Guy Lafleur, Montreal
1978	Guy Lafleur, Montreal
1979	Marcel Dionne, Los Angeles
1980	Marcel Dionne, Los Angeles
1981	Mike Liut, St. Louis
1982	Wayne Gretzky, Edmonton
1983	Wayne Gretzky, Edmonton
1984	Wayne Gretzky, Edmonton
1985	Wayne Gretzky, Edmonton
1986	Mario Lemieux, Pittsburgh
1987	Wayne Gretzky, Edmonton
1988	Mario Lemieux, Pittsburgh
1989	Steve Yzerman, Detroit
1990	Mark Messier, Edmonton
1991	Brett Hull, St. Louis

Pedestrianism

Race running and race walking were both known as "pedestrianism" during the 19th century, until they were absorbed by modern track and field meets. The

The fifth Astley Belt race for the world pedestrian championship was held at Madison Square Garden in 1879.

sports became popular in England in the late 18th century, but in North America running races were purely local events, usually spurred by challenges and wagers. The first major pedestrian meet was conducted by the Hoboken Ferry Company at a new track in Hoboken on July 5, 1824, with a $100 prize for a half-mile race and $50 for 220 yards. The ferry company made enough money selling tickets to hold another running race, a half-mile, three-heat event, on July 22. The judges decided that the first- and second-place finishers were in collusion and awarded the $125 prize to the runner who finished third.

Pedestrianism fell into some disrepute for a while, but John Cox Stevens revived the sport at Union Race Course in June of 1835, offering a $1,000 prize to an entrant who ran 10 miles in less than an hour, with a $300 bonus if no one else in the field matched the feat. An estimated 20,000 spectators turned out; Philip Hone confided to his diary, "immense sums were betted by men who find it difficult to pay their honest debts." Only three of the nine runners finished, but Henry Stannard won the prize and the bonus by running the 10 miles in 59 minutes 48 seconds. He became a celebrity, and within a year had won enough money to buy a hotel in Connecticut; he renamed it "The Pedestrian."

The Beacon Race Course held what amounted to a small-scale track meet in August of 1838, with a total of $1,000 in prizes for the 220-yard, quarter-mile, 1-mile, and 2-mile runs, the 1-hour walk, pitching the bar, high jumping, hammer throwing, a sack race, and the "farthest three jumps," which may have been the triple jump or a series of three long jumps.

New interest in pedestrianism was aroused when the Beacon Course again hosted a major race on June 3, 1844, with a prize of $500 to anyone who could run 10¼ miles in an hour. About 30,000 spectators watched, and bet on, the nine runners. Again there

Men on horseback rode the course to keep the crowd away from the runners at a 10-mile running race at the Elysian Fields in Hoboken in 1845. Frank Leslie's Illustrated Weekly

were only three finishers, and again Stannard won, but he failed to cover the distance. He got a $300 prize for placing first. The Beacon then offered another $300 prize for a 1-hour race, with a $700 bonus if the winner covered more than 10 miles. The result was one of the first international sporting events, as 3 English runners joined entrants from seven states in a 17-runner field on October 14. The crowd numbered about 30,000, and it looked as if the race might not be run because so many of them crowded onto the track. But at last it got under way. The winner was John Gildersleeve of New York, who covered a little more than 10½ miles.

The American victory over the British was hailed by the press, but English runners won the next two big races, with John Barlow setting a record of 54 minutes 21 seconds for 10 miles on November 18 and John Greenhalgh edging Gildersleeve in a $500, 12-mile race on December 15. Interest was not as great in a series of races at the Beacon course in 1845, in part at least because it was an unusually hot summer. Another English runner, William Jackson, ran a number of challenge races that year in New York, Montreal, Toronto, Baltimore and Metairie, LA, where his narrow defeat by Gildersleeve again raised questions about the sport's honesty. One observer from Kentucky commented, "I can't afford to bet a red cent on anything that talks."

In addition to the doubts about whether races were honest, it was becoming harder for good runners to

find opposition. Jackson returned to North America in 1849 and began running against horses for lack of human challengers. John Grindall, a New York butcher who emerged as a top distance runner in the 1850s, had the same problem. Public challenges by other runners specifically excluded Grindall, and after he was refused entry into a 5-mile race at Boston he also began racing against horses. As 1860 approached, there was growing criticism of professionalism in general, which also led to declining interest in pedestrianism.

The most celebrated runner of the period was a Seneca Indian from New York, Lewis Bennett, who went to England in 1861 to run under the name of "Deerfoot". Although his performances were unpredictable because of a heavy schedule, he turned in some outstanding times, including records of 51 minutes, 26 seconds for 10 miles and 62 minutes 2¼ seconds for 12 miles. In 1867 Deerfoot and another Seneca, John Steeprock, went on tour running handicap races against horses.

The rise of athletic clubs and the growth of amateur track and field virtually wiped out the running side of pedestrianism in the 1870s, but race walking became a craze. Long popular in England, race walking had had only a couple of brief moments of attention in North America. In 1842, Thomas Elsworth claimed to have equaled Englishman Robert Barclay's record by walking 1,000 miles in 1,000 consecutive hours, and in 1856 and 1857,

William Hughes traveled through the East and Midwest staging 100-mile walks on a 3-foot-wide plank. Hughes' exhibitions were generally staged in saloons. A Mrs. Bentley of Ohio also did plank walking in New York saloons, doing 30 miles at a time.

The postwar "walking mania" or "foot fever," as newspapers called it, was largely inspired by the exploits of Edward Payson Weston. He first attracted notice in 1861 by walking from Boston to Washington, DC between February 22 and March 4, averaging 51 miles a day despite running into a snowstorm. After serving in the Civil War, Weston won a $10,000 bet in 1867 by walking from Portland, ME to Chicago in a 30-day period, which included only 26 days of walking because he rested on Sundays. Crowds met him at every stop along the way, and he became a national celebrity. In 1868 he and English champion George Topley met in a 100-mile race. Weston, leading, dropped out after 75 miles and Topley quit after 74, giving Weston the victory. The *New York Clipper* called the race a "palpable fraud."

Nevertheless, Weston remained popular. In 1870, he tried to walk 400 miles in five days at the Empire Skating Rink, but fell 80 miles short. The following year, he accomplished the 400-mile goal and also set a new record of 112 miles in a single day. And in May of 1874 he tried to walk 500 miles in six days. Again he failed, but collected $6,000 in gate receipts and, incidentally, invented what was to become a true craze in both walking and bicycling—the six-day race.

Weston generally avoided competition, preferring to race alone against time, but a persistent challenger, Daniel O'Leary of Chicago, finally caught up with him in England in 1877. English promoters raised a $5,000 prize for a six-day race between the two, and Weston couldn't refuse. The race began on April 7 at the London Agricultural Hall; O'Leary won, 520 miles to 510. Both were cheered wildly after the finish.

Lord Astley in 1878 offered a silver and gold championship belt for a six-day "go-as-you-please" race, in which competitors were allowed to walk or run. O'Leary won, covering 520½ miles. Weston missed the race because of illness. O'Leary defended the belt before large crowds in New York, then lost it to Charles Rowell of England in February 1879. Four months later, Rowell was challenged by Weston and two other competitors. To everyone's surprise, Weston won with a record 550 miles, well ahead of the Englishman. Thousands of people thronged New York's Printing House Square to watch bulletin boards when it became known that he was within reach of the record.

The biggest race of all began at Madison Square Garden at 1 A.M. on September 23, 1879. There were 13 entrants, including Rowell and Weston. This time Rowell won, collecting $27,721, while Weston finished sixth and earned just $1,663. That was just one of many six-day races throughout North America that year, including major events in Boston, San Francisco, and Toronto. Women also got involved in the sport. In a Madison Square Garden race that began on December 20, Amy Howard set a new record of 393¾ miles. In addition to the six-day races, many shorter races were held, at 25, 50, and 100 miles, and for 24-, 48-, and 72 hours.

Daniel O'Leary became a major promoter of the distance events, including 75-mile races at Boston and Providence and six-day races for the O'Leary Belt at Madison Square Garden. John Ennis, who had competed in the first Astley Belt race, also began promoting six-day races in 1881. But a big race at Madison Square Garden in 1882 had a disappointing gate, despite many outstanding entrants, and the Garden didn't have another six-day race until April 1884. When that also failed to attract much interest, six-day racing seemed extinct, although many shorter races with small purses were staged in the Midwest and West, from Detroit to Carson City, NV. These events were often put together by groups of itinerant pedestrians in search of paying spectators; sometimes the spectators showed up and sometimes they didn't, because of growing skepticism: The word "contest" was put in quotation marks by many newspapers covering one such race.

The top performer in the late 1880s was Anton Strokel, an Austrian native who had emigrated to Saginaw, MI. After easy victories in three 72-hour races, Strokel won a six-day race in May 1887 at Philadelphia, beating top competition. He was a disappointing sixth in another Madison Square Garden six-day event in February 1888; the winner was James Albert, with a record of 621 miles, 1,350 yards. Albert retired, and Englishman George Littlewood won a six-day race at the Garden in May. The Garden's last major six-day race, which began on November 26, attracted several English runners and good crowds, who saw Littlewood break Albert's record with a distance of 623 miles, 1,320 yards. There was one more race at the Garden, in May of 1889, but none of the top runners took part. A cycling craze was beginning to sweep the country, and six-day bicycle races replaced the pedestrian events during the 1890s. A few itinerant runners hung on into the early 20th century, but crowds and purses continually declined; the age of amateur track and field had arrived.

Further Reading: Cumming, John. *Runners and Walkers: A Nineteenth Century Sports Chronicle.* Chicago: Regnery Gateway, 1981.

See also SIX-DAY RACES.

Pennsylvania International Raceway
Nazareth, PA

This 1-mile oval track, opened in 1987, annually hosts a 200-mile race in the Championship Auto Racing Teams' Indy car series. Since 1988 a 300-mile NASCAR Grand National race has also been held at the track.

Address: P.O. Drawer F, Highway 191, Nazareth, PA 18064 (215) 759–8000

Penske, Roger S. (1937–)
Auto Racing
Born February 20, 1937, Shaker Heights, OH

One of the most influential figures in auto racing, Penske was named driver of the year by *Sports Illustrated* in 1961 after winning the Sports Car Club of America D Modified title. In 1966, he founded Penske Racing with Mark Donohue as his engineer-driver. The team has won more than 50 Indy Car races, including five Indianapolis 500s, as well as eight national championships.

Dissatisfied with the U.S. Auto Club's administration, Penske in 1978 joined with another car owner, U. E. "Pat" Patrick, to form Championship Auto Racing Teams, which has overseen Indy car racing since 1979. The Penske Corporation, which operates Cadillac dealerships, manages Hertz Penske Truck Leasing and owns the Michigan International Speedway and the Pennsylvania International Raceway. The corporation also promotes CART's Cleveland Grand Prix.

Pentathlon

This five-event test of all-around ability included the 200- and 1,500-meter run, the discus and javelin throws, and the long jump. It was on the Olympic track and field program for men in 1906, 1912, 1920, and 1924, and it was a championship event at the AAU outdoor meet from 1920 through 1978. The women's pentathlon originally included the 100-meter hurdles, 200-meter run, shot put, high jump, and long jump; the 800-meter run replaced the 200-meter in 1971. It was a national championship event from 1950 through 1980, then was replaced by the heptathlon. The event was also on the Olympic program from 1964 through 1980.

Petanque

A kind of outdoor bowling game developed in France, petanque is played by fewer than 1,000 people in the United States. The Federation of Petanque U.S.A., founded as the American Petanque Association in 1976, oversees the sport.

Address: Federation of Petanque U.S.A., P.O. Box 19234, Washington, DC 20036 (202) 741–2494

Peterson Tournament
Bowling

Louis C. Peterson established this match-game bowling tournament in 1922. It used the Peterson Point System, which awards one point for each game won, one point for each 50 pins (or fraction thereof) knocked down, and one-half point for the highest pinfall in a three-game series. The Peterson became the Bowling Proprietors' Association of America match play tournament in 1933 and the BPAA All-Star Tournament in 1941. Since 1971 it has been the BPAA-PBA Open, an event on the Professional Bowlers Association tour.

Pettit, "Bob" Robert L. (1932–)
Basketball
Born December 12, 1932, Baton Rouge, LA; Basketball Hall of Fame

Pettit was the first big man with an accurate outside jump shot. Though some thought he was too slender, at 6-foot-9 and 216 pounds, to star in professional basketball, he was also a fine rebounder who used intelligence and finesse to beat bigger men to the ball. An All-American forward at Louisiana State University in 1954, Pettit joined the Milwaukee Hawks of the National Basketball Association for the 1954-55 season and became Rookie of the Year, averaging 20.4 points a game.

The Hawks moved to St. Louis the following season, when Pettit led the NBA in scoring with 25.7 points a game and in rebounding with 16.2 a game to win the league's Most Valuable Player award. He led the Hawks to the 1957–58 NBA championship in a six-game series against the Boston Celtics, scoring 50 points in the decisive game. Pettit won another scoring title in 1958–59, averaging 29.2 points, and was MVP for the second time. In his 11-season career, he was a first-team all-star nine times. He scored a total of 20,880 points, an average of 26.4 a game, and had a playoff scoring average of 25.5 points a game.

Petty, Richard L. (1937–)
Stock Car Racing
Born July 2, 1937, Randleman, NC

Undoubtedly the greatest stock car driver of all time, Petty won an even 200 races and had 356 other top-five finishes, winning nearly $7 million. He began his career in 1958, when one of the top drivers was

Richard Petty has 200 career Winston Cup victories, nearly 100 more than the runner-up. Courtesy of NASCAR Photo

his father, Lee, and in 1979 his son Kyle also became a NASCAR driver. He won the sport's top race, the Daytona 500, in 1964, 1966, 1971, 1973, 1974, 1979, and 1981, and was the Winston Cup champion in 1964, 1967, 1971, 1972, 1974, 1975, and 1979.

PFRA
See PROFESSIONAL FOOTBALL RESEARCHERS ASSOCIATION.

PGA
See PROFESSIONAL GOLFERS ASSOCIATION OF AMERICA.

PGA Championship
Golf
The first PGA Championship was a match play tournament held October 10–16, 1916, at the Siwanoy Country Club in Bronxville, NY. Thirty-one golfers competed for $2,580 in prize money, donated by department store magnate Rodman Wanamaker. It was not held in 1917 and 1918 because of World War I, but it resumed in 1919. The tournament

remained at match play until 1957, when it was changed to stroke play to accommodate television coverage.

PGA Champions

1916	James M. Barnes
1917–18	Not Played
1919	James M. Barnes
1920	Jock Hutchison
1921	Walter Hagen
1922	Gene Sarazen
1923	Gene Sarazen
1924	Walter Hagen
1925	Walter Hagen
1926	Walter Hagen
1927	Walter Hagen
1928	Leo Diegel
1929	Leo Diegel
1930	Tommy Armour
1931	Tom Creavy
1932	Olin Dutra
1933	Gene Sarazen
1934	Paul Runyan
1935	John Revolta
1936	Denny Shute
1937	Denny Shute
1938	Paul Runyan
1939	Henry Picard
1940	Byron Nelson
1941	Vic Ghezzi
1942	Sam Snead
1943	Not Played
1944	Bob Hamilton
1945	Byron Nelson
1946	Ben Hogan
1947	Jim Ferrier
1948	Ben Hogan
1949	Sam Snead
1950	Chandler Harper
1951	Sam Snead
1952	Jim Turnesa
1953	Walter Burkemo
1954	Chic Harbert
1955	Doug Ford
1956	Jack Burke, Jr.
1957	Lionel Hebert
1958	Dow Finsterwald
1959	Bob Rosburg
1960	Jay Hebert
1961	Jerry Barber
1962	Gary Player
1963	Jack Nicklaus
1964	Bob Nichols
1965	Dave Marr
1966	Al Geiberger
1967	Don January

1968	Julius Boros
1969	Ray Floyd
1970	Dave Stockton
1971	Jack Nicklaus
1972	Gary Player
1973	Jack Nicklaus
1974	Lee Trevino
1975	Jack Nicklaus
1976	Dave Stockton
1977	Lanny Wadkins
1978	John Mahaffey
1979	David Graham
1980	Jack Nicklaus
1981	Larry Nelson
1982	Ray Floyd
1983	Hal Sutton
1984	Lee Trevino
1985	Hubert Green
1986	Bob Tway
1987	Larry Nelson
1988	Jeff Sluman
1989	Payne Stewart
1990	Wayne Grady

Philadelphia, PA

Baseball Philadelphia had a team in the National League during its first season, 1876, then dropped out until 1883, when the present franchise was established. The Phillies were World Series champions in 1980 and also won pennants in 1915, 1950, and 1983.

Philadelphia was also in the American Association from 1882 through 1891, winning the pennant in 1883; in the Union Association and the Players' League during their only seasons, 1884 and 1890 respectively; and in the American League from its founding in 1901 until 1955, when the team moved to Kansas City. The American League's Athletics won the World Series in 1910, 1911, 1913, 1929, and 1930, and were also pennant winners in 1914 and 1931.

Basketball The Philadelphia Warriors won the Basketball Association of America's playoffs in its first season, 1946–47. The team moved to San Francisco in 1962, after the BAA had become the National Basketball Association, and the following year the Syracuse Nationals became the Philadelphia 76ers. The 76ers won NBA championships in 1967 and 1983.

Football The Frankford Yellowjackets, representing a section of Philadelphia, entered the National Football League in 1924. They won the 1926 NFL championship. The team became the Philadelphia Eagles in 1933 and won titles in 1948, 1949, and 1960.

Hockey The National Hockey League admitted the Philadelphia Flyers as an expansion team in 1967. They were Stanley Cup champions in 1974 and 1975.

See also CONNIE MACK STADIUM; SPECTRUM, THE; VETERANS STADIUM.

Phoenix, AZ

Basketball The Phoenix Suns entered the National Basketball Association as an expansion franchise in 1968. They won the Pacific Division championship in 1981 but were eliminated in the semifinal playoff round.

Football Phoenix got a long-sought-after National Football League team in 1988, when the Cardinals moved from St. Louis.

See also SUN DEVIL STADIUM; VETERANS MEMORIAL COLISEUM.

Phoenix International Raceway

A 1-mile oval track, Phoenix opened in 1964 and hosted two Indy car races, of 100 and 200 miles, that year. The raceway is now the site of two 200-mile Championship Auto Racing Teams races annually. Since 1988, it has also hosted a 500-mile race in the National Association for Stock Car Racing's Winston Cup Series.

Address: 1313 North Second Street, Suite 1300, Phoenix, AZ 85004 (602) 252–3833

Physical Education

Benjamin Franklin espoused the value of exercise in a 1749 pamphlet, *Proposals Relating to the Education of Youth in Pennsylvania,* but physical education was little thought of until 1825, when Dr. Charles Beck was hired as instructor of gymastics at Round Hill School in Northampton, MA. Beck, a native of Germany, was a member of Friedrich Jahn's Turner Movement, and other Turners who arrived in the late 1840s and 1850s promoted gymnastics for school curricula. Horace Mann had recommended that every school should have some type of exercise on its daily curriculum, and medical textbooks of the early 19th century called for regular exercise, but schools largely ignored physical education until late in the century.

There were a few pioneering cities, led by Boston, which required daily exercise beginning in 1853. By 1860, Brooklyn, Cincinnati, Hartford and Toledo had high school gyms and physical exercise programs. On the college level, Amherst College pioneered the movement in 1861, when Edward Hitchcock, newly appointed professor of hygiene and physical education, was placed in charge of the school's new gymnasium. The North American Turnerbund opened a training school for physical education teachers in Rochester, NY, also in 1861. The school was shut down during the Civil War and reopened afterward.

Dudley A. Sargent, who became director of the Harvard gymnasium in 1879, was a leading proponent of physical education. He wrote in 1883 that physical education was vital for creating "fitness for work, fitness for play, fitness for anything a man may be called upon to do." The YMCA shortly afterward began emphasizing sports and physical education to develop the all-around Christian man, "with his physical nature healthy, strong, evenly developed and well disciplined; his spiritual nature strong, well balanced and trained." The YMCA founded its first training school at Springfield, MA in 1887 and opened a second in Chicago three years later.

The Association for the Advancement of Physical Education was founded in 1885 with a number of German-American Turner leaders as members, and during the 1890s the Turner system of gymastics was introduced into many school programs. Swedish gymastics, brought to North America by Hartvig Nissen in 1883, was also added to many curricula. Another Swede, Baron Nills Posse, in 1889 founded the Boston Normal School of Gymnastics with the support of several prominent Bostonians. As a result, Boston schools adopted the Swedish system, followed by many other eastern cities.

California had passed a law requiring two daily 5-minute periods for gymnastics and "breathing exercises" as early as 1866. In 1892 Ohio required physical education in larger schools, largely because of lobbying by the Turners, and a few other states followed suit in the 1890s and early 1900s. During the early 20th century, physical educators began to replace rigid calisthenics and exercise programs with recreational and sports activities, including intramurals. Physical educators were asked by the War Department to develop training programs in military camps during World War I, because the general level of physical fitness was so poor. That led to a much greater awareness of physical education's importance; from 1914 through 1921, 25 states passed physical education laws, and several other states revised existing laws.

There weren't enough physical education teachers available to meet the sudden demand, and many colleges began adding curricula in physical education. New York University and Columbia were the first schools to offer doctorates in the field, in 1924. By 1933, graduate courses were being offered by 31 colleges.

The emphasis of physical education changed considerably during the 1930s. Its chief goals were seen as helping develop social skills, including good sportsmanship, and teaching students how to use their leisure time productively. However, World War II again brought an emphasis on physical fitness that carried over after the war, as most states enacted new laws requiring longer periods of physical education as well as health and safety education. Again, there was a demand for more physical educators. By 1950, more than 400 colleges and universities were offering a major in physical education and the American Association for Health, Physical Education and Recreation (originally the American Physical Education Association) reached a new peak of 18,000 members.

See also GYMNASIUM MOVEMENT.

Pimlico Race Course
Baltimore, MD

Pimlico, established by the Maryland Jockey Club, held its first races on October 25, 1870, and a horse named Preakness won the first stakes race held that day. Three years later, the Preakness Stakes, now one of the Triple Crown races for three-year-olds, was inaugurated. The main track at Pimlico is a 1-mile loam oval, and there is an inner 7/8-mile turf course, added in 1954. Total seating is about 20,000, and the infield, which has been used since 1967 only for the Preakness, holds an estimated 60,000 people.

Address: Maryland Jockey Club, Pimlico Race Course, Baltimore, MD 21215 (301) 542–9400

Ping Pong
See TABLE TENNIS.

Pistol Shooting
See SHOOTING.

Pittsburgh, PA

Baseball Baseball teams represented Pittsburgh in the American Association from 1882 through 1886, the Union Association in its one season, 1884, and the Players' League in its single season, 1890. The National League team, formed in 1887, became known the Pirates in 1891 after signing second baseman Louis Bierbauer, who belonged to the new Philadelphia team in the American Association. The Pirates won National League pennants in 1901, 1902, 1903, 1927, 1971, and 1979. They were World Series champions in 1960, 1971, and 1979.

Basketball The Pittsburgh Ironmen were in the Basketball Association of America when it was founded in 1946, but the team lasted only one season. The Pittsburgh Pipers won the first American Basketball Association championship in 1967–68; that franchise moved to Minnesota the following season. In 1969, the team moved back to Pittsburgh and became known as the Condors. The team folded when the ABA merged with the National Basketball Association in 1976.

Football Founded in 1933, the Pittsburgh team in the National Football League was originally called the Pirates, after the baseball team. It was renamed the Steelers in 1940. The Steelers moved into the American Football Conference after the 1970 merger of the NFL and the American Football League. They were AFC champions in 1974, 1975, 1978, and 1979, and won four Super Bowls.

Hockey The Pittsburgh Pirates entered the National Hockey League in 1925. The franchise moved to Philadelphia after the 1929–30 season. In 1967, the Pittsburgh Penguins joined the league as an expansion team. They won the 1991 Stanley Cup.

See also FORBES FIELD; PITTSBURGH CIVIC ARENA; THREE RIVERS STADIUM.

Pittsburgh Civic Arena
Pittsburgh, PA

Built by the city of Pittsburgh at a cost of about $22 million, the Civic Arena formally opened on September 17, 1961. Capacity was expanded by 1,800 seats in 1966, 1,100 seats in 1972, and 1,000 seats in 1973. Two balconies were added in 1974, adding another 3,000 seats, and in 1988 and 1989 about $11 million was spent on renovation, including the addition of superboxes. Seating capacity is now 16,025. The arena since 1967 has been the home rink of the National Hockey League's Pittsburgh Penguins. It hosts many other sports events, including boxing matches, high school and college basketball, indoor football, lacrosse, and wrestling.

Plante, "Jake the Snake" J. Jacques O. (1929–   )
Hockey

Born January 17, 1929, Shawinigan Falls, Quebec; Hockey Hall of Fame

He was one of the greatest goaltenders of all time, but Plante may well go down in history as the man who invented the goalie mask after being hit in the face by a shot on November 1, 1959. He had been trying out a mask in practice before the injury; when he returned to hockey after recovering, he wore it all the time and other goaltenders began to follow his example. Originally, the mask was form-fitting and made of hard plastic, but in the 1970s the "cage," an iron grid similar to the baseball catcher's mask, was developed, and all goalies now wear that type.

Plante also pioneered the technique of skating well out of his net to get the puck and pass it. Other goalies now use the technique, but not to the extent Plante did, because he was an excellent skater. He joined the Montreal Canadiens during the 1952–53 season and played for six Stanley Cup champions, in 1953 and from 1956 through 1960. He was traded to the New York Rangers in 1963, to the St. Louis Blues in 1968, to the Toronto Maple Leafs in 1970, and to the Boston Bruins during the 1972–73 season. He retired in 1973, but returned briefly with the Edmonton Oilers of the World Hockey Association in 1974–75 before retiring for good. Plante won the Vezina Trophy as the NHL's best goalie from 1956 through 1960 and in 1962; he shared the award with Glenn Hall in 1969. He won the Hart Trophy, the league's Most Valuable Player Award, in 1962.

Platform Tennis

This sport was almost accidentally created by two Scarsdale, NY tennis players in the winter of 1928–29. Fessenden S. Blanchard and James K. Cogswell built an elevated platform in Cogswell's backyard, reasoning it would be easy to clear of snow. The court was the right size for badminton, but the windy winter weather wasn't right. Finally, they found some paddle tennis paddles and a couple of sponge rubber balls. They called their new sport "mini-tennis." But chasing the ball when it went off the platform was a problem, so they put a fence around the court and decided that the ball was still in play if it hit the fence—as with the walls in squash or racquetball.

Now the sport was called "paddle tennis," which was confusing, because the paddles they used were from a different sport, also called paddle tennis. The American Paddle Tennis Association was founded in 1934; it became the American Platform Tennis Assocation in 1950, when the name of the sport also changed. The APTA held its first national championship tournaments in 1935. There was a men's singles event, as well as men's, women's, and mixed doubles, but the singles competition was dropped in 1938 and since then all formal competition has been in doubles.

Platform tennis went through a kind of boom in the early 1970s, when many courts were built at municipal parks, playgrounds, colleges, and resorts. Two major tournaments, in 1973 and 1974, were nationally televised, and in 1975 a grand prix tour was established for men, followed by a similar tour for women players in 1976.

Address: American Platform Tennis Association, Box 901, Upper Montclair, NJ 04073 (201) 744–1190

See also PADDLE TENNIS.

Playdays

The people in charge of women's scholastic and collegiate sports were generally opposed to all-out competition during the early part of this century. During the 1920s, the playday evolved as a substitute. On playdays, women from several schools were assembled for a wide range of activities from hopscotch to field hockey, and even the appearance of interschool competition was avoided by forming teams randomly made up of women from different schools. The emphasis was more on socialization than competition, with frequent breaks for tea, juice, and cookies. One woman athlete said of that era, "We had fun at these playdays, and we enjoyed the tea and the sociability—but the better players among us felt frustrated by the lack of meaningful team play." A 1926 survey of colleges showed that only 12 percent took part in intercollegiate competition, but 80 percent participated in playdays. During the 1950s, playdays were gradually replaced by intramural and intercollegiate competition.

See also WOMEN IN SPORTS.

Player Drafts

Although the player draft is most commonly associated with modern professional basketball and football, the idea originated in baseball in 1892, when the National League and a group of minor league, signed a National Agreement that set up two minor-league classes, A and B. Major-league teams could draft Class A players for $1,000 each, and Class A teams could draft Class B players for $500 apiece. The basic purpose of the system was to prevent the majors from raiding the minors for players, as had happened during the 1891 war between the National League and the American Association.

Because of the development of the farm system, with most minor-league teams controlled by major-league teams through either outright ownership or a working agreement, that draft system was replaced in 1965 by a draft of amateur players. Once a team drafts an amateur player, it has the exclusive right to sign him until the next annual draft; if he has not signed, his name goes back into the pool and he can be drafted by another team.

The National Hockey League has a similar draft of amateur players. Most of the players chosen are from junior leagues in Canada, but an increasing number of draftees are college players.

In 1936, the National Football League adopted its draft of college players. The team with the worst record is given the first choice, the defending champion the last choice. The league's official position is that the draft helps strengthen weaker teams to keep a good competitive balance, but of course it also works to limit salaries by eliminating competition among teams for top players. The first player chosen was Heisman Trophy winner Jay Berwanger of the University of Chicago, by the Philadelphia Eagles, who traded the rights to the Chicago Bears. Berwanger chose not to play professionally.

The draft was originally limited to players who had no college eligibility remaining, but in 1990 the NFL began to allow a college junior to enter the pool, provided that he signs a certificate giving up his remaining eligibility.

When the Basketball Association of America (now the National Basketball Association) was organized in 1946, it adopted a college draft patterned after the NFL's. The rival American Basketball Association, which began operating in 1967, originally had the same kind of draft, but in 1969 it allowed an undergraduate to enter the draft as a "hardship case" by filing a declaration that he needed the money he could earn in professional basketball—a transparent ploy allowing ABA teams to sign outstanding college players before the NBA could have a chance. The hardship rule stayed in effect for the NBA draft after the two leagues merged in 1976. Like the NFL, the NBA now allows a college player to announce he wants to enter the draft before he's used up his eligibility.

Players' Associations

Major-league baseball players formed three short-lived "unions," the Brotherhood of Professional Base Ball Players in 1885, the Protective Association of Professional Baseball Players in 1900, and the Base Ball Players' Fraternity in 1912 (see individual entries). In 1953, the Major League Baseball Players Association was founded, primarily to negotiate a pension plan. The MLBPA became much more militant in 1966 when Marvin Miller, an experienced labor professional who had worked for the United Steelworkers of America, was hired as full-time executive director.

One of Miller's first victories was winning more money for the players from the Topps Chewing Gum Company, which had been paying just $125 for the right to use a player's photo on bubble-gum cards. Miller in early 1968 persuaded the players to hold out and ultimately won a contract worth several million dollars a year in royalties. Shortly afterward, the first basic agreement was signed, raising the minimum salary from $7,000 to $10,000 and establishing a formal procedure for settling grievances.

The second basic agreement, signed in May of 1970 after bitter negotiation, was a major landmark in player relations. For the first time, the MLBPA was formally recognized as the collective bargaining agent for all players; the minimum salary was raised to $12,000 in 1970, with an increase to $15,000 in 1972; players were given the right to be represented by agents or lawyers during contract negotiations; and, most important in the long run, a provision was made for a neutral arbitrator to settle any disputes arising from the agreement.

The first general strike in professional sports history began on April 1, 1972, when the players walked out of spring training because of the owners' refusal to add a cost-of-living increase to medical benefits and the pension plan. They got the increase, but only after 86 regular-season games were canceled. Another strike was threatened before a new basic agreement was signed in March of 1973. This agreement gave the players the right to salary arbitration, another landmark. Under the arbitration system, which is still in use, the team and the player each submits a figure to an arbitrator, who then selects one or the other. The right to arbitration was extended to any player with two or more years of major-league experience.

The last big breakthrough came in 1975, when the association filed grievances on behalf of pitchers Dave McNally and Andy Messersmith, who had played the season without signing contracts. Under baseball's reserve clause, they were still bound to their teams—Messersmith to the Los Angeles Dodgers, McNally to the Baltimore Orioles—but the MLBPA contended that after a single year they should be free agents, while the owners insisted that the clause bound them to a team perpetually. Arbitrator Peter Seitz in December ruled that they were free agents. The Basic Agreement signed in July of 1976 was a compromise, granting free agency to a player after six years of major-league service.

That was a five-year agreement, two years longer than its predecessors. During negotiation for the next agreement in 1981, the owners insisted that a team losing a free agent should receive a player from his new team in compensation. The players, naturally, were adamantly opposed to that idea, and on June 12 they went on strike. They were out for 50 days, finally agreeing to a three-year contract on July 31. The result was the only split season in modern major-league history. The teams who had been leading their divisions at the time of the strike were declared first-half champions and all teams started

the second half with clean slates. After the season, the first-half champions played the second-half champions in division playoff series.

Negotiations in 1984 again went slowly, and the association went on strike on August 6. However, a five-year agreement was reached the following day, and the season resumed on August 8. The amount of experience required to go into arbitration was increased from two years to three years. That became a major sticking point in 1990, when the players wanted to go back to a two-year minimum. Anticipating a spring training lockout by the owners, the association had built a $60 million reserve fund, mostly from royalties on trading cards, action figures, and other items bearing players' names or likenesses. The lockout ended after a compromise was reached; two-year players with at least 86 days of service the previous season were allowed to go to arbitration under a four-year contract that was signed on March 18. Although the beginning of the season was postponed for a week, the missed games were rescheduled later.

Like the MLBPA, the National Football League Players Association was mainly interested in getting a pension plan when it was organized in 1957. But the association in 1968 sought a higher minimum salary and the right to representation during salary negotiations, and threatened to strike over the issues. In response, the owners said they would lock the players out by not opening training camps. But CBS, not wanting to lose any televised games, pressured the owners to give in; the minimum salary was increased from $5,000 to $12,000, and players did get the right to representation.

In 1970, the players won increased pension benefits by once again threatening to strike, but four years later the sides couldn't agree at all. Despite brief preseason strikes in 1974 and 1975, a new collective bargaining agreement wasn't reached until 1977. In the meantime, the players won an important court case. The standard NFL contract included the so-called option clause, which gave a team an option on a player's services for one year after his contract expired. By "playing out his option," a player could become a free agent. Commissioner Pete Rozelle had ruled that his former team should receive compensation from his new. But in 1975, a federal court decided that the Rozelle rule was a violation of antitrust laws. When the new collective bargaining agreement was finally signed on February 16, 1977, it provided for compensation in the form of a draft choice or choices.

NFLPA Executive Director Ed Garvey made a radical proposal in 1982, asking that the players receive

55 percent of the teams' gross receipts, with each player's years in the league and incentive bonuses to determine his share. The owners balked, and two weeks into the season the players went on strike. However, the new agreement, signed on November 16 after a 57-day strike, made no essential changes in the system.

Free agency was the major issue in 1987, when the association once more called a strike during the season. This time, the owners were prepared. After a one-week delay, they played games with replacement teams made up of free agents and some regular players who refused to strike. Other veterans began to cross the picket lines, and after three weeks the strike was called off.

There was still no agreement in February of 1989, when the owners unilaterally made a major change in the league's labor policy by adopting their own free-agency plan, allowing each team to protect 37 players, with the other 10 players on the regular-season roster becoming "Plan B" free agents. In the meantime, the NFLPA had sued the league on antitrust grounds, seeking to overturn the option clause, which would have made every player a free agent after his contract expired. A federal court ruled that the option clause should be a collective bargaining issue. In response, the NFLPA asked to be decertified as a collective bargaining unit, an action unprecedented in labor history. Lacking both the strong leadership and solid common sense of the MLBPA, the association was in complete disarray and in serious financial trouble because it had lost the power to have dues automatically deducted from players' pay with the expiration of the agreement.

Boston Celtics star Bob Cousy almost single-handedly organized the National Basketball Players Association in 1952. Like its counterparts in baseball and football, the association was not very active until it hired a full-time executive director, Lawrence Fleisher, in 1962. Fleisher won his first victory, an improved pension plan, with the threat of a ministrike at the 1964 all-star game. The all-star players refused to come out of their locker rooms until the owners promised to improve the plan, and the owners agreed at the last moment in order to avoid losing the game, an important television showcase for the NBA.

NBA players got a minimum salary for the first time in 1968. The minimums were set at $10,000 for rookies, to increase to $13,000 in 1970, and $12,500 for veterans, to increase to $13,500 in 1970—extremely modest figures compared with today's salaries. They were helped by the formation in 1967 of the rival American Basketball Association, which forced salaries to increase by bidding for college talent and some established stars. ABA competition was so helpful that, when the leagues announced plans to merge in 1970, the NBAPA brought suit to prevent the merger on antitrust grounds and won a restraining order on April 16. The association finally agreed to drop its suit in 1975 in exchange for $5 million in damages. It also won a qualified kind of free agency: A player can now sign an offer sheet from any team after his contract expires, but his former team is given a chance to match the offer in order to keep him.

See also BASE BALL PLAYERS FRATERNITY; BROTHERHOOD OF PROFESSIONAL BASE BALL PLAYERS; NATIONAL BASEBALL PLAYERS ASSOCIATION OF THE U.S.; PROTECTIVE ASSOCIATION OF PROFESSIONAL BASEBALL PLAYERS.

Players' League
Baseball

For the 1889 season, baseball's owners adopted a Classification Plan that set maximum salaries for players in each of five classifications, ranging from $1,500 for Class E to $2,500 for Class A. The Brotherhood of Professional Base Ball Players immediately objected and actually considered a strike on July 4, but their president, John Montgomery Ward, came up with a better idea. He and Albert L. Johnson, owner of a streetcar line in Cleveland, met on July 14 to talk about forming a new league that would operate as a cooperative combining players and backers rather than owners.

The Players' National League of Base Ball Clubs, as it was formally known, was organized on November 4. Originally, there were to be teams in Boston, Chicago, Cleveland, Indianapolis, New York, Philadelphia, Pittsburgh, and Washington, but Brooklyn and Buffalo eventually replaced Indianapolis and Washington. An eight-man board, with four representatives of the players and four representatives of the backers, ran each team. The league itself was governed by a senate made up of two representatives from each team, one chosen by the players, the other by the backers.

Player signed three-year contracts at their 1889 salaries, except that a player who had taken a pay cut because of the Classification Plan would receive his 1888 salary. The backers of a team were allowed to keep the first $10,000 in profits, with the next $10,000 going into a pool to be divided equally among all the league's players. Any profit over $20,000 would be shared among all the backers and all the players.

While local newspapers in major-league cities predictably attacked the Players' League, the sporting press was generally favorable. *Sporting News* commented, "The child is born. It is a big, strong, lively kicking infant."

To avoid a two-front war against both existing leagues, Ward's strategy was to keep the American Association neutral by raiding only National League teams. One estimate is that the league retained fewer than 40 of its players, while the association lost a relatively small number of players whose contracts had expired. There were even secret talks about a possible merger of the association and the Players' League into a single ten-team circuit, but they fell through.

Despite its wealth of talent and the fact that it probably drew more fans than the National League, the Players' League lasted only one season. In July, each team had to be assessed $2,500 to keep it afloat. A good pennant race had developed between Boston and Brooklyn, but a rainy September forced cancellation of many games down the stretch. The league lost about $340,000. The National League may have lost even more money—estimates range as high as $500,000—and it even lost its Cincinnati team in October when the owner sold out to the Players' League.

Allan W. Thurman, owner of the American Association's Columbus team, proposed a consolidation of the three leagues into two eight-team circuits. At a peace conference a few days later, Players' League representatives made the mistake of telling Albert G. Spalding exactly how big their losses had been. Spalding, the sporting goods magnate and owner of the Chicago team in the National League, then orchestrated the piece-by-piece dismantling of the Players League. He bought the league's New York and Chicago franchises, merging them into the existing National League franchises. The Pittsburgh Players' League team was similarly merged with its National League counterpart, and the owners of the Philadelphia franchise agreed to give it up in exchange for the National League's Washington team.

Some of the remaining backers and most of the players wanted to keep fighting, but the Players' League was moribund. It was officially dissolved in January of 1891, and its players were reassigned to the teams that had reserved them in 1889.

See also BROTHERHOOD OF PROFESSIONAL BASE BALL PLAYERS.

Playground Movement

The playground movement of the late 19th and early 20th centuries had its roots in the 1850s, when the park movement grew out of increasing concerns about the health of city dwellers and the increase in juvenile crime. The Massachusetts Medical Society expressed the rationale in 1850: "Open spaces would afford to the artisan and the poorer classes the advantages of fresh air and exercise . . ." Many major cities, including Baltimore, Brooklyn, Cincinnati, Hartford, New Haven, New Orleans, St. Louis and San Francisco, established public parks during the decade.

When Frederick Law Olmsted proposed construction of Central Park in New York City, the idea was immediately supported by William Cullen Bryant of the *New York Post* and by other editors. Most of its proponents saw the park as a pastoral refuge that would allow people to "enjoy at once the excitement of the streets and the charm of woods and fields," as the *Tribune* put it, and a few noted its potential for recreation as well. After Central Park opened in 1860, the *Spirit of the Times* enthused that it would bring sports "within the reach of every man in New York."

The park movement was stalled by the Civil War, but it received new impetus in the 1880s, as more and more people moved into the cities. However, those who favored the construction of parks weren't necessarily in favor of playgrounds. A report by New York's Small Parks Committee proposed, as late as 1897, that "the law should be amended as to *require* playgrounds to be made part of a park."

The playground movement *per se* is usually dated to 1885, when the Massachusetts Emergency and Hygiene Association put sand heaps at the Parmenter Street Chapel and the West End Nursery. During the next two years, sand piles were set out at eight other locations and by 1893 each sand garden was supervised. By 1899, the MEHA was sponsoring 21 playgrounds throughout the city of Boston. The association was also instrumental in persuading the city to build the Charlesbank outdoor gymnasium in 1889. Philadelphia opened two playgrounds in 1893. A playground had been established in New York in 1891, and in 1897 the city appropriated $30,000 for playgrounds and vacation schools.

Chicago soon became the model for other cities attempting to establish playground systems. Jane Addams' Hull House in 1893 opened a large playground, and three years later both the University Settlement of Northwestern University and the University of Chicago Settlement opened well-equipped playgrounds supported by private donations.

Six temporary school playgrounds were established in Chicago with a combination of public and private money during the summer of 1898. With many women's clubs, charitable organizations, and settlement houses backing playgrounds, the city formed a Special Parks Commission in the fall of 1899. An initial appropriation of $11,000 in 1900 grew to $110,000 by 1907, and the city in 1903 also approved a $5 million bond issue to build and equip new playgrounds. These playgrounds included field houses and gyms for boys and girls, and two instructors at each playground supervised activities ranging from folk dancing for the whole neighborhood to organized summer athletic leagues.

The early playground movement had focused on sand boxes, swing sets, slides, and other paraphernalia for young children. But Chicago's growing playground system also offered organized games and sports for older youths, and other cities began to follow that example in the early part of the 20th century, in part because of the leadership of the Playground Association of America, founded in 1906 by Luther Gulick and Joseph Lee. There were just 41 cities with supervised playgrounds in 1906; by 1917, there were 504.

Supervised play and moral leadership were vitally important in this phase of the playground movement. Joseph Lee expressed the philosophy: "What is wanted on the playground is not the teaching of baseball . . . but the influence of a man or woman of high character. . . . It is the incidental teaching by example that counts, especially on the moral side, and nowhere else does example count more than on the playground." Gulick's evolutionary theory of play held that certain specific activities were required at certain ages, so supervision was also necessary to ensure that the children were playing the sports and games that would contribute to their proper development.

By 1920, many public parks in medium-sized and large cities were in fact playgrounds in the newer meaning of the term, with softball and baseball diamonds, tennis courts, wading and swimming pools, basketball courts, and facilities for table tennis, croquet, horseshoes, tetherball and other sports. Growth slowed during the 1920s, but received a tremendous boost during the Great Depression when the federal government built or helped to build many recreational facilities. The number of communities with organized recreation programs more than doubled between 1934 and 1935, from 1,036 to 2,190, and the amount of money spent on the programs increased even more dramatically, from just over $7 million to nearly $42 million. To a great extent, the playground movement had reached its goal, and the Playground Association of America shifted its emphasis from getting playgrounds built to working for increased funding of programs.

Pocket Billiards
See BILLIARDS.

Pocono International Raceway
Long Pond, PA

This unique 2.5-mile "tri-oval" is a triangular course with curved turns of three different lengths. The track has hosted a 500-mile Indy car race since 1971. NASCAR established a 500-mile stock car race at Pocono in 1974, and a second NASCAR 500-mile event was added in 1982.

Address: P.O. Box 500, Long Pond, PA 18334 (717) 646–2300

Podoloff Trophy
Basketball

Named for Maurice Podoloff, president of the National Basketball Association from 1946 until 1963, this is the league's Most Valuable Player trophy. The winner is selected by a vote of the NBA players.

Podoloff Trophy Winners

1956	Bob Pettit, St. Louis
1957	Bob Cousy, Boston
1958	Bill Russell, Boston
1959	Bob Pettit, St. Louis
1960	Wilt Chamberlain, Philadelphia
1961	Bill Russell, Boston
1962	Bill Russell, Boston
1963	Bill Russell, Boston
1964	Oscar Robertson, Cincinnati
1965	Bill Russell, Boston
1966	Wilt Chamberlain, Philadelphia
1967	Wilt Chamberlain, Philadelphia
1968	Wilt Chamberlain, Philadelphia
1969	Wes Unseld, Baltimore
1970	Willis Reed, New York
1971	Lew Alcindor (Kareem Abdul-Jabbar), Milwaukee
1972	Kareem Abdul-Jabbar, Milwaukee
1973	Dave Cowens, Boston
1974	Kareem Abdul-Jabbar, Milwaukee
1975	Bob McAdoo, Buffalo
1976	Kareem Abdul-Jabbar, Los Angeles
1977	Kareem Abdul-Jabbar, Los Angeles
1978	Bill Walton, Portland
1979	Moses Malone, Houston
1980	Kareem Abdul-Jabbar, Los Angeles
1981	Julius Erving, Philadelphia
1982	Moses Malone, Houston
1983	Moses Malone, Houston
1984	Larry Bird, Boston
1985	Larry Bird, Boston
1986	Larry Bird, Boston

Pole Vault

During the early and middle 19th century, pole-vaulters sometimes competed for both distance and height. When the event became standard on the modern track and field program, it was for height only, and vaulting for distance died out. Originally, the pole was made of ash, cedar, or hickory and had three iron spikes in the base to allow the vaulter to plant it in the ground. Early in this century bamboo poles were brought in from Japan. The aluminum pole arrived after World War II, and the fiberglass pole, introduced in the early 1960s, revolutionized the event because its flexibility allows the vaulter to use it as a kind of catapult.

Until 1892, English vaulters used an unusual style, climbing up the pole while in flight, but elsewhere it was against the rules for the vaulter to move the upper hand after leaving the ground. The first man to exceed 11 feet using that restricted technique was Hugh Baxter of the United States in 1883. The record climbed quickly early in the century, as Norman Dole cleared 12 feet in 1904, Robert Gardner 13 feet in 1912, and Sabin Carr 14 feet in 1927. Like the 4-minute mile, the 15-foot pole vault seemed an insurmountable barrier until Cornelius Warmerdam finally broke it in 1940.

John Uelses, a German native and American citizen, exceeded 16 feet in 1962. He was one of the pioneers of the fiberglass pole. John Pennel, another American, cleared 17 feet in 1964. The first 18-foot vaulter was Chris Papanicolaou of Greece in 1970. The 19-foot barrier was broken in 1984 by the Soviet Union's Sergei Bubka, who cleared 20 feet in 1991.

See also RICHARDS, BOB; WARMERDAM, CORNELIUS.

Police Gazette
See NATIONAL POLICE GAZETTE.

Pollard, "Fritz" Frederick D. (1894–1986)
Football
Born January 27, 1894, Chicago, IL; died May 11, 1986; National Football Foundation Hall of Fame

The only black coach in the National Football League until 1989, Pollard was an All-American halfback at Brown University in 1916. He joined the Akron Pros in 1919, the year before the team entered the new American Professional Football Association, which

An 1876 match at the Westchester Polo Club's field was depicted by Harper's Weekly.

became the NFL in 1922. He was one of just four black players in the league during the early 1920s. Pollard was co-coach of the team with Elgie Tobin in 1921. He also played for Akron in 1922 and went to the Milwaukee Badgers in 1923. After a year out of football, Pollard was player-coach with Akron for two games and with Hammond for one game in 1925, then finished the season with Providence. He then became a successful businessman. At one time, he was theatrical agent for the great black singer-actor Paul Robeson, who had been a teammate of his in 1920.

Polo

Polo originated in Persia between the sixth century B.C. and the first century A.D. The sport spread to Arabia, China, Japan, and Tibet, where it got its name—the ball is made of willow wood, and *pulu* is the Tibetan word for willow. About 700 years ago, it arrived in India. The first Europeans to play polo were British tea planters in Assam, who founded a polo club in 1859. Then the sport was discovered by British Army officers, who in 1863 organized three clubs. Shortly afterward polo was brought to England by returning officers.

James Gordon Bennett, Jr. saw a match at Hurlingham in the spring of 1875 and brought mallets and balls back to the United States. He persuaded some wealthy friends to try the sport and had a railcar load of cow ponies shipped from Texas to New York. After practicing at Dickel's Riding Academy in New York City, Bennett and his friends played their first game there early in 1875. The first two U.S. polo clubs were the Westchester, formed in 1877 to play at Jerome Park Race Course, and the Meadow Brook, established in 1881. In 1890, when the U.S. Polo Association was organized, there were 8 clubs, and that increased to 33 by 1904.

Originally, there were eight players on a team. That was soon reduced to five and then to four, the present number, in 1881. The Hurlingham Club, which was the governing body in England, adopted an offside rule similar to that used in soccer, but the United States did away with the rule, allowing a player to receive a forward pass, which ultimately changed polo from a slow, cautious game to a fast-moving sport. Another innovation was the handicapping system adopted by the USPA in 1890. With handicapping, each player is rated at a certain number of goals, from 0 for a novice to 10 for an outstanding player, and a team is limited in the number of goals it can have on its roster. In a 12-goal match, for example, a team could have four 3-goal players or three 4-goal players and one novice.

The first international match was played at Newport on August 25, 1886, between England and the United States for the International Polo Challenge Cup. England won that game handily, 10–2, and took the cup home with a 14–2 victory in the second game. The United States traveled to England in 1902 to challenge for the cup, but, after winning the first game, lost the next two. In the meantime, top United States players developed a different style of play, featuring fast riding and long passes, as opposed to the slower, short-passing game of the British. That style won the cup in two straight games in 1909. After successful defenses in 1911 and 1913, the cup went back to England in 1914. The U.S. reclaimed it in 1921 and beat back British challenges in 1924, 1927, 1930, 1936, and 1939.

Another major international trophy was Copa de las Americas (the Cup of the Americas), for competition between Argentina and the United States. The United States won that cup in 1928 and 1932, Argentina won in 1936 and 1950, the last year of competition. The United States and Mexico played for the General Manuel Avila Camacho Cup in 1941 and twice in 1946, the United States winning each time.

After a long lapse, international polo began a comeback in 1971, when the Coronation Cup was offered for competition between the United States and England. European championships were established in 1980, and the first world tournament was held in 1985. Canadian teams had long been members of the USPA, but the International Polo Federation requires a country to have its own governing body to take part in the world championships, so the Canadian Polo Association (also known as Polo Canada) was founded in 1985. At the time, Canada

had only two polo clubs, in Toronto and Calgary, but there are now 16.

The USPA held its first National Open championship in 1904. After a five-year lapse, the tournament was held again in 1910 and in 1912. Since then, it has been held annually except for 1915, 1917–18, and 1942–45. Other major tournaments include the National Intercircuit, begun in 1925, the National 20-Goal (1939), the National 12–Goal (1924), and the Monty Waterbury Memorial Cup handicap tournament (1922).

Address: U.S. Polo Association, 4059 Iron Works Pike, Lexington, KY 40511 (606) 255–0593

See also BICYCLE POLO; CANADIAN POLO ASSOCIATION; HITCHCOCK, TOMMY; INDOOR POLO.

Polo Grounds
New York, NY

James Gordon Bennett in 1883 allowed John B. Day to build a baseball park on a large plot of land where he and his friends often played polo. The site, between Fifth and Six Avenues, was bordered by 110th and 112th Streets. Day owned two major-league teams, the Metropolitans of the American Association and a National League team that was soon to become known as the Giants. Both teams played at the new park, which was called the Polo Grounds after its former use.

In 1889, the city tore down Day's grandstand to make way for what is now Douglass Circle. The Giants played in Jersey City and at the St. George Cricket Grounds until their new park at Manhattan Field opened on July 8. Day also named this park the Polo Grounds. The wooden grandstand and bleachers held about 15,000 people. In 1890, the New York Players' League team built its own, larger grandstand just north of the Polo Grounds, and on May 12 the Giants' Mike Tiernan hit a mammoth home run that cleared the center field fence of the Polo Grounds and landed in the other park, where there was also a game going on. He was cheered by fans in both parks as he circled the bases.

The Players' League folded after one season; Day bought the larger park and the Giants began playing there in 1891. They were there for 20 seasons and two games, until a fire destroyed the grandstand on April 14, 1911. John T. Brush, who had become the Giants' owner in 1902, immediately negotiated a long-term lease with Harriet Coogan, owner of the land, and began building again. He said he wanted his new park to be "a model for all subsequent Base Ball structures." It was a concrete and steel structure with a horseshoe-shaped grandstand, allegorical bas-relief friezes on double-decked facade, and box seats designed after the royal boxes in the Roman Colosseum.

When it opened on June 28, 1911, it had only 16,000 seats, but by the time the Giants played in the World Series that year, the park could seat 34,000. Capacity was increased to 55,000 in 1924 by adding a second deck almost all the way around the outfield, leaving just some center field bleachers. Lights were installed in 1940, and the first night game was played there on May 24.

The Polo Grounds was probably home to more teams than any other stadium. The New York Yankees of the American League rented the park from the Giants for home games from 1913 through 1922, and after the Giants had moved to San Francisco in 1958 the expansion New York Mets spent their first two seasons, 1962 and 1963, there. The National Football League's New York Giants played there from 1925 through 1955, and the American Football League's New York Titans (now the Jets) also played at the Polo Grounds from 1960 through 1963. After Shea Stadium was completed in 1964, the park was torn down to allow expansion of a neighboring housing project.

Pontiac Silverdome
Pontiac, MI

Originally opened on August 23, 1975, as Pontiac Metropolitan Stadium, the Silverdome took its present name in 1976. The $55.7-million all-purpose facility has been the home field of the National Football League's Detroit Lions since it opened, and it was also the home court of the National Basketball Association's Detroit Pistons from 1978 until after the 1987–88 season. It was the first stadium to have an inflatable roof, made of Teflon-coated fiberglass. The Silverdome has also hosted college basketball, boxing matches, motocross racing, rodeos, and soccer. It seats 80,638 for football, 22,366 for basketball.

PONY Baseball

The name is an acronym of Protect Our Nation's Youth. PONY baseball was established in Washington, PA in 1951 as a six-team league for 13- and 14-year-old graduates of the Little League. The idea spread rapidly; in 1952, there were 106 leagues and more than 500 teams, and the first PONY League World Series was held. The following year, the Colt League was established in Martins Ferry, OH for 15- and 16-year-olds; it merged into the PONY League in 1959.

The PONY League broke away from its original idea in 1961 by organizing the Bronco League for 11- and 12-year-old players, overlapping with the Little League age group. The Bronco League, however, uses 90-foot base paths, whereas Little League base paths are 60 feet long. In 1970, the Mustang League was developed for 9- and 10-year-olds, using 60-foot base paths, and the Pinto League began for 7- and 8-year-olds, using 50-foot base paths. PONY Baseball then moved up in age, adding the Thorobred League for 17- through 20-year-olds in 1973. The ages were changed to 19 through 21, and the Palomino League was added for the 17–18 age group in 1977. The Thorobred League was dropped in 1984.

Girls can play PONY League baseball, and a separate softball for girls program was added in 1976. Generally, Bronco League is for girls 12 and under, and Colt League for 16 and under. In larger cities, the Mustang League is for players under 10, Bronco League for ages 11–12, PONY League for 13–14, Colt League for 15–16, and Palomino League for 17–18.

Address: P.O. Box 225, Washington, PA 15301 (412) 225–1060

See also BABE RUTH BASEBALL; LITTLE LEAGUE.

Pool
See BILLIARDS.

Portland, OR

Basketball The Portland Trail Blazers joined the National Basketball Association as an expansion franchise in 1970. They won the Pacific Division championship in 1973.

See also PORTLAND MEMORIAL COLISEUM.

Portland International Raceway
Portland, OR

This 1.915-mile, nine-turn road racing course was first used in 1984. It hosts an annual 200-mile race on the Championship Auto Racing Teams tour.

Address: 220 NW Second Avenue, Portland, OR 97209 (503) 227–8200

Portland Memorial Coliseum
Portland, OR

Opened in 1960, the Coliseum has been the home of the National Basketball Association's Portland Trail Blazers since the team was established in 1970. Seating capacity is 12,880.

Portsmouth, OH

Football The Portsmouth Spartans joined the National Football League in 1930 and played in the league for four seasons. The team moved to Detroit and became known as the Lions in 1934.

Pottsville, PA

Football In 1925, the Pottsville Maroons apparently had the National Football League championship wrapped up with a 10–2–0 record. But the franchise was suspended after the Maroons violated the Frankford Yellowjackets' territorial rights by playing a game in Philadelphia against a team of Notre Dame all-stars. Meanwhile, the Chicago Cardinals won two hastily scheduled games to finish with an 11–2–1 record and the championship. Pottsville was in the league only from 1925 through 1928, but some diehard fans periodically petition the NFL to award the 1925 title to the team.

Powder Puff Derby
Air Racing

Formally the International Air Race for Women, this race was established in 1947 by the Ninety-Nines, an organization of female pilots. Sportswriters sarcastically called it the Powder Puff Derby, and that name was proudly accepted by the organizers. The transcontinental race of about 2,500 miles is based on elapsed time. Night flying and instrument flying are prohibited, and the pilots have to land at designated airports for overnight stays.

Powerboat Racing

The first powered pleasure boats were so-called steam yachts. The name was evidently coined by Cornelius Vanderbilt, who applied it to his 2,000-ton sidewheel passenger steamer *North Star*, built in 1853. Other wealthy men began building steam yachts after the Civil War. Like sailing yachts, they were used primarily for cruising, but there were occasional challenge races and time trials. For efficiency, steam-powered boats had to be large, but the development of the naphtha engine in 1885 allowed construction of powerboats in the 30- to 40-foot range.

During the 1890s and early 1900s, boats powered by internal combustion engines proliferated, especially on Long Island Sound. They were generally custom-made, and owners often had impromptu races to determine which had the faster design. The American Power Boat Association was founded in 1903 by about 20 clubs that attended a meeting called by the Columbia Yacht Club. The APBA established a system of time allowances, based on yacht racing rules, to equalize competition, and in June of 1904 the association held its first major race, for the Challenge Cup. A second Challenge Cup race was held in September. The trophy, now known as the Gold

Cup, has been in competition ever since. Another major trophy was offered by Sir Alfred Harmsworth of England in 1903 for international competition. Races were held sporadically through 1933, and there were three races after World War II, but the trophy is no longer in competition.

A special racing commission appointed by the APBA in 1913 set up five competitive classifications: cruisers, express cruisers, displacement racers, hydroplanes, and open boats. The system was extensively revised ten years later by establishing classes based on engine displacement for hydroplanes and runabouts. There are now nine major racing categories and a large number of subclassifications within each category.

See also AMERICAN POWER BOAT ASSOCIATION.

Powerlifting

During the 1950s, bodybuilding and physique competitions started to gain some popularity among weight lifters, largely through the efforts of Joseph Weider, owner of the Your Physique Equipment Company in Montreal and founder of the International Federation of Body Builders (IFBB) in 1946. Bodybuilders use powerlifts, as opposed to the classic Olympic lifts. In addition to physique competitions, such as the Mr. Universe contest, they compete in three lifting events: the bench press, the dead lift, and the squat. The first U.S. powerlifting championship was held in 1964 in York, PA. More than 130 countries now belong to the IFBB, which has been attempting to have power lifting accepted as an Olympic sport. At one time the sport was widely associated with steroid use, but both the IFBB and the U.S. Powerlifting Federation, which was established in 1981, have adopted stringent testing programs.

Addresses: International Federation of Bodybuilders, 2875 Bates Road, Montreal, Quebec, Canada H3S 1B7; U.S. Powerlifting Federation, P.O. Box 18485, Pensacola, FL 32523 (904) 477–4863

See also WEIGHT LIFTING.

Preakness Stakes
Horse Racing

Established in 1873, the Preakness is the second oldest of the three Triple Crown races for thoroughbreds. It offers the richest trophy in North American sports, the Woodlawn Vase, created by Tiffany in 1860 and appraised at $1 million in 1983. The Preakness is run at Pimlico Race Course and is named for the first horse to win a stakes race at Pimlico. Originally 1½ miles, the distance was changed several

The unlimited hydroplane is the fastest powerboat. Dr. Robert Magoon drove this one to three U.S. offshore championships. Courtesy of Kiekhafer Aeromarine Motors, Inc.

times until 1925, when it was established at its present 1³⁄₁₆ miles.

Presidents' Trophy
Hockey

The National Hockey League board of directors presented this trophy to the league during the 1985–86 season. Named in honor of the league's past presidents, it is awarded to the team that has the NHL's best regular-season record.

Presidents' Trophy Winners

1986 Edmonton Oilers
1987 Edmonton Oilers
1988 Calgary Flames
1989 Calgary Flames
1990 Boston Bruins
1991 Chicago Black Hawks

Prince of Wales Trophy
Hockey

The Prince of Wales in 1924 gave this trophy to the National Hockey League for the team that had the best regular-season record. From 1927 through 1938, it was awarded to the team finishing first in the American Division. The NHL dropped its two-division setup for the 1938–39 season, and the trophy again went to the regular-season champion until expansion in 1966–67, when it became the eastern division championship trophy. With further expansion in 1981–82, the league split into four divisions and two conferences; since then, the trophy has been awarded to the team with the best record in the Prince of Wales Conference.

Prince of Wales Trophy Winners

1925 Montreal Canadiens
1926 Montreal Maroons
1927 Ottawa Senators
1928 Boston Bruins
1929 Boston Bruins
1930 Boston Bruins
1931 Boston Bruins
1932 New York Rangers
1933 Boston Bruins
1934 Detroit Red Wings
1935 Boston Bruins
1936 Detroit Red Wings
1937 Detroit Red Wings
1938 Boston Bruins
1939 Boston Bruins
1940 Boston Bruins
1941 Boston Bruins
1942 New York Rangers
1943 Detroit Red Wings

1944	Montreal Canadiens
1945	Montreal Canadiens
1946	Montreal Canadiens
1947	Montreal Canadiens
1948	Toronto Maple Leafs
1949	Detroit Red Wings
1950	Detroit Red Wings
1951	Detroit Red Wings
1952	Detroit Red Wings
1953	Detroit Red Wings
1954	Detroit Red Wings
1955	Detroit Red Wings
1956	Montreal Canadiens
1957	Detroit Red Wings
1958	Montreal Canadiens
1959	Montreal Canadiens
1960	Montreal Canadiens
1961	Montreal Canadiens
1962	Montreal Canadiens
1963	Toronto Maple Leafs
1964	Montreal Canadiens
1965	Detroit Red Wings
1966	Montreal Canadiens
1967	Chicago Black Hawks
1968	Montreal Canadiens
1969	Montreal Canadiens
1970	Chicago Black Hawks
1971	Boston Bruins
1972	Boston Bruins
1973	Montreal Canadiens
1974	Boston Bruins
1975	Buffalo Sabres
1976	Montreal Canadiens
1977	Montreal Canadiens
1978	Montreal Canadiens
1979	Montreal Canadiens
1980	Buffalo Sabres
1981	Montreal Canadiens
1982	New York Islanders
1983	New York Islanders
1984	New York Islanders
1985	Philadelphia Flyers
1986	Montreal Canadiens
1987	Philadelphia Flyers
1988	Boston Bruins
1989	Montreal Canadiens
1990	Boston Bruins
1991	Boston Bruins

Pro Bowl

See ALL-STAR GAMES.

Professional Bowlers Association of America (PBA)

The PBA was founded in 1958 by Eddie Elias, an attorney from Akron, OH. There were 33 charter members. The first PBA tour, in 1959, included only three tournaments with a total of $49,500 in prize money. But Elias kept lining up sponsors, and the tour grew to 7 tournaments in 1960, 11 in 1961, 32 in 1962, and 38 in 1963, when prize money reached $1 million. Although the number of tournaments dropped to 31 the following year, prize money increased to about $1.2 million. The first real big-money event, the $100,000 Firestone Tournament of Champions, was added to the tour in 1965.

In 1969, the PBA inaugurated its National Resident Professional Championship at Cincinnati, for bowling pros who work as instructors at lanes, and in 1970 it set up a regional tournament program as a stepping-stone to the pro tour for younger professional bowlers. Major additions to the tour in 1971 were the Brunswick World Open, with 20 top foreign bowlers competing against the best American professionals, and the BPAA-PBA Open, which had previously been the BPAA All-Star Tournament, not affiliated with the professional tour.

Earl Anthony in 1975 became the first bowler ever to earn more than $100,000 in a year—more than twice the total prize money available just 17 years earlier. Like other professional sports, bowling profited greatly from television. ABC has been the major network for the PBA, beginning with the finals of the National PBA invitational in 1961. Thirty-three of the 34 national championships were televised in 1979, with ABC covering the winter tour, CBS the summer tour, ESPN five of the six fall tour events, and NBC the PBA Doubles Classic.

Seagram's took over sponsorship of the BPAA-PBA Open in 1987, turning it into the first $500,000 tournament in history. The tours now offer an average total of about $200,000 per tournament; ABC still does the winter tour and part of the spring tour, and ESPN covers the summer tour.

Address: 1720 Merriman Road, P.O. Box 5118, Akron, OH 44313 (216) 836–5568

Professional Football Researchers Association (PFRA)

The PFRA was established during a meeting June 21–23, 1979, in Canton, OH, the home of the Pro Football Hall of Fame, by about two dozen researchers concerned by the amount of misinformation being disseminated on the early history of the sport. Membership is now about 220. The association issues a bimonthly newsletter, Coffin Corner, and has also published several monographs and booklets. (A "coffin corner" is an area of the sideline, near the opponent's goal line, where a punter attempts to kick the ball out of bounds to put the opponent in dangerous territory.)

Address: 12870 Route 30, North Huntingdon, PA 15642

Professional Golfers' Association of America (PGA)

Rodman Wanamaker, the Philadelphia department store magnate, called a meeting of professional golfers at the Teplow Club in New York City on January 17, 1916. "Gentlemen," he told them, "I think you should have a national organization. If you are interested, I will donate $2,580 as prize money for a tournament." With that incentive, the PGA was formally established by 82 charter members on April 10, 1916, at the Hotel Martinique, and the first PGA championship tournament was held October 10–16 at the Siwanoy Country Club in Bronxville. "Long Jim" Barnes beat Jock Hutchison, Sr. in the final of the match-play tournament.

In the early years of the PGA, virtually every professional golfer worked for a club as an instructor. The professional tour wasn't really established until 1936, when the PGA hired Fred Corcoran as its first tournament director. In ten years, Corcoran built the tour from 11 tournaments with a total of about $50,000 in prize money to more than 30 tournaments worth about $750,000, and the top professional golfers were full-time tour competitors.

The association now has about 9,800 members and more than 5,000 apprentices. Most members are club pros or assistant pros. Only about 225 of them play golf for a living on the PGA Tour, which has been a separate entity with its own governing body, the Tournament Players Division, and its own commissioner since 1968. Prize money is now approaching $100 million.

The PGA has several operating areas, including club operations, management and administration, marketing and communications, and member services. It conducts training for its members in business schools and workshops across the country, hosts the golf industry's largest annual trade event, the PGA Merchandise Show, publishes a monthly magazine, and presents a variety of awards. Among its tournaments are the Club Professional Championship, inaugurated in 1968; the Seniors' Championship (1937); the World Series of Golf (1962); the PGA Assistants' Championship (1977); the National Junior Championship (1976); and the PGA Cup Matches (1973).

Since 1961, the PGA has been based in Palm Beach Gardens, FL at the PGA National Golf Club, which includes a 72-hole course. The association also administers the World Golf Hall of Fame in Pinehurst, NC.

Address: P.O. Box 109601, Palm Beach Gardens, FL 33410–9601 (305) 626–3600

See also PGA CHAMPIONSHIP; TOURNAMENT PLAYERS DIVISION.

Professional Rodeo Cowboys Association (PRCA)

The PRCA had its roots in an informal organization of rodeo cowboys who got together in 1936 to work for better purses and better judges. They called themselves the Cowboys' Turtle Association because progress was so slow. In 1945, the group became the Rodeo Cowboys Association. Undoubtedly the biggest step toward its present prosperity was the establishment of the National Finals Rodeo in 1959.

Despite the name, which it took in 1975, the PRCA now includes members from all facets of the sport, including rodeo organizing committees and stock contractors. The association sanctions more than 600 rodeos a year and has 6,000 contestant members and another 3,000 permit-card holders who compete in smaller rodeos. A permit-card holder must earn at least $2,500 before being entitled to full membership.

Since 1976, the PRCA has operated Procom, a computerized system that allows cowboys to enter sanctioned rodeos by making a phone call to the association's headquarters in Colorado Springs. The association also operates a computerized news service for the media, assigns professional officials to rodeos, and publishes a weekly newspaper, *Prorodeo Sports News*. The PRCA shares a $2.5 million building with the Prorodeo Hall of Champions and Museum of the American Cowboy.

Address: 101 Prorodeo Drive, Colorado Springs, CO (719) 593–8840

Professional Women's Bowling Association
See LADIES PROFESSIONAL BOWLERS TOUR.

Pro Football Hall of Fame
Canton, OH

Because the National Football League was formally organized in a meeting at Canton, OH in 1920, the city was chosen as the site for the Pro Football Hall of Fame in 1961. The hall formally opened on September 7, 1963, with the induction of 17 charter members. There were originally two buildings in the complex; a third building was added in 1971 and a fourth in 1978 to bring the total area to 51,000 square feet. The hall includes an area tracing the history of professional football, an art gallery, a room devoted to enshrinees and the teams they played for, an "adventure room" that has special exhibits on such subjects as blacks in pro football, and a 350-seat movie theater. Its library contains many original documents on the sport, including a ledger from the Allegheny Athletic Association of Pittsburgh that shows W. W. "Pudge" Heffelfinger was paid $500 for one game in 1892, thus becoming the first known professional player.

Address: 2121 George Halas Drive, N.W., Canton, OH 44708 (216) 456–8207

Protective Association of Professional Baseball Players

The Protective Association was organized on June 10, 1900, by three delegates from each of the eight National League teams. Dave Harris of the American Federation of Labor attended the meeting, but the players decided not to become affiliated with the AFL. In late July, they approved a constitution drawn up by lawyer Harry L. Taylor, a former major-league pitcher. The document was virtually a manifesto. It called for player approval of any trade or sale, an end to unjust fines, and a limitation on the reserve clause. The players agreed not to sign contracts for the 1901 season until their demands were met, except with Taylor's approval of the contract language.

Predictably, owners were furious. John Rogers of Philadelphia said, "When the players band together in an effort to dictate to us the manner in which we shall conduct our business, it will be time for the magnates to retire," and Arthur H. Soden of Boston said he simply didn't believe in any sort of union. But the press was generally favorable. *Sporting Times* said, "The wonder is that the union for self-protection against intolerable oppression has been so long delayed," while *Sporting News* suggested that players were in the right on their chief demands because "civil law does not permit the sale of a personal contract."

Taylor was asked to put the players' demands in writing, and he responded by adding several things to the list, including a board of arbitration to settle disputes, team payment of medical bills, and a player's right to "release" his team, just as the team could release him, with ten days' notice. The National League rejected the entire set of demands. But the American League was now claiming major-league status, and its president, Ban Johnson, agreed to recognize the association and accept its demands. Charles "Chief" Zimmer, a Pittsburgh catcher and the association president, was acting as spokesman because Taylor had other legal business to handle. Zimmer then went back to the National League to renegotiate; the league agreed to limit the reserve clause and to prohibit the sale or farming out of a player without his consent, but only if the Association agreed to expel any player who went to the American League.

The players were upset by Zimmer's apparent sellout, but, as *Sporting Life* pointed out, he had left a loophole. The agreement provided that a player who jumped to the American League would be expelled "pending action on the case by the Association as a body." There was no way that the association, meeting as a body, would actually vote to expel a player who changed leagues for more money. But the question was academic, anyway. Johnson was just as strongly opposed to a players' union as the National League, and was only using the Protective Association to help his new major league land more players, while the National League conceded some of its demands only to keep players from jumping. By the end of the year, the two major leagues had made peace, and the Protective Association was out of business.

See also PLAYERS' ASSOCIATIONS.

Providence, RI

Baseball Providence had a team, the Greys, in the National League from 1878 through 1885. The team won pennants in 1879 and 1884.
Football The Providence Steamroller played in the National Football League from 1925 through 1931 and won the 1928 NFL championship.

Psychology, Sports

Athletes and others have long known that the right mental attitude can improve performance. As early as 1908, Arnold Haultain offered psychological tips for better putting in his book *The Mystery of Golf*, and Alex Morrison, in *Better Golf without Practice* (1940), advocated a method of visualizing the perfect shot before swinging the club. But those were intuitive approaches. There was no genuine attempt to study the psychology of sports until after World War II, and in the early years psychologists generally focused on testing to determine the psychological makeup of the successful athlete.

Meanwhile, some athletes had already developed their own psychological approaches. Former Boston Celtic Bill Russell, whose professional career began in the mid-1950s, described his method of "mental rehearsal" in his book *Second Wind*. Similarly, golfer Jack Nicklaus wrote in *Golf My Way*: "I never hit a shot, not even in practice, without having a very clear, in-focus picture of it in my head." Both practiced a technique known in sports psychology as "visualization" or "imaging."

Both the space program and interest in Eastern meditation techniques contributed to sports psychology in the early 1960s, especially in the Soviet Union. Alexander Romen, after studying yoga methods, developed "self-regulation training" to teach Soviet cosmonauts voluntary control of their heart rates, body temperatures, muscle tension, and emotional reactions, and then realized that the technique could also be of value to athletes. Similar developments took place, though more slowly, in North America. Alyce and Elmer Green in 1964 began researching biofeedback, the use of the mind to control the autonomic functions, which are theoretically self-regulating. Their work, like Romen's, eventually had important applications in sports psychology.

Modern sports psychology recognizes a variety of training methods, some as simple as relaxation and anxiety management. Relaxation is often a prelude to imaging, through which an athlete is taught to recall success and visualize a perfect performance leading to victory. This practice was given a scientific basis by Swedish sport psychologist Lars-Eric Unestahl and V. M Melnikov of the Soviet Union. Unestahl in 1978 studied Sweden's best downhill skiers and discovered that "the best skiers seem to have better ability to experience the actual course visually" before making their runs. Another technique is called modeling: An athlete watches a film or videotape of a top-level performer, and the visual image is then transferred to motor memory during practice. Subliminal audiotapes meant to build self-confidence are being marketed for recreational athletes, although there's some doubt about how effective they actually are; and some sports psychologists emphasize a holistic mind-body approach using hypnosis.

There are two major organizations in the field: the North American Society for the Psychology of Sport, and Physical Activity and the International Society of Sports Psychology, which publishes the *International Journal of Sport Psychology*.

Further Reading: Klavora, Peter, and Juri V. Daniel. *Coach, Athlete, and the Sports Psychologist.* Toronto: University of Toronto School of Physical Education and Health Education, 1979.

Address: North American Society for the Psychology of Sport and Physical Activity, c/o Mary J. Carlton, Department Of Kinesiology, 906 S. Goodwin, University of Illinois, Urbana, IL 61801 (217) 244–3986

Public Schools Athletic League (PSAL)

Luther H. Gulick became director of physical training for Greater New York public schools in 1903.

One of his first acts was to meet with Superintendent William H. Maxwell, AAU secretary James E. Sullivan, and General George W. Wingate to form the Public Schools Athletic League. The PSAL was privately financed by donations from a variety of people, including Andrew Carnegie, S. R. Guggenheim, John D. Rockefeller, and Henry Payne White, but it required the cooperation of 630 schools to operate its program. It offered three levels of performance. On the first level, students could win badges by performing specified athletic tasks. On the second, classes competed against one another on the basis of their average performances in athletic event. The third level was interscholastic competition in a variety of team sports, leading to city championships. The PSAL added a Girls' Branch in 1905, but didn't include interscholastic competition in girls' sports.

Teachers and administrators generally favored the league because students had to have good grades and certificates for good conduct to compete, so discipline improved. The success of the PSAL led other large cities to adopt the idea. In 1907, about 15,000 spectators attended the city's championship baseball game, more than a major-league game usually drew at the time, and by 1910 there were similar leagues in 17 other cities. Late in 1914, the PSAL formally became part of the New York school system. The league still conducts city-wide championships in several sports.

See also HIGH SCHOOL SPORTS.

Pulitzer Trophy
Air Racing

The publishers of the *New York World* and *St. Louis Post-Dispatch* on August 2, 1919, offered the Pulitzer trophy for an international air race. The first trophy race was held November 25, 1920, at Mitchel Field, Long Island. In 1921, the race became the major event at an annual air meet, which in 1923 became the International Air Races and in 1924 the National Air Races. The Pulitzer Trophy remained in competition only through 1925.

Puritanism

The Puritans of England and North America looked at time as a precious commodity that was not to be wasted, and thus generally opposed play and amusements as unproductive activities. They also did not observe England's folk holidays, and Sunday was considered a day on which people were to devote themselves to religion. William Penn expressed the Puritan point of view well when he said that Quakers should not "eat, drink, play, game, and sport away their irrevocable precious time, which should be dedicated to the Lord."

During the 17th century, every colony enacted laws forbidding frivolity on Sunday. When Sir Thomas Dale became governor of Virginia in 1611, he enacted a criminal code that banned "gaming" on the Sabbath, with death as the penalty for a third offense. And in 1621 Governor William Bradford of the Plymouth Colony in Massachusetts was enraged at seeing colonists "at play, openly, some pitching the bar and some at stool-ball, and such-like sports"; he confiscated their equipment and gave them a tongue-lashing. Even the New Amsterdam Dutch, who were more tolerant of play than the Puritans, prohibited amusements on Sunday morning in 1656.

However, the Puritans were not entirely opposed to play. They never prohibited it on weekdays; boys who behaved well and had free time were usually allowed to take part in games; and some diversions could be seen as recreation (that is, "re-creation") that might actually promote religion by helping to restore the proper frame of mind for religiousness. The continual enactment of laws prohibiting gaming and play shows that they were going on, in large part because, although the Puritans usually controlled the government, they were in the minority. During the "Great Migration" of 1629–40, about 75 percent of the immigrants from England were non-Puritans looking for a better way of life. Nevertheless, Puritanism persisted into the 20th century in the Blue Laws that forbade sports on Sunday, especially in Connecticut and Pennsylvania.

See also COLONIAL SPORTS.

PWBA

Professional Women's Bowling Association; see LADIES PROFESSIONAL BOWLERS TOUR.

Quadrilateral Trotting Combination
See GRAND CIRCUIT.

Quarter-Horse Racing
Horse racing in colonial Virginia was quarter-horse racing: A straight-line course of a quarter-mile or so was laid out on a town street or a country road, the start and finish lines marked by poles, and two horses raced from one pole to the other. The horses were not Thoroughbreds—the word had not even been coined yet—but usually the progeny of English mares and the "Indian ponies" that were descended from horses originally brought to North America by the Spanish conquistadors.

While the quarter-mile race on a straight track was being supplanted in the East and Mid-Atlantic by Thoroughbred racing on circular or oval courses, it moved into Kentucky and Tennessee with settlers from Virginia. In Lexington, later to become the center of Thoroughbred breeding in North America, quarter-horse races were run along Main Street to Henry Clay's home as early as 1787.

The cow pony of the American cowboy was closely related to those early quarter horses: small but tough, very intelligent, gifted with great acceleration and exceptional speed over short distances. Like the Virginia planters of the late 17th and early 18th centuries, the cowboys were given to boasting about their horses, and they, too, arranged informal match races over short, straight-line courses. Quarter-horse racing became a staple at county fairs in the Southwest, as harness racing was in the Midwest.

Although relatively unknown outside of the area, quarter-horse racing went big time in 1959, when the All-American Futurity was first run at Ruidoso Downs in New Mexico. Until the Breeders' Cup races for Thoroughbreds came along, this was the richest horse race in the world, with a total purse of more than $1 million. The All-American is the chief race in the quarter-horse Triple Crown; the others are the Kansas Futurity and the Rainbow Futurity. All three races are for two-year-olds, while the Thoroughbred Triple Crown is for three-year-old horses.

Quebec, Quebec
Hockey   The Quebec Aces played in the National Hockey League for just one season, 1919–20, and then moved to Hamilton, Ontario. The Quebec Nor-diques joined the World Hockey Association when it was founded in 1972, and they were taken into the NHL when the leagues merged before the 1979–80 season.
See also QUEBEC COLISEUM.

Quebec Coliseum
The original Quebec Coliseum was built in 1930 and hosted hockey for the first time in 1942. It was destroyed by fire on March 15, 1942. The City of Quebec then constructed a new 10,000-seat coliseum, which opened on December 8, 1949, with a game between the Quebec Aces and the Quebec Citadelles, both minor-league teams. Since 1972, the Coliseum has been the home of the Quebec Nor-diques, originally in the World Hockey Association. After the Nordiques joined the National Hockey League in 1979, the Coliseum was expanded to 15,250 seats.

Queen's Plate
Horse Racing
The oldest Thoroughbred race in North America, this was originally the King's Plate, run in 1836 at Trois Rivieres, Quebec. It became an annual event in 1860 when Queen Victoria donated a trophy for a race on June 27 at the Toronto Turf Club, a short time after her consort, Prince Albert, had urged Canada to breed better horses. The race was run at Old Woodbine in Toronto from 1883 to 1955. Since it opened in 1956, the present Woodbine has hosted the Queen's Plate. (Old Woodbine, originally known simply as Woodbine, changed its name to Green-wood in 1956.)
See also WOODBINE RACE TRACK.

Queens Tournament
Bowling
Established in 1961, the WIBC Queens Tournament was originally at match play, the counterpart of the ABC Masters Tournament. In 1976, the tournament went to the "stepladder" format used in most ABC and WIBC events. The Queens and the U.S. Open are the two most prestigious tournaments in women's bowling.

Queens Tournament Champions

1961   Janet Harman
1962   Dorothy Wilkinson

1963 Irene Monterosso
1964 D. D. Jacobson
1965 Betty Kuczynski
1966 Judy Lee
1967 Mildred Martorella
1968 Phyllis Massey
1969 Ann Feigel
1970 Mildred Martorella
1971 Mildred Martorella
1972 Dorothy Fothergill
1973 Dorothy Fothergill
1974 Judy Cook Soutar
1975 Cindy Powell
1976 Pamela Buckner
1977 Dana Stewart
1978 Loa Boxberger
1979 Donna Adamek
1980 Donna Adamek
1981 Katsuko Sugimoto
1982 Katsuko Sugimoto
1983 Aleta Sill
1984 Kazue Inahashi

1985 Aleta Sill
1986 Coral Flebig
1987 Cathy Almeida
1988 Wendy Macpherson
1989 Carol Gianotti
1990 Patty Ann

Quoits

Quoits appears to have been invented by Roman soldiers early in the Christian era. They bent discarded horseshoes into a circular shape and threw them for distance. The Romans brought the sport to England and the English began throwing the shoes at a stake. Quoits arrived in North America with English settlers, but was generally replaced by modern horseshoe pitching by the end of the 19th century, although it remains relatively popular in England. A shipboard form of the sport, using a quoit of braided rope, eventually turned into a children's game, usually called ring toss.

See also HORSESHOE PITCHING.

Racine, WI

Football   The Racine Legion, sponsored by the local American Legion post, was in the National Football League from 1922 through 1924 and in 1926.

Racquetball

Joseph G. Sobek, a tennis and squash instructor, took up handball in the late 1940s but found it too hard on the hands. He thought the sport might be just as good, maybe even better, if a racquet were used. So he designed a racquet based on those used in paddleball, paddle tennis and platform tennis. Twenty-five of the racquets were manufactured in late 1950, and the new sport, then called "paddle rackets," was first played at the Greenwich (CT) YMCA. In 1952, Sobel founded the National Paddle Rackets Association and developed official playing rules.

The handball was much too lively with the speed added by the racquet, and Sobel spent several years looking for the right ball. Finally he found a manufacturer to design a slower ball, and Sobek began selling equipment and rules books by mail to YMCAs, colleges, YMHAs, and other organizations with handball courts. As with paddleball, paddle rackets faced opposition from handball players who didn't want to share their courts with another sport. But Robert Kendler, founder of the U.S. Handball Association, in 1969 organized the International Racquetball Association, thereby renaming the sport. The IRA held the first national tournament that year.

The national racquetball tournament was first held in 1969. Charles Brumfield, right, won four of the first seven championships. Courtesy of the American Amateur Racquetball Association

Racquetball was one of the fastest growing sports of the 1970s. The number of players increased from about 50,000 in 1970 to 350,000 in 1974 and about 3 million in 1980, of whom an estimated 35 percent were women. The IRA was renamed the American Amateur Racquetball Association in 1980. It now boasts 9 million members and sanctions more than 1,000 amateur events. The world racquetball championship was inaugurated in 1985.

Addresses: American Amateur Racquetball Association, 815 North Weber, Colorado Springs, CO 80903 (719) 635–5396; Canadian Racquetball Association, 333 River Road, Vanier, Ontario, Canada K1L 8H9 (613) 748–5653

Racquets

Also called "hard rackets," this sport dates at least to 1760, but it is commonly associated with London's Fleet Street Debtors' Gaol, where prisoners began playing in the early 19th century, using balls from "fives," an English version of handball, and court tennis racquets with chopped-down handles. Charles Dickens described the setting in *The Pickwick Papers* (1836): "The area formed by the wall in that part . . . in which Mr. Pickwick stood was just wide enough to make a good racket court; one side formed, of course, by the wall itself, and the other by that portion of the prison which looked toward St. Paul's Cathedral." When the first indoor court was built at the Prince's Club in London in 1853, racquets became a four-wall sport for the elite.

Meanwhile, a form of racquets was played as early as 1750 in New York, where it was generally associated with taverns. An outdoor court was built in Montreal in 1836 and the Montreal Racquets Club was founded in 1840. The first genuine court in the United States, the Allen Street Court in New York, was built in the early 19th century. Several of its members, who objected to gambling on the sport, formed the Racket Court Club in 1845. The sport spread to major cities such as Boston, Chicago, Cleveland, Detroit, Philadelphia, Pittsburgh, and St. Louis late in the century, but interest began to decline during the 1920s, in part because of the growing popularity of lawn tennis and squash. As with court tennis, the high cost of building courts has kept racquets from gaining any measure of popularity.

See also SQUASH RACQUETS; SQUASH TENNIS.

Radbourn, Charles G. (1853–1897)
Baseball
Born December 9, 1853, Rochester, NY; died February 5, 1897; Baseball Hall of Fame

"Old Hoss" earned his nickname during the 1884 season, when he won 60 games, the major-league record, while losing only 12 to lead the Providence Grays to the National League pennant. He then won all three games in a postseason championship series against New York of the American Association. Providence had started the season with two pitchers, Radbourn and Charles Sweeney. Radbourn was suspended on July 16, but shortly afterward Sweeney was also suspended, and Radbourn was reinstated on July 23 with a salary increase for agreeing to pitch every game the rest of the season.

Radbourn played briefly as a right fielder for Buffalo of the National League in 1880. He went to Providence in 1881 and played the outfield and shortstop in addition to compiling a 25–11 record as a pitcher. He followed that with a 33–20 record in 1882 and a 48–25 record in 1883, when he pitched a no-hitter against Cleveland on July 25. During his record-setting 1884 season, he pitched 11 shutouts and had a 1.38 earned run average. After winning 28 and losing 21 in 1885, Radbourn went to Boston for four seasons, then jumped to the Boston Players' League team in 1890. He spent the 1891 season with Cincinnati in the National League, then retired.

During Radbourn's career, the pitching distance was only 50 feet. Until 1884, pitchers had to throw underhand, but he continued to throw underhand even after sidearm and overarm deliveries were allowed. In his 11 seasons as a pitcher, he won 310 games, lost 195, pitched 34 shutouts, and had 489 complete games in 503 starts.

Radio

KDKA of Pittsburgh, founded by Westinghouse Electric and Manufacturing Company in 1920 as the first commercial radio station, was also the first to cover a sports event when it broadcast the April 11, 1921, fight between Johnny Dundee and Johnny Ray. The station's pioneering sportscaster was Harold Arlin, who did the first radio broadcasts of a major-league game (Pittsburgh vs. Philadelphia, August 5), a tennis match (August 6), and a football game (Pittsburgh vs. West Virginia, October 8).

David Sarnoff of the Radio Corporation of America founded WJY in Hoboken in 1921, and on July 2 of that year the station broadcast the heavyweight championship fight between Jack Dempsey and Georges Carpentier into about 100 dance halls, fraternal lodges, and theaters in the Northeast. The fight was heard by an estimated 300,000 people, most of whom paid a dollar as a contribution for "aid to devastated France." A relay system was used, with Major J. Andrew White, at ringside, sending a blow-by-blow account by telephone to an engineer who repeated the account over the air. WJZ of Newark used a similar relay system to cover the 1921 World Series.

In 1922, there were about 60,000 radio receiving sets in the United States. That fall, sportswriter Grantland Rice did play-by-play of the World Series for WJZ, and WEAF in New York City, which was owned by AT&T, used long-distance lines from Chicago to broadcast the Princeton–University of Chicago football game. WEAF also did the Harvard-Yale game that year.

WEAF sent the World Series broadcast to a small network of stations across the country in 1924, when college football became a weekly staple. Rice had left the microphone during the third game of the 1923 Series, and Graham McNamee took over as the first genuine full-time sportscaster. He was to become the best-known voice in America, doing ten different sports, including major horse races, boxing matches, and football games. There were 6.5 million radios in use by 1927, when an estimated 50 million listeners heard his broadcast of the second Jack Dempsey–Gene Tunney fight on 73 NBC stations.

The number of licensed stations had grown to 690 by the end of 1922, and they all faced the same problem: how to pay operating expenses. Many of the stations were run by newspapers as public relations vehicles, and many others were owned by corporations like RCA (which in 1926 formed the NBC network) that wanted to furnish programming in order to sell radios. After much controversy and struggle, the idea of "toll broadcasting" was generally accepted by the late 1920s. At first, advertisers paid for brief commercial announcements, but with the growth of network radio companies began to sponsor entire shows. The first major sports sponsor was the Ford Motor Company, which in 1934 paid $400,000 to organized baseball for World Series broadcasts on the CBS, NBC, and Mutual networks.

The Chicago Cubs had allowed all of their games to be broadcast in 1925 and attendance actually increased, but during the 1930s there was growing concern about radio's possible adverse effect on live gates. Jim Tierney, secretary of baseball's New York Giants, rejected a broadcast proposal, saying "it would cut into our attendance. . . . We want the fans following the game from the grandstand, not from their homes." And the Baseball Writers' Association protested play-by-play broadcasts with the threat that "it would kill circulation of afternoon papers and in the end will result in curtailment of baseball publicity." The Dodgers, Giants, and Yankees in 1934 agreed among themselves to ban broadcasts of their games, but Larry MacPhail became general

manager of the Dodgers in 1937 and two years later he sold radio rights to the team's games for $70,000.

College football attendance declined during the Great Depression, and the NCAA in 1935 established a committee to determine whether radio broadcasts contributed to the decline. The committee reported that the question couldn't be definitely answered, but recommended that the home team should have the right to sell games to radio stations and that the visiting team should not be allowed to sell broadcast rights without the permission of the home team. That became NCAA policy in 1936.

Because of the high cost of leasing telephone lines, many stations did "re-creations" of games on the road. A Western Union operator in the park would telegraph a coded pitch-by-pitch account to the station's studio, where an announcer translated for the audience. For example, the operator would send the message "B1L," and the announcer would say, "Here comes the pitch—it's low for ball one." Some stations did everything possible to make a re-creation sound like a live broadcast, using sound effects and recordings of crowd noise and cheering.

Radio reached its peak of popularity after World War II. In 1946 there were 56 million radios in the United States, and sets were selling at the rate of more than 15 million a year. By 1952, there were more than 2,000 stations and four major national networks (ABC, CBS, Mutual and NBC), with total revenues of more than $2 billion. A fifth, the Liberty Network, suddenly appeared in 1949. The brainchild of Gordon McLendon, Liberty specialized in re-creations on its "Game of the Day" broadcasts. It had 300 stations by the end of the season, and that increased to 431 in 1950, when Mutual also began "Game of the Day" broadcasts. Unlike Liberty, Mutual did all of the games live and paid for rights fees, which averaged $210,000 for each major-league team that year. In 1952, organized baseball banned re-creations, and Liberty went out of business. By 1955, more than 500 stations were carrying Mutual's daily broadcasts. That was the final season of a 10-year, $14 million contract from the Gillette Razor Company for exclusive sponsorship of the all-star game and the World Series.

Mutual lost the World Series to NBC in 1957 and ended baseball coverage entirely in 1959. With the ascent of television during the 1960s, the structure of radio broadcasting changed entirely. The network system gave way to fragmentation, with independent stations struggling to find a niche and network series yielding to local disc jockeys. NBC, which did baseball's all-star game and the World Series through 1975, couldn't depend on its affiliates alone to support the broadcasts, and each year it put together an ad hoc network of independent stations to carry the games.

Beginning in the mid-1970s, sports on radio began to make a comeback. Baseball in particular had a resurgence. CBS in 1976 began coverage of the all-star game, both league championship series, and the World Series; over a ten-year period, the World Series radio audience grew from 41 million listeners to 56 million. In 1985, the network signed a five-year, $32 million contract to do a game of the week on radio. But the popularity of local announcers, such as Johnny Most on the Boston Celtics' basketball broadcasts and Vin Scully with the Brooklyn and Los Angeles Dodgers, was a major factor in the medium's growth. Led by the Dodgers, who pioneered the idea in 1953, teams put together their own regional networks. In 1976, nearly 900 stations belonged to regional baseball networks, and that grew to more than 1,300 in 1985.

Although there's never been a formal study done, it is known that some fans turn off television sound and listen to the radio broadcast while watching games, often because of the popularity of a local sportscaster. Reportedly, dislike of Howard Cosell when he was doing "Monday Night Football" on ABC spurred many fans to listen to the CBS radio broadcast. With the trend toward cable television of home games in baseball, basketball, and hockey, fans who don't have access to cable have to follow their teams via radio much of the time. And millions of fans bring transistor radios to ballparks and stadiums to listen to the game while they watch. There are so many radios in the crowd at Dodger Stadium that engineers have to control the volume very carefully to keep Scully's voice from being overwhelmed by feedback.

Further Reading: Barnouw, Eric. *A Tower in Babel.* New York: Oxford University Press, 1966; Smith, Curt. *Voices of the Game.* South Bend: Diamond Communications, 1987.

See also BARBER, RED; JOURNALISM, SPORTS; MCNAMEE, GRAHAM; TELEVISION.

Raisin Bowl
Football

Played in Fresno, CA on New Year's Day from 1946 through 1949 and on December 31, 1949, the Raisin Bowl matched a California team against a team from the Midwest or Southwest.

Raisin Bowl Results

1946 Drake 13, Fresno State 12
1947 San Jose State 20, Utah State 0
1948 Pacific 26, Wichita State 14
1949 (Jan.) Occidental 21, Colorado State 20
1949 (Dec.) San Jose State 20, Texas Tech 13

Rawls, "Betsy" Elizabeth E. (1928–)
Golf

Born May 4, 1928, Spartanburg, SC; World Golf Hall of Fame

She didn't begin playing golf until she was 17, but five years later Rawls finished second in the U.S. Women's open as an amateur. A Phi Beta Kappa in physics at the University of Texas, she turned professional after graduating in 1951. She won the Open that year and in 1953, 1957, and 1960. She was the LPGA champion in 1959 and 1969. The winner of more than 50 LPGA tournaments and nearly $250,000 in prize money, Rawls led in winnings in 1952 and 1959 and received the Vare Trophy for the lowest stroke-per-round average in 1959.

Ray, "Shorty" Hugh (1884–1956)
Football

Born September 21, 1884, Highland Park, IL; died September 16, 1956; Pro Football Hall of Fame

The smallest man in the Pro Football Hall of Fame at 5-foot-6 and 136 pounds, Ray made his mark as the National Football League's supervisor of officials and technical advisor on rules from 1938 until 1952. A four-sport star at the University of Illinois, Ray was a high school coach for 20 years before organizing the American Association of Officials, which conducted clinics to standardize officiating and rules interpretation. In 1929, he drafted a new football code for the National Federation of State High School Associations that became the model for all future rulebooks, including the NFL's.

Later, Ray also recodified the college and NFL rules. He was brought into the NFL in 1938 by an old friend, George Halas of the Chicago Bears, and he immediately began preseason testing of the league's officials, requiring scores of better than 95 percent on their knowledge of the rules. He also recommended rules changes after each season; his primary goals were to decrease injuries and speed up play. It is estimated that one of his innovations, having officials relay the ball with tosses from the sidelines instead of carrying it back into the field of play, added an average of 12 plays to every game.

Regina
See SASKATCHEWAN.

Renaissance Big Five
See HARLEM RENAISSANCE BIG FIVE.

Reserve Clause

The "backbone of baseball," as Washington Senators owner Clark Griffith once called it, the reserve clause had its beginning on September 26, 1879, when major-league owners entered into a secret agreement that each team could reserve five players that other teams would not attempt to sign. The number was increased to 11 in 1883, 12 in 1886, and 14 in 1887, when a committee of players persuaded the owners that the reserve clause should be specifically written into the standard player's contract rather than existing only as a gentleman's agreement.

In protest against the clause and a new Classification Plan that would limit salaries, some players formed their own league in 1890. Most established major-leaguers jumped to the Players League. The New York Giants sought an injunction to prevent John Montgomery Ward, the leader of the revolt, from leaving the team, but Judge Morgan J. O'Brien of the New York State Supreme Court refused to uphold the reserve clause because it was "indefinite and uncertain." In a similar case involving the Giants' Buck Ewing, a federal district judge ruled that the clause was "unenforceable."

Nevertheless, the reserve clause remained in the standard contract, and owners continued to enforce it after the Players League collapsed. While many players grumbled about it in ensuing years, other issues were more important to the Players Protective Association, organized in 1900. Its lawyer, Harry L. Taylor, called the reserve clause the "bulwark" of professional baseball, but he objected to players being farmed out without their permission, and he also proposed that a player should be given half the price when sold by one team to another. The association won some minor concessions from the National League because of the salary war with the new American League in 1901, but the association folded late in 1902, shortly before the two leagues and the National Association of Professional Minor Leagues entered into a new National Agreement under which all teams agreed to honor the reserve clause.

The Fraternity of Professional Baseball Players of America, formed in 1913 and headed by Dave Fultz, a former major-league pitcher who had become a lawyer, also took a moderate approach to the reserve clause. Fultz did suggest that teams should be allowed to reserve players for a maximum of five years, and he attacked the owners' common practice of cutting a player's salary drastically when invoking the clause.

The Federal League, established as a minor league in 1913, claimed major-league status the following season and attracted about 90 players from the National and American Leagues. The Federal League was unique in that players were hired by the league and assigned to teams. Instead of using the reserve clause, the league gave its players three-year contracts guaranteeing a raise each year. The Chicago White Sox sued to keep their first baseman, Hal Chase, from jumping to the Federal League's Buffalo team, and once again a New York Supreme Court judge found the reserve clause untenable because it led to "a species of quasi peonage."

After just two seasons as a supposed major league, the Federal League settled with organized baseball, receiving $600,000 in exchange for dropping an antitrust suit. Two of its owners were allowed to buy into existing franchises after the league went out of business. However, Baltimore's Federal League team was left out of the settlement and its owners brought their own antitrust suit. It ultimately led to the landmark Supreme Court decision of 1922 granting organized baseball an exemption from antitrust laws. Oddly enough, baseball's chief attorney, George Wharton Pepper, told the Court that the reserve clause was not legally binding, but Justice Oliver Wendell Holmes disagreed. Writing for a unanimous Court, Holmes ruled that the clause "was intended to protect the rights of clubs . . . to retain the services of sufficient players." The definition of "sufficient" was implicitly left to the owners themselves.

Judge Kenesaw Mountain Landis, who became the first commissioner of baseball in 1921, was ambivalent about the reserve clause. He opposed major-league teams' increasing use of minor-league farm systems during the 1930s because too often it placed "a stone wall in the advancement of a ballplayer," as he told a minor-league meeting in December of 1921. He favored a universal annual draft of minor-league players, which in effect would have eliminated the reserve clause below the major-league level. On several occasions, Landis also released minor-league players from their contracts on the grounds that they were being illegally "hidden" by the major-league teams that actually controlled them.

Although Landis never spoke out publicly against the clause, he periodically warned the owners that he saw serious legal difficulties with it, and his secretary, Leslie O'Connor, said that Landis would have granted a contract without a reserve clause to any player who asked for it, in defiance of the National Agreement, which specifically prohibited such contracts. The issue was moot, however, since no one ever asked for such a contract.

After the collapse of the fraternity in 1917, players were generally quiet. But Robert F. Murphy in 1946 established a labor organization, the American Baseball Guild, and called for a modification of the reserve clause. A perpetual reserve on a player's services was unnecessary, he suggested, since he estimated that 95 percent of them were either sold or traded during their careers. The Pittsburgh Pirates formed the first ABG chapter and threatened a strike after the team refused to recognize the union as a collective bargaining unit. The ABG barely lasted the season, but owners made a couple of major concessions, limiting salary cuts to 25 percent when the reserve clause was invoked. A 30-day severance period replaced the former clause that allowed a team to release a player with just ten days' notice.

Just a year later, the reserve clause faced a major legal challenge. Danny Gardella, an outfielder with the New York Giants in 1944 and 1945, had jumped to the Mexican League in 1946, and he was blacklisted by organized baseball when he returned to the United States in 1947. Frederic A. Johnson, a constitutional lawyer, who in 1939 had written a paper, "Baseball Law," for the *United States Law Review*, agreed to take Gardella's case.

A federal district court judge dismissed the case, but the Second Circuit Appellate Federal Court ruled 2-1 that Gardella deserved a trial on the issues. Judge Jerome Frank agreed with Johnson that the reserve clause created a form of peonage and, to organized baseball's argument that major-league players were well paid, he replied, "Excusing virtual slavery because of high pay is only an excuse for the totalitarian-minded." The case was settled out of court in October 1949.

In 1951 Brooklyn congressman Emmanuel Celler, chairman of the House Judiciary Committee, launched an investigation of organized baseball. Very few players were willing to testify for fear of reprisal; those who did generally said they favored the reserve clause. A notable exception was Ned Garver, a very good pitcher with a very bad team, the St. Louis Browns, who wrote to the committee with a suggestion for a kind of salary arbitration. Garver recommended that after a player had been with a second-division team for three consecutive seasons, every other team in the league should be allowed to bid for his contract. If his present team didn't agree to pay him at least the average of the bids, he should become a free agent. Most of the witnesses were representatives of organized baseball who carried the message that the reserve clause was vital to the sport and that it should be explicitly legalized. But the hearings didn't result in any legislation.

The beginning of the end for the reserve clause came in 1966, when the 13-year-old Major League Baseball Players Association chose Marvin Miller as full-time executive director. While Miller was touring spring training camps to talk to the players, Los Angeles Dodger pitchers Sandy Koufax and Don Drysdale were staging a joint holdout. Among their bargaining chips was a California law that prohibited a personal services contract lasting more than seven years, a direct blow at the theoretically perpetual reserve clause.

Koufax and Drysdale finally settled for sizable contracts, so the statute was never invoked against the reserve clause. But Miller, experienced in labor law and negotiations, immediately began attacking the clause. When the first basic agreement between organized baseball and the MLBPA was signed in 1968, the owners promised to study the issue, but nothing came of the study, if there even was one.

Miller got his chance for a head-on attack when center fielder Curt Flood was traded by the St. Louis Cardinals to the Philadelphia Phillies in 1969. After 12 years in St. Louis, Flood didn't want to go to Philadelphia, and he felt he should be free to make his own deal if St. Louis didn't want him. The MLPBA decided to back an antitrust suit aimed primarily at the reserve clause. To avoid the litigation, organized baseball offered to make Flood a free agent, but he pressed on. Ultimately, he lost the case, but it paved the way for the virtual end of the clause, because one of the owners' arguments was that it should be "a mandatory collective bargaining issue."

The LPBA adopted a new strategy in 1973, advising some players not to sign new contracts in order to test the duration of the reserve clause. From 1973 through 1975, 17 players began a season without contracts. Two of them, pitchers Dave McNally of the Montreal Expos and Andy Messersmith of the Los Angeles Dodgers, claimed free agency after having played an entire season without re-signing, and their case went to arbitration. The owners argued that the arbitration panel had no right to consider a grievance involving the reserve clause, but Chairman Peter Seitz rejected that position, since the owners had gone on record in the Flood case as saying that the clause was a collective bargaining issue. On December 23, 1975, Seitz ruled that a team couldn't bind a player in perpetuity and that McNally and Messersmith were indeed free agents.

The owners fired Seitz and went to court in an attempt to overturn his decision, but they were rebuffed. When a new basic agreement was signed in July 1976, the players gave back some of their newfound freedom in exchange for a clause allowing any player with six years of major-league experience to become a free agent. The perpetual reserve clause was dead.

The Flood case, incidentally, helped to do away with the National Hockey League's reserve clause.

When players jumped from the NHL to the new World Hockey Association in 1972, courts persistently ruled that the clause was invalid, because the Supreme Court had stated unequivocally that only baseball among the professional sports had an antitrust exemption as a result of the 1922 decision in the Baltimore Federal League case. On December 3, 1973, the league voted to replace the reserve clause with a one-year option clause similar to that used by the National Football League.

Further Reading: Lowenfish, Lee, and Tony Lupien. *The Imperfect Diamond: The Story of Baseball's Reserve System and the Men Who Fought to Change It.* New York: Stein and Day, 1980.

See also OPTION CLAUSE; PLAYERS' ASSOCIATIONS.

Reunion Arena
Dallas, TX

Built by the city of Dallas at a cost of about $27 million, Reunion Arena opened in April of 1980 and became the home court of the new Dallas Mavericks that fall. The Dallas Sidekicks of the Major Indoor Soccer League also play at the arena. Seating capacity is 17,007.

Rhythmic Gymnastics

Although one of the newest sports on the Olympic program, rhythmic gymnastics has its roots in the 19th century. Between 1880 and 1890, French physiologist George Demeney developed a form of gymnastics for women that replaced strenuous calisthenics with exercises designed to develop graceful movement, good posture, and muscular flexibility, and Emil Dalcroze of Switzerland came up with eurhythmics for training dancers and musicians. About 1900, the two disciplines were combined into the Swedish School of rhythmic gymnastics. The Finns added dance elements, the Germans expressive body movements, and Ernest Idla of Estonia contributed some of his own ideas, including a degree of difficulty for each movement.

The young sport was introduced to North America in 1906 by Yritys, a Finnish-Canadian athletic club in Toronto. But it didn't really take root until the 1960s, when it was known as modern gymnastics. Evelyn Koop, who taught rhythmic gymnastics at the Kalev-Estienne Club in Toronto, took her team on several long tours of Canada to give exhibitions and conduct clinics to popularize the sport. The Canadian Modern Gymnastics Federation was founded in 1969, and the first national championships were held in Toronto on June 19, 1970. The CMGF became the Canadian Modern Rhythmic

Gymnastics Federation the following year and dropped the word "modern" in 1981.

Rhythmic gymnastics became an Olympic sport in 1984, and Canada's Lori Fung won the first Gold Medal.

Further Reading: Schmid, Andrea Bodo. *Modern Rhythmic Gymnastics.* Palo Alto: Mayfield Publishing Co., 1976.

Address: Canadian Rhythmic Gymnastics Federation, 333 River Road, Vanier, Ontario, Canada K1L 8H9 (613) 748–5654

See also GYMNASTICS.

Rice, H. Grantland (1880–1954)
Sportswriter

Born November 1, 1880, Murfreesboro, TN; died July 13, 1954; National Sportswriters and Sportscasters Hall of Fame

After playing football at Vanderbilt University, Rice became sports editor of the *Nashville Daily News* and worked for the *Atlanta Journal, Cleveland News,* and *Nashville Tennesseean* before taking a $20-a-week pay cut to join the *New York Mail* in 1911. He moved to the *New York Tribune* in 1914 and within a few years was more famous than most of the athletes he wrote about in his syndicated column, "Sportlight." He frequently included Kiplingesque verse in his column, including the often quoted (and misquoted) lines:

> When the One Great Scorer comes
> to write against your name—
> He marks—not that you won
> or lost—but how you played the game.

Another Rice specialty was assigning nicknames, often alliterative, to athletes: the "Galloping Ghost" for Red Grange, and the "Big Train" for Walter Johnson because of the speed of his fastball. The most famous of all, the "Four Horsemen" for the 1924 Notre Dame backfield, was actually coined by George Strickler, a student publicist at the school, but Rice popularized it after a Notre Dame victory over Army with the lead, "Outlined against a blue-grey October sky, the Four Horsemen rode again."

In the "Golden Age of Sports," also known as the "Era of Wonderful Nonsense," Rice was a fan with a typewriter, a troubadour who not only sang of heroic exploits but helped to create new heroes. Because of his fame, he was hired to do the play-by-play on the second World Series ever broadcast on radio in 1922. He quit that job after the fourth inning of the third game in 1923, giving way to Graham McNamee, but he did a weekly radio commentary during the 1920s and 1930s, and, beginning in 1925, he also hosted a monthly movie sports newsreel for Paramount, which won two Academy Awards.

By the time of his death, Rice's hero-worshiping approach and style had become passé; a new breed of sportswriters were viewing their field more critically and more cynically. But "Granny" had perhaps served an important purpose. As Bruce Barton said in a eulogy at Rice's funeral, "He was the evangelist of fun, the bringer of good news about games . . . (B)y the sheer contagion of his joy in living, he made us want to play. And in so doing he made us a people of better health and happiness in peace; of greater strength in adversity."

Further Reading: Rice, Grantland. *The Tumult and the Shouting: My Life in Sport.* New York: A. S. Barnes, 1954.

See also JOURNALISM, SPORTS.

Rich Stadium
Orchard Park, NY

The Buffalo Bills of the National Football League moved into Rich Stadium when it opened in 1973. It was built by Erie County and the city of Buffalo and was originally to be called Erie County Stadium, but the Rich Products Corporation paid $1.5 million to have it renamed. The stadium seats 80,290.

Richard, "Rocket" Joseph Henri Maurice
(1921–   )
Hockey
Born August 4, 1921, Montreal, Quebec; Hockey Hall of Fame

The fiery, flamboyant Richard astounded hockey fans in 1944–45, when he scored 50 goals in 50 games for the Montreal Canadiens, becoming the first player to average a goal a game over an entire season. Only Wayne Gretzky has ever had a higher scoring average. Called by one sportswriter "the epitome of recklessness, of untrammeled fire and fury and abandon on the ice," Richard was known for his rink-long rushes and for his temper. After he attacked a linesman on March 13, 1955, he was suspended for the rest of the season and the playoffs by NHL President Clarence Campbell. Four days later, Campbell attended a game in Montreal, and his presence touched off a riot that lasted into early morning and caused more than $100,000 damage to downtown Montreal.

The "Rocket," as he quickly became known, joined the Canadiens in 1942 but missed much of the season with a broken ankle. He established himself as a genuine star in 1943–44, when he scored 32 goals and was named a second-team all-star. He was named first team right wing six consecutive years, 1945–

Known as "Rocket" because of his speed and fiery temperament, Maurice Richard scored a Stanley Cup record of 18 game-winning goals. He had 544 regular-season goals in his 18 years with the Montreal Canadiens. Courtesy of the Hockey Hall of Fame

50, and he won the Hart Trophy as the Most Valuable Player in 1947.

Richard was especially dangerous in Stanley Cup play. In 133 playoff games, he had 82 goals, and 18 of them won games for Montreal. Against Detroit in the 1951 Stanley Cup semifinals, Richard scored all four of Montreal's game-winning goals, two of them in overtime. He scored a record five goals in one playoff game against Toronto in 1944, and three times he scored three goals in a single period of a playoff game. Often injured because of his breakneck style and frequently suspended or given game misconduct penalties, Richard played 978 regular-season games in 18 seasons, all with Montreal, and scored 965 points on 544 goals and 421 assists.

Richards, "Bob" Robert E. (1926–   )
Track and Field
Born February 20, 1926, Champaign, IL; National Track and Field Hall of Fame

The "Vaulting Vicar," as sportswriters nicknamed Richards after he became a minister in 1948, was the second man in history to pole vault more than 15 feet (the first was Cornelius Warmerdam); during his career he exceeded that height 126 times. At the University of Illinois, Richards tied for the NCAA championship in 1947. The following year, he won the first of nine AAU outdoor pole-vaulting championships and the first of eight indoor titles. He was the Olympic Gold Medalist in the event in 1952 and 1956. Like many pole-vaulters, Richards was an excellent all-around athlete. He won the AAU decathlon championship in 1951, 1954, and 1956. His highest score in the event was 7,834 points in 1951, when he won the Sullivan Award as outstanding athlete of the year. After retiring in 1957, Richards worked on several Olympic television and radio broadcasts, was the official spokesman for Wheaties breakfast food for 15 years, and founded the Bob Richards Motivational Institute.

Richmond International Raceway
Richmond, VA

Formerly the Richmond Fairgrounds Raceway, this track was completely rebuilt during 1988, between NASCAR Winston Cup races in February and September. The length was extended from a little more than a half-mile to three-quarters of a mile, and the average speed increased from about 66.5 miles per hour to 95.8 miles per hour. A crowd estimated at 60,000 attended the September race after the rebuilding.

Address: P.O. Box 9257, Richmond, VA 23227 (804) 329–6796

Rickard, "Tex" George L. (1870–1929)
Boxing
Born January 2, 1870, Kansas City, MO; died January 6, 1929

The man who made boxing respectable and profitable, Rickard rode a financial roller coaster early in his career. He made $60,000 in the Yukon Gold Rush, built a gambling casino, and lost it to miners who were on a winning streak. Then he built another casino, made $500,000 in four years, and lost most of the money on bad mining claims. Rickard next opened a casino in Goldfield, NV and promoted the lightweight title fight between Joe Gans and Battling Nelson on September 3, 1906. He guaranteed a purse of $30,000 in gold coins, which was displayed in the window of a local bank to publicize the fight. Although Rickard insisted the only purpose of the promotion was to draw attention to Goldfield, he made a profit of about $13,000.

The great boxing promoter "Tex" Rickard is shown testifying before a congressional committee on March 20, 1924. The committee was investigating possible violations of a federal law banning the interstate transportation of fight films.

His next venture into prizefighting was the July 4, 1910, heavyweight title fight between former champion Jim Jeffries and the first black champion, Jack Johnson. Rickard won the bidding by guaranteeing the fighters $101,000 plus two thirds of the movie rights. The winner would get 75 percent, the loser 25 percent. Originally scheduled for San Francisco, the bout had to be moved to Reno after a public outcry over allowing a black fighter to challenge for the title and the resulting political pressure. Rickard billed Jeffries as the "Hope of the White Race," Johnson as the "Negroes' Deliverer." More than 20,000 spectators and 500 newspaper reporters were on hand to see Johnson knock Jeffries out in the 15th round.

That match set the pattern for all of Rickard's future promotions. Although others usually offered fighters only a share of the receipts, Rickard always guaranteed a purse. And he always created what would now be called "a story line" that attracted publicity. His biggest matches all involved Jack

Dempsey, billed as "Jack the Giant Killer" after winning the heavyweight title by knocking out the 6-foot-7, 250-pound Jess Willard. In later fights against French war hero Georges Carpentier and U.S. Marine veteran Gene Tunney, Dempsey became the villain because of accusations that he had dodged the draft during World War I.

But Rickard had other strengths as a promoter. All seats were reserved at his fights—"A seat for every customer and every customer in his seat," he proclaimed—and he trained crews of ushers skilled in crowd control. The reserved seat system allowed Rickard to make high-priced ringside seats attractive to the elite after he began promoting fights in New York, and he also made special efforts to draw women spectators, beginning with a "Jenny Wren" section specifically set aside for women at the Dempsey-Willard fight on July 4, 1919.

Although a shrewd promoter who made phony press releases a stock in trade to boost a fight, Rickard was known for his honesty in financial dealings and was therefore often able to obtain sizable loans without security to pay prefight expenses. Thomas F. Cole, a Minnesota millionaire for whom Rickard had acted as agent in buying some mining properties, gave him unlimited backing for the Johnson-Jeffries fight, and Frank Flournoy, a Memphis cotton broker, advanced him $150,000 for the Dempsey-Willard match.

That was Rickard's first losing venture, mainly because of a terrific heat wave that kept spectators away. He built an 80,000-seat temporary arena in Toledo, OH, but sold only 19,650 tickets. Although Rickard claimed a profit of $85,000, he admitted privately to a small loss, according to his biographer.

In 1920, two months after passage of the Walker Law, which made prize fighting legal in New York, Rickard signed a ten-year, $350,000 lease for Madison Square Garden with the backing of circus owner John Ringling. Rickard promoted lesser fights in the Garden, but he preferred to use outdoor arenas for the major bouts because of their greater capacity. He built an arena at Boyle's Thirty Acres in Jersey City for the first major international championship fight, between Dempsey and Carpentier, on July 2, 1921.

Two copromoters pulled out of that fight, leaving Rickard short of money. Again, however, he was able to get an advance from another backer, ticket speculator Mike Jacobs. Rickard's skillful ballyhooing of the matchup between the "Manassa Mauler" and the handsome Frenchman, nicknamed the "Orchid Man," made it the first fight ever to draw a million-dollar gate. It was a mismatch, but Dempsey collected $300,000 for winning, Carpentier $200,000, and Rickard turned a profit of $400,000.

Next it was the "Giant Killer" once more against the "Wild Bull of the Pampas," Luis Firpo, a 6-foot-3, 216-pound Argentinian. The fight, staged at the Polo Grounds on September 14, 1923, drew 80,000 and grossed more than $1 million. It was a short but sensational bout. Firpo knocked down Dempsey early in the first round. Dempsey came back to knock down Firpo seven times, but then the Argentinian threw a terrific right and sent the champion through the ropes and onto the typewriter of sportswriter Jack Lawrence. Helped by Lawrence and other writers, he scrambled back into the ring, avoided Firpo for the rest of the round, and knocked him out in the second.

Rickard had turned the Garden into a money-maker by adding wrestling matches and six-day bicycle races to the regular boxing matches, but in 1925 he decided to build a new Garden of his own, backed by several millionaires, including New York Governor W. Averill Harriman. It opened with a six-day bicycle race in late November, and on December 15 the New York Americans, organized by Rickard, played their first National Hockey League game.

Although Rickard's first two fights, Gans-Nelson and Johnson-Jeffries, had featured black fighters against white fighters, he ignored the New York Athletic Commission's insistence that Dempsey be matched against black challenger Harry Wills. (Rickard told friends that state officials privately opposed such a match because they were afraid of riots if Wills won the title.) Instead, he staged a fight between Dempsey and Gene Tunney at Philadelphia's Sesquicentennial Stadium on September 23, 1926. The gate was nearly $2 million, and more than 120,000 spectators were astounded when Tunney went the ten rounds and won the championship on a unanimous decision.

The second Dempsey-Tunney fight, at Chicago's Soldier Field on September 22, 1927, had an incredible gate of more than $2.5 million, still the largest in boxing history. This was the famous "long count" bout. Dempsey knocked down Tunney in the seventh round, but stood over him for several seconds, and the referee didn't begin counting until Dempsey finally went to a neutral corner. Tunney got up at the count of nine, after having been down for 14 or 15 seconds, and went on to win another ten-round decision.

Rickard's last major promotion, Tunney against New Zealander Tom Heenan on July 26, 1928, was a flop. Tunney was guaranteed $500,000 and the fight grossed only $691,000, resulting in a loss of more than $150,000. Less than six months later, the promoter died of appendicitis in Miami. Fifteen thousand people filed past his casket in Madison

Square Garden on January 8, 1929, and 9,000 attended his funeral the following day. Dempsey, his face streaming with tears, told reporters, "I've lost the best friend I ever had."

Further Reading: Samuels, Charles. *The Magnificent Rube: The Life and Gaudy Times of Tex Rickard.* New York: McGraw-Hill, 1957.

Rickey, Branch (1881–1965)
Baseball
Born December 20, 1881, Lucasville, OH; died December 9, 1965; Baseball Hall of Fame

The most influential executive in the history of baseball, Rickey created the modern farm system and broke the sport's unofficial ban on black players when he signed Jackie Robinson to a Brooklyn Dodger contract in 1947. He also introduced practice sliding pits and batting cages, and was probably the first manager to give his players classroom instruction in the finer points of the game.

Rickey played minor-league ball while attending Ohio Wesleyan College. After graduating, he played in some exhibition games with the Cincinnati Reds in 1904, but was cut for refusing to play on Sundays. He earned a second bachelor's degree from Allegheny College in 1906, and also hit .284 with the St. Louis Browns. A catcher, he played briefly with the New York Highlanders (now the Yankees) in 1907 before entering Ohio State to study law. He received his law degree in 1911 from the University of Michigan, where he coached baseball from 1910 through 1913, then became manager of the Browns late in the season. He held the job through 1915 and spent a year in the team's front office before going to the St. Louis Cardinals as club president.

The Cardinals were $175,000 in debt, and Rickey wrestled with the problem of how to improve the team, which finished last in the National League in 1918. Gradually, he developed the idea of the farm system. In 1919, he bought 50 percent of the Ft. Smith, AR team, an 18-percent interest in the Houston team of the Texas League, and a 50-percent interest in Syracuse of the International League. His contacts with college coaches allowed Rickey to hear about many promising young players who could be signed and developed on the farm clubs. Not only did the system furnish top players for the Cardinals, but the surplus "crop" could be sold to other teams.

By 1941, the Cardinals had more than 600 players with 32 minor-league teams, and from 1926 through 1946 the team won eight National League pennants and finished second six times. Rickey went to the Dodgers in 1943 and immediately strengthened a farm system that was already in place. His chief strategy was to sign promising players too young to be drafted by the military. When the war ended in 1945, those young players were beginning to mature, and several of them combined with returning veterans to lead Brooklyn to pennants in 1947 and 1949. Rickey in 1951 became general manager of the Pittsburgh Pirates, but he left the Dodgers a legacy of five more pennants during the 1950s.

Black players, such as Robinson, Roy Campanella, Don Newcombe, and Joe Black, formed a large part of his legacy to the Dodgers. Rickey's motives in integrating the team and, ultimately, all major-league teams were unquestioably complex. In 1945, after being forced to give two black players a tryout, Rickey as much as called the action a Communist plot, denied that the Dodgers would sign a black, denounced the Negro major leagues as rackets, and announced the formation of the United States League, for black players only.

Rickey was undoubtedly opposed to racism. Later, he told of a black player he had known at Ohio Wesleyan, Charlie Thomas, who had been denied a hotel room when the team went to South Bend, IN to play Notre Dame. Thomas slept on a cot in Rickey's room that night, and Rickey remembered the young black crying and rubbing his hands, saying "Black skin! If I could only make them white!" Although there were some doubters, Thomas, who had become a dentist, corroborated Rickey's story. Rickey also saw integration as a way of improving his team. "The Negroes will make us winners for years to come, and for that I will happily bear being called a bleeding heart and a do-gooder and all that humanitarian rot," he told his family.

He moved cautiously toward his goal. The USL was only a smokescreen that gave Rickey the chance to scout black players in order to find one who could break the "color barrier." He finally zeroed in on Robinson, an all-around athlete at UCLA who had served as an army lieutenant during World War II and was, in 1945, playing shortstop for the Kansas City Monarchs, a black barnstorming team. On August 28, Dodger scout Clyde Sukeforth brought Robinson into Rickey's office, where a famous scene took place. Rickey warned Robinson that, until he established himself as a major-league player, he would have to avoid confrontations. He hurled racial epithets and profanity at Robinson, demonstrating what he would face from some players and fans. Finally, Robinson asked, "Mr. Rickey, do you want a ballplayer who's afraid to fight back?" Rickey replied, "I want a player with guts enough not to fight back."

The Dodgers' top farm club, the Montreal Royals, on October 23 announced that Robinson had signed a contract to play in 1946. In the meantime, Rickey had bought a 25-percent interest in the Dodgers. Shortly afterward, he began to suffer from Meniere's disease, which was to trouble him for the rest of his life. An inner-ear disturbance symptomized by dizziness and nausea, the disease may have been brought on in part by the stresses Rickey was under because of the Robinson signing and the debt he had incurred to become a part owner of the team.

To avoid segregation of his players, Rickey moved the Dodgers' training camp from Florida to Cuba in 1947, when Robinson and three other black players joined the major-league club. However, fearing racial dissension on the team, he imposed his own segregation, putting the blacks in a cheap hotel. Shortly after their arrival, Rickey learned that some southern players were circulating a petition to keep Robinson off the team; he immediately called the suspects together, lectured them on Americanism, and told them that anyone who refused to play with a black teammate would be traded. Three players requested trades, but two later withdrew their requests. The third was traded to Pittsburgh early in the season.

On April 10, Rickey formally announced that Robinson would be with the Dodgers for the 1947 season. Five days later, Robinson started at first base on opening day at Ebbets Field. He helped lead the team to a pennant and was given the major leagues' first Rookie of the Year award. The door was open. Rickey sold his share of the Dodgers for $1 million to become general manager of the Pittsburgh Pirates in 1951, but his legacy remained. From 1949 through 1956, three black Dodgers won a total of five Most Valuable Player awards—Robinson in 1949, Roy Campanella in 1951, 1953, and 1955, and Don Newcombe in 1956. Newcombe also won the first Cy Young Award in 1956. In large part because of their black players, the Dodgers won pennants in 1949, 1952, 1953, 1956, and 1959.

Rickey left the Pirates in 1959 to head a proposed third major league, the Continental. The league never became a reality, but its threat forced the existing major leagues to expand in 1961, and some observers thought that was exactly what Rickey had intended. Making a speech at his induction into the Missouri Sports Hall of Fame on November 13, 1965, he suffered a heart attack and died less than a month later.

Dubbed the "Mahatma" after India's Mahatma Gandhi, "a combination of God, your father, and a Tammany Hall leader," Rickey was a paradoxical figure. Although he refused to play or even attend a game on Sunday, he created the Sunday doubleheader because it was profitable; religious and self-righteous, he was, as Red Smith put it, "so good at evasion, at circumlocution, that he didn't have to lie"; a brilliant man trained in the law, he devoted his life to what many sportswriters are fond of calling "a little boy's game"; a gifted speaker, he could turn a good phrase—"Luck is preparedness meeting opportunity"—but he could also be pompous and bombastic. Though he demanded formality and was always called "Mr. Rickey" by players and club personnel, he liked aggressive, hard-nosed competitors.

Further Reading: Mann, Arthur. *Branch Rickey, American in Action.* Boston: Houghton Mifflin, 1957; Frommer, Harvey. *Rickey and Robinson: The Men Who Broke Baseball's Color Barrier.* New York; Macmillan, 1982.

See also ROBINSON, JACKIE.

Rifle Shooting
See SHOOTING.

Ringette
Sam Jacks, director of recreation in North Bay, Ontario, developed ringette as a version of ice hockey for girls. Instead of a puck, the sport uses a ring, and players carry or pass the ring with bladeless sticks. Ringette quickly spread from Ontario into Western Canada, and a national governing body, Ringette Canada, was established in 1974. The first national championships were held in 1979. The number of registered players passed 20,000 in 1985 and is now approaching 30,000. Ringette Canada estimates that another 35,000 girls play the sport recreationally, without registering.

Address: Ringette Canada, Tower C, 6th Floor, 333 River Road, Vanier, Ontario, Canada K1L 8H9 (613) 748–5655

Riverfront Stadium
Cincinnati, OH
The first baseball park to use sliding pits in artificial turf around the bases, rather than having a complete dirt infield, Riverfront became the home of the National League's Cincinnati Reds during the 1970 season. After drawing only 567,937 fans in their first 34 home games at Crosley Field, the Reds drew 1,235,610 in the 43 remaining games at their new park. Built on a 48-acre site between downtown Cincinnati and the Ohio River, Riverfront is atop a giant underground parking garage. The stadium seats 52,392 for baseball; home run dimensions are 330 feet down the lines and 404 feet to center field. The Cincinnati Bengals of the National Football League have also played in Riverfront since 1970. The football capacity is 60,311.

Riverside International Raceway
Riverside, CA

Opened in 1963, Riverside was a 2.62-mile road style track that hosted two major NASCAR races in its inaugural year, one from 1964 through 1969, and two from 1970 through 1987. The track closed in 1988 after the running of NASCAR's Riverside International Raceway Winston Cup event. It was also the site of USAC 300-mile races from 1967 through 1969 and CART 313.5-mile races from 1981 through 1983.

Road America
Elkhart Lake, WI

A twisting, 14-turn, 4-mile road course, Road America opened in 1955 with a major Sports Car Club of America race. The first professional event was a NASCAR race the following year. In early 1990, a $1.1 million renovation of the paddock area was completed. There is a 2,000-seat grandstand at the start/finish line and an 800-seat grandstand at the third turn, along with many viewing areas throughout the course. Crowds have been estimated as high as 65,000. Road America currently hosts a 200-mile CART race, a Formula One Grand Prix event, a weekend of motorcycle racing, and the SCCA June Sprints, as well as SCCA regional competition.

Address: 81 Lake Street, Elkhart Lake, WI 53020 (414) 876-3366.

Road Racing
See MARATHON; PEDESTRIANISM; SPORTS CAR RACING; TRACK AND FIELD.

Robbie Stadium
See JOE ROBBIE STADIUM.

Robert F. Kennedy Stadium
Washington, DC

In its role as the local government of the District of Columbia, the federal government built the $24 million D.C. stadium as the home of the American League's Washington Senators. While construction was underway in 1961, the Senators became the Minnesota Twins, but the American League promptly granted the city a new franchise. The expansion team, also called the Senators, played in old Griffith Park for one season.

Meanwhile, Secretary of the Interior Stewart L. Udall used the stadium as leverage to force the Washington Redskins to integrate. The Redskins were the last team in the National National Football League to have black players. After the team had signed a 30-year lease for District of Columbia, Udall informed owner George Preston Marshall that the Department of the Interior had adopted regulations prohibiting job discrimination by any party using a federally owned park facility. He threatened to cancel the lease if the Redskins didn't end their ban on blacks. Eventually, the Redskins were allowed to use the stadium in 1961 in exchange for a promise that they would have at least one black player the following season. In fact, they added four black players, running back/wide receiver Bobby Mitchell, guard John Nisby, fullback Ron Hatcher, and running back Leroy Jackson.

The new Washington Senators opened their first season in the stadium on April 10, 1962. They stayed just ten years before becoming the Texas Rangers in 1972.

D.C. Stadium was renamed Robert F. Kennedy Stadium in 1968. Home run dimensions are 335 feet down the lines and 410 feet to center; capacity is 45,016 for baseball and 55,750 for football.

Robertson, Oscar (1938–)
Basketball
Born November 24, 1938, Charlotte, TN; Basketball Hall of Fame

The "Big O" was a three-time All-American and twice College Player of the Year (1959 and 1960) at the University of Cincinnati, where he led the nation's major colleges in scoring three years in a row. When he graduated, his 2,973 points was the NCAA career record. But Robertson was much more than a scorer, as he demonstrated in the 1961–62 season with the Cincinnati Royals, averaging in double figures in scoring, rebounding, and assists, a feat that has never been matched. Large enough at 6–5 and 215 pounds to play forward, he was also skilled enough at ball handling and passing to play guard. Although he was primarily a guard during his professional career, he often moved to forward in the course of a game.

After captaining the 1960 Olympic Gold Medal team, he joined Cincinnati and won the Rookie of the Year award. The Royals in 1970 traded him to Milwaukee, where he teamed up with Kareem Abdul-Jabbar to lead the Bucks to the National Basketball Association championship in 1971. Robertson was named an All-NBA guard nine consecutive times, 1960–1969, and was the league's Player of the Year in 1964. In 14 NBA seasons, he scored 26,710 points, an average of 25.7 per game, and had 7,804 rebounds and 9,887 assists.

Robinson, Brooks C. (1937–)
Baseball
Born May 18, 1937, Little Rock, AR; Baseball Hall of Fame

Probably the greatest third baseman of all time, Robinson was sometimes called the "Human Vacuum Cleaner" because of his outstanding fielding ability. His teammates had a name for his backhanded stops to the right and diving stabs to the left: "Brooksies." And, though he wasn't an outstanding hitter, he was a good batter with some power who could drive in runs in crucial situations. Baltimore Oriole Manager Earl Weaver, asked if he enjoyed the challenge of managing, replied, "I don't want a challenge. I'd rather have a whole team of Robinsons"—referring to Brooks and Frank, who were Oriole teammates for six years.

Robinson joined the Orioles in 1955 and became a starter in 1958. A knee injury limited his playing time in 1959, but from 1960 through 1977 he was a fixture at third base for Baltimore. His best season as a hitter was 1964, when he batted .317 and led the American League in runs batted in with 118. He was named the league's Most Valuable Player that season, and in 1970 he was the Most Valuable Player in the World Series.

He didn't quite beat the Cincinnati Reds single-handedly in that Series, but he came close. In the first game, he prevented at least one run and probably two by making a brilliant backhanded play down the line in the sixth inning, then hit a seventh-inning home run that gave Baltimore a 4–3 victory. With the Reds leading 4–0 in the second game, he turned an apparent hit that would have scored two more runs into a double play, and singled home a run as the Orioles rallied to win 6–5. He got two doubles and made three outstanding defensive plays in a 9–3 victory in the third game, and he collected four hits, including a home run, in a 6–5 loss in the fourth game. The Orioles won the fifth and final game easily, 9–3. The first Reds' hitter in the ninth inning hit a line drive over third base that looked like a sure double, but once again Robinson came up with a diving catch. Pete Rose of the Reds was moved to remark, "He could play third base with a pair of pliers."

Among nonpitchers, Robinson holds the record for the most Gold Glove awards as the top fielder at his position with 16, four more than anyone else. In his 23 seasons with Baltimore, he played in 2,896 games, batted .267, had 268 home runs, and drove in 1,357 runs.

Robinson, Frank (1935–   )
Baseball

Born August 31, 1935, Beaumont, TX; Baseball Hall of Fame

The only player ever to win the Most Valuable Player award in both major leagues, Robinson was also the sport's first black manager. He arrived in the major leagues with the Cincinnati Reds in 1956 and immediately became a starting outfielder. He led the National League in runs scored and was named Rookie of the Year. The Reds won the pennant in 1961 and Robinson was named MVP; he batted .323 with 37 home runs, 124 runs batted in, and 117 runs scored. However, he hit only .200 as the Reds lost the World Series in five games to the New York Yankees. Robinson had an even better year in 1962, batting .342 with a league-leading 51 doubles and 134 runs scored, along with 39 home runs and 136 runs batted in.

Traded to the Baltimore Orioles in 1966, Robinson won the Triple Crown, leading the league with a batting average of .316, 49 home runs, and 122 runs batted in, and was named the league's MVP. His two-run home run in the first game of the World Series against the Los Angeles Dodgers gave the Orioles the lead for good, as they won 5–2, and he hit a home run to win the fourth and final game 1–0. Robinson played with the Orioles through 1971, batting over .300 each season. He played only part time his last two seasons there, but managed to hit 25 home runs in just 132 games in 1970 and 28 in 133 games the following season. He was with the Los Angeles Dodgers in 1972, then went to the California Angels as a designated hitter for the next two seasons. Robinson was named playing manager of the Cleveland Indians in 1975. After two respectable seasons, he was fired during the 1977 season. He managed the San Francisco Giants from 1981 into the 1984 season. Robinson got his third managing job with the Orioles in 1989. Taking over a team that had finished last the previous season, he came close to winning the eastern division title; ironically, the Orioles were edged by the Toronto Blue Jays, another team with a black manager, Cito Gaston.

During his 22 seasons in the major leagues, Robinson batted .294 with 586 home runs and 1,812 runs batted in. He also stole 204 bases.

Robinson, "Jackie" Jack R. (1919–1972)
Baseball

Born January 31, 1919, Cairo, GA; died October 24, 1972; Baseball Hall of Fame

The man handpicked by Branch Rickey to become the first black player in modern major-league history was considered by many an unlikely candidate for the task. There were players in the black major leagues such as Satchel Paige, Josh Gibson, and Monte Irvin who were proposed as better prospects. Robinson, The Sporting News suggested, was probably qualified only to play Class C minor-league baseball. Even many black players questioned the choice. Robinson had been with the Kansas City

Monarchs for less than a season, and he had been the team's second-string shortstop for part of that time. Some blacks thought that a inferior player had deliberately been chosen to delay the integration of baseball for as long as possible.

But Rickey had made his choice well. Robinson was an intelligent, articulate man who had lettered in four sports at UCLA and had served as an officer in World War II. He was not only an outstanding athlete, but a very competitive one who, nevertheless, understood his place in history and, as Rickey put it, had "the guts not to fight back" against racial slurs until he had definitely established himself as a player of major-league caliber.

Robinson actually entered organized baseball by signing a contract with the Brooklyn Dodgers' top farm team, the Montreal Royals, on October 23, 1945, and he played second base for the Royals in 1946, dispelling any doubts about his ability. He led the International League in hitting at .349 and in runs scored with 113, and he finished second in stolen bases.

When he went to spring training in 1947, though, he received a couple of shocks. Although the Dodgers had moved their training camp from Florida to Cuba to avoid segregation, Rickey had decided the four black players (the other three were Roy Campanella, Don Newcombe, and Roy Partlow) would stay in a third-rate hotel. And Robinson, who had already changed positions once, was going to be tried at first base. Despite those problems, he was formally promoted to the Dodgers and opened the season at first base on April 15, 1947.

Robinson faced verbal and physical abuse from some opponents, especially the Philadelphia Phillies and the St. Louis Cardinals, as well as verbal abuse from fans in many cities. But Brooklyn fans, by and large, welcomed him. And he drew crowds in every city he played in; so many blacks turned out in St. Louis that they overflowed into the area traditionally reserved for whites, and the team's segregation of its fans was ended in fact, if not in word. Despite the incredible pressures, Robinson performed well above average major-league levels, and as a vitally important player in the Dodgers' pennant drive he also quietly developed good relationships with most of his teammates, even with a couple of southern players who had earlier asked to be traded rather than play alongside a black man. Robinson batted .297, led the league in stolen bases with 29, and was second in runs scored. The Dodgers won the pennant and, at the age of 28, Robinson became baseball's first Rookie of the Year.

In 1948, Robinson moved back to second base, where he spent most of the rest of his career. After

hitting .296 that season, he had an outstanding year in 1949, leading the league in batting at .342 and in stolen bases with 37. He had 203 hits, 122 runs scored, and 124 runs batted in, and was the first black to be named Most Valuable Player of his league, as the Dodgers won their second pennant in his three seasons. For the second time, they lost to the New York Yankees in the World Series.

Robinson batted over .300 each of the next four seasons. But he played just 105 games in 1955, most of them at third base, and he hit only .256. After a .275 season in 1956, the Dodgers traded Robinson to the New York Giants. Rather than report, he announced his retirement early in 1957. He had played only nine seasons in the major leagues, but he was almost 38 years old. In 1,382 games, he batted .311 with 273 doubles, 54 triples, 137 home runs, 947 runs scored, 734 runs batted in, and 197 stolen bases.

The statistics don't show Robinson's fierce competitiveness. One of his managers, Leo Durocher, summed it up: "If I go to war, I want Jackie Robinson on my side." The competitiveness carried over into life off the playing field. By 1949, his MVP year, Robinson knew that he had proven himself, and he began campaigning for better conditions for black players. Appearing on the television show "Youth Wants To Know" in 1952, Robinson ignited a public feud by charging New York Yankee management with prejudice because, he pointed out, "There isn't a single Negro on the team now and very few in the entire Yankee farm system."

After retiring from baseball, Robinson worked for the Chock Full O' Nuts restaurant chain, wrote a column for the *New York Post*, and became involved in politics, usually on the Republican side. During the 1960s, he fought for school desegregation in the South. He also spoke bitterly about baseball's failure to hire black managers and front-office personnel. He suffered from diabetes, and in 1968 he had a heart attack. The Dodgers, now in Los Angeles, retired his number, 42, in 1972. Later that year, the 25th anniversary of his groundbreaking appearance, he threw out the first ball at the second game of the World Series in Cincinnati. He died just ten days later. His eulogy was given by a young minister named Jesse Jackson.

Further Reading: Allen, Maury. *Jackie Robinson: A Life Remembered*. New York: Franklin Watts, 1987; Tygiel, Jules. *Baseball's Great Experiment: Jackie Robinson and His Legacy*. New York: Oxford University Press, 1983.

See also RICKEY, BRANCH.

Robinson, Sugar Ray (Walter Smith) (1920–1989)
Boxing

Born May 3, 1920, Detroit, MI; died April 12, 1989;
Boxing Hall of Fame

Sugar Ray's quickness and boxing ability sometimes obscured the fact that he was an outstanding puncher and a tough competitor. Joe Louis called him the "greatest fighter ever to step into the ring," and Archie Moore said, "Generations of fighters copied his style, including Muhammad Ali."

He won Golden Gloves championships as a featherweight and as a lightweight and had 69 knockouts in 85 amateur fights before becoming a professional in 1940. On December 20, 1946, Robinson won the vacant world welterweight title with a 15–round decision over Tommy Bell, and he held the title until February 14, 1951, when he became middleweight champion by knocking out Jake LaMotta in the 13th round. Later that year, Robinson went to Europe for seven fights in a three-month period. He lost the title in the seventh fight, on July 10, to Randy Turpin of England on a 15–round decision. In a rematch against Turpin on September 12 in New York, referee Ruby Goldstein was about to call the ringside doctor in to examine a cut over Robinson's eye. "Give me one more round," Robinson asked, and then knocked out Turpin to regain the title.

After being knocked out by Joey Maxim in a fight for the light-heavyweight championship on June 25, 1952, Robinson retired. But he returned to the ring late in 1954, and on December 9, 1955, he regained the middleweight title by knocking out Bobo Olsen in the second round. That began a roller-coaster ride: Robinson lost the title to Gene Fullmer in 15 rounds on January 2, 1957, regained it by knocking out Fullmer in the the fifth round on May 1, lost it to Carmen Basilio on September 23, and won it back with a decision over Basilio on March 25, 1958.

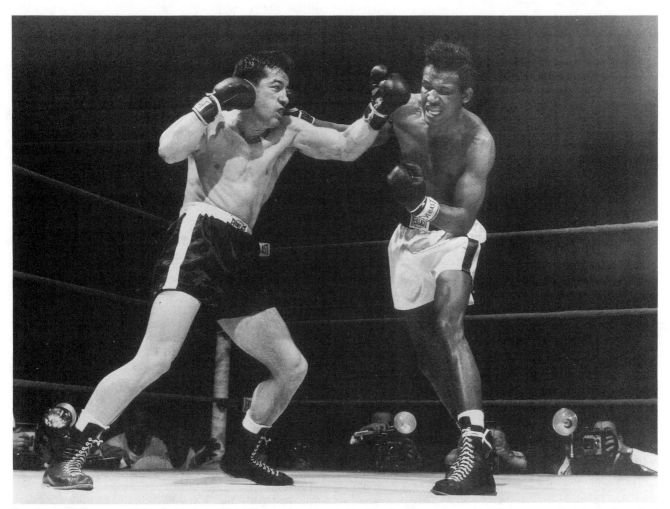

Sugar Ray Robinson, right, defends his middleweight title against Rocky Graziano on April 16, 1952. Robinson knocked out Graziano in the third round. Courtesy of the Public Broadcasting System

Robinson lost the middleweight championship for good when Paul Pender decisioned him on January 22, 1960. But he continued fighting until 1965, when he announced his retirement. He won 174 of his 201 professional bouts, with 109 knockouts. Of his 19 defeats, only 1 was by knockout. Robinson also had six draws and two no-contests.

Rochester, NY

Football The Rochester Jeffersons joined the National Football League in 1920, its first season, and remained through the 1925 season.

Rock Island, IL

Football From 1920 through 1925, the Rock Island Independents played in the National Football League. The team moved into the first American Football League for its only season, 1926.

See also TRI-CITIES.

Rockne, Knute K. (1888–1931)
Football
Born March 4, 1888, Voss, Norway; died March 31, 1931; National Football Foundation Hall of Fame

Rockne was never involved with a losing team. During his three seasons as a starting end at Notre Dame, the team won 20 games and tied 2 without a loss; in his four seasons as an assistant coach under Jess Harper, the team went 26–5–1; and in 13 seasons as the team's head coach, he won 105 games with 12 losses and 5 ties.

A charismatic figure known for his inspiring pep talks, Rockne was also an innovative coach. Inheriting the "Notre Dame shift" from Harper, Rockne turned it into a versatile system of attack. His offense lined up in a T-formation and usually shifted into one of three formations. The shifting, and the fact that Rockne used a balanced line (the single wing of the time used an unbalanced line, usually strong to the right), made it difficult for defenses to guess what was coming. He also developed the technique of "stunting," in which defensive linemen charge diagonally rather than straight ahead. Although Harper had an outstanding record, Rockne turned Notre Dame into a genuine football power by building up a "suicide schedule" against strong teams from throughout the country.

Though only 5 feet 8 inches and 145 pounds, Rockne first attracted public notice in Notre Dame's surprise 35–13 victory over Army in 1913, when Notre Dame unveiled the forward pass as a primary weapon for the first time. Rockne caught several passes from his good friend, quarterback Gus Dorais, in the victory. After graduating in 1914, Rockne remained at Notre Dame as chemistry instructor, head track coach, and assistant football coach. Harper resigned after the 1917 season, and Rockne replaced him.

Because of World War I, there were only six games on the 1918 schedule; Notre Dame won 3, lost 1, and tied 2. Led by George Gipp, Rockne's next two teams were undefeated, winning all 18 of their games, and the 1921 team won 10 of 11, losing only to Iowa. With the Four Horsemen in the backfield and the Seven Mules in the line, Rockne's 1924 squad was also unbeaten, winning all nine regular-season games and beating Stanford 27–10 in the Rose Bowl. Rockne pulled one of his many psychological ploys that season: Afraid that the Four Horsemen were getting lackadaisical because of all their publicity, he put a third-string line in front of them for several plays. After the backs had floundered for a while because of inadequate blocking, he replaced them all, called them together on the sidelines, and asked sarcastically, "Why didn't you show them your press clippings?"

From 1925 through 1928, Notre Dame won 28, lost 8, and tied 1. Rockne's worst year was a 5–4–0 record in 1928. He might have had a losing season but for a 12–6 upset of Army. That was the game when Rockne give his most famous talk: George Gipp had died of pneumonia shortly after the end of the 1920 season and, Rockne now told his players, on his deathbed he had said, "Rock, someday when the going is real tough, ask the boys to go out and beat Army for me." The outmanned but inspired Notre Dame team did just that. Despite the toughest schedule in the nation, Rockne followed that with unbeaten, untied teams in 1929 and 1930.

On March 31, 1931, Rockne was one of six passengers on a flight from Kansas City to Los Angeles when the plane lost a wing and crashed near Bazaar, KS, killing all aboard. His death was front-page news across the country, and 10,000 crowded into a Chicago station to see the train carrying Rockne's casket back to South Bend. Among the many tributes was this from James L. Knox of Harvard: "One man like Rockne means more to our country than a million reformers; and if football produces one Rockne in each generation, the nation can ill afford to curtail football."

A charismatic figure, Rockne was an outstanding public speaker who was hired by Studebaker to give motivational talks to salesmen. He wrote many magazine and newspaper articles as well as three books, appeared in movie shorts, and, just before his death, was being offered $50,000 by RKO to play a football coach in a movie musical and $75,000 by Hearst to write a daily column. He was, wrote Grantland Rice, "a man of great force, deep charm and an amazing personality . . . Whenever there was a gathering of coaches in any city there was usually one question: 'Where's Rock staying?' That's where they all gathered."

Further Reading: Wallace, Francis. *Knute Rockne*. Garden City: Doubleday, 1960.

Rodeo

As early as 1872, cowboys demonstrated their skill in steer riding and bronco busting at Cheyenne, TX. True competition began in the 1880s: When cowboys from different ranches met at common stopping places during cattle drives, ranchers would bet among themselves on their best cowboys. The first real rodeo (then called a "cowboy tournament") was staged in 1888 at Prescott, AZ, where citizens built a grandstand, sold tickets, and awarded silver belt buckles to the winners. Other cow towns adopted the idea, and soon professional organizers got involved, establishing an informal circuit of tournaments. (The word "rodeo," from the Spanish for "cattle ring," apparently wasn't applied to the sport until early in this century.)

When promoters organized the Rodeo Association of America in 1928, few cowboys were riding the range, and most contestants were professionals who traveled from one rodeo to the next. In 1929, the RAA began naming an all-around champion based on performances in the five standard events: bareback riding, bull riding, calf roping, saddle bronc riding, and steer wrestling. The contestants themselves banded together in 1936 as the Cowboys' Turtle Association to work for larger purses and fair judging. That informal group became the Rodeo Cowboys Association in 1945 and the Professional Rodeo Cowboys Association in 1975. A similar group, the Canadian Professional Rodeo Association, originally the Cowboys' Insurance Association, was organized in 1944.

Both associations gradually took over more and more responsibility for operating rodeos and eventually became sanctioning and governing bodies. Thousands of rodeos are held annually in North America, but only about 700 of them are sanctioned. At the end of the season, the Canadian Finals Rodeo and the National Finals Rodeo are held to determine national champions. The NFR was established in 1959, the CFR in 1974.

Women have long been involved in rodeo, but for years they competed only in barrel racing, in which competitors race ponies through an obstacle course marked by barrels. The Women's Professional Rodeo Association, founded in 1947, now offers a full range of competition, including national finals. Competition for younger age groups is conducted by the National Intercollegiate Rodeo Association, the National High School Rodeo Association, and the Little Britches Rodeo Association, for ages 8 through 18.

Addresses: National High School Rodeo Association, 12200 Pecos Street, Suite 120, Denver, CO 80234 (303) 452–0800; National Intercollegiate Rodeo Association, 1615 Portland Street, Walla Walla, WA 99362 (509) 529–4402; National Little Britches Rodeo Association, 1045 West Rio Grande, Colorado Springs, CO 80906 (303) 389–0333; Women's Professional Rodeo Association, Route 5, Box 698, Blanchard, OK 73010 (405) 485–2277

See also CANADIAN PROFESSIONAL RODEO ASSOCIATION; NATIONAL FINALS RODEO; PROFESSIONAL RODEO COWBOYS ASSOCIATION.

Roller Derby

The original roller derby was patterned after six-day bicycle races. Leo Seltzer of Chicago conceived the idea of a roller skating marathon in 1935 and trademarked the name. The first roller derby was a "transcontinental race" at the Chicago Coliseum on August 13, 1935, with two-person teams. Each team had a man and a woman, one of whom had to be on the track at all times. Contestants skated about 4,000 miles in the course of the race, which drew about 20,000 spectators. Lights on a huge map of the country showed where the skaters were on their supposed transcontinental journey.

Seltzer staged several similar races at shorter distances, and some competitors began working as teams to block opponents from passing. At the suggestion of sportswriter Damon Runyon, Seltzer in 1938 turned the roller derby into a new sort of sport, emphasizing blocking and body contact, with two five-person teams competing. The two teams always had the same skaters, but their names changed on tour. The visiting team would usually be called "Chicago" in the Midwest, "New York" in the East, and the home team took the name of whatever city they happened to be appearing in.

In 1948, CBS broadcast part of the roller derby during a New York appearance, and the sport became popular. Seltzer organized a league with teams representing Brooklyn, Chicago, New Jersey, New York, Philadelphia, and Washington-Baltimore. Within a couple of years, though, interest waned, and by 1958 the sport was confined to the San Francisco Bay area. Seltzer's son Richard then took over the operation. To regain television exposure, he distributed the videotapes of competition to stations without charge. Many stations were delighted

Roller skating became a craze for about a decade after the four-wheeled skate was invented in 1875. This is a New York rink in 1880.

to carry free programming, and the sport once again gained a measure of popularity in the late 1960s and early 1970s.

The great increase in live programming of many other sports, along with relatively inexpensive syndicated programming, led to the death of the roller derby in 1975. The International Roller Derby League merged with the rival National Skating Derby Roller Games under a new name, World Skating Derby Roller Races, but that venture folded after drawing only 600 fans to its first event. A similar made-for-television sport is now syndicated under the name "Roller Games."

Roller Skating

The roller skate was apparently invented in Holland during the 18th century when someone attached wooden wheels to ice skates, and similar roller skates were made in Belgium and France late in the century. These early skates had only two wheels, front and back. James L. Plimpton developed the modern skate in 1863, using four wheels, and roller skating soon became popular among the upper classes in England, Europe, and North America. The New York Skating Association was founded in 1869.

An improved roller skate with metal wheels and roller bearings was invented in 1875, greatly increasing the sport's popularity. Rinks were established in old warehouses and factory buildings, where people could rent skates and do figures to dance music. As with ice skating, girls and women quickly got involved, and competition began to develop in both figures and racing. Roller polo, roller hockey, and basketball on skates were also promoted at many rinks. By 1885, more than $20 million had been invested in rink properties, but the fad died out as suddenly as it had sprung up.

It came back early in the 20th century, when the ball-bearing skate was developed. After another decline, the sport reached a new peak in the 1930s. The Roller Skating Rink Operators Association was organized in 1937 to develop standard rules and conduct national championships for speed skating. In 1939, the RSROA also standardized figure skating competition. A rival group, the U.S. Amateur Roller Skating Association, was founded that year to conduct its own figure skating championships, and it added speed skating championships in 1942.

After World War II, many rinks were built throughout North America, and the number of skaters grew to an estimated 17 million. The RSROA and USARSA merged into the United States of America Confederation of Amateur Roller Skating in 1972. The confederation has three divisions: the Artistic Skating Union, the Speed Skating Union, and the Hockey Skating Union, which oversees competition in roller polo, played with a ball, and roller hockey, played with a puck. There are more than 5,000 roller rinks and an estimated 25 million skaters in North America.

Addresses: Canadian Federation of Amateur Roller Skaters, 1220 Sheppard Avenue E., Willowdale, Ontario, Canada M2K 2X1; U.S. of A. Confederation of Amateur Roller Skating, P.O. Box 6579, Lincoln, NE 68506 (402) 483–7551

See also ROLLER DERBY.

Rookie of the Year

The idea of a Rookie of the Year award originated in the National Hockey League in 1937, when Frank Calder, the league's president, donated a trophy for the player named "the most proficient in his first year of competition." Other sports were slow to adopt the idea. The Baseball Writers Association of America in 1947 and 1948 gave a trophy to the player selected as the best rookie in the major leagues. Since 1949, there has been an award in each league. The Eddie Gottlieb Trophy, for the Rookie of the Year in the National Basketball Association, was first presented in 1953. United Press International began choosing a National Football League Rookie of the Year in 1955 and an American Football League winner in 1960, that league's first year. Since the leagues merged in 1970, awards have been presented for rookies of the year in the American and National Football Conferences by UPI, the Associated Press, the *Sporting News,* and various football periodicals.

Roosevelt Raceway
Westbury, NY

Roosevelt pioneered night harness racing when it opened in 1940, and by 1952 the track had racing more than 100 nights of the year, attracting 1.7 million fans, who bet a total of $85 million. Long one of the premier tracks in the country, Roosevelt in 1956 inaugurated the Messenger Stakes, which became one of the races in the Triple Crown of pacing. However, the track began having financial problems in the late 1970s. A group of investors bought Roosevelt in 1984, with financing of about $54 million in municipal bonds issued by the town of Hempstead, on Long Island, where the track was located. Attendance declined from 1.25 million in 1983 to just over 732,000 in 1987, and total betting dropped from $210.5 million to $157.5 million during the same period. The track closed in early 1988, and the Messenger Stakes moved to Yonkers Raceway.

Roque

See CROQUET.

Rose Bowl
Football

The Tournament of Roses in Pasadena, CA, inaugurated in 1889 as a parade and sports activities, added a football game as a sidelight in 1902. Perhaps because of Michigan's lopsided 49–0 victory over Stanford, the next game wasn't played until 1916. Originally known as the Tournament of Roses game or the East-West Classic, it has been called the Rose Bowl since 1923. The Tournament of Roses Committee invited a West Coast team, and the West Coast team invited a team from the East until 1947. Because the War Department forbade large gatherings of people on the West Coast in 1942, Duke University hosted Oregon State at Durham, NC. Beginning in 1947, the champions of the Pacific Coast Conference and the Western Conference (Big Ten) played in the game. The PCC was supplanted in 1960 by the Athletic Association of Western Universities, now the Pacific 10.

Rose Bowl Results

1902	Michigan 49, Stanford 0
1916	Washington State 14, Brown 0
1917	Oregon 14, Pennsylvania 0
1918	Mare Island 19, Great Lakes 7
1919	Great Lakes 17, Mare Island 0
1920	Harvard 7, Oregon 6
1921	California 28, Ohio State 0
1922	Washington & Jefferson 0, California 0
1923	Southern California 14, Penn State 3
1924	Navy 14, Washington 14
1925	Notre Dame 27, Stanford 10
1926	Alabama 20, Washington 19
1927	Alabama 7, Stanford 7
1928	Stanford 7, Pittsburgh 6
1929	Georgia Tech 8, California 7
1930	Southern California 47, Pittsburgh 14
1931	Alabama 24, Washington State 0
1932	Southern California 21, Tulane 12
1933	Southern California 35, Pittsburgh 0
1934	Columbia 7, Stanford 0
1935	Alabama 29, Stanford 13
1936	Stanford 7, Southern Methodist 0
1937	Pittsburgh 21, Washington 0
1938	California 13, Alabama 0
1939	Southern California 7, Duke 3
1940	Southern California 14, Tennessee 0
1941	Stanford 21, Nebraska 13
1942	Oregon State 20, Duke 16
1943	Georgia 9, UCLA 0
1944	Southern California 29, Washington 0
1945	Southern California 25, Tennessee 0
1946	Alabama 34, Southern California 14
1947	Illinois 45, UCLA 14
1948	Michigan 49, Southern California 0
1949	Northwestern 20, California 14
1950	Ohio State 17, California 14
1951	Michigan 14, California 6
1952	Illinois 40, Stanford 7
1953	Southern California 7, Wisconsin 0
1954	Michigan State 28, UCLA 20
1955	Ohio State 20, Southern California 7
1956	Michigan State 17, UCLA 14
1957	Iowa 35, Oregon State 19
1958	Ohio State 10, Oregon 7
1959	Iowa 38, California 12
1960	Washington 44, Wisconsin 8
1961	Washington 17, Minnesota 7
1962	Minnesota 21, UCLA 3
1963	Southern California 42, Wisconsin 37
1964	Illinois 17, Washington 7
1965	Michigan 34, Oregon State 7
1966	UCLA 14, Michigan State 12
1967	Purdue 14, Southern California 13
1968	Southern California 14, Indiana 3
1969	Ohio State 27, Southern California 16
1970	Southern California 10, Michigan 3
1971	Stanford 27, Ohio State 17
1972	Stanford 13, Michigan 12
1973	Southern California 42, Ohio State 17
1974	Ohio State 42, Southern California 21
1975	Southern California 18, Ohio State 17
1976	UCLA 23, Ohio State 10
1977	Southern California 14, Michigan 6
1978	Washington 27, Michigan 20
1979	Southern California 17, Michigan 10
1980	Southern California 17, Ohio State 16
1981	Michigan 23, Washington 6
1982	Washington 28, Iowa 0
1983	UCLA 24, Michigan 14
1984	UCLA 45, Illinois 9

1985	Southern California 20, Ohio State 17
1986	UCLA 45, Iowa 28
1987	Arizona State 22, Michigan 15
1988	Michigan State 20, Southern California 17
1989	Michigan 22, Southern California 14
1990	Southern California 17, Michigan 10
1991	Washington 46, Iowa 34

Rose, Mauri (1906–1981)
Auto Racing

Born May 26, 1906, Columbus, OH; died January 1, 1981; Racing Hall of Fame

Rose made his reputation almost entirely in the Indianapolis 500, for good reason: He was, for most of his career, a part-time driver who specialized in that one big race. An engineer, he spent most of his time working for automobile companies, including Hupmobile, Chevrolet, and General Motors. He qualified for 15 consecutive Indy races, was the first driver to win the race three times and the first to win it two years in a row. After being the top qualifier in 1941, he lost his car to mechanical problems on the 60th lap, but then took over a car running in 14th place to win the race. He won again in 1947 and 1948, and he was leading in 1949 when engine problems forced him out with only eight laps to go. Despite his part-time status, he won the national driving championship in 1936 and finished second in 1934.

Ross Trophy
Hockey

Arthur H. Ross, the first manager-coach of the Boston Bruins, in 1947 donated this trophy to the National Hockey League to be awarded to the player scoring the most points. In case of a tie, the trophy goes to the player who scored the most goals. The trophy was made retroactive to 1917–1918, the league's first season.

Ross Trophy Winners

1918	Joe Malone, Montreal
1919	Newsy Lalonde, Montreal
1920	Joe Malone, Quebec
1921	Newsy Lalonde, Montreal
1922	Punch Broadbent, Ontario
1923	Babe Dye, Toronto
1924	Cy Denneny, Ottawa
1925	Babe Dye, Toronto
1926	Nels Stewart, Montreal Maroons
1927	Bill Cook, New York Rangers
1928	Howie Morenz, Montreal Canadiens
1929	Ace Bailey, Toronto
1930	Cooney Weiland, Boston
1931	Howie Morenz, Montreal
1932	Harvey Jackson, Toronto
1933	Bill Cook, New York Rangers
1934	Charlie Conacher, Toronto
1935	Charlie Conacher, Toronto
1936	Dave Schriner, New York Americans
1937	Dave Schriner, New York Americans
1938	Gordie Drillon, Toronto
1939	Toe Blake, Montreal
1940	Milt Schmidt, Boston
1941	Bill Cowley, Boston
1942	Brian Hextall, New York
1943	Doug Bentley, Chicago
1944	Herbie Cain, Boston
1945	Elmer Lach, Montreal
1946	Max Bentley, Chicago
1947	Max Bentley, Chicago
1948	Elmer Lach, Montreal
1949	Roy Conacher, Chicago
1950	Ted Lindsay, Detroit
1951	Gordie Howe, Detroit
1952	Gordie Howe, Detroit
1953	Gordie Howe, Detroit
1954	Gordie Howe, Detroit
1955	Bernie Geoffrion, Montreal
1956	Jean Beliveau, Montreal
1957	Gordie Howe, Detroit
1958	Dickie Moore, Montreal
1959	Dickey Moore, Montreal
1960	Bobby Hull, Chicago
1961	Bernie Geoffrion, Montreal
1962	Bobby Hull, Chicago
1963	Gordie Howe, Detroit
1964	Stan Mikita, Chicago
1965	Stan Mikita, Chicago
1966	Bobby Hull, Chicago
1967	Stan Mikita, Chicago
1968	Stan Mikita, Chicago
1969	Phil Esposito, Boston
1970	Bobby Orr, Boston
1971	Phil Esposito, Boston
1972	Phil Esposito, Boston
1973	Phil Esposito, Boston
1974	Phil Esposito, Boston
1975	Bobby Orr, Boston
1976	Guy Lafleur, Montreal
1977	Guy Lafleur, Montreal
1978	Guy Lafleur, Montreal
1979	Brian Trottier, New York Islanders
1980	Marcel Dionne, Los Angeles
1981	Wayne Gretzky, Edmonton
1982	Wayne Gretzky, Edmonton
1983	Wayne Gretzky, Edmonton
1984	Wayne Gretzky, Edmonton
1985	Wayne Gretzky, Edmonton
1986	Wayne Gretzky, Edmonton
1987	Wayne Gretzky, Edmonton

1988   Mario Lemieux, Pittsburgh
1989   Mario Lemieux, Pittsburgh
1990   Wayne Gretzky, Los Angeles
1991   Wayne Gretzky, Los Angeles

Rounders

American baseball evolved from rounders and similar sports. The bases in rounders were posts or flat stones, 12–20 yards apart. The striker—"batter," we would say—tried to hit a ball tossed by the "pecker" or "feeder." Bases were run clockwise. The striker was out if he swung and missed three times, hit a foul ball, or had his batted ball caught while in the air. He could also be put out if hit by a thrown ball while between bases.

Rowing

Competitive rowing in North America began in the South during the 18th century, with southern gentlemen steering boats while black slaves rowed. Slaves sometimes arranged boat races of their own during their leisure time. The modern sport, however, originated in the Northeast, where crews originally competed against one another to bring news and supplies to incoming ships. That kind of competition led to betting on challenge races; one such race, for a $20 bet, was recorded as early as 1756 by the *New York Mercury.*

Crew racing became relatively popular in the early part of the 19th century. Two New York boat builders, John Baptist and John Chambers, had a match race in 1807 between four-oared crews, with Baptist's boat winning. They met again in 1811, Baptist's *Knickerbocker* beating Chambers' *Invincible,* and a third time in 1820 for an $800 bet. New York newspapers reported that a large crowd bet a total of $8,000 to $10,000 on the outcome of the 1820 race.

Rowing was the first popular intercollegiate sport. This newspaper illustration shows the 1881 Harvard-Yale race at New London.

The Savannah Boat Club and the Whitehall Aquatic Club of New York were both organized in 1820, and a regatta was held that year on Quidi Vidi Lake near St. John's, Newfoundland. When the English frigate *Hussar* docked in New York in late 1824, Captain George Harris issued a newspaper challenge for a race, and the Whitehall crew accepted. Racing on December 9 in a Chambers-built boat, *American Star,* the Whitehallers won the 4-mile competition before a crowd estimated at from 20,000 to 50,000. On May 20 of the following year, about 30,000 spectators watched Whitehall beat the Richmond crew from Staten Island in a 5-mile race.

Rowing declined in popularity toward the end of the decade, but had a resurgence in the 1830s. Young New York gentlemen formed several rowing clubs; nine of the clubs established the Castle Garden Boat Association in 1834, and the association's annual regatta became a major social event. Rowing also prospered in Boston, Charleston, Detroit, New Orleans, Philadelphia, and Savannah during the late 1830s. Most racing during this period was between four-oared barges or six-oared cutters, but single sculling began to come into its own with a series of races between professional New York oarsmen Sydney Dolan and Stephan Roberts in 1837 and 1838.

A regatta in the Bay of Toronto in August of 1840 included rowing and sailing races. Although the sport once again declined in major cities during the 1840s, it took root at several eastern colleges, led by Yale in 1843 and Harvard in 1844. Collegiate rowing clubs were at first primarily social, although both colleges took part in some local regattas. The first intercollegiate sports competition ever staged in North America was the August 3, 1852, race between eight-oared barges from Harvard and Yale on Lake Winnepesaukee in New Hampshire. Harvard won the 2-mile race, sponsored by the Boston, Concord, and Montreal Railroad, which ran excursion trains to the area.

Meanwhile, rowing was again making a comeback in New York. The *Times* in 1854 called for a July 4 rowing regatta "to beguile young men from the sedentary relaxation of gaming, or the semi-effeminate skill of the billiard table, and lead them out in God's open air . . ." The Empire City Regatta Club was organized in 1855 by boat builders to offer prize money for rowing races, and in 1859 the New York Regatta Club began holding a regatta on July 4. Meanwhile, a group of clubs in the Philadelphia area banded together in 1858 as the Schuylkill Navy, which was to become important in the history of amateurism as well as the history of rowing.

The second Harvard-Yale race wasn't held until 1855. By then, the University of Pennsylvania had a barge club, and more colleges got involved in

Rowing clubs proliferated in New York during the 1870s. This magazine illustration shows scenes from the second annual regatta of the Union Boat Club of Harlem in 1880.

rowing during the next several years. Brown, Harvard, Trinity College of Connecticut, and Yale in 1858 gathered at Springfield, MA for a proposed race, but it was canceled when a Yale crew member drowned. They organized the College Union Regatta Association the following year and did stage a race at Lake Quinsigamond in Worcester, MA, although Trinity didn't take part. A crowd estimated at 15,000 to 20,000 watched Harvard's victory, which was front-page news in the *New York Herald*. The following day, about 10,000 spectators saw Yale beat Harvard in a race for a $100 prize donated by the city of Worcester.

Harvard also won in 1860 and 1861, but the Yale faculty in 1862 prohibited racing during term time. In 1864 Yale hired a professional trainer, William Wood—we would now call him a coach—and challenged Harvard to another contest. Wood was the first professional coach ever hired by an American college. Yale won that race, also at Worcester, and repeated in 1865.

That was the major sports activity in the United States during the Civil War. However, rowing grew rapidly in Canada, with several clubs formed be-

tween 1860 and 1865. One of the historic highlights of Canadian sports was the victory of a St. John, New Brunswick, crew in the 1867 world four-oared championship in Paris. The "Paris crew," as it became known, lost an 1870 race against a crew from Tyne, England, for a £1,000 prize.

Harvard and Yale continued their races after the Civil War, and in August 1869 the Harvard crew rowed against Oxford University in England, losing by about 3 lengths. A crowd estimated at as many as 1 million people lined the Thames for the 4¼-mile race, and American reporters cabled lengthy stories home on this major international sports event.

The 1870 Harvard-Yale race ended in a dispute: Harvard won when Yale was disqualified after having finished first, and Yale refused to race the following year. Harvard hosted Bowdoin, Brown, and Massachusetts Agricultural College (now the University of Massachusetts) at an April meeting at which the Rowing Association of American Colleges was formed. Massachusetts won the first RAAC regatta in an upset. Brown left the association, but Amherst, Williams and Yale joined in 1872. The regatta moved to Saratoga Lake, NY in 1874, and there were 13 crews in the 1875 race, which drew about 30,000 spectators. However, Harvard and Yale withdrew from the six-oared competition to begin their own series in eight-oared shells in 1876. College crew had been replaced by football as the premier intercollegiate sport, and the RAAC collapsed.

After the Civil War, amateur rowing made a strong comeback. There were 48 match races or regattas in 1867, 65 in 1869, and more than 150 in 1872. According to the *Boating Almanac* and *Boat Club Directory*, in 1873 there were 289 boat clubs in 25 states and 159 scheduled races or regattas. Professional sculling also prospered during the 1870s. (In sculling, a scull is held in each hand, as in ordinary rowboating; in rowing, each oarsman uses two hands on a single oar.) Edward "Ned" Hanlan of Canada won the professional single sculls race at the Philadelphia Centennial Exposition in 1876 and was generally considered the world champion until losing to Australian William Beach in 1884. Hanlan reportedly won about $12,000 in 1879.

A clear line between amateurism and professionalism was drawn by the Schuylkill Navy, which held the first major noncollegiate regatta in 1872. Many potential entrants were banned because they had raced for side bets. The National Association of Amateur Oarsmen, organized in August 1872, took over the regatta the following year and also adhered to stringent standards of amateurism. Professionals kept competing for side bets and attracting crowds for a time. Charles E. Courtney of the U.S., the amateur champion at the Philadelphia Exposition, became a professional in 1877 to row against Hanlan. He narrowly lost. The same year, about 30,000 people watched Michael Davis beat George Faulkner on the Charles River for a $1,000 side bet. But gambling and the rise of other spectator sports killed off professional rowing before the 20th century began.

Collegiate crew racing was sporadic, except for the annual Harvard-Yale race, but Columbia in 1878 became the first foreign crew ever to win a trophy at England's prestigious Henley Regatta. There was another major revival when the first Intercollegiate Rowing Association regatta was held in 1895. By then, college crews were all racing in eight-oared shells. Many colleges were still debating the wisdom of hiring professional football coaches, but most of the rowing colleges had professional crew coaches, chief among them Courtney at Cornell, which won 13 of the first 19 IRA races.

The IRA regatta became truly national early in this century. Wisconsin first entered the regatta in 1897, Stanford in 1912, Washington in 1913, and California in 1921. But colleges raced almost entirely in eight-oared shells; rowing and sculling in smaller

vessels became the province of amateur boat clubs, and their numbers declined. To bolster its numbers, the NAAO in 1929 decided to accept colleges and individuals as members rather than just clubs.

Rowing became an Olympic sport in 1904, with five events: single and double sculls, pair-oared and four-oared without coxswain, and eight-oared shells. The U.S. won all five Gold Medals. Racing for four-oared and pair-oared shells with coxswain were added in 1912 and 1920, respectively. International rowing is under the jurisdiction of the Federation International des Sociétés d'Aviron (FISA), organized in 1892. However, the NAAO didn't join until 1929, and then only because the 1932 Olympics were to be held in Los Angeles.

American women began rowing in college intramural competition during the 1930s. Only in the 1960s did they really become involved in the sport. Largely ignored or turned away by male-dominated clubs, they formed their own clubs and, in 1964, the National Women's Rowing Association. The NWRA held its first national championships in 1966, with just 45 boats and fewer than 100 competitors in 11 events. By 1978, the numbers were up to 130 boats and 650 competitors from about 60 clubs. Women's rowing was added to the Olympic program in 1976. The NAAO and NWRA merged in 1982 to form the U.S. Rowing Association.

Further Reading: Mendenhall, Thomas C. *A Short History of American Rowing.* Boston: Charles River Books, [1980].

Addresses: Canadian Amateur Rowing Association, 333 River Road, Vanier, Ontario, Canada K1L 8H9 (613) 748–5656; Intercollegiate Rowing Association, P.O. Box 3, Centerville, MA 02632 (508) 771–5060; U.S. Rowing Association, 201 South Capitol Avenue, Suite 400, Indianapolis, IN 46225 (317) 237–5656

Royals Stadium
Kansas City, MO

Part of the Harry S. Truman Sports Complex, Royals Stadium opened on April 10, 1973, when the Kansas City Royals beat the Texas Rangers 12–1. It was the first stadium built solely for baseball since Dodger Stadium in 1962. One of the most beautiful of the modern parks, the stadium has a 322-foot-wide illuminated water show running from center field to the right field corner and featuring a 10-foot-high waterfall cascading from an upper pool and two giant fountains. The 12-story-high, computer-operated scoreboard has 16,320 light bulbs. Royals Stadium seats 40,625 and has home run distances of 330 feet down the lines and 410 feet to center field.

Rozelle, "Pete" Alvin R. (1926–)
Football
Born March 1, 1926, South Gate, CA; Pro Football
Hall of Fame

After the death of Commissioner Bert Bell in 1959,
National Football League owners were deadlocked
in their attempts to choose a replacement. After 23
ballots, on January 26, 1960, they made a surprising
compromise choice: Rozelle, the 33-year-old general
manager of the Los Angeles Rams. Many thought he
would be an interim commissioner, serving only
until the owners could agree on someone better
suited for the job. He lasted nearly 30 years and
helped transform professional football.

"We sell an experience," Rozelle once said, and
perhaps his major goal as commissioner was to make
that experience—an NFL game—as interesting as
possible by making the teams as equal as possible.
He took a giant step toward that goal in 1961 by
lobbying successfully for the Sports Antitrust Broadcast Act, which allows sports leagues to sell television rights to all games as a package; more important, he also persuaded the owners to share television
money equally. The two-year contract he negotiated
with CBS paid each team about $330,000 a year;
when he retired in 1989, the revenue was more than
$17 million per team. Vince Lombardi, coach and
general manager of the Packers, said in tribute, "What
Rozelle did with television receipts probably saved
football at Green Bay," pro football's smallest market.

Rozelle also conceived the idea of a weekly Monday night telecast; turned down by both CBS and
NBC, it helped make ABC a successful network.
Some of his moves were more controversial, however. To lay the groundwork for the merger of the
NFL and its rival, the American Football League,
Rozelle again lobbied in Washington, this time for
legislation exempting the merger from antitrust action. According to the *New York Times*, he "dangled
an NFL expansion team for New Orleans" before
Senator Russell Long and Congressman Hale Boggs,
both of Louisiana. Three weeks after Congress passed
the merger exemption, New Orleans had its franchise, and there was considerable criticism—most
of it, however, from editorial writers rather than
sportswriters.

In 1974, he laid down the "Rozelle rule," requiring
that a team signing a free agent who had played out
his option would have to compensate the player's
previous team; that was abolished in 1976 after a
federal court agreed with the NFL Players' Association that it was a violation of antitrust laws. His
"parity schedule," adopted by the NFL in 1977,

drew wide criticism from sportswriters and from
some NFL coaches; under that scheduling system,
the weak teams in one division play the weak teams
in other divisions, while the stronger teams are also
pitted against one another.

A long-standing feud with Al Davis, managing
general partner of the Raiders, caused Rozelle his
biggest problems. At Rozelle's insistence, the NFL
in 1976 adopted a rule requiring that any franchise
move be approved by three-quarters of the teams.
When Davis in 1980 decided to move the Raiders
from Oakland to Los Angeles, he refused to abide
by the rule. In the meantime, the Los Angeles Coliseum Commission brought a suit complaining that
the rule was another antitrust violation, and the
Raiders joined the suit. The NFL lost that suit, too,
and the Raiders moved in 1982.

Despite those problems and setbacks, the NFL
grew remarkably during Rozelle's reign. In 1960,
there were 13 teams with a total of about 500 players,
averaging about 40,000 spectators per game; when
he retired, there were 28 teams, more than 1,500
players, and average attendance was well over 60,000.
The price of a franchise had gone from $1 million
to about $50 million in the same period. His chief
contribution may have been his ability to act as an
arbiter among the rival owners who are, in effect,
partners when it comes to league business. Jack Kent
Cooke of the Washington Redskins once commented,
"His capacity to conjure up agreement is sometimes
nothing short of miraculous."

Rubberband Duckpin Bowling

Shortly before World War II, rubberband duckpin
bowling was developed in the Middle Atlantic states.
The wooden pins are encircled with hard rubber
bands that increase pin action and, therefore, scores.
The American Rubberband Duckpin Bowling Congress was organized on August 16, 1946, to sanction
league play and conduct a national tournament. The
ARDBC is affiliated with the National Duckpin
Bowling Congress. As with the parent sport, rubberband duckpin bowling is played in a small geographical area, including Maryland, eastern Pennsylvania,
Virginia, and the District of Columbia.

See also DUCKPIN BOWLING.

Rudolph, Wilma G. (1940–)
Track and Field
Born June 23, 1940, St. Bethlehem, TN; National
Track and Field Hall of Fame

Rudolph lost the use of her left leg after suffering
from scarlet fever and double pneumonia when she
was four years old. She wore a brace until she was

8 and then a special shoe until she was 11. Five years after abandoning the special shoe, she was a member of the U.S. 400-meter relay team that won a Bronze Medal in the 1956 Olympics.

Rudolph was the U.S. hero of the 1960 Olympics, easily winning the 100- and 200-meter dashes and anchoring the 400-meter relay team to victory. She was the first woman ever to win three track and field Gold Medals at one Olympic Games. Rudolph's time in the 100 was 11.18 seconds, nearly 2 seconds below the world record, but it was disallowed because of a trailing wind slightly over the permissible limit.

Representing Tennessee State College, Rudolph won the U.S. outdoor 100-meter in 1959 and 1960, the 100-yard dash in 1961 and 1962, and the 200-meter dash in 1960. Her time of 22.9 in the 200 meters was a world record, and in 1961 she set a record of 11.2 in the 100 meters. She retired from competition after the 1964 season, and in 1982 she established the Wilma Rudolph Foundation to help disadvantaged youngsters.

Rugby

Though now little known in North America, rugby is very important historically as the ancestor of both American and Canadian football. The sport was originally developed at and named for England's Rugby School in 1823, when a student named William Webb Ellis picked up a soccer ball and ran with it, possibly because he wasn't skilled at kicking. Standard rules were drawn up by a group of English colleges in 1841.

Whether related to rugby or not, a kind of football (soccer) in which a player could carry the ball was popular in the Boston area by the middle of the 19th century, and a team of British officers played a rugby match against Montrealers in 1865. Among the Montreal players were a number of students from McGill University, where the sport soon became popular.

Princeton, Rutgers, and Yale met to standardize football rules in 1873, while Harvard remained independent. Left without anyone to play against in the United States, Harvard in 1874 challenged McGill to play two games, one under Harvard's rules and one under McGill's rules. After the two games, Harvard students adopted rugby as their own. In 1875 Harvard and Yale agreed to play a game under the so-called "concessionary rules," which were pretty much the McGill rugby rules. Columbia and Princeton joined them in forming the Intercollegiate Football Association in 1876.

In 1875, Yale and Harvard agreed to play under a set of "concessionary rules," actually pretty much

Harvard's, and Harvard won, four goals and four touchdowns to nothing. Columbia, Harvard, Princeton, and Yale formed the Intercollegiate Football Association in a meeting at Springfield, MA in the fall of 1876. They agreed to play McGill's version of rugby, with some modifications.

The sport spread rapidly through Canada. The Quebec and Canadian Rugby Football Unions were both organized in 1882, the Ontario Rugby Football Union the following year. The first championship game between the QRFU and the ORFU was played in 1884. Rugby was already beginning to evolve into something different. Disputes over rules led to the demise of the CRFU in 1886, and when rules were standardized by the newly formed Canadian Rugby Union in 1891, the sport was well on its way to becoming Canadian football.

Rugby did have a brief spurt of popularity on the college level in 1905 and 1906, when football was under attack for its violence. A number of colleges, especially on the West Coast, briefly dropped football and took up rugby instead, but they went back to football after a series of rules changes designed to reduce violence.

The United States of America Rugby Football Union, founded in 1975, comprises four regional groups, the Midwest and Pacific Coast Rugby Football Unions, USA Rugby East, and the Western Rugby Union of the U.S. They have a combined membership of about 1,200 clubs representing some 50,000 players. The USARFU conducts national club and collegiate championships.

Addresses: Canadian Rugby Union, 333 River Road, Vanier, Ontario, Canada K1L 8H9 (613) 748–5657; U.S. of A. Rugby Football Union, 830 North Tajon, #104-B, Colorado Springs, CO 80903 (719) 632–1022

See also CANADIAN FOOTBALL; FOOTBALL.

Running
See PEDESTRIANISM; TRACK AND FIELD.

Rupp, Adolph F. (1901–1977)
Basketball
Born September 2, 1901, Halstead, KS; died December 10, 1977; Basketball Hall of Fame

"The Baron" ruled University of Kentucky basketball for 41 seasons and is the all-time collegiate leader in coaching victories with 875, against only 190 losses. After playing at the University of Kansas under Phog Allen, he coached high school teams in Iowa and Illinois before going to Kentucky in 1931. Although Rupp had some tall players through the years, he used a series of set offenses that called for

Both American and Canadian football sprang from rugby, which has survived primarily as an amateur club sport played by a small number of enthusiasts. Courtesy of Huey Photo Systems

speed and toughness, and he usually preferred the smaller, more aggressive player.

Rupp took 20 teams to the NCAA tournament, a record broken by Dean Smith in 1991. Kentucky won the championship, in 1948, 1949, 1951, and 1958; Rupp was the first coach to win the title two years in a row. Kentucky also won the National Invitation Tournament in 1946. Rupp was named Coach of the Year by UPI in 1959 and 1966. Crusty and outspoken, he once said, "I know I have plenty of enemies, but I'd rather be the most hated winning coach in the country than the most popular losing one."

Rupp Trophy
Basketball

The Commonwealth Athletic Club of Kentucky in 1961 began presenting this award to the Associated Press collegiate basketball player of the year. It is named for former University of Kentucky coach Adolph Rupp.

Rupp Trophy Winners

1961	Jerry Lucas, Ohio State
1962	Jerry Lucas, Ohio State
1963	Art Heyman, Duke
1964	Gary Bradds, Ohio State
1965	Bill Bradley, Princeton
1966	Cazzie Russell, Michigan
1967	Lew Alcindor (Kareem Abdul-Jabbar), UCLA
1968	Elvin Hayes, Houston
1969	Lew Alcindor (Kareem Abdul-Jabbar), UCLA
1970	Pete Maravich, Louisiana State
1971	Austin Carr, Notre Dame
1972	Bill Walton, UCLA
1973	Bill Walton, UCLA
1974	David Thompson, North Carolina State
1975	David Thompson, North Carolina State
1976	Scott May, Indiana
1977	Marques Johnson, UCLA
1978	Butch Lee, Marquette
1979	Larry Bird, Indiana State
1980	Mark Aguirre, DePaul

1981   Ralph Sampson, Virginia
1982   Ralph Sampson, Virginia
1983   Ralph Sampson, Virginia
1984   Michael Jordan, North Carolina
1985   Patrick Ewing, Georgetown
1986   Walter Berry, St. John's
1987   David Robinson, Navy
1988   Hersey Hawkins, Bradley
1989   Sean Elliott, Arizona
1990   Lionel Simmons, La Salle
1991   Larry Johnson, Nevada-Las Vegas

Rural Sports

During the first half of the 19th century, small villages and towns continually sprang up just behind the westward-moving frontier. While frontiersmen liked rough, even violent games, the family-oriented people in these rural settlements preferred quieter, gentler forms of recreation, including participatory sports such as fishing, hunting, skating, sledding, and swimming. Town ball, an early version of baseball, was popular in many communities, and there was also impromptu horse racing on village streets and country roads. Lumbermen competed in logrolling in areas where timber was an important product, and farmers took part in plowing matches after the county agricultural fair achieved prominence in the 1840s. The village smithy, a gathering place for farmers from miles around, was often the center for horseshoe pitching and quoits contests (the difference being that a quoit was an old horseshoe bent into a complete ring by the smith). Harness racing also became a staple at many county fairs, but not without protest. The magazine *Working Farmer* complained in 1856 about racing, "If we cannot have Agricultural Fairs without this accompaniment, let us wait until we can."

Russell, "Bill" William F. (1934–)
Basketball

Born February 12, 1934, Monroe, LA; Basketball Hall of Fame

There have been many great scorers in the history of basketball, but the man named in 1980 as the greatest player in National Basketball Association history was known for his defensive abilities and his rebounding. The Boston Celtics' dynasty that won 11 championships in his 13 seasons, including 8 in a row, was built around Russell's skills. The 6-foot-10 center had great leaping ability and outstanding reflexes that made him a very intimidating shot blocker. That allowed other Celtic defenders to play their men close, knowing that if they drove to the basket they'd confront Russell. His rebounding,

Bill Russell, five times named the Most Valuable Player in the National Basketball Association, became the NBA's first black coach in 1966. Courtesy of the Basketball Hall of Fame

combined with the ability to make good outlet passes, triggered the Celtics' fast break.

Russell played for two NCAA championship teams at the University of San Francisco in 1955 and 1956. The Celtics traded a fine center, Ed Macauley, to the St. Louis Hawks for the draft choice that brought them Russell. They also had to wait for him, because Russell played for the U.S. Gold Medal Olympic team before beginning his professional career. It was worth the wait. Because of his shortened season, Russell finished only fourth in rebounding, but he topped the league in average rebounds per game at 19.6, and he led the Celtics to their first NBA championship.

His value to the team was dramatically displayed the following season, when he was named the league's Most Valuable Player, even though he was only a second-team All-NBA selection. Russell sprained his ankle in the third game of the NBA finals and the Celtics lost the championship series in six games. Beginning in 1959, they won an unmatched eight championships games in a row. Russell became player-coach of the Celtics for the 1966–67 season, when they finished second in their division and lost in the playoff semifinals. But they won championships again in 1968 and 1969, after which Russell retired. He also coached the Seattle Supersonics in

1974–75 and the Los Angeles Clippers for part of the 1988–89 season

Russell was named the NBA's Most Valuable Player in 1961, 1962, 1963, and 1965. In his 13 seasons, he scored 14,522 points, an average of 15.1 a game, and had 21,620 rebounds, 22.5 a game. He's the all-time leader in playoff rebounds, with 4,104 in 165 games, an average of 24.9.

Ruth, "Babe" George H. (1895–1948)
Baseball

Born February 6, 1895, Baltimore, MD; died August 16, 1948; Baseball Hall of Fame

The fact that an entire room at the Baseball Hall of Fame is devoted to his exploits is just one measure of Babe Ruth's stature. He may well have been the greatest player of all time; certainly he was the best-known and the best-paid, in terms of purchasing power. The New York Yankees paid him $80,000 a year in 1930 and 1931, and he was the first athlete to earn large sums off the field for public appearances and endorsements. It's been estimated that he made about $1 million in salaries and World Series money and another $1 million from outside income.

His troubled childhood helped feed the legend. Neglected by his parents, he was placed in St. Mary's Industrial School at the age of eight. He learned to play baseball there, and Brother Matthias, the team's coach, in 1914 persuaded Jack Dunn of the minor-league Baltimore Orioles to scout him. Dunn not only signed Ruth to a contract, he became the 19-year-old's legal guardian. Then a left-handed pitcher, Ruth joined the Boston Red Sox at the end of the season. At 20, he won 18 games and lost 8 in 1915 and followed that with a 23–12 record and a league-leading 1.75 earned run average in 1916. He also had a 14-inning 2–1 victory in the second game of the World Series.

After going 24–13 with a 2.02 earned run average in 1917, Ruth began playing the outfield and first base on his nonpitching days in 1918. He hit 11 home runs to tie for the American League lead. He also set a World Series record (broken by Whitey Ford in 1961) by extending his scoreless inning streak to 29⅔. By 1919, he was spending much more time in the outfield than on the mound, and he hit a record 29 home runs. After that season, the Red Sox sold him to the New York Yankees for $125,000 plus a $300,000 loan.

As a full-time player with the Yankees, Ruth hit an incredible 54 home runs in 1920 and he followed that with 59 in 1921. Aside from the Yankees, no *team* in the major leagues surpassed those figures. Because of illness, he appeared in only 110 games

With his mighty swing and incredible power, Babe Ruth transformed baseball from a running game to a slugging game. In 1920, he hit 54 home runs for the New York Yankees—more than any other team hit that season. Courtesy of Wide World

in 1922, but came back to lead the league in home runs again with 41 in 1923 and 46 in 1924.

Ruth's exploits off the field were as gargantuan as his statistics. He missed the first two months of the 1925 season with "the stomach-ache heard round the world," as a sportswriter called it. One apocryphal story was that he'd eaten a couple of dozen hot dogs and washed them down with as many bottles of soda. But Ruth's appetite was not for soda. Many sportswriters suspected he had a venereal disease, though that suspicion never appeared in print. The official report was that he was operated on for an intestinal abcess. In any event, he returned to the Yankee lineup in June, but in August Manager Miller Huggins fined him $5,000 and suspended him for "misconduct." A sportswriter asked if that meant drinking, and Huggins replied, "Of course it means drinking, and it means a lot of other things besides."

Ruth eventually apologized and was reinstated. He proceeded to lead the league in home runs for six consecutive seasons, 1926 through 1931, establishing the 154-game record of 60 in 1927. Although the ball had become livelier and more home runs were being hit, that figure accounted for nearly 14 percent of all home runs in the American League that season, and was more than 12 entire major-league teams hit.

His home run figures begin to decline in 1932, when he hit 41 and failed to lead the league, although he did lead in runs batted in with 130, and he led in that category again in 1933 with 114, though he hit only 34 home runs, his lowest total since 1925. After the 1934 season, the Yankees released him, and he was signed by the Boston Braves of the National League. In a final flourish, he hit three home runs in a game on May 25, 1935, and retired a few days later.

Myths and legends inevitably accumulated around Ruth. The most famous, still disputed, was the "called shot" home run in the 1932 World Series against the Chicago Cubs. Reportedly, Ruth pointed to the center field bleachers after taking two called strikes, and then hit a home run to the exact spot he had indicated. Many who were there, however, said that Ruth simply pointed at the Cubs' pitcher, Charlie Root, and yelled an epithet at him because of Root's bench jockeying during the previous half-inning.

Sportswriters also wrote saccharine stories of his visits to children in hospitals and of home runs he hit in response to requests. But it's undeniable that he did love children, and he did spend a lot of time with them, cheerfully signing thousands of autographs. He was no role model, however; he and his first wife adopted a baby girl, undoubtedly Ruth's illegitimate daughter, and his capacity for women was as great as his capacity for alcohol. After his first wife died in a fire in 1929, he married a showgirl who seemed to have tamed him somewhat.

At first bitter because he had hoped to become the Yankees' manager, Ruth eventually settled into a fairly happy retirement, enjoying his wealth. He played himself in the movie *Pride of the Yankees*, a biography of his long-time teammate, Lou Gehrig, in 1942. Suffering from cancer of the larynx, he made his final appearance at Yankee Stadium on June 13, 1948, giving a brief speech. He died less than two months later.

In 22 major-league seasons, Ruth batted .342, with 2,873 hits, including 506 doubles, 136 triples, and 714 home runs. He scored 2,174 runs and drove in 2,204. Although Henry Aaron broke his home run record in 1974, Ruth still holds the American League career record with 708. He also holds records for most seasons leading a league in home runs (12), most years with 50 or more home runs (4), and most times hitting two or more home runs in a game (72). As a pitcher, he won 94 games and lost 46, with an earned run average of 2.28. Ruth played in 10 World Series, batting .326 with 15 home runs, 33 runs batted in, and 37 runs scored.

Further Reading: Creamer, Robert W. *Babe: The Legend Comes to Life*. New York: Simon & Schuster, 1974.

Ryder Cup
Golf

Golfers from the American and British Professional Golfers Associations played a match in England in 1926, after which English merchant Samuel A. Ryder donated a trophy for biennial competition alternating between the two countries. The first Ryder Cup match was held in Worcester, MA in 1927. There were four 36-hole foursome matches the first day and eight 36-hole singles matches the next day until 1961, when the format changed to eight 18-hole foursomes the first day and sixteen 18-hole singles matches the following day. Since 1963, there has also been a day of eight four-ball matches.

Sacramento, CA

Basketball The Kansas City Kings of the National Basketball Association moved to Sacramento in 1985. It is their fifth stop since originating as the Rochester Royals in the National Basketball League in 1945.

See also ARCO ARENA.

Sailing

See YACHTING.

St. Louis, MO

Baseball St. Louis has had a baseball team in every major league except the Players' League of 1890. The first was a National League team in 1876 and 1877. Then came the Browns in the American Association from 1882 through 1891. They won four straight pennants, from 1885 through 1888. There was another National League team in 1885 and 1886. After the American Association folded, the Browns moved into the National League in 1892. They became the Cardinals in 1900. The Cardinals won the World Series in 1926, 1931, 1934, 1942, 1944, 1946, 1964, 1967, and 1982, and they were also National League champions in 1928, 1930, 1943, 1968, 1985, and 1987.

St. Louis got an American League team in 1902, when the Milwaukee franchise moved. This team, also named the Browns, won the American League pennant in 1944. The franchise moved to Baltimore in 1954.

Basketball The Milwaukee Hawks of the National Basketball Association moved to St. Louis in 1955 and won the 1958 NBA championship. The franchise went to Atlanta in 1968.

Football The St. Louis Browns played in the National Football League for just the 1923 season. During the 1934 season, the Cincinnati Reds moved to St. Louis and became known as the Gunners, but they played only three games and folded after the season. The Chicago Cardinals' franchise was moved to St. Louis in 1960; the franchise went to Phoenix in 1988.

Hockey The Ottawa Senators of the National Hockey League became the St. Louis Eagles in 1934, but the franchise was deactivated after one season. The St. Louis Blues entered the NHL as an expansion franchise for the 1967–68 season and won the first three western division championships, from 1968 through 1970, but lost in the Stanley Cup finals each time.

See also BUSCH STADIUM; ST. LOUIS ARENA; SPORTSMAN'S PARK.

St. Louis Arena
St. Louis, MO

When it opened in 1929, St. Louis Arena was the largest building of its kind in the world, with a seating capacity of 21,000. Built at a cost of about $2 million, its major purpose was to house the annual National Dairy Show, but it also hosted many other events, including minor-league hockey. The building was extensively remodeled in 1967, when it became the home rink of the St. Louis Blues, a National Hockey League expansion team. Current capacity is 17,188. The Ralston Purina Corporation owned the team from 1977 to 1982, and during that period the arena was called the Checkerdome.

St. Paul, MN

St. Paul can be said to share Minnesota's major-league franchises with its sister city, Minneapolis, which is why most of the teams have "Minnesota" in their names. However, St. Paul did have its own baseball team in the Union Association during that league's only season in 1884.

See also MINNEAPOLIS; MINNESOTA.

Salad Bowl
Football

Phoenix hosted this postseason college game on New Year's Day from 1948 through 1951.

Salad Bowl Results

1948	Nevada-Reno 13, North Texas State 6
1949	Drake 14, Arizona 13
1950	Xavier (OH) 33, Arizona State 21
1951	Miami (OH) 34, Arizona State 21
1952	Houston 26, Dayton 21

Salt Lake City, UT

Basketball The National Basketball Association's New Orleans Jazz moved to Salt Lake City in 1979, becoming the Utah Jazz.

See also SALT PALACE.

Salt Palace
Salt Lake City, UT

The original Salt Palace, opened in 1899, was actually built of blocks of salt. It was a kind of museum, with displays of Utah's agricultural products and mineral resources, but on its grounds was a ⅛-mile velodrome where bicycle races were held twice a week. Because of the low air resistance at Salt Lake City's high altitude, many sprint records were set there. The velodrome shut down in 1914.

The City of Salt Lake built the new Salt Palace in 1969 as a convention center and sports arena. The Utah Jazz of the National Basketball Association has played there since moving to Salt Lake City from New Orleans in 1979. The arena seats 12,444.

Samuelson, Joan Benoit
See BENOIT, JOAN.

San Antonio, TX
Basketball The Dallas Chapparals of the National Basketball Association moved to San Antonio and became the Spurs before the 1973–74 season.

See also HEMISFAIR ARENA.

San Diego, CA
Baseball The San Diego Padres entered the National League as an expansion franchise in 1969. They won the league's pennant in 1984.
Basketball The National Basketball Association's Buffalo Braves moved to San Diego in 1978 and became known as the Clippers. The franchise went to Los Angeles in 1984.
Football One of the founding members of the American Football League, the Los Angeles Chargers moved to San Diego in 1961. They were AFL champions in 1963.

See also JACK MURPHY STADIUM.

San Diego East West Christmas Classic Bowl
Football
This postseason college bowl game was played just twice. Centre beat Arizona 38–0 in 1921, and West Virginia beat Gonzaga 21–13 in 1922.

San Diego Stadium
See JACK MURPHY STADIUM.

Sande, Earl H.
Horse Racing (1898–1968)
Born November 13, 1898, Groton, SD; died August 19, 1968; National Racing Hall of Fame

A tough jockey known as "Big Feet" because of his practice of nudging rival jockeys with his feet when their horses were running side by side, Sande began as a rodeo broncobuster in Idaho before switching to Thoroughbred riding. The best-known jockey dur-

ing the 1920s, the so-called Golden Age of Sports, he won his first Kentucky Derby aboard Zev in 1923. The following year he fell on the backstretch of a race at Saratoga, suffering a fractured skull, internal injuries, and several broken bones. For a time he was not expected to live, but he was riding again less than a year later, and he won the 1925 Kentucky Derby with Flying Ebony.

Sande retired in 1928 to start his own stable of horses, but he lost money and began jockeying again in 1930. He rode Gallant Fox to the Triple Crown that year; together, horse and rider won $308,275. Sande retired again in 1931 and became a trainer. In 1938, he led all trainers in winnings with $229,495. After a brief comeback as a jockey in 1953, Sande retired from riding for the third and last time. He had a total of 968 winners in 3,673 rides.

San Francisco, CA
Baseball Shortly after the Brooklyn Dodgers of the National League announced plans to move to Los Angeles in 1958, the New York Giants decided to follow suit by going to San Francisco. The Giants won pennants in 1962 and 1989, but lost both World Series.
Basketball The Philadelphia Warriors of the National Basketball Association moved to San Francisco in 1962. The franchise went to Oakland in 1971 and became the Golden State Warriors.
Football The San Francisco 49ers joined the All America Football Conference when it was formed in 1946. The AAFC merged into the National Football League in 1950, and San Francisco was one of only four franchises to survive the merger. They have won four Super Bowls, in 1982, 1985, 1989, and 1990, only the second team to do so. (Pittsburgh was the first.)

See also CANDLESTICK PARK.

Sanity Code
The NCAA Conference of Conferences at a special meeting in Chicago July 22–23, 1946, drew up "Principles for the Conduct of Intercollegiate Athletics" in questionnaire form, and it was sent to all member institutions. Tabulation revealed that there was general agreement with the principles, and in 1948 they were embodied in Article 3 of the NCAA Constitution, generally known as the "Sanity Code" because its supporters viewed it as a means of restoring sanity to college sports. The article required colleges to hold athletes to the same academic standards as other students and forbade overt recruiting and financial aid awarded for athletic ability alone. A three-member Constitutional Compliance Commit-

tee was appointed to investigate charges and make rulings. In its first year, the committee looked into 20 complaints.

Opposition to the code arose quickly. One problem was that the only penalty allowed was expulsion from the NCAA. The NCAA's 1950 convention was asked to terminate membership of seven institutions for violating the code. The vote was 111 to 93 in favor, short of the two-thirds majority required. The code was repealed in 1951 and eventually replaced by a 12-point code.

See also NATIONAL COLLEGIATE ATHLETIC ASSOCIATION.

Santa Anita Race Track
Arcadia, CA

A dentist named Charles H. Strub was the impetus behind the construction of Santa Anita, California's first major Thoroughbred track, in 1934. He organized a group of investors as the Los Angeles Turf Club and announced that the track would offer a $100,000 purse for the Santa Anita Handicap, which drew more than 20 horses for its inaugural running in 1935. Santa Anita went through some early struggles because of the Great Depression, but after World War II became the most successful Thoroughbred track in the country, annually at or near the top in average daily attendance and handle (total amount bet). In 1988, the track became the first to average more than $6 million a day.

The track was built on part of Rancho Santa Anita, which had been the site of an earlier racetrack, opened in 1907 by Elias J. "Lucky" Baldwin. That track closed after Baldwin's death in 1909. The modern Santa Anita, which opened on Christmas Day of 1934, has pioneered several racing innovations, including the photofinish camera and the magnetically controlled starting gate. The track seats 15,589 in its grandstand, 2,660 in the clubhouse, and can accommodate more than 25,000 when the infield is opened to spectators. It has a 1-mile dirt track and a turf course totalling 1¾ miles. The overall turf course, rated one of the best in North America, combines the 6-furlong Hillside Course with an inner course of just over 7 furlongs.

Address: 285 W. Huntington Drive. Arcadia, CA 91006 (818) 574–7223

Saperstein, Abraham M. (1901–1966)
Basketball

Born July 4, 1901, London, England; died March 15, 1966; Basketball Hall of Fame

The 5-foot-tall Saperstein wanted to play basketball at the University of Illinois, but the coach wouldn't even let him try out. After graduating, Saperstein was coaching a boys' team in a Chicago suburb when he was asked to help organize a black American Legion team in 1926. That was the beginning of the world-famous Harlem Globetrotters. The team played its first game in Hinckley, IL in January 1927. For a time they were known as the Savoy Five, because they played all challengers in Chicago's Savoy Ballroom, then went on the road after the ballroom became a skating rink.

That was when Saperstein came up the name—"Harlem," because all of the players were black (though none of them had ever been in Harlem), "Globetrotters," because he wanted to give the impression they had traveled all over the world, as they eventually did.

The Globetrotters became such a dominant team that Saperstein began to put more emphasis on showmanship than on basketball after World War II. The team developed a variety of trick shots and ball-handling skills, mixed with a fair amount of buffoonery, and the combination made the Globetrotters probably the best-known sports team in the world. Saperstein made several million dollars.

In 1961, he applied for a Los Angeles franchise in the National Basketball Association. After being turned down, he organized his own American Basketball League. He was the ABL's chief financial backer, and he lost more than $1 million when the league folded halfway through its second season. But one of Saperstein's innovations, the three-point shot, found its way into the American Basketball Association in 1967 and eventually into the NBA and college basketball as well.

See also AMERICAN BASKETBALL LEAGUE; HARLEM GLOBETROTTERS.

Saratoga Racetrack
Saratoga Springs, NY

John C. Morrissey, a former prizefighter who owned a gambling house in New York City, held the first Saratoga race meeting, beginning August 15, 1863, with the backing of William R. Travers and John R. Hunter of the prestigious New York Jockey Club. When the four-day meeting was a success, the Saratoga Association for the Improvement of the Breed formed to build a permanent track and conduct annual meetings. Saratoga's success marked the comeback of Thoroughbred racing in New York and inspired the construction of Jerome Park two years later.

Saratoga's major race is the Travers, the oldest continuously run stakes race in the country. Other important races are the Sanford Stakes, the Forego

Handicap and the Test Stakes. The track has a 1⅛-mile oval course, a 1-mile, 98-foot turf course, and a 7-furlong, 304-foot infield course that doubles as a six-jump steeplechase course. The grandstand seats 6,224, the clubhouse 465, but total attendance has run over 50,000 on Travers Day, when the infield is opened to spectators.

See also NEW YORK RACING ASSOCIATION.

Saskatchewan

The Regina Roughriders were organized in 1910, along with the Saskatchewan Rugby Football Union, and Saskatchewan joined the newly formed Western Canada Rugby Football Union in 1911. The team moved into the Western Interprovincial Football Union when it was organized in 1936 and became known as the Saskatchewan Roughriders in 1946. Regina/Saskatchewan has been in the Grey Cup finals 13 times, winning only in 1966.

See also TAYLOR FIELD.

Sayers, Gale (1943–   )
Football
Born May 30, 1943, Wichita, KS; National Football Foundation, Pro Football Hall of Fame

The youngest person ever elected to the Pro Football Hall of Fame, at 34, Sayers played only five full seasons with the Chicago Bears, but during that time he put up some amazing numbers. Twice an All-American halfback at the University of Kansas, he joined the Bears in 1965. As a rookie, he scored four touchdowns against the Minnesota Vikings, one of them on a 96-yard kickoff return, and he had six against the San Francisco 49ers to tie the NFL record. Sayers totaled 2,272 yards that season and scored a record 22 touchdowns, 14 rushing, 6 on pass receptions, 1 on a kickoff return, and 1 on a punt return.

In 1966, he rushed for 1,231 yards to lead the league, averaging 5.4 yards per carry, and he also led in kickoff return average, 31.2 yards. His total of 2,440 yards rushing, receiving, and returning kicks is a record for a 14-game season. Sayers returned just 16 kickoffs in 1967, 3 of them for touchdowns to lead the league, and he had only 3 punt returns, but 1 of those was for a touchdown. He also rushed for 880 yards. He was on his way to a sensational year in 1968 when his right knee was seriously injured. His 6.2 yards per carry again led the league, but he was stopped short of another 1,000-yard season—his total was 856.

After an intensive off-season rehabilitation program, Sayers came back with a league-leading 1,032 yards in 1969. But his left knee was injured early in the 1970 season, and he carried the ball just 23 times

that year and 13 times in 1971 before retiring. The "Kansas Comet" had a total of 991 rushing attempts for 4,956 yards, a 5.0 average, and 39 touchdowns. He caught 112 passes for 1,307 yards and 9 touchdowns; returned 91 kickoffs for 2,781 yards, a 30.6 average, and 6 touchdowns; and returned 28 punts for 391 yards, a 14.0 average, and 2 touchdowns.

SCCA
See SPORTS CAR CLUB OF AMERICA.

Schmidt, Joseph (1932–   )
Football
Born January 18, 1932, Pittsburgh, PA; Pro Football Hall of Fame

Playing at a time when there were many outstanding middle linebackers in the National Football League, Schmidt may have been the best of them all. Running back John Henry Johnson once summed him up: "He is *always* in the way." Because he suffered many injuries at the University of Pittsburgh, he wasn't well known as a college player, and the Detroit Lions chose him on the seventh round of the 1953 college draft. He was a starter well before the season ended. An All-Pro in 1955, 1956, 1957, 1958, 1959, 1961, and 1962, the 6-foot-2, 220-pound Schmidt was a devastating tackler who also had the speed to cover potential pass receivers out of the backfieled, and he was a very intelligent captain, calling defensive alignments after sizing up the offensive formation. In his 13 seasons, he intercepted 24 passes, returning them for 294 yards and 2 touchdowns.

Sculling
See ROWING.

Seabiscuit (1933–1947)
Horse Racing
A late bloomer, Seabiscuit won just 5 out of 35 races as a two-year-old and 9 of 23 the following year, when Charles S. Howard bought him, "Silent Tom" Smith became his trainer, and Red Pollard took over as his jockey. Seabiscuit was the nation's top money-winner with $168,642.50 in 1937, but Triple Crown winner War Admiral was named Horse of the Year. After winning the Hollywood Gold Cup in 1938, Seabiscuit and War Admiral were matched in a 1³⁄₁₆-mile race at Pimlico. An 11–5 underdog, Seabiscuit won by three lengths in a track record 1 minute 56⅗ seconds. The victory brought him Horse of the Year honors. An injury limited his racing in 1939, but Seabiscuit came back to win the San Antonio and Santa Anita Handicaps in 1940 to finish his career

with a record $437,730 in winnings. The record was broken by Whirlaway in 1943.

Sears, Eleonora R. (1881–1968)
Squash, Tennis
Born September 28, 1881, Boston, MA; died March 29, 1968

Probably the greatest all-around woman athlete before Babe Didrikson Zaharias, Sears was a great-great-granddaughter of Thomas Jefferson and a member of Boston and Newport society. She was one of the first women to drive a car, fly an airplane, and race a speedboat. A fearless horsewoman, she rode in hunting meets and steeplechases for more than 60 years. When she wasn't allowed to join an all-male polo team, she organized her own team. She won four national doubles tennis titles, with Hazel Hotchkiss Wightman in 1911 and 1915 and with Molla Bjurstedt Mallory in 1916 and 1917. She and Willis E. Davis won the mixed doubles in 1916. Twice she was a finalist in the national singles tennis championship and in 1928, when she was 46 years old, she won the first women's national squash racquets championship.

Sears actually took part in more sports than Didrikson. She regularly swam distances of 3 to 6 miles, was a very good golfer, a fine shot with rifle or pistol, and an excellent canoeist, and she once sparred vigorously with a professional boxer in Boston. She skippered a yacht to victory over Alfred Vanderbilt's *Walthra*, and she also played baseball and football at one time or another. In her forties, she became interested in long-distance walking; at the age of 44, she won a $2,000 bet by walking from Providence to Boston, about 50 miles, in less than 10 hours.

Sears, Richard D. (1861–1943)
Tennis
Born October 26, 1861, Boston, MA; died April 8, 1943; International Tennis Hall of Fame

Sears learned to play tennis on the second court built in the United States, at Nahant, MA. At the time he played, the net was a foot lower in the middle than at the posts. By watching Englishman Spencer W. Gore play, Sears learned the serve-and-volley method of attacking. The volleyer could comfortably position himself at the center of the net, since his opponent would be unlikely to try returning the ball down the lines, where the net was higher. "All I had to do," he later wrote, "was to tap the balls as they came over, first to one side and then to the other, running my opponent all over the court."

It was a successful strategy. Sears won the first seven national singles titles, from 1881 through 1886.

He also teamed with James Dwight to win six doubles titles in seven years, giving him 13 championships in 14 tournaments before retiring from competition. In 1892, Sears won the first national court tennis championship.

Seattle, WA
Baseball The Seattle Pilots entered the American League as an expansion team in 1969, but attendance was poor, in part because the city had no adequate major-league stadium, and the team became the Milwaukee Brewers in 1970. Another expansion franchise, the Mariners, came to the city in 1977 to play in the brand-new Kingdome. The Mariners have yet to win a pennant.
Basketball The Supersonics joined the National Basketball Association in the 1967–68 expansion. The team won the NBA championship in 1979.
Football An expansion franchise, the Seahawks became a National Football League team in 1976.

See also KINGDOME; SEATTLE COLISEUM.

Seattle Coliseum
Seattle, WA

Since 1985, the Coliseum has been the home court of the National Basketball Association's Seattle Supersonics. The arena has seating for 14,200.

Seattle Slew (1974–   )
Horse Racing
The only undefeated winner of the Triple Crown, Seattle Slew was bought for just $17,500 by Karen and Mickey Taylor; they nicknamed him Baby Huey, after the cartoon character, because he was so lazy. But he won 14 of 17 races and total purses of $1,208,726 before being put out to stud. A horse who liked to take the lead early and hold onto it, Seattle Slew made his first start on September 20, 1976, and won by 5 lengths. After setting a stakes record in the Champagne, he was named two-year-old of the year.

He literally got off to a bad start in the Triple Crown. Left in the gate, he managed to work through the whole field and win the 1977 Kentucky Derby by nearly 2 lengths. He and Cormorant had a long stretch duel in the Preakness, Seattle Slew winning by a length and a half. Then he had a relatively easy 4-length victory in the Belmont. He also won the Flamingo Stakes and the Wood Memorial and was named Horse of the Year. A virus kept him out of action early in 1978, and he missed the Metropolitan Handicap with a leg injury, but he beat Affirmed by 3 lengths in the Marlboro Cup, took the Woodward Stakes, suffered a narrow defeat in the Jockey Club

Gold Cup, and carried 134 pounds to victory in his last start, the Stuyvesant Handicap. He was syndicated for $12 million after that win.

Secretariat (1970–1989)
Horse Racing

The owner of "Big Red" during his racing days, Peggy Chenery, said of him, "Maybe he was not the world's greatest racehorse, but he was a charismatic *person*. This red horse with the blue-and-white blinkers and silks seemed to epitomize an American hero." Secretariat was the only two-year-old ever named Horse of the Year, in 1972, and he repeated after winning the Triple Crown spectacularly in 1973. In the Kentucky Derby, he came from last to win in a record 1 minute 59⅖ seconds. He was 6 lengths behind in the Preakness when his jockey let him run, and he won by more than 2 lengths. Finally, in the Belmont, he pulled away from the field to win by an incredible 31 lengths, shattering the race record by 2 full seconds in 2:24, a world record for a 1½-mile race on a dirt track. He won 16 of his 21 starts and earned $1,316,608, and was syndicated for more than $6 million. Suffering from a painful and incurable hoof inflammation, he was humanely destroyed on October 4, 1989.

Selke Trophy
Hockey

Named in honor of Frank J. Selke, this trophy was presented by the National Hockey League Board of Governors in 1977. It goes to the player chosen by the Professional Hockey Writers' Association as the best defensive forward in the league.

Selke Trophy Winners

1978	Bob Gainey, Montreal
1979	Bob Gainey, Montreal
1980	Bob Gainey, Montreal
1981	Bob Gainey, Montreal
1982	Steve Kasper, Boston
1983	Bobby Clarke, Philadelphia
1984	Doug Jarvis, Washington
1985	Craig Ramsay, Buffalo
1986	Troy Murray, Chicago
1987	Dave Poulin, Philadelphia
1988	Guy Carbonneau, Montreal
1989	Guy Carbonneau, Montreal
1990	Rick Meagher, St. Louis

Shaughnessy, Clark D. (1892–1970)
Football

Born March 6, 1892, St. Cloud, MN; died May 15, 1970; National Football Foundation Hall of Fame

Shaughnessy didn't invent the T-formation, as has sometimes been written—it dates at least to 1906—but his innovations made the T and its many variations the offensive formation used by virtually every high school, college, and professional team today. After playing at the University of Minnesota, Shaughnessy coached at Tulane, 1915–20 and 1922–25, Loyola of the South 1926–1932, and the University of Chicago, 1933–39. When Chicago dropped football, Shaughnessy went to Stanford in 1940. Studying game films, he saw Frankie Albert, a left-handed tailback who was a good passer but not an exceptional runner; a big fullback, Norm Standlee; and two very quick halfbacks, Hugh Gallarneau and Pete Kmetovic. He decided they could best be used in a new version of the T-formation.

The new formation Shaughnessy created used line splits to open up the offense, had the fullback either running up the middle or faking up the middle and making a block, with the halfbacks hitting quickly over tackle or taking pitchouts to run the ends. And, after a fake or two, the quarterback could also drop back and throw a pass. Speed and deception replaced the sheer power of the single wing. Stanford won all nine of its games and the national championship in 1940, then beat Nebraska 21–13 in the Rose Bowl.

While at the University of Chicago, Shaughnessy had become friendly with George Halas, owner-coach of the Chicago Bears. Halas asked him to help install the new system with the Bears, who were about to play the Washington Redskins for the National Football League championship. The Bears had used the T-formation most of the time since 1920, but the changes Shaughnessy introduced proved devastating, at least to the Redskins. The Bears beat them 73–0.

Shaughnessy was suddenly famous, and he spoke at many banquets in the off-season. He liked to explain, "The secret of the T-formation's success is simple: Get a quarterback like Albert, a fullback like Standlee, and halfbacks like Gallarneau and Kmetovic." That was the secret of Shaughnessy's coaching success: designing a system built around the talent available. When he became head coach of the Los Angeles Rams in 1948, he had three dangerous pass receivers, so he created the "three-end" offense, using a fast halfback as a flanker. The Rams won the western division championship in 1949 but lost the NFL championship game 14–0 to the Philadelphia Eagles.

Ironically, during the 1950s Shaughnessy was a defensive consultant for the Bears, where he developed sophisticated defenses to stop the T-formation that eventually turned it back into a power offense, similar to the single wing, that emphasized double-teaming, cross-blocking, and pulling guards instead of the relatively simple blocking that Shaughnessy's original T had emphasized.

Shaw, W. Wilbur (1902–1954)
Auto Racing

Born October 31, 1902, Shelbyville, IN; died October 30, 1954; Auto Racing Hall of Fame

After building his own car when he was 18, Shaw won a number of local and regional races in the Midwest. He suffered a skull fracture in a 1923 race and then helped design a crash helmet. Other drivers kidded him about it, but Shaw survived another crash in which he was thrown from his car and landed on his head, and the American Automobile Association—then the governing body for auto racing in this country—made helmets mandatory racing gear. He had a long run of bad luck in the Indianapolis 500, finishing second in 1933 and 1935, but finally won it in 1937, when he was 35. After another second-place finish in 1938, he won again in 1939 and 1940. Shaw served as president and general manager of the Indianapolis Speedway Corporation from 1945 until his death in a plane crash in 1954.

Shea Stadium
New York, NY

Named for William A. Shea, a lawyer who worked hard to get a National League expansion team for New York after the Giants and Dodgers had moved out, the stadium was built for that expansion team,

Winner of the Indianapolis 500 in 1937, 1939, and 1940, Wilbur Shaw pioneered the use of the crash helmet in auto racing. Courtesy of the Indianapolis Motor Speedway

the New York Mets, at a cost of about $24 million. It opened in Flushing Meadows in 1964, after the Mets had spent their first two seasons at the Polo Grounds. Finishing tenth in a ten-team league, the Mets attracted 1,732,597 fans that season, 400,000 more than the Yankees, who won the American League pennant.

The stadium was also home to the Yankees in 1974 and 1975, when Yankee Stadium was being completely rebuilt; to the National Football League's New York Giants in 1975, when Giants Stadium was being constructed in East Rutherford, NJ; and to the New York Jets from 1964 until 1984, when the Jets also moved to Giants Stadium. Shea has a capacity of 55,601 for baseball, 60,372 for football. Its home run distances are 338 feet down the lines and 410 feet to center field.

Sheridan, Martin J. (1881–1918)
Track and Field

Born March 21, 1881, Bohola, Ireland; died March 27, 1918; National Track and Field Hall of Fame

Probably the greatest athlete of his era, Sheridan won nine Olympic medals in six different events, including Gold Medals in the discus in 1904, 1906, and 1908, the Greek-style discus in 1908, and the shot put in 1906. He also won three Silver Medals and a Bronze in the stone throw, the standing high jump, and the standing long jump. He won the U.S. all-around championship each time he entered, (1905, 1907, and 1909). His world record of 7,385 points in the decathlon was broken by Jim Thorpe in 1912.

Sheridan was unquestionably the world's premier discus thrower in the early part of the century. He held the world record from 1901 until 1912. He was the first to break 120 feet, in 1901; 130 feet, in 1904; and 140 feet, in 1911. Sheridan won the U.S. championship in 1901, 1902, 1904, 1906, 1907 and 1911. He was hammer throw champion in 1901 and shot put champion in 1904.

Sheridan came to the United States when he was 16. He was one of the "Irish whales," New York policemen who starred in the weight events. During the 1904 London Olympics, Sheridan helped start a tradition that continues to this day. He and some other American athletes, several of Irish descent, decided the night before the opening ceremony that the U.S. flag should not be dipped to the King of England during the parade of competitors. After the parade, Sheridan explained to English journalists, "This flag dips to no earthly king."

Shibe Park
See CONNIE MACK STADIUM.

Shoemaker, "Willie" William L. (1931–   )
Horse Racing

Born August 19, 1931, Fabens, TX; National Racing Hall of Fame

The winningest jockey of all time, Shoemaker was probably also the greatest, as the subtitle of his autobiography proclaims. Born prematurely at home, he was not expected to live more than a day, but his grandmother wrapped him in blankets and laid him on the open door of an oven to keep him warm, and he survived.

He rode his first race March 19, 1949, and that year he finished second among all jockeys with 219 wins. He tied for first with 388 victories in his second year of riding. He went on to lead all jockeys in wins five times, in 1951, 1953, 1954, 1958, and 1959, and in money won ten times, including a record seven years in a row, from 1958 through 1964. Shoemaker rode in a record 24 Kentucky Derbies, winning four, aboard Swaps in 1955, Tomy Lee in 1959, Lucky Debonair in 1965, and Ferdinand in 1986. With Ferdinand, he became the oldest jockey to win the Derby, at 54. He also won the Belmont Stakes five times and the Preakness twice, and he was the top jockey at Santa Anita 17 years in a row, 1951 through 1967. During his career, Shoemaker rode a record 8,833 winners and won more than $120 million.

Shoemaker announced his retirement early in 1990 and spent the rest of the year making farewell appearances at tracks across the country, culminating in a second-place finish at Santa Anita in December. Although he suffered fractures of the neck and the lower spine in a car crash on April 8, 1991, and has been paralyzed below his upper chest since then, Shoemaker continues to work as a horse trainer.

Further Reading: Shoemaker, Bill, with Barney Nagler. *Shoemaker: America's Greatest Jockey*. New York: Doubleday, 1988.

Shooting

Target shooting, or "shooting at the mark," was a common feature of training days for colonial militia during the 18th century. As early as 1704, a traveler saw a contest in Connecticut at which the winner was presented with several yards of red ribbon. Later in the century, frontiersman often had impromptu challenge matches for side bets, and early in the 19th century turkey shoots became customary after the harvest in rural areas. A competitor paid an entry fee and shot a specified number of rounds at a staked bird. If he killed the bird, it became his prize. The distance was usually 110 yards for muskets and 165 yards for rifles.

Women compete on an equal basis with men in shooting. Margaret Murdock was the Silver Medalist in free rifle at the 1976 Olympics. Courtesy of the National Rifle Association

Originally a practical way of developing hunting skills, target shooting became a competitive sport at least as early as 1833, when *Spirit of the Times* reported a match in New York City, but it was at best sporadic. Tavern owners occasionally promoted meets with entry fees and cash prizes, and target companies, many of them associated with militia units, held annual contests during the 1830s, although competition seems to have declined during the next decade. The first pure target rifles were developed during the 1840s. They were heavy weapons that had to be rested on benches or logs, and the object was to get the closest possible grouping of shots on the target. About 1850, German immigrants brought small-bore rifle shooting to the American Midwest, where "varmint shooting" and target shooting from the standing position at distances of up to 200 yards became popular.

Like many other sports, competitive shooting grew rapidly after the Civil War. One reason was the publicity given Union sharpshooters during the war. Another was increased interest among German and Swiss Americans, who established many *Schutzen*

clubs. A *Schutzenfest*, or shooting festival, had been held in New York City as early as 1863; in 1868 it became a ten-day event that drew competitors from all over the country.

The National Rifle Association was incorporated on November 17, 1871, primarily to improve marksmanship among its member clubs. The first major international match also took place that year, when the Kolapore Cup was offered for competition between Canada and England. Canada won the cup in 1871 and 1872. With financial help from the State of New York, the NRA opened its 90-acre Creedmoor rifle range on Long Island on April 25, 1873, and held its first annual matches on October 8.

Another major international match took place in 1874, when the Amateur Rifle Club of New York accepted a challenge from the Irish shooting team that had won the championship of Great Britain. Colonel John Bodine hit three bull's-eyes on his final three shots to give the United States a 934–931 victory. The Americans won again, at Ireland, in 1875, and the following year the Palma Trophy was established for international competition at Philadelphia's Centennial Exposition. Competing against teams from Australia, Canada, Ireland, and Scotland, the United States won the trophy and repeated in 1877 and 1878. There was no challenge in 1879.

Pistol shooting was popularized during 1870s and 1880s by Buffalo Bill's Wild West Show and similar troupes and by Ira Paine, an outstanding marksman who toured the East giving exhibitions. The U.S. Revolver Association was organized in 1900 to oversee this version of the sport. It held its first national championship that year, and its 1901 championship was held in conjunction with the NRA's national matches. The NRA began holding its own pistol competition in 1906. Two years later, the NRA added small-bore rifle events to its program, chiefly for high school and college marksmen. By 1912, there were at least 65 collegiate teams in the country. New York's Public School Athletic League also featured small-bore target shooting, and was imitated by the many similar interscholastic leagues that sprang up in other large cities.

Small-bore shooting became increasingly popular during the 1920s and 1930s because the ammunition is less expensive and indoor shooting galleries require much less space than outdoor ranges. All large-caliber ammunition was reserved for military use during World War II. When the NRA championship matches resumed in 1946, there was competition only in small-bore and pistol shooting. However, high-power rifle shooting was restored to the program in 1951.

There were several shooting events on the first modern Olympic program in 1896, and the NRA began sending an official U.S. team in 1908. The Olympic events now include free pistol, rapid-fire pistol, free small-bore rifle, standard smallbore rifle, air pistol, air rifle, and running target shooting for men, and sport pistol, air pistol, small-bore standard rifle, and air rifle for women.

See also NATIONAL RIFLE ASSOCIATION OF AMERICA; SKEET SHOOTING; TRAPSHOOTING.

Shore, "Eddie" Edward W. (1902–1985)
Hockey

Born November 25, 1902, St. Qu'Appelle-Cupar, Saskatchewan; died March 16, 1985; Hockey Hall of Fame

Shore was a legendary figure in western Canada by the time he reported to the Boston Bruins in 1926. A defenseman, he was known for his end-to-end rushes, his hard shot, and his brawling. In Boston, he added a reputation for showmanship. Occasionally, he would stay off the ice until the last second when the players came out before a game; then, while Bruins' fans sang "Hail to the Chief," he'd appear in a matador's cloak, accompanied by a valet who would take the cloak away after Shore's ovation.

Fans in other National Hockey League cities hated him as much as the Bruins' fans loved him. In 1933, he charged into Toronto's Ace Bailey from behind. Tossed into the air, Bailey landed on his head and suffered a skull fracture that required two operations. Shore was suspended by the league, but the suspension was soon lifted because, despite his reputation for violence, that was the first time he'd been penalized for deliberately injuring an opponent. Two months after the incident, Shore played in an all-star game to raise money for Bailey, and the two met on the ice before the game and embraced.

Shore could take punishment as well as give it out. He once broke three ribs in a collision with a goalpost at Madison Square Garden. A doctor treated him at the Bruins' hotel, then left to arrange for a hospital room. When the doctor returned, Shore was gone. He'd taken the train to Montreal, where he scored two goals and had an assist the following night against the Canadiens. Another time, the Montreal Maroons ganged up on him, and Shore was unconscious on the ice for 14 minutes. He had a broken nose, two black eyes, gashes in his cheek and over his left eye, and three broken teeth. But he played in the Bruins' next game. "This is all part of hockey," he told his teammates.

A first-team all-star seven times, Shore won the Hart Trophy as the NHL's Most Valuable Player in 1933, 1935, 1936, and 1938. In 1939, he bought his own team, the Springfield (MA) Indians of the International-American Hockey League. He finished the 1939–40 season with the New York Americans, then became Springfield's player-coach. In his 14 NHL seasons, Shore played in 553 games, scoring 105 goals and 179 assists for a total of 284 points.

Shorter, Frank (1947–)
Track and Field

Born October 31, 1947, Munich, Germany; National Track and Field Hall of Fame

The top marathoner in the world during the early 1970s, Shorter in 1972 became the first American since 1904 to win the Olympic Gold Medal in the event, and he was the Silver Medalist in 1976. He was also the Pan-American Games champion in 1971. Representing Yale, he won the NCAA and AAU 6-mile events in 1969. He tied for the AAU championship in 1970, won the event in 1971, and was AAU 10,000-meter champion in 1974 and 1975. Four years in a row, 1971 through 1974, Shorter won Japan's Fukouku Marathon, then generally considered the world championship. A broken bone in his left foot forced him out of the 1977 New York City Marathon, and he retired from competitive running after 1978. Since then he has been designing and marketing running attire in addition to other business enterprises.

Shot Put

The shot was originally a small cannonball thrown for distance by English soldiers during leisure periods. It became a standard event in Scotland's Caledonian Games and from there entered track and field programs in England and North America. The modern shot is a ball or shell of iron or brass; if a shell, it's filled with lead to bring it up to 16 pounds for men and 8 pounds 13 ounces for women. The shot put has been on the Olympic program for men since the first modern Olympics in 1896, and the women's event was added in 1948.

Ralph Rose of the United States was the first man to break the 50-foot barrier, with a put of 51 feet in 1909. That remained the world record until 1928, when it was broken by Emil Hirschfeld of Germany. Jack Torrance of the United States pushed the record beyond 55 feet and then over 57 feet in 1934. The

The shot was originally a small cannonball thrown or put for distance, but has long been stylized, like the discus, hammer, and javelin. Here Peter Shmock of the United States watches his put during a dual meet with the Soviet Union. Courtesy of William J. Wallace/Duke University

60-foot mark was finally broken by Parry O'Brien in 1954. Twenty years later, Al Feurbach became the first American to put the shot more than 70 feet.

See also O'BRIEN, PARRY.

Show Jumping
See EQUESTRIAN SPORTS.

Shrine Bowl
Football

The Shrine Bowl was played only once, in Little Rock, AR on December 18, 1948. Hardin-Simmons beat Ouachita 40–12.

Shuffleboard

Shakespeare referred to "shovel board" and "shove groat," both games in which coins were slid along a table, and similar games were played in colonial taverns, but the sport seems to have disappeared until the 1870s, when it was revived as a shipboard game in which players used a stick to propel wooden pucks along the deck toward a scoring triangle. The sport became popular in the Daytona, FL area beginning in 1913, and the first formal shuffleboard club was organized in St. Petersburg in 1924. The Na-

The National Masters shuffleboard tournament was inaugurated in 1960, when Mary Luhn, right, won the women's championship. Courtesy of the St. Petersburg (FL) Shuffleboard Club

tional Shuffleboard Association was founded in 1929 to standardize rules; it held the first national tournament in 1931. Women's competition was added the following year.

Many shuffleboard courts were built in playgrounds by the Works Progress Administration during the 1930s, and after World War II the game was adapted for indoor play on smaller surfaces. An offshoot is a tavern game played with small metal pucks on a polished table. The NSA now has about 156,000 members, but it has been estimated that more than 5 million people play various forms of shuffleboard in informal competition.

Address: National Shuffleboard Association, c/o Harold Edmondson, 3816 Northbrook Drive, Columbus, OH 43220

Silverdome
See PONTIAC SILVERDOME.

Simmons, Al (Aloysius H. Szymanski) (1903–1956)
Baseball
Born May 22, 1903, Milwaukee, WI; died May 26, 1956; Baseball Hall of Fame

Despite the bad habit of striding toward third base instead of toward the pitcher, which won him the nickname "Bucketfoot Al," Simmons was one of the all-time great hitters. He joined the Philadelphia Athletics in 1924, played every game in left field and batted .308 with 102 runs batted in. In 1925, he collected 253 hits, 4 short of the major-league record, but finished third in hitting despite a .384 average; Harry Heilmann led the American League with .393 that season. After a .343 average in 1926, he hit .392 in 1927, but Heilmann again won the batting title, at .398.

Simmons was named the league's Most Valuable Player in 1929, when he batted .365 with 34 home runs and 157 runs batted in, tops in the league. The Athletics beat the Chicago Cubs in the 1929 World Series, Simmons batting an even .300 with two home runs. He finally won a batting championship in 1930, hitting .381 and also leading in runs scored with 152, and he again had two home runs, along with a .364 average, in a six-game World Series victory over St. Louis. Simmons held out for more money the following year, missing all of spring training, but he hit a home run his first time at-bat and went on to win his second consecutive batting title, with a .390 average. The Athletics lost the World Series to St. Louis in seven games despite Simmons' .333 average, two home runs, and eight runs batted in.

After he hit .322 in 1932, Simmons was sold to the Chicago White Sox. He spent three seasons there, hitting over .300 the first two years and driving in more than 100 runs for the 11th consecutive season in 1934. But he dropped to .267 the following year and was sold to Detroit. Despite a .327 average, the Tigers sold him to Washington in 1937. He also played for Boston and Cincinnati in the National League in 1939, went back to Philadelphia as a player-coach in 1940, and played briefly for the Boston Red Sox in 1943 and for Philadelphia again in 1944.

During his 20 major-league seasons, Simmons batted over .300 15 times. He had a lifetime average of .334, with 2,927 hits, 539 doubles, 149 triples, 307 home runs, 1,507 runs scored, and 1,827 runs batted in.

Simpson, "O. J." Orenthal J. (1947–   )
Football
Born July 9, 1947, San Francisco, CA; National Football Foundation, Pro Football Hall of Fame

A two-time All-American halfback at the University of Southern California, Simpson won the Heisman Trophy in 1968. But he had a relatively slow start after joining the Buffalo Bills of the National Football league, primarily because the team didn't make him an integral part of the offense. He gained a total of less than 2,000 yards in his first three seasons, and considered retirement after suffering a serious knee injury while playing on special teams in 1970.

The following season, however, Lou Saban took over as head coach, and in 1972 he built a new offense around Simpson and a strong offensive line. "Orange Juice," as he was sometimes called, responded by leading the league with 1,251 yards and a 4.3 yards-per-carry average. It was the first of five consecutive seasons in which he rushed for more than 1,000 yards. He is the only runner ever to gain more than 2,000 yards in a season, in 1973, when he averaged 6.0 yards per carry and also led the league in rushing touchdowns with 12. An injury limited him to 1,125 yards in 1974, but he led the league again the following two seasons, with 1,817 yards in 1975 and 1,503 in 1976. Simpson also led the NFL in rushing average, 5.5 yards, and rushing touchdowns, 16, in 1975.

After limited action in 1977, Simpson spent two seasons as a part-time player with the San Francisco 49ers before retiring. In 11 NFL seasons, he rushed 2,404 times for 11,236 yards, a 4.7 average, and scored 61 touchdowns. He also caught 203 passes for 2,142 yards and 14 touchdowns, and he returned 333 kickoffs for 990 yards, a 30.0 average, and 1 touchdown.

Sisler, George H. (1893–1973)
Baseball

Born March 24, 1893, Nimisila, OH; died March 26, 1973; Baseball Hall of Fame

Sisler was such a great hitter that his outstanding defensive ability often went unnoticed. He led American League first basemen in assists six times. One play he made has become a baseball legend. With a runner on third, the batter tried a squeeze bunt. Sisler charged in, fielded the ball, tagged the batter in the base line, and then made a diving tag to get the runner attempting to score for an unassisted double play.

Branch Rickey figured prominently in Sisler's career. As a high school student, Sisler signed a minor-league contract, but he decided to go to the University of Michigan, where Rickey was baseball coach. The contract finally ended up with the Pittsburgh Pirates, who listed Sisler on their roster. Rickey, a lawyer, persuaded the National Commission to void the contract. He then became manager of the St. Louis Browns and signed Sisler as a pitcher. In 1915, Sisler had a 4–4 record and a 2.83 earned run average, but Rickey decided to make him a first baseman because of his hitting ability.

He hit .305 in 1916, his first full season, .353 in 1917, .341 in 1918, and .352 in 1919. But he was just getting warmed up. He had three remarkable seasons in a row beginning in 1920, when he led the league in hitting at .407 and set a major-league record with 257 hits, including 49 doubles, 18 triples, and 19 home runs. He also stole 42 bases, drove in 122 runs, and scored 137. He batted .371 in 1921, collecting 216 hits, although injuries limited him to 138 games. Then came the most sensational of all, a .420 average, the second highest in major-league history, a league-leading 18 triples, 246 hits, 51 stolen bases, and 134 runs scored. Sisler hit safely in 41 games, an American League record later broken by Joe Dimaggio, and was named the league's Most Valuable Player.

A severe sinus infection that caused double vision kept him out of the entire 1923 season. Although he had some fine years after returning in 1924, he was never quite the same hitter. He did hit over .300 in six of his final seven seasons, however, with a high of .345 in 1925. He was sold to the Washington Senators in 1928, but played only 20 games there before being sold again, to the Boston Braves of the National League. He retired after the 1930 season with a lifetime average of .340 and 2,812 hits, including 425 doubles, 164 triples, and 100 home runs. He scored 1,284 runs, drove in 1,180, and stole 375 bases.

Six-Day Races

Six-day racing originated with race walker Edward Payson Weston in 1874. For Weston, it was a one-week race, since he took Sundays off. He tried to walk 500 miles at the Empire Skating Rink that year and failed, but still collected $6,000 in gate receipts. In 1878, Lord Astley of England presented a championship belt for a six-day "go-as-you-please" race. Six-day races were held in a number of cities in 1879, including Boston, San Francisco, and Toronto. By 1884, six-day racing seemed extinct, but it made a brief comeback late in the decade.

Then six-day bicycle racing took over in 1895 at Madison Square Garden. It died out by the turn of the century. Tex Rickard, better known as a boxing promoter, revived six-day races at the Garden in 1920, and a whole circuit spring up. Rickard in 1925 had a six-day race for the grand opening of his new Madison Square Garden. The last "six-day" race was held in December of 1939, and actually lasted only five days.

See also CYCLING; PEDESTRIANISM.

Six-Man Football

Stephen T. Epler, coaching at an undermanned Nebraska high school, invented six-man football in 1934. The ball has to be thrown, forward or backward, before it can cross the line of scrimmage, and all six players are eligible to receive a forward pass. The sport was common at small high schools into the 1950s, when the advent of large regional high schools serving many communities made it obsolete.

Skating
See FIGURE SKATING; ICE SKATING; ROLLER SKATING; SPEED SKATING.

Skeet Shooting

Charles E. Davies of Andover, MA invented skeet shooting as practice for hunting in 1915. He and his son set up a circle with a 25-yard radius, 12 shooting stations, and a trap that threw clay targets across the circle. They called the sport "shooting around the clock." When a neighbor built henhouses within range of the shooting circle, they reduced it to a semicircle with six shooting stations aiming away from the henhouses. A friend, outdoor writer Bill Foster, suggested using two traps, one at each end of the semicircle. He also publicized the sport, and in 1926 he offered a $100 prize for the best name. Gertrude Hurlbutt of Dayton, MT won by suggesting "skeet," the old Norse word for "shoot."

The National Skeet Shooting Association, founded in 1927, currently has more than 16,000 registered shooters. It held the first national tournament in 1935, and competition for women was added in 1939. There are now eight shooting stations, one of them in the center of the semicircle's 120-yard radius. The "high house" is at the shooter's left, the "low house" on his or her right. Targets are thrown from the high house at a height of 10 feet and in a nearly horizontal path. Targets from the low house begin at a height of 3½ feet and follow a rising trajectory.

As skeet became more refined through the years, it became less valuable as training for the hunter. International skeet, developed after World War II, is much closer to Davies' original version. It has been on the Olympic program since 1968, and the National Rifle Association, which is responsible for selecting U.S. teams for international competition, conducts a national championship in this form of the sport.

Address: National Skeet Shooting Association, P.O. Box 680007, San Antonio, TX 78268 (512) 688–3371

See also TRAPSHOOTING.

Skiing

Immigrants from Norway brought skiing to North America during the 1850s. There were "ski running" races in Onion Valley, CA in 1853, but snowshoes were also called skis at the time, and those were probably snowshoe races. The first definitely known ski competition was a cross-country race held in 1885 by the Norwegian Ski Club of Minneapolis. The following year, Norwegian immigrants also held races in Red Wing, MN and Eau Claire, WI. Members of the Red Wing club took part in a ski jumping exhibition at Ishpeming, MI in 1892. Many ski clubs were organized in the Upper Midwest during the 1890s, and the National Ski Association was founded in Ishpeming in 1904. The NSA held its first national jumping championship that year; cross-country racing was added in 1907.

Nordic skiing took root in Canada about the same time. The Montreal Ski Club, founded on February 11, 1904, held a jumping competition in 1907, and a national jumping championship took place in 1909. The Montreal club introduced cross-country competition in 1914.

Alpine skiing developed later, primarily in Austria. Hannes Schneider, from that country's Arlberg region, developed a system of downhill skiing that came to be known as the Arlberg technique. Englishman Arnold Lunn, one of Schneider's students, invented modern slalom racing in 1921 to demonstrate the technique. (An Austrian, Mathias Zardsky, had invented single-pole slalom about 1907; the modern slalom developed by Lunn uses two-pole gates.)

Dartmouth College was instrumental in the early growth of the sport. A group of Dartmouth students visited the Montreal Ski Club in 1909, and, on their return, they organized the Dartmouth Outing Club. The first intercollegiate meet ever held was between Dartmouth and McGill University of Montreal in 1913. Charles Proctor of Dartmouth laid out North America's first slalom course in 1923, and in 1929 Katharine Beckett hired a staff of European instructors for the continent's first skiing school at nearby Franconia, NH. The Canadian Amateur Ski Association, formed in 1921, established its own school in 1930.

Ironically, skiing's popularity increased dramatically during the Great Depression. The Boston and Maine Railroad began running ski trains from Massachusetts to New Hampshire in 1931, and the Winter Olympics at Lake Placid, NY the following year helped stir interest in the sport. The downhill, an Alpine event, was added to the national championship program in 1933, followed by the slalom in 1935. The first Alpine trails were developed at Mount Greylock in Massachusetts and at Franconia in 1935.

Many ski resorts were developed during the 1930s, the biggest of them Sun Valley in Idaho, where the Union Pacific Railroad invested more than $3 million. The Works Progress Administration also built many ski trails in state and national parks. Methods of transporting skiers up the mountain were vital to popularizing the sport. The rope tow, invented by a Swiss engineer in 1932, was first installed at Woodstock, VT in 1934. Fred Pabst of Wisconsin invented the J-bar in 1936, and Union Pacific engineers designed the ski lift for Sun Valley the same year.

Many women took up the sport during the 1930s. Spurned by men's clubs, a group of Canadian women founded the Penguin Ski Club in 1933. Women's events were added to the Canadian national championship in 1935 and to the U.S. championships in 1938. The Great Depression had eased somewhat by that year, when more than $3 million was spent on ski equipment and more than $6 million on ski clothing.

There were 75 ski clubs with about 3,500 members in the United States in 1930; by 1940, there were an estimated 2 million recreational skiers in the country, and membership in the CASA had grown to 200 clubs with more than 30,000 members. After World War II, many servicemen discovered skiing in central Europe and returned to North America as enthusiasts. The postwar economic boom and increased leisure time also contributed to the sport's growth.

Although cross-country skiing was the original form of the sport, it was largely superseded by Alpine skiing during the 1920s. Television exposure during the Winter Olympics of 1972 and 1976 brought a mild resurgence, but it is still much more popular as a recreation than as a competitive sort. Courtesy of F. Kelly MacNeill

Nordic skiing was on the Winter Olympic program in 1924, but Alpine skiing wasn't added until 1948. North American women had some early success in the sport: Gretchen Fraser and Andrea Mead Lawrence of the United States were the first two Gold Medalists in the slalom; Lawrence also won the giant slalom in 1952, the first year it was held. Canada's Anne Heggtveit was the slalom champion in 1960. The Alpine World Cup was inaugurated in 1967, and Nancy Greene of Canada won the women's championship the first two years. She was also Olympic Gold Medalist in the giant slalom in 1968.

United States skiers blossomed on the international circuit in the 1980s, when skiing had a tremendous increase in popularity. Phil Mahre won World Cups from 1981 through 1983, Tamara McKinney was the women's World Cup champion in 1983, and the United States won three Gold Medals at the 1984 Winter Olympics. But injuries depleted the 1988 Olympic team, and few promising young skiers appeared on the horizon although recreational skiing had reached new heights. The number of lift tickets sold increased from 51.4 million in the 1984–85 season to more than 60 million in 1985–86, and ski shop sales climbed from $1.07 billion to $1.30 billion during the same period. Then a decline set in. Lift ticket sales went over $1 billion for the first time in 1986–87, but dropped to $926 million in 1987–88. Ski shop sales fell to just over $1 billion that season.

Further Reading: Berry, I. William. *The Great North American Ski Book.* New York: Scribner's, 1981; Needham, Richard, editor. *Ski Magazine's Encyclopedia of Skiing.* New York: Harper and Row, 1979.

Addresses: Canadian Ski Association, 333 River Road, Vanier, Ontario, Canada K1L 8H9 (613) 748–5660; U.S. Ski Association, P.O. Box 100, Park City, UT 84060 (801) 649–9090

See also FREESTYLE SKIING; U.S. NATIONAL SKI HALL OF FAME; WINTER OLYMPICS; WORLD CUP.

Skin Diving

The only essential piece of equipment for skin diving is a pair of goggles. Polynesian pearl divers evidently made the first such goggles, out of transparent tortoise shells, centuries ago. They also made flippers out of reeds to improve their underwater swimming. The Japanese developed a single-lens mask, or faceplate, with a bamboo frame in the 1920s and later came up with the rubber-framed mask. Jacques-Yves Cousteau and Emil Gagnan invented the aqualung, the first self-contained underwater breathing apparatus (SCUBA) in 1943. As a recreation, skin diving and SCUBA diving had enormous growth during the 1950s.

Several games have been adapted for underwater play, but the major form of competition is spearfishing, which was brought to North America from the Mediterranean during the 1930s by Guy Kilpatric. Three types of weapons are used: the sea gig, or trident, which has three or five prongs; the sea spear, which is 50–70 inches long and has a single sharp head, as on an arrow; and the sea lance, which is a longer version of the lance, ranging from 90 inches to as much as 12 feet. All are propelled by hand. The spear can also be launched by a sling, based on an old Hawaiian method of fishing, by a kind of crossbow, or by a gun that uses compressed air or carbon dioxide. Spearfishing contests are similar to fishing derbies, with prizes awarded for the most fish, the largest, the heaviest total catch, and so forth.

Skin divers have created other games, ranging from underwater tag to underwater versions of hockey and rugby, as well as fin swimming races. The Underwater Society of America, founded in 1955, coordinates competition in these sports, but they remain more or less informal.

Address: Underwater Society of America, P.O. Box 628, Daly City, CA 94017 (415) 583–8492

Ski Orienteering

Ski orienteering is perhaps the newest sport around. Based on orienteering, this sport lets the competitors use a map and compass to negotiate a course. The first U.S. championships were held by the Cambridge (MA) Sports Union on February 11–12, 1989, in Graftsbury, VT. Most of the 90 competitors were experienced cross-country skiers who had never tried ski orienteering. Among them was Bill Spencer, a member of the 1988 U.S. Olympic team, who won the men's event. Men skied a 20-kilometer course the first day and 14 kilometers the second; women skied 14 and 8 kilometers on the two days of competition.

See also ORIENTEERING.

Skittles

Skittles was brought to North America by the Dutch and the English. The name and the game may have originated in Holland or even in Scandinavia, since the root is Old Norse. Also known as nine-pins, skittles was a kind of bowling game in which the nine pins were set up in a diamond shape and bowlers attempted to knock them down with a ball. Since it was a folk game, nothing was standardized. Pins might be tall and thin, like today's candlepins, or oval-headed, as in modern ten-pin bowling; the ball could vary in size and weight, and the distance between bowler and pins could also change from one alley to the next. Like billiards, skittles was frowned upon in public places during the colonial period because it was associated with taverns and gambling, but was tolerated as a game at home among family and friends.

See also BOWLING.

Skydiving
See SPORT PARACHUTING

Skydome, The
Toronto, Ontario

The newest and, at $500 million, the most expensive of the modern domed stadiums, the Skydome opened on June 5, 1989. The 310-foot-high structure is the home of the American League's Toronto Blue Jays and the Canadian Football League's Toronto Argonauts. It has a four-section, 8-acre retractable roof and a 35-by-115-foot scoreboard. The roof can be opened or closed in about 20 minutes. A 350-room hotel attached to the complex has rooms overlooking the field, and a restaurant is located between the upper and lower decks in right center field. The Skydome seats 53,595 for football and 49,500 for baseball. Its home run distances are 328 feet down the lines and 400 feet to center field.

Slaney, Mary Decker
See DECKER, MARY.

Slater, "Duke" Frederick W. (1898–1966)
Football

Born December 9, 1898, Normal, IL; died August 14, 1966; National Football Foundation Hall of Fame

One of the first great black football players, the 6-foot-2, 210-pound Slater was a four-year starter at tackle for the University of Iowa and was named to some All-American teams in 1921, his senior season. He turned in an outstanding performance that year when Iowa upset previously unbeaten Notre Dame 10–7. Matched against consensus All-American Hunk Anderson, Slater continually opened holes for halfback Gordon Locke, who scored Iowa's only touchdown in the victory. Slater played professionally for ten seasons with the Milwaukee Badgers, Rock Island Independents, and Chicago Cardinals. He was named to unofficial All-Pro teams in 1926, 1928, and 1929. While playing pro football, Slater attended law school and became a Cook County Superior Court judge in 1949, serving until his death.

Sled Dog Racing

Like horse racing, sled dog racing undoubtedly began with challenge races, probably during the late 19th century in Alaska and the Yukon. The first known organized race was the All-Alaska Sweepstakes in 1908, a 408-mile run from Nome to Candle and back to Nome. The Hudson Bay Derby began in 1916, and the Banff, Alberta, Dog Derby in 1923. The Laconia (NH) Sled Dog Club, organized in 1933, held its first World Championship Derby that year. The club was inactive from 1934, when it resumed the race.

The International Sled Dog Racing Association was established in 1966 to standardize rules for the sport. That led to a small circuit of races. The best-known sled dog race is the Iditarod, inaugurated in 1973. This 1,160-mile race was won by women drivers five times in a six-year period from 1984 through 1990.

Address: International Sled Dog Racing Association, P.O. Box 446, Nordman, ID 83848 (208) 443–3153

Sloan, "Tod" James F. (1874–1933)
Horse Racing

Born August 10, 1874, Bunker Hill, IN; died December 21, 1933; National Racing Hall of Fame

Sloan had unusually short legs and was called "Toad" as a youngster. Later he adapted the nickname to "Tod," and, after becoming a successful jockey, he had his name legally changed to J. Todhunter Sloan to explain the nickname. Because of his short legs, Sloan revolutionized riding by using short stirrups and the "monkey crouch," now used universally by jockeys because it reduces air resistance. He was also one of the first jockeys to study his rivals in order to plan his strategy and tactics before a race.

After winning 132 races in 1896 and 137 in 1897, he had an incredible 186 winners in just 362 rides in 1898. Sloan often traveled to England, riding three winners for the royal stable in 1897, though the English at first ridiculed his riding style. He won a lot of money and spent it almost as fast as he won it, going through about $1 million in a two-year period, during which he traveled in England and Europe with 38 trunks of clothing, changing his costume every hour. His arrogance brought the disapproval of the English Jockey Club, which in 1900 told him not to apply for a renewal of his license. Sloan never raced again.

Slow Pitch Softball
See SOFTBALL.

Smith, "Red" Walter W. (1905–1982)
Sportswriter
Born September 25, 1905, Green Bay, WI; died January 15, 1982; National Sportswriters and Sportscasters Hall of Fame

Red Smith's writing, like Joe Dimaggio's fielding, was so graceful that it seemed effortless. But he was fond of saying that to write a column, "I just open a vein and bleed."

Generally considered the best sportswriter of his era, and probably of all time, Smith was a self-deprecating man who called himself "a working stiff." After majoring in journalism at Notre Dame, he simply wanted to be a newspaperman. But he was moved to the sports desk at his second paper, the *St. Louis Star,* in 1929, and he soon became the paper's top sportswriter, covering the National League Cardinals. He went to Philadelphia in 1936 and began to attract attention. Then Stanley Woodward, sports editor of the *New York Herald Tribune,* hired him in 1945, and Smith became genuinely famous within a few years.

By 1948, his syndicated column was second only to Grantland Rice's in national readership. A collection of his columns, *Out of the Red,* was published by Alfred A. Knopf in 1950. There were to be six more collections, two of them published posthumously. The *Herald Tribune* briefly became the *World Journal Tribune* in 1966, then folded, and Smith did most of his writing for *Women's Wear Daily* until 1971, when he was hired by the *New York Times* to write three columns a week. His last column appeared just four days before he died of congestive heart failure.

Smith won the second Grantland Rice Memorial Award in 1956, and in 1976 he became the second sportswriter to win the Pulitzer Prize for Distinguished Commentary. His citation read, in part, "Mr. Smith is unique in the erudition, the literary quality, the vitality and freshness of viewpoint he brings to his work and in the sustained quality of his columns."

Further Reading: Berkow, Ira. *Red: A Biography of Red Smith.* New York: Times Books, 1986.

Smoke, Marcia (Jones) (1941–   )
Canoeing
Born July 18, 1941, Oklahoma City, OK

Marcia Jones Smoke and her sister, Sperry Jones Rademaker, dominated U.S. canoeing for nearly a decade. As Marcia Jones, she won the women's kayak championship in 1964, and as Marcia Smoke she paddled to a tie with her sister in 1965, then won five titles in a row, 1966–70. All women's racing was at 500 meters until 1971, when a 5,000-meter race was added. Smoke won both events that year, and she was 500-meter champion in 1972 and 1973. Her sister won the 5,000-meter race from 1972 through 1974.

Smythe Trophy
Hockey
Presented by Maple Leaf Gardens in 1964 to honor Conn Smythe, the Toronto Maple Leafs' former coach, manager, and owner, this trophy is presented to the player chosen by the Professional Hockey Writers' Association as the most valuable in the Stanley Cup playoffs.

Smythe Trophy Winners

1965	Jean Beliveau, Montreal
1966	Roger Crozier, Detroit
1967	Dave Keon, Toronto
1968	Glenn Hall, St. Louis
1969	Serge Savard, Montreal
1970	Bobby Orr, Boston
1971	Ken Dryden, Montreal
1972	Bobby Orr, Boston
1973	Yvan Cournoyer, Montreal
1974	Bernie Parent, Philadelphia
1975	Bernie Parent, Philadelphia
1976	Reggie Leach, Philadelphia
1977	Guy Lafleur, Montreal
1978	Larry Robinson, Montreal
1979	Bob Gainey, Montreal
1980	Brian Trottier, New York Islanders
1981	Butch Goring, New York Islanders
1982	Mike Bossy, New York Islanders

1983   Bill Smith, New York Islanders
1984   Mark Messier, Edmonton
1985   Wayne Gretzky, Edmonton
1986   Patrick Roy, Montreal
1987   Ron Hextall, Philadelphia
1988   Wayne Gretzky, Edmonton
1989   Al MacInnis, Calgary
1990   Bill Ranford, Edmonton
1991   Mario Lemieux, Pittsburgh

Snead, Samuel J. (1912–   )
Golf
Born May 27, 1912, Hot Springs, VA; World Golf
Hall of Fame

Perhaps the greatest natural swinger in golf's history, Snead taught himself to play when he was a caddy by whittling a single club out of a tree branch. Although he won 37 tournaments, including the 1942 PGA Championship, between 1936 and 1945, Snead didn't emerge as a genuine star on the pro tour until 1946, when he won the British Open and the World Championship. He won both the Masters and the PGA in 1949, the PGA in 1951, and the Masters in 1952 and 1954. But he was haunted by his inability to win the U.S. Open. Snead finished second in 1937, the first time he entered the tournament. In 1939, he needed only a 5 on the final hole to win, but he ended up shooting an 8 and finishing in third place. He and Lew Worsham tied for the lead in 1947, but Worsham won the playoff; Snead also finished second in the Open in 1949 and 1953.

Snead was the tour's top money-winner in 1938, 1949, and 1950, and he won a total of $541,514 in official tour events, a remarkably high figure for his era. He won the Vardon trophy for the fewest strokes per round in 1938, 1949, 1950, and 1955. A great hitter from tee to green, Snead was only an average putter, which undoubtedly cost him many tournaments.

Snowmobiling
The first snowmobile was built by Joseph-Armand Bombardier of Quebec in 1922. It had two motorized tracks in back and two skis in front. Carl Eliason of Wisconsin developed a similar vehicle in 1928, and by 1932 he had increased its speed over snow to 40 miles an hour. But snowmobiling was virtually unknown until 1958, when Bombardier began to market the Ski-Doo. He sold only 225 vehicles in 1959, but sales were averaging about 300,000 a year by the early 1960s.

Racing had begun in a tentative way somewhat earlier. The U.S. Snowmobiling Association was or-
ganized in 1956 to establish racing rules, with help from the U.S. Ski Association. By the early 1970s, there were a number of competing manufacturers with racing teams to publicize their vehicles, and the Sno-Pro Racing Circuit was established by the USSA in 1973. The circuit includes races on several tracks in the United States and Canada. Amateur racing is also held in many categories, based on vehicle horsepower and the driver's experience.

Snowshoe Racing
Although snowshoes of a sort date to ancient times in Scandinavia, the North American snowshoe was developed by native Americans, who undoubtedly did some racing among themselves. In 1840, a group of about a dozen well-to-do Montrealers began going on informal "tramps," and they organized the Montreal Snow Shoe Club in 1843. The first recorded race was held by the MSSC that year, with two of its members competing against some voyageurs from the Northwest and some Indians from the nearby Caughnawaga reserve. A voyageur won the 4-mile event at the St. Pierre race course. A 1-mile race over 4-foot-high hurdles was also held.

The Quebec Snow Shoe Club, founded in 1847, held races that year. The MSSC in 1851 began offering a cash prize for its feature race, but toward the end of the decade trophies were offered for major races, sashes, belts, and medals for the lesser events. The first trophy was the Eyre Cup, presented in 1859 for a 3-mile race. It was followed by the Sir Frederick Williams Cup in 1861, and the General Lord Paulet Trophy in 1863. The sport grew tremendously in the late 1860s and into the 1870s. The number of clubs in Canada increased from just 9 at the beginning of 1867 to 80 by the end of the year, and in 1869 an estimated 5,000 spectators watched the annual Ottawa Snow Shoe Club races.

By 1885, there were 25 clubs in Montreal alone, and the MSSC had 1,000 members. But the sport began to decline shortly afterward, in large part because of the rise of ice skating and ice hockey. Somewhat like cricket in the United States, snowshoeing suffered from its generally upper-class orientation and the fact that most of the clubs were as interested in social activities as they were in sport. Snowshoe racing barely lasted into the 20th century. Manitoba held a "world championship" in 1911, but that was ended after 1914.

The sport began a comeback about 1970, just as cross-country skiing was also regaining popularity. The U.S. Snowshoe Association was founded in 1977, and the International Snowshoe Federation in 1981. Snowshoeing is primarily a social and recreational sport, but there is some racing.

Addresses: International Snowshoe Federation, 8720 28th Avenue, Merrill, WI 54452 (715) 536–1230; U.S. Snowshoe Association, R.D. 1, Box 170, Corinth, NY 12822 (518) 654–7165

Soap Box Derby

A photographer, Myron Scott, covered a race of "cars" built by boys in Dayton, OH in 1933 and persuaded his newspaper to sponsor a citywide race the following year. The Soap Box Derby was so named because most of the cars had bodies made of crates similar to those used to ship soap to grocery stores—probably influenced by the phrase "soap box orator." The race was moved to Akron in 1935 because of its hillier terrain, and in 1936 a permanent site, Derby Downs, was built in Akron by the Works Progress Administration.

Competition is held at the local level, often sponsored by newspapers, and winners move on to regional competition and then to the championship event in Akron. Competitors were expected to build their own cars from scratch until 1976, when a kit car division was introduced for those who want to buy patterns and hardware from the All-American Soap Box Derby, the sponsoring organization. Boys and girls aged 9 through 16 now compete.

Address: All-American Soap Box Derby, P.O. Box 7233, Akron, OH 44306 (216) 733–8723

Soaring

Gliders were widely used early in the century to test the aerodymanics of airplane designs. Soaring, as the sport of glider flying is known, developed during the late 1920s, and the Soaring Society of America was founded in 1932 to oversee the sport. The SSA and the Soaring Association of Canada both conduct national championships. Competition is based on a series of events, including speed on a triangular course, straightaway distance flight, and accuracy in returning to the starting point.

Addresses: Soaring Association of Canada, 485 Bank Street, 2nd Floor, Ottawa, Ontario, Canada K2P 1Z2 (613) 232–1243; Soaring Society of America, Inc., P.O. Box E, Hobbs, NM 88241–1308

See also HANG GLIDING.

Soccer

Although a kind of football was played in North America in Colonial times, soccer wasn't codified until 1863, with the formation of the London Football Association. The sport arrived in North America shortly afterward. In 1866, the *New York Times* reported that football was very popular at Columbia University, though that might have been an earlier version of the sport that had been played at several other colleges beginning in the late 18th century. The first intercollegiate "football" game, between Princeton and Rutgers on November 6, 1869, was actually a soccer match. However, soccer was supplanted by rugby at eastern colleges when the Intercollegiate Football Association was established in 1876.

Soccer had a similar fate in Canada. The Montreal Football Club, organized in 1868, played English soccer, and Upper Canada College also played soccer during the early 1870s before switching to rugby in 1876. The Dominion Football Association, founded in 1873, is still the governing body for the sport. But in Canada, as in the United States, rugby became the preferred type of football.

Soccer never became completely extinct; it was kept alive primarily by textile workers from England. A group of cricket clubs in Philadelphia formed a soccer league in 1886, and about the same time Scottish immigrants were playing the sport in New York. The New England Association Football League was established in 1887. In the Midwest, Chicago, Cincinnati, and St. Louis all had leagues by 1890. There was something of a revival on the college level beginning in 1901, when Haverford College organized a team. Haverford and Harvard played a match in 1905, and the following year those two schools joined with Columbia, Cornell, and Pennsylvania to found the Intercollegiate Association Football League.

The American Football Association, which controlled professional soccer in the East, and the American Amateur Football Association, an outgrowth of the New York State Amateur Association Football League, merged into the U.S. Football Association on April 5, 1913. The USFA took over the National Challenge Cup, which had been established by the AAFA in 1912. The Dominion Challenge Cup, for the Canadian championship, was first awarded in 1913.

Professional soccer gained some popularity after World War I, and the professional American Soccer League was organized in 1921. Because the pro teams dominated competition, the National Challenge Cup in 1923 became the trophy for the winner of an open tournament, and the National Amateur Challenge Cup was established for nonprofessional teams. During this period, most soccer players were immigrants or their second-generation descendants, and as immigration declined, so did soccer.

The sport began a comeback after World War II, largely because of returning servicemen who had learned to play soccer in Europe. Both the NCAA and the NAIA inaugurated national collegiate championships in 1959, and two professional leagues, the

United Soccer Association and the National Professional Soccer League, began play in 1967. They relied heavily on foreign players, but the two leagues merged into the North American Soccer League in 1968, and the NASL soon adopted a policy of encouraging amateur soccer in this country by giving financial aid to the USFFA and by requiring each team to have a certain number of American-born players.

Many parents during the 1960s and 1970s got their sons—and, eventually, their daughters—into soccer as a less violent alternative to football, and a number of youth soccer programs sprang up during that period. Soccer's heyday in the United States probably came in the 1971–72 season, when the NASL Rookie of the Year, Goalie of the Year, and Coach of the Year were all Americans. The NASL folded after the 1984 season. However, youth soccer and college soccer are still flourishing. More than 600 colleges and universities have teams, and the NCAA in 1982 began a national women's championship tournament. There are an estimated 500,000 players in youth and high school programs.

Addresses: Canadian Soccer Association, 333 River Road, Vanier, Ontario, Canada K1L 8H9 (613) 748–5667; U.S. Soccer Federation, 1750 East Boulder Street, Colorado Springs, CO 80909 (719) 578–4678

See also AMERICAN INDOOR SOCCER ASSOCIATION; AMERICAN SOCCER LEAGUE; INDOOR SOCCER; MAJOR INDOOR SOCCER LEAGUE; NATIONAL CHALLENGE CUP; NATIONAL PROFESSIONAL SOCCER LEAGUE; NATIONAL SOCCER HALL OF FAME; NORTH AMERICAN SOCCER LEAGUE; WORLD CUP.

Softball

It is possible that modern softball grew out of two versions of "indoor baseball" that were developed independently. The first such sport was created in 1887 by George Hancock of Chicago's Farragut Boat Club. Hancock's indoor baseball used a broomstick as a bat, a boxing glove as a ball, a pitching distance of 40 feet, and base lines of 60 feet. Minneapolis firefighter Lewis Robey came up with a similar sport in 1895; it may have been an independent invention, or he may have known of Hancock's game. Robey did develop a soft, oversized ball similar to today's softball, and he called it kittenball. The dimensions of his diamond were about the same as Hancock's, but pitchers were at first allowed to throw overhand in kittenball. Within a few years, however, underhanded pitching was required, as in indoor baseball.

Whether one sport or two at the beginning, softball spread rapidly through the Midwest in the early part of the century, and it got a real boost from World War I, when thousands of American soldiers played

it in army gyms as an alternative to baseball. Still called indoor baseball or kittenball, the sport continued to grow after the war, but rules varied widely from one place to another. Sportswriter Leo H. Fischer and sporting goods salesman Michael J. Pauley decided to hold a national tournament in conjunction with the 1933 Century of Progress Exposition in Chicago, and they developed standardized rules for the first time. That led to the formation of the Amateur Softball Association of America, which still oversees the sport.

The sport became very popular among women during the 1930s, largely because of company-sponsored teams. There was a women's championship event at that first national tournament in 1933, and after World War II many high schools and colleges added women's softball to their sports programs. Because pitchers dominate fast-pitch softball, a slow-pitch version was developed during the early 1950s. There is also a slow-pitch softball that uses a very large (16-inch diameter as opposed to the normal 12-inch diameter) ball, which is especially popular in the Chicago area.

There are more than 220,000 teams represented in the ASA membership, and the number of players on all levels is probably about 30 million. Canada has an estimated 2.5 million players, and the International Softball Federation has 47 member countries, most of them in the Americas or the Orient, with a total of nearly 50 million active players.

See also INTERNATIONAL SOFTBALL CONGRESS; NATIONAL SOFTBALL HALL OF FAME AND MUSEUM.

Soldier Field
Chicago, IL

Opened in 1924 as a war memorial, Soldier Field was the site of the College All-Star football game from 1934 through 1976. Notre Dame played some "home" games there during the 1920s and 1930s, it was the site of several Army-Navy games, and the University of Chicago also played some of its home games there. In 1971, seating capacity was increased from 55,049 to 66,946, and it became the home field of the National Football League's Chicago Bears.

Southeastern Conference

The Southern Intercollegiate Conference, organized in 1921, had grown to an unwieldy 23 members by 1932, when 13 of its members split away to form the Southeastern Conference. The original members were Alabama, Alabama Polytechnic Institute (now Auburn University), Florida, Georgia, Georgia Tech, Kentucky, Louisiana State, Mississippi, Mississippi State, Tennessee, Tulane, University of the South, and Vanderbilt. The University of the South dropped out in 1940. Georgia Tech moved into the Atlantic Coast Conference in 1978, and Tulane left in 1985 after dropping basketball because of a gambling scandal. The University of South Carolina joined the conference in 1991, and the University of Arkansas is to join in 1992, when the conference will split into two divisions of six teams each.

Address: 900 Central Bank Building, Birmingham, AL 35233 (205) 252-7415

Southern Ocean Racing Conference (SORC)

The SORC began by conducting a yacht race from St. Petersburg, FL to Havana, Cuba, in 1930. By the 1970s, the conference was running a major series of six ocean races, including a 184-mile, three-leg Miami-to-Nassau and a 403-mile from St. Petersburg to Fort Lauderdale, around the Florida peninsula. The series reached its peak with 135 entries in 1974, but that was down to 44 by 1988. The following year the Miami-Nassau race was discontinued, and the length of the race meeting was cut from 23 days to 13. The St. Petersburg–Ft. Lauderdale race is still a major event, and sponsorship from Audi has increased prize money, which may help the SORC attract more entries in the future.

Southwest Athletic Conference (SAC)

The original members of the SAC when it was chartered on December 8, 1914, were Arkansas, Baylor, Oklahoma, Oklahoma A & M (now Oklahoma State), Rice, Southwestern University, Texas, and Texas A & M. The original name was the Southwest Intercollegiate Athletic Conference; the word "Intercollegiate" was dropped in 1916, when Southwestern University left the conference. Southern Methodist joined the SAC in 1918, and Phillips University was a member from 1919 through 1921. Oklahoma dropped out in 1920, Texas Christian was added in 1922, and Oklahoma A & M withdrew in 1925. Texas Tech became a member of the conference in 1958, the University of Houston in 1976. Arkansas planned to withdraw and play as an independent school in 1991, before joining the Southeastern Conference in 1992, but later decided to remain in the SAC during the 1991–92 academic year.

Address: P.O. Box 569420, Dallas, TX 75356 (214) 634-7353

Spahn, Warren E. (1921–   )
Baseball

Born April 23, 1921, Buffalo, NY; Baseball Hall of Fame

Because he served in World War II, winning a Purple Heart and a citation for bravery, Spahn didn't get his first major-league victory until he was 25 years old. Nevertheless, he won more games than any left-handed pitcher in history, 363.

He appeared briefly in two games with the Boston Braves in 1942 and rejoined the team in 1946. A full-time starter, he had a 21–10 record and led the National League with a 2.33 earned run average in 1947, the first of 13 seasons in which he won 20 or more games. He slumped to 15–12 in 1948, when the Braves won the pennant but lost to the Cleveland Indians in the World Series, where Spahn had a 1–1 record.

Although the Braves finished fourth or worse during the next three seasons, Spahn won more than 20 games each year, and in 1952 he led the league in strikeouts for the fourth straight time despite a 14–19 record. The following season, the team moved to Milwaukee and Spahn responded with 23 victories and a league-leading 2.10 earned run average. He had two more 20-victory seasons in the next three years, then won the Cy Young Award in 1957 with a 21–11 record and a 2.69 ERA. The Braves won the pennant that year and beat the New York Yankees in the World Series, Spahn winning 1 and losing 1. He won 22 games the following season, when the Braves again won the pennant. Spahn had a 2–1 record in the Series, including a 2-hit shutout, but the Braves lost to the Yankees this time.

Once basically a fastball pitcher with excellent control, Spahn was now in his late thirties and he was relying on guile more than speed. Yet he won 20 or more games from 1959 through 1961. He pitched his first no-hitter in 1960, when he was 39, and added a second the following year. After slipping to 18 wins in 1962, he had his final 20-victory season in 1963, with a 23–7 record, the best of his career.

Spahn hoped to break the National League record of 373 wins, but he was only 6–13 in 1964. The Braves sold him to the New York Mets the following year; released in July, he ended the year and his major-league career with the San Francisco Giants. Spahn unfortunately delayed his induction into the Hall of Fame by pitching three games for a minor-league team in 1967, but he was elected in his first year of eligibility, 1973. In 21 major-league seasons, he had a 363–245 record with a 3.09 ERA. He pitched 57 shutouts and struck out 2,583 hitters while walking only 1,434 in 5,243⅔ innings.

Spalding, Albert G. (1850–1915)
Baseball

Born September 2, 1850, Byron, IL; died September 9, 1915; Baseball Hall of Fame

Spalding was a successful pitcher in the early years of professional baseball, and in 1876 he became the first manager of the Chicago White Stockings in the American League. He also pitched the team's first victory, 4–0 over Louisville. However, he retired after the 1877 season to devote himself to the sporting goods store he and his brother, J. Walter Spalding, had opened the previous year. His contacts within organized baseball were valuable; he published the first official *Baseball Guide* in 1877, with Henry Chadwick as its editor, and in 1878 the Spalding baseball became the National League's official ball.

The business expanded greatly during the next two decades. Spalding published guides, manuals, and rule books for many other sports. In 1885 he bought a half-interest in A. J. Reach and Company of Philadelphia, and six years later he also bought a share of Wright and Ditson of Boston. His company imported golf equipment and bicycles and began manufacturing basketballs soon after that sport was invented in 1891.

Spalding was also involved in baseball during that period. He became president of the White Stockings in 1882; the team won pennants that season and in 1885 and 1886. Spalding organized a world tour after the 1888 season, taking 20 players to Australia, Ceylon, England, Egypt, France, Hawaii, Italy, and New Zealand, and seizing the opportunity to open a London branch of his business during the trip. Spalding resigned as president of the Chicago team after the 1890 season, but remained as a major stockholder. In 1911 he wrote the first history of baseball, *America's National Game.*

Speaker, Tristram (1888–1958)
Baseball
Born April 4, 1888, Hubbard City, TX; died December 8, 1958; Baseball Hall of Fame

Speaker was the first center fielder to play very shallow, depending on his speed to catch up to balls hit over his head. He also had a strong arm and he was an outstanding hitter as well as the best defensive outfielder of his day. "The Gray Eagle," as he became known, played briefly for the Boston Red Sox in 1907 and 1908, then became a starter in 1909, when he hit .309 and had 35 assists, still the American League record for an outfielder. That was the first of ten consecutive seasons in which he hit over .300.

His finest year was 1912, when he won the Chalmers Award as the American League's Most Valuable Player. Speaker hit .383, with 222 hits, 53 doubles, 13 triples, 136 runs scored, and 90 runs batted in to lead the Red Sox to the pennant. He then batted .300 and scored four runs in a World Series victory over the New York Giants. After he

hit .363 in 1913, .338 in 1914, and .322 in in 1915, another World Series championship year for Boston, the team wanted to cut his salary from $18,000 to $9,000. Speaker held out most of the spring, then was sent to the Cleveland Indians for $50,000 and two players. He continued to hold out, demanding $10,000 of the sales price, and he finally got it.

He won his only batting championship in his first year with Cleveland, hitting .388, and he also led the league with 211 hits and 41 doubles. He hit .352 in 1917 and .318 in 1918, then was named the Indians' playing manager during the 1919 season. He slumped to .296 in the dual role, but bounced back with a .386 average in 1920, when the Indians won the pennant. Speaker scored the only run in a 1–0 victory over Brooklyn in the sixth game of the World Series, which the Indians won in seven games.

Speaker continued as player-manager for six more seasons, hitting over .300 each time. But he suddenly resigned in December of 1926, about a month after the Detroit Tigers had released their player-manager, Ty Cobb. It transpired that a retired pitcher had accused the two of fixing a game between their teams in 1919. Baseball Commissioner Kenesaw Mountain Landis cleared them of the charge after an investigation, and Speaker played for the Washington Senators in 1927. He retired after playing one more season, with the Philadelphia Athletics. Speaker was among the second group of players elected to the Baseball Hall of Fame in 1937.

Speaker holds the major league record for career doubles, 793, and his lifetime average of .344 is the sixth best in history. He had 3,514 hits, scored 1,881 runs, drove in 1,528 runs, and stole 433 bases.

Special Olympics

Frank Hayden, a professor at McMaster University in Canada, proposed conducting organized sports and recreation programs for the mentally handicapped and the Joseph P. Kennedy Foundation adopted the idea in 1968. About 1,000 athletes took part in the first Special Olympics, held in Chicago in 1968 and Canada held its first national competition the following year. While track and field is the most publicized event, the Special Olympics includes many other sports, among them bowling, figure and speed skating, gymnastics, skiing, softball, swimming, and weight lifting. The Special Olympics oath is "Let me win, but if I cannot win, let me be brave in the attempt," and every competitor is awarded a medal or a ribbon. Competition begins on the local level, with state and regional championships leading to national Summer and Winter Games. More than 1.5 million athletes in more than 70 countries now take part.

Address: Special Olympics International, 1350 New York Avenue, NW, Suite 500, Washington, DC 20005 (202) 628–3630

Spectrum, The
Philadelphia, PA

The Spectrum opened in the fall of 1967 as the home of the National Basketball Association's Philadelphia 76ers and the National Hockey League's Philadelphia Flyers. Part of the roof blew off in March of 1968 and the Flyers had to play their last seven regular-season home games elsewhere; the 76ers weren't affected, because they were scheduled to be on the road during that period. The roof was fixed by the beginning of the NHL playoffs. The Spectrum seats 17,425 for hockey, 18,168 for basketball.

Speedball

Elmer Mitchell of the University of Michigan invented speedball, a kind of mixture of football and soccer, in 1921. The game is played with a soccer ball on a football field. If the ball is on the ground, it has to be kicked, but if a player catches it on the fly, it can be thrown, punted, or dropkicked. It had a brief flurry of popularity in the Upper Midwest shortly after it was introduced, but never really caught on and is now virtually unknown.

Speed Skating

Speed skating was popular in Holland as early as the 16th century, and it spread to England and Scotland during the early 18th century. The first true speed skate was developed about 1850 by two Norwegian skaters, who made a blade of a hollow metal tube and attached it to a boot. Although there was some informal competition on the Hudson River during the late 1830s, and three British officers had a highly publicized race from Montreal to Quebec City in 1854, skating didn't really become popular in North America until the 1860s, primarily as a recreational sport. Many of the skating clubs formed during the period did hold occasional races, though.

After the Civil War and into the 1870s, skaters often competed for cash prizes or side bets and promoters organized sweepstakes races, in which competitors put up entry fees that became part of the purse. The American Skating Congress, organized in 1868, tried to enforce amateurism and standardize rules, but was not generally successful. The U.S. Skating Association replaced the ASC in 1886, but didn't hold its first national championships until 1891. In Canada, on the other hand, a national championship event was held in 1883 at the Victoria Rink in New Brunswick, although the Amateur Skating

Association of Canada wasn't founded until November 30, 1878. The associations governed both figure skating and speed skating.

Because of wide variations in rules, clubs from Canada and the United States met on February 3, 1907, to organize the International Skating Union of America, which served as the governing body in both countries until 1926, when the Amateur Skating Association of Canada withdrew. The Amateur Skating Union of the U.S. was then organized to oversee both forms of the sport in this country. Canada decided in 1960 to have separate governing bodies, and the Canadian Amateur Speed Skating Association was established. The United States followed suit after the 1964 Winter Olympics by organizing the U.S. International Speed Skating Association. Speed skating has been on the Winter Olympic program since the first Games in 1924; events for women were added in 1960.

Although the pack start, with all skaters racing against one another, is used in a unique American event called short-track racing, most competition is against the clock. Competitors skate in pairs, and after each skater has competed the one with the best time for the distance wins. Short-track racing was a demonstration sport at the 1988 Winter Olympics.

Addresses: Canadian Amateur Speed Skating Association, 333 River Road, Vanier, Ontario, Canada K1L 8H9 (613) 748–5669; U.S. International Speed Skating Association, 2005 North 84th Street, Wauwatosa, WI 53226 1–800–872–1423

See also AMATEUR SKATING UNION OF THE U.S.; CANADIAN AMATEUR SPEED SKATING ASSOCIATION; ICE SKATING; WINTER OLYMPICS.

Spirit of the Times

William T. Porter and printer James Howe published the first issue of Spirit of the Times and Life in New York on December 10, 1831. A weekly, it was the first newspaper devoted primarily to sports, with a heavy emphasis on harness and Thoroughbred racing. Spirit of the Times, as it is more commonly known, was patterned after Bell's Life in London, and it reprinted many articles about English sports from that paper. The four-page weekly had a subscription price of $3 a year. It wasn't successful at first, and in November of 1832 it was bought by the owners of the New York Traveller, who merged it with their newspaper and hired Porter as sporting editor.

On January 3, 1835, Porter bought the rights to Spirit of the Times and began publishing the paper again, numbering it as though publication had never ceased. As a result, for many years it was believed that more than three years' worth of issues had mysteriously vanished. *Spirit* was a success on this second try. It soon became accepted as the authority on sports, and many of its articles were reprinted by newspapers across the country. By 1840, it carried 8 or 12 pages per issue, cost $10 a year, and had a circulation of more than 40,000. Its readership was much larger than that, since barbershops, taverns, and other male gathering places had copies available for customers to read. In addition to coverage of sports events, *Spirit* carried many accounts of sportsmen's travels and experiences, along with backwoods humor and tall tales.

The paper's office became a gathering place for sportsmen, who often negotiated and settled bets there. In addition to printing racing summaries from many tracks, *Spirit* published pedigrees of horses, a valuable service in the days before the *American Stud Book* was established. Porter sold the paper to printer John Richards in 1842, but continued as editor until September of 1856, shortly after it was purchased by George Wilkes, who renamed it *Wilkes' Spirit of the Times*. The pre-Wilkes version is sometimes retroactively called *Porter's Spirit of the Times*, although that wasn't its real name.

Further Reading: Yates, Norris. *William T. Porter and the Spirit of the Times: A Study of the Big Bear School of Humor*. Baton Rouge: Louisiana State University Press, 1957.

Spitz, Mark (1950–)
Swimming
Born February 10, 1950, Modesto, CA; International Swimming Hall of Fame

Spitz won seven Gold Medals in the 1972 Olympics, breaking the record of five that had been set by Italian fencer Nedo Nadi in 1920. His individual medals came in the 100- and 200-meter freestyle swimming and the 100- and 200-meter butterfly. He was also a member of the winning 400-meter freestyle, 800-meter freestyle, and 400-meter medley relay teams. Representing the University of Indiana, Spitz was the NCAA champion in the 200- and 500-yard freestyle in 1969, the 100-yard butterfly in 1969, 1970, 1971, and 1972, and the 200-yard butterfly in 1971 and 1972. He won AAU long-course championships in the 100-meter freestyle in 1968 and 1971, the 200-meter freestyle in 1968, 1970, and 1971, the 100-meter butterfly in 1966, 1967, 1968, 1970, and 1971, and the 200-meter butterfly in 1967 and 1971.

In 1991, Spitz began swimming competitively again, after nearly 20 years of retirement, in hopes of making the 1992 Olympic team.

Sport Parachuting

Leonardo da Vinci designed a parachute in the late 15th century, but the first practical one was made in 1783 by the Montgolfier brothers, inventors of the hot-air balloon, who tested it on a sheep. The first emergency jump was made in 1808 by Jodaki Kuparento, who bailed out of a burning balloon in Warsaw.

Sport parachuting originated during the early part of the 20th century, when touring parachutists, like balloonists and stunt fliers, began performing at fairs and carnivals. One of the pioneers was Georgia "Tiny" Thompson, who made her first jump in 1908, at the age of 15, from a balloon over Raleigh, NC. She also made the first free-fall in 1914, while demonstrating the use of the parachute to U.S. government officials. Until then, a static line attached to the aircraft opened the chute. After her static line got tangled up in the plane's tail section, she made her next jump without it and pulled the ripcord manually while in free-fall.

The first sport parachuting competition was held in 1930 as part of a Russian sports festival, and two years later 40 parachutists took part in a competition at the National Air Races. Target jumping was the only form of the sport at that time, but after World War II French parachutists developed methods of body control in free-fall, and two other types of competition evolved: style and relative jumping. Style involves aerobatic maneuvers by a single parachutist. In relative jumping, groups of jumpers work together to display formations during free-fall.

The National Parachute Jumpers Association, founded in 1946, became the National Parachute Jumpers and Riggers, Inc., in 1957 and the U.S. Parachute Association in 1967. The USPA is the governing body for competitive jumping in the United States. It is affiliated with the Federation Aeronautique Internationale, which has governed international sport parachuting since 1952. Five European nations competed in the first world championships in France in 1951. Under FAI auspices, world championships have been held every two years since 1954. Another major international meet, the Adriatic Cup, is held in even-numbered years at Portoroz, Yugoslavia.

Addresses: Canadian Sport Parachuting Association, 333 River Road, Vanier, Ontario, Canada K1L 8H9 (613) 748–5650; U.S. Parachute Association, 1440 Duke Street, Alexandria, VA 22314 (703) 836–3495

Sporting Goods

Sports equipment was originally either handmade for the moment or brought to North America from

The winner of a record seven Gold Medals at the 1972 Olympics, Mark Spitz is shown here with his Indiana University coach, James Counsilman. The swimmer standing in the water is teammate Gary Hall. Courtesy of the International Swimming Hall of Fame

England. An advertisement in the *Pennsylvania Gazette* during the 1830s reported that hooks and other fishing tackle were imported from England, and in 1866 James Rivington advertised imported battledores, shuttlecocks, cricket balls, tennis and fives racquets, and backgammon tables. Hunting and fishing equipment were the first kinds of sporting goods actually manufactured in North America. Early in the 19th century, gunsmiths were making a variety of hunting rifles. The famed Kentucky rifle, based on a German weapon, was used primarily for hunting. George Snyder of Kentucky was manufacturing fishing reels early in the century, and in 1848 Samuel Philippe of Easton, PA began making multisection bamboo rods.

About 1850, J. W. Brunswick and Brothers of Cincinnati began making billiards tables, and shortly afterward Michael Phelan and Hugh Collender formed a partnership to manufacture tables, balls, and cues. They were probably the first sporting goods manufacturers to promote competition in order to help sales. By 1858, there were four billiards manufacturers in New York alone, and in 1872 one source said that billiards had spawned "a manufacturing and commercial enterprise hardly second to that which the *piano-forte* creates."

The tremendous growth of sports after the Civil War naturally spurred a boom in sporting goods. Baseball "emporiums" that sold equipment for the sport sprang up in major cities. Several former players got into the manufacturing end, among them Albert J. Reach, who had played in the first professional league, the National Association; George Wright, organizer and manager of the first professional team and a parter in Wright and Ditson; and Albert G. Spalding, who retired from baseball in 1876 to devote his time to a Chicago sporting goods store that he and his brother owned.

Spalding at first specialized in baseball uniforms and equipment, Wright and Ditson in tennis and croquet, Reach in manufacturing baseballs. Reach's partner, Ben Shibe, who was also a co-owner of the Philadelphia Athletics with Connie Mack, invented machines to wind yarn around the core of the ball and to punch holes in the covers so they could be stitched on. The J. F. Hillerich Company (now Hillerich and Bradsby) turned baseball bats on lathes in its Kentucky factory.

The A. G. Spalding Company was reorganized in 1892, taking Reach and Wright & Ditson under its corporate umbrella. Those companies kept concentrating on their specialties, however. Spalding also began importing golf clubs from England in 1892, and in 1894 the company imported craftsmen from Scotland to make clubs. Four years later, Spalding became the first North American company to manufacture the new gutta-percha ball, the "Vardon Flyer," named for and endorsed by the great English golfer, Harry Vardon.

Technology has helped improve performance in many sports, and the sporting goods industry furnishes the technology. One reason for the live ball that helped transform baseball from a game of singles and stolen bases into a game of home runs was a machine that could wind the yarn more tightly. A similar machine, invented in 1898, also produced the first modern rubber golf balls, which replaced the short-lived gutta-percha balls early in this century. Spalding improved the rubber ball by developing the hard balata cover in 1903, and in 1905 the company produced the first genuinely white golf balls.

The U.S. Business Census of 1880 showed 86 sporting goods manufacturers producing $1,556,358 worth of goods. (The figure doesn't include recreational products such as bicycles, boats, firearms and ammunition, and playground equipment.) By 1890, the numbers had increased to 136 companies and $2,709,449 in goods, and the value of goods produced reached $11,052,000 in 1909. There was a tremendous boom during the sports-happy 1920s. From 1919 to 1929, the value of sporting goods produced increased by about 250 percent, from $22,890,000 to $58,289,000. The rate of growth naturally slowed during the Great Depression, but there was another boom immediately after World War II. In 1947, the value of goods reached $163,039,000.

Spalding had set out to create a monopoly in the market, but many more companies entered the sporting goods field after the war. The Pennsylvania Rubber Company and the Dunlop Tire Company both began manufacturing tennis balls, for example. Other companies expanded into new kinds of equipment: Hillerich and Bradsby began producing golf clubs as well as baseball bats; the Shakespeare Company, long a manufacturer of fishing equipment, adapted the technology it had developed for making fiberglass fishing rods to produce the first fiberglass golf clubs in the early 1950s; and Le Fiell Products introduced the aluminum-shafted club in 1965.

The major trend during the 1970s and 1980s was toward prestigious brand names and designer names in sports apparel. Keds and Converse, previously the biggest names in athletic shoes, were challenged by Adidas, New Balance, Nike, Puma, Reebok, and other newcomers. "Nike made high tech fashionable," according to Tom Doyle of the National Sporting Goods Association. "It made wearing technologically advanced shoes fashionable and it made it fashionable for other sporting goods companies to use technology as a selling point." The new emphasis on health and fitness in fitness during the 1980s led to increased sales of running shoes, sweatsuits (now often called "workout suits"), weights, and specialized exercise equipment. In 1988, sporting goods sales reached an all-time high of $19,012,800,000, up 21.1 percent over 1987. Clothing represented nearly a quarter of the total, at $4.8 billion, and footwear was nearly 20 percent, at just under $3.8 billion.

Sports Antitrust Broadcast Act

When the National Football League signed a contract granting CBS exclusive coverage of all NFL games in 1961, federal district court Judge Alan K. Grim ruled that it was an undue restraint of trade. NFL Commissioner Pete Rozelle then successfully lobbied for the Sports Antitrust Broadcast Act, which was passed by Congress on September 30, 1961. The act specifically granted professional sports leagues an exemption from antitrust laws, allowing them to pool television rights for package sales.

Sports Car Racing

Although not nearly as popular as Indy car and NASCAR racing in North America, sports car racing is big in terms of the number of participants, most of them amateurs. It includes a wide variety of races for more than 20 classes of cars, usually rated either on engine displacement or on lap-speed potential. The cars range from converted pre-1969 Volkswagens to the high-powered two-seaters that race for the Canadian-American Challenge Cup.

The Sports Car Club of America, organized in 1944, sanctions local and regional competition in gymkhanas and rallies as well as racing. (In gymkhana, also known as autocross or slalom, cars are maneuvered through a serpentine course marked by traffic control pylons. In a rally, a driver and navigator attempt to negotiate a course marked on a road map at a given average rate of speed.) The highest level of SCCA racing is in "Trans-American" cars, small sporty sedans divided into two classes based on engine displacement.

The SCCA, which has about 50,000 members, sanctions an estimated 300 racing weekends annually. Because of the many classes involved, a weekend can include more than 20 races. Thousands of gymkhanas and rallies are conducted by local and regional affiliates.

Address: Sports Car Club of America, 9033 East Easter Place, Englewood, CO 80112 (303) 694-7222

Sports Law
See LAW, SPORTS.

Sportsman's Park
Cicero, IL

Opened in 1930, Sportsman's Park is operated by the National Jockey Club. The ⅝-mile oval track has a total capacity of about 40,000. Its most important race is the $500,000 Illinois Derby, the only Grade II race run at a track of less than 1 mile.

Address: 3301 Laramie Avenue, Cicero, IL 60650 (312) 652-4709

Sportsman's Park
St. Louis, MO

The Sportsman's Park and Club Association was formed in 1880 by Alfred H. Spink (later the founder of The Sporting News) to improve the Grand Avenue Grounds in St. Louis, renamed Sportsman's Park. Brewer Chris Von der Ahe, the association's major financial backer, in 1882 became the owner of the St. Louis Browns in the newly formed American Association, and the Browns played in the renovated park. The association folded after the 1891 season, and von der Ahe's team moved into the National League. They also moved to a different park, formerly the home of a Union Association team.

In 1902, Sportsman's Park was hastily renovated to become the home of a new American League club,

also called the Browns, and it was completely rebuilt after the 1908 season. The single-decked wooden grandstand from first base to third was replaced by a double-decked concrete and steel stand, only the second of its kind in the major leagues, with adjoining pavilions and outfield bleachers, bringing capacity to about 18,500.

The St. Louis National League team, now called the Cardinals, began playing in Sportsman's Park in 1920, and the additional income allowed the Browns to extend the grandstand into the outfield corners, adding nearly 12,000 seats, in 1925. After World War II, the team was in desperate financial trouble, and the park was sold in 1953 to Augustus Busch, owner of the Cardinals. He promptly renamed it Busch Stadium, but St. Louis fans continued to use the old name for years. Busch spent $1.5 million on rehabilitation during 1953 and 1954, adding box seats and improving the dugouts and clubhouses. Home run distances were reduced somewhat, to 351 feet in left field, 422 in center, and 310 in right. The park was abandoned early in 1966, when the new Busch Memorial Stadium opened, and it was later torn down.

Sportsman's Park was also the home field of the National Football League's St. Louis Cardinals from 1960 through 1965.

Sports Medicine
See MEDICINE, SPORTS.

Sports Psychology
See PSYCHOLOGY, SPORTS.

Squash Racquets

Students at the Harrow School in England created squash racquets as an alternative to racquets about 1850. They began by playing racquets on a smaller court, usually used for fives, a type of handball. But the ball was too lively, so they substituted a softer ball of India rubber. The name of the sport probably came from the sound of the softer ball hitting the wall, a contrast to the louder, riflelike crack of the racquets ball.

The sport quickly spread to other schools, and in 1882 it arrived at St. Paul's School in Concord, NH. The first genuine court was built in 1893 at the Racquet Club in Philadelphia; for reasons unknown, it was 2½ feet narrower than the standard English court, but that became the standard North American size, which still causes some international disputes. Because of the size difference, Canada and the United States were banned from membership in the International Squash Racquets Federation when it was organized in January of 1967, but later that year the ISRF reversed its stand and allowed both countries to join.

For years, squash tennis was the preferred sport in the United States, but Canadians evidently preferred squash racquets. The Hamilton, Montreal, and Toronto clubs formed the Canadian Squash Racquets Association in 1913 to standardize rules and conduct a national championship. The sport began to achieve some popularity in New York City in 1915 when the Racquet and Tennis Club added a court. The U.S. Squash Racquets Association was founded in 1930, and it took over supervision of the national championship tournament, which had begun in Philadelphia in 1907; the women's championship began in 1928.

Doubles competition is unique to North America. The Philadelphia Racquets Club built the first doubles court in 1907; others were built by the Germantown Cricket Club in 1923 and the Merion Cricket Club in 1925. The first national doubles championship was held in 1933.

The number of players in Canada more than quadrupled during the 1970s; more than 40 courts were built just in Toronto, where the number of participants increased from about 3,000 to nearly 50,000 during the decade. Growth was not quite so dramatic in the United States, but participation did increase by about 20 percent a year, and in 1980 there were about 5,000 courts and an estimated 1 million players in the country. However, growth slowed almost to a halt during the 1980s because of the advent of racquetball. The USSRA now has a membership of about 10,000. The World Professional Squash Association conducts a tour of more than 40 tournaments for its 300 members, and the National Intercollegiate Squash Association oversees a national collegiate tournament.

Addresses: Canadian Squash Racquets Association, 333 River Road, Vanier, Ontario, Canada K1L 8H9 (613) 748–5672; National Intercollegiate Squash Racquets Association, Athletic Department, P.O. Box 402, Vassar College, Poughkeepsie, NY 12601 (914) 437–7467; U.S. Squash Racquets Association, P.O. box 216, 23 Cynwyd Road, Bala-Cynwyd, PA 19004 (215) 667–4006; World Professional Squash Association, 12 Sheppard Street, Suite 401, Toronto, Ontario, Canada M5H 3A1 (416) 869–3499

See also RACQUETS; SQUASH TENNIS.

Squash Tennis

The first squash racquets courts in North America were unheated, and the ball wasn't as lively in the cold as it should have been. Students at St. Paul's School, where the sport had been introduced, soon began playing a faster version by using tennis rackets and balls. Stephen J. Feron, a New York professional, created the modern version of squash tennis in the early 1890s by simply wrapping some webbing around a tennis ball so that more spin could be put on it. The new sport was taken up by a number of wealthy New Yorkers who could afford to build courts, among them August Belmont, Herbert Harriman, J. P. Morgan, and William C. Whitney, who had two courts in his home.

The prestigious Tuxedo Club installed courts in 1898, and shortly afterward the Racquet and Tennis Club, the Columbia, Harvard, and Princeton Clubs in New York City, and the Heights Casino and Crescent Athletic Clubs in Brooklyn followed suit. The Metropolitan Squash Tennis League was founded in 1908 to conduct interclub competition, and two years later the National Squash Tennis Association was organized. The first national tournament was held in April of 1911. The sport was largely confined to New York, Boston, and Philadelphia, although there were a few other courts in large cities such as Chicago, Cincinnati, and St. Louis. The NSTA in 1918 adopted an even livelier ball, making squash tennis so fast and so strenuous that recreational play was discouraged, and the racquets version of the sport began to gain popularity at the expense of the tennis version. There was a brief revival of squash tennis in New York City in 1965, when the NSTA held a series of demonstrations to attract new players. The association now has just over 100 members.

Address: National Squash Tennis Association, c/o Gary Squires, Greenwich Country Club, Doubling Road, Greenwich, CT 06830 (203) 869–1000

See also RACQUETS; SQUASH RACQUETS.

Stadiums

The popularity of college football, along with the advent of steel-and-concrete construction, led to the building of huge stadiums during the 1920s, although Harvard led the way in 1903 with its 38,000-seat Roman style stadium; the 67,000-seat Yale Bowl, built at a cost of nearly $1 million, opened ten years later; and Georgia Tech's 46,000-seat stadium opened in 1914. More than 20 major football colleges built stadiums seating 40,000 or more during the 1920s, among them the University of Washington (1920, 46,000), Stanford (1921, 86,011), Tennessee (1921, 91,429), Ohio State (1922, 85,339), Nebraska (1923, 73,650), Oklahoma (1923, 75,004), Illinois (1923, 70,538), California (1923, 75,630), Purdue (1924, 67,861), Louisiana State (1924, 80,140), Texas (1924, 80,000), Texas A & M (1925, 72,387), Missouri (1926,

62,000), Michigan (1927, 101,701), and Alabama (1929, 70,123). Two other stadiums seating more than 100,000 fans and used by college football teams were built by cities—the Rose Bowl in Pasadena, used by UCLA, and the Los Angeles Coliseum, used by Southern California.

New college stadiums continued to rise during the 1930s, though at a slower pace because of the Great Depression. Construction stopped during World War II, but it resumed immediately after the war. In 1924, there were only about 20 stadiums seating more than 20,000; that number had reached more than 130 by 1952. The growth of professional football helped fuel stadium construction beginning in the late 1950s, as many cities built stadiums either to attract new teams or to keep existing teams. Of the 28 stadiums used by National Football League teams, only 4 predate 1957, when the city of Green Bay built Lambeau Field for the Packers. Seven of the stadiums were built during the 1960s, 12 during the 1970s, and 3 during the 1980s.

The Houston Astrodome, opened in 1965, ushered in the era of the domed stadium, although it was the only one of its kind for ten years. The Superdome in New Orleans and the Silverdome in Pontiac, MI both opened in 1975, followed by Seattle's Kingdome and Montreal's Olympic Stadium in 1976, the Carrier Dome at Syracuse University in 1980, the Metrodome in Minneapolis in 1982, the Hoosier Dome in Indianapolis in 1984, Toronto's Skydome in 1989, and St. Petersburg's Suncoast Dome in 1990. Two others, the Georgia Dome in Atlanta and the Alamodome in San Antonio, are scheduled to open during the early 1990s.

Both domes in Canada, Olympic Stadium and the Skydome, have retractable roofs. The Hoosier Dome, Metrodome, and Silverdome all have inflatable roofs made of Teflon-coated fiberglass. Two of them have had problems. The Silverdome was extensively damaged by a snowstorm on March 4, 1985, and the Hoosier Dome's roof collapsed completely on February 2, 1988, when heavy rain caused a 40-foot rip in the fabric. Fortunately, both stadiums were empty, and there were no injuries.

Public funding of stadiums has had its critics. Charles Maher wrote in the *New York Times* of November 14, 1971, "If you are going to build a major sports stadium today, you start out by digging a hole. That is where you are going to put the stadium. And that is probably where the stadium is going to put you." And Robert C. Byrd of Virginia complained in a speech to the Senate, "In many cities across this nation, citizens are placing their lives, their children's lives, and even their grand-children's lives in hock so that they can sit on cushioned seats watching professional athletes who dress in carpeted rooms."

There has been a certain trend back toward private funding and construction. The Boston Patriots, unable to get a new stadium in Boston, built their own in nearby Foxboro in 1971, and the Miami Dolphins, dissatisfied with the city of Miami's Orange Bowl, financed Joe Robbie Stadium, which opened in 1987. But the Suncoast Dome was built by the city of St. Petersburg on speculation; it still has no professional tenant. And the Alamodome is also being built as a means of attracting a franchise, without a prior commitment from any team.

The "superstadiums" are multipurpose facilities, but they're much better suited to baseball and football than to basketball and hockey. The New Orleans Jazz of the National Basketball Association did play in the Superdome until moving to Utah in 1979. The Detroit Pistons spent ten seasons in the Silverdome, but moved to a new arena, the Palace in Auburn Hills, in 1988. The Seattle Supersonics played in the Kingdome from 1978 until 1985, when they went to the Seattle Center Coliseum. And the expansion Minnesota Timberwolves made the Metrodome their home for just one season, while awaiting completion of a new arena in Minneapolis.

See also ARENAS; BASEBALL PARKS.

Stagg, Amos Alonzo (1862–1965)
Basketball, Football
Born August 16, 1862, West Orange, NJ; died March 17, 1965; Basketball and National Football Foundation Hall of Fame

"The Grand Old Man of Football" was also a major figure in the early history of basketball. An end at Yale, he was named to the first All-American team in 1889, and the following year he enrolled at the YMCA's Training School (now Springfield College) in Springfield, MA. He organized and coached a football team of students and faculty members, most of whom had never played the sport before. "Stagg's Stubby Christians," as they were called, lost 16–10 to Yale at Madison Square Garden in the first indoor football game ever played. One of the players was James Naismith, who invented basketball in 1891, and Stagg scored the only basket in the first public basketball game on March 11, 1892.

When the University of Chicago was endowed by John D. Rockefeller in 1892, Stagg was hired as football coach, the first in the country to have faculty status. He introduced and coached basketball at the school, and at one time or another he also coached baseball and track. In 41 seasons at Chicago, he coached four undefeated football teams and had a record of 244 wins, 113 losses, and 27 ties. Forced to retire at the age of 70, he became head coach at the College of the Pacific in 1933; he was named Coach of the Year in 1943, when his team won seven of nine games, including victories over UCLA and the University of California. He retired after the 1946 season with an overall record of 314–199–35.

In 1917, Stagg organized the National Interscholastic Basketball Tournament in Chicago, an annual event until 1931. By bringing together high school players and coaches from throughout the country, the tournament was instrumental in standardizing rules. Stagg and Henry L. Williams wrote the first technical book on football, *A Scientific and Practical Treatise on American Football for Schools and Colleges,* in 1893.

Stanley Cup
Hockey

The sixth governor of Canada, Lord Stanley of Preston, bought this trophy for 10 pounds (about 50 Canadian dollars at the time) in 1893, and offered it for the hockey championship of Canada. He selected the Montreal Amateur Athletic Association as the first champion. Stanley returned to England that year and from 1894 through 1909 two trustees were in charge of the trophy. Theoretically, any team could challenge the cup holder any time during the hockey season, but in practice the trustees sorted out the challenges to pick a qualified team. A single championship game was played until 1901, when the best-of-three format was adopted.

From 1903 through 1909, a two-game series was played, with the cup going to the team that scored the most total goals. A single championship game was played in 1910 and 1911, and the best-of-three format was used once again in 1912 and 1913. From 1914 through 1917, the championship was decided by a best-of-five series between eastern and western champions. The two regions used different rules, so the series used the eastern rules in odd-numbered games and western rules in even-numbered games.

The National Hockey League began play in the 1917–18 season and from then through 1926 the NHL champion played a challenger from the Pacific Coast Hockey Association, the Western Canada Hockey League, or the Western Hockey League. After the Western Canada Hockey League folded in 1926, the Stanley Cup became the NHL's championship trophy.

Stanley Cup Champions

1893	Montreal Amateur Athletic Association
1894	Montreal Amateur Athletic Association
1895	Montreal Victorias
1896	(Feb.) Winnipeg Victorias
1896	(Dec.) Montreal Victorias
1897	Montreal Victorias
1898	Montreal Victorias
1899	Montreal Shamrocks
1900	Montreal Shamrocks
1901	Winnipeg Victorias
1902	Montreal Amateur Athletic Association
1903	Ottawa Silver Seven
1904	Ottawa Silver Seven
1905	Ottawa Silver Seven
1906	Montreal Wanderers
1907	(Jan.) Kenora Thistles
1907	(Mar.) Montreal Wanderers
1908	Montreal Wanderers
1909	Ottawa Senators
1910	Montreal Wanderers
1911	Ottawa Senators
1912	Quebec Bulldogs
1913	Quebec Bulldogs
1914	Toronto Blueshirts
1915	Vancouver Millionaires
1916	Montreal Canadiens
1917	Seattle Metropolitas
1918	Toronto Arenas
1919	(No Decision)
1920	Ottawa Senators
1921	Ottawa Senators
1922	Toronto St. Pats
1923	Ottawa Senators
1924	Montreal Canadiens
1925	Victoria Cougars
1926	Montreal Maroons
1927	Ottawa Senators
1928	New York Rangers
1929	Boston Bruins
1930	Montreal Canadiens
1931	Montreal Canadies
1932	Toronto Maple Leafs
1933	New York Rangers
1934	Chicago Black Hawks
1935	Montreal Maroons
1936	Detroit Red Wings
1937	Detroit Red Wings
1938	Chicago Black Hawks
1939	Boston Bruins
1940	New York Rangers
1941	Boston Bruins
1942	Toronto Maple Leafs
1943	Detroit Red Wings
1944	Montreal Canadiens
1945	Toronto Maple Leafs
1946	Montreal Canadiens
1947	Toronto Maple Leafs
1948	Toronto Maple Leafs

1949	Toronto Maple Leafs
1950	Detroit Red Wings
1951	Toronto Maple Leafs
1952	Detroit Red Wings
1953	Montreal Canadiens
1954	Detroit Red Wings
1955	Detroit Red Wings
1956	Montreal Canadiens
1957	Montreal Canadiens
1958	Montreal Canadiens
1959	Montreal Canadiens
1960	Montreal Canadiens
1961	Chicago Black Hawks
1962	Toronto Maple Leafs
1963	Toronto Maple Leafs
1964	Toronto Maple Leafs
1965	Montreal Canadiens
1966	Montreal Canadiens
1967	Toronto Maple Leafs
1968	Montreal Canadiens
1969	Montreal Canadiens
1970	Boston Bruins
1971	Montreal Canadiens
1972	Boston Bruins
1973	Montreal Canadiens
1974	Philadelphia Flyers
1975	Philadelphia Flyers
1976	Montreal Canadiens
1977	Montreal Canadiens
1978	Montreal Canadiens
1979	Montreal Canadiens
1980	New York Islanders
1981	New York Islanders
1982	New York Islanders
1983	New York Islanders
1984	Edmonton Oilers
1985	Edmonton Oilers
1986	Montreal Canadiens
1987	Edmonton Oilers
1988	Edmonton Oilers
1989	Calgary Flames
1990	Edmonton Oilers
1991	Pittsburgh Penguins

See also HOCKEY; NATIONAL HOCKEY LEAGUE.

Staten Island, NY

The Staten Island Stapletons played in the National Football League from 1929 through 1932.

Steamboat Racing

Mark Twain wrote, in *Life on the Mississippi*, "In the 'flush' times of steamboating, a race between two notoriously fleet steamers was an event of vast im-portance. The date was set for it several weeks in advance, and from that time forward, the whole Mississippi Valley was in a state of consuming excitement." Steamboats and steamboat racing flourished especially on the Mississippi from about 1830 to 1860. A single boat often set out to break a point-to-point record as a kind of advertising, since there was a great deal of competition for business. In 1836 and 1837, several boats exploded or were set afire by overheated boilers during races, calling for demands that racing be prohibited, but the practice went on. Promoters brought steamboat racing to California, the Great Lakes, and the Hudson River during the 1850s. The last great race, between *Robert E. Lee* and *Natchez* from New Orleans to St. Louis in 1870, received extensive newspaper coverage. *Robert E. Lee* won in 3 days, 18 hours, and 14 minutes.

Steeplechase

Steeplechasing was originally cross-country racing on horseback over the same kind of terrain where foxes are hunted. It originated in Ireland during the 18th century; the goal was often a church steeple that could be seen by riders throughout the race, hence the name. There are now two types of steeplechases: point-to-point races run over natural terrain and natural obstacles, and closed-circuit races on tracks with artificial fences, hurdles, and water jumps.

Steeplechasing became relatively popular in Canada beginning in 1838, and some races were run at New York's Beacon Race Course in the early 1840s, but that ended after Cyril Browning, the owner of the course, was killed in a fall. The American Jockey Club revived the sport at Jerome Park in 1865. New York newspapers spoke out against steeplechasing after another death in 1867, the *Times* calling it "at best a dangerous sport," but it continued, though it never became very popular.

Point-to-point races were often held in association with fox hunting, during hunt meets in Maryland, Virginia, and other Middle Atlantic states during the early part of the century. But the sport in general languished until the 1970s. The Colonial Cup was established as the first $100,000 race in 1972. The Colonial is run at Camden, SC over a 17–obstacle course that's 2 miles 6½ furlongs in length. A few northern tracks gradually added a steeplechase or two to their programs.

Sponsorship by companies looking for an upscale audience gave steeplechasing a tremendous boost in the late 1980s. Purses climbed over $1 million for the first time in 1984, went over $2 million in 1986, and increased to more than $5 million in 1989. The

Steeplechasing was popular in Canada beginning in the late 1830s. This painting shows a race at London, Ontario, on May 9, 1843.

circuit includes both hunt meets and track racing. The spring meet begins in late March with hunt meets in the Carolinas and track racing in the Middle Atlantic States, culminating at Belmont Park in New York with the Temple Gwathney. During the summer, most racing is at eastern tracks, ending at Saratoga with the $100,000 Turf Writers' Handicap. Most autumn racing is again in the Middle Atlantic region. The country's top races conclude the season, the $250,000 Breeders' Cup in early November and the Colonial Cup in early December.

The steeplechase is also a track and field event. Since 1920, when it was added to the Olympic program, the distance has been internationally standardized at 3,000 meters, with 28 hurdles and seven water jumps, although in North America the distance is sometimes 2 miles. The steeplechase has been an event in the U.S. national outdoor track and field championships since 1889.

See also NATIONAL STEEPLECHASE AND HUNT ASSOCIATION.

Steers, George "Pop" (1820–1856)
Rowing, Yachting
Born July 20, 1820, Washington, DC; died September 25, 1856

When he was only 18, Steers designed and built a 30-foot-long, four-oared boat with outriggers that weighed only 40 pounds and drew only 4 inches of water. Known as the "whirlwind," it was the prototype of the modern racing shell. He then developed a reputation for designing fast pilot boats. When a group of New York Yacht Club members headed by John C. Stevens decided to build a racing yacht to take to England, Steers was chosen to design it. The result was *America,* which won the Hundred-Guinea

Cup in an 1851 race around the Isle of Wight. The trophy is now known as the America's Cup. Steers also designed other fast yachts as well as the steamship *Adriatic* and the warship *Niagara,* which helped lay the first trans-Atlantic cable.

Stengel, "Casey" Charles D. (1889–1975)
Baseball
Born July 30, 1889, Kansas City, MO; died September 29, 1975; Baseball Hall of Fame

One of baseball's great managers, the free-spirited Stengel was also one of its great comedians. A left-handed outfielder, Stengel joined the Brooklyn Dodgers late in the 1912 season and became a starter the following year. He had a solid but unspectacular 14-season playing career with the Dodgers, Pittsburgh Pirates, Philadelphia Phillies, Boston Braves, and New York Giants. His career batting average was .284. As a player, he was best known for two disparate exploits. Brooklyn fans booed him in his first game there with the Pirates; the following day, Stengel bowed and tipped his cap to the crowd—and a sparrow flew out. With the Giants in 1923, he hit an inside-the-park home run to beat the Yankees 5–4 in the first game of the World Series, losing a shoe while running the bases to make it even more interesting.

His career as a major-league manager didn't begin auspiciously. The Brooklyn Dodgers hired him in 1934 and fired him after three second-division finishes. With the Boston Braves beginning in 1938, he had six second-division finishes in six years before being fired. But the New York Yankees surprised the baseball world by hiring him in 1949. The team was in a transition period, with a mixture of aging stars and young players, and many sportswriters thought he was just an interim manager. But by shrewdly platooning players and juggling his pitchers, Stengel brought the Yankees home in first place and they beat the Brooklyn Dodgers in a five-game World Series. He was named American League Manager of the Year, an award he also won in 1953 and 1955.

Stengel managed the Yankees for 12 seasons, winning ten pennants and seven World Series. Despite his success as a manager, he was always probably better known for his idiosyncrasies. He had a problem remembering names—even Mickey Mantle, at times, became just "that big blond kid from Oklahoma"—and he often talked in a kind of Joycean stream-of-consciousness. He was once quoted in the *New York Times:* "Mr. Kryhoski played on our ball club part of the year and he lives in New Jersey where a lotta writers and ballplayers live. He once hit 16 home runs in the American League which ain't the American Association but the big leagues although he only hit one homer last year with Baltimore which is a bad ball park."

Fired by the Yankees after a seven-game loss to Pittsburgh in the 1960 World Series, Stengel spent a year out of baseball before returning to New York as manager of the Mets, a National League expansion team. It was basically a public relations move, since fans and sportswriters alike loved Stengel. The team was so bad that fans came out to see what would happen next. "The amazin' Mets," Stengel called them, and the name stuck through several seasons of futility. But the futility began to get to Stengel. "Can't anyone here play this game?" he once asked in exasperation. After three tenth-place finishes, Stengel broke his hip in a fall during the 1965 season and retired. In 25 seasons as a manager, his teams won 1,926 games and lost 1,867. He was 37 and 26 in World Series play.

Further Reading: Creamer, Robert W. *Stengel: His Life and Times.* New York: Simon & Schuster, 1984.

Steroids

See ANABOLIC STEROIDS.

Stevens, John Cox (1785–1857)
Yachting
Born in 1785, Hobokin, NJ, died June 10, 1857

As a promoter and investor, John Cox Stevens was one of the most important men in 19th-Century American sport. Not only did he help bring public attention to a variety of sports, he made them acceptable to the social elite. His father was a wealthy engineer and inventor, and Stevens had the tastes so common in an inheritor of wealth: good food, good wine, and sports. In the biggest horse race of the century—American Eclipse against Sir Henry in 1823—Stevens bet large amounts of money on American Eclipse, and won. He then bought both horses and put them to stud.

In 1831, he opened an amusement park called Elysian Fields on the Hoboken waterfront. It became the site of the first American baseball game, the home of the New York Yacht Club, and the first playing field for the New York Athletic Club.

Footracing, called "pedestrianism" then, was a very popular sport, and Stevens became involved as a promoter. In 1835, he offered a $1,000 prize to any runner who could cover 10 miles in less than an hour, with a $300 bonus if that runner was the only one in the field who did it. About 20,000 spectators paid admission to watch the well-publicized "Great Race" at Union Race Course. There were nine runners, including an Irishmen and a Prussian, in the field. Henry Stannard of Connecticut won the prize and the bonus by running 10 miles in just 12 seconds less than an hour.

On July 30, 1844, nine men met aboard Stevens' yacht, *Gimcrack*, to found the New York Yacht Club. Stevens was elected commodore and oversaw the club's first regatta in the summer of 1845. Shortly afterward, he gave the NYYC a piece of land at Elysian Fields for a clubhouse, which opened the following year. Stevens' most enduring legacy was the America's Cup. He headed the syndicate of NYYC members who commissioned the construction of the yacht *America*, which sailed to England in 1851 to win the Hundred-Guineas Cup, now known as the America's Cup.

See also AMERICAS CUP; ELYSIAN FIELDS; NEW YORK YACHT CLUB.

Stock Car Racing

During Prohibition, illegal moonshine was often carried in "souped-up" cars in the Southeast. Because of the many hills and winding roads in the region, suspensions and shock absorbers had to be carefully adjusted, and preparing a car became something of a craft. Inevitably, informal match races took place, usually with money as well as pride on the line. There was even racing as early as 1936 on a 3.2-mile hard-packed sand course at Daytona Beach, FL. The National Association for Stock Car Racing was founded in 1947 at Daytona Beach to bring order to the sport. Despite the name, modern stock cars are anything but "stock." They're carefully prepared for speed and safety, with special engines that cost $10,000 or more, although amateur racers drive cars that are much more like ordinary street vehicles.

NASCAR launched its first major race series, the Grand National, in 1949. The following year, the Southern 500 was inaugurated at Darlington (SC) Raceway, the first paved stock car speedway. A group of ten California tracks joined NASCAR in 1954 and were given their own circuit, the Grand National West. The Convertible Division was added in 1955, when SAFE, a midwestern stock car racing organization, merged into NASCAR. Beach racing at Daytona continued until 1959, when Daytona International Speedway opened with the Daytona 500, the sport's premier event.

The trend toward long, paved "superspeedways" continued with the addition of Atlanta International Speedway and Charlotte Motor Speedway in 1960, North Carolina Motor Speedway in 1965, Michigan International Speedway in 1968, the 2.66-mile Alabama International Speedway at Talladega and Dover Downs International Speedway in Delaware in 1969.

Richard Petty drives to victory in the 1973 Daytona 500, the premiere event in stock car racing. Courtesy of NASCAR Photo

When R. J. Reynolds Tobacco Company took over sponsorship in 1970, the Grand National series became the Winston Cup series, although the Grand National name was retained for a series of races on shorter tracks. Reynolds and NASCAR also established Winston Cup series for the Grand American and Modified divisions. (Grand American cars are small, sporty sedans, and Modified embraces a wide variety of cars, all at least four years old.)

The Winston Racing Series format became regional in 1982, with short-track championships awarded in each of five geographic regions and a national championship for the top scorer among the regional winners. That expanded to eight regions in 1989.

In addition to Reynolds, many other sponsors have become involved in stock car racing. Posted awards on the Winston Cup schedule alone in 1980 totaled $6.1 million. That reached $12.5 million in 1985 and $16.7 million in 1988. Attendance has also increased steadily. About 10 million spectators attended all NASCAR races in 1983; the total climbed to 15 million in 1986 and to nearly 18 million in 1989.

See also NATIONAL ASSOCIATION FOR STOCK CAR AUTO RACING.

Stoolball

A game played by English milkmaids at least as early as the 14th century—when a clergyman urged banning it, along with many other games, as well as dancing—stoolball was the ancestor of cricket, rounders, and, ultimately, baseball. In stoolball, only two players competed. One of them, the pitcher in modern terms, tried to knock down a milking stool with a round stone or ball while the other protected the stool with her hand. When the pitcher succeeded in knocking the stool down, the two players changed places. The game was later taken up by boys and young men, and a stick or bat was often used. It came to North America very early. On Christmas Day of 1621 Governor William Bradford of Plymouth saw some recent arrivals playing games, including "stoole-ball," and he ordered them to stop because the Pilgrims didn't celebrate Christmas and they should have been working.

See also CRICKET.

Sugar Bowl
Football

Inaugurated in New Orleans in 1935, the Sugar Bowl is one of the four major college football games, along with the Cotton, Orange, and Rose Bowls. It is usually played on New Year's Day. From 1972 through 1975, however, it was played on New Year's Eve, and when New Years Day falls on a Sunday, it is played on January 2. Since 1977, the Southeastern Conference champion has been one of the teams. The Sugar Bowl was played at Tulane Stadium from 1935 through 1974, when it moved to the Louisiana Superdome.

Sugar Bowl Results

1935	Tulane 20, Temple 14
1936	Texas Christian 3, Louisiana State 2
1937	Santa Clara 21, Louisiana State 14
1938	Santa Clara 6, Louisiana State 0
1939	Texas Christian 15, Carnegie Tech 7
1940	Texas A & M 14, Tulane 1
1941	Boston College 19, Tennessee 13
1942	Fordham 2, Missouri 0
1943	Tennessee 14, Tulsa 7
1944	Georgia Tech 20, Tulsa 18
1945	Duke 29, Alabama 26
1946	Oklahoma A & M 33, St. Mary's (CA) 13
1947	Georgia 20, North Carolina 10
1948	Texas 27, Alabama 7
1949	Oklahoma 14, North Carolina 6
1950	Oklahoma 35, Louisiana State 0
1951	Kentucky 13, Oklahoma 7
1952	Maryland 28, Tennessee 13
1953	Georgia Tech 24, Mississippi 7
1954	Georgia Tech 42, West Virginia 19
1955	Navy 21, Mississippi 0
1956	Georgia Tech 7, Pittsburgh 0
1957	Baylor 13, Tennessee 7
1958	Mississippi 39, Texas 7
1959	Lousiana State 7, Clemson 0
1960	Mississippi 21, Louisiana State 0
1961	Mississippi 14, Rice 6

1962	Alabama 10, Arkansas 3
1963	Mississippi 17, Arkansas 13
1964	Alabama 12, Mississippi 7
1965	Lousiana State 13, Syracuse 10
1966	Missouri 20, Florida 18
1967	Alabama 34, Nebraska 7
1968	Lousiana State 20, Wyoming 13
1969	Arkansas 16, Georgia 2
1970	Mississippi 27, Arkansas 22
1971	Tennessee 34, Air Force 13
1972	(Jan.) Oklahoma 40, Auburn 22
1972	(Dec.) Oklahoma 14, Penn State 0
1973	Notre Dame 24, Alabama 23
1974	Nebraska 13, Florida 10
1975	Alabama 13, Penn State 6
1977	Pittsburgh 27, Georgia 3
1978	Alabama 35, Ohio State 6
1979	Alabama 14, Penn State 7
1980	Alabama 24, Arkansas 9
1981	Georgia 17, Notre Dame 10
1982	Pittsburgh 24, Georgia 20
1983	Penn State 27, Georgia 23
1984	Auburn 9, Michigan 7
1985	Nebraska 28, Louisiana State 10
1986	Tennessee 35, Miami (FL) 7
1987	Nebraska 30, Louisiana State 15
1988	Syracuse 16, Auburn 16
1989	Florida State 13, Auburn 7
1990	Miami (FL) 33, Alabama 25
1991	Tennessee 23, Virginia 22

Sullivan Award
Amateur Sports

The Amateur Athletic Union in 1930 established this award in memory of James E. Sullivan (1860–1914). Sullivan was a founder of the AAU in 1888 and served as its secretary (1889–96), president (1906–09), and secretary-treasurer (1909–14). The AAU, which began as a governing body for track and field, gained control of many amateur sports under his leadership. The award is presented to the athlete who "by his or her performance, example and influence as an amateur has done the most during the year to advance the cause of sportsmanship." A person can win the award only once.

Sullivan Award Winners

1930	Bobby Jones, golf
1931	Barney Berlinger, track
1932	Jim Bausch, track
1933	Glenn Cunningham, track
1934	Bill Bonthron, track
1935	Lawson Little, golf
1936	Glenn Morris, track
1937	Don Budge, tennis

Rick Wohlhuter, who won the Sullivan Award in 1974, is shown finishing an easy victory in the 1,500-meter run. Courtesy of W.J. Wallace/Duke University

1938 Don Lash, track
1939 Joe Burk, rowing
1940 Greg Rice, track
1941 Leslie MacMitchell, track
1942 Cornelius Warmerdam, track
1943 Gil Dodds, track
1944 Ann Curtis, swimming
1945 Doc Blanchard, football
1946 Arnold Tucker, football
1947 John B. Kelly Jr., rowing
1948 Bob Mathias, track
1949 Dick Button, figure skating
1950 Fred Wilt, track
1951 Bob Richards, track
1952 Horace Ashenfelter, track
1953 Sammy Lee, diving
1954 Mal Whitfield, track
1955 Harrison Dillard, track
1956 Patricia Keller McCormick, diving
1957 Bobby Morrow, track
1958 Glenn Davis, track
1959 Parry O'Brien, track
1960 Rafer Johnson, track
1961 Wilma Rudolph, track
1962 Jim Beatty, track
1963 John Pennel, track
1964 Don Schollander, swimming
1965 Bill Bradley, basketball
1966 Jim Ryun, track
1967 Randy Matson, track

1968 Debbie Meyer, swimming
1969 Bill Toomey, track
1970 John Kinsella, swimming
1971 Mark Spitz, swimming
1972 Frank Shorter, track
1973 Bill Walton, basketball
1974 Rich Wohlhuter, track
1975 Tim Shaw, swimming
1976 Bruce Jenner, track
1977 John Naber, swimming
1978 Tracy Caulkins, swimming
1979 Kurt Thomas, gymastics
1980 Eric Heiden, speed skating
1981 Carl Lewis, track
1982 Mary Decker, track
1983 Edwin Moses, track
1984 Greg Louganis, diving
1985 Joan Benoit Samuelson, track
1986 Jackie Joyner-Kersee, track
1987 Jim Abbott, baseball
1988 Florence Griffith-Joyner, track
1989 Janet Evans, swimming
1990 John Smith, wrestling

Sullivan, John L. (1858–1918)
Boxing

Born October 15, 1858, Boston, MA; died February 2, 1918; Boxing Hall of Fame

The "Boston Strong Boy," Sullivan was known as a drinker and brawler, but he almost single-handedly dragged American boxing from the bareknuckle era into the Marquis of Queensbury era. Sullivan became famous among fight fans before he was champion. After knocking out Canadian champion Jack Stewart in the second round on January 3, 1881, he fought some exhibitions and then appeared at Harry Hill's Dance Hall and Boxing Emporium in New York City, where he offered to give $50 to anyone who could last four rounds with him. That drew the attention of Richard Kyle Fox, publisher of the *National Police Gazette* and frequent backer of fighters. Sullivan snubbed Fox, creating an enemy who, ironically, did a great deal to publicize his career.

On October 5, Sullivan put up $500 and challenged Paddy Ryan, an Irish native who was considered the American heavyweight champion, for a $2,500 side bet. The fight took place in Mississippi City, MS on February 7, 1882. Sullivan won on a ninth-round knockout. Fox then began using his newspaper to promote various challengers, while Sullivan went on tour to exploit his fame. He didn't have a formal championship fight for more than seven years, but he did beat some of Fox's favorites while traveling around the country. In 1887, Sullivan rejected a challenge to fight Fox's latest challenger, Jake Kilrain. Fox declared that Sullivan had forfeited his title, and he presented Kilrain with a diamond-studded silver belt emblematic of the *National Police Gazette* heavyweight championship. Enraged Boston fans donated money to give Sullivan an even more ornate belt that was presented to the champion at the Boston Theater on August 8, 1887. He delighted 3,500 spectators by declaring, "I wouldn't put Fox's belt around the neck of a goddamn dog!"

Later that year he sailed to England, where he fought exhibitions and sparred with Jack Ashton while the Prince of Wales looked on. After a 39–round draw with English fighter Charlie Mitchell in Chantilly, France, early in 1888, he returned to Boston. On December 7 he agreed to fight Kilrain. Sullivan was badly overweight, and his draw with Mitchell had cast some doubt on his ability. William P. Muldoon, a noted amateur wrestler and professional trainer, was brought in to help whip him into shape for the fight on July 8, 1889, with a $10,000 side bet and the heavyweight championship at stake. Because prizefighting was illegal almost everywhere, the location of the fight was kept secret until July 7, when fans boarded special trains in New Orleans to travel to Richburg, MS.

The fight began at 10:30 the following morning, and for a long time it looked as though the challenger would win. He drew first blood from Sullivan in the seventh round. The champion seemed to be in desperate trouble when he vomited in the 44th round. (According to some accounts, the vomiting was caused by a mixture of whisky and water that Muldoon was administering between rounds.) But that seemed to restore him. He began battering Kilrain so badly that the challenger's manager threw in the sponge after the 75th round. The manager told the press afterward that he "did not wish to be a party to murder."

That was the last important bareknuckle fight. Sullivan had worn gloves and demonstrated the newer Marquis of Queensbury Rules in many of his exhibitions. After spending three years fighting a few more exhibitions and touring in a show, "Honest Hearts and Willing Hands," he agreed to fight James Corbett, but insisted that the Queensbury rules be used. On September 21, 1892, Corbett knocked out Sullivan in the 21st round at the New Orleans Olympic Club. It was the only defeat of his career.

Still popular, Sullivan continued to appear in exhibitions now and then, and from 1893 to 1895 was on theatrical tours. Although he had a reputation as a heavy drinker, he spent his last years giving temperance lectures as part of a vaudeville performance. From 1876 through 1915, Sullivan had earnings of $1,221,470 from his fights, exhibitions, and theatrical appearances. In addition to countless exhibitions, he won 31 fights, 16 by knockout, lost just once, and fought 3 draws and 40 no-decisions.

Further Reading: Isenberg, Michael T. *John L. Sullivan and His America*. Urbana: University of Illinois Press, 1988.

Sullivan Stadium
Foxboro, MA

After 11 years of trying to find a permanent home in Boston, the National Football League's Boston Patriots in 1971 built their own stadium in Foxboro, about 40 miles away, and became known as the New England Patriots. Originally called Schaefer Stadium because the Schaefer Brewing Company underwrote some of the costs, the field in 1982 was renamed after Billy Sullivan, the team's founder and longtime owner.

Summit, The
Houston, TX

The Summit opened as the home of the National Basketball Association's Houston Rockets in 1975. It was also the Houston Aeros' home rink from 1975 until the team folded after the 1977–78 season. The arena seats 16,611 for basketball.

Sun Bowl
See JOHN HANCOCK BOWL.

John L. Sullivan is at the center of this 1883 lithograph by J. G. Hyde showing the top fighters of the day.

Sun Devil Stadium
Tempe, AZ

The home field of the Arizona State University Sun Devils, this stadium opened in 1958. It is now also the home of the National Football League's Phoenix Cardinals, who moved from St. Louis in 1988. The stadium seats 73,500.

Super Bowl
Football

The Green Bay Packers of the National Football League beat the American Football League's Kansas City Chiefs 35–10 in the first Super Bowl on January 15, 1967, in the Los Angeles Coliseum.

For the first four years, the Super Bowl was formally called the World Championship, and the competing teams were the AFL and NFL champions. It became the NFL Championship Game in 1971, after the leagues merged. With the merger, the new NFL was reorganized into the American and National Football Conferences, and the Super Bowl is now played between the AFC and NFC champions, determined by a series of conference playoff games.

Super Bowls are designated by Roman numerals and actually take place in the year following the NFL regular season. Thus Super Bowl XXII, in 1988, determined the 1987 NFL championship.

One reason for the success of the Super Bowl, at the outset, was the bitter seven-year rivalry between the competing leagues, and the resultant debate among fans of professional football about whether the AFL would ever become equal to the older NFL. The first four games were on the order of David and Goliath contests. And David won twice.

The Packers followed their victory in Super Bowl I with a 33–14 win over the Oakland Raiders the following year, which seemed to establish the NFL's superiority beyond a doubt.

The NFL's Baltimore Colts were favored by 18 points over the New York Jets in Super Bowl III. Three days before the game, the Jets' brash young quarterback, Joe Namath, violated an unwritten rule of professional sports by criticizing the opposition. He said that there were at least five quarterbacks in the AFL who were better than the Colts' Earl Morrall, the NFL's Most Valuable Player. And he added, "We're going to win. I guarantee it."

His comments infuriated the Colts, and brought derision from most sportswriters. But Namath delivered on his guarantee with pinpoint passing, assisted by solid defense, as the Jets won 16–7.

In the final Super Bowl before the merger, Kansas City easily defeated the favored Minnesota Vikings 23–7, evening the record at two victories for each league.

Some sportswriters have called the game "the stupor bowl," because it has often been anticlimactic after the long buildup. Walter Bingham of *Sports Illustrated* wrote, "Perhaps we expect too much. For two weeks we are fed a junk-food diet of information about the participants . . . and starting at dawn on game day the guys in the network blazers saturate us with more trivia. No wonder hopes are high."

The first game after the merger, Super Bowl V in 1971, was among the closest ever. The Colts, now in the AFC, edged the Dallas Cowboys, 16–13, on a field goal with 5 seconds to play. However, that game was called the "Blooper Bowl" or "Stumble Bowl" because it was so sloppily played, with a total of six interceptions, six fumbles, and 164 yards in penalties, but only 222 yards in total offense.

The Pittsburgh Steelers and the Dallas Cowboys played two exciting games, the Steelers winning both, 21–17 in 1976 and 35–31 in 1979. But in 1980 when the Steelers won their record fourth Super Bowl 31–19 over the Los Angeles Rams, it started a streak of one-sided games. Since then, the average margin of victory has been nearly 20 points, and only three games have been decided by fewer than 10 points.

But, despite the frequently disappointing quality of the game itself, Super Sunday, when the game is played, has been called "the most authentically American holiday," and the Super Bowl itself has been called "the ultimate game." (Running back Duane Thomas of the Dallas Cowboys once asked,

"If it's the ultimate game, why are they going to play another one next year?")

In part, this is a reflection of pro football's emergence as *the* television sport. According to the Gallup Poll, pro football in 1973 passed baseball, the national pastime, as the most popular spectator sport in the United States. But the great majority of fans watch games only on television, not at the stadium.

The Super Bowl has accounted for five of the ten highest-rated programs in television history. The 1982 Super Bowl was watched by 49.1 percent of all American households, and 73 percent of all TV sets that were on at the time were tuned to the game. It attracted the most viewers ever for a live event, and the third most in history for any type of program.

Ratings have declined somewhat since that peak, but the Super Bowl is still consistently one of the highest-rated TV shows of the year. And it's likely that audiences are actually higher than the ratings show, because there are large gatherings around TV sets at homes, restaurants, and bars all over the country on Super Sunday.

According to Bowling Green University sociologist Eldon Snyder, the Super Bowl "is one of the great integrating events of our country, one of the things that seem to bring a lot of different parts of American culture together."

See also AMERICAN FOOTBALL LEAGUE; NATIONAL FOOTBALL LEAGUE.

Super Bowl Results

1967	Green Bay (NFL) 35, Kansas City (AFL) 10
1968	Green Bay (NFL) 33, Oakland (AFL) 14
1969	New York (AFL) 16, Baltimore (NFL) 7
1970	Kansas City (AFL) 23, Minnesota (NFL) 7
1971	Baltimore (AFC) 16, Dallas (NFC) 13
1972	Dallas (NFC) 24, Miami (AFC) 3
1973	Miami (AFC) 14, Washington (NFC) 7
1974	Miami (AFC) 24, Minnesota (NFC) 7
1975	Pittsburgh (AFC) 16, Minnesota (NFC) 6
1976	Pittsburgh (AFC) 21, Dallas (NFC) 17
1977	Oakland (AFC) 32, Minnesota (NFC) 14
1978	Dallas (NFC) 27, Denver (AFC) 10
1979	Pittsburgh (AFC) 35, Dallas (NFC) 31
1980	Pittsburgh (AFC) 31, Los Angeles (NFC) 19
1981	Oakland (AFC) 27, Philadelphia (NFC) 10
1982	San Francisco (NFC) 26, Cincinnati (AFC) 21
1983	Washington (NFC) 27, Miami (AFC) 17
1984	Los Angeles (AFC) 38, Washington (NFC) 9
1985	San Francisco (NFC) 38, Miami (AFC) 16
1986	Chicago (NFC) 46, New England (AFC) 10
1987	New York (NFC) 39, Denver (AFC) 20
1988	Washington (NFC) 42, Denver (AFC) 10

1989 San Francisco (NFC) 20, Cincinnati (AFC) 16
1990 San Francisco (NFC) 55, Denver (AFC) 10
1991 New York (NFC) 20, Buffalo (AFC) 19

Superdome

See LOUISIANA SUPERDOME.

Surfing

Hawaiians were probably surfing as early as A.D. 1000. Many ancient legends tell of surfing contests between mythical figures, often rulers, and the surfboard was linked to religious ritual. After a tree was selected, an offering of fish was placed at its base; the tree was then cut down, shaped, stained, and dedicated with a prayer. Captain James Cook, who discovered the islands in 1778 and named them for the Earl of Sandwich, left a description of surfing: "Twenty or thirty of the natives, taking each a long narrow board, rounded at the ends, set out together from shore. The first wave they meet, they plunge under, and suffering it to roll over them, rise again beyond it, and make the best of their way by swimming, out into the sea. . . . The boldness and address, with which we saw them perform these difficult and dangerous manoeuvres, was altogether astonishing, and is scarce to be credited."

When Christianity and the Protestant ethic spread through the islands, beginning in 1821, surfing almost became extinct. By 1853, the sport was popular in only one community, Lahaina on Maui Island. However, a revival began about 1900, and in 1908 George Freeth discovered surfing in Hawaii and introduced it at Redondo Beach, CA. The same year the Outrigger Canoe Club was organized at Waikiki, and by 1910 surfboard riding had become one of the club sports, along with canoeing. During the 1920s, many visitors from California watched surfing in Hawaii and returned to the mainland as enthusiasts.

At that time, most surfers simply lay on their stomachs and paddled the board with their hands, although some sat and used a canoe paddle. Many native Hawaiians, however, stood on their boards and maneuvered along the waves rather than simply riding them in to shore. Among them was Duke Kahanamoku, an Olympic Gold Medalist as a swimmer, who demonstrated the skill in California and Australia. This kind of surfing became especially popular in the Malibu area of California during the late 1930s, and many surfboard clubs sprang up along the coast near Malibu during that period.

But modern surfing awaited a lighter, more maneuverable board. After World War II, the balsa board was developed in Malibu, and Bob Simmons, a student at California Institute of Technology, added a fiberglass coating for durability and an underwater fin for improved maneuverability about 1949. A board of polyurethane foam with a fiberglass skin was invented by two California surfers, Hobie Alter and Dave Sweet, in 1956. Those developments made standup surfing popular. There had been informal paddle racing early, but a new kind of competition, with subjective judging of the surfer's form while riding a wave, became predominant. The United States Surfing Association, founded in 1960 to govern the new sport, was renamed the American Surfing Association in 1966 and it became the U.S. Surfing Federation in 1980.

The first major competitive event was the Makaha International Surfing Championship in Hawaii, which originated in 1963. The ASA held its first U.S. Invitational Championships in 1964, and the first World Championships, conducted by the International Surfriding Federation, took place in Australia the same year. The ISF has been supplanted by the International Council of Associations of Surfing, which has more than 100 member nations representing nearly 300,000 competitors. The ICAS conducts both amateur and professional competition. The USSF oversees U.S. open and amateur championships as well as the All-American Championships for college and high school surfers.

Address: U.S. Surfing Federation, 7104 Island Village Drive, Long Beach, CA 90803 (213) 596–7785

Swimming

Beginning in the Middle Ages, swimming was considered hazardous to health throughout Europe and England, and that belief was brought to North America. As recreations, swimming and ocean bathing came into vogue in England late in the 18th century. Despite Benjamin Franklin's advocacy of swimming as both healthful and practical, the sport lagged behind in North America, although it received sporadic support. As early as 1826, the *New York American* recommended that every boy should be taught to swim, and in 1863 *Spirit of the Times* lamented that New York had so few swimming clubs and schools compared with England and Europe.

YMCAs spread across the continent during the last quarter of the century, and those in larger cities often had indoor pools as well as gymnasiums. Many athletic clubs also added pools. The first swimming club was the Dolphin Club of Toronto, established in May of 1875, and the Montreal Swim Club was formed the following year. Seven swimmers entered a Toronto race for the Governor General's silver

Surfing originated in Hawaii about 1,000 years ago. Four-time world champion Frieda Zamba demonstrates modern technique. Courtesy of Peter Brouillet/Surfing Magazine.

medal in 1877; on August 13 of that year, the Montreal club conducted races. The first major race in the United States, billed as being for the national championship, was held by the New York Athletic Club in 1883.

The breaststroke was the most commonly used stroke in competition until nearly the end of the century, when the crawl became popular among racers. The crawl was first discovered in the early 1870s by an English swimmer, J. Arthur Trudgen, who saw South Americans using it. He combined the hand-over-hand arm action with the scissors kick used by most English swimmers. Another Englishman, Frederick Cavill, went to Australia in 1878 to teach swimming and saw natives using a similar stroke, but with a "flutter kick," the legs moving alternately up and down. Cavill's son Richard returned to England in 1902 and became the first to swim 100 yards in less than 60 seconds. A British newspaper described it as "like crawling over the water," and the stroke became known as the Australian crawl.

Another of Cavill's sons, Sydney, became swimming coach at San Francisco's Olympic Club in 1903. One of his students, J. Scott Leary, broke the U.S. record by 4 seconds, swimming the 100 yards in 60 seconds flat. Charles M. Daniels of the NYAC then began experimenting with the stroke; he synchronized the kick with the arm action, using six kicks for every cycle. He set a world record of 56 seconds in 1906, and the American crawl became the dominant stroke, although some experi-

In synchronized swimming, competitors perform to music. Beulah Gundling, shown here, won the first four U.S. outdoor singles championships, 1950–1953. Courtesy of the International Swimming Hall of Fame

mentation with the kick continued well into the 1930s.

The Amateur Athletic Union in 1888 took over the national meet from the NYAC. Since the crawl was being used by virtually every swimmer, breaststroke competition was added in 1906. The first women's events were on the program in 1916, and the backstroke was added in 1934. The butterfly was introduced as a type of breaststroke after World War II, but it was so much faster than the regular breaststroke that it became a separate event in 1952.

The Canadian Amateur Swimming Association was organized on May 1, 1909, to govern swimming, diving, and water polo in that country. It held the first national championships in 1911 and added women's competition in 1920. The CASA, also known as Swimming Canada, now oversees swimming only. In the United States, the AAU governed the sport until 1980, when U.S. Swimming, Inc., was formed as an independent governing body. The National Collegiate Athletic Association has held national championships since 1925 for men, since 1982 for women.

There was one swimming event, the 100-meter race, at the first modern Olympics in 1896. The sport was not on the 1900 program, but it was restored with many events, including the plunge for distance, at London in 1904. Women's swimming was added in 1912.

Addresses: Swimming Canada, 333 River Road, Vanier, Ontario, Canada K1L 8H9 (613) 748–5673; U.S. Swimming, Inc., 1750 East Boulder Street, Colorado Springs, CO 80909 (719) 578–4578

See also DIVING; ENGLISH CHANNEL SWIM; INTERNATIONAL SWIMMING HALL OF FAME.

Synchronized Swimming

Inspired by water ballets at shows such as Billy Rose's Aquacade during the 1930s, synchronized swimming became a competitive sport immediately after World War II. The AAU held the first national championships for duets and teams in 1946, and solo competition was added in 1950. Swimmers synchronize their movements to accompanying music, as in figure skating, and they are judged subjectively. The sport was added to the Olympic program in 1984.

Addresses: Synchro Canada, 333 River Road, Vanier, Ontario, Canada K1L 8H9 (613) 748–5674; U.S. Synchronized Swimming, Inc., Pan-Am Plaza, 201 South Capitol, Suite 510, Indianapolis, IN 46275 (317) 237–5700

Synthetic Turf
See ARTIFICIAL TURF.

Syracuse, NY

Baseball Syracuse had two short-lived major-league teams, in the National League in 1879 and in the American Association in 1890.

Basketball The Syracuse Nationals were in the National Basketball League when the rival Basketball Association of America was organized in 1946. The two leagues merged into the National Basketball Association before the 1949–50 season, and Syracuse won the 1955 NBA championship. The team became the Philadelphia Warriors in 1963.

Table Tennis

It appears that British officers began playing a sport called "indoor tennis" in the 1890s, using a small ball covered with net and small racquets. The "net" was a row of books laid across a table. In various informal versions, the new game became known as "whiff whaff" or "gossima." A British promoter named Gibb in 1902 returned from the United States with a supply of hollow celluloid balls. He packaged the balls with a table and racquets of stretched vellum, and called the product "Ping Pong"—"ping" being the sound of the ball hitting the table, "pong" the sound of the racquet hitting the ball. He sold U.S. distribution rights to Parker Brothers.

Ping Pong became popular in both England and North America early in the century, but it was primarily an informal game for children and families, and rules were not standardized. By 1914, the fad was over. But the introduction of a wooden paddle with a textured rubber surface in the early 1920s led to a revival. The English Table Tennis Association was formed in 1923 to standardize the rules, and in 1926 eight countries established the International Table Tennis Federation, which held the first world championship in 1927.

The sport lagged somewhat in North America. The American Ping Pong Association was organized in 1930, but, because it used a trademarked name, only Parker Brothers equipment was allowed in its tournaments, and other companies were now in the market. The U.S. Table Tennis Association was founded in 1932, and by 1935 it had replaced the APPA. The following year, the Canadian Table Tennis Association was organized.

The growth of table tennis in Asia and, to a lesser extent, in Africa, was truly astonishing. Cairo hosted the 1939 world tournament, the first time the world championship in any sport was held in Africa. The 1952 tournament took place in Bombay, the first world championship of any kind ever hosted by an Asian country. Table tennis became remarkably popular in China after World War II, and Beijing hosted the 1961 championship, quite a breakthrough for a country that had alternately isolated itself from, and been isolated by, most other countries.

Like badminton, table tennis is a major recreational sport in North America, but has never become a serious competitive sport. An estimated 25 million people play table tennis in the United States, but only 295 clubs, representing fewer than 10,000 competitors, are registered with the USTTA.

Addresses: Canadian Table Tennis Association, 333 River Road, Vanier, Ontario, Canada K1L 8H9 (613) 748–5675; U.S. Table Tennis Association, 1750 East Boulder Street, Colorado Springs, CO 80909 (719) 578–4583

TAC
See THE ATHLETICS CONGRESS.

Talladega Superspeedway

Opened in 1969, this 2.66-mile auto racing track was originally called Alabama International Speedway. It was given its present name in 1989. The track seats about 70,000 spectators and has an infield capacity of another 70,000. It hosts two major NAS-CAR 500-mile races each year.

Address: P.O. Box 777, Talladega, AL 35160 (205) 362-2261

Tampa, FL

Football   The Tampa Bay Buccaneers entered the National Football League as an expansion franchise in 1976.

See also TAMPA STADIUM.

Tampa Stadium
Tampa, FL

Built in 1967, Tampa Stadium became the home field of the Tampa Bay Buccaneers when that team came into existence in 1976. Since 1986, the stadium has hosted the college football Hall of Fame Bowl. It seats 74,314 and has a grass field.

Tangerine Bowl
See CITRUS BOWL.

Target Parachuting
See SPORT PARACHUTING.

Taylor, "Major" Marshall W. (1878–1932)
Cycling
Born November 26, 1878; died July 6, 1932

Taylor was the first well-known black athlete and the first American athlete who was not a boxer to be recognized internationally. He won his first cycling race in Indianapolis when he was 13, and two years later he set an Indianapolis track record for the mile. Taylor was then banned from the track because white cyclists threatened to boycott races. Louis Munger, owner of a bicycle manufacturing company, supported Taylor and helped him train. Munger moved his company to Worcester, MA in 1895, taking Taylor with him as an employee.

After a year of racing in the Northeast, Taylor became a professional late in 1896 and entered a Madison Square Garden six-day race and finished eighth. His forte, though, was sprinting, and in 1897 he became a crowd favorite in the New York City area. His fame soon spread into the Midwest as well, but he had to skip all the southern races on the national championship circuit, and he was often victimized by white riders and judges.

A major breakthrough came when the 1899 world championships were held in Montreal. Before 18,000 fans, Taylor won the ½-mile, 1-mile, and 2-mile races. He was then given a $1,000 contract to ride for a Massachusetts manufacturer in 1900. He won the National Cycling Association's sprint championship that year and was paid $5,000 plus expenses to compete in Europe in 1901. He won 42 races in five countries against most of Europe's national champions. The culmination was a $7,500 match race against world champion Edmund Jacquelin. Taylor won the best-of-three sprint in two straight races.

After winning another 40 races in Europe early in 1902, Taylor returned to the United States. A celebrity in Europe, he was still subjected to bigotry from other riders, who often combined to box him in or even knock him from his bike to prevent his winning a race. Taylor thought of retiring after the season, but accepted an offer of $5,000 to race in Australia, where he won $23,000 in four months. But the strain of almost constant competition, combined with the prejudice he faced, not only on the track but in everyday life in the United States, combined against him. Taylor suffered a nervous breakdown early in 1904 and was suspended for breaking his contract to race in Europe again. He retired from racing and settled in Worcester with his wife and baby daughter.

Further Reading: Taylor, Marshall W. *The Fastest Bicycle Rider in the World.* Worcester, MA: Wormley Publishing Company, 1928.

Taylor Field
Regina, Saskatchewan

This stadium was named for N. J. Piffles Taylor, a former player with the Regina Roughriders, who was president of the team from 1934 to 1936. It opened in 1948 as the home field of the team, which since 1950 has been called the Saskatchewan Roughriders. Capacity is 27,637.

Team Handball

Team handball was originally based on soccer, but hands instead of feet were used to advance the ball. It was developed in 1904 by a Danish physical education teacher, Holger Nielsen, who published the rules for the sport two years later. Eleven European countries founded the International Amateur Handball Association in 1926. Called simply handball in Europe, the sport was introduced into North America during the 1930s and became known as team handball to distinguish it from the court game. (A somewhat different variety, called fieldball or field handball, was adapted for play by women and became a fairly popular intramural sport in high schools and colleges.) The U.S. Team Handball Federation was organized in 1947, after many World War II veterans had discovered the sport in Europe.

In the meantime, an indoor version had been developed in the Scandinavian countries, with a smaller ball, a smaller playing area, and only 7 players on a team, rather than 11. Indoor team handball was brought to the New York City area by immigrants during the late 1950s. Often played outdoors, this version of the sport has now supplanted the original game. It became an Olympic sport in 1972.

Addresses: Canadian Team Handball Federation, 333 River Road, Vanier, Ontario, Canada K1L 8H9 (613) 748–5676; U.S. Team Handball Federation, 1750 East Boulder, Colorado Springs, CO 80909 (719) 578–4582

Television

The first televised sports event was the Princeton-Columbia baseball game at Baker Field, Manhattan, on May 17, 1939. It was covered by a single camera from NBC's New York station, W2XBS, with Bill Stern doing the play-by-play. Princeton won an exciting 10-inning game, 2–1, but not many people watched. There were fewer than 400 sets in the New York area. It was admittedly experimental. Stern said later, "In that one game, we learned a complete lesson about how not to televise a sports event." Three days later, Stern did a live report on a six-day bicycle race from Madison Square Garden, and on June 1, W2XBS broadcast a boxing match between Lou Nova and Max Baer from Yankee Stadium, still using just one camera. Televised sports had a long way to go, but it was here to stay.

Also in 1939, Red Barber did the first telecast of a major-league game, between the Brooklyn Dodgers and the Cincinnati Reds, and the following season the Dodgers had a weekly telecast. That year, the Mutual Broadcasting System paid $2,500 for the National Football League championship game. World War II held up development of the medium, but immediately after the war it began its inexorable growth. Owners were at first wary, as they had been about radio. In 1946, major-league baseball adopted a rule that a team couldn't broadcast a game into another team's territory. When the Justice Department threatened antitrust action in 1950, the rule was modified, and in 1952 it was abandoned entirely. NFL commissioner Bert Bell, in 1951, established a blackout rule prohibiting broadcasts into a team's territory when it was playing a home game, and the rule was upheld by federal judge Alan K. Grim.

The Los Angeles Rams, who drew 205,000 fans in 1949, allowed all of their games to be televised in 1950 and saw attendance shrink to 110,000. Without television in 1951, attendance climbed back to its previous level. The NCAA also grew concerned about the effect of television on attendance; after a study, the association in 1952 sold rights to selected college games to Westinghouse for $700,000, and Westinghouse sponsored the games on NBC. That kind of arrangement was not unusual at the time: Gillette and Ford bought rights to the 1947 World Series for $30,000 apiece and had it televised on three networks, reaching an audience of about 3 million, and Ford held exclusive rights to Madison Square Garden boxing matches for several years.

The NCAA package deal, the first of its kind, established a pattern for professional sports, but only after a legal struggle. The National Basketball Association led the way in 1954 with an NBC television package that went unchallenged. The new American Football League in 1960 negotiated a four-year contract with ABC for $1.7 million a year, and the NFL the following year sold a $4.6 million package to CBS. Judge Grim this time ruled that the package was a restraint of trade, but Congress passed the Sports Antitrust Broadcast Act, specifically allowing professional basketball, football, and hockey leagues to sell television rights as a package. (Baseball wasn't included because it had been granted an exemption from antitrust laws by the Supreme Court in 1922.)

Pro football soon became the highest-rated sport on television. NFL ratings grew by 50 percent during the three years of the CBS contract. In 1964 the network signed a new two-year contract paying $14.1 million year, and NBC signed a five-year contract

with the AFL at just over $8 million a year. The two leagues merged in 1970, and the new NFL was realigned to help equalize television markets for the two networks. After Baltimore, Cleveland, and Pittsburgh agreed to join the former AFL teams in the American Football Conference, the CBS advantage in potential audience was cut from 2-to-1 to 7-to-5. And the third major network, ABC, got into the act by paying $8 million to televise 13 Monday night games.

The NFL's television money escalated to $144 million a year in 1977, about $400 million in 1982, and nearly $470 million in 1987, when ESPN also began televising Sunday night games. And that was just for the regular season. The Super Bowl, as the annual championship game had become known, was one of the most-watched television shows every year; from 1987 through 1989, CBS paid $18 million a year for the Super Bowl, and CBS and NBC together paid a total of $26 million for the other playoff games leading up to the Super Bowl. Despite stagnant ratings for regular-season games, contracts negotiated in 1990 were to bring in a total of $3.6 billion over a four-year period, with Turner Broadcasting System, a so-called superstation, joining the three major networks and ESPN.

College football also had a long period of growth in television revenue before running into difficulties with its own members. The 1952 NCAA television contract was worth $1.2 million a year. That climbed to $5.1 million in 1962, $6.5 million in 1964, $12 million in 1970, $30 million in 1977, and $74 million in 1981, when ABC, CBS, and TBS all televised games. But the college football powers were unhappy about the way money was shared; they formed the College Football Association in 1976 and, through two member schools, brought an antitrust suit against the NCAA. In 1983, the Supreme Court ruled that the association's package deal did violate antitrust laws, and the CFA negotiated its own contracts, receiving $16 million a year each from CBS and ESPN from 1987 through 1990. In addition, the Pacific Ten and Big Ten assigned their games to ABC for $13 million a year, and other major conferences went with regional networks.

The NCAA basketball tournament more than made up for the loss in football revenue. CBS paid $55.3 million a year for the tournament from the 1987–88 season through the 1989–90 season; that increased to $142.9 million a year in 1990–91. Professional basketball didn't do so well for a number of years, but an influx of very popular stars during the 1980s boosted its stock enormously, and television money more than tripled, from $72 million in 1989–90 to nearly $220 million the following season. Major-league baseball also spent a time in the doldrums; its television money increased, but at a considerably slower pace than NFL and college football. Its "Game of the Week" package was worth just $1 million a year from 1951 through 1956. That increased to $3.25 million in 1960, $16 million in 1970, $23 million in 1976, and $46 million in 1980. It leaped to $183 million in 1986 and $365 million in 1990. (In addition, individual teams sell their own television rights locally and regionally, as in professional basketball.)

The biggest television package of all, though, is the Olympics. Olympic television coverage really began in 1960, when CBS paid $394,000 for the Summer Games and $50,000 for the Winter Games. The 1964 Summer Games went to NBC for just $1.5 million. Then ABC, trying to build prestige as a sports network, paid $4.5 million for the 1968 Summer Games and $2.5 million for the Winter Games. Summer Games fees went up to $7.5 million in 1972, then escalated to $25 million in 1976. NBC, now battling ABC for sports supremacy, bid $85 million for the 1980 Moscow Games, but there was no coverage because of the U.S. boycott. That didn't deter the network from paying $225 million in 1984 and $401 million in 1988—16 times the 1976 figure.

One reason for the great increase in rights fees during the 1980s was that the structure of television was changing. Cable television's coverage of sports began very quietly on November 28, 1953, when Telemeter brought the Notre Dame–Southern California football game to 200 subscribers in Palm Springs, CA. The new medium was originally a way of bringing television to isolated areas that had poor reception. A single large antenna picked up signals and distributed them by cable, hence the name "community antenna television," or CATV. The advent of satellite communications during the 1970s greatly increased the number of signals that the central antenna could receive, making cable TV attractive to almost any community.

Home Box Office was the first major cable service. It began as a regional cable service and went national in 1975, with championship boxing as its major sports attraction. Then came the Entertainment and Sports Programming Network in 1979. ESPN began with minor sports that none of the major networks wanted, but became a major player with a piece of the NFL television pie in 1987. Cable also created the superstation, a local station that becomes a national station by transmitting its signal via satellite. The first was Ted Turner's WTBS in Atlanta, which became a superstation in 1976. It was followed by WPIX and WWOR in New York, WGN in Chicago, and KTVT in Los Angeles.

The regional sports channel is another recent development. The leader in this field is SportsChannel, actually an amalgam of outlets in Chicago, Detroit, Florida, New England, New York, and Philadelphia. The New England station, for example, carries the Boston Celtics and Hartford Whalers home games. When those teams are not playing at home, the station can pick up the feed from another region to bring New England fans another game of interest, such as Philadelphia 76ers basketball or New York Rangers hockey.

Prestige has always been a factor in the bidding for sports programming. For years, ABC took a loss on NCAA football because it was a prestige item, and the Olympics has been a "loss leader" at least since 1976. But the competition between the three major over-the-air networks and cable outlets made prestige even more important at a time when ratings were stagnant. CBS disdained high bids while it was the dominant network. But, with its ratings down and its news division in disarray, CBS in 1990 bid more than $1 billion for four years of major-league baseball, $142.9 million a year for exclusive rights to the NCAA basketball tournament (previously shared with ESPN), and a total of $543 million for the 1992 and 1994 Winter Olympics.

Television money isn't as important to sports such as auto racing, golf, and tennis, because most of their events are sponsored, but television coverage is. Golf has been the only sport to show substantial growth in recent years, climbing from 70 events and 146 hours of programming in 1984 to 104 events and 218 hours in 1988. Tennis coverage reached a peak of 115 hours in 1987 but dropped sharply to 90 hours the following year, and auto racing went from just 17 hours in 1984 to a high of 53 hours in 1987, but declined to 46 hours in 1988.

Further Reading: Klatell, David A., and Norman Marcus. *Sports for Sale: Television, Money and the Fans.* New York: Oxford University Press, 1988; Powers, Ron. *Super Tube.* New York: Coward-McCann, 1984.

See also JOURNALISM, SPORTS; RADIO.

Temple Cup
Baseball

The champions of the National League and the American Association played an annual postgame series in 1882 and from 1884 through 1890. There was no series in 1891 because the leagues were involved in a battle for players, and the association folded after that season. National League owners adopted a split-season schedule in 1892, with the first- and second-half champions meeting in a postseason playoff, but fans weren't crazy about that idea, so it was dropped in 1893. The following season, William C. Temple, owner of the Pittsburgh team, offered a trophy worth $800 to the winner of a series between the first- and second-place teams. He specified that the winning team should get 65 percent of the gate receipts, the losing team 35 percent. The Temple Cup series was played through 1896.

Tennis

Originally played in a courtyard, tennis was informally adopted for outdoor play in England during the first half of the 19th Century. But modern lawn tennis can trace its roots to Major Walter Clopton Wingfield, who late in 1873 developed a game he eccentrically called *sphairistike*, a Greek word that can be roughly translated as "play ball." The game was as eccentric as the name. The court was hourglass-shaped, narrower at the net than at the ends, the net was nearly 5 feet high, and there were "wing nets" stretched along the sidelines near the net.

Game was 15 points, as in badminton and most other racquet sports.

Wingfield introduced the sport to friends and put together a package, including net, stakes, racquets, balls, and an eight-page pamphlet containing a diagram of the court and the rules, to be sold for 5 guineas (approximately $26 at the time). He patented *sphairistike* in February 1874. Lawn tennis was undoubtedly an idea whose time had come, but Wingfield's invention was not quite the right idea. The Marylebone Cricket Club issued a revised set of rules in 1875, and two years later the All England Croquet and Lawn Tennis Club rewrote them completely: The court became rectangular, the wing nets were eliminated, the net was lowered, and the court tennis system of scoring, still in use today, was adopted.

The new sport reached North America with remarkable speed. Mary Ewing Outerbridge, a young woman from Staten Island, saw lawn tennis in Bermuda, where it had been introduced by British officers, and she brought some equipment home just about the time Wingfield was getting his patent. A little later, the sport was being played at the Staten Island Cricket and Base Ball Club. That summer, James Dwight of Nahant, MA, brought equipment

The West Side Tennis Club at Forest Hills, NY, hosted the U.S. national tennis championships from 1915 through 1920 and from 1923 through 1977. Here Helen Wills, left, plays Helen Jacobs in the 1928 finals; Wills won. Courtesy of the U.S. Tennis Association

back from England and laid out a court. It is believed that tennis was also introduced to the Toronto area during 1874.

In 1878, just four years later, *Harper's Weekly* carried a long article explaining the rules of tennis and discussing some of its finer points, indicating that the sport had already gained a fair amount of popularity. (Interestingly, the article said it could be played by two, four, or eight people.) However, it hadn't been standardized in North America. The Staten Island club held a "national" tournament beginning September 1, 1880. James Dwight and his second cousin, Dick Sears, arrived from Nahant, but refused to play in the singles because they said the balls were too small, too light, and too soft. A little later that year Philadelphia's Young America Cricket Club sent a team to play against Staten Island and lost, in part because the net was six inches lower than the net used in Philadelphia.

Nineteen clubs were represented at the organizational meeting of the U.S. National Lawn Tennis Association on May 21, 1881, in New York City. Fourteen other clubs sent proxies. The All-England rules and the English ball were adopted, and the new association decided to conduct national championship tournaments in men's singles and doubles at the Casino in Newport, RI, beginning August 31. A women's singles tournament was added in 1888, women's doubles in 1890, and mixed doubles in 1891. The Canadian Lawn Tennis Association held its first championships in 1894.

Many students at colleges in the Northeast took up tennis soon after its introduction. Amherst, Brown, Trinity College of Connecticut, and Yale formed the Intercollegiate Lawn Tennis Association in 1883, and the USNLTA held a national intercollegiate tournament that year. In 1899 a group of Harvard tennis players accepted an invitation to demonstrate their skills on the West Coast. They played matches in California, Oregon, Washington, and British Columbia. One of them was Dwight F. Davis, who a year later presented the International Lawn Tennis Challenge Trophy, better known as the Davis Cup. The British challenged, but lost to the United States that first year.

Like golf, tennis was a sport for the wealthy in its early years, since it was played only by those who belonged to exclusive clubs or who could build their own courts. But during the early part of the century, many cement and asphalt courts were built in California, in part because of that visit by the Harvardians. In 1909 the "California Comet," Maurice McLoughlin, suddenly appeared from the West. Trained on those hard courts, McLoughlin played a different kind of game, rushing to the net behind a cannonball serve and hitting long, hard ground strokes. Although he lost in his first three attempts to win the national championship, he won many converts to his style of play; when he won the title in 1912, he was the first champion to come from west of the Mississippi.

Another Californian, Hazel Hotchkiss (later, as Mrs. Wightman, donor of the Wightman Cup), also made her first appearance in the nationals in 1909, and she won three consecutive championships. Although too short to have a strong first serve, she nevertheless played a volleying game at net, using her speed and quickness to overcome harder-hitting opponents. Between them, Hotchkiss and McLoughlin not only changed the style of tennis, they helped popularize it somewhat among the middle class, as Francis Ouimet did for golf in 1913.

The rapid increase in public facilities also helped. The first national Public Parks championship was held in 1923. The two top American men in the sport during the first half of the 1920s were almost perfect opposites: "Big Bill" Tilden, trained at Philadelphia's exclusive Germantown Cricket Club, and "Little Bill" Johnston, another product of the California public courts. Between 1919 and 1925, they met in the national finals six times, Johnston winning only once, and they won the Davis Cup for the United States from 1921 through 1926.

Tilden's skill and showmanship, combined with greater public awareness of tennis, helped bring out crowds during the 1920s. The national tournament had moved from Newport to the West Side Tennis Club at Forest Hills, NY in 1915 and then to the Germantown Cricket Club in 1921. The WSTC in 1923 built a permanent concrete stadium to replace its temporary wooden grandstands. The 14,000-seat stadium was the first of its kind for tennis. It hosted the first Wightman Cup competition between British and American women in 1923, and the following year the United States Nationals returned to Forest Hills.

The first well-known women athletes were tennis players, chief among them Helen Wills, Helen Jacobs, and Alice Marble of the United States and Suzanne Lenglen of France. In 1926, Promoter C. C. Pyle organized the first professional tour around Lenglen, who was paid $50,000 for the season. The tour was a success, but Pyle got out of it when Lenglen demanded more money for 1928; one of the players, Vincent Richards, then organized the U.S. Professional Lawn Tennis Association. The pro tour during the sport's amateur period consisted of just a handful of players, sometimes only two, traveling around the country playing matches. It was intermittently successful. Tilden and Czech pro Karel Kozeluh grossed nearly $250,000 in 1931, and matches between Fred Perry of England and Ellsworth Vines of the United States took in more than $400,000 in 1937. But in most other years the tour lost money or barely broke even.

Tennis had become the most international of sports. Australasia (Australia and New Zealand) won the Davis Cup six times between 1908 and 1914, then won again in 1919 after a four-year hiatus because of World War I, but the United States dominated from 1920 through 1926. Then France took over, winning the cup from 1927 through 1932, and Australia emerged as a major challenger in the late 1930s, winning in 1939. Japan had been the cup challenger in 1921, and Germany produced some top-ranked players, led by Baron Gottfried von Cramm, who reached the Wimbledon finals in 1937.

After World War II, Australian men and American women dominated the sport. With the rise of professional sports in the United States, there was not much incentive for male athletes to play serious tennis. The pro tour was still shaky and could accommodate only a few players. Jack Kramer, a former star who promoted the tour, began a campaign for open tennis to awaken public interest in the sport, but it was a long campaign. From 1953 through 1967, U.S. men failed to win a singles championship at their own national tournament.

During the early 1960s, Australia, Britain, and France joined Kramer's campaign for open tennis, but the International Lawn Tennis Association balked at the idea. Suddenly, the All-England Club announced that world's most prestigious tournament, Wimbledon, would be open to amateurs and professionals in 1968. The USLTA didn't go quite so far; it held an open tournament in conjunction with the 1968 and 1969 national amateur championships before going to a completely open national championship in 1970.

It was as if a floodgate had opened. World Championship Tennis was organized as a small professional tour in 1967. In 1970 Jack Kramer established the Grand Prix tour, which awarded points for high finishes in major tournaments. Prize money was distributed among the players with the most points, and the eight best played in a season-ending Masters Tournament. Prize money has always helped to attract spectators; with the best players in the world competing, television was suddenly interested. From 1970 to 1973, the amount of television time for tennis tripled. NBC paid $100,000 for eight WCT tournaments. The 1972 WCT final lasted 4 hours, forcing the network to preempt prime-time shows.

The reward was an audience of 23 million, the largest ever to watch tennis up to that time.

Women were left out by both the WCT and the Grand Prix. Led by Billie Jean King and Gladys Heldman, publisher of *World Tennis* magazine, in 1971 they formed their own professional body, the Women's International Tennis Association, and their own tour, the Virginia Slims Circuit. King became the first woman to win more than $100,000 that year. By 1975, the circuit's total prize money was nearly $1 million, and Chris Evert won more than $300,000 (including noncircuit winnings). As a kind of sideshow to these very real gains, the 55-year-old Bobby Riggs announced that he could beat any woman. He did beat Margaret Court Smith easily on Mothers' Day, but King emerged as the true women's champion as she so often had, and wiped out Riggs, 6–4, 6–4, 6–3, before an audience of 30,492 in the Houston Astrodome while millions more watched on prime-time television.

Tired of being controlled by the ILTF, men also formed their own organization, the Association of Tennis Professionals, in 1972. In response, the ILTF established a Grand Prix Committee to oversee men's professional tennis. The six-man committee had three player members. It became the Men's International Professional Tennis Council in 1974, the Men's Tennis Council in 1988. In 1989, the men's tour, with sponsorship from Nabisco, embraced more than 70 tournaments in 23 countries, with total prize money of more than $37 million.

The last two decades brought an influx of greatly talented players of both sexes from almost everywhere: Martina Navratilova, Jan Kodes, Hana Mandlikova, and Ivan Lendl from Czechoslovakia, Bjorn Borg, Stefan Edberg, and Mats Wilander from Sweden, Evonne Goolagong from Australia, Guillermo Vilas from Argentina, Yannick Noah from the Cameroons by way of France, Ilie Nastase from Rumania, Manuel Orantes from Spain, Helena Sukova of the Soviet Union, and Germany's Boris Becker and Steffi Graf, the 1989 Wimbledon singles champions. In addition to Evert and King, the United States produced Jimmy Connors, Tracy Austin, Pam Shriver, John McEnroe, and Vitas Gerulaitis. Professionalism may not be the only reason for these stars, but it is certainly an important reason.

Tennis had been on the Olympic program in 1896 and from 1904 through 1924. It was restored to the Olympics in 1988, and professionals were allowed to play, since amateur competition would have drawn very little interest. From the supposed lily-white amateurism of its long past, tennis had become a major professional sport in a relatively short period. And, belatedly, the organizations that control it had finally recognized that the sport is simply called "tennis," by dropping the word "lawn" from their names. The USLTA is now the USTA, and the ILTF has become the ITF.

Further Reading: Cummings, Parke. *American Tennis: The Story of a Game and Its People.* Boston: Little, Brown, 1957; Evans, Richard. *Open Tennis 1968–1988.* Lexington, MA: Stephen Greene Press, 1989; Grimsley, Will. *Tennis: Its History, People and Events.* Englewood Cliffs, NJ: Prentice-Hall, 1971.

See also ASSOCIATION OF TENNIS PROFESSIONALS; DAVIS CUP; FEDERATION CUP; GRAND PRIX OF TENNIS; INTERNATIONAL TENNIS HALL OF FAME; U.S. TENNIS ASSOCIATION; VIRGINIA SLIMS CIRCUIT; WIGHTMAN CUP; WOMEN'S INTERNATIONAL TENNIS ASSOCIATION; WORLD CHAMPIONSHIP TENNIS; WORLD TEAM TENNIS.

Texas

Baseball   After 11 years in Washington as an American League expansion franchise, the Washington Senators became the Texas Rangers in 1972. The Rangers play in Arlington (TX) Stadium, about halfway between Dallas and Ft. Worth.
See also ARLINGTON STADIUM.

Texas Stadium
Irving, TX

The Dallas Cowboys of the National Football League built Texas Stadium and moved there from the Cotton Bowl in 1971. The stadium has a roof with a large opening that can be closed to keep rain or snow out. It seats 65,024.

The Athletics Congress/USA (TAC)
Track and Field

The Amateur Athletic Union governed track and field from 1888 until 1979. The Amateur Sports Act of 1978 required that all governing bodies for Olympic or Pan-American Games sports should be autonomous by November of 1980, and the TAC took over control of track and field in August 1979. It was essentially a direct spinoff; its first executive director, Ollan Cassell, had been the AAU's executive director, and the TAC is headquartered in Indianapolis, which is also the home of the AAU. In addition to the traditional track and field events, the TAC governs road running, cross-country, and race walking. The TAC has more than 2,500 member clubs, schools, colleges, and universities, representing more than 150,000 athletes.

Address: 2000 South Capitol Avenue, Suite 140, Indianapolis, IN 46225 (317) 638–9155

Thoroughbred Racing
See HORSE RACING.

Thoroughbred Racing Associations

Representatives of 22 racetracks met in Chicago in March 1942 to form Thoroughbred Racing Associations of the U.S., Inc. When the TRA held its first annual meeting in December, there were 32 member tracks. One of the association's short-range goals was to keep racing alive during World War II by raising money for a variety of war-related charities through an affiliate, the Turf Committee of America. Longer-range goals were to act as a liaison agency between the tracks and many other racing interests and to ensure the sport's integrity.

On January 15, 1946, the TRA created the Throughbred Racing Protective Bureau, an investigatory body. The TRPB oversees lip tattooing of horses, which has virtually eliminated the practice of running a horse under the wrong name, and investigates would-be jockeys, trainers, and others who want to become involved in the sport.

Address: 3000 Marcus Avenue, Suite 2W4, Lake Success, NY 11042 (516) 328–2660

Thorpe, "Jim" James F. (1888–1953)
Football
Born May 28, 1888, Prague, OK; died March 28, 1953; National Football Foundation, Pro Football Hall of Fame

Voted the greatest American athlete of the first half of the 20th century in 1950 and named to the all-time all-pro team in 1969, Thorpe was of Irish, French, and Sac-Fox Indian ancestry. A halfback at Carlisle Institute, he was an All-American in 1911 and 1912, when he scored 25 touchdowns and 198 points in 14 games. Thorpe won the pentathlon and the decathlon at the 1912 Olympics in Stockholm, and the King of Sweden, presenting the Gold Medals, told him, "Sir, you are the greatest athlete in the world." A year later, he had to return the medals because he had earned $15 a week playing semipro baseball while attending Carlisle. (In 1982, the International Olympic Committee decided that the medals should be restored to Thorpe posthumously. Replicas of the original medals were presented to one of his daughters in 1983.)

Paid $250 a game by the Canton Bulldogs in 1915, Thorpe became the first professional football player to sign a contract to play the entire season with a single team the following season. He was Canton's player-coach in 1920, when the team joined the new American Professional Football Association, and he was named APFA president because he had the best-

Shown here attempting a dropkick for the Canton Bull-dogs in 1920, Jim Thorpe was one of the greatest athletes of all time. He won the pentathlon and the decathlon in the 1912 Olympics, was a charter member of the Pro Football Hall of Fame, and played major-league baseball with the New York Giants. Courtesy of the Pro Football Hall of Fame

known name in football. The Canton team became the Cleveland Indians in 1921. After one season in Cleveland, Thorpe organized his own team, the Oorang Indians, playing out of Marion, OH. That team folded after the 1923 season, and Thorpe played for the Rock Island Independents in 1924, the New York Giants in 1925, and Canton in 1926. After a year out of football, he spent a final season with the Chicago Cardinals in 1928.

Thorpe also played major-league baseball for parts of six seasons, mostly with the New York Giants. He hit .327 in 62 games with the Giants and the Boston Braves in 1919, his final season in the majors.

Thorpe Trophy
Football

Named for Jim Thorpe, this award goes to the National Football League's Player of the Year, as chosen by a vote of the players.

1955	Harlon Hill, Chicago Bears
1956	Frank Gifford, New York Giants
1957	John Unitas, Baltimore
1958	Jim Brown, Cleveland
1959	Charlie Conerly, New York Giants
1960	Norm Van Brocklin, Philadelphia
1961	Y. A. Tittle, New York Giants
1962	Jim Taylor, Green Bay
1963	Jim Brown, Cleveland
	Y. A. Tittle, New York Giants (tie)
1964	Lenny Moore, Baltimore
1965	Jim Brown, Cleveland
1966	Bart Starr, Green Bay
1967	John Unitas, Baltimore
1968	Earl Morrall, Baltimore
1969	Roman Gabriel, Los Angeles Rams
1970	John Brodie, San Francisco
1971	Bob Griese, Miami
1972	Larry Brown, Washington
1973	O. J. Simpson, Buffalo
1974	Ken Stabler, Oakland
1975	Fran Tarkenton, Minnesota
1976	Bert Jones, Baltimore
1977	Walter Payton, Chicago Bears
1978	Earl Campbell, Houston
1979	Earl Campbell, Houston
1980	Earl Campbell, Houston
1981	Ken Anderson, Cincinnati
1982	Dan Fouts, San Diego
1983	Joe Theismann, Washington
1984	Dan Marino, Miami
1985	Walter Payton, Chicago Bears
1986	Phil Simms, New York Giants
1987	Jerry Rice, San Francisco
1988	Roger Craig, San Francisco
1989	Joe Montana, San Francisco
1990	Jim Kelly, Buffalo

Three-Day Event
See EQUESTRIAN SPORTS.

Three Rivers Stadium
Pittsburgh, PA

One of several modern circular stadiums, Three Rivers is near the conjunction of the Monongahela, Pittsburgh, and Ohio Rivers. The stadium opened on July 16, 1970. After having drawn only 386,907 fans in 40 games at Forbes Field that season, the Pittsburgh Pirates drew 955,040 in 41 games at the new park. The park's seating capacity for baseball is 58,729. Home run distances are 335 feet down the lines and 400 feet to center field. The stadium, also the home of the National Football League's Pittsburgh Steelers, seats 59,030 for football.

Tiger Stadium
Detroit, MI

Frank Navin, president of the Detroit Tigers from 1911 until his death in 1935, built this stadium in 1912. Originally known as Navin Field, it had a concrete and steel grandstand with a capacity of about 29,000. After Navin's death, Walter O. "Spike" Briggs took over the team and expanded capacity to 54,900 by building double-decked stands around the entire field before the 1938 season. The park then became known as Briggs Stadium; the name was changed to Tiger Stadium in 1961. The stadium now seats 52,416. Home run distances are 340 to left, 440 feet to center, and 325 feet down the right field line. The Detroit Lions of the National Football League also played in the stadium from 1938 through 1974.

Tilden, "Big Bill" William T. II (1893–1953)
Tennis

Born February 10, 1893, Germantown, PA; died June 5, 1953; International Tennis Hall of Fame

For years, Tilden was a player who showed promise without fulfilling it. He reached the finals of the U.S. Nationals for the first time in 1918, but lost to R. Lindley Murray. The following year, "Little Bill" Johnston beat him in the finals by working on Tilden's weak backhand. Tilden practiced his backhand at an indoor court that winter, and in 1920 he became the first American man to win the singles at Wimbledon. He went on to beat Johnston in a dramatic five-set match for the U.S. Championship, and in December he and Johnston won the Davis Cup from Australia without losing a match.

Tilden won the national title five years in a row, 1921 through 1925, beating Johnston in the finals four of those years, and he won it for a seventh time in 1929, when he was 36. He also won the Wimbledon title in 1921 and 1930. He was the U.S. clay court champion from 1921 through 1927, the indoor singles champion in 1920, and the world hard court champion in 1921.

He teamed with a variety of partners to win doubles championships, beginning with Mary K. Browne in the national mixed doubles in 1913 and 1914. He and Molla Bjurstedt Mallory won that title in 1922 and 1923. Tilden also won the men's doubles at Wimbledon in 1927, the U.S. men's doubles in 1918, 1921, 1922, 1923, and 1927.

A dramatic and temperamental player, Tilden was known for the withering glare he directed at officials when he didn't agree with a call—even if the call went in his favor. On several occasions, after an official called an opponent's shot out when Tilden thought it was in, he delivered the glare and then

The colorful, often controversial, "Big Bill" Tilden in 1920 was the first American tennis player to win a singles championship at Wimbledon. Courtesy of the International Tennis Hall of Fame

deliberately blew the next point. He also defied the sport's higher officialdom in 1928 by writing articles about the Wimbledon tournament, violating a U.S. Lawn Tennis Association rule. The USLTA suspended him shortly before the Davis Cup match against France, igniting a furor. The French had just built an enormous stadium, and Tilden was the chief gate attraction. The U.S. ambassador to France finally intervened with the president of the USLTA to have the suspension lifted.

Tilden became a professional in 1931, and 13,600 people turned out at Madison Square Garden on February 18 to watch his pro debut against the Czech, Karel Kozeluh. The tour grossed $238,000 that year, with Tilden winning the championship, but it lost money the next two years, partly because of the Great Depression and partly because Tilden was just too good for the competition he faced. But he and Ellsworth Vines grossed $243,000 in 1934 and $188,000 in 1935. Tilden sponsored his own tour in 1936, losing money, and played just a few times in 1936 before retiring. But he returned in 1945, at the age of 52, to win the professional doubles title with Vince Richards.

Like many of the other great athletes of the 1920s, Tilden seemed to be created for the time. As Red Smith wrote, "He would have been great in any age;

he lived in the age that was exactly right for him. He was one of the company of giants whose personalities transcended their own narrow fields and left an indelible mark on their time." John Kieran summed Tilden up: "He was a great artist and a great actor. . . . He strode the court like a confident conqueror. . . . He was the most striking and commanding figure the game of tennis ever had put in court."

Further Reading: DeFord, Frank. *Big Bill Tilden: The Triumphs and Tragedy.* New York: Simon and Schuster, 1976.

Title IX

Women's sports got its greatest single boost from Title IX of the Educational Amendments Act of 1972, prohibiting sexual discrimination by any school or college receiving federal aid. There was no immediate impact until 1975, when the Department of Health, Education and Welfare adopted an implementing regulation that set up an adjustment period for sports programs, requiring that all institutions must be in compliance by July 21, 1978. Many schools and colleges had already begun to expand women's sports programs as a result of Title IX, and many more of them took action after the regulation was adopted.

There was still considerable confusion about what Title IX actually required, and the HEW in 1977 began drafting specific enforcement principles, which were released on December 6, 1978. A "financial-proportionality" standard in scholarship money was adopted as the major test of compliance. "If 70 percent of a school's athletes are male," HEW Secretary Patricia Harris explained, "they are entitled to 70 percent of the financial aid their school makes available." Equivalency tests were also established for travel allowances, scheduling, coaches' pay, and the availability of sports equipment and facilities.

Even before the standards were established, Title IX had a major impact. In 1970–71, only 7.4 percent of high school students participating in interscholastic sports were girls; that increased to 17.2 percent in 1972–73, 23.5 percent in 1974–75, and 31.9 percent in 1978–79. Girls' basketball was offered at 4,856 schools in 1970–71; that figure grew to 17,617 in 1978–79. Figures for individual participation in college sports aren't available, but the average number of intercollegiate sports offered for women doubled from 2.5 in 1973–74 to 5.0 in 1978–79 (the men's average increased from 7.3 to 7.4 during the same period). It was estimated that women's intercollegiate sports received 1 percent, or less, of the average college's total budget in 1970–71; that was up to 16.4 percent in 1978–79.

The new emphasis on women's sports programs led the NCAA to inaugurate national championships for women, beginning with cross-country, field hockey, and volleyball in 1981, followed by basketball, fencing, golf, gymnastics, lacrosse, soccer, softball, swimming and diving, tennis, and outdoor track and field in 1982, and indoor track and field in 1983.

Further Reading: "The Impact of Title IX: Participation in High School and College Competitive Athletics," in Riess, Stephen A., *The American Sporting Experience: A Historical Anthology of Sport in America.* Champaign, IL: Leisure Press, 1984, pp. 386–397.

See also WOMEN IN SPORTS.

Tobogganing
See BOBSLEDDING; LUGE.

Toledo, OH
Toledo had a baseball team in the American Association in 1884 and 1890.

Toronto, Ontario
Baseball The Toronto Blue Jays entered the American League as an expansion team in 1977. They won eastern division championships in 1985 and 1989, but lost in the league championship series both years.

Football Members of the Argonaut Rowing Club in Toronto began playing rugby in 1873, and the following year they formally organized a team. The Toronto Argonauts entered the Ontario Rugby Football Union when it was founded in 1883, and they won the first ORFU championship. In 1907, the team joined the new Interprovincial Rugby Football Union, also known as the Big Four. The IRFU in 1960 became the Eastern Football Conference of the Canadian Football League. The Argonauts won the Grey Cup in 1914, 1921, 1933, 1937, 1938, 1945, 1946, 1947, 1950, 1952, and 1983. Another Toronto team, Balmy Beach, won the Grey Cup in 1927 and 1930 and Toronto's Royal Canadian Air Force Hurricanes won in 1943.

Hockey The Toronto Arenas joined the National Hockey League when it was founded in 1917. They were renamed the St. Pats in 1919, the Maple Leafs in 1926. Toronto won the Stanley Cup in 1918, 1922, 1932, 1942, 1945, 1947, 1948, 1949, 1951, 1962, 1963, 1964, and 1967. The Toronto Blueshirts won the Cup in 1914, before the NHL existed.

See also MAPLE LEAF GARDENS; SKYDOME, THE.

Touch Football

The origin of touch football can't be pinned down. There's some evidence that U.S. soldiers played a kind of touch football during both the Spanish-American War and World War I. Coach John W. Heisman at Georgia Tech had his teams scrimmage at touch football to avoid injury, but as an organized sport it developed during World War II as "the new army game." Millions of soldiers played it in all seasons at camps around the world, and when the war ended they brought the sport to colleges and playgrounds. It was originally an 11-player sport, but versions using anywhere from 6 to 9 players on a team were soon developed. (For some reason, there never seems to have been a 10-player version.) Touch football quickly became a very popular intramural sport on both the high school and college levels, and leagues were also organized in many communities. There are variations, such as two-hand touch and flag football, in which a defender "tackles" the ball-carrier by removing one of two flags that are tucked into his waistband.

The National Touch Football League, established in 1969, has 1200 member clubs in various community leagues across the country, and it sponsors a national tournament. The U.S. Flag Football League, founded as the U.S. Touch and Flag Football Association in 1982, has member leagues in about a dozen states.

Address: National Touch Football League, 1039 Coffey Court, Crestwood, MO 63126 (314) 621–0777

Tour de Trump
Cycling

Patterned after the Tour de France, this long-distance bicycle race was held for the first time in May 1989. The 837-mile race began May 5 in Albany, NY and finished May 14 at the Trump Plaza Hotel and Casino in Atlantic City, NJ. The 1990 race covered more than 1,100 miles in 11 days, winding through six northeastern states before finishing in Boston on May 13. Total prize money is $250,000.

Tournament Players Division
Golf

Golfers on the professional tour are far outnumbered by club professionals in the Professional Golfers Association. In 1968 they formed their own organization, American Professional Golfers, and announced plans to operate their own tour in 1969. Eventually a compromise was worked out with the PGA, and the Tournament Players Division was created as an autonomous affiliate. Under the leadership of a commissioner, the TPD has virtually total control over the tour, except for a few special tournaments such as the U.S. Open, which is conducted by the U.S. Golf Assocation.

See also PROFESSIONAL GOLFERS ASSOCIATION.

Town Ball
See MASSACHUSETTS GAME.

TPD
See TOURNAMENT PLAYERS DIVISION.

Track and Field

Track meets, including running and jumping events, were held in England early in the 19th century, and in 1842 the Olympic Club of Montreal was founded to conduct running races and other outdoor sports. Most of the weight-throwing events of modern track and field were taken from the traditional Caledonian Games, transplanted from Scotland. In addition to running and jumping, the Caledonian Games included hammer throwing, vaulting, and stone- or shot-putting. Brought to North America by Scottish immigrants during the 1850s, the Caledonian Games became popular spectator events. In 1857, more than 4,000 people watched the Montreal Caledonian Society's games in Guilbault's Gardens.

Princeton, which had many Scottish-American and Scots-born students, held a meet in 1859 which was probably the first in the United States. The New York Athletic Club was founded in 1868 to promote track competition. It held its first meet on November 11, 1868, and the New York Caledonian Club was invited to compete. From that point on, the Caledonian field events were a regular feature of meets.

Intercollegiate track began in 1873, when James Gordon Bennett offered a trophy worth $500 for a 2-mile run held in conjunction with the annual rowing regatta at Springfield, MA. There was so much interest that Bennett offered prizes for the 100-yard dash, 1-mile and 3-mile runs, 120-yard hurdles, and 7-mile walk in 1874. Ten colleges met on December 10, 1875, to form the Intercollegiate Association of Amateur Athletes of America (IC4A), which held its first meet in 1876.

The NYAC meet of 1876 was billed as the first national amateur track and field championships, and participation increased dramatically in 1878, when many college athletes entered. The National Association of Amateur Athletes of America, organized in 1879, took over the national championships that year. Professionalism was rampant, and the NAAAA couldn't deal with it. Establishing separate categories for professionals and amateurs brought criticism from the *New York Clipper*, which said in 1883 that

Organized in 1875, the Intercollegiate Association of Amateur Athletes of America still conducts a major track and field meet. This illustration of an early meet is from the June 18, 1881, Harper's Weekly.

the practice "will thereby cheapen their [amateurs'] popularity to such an extent that the public will not flock to see them at games given by their own clubs."

NAAAA member clubs continually bickered with one another about recruiting and illegal payments, and the 1883 meet had so few entrants that there was no competition in several events. After an NYAC athlete was barred for professionalism, the club withdrew from the NAAA in 1887 and joined with about a dozen other clubs to organize the Amateur Athletic Union. The AAU won the short struggle when the NAAAA disbanded in 1888.

Track and field became international in 1894, when a Yale team competed against Oxford at Queen's Grounds in London. Oxford narrowly won the meet with a victory in the final event. The following year, the NYAC hosted the London Athletic Club at a meet in New York and won all 11 events. In part because of the competition between the two countries, track and field events were on the first Olympic program in 1896, and have remained a staple of the Games.

The AAU held its first indoor championships meet in 1906. Women's events were added to the outdoor championships in 1923 and to the indoor championships in 1927, one year before women's track and field became an Olympic sport. The IC4A meet was the major intercollegiate championship event until 1921, when the NCAA held its first championship. The NCAA has also held an indoor meet since 1965, an outdoor meet for women since 1982, and an indoor women's meet since 1983.

See also AMATEUR ATHLETIC UNION; INTERCOLLEGIATE ASSOCIATION OF AMATEUR ATHLETES OF AMERICA; INTERNATIONAL TRACK ASSOCIATION; NATIONAL TRACK AND FIELD HALL OF FAME; NEW YORK ATHLETIC CLUB; PEDESTRIANISM; THE ATHLETICS CONGRESS.

Training Days

During the colonial period, New England towns periodically mustered the local militia for drill and target practice. Early in the 18th century, training days became virtual holidays, as spectators gathered to watch the drill. Target practice often became a true competition, with prizes ranging from a ribbon to a silver cup, and the men also took part in running and jumping contests, wrestling matches, and rough-and-tumble fighting. The training day was as close as colonial New England came to the traditional English holiday with its entertainment and folk games.

See also COLONIAL SPORTS.

Trampoline and Tumbling

Tumbling was an event on the national gymnastics championship program from 1885 until 1964. It became associated with trampoline after World War II because many competitors took part in both. The trampoline was originally created for circus entertainers, but the modern apparatus was developed by George Nissen in 1926. He patented an improved model in 1939, and trampolines were introduced into many gymnasiums after World War II. Trampoline and tumbling split off from the parent sport in 1964, and they are now governed by the Federation of International Trampoline's U.S. Technical Committee.

Address: U.S. Technical Committee, Federation of International Trampoline, 3121 Raintree, Rockford, IL 61111 (815) 877–9426

See also GYMNASTICS.

Trapshooting

Trapshooting is so called because birds were originally imprisoned in traps and then released as targets for hunters practising their marksmanship. The sport originated in England, where it was "a well established recreation" by 1793, according to a magazine article that year. In 1831, the Sportsmen's Club of Cincinnati began competitive shooting of quail and wild pigeons released from traps, and the Long Island Gun Club inaugurated trap shooting in 1840.

The sport declined during the 1850s, but after the Civil War Adam H. Bogardus helped reestablish its popularity. Better rifles also helped, as did the automatic trap, developed by Charles Portlock of Boston in 1866. The trap threw glass balls, 2½ inches in diameter, which made the sport humane and more accessible. Bogardus toured the Midwest, beating most local and regional champions, and was then matched against Ira Paine, generally considered the national champion. Bogardus lost to Paine early in 1871, but beat him later that year. He gave exhibition matches at Dexter Park in Chicago, attracting many sportsmen, and also wrote many newspaper and magazine articles promoting trapshooting.

George Ligowsky of Cincinnati developed the first practical clay pigeon in 1880, and an Englishman named McCaskey improved it by using a mixture of river silt and pitch. McCaskey also designed a better trap that helped make the sport internationally popular. The National Gun Club held the first national tournament at New Orleans in 1885, and by the end of the century there were hundreds of local trapshooting clubs throughout the country.

The Interstate Manufacturers' Trapshooting Association was founded in the late 1880s. The IMTA organized state leagues, each of which held a tournament, with the winners going to the national championship tournament. Renamed the American Trapshooting Association in 1922 and the Amateur Trapshooting Association in 1924, the organization is headquartered in Vandalia, OH, where it has a 97-acre site with more than 50 traps. The ATA conducts the Grand American tournament at Vandalia.

As an international sport, trapshooting is very different from the North American version, which uses just a single trap. International trap, also known as Olympic trench shooting, has 15 traps set in a trench. They're arranged in five groups of three each, and the shooter moves from one station to the next. The targets are smaller and thrown at a much greater variety of angles. To train shooters for that international competition, the National Rifle Association conducts "modified clay pigeon" shooting, which uses the smaller target and a single trap that can duplicate almost all of the angles of international trap.

Address: Amateur Trapshooting Association, 601 West National Road, Vandalia, OH 45377 (513) 898-4638

See also SHOOTING; SKEET SHOOTING.

Traynor, "Pie" Harold J. (1899–1972)
Baseball

Born November 11, 1899, Framingham, MA; died March 16, 1972; Baseball Hall of Fame

Generally considered the greatest third baseman before Brooks Robinson came along, Traynor played briefly at shortstop for the Pittsburgh Pirates in 1920 and 1921, and he opened the 1922 season at that position. But in June he was moved to third, where he spent the rest of his career. Traynor had great range to his left, allowing the Pittsburgh shortstop to play closer to second base than normal, and he

was also expert at making diving stops of balls hit down the line.

And he could hit. Traynor batted .338 in 1923, with 208 hits, 108 runs scored, 101 runs batted in, and a league-leading 19 triples. That was the first of ten seasons in which he batted over .300, and the first of seven in which he had more than 100 runs batted in. He had four straight outstanding seasons from 1927 through 1930, hitting .342, .337, .356, and .366, driving in more than 100 runs each year.

Traynor become Pittsburgh's playing manager during the 1934 season, when he hurt his throwing arm while sliding. The injury limited his playing time in 1935. He didn't play at all in 1936 and appeared in only five games the following season. Traynor managed the club through the 1939 season. In his 16 major-league seasons, he had a .320 average. Sportswriters in 1969 named him the greatest third baseman of baseball's first 100 years.

Triathlon

This grueling sport began with a bet in 1978, when 15 men decided to compete in the Waikiki Roughwater Swim, the Around Oahu Bike Race, and the Honolulu Marathon all in the same day. That informal event soon became the Hawaii Ironman Triathlon. After ABC televised portions of the 1982 race, the sport took off; there are now an estimated 750,000 triathletes and more than 2,000 races worldwide. The Hawaii triathlon includes a 2.4-mile swim, a 112-mile bike race, and a standard 26-mile, 385-yard marathon. There is also a short-course triathlon, which includes a 1.5-kilometer swim, 40-kilometer bike ride, and 10-kilometer run.

Address: Triathlon Federation/U.S.A., P.O. Box 1010, Colorado Springs, CO 80901 (719) 630–2255

Tri-Cities

Basketball The Tri-Cities Blackhawks, representing Moline, IL, Rock Island, IL, and Davenport, IA, were in the National Basketball League beginning in 1946. The NBL merged with the Basketball Association of America in 1949 to create the National Basketball Association. The Tri-Cities team was in the NBA until 1951, when the franchise moved to St. Louis and became the Hawks.

Tripartite Pact
See NATIONAL AGREEMENT.

Triple Jump

The modern triple jump originated as the hop, step, and jump, a more-or-less standard event in the Caledonian Games. It has been on the Olympic program since the first modern Games in 1896. The triple jump was in the U.S. national track and field championships in 1893, then was dropped until 1906. Daniel Ahearn of the United States was the first to break the 50-foot mark, in 1909; no one has ever exceeded 60 feet.

Trotting

See HARNESS RACING.

Trotting Register

John H. Wallace established the *Trotting Register* in 1871 as harness racing's stud book. It originally listed any horse that had trotted or paced a mile in less than 2 minutes 30 seconds, or had produced progeny that met that standard, and the harness breed became known as the Standardbred. The *Register* was taken over by the National Association of Trotting Horse Breeders in 1879 and later the American Trotting Register Association was organized to maintain it. The ATRA became defunct in 1924; two years later, the *Register* was taken over by the Trotting Horse Club of America, which turned it over to the U.S. Trotting Association when it was founded in 1938. The current standard is 2:20 for a two-year-old and 2:15 for an older horse.

Troy, NY

Baseball The Troy Haymakers were notorious for throwing games during the late 1860s and early 1870s. Controlled by a group of gamblers headed by John C. Morrissey, the team walked off the field after the sixth inning of an 1869 game with the Cincinnati Red Stockings so their owners wouldn't lose a bet. The Haymakers played in the National League from 1879 through 1882.

Tumbling

See TRAMPOLINE AND TUMBLING.

Turner Movement

The Turner movement was founded by Friedrich Ludwig Jahn in 1811, when he opened a *Turnplatz* in Berlin. Jahn coined the word *turnen*, meaning gymnastics or, as a verb, to do gymnastics. Jahn also campaigned for a united Germany under a constitution, and that campaign became associated with turners in general.

Two of Jahn's disciples, Carl Beck and Carl Follen, came to the United States in 1824. Beck was a founder of the Round Hill School in Northampton, MA, where he established the first gym in North America. Follen taught there until 1826, when he went to Harvard and built the first college gym. The Jahn system of gymnastics used a variety of apparatus, much of which is still part of gymnastics: single and parallel bars, a wooden horse, rope ladders, and dumbbells.

In Germany, most Turners supported the revolution of 1848 and many of them emigrated to the United States when it failed. The Cincinnati Turngemeinde was organized in November of 1848, and societies were established in Baltimore and Philadelphia the following year. In 1851 the Philadelphia society held a gymnastics festival for all the country's societies, and they formed a national organization, the *Socialistischer Turnerbund*. By the end of that year, there were 22 societies in the country.

Internal dissension reduced membership in the national organization during the late 1850s, but the movement made a comeback after the Civil War, and in 1867 there were 108 societies with more than 10,000 members. The Turner movement was largely responsible for the rise of gymnastics beginning in the 1870s, and Turners also helped establish physical education programs in many schools. Dr. Edward M. Hartwell, in a report to the U.S. Commissioner of Education in 1898, commented, "The more or less successful introduction of school gymnastics, since 1884, by the cities of Chicago, Kansas City, Cleveland, Denver, Indianapolis, St. Louis, Milwaukee, Cincinnati, St. Paul, San Francisco, and Boston . . . has been chiefly due to the zeal and insistence of the advocates of the German and Swedish systems of gymnastics. . . . In every city named above, except Boston, German free and light gymnastics had been adopted, and the directors of physical education were graduates of the Seminary or Normal School of the American *Turnerbund*."

Further Reading: Metzner, Henry. *History of the American Turners*. Rochester, NY: National Council of the American Turners, 1974.

Address: American Turners, 2503 South Preston Street, P.O. Box 17345, Louisville, KY 40217 (502) 636–2395.

USAC
See U.S. AUTO CLUB.

Ultimate Frisbee
See FRISBEE.

Union Association
Baseball

Henry V. Lucas of St. Louis was the driving force behind the Union Association, which was organized on September 12, 1883. Lucas had hoped to get a St. Louis franchise in an existing major league, but was blocked because the city already had a team in the American Association. The new league, which honored existing contracts but not the reserve clause, signed about 30 major-league players, although some of them went back to their original teams when organized baseball threatened to blacklist anyone who jumped to the unions. The National League and American Association also set up "reserve teams" of young amateur and semiprofessional players to keep them away from the Union Association.

The Association began play in 1884 with teams in Altoona, Baltimore, Boston, Chicago, Cincinnati, Philadelphia, St. Louis, and Washington. Altoona lasted only six weeks and was replaced by Kansas City; the Chicago team moved to Pittsburgh in August and was replaced by a St. Paul team in September; and the Philadelphia team, which folded in August, was replaced by Wilmington, which in turn was replaced by Milwaukee. Lucas' St. Louis team won the pennant easily with a 91–16 won-lost record, 21 games ahead of its nearest competitor, which virtually destroyed fan interest by midseason. Only two clubs were represented at the Union Association's meeting on January 15, 1885, and they voted to disband. Lucas was given a St. Louis franchise in the National League that season.

Union Course
Long Island, NY

The New York Legislature in 1821 passed a bill legalizing horse racing for two meets a year in Queens County, after the sport had been prohibited for nearly 20 years. The New York Association for the Improvement of the Breed built the Union Course, which opened in October of 1821. The biggest race ever held at the track was the May 27, 1823, contest between American Eclipse, representing the North, and Henry, representing the South. The underdog Henry won the first 4-mile heat, but Eclipse won the next two heats and the race. Horse racing declined during the latter part of the decade, and the Union Course fell into disrepair. An NYAIB member, Cadwallader Colden, took the track over in 1829. He enclosed it and began charging admission, a novelty at the time, and offered prize money of $5,000 a year. On October 20, 1830, the scheduled race was canceled because money wasn't available for the purse, and the spectators rioted. Colden then resigned, and the NYAIB resumed control of the course.

Alexander L. Botts of Virginia bought the Union Course in 1833 and shortly afterward took another Virginian, David H. Branch, as a partner. They operated the track successfully for nine years, running 107 races for purses totaling $54,000. But racing again fell on hard times about 1840, and Henry K. Toler of New Jersey took over in 1842, after Botts and Branch had returned to Virginia. The course hosted a second major intersectional race, between the North's Fashion and the South's Boston, on May 20, 1842. According to New York newspapers, more than 50,000 people watched Fashion win in two straight heats, the first of them with a world record for 4 miles.

There was a third and final intersectional contest at the Union Course in 1845, Fashion again representing the North against a new Southern challenger, Peytona. This time the southern horse won in straight heats. The crowd was estimated at 70,000 to 100,000. However, the capacity of Union Course is believed to have been only about 5,000, including 2,000 in the grandstand and 3,000 standing, so the newspaper estimates were probably greatly inflated.

During the 1850s, Union Course became a successful harness racing track, as that sport replaced Thoroughbred racing in popularity.

Union Grounds
Brooklyn, NY

William H. Cammeyer converted a skating rink into the first enclosed baseball field in 1862. He allowed baseball clubs to use the Union Grounds free of charge, but he collected a 10-cent admission fee. It was the first time admission was regularly charged for the sport (there had been a 50-cent admission for an 1858 game between all-star teams from New York and Brooklyn). In 1867, the price rose to 25 cents, with Cammeyer collecting 40 percent of the gate receipts plus expenses from the Brooklyn Atlantics, one of the top teams of the period. Cammeyer later became president of the New York Mutuals, a National Association team, which also played at the Union Grounds.

Unions

See PLAYERS ASSOCIATIONS.

United Golfers Association (UGA)

Banned from most country clubs, a group of black black golf-playing doctors from Washington, DC met at Stowe, MA in 1926 to organize their own tournament. Two years later the United Golfers Association was founded to run the tournament and a small professional tour. The UGA added a women's championship in 1930. Most of the black golfers who eventually joined the Professional Golfers' Association tour, including Lee Elder, Calvin Peete, and Jim Thorpe, got their early training in UGA tournaments.

Address: 321 Congress, Indianapolis, IN 46208 (317) 925–8135

United States

See entries beginning with U.S.

U.S. Auto Club

The American Automobile Association controlled auto racing in the United States until 1957, when USAC was founded. USAC inherited a broad schedule of racing, including the Indianapolis 500 and other races for Indy cars. A group of car owners in 1978 formed Championship Auto Racing Teams, Inc., and CART began its own racing for Indy cars the following year. USAC then voted to reject Indianapolis 500 entries from any owners who had entered the first CART race, but a federal district judge enjoined the banning on antitrust grounds. CART and USAC briefly cooperated as the Championship Racing League in 1980, but the partnership folded after five races and CART took over the rest of the schedule. The following year, CART took over all Indy car racing except for the Indianapolis 500 itself, which is cosanctioned by the two groups. USAC also sanctions about 200 races annually for midget, sprint, and late model cars.

Address: 4910 West 16th Street, Speedway, IN 46224–0001 (317) 247–5151.

See also CHAMPIONSHIP AUTO RACING TEAMS, INC.; INDIANAPOLIS MOTOR SPEEDWAY.

U.S. Basketball Writers Association (USBWA)

The USBWA was founded on September 14, 1956, in Chicago, primarily to work for better press box facilities and standardized compilation of statistics. Open to professional writers who cover college and professional basketball, the association has about 1,000 members. Since 1959, the USBWA has presented awards to the College Coach of the Year and the College Player of the Year.

Address: 200 North Broadway, Suite 1905, St. Louis, MO 63102 (314) 421–0339

U.S. Golf Association (USGA)

The U.S. Golf Association of America was founded in 1895, a year after the Newport (RI) Golf Club and the St. Andrew's Golf Club of Yonkers had both held what they called national championships. The USGA held the first true national amateur championship at Newport in October of 1895, followed by the first U.S. Open, and in November the first women's amateur championship was conducted at the Meadowbrook Golf Club on Long Island.

The USGA still conducts those three championships, and in 1953 it took over the U.S. Women's Open from the Women's Professional Golfers' Association. It inaugurated the Junior Amateur championship in 1948, the Girl's Junior Amateur in 1949, the Senior Amateur in 1955, and the Senior Women's Amateur in 1962. The association also selects and funds national teams for the Walker and Curtis Cup matches, operates a museum and golf library, and maintains a national handicapping system. There are now about 5,500 member clubs and courses.

Address: Golf House, Far Hills, NJ 07931 (201) 234–2300

See also U.S. NATIONAL AMATEUR CHAMPIONSHIP; U.S. OPEN; U.S. WOMEN'S AMATEUR CHAMPIONSHIP; U.S. WOMEN'S OPEN.

U.S. Hockey Hall of Fame

Eveleth, MN calls itself the "amateur hockey capital of the United States," and in 1973 the city's civic association received permission from the Amateur Hockey Association to establish the U.S. Hockey Hall of Fame. The hall is housed in a city-owned three-story building that includes many exhibits on the history of U.S. hockey.

Address: P.O. Box 657, Hat Trick Avenue, Eveleth, MN 55734 (218) 744–5167

See also HOCKEY HALL OF FAME.

U.S. Lawn Tennis Association

See U.S. TENNIS ASSOCIATION.

U.S. National Amateur Championship
Golf

The U.S. Golf Association held its first National Amateur Championship at the Newport (RI) Golf Club in 1895. The tournament was at match play until 1965, when it became a 72-hole medal play event.

National Amateur Champions

1895	Charles B. MacDonald
1896	H. J. Whigham
1897	H. J. Whigham
1898	Findlay Douglas
1899	H. M. Harriman
1900	Walter Travis
1901	Walter Travis
1902	Louis James
1903	Walter Travis
1904	H. Chandler Egan
1905	H. Chandler Egan
1906	Eben Byers
1907	Jerome Travers
1908	Jerome Travers
1909	Robert Gardner
1910	W. C. Fownes, Jr.
1911	Harold Hilton
1912	Jerome Travers
1913	Jerome Travers
1914	Francis Ouimet
1915	Robert Gardner
1916	Chick Evans
1917	Not Held
1918	Not Held
1919	Davidson Herron
1920	Chick Evans
1921	Jesse Guilford
1922	Jess Sweetser
1923	Max Marston
1924	Bobby Jones
1925	Bobby Jones
1926	George Von Elm
1927	Bobby Jones
1928	Bobby Jones
1929	Harrison Johnson
1930	Bobby Jones
1931	Francis Ouimet
1932	Ross Somerville
1933	George Dunlap
1934	Lawson Little
1935	Lawson Little
1936	John Fischer

1937	John Goodman
1938	William Turnesa
1939	Bud Ward
1940	Richard Chapman
1941	Bud Ward
1942	Not Held
1943	Not Held
1944	Not Held
1945	Not Held
1946	Ted Bishop
1947	Skee Riegel
1948	William Turnesa
1949	Charles Coe
1950	Sam Urzetta
1951	Billy Maxwell
1952	Jack Westland
1953	Gene Littler
1954	Arnold Palmer
1955	Harvie Ward
1956	Harvie Ward
1957	Hillman Robbins
1958	Charles Coe
1959	Jack Nicklaus
1960	Deane Beman
1961	Bill Campbell
1962	Labron Harris
1963	Deane Beman
1964	Bill Campbell
1965	Bob Murphy
1966	Gary Cowan
1967	Bob Dickson
1968	Bruce Fleisher
1969	Steve Melnyk
1970	Lanny Wadkins
1971	Gary Cowan
1972	Vinnie Giles
1973	Craig Stadler
1974	Jerry Pate
1975	Fred Ridley
1976	Bill Sander
1977	John Fought
1978	John Cook
1979	Mark O'Mara
1980	Hal Sutton
1981	Nathaniel Crosby
1982	Jay Sigel
1983	Jay Sigel
1984	Scott Verplank
1985	Sam Randolph
1986	Buddy Alexander
1987	Billy Mayfair
1988	Eric Meeks
1989	Chris Patton
1990	Phil Mickelson

U.S. National Ski Hall of Fame

Founded by the U.S. Ski Association in 1954, the USSA's 50th anniversary, this hall of fame is misnamed, because many of its inductees are Canadians. Located at the USSA complex in Ishpeming, MI, the hall boasts the 1,000-volume Roland Palmedo National Ski Library. A fund-raising drive is underway to construct a $1.3 million building.

Address: P.O. Box 191, Ishpeming, MI 49849–0191 (906) 486–9281

U.S. Olympic Committee (USOC)

The American Olympic Committee was created by the Amateur Athletic Union in 1896, the year the first modern Olympics were held, but the committee was essentially inactive until the 1906 "intercalated" Games in Greece, when it selected an official team for the first time. Teams were at first dominated by track and field athletes. At a meeting on December 12, 1918, the AOC decided to reorganize by adding representatives from various organizations involved in Olympic sports, including the armed services and the National Collegiate Athletic Association. The AAU dominated the new committee with nine representatives, while no other organization had more than one.

The 1920 track and field team sailed to Antwerp aboard an army transport ship with limited accommodations and poor food. When the athletes arrived, they learned that they were to be quartered in an abandoned schoolhouse. One of them wrote, "Sanitation was conspicuously absent . . . drinking water was terrible." Triple jumper Dan Ahearn rented a room elsewhere and was suspended by the AOC. More than 200 athletes then signed a petition demanding better accommodations and Ahearn's reinstatement, threatening to stay out of the competition.

Judge Bartow S. Weeks met with the team. "You must carry on," he told them. "The committee must carry on. What would you do if the committee quit?" One of the athletes shouted, "Get a better one." Ahearn was eventually reinstated, and the athletes took part in the Olympics, even though their accommodations weren't improved. But after the Games, there was a move to get a better committee. The AOC had been inactive between Olympiads; it now formed the American Olympic Association as an ongoing organization to raise funds and oversee the U.S. Olympic effort. Again, the AAU was dominant, with a total of 33 votes, while each other member organization had only 3 votes. The army, navy, NCAA, and YMCA refused to join the AOA until 1922, when it was restructured to give them more representation.

However, feuding continued until 1927, when the navy, the NCAA, the YMCA, the National Amateur Athletic Federation, and other organizations resigned from the AOA. Representatives of the NCAA and AOA met on December 30, 1929, to resolve their differences, and the AOA once again reorganized in 1930. The executive committee had three representatives each from the AAU and the NCAA, while other member groups each had one representative; ten other representatives were to be selected by a two-thirds vote. After the 1936 Olympics, the AOA established separate committees to select and administer teams in boxing, gymnastics, swimming, track, and wrestling.

The Pan-American Games, scheduled to begin in 1941, were canceled because of World War II, but the AOA that year became the United States of America Sports Federation, with separate Olympic and Pan-American Games Committees. In 1946, the name changed once again, to the U.S. Olympic Association; it became the U.S. Olympic Committee in 1952.

Relations between the USOC and the NCAA began to break down again during the late 1950s. The NCAA backed the formation of individual sports federations independent of the AAU. Federations were established for baseball, men's and women's basketball, gymnastics, track and field, and wrestling, but they were denied representation on the USOC in 1969. After the 1972 Olympics, the NCAA voted to withdraw from the committee. Walter Byers, executive director of the NCAA, commented, "The situation is worse now than in the Sixties. The only external force that has the clout to bring about reorganization is the agency that gave the USOC its original charter, Congress."

The Senate in 1974 passed the Amateur Athletic Act that would have created a five-member national Amateur Sports Board appointed by the president. The board would have had the power to revoke the charters of any national governing bodies, including the IOC, and to issue new charters to qualified organizations. The House of Representatives never voted on the act, however, and Lord Killanin, president of the International Olympic Committee, pointed out that the IOC opposes direct government intervention in Olympic matters.

President Gerald Ford in 1975 appointed a Commission on Olympic Sports to study the problem. After a year of study, the commission issued a 613-page report. Most of its recommendations were incorporated into the Amateur Sports Act of 1978. The act completely reorganized the USOC as a central policy-making and coordinating body for U.S. involvement in international competition. It also required that the national governing body for each Olympic sport must be autonomous and separately incorporated by the end of 1980. That effectively ended the AAU's long reign over many amateur sports, giving control to the NCAA-supported federations and other independent groups.

The USOC, headquartered in Colorado Springs, is now a federation of governing bodies representing all Olympic and Pan-American Games sports. It also includes representation from several other groups, including the AAU, NCAA, and YMCA. The committee operates three Olympic training centers and conducts the U.S. Olympic Festival, which is held in every non-Olympic year.

Address: 1776 East Boulder Street, Colorado Springs, CO 80909 (719) 632–5551

U.S. Open
Golf

The first U.S. Open tournament was held on October 4, 1895, at the Newport (RI) Golf Club. One amateur and ten professionals entered the one-day, 36-hole tournament. It became a 72-hole event in 1898. There were so many entries by 1924 that sectional qualifying rounds were introduced to narrow the field. All 150 starters play the first 36 holes, and the field is then cut to the top 60, including any players tied for 60th.

U.S. Open Champions

1895	Horace Rawlins
1896	James Foulis
1897	Joe Lloyd
1898	Fred Herd
1899	Willie Smith
1900	Harry Vardon
1901	Willie Anderson
1902	Lawrence Auchterlonie
1903	Willie Anderson
1904	Willie Anderson
1905	Willie Anderson
1906	Alex Smith
1907	Alex Ross
1908	Fred McLeod
1909	George Sargent
1910	Alex Smith
1911	John McDermott
1912	John McDermott
1913	Francis Ouimet
1914	Walter Hagen
1915	Jerome Travers
1916	Chick Evans
1917	Not Held
1918	Not Held
1919	Walter Hagen
1920	Edward Ray
1921	James Barnes
1922	Gene Sarazen
1923	Bobby Jones
1924	Cyril Walker
1925	William Macfarlane
1926	Bobby Jones
1927	Tommy Armour
1928	Johnny Farrell
1929	Bobby Jones
1930	Bobby Jones
1931	Billy Burke
1932	Gene Sarazen
1933	John Goodman
1934	Olin Dutra
1935	Sam Parks, Jr.
1936	Tony Manero
1937	Ralph Guldahl
1938	Ralph Guldahl
1939	Byron Nelson
1940	Lawson Little
1941	Craig Wood
1942	Not Held
1943	Not Held
1944	Not Held
1945	Not Held
1946	Lloyd Mangrum
1947	Lew Worsham
1948	Ben Hogan
1949	Cary Middlecoff
1950	Ben Hogan
1951	Ben Hogan
1952	Julius Boros
1953	Ben Hogan
1954	Ed Furgol
1955	Jack Fleck
1956	Cary Middlecoff
1957	Dick Mayer
1958	Tommy Bolt
1959	Billy Casper, Jr.
1960	Arnold Palmer
1961	Gene Littler
1962	Jack Nicklaus
1963	Julius Boros
1964	Ken Venturi
1965	Gary Player
1966	Billy Casper, Jr.
1967	Jack Nicklaus
1968	Lee Trevino
1969	Orville Moody
1970	Tony Jacklin
1971	Lee Trevino

1972	Jack Nicklaus	1898	Malcolm D. Whitman
1973	Johnny Miller	1899	Malcolm D. Whitman
1974	Hale Irwin	1900	Malcolm D. Whitman
1975	Lou Graham	1901	William A. Larned
1976	Jerry Pate	1902	William A. Larned
1977	Hubert Green	1903	Hugh L. Doherty
1978	Andy North	1904	Holcombe Ward
1979	Hale Irwin	1905	Beals C. Wright
1980	Jack Nicklaus	1906	William J. Clothier
1981	David Graham	1907	William A. Larned
1982	Tom Watson	1908	William A. Larned
1983	Larry Nelson	1909	William A. Larned
1984	Fuzzy Zoeller	1910	William A. Larned
1985	Andy North	1911	William A. Larned
1986	Ray Floyd	1912	Maurice E. McLoughlin
1987	Scott Simpson	1913	Maurice E. McLoughlin
1988	Curtis Strange	1914	R. Norris Williams II
1989	Curtis Strange	1915	William Johnston
1990	Hale Irwin	1916	R. Norris Williams II
1991	Payne Stewart	1917	R. Lindley Murray
		1918	R. Lindley Murray

U.S. Open

Tennis

The U.S. Lawn Tennis Association held its first national championships in men's singles and doubles on August 31, 1881, at the Casino Club in Newport, RI. There were 26 entrants. The women's singles championship was added in 1887, women's doubles in 1890, and mixed doubles in 1892. From 1885 until 1912, the winner of the tournament became the challenger, who then played the defending champion for the national title. In 1968 and 1969, there was a national tournament, from which contract professionals were barred, and an open tournament. Since 1970, the tournament has been the U.S. Open, for amateurs and professionals.

U.S. Open Champions—Men's Singles

1881	Richard D. Sears	1919	William Johnston
1882	Richard D. Sears	1920	William T. Tilden II
1883	Richard D. Sears	1921	William T. Tilden II
1884	Richard D. Sears	1922	William T. Tilden II
1885	Richard D. Sears	1923	William T. Tilden II
1886	Richard D. Sears	1924	William T. Tilden II
1887	Richard D. Sears	1925	William T. Tilden II
1888	Henry W. Slocum, Jr.	1926	Rene Lacoste
1889	Henry W. Slocum, Jr.	1927	Rene Lacoste
1890	Oliver S. Campbell	1928	Henri Cochet
1891	Oliver S. Campbell	1929	William T. Tilden II
1892	Oliver S. Campbell	1930	John H. Doeg
1893	Robert D. Wrenn	1931	H. Ellsworth Vines, Jr.
1894	Robert D. Wrenn	1932	H. Ellsworth Vines, Jr.
1895	Fred H. Hovey	1933	Frederick J. Perry
1896	Robert D. Wrenn	1934	Frederick J. Perry
1897	Robert D. Wrenn	1935	Wilmer L. Allison
		1936	Frederick J. Perry
		1937	J. Donald Budge
		1938	J. Donald Budge
		1939	Robert L. Riggs
		1940	Donald McNeill
		1941	Robert L. Riggs
		1942	Frederick R. Schroeder, Jr.
		1943	Joseph R. Hunt
		1944	Frank A. Parker
		1945	Frank A. Parker
		1946	John A. Kramer
		1947	John A. Kramer
		1948	Pancho Gonzalez
		1949	Pancho Gonzalez
		1950	Arthur Larsen
		1951	Frank Sedgman
		1952	Frank Sedgman

1953	Tony Trabert
1954	E. Victor Seixas, Jr.
1955	Tony Trabert
1956	Ken Rosewall
1957	Mal Anderson
1958	Ashley Cooper
1959	Neale Fraser
1960	Neale Fraser
1961	Roy Emerson
1962	Rod Laver
1963	Rafael Osuna
1964	Roy Emerson
1965	Manuel Santana
1966	Fred Stolle
1967	John Newcombe
1968	Arthur Ashe (Open and National)
1969	Rod Laver (Open)
1969	Stan Smith (National)
1970	Ken Rosewall
1971	Stan Smith
1972	Ilie Nastase
1973	John Newcombe
1974	Jimmy Connors
1975	Manuel Orantes
1976	Jimmy Connors
1977	Guillermo Vilas
1978	Jimmy Connors
1979	John McEnroe
1980	John McEnroe
1981	John McEnroe
1982	Jimmy Connors
1983	Jimmy Connors
1984	John McEnroe
1985	Ivan Lendl
1986	Ivan Lendl
1987	Ivan Lendl
1988	Mats Wilander
1989	Boris Becker
1990	Pete Sampras

U.S. Open Champions—Women's Singles

1887	Ellen F. Hansell
1888	Bertha L. Townsend
1889	Bertha L. Townsend
1890	Ellen C. Roosevelt
1891	Mabel E. Cahill
1892	Mabel E. Cahill
1893	Aline M. Terry
1894	Helen R. Helwig
1895	Juliet P. Atkinson
1896	Elisabeth H. Moore
1897	Juliet P. Atkinson
1898	Juliet P. Atkinson
1899	Marion Jones
1900	Myrtle McAteer

1901	Elisabeth H. Moore
1902	Marion Jones
1903	Elisabeth H. Moore
1904	May G. Sutton
1905	Elisabeth H. Moore
1906	Helen Homans
1907	Evelyn Sears
1908	Maud Barger-Wallach
1909	Hazel V. Hotchkiss
1910	Hazel V. Hotchkiss
1911	Hazel V. Hotchkiss
1912	Mary K. Browne
1913	Mary K. Browne
1914	Mary K. Browne
1915	Molla Bjurstedt
1916	Molla Bjurstedt
1917	Molla Bjurstedt
1918	Molla Bjurstedt
1919	Hazel Hotchkiss Wightman
1920	Molla Bjurstedt Mallory
1921	Molla Bjurstedt Mallory
1922	Molla Bjurstedt Mallory
1923	Helen Wills
1924	Helen Wills
1925	Helen Wills
1926	Molla Bjurstedt Mallory
1927	Helen Wills
1928	Helen Wills
1929	Helen Wills
1930	Betty Nuthall
1931	Helen Wills Moody
1932	Helen Hull Jacobs
1933	Helen Hull Jacobs
1934	Helen Hull Jacobs
1935	Helen Hull Jacobs
1936	Alice Marble
1937	Anita Lizana
1938	Alice Marble
1939	Alice Marble
1940	Alice Marble
1941	Sarah Palfrey Cooke
1942	Pauline M. Betz
1943	Pauline M. Betz
1944	Pauline M. Betz
1945	Sarah Palfrey Cooke
1946	Pauline M. Betz
1947	Louise Brough
1948	Margaret Osborne duPont
1949	Margaret Osborne duPont
1950	Margaret Osborne duPont
1951	Maureen Connolly
1952	Maureen Connolly
1953	Maureen Connolly
1954	Doris Hart
1955	Doris Hart

1956	Shirley Fry
1957	Althea Gibson
1958	Althea Gibson
1959	Maria Bueno
1960	Darlene Hard
1961	Darlene Hard
1962	Margaret Smith
1963	Maria Bueno
1964	Maria Bueno
1965	Margaret Smith
1966	Maria Bueno
1967	Billie Jean King
1968	Virginia Wade (Open)
1968	Margaret Smith Court (National)
1969	Margaret Smith Court (Open and National)
1970	Margaret Smith Court
1971	Billie Jean King
1972	Billie Jean King
1973	Margaret Smith Court
1974	Billie Jean King
1975	Chris Evert
1976	Chris Evert
1977	Chris Evert
1978	Chris Evert
1979	Tracy Austin
1980	Chris Evert Lloyd
1981	Tracy Austin
1982	Chris Evert Lloyd
1983	Martina Navratilova
1984	Martina Navratilova
1985	Hana Mandlikova
1986	Martina Navratilova
1987	Martina Navratilova
1988	Steffi Graf
1989	Steffi Graf
1990	Gabriela Sabatini
1991	Steffi Graf

U.S. Tennis Association (USTA)

The rules of tennis were changing so rapidly during its early years that many clubs couldn't keep up with them. On May 21, 1881, 19 clubs were represented at a meeting in New York at which the U.S. Lawn Tennis Association was founded. Members agreed to adopt the rules of the All-England Croquet and Lawn Tennis Club and to use the standard English ball. The USLTA also decided to hold the first national championships at the Casino Club in Newport, RI on August 31.

Like the Amateur Athletic Union, the USLTA was committed to simon-pure amateurism, at least in theory, and its officials often got involved in controversy over the issue. The most celebrated case arose in 1928, when Bill Tilden was suspended for writing accounts of the Wimbledon tournament, where he was playing, a violation of the USLTA's "player-writer" rule. Tilden was suspended shortly before he was to play for the U.S. Davis Cup team in France. The French were outraged, and the U.S. ambassador finally intervened to get the suspension lifted until after the Davis Cup matches.

The association also developed a reputation for treating players high-handedly, especially after World War II, when tennis began to develop as a popular sport. Officials once tried to break up a romance between two players, Karen Hantze and Rod Susman, because they were afraid Hantze's tennis would suffer. Instead, they got married and retired from competitive tennis. In 1967, the USLTA refused to give Billie Jean King permission to play in Europe because she was needed to draw spectators to the association's grass court tournaments. "Tournament promoters used us as cheap labor," King later wrote.

The USLTA lost much of its control over the sport when Wimbledon became an open tournament in 1967, followed by the U.S. national tournament a year later. Most of the world's top players quickly turned professional, and they put together their own organizations—the men's Association of Tennis Professionals in 1972 and the Women's International Tennis Association in 1973. These groups were essentially independent of the USLTA, since as international organizations they could work directly with the International Lawn Tennis Federation.

The USLTA became simply the U.S. Tennis Association in 1975. With professional tennis players by and large controlling their own destiny, the USTA now conducts just a few major tournaments, including the U.S. Open; its chief strength is in junior tennis, since players must remain amateurs at least until they turn 14.

Address: 1212 Avenue of the Americas, New York, NY 10036 (212) 302-3322

U.S. Women's Amateur Championship
Golf

The first U.S. Women's Amateur Championship was held by the U.S. Golf Association at the Meadowbrook Club in Westbury, Long Island, on November 9, 1895. Thirteen competitors took part in the 18-hole stroke play tournament. Since 1896, it has been a match play tournament preceded by two 18-hole qualifying rounds.

Women's Amateur Champions

1895	Mrs. Charles S. Brown
1896	Beatrix Hoyt
1897	Beatrix Hoyt
1898	Beatrix Hoyt
1899	Ruth Underhill

1900	Frances Griscom
1901	Genevieve Hecker
1902	Genevieve Hecker
1903	Bessie Anthony
1904	Georgianna Bishop
1905	Pauline Mackay
1906	Harriot Curtis
1907	Margaret Curtis
1908	Katherine Harley
1909	Dorothy Campbell
1910	Dorothy Campbell
1911	Margaret Curtis
1912	Margaret Curtis
1913	Gladys Ravenscroft
1914	Katherine Harley
1915	Florence Vanderbeck
1916	Alexis Stirling
1917	Not Held
1918	Not Held
1919	Alexis Stirling
1920	Alexis Stirling
1921	Marion Hollins
1922	Glenna Collet
1923	Edith Cummings
1924	Dorothy Campbell Hurd
1925	Glenna Collet
1926	Helen Stetson
1927	Miriam Burns Horn
1928	Glenna Collet
1929	Glenna Collet
1930	Glenna Collet
1931	Helen Hicks
1932	Virginia Van Wie
1933	Virginia Van Wie
1934	Virginia Van Wie
1935	Glenna Collet Vare
1936	Pamela Barton
1937	Estelle Lawson
1938	Patty Berg
1939	Betty Jameson
1940	Betty Jameson
1941	Elizabeth Hicks
1942	Not Held
1943	Not Held
1944	Not Held
1945	Not Held
1946	Babe Didrikson Zaharias
1947	Louise Suggs
1948	Grace Lenczyk
1949	Dorothy Porter
1950	Beverly Hanson
1951	Dorothy Kirby
1952	Jacqueline Pung
1953	Mary Lena Faulk
1954	Barbara Romack

1955	Patricia Lesser
1956	Marlene Stuart
1957	JoAnne Gunderson
1958	Anne Quast
1959	Barbara McIntire
1960	JoAnne Gunderson
1961	Anne Quast Decker
1962	JoAnne Gunderson
1963	Anne Quast Welts
1964	Barbara McIntire
1965	Jean Ashley
1966	JoAnne Gunderson Carner
1967	Mary Lou Dill
1968	JoAnne Gunderson Carner
1969	Catherine Lacoste
1970	Martha Wilkinson
1971	Laura Baugh
1972	Mary Budke
1973	Carol Sempel
1974	Cynthia Hill
1975	Beth Daniel
1976	Donna Horton
1977	Beth Daniel
1978	Cathy Sherk
1979	Caroline Hill
1980	Julie Inkster
1981	Julie Inkster
1982	Julie Inkster
1983	Joanne Pacillo
1984	Deb Richard
1985	Michiko Hattori
1986	Kay Cockerill
1987	Kay Cockerill
1988	Pearl Sinn
1989	Vicki Goetze
1990	Pat Hurst

U.S. Women's Open Golf

The Women's Professional Golfers' Association established the U.S. Women's Open in 1946, when it was held at the Spokane (WA) Country Club. The Ladies' Professional Golfers' Association took over in 1949. Since 1953, the U.S. Golf Association has conducted the tournament. It was a match play event in its first year, but has been a 72-hole stroke play tournament since 1947.

U.S. Women's Open Champions

1946	Patty Berg
1947	Betty Jameson
1948	Babe Didrikson Zaharias
1949	Louise Suggs
1950	Babe Didrikson Zaharias
1951	Betsy Rawls

1952	Louise Suggs
1953	Betsy Rawls
1954	Babe Didrikson Zaharias
1955	Fay Crocker
1956	Kathy Cornelius
1957	Betsy Rawls
1958	Mickey Wright
1959	Mickey Wright
1960	Betsy Rawls
1961	Mickey Wright
1962	Murie Lindstrom
1963	Mary Mills
1964	Mickey Wright
1965	Carol Mann
1966	Sandra Spuzich
1967	Catherine Lacoste
1968	Susie Maxwell Berning
1969	Donna Caponi
1970	Donna Caponi
1971	JoAnne Carner
1972	Susie Maxwell Berning
1973	Susie Maxwell Berning
1974	Sandra Haynie
1975	Sandra Palmer
1976	JoAnne Carner
1977	Hollis Stacy
1978	Hollis Stacy
1979	Jerilyn Britz
1980	Amy Alcott
1981	Pat Bradley
1982	Janet Anderson
1983	Jan Stephenson
1984	Hollis Stacy
1985	Kathy Baker
1986	Jane Geddes
1987	Laura Davies
1988	Liza Newman
1989	Betsy King
1990	Betsy King

U.S. Yacht Racing Union

The North American Yacht Racing Union was organized on October 30, 1897, by several U.S. and Canadian racing associations. Very little is known about its early history, and it seems to have been largely inactive until it was revived in 1925. The NAYRU worked with the International Yacht Racing Union during the late 1920s to develop the International Rule for measuring and rating yachts and to develop a uniform code of right-of-way rules. The union didn't become a full-fledged member of the IYRU until 1962. Because of the growth of the Canadian Yachting Association, which had been established in 1931, the NAYRU became the U.S. Yacht Racing Union in January 1976. The USYRU conducts many U.S. and North American championships.

Address: Box 209, Newport, RI 02840 (401) 849–5200

Utah

See SALT LAKE CITY, UT.

Vancouver

Football The Vancouver Grizzlies played just one season in the Western Interprovincial Football Union, in 1941. The British Columbia Lions, based in Vancouver, joined the WIFU in 1954. The WIFU is now the Western Football Conference of the Canadian Football League, and the Lions won the Grey Cup, representative of the CFL championship, in 1964 and 1985.

Hockey The Vancouver Canucks entered the National Hockey League as an expansion team in 1970.

See also B.C. PLACE STADIUM; PACIFIC COLISEUM.

Vanderbilt Cup
Auto Racing

William K. Vanderbilt, an early aficionado of the automobile, established a 300-mile race over Long Island roads in 1904, with the Vanderbilt Cup as the trophy. There were 18 entrants and more than 30,000 spectators. The race was held through 1908.

Vardon Trophy
Golf

From 1934 through 1936, the Harry E. Radix Trophy was awarded to the professional with the best overall tournament record for the year. It was replaced in 1937 by the Vardon Trophy, named for British golfer Harry Vardon, whose tours and exhibitions helped popularize golf in North America early in the century. The award was based on a point system from 1937 through 1941. The Radix Trophy was given in 1942, 1945, and 1946, but the Vardon Trophy was restored in 1947. Since then, it has gone to the player on the PGA tour with the lowest average number of strokes per round.

Vare, Glenna (Collett) (1903–1989)
Golf

Born June 20, 1903, New Haven, CT; died February 3, 1989; World Golf Hall of Fame

When she was 12 years old, Glenna Collett went to the course to watch her father and some friends play golf. She asked if she could try hitting the ball and drove it right down the middle of the fairway. Seven years later, in 1922, she won the first of her six U.S. Women's Amateur championships, a record. The others came in 1925, 1928, 1929, 1930, and 1935. She was noted for her long drives—she was said to have driven the ball more than 300 yards when she was 18—but she was also very consistent off the fairway and on the green. A supporter of international golf, she won the Canadian Women's Amateur in 1923 and 1924 and was runner-up in the British Ladies' Amateur championship in 1929 and 1930. After Curtis Cup play lapsed for a year, she revived it by taking a team of eight American women to England in 1930. At the age of 85, she was still playing frequently, with a 15 handicap.

Vare Trophy
Golf

Named for Glenna Collett Vare, this trophy was given to the Ladies' Professional Golf Association in 1952 by Betty Jameson. The award is presented to the LPGA member with the lowest average strokes per round.

Vaulting

A sport that involves performing gymnastics while riding a horse, vaulting is said to have originated with the Romans, but as we know it was a kind of exercise for cavalrymen that grew up along with other equestrian sports during the late 19th century, and was especially popular in Germany. Vaulting was on the 1920 Olympic program, but only Belgium, France, and Sweden took part. (As an aggressor in World War I, Germany was barred from the Olympics in 1920.) The sport has achieved some recent popularity in North America, particularly among girls who belong to pony clubs. The American Vaulting Association, founded in 1969, has about 1,000 member groups.

Address: American Vaulting Association, P.O. Box 3663, Saratoga, CA 95070 (408) 867–6402

Veterans Memorial Coliseum
Uniondale, NY

Built by Nassau County, the Coliseum opened in 1971 as the home of the American Basketball Association's New York Nets. The following year it became the home rink of the New York Islanders, an expansion team in the National Hockey League. The Nets moved to New Jersey in 1977, but the Islanders still play at the Coliseum, which seats 16,297 for hockey.

Veterans Stadium
Philadelphia, PA

When Veterans Stadium opened as the new home of the Philadelphia Phillies in 1971, the outfield fences were only 8 feet high. They were raised to 12 feet during the season because so many balls were bouncing off the AstroTurf surface and into the stands. The original capacity of 56,371 was increased to 62,382 in 1978, making Veterans the largest park in the National League. Home run distances are 330 feet down the lines and 408 feet to center field. As the home field of the National Football League's Philadelphia Eagles, the stadium seats 66,945.

Vezina, Georges (1887–1926)
Hockey

Born January 1887, Chicoutimi, Quebec; died March 24, 1926; Hockey Hall of Fame

"Georges has a calmness not of this world," one sportswriter said of Vezina, whose coolness under pressure won him the nickname, the "Chicoutimi Cucumber." His coolness was all the more remarkable in that he spent at least three seasons playing goal for the Montreal Canadiens while suffering from tuberculosis.

Vezina joined the Canadiens during the 1916–17 season, the year before the National Hockey League was organized. He was soon recognized as one of the NHL's very best goaltenders, although Montreal was not a top team during his early years. He had a sensational victory over Ottawa in 1922–23, stopping 79 of 80 shots despite a broken nose and a severe cut in the head suffered just a few days before.

In 1923–24, Vezina had three shutouts and allowed only 48 goals in 24 games. The Canadiens finished second that year, but they beat first-place Ottawa in the NHL playoffs, 1–0 and 4–2. Then they had to play two western teams, Vancouver and Calgary, for the Stanley Cup. They won all four games, Vezina giving up only 4 goals. The Canadiens slipped to third place in 1924–25, but Vezina's goals-against average of 1.90 led the league, and he gave up just two goals in two playoff victories over Toronto. Vancouver beat Montreal three games out of four in the Stanley Cup final.

On November 28, 1925, the Canadiens opened a new season against Pittsburgh at Montreal. Vezina was not scored on in the first period. Early in the second period, he suddenly collapsed in his goal crease and was carried from the ice. He had a 105-degree temperature and internal hemorrhaging had begun, brought on by his tuberculosis. He died less than four months later.

Vezina Trophy
Hockey

The owners of the Montreal Canadiens presented this trophy to the National Hockey League in 1926 in memory of their great goaltender, Georges Vezina. It was intended as an award for the league's best goalie, judged by the number of goals given up by his team. As the season lengthened with expansion, most teams began to use at least two goalies more or less alternately, so two goaltenders often shared the award beginning in the mid-1960s. Since the 1981–82 season, the Vezina Trophy has gone to the league's best goalie as chosen by a vote of general managers.

Vezina Trophy Winners

1927 George Hainsworth, Montreal Canadiens
1928 George Hainsworth, Montreal Canadiens
1929 George Hainsworth, Montreal Canadiens
1930 Tiny Thompson, Boston
1931 Roy Whorters, New York Americans
1932 Charlie Gardiner, Chicago
1933 Tiny Thompson, Boston
1934 Charlie Gardiner, Chicago
1935 Warren Chabot, Chicago
1936 Tiny Thompson, Boston
1937 Normie Smith, Detroit
1938 Tiny Thompson, Boston
1939 Frank Brimsek, Boston
1940 Dave Kerr, New York Rangers
1941 Turk Broda, Toronto
1942 Frank Brimsek, Boston
1943 John Mowers, Detroit
1944 Bill Durnan, Montreal
1945 Bill Durnan, Montreal
1946 Bill Durnan, Montreal
1947 Bill Durnan, Montreal
1948 Turk Broda, Toronto
1949 Bill Durnan, Montreal
1950 Bill Durnan, Montreal
1951 Al Rollins, Toronto
1952 Terry Sawchuk, Detroit
1953 Terry Sawchuk, Detroit
1954 Harry Lumley, Toronto
1955 Terry Sawchuk, Detroit
1956 Jacques Plante, Montreal
1957 Jacques Plante, Montreal
1958 Jacques Plante, Montreal
1959 Jacques Plante, Montreal
1960 Jacques Plante, Montreal
1961 Johnny Bower, Toronto
1962 Jacques Plante, Montreal
1963 Glenn Hall, Chicago
1964 Charlie Hodge, Montreal
1965 Terry Sawchuk–Johnny Bower, Toronto

1966   Loren Worsley–Charlie Hodge, Montreal
1967   Glenn Hall–Denis Dejordy, Chicago
1968   Lorne Worsley–Rogatien Vachon, Montreal
1969   Jacques Plante–Glenn Hall, St. Louis
1970   Tony Esposito, Chicago
1971   Ed Giacomin–Gilles Villemeure, New York Rangers
1972   Tony Esposito–Gary Smith, Chicago
1973   Ken Dryden, Montreal
1974   Bernie Parent, Philadelphia
          Tony Esposito, Chicago (Tie)
1975   Bernie Parent, Philadelphia
1976   Ken Dryden, Montreal
1977   Ken Dryden–Michel Larocque, Montreal
1978   Ken Dryden–Michel Larocque, Montreal
1979   Ken Dryden–Michel Larocque, Montreal

1980   Bob Sauve–Don Edwards, Buffalo
1981   Richard Sevigny–Denis Herron–Michel Larocque, Montreal
1982   Bill Smith, New York Islanders
1983   Pete Peeters, Boston
1984   Tom Barrasso, Buffalo
1985   Pelle Lindbergh, Philadelphia
1986   John Van Biesbrouck, New York Rangers
1987   Ron Hextall, Philadelphia
1988   Grant Fuhr, Edmonton
1989   Patrick Roy, Montreal
1990   Patrick Roy, Montreal
1991   Ed Belfour, Chicago

Vince Lombardi Award
See LOMBARDI AWARD; LOMBARDI TROPHY.

Invented in 1895 as a rather slow sport for older men, volleyball has become a very fast, highly competitive sport. Courtesy of the U.S. Volleyball Association

Virginia Slims Circuit
Tennis

Because tournaments sanctioned by the U.S. Lawn Tennis Association paid so little money to women, Billie Jean King in 1970 threatened to lead a boycott by women players. Gladys Heldman, publisher of *World Tennis* magazine, persuaded them to set up their own tournament instead. The result was the $5,000 Houston Women's Invitation tournament, which soon became the $7,500 Virginia Slims Invitation, with sponsorship from Philip Morris. The tournament was a success, and in 1971 the Virginia Slims tour was established, with 24 tournaments and prize money of $250,000.

By 1972, there were 60 women playing the tour for total prize money of $660,000. After several threats to suspend the tour's players, the U.S. Lawn Tennis Association surrendered; in 1974, most of the USLTA's women's tournaments became part of the Virginia Slims circuit. Virginia Slims was replaced by Avon as the tour's major sponsor in 1979, but returned in 1983. Prize money was up to $10.2 million that year, and it grew to $16.2 million in 1988. The top 16 women on the tour compete for more than $1 million in the season-ending Virginia Slims Championship tournament.

See also WOMEN'S INTERNATIONAL TENNIS ASSOCIATION.

Volleyball

Shortly after basketball was invented, William G. Morgan, director of the YMCA in Holyoke, MA, decided there should be an indoor sport for older men who didn't want to run up and down the court. Inspired by badminton, in 1895 Morgan created a sport that he called "mintonette." When it was demonstrated at a conference of YMCA directors, Dr. A. T. Halsted suggested the name "volleyball," and it stuck. Rules for YMCA play were standardized in 1897, and volleyball soon spread across the country, although it didn't catch on the way basketball had.

Playground leaders discovered that volleyball was a good sport for youngsters as well as older men, and many outdoor courts were set up during the 1920s. The sport also became popular at many colleges. Instead of being the relatively slow, recreational game Morgan had envisioned, volleyball for many skilled younger players became a very fast-paced competitive sport. The U.S. Volleyball Association was organized in 1928 to conduct tournaments leading up to national championships.

American servicemen introduced volleyball to many countries during and after World War II, and it became especially popular in China, Japan, and Korea. The International Volleyball Federation, founded in 1947, held the first world championships in 1949. Volleyball became an Olympic sport for both men and women in 1964. The Soviet Union and Japan dominated the sport internationally until the early 1980s when it had a surge of popularity in North American colleges. The U.S. men won Olympic Golds in 1984 and 1988, and they won the 1986 world championship. There have been national collegiate championships for men since 1970 and for women since 1981.

Beach volleyball is often played in California with teams of just one or two players. The U.S. Outdoor Volleyball Association controls that version of the sport, which is often televised by ESPN. An unusual offshoot is "wallyball," created by racquetball pro Joe Garcia in 1979. Wallyball is played on a racquetball court; in general, it follows the rules of volleyball except that the walls are in play.

Addresses: Canadian Volleyball Association, 333 River Road, Vanier, Ontario, Canada K1L 8H9 (613) 748–5681; U.S. Volleyball Association, 1750 East Boulder, Colorado Springs, CO 80909 (719) 578–4750

WAC

See WESTERN ATHLETIC CONFERENCE.

Wade, L. Margaret (1912–   )
Basketball

Born December 30, 1912, McCool, MS; Basketball Hall of Fame

One of the first two women elected to the Basketball Hall of Fame, Wade starred in the sport at Delta State University, graduating in 1933, and then went into high school coaching. In 19 years at Cleveland (MS) High School, her teams won 453 games and lost 89. She returned to Delta State in 1973 to revive the basketball program, compiling a 16–2 record in her first season. Delta State then won three consecutive national collegiate championships, in 1975, 1976, and 1977. Her 1974–75 team won 28 consecutive games, her 1975–76 team had a 33–1 record, including a victory over the touring Chinese national team, and her 1976–77 team won 32 out of 35 games. Wade retired in 1979 with an overall record of 633 wins and 117 losses.

Wade Trophy
Basketball

Named for L. Margaret Wade, this award is given by National Association for Girls and Women in Sports to the outstanding women's collegiate basketball player of the year.

Wade Trophy Winners

1978	Carol Blazejowski, Montclair State
1979	Nancy Lieberman, Old Dominion
1980	Nancy Lieberman, Old Dominion
1981	Lynette Woodward, Kansas
1982	Pam Kelly, Louisiana Tech
1983	LaTaunya Pollard, Long Beach State
1984	Janice Lawrence, Louisiana Tech
1985	Cheryl Miller, Southern California
1986	Kamie Ethridge, Texas
1987	Shelly Pennefather, Villanova
1988	Teresa Weatherspoon, Louisiana Tech
1989	Clarissa Davis, Texas
1990	Jennifer Azzi, Stanford
1991	Dawn Staley, Virginia

Wagner, "Honus" John P. (1874–1955)
Baseball

Born February 24, 1874, Mansfield, PA; died December 6, 1955; Baseball Hall of Fame

A lifetime .329 hitter, Honus Wagner was also an outstanding shortstop. He won eight National League batting titles and had 3,430 career hits. Courtesy of the National Baseball Library, Cooperstown, NY

Wagner met all the criteria for a truly great player. He could hit for average and for power, he could steal bases, and he was an outstanding defensive shortstop. He arrived in the major leagues with Louisville in 1897 and hit .338 as an outfielder. The following season he played first base and third base, batting .299 and tying for the National League lead in home runs with 10. After he hit .336 in 1899, the Louisville team folded and Wagner went to Pittsburgh with most of the team's players. He led the league in hitting at .381, in doubles with 45, and in triples with 22 in 1900. That was the first of his eight batting titles.

In 1901, Wagner played shortstop for the first time, but he also played the outfield and third base. Shortstop finally became his full-time position in 1903. That year he won his second batting title with a .355 average and again led the league in triples with 19. The Pirates won the pennant, but lost an eight-game World Series to the Boston Red Sox. Wagner hit only .222, although he did have three stolen bases and three runs batted in.

During the next eight seasons, Wagner was the league's leading hitter six times. His lowest average during that period was .320; his highest, .363. He also led in doubles five times, in triples once, in runs scored once, in runs batted in twice, and in stolen bases three times. When the Pirates won their second pennant in 1909, Wagner and young Ty Cobb of Detroit had a much-publicized showdown in the World Series. The fiery Cobb threatened to spike the easygoing Wagner when stealing second base, but Wagner cut Cobb's lip with a hard tag and never did get spiked. He also won the confrontation handily, batting .333 and stealing six bases to Cobb's .231 and two steals.

After hitting .324 in 1912 and .300 in 1913, his 15th consecutive season at .300 or better, Wagner began to suffer from arthritis in his often-battered legs. He played three more full season and was the Pirates' playing manager briefly in 1917 before retiring. He was one of the first five players elected to the Baseball Hall of Fame in 1936.

At 6 feet 1 inch and 205 pounds, Wagner was big for his time, and he had very large hands. A former teammate recalled, "He just ate the ball up with his big hands, like a scoop shovel, and when he threw it to first base you'd see pebbles and dirt and everything else flying over there along with the ball. . . . The greatest shortstop ever. The greatest *everything* ever." During the 1920s, fans and sportswriters debated about whether Cobb or Babe Ruth was the best player in the history of baseball. But John McGraw insisted that Wagner was the best all-around player ever.

In 21 major-league seasons, Wagner had an average of .327, with 3,415 hits, including 640 doubles, 252 triples, and 101 home runs. He stole 722 bases, scored 1,736 runs, and drove in 1,732 runs.

Walker Cup
Golf

George H. Walker, president of the U.S. Golf Association, presented this trophy in 1922 for competition between teams of amateur male golfers representing the United States and Great Britain. Each team consists of eight players, two alternates, and a nonplaying captain. There are four 18-hole foursomes and eight 18-hole singles matches on each of the two days of competition. A victory in a match is worth a point. Walker Cup matches were played annually from 1922 through 1924 and became biannual in 1926. Play was suspended during World War II and resumed in 1947. The site alternates between the United States and Great Britain.

Walking

See PEDESTRIANISM; TRACK AND FIELD.

Ward, "Monte" John Montgomery (1860–1925)
Baseball

Born March 3, 1860, Bellefonte, PA; died March 4, 1925; Baseball Hall of Fame

Although little known today, Ward was one of the most versatile players of his era, and he was also a successful manager, an owner, and the leader of the first players' association. He began playing for the Providence Grays in the National League in 1878, when he was 18. He pitched shutouts in his first two starts and went on to win 22 while losing 13. The following season, he had a 47–19 record to lead the Grays to the pennant, and on June 17, 1880, he pitched the second perfect game in history en route to a 39–24 record. (The first had been pitched five days before by John Richmond of Worcester.)

Ward developed a sore arm shortly after being traded to the New York Giants in 1883 and was moved to shortstop the following year. While playing, he studied law at Columbia and received his degree in 1885. That year, the Brotherhood of Professional Base Ball Players was organized, with Ward as its president. The duties didn't distract him from the game. He hit .338 and led the league with 111 steals in 1887, and was captain of one of the teams taken on a world tour by Albert G. Spalding after the 1888 season.

While the players were on tour, the owners adopted the Classification Plan, limiting salaries to a maximum of $2,500. Ward persuaded Albert Johnson of Cleveland to organize backing for a Players' League, to be run as a cooperative, in 1890. The league attracted most of the top players of the day, but lasted only one season. Ward, as playing manager of its Brooklyn team, batted .337. In 1891, he became playing manager of the National League's Brooklyn team. After three seasons, he was New York's playing manager in 1894, then retired to practice law. His last foray into baseball was as part owner of the Boston Braves from 1911 until midway through the 1912 season.

An articulate and often outspoken man, Ward wrote a book for boys, *Baseball, How to Become a Player*, in 1888, and he was also the author of an attack on baseball's labor practices in the August 1887 issue of *Lippincott's* magazine. "Like a fugitive slave law, the reserve rule denies him [the player] a harbor or a livelihood, and carries him back, bound and shackled, to the club from which he attempted to escape," he wrote. "He goes where he is sent, takes what is given him, and thanks the Lord for life."

Warmerdam, Cornelius (1915–   )
Track and Field

Born June 22, 1915, Long Beach, CA; National Track and Field Hall of Fame

Like the 4-minute mile, the 15-foot pole vault was long considered an insurmountable barrier until Warmerdam exceeded it in 1940. He jumped over 15 feet a total of 43 times, eventually raising the world records to 15–7¾ outdoors in 1942 and 15–8½ indoors. He retired from competition in 1944, and remained the only man ever to vault more than 15 feet until 1951, when Bob Richards did it. Warmerdam's outdoor record stood until 1957.

Something of a late bloomer, Warmerdam attended Fresno State College, but never won the collegiate championship in his event. However, he won the national championship shortly after graduating, in 1938, and repeated from 1940 through 1944. He was also the national indoor champion in 1939 and 1943. He was track coach at Stanford in 1946 and 1947 and at Fresno State from 1948 until 1980. His 1964 team won the NCAA Division II outdoor championship.

Warner, "Pop" Glenn S. (1871–1954)
Football

Born April 5, 1871, Springville, NY; died September 7, 1954; National Football Foundation Hall of Fame

Warner was one of the great technical innovators in football. He developed offensive formations that were used, with variations, for nearly 50 years. He was the first coach to teach players to kick spiral punts for greater distance, the first to teach the cross-body block, and the inventor of the trap play.

Warner graduated from Cornell with a law degree in 1895, coached Georgia to a 7–4–0 record for two seasons, then returned to Cornell for two years, compiling a 15–5–1 record. In 1899, Warner began coaching at Carlisle Institute. He went back to Cornell for three seasons beginning in 1904, then to Carlisle again in 1907. With players like Jim Thorpe and Joe Guyon, Carlisle became a football power, winning 70 games while losing 16 and tying 4, during the next seven seasons.

At Carlisle, Warner developed the single-wing and double-wing formations, which were used by most college and professional teams until the T-formation

came into vogue during the 1940s. He went to the University of Pittsburgh in 1915 and coached there for nine seasons, producing unbeaten teams in 1915, 1916, and 1917. In one of the most unusual coaching changes ever, Warner agreed in 1922 to coach at Stanford, but not until 1924. He sent his assistant, Andy Kerr, to install the Warner system. Kerr had an 11–7–0 record in his two years before Warner's arrival. In 12 seasons, Warner took Stanford to three Rose Bowls and compiled a 71–17–8 record. He finished his career at Temple, winning 31 games, losing 18, and tying 9 from 1933 through 1938. In 44 years of college coaching, he had a 312–104–32 record.

Washington, DC

Baseball Washington has had an on-and-off relationship with the major leagues since 1884, when it had teams in both the American Association and the Union Association for one season. In 1886, Washington joined the National League for four seasons, dropping out after 1889. After a year's absence from major-league baseball, the city had a team in the American Association in 1891, but the league folded and Washington ended up in the National League again from 1892 through 1899. The Senators entered the American League in 1901. That team became the Minnesota Twins in 1961, when Washington got an expansion franchise, also called the Senators. Those Senators lasted 11 seasons before moving to Arlington, TX as the Texas Rangers, in 1972. The original Senators won American League pennants in 1924, 1925, and 1933; their only World Series victory was in 1924.

Basketball The Washington Capitols joined the Basketball Association of America when it was organized in 1946, and they finished first in the western division but were eliminated in the first round of the 1946–47 playoffs. By the 1950–51 season, the team was in bad shape, and disbanded on January 10, 1951, after having won only 10 of 35 games. The BAA had become the National Basketball Association by then.

The NBA's Baltimore Bullets began playing in the Capital Centre in Landover, MD, in 1973, and were renamed the Capital Bullets, representing both Baltimore and Washington. The became the Washington Bullets before the 1974–75 season. The Bullets won the 1978 NBA championship.

Football The Boston Redskins won the National Football League's eastern division in 1936, but attendance was so poor that owner George Marshall moved the team's championship game with the Green Bay Packers to the Polo Grounds in New York, and the following season he moved the team to Washington.

The Redskins won NFL championships in 1937 and 1942, and they won Super Bowls XVII and XXII. They were National Football Conference champions in 1983, but lost Super Bowl XVIII to the Oakland Raiders.

Hockey The Washington Capitals entered the National Hockey League as an expansion franchise for the 1974–75 season. They have never won a division title.

See also CAPITAL CENTRE; GRIFFITH STADIUM; ROBERT F. KENNEDY MEMORIAL STADIUM.

Water Polo

As swimming in indoor pools became popular around the turn of the century, there were several attempts to develop a team water sport, including water basketball, water football, and water handball. In the original water polo, players actually rode on floating barrels, decorated to look like horses, and hit the ball with sticks. Thus, the name was attached to a sport that now looks more like an aquatic version of team handball.

The first set of American rules was drawn up by Harold Roeder of the Knickerbocker Athletic Club in 1897, and water polo was on the Olympic program in 1900. A different version of the sport, softball water polo, developed in the United States. It used a partially deflated ball so a player could grip it and carry it; a common defensive tactic was to hold a player under water until he released the ball for fear of drowning. That was a demonstration sport on the 1904 Olympic program in St. Louis, but other countries were not impressed.

The Amateur Athletic Union, which began supervising water polo in 1906, banned the softball version in 1910, although some clubs continued to play it informally into the 1930s. The New York and Illinois Athletic Clubs, both of which had fine swimming teams, dominated water polo in the United States until after World War II, when the sport became very popular in California and among colleges. The NCAA held the first collegiate championship tournament in 1969.

The sport is now governed by U.S. Water Polo, founded in 1980.

Address: U.S. Water Polo, 1750 East Boulder, Colorado Springs, CO 80909 (719) 578–4549

Water Skiing

The original form of water skiing was aquaplaning, in which a rider was towed on a surfboard. It was especially popular on the French Riviera in the early

Water polo was originally played in England by men riding on barrels painted to look like horses. The modern version of the sport, however, is an American adaptation of "water soccer." Courtesy of the Water Polo Scoreboard

Tricks competition is just one component of a water skiing tournament. This is Carl Lyman performing a single-ski flip at the 1974 national championships. Courtesy of the American Water Ski Association

1920s, and there is an unsubstantiated story that Count Maximilian Pulaski came up with the idea of putting a small surfboard on each foot about that time.

Fred Waller, the inventor of Cinerama movies, also invented modern water skis. He began marketing them as "Dolphin Akwa-Skees" in 1924. Originally, each ski had a tow line and a hand rope, and the skier simply stood on the skis. Later, Waller improved his invention by putting bindings on the skis and substituting a single tow line, held by the skier.

The idea may have been in the air, because others came up with their own types of water skis. Dan Ibsen in 1928 made them out of curved boards with sneakers stapled to them and sold them on a small scale. And Bruce Parker tried using snow skis unsuccessfully in 1935, then made his own primitive water skis out of a pair of boards from the side of a barn.

Parker became the first professional water ski instructor and did a great deal to popularize the sport. In 1938, he was filmed water skiing at 90 miles an hour, towed by an airplane, and he and Evie Wolford attracted nationwide publicity by twice water skiing from the Bahamas to Florida.

Aquaplaning and water skiing existed side by side for a number of years. But when Jack Andresen demonstrated a jump on water skis at a meeting of aquaplanists in 1936, most of them were converted to skiing. However, water skiers still sometimes perform on aquaplanes. They may also ski barefoot, on circular saucers ranging from 3 to 4 feet in diameter, or on shoe skis about 15 inches long and 6 inches wide.

The American Water Ski Association was founded in 1939 to oversee the sport and to establish uniform rules for competition. Ten years later, the World Water Ski Union was organized and began conducting the world championships, which are held biannually. A meet includes jumping, slalom, and tricks competition. At major meets, there may be a mixed doubles event, in which a male and a female skier perform a set routine together.

Further Reading: Scharff, Robert. *The Complete Book of Water Skiing.* New York: G. P. Putnam's Sons, 1959.

Addresses: Canadian Water Ski Association, 333 River Road, Vanier, Ontario, Canada K1L 8H9 (613) 748–5663; American Water Ski Association, 799 Overlook Drive, Winter Haven, FL 33884 (813) 324–4341

Waterloo, IA

Basketball Waterloo had a team in the National Basketball League during its final season, 1948–49. When the NBL and the Basketball Association of America merged to become the National Basketball Association in 1949, Waterloo joined the NBA, but the team folded after one season.

Watkins Glen International
Watkins Glen, NY

In 1948, Watkins Glen began holding a road race for sports cars, and in 1957 a road-type track was built. The 2.428-mile circuit hosted the U.S. Grand Prix from 1960 through 1980. NASCAR races were held at Watkins Glen in 1957, 1964, and 1965. Stock car racing returned to the track with a 219-mile NASCAR event in 1986.

Address: Box 500, Watkins Glen, NY 14891 (607) 535–2481

WBA
See WORLD BOXING ASSOCIATION.

Weight Lifting

Exercising with dumbbells was part of the Turners' gymnastic routine, and wrestlers began working with weights to build up their bodies late in the 19th Century. Louis Cyr, Eugen Sandow, and other professional strongmen helped popularize the sport with stage demonstrations of weight-lifting feats. The chief promoter of weight lifting in the early part of the century was the Milo Barbell Company of Philadelphia, founded by Alan Calvert in 1902. Calvert's magazine, *Strength,* carried many instructional and technical articles, as well as news of the sport.

There were two weight-lifting events on the original modern Olympic program in 1896, and weight lifting became a permanent Olympic sport in 1920. It was slow to catch on in North America, though. The Amateur Athletic Union conducted the first national championships in 1929.

The sport got a major boost from another manufacturer, the York (PA) Barbell Company. Bob Hoffman founded the company in 1932. He attended the Los Angeles Olympics that year and was dismayed by the U.S. performance. Foreign weight lifters, he wrote later, "looked upon the U.S. team as something of a joke." Hoffman began hiring young weight lifters to work for his company, offering them training facilities and instruction, and he also financed trips to international meets. The U.S. dominated the sport from 1946 through 1952, and most of its top competitors were Hoffman's protégés.

During the early 1950s, the sport began to decline in North America, in part because of the growth of powerlifting. Classical weight lifting involves good technique and balance, whereas powerlifting emphasizes sheer strength and building muscle bulk. The sport is closely linked with bodybuilding, which has its own competitions. The United States Weight-lifting Federation, now the governing body for Olympic weight lifting, has only about 2,000 registered members, while the U.S. Powerlifting Federation has more than 10,000.

Addresses: Canadian Weightlifting Federation, 333 River Road, Vanier, Ontario, Canada K1L 8H9 (613) 748–5684; U.S. Weightlifting Federation, 1750 East Boulder, Colorado Springs, CO 80909 (719) 578–4508

Weissmuller, Johnny (1904–1984)
Swimming
Born June 2, 1904, Chicago, IL; died January 20, 1984; International Swimming Hall of Fame

Weissmuller, the most famous of the movie Tarzans, was unquestionably the greatest swimmer of the 1920s. Although his best event was the 100-yard or 100-meter freestyle, he set world records at every distance up to 880 yards. His record of 51.0 seconds for 100 yards, set in 1927, wasn't broken until 1943. The tall, broad-chested Weissmuller won Olympic Medals in the 100- and 400-meter freestyle in 1924, and he repeated in the 100-meter in 1928. He also swam the anchor leg on the winning 800-meter relay team in both 1924 and 1928, giving him a total of five Gold Medals.

Weissmuller was the U.S. outdoor champion at 100 yards in 1922, 1923, and 1925; at 100 meters in 1926, 1927, and 1928; at 220 yards in 1921 and 1922; at 440 yards in 1922, 1923, 1925, 1926, 1927, and 1928; and at 880 yards in 1925. He won indoor titles at 100 yards in 1922, 1923, 1924, 1925, 1927, and 1928, and at 220 yards in 1922, 1923, 1924, 1927, and 1928. Just for variety, he was also the indoor 150-yard backstroke champion in 1923. From

Johnny Weissmuller, right, became famous as Hollywood's Tarzan after winning five Olympic Gold Medals in 1924 and 1928. He's shown here with Mark Spitz, who won seven Gold Medals in 1972. Courtesy of the International Swimming Hall of Fame

1934 through 1948, Weissmuller starred in 19 Tarzan movies.

Western Athletic Conference (WAC)

The Skyline Conference disbanded in 1962, and five of its former members—Brigham Young, Colorado State, New Mexico, Utah, and Wyoming—formed the Western Athletic Conference. An NCAA Division 1A football conference, the WAC now has nine members, the five original schools plus Air Force, Hawaii, San Diego State, and Texas-El Paso.

Address: 14 West Dry Creek Circle, Littleton, CO 80120 (303) 795–1962

Western Conference

See BIG TEN CONFERENCE.

Western League
Baseball

The Western, a minor league, was pieced together in 1892 from the remnants of the old Northwestern League. It was faltering when Ban Johnson became league president in 1894. Detroit, Grand Rapids, Indianapolis, Kansas City, Milwaukee, Minneapolis, Sioux City, and Toledo were in the league at that time. Johnson in 1895 persuaded Charles Comiskey to buy the Sioux City franchise and move it to St. Paul. By 1898 the league was so successful that Johnson decided to turn it into a second major league. The Western League was renamed the American League in 1900.

See also AMERICAN LEAGUE.

WFL

See WORLD FOOTBALL LEAGUE.

White House Conference on Football

At the urging of Endicott Peabody, headmaster of the Groton School, President Theodore Roosevelt in 1905 invited two representatives each from Harvard, Princeton, and Yale to meet with him and Secretary of State Elihu Root to discuss the problem of violence in college football. The luncheon meeting took place at the White House in early October. The representatives were coach William Reid and team physician Dr. Edward Nichols of Harvard, coach Arthur Hildebrand and Professor John B. Fine from Princeton, and coach John Owsley and the ubiquitous Walter Camp from Yale. After a discussion, Roosevelt asked for an agreement that the three schools would play football cleanly in the future.

On the train back from Washington, the message was written. Camp immediately wired it to Roosevelt and released it to the press. It read: "At a meeting with the President of the United States, it was agreed that we consider an honorable obligation exists to carry out in letter and in spirit the rules of the game of football, relating to roughness, holding, and foul play, and the active coaches of our universities being present with us, pledge themselves to so regard it and to do their utmost to carry out that obligation."

Although the *New York Times* and other newspapers praised the statement, many college leaders were skeptical, including Harvard President Charles W. Eliot, who noted that the signers of the agreement were the men chiefly responsible for college football's problems. Major rules changes were needed, and they would come in 1906, after many colleges seriously considered abolishing football.

See also CAMP, WALTER; INTERCOLLEGIATE SPORTS.

White Sox Park

See COMISKEY PARK.

Whitfield, Malvin G. (1924–)
Track and Field

Born October 11, 1924, Bay City, TX; National Track and Field Hall of Fame

The first black to win the Sullivan Award, Whitfield was a very intelligent middle-distance runner who relied on tactics as well as sheer speed to win races. He never held a world record, but he won Olympic Gold Medals in the 800-meter run in 1948 and 1952, running 1:49.2 both times. He also anchored the winning 1,600-meter relay team at the 1948 Olympics. Whitfield was the AAU outdoor champion at 800 meters in 1949, 1950, and 1951, at 880 yards in 1953 and 1954, and at 400 meters in 1952. Representing Ohio State, he was NCAA 880-yard champion in 1948 and 1949.

Whitfield went to Kenya in 1955 as a youth officer with the U.S. Information Agency, and he remained in the country as a recreation director. He also operates a training camp for African track and field athletes in Ethiopia, where he has helped to train many of the stars who have represented African countries in recent Olympics.

WIBC

See WOMENS INTERNATIONAL BOWLING CONGRESS.

WIBC Queens

See QUEENS TOURNAMENT.

Wightman Cup
Tennis

Hazel Hotchkiss Wightman paid $300 for a silver cup at a Boston jewelry store in 1919 and presented it to the U.S. Lawn Tennis Association as a trophy for an international women's tennis championship. The USLTA did nothing with it until 1923, when a match was arranged between England and American players to mark the opening of the West Side Tennis Club's new stadium in Forest Hills, NY. The Wightman Cup was formally named the Ladies International Lawn Tennis Trophy, but it has almost always been referred to by its informal name. England and the United States have played annual matches for the trophy since 1923, except for a hiatus during World War II.

Wightman, Hazel Hotchkiss
See HOTCHKISS, HAZEL.

Williams, "Ted" Theodore S. (1918–　　)
Baseball
Born August 30, 1918, San Diego, CA; Baseball Hall of Fame

Despite missing most of five seasons while serving as a pilot in both World War II and the Korean conflict, Williams was the American League batting champion six times. He batted .406 in 1941; no player since has hit over .400 for a season. "The Splendid Splinter," as he was known in his younger, skinnier days, was the starting right fielder for the Boston Red Sox at the beginning of the 1939 season, but he was soon moved to left field, where he spent most of his career. In his rookie year, he hit .327 with 31 home runs and led the American League in runs batted in with 145.

After hitting .344 in 1940, he had his remarkable .406 season. Williams was batting .400 on the last day of the season, with just a double-header remaining, and Red Sox manager Joe Cronin suggested he take the day off to avoid slipping below .400. Williams insisted on playing both games and collected six hits in eight at-bats. He also led the league in home runs with 37 and in runs scored with 135.

Williams won the Triple Crown in 1942 with a .356 average, 36 home runs, and 137 runs batted in. He then spent three years as a marine pilot. He returned to the Red Sox in 1946 to hit .342 and win the league's Most Valuable Player award. He won his second Triple Crown in 1947 by batting .343 with 32 home runs and 142 runs batted in, and he collected his fourth batting title with a .369 average in 1948.

Though he didn't lead the league in hitting, 1949 was an outstanding season for Williams: He did lead in doubles (39), home runs (43), runs scored (150), runs batted in (159), walks (162), and slugging percentage (.650). A broken elbow suffered when he ran into the fence during the all-star game limited him to only 89 games in 1950. After hitting just .318

in 1951, he saw limited action again in the next four seasons. He served in the marines for most of 1952 and 1953 and broke his shoulder in 1954. The shoulder injury kept him out of action for all but 98 games in 1955, and many observers thought his career was just about over.

But Williams hit .345 in 1956, then won two more batting titles, with a .388 average in 1957 and a .328 average in 1958. At 40, he was the oldest player ever to lead either league in hitting. Suffering from a pinched nerve in his neck, Williams slipped to .254 in 1959, his only season under .300. He played one more year, batting .318, and he hit a dramatic home run in his final at-bat—an event chronicled by John Updike in a famous *New Yorker* article.

In 1969, Williams became manager of the hapless Washington Senators and won the Manager of the Year Award for finishing fourth. He went with the Senators when they became the Texas Rangers in 1972, but that was his last season as a manager.

Gifted with great eyesight and natural ability, Williams was also a thinking hitter who explained his principles in a book, *The Science of Hitting*, published in 1981. His basic premise was that, on the first two strikes, a batter should swing only at a pitch in what Williams called "the power portion of the strike zone," the inside half of the plate at about belt level. It certainly worked for him. In his 19 seasons, he batted .344 with 2,654 hits, including 521 home runs. He scored 1,798 runs, drove in 1,839 runs, walked 2,018 times, and struck out only 709 times. His career slugging percentage of .634 is second only to Babe Ruth's.

Wills, Helen N. (Mrs. Moody) (1905–　　)
Tennis
Born October 6, 1905, Centerville, CA; International Tennis Hall of Fame

Wills dominated women's tennis during the 1920s. From 1923 through 1931, she won seven national singles championships. She won eight singles titles at Wimbledon from 1927 through 1938, and she also won the French championship from 1928 through 1930 and in 1932. Her total of 19 major titles could have been even higher, but she didn't play in the U.S. Nationals after 1933, she didn't play in any major tournaments in 1936 or 1937, and injury or illness kept her out of the major events in 1926 and 1934. Wills also won the U.S. women's doubles title in 1922, 1924, 1925, and 1928, the Wimbledon doubles in 1924, 1927, and 1930, and the French doubles in 1930 and 1932. She won Olympic Gold Medals in both singles and doubles in 1924.

Dubbed "Little Miss Poker Face" by sportswriter Grantland Rice because of her apparent lack of emotion while playing, Wills was a strong, steady base line player who rarely made an unforced error. She wrote in her autobiography, "I know that I would hate life if I were deprived of trying, hunting, working for some objective within which there lies the beauty of perfection." She may have come as close to perfection as any athlete ever has. During one period, she not only won 158 consecutive matches, she won every set she played. A Phi Beta Kappa at the University of California, she was also a talented artist whose work was often displayed in major galleries.

Further Reading: Wills, Helen. *Fifteen-Thirty.* (London: Scribner's, 1937.

Wilmington, DE

Baseball Wilmington had a team in the minor Eastern League that moved into the Union Association during the 1884 season to replace the Philadelphia Keystones. After a month, Wilmington was in turn replaced by Milwaukee. The Union Association folded when the season was over.

Winnipeg, Manitoba

Football Winnipeg had two teams, the St. John's Football Club and the Winnipegs, during the early 1930s. They merged in 1933 to form a team called the 'Pegs. That team became known as the Blue Bombers when it joined the Western Interprovincial Football Union in 1936. The 'Pegs won the Grey Cup in 1935, and the Blue Bombers won it in 1939, 1941, 1958, 1959, 1961, 1962, and 1984.

Hockey The Winnipeg Jets joined the new World Hockey Association in 1972, and they won WHA championships in 1976, 1978, and 1979. The WHA merged into the National Hockey League before the 1979–80 season.

See also WINNIPEG ARENA AND STADIUM.

Winnipeg Arena and Stadium
Winnipeg, Manitoba

Winnipeg Stadium, built as part of the city's sports complex, opened in 1953. The home field of the Canadian Football League's Blue Bombers, it seats 32,694. The arena, which opened the following year, since 1972 has been the home rink of the Winnipeg Jets. Its capacity is 15,401.

Winston Cup

The Grand National was the top series in stock car racing from 1949 until 1971, when R. J. Reynolds began sponsoring it as the Winston Cup series. NASCAR's listing of Winston Cup champions, was made retroactive to 1949.

Winston Cup Champions

1949	Red Byron
1950	Bill Rexford
1951	Herb Thomas
1952	Tim Flock
1953	Herb Thomas
1954	Lee Petty
1955	Tim Flock
1956	Buck Baker
1957	Buck Baker
1958	Lee Petty
1959	Lee Petty
1960	Rex White
1961	Ned Jarrett
1962	Joe Weatherly
1963	Joe Weatherly
1964	Richard Petty
1965	Ned Jarrett
1966	David Pearson
1967	Richard Petty
1968	David Pearson
1969	David Pearson
1970	Bobby Isaac
1971	Richard Petty
1972	Richard Petty
1973	Benny Parsons
1974	Richard Petty
1975	Richard Petty
1976	Cale Yarborough
1977	Cale Yarborough
1978	Cale Yarborough
1979	Richard Petty
1980	Dale Earnhardt
1981	Darrell Waltrip
1982	Darrell Waltrip
1983	Bobby Allison
1984	Terry Labonte
1985	Darrell Waltrip
1986	Dale Earnhardt
1987	Dale Earnhardt
1988	Bill Elliott
1989	Rusty Wallace
1990	Dale Earnhardt

Winter Olympics

Figure skating was so popular in England early in this century that it was on the Olympic program in 1908, when the Games were held in London. Antwerp, hosting the 1920 Olympics, offered both figure skating and hockey. The sports proved so popular that there was a move to create a separate Winter Olympics. The International Olympic Committee at first opposed the idea, but France, which was to host the 1924 Games, was in favor. The French organizers suggested holding an "Olympic winter carnival" in Chamonix, and the IOC reluctantly gave its approval.

Bobsledding, figure skating, hockey, Nordic skiing, and speed skating were on the program, and 293 athletes took part, representing 16 countries. The IOC was applauded, and the Winter Olympics became a permanent fixture. It was decided that the same country would host the Summer and Winter games in each Olympiad, but the Netherlands backed out in 1928 because it had no skiing facilities and Switzerland took over. Norwegian figure skater Sonja Henie, only 15, was the star of the Winter Games at St. Moritz, winning a Gold Medal with a dazzling performance.

Bad weather—that is, warmth instead of cold, rain instead of snow—has often bedeviled the Winter Olympics, beginning at Lake Placid, NY in 1932. But, despite the weather and the Great Depression, 80,000 spectators turned out and were rewarded by U.S. victories in all four speed skating events and both bobsledding events. Sonja Henie, already world-famous at 19, won her second Gold Medal in figure skating.

The 1936 Winter Games were held in Garmisch-Partenkirchen, Germany, as a kind of prelude to the Berlin Summer Games later that year. Alpine skiing was on the program for the first time, as a combined event (downhill and slalom) for both men and women. Sonja Henie again won a Gold Medal. Another Norwegian, Birger Ruud, won his second consecutive Gold Medal in ski jumping. Within a few years, he and his two brothers were in a Nazi prison camp. (They survived imprisonment and were still alive in 1990.)

After World War II, the idea of holding both sets of Games in the same country was abandoned. The 1948 Summer Olympics were held in London, the Winter Olympics in St. Moritz again. Alpine skiing was now a major feature, with the downhill and slalom for both men and women, along with the Alpine combined. Barbara Ann Scott of Canada won a Gold in figure skating, and Gretchen Fraser became the first U.S. Gold Medalist in skiing by winning the slalom. For the first time, there was a major controversy at the Winter Games: The United States sent two hockey teams, one chosen by the AAU, the other by the Amateur Hockey Association. The IOC first wanted to cancel the hockey tournament entirely, but the Swiss organizers protested. Finally, the AHA team was allowed to compete, but none of its games counted. After the Olympics, the AHA and AAU worked out a method of jointly choosing a national team.

Snow was scarce in Oslo, Norway, almost until the 1952 Games began, and then it arrived to save the day, and the Games. The giant slalom became an Olympic event for the first time, and women's cross-country skiing was also added to the program.

A record 30 countries competed, and crowds totaled more than 750,000. Andrea Mead Lawrence of the U.S. became the first woman to win two Gold Medals in skiing, in the slalom and the giant slalom.

The 1956 Winter Games were held in Cortina, Italy, in the Dolomite Alps. Although Europe in general was suffering one of the worst winters in history, Cortina went nearly a month without snow, and Italian soldiers trucked it in from the upper Alps. Two feet of snow finally fell just a couple of weeks before the opening ceremony, but warm weather arrived a few days later and practice skiing became treacherous. Nearly 30 skiers were injured, and a dozen of them missed the Games entirely; among them was Katy Rodolph, the top American woman, who broke a vertebra in her neck. A Frenchman warned, "The Olympic downhill will be a race to the death if it doesn't snow soon." Again the Italian army was put to work, and the Games went on.

The Soviet Union entered the Winter Olympics for the first time in 1956 and claimed three Gold Medals in speed skating and two in cross-country skiing. The biggest surprise of the Games was the Soviets' 2–0 victory over Canada to win the hockey championship. Toni Sailer of Austria was the individual star, winning three Golds in Alpine skiing. Tenley Albright became the first U.S. woman to win a figure skating Gold, and Hayes Alan Jenkins was the men's figure skating champion.

Europeans were unhappy about the choice of Squaw Valley, CA as the site for the 1960 Winter Games. California spent more than $9 million building facilities at the desolate resort area. But all that money couldn't buy snow. A month before the Olympics, a reporter wrote, "If rain and thaw hit Squaw Valley full force, it will be worse than the Johnstown flood." Two weeks later, it almost happened. A torrential rainstorm, with winds up to 100 miles a hour, struck the area. After 6 hours of rain, the temperature had dropped 30 degrees, the rain turned to snow, and the Olympics went on as planned.

The Soviet Union again dominated in 1960. Women's speed skating was on the program for the first time; the Russians won three Gold Medals there and three more in men's speed skating. Carol Heiss and David Jenkins gave the U.S. another sweep of the figure skating Golds, and the U.S. hockey team upset both Canada and the Soviet Union to win that Gold Medal.

Innsbruck, Austria, hosted the 1964 Games. Weather was again a problem. Austrian soldiers carved 10,000 blocks of ice from the upper Alps for the bobsled and luge runs, and they trucked in 60,000 cubic meters of snow. Rain and warm weather destroyed much of their work. A skier and a luger were killed in practice. More snow was trucked in. When competition began, speed skaters sloshed around a soft course. Luge and bobsled runs were closed until cold weather finally arrived on the next to the last day of the games. Skiing medals went to competitors who had early runs, before the courses became treacherous. The U.S. Olympic Committee had said that the country was about to become a winter sports power, but the U.S. team won only one Gold Medal, an upset victory by Terry McDermott in speed skating. (The entire U.S. figure skating team had been killed in a 1961 plane crash, en route to the world championships.) The top U.S. skater in Innsbruck was 14-year-old Scott Ethan Allen, who won a Bronze Medal.

Rain struck once more at Grenoble, France, during the 1968 Winter Olympics. Bobsledding was delayed several times, but none of the other events was badly affected. Jean-Claude Killy, already a French national hero, won all three Alpine skiing events. This was the first Winter Olympics to get extensive television coverage, and the handsome, dashing Killy won many fans in North America, as did figure skater Peggy Fleming, the only U.S. Gold Medalist.

Aside from unpredictable weather, the Winter Games were relatively trouble-free until 1972, when IOC President Avery Brundage threatened to ban virtually every world-class Alpine skier from competition. The practice of taking money from equipment manufacturers was accepted throughout Europe, but not by Brundage. The skiers were already practicing at the Olympic site in Sapporo, Japan, and the Japanese organizers protested this last-minute threat to the most glamorous sports of the Winter Games. Brundage decided to make an example of just one athlete, Austria's Karl Schranz. Other skiers talked of boycotting the Games, but nothing came of it. Austria and France, previously the powers in the sport, failed to win a single Alpine medal, and Barbara Cochran won the slalom to bring the United States its first Gold Medal in skiing since 1952.

Denver, CO was chosen to host the 1976 Winter Games, but Colorado voters overwhelmingly approved a referendum prohibiting the state from spending money to develop the proposed site. The IOC turned to Innsbruck for the third time. And, for the second time, the Austrian army had to truck snow to the site. U.S. speed skaters were spotlighted on television, winning six medals in the eight events; Sheila Young won three of them, including a Gold in the 500-meter race. Dorothy Hamill was the women's figure skating champion and Kathy Kreiner of Canada won an upset victory in the giant slalom.

Eric Heiden of the United States starred in the 1980 Games, at Lake Placid, winning all five Gold Medals in men's speed skating. But the biggest story for the United States was the Gold Medal in hockey: The young American team knocked the Soviet Union from contention with an upset victory and then beat Finland in the final game. Because the Games were in North America, there was much more live television coverage than there had been in the past, and those two games received the highest ratings ever for hockey in the United States.

Although the Winter Olympics aren't nearly as large as the Summer Games, they've shown steady growth. Forty-nine countries, including unlikely entries such as Senegal and the British West Indies, sent athletes to Sarajevo, Yugoslavia, in 1984. This time, snow was the problem: Blinding storms delayed Alpine skiing for several days, and it looked for a while as if the races might have to be canceled entirely, but the weather finally improved. U.S. skiers made their best showing ever, claiming three Gold Medals, and Scott Hamilton won a Gold in figure skating, the first victory by an American male since 1960.

Calgary, Alberta, was the site of the 1988 Games, which again set records with 1,750 athletes from 57 countries. Unseasonably warm weather once again marred the competition, along with high winds that delayed some of the skiing events, but Calgary staged a magnificent show. Two figure skating duels highlighted the competition. Brian Boitano of the United States edged Brian Orser of Canada in the men's finals, while Katerina Witt of East Germany won the Gold Medal in women's figure skating for the second consecutive time. Witt was expected to face a strong challenge from Debi Thomas of the United States, but Thomas faltered and settled for the bronze. The women's finals drew a television audience of 60 million, the largest for a Saturday night since the series "Roots" in 1977.

The Winter Games will be held in the same year as the Summer Games in 1992, and then will be moved to even-numbered years in which the Summer Olympics are not held. After the 1992 Games in Albertville, France, the 1994 Winter Olympics will be hosted by Lillehammer, Norway.

See also OLYMPIC GAMES.

Women in Sports

During the Victorian period, women were discouraged from taking part in sports because it was believed that they were physically and emotionally weaker than men and that their energies should be channeled into developing their "special apparatus" for childbearing. (The same arguments were advanced against education for women.) However, physical strength and health were also seen as necessary for motherhood, so some kinds of exercise were approved. Vassar, founded in 1861 as the first women's college in North America, offered regular physical activities for its students; in addition to a well-equipped gym, the school had facilities for boating, bowling, horseback riding, skating, and swimming.

Less strenuous sports came to be accepted late in the 19th century. Women competed in the first national archery championships in 1879, and during the 1880s women played croquet and tennis, which was a very sedate sport at the time. Many golf clubs set aside an afternoon or two a week for wives and daughters of members. The bicycle had a distinctly liberating influence. Women's cycling began with the tricycle during the early 1880s. The New York City Ladies' Tricycle Club was organized in 1884, and the vehicle was relatively popular among women in other large cities. But a tricycle could cost as much as $300, well out of reach of most families. The "safety bicycle," introduced late in the decade, was less expensive. For riding, women began wearing shorter, more comfortable skirts, and some even dared to don knickers or bloomers. The bicycle craze ended early in the 20th century, but the fashions lingered on.

Attitudes toward women and the feminine ideal had changed somewhat by 1890. The "new woman" of the period sought education, backed the women's suffrage movement, and possibly even entered a career—most likely in social work or teaching, two of the few professions open to women at the time. More and more women's colleges were established by the end of the century, and they offered a greater variety of sports, including crew racing, baseball, track and field, and swimming. The national women's tennis championship began in 1887, the national amateur women's golf tournament in 1895.

But there was a backlash early in the 20th century. In 1902, the standard women's tennis match was reduced from five sets to three to limit physical strain. Basketball had been taken up by women less than a year after its invention in 1891 and had become a popular team sport. But women physical educators designed a new version of the sport to minimize exertion. The court was divided into three sections, and each player was permanently assigned to a section; the dribble was limited to three bounces, and stealing the ball was prohibited. Originally drawn up by Senda Berenson of Smith College in 1899, these rules were adopted by the Women's Basketball Rules Committee in 1908.

Nevertheless, there was progress in the early part of the century. Field hockey and volleyball became very popular at women's colleges. Tennis was an Olympic sport beginning in 1904, and the women's singles championship was added at the 1906 "intercalated Olympics"; women's doubles followed in 1908, the mixed doubles in 1912. Figure skating was on the Olympic program in 1908, and swimming and diving events for women were added in 1912. Women competed in both singles and doubles at the first U.S. national figure skating championships in 1916, and the Amateur Athletic Union inaugurated national women's swimming and diving championships in 1916.

Genuine women stars emerged during the 1920s, the "Golden Age of Sports." Golfer Glenna Collett Vare and tennis player Helen Wills dominated their sports, and Wills' match against Suzanne Lenglen in 1926 was one of the most publicized international events of the decade. Internationally, there was a campaign to have women's track and field added to the Olympics. The Federation Sportive Féminine Internationale held its own "Women's Olympics" in 1922 and 1926. The IOC reluctantly included five track and field events for women in the 1928 Olympic Games, in exchange for an agreement that the FSFI would change the name of its quadrennial competition to the "International Ladies' Games," dropping the word "Olympic."

Most female physical educators, however, didn't believe that all-out competition was good for their sex. The Women's Division of the National Amateur Athletic Federation at its first conference in 1923 adopted two principles: "play for play's sake" and "a game for every girl and a girl in every game." Most women's colleges abandoned intercollegiate competition in favor of "play days," which emphasized socialization and participation. A 1931 survey of colleges showed that only 12 took part in intercollegiate sports, while 80 of them had play days. This point of view was, in large part, an egalitarian reaction against the elitist, sports-for-the-few development of male intercollegiate sports. Agnes R. Wyman of Barnard College wrote in 1934, "It isn't the competition which so many of us decry, but the highly intense type of 'do-or-die' play."

Many male physical educators agreed. Intramural programs for male students expanded greatly during the 1930s in both high schools and colleges. But the "play for play's sake" idea was also opposed by some women, especially by the best athletes among them. One college teacher, Mary K. Baker, pointed out in 1939 that most women students hated gym class and stayed away from sports because the games offered them were "trivial and boring." A few women

Senda Berenson is about to toss the ball up in the first public basketball game played by women, at Smith College on March 22, 1863. Courtesy of the Basketball Hall of Fame

coaches, led by Gladys Palmer of Ohio State, organized the first national collegiate women's golf championship in 1941. Palmer later recalled that they were virtually ostracized for years by other members of the Division of Girls' and Women's Sports.

Babe Didrikson emerged during the 1930s as the greatest woman athlete ever. She led her team, the Golden Cyclones of the Employers Casualty Company of Dallas, to the 1931 AAU basketball championship and the 1932 national track and field title; the only member of the track team, she won six events and set four world records. She also won two Gold Medals at the Olympics that year. In 1934 she toured the country with a mixed-sex basketball team, and the following year she toured with the otherwise all-male House of David baseball team. Later she became the world's best woman golfer. Despite her prowess—or perhaps because of it—she didn't do

much for women's sports in general. Tall, large-framed, hatchet-faced, and rough in her speech, "she was used as a kind of bogeywoman by mothers who wished to prevent their budding tomboy daughters from pursuing sports," according to William Oscar Johnson and Nancy Peterson in their biography of Didrikson.

The extension of the cold war into the Olympics after World War II gave women's sports considerable impetus. There were only ten track and field athletes on the U.S. women's team in 1952, when the Soviet Union entered the Olympics for the first time. The U.S. Olympic Committee in 1958 formed a Women's Advisory Board to discuss ways of developing more and better athletes, and in 1960 Doris Duke Cromwell gave the USOC $500,000 to help. The women's liberation movement of the early 1960s also had its impact on sports. In 1966 the Commission of Intercollegiate Athletics for Women was organized by the

Division of Girls' and Women's Sports. In an attempt to prevent the NCAA from assuming control of women's sports, the commission held its first national collegiate championships in 1968, and it became an autonomous group, the Association of Intercollegiate Athletics for Women, in 1971.

Tennis player Billie Jean King probably did more for women's sports than any other single person. Campaigning for equal prize money for women, she and Gladys Heldman of *World Tennis* magazine organized a $7,500 tournament in 1970; that grew into the Virginia Slims circuit, which offered purses totaling $16.2 million in 1988. King was also the major force behind the founding of the Women's Tennis Association in 1973. The WTA tour's prize money grew from about $1 million in 1974 to $14.2 million in 1986. King's crowning achievement on behalf of the women's cause may have been her victory over Bobby Riggs, a former U.S. and Wimbledon champion, who proclaimed that at the age of 55 he could defeat any woman. He did beat Margaret Court Smith on Mothers Day of 1973, but King took him apart in their September match at the Houston Astrodome.

Interscholastic and intercollegiate sports for girls and women got a major boost from Title IX of the Education Amendments Act of 1972, which prohibited sexual discrimination in schools receiving federal aid—meaning virtually every high school and college in the country. Although the NCAA fought the application of Title IX to sports as "disruptive, often destructive, and surely counterproductive," the Department of Health, Education and Welfare promulgated regulations requiring that men's and women's athletic budgets must be proportional to the number of participants. Even before the regulations were adopted in 1975, many schools began expanding women's sports programs. The number of girls participating in high school sports rose from 294,000 in the 1970–71 school year to nearly 2 million in 1979–80, and the women's share of the average college athletic budget grew from less than 1 percent in 1970–71 to 16.4 percent in 1978–79.

The AIAW, still opposed to big-time collegiate sports for women, banned athletic scholarships. But a court ruled in 1973 that the ban was discriminatory, and colleges with major men's sports programs began expanding their women's programs. The NCAA began holding women's championships during the 1981–82 school year. The AIAW disbanded the following year. Many colleges merged their men's and women's athletic departments, usually under the control of a male athletic director, and the number of male coaches in charge of women's teams in-creased as programs went big-time. By the early 1980s, women's collegiate athletics faced many of the problems previously associated with men's sports, including intensive recruiting and, in some cases, charges that illegal inducements were offered to promising prospects.

Television sponsors discovered women's golf, as well as tennis, during the 1970s. Colgate-Palmolive was a leader, establishing the Dinah Shore Classic in 1972 as the richest tournament on the women's tour. Nabisco took over sponsorship of the tournament in 1982. First prize is now $80,000, more than the tour's top money-winner collected in the entire 1972 season. The U.S. Women's Open also has an $80,000 first prize.

Women have also moved into sports that were previously for men only. Diane Crump became the first woman jockey to ride in the Kentucky Derby in 1970. During the 1980s, Diane Krone emerged as one of the best jockeys in the country. She rode 363 winners in 1988 to finish fourth among all jockeys, and on February 11, 1989, she rode five winners on a single card at Aqueduct. The most macho sport of all, auto racing, has also attracted a few women. Shirley Muldowney is a genuine drag racing star. Janet Guthrie was the first woman to drive in the Indianapolis 500, in 1977, and Desire Wilson won more than $50,000 in Indy car racing in 1983. Shawna Robinson in 1988 became the first woman to win a major stock car race and was named Rookie of the Year in NASCAR's touring division.

While women may never play the major professional team sports with men, they are competing in intercollegiate basketball, lacrosse, and soccer in unprecedented numbers. The NCAA has conducted national women's championships in those sports, and in field hockey, since the 1981–82 school year.

Further Reading: Gerber, Ellen W. *et al. The American Woman in Sport.* Reading, MA: Addison-Wesley, 1974; Kaplan, Janis. *Women and Sports.* New York: Viking, 1979.

See also ALL-AMERICAN GIRLS PROFESSIONAL BASE-BALL LEAGUE; ASSOCIATION FOR INTERCOLLEGIATE ATHLETICS FOR WOMEN; BERENSON, SENDA; CANADIAN ASSOCIATION FOR THE ADVANCEMENT OF WOMEN AND SPORT; CHADWICK, FLORENCE; DIDRIKSON, "BABE"; EDERLE, GERTRUDE; GUTHRIE, JANET; INTERNATIONAL LADIES' GAMES; INTERNATIONAL WOMEN'S PROFESSIONAL SOFTBALL LEAGUE; KING, BILLIE JEAN; LADIES PROFESSIONAL BOWLERS TOUR; LADIES PROFESSIONAL GOLF ASSOCIATION; OAKLEY, ANNIE; PLAY DAYS; SEARS, ELEONORA; TITLE IX; VIRGINIA SLIMS TOURNAMENT; WADE, L. MARGARET; WADE TROPHY; WOMEN'S INTER-

NATIONAL TENNIS ASSOCIATION; WOMEN'S INTERNATIONAL BOWLING CONGRESS; WOMEN'S SPORTS FOUNDATION.

Women's International Bowling Congress (WIBC)

The American Bowling Congress ruled women's bowling until 1916, when the WIBC was organized with 40 members. It held its first national tournament, patterned after the ABC tournament, in 1917. Only 24 bowlers entered the individual events. Membership grew rapidly, to 5,357 in 1926, 23,308 in 1936, and 301,064 in 1946. By 1957, there were more than 1 million members in nearly 37,000 leagues. WIBC membership peaked at 4.2 million in 1977, but has since dropped to about 3.3 million.

In 1956 the WIBC divided its annual tournament into two divisions, based on averages. Division I is for bowlers with averages between 151 and 170, Division II for those with averages of 150 or lower. In 1969 an Open Division was added for bowlers with averages over 170. Since 1961, the WIBC has also conducted the Queens Tournament for professional bowlers.

Address: 5301 South 76th Street, Greendale, WI 53129 (414) 421–9000

See also QUEENS TOURNAMENT.

Women's International Tennis Association

After the Virginia Slims circuit was launched, Billie Jean King led a group of women players who founded the Women's Tennis Association during the 1973 Wimbledon tournament. Conceived as a union of tennis professionals, the WTA began organizing its own tournaments in 1974, when Jerry Diamond became its full-time executive director. The organization became the Women's International Tennis Association in 1986. It now offers nearly $20 million in prize money for its tournaments.

See also VIRGINA SLIMS CIRCUIT.

Women's Olympics
See INTERNATIONAL LADIES GAMES.

Women's Sports Foundation

Tennis player Billie Jean King and Olympic swimmer Donna de Varona were founding members of the Women's Sports Foundation in 1974. The major goal of the WSF is to raise public awareness of the benefits of sports and fitness for girls and women. The foundation publishes *Women's Sports and Fitness* magazine and a guide listing athletic scholarships available to women. It offers travel and training grants to female athletes and selects an amateur and professional sportswoman of the year. The WSF Up and Coming Awards are given annually to ten young athletes. In 1986, the foundation launched an "Aspire Higher" campaign to give financial aid to programs training women for careers in coaching, physical education, officiating, and sports administration. The campaign was announced by Martina Navratilova immediately after she won the U.S. Open tennis championship that year; she donated $150,000 and called upon other women athletes to donate 1 percent of their earnings to the cause.

Address: 342 Madison Avenue, Suite 728, New York, NY 10173 (212) 972–9170

Woodbine Race Track
Toronto, Ontario

The original Woodbine opened in 1874 and in 1883 it began hosting the Queen's Plate, North America's oldest continuously run stakes race. The new course, built by the Ontario Jockey Club at a cost of $13 million, opened in June of 1956. The old track still exists; it was called Old Woodbine until 1963, when it became known as Greenwood. In addition to the Queen's Plate, Woodbine hosts the Rothman's International, founded in 1956 as the Canadian National Championship. A 1⅝-mile turf race, the International is one of the world's premier racing events, with a guaranteed purse of $700,000.

Address: P.O. Box 156, Rexdale, Ontario, Canada M9W 5L2 (416) 675–6110

See also QUEEN'S PLATE.

Wooden Award
Basketball

The Los Angeles Athletic Club presents this award to the college basketball Player of the Year, as chosen by a panel of coaches, broadcasters, and sportswriters. It's named for John Wooden, long-time UCLA coach.

Wooden Award Winners

1977	Marques Johnson, UCLA
1978	Phil Ford, North Carolina
1979	Larry Bird, Indiana State
1980	Darrell Griffith, Louisville
1981	Danny Ainge, Brigham Young
1982	Ralph Sampson, Virginia
1983	Ralph Sampson, Virginia
1984	Michael Jordan, North Carolina
1985	Chris Mullin, St. John's
1986	Walter Berry, St. John's
1987	David Robinson, Navy
1988	Danny Manning, Kansas

The only person named to the Basketball Hall of Fame both as a coach and as a player, John Wooden was an All-American at Purdue from 1930 through 1932. He coached UCLA to ten national championships from 1964 through 1975. Courtesy of the Basketball Hall of Fame

1989   Sean Elliott, Arizona
1990   Lionel Simmons, LeSalle
1991   Larry Johnson, Nevada-Las Vegas

Wooden, John R. (1910–   )
Basketball
Born October 14, 1910, Martinsville, IN; Basketball Hall of Fame

Wooden was a three-time All-American guard at Purdue from 1930 through 1932 and was College Player of the Year as a senior. As a professional with the Kautsky Grocers of Indianapolis, he made 138 consecutive free throws. After winning 83 percent of his games as a high school coach in Kentucky and Indiana, he took over at Indiana State college in 1948 and had a 47–14 record in two seasons before becoming head coach at UCLA. Wooden's UCLA teams dominated college basketball from 1964 through 1975, winning ten NCAA tournament championships, including seven in a row from 1967 through 1973. He was named Coach of the Year in 1964, 1967, 1969, 1970, 1972, and 1973. Although he coached two of the greatest centers in history, Lew Alcindor (later Kareem Abdul-Jabbar) and Bill Walton, Wooden also won championships with less-talented teams. His 1970 champions, for example,

didn't have a single All-American player. In 29 seasons, Wooden had a record of 667 wins and 161 losses, an .806 percentage, and he was 47 and 10 in NCAA tournament competition.

Worcester, MA
Baseball Worcester had a team in the National League from 1880 through 1882.

World Boxing Organization
The National Boxing Association was founded in 1920 as an organization of state athletic commissions to standardize boxing rules and regulations. However, California, New York, and Pennsylvania refused to join. As John Kieran of the *New York Times* pointed out in 1930, "A fighter banned in New York can fight in National Boxing Association territory, and that includes twenty-six states. A fighter banned in NBA territory can fight in New York or Pennsylvania." On a number of occasions, the NBA recognized a fighter as a champion while New York State recognized a different champion. The NBA became the World Boxing Association in 1956, when several Central and South American countries joined. It took its present name in 1988.
Address: 412 Colorado Avenue, Aurora, IL 60506 (312) 897–4765

World Championship Tennis (WCT)
Conceived in 1967 by businessmen Dave Dixon of New Orleans and Lamar Hunt and Al Hill, Jr. of Dallas, WCT signed the "Handsome Eight"—Pierre Barthes, Butch Buchholz, Cliff Drysdale, John Newcombe, Nikki Pilic, Dennis Ralston, Tony Roche, and Roger Taylor—to contracts and began a small circuit of professional tournaments. It became a worldwide tour in 1971, with the eight top players meeting in the WCT Finals at Dallas. Frustrated by financial losses, the backers withdrew their support in August of 1990 and the WCT folded.

World Cup
Golf
Originally the Canada Cup, this trophy was donated in 1953 by Canadian industrialist John Jay Hopkins for international competition among two-man professional teams. It was renamed the World Cup in 1967.

World Cup
Skiing
Established by the Federation of International Skiing in 1967, the World Cup is based on season-long

competition among men and women in Alpine skiing. Points are awarded to the top ten finishers in each of a series of races, and bonus points are also given for finishing in the top ten in the Alpine combined event at three of the races. Only three North Americans have ever won the World Cup: Nancy Greene of Canada in 1967 and 1968, Phil Mahre of the United States in 1981, 1982, and 1983, and Tamara McKinney of the United States in 1983.

World Cup
Soccer

Formally the Jules Rimet Trophy, the World Cup is awarded every four years to the winning nation in a worldwide soccer tournament. After preliminary rounds, 16 teams qualify for the final tournament. The 1994 World Cup finals will be held in the United States for the first time.

World Eskimo-Indian Olympics

Pilot Sam Houston of Wien Airways saw native games in 1961, when his plane was broken down in Point Hope, Alaska. He persuaded his employer to sponsor the World Eskimo-Indian Olympics as an annual event on the banks of the Chena River near Fairbanks. Held in late July, the games are now conducted by a nonprofit corporation. In addition to the competition, some sports are demonstrated nightly at the Alaskaland theme park in Fairbanks. Among the events are the arm pull, in which two competitors lock arms while sitting and attempt to pull one another over, and the high kick, in which the athlete stands on one foot and kicks a ball suspended at a predetermined height with the foot he's standing on. The ball is continually raised higher until only one competitor is able to kick it.

See also ESKIMO SPORTS; NATIVE AMERICAN SPORTS.

World Figure Skating Hall of Fame
Colorado Springs, CO

Founded in 1979 as the U.S. Figure Skating Hall of Fame and Museum, this facility was recognized by the International Skating Union in 1984 as a worldwide hall of fame. Its centerpiece is the Gillis Grafstrom "Skating in Art" collection, which features prints, etchings, figurines, literature, and music covering more than 200 years of the sport. The Gallery of Skates traces the development of the skate from carved bones to modern steel blades. The hall of fame also has a large collection of films and videotapes, as well as a reference library. It is located next to the U.S. Figure Skating Association's headquarters in Colorado Springs.

Address: 20 First Street, Colorado Springs, CO 80906–3697 (303) 635–5200

World Football League

Garry Davidson, who had organized the American Basketball Association and the World Hockey Association, was also the man behind the WFL, which began play in 1974. To avoid head-to-head competition with the National Football League, the WFL began its season in mid-July, with most of its games on Wednesday and Thursday nights rather than Sunday afternoon. The league adopted five rules changes to increase scoring. Kickoffs were from the 30- rather than the 40-yard line; goalposts were on the end line rather than the goal line; the ball was returned to the original line of scrimmage on a missed field goal from beyond the 20-yard line; a pass reception was allowed if the player had just one foot in bounds; and teams had the option of running or passing for a two-point conversion after a touchdown. In addition, the WFL adopted a 15-minute extra period, with a kickoff at the beginning of the period and at the 7½-minute mark, if a game was tied after the regulation four quarters.

The league had teams in Birmingham, Chicago, Detroit, Florida, Hawaii, Houston, Jacksonville, Memphis, New York, Philadelphia, Portland, and Southern California. At first, attendance seemed good, but it was then revealed that figures had been greatly inflated. The WFL folded after its 1975 season.

World Golf Hall of Fame
Pinehurst, NC

Formally opened on September 11, 1974, the World Golf Hall of Fame was originally privately owned by the Diamondhead Corporation, which also owned and operated Pinehurst Resort. Because of financial difficulties, ownership was transferred to a consortium of banks in the late 1970s. The Professional Golfers Association of America was given control in 1983, and three years later the PGA acquired full ownership. The hall overlooks the fourth hole of Pinehurst Number 2, one of the country's finest golf courses. The 25,000-square-foot facility includes a gallery of golf art, the Laurie Auchterlonie Collection of golf artifacts and memorabilia, exhibits on major tournaments and the Ryder Cup, and the Hall of Fame itself. Inductees are selected by the National Golf Writers Association.

Address: PGA Boulevard, P.O. Box 1908, Pinehurst, NC 28374 (919) 295–6651

World Hockey Association (WHA)

The WHA began play in the 1972–73 season with teams in Alberta, Boston, Chicago, Cleveland, Houston, Los Angeles, Minnesota, New York, Ottawa, Philadelphia, Quebec, and Winnipeg. It also landed several stars from the rival National Hockey League, including high-scoring forward Bobby Hull with Winnipeg and goalie Gerry Cheevers with Cleveland. In the second season, Houston persuaded hockey legend Gordie Howe to come out of retirement to play alongside his sons, Mark and Matt. Howe was named the league's most valuable player, Mark was rookie of the year, and Houston won the Avco World Trophy, the WHA's equivalent of the Stanley Cup.

An antitrust suit brought by the WHA against the NHL was settled out of court in 1974. The leagues agreed to honor one another's player contracts, the NHL paid the WHA an indemnity of $1.75 million, and plans were made for interleague exhibition games beginning in 1975. The salary war for young players continued, however, and several teams ran into financial problems. Among them were the Denver Spurs and the Toronto Toros, which had entered the league in 1975, and the Minnesota Fighting Saints. The Denver and Minnesota franchises folded after the 1975–76 season, the Toros became the Birmingham Bulls, and the Cleveland Crusaders moved to Minnesota to become the new Fighting Saints. The WHA merged into the NHL in 1979, but only four teams survived: Edmonton Oilers, New England Whalers, Quebec Nordiques, and Winnipeg Jets.

WHA Champions

1973	New England Whalers
1974	Houston Aeros
1975	Houston Aeros
1976	Winnipeg Jets
1977	Quebec Nordiques
1978	Winnipeg Jets
1979	Winnipeg Jets

See also NATIONAL HOCKEY LEAGUE.

World League of American Football

The National Football League in 1988 announced plans for what was then called the International League of American Football. The league was to begin with teams in six European cities playing a 12-game schedule beginning in April of 1990, with 6 U.S. cities to be added in the second season. The name was changed to the World League of American Football in 1989, and it was announced that the six European teams would be the Amsterdam Lions, Barcelona Olympics, Birmingham Bears, London Lightning, Helsinki Blue Fox, and Munich Falcons.

Because the league couldn't land a television contract with a major network, its inaugural season was postponed to 1991.

When the WLAF began play in March of 1991, there were only three European teams, in Barcelona, Frankfurt, and London, along with teams representing Birmingham, Montreal, New York-New Jersey, Orlando, Raleigh-Durham, Sacramento, and San Antonio. The league has a two-year, $50 million contract with ABC, as well as coverage by the USA cable network, the British Sky Eurosport Network, Germany's Tele 5 Network, and Spain's Catalunya Network.

World Series
Baseball

The phrase "World Championship Series" was in use nearly 20 years before the modern World Series came into existence. It was first applied to an 1884 postseason series between the New York Metropolitans of the American Association and the Providence Grays of the National League. Informal competition between the pennant winners of the two leagues continued through 1890. The number of games ranged from just 3 in 1884 to 15 in 1887, when the Association's St. Louis team and the League's Detroit team went on tour, playing at eight major-league parks in addition to their own. The leagues were at war in 1891, the American Association's final season.

The World Series as we know it, a contest between the American and National League champions, began in 1903 after the two leagues decided to end their two-year battle for players by signing a new National Agreement. When the season ended, the two pennant winners, Boston of the American and Pittsburgh of the National League, agreed to play for the world championship in a nine-game series, the winning team to get 75 percent of the gate receipts. Boston beat Pittsburgh, five games to three.

The New York Giants won the National League pennant in 1904, but refused to play such a series because owner John T. Brush and manager John McGraw held grudges against American League president Ban Johnson. The following year, National League owners voted to require their champion to play the American League pennant winner after the season; ironically, Brush drew up the rules governing the series. The rules called for a best four-of-seven series. Baseball went back to the five-of-nine format from 1919 through 1921, but since 1922 it has been four-of-seven, as Brush had specified.

Under Brush's plan, 60 percent of the gate receipts from the first four games went to the players, with the winners getting 75 percent of that amount. The other 40 percent was divided equally between the two teams. Because of the great difference between a winner's share and a loser's share, players began to make secret agreements for a 50–50 split, regardless of the outcome. As a result, the split became a more equitable 60–40, and it's the same today, although revenues are obviously much higher because of television.

The owners in 1918 decided to allow the second-, third-, and fourth-place finishers in each league to share in World Series receipts, which almost brought about a strike. Attendance was lower than normal because of World War I, and after three games in Chicago the National Commission announced that Series shares would be $1,200 and $800 for the winners and losers, respectively, rather than the $2,000 and $1,400 that had been projected. The Red Sox and Cubs discussed the matter on the train from Chicago to Boston and decided not to play the rest of the Series unless their shares were restored. The strike lasted an hour, while fans waited, and then the players gave in.

Within a short time after its establishment, the World Series was a major event. Receipts increased from about $50,000 in 1905 to nearly $500,000 in 1912 and to more than $1 million in 1923, when the two New York teams met for the third year in a row. The interest in that series showed that baseball had recovered very quickly from the "Black Sox scandal," which broke in September of 1920 with the revelation that gamblers had paid a number of Chicago White Sox players to throw the 1919 World Series against Cincinnati.

There were a couple of untoward events during the long reign of Commissioner Kenesaw Mountain Landis. The Giants won the first game of the 1922 Series against the Yankees, and the second game was tied 3–3 after ten innings when the umpires called it off, supposedly because of darkness, although the sun was still shining on the edge of the outfield grass. Angry fans stormed onto the field, and baseball was accused of trying to make extra money by stretching out the Series. Landis impounded the gate receipts and gave the money to charity.

The St. Louis Cardinals were beating the Detroit Tigers 11–0 in the seventh game of the 1934 Series when Joe Medwick of St. Louis hit a seventh-inning triple, sliding hard into the Tigers' third baseman. When Medwick took his position in left field in the bottom half of the inning, Detroit fans showered him with fruit, vegetables, and bottles. Landis had Medwick taken out of the game for his own protection, and some sportswriters criticized his high-handedness. Medwick and St. Louis manager Frankie Frisch

didn't complain, though, because of the almost insurmountable Cardinal lead at the time—11–0 was the final score.

When both major leagues expanded to 12 teams in 1969, they were split into two 6-team divisions, with the division champions meeting in the league championship series to determine the pennant winners. Many writers feel that the playoff format takes some of the luster from the World Series, although the National Football League has an extended series of playoffs leading up to the Super Bowl, which is the most ballyhooed and most watched of all sports events.

The American League in 1973 began using the designated hitter, who bats in place of the pitcher but doesn't play defensively. The DH rule didn't apply to the World Series until 1976; from then until 1983, it was used in even-numbered years. Since 1984, the pitcher bats in games played in the National League park, and the designated hitter is used in the American League park.

Night games were first played in the 1971 World Series, for the sake of higher television ratings. For 15 seasons, weekend games were still staged in the afternoon, but games played during the week were in prime time. NBC television in 1985 insisted that the weekend games be played at night as well. The network was rewarded with an increase from an 18.9 rating in 1984 to 25.3 in 1985 and 28.6 in 1986. More important—to NBC, at least—the prime-time ratings meant that a 30-second commercial was worth $250,000, double the price of a weekend afternoon spot.

World Series Results
(Figures indicate the number of games won by each team)

1903 Boston (AL) 5, Pittsburgh 3
1904 Not Played
1905 New York (NL) 4, Philadelphia 1
1906 Chicago (AL) 4, Chicago (NL) 2
1907 Chicago (NL) 4, Detroit 0
1908 Chicago (NL) 4, Detroit 1
1909 Pittsurgh (NL) 4, Detroit 3
1910 Philadelphia (AL) 4, Chicago 1
1911 Philadelphia (AL) 4, New York 2
1912 Boston (AL) 4, New York 3
1913 Philadelphia (AL) 4, New York 1
1914 Boston (NL) 4, Philadelphia 0
1915 Boston (AL) 4, Philadelphia 1
1916 Boston (AL) 4, Brooklyn 1
1917 Chicago (AL) 4, New York 2
1918 Boston (AL) 4, Chicago 2
1919 Cincinnati (NL) 5, Chicago 3
1920 Cleveland (AL) 4, Brooklyn 3

1921	New York (NL) 5, New York 3		1976	Cincinnati (NL) 4, New York 0
1922	New York (NL) 4, New York 3		1977	New York (AL) 4, Los Angeles 2
1923	New York (AL) 4, New York 2		1978	New York (AL) 4, Los Angeles 2
1924	Washington (AL) 4, New York 3		1979	Pittsburgh (NL) 4, Baltimore 3
1925	Pittsburgh (NL) 4, Washington 3		1980	Philadelphia (NL) 4, Kansas City 2
1926	St. Louis (NL) 4, New York 3		1981	Los Angeles (NL) 4, New York 2
1927	New York (AL) 4, Pittsburgh 0		1982	St. Louis (NL) 4, Milwaukee 3
1928	New York (AL) 4, St. Louis 0		1983	Baltimore (AL) 4, Philadelphia 1
1929	Philadelphia (AL) 4, Chicago 1		1984	Detroit (AL) 4, San Diego 1
1930	Philadelphia (AL) 4, St. Louis 2		1985	Kansas City (AL) 4, St. Louis 3
1931	St. Louis (NL) 4, Philadelphia 3		1986	New York (NL) 4, Boston 3
1932	New York (AL) 4, Chicago 0		1987	Minnesota (AL) 4, St. Louis 2
1933	New York (NL) 4, Washington 1		1988	Los Angeles (NL) 4, Oakland 1
1934	St. Louis (NL) 4, Detroit 3		1989	Oakland (AL) 4, San Francisco 0
1935	Detroit (AL) 4, Chicago 2		1990	Cincinati (NL) 4, Oakland 0
1936	New York (AL) 4, New York 2			
1937	New York (AL) 4, New York 1			

1921 New York (NL) 5, New York 3
1922 New York (NL) 4, New York 3
1923 New York (AL) 4, New York 2
1924 Washington (AL) 4, New York 3
1925 Pittsburgh (NL) 4, Washington 3
1926 St. Louis (NL) 4, New York 3
1927 New York (AL) 4, Pittsburgh 0
1928 New York (AL) 4, St. Louis 0
1929 Philadelphia (AL) 4, Chicago 1
1930 Philadelphia (AL) 4, St. Louis 2
1931 St. Louis (NL) 4, Philadelphia 3
1932 New York (AL) 4, Chicago 0
1933 New York (NL) 4, Washington 1
1934 St. Louis (NL) 4, Detroit 3
1935 Detroit (AL) 4, Chicago 2
1936 New York (AL) 4, New York 2
1937 New York (AL) 4, New York 1
1938 New York (AL) 4, Chicago 0
1939 New York (AL) 4, Cincinnati 0
1940 Cincinnati (NL) 4, Detroit 3
1941 New York (AL) 4, Brooklyn 1
1942 St. Louis (NL) 4, New York 1
1943 New York (AL) 4, St. Louis 1
1944 St. Louis (NL) 4, St. Louis 2
1945 Detroit (AL) 4, Chicago 3
1946 St. Louis (NL) 4, Boston 3
1947 New York (AL) 4, Brooklyn 3
1948 Cleveland (AL) 4, Boston 2
1949 New York (AL) 4, Brooklyn 1
1950 New York (AL) 4, Philadelphia 0
1951 New York (AL) 4, New York 2
1952 New York (AL) 4, Brooklyn 3
1953 New York (AL) 4, Brooklyn 2
1954 New York (NL) 4, Cleveland 0
1955 Brooklyn (NL) 4, New York 3
1956 New York (AL) 4, Brooklyn 3
1957 Milwaukee (NL) 4, New York 3
1958 New York (AL) 4, Milwaukee 3
1959 Los Angeles (NL) 4, Chicago 2
1960 Pittsburgh (NL) 4, New York 3
1961 New York (AL) 4, Cincinnati 1
1962 New York (AL) 4, San Francisco 3
1963 Los Angeles (NL) 4, New York 0
1964 St. Louis (NL) 4, New York 3
1965 Los Angeles (NL) 4, Minnesota 3
1966 Baltimore (AL) 4, Los Angeles 0
1967 St. Louis (NL) 4, Boston 3
1968 Detroit (AL) 4, St. Louis 3
1969 New York (NL) 4, Baltimore 1
1970 Baltimore (AL) 4, Cincinnat 1
1971 Pittsburgh (NL) 4, Baltimore 3
1972 Oakland (AL) 4, Cincinnati 3
1973 Oakland (AL) 4, New York 3
1974 Oakland (AL) 4, Los Angeles 1
1975 Cincinnati (NL) 4, Boston 3

1976 Cincinnati (NL) 4, New York 0
1977 New York (AL) 4, Los Angeles 2
1978 New York (AL) 4, Los Angeles 2
1979 Pittsburgh (NL) 4, Baltimore 3
1980 Philadelphia (NL) 4, Kansas City 2
1981 Los Angeles (NL) 4, New York 2
1982 St. Louis (NL) 4, Milwaukee 3
1983 Baltimore (AL) 4, Philadelphia 1
1984 Detroit (AL) 4, San Diego 1
1985 Kansas City (AL) 4, St. Louis 3
1986 New York (NL) 4, Boston 3
1987 Minnesota (AL) 4, St. Louis 2
1988 Los Angeles (NL) 4, Oakland 1
1989 Oakland (AL) 4, San Francisco 0
1990 Cincinati (NL) 4, Oakland 0

See also TEMPLE CUP.

World Team Tennis (WTT)

The WTT was founded in 1974 as a 16-team league. At first, teams played one another head-to-head in six sets, two sets each of men's singles, women's singles, and mixed doubles. Just two weeks into the season, the format was changed to one set each of men's singles, women's singles, men's doubles, women's doubles, and mixed doubles because matches were running too long.

The original teams were the Baltimore Banners, Boston Lobsters, Chicago Aces, Cleveland Nets, Denver Racquets, Detroit Loves, Florida Flamingos, Golden Gaters, Hawaii Leis, Houston EZ Riders, Los Angeles Strings, Minnesota Buckskins, New York Sets, Philadelphia Freedoms, Pittsburgh Triangles, and Toronto-Buffalo Royals. The number of teams shrank to ten in 1975, and in 1977 a touring team from the Soviet Union replaced Pittsburgh. They were replaced by the Anaheim Oranges in 1978, the league's final season.

The WTT attracted some of the best players in the world, including Bjorn Borg, Jimmy Connors, Chris Evert, Evonne Goolagong, Billie Jean King, and Martina Navratilova and matches generally drew good crowds. The main reason the WTT folded was that professional tennis had developed some strong worldwide tours by the late 1970s and the WTT money simply wasn't worth the trouble to most players.

Wrestling

Informal wrestling without rules is common among young animals as well as human children, so in a sense it is probably one of the oldest sports. A statue of two wrestlers found in Iraq dates to about 5,000 years ago. The ancient Egyptians codified the sport as early as 1850 B.C. and the Greeks adapted the

Egyptian style of wrestling. The Romans developed a somewhat different style that eventually merged with the Greek into "stand-up" wrestling, now known as Greco-Roman.

By the Middle Ages, forms of Greco-Roman wrestling were popular in the Cumberland-Westmoreland and Cornwall-Devon regions of England, while a less restrictive style, called "catch as catch can" or "no holds barred," was favored in Scotland, Ireland, and the Lancashire region.

Frontiersmen engaged in rough-and-tumble fighting in which everything was allowed, including biting, scratching, and eye gouging. But there were also more formal matches, often arranged between the acknowledged champions of two neighboring towns or settlements, in which the Lancashire catch-as-catch-can rules were used. As a genuine organized sport, however, wrestling had to await the arrival of gymnasiums and athletic clubs during the last quarter of the 19th century. At first, gym instructors taught the Greco-Roman style, in which the wrestlers stand; holds below the waist and tripping are prohibited, and the object is to throw the opponent down. But freestyle wrestling, a form of catch-as-catch-can, was far more popular, and it began spreading into the gyms and, gradually replaced Greco-Roman. When the Amateur Athletic Union held its first championship tournament in 1889, it was for freestyle; Greco-Roman wrestling didn't become a national championship sport until 1953.

Several touring professionals helped popularize wrestling around the turn of the century. Martin "Farmer" Burns won the heavyweight championship by beating Evan "Strangler" Lewis in 1895. Two years later, Tom Jenkins took the title from Burns. He held it until 1904, when Frank Gotch beat him. Gotch was an outstanding wrestler who won 154 of 160 professional matches. His 1909 contest with the European champion George Hackenschmidt drew a crowd of 40,000 people in Chicago. Gotch retired in 1913, and after World War I professional wrestling fell into disfavor because there was so much fakery involved, as there is today.

The Intercollegiate Wrestling Association was founded by Columbia, Pennsylvania, Princeton, and Yale in 1903. Cornell, Lehigh, Penn State, and Syracuse soon joined the IWA. Colleges usually took part in dual meets; the first major college tournament was the national championship established by the NCAA in 1928. That was only the third NCAA championship event—the first two were track and field in 1921 and swimming in 1924.

There was a single freestyle wrestling event on the original modern Olympic program in 1896, but it was dropped in 1900. There were seven freestyle weight divisions in 1904, and the "intercalated" Games of 1906 had Greco-Roman wrestling in three weight classes but no freestyle wrestling. However, freestyle was restored to the program in 1908, and Greco-Roman was expanded to six weight classes in 1920.

USA Wrestling, founded as the U.S. Wrestling Federation in 1969, replaced the AAU as the sport's national governing body in 1979. Under its leadership, the United States has gained international respectability in the sport, winning two Gold Medals in freestyle and its first ever in Greco-Roman at the 1988 Olympics. The organization has 90,000 registered wrestlers, 80,000 of them 18 or younger, and in 1989 it increased its revenues by 80 percent, to $4.5 million, through sponsorship and a $400,000 television contract with TBS.

Addresses: Canadian Amateur Wrestling Association, 333 River Road, Vanier, Ontario, Canada K1L 8H9 (613) 748–5686; U.S.A. Wrestling, 225 South Academy Boulevard, Colorado Springs, CO 80910 (719) 597–8333

Wright, "Harry" William Henry (1835–1895)
Baseball

Born January 10, 1835, Sheffield, England; died October 3, 1895; Baseball Hall of Fame

The son of a professional cricket player, Wright was brought to the United States by his parents when he was just a year old. He became known as one of the country's best cricketers during the 1850s, and in 1858 he also began playing baseball with the Knickerbocker Club. The Union Cricket Club of Cincinnati hired Wright as an instructor in August of 1865, and a year later he organized the Cincinnati Red Stockings. He made them the first openly professional basketball team in 1869. Among the players was his younger brother, George, one of the country's best shortstops. Harry usually played the outfield, but he occasionally pitched. The Red Stockings toured throughout the Midwest and the East in 1869 and 1870, playing 130 consecutive games without a loss until the Brooklyn Atlantics beat them 8–7 in 11 innings.

Wright in 1871 became the manager of the Boston team in the new National Association, with brother George again at shortstop. The Boston team, also called the Red Stockings, won four consecutive pennants from 1872 through 1875. The association collapsed and was replaced by the National League in 1876, with Harry again managing Boston and George still playing shortstop. That team won the pennant in 1877 and 1878. Wright managed the Providence Grays in 1882 and 1883 and Philadelphia from 1884 through 1893, then became the league's chief of umpires until his death.

Wright, "Mickey" Mary K. (1935–   )
Golf
Born February 14, 1935, San Diego, CA; World Golf Hall of Fame

As an amateur, Wright was paired with Babe Didrikson Zaharias during the 1954 U.S. Women's Open. Zaharias watched her hit practice drives for a while and said to her husband, George, "Get a load of that young dame. I didn't think anyone could hit 'em that far except the old Babe." Zaharias won the tournament, and Wright was the top amateur finisher. She turned professional the following year and replaced Zaharias as the tour's top golfer during the late 1950s. She won both the LPGA Championship and the Women's Open in 1958 and 1961. Wright was also the Open champion in 1959 and 1964 and the LPGA champion in 1960 and 1963.

Wright won a record 13 tournaments in 1963, when she was named the Associated Press Female Athlete of the Year. She was the tour's leading money-winner from 1961 through 1964, and she won the Vare Trophy five times, from 1960 through 1964. At the age of 30, she curtailed her playing schedule to return to college at Southern Methodist University.

Wrigley Field
Chicago, IL

The oldest park in the major leagues, Wrigley was built in 1914 by Charles Weeghman, owner of the Chicago Federal League team, who named it Weeghman Field. At that time, the park had a capacity of about 14,000 in a single-level grandstand behind home plate and bleacher seats in right field. Weeghman acquired the National League's Chicago Cubs in 1916, after the Federal League folded, and promptly moved the team to his field. William Wrigley, Jr. led a group of Chicago businessmen who bought the team in 1921, when capacity was expanded to about 20,000.

A major renovation took place during the winter of 1926–27. A double-decked grandstand was built from the right field corner to the left field corner, nearly doubling seating capacity. The park was then renamed Wrigley Field. It took on its present configuration in 1937, when bleachers were added around the entire outfield. At that time, the famous ivy-covered brick wall was also added. Beginning in 1967 and continuing into the winter of 1970–71, the upper deck was completely rebuilt in sections, the work being done in the off-season.

Wrigley Field was the last major-league park to get lights. The team had planned to install lights in 1942, but after the Japanese attacked Pearl Harbor on December 7, 1941, it was assumed that baseball would not be played for the duration of the war, and the Cubs donated the structural steel and electric cable to the War Department. Shortly afterward, President Franklin D. Roosevelt said major-league baseball should be played during the war because it would aid national morale, and he also called on teams to play more night games as recreation for wartime factory workers.

The Chicago Tribune Company acquired the Cubs in 1981 and shortly afterward announced plans to install lights at the field. A neighborhood citizens' group called Chicagoans United for Baseball in Sunshine (CUBS) opposed the idea, and in 1982 the Illinois Legislature passed a new noise pollution law that, in effect, prohibited games in Wrigley Field after 10 P.M. The following year, the Chicago City Council enacted an ordinance that would have prevented night games at the park. The ordinance and law were both repealed in 1988 under a compromise allowing just eight night games. The Cubs finally played their first home game under the lights on August 8 against the Philadelphia Phillies, but the game was suspended because of rain after 2 hours and 10 minutes. The first official night game at Wrigley was a 6–4 victory over the New York Mets on August 9.

Wrigley Field is one of the smallest parks in the majors, seating just 39,012. Its home run distances are 355 to left field, 400 feet to center, and 353 feet to right.

Yachting

Like most racing, yachting began with impromptu match races that often involved bets. The first recorded race of that kind was in 1662, when King Charles II of England's *Jamie* beat the Duke of York's *Anne* for a wager of 100 pounds. There was some pleasure boating in North America as early as the 17th century, but the first real yacht was *Jefferson*, a 22-ton sloop built in 1801 by George Crowninshield of Salem, MA. Crowninshield also built a 200–ton schooner-rigged yacht, *Cleopatra's Barge*, in 1816. There was a brief flurry of yachting activity in the Boston area during the early 1830s, but it died in the financial panic of 1837.

The first recorded yacht race in North America took place in 1835, when John Cox Stevens of New York sailed his schooner *Wave* to Nantucket to challenge Robert Bennett Forbes' *Sylph*. Stevens won an easy victory. Later, he commissioned a yacht called *Gimcrack* from builder George Steers; on July 30, 1844, the New York Yacht Club was founded by nine men meeting aboard *Gimcrack*. The NYYC in 1847 developed a handicap system based on a vessel's size to allow boats of different types to compete against one another.

Other yacht clubs were soon established along the East Coast. In 1851 the Steers-designed *America*, commissioned by a syndicate headed by Stevens, sailed to England; on August 22 she won the Hundred Guinea Cup in a Royal Yacht Squadron race around the Isle of Wight. The trophy later became known as the America's Cup.

Many pleasure yachts were built after the Civil War, most of them schooners requiring sizable crews. In 1866, Pierre Lorillard, Jr. challenged George and Franklin Osgood to a trans-Atlantic race from Sandy Hook Lightship to the Needles in England. James Gordon Bennett, Jr. also got involved in the race for a winner-take-all bet of $90,000. The race began on December 11 and ended on Christmas Day when Bennett's *Henrietta* finished 8 hours ahead of the Osgood's *Fleetwing*. The race aroused so much publicity that membership in the NYYC doubled during the following year.

The first America's Cup race in 1870 also stirred a lot of interest in yachting, but the sport was basically for the very wealthy during this period. Some sailing was taking place in smaller, less expensive boats, however. As early as the 1830s, the "sandbag-

The first challenge for the America's Cup was in 1870, when Herbert Ashbury's Cambria faced the entire New York Yacht Club fleet. Magic won and Cambria finished eighth. This Currier & Ives lithograph depicts the race.

ger," a shallow sloop ballasted with sandbags, was developed in New York Harbor. The Seawanhaka Corinthian Yacht Club in 1871 organized sailing for smaller boats, generally sloops, around Oyster Bay, Long Island, and the catboat was developed in Rhode Island about the same time. At first a working boat, the catboat soon became a popular pleasure boat in New England.

It was the one-design, though, that really gave sailing a boost during the early 20th century. In one-design racing, all boats are built to the same specifications, eliminating the need to work out ratings and use handicaps. The Seawanhaka CYC pioneered in this area, as well, building four catboats of a single design in 1892. In 1896, Nathaniel Herreshoff began producing 30-foot one-design boats for Newport sailors. Soon there were many one-design sailboats around, on inland lakes as well as on the ocean.

Several major long-distance races had tentative beginnings early in the century. The first actually took place in 1898, between Chicago and Mackinac Island, a distance of 333 miles. Like the trans-Atlantic race of 1866, it began with a bet. The second race was held in 1904, and it is now an annual event conducted by the Chicago Yacht Club. A New York-to-Bermuda race was held in 1906, 1907, and 1910. Revived in 1923, it became the Newport-to-Bermuda race in 1924 and is now held biannually. A trans-Pacific race was held biannually from 1906 through 1912. It was also revived in 1923 and has become a biannual 2,200-mile race from Los Angeles to Hawaii. The Southern Ocean Racing Conference in

1930 began a St. Petersburg-to-Havana race, which eventually grew into a series of six major ocean races.

Like golf and tennis, sailing grew rapidly during the 1920s, with the growth of a prosperous middle class. More one-design sailboats also appeared. The most popular was the *Star*, a 22-foot, 7½-inch sloop designed in 1911 by Francis Sweisguth. The Star Class Association, organized in 1922, soon had its own regatta, yearbook, and monthly magazine. Other early one-designs that are still popular are the 15½-foot *Snipe* and the 16-foot *Comet*.

Sailing declined during the Great Depression, but came back strong after World War II. Like most sports, it was boosted by increases in leisure time and discretionary income, but another major factor was the fiberglass hull. Fiberglass hulls can be molded in large quantities, thus lowering costs, and they require less maintenance than wood. More and more one-designs came to market during the 1950s. They made the sport more affordable, and thus moved it out of the exclusive yacht clubs. Following the *Star* class example, associations were established to organize regattas for the more popular designs. There are about 50 such associations in North America now, the number of sailboat owners has reached about 1 million, and more than 5 million people take part in the sport, at least as a recreation.

The advent of the one-design has also made international competition meaningful. While millions of dollars are spent to develop America's Cup boats every three or four years, the relatively inexpensive one-design boats compete in the Olympics, the Pan-American Games, and in their own international championships. Yachting was added to the Olympic program in 1932 with the Star Class. The Dragon Class was added in 1948, the Finn Class in 1952, the Flying Dutchman Class in 1960, the Tempest and Soling Classes in 1972, and the Tornado and 470 Classes in 1976. The Pan-American Games have competition in the Finn, Flying Dutchman, Lightning, Star, and Snipe Classes.

Further Reading: *Encyclopedia of Sailing.* Editors of *One Design and Offshore Racing.* New York: Harper & Row, 1971; Robinson, Bill. *World Yachting.* New York: Random House, 1967.

See also AMERICA'S CUP; FISHERMAN'S CHALLENGE CUP; NEW YORK YACHT CLUB; SOUTHERN OCEAN RACING CONFERENCE; U.S. YACHT RACING UNION.

Yankee Stadium
New York, NY

The American League Yankees played in the Polo Grounds, owned by the National League's New York Giants, from 1913 through 1922. By 1920, they were drawing more fans than the Giants, and they were told that their lease wouldn't be renewed. The club bought a former lumberyard at 161st Street in the Bronx and built an enormous stadium with a triple-decked concrete and steel grandstand and huge wooden bleachers in the outfield. Seating capacity was about 80,000, easily the largest in baseball. Known as "the house that Ruth built," the stadium opened in 1923, and, fittingly, Babe Ruth hit a three-run home run to beat Boston 4–1 in the first game.

The grandstand was gradually extended into the outfield. The left field stands were completed in 1928, the right field stands in 1937, when the wooden bleachers in center field were replaced by concrete and steel bleachers. The changes reduced capacity to 67,163. Lights were installed in 1946, and the first night game was played on May 28. During the 1960s, further structural changes cut capacity to 65,010.

The stadium was sold to New York City in 1973, and it was closed down for complete reconstruction after that season. The Yankees played at Shea Stadium in 1974 and 1975 during the refurbishing. Yankee Stadium reopened on April 15, 1976, with a capacity of 58,028 because wider seats were installed. The total cost to the city, originally estimated at $24 million, was between $54 million and $97 million, depending on which source you believe. The higher figure, from the city's Public Works Department, includes extensive street renovations, including an expressway ramp.

The reconstruction reduced the home run distance from 312 feet to 310 down the left field line, and from 461 feet to 417 in center field. It increased the distance from 296 to 310 down the right field line. The statues of Lou Gehrig, Miller Huggins, and Babe Ruth that were formerly on the playing surface in deep center field are now in a "memorial park" area beyond the center field fence. The new Yankee dugout is air-conditioned, but the visiting team's dugout is not.

Yonkers Raceway
Yonkers, NY

The original Yonkers Raceway opened in 1899, but it was completely rebuilt for a grand reopening in 1950. The ½-mile track has seating for 15,000 in the grandstand and another 15,000 in the clubhouse. It hosts three of the top six races for three-year-old harness horses: the Yonkers Trot in July, the Cane Pace, also in July, and the Messenger Stakes in October.

Address: Yonkers Raceway, Yonkers, NY 10704 (914) 968–4200

Yonkers Trot
Harness Racing

Established in 1955 as the Yonkers Futurity, this is the first race in the Triple Crown for trotters. It was a 1¹⁄₁₆-mile dash until 1963, when it became a 1-mile dash. The race is run at Yonkers Raceway.

Yost, "Hurry Up" Fielding H. (1871–1946)
Football

Born April 30, 1871, Fairview, WV; died August 20, 1946; National Football Foundation Hall of Fame

Yost played and coached during a period when college eligibility rules were almost nonexistent, and he took full advantage of the fact. A tackle at the University of West Virginia in 1896, he suddenly became a special student at Lafayette, helped the team beat Pennsylvania 6–4 to claim the national championship, and returned to West Virginia to get his law degree. He coached at Ohio Wesleyan in 1897, Nebraska in 1898, and Kansas in 1899. In 1900 he coached both Stanford and San Jose State as well as two high school teams. All four of them won league championships.

He was hired by the University of Michigan in 1901, and he began recruiting players who had already graduated from other colleges to attend graduate school at Michigan to continue their football careers, which was permissible at the time. Among his recruits was Willie Heston, a halfback who scored 100 touchdowns in four seasons at Michigan, according to Yost (Heston took credit for only 93). Heston was the leader of Yost's "point-a-minute" teams. From 1901 through 1905, Michigan scored 2,821 points in 57 games, an average of 49.5 a game and they won 55 while losing just 1 and tying 1.

The Western Conference (now the Big Ten) in 1906 adopted a rule limiting players to three years of eligibility. As a result, Michigan left the conference and began playing most of its games against the best eastern colleges. Yost's record wasn't quite as outstanding during that period, but he never had a losing season until Michigan rejoined the conference in 1919, when he went 3–4–0. Yost's 1923 team won all eight of its games. He missed the 1924 season because of illness, then coached for two more seasons before retiring to become athletic director.

In 25 seasons at Michigan, Yost won 165 games while losing 29 and tying 10. His overall record was 196–36–12.

Young, "Cy" Denton T. (1867–1955)
Baseball

Born March 29, 1867, Gilmore, OH; died November 4, 1955; Baseball Hall of Fame

As a minor-league pitcher, Young was warming up before a game by throwing the ball against an outfield fence. Someone remarked that it looked as if a cyclone had hit the fence, and Young was immediately nicknamed "Cyclone," soon shortened to "Cy." He joined the Cleveland National League team late in the 1890 season and pitched a three-hit shutout in his first start. The following season, he was 27–22, the first of 16 seasons in which he won 20 or more games, and in 1892 he had a 36–12 record with 9 shutouts.

A typical, wild fastball pitcher at first, he developed outstanding control by 1895. From then through 1911, his final season, he never walked more than 62 batters, but he struck out more than 100 a dozen times and more than 200 twice.

After two seasons with St. Louis in the National League, Young jumped to the Boston team in the American League in 1901. He led the league in victories in its first three seasons, with 33 in 1901, 32 in 1902, and 28 in 1903, and he had a league-leading 10 shutouts in 1904. After three below-average seasons, Young won 21 games in 1908. Traded to Cleveland in 1909, he was released in 1911, but he finished the season with the Boston Braves before retiring.

In 22 seasons, Young had 511 victories, 95 more than runner-up Walter Johnson. He also holds career records for starts (815), complete games (749) and innings pitched (7357). His 77 career shutouts ranks third all-time. The Cy Young Award, given annually to the best pitcher in each league, was established shortly after his death in 1955.

See also CY YOUNG AWARD.

Young, Sheila (1950–   )
Cycling, Speed Skating

Born October 14, 1950, Detroit, MI

A world champion and Olympic competitor in cycling and speed skating, Young won the national outdoor speed skating championship in 1970. She repeated in 1971 and won the national cycling sprint championship, too. It was only her second year of competition in that sport. She was the world 500-meter speed skating champion in 1972, shortly after she missed the Bronze Medal by .08 second at the Winter Olympics.

In 1973, Young won the U.S. speed skating titles at 500, 1,000, and 3,000 meters along with the world sprint title and the world 500-meter championship. She won no major skating championships in 1974, but she was U.S. and world cycling sprint titlist. Young won the world speed skating sprint championship again in 1975, and the following year she won a Gold Medal at 500 meters, a Silver at 1,500 meters, and a Bronze at 1,000 in the Winter Olympics. She also set a world record of 40.91 seconds in the speed skating 500-meter that year. Later in the year she won the U.S. and world sprint titles.

Young married cyclist Jim Ochowicz in 1976 and stopped competing to have their first child in 1977. She returned in 1981 to win the world cycling championship. After placing second in the 1982 world championship, she retired to have her second child.

Z

Zaharias, "Babe" Didrikson

See DIDRIKSON, "BABE" MILDRED.

Zuppke, "Bob" Robert C. (1879–1957)
Football

Born July 2, 1879, Berlin, Germany; died December 22, 1957; National Football Foundation Hall of Fame

"The Little Dutchman" was an unlikely looking football coach, but he had an inventive mind that often helped his teams beat more talented teams. His family moved from Germany to Milwaukee, WI when he was two years old. Too light for football, he became a basketball star at the University of Wisconsin despite his lack of height. He also developed an interest in art that led him to spend a summer studying at the Chicago Art Institute.

He coached several sports at high schools in Michigan and Illinois before the University of Illinois hired him as head football coach in 1913. He won Western Conference (Big Ten) titles in 1914, 1915, 1918, 1919, 1923, 1927, and 1928, but his teams were probably best known for their upsets. In 1913, Illinois surprised everyone by holding Purdue to a scoreless tie, and in 1918 the Illini beat Minnesota 14–9 after Minnesota had won three games in a row by a combined score of 170–0.

Red Grange entered Illinois in 1921, thinking he wasn't good enough to play college football. But Zuppke knew about him and talked him into coming out for the team, and Grange became a three-time All-American. During Grange's career, the Illinois offense was pretty straightforward, but in other seasons Zuppke came up with unusual plays to confuse the defense. He is credited with inventing the screen pass and the flea-flicker.

After Grange's departure, Illinois football began to go downhill. Under pressure for several years, Zuppke retired from coaching after the 1941 season and spent much of his retirement in Arizona, painting landscapes. In 29 seasons, his teams won 131 games, lost 81, and tied 12.

BIBLIOGRAPHY

Only works frequently consulted for a variety of entries are included. Works on special topics are listed under those topics. There is some duplication, since a few books on specific sports or broad general topics were used for several other entries as well.

REFERENCE BOOKS

Arlott, John, ed. *The Oxford Companion to Sports and Games*. London: Oxford University Press, 1975.

Hickok, Ralph. *The New Encyclopedia of Sports*. New York: McGraw-Hill, 1977.

Menke, Frank G. *The Encyclopedia of Sports*. New York: A. S. Barnes, 1978, sixth revised edition.

Meserole, Mike, ed. *The 1990 Information Please Sports Almanac*. Boston: Houghton Mifflin, 1989.

GENERAL SPORTS HISTORY

Baker, William J. *Sports in the Western World*. Urbana and Chicago: University of Illinois, 1988, revised edition.

Baker, William J., and John M. Carroll, eds. *Sports in Modern America*. St. Louis: River City, 1981.

Betts, John R. *America's Sporting Heritage, 1850–1950*. Reading, MA: Addison-Wesley, 1974.

Howell, Nancy, and Max L. Howell. *Sports and Games in Canadian Life: 1700 to the Present*. Toronto: Macmillan of Canada, 1969.

Krout, John A. *Annals of American Sport*. New Haven: Yale University Press, 1929.

Lucas, John A., and Ronald A. Smith. *Saga of American Sport*. Philadelphia: Lea and Febiger, 1978.

Rader, Benjamin G. *American Sports: From the Age of Folk Games to the Age of Televised Sports*. Englewood Cliffs, NJ: Prentice Hall, 1990, second edition.

Riess, Steven A., *The American Sporting Experience: A Historical Anthology of Sport in America*. Champaign, IL: Leisure Press, 1984.

Spivey, Donald, ed. *Sport in America: New Historical Perspectives*. Westport, CT: Greenwood Press, 1985.

REGIONAL AND PERIOD SPORTS HISTORY

Adelman, Melvin L. *A Sporting Time: New York City and the Rise of Modern Athletics, 1820–70*. Urbana and Chicago: University of Illinois Press, 1986.

Carson, Jane. *Colonial Virginians at Play*. Charlottesville: University Press of Virginia, 1965.

Hardy, Stephen. *How Boston Played: Sport, Recreation and Community 1865–1915*. Boston: Northeastern University Press, 1982.

Henderson, Robert W. *Early American Sport*. Rutherford, NJ: Fairleigh Dickinson, 1976, third edition.

Holliman, Jennie. *American Sports, 1785–1835*. Durham, NC: Seeman, 1931.

Metcalfe, Alan. *Canada Learns to Play: The Emergence of Organized Sport, 1807–1914*. Toronto: McClelland and Stewart, 1987.

Smith, Ronald A. *Sports and Freedom: The Rise of Big-Time College Athletics*. New York: Oxford University Press, 1988.

Somers, Dale A. *The Rise of Sports in New Orleans, 1850–1900*. Baton Rouge; Louisiana State University Press, 1972.

MULTISPORTS HISTORY

Bass, Howard. *International Encyclopedia of Winter Sports*. Cranbury, NJ: Great Albion Books, 1972.

Brown, W. A. Nigel. *Ice-Skating: A History*. New York: A. S. Barnes, 1959.

Emrich, Linn. *The Complete Book of Sky Sports*. New York: Macmillan, 1970.

Flowers, Raymond. *The History of Skiing and Other Winter Sports*. New York: Methuen, 1977.

Heller, Mark, ed. *The Illustrated Encyclopedia of Ice Skating*. New York: Paddington Press, 1979.

Liebers, Arthur. *The Complete Book of Water Sports*. New York: Coward-McCann, 1972, revised edition.

Sparano, Vin T. *Complete Outdoors Encyclopedia*. New York: Harper and Row, 1980, second edition.

Squires, Dick. *The OTHER Racquet Sports*. New York: McGraw-Hill, 1978.

HEALTH, PHYSICAL EDUCATION, AND RECREATION

Dulles, Foster Rhea. *America Learns to Play: A History of Popular Recreation, 1607–1940*. New York: Appleton-Century, 1940.

Van Dalen, Bruce B., and Bruce L. Bennett. *A World History of Physical Education*. Englewood Cliffs, NJ: Prentice-Hall, 1971, second edition.

Zeigler, Earle F., ed. *A History of Sport and Physical Education to 1900 (Selected Topics)*. Champaign, IL: Stipes, 1973.

COLLECTIVE BIOGRAPHY

Appel, Martin, and Burt Goldblatt. *Baseball's Best: The Hall of Fame Gallery*. New York: McGraw-Hill, 1980, updated edition.

Burrill, Bob. *Who's Who in Boxing*. New Rochelle, NY: Arlington House, 1974.

Elliott, Len, and Barbara Kelly. *Who's Who in Golf*. New Rochelle, NY: Arlington House, 1976.

Hanley, Reid M. *Who's Who in Track and Field*. New Rochelle, NY: Arlington House, 1973.

Hickok, Ralph. *Who Was Who in American Sports*. New York: Hawthorn, 1971.

Kariher, Harry C. *Who's Who in Hockey*. New Rochelle, NY: Arlington House, 1973.

Mendell, Ronald L. *Who's Who in Basketball*. New Rochelle, NY: Arlington House, 1973.

Mendell, Ronald L., and Timothy B. Phares. *Who's Who in Football*. New Rochelle, NY: Arlington House, 1974.

Padwe, Sandy. *Basketball's Hall of Fame*. Englewood Cliffs, NJ: Prentice-Hall, 1970.

Porter, David L., ed. *Biographical Dictionary of American Sports: Basketball and Other Indoor Sports*. New York: Greenwood Press, 1989.

Porter, David L., ed. *Biographical Dictionary of American Sports: Football*. New York: Greenwood Press, 1987.

Porter, David L., ed. *Biographical Dictionary of American Sports: Outdoor Sports*. New York: Greenwood Press, 1988.

THE BUSINESS AND LAW OF SPORTS

Berry, Robert C., William B. Gould, and Paul B. Staudohar. *Labor Relations in Professional Sports*. Dover, MA: Auburn House, 1986.

Gallner, Sheldon M., with contributions by Michael Dennis. *Pro Sports: The Contract Game*. New York: Scribner's, 1974.

Lineberry, William P., ed. *The Business of Sports*. New York: H. W. Wilson, 1973.

Noll, Roger G., ed. *Government and the Sports Business*. Washington, DC: Brookings Institute, 1974.

STATISTICAL SOURCES

It seems strange at a time when sports researchers are using computers to discover more and more ways to manipulate statistics, that numbers have not always been so important in sports—except, of course, for the final score and the won-lost record. When Beattie Feathers in 1934 became the first professional football player to rush for more than 1,000 yards, the milestone was barely noticed. Events such as Christy Mathewson's 300th victory (not to mention Cy Young's 500th) and Cap Anson's 3,000th hit, which today would be eagerly awaited and breathlessly reported, went unnoticed by press and public alike. When Babe Ruth hit 29 home runs in 1919, everyone was sure it was a record, but it took weeks of painstaking research to discover that the old record belonged to a long-forgotten player named Ned Williamson, who hit 27 in 1884.

The National Football League didn't begin keeping official statistics until 1932, its 13th season. The National Collegiate Athletic Association's official football statistics date only to 1938, its basketball statistics to 1948. The National Basketball Association has kept official records since its founding as the Basketball Association of America in 1946, but its predecessors had been too concerned about survival to worry much about numbers. Even major-league baseball, known for its wealth of statistics almost from time immemorial, has not been perfect. Until about 1920, record keeping lagged far behind the event. Official scorers sent box scores to league secretaries at their leisure, and the secretaries were just as leisurely in compiling official statistics. Final figures were usually not released until a month or more after the end of the season. Newspapers, meanwhile, kept their own box scores and compiled their own unofficial statistics.

The resultant confusion was highlighted by the 1910 batting race between Ty Cobb and Napoleon Lajoie, when a new Chalmers automobile was at stake. (See CHALMERS AWARD for the full story.) On October 10, the day after the season ended, the *New York Times* reported that Lejoie had won the title, .3868 to .3834. The official statistics were not available until November 21, six weeks later. They gave Cobb the victory, .385 to .384.

When Macmillan's landmark *Encyclopedia of Baseball* was published in 1969, it carried the imprimatur of Commissioner Bowie Kuhn as the sport's official record book. Some long-standing numbers changed, but none was particularly significant to the history of the sport. In fact, the Special Baseball Records Committee that worked on the project originally made a decision that would have given Babe Ruth one more home run; but, when committee members realized that one of baseball's best-known records, Ruth's 714 career home runs, would be increased to 715, they reversed their decision.

Later editions of the encyclopedia have not been so careful about preserving "sacrosanct" numbers. In recent years, many researchers have been poring over old game accounts and box scores to reconstruct early baseball statistics, resulting in many changes that have been incorporated into subsequent editions of Macmillan's *Baseball Encyclopedia,* as it is now called.

Such revisionism is not bad in itself. To draw an analogy from another field, if documentation were found proving that Shakespeare was born on April 22, 1564, rather than April 23 (a date long accepted but never documented), it should obviously become part of the record. But no scholar making such a discovery would suddenly produce a new biography of Shakespeare using the new birthdate without explanation. The documentation would first be produced and made available for inspection and verification by other scholars.

The editors of the Macmillan encyclopedia have, unfortunately, introduced many changes without explanation. The eighth edition, published in 1990, was the source of much controversy, in large part because Honus Wagner was suddenly deprived of 12 hits. The questions naturally arise: What hits previously credited to Wagner were spurious? What box scores were found to be in error? What evidence was discovered documenting the errors? And who, specifically, discovered that evidence? Macmillan is silent on such questions.

Changes in individual statistics have created other problems, as pointed out by Frank V. Phelps in an excellent critique ("Macmillan," in *The National Pastime* (Winter 1987), pp. 28–35). A box score, like a bank statement, must balance; and a season's statistics, like the figures in an annual report, must also balance. If a hit is subtracted from a player's record, it must be subtracted from his team's record and from his league's record. *And* it must be subtracted from the record of the pitcher who had originally been charged with giving up the hit, and from the pitching statistics for that pitcher's team. As Macmillan has changed individual statistics, many of its other records have been thrown out of balance, rendering it unreliable.

All this is by way of preface to the following list of statistical sources. For the sake of consistency, my editor, Nick Bakalar, and I agreed that *Total Baseball* would be used for all baseball statistics. However, the figures in *Total Baseball* are not accepted as official by major-league baseball, so the reader may note occasional discrepancies between statistics shown in my text and those shown in official listings of, for example, league batting leaders.

Neft and Cohen (both of whom, incidentally, worked on the original Macmillan *Encyclopedia of Baseball*) reconstructed partial National Football League statistics for seasons prior to 1932 in the first volume of their encyclopedia. The Baker work contains a wealth of statistical material on collegiate football before the NCAA began its record keeping. The other books cited are standard, reliable modern sources.

Baker, L. H. *Football: Facts and Figures.* New York: Farrar and Rinehart, Inc., 1945.

Bateman, Hal, ed. *American Athletics Annual 1989.* Indianapolis; The Athletics Congress of the United States, 1989, annual.

National Collegiate Championships 1987–88. Mission, KS: National Collegiate Athletic Association, 1988, annual.

NCAA Basketball. Mission, KS: National Collegiate Athletic Association, 1989, annual.

NCAA Football. Mission, KS; National Collegiate Athletic Association, 1989, annual.

National Hockey League Official Guide and Record Book. Philadelphia: Running Press, 1989, annual.

Neft, David S., and Richard M. Cohen. *Pro Football: The Early Years, 1895–1959.* Ridgefield, CT: Sports Products, Inc., 1978.

Neft, David S., and Richard M. Cohen. *The Sports Encyclopedia—Pro Football: The Modern Era, 1960 to the Present.* New York: Grosset and Dunlap, 1988.

Thorn, John, and Pete Palmer, eds. *Total Baseball.* New York: Warner Books, 1989.

INDEX